Environmental Law

Environmental Law

4th edition

David Hughes LLB (Liverpool), LLM (Cantab), FRSA
Professor of Housing and Planning Law,
De Montfort Law School, De Montfort University, Leicester

Tim Jewell LLB, MPhil (Leicester)
Barrister, Senior Visiting Fellow,
Faculty of Law, University of Southampton

Jason Lowther LLB (Middlesex Polytechnic), LLM (Southampton), PGCE
Lecturer in Law,
School of Legal Studies, University of Wolverhampton

Neil Parpworth LLB (Leicester), MA (London)
Senior Lecturer in Law,
De Montfort Law School, De Montfort University, Leicester

Paula de Prez LLB, PhD (Wolverhampton)
Lecturer in Law,
Liverpool Law School, University of Liverpool

Butterworths
LexisNexis™

Members of the LexisNexis Group worldwide

United Kingdom	LexisNexis Butterworths Tolley, a Division of Reed Elsevier (UK) Ltd, Halsbury House, 35 Chancery Lane, LONDON, WC2A 1EL, and 4 Hill Street, EDINBURGH EH2 3JZ
Argentina	LexisNexis Argentina, BUENOS AIRES
Australia	LexisNexis Butterworths, CHATSWOOD, New South Wales
Austria	LexisNexis Verlag ARD Orac GmbH & Co KG, VIENNA
Canada	LexisNexis Butterworths, MARKHAM, Ontario
Chile	LexisNexis Chile Ltda, SANTIAGO DE CHILE
Czech Republic	Nakladatelství Orac sro, PRAGUE
France	Editions du Juris-Classeur SA, PARIS
Hong Kong	LexisNexis Butterworths, HONG KONG
Hungary	HVG-Orac, BUDAPEST
India	LexisNexis Butterworths, NEW DELHI
Ireland	Butterworths (Ireland) Ltd, DUBLIN
Italy	Giuffrè Editore, MILAN
Malaysia	Malayan Law Journal Sdn Bhd, KUALA LUMPUR
New Zealand	LexisNexis Butterworths, WELLINGTON
Poland	Wydawnictwo Prawnicze LexisNexis, WARSAW
Singapore	LexisNexis Butterworths, SINGAPORE
South Africa	Butterworths SA, DURBAN
Switzerland	Stämpfli Verlag AG, BERNE
USA	LexisNexis, DAYTON, Ohio

© Reed Elsevier (UK) Ltd 2002

A CIP Catalogue record for this book is available from the British Library.

ISBN 0 406 94291 9

Printed and bound in Great Britain by The Bath Press, Bath

Visit Butterworths LexisNexis *direct* at www.butterworths.com

Preface

This book is a descendant from the first edition of this title, which appeared in 1986. The prime object of the work remains to examine the current state of environmental law with particular regard to England and Wales, within the context of both EC and international environmental law, and also with reference to wider policy and ethical issues. In this respect I repeat what I wrote in the preface to the 3rd edition of 1996: those who write about environmental law without setting it in the context of policy run the risk of either the Scylla of producing a dry-as-dust legal tome divorced from reality, or the Charybdis of a work which fosters the belief that simply making laws 'magics away' problems. As with the previous edition of this work, constraints of space have limited the coverage that can be given to international environmental law and EC law, and similarly those constraints continue to confine the coverage of the text to an examination of those laws which relate to the three 'environmental media' of land, air and water. I am happy to note, however, that there are now a number of excellent texts on those issues to which this book can give only general or transient attention.

What readers will note about this current edition is that it is in very many ways new. The most noticeable feature is that the old order of chapters has been broken up. While the order of treatment of topics remains in the form of a general introductory section, chapters 1 to 7, followed by a section concerned with land, chapters 8 to 15, which in turn is followed by the section on atmospheric issues, chapters 16 to 18, and then the section on water, chapters 19 to 20, it will be noted that the numbers of chapters have increased. In previous editions the old chapter structure had been retained with each chapter growing in itself to accommodate new material. This time it was clear a new approach was needed and so the chapters have been recast and rewritten. This has enabled full account to be taken of the very considerable developments that have taken place in environmental law since 1996, for example the introduction of the IPPC regime, the growing impact of human rights issues, new countryside access provisions and considerable policy and other legal changes with regard to planning control. Just as the law of the environment seems constantly to grow and develop, so this book has had to change, and arguably mutate. The consequence is that this edition is very much a new book with new emphases as well as new patterns of presentation.

The revision of the work has benefited from the collaboration of a number of colleagues. I am delighted to record the continued involvement of Neil Parpworth and Tim Jewell, who have been responsible for chapters 16, 18, 19, 20 and 13, 14 and 15 respectively. I am similarly delighted to welcome two new collaborators, Paula de Prez and Jason Lowther, who have been responsible for chapters 3, 6, 7, 12 and 4, and 17 respectively. I have undertaken chapters 1, 2, 5, 8, 9, 10 and 11, and have also been responsible for the allocation of the work. There are a number of connections between the various collaborators, first of which is our joint involvement in various editorial capacities with the journal 'Environmental Law and Management'. However, there is another circle of acquaintance at work. Both Neil Parpworth and Tim Jewell are former students of mine at the University of Leicester. Jason Lowther is a former student of Tim Jewell's at the University of Southampton. Jason Lowther is in turn married to Jo Sellick, another former student of mine, who taught Paula de Prez at the University of Wolverhampton. Paula de Prez has now taken up a lecturing post at the University of Liverpool where I began my undergraduate career in 1964. While I never contemplated all those years ago the production of this book nor indeed any other of my writings – my head was then full of being in one of the world's most exciting cities in the immediate post-Beatles era – I am content to believe now that in a very real sense an academic wheel has come full circle. I also take this opportunity of thanking all of my collaborators for their very hard work and the great pleasure I have gained from working with them. It is not an exaggeration to say it has been a privilege to work with such a committed group of people. Equally I am sure all of us would wish to place on record our grateful thanks to our publishers and their staff for all their help and support in the publication of this book.

Mention of book publishing leads me to make one final and very personal set of observations. There is a very real danger, I believe, that the pressures of research assessment exercises to which, for good or ill, academics have been subject for a number of years will distort academic publishing. It is, I maintain, indisputable that one of the great achievements of our university law schools has been the development of the high quality textbook. Other disciplines may rely to a lesser extent on such works, but we should not be seduced by the false allure of homogeneity into believing that what is good for other academics is necessarily good for academic lawyers or our students. If, in the name of ever-increasing assessment scores, the brightest and best academics are diverted away from the production of the most stimulating and challenging texts and are set solely to the task of producing ever more journal articles, then it is my belief that law teaching and law students will suffer. This is not to denigrate in any way or to diminish the importance of journal production, nor would it be appropriate in the preface to a book which is the fruit of collaboration by a team all of whom are active in writing for and editing journals: rather it is a plea for the continuing importance of book production to be recognised and indeed celebrated. I rest my case.

David Hughes

April 2002

Contents

PART I

The overall structure and development of environmental law

CHAPTER 1

Environmental law – past, present and future   3

CHAPTER 2

The ethical basis of environmental law and its principles   17

CHAPTER 3

The players: bodies responsible for the formulation and implementation of environmental policy and regulation   33

CHAPTER 4

Environmental law: the international and European dimension   63

CHAPTER 5

Human rights and the environment   95

CHAPTER 6

Civil liability for environmental damage   117

PART II

Protection of the land

CHAPTER 8

The basic structure of planning control   179

CHAPTER 9

The use of land in rural areas and powers to deal with derelict land   251

CHAPTER 10

Access to the countryside and public rights of way   297

CHAPTER 11

Controversial uses of land   311

CHAPTER 12

Genetic modification technology and the environment   351

CHAPTER 13

Mineral extraction   373

CHAPTER 14

Waste management   405

CHAPTER 17

Atmospheric pollution   543

CHAPTER 18

Noise   579

PART IV

Protection of the aqueous environment

CHAPTER 19

Marine pollution   625

CHAPTER 20

Riverine pollution   647

Terms and abbreviations regularly encountered

ACBE	Advisory Committee on Business and the Environment
ACNFP	Advisory Committee on Novel Foods and Processes
ACRE	Advisory Committee on Releases to the Environment
ADAS	Agricultural Development and Advisory Service
ALARA	As Low as Reasonably Achievable
ALARP	As Low as Reasonably Praciticable
ALATA	As Low as Technically Achievable
AONB	Areas of Outstanding Natural Beauty
BATNEEC	Best Available Techniques Not Entailing Excessive Cost
BNFL	British Nuclear Fuels Ltd
BoD	Biological/Biochemical Oxygen Demand
BPEO	Best Practicable Environmental Option
BPM	Best Practicable Means
BS	British Standard, eg 5750 (quality systems) and 7750 (environmental management systems)
CAP	Common Agricultural Policy
CARPE	Common Agriculture and Rural Policy for Europe
CFCs	Chloroflurocarbons
CPRE	Council for the Protection of Rural England
CROWA	Countryside and Rights of Way Act 2000
DBA	Decibel scale — an international scale of sound levels
DEFRA	Department for Environment, Food and Rural Affairs
DETR	Department of Environment, Transport and the Regions
DoE	Department of the Environment
DTLR	Department for Transport, Local Government and the Regions
DWI	Drinking Water Inspectorate
EAC	Environment Audit Committee
EIA	Environmental Impact Assessment
EC	European Communities
ECJ	European Court of Justice
EConHR	European Convention on Human Rights
EINECS	European Inventory of Existing Commercial Chemical Substances
ELINCS	European List of Notified Chemical Substances

EMAS	Eco-management and Auditing Scheme
EMF	Electro magnetic fields
EQS	Environmental Quality Standard
ES	Environmental Statement
ESA	Environmentally Sensitive Area
EU	European Union
FSA	Food Standards Agency
GATT	General Agreement on Tariffs and Trade
GDPO	General Development Procedure Order
GMO	Genetically Modified Organism
GPDO	General Permitted Development Order
HBFCs	Hydrobromoflurocarbons
HCFCs	Hydrochloroflurocarbons
HFCs	Hydroflurocarbons
HMIP	Her Majesty's Inspectorate of Pollution
HSC	Health and Safety Commission
HSE	Health and Safety Executive
ICRCL	Inter Departmental Committee on the Redevelopment of Contaminated Land
ICRP	International Commission on Radiological Protection
IEHO	Institution of Environmental Health Officers
IMO	International Maritime Organisation
IMPEL	European Union Network for the Implementation and Enforcement of Environmental Law
IPC	Integrated Pollution Control
IPPC	Integrated Pollution Prevention and Control
LAAPC	Local Authority Air Pollution Control
LAWDC	Local Authority Waste Disposal Company
LDF	Local Development Framework
LFG	Land Fill Gas
LPA	Local Planning Authority
MAFF	Ministry of Agriculture Fisheries and Food
MARPOL	Maritime Convention for the Prevention of Pollution from Ships
MPG	Minerals Policy Guidance
NAWDC	National Association of Waste Disposal Contractors
NCC	Nature Conservancy Council
NFFO	Non Fossil Fuel Obligation
NGO	Non Governmental organisation
NNR	National Nature Reserve
NRA	National Rivers Authority
NRPB	National Radiological Protection Board
NSCA	National Society for Clean Air and Environmental Protection
OECD	Organisation for Economic Co-operation and Development
OFFER	Office of the Director General of Electricity Supply
OFGAS	Office of Gas Services
OFWAT	Office of Water Services
PAH	Polycyclic Aromatic Hydrocarbons
PCB	Polychlorinated Biphynyls
PFA	Pulverised Fuel Ash
PIC	Prior Informed Consent
PPG	Planning Policy Guidance

RCEP	Royal Commission on Environmental Pollution
RPG	Regional Planning Guidance
RSPB	Roayl Society for the Protection of Birds
RWMAC	Radioactive Waste Management Advisory Committee
SAC	Special Area of Conservation
SPA	Special Protection Area
SPA	Supplementary Planning Guidance
SSSI	Site of Special Scientific Interest
SWQO	Statutory Water Quality Objective
TOVALOP	Tanker Owners Voluntary Agreement Concerning Liability for Oil Pollution
TPO	Tree Preservation Order
UCO	Use Classes Order
UKAEA	United Kingdom Atomic Energy Authority
UKELA	United Kingdom Environmental Law Association
UNCED	United Nations Conference on Environment and Development (Rio '92)
UNCLOS	United Nations Convention on the Law of the Sea
UNEP	United Nations Environment Programme
VOCs	Volatile Organic Compounds
WAMITAB	Waste Management Industry Training Board
WCA	Waste Collection Authority
WDA	Waste Disposal Authority
WML	Waste Management Licence
WQO	Water Quality Objective
WRA	Waste Regulation Authority
WTO	World Trade Organisation

Web-based resources

NB All the URLs listed below begin with http://, but this is *generally* omitted in this work.

UK: GENERAL

Index of national and local government,
 and government agencies in the UK   www.open.gov.uk
Guide to Official Information in the UK   www.clickso.com
The Stationery Office web site
National Statistics for the UK, including
 the Office for National Statistics   www.statistics.gov.uk

UK: LAW

BAILII, Case and legislation   www.bailli.org/

Legislation

UK Public General Acts from 1988,
 and Statutory Instruments from 1987   www.hmso.gov.uk/legis.htm
Official documents including White Papers,
 Green Papers (operational from 1 January
 2002, but an archived selection before
 this date is available)   www.official-documents.co.uk/
Net Regs, the Environment Agency's Guide
 to Law and Practice and who does what   www.netregs.environment-
                     agency.gov.uk/

INTERNATIONAL: GENERAL

Environmental organisations web directory   www.webdirectory.com
Planum (Europe)   www.planum.net

EUROPEAN OFFICIAL SOURCES

Europa, The main site of the European Union	europa.eu.int/
The European Commission Office in the UK	www.cec.org.uk.index.htm
Council of the European Union	ue.eu.int/
EU Environmental Directorate	europa.eu.int/comm/environment
EU Regional Policy Directorate	europa.eu.int/comm/dgs/ regional_policy/index_en.htm
Inforegio, Regional policy and EU Structural Funds	www.inforegio.cec.eu.int/ dg16_en.htm
Eurostat – EU Statistics	europa.eu.int/comm/eurostat
European Parliament	www.europarl.eu.int
Committee of the Regions (EU)	www.cor.eu.int
European Environment Agency	www.eea.dk
Catalogue of Free Publications from the EU	w w w . c e c . o p r g . u k / s o u r c e d i / catalog1.htm
Office for the Official Publications of the European Union	eur-op.eu.int/general/en/
Local Government International Bureau	www.1gib.gov.uk
European Environment Bureau	www.eeb.org

HUDOC

The European Court of Human Rights	www.echr.coe.int/

ENGLAND: GOVERNMENT AGENCIES AND BODIES

UK Online, general web site (government bodies and documents)	www.ukonline.gov.uk
Department of Transport, Local Government and the Regions	www.dtlr.gov.uk
Department of Environment, Food and Rural Affairs	www.defra.gov.uk
Central Office of Information	www.nds.coi.gov/uk/
Environment Agency	www.environment-agency.gov.uk
Royal Commission on Environmental Pollution	www.rcep.org.uk
The New Deal for Communities	www.newdeal.gov.uk
English Partnerships	www.englishpartnerships.co.uk
English Nature	www.english-nature.org.uk
Heritage Lottery Fund	www.hlf.org.uk
English Heritage	www.english-heritage.org.uk
National Land Use Database	www.nlud.org.uk
Countryside Agency	www.countryside.gov.uk
Home Office Human Rights Unit	www.homeoffice.gov.uk/hract
The Planning Inspectorate	www.planning-inspectorate.gov.uk

WALES: GOVERNMENT AND AGENCIES

National Assembly for Wales	www.wales.gov.uk/index_e.html
Countryside Council for Wales	www.ccw.gov.uk/
Environment Agency Wales	www.environment-agency.wales.gov.uk/

REGIONAL AND LOCAL GOVERNMENT

Directory of regional bodies and local authorities	www.open.gov.uk/index/orgindex.htm
Local Government Association	www.lga.gov.uk
Greater London Authority	www.london.gov.uk

INTERNATIONAL SOURCES

United Nations	www.un.org
UN Environment Programme	www.unep.org/
UN Commission for Sustainable Development	www.un.org/esa/sustdev/csd.htm
UN Economic Commission for Europe	www.unece.org
RIO + 10 2001 Summit	www.johannesburgsummit.org

PLANNING ASSOCIATIONS, ETC

Royal Town Planning Institute	www.rtpi.org.uk/
Town and Country Planning Association	www.tcpa.org.uk

NON-GOVERNMENTAL ORGANISATIONS

Association of National Park Sites	www.anpa.gov.uk
Brownfield land	www.brownfieldsites.com
Civic Trust	www.civictrust.org.uk
Council for the Protection of Rural England	www.cpre.org.uk
Friends of the Earth, UK	www.foe.co.uk
Greenpeace	www.greenpeace.org
House Builders' Federation	www.hbf.co.uk
Local Agenda 21 in the UK	www.la21-uk.org.uk
National Retail Planning Forum	www.nrpf.org
National Trust	www.nationaltrust.org.uk
Royal Society for the Protection of Birds	www.rspb.org.uk/education
The Campaign for the Protection of Rural Wales	www.cprw.org.uk
Transport 2000	www.transport2000.org.uk
Sustainable Development Commission	www.sd-commission.gov.uk/index.htm
Entri	
This is an online search service for finding information about environmental treaties and resource indicators	http://sedac.diesin.org/entri/

European Environmental Law (Publishers' site)
A site giving access to full text cases,
    legislation and other materials on
    European Environmental Law.   http://Struiken.ic.ura.nl:88/

Table of statutes

List of cases

Decisions of the European Court of Justice are listed both alphabetically and numerically. The numerical list follows the alphabetical.

C

M

X

Y

Z

Decisions of the European Court of Justice are listed below numerically.
These decisions are also included in the preceding alphabetical list.

Part I

The overall structure and development of environmental law

Chapter 1

Environmental law – past, present and future

'The past indicative, the present imperfect and the future uncertain'

Increasing environmental consciousness over the last 30 years should not blind us to the fact that there have been laws concerning the environment for centuries. What we had was a number of *diverse laws relating to* the environment. The oldest sources of law on the topic were the law of public health, the law of town and country planning and the law of torts. From these, together with international and European Community law, it has been possible to see the emergence of a more coherent system. We shall examine the history, development and current state of the law, and in chapter 2 give time to an examination of the philosophy, ethics and principles of the law. But first a basic definition of environmental law for the purpose of this work must be given. It is the law relating to the use, protection and conservation of the three environmental media of earth, air and water. This law expresses itself in rules of environmental regulation (primarily the domain of public authorities) and environmental liability which are concerned with attributing responsibility to meet the costs and consequences of environmental harm, and for past environmental wrong doing, intentional or otherwise.

A THE HISTORICAL DEVELOPMENT OF THE LAW RELATING TO PUBLIC HEALTH

'Matters of Imperial interest, which we cannot with impunity neglect' (Stewart & Jenkins, *The Medical and Legal Aspects of Sanitary Reform*, 1867)

The need for public intervention by law arose largely from the public health problems of the nineteenth century. The vast expansion of towns and cities, and the eruption of acre upon acre of filthy insanitary slums and factories across the face of the land, led to the passage of the great Public Health Act 1875 which was designed to protect health and secure, inter alia, minimum standards of housing. However, the fact that the century was almost gone before this monumental legislation was put on the statute book is indicative of a considerable body of public and private resistance to state intervention in environmental matters. In 1875 the death rate was still almost as high as it had been 40 years previously, and the appallingly high level of infant mortality did not begin to reduce greatly until the end of the century. The enactment of the PHA 1875 achieved a rationalised and codified law of sanitation and health, but it only ushered in a period when mortality could begin to fall. An account of how that national code reached the statute book follows.

In 1838 Edwin Chadwick sent Poor Law medical investigators into the London slums and in 1842 his 'Report on an Enquiry into the Sanitary Condition of the Labouring Population of Great Britain' was issued. In due course Parliament passed the Public Health Act 1848. But few of the Act's provisions were mandatory. Throughout the 1850s and 60s public health administration was not properly centrally directed, while the various local government bodies that littered the map reacted, often in a less then interested fashion, to the responsibilities increasingly laid upon them. Between 1848 and 1872 a multiplicity of enactments covering issues such as nuisances, sewage and sanitation, vaccination, diseases, general public health and common lodging houses were put on the statute book. The essential basics of modern public health law were created in this period, but, sadly, in a confused and tangled manner which was beyond the comprehension even of trained minds.

Furthermore the division of responsibility between urban and rural authorities made the operation of law unnecessarily unwieldy. Added to this complexity was the fact that most of the law was permissive and not mandatory. These basic defects made the law unworkable. It is easy to criticise the Victorians for their cumbersome administrative arrangements; as will become apparent from this and subsequent chapters the twentieth century also signally failed to create either a comprehensive system of environmental law or integrated machinery to enforce it. Whether the twenty first century will achieve more remains to be seen.

From the mid 1860s reform was clearly essential, while coherent duties needed to be imposed on local government. In 1868 the government agreed to set up a Royal Sanitary Commission to consider all sanitary laws. This body reported in 1871 and that led, ultimately, to the Public Health Act 1875. Subsequent attention has focused on amendment or codification. Various enactments relating to public health in the years after 1875 were consolidated in the Public Health Act 1936, supplemented by the Public Health Act 1961 and the Public Health (Recurring Nuisances) Act 1969. Other legislation has been passed to deal with *particular issues* affecting public health, or the health of *particular sections* of the community, for example statutes relating to refuse disposal, water, clean air, litter and health and safety at work, see, for example, the Clean Air Act 1993 consolidating earlier legislation.

The Control of Pollution Act 1974 marked a further major development in public health legislation in that it attempted to protect the public by ensuring certain basic standards of *environmental* protection. It was put on the statute book after an extensive series of reports and consultations by the concerned Departments of State on issues such as refuse collection, storage and disposal, and disposal of solid toxic waste, sewage disposal, noise, clean air and industrial emissions into the atmosphere. The initiatives of the 1974 legislation were continued by the Water Act 1989 which is now found as the Water Industry Act 1991 and the Water Resources Act 1991.

The Environmental Protection Act 1990 marked a further major step forward in this process in that it was concerned with protection of the environment and not just public health, and it introduced a generalised concept of 'the environment', which applies throughout many of its provisions, as being the media of air, land and water. Likewise pollution of the environment and harm to the environment are broad concepts embracing both harm to humankind *and* other living things supported by the environment, while 'harm' extends to harming the health of living organisms, or interference with the ecological system of which they form part, including harm to any human senses, or harm to human property; see the EPA 1990, s 1(2)–(4) and also s 29. This process continued as a result of the Environment Act 1995, with an encouragingly more integrated notion of environmental protection being introduced by further legislation in 1999; see chapter 16 below.

Pour encourager les autres

The prime legacy bequeathed to environment law by its public health origins is the use of penal sanctions for infringements of legal requirements – very often on the basis that it is not necessary for the enforcing body to prove any mens rea or guilty intent on the part of the wrongdoer. Both the courts and Parliament accept that there are incidents which 'are not criminal in any real sense, but are acts which in the public interest are prohibited under a penalty' per Wright J in *Sherras v De Rutzen.*[1] The purpose of the law is to *prevent* the occurrence of prohibited events by visiting them with strict consequences. The object is to prompt operators to do all in their power to avoid penalties by conducting their activities as well as they can.

However, there is a disbenefit in that to escape criminal liability for many regulatory offences – particularly those concerned with water – an operator has to undertake positive, and often expensive, burdens of a preventive nature, and even if such burdens are assumed liability may still be imposed if a polluting incident occurs. Many object to a system capable of imposing legal blame in the absence of moral fault. Others argue that the money spent on implementing legislation could be better spent on educating and advising operators.

This issue will be returned to in detail in the subsequent chapters.

B THE GROWTH AND CURRENT STATE OF PLANNING LAW

The planned development of land, for economic, military and social reasons, has gone on for centuries. Such activity usually resulted in the creation of new settlements. The need, however, for public control of land use and development initially grew out of the same public health problems we have already encountered. but, as with the law relating to public health, planning law took a long time to emerge and develop. It differs from public health law in that the period of its emergence and development is much longer. Also, because of the differing land use policies of various governments, the law is not securely based on any one coherent, nationally agreed, politically irreproachable and generally acceptable philosophy as to why it exists and what aims and objectives it should seek to promote.

From slum to Utopia?

The history of planning law can also be traced back to Edwin Chadwick. He called for the development of a new class of 'town surveyors' trained in science and engineering, able to build healthy towns with adequate protection for health. In 1873 the Association of Municipal Engineers was founded. This was an attempt to professionalise the 'town surveyor' ideal – an ideal that was subsequently to give rise to the profession of planning. Initially, under the Public Health Act 1875, all efforts were directed to secure public health and building standards. It was soon realised that this alone was not enough. In 1909 Unwin said in *Town Planning in Practice: An Introduction to the Act of Designing Cities and Suburbs:*

---

1   [1895] 1 QB 918 at 922.

'We have, indeed … laid a good foundation and have secured many of the
necessary elements for a healthy condition of life; and yet the remarkable fact
remains that there are growing up around our big towns vast districts … which
for dreariness and sheer ugliness it is difficult to match anywhere.'

Decent main drainage alone was insufficient: existing slums had to be demolished and
replaced, and there was growing realisation that a poor environment flowed from a
general lack of systematised co-ordination in town development: *planning was
necessary.*

The expression 'town planning' seems to have emerged in a report of the City of
Birmingham Housing Committee in 1906. It acquired legal recognition in the Housing,
Town Planning, etc Act 1909. The 1909 Act allowed local authorities to prepare schemes
to control the development of new housing, but little use was made of these powers.
The making of planning schemes was made compulsory by the Housing, Town Planning,
etc Act 1919 and further planning powers were conferred by the Town and Country
Planning Act 1932 and the Restriction of Ribbon Development Act 1935. It soon became
obvious that a system of planning control wider than local schemes was needed;
something to cope with the emergence of conurbations straddling local areas and
spreading along major trunk routes was essential. The RRDA 1935 was a stop-gap
measure to impose some control while a better system could be devised. The Barlow
Report of the 'Royal Commission on the Distribution of the Industrial Population',[2]
the Beveridge Report on 'Social Insurance and Allied Services',[3] the Uthwatt 'Report
of the Expert Committee on Compensation and Betterment'[4] and the Scott 'Report of
the Committee on Land Utilisation in Rural Areas'[5] produced a new pattern of thinking
and new principles on which to base the law:

1   An end had to be made to the haphazard distribution of industry, population and
     urban sprawl.
2   Urban squalor had to be eliminated and public health improved by the creation of
     healthy, new, planned communities.
3   Older urban areas were to be revived.
4   National parks and forests had to be created and access to the countryside
     guaranteed.
5   A new national communications system based on planned roads and airports had
     to be created.
6   The emphasis in all this new work was to be on planning initiatives from central
     and local government. These would exist within the framework of a nationwide
     system of planning control in which land planning would be integrated with social
     and economic planning.

'We'll keep the red flag flying here?'

It fell to the 1945 Labour government to translate these principles into legislative practice.
This they did in an impressive package which included the creation of a new system of
social insurance and national assistance, the setting up of the National Health Service,
and the passing of the New Towns Act 1946, the National Parks and Access to the
Countryside Act 1949 and the Town and Country Planning Act 1947. The 1947 Act
enshrined certain principles:

2   (1940 Cmd 6153).
3   (1942 Cmd 6404).
4   (1942 Cmd 6386).
5   (1942 Cmd 6378).

1   All land is subject to the jurisdiction of planning authorities.
2   As a general rule land development may not take place without a grant of planning permission.
3   Such permission should not generally be granted unless the proposed development accords with a publicly prepared plan for the land in question. This last principle has always been the least honoured of the first three.
4   The development value of land should be nationalised for the public good. This did not long survive the return of the Conservatives to power in 1951.

It has never been easy for planners to ensure that development accords with prepared plans. The time taken in drawing up plans is one important factor in this. Another is that planners as a profession have felt constrained to base their plans on predictions of what they have thought *would* be the future pattern of land demand, an activity frequently outpaced by changes in economic circumstances. It is arguable that the only sure way to marry actual development with statutory plans would be, first, to give planning authorities vastly increased powers to direct and manipulate land development, that is, to draw up plans based on what planners believe *ought* to happen, and, second, to build up publicly owned 'land banks' to ensure an ample supply of land for controlled development. Neither of these processes has been politically or administratively workable in the UK. So far as the *law* of planning is concerned, the *general* rule is that the various statutory plans are only factors, admittedly very important factors, amongst many others in deciding whether planning permission should be granted. (The impact of s 54A, Town and Country Planning Act 1990 and Planning Policy Guidance (PPG) will be considered in chapter 8.) The result is a clear separation between the original impetus for forward planning according to plans and the *actual practice* of development control. This is a far cry from the intention of the framers of the 1947 legislation who believed that planning authorities should hold and be held closely to their plans.

It is to the credit of the system set up in 1947 that we have something of 'a green and pleasant land', yet there is widespread dissatisfaction with planning. Why should this be so? The answer is far from certain: the following may be reasons.
1   Planners as a profession have tended to fly somewhat indiscriminately after each passing architectural fashion. The result has been the construction of unlovely and unloved tower blocks of housing and offices which have altered beyond recognition a centuries-old skyline in too many places. The building of urban motorways has failed to solve the problem of how to provide a suitable traffic system for towns and has also led to the destruction of whole communities. At the same time developers have made great profits from the carrying out of such works.
On the other hand it would be wrong to single out planners alone for criticism. Architects, builders, administrators and politicians have been equally, and maybe even more, to blame, and the planning profession has been made a convenient scape-goat for the mistakes of others.
2   Planners have often been seen as miniature 'big brothers', and there has been a feeling that a superiority of assumption amongst planners has to be resisted.
3   Despite legislative attempts to open up the planning system to public participation, the general public is not, *on the whole*, involved in planning. Those members of the public who do involve themselves tend to represent only certain narrowly defined, sectional interest groups.
4   The planning system is often accused of being cumbersome and slow moving.
5   Planning law has become a 'killing field' for lawyers who have made it one of the most highly technical and complex branches of legal regulation. This has made the job of the planning profession vastly more difficult.
6   There us a general feeling of disenchantment in that, despite public planning, we still have urban squalor, bad health conditions and unemployment. Many people

believe there has been too much planning and that this has strangled initiatives
that would have improved the environment.
By the early 1980s there was a general feeling that society had forgotten the reasons
behind land use planning, while an increasingly strong body of opinion suggested
that planning should exist as the handmaid of private sector enterprise and economic
regeneration. Out of this we seem to have arrived at a situation where there is *no*
generally agreed single reason for the existence of planning. Notions of 'the orderly
management of change' command quite a degree of support, but onto this are grafted
other ideas – not always compatible – of employment creation and protection, urban
containment and rural preservation. Planning *as a system*, however, survives in that it
provides a known structure within which developers, builders, authorities, neighbours,
workers and financiers can operate.

Land, social and economic planning have also not gone hand in hand, while no
system of planning yet devised has been able to stop the ever escalating price of land
and to prevent profiteering from land speculation. The basic problems involved are
whether land values should be pegged or taxed so that increases in value consequent
on the granting of planning permission should be netted for the public good, and
whether the initiative in providing land for development should come from the public
or the private sector of the economy. The Labour and Conservative parties were
fundamentally divided over these issues, and the law after 1947 was often in a state of
flux and confusion as first one party and then the other imposed its policies via legislation.

The years of 'one of us' – planning under the Thatcher governments

After 1979 the law was greatly changed in order to enshrine the philosophy that
development initiatives should come mainly from the private sector of the economy.
The emphasis on privatisation of public assets and on land holding for development
as a private enterprise function is a very different policy from that envisaged in 1947.
Official thinking believes that over stringent public control of land use adds to other
problems of dereliction and industrial decline. For a government committed to releasing
the so-called 'spirit of enterprise', public controls over land use had to be relaxed as
part of a general subordination of planning to economic regeneration. In the greatest
injection of *laissez-faire* thinking into planning in 30 years, the Thatcher government
introduced the notion that planning authorities should allow commerce and industry
to go and expand in those locations where they found the best prospects for growth
and prosperity. Central planning policy, as enunciated in DoE Circular 22/80, encouraged
planning authorities, except in environmentally sensitive areas, to pick out for priority
handling applications that would contribute most to economic regeneration. Authorities
were also encouraged to give planning permission for development unless there were
clear-cut reasons for refusal. They were requested to relax controls over land uses which
did not conform to the various plans that have been made, to withdraw from detailed
control of the external appearance of buildings except where the character of the area
or of the particular building justified intervention, and to use planning enforcement
procedures only where there was no alternative. The message for urban authorities
was clear: a general relaxation of planning control and a streamlining of control
procedures was essential for national economic recovery.

The desire for unified, socio-economic planned public control of land use policy
which lay behind the TCPA 1947 was no longer enshrined in our planning law. Planning
was made subservient to economic goals. The work of planners during this century,
and particularly since 1947, was set at risk by this change in emphasis.

Though DoE Circular 22/80 stated: '... authorities are now asked to pick out for
priority handling those applications [for planning permission] which in their judgment

will contribute most to national and local economic activity', it continued: 'This does not mean, of course, that health and safety standards, noise, smell or other pollution problems should be given less weight.' Other guidance, such as the original PPG1 of January 1988, added that the planning system 'is an important instrument for the protection and enhancement of the environment in town and country'.

The large measure of discretion enjoyed by planning authorities, coupled with the fact that environmental concerns are only relevant *not* overriding considerations, make planning law an imperfect agent of environmental control. Planning law, however, has other defects such as the lengthy and cumbersome nature of its procedures, the principle that an authorised development or activity can only be halted following the payment of compensation, historically slow moving and somewhat ineffective enforcement systems, and a failure to rationalise the legislative overlap between planning law and other industrial safety, environmental and public health measures that have grown up around it. The principal bequest to environmental law from its planning origins is the use of managerial discretion vested in a public body whereby various activities are licensed or permitted, usually subject to conditions, on the application of an operator, *possibly* with a degree of public consultative involvement and subject to the appellate oversight of the Secretary of State.

Sustainable development notions (see further chapter 2) are now influencing planning, however, a desire to encourage redevelopment of already used ('brownfield') sites and to protect 'greenfield' land is prompted as much by a desire to conserve scarce resources as by the traditional need to protect amenity by preventing urban sprawl.

C TO SUM UP SO FAR …

From its past development the current law inherits a number of characteristics, not all of which are easily compatible. Broad managerial discretion is planning's bequest, while that from public health law is the imposition of criminal 'pains and penalties' on those who fail to meet legal requirements. However, even these can reflect old legal values derived from the common law. This is very true with regard to statutory nuisances which may be conveniently considered at this point.

D THE CURRENT LAW RELATING TO STATUTORY NUISANCES

Action taken by local authorities or by aggrieved individuals can be a most effective means of local environmental control, and though the concept of 'statutory nuisance' is derived from nineteenth century common law it is still relevant today. It should, however, be noted that once the IPPC regime is fully in place (see chapter 16 below) the rôle of statutory nuisances in dealing with environmental issues will be diminished.

It is the duty under the Environmental Protection Act 1990, s 79 as amended, of local authorities (districts and London boroughs, and, in Wales, county and county borough councils, while port health authorities may also exercise powers under the EPA 1990, s 79(8)) to inspect their areas from time to time, and to investigate complaints from the inhabitants, in respect of 'statutory nuisances'. These are: premises prejudicial to health, or a nuisance, smoke from premises prejudicial to health or a nuisance, fumes or gases from premises, dust, steam, smell or other effluvia arising on industrial trade or business premises, accumulations or deposits, animals, noise emitted from premises, or from or caused by a vehicle, machinery or equipment in a street, any other matter declared by statute to be a statutory nuisance, provided in each case the matter is prejudicial to health, ie actually injurious, or likely to cause injury, to health, or a nuisance. The question of whether a matter is 'prejudicial to health' *appears* to require a decision taken on an objective basis, as opposed to the subjective opinion of the person suffering from the nuisance and their particular needs.[6] Note: contaminated land falling within Part IIA of the EPA 1990 as inserted in 1995 is not to be dealt with as a statutory nuisance, see the EPA 1990, s 79 (1A)–(1B).

Health seems to mean physical as opposed to mental health, see *Coventry City Council v Cartwright*,[7] while nuisance bears its common law meaning of a deleterious affectation of land or its use and enjoyment which arises outside that land and then proceeds to invade it.[8] However, a single instance of a deleterious act may be sufficient to ground a statutory nuisance action.[9] It should also be noted that 'dust' does not include dust emitted as a constituent of smoke, while fumes are 'airborne solid matter smaller than dust'. Likewise 'noise' includes vibration, 'premises' includes land and vessels, and 'smoke' includes soot, ash, grit and gritty particles, though statutory nuisance proceedings in respect of smoke are excluded where the smoke is emitted from the chimney of a private dwelling in a smoke control area, where smoke and steam is emitted from a railway locomotive steam engine (a merciful exemption for railway preservation buffs!) and where dark smoke is emitted from, inter alia, boiler furnaces or from industrial or trade premises, control here existing under other legislation. 'Smoke' means primarily 'the visible volatile product given off by burning or smouldering substances', but also extends to the *smell* of smoke, thus enabling authorities to deal with smoke in all its aspects under both s 79(1)(b) and 79(1)(c) of the EPA 1990.[10] Without the consent of the Secretary of State *local authorities* may not take action in respect of smoke, dust, smell or effluvia nuisances arising on trade premises, or accumulation or deposit nuisances where proceedings *could* also be taken under the IPC/LAAPC provisions of the EPA 1990, Part I. Likewise proceedings cannot be taken in respect of smoke or noise emitted from premises occupied by the Crown for military or defence purposes, or by visiting overseas forces. Furthermore, proceedings in respect of fumes, etc, can only be taken in respect of premises which are private dwellings. For specific details on noise nuisance see chapter 18 below.

Authorities *have* to follow the statutory procedure once they decide to act,[11] but appear to have a discretion whether to act.[12] They do not *have* to consult the alleged perpetrator of the nuisance before acting, though may find they have to if they give that person a legitimate expectation consultation will take place.[13]

The procedure for taking action in respect of a statutory nuisance: local authorities

The EPA 1990, s 80 provides that where an authority is satisfied a statutory nuisance *exists, is likely to occur or recur*, they must serve an abatement notice which will require the nuisance's abatement or prohibit or restrict its occurrence or recurrence, and may require the execution of works or taking of steps for such purposes, specifying the time within which compliance is required.[14]

6 . *Cunningham v Birmingham City Council* (1997) 96 LGR 231, and see *R (on the Application of Anne) v Test Valley Borough Council* [2001] EWHC Admin 1019, [2001] All ER (D) 245 (Nov), [2001] 13 ELM 278.
7 [1975] 2 All ER 99, [1975] 1 WLR 845.
8 *National Coal Board v Neath Borough Council* [1976] 2 All ER 478.
9 *East Northamptonshire District Council v Fossett* [1994] Env LR 388.
10 *Griffiths v Pembrokeshire County Council* [2000] All ER (D) 443.
11 *Cocker v Cardwell* (1869) LR 5 QB 15.
12 *Nottingham Corpn v Newton* [1974] 2 All ER 760, [1974] 1 WLR 923.
13 *R v Falmouth and Truro Port Health Authority, ex p South West Water Ltd* [2001] QB 445, [2000] All ER (D) 429.
14 *Bristol Corpn v Sinnott* [1918] 1 Ch 62.

Notices under the EPA 1990 must, as with those under the previous legislation, be clear and certain.[15] While a specific period of time for taking action does not *have* to be stated[16] notices must tell their recipients what needs to be done.[17] Where works are required, however, they must be specified, as must the time for doing them, though where the notice merely requires a cessation of activity, or the doing of some simple task such as closing a pollution prevention barrier there seems to be no such need.[18] Notices must, in all fairness therefore, tell recipients what is amiss and what remedial action will be needed, though over-particularity will not be required where it is clear from the notice and the surrounding circumstances what is wrong.[19] It is not necessary for the notice to specify whether the nuisance is 'prejudicial to health' or 'a nuisance',[20] and in construing an abatement notice it is permissible to refer to letters accompanying it in any case of ambiguity to determine how its recipient may understand it, though that does not remove the overriding requirement of clarity.[21] In appropriate cases the choice of the means of abatement may be left to the perpetrator.[22] Though special circumstances may apply in the case of noise nuisances (see chapter 18 below), the overall effect of the case law is that a notice should be sufficiently particular to make it certain what is needed to remedy the clearly defined wrong in *one* 'package' of remedial measures.

Against whom is action taken?

Notice is to be served on the person responsible for the nuisance, save in cases of nuisances arising from structural defects, or where the person responsible cannot be found, in which case the owner is to be served. The 'owner' is the person who receives the 'rack' (economic) rent of the property, or who would receive it if the property was let, either on his/her own account or as an agent.[23] Failure to comply with a notice is an offence, and in respect of offences committed on industrial, trade or business premises the fine on summary conviction may be up to £20,000. However, it should be noted that authorities are not statutorily bound to prosecute offences, even though they may have taken default action themselves under the EPA 1990, s 81(3), which enables them, under s 81(4), to recover their expenses with interest, both constituting a charge on relevant premises, see s 81A and B. The EPA 1990, s 81(5) further empowers authorities to commence High Court proceedings where they are of the opinion that statutory nuisance proceedings before the justices would provide an inadequate remedy.

A person served with an abatement notice may, under the EPA 1990, s 80(3), appeal to the justices within a period of 21 days beginning with the date of service of the notice. Schedule 3 to the EPA 1990 enables regulations to be made concerning such appeals. The Statutory Nuisance (Appeals) Regulations SI 1995/2644, provide in reg 2 as grounds of appeal that: the abatement notice was not justified; there has been an

---

15 *R v Secretary of State for the Environment, ex p Watney Mann (Midlands) Ltd* [1976] JPL 368.
16 *Strathclyde Regional Council v Tudhope* [1983] JPL 536.
17 *Network Housing Association v Westminster City Council* (1994) 27 HLR 189.
18 *Brighton and Hove Council v Ocean Coachworks (Brighton) Ltd* [2000] All ER (D) 521.
19 *Myatt v Teignbridge District Council* [1994] Env LR D18.
20 *Lowe v South Somerset District Council* (1997) LGR 487.
21 *Camden London Borough Council v London Underground Ltd* [1999] All ER (D) 1439.
22 *R v Falmouth and Truro Port Health Authority, ex p South West Water Ltd* [2001] QB 445, [2000] All ER (D) 429.
23 *Pollway Nominees Ltd v Havering London Borough Council* (1989) 21 HLR 462, and *Camden London Borough Council v Gunby* [1999] 4 All ER 602.

informality, defect or error in, or in connection with the notice, or with any copy of a notice served under the EPA 1990, s 80A(3); the authority has unreasonably refused compliance with alternative requirements, or the notice's requirements are otherwise unreasonable in character or extent or unnecessary; a reasonable amount of time has not been specified for compliance; the best practicable means defence applies (see further below); the notice should have been served on some other person as the person responsible for the nuisance, or, in structural defect cases, as the owner of the premises, or as the owner of premises where the person responsible cannot be found, or it might lawfully have been served on someone else as an occupier of the premises in question or as their owner and it is equitable for the notice to be so served, or on someone else in addition to the appellant as a person responsible, or as an owner or occupier of the premises, etc. Other grounds of appeal apply in respect of noise nuisances, see further chapter 18 below.

Where an appeal is made on the basis of informality, defect or error in a notice, or a copy thereof as the case may be, the court is to dismiss the appeal where satisfied that the informality is not material. Otherwise the court has a wide discretion to quash the notice, vary the notice as it thinks fit, but only in the appellant's favour, or dismiss the appeal. However, the court must consider whether the notice was justified as at the date of service, not the date of the hearing.[24] The court may make any order with regard to the person by whom work is to be executed or who is to contribute towards that work, or as to the proportions in which expenses recovered by an authority which has done work are to be borne by the appellant and other persons. In such cases the court is to take into account the terms of any tenancy existing between the owner and occupier of any premises, and whether, in a case where the ground of appeal is that the notice might lawfully have been served on some person other than the appellant, or in addition to the appellant, that other person has received a copy of the notice of appeal as if required under the regulations.

Where an appeal is made and compliance with the notice would involve any person in expenditure on carrying out works before the appeal is heard, the notice is suspended by the appeal until it has either been abandoned or decided. However, where the nuisance in question is one which is injurious to health, or is likely to be of limited duration so that the notice's efficacy would be rendered nugatory by suspension, or the expenditure referred to above would not be disproportionate to the public benefit to be expected pending the determination of the appeal in consequence of compliance, suspension may be avoided. The abatement notice *must* include a statement, eg that the nuisance is injurious to health. In such a case the notice has effect notwithstanding the appeal. The statement must also be specific as to the ground on which it is based.

It is a defence in respect of statutory nuisance proceedings to show that the 'best practicable means' (bpm) were used to prevent or counteract the effects of the nuisance. This defence is *not* available in respect of nuisances comprised of fumes or gases emitted from premises, nor in respect of smoke nuisances *unless* the smoke is emitted from a chimney, nor in respect of nuisances comprising premises, dust, steam, smell or effluvia, accumulations and deposits, animals or noise, *except* where the nuisance arises on industrial trade or business premises. Following *Scholefield v Schunck*[25] it seems that 'bpm' means those means that are the best available to secure the end in view, and not merely those ordinarily accepted in the trade in question. However, in *National Smokeless Fuels v Perriman*,[26] an industrial tribunal case on similar wording under the Alkali, &c, Works Regulation Act 1906 and the Health and Safety at Work etc Act

---

24   *Surrey Free Inns plc v Gosport Borough Council* (1998) 96 LGR 369.
25   (1855) 19 JP 84.
26   (1987) 1 Environmental Law No 2 p 5.

1974, it was indicated that not only technical factors should be taken into account in deciding whether bpm has been used, but also social and economic factors such as working agreements made with trades unions, and the cost, excessive or otherwise, of introducing abating technology. However, mere lack of finance on the part of the party served is no reason for setting aside a notice,[27] as neither is increased expenditure or the resulting unprofitability of an activity,[28] and see the EPA 1990, s 79(9).

It is a defence to a prosecution under the EPA, s 80 to show that there was a 'reasonable excuse': see s 80(4). If evidence of such an excuse is put forward by the defence it is for the prosecution to disprove it according to the criminal burden of proof.[29]

Taking of action in respect of statutory nuisances by private citizens

The majority of statutory nuisances are dealt with by local authorities but an individual wishing to proceed may rely on the EPA 1990, s 82. This provides that the magistrates may act on a complaint made by a 'person aggrieved', and where they are convinced the alleged nuisance *exists, or is likely to recur*, they may require the defendant to abate the nuisance, and execute any necessary works, and may further prohibit a recurrence of the nuisance. Where a recurrence is forbidden there is no need to state a specific compliance date.[30] The magistrates may also fine the defendant and have powers to direct the local authority to institute abatement measures where the defendant defaults: see the EPA 1990, s 82(1) and (3). Indeed the court has no option but to make the relevant order against the defendant once convinced under the EPA 1990, s 82(2), that a statutory nuisance exists or is likely to recur, *but* the court does have considerable discretion as to the content of the order, and should not require the doing of excessive works, merely those needed to abate the nuisance. As with local authority proceedings it is the person responsible for the nuisance who is generally to be proceeded against, though where the nuisance is of a structural character, or where the 'person responsible' cannot be found, it is the owner of the premises who will be liable. Before complaining to the magistrates, however, the person aggrieved must give the potential defendant written notice of intention to commence proceedings, specifying the matter complained of. In the case of alleged noise nuisances three days' notice must be given, in all other cases not less than 21 days' notice is required, see the EPA 1990, s 82(6) and (7). Such a notice is *not* the equivalent of an abatement notice, and does not have to state formally whether the recipient will be proceeded against as either 'owner' or 'person responsible'. However, the notice must specify the matter complained of, so that the recipient has a chance to remedy the situation. The courts are unwilling, however, to tie up this 'citizens' remedy' in too much red tape and technicality, for example niceties as to place of service of the notice.[31]

Where the magistrates make an order, it is an offence to contravene it, though where proceedings are commenced 'bpm' may be available as a defence in the case of premises, dust, steam, smell, effluvia, accumulations, deposits, or noise constituting a nuisance *provided* the nuisance arises on industrial, trade or business premises. It may also be available in respect of smoke nuisances where the smoke is emitted from a chimney.

27 *Saddleworth UDC v Aggregate and Sand Ltd* (1970) 114 Sol Jo 931.
28 *Wivenhoe Port Ltd v Colchester Borough Council* [1985] JPL 175 and 396.
29 *Polychronakis v Richards and Jerrom Ltd* [1998] Env LR 347.
30 *R v Tunbridge Wells Justices, ex p Tunbridge Wells Borough Council* (1995) 160 JP 574.
31 *East Staffordshire Borough Council v Fairless* (1998) 31 HLR 677, *Pearshouse v Birmingham City Council* (1998) 31 HLR 756, *Hewlings v McLean Homes East Anglian Ltd* [2001] 2 All ER 281, and *Hall v Kingston upon Hill City Council* [1999] 2 All ER 609.

Where on the hearing of proceedings in respect of an alleged nuisance it is shown that the nuisance did exist when the initial complaint was made, then, irrespective of whether it still exists or is likely to recur at the date of the hearing, the court *must* order the defendant to compensate the complainant for expenses incurred in bringing the proceedings, see the EPA 1990, s 82(12), though they have a discretion as to the amount of compensation, which must be 'reasonably sufficient' to compensate for expenditure incurred in bringing the action.[32] Compensation *may* also be ordered under the Powers of Criminal Courts Act 1973, s 35, though this is unlikely to be a substantial sum unlike damages in a Civil action.[33] Orders made must be clear and precise.

Proceedings may, as has been stated, be commenced by a person aggrieved. This would include anyone whose health had been injured or threatened by the nuisance, or whose premises had been deleteriously affected.[34] Whether a trespasser could take action remains an open point, see *Coventry City Council v Cartwright.*[35] The EPA 1990, s 82 proceedings can, however, only be taken where a nuisance *exists*, while local authorities may, under s 80, take action in respect of *threatened* nuisances. It should further be noted that the proceedings are criminal in nature, with the appropriate burden of proof.[36]

It is clear that a local authority may be proceeded against under this provision. In *Scarborough Corpn v Rural Sanitary Authority of Scarborough Poor Law Union,*[37] an order was made against the Corporation for having created a nuisance by collecting refuse, manure, cinders, etc, and depositing the same in a dump whence farmers could take the matter for their land. Also in *R v Epping (Waltham Abbey) Justices, ex p Burlinson,*[38] it was held that a private citizen can proceed against a defaulting authority.

Further reading

Each chapter will end with a list of further reading. General reference should be made to the periodical literature contained in:
The Journal of Planning and Environment Law (Sweet and Maxwell);
The Journal of Environmental Law (OUP);
Environmental Liability (Lawtext Publishing Ltd);
Environmental Law and Management (Lawtext Publishing Ltd);
Water Law (Lawtext Publishing Ltd);
Environmental Data Services (ENDS) Report (Environmental Data Services Ltd).

HISTORY AND DEVELOPMENT OF THE LAW
Bell, C and R, City Fathers: The Early History of Town Planning in Britain (1972) Penguin Books.
Cullingworth, JB, Town and Country Planning in Britain (13th Ed) Routledge.

32   *Hollis v Dudley Borough Council* [1998] 1 All ER 759, [1999] 1 WLR 642; *Davenport v Walsall Metropolitan Borough Council* (1995) 28 HLR 754; *R v Southend Stipendary Magistrate, ex p Rochford District Council* [1994] Env LR D15; *Taylor v Walsall and District Property and Investment Co Ltd* (1998) 30 HLR 1062.
33   *Herbert v Lambeth London Borough Council* (1991) 24 HLR 299; *R v Liverpool Crown Court, ex p Cooke* [1996] 4 All ER 589, [1997] 1 WLR 700.
34   *Sandwell Metropolitan Borough Council v Bujok* [1990] 3 All ER 385.
35   [1975] 2 All ER 99, [1975] 1 WLR 845.
36   *Botross v Hammersmith and Fulham London Borough Council* (1994) 27 HLR 179. This is so even in relation to noise nuisances it appears: *Lewisham London Borough v Fenner* [1996] 8 ELM 11 (Knightsbridge Crown Court).
37   (1876) 1 Ex D 344.
38   [1948] 1 KB 79, [1947] 2 All ER 537.

Finn, MW, (Ed) The Medical and Legal Aspects of Sanitary Reform (Alexander P Stewart and Edward Jenlaus) (1969) Leicester University Press.

THE CURRENT LAW OF STATUTORY NUISANCES

Reference should be made to the Encyclopaedia of Environmental Health Law and Practice, and the Companion series of Environmental Health Law Reports, both published by Sweet and Maxwell.

Chapter 2

The ethical basis of environmental law and its principles

The roots of environmental regulation in the United Kingdom lie in planning law, whose task is to provide a framework for the orderly management of the changing use of land, and in public (or environmental) health law which is virtually exclusively concerned with protection of human beings. Over the last decade and half these roots have become entwined with the growth of ideas – often emanating from Brussels – that the environment itself is deserving of protection, and indeed the Environmental Protection Act 1990 was specifically declared to be a measure to protect the environmental media of land, air and water in addition to human health.

But does it matter whether the rules of environmental law reflect underlying principles and, ultimately, moral concerns? The answer must be 'yes', for without some basis in principle individual laws are no more than mere reactions to individual perceived problems lacking coherence, and likely to result in anomalies.

The search for a moral basis for the law

It is tempting to think of the law as being based on principles which are themselves derived from moral precepts: tempting, but unsatisfactory, for what may be morally desirable is often not translated into law. A rather better way of thinking is that laws, principles and moral precepts do not exist as a hierarchy, but interact fluidly. Even this model, however, assumes that this is a moral basis for the law – is that justified?

Our world is diversely plural with regard to religious, political and economic systems. We can identify a whole range of perceptions of the environment each one of which is affected by, and in turn reflects, moral concerns. These range from intense utilitarianism through to the polar opposite of deep ecology. These moral positions can be variously classified. Alder and Wilkinson in *Environmental Law and Ethics* (to which indebtedness is acknowledged and to which interested readers are referred) identify the following: anthropocentrism (ie human-centred), enlightened anthropocentrism, extended anthropocentrism, non-anthropocentric individualism, concern for animal welfare, biocentrism, ecocentrism, land ethics, and deep ecology. However, it is possible in this spectrum to find a number of 'staging posts' as Professor Kerry Turner found in *Blueprint 2* (1991), chapter 11.

Human-centred (anthropocentric) utilitarianism is the least environmentally concerned moral viewpoint. It stresses achieving the greatest happiness of the greatest number of humans – tending to define them as those who are currently alive. Those adhering to this point of view are usually economic liberals who are desirous of economic growth within an unfettered free market. The world is seen as an instrument which exists for the benefit of humans, and they are best served by the creation of wealth which will lift them out of poverty, ignorance and want. Human activity, on this view, should be restrained only where positive harm to other humans can be shown to flow from that activity.

Somewhat related to this position is that of stewardship which, while primarily anthropocentric, accepts the need for a degree of resource conservation and environmental management based on notions of sustainable development and intergenerational equity (see further below). However, this position is resistant towards according a moral significance to non-human entities – they receive protection only a consequence of the need to preserve resources for future human generations. Biocentrism is concerned also with resource conservation, but moves away from anthropocentrism towards more holistic patterns of thinking, adopting restrictive attitudes towards economic growth, and eroding moral distinctions between humans and the rest of the ecosystem. Animals and plants can be seen as having rights – often with the collective interests of all biota being given preference over the individual interests of species and individual specimens. Finally there is 'deep ecology', the most holistic and preservationist position, opposed to economic growth, favouring reduced use of natural resources and human populations. The natural world is seen as having its own absolute intrinsic value, irrespective of human experience, with all parts of the ecosystem – whether biotic (eg plants) or abiotic (eg geological features) having 'rights' – though what those 'rights' could be is the subject of great uncertainty.

Inevitably the foregoing descriptions are something of a caricature which do violence to the subtlety of the various groups of opinions and arguments, and many people would not claim to adhere exclusively to one point of view, for moral perceptions can be eclectic. Nevertheless those four 'staging posts' do represent broadly recognisable and widely held points of view and moral perceptions with regard to the environment, and thus it appears fruitless to search for a single, unified, morally imperative basis for the law. However, even if there were to be universal agreement on the moral desirability of doing (or not doing) something that would not automatically represent the legal position. Law and morality are different entities and simply because a matter is something that is regarded as generally morally desirable does not mean that it will be translated into law. So far as the environment is concerned moral desirables are only likely to become legal actualities where there is (a) a generally agreed social, political and scientific perception of the existence of a problem, (b) traceability of that problem to a particular cause, (c) an economic justification for taking action and (d) a sufficient body of social and political feeling that action should be taken. Moral issues thus play an important, but by no means decisive, part in the creation and formulation of the law (and also its implementation and application – see further chapter 3). Furthermore it is important to remember, as Professor Merills pointed out in his chapter in Boyle and Anderson's collection of essays *Human Rights Approaches to Environmental Protection* (1996) OUP, that not only must legal rights and moral rights be kept conceptually apart, it is also as important to separate moral rights and moral preferences, for the latter can vary, as we have seen, from individual to individual with little consensus. Where individuals choose to take their morally preferred stand on environmental issues will depend on a whole range of issues – educational, experiential, instructional emotional and personal. Thus while Dobson in *Green Political Thought* (1990) Harper Collins, argues for a consensus of radical, ecological and feminist thinking as *the* acceptable basis for environmental protection, Allison in *Ecology and Utility* (1991) Leicester University Press, denounced environmental radicalism as 'fanatical' and 'the revenge of the unhappy ... premised on a hatred of life and driven by malice'.

Many people find stewardship notions to be an acceptable moral basis for environmental protection and regulation. This recognises that human beings as purposive, self-aware creatures have during our comparatively short time on this planet developed a collective power to alter it drastically and dramatically in a way other living things cannot. To that extent we are separate from the rest of the natural order, and, as Alder and Wilkinson argue, our ethics can:

> 'only be human centred ... the concept of nature's rights is no more than a fiction, although as such it may be very useful. Many anthropocentric values are capable of being elaborated in ways which benefit environmental protection, although these may ultimately result only in the protection of aspects of the environment that are considered important for human well being.'

The attractions of this position cannot be denied. It is quite easy for people to conceive of themselves as part of a generational matrix extending backwards and forwards in time – from grandparents through to grandchildren. The 'here and now' thus takes on a past and future significance – we can have both in reasonable contemplation. From there it is but an apparently small step for lawyers, at least, to accept that there is a degree of reasonable foresight involved – albeit in a temporal as opposed to the spatial mode more usually encountered. If future generations – as opposed to future individuals – lie within our reasonable foresight, is not that a basis for arguing we might owe them some sort of duty? Quite what the content of that duty could be and how it would translate into law are matters of uncertainty, but that does not invalidate the basic argument which can be used to ground an argument for the existence of duties between human generations.

Before, however, concluding consideration of this matter (at least for a while for it will be returned to in chapter 5 when human rights and the environment are dealt with) it has to be said that not all commentators accept the inevitability of an anthropocentric environmental morality. In her contribution to *Human Rights Approaches to Environmental Protection* Catherine Redgwell ('Life, The Universe and Everything: A Critique of Anthropocentric Rights') argued that the moral basis for environmental law need not be exclusively human-centred, and that there can be *additional* moral underpinnings based on recognising that other biotic and abiotic entities have a degree of moral status. This may come about because, for example, we recognise that status as being as inherent as our own, arising from the simple fact that we all share a common existence, or may be because some religious impulse forces the conclusion that everything shares in the status of being created. Such a broadening out of the law's moral base does *not* determine what the law's content should be, nor does it provide an easy answer when questions of conflict arise between the various entities recognised as being morally 'considerable'. But it gives those who wish to extend the law's realm (both as to coverage *and* application) a greater range of *reasons why* action should be taken. This is important because moral choices on environmental issues are rarely between the clearly good and the clearly bad – they are usually between conflicting 'goods' – ease of individual transport and freedom of movement for example versus the pollution that possession of motor cars causes.

Nowadays we may therefore find an appeal to the wider moral worthiness of the environment in documents making declarations of rights. The UN report 'Human Rights and the Environment' (The Ksentini Report 1994) while accepting that environmental protection is consequential on the protection of human rights, nevertheless appears to presuppose that the environment has a degree of moral worth in its principles 19 and 21 which declares the right – and indeed the *duty* – of persons individually and collectively to protect and preserve the environment. The draft International Covenant on Environment and Development (IUCN, 1995) went further and declared 'humanity is part of nature' and that 'nature as a whole warrants respect ... peace, development, environmental protection and respect for human rights and fundamental freedoms are interdependent ...'. Thus while life for humans without rights is intolerable, rights alone in the abstract are meaningless without a life enabling them to be enjoyed, and what life can there be if the resource base upon which it all depends is degraded and destroyed? Thus while we may find Alder and Wilkinson's arguments very attractive, along with Redgwell we may find our anthropocentric views either modified, or at least supplemented, by an acknowledgment that all that which exists beyond humanity has a claim to consideration when we are making and applying the law.

From morality to legal principle

If there is no one single moral basis on which environment law rests but rather a number, can we nevertheless discern fundamental principles which, while not law in themselves, nevertheless serve to underpin and guide the development and application of rules of law? The answer is yes, and to these attention must now turn.

   These principles are: *sustainable development*, *the precautionary principle*, and *the 'polluter pays' principle*. These are supplemented by a number of subsidiary principles to be considered in due course.

Sustainable development

The development of an idea

Humanity's numbers, styles of living and needs for adequate provision of food, shelter, employment, recreation, and that elusive concept 'quality of life', have to be considered globally, not in isolation, *and* in relation to the ability of the planet and its atmosphere to meet the demands made upon it. In this context there emerges the concept of 'sustainable development'. Many argue that while the world's population cannot continue to grow without unacceptable consequences for wildlife, urban congestion, pollution and energy and other resource demands, it is neither possible nor desirable to argue that economic growth must cease. If it did there would be disastrous consequences for the poorest nations of the world. *The World Conservation Strategy* (IUCN 1980) argued that: 'development and conservation are equally necessary for our survival' and the report of the World Commission on Environment and Development (Brundtland Commission), *Our Common Future* (1987) argued that sustainable development means global economic development sufficient to meet current needs while allowing future generations to achieve their needs: what is done now should not prevent future generations from pursuing their legitimate options. So, for example, where natural resources are used now there should be a compensating creation of some other form of asset – perhaps intellectual or technical – sufficient to enable future generations to have the same standard of living currently derived from the use of natural resources. Where an irreplaceable asset would be used up by an activity, sustainable development requires that activity's cessation.

The relationship with environmental economics

Lawyers and economists have given considerable thought to the evolution of the concept of sustainable development within the context of their own disciplines. In a book devoted to law it is not possible to do full justice to the very considerable development of economic thinking, and the interested reader must be referred to *Blueprint for a Green Economy* (Pearce, Markandya and Barbier, to whose work the author acknowledges his indebtedness). However, in the hope that for once a little knowledge will *not* be a dangerous thing, the following outline may be helpful. Economic thinking stresses the following issues:

1 Sustainable development is a concept of rising real incomes coupled with increases in educational standards, the enhanced health of individuals and communities and improvements in the general quality of life.

2 It involves placing a substantial value on the environment, natural, built and cultural, and the realisation that environmental resources are not 'free', ie they are not 'there for the taking'.

3 The concept involves planning and forecasting over both the medium (5–10 years) and long term (30–60 years) timescales, while future disbenefits will *not* be discounted as 'too remote to consider'.

4 It stresses that those who are least advantaged in society should have provision made for their needs (the 'intra-generational principle'), and that there should be fair treatment for future generations (the 'intergenerational principle').

5 In sum, the concept is based on three key ideas, namely, '*environment, futurity and equity*'. This means that 'future generations should be compensated for reductions in the endowments of resources brought about by the actions of present generations.' (*Blueprint for a Green Economy*, p 3.)

6 Sustainable development accepts that it is not possible to separate economic activity from the human environment, and argues that simply because the environment provides us with resources such as the ozone layer which have no market place in which they are traded, this does not mean that those resources are free. If those resources are used up by the current generation then future generations will have been permanently impoverished.

7 Sustainable development embraces an anticipatory approach to environmental issues under which an attempt is made to determine the likely nature and cost of environmental problems in advance of their occurrence, so that appropriate measures can be taken to prevent the impoverishment of the future. This predicates a 'precautionary principle' (see further below) being an integral feature of all projects.

8 The concept does not pit 'growth' against 'environment', but rather accepts that in some cases environmental protection and conservation can promote growth in the economy, and also stresses that the real issue is *not* 'growth or no growth', but *how* growth is to be attained. In particular instances this may mean trading off environmental quality for growth, but only after a fully informed decision of the true environmental costs has been made; in other cases growth will be sacrificed in favour of environmental quality.

9 Sustainable development involves taking a broad view of development that values the well being of individuals, their freedom and self respect, and stresses co-operation.

10 There is room within the overall concept for debate as to how intergenerational equity may be achieved. Some argue that future generations should be left with the same amount of 'capital wealth' (eg goods and facilities created by humankind together with human intelligence) as that which the current generation holds. Others argue that they should be left an equal stock of environmental capital (eg water, land and air) as that currently enjoyed. The distinction between the two views is that, under the former, environmental quality and resources may be sacrificed provided there is a commensurate return of capital wealth, while the latter view

inclines against such trade-offs. Overall it appears that the balance of the argument favours the view that 'the stock of environmental assets as a whole should not decrease' (*Blueprint for a Green Economy*, p 48), and that there is a notion of 'critical environmental capital' which should not be depleted, ie critical natural assets such as species, resources and habitats.

Further legal development

In the wake of the Brundtland Commission, the experts' group on environmental law of the World Commission on Environment and Development, in *Environmental Protection and Sustainable Development*, set down certain general principles with regard to rights and obligations relating to environmental resources and interests. In some cases these mirror the thinking of economists outlined above.

1   There is a human right to have an environment adequate to support life and well being.
2   Nations should adopt principles of intergenerational equity in the use of the environment and its national resources.
3   There is a principle of conservation, ie the management of use of the environment and its resources so as to give the greatest sustainable benefit to the current generation while maintaining the ability of the resource base to meet the needs of future generations. In this context 'conservation' subsumes notions of 'preservation', 'maintenance', 'utilisation', 'restoration' and 'enhancement'. This principle should be an integral part of planning processes.
4   The essential ecosystems and ecological processes of the biosphere should be subject to conservation, and the need to preserve biological diversity.
5   Nations should adopt adequate standards of environmental protection, and should monitor changes in the quality and use of environmental resources, publishing relevant data obtained.
6   Where an activity may result in significant impact on the environment or use of its resources, that activity should be subject to *environmental assessment* of its effects before a decision is taken as to whether it should be allowed to proceed, and *environmental impact assessment* of its subsequent effects.
7   Those likely to be affected by activities of the foregoing kind should be informed of the issue in good time and given access to any relevant administrative or judicial proceedings.
8   Nations should co-operate in promoting the concept of sustainable development, and those nations which are more developed should assist those which are still developing.
9   Where natural resources traverse national boundaries (as, for example, does the atmosphere) they should be used by nations in a reasonable and equitable way, while nations should generally prevent environmental interferences from causing significant transboundary harm.

Sustainable development, particularly where it is broadly defined to include decisions on resource allocation and requirements that any changes and developments should not have an adverse effect on human health, is undoubtedly the basic principle of environmental law. But too much should not be read into that. It is easy to say that we should act to meet the needs of the present generation without compromising the ability of future generations to meet their needs – but what does that actually mean? In itself the principle states the problem, it does not solve it, and in any case what is meant by 'needs' – are they not too easily confused with 'wants'? Most people would accept the argument that both the present generation and its successors have a claim to live in an environment that is capable of sustaining an acceptable quality of life, but that does not bring us closer to reconciling the claims of the present with those of the future, nor does it show us the means of doing so.

How might sustainability as a notion further express itself?

A number of applications of sustainability *could* be developed, for example:
1   Non-irreveresability – as little as possible should be done that is not reversible.
2   Substitutionality – resources should be so used and developed so that substitutes can be found for them, while less or non-polluting technologies and uses of resources should be substituted for the more polluting consumptive ones.
3   Replaceability – resources should be used on the basis of their equivalent replacement.
4   Recyclability – material should be so used as to be capable of reuse over again, but not just in a 'cradle to grave' sense, ie creation to disposal, but rather in the sense of 'conception to resurrection' so that where materials are used that is done in a way that ensures their ability to be reused over and over again.

For the future?

As pointers to the future development of the law, the attention of readers is drawn to a work by Decleris, *The Law of Sustainable Development: General Principles*, to which indebtedness is acknowledged.

Decleris identifies 'sustainability' not just as a principle of environmental law, but also as a basic principle of justice within society and between states. It calls for whole new ways of decision-taking requiring a greater flow of information so that all participants in society can take a responsible part in decision taking (see also chapter 5), relying on popular participation and ensuring greater transparency in decision-taking and accountability for decisions. He sees the role of the state as being the strategic controller and supervisor of a system of 'public environmental order' in which all individuals, groups and institutions in society *collaborate* in achieving sustainable development. In this context, however, every state would need to produce its own 'national strategic plan for sustainable development', in which all public policies should converge towards sustainable development – and this must operate within the context of each state's international obligations. In addition Declaris identifies the need for the 'finite capacity' and 'finite tolerance' of ecosystems to be accepted as a fundamental principle by which to judge proposals for human developments and projects. Thus: 'the construction and management of man-made systems must not transcend their own carrying capacity or that of the ecosystems (land or water based or marine) influenced by them'. He points out, however, that natural systems have a degree of elasticity and 'resilience', and thus humanity can continue to change and develop new ideas – but only up to the limit of the carrying capacity of the natural world. This leads Decleris to go on to say, as an application of sustainable development, that where ecosystems have been destroyed and the essential equilibrium between humanity and the rest of the natural world has been disturbed, restorative action should take place where this is physically possible. He also lays stress on the need to preserve biodiversity of animals, plants, etc, as 'the greater an ecosystem's biodiversity, the greater is its stability'.

As an example of the finite capacity of an ecosystem we may think of fish stocks. According to the Decleris view – and indeed the rapidly emerging theory and practice of international fishery conservation law – fish stocks must not be exploited beyond their capacity to recover. In determining what that capacity is, sustainable development thinking would argue that it is not just the effect of over-fishing on a particular fish species that must be resisted, it is the impact that exploitation has on other fish and marine populations – for example predatory fish who themselves depend on the availability of the same threatened fish stocks. Moreover, the limit of exploitation has to be set on a precautionary basis to allow a wide margin of error for recovery – to protect a species there is little point in waiting to take precautionary steps until it is clear beyond any question that the species has gone into irreversible decline.

It is impossible in so short a space as this to do proper justice to Decleris's challenging ideas, though much of what he argues for is, arguably, implicit in the notions of non-irreversibility, substitutionality, replaceability and recyclability outlined above. But it is important to remember that a system of laws that incorporates and applies those values is very different from traditional legal systems which generally favour individual over collective rights and which attribute responsibility generally only after a deleterious activity has occurred and 'the damage has been done'. The entire culture within which law and policy are made has to change, at the international and national level. As Decleris concludes:

> 'It is ... impossible to create the new ethos unless, in parallel, citizens participate in the process of public decision-making. In reality, the development of the new ethos among citizens entails transforming them from selfish individuals lured by hedonistic and utilitarian motives into responsible people who are organically involved in the social and public systems and who play their part with a sense of responsibility and mission.'

Sustainable development may yet, however, become a basic constitutive underpinning for law and policy making, thus acquiring a constitutional significance and enabling courts to interpret, and even modify – perhaps declare invalid – other laws and policies. Decleris sees evidence of this at a European level – a matter to be generally returned to in chapter 4 – though within the United Kingdom it would as yet be hard to agree.

As a further thought on the future role of sustainable development, the arguments of those who see the principle not just as a goal to be achieved by law, but also as a process, should be noted. In the UK much of the thinking on this issue is associated with the work of Professor Richard McRory and his group of environmental scientists and lawyers at Imperial College, London – to whom indebtedness is acknowledged. As a *process* sustainable development is a means of integrating environmental perspectives into economic, political and social policies so that all of these are directed towards, inter alia, the efficient use of resources, the management of demand and the minimisation of environmental impact. The thinking of this group and that of Decleris is, of course, informed by the principles that came out of the Earth Summit Conference at Rio (UNCED) that all those who are affected by environmental decision-taking should be able to participate and that they should have effective remedies and redress for the wrongs they suffer as a result of environmental degradation. This gives sustainable development a procedural aspect, but also reinforces its position as a tool to ensure the rule of law with regard to environmental issues.

The precautionary principle

It is not always possible, and rarely easy, to know what environmental consequences may, at some unknown future date, flow from particular uses of the environment and its resources, or from particular industrial, or agricultural processes, nor the ways in which they may happen. This may be labelled the 'principle of uncertainty,' the law could require:

1　cautious progress until a process/project is judged 'innocent';
2　ordinary progress until findings of 'guilt' are made; or
3　*no* progress until intensive research has been conducted into a proposed process and its innocence has been demonstrated.

It is 3 which represents the strongest formulation of the 'precautionary principle'. It is 2, however, which represents the historic British response to the problem. However, the White Paper, 'This Common Inheritance'[1] now states, at p 11:

> 'Where there are significant risks of damage to the environment, the Government will be prepared to take precautionary action to limit ... use of potentially dangerous pollutants, even where scientific knowledge is not conclusive ... particularly where there are good grounds for judging either that action taken promptly at comparatively low cost may avoid more costly damage later, or that irreversible effects may follow if action is delayed.'

'Sustainable Development: the UK Strategy'[2] repeats this, and further adds from the Rio Declaration of 1992 'where there are threats of serious or irreversible damage, lack of full scientific certainty shall not e used as a reason for postponing cost-effective measures to prevent environmental degradation'. However, the implications of the oblique reference to cost/benefit equations should not be ignored, while Cm 2426 elsewhere states that the government 'remains committed to basing action on fact, not fantasy, using the best scientific information available; precipitate action on the basis of inadequate evidence is the wrong response' (para 3.12).

It is easy for views on the merits/demerits of policies and processes to polarise where there is apparently conflicting data as to consequences: where, for example, a proposal's proponents rely on demand forecasts to support their project. Demand forecasting has a history of unreliability. Likewise predictions as to the consequences of a particular process may have a strong element of subjectivity in them. There may be initial disagreement as to the test parameters to be used in the initial collection of data, and once it has been collected it needs evaluation, and hence a further departure from strict objectivity. If the results obtained indicate a degree of danger flowing from the process it may be felt necessary to build a further safety factor, or margin of error, into any recommendations made as to safety or other applicable standards of regulation. This will be another evaluative step, though it may also be seen as an application of the precautionary principle. These matters were considered by the courts in *R v Secretary of State for Trade and Industry, ex p Duddridge*,[3] a case arising from allegations that the Secretary of State should take precautionary action to prevent risks of childhood leukaemia arising from exposure to electromagnetic fields generated by power cables. Smith J pointed out there is 'no comprehensive and authorative definition of the precautionary principle' but rejected arguments that precautionary action is needed where there is 'evidence of a possible risk even though the scientific evidence is presently unclear and does not prove the casual connection', ie 'where the mere possibility exists of a risk of serious harm to the environment or to human health'. On the contrary, Smith J considered that the government was perfectly entitled to formulate

---

1　Cm 1200.
2　Cm 2426.
3　[1995] 7 JEL 224. On 6 October 1995 the Court of Appeal in a short judgment upheld the Divisional Court's decision.

the much more restricted notion of precautionary action found in C, 1200 which makes the threshold for taking action the perception of a *significant* risk of harm – though it is not clear who must have that perception, the government or some other agency. Where, however, there is a perception of a significant risk then the precautionary principle as enunciated in Cm 1200 will enter into the decision making equation as a relevant factor to be taken into account.

The 'polluter pays' principle

Where a process is found to have unwanted consequences questions arise as to who should 'pay' for them. In some cases it may not be easy to identify a responsible individual and it may be considered to be economically and administratively more efficient in such circumstances to place the responsibility for, and costs of 'clean up' measures, on some other body. This has been true of the water industry where water suppliers have borne the cost of purifying water affected by nitrates, applied by farmers, which have leached into ground and surface waters. It has been thought preferable to impose costs on water suppliers rather than to disrupt food production.

However, the principle usually argued for is, 'the polluter pays', which was developed by the Organisation for Economic Co-operation and Development (OECD) in 1902. This can be a vague notion. Some argue that it is satisfied when a polluter has to meet at least some of the administrative costs of the agencies who regulate polluting activities; an example of this is provided by provisions on administrative costs of regulation originally in the 1990 Act, now the Environment Act 1995. Others argue that it can only be satisfied by polluters having to pay the full reinstatement costs of their activities, while yet others appeal to the principle of legitimising taxation of particular activities to indicate that the use which those activities make of environmental resources is not 'free'. An example of this is provided by the arguments for 'carbon taxes' on the use of fossil fuels which produce atmospheric warming or 'greenhouse gases'. Cm 2426 contents itself with declaring that where 'production processes threaten or cause damage to the environment, the cost of necessary environmental measures should be borne by the producer, and not by society at large ...' (para 3.16).

But is it the polluter pays or the user pays?

However, there is debate whether the 'polluter pays' principle is adequately satisfied if the polluter is allowed simply to treat pollution costs as mere overheads which are then passed on to customers as increased charges. This is a particular problem where a polluter is a large corporate organisation and the 'cost' is in the form of a fine for an offence involving breaches of environmental protection laws. This issue was examined by Professor Fisse in 'Sentencing Options Against Corporations',[4] to which the author acknowledges indebtedness. The problems, as elucidated by Fisse are: historic unwillingness on the part of courts to impose real, deterrent level fines on corporate offenders; the financial inability of some corporations to pay appropriately high fines so that the deterrence value of the fine becomes entirely notional; the fact that fines impinge only on a corporation's money making activities, as opposed to the desires for power, prestige and control, and creative urges which exist within corporations; the argument that fines convey no clear message that a corporate offence is socially intolerable, but may instead indicate that an offence is permissible provided a 'tariff' is

4   [1990] 1 Criminal Law Forum 211.

paid, thus reducing criminal law to an accounting exercise; the fear that fining a corporation may divert attention from those individuals who are responsible for wrongful activities committed in the corporation's name; the argument that, following imposition of fines, there is no guarantee that the corporation will discipline itself, its members and employees to ensure no recurrence of the behaviour in question; the problem of 'spillover' whereby fines may simply be passed on to innocent persons such as shareholders, employees or consumers as opposed to the responsible managers. Against this, however, it may be argued that those who derive benefits from a corporation's activities, either by way of share dividends or remuneration, should bear the financial burdens of any wrongdoing by 'their' corporation.

Fisse goes on to point to alternative sanctions which may be more appropriate: enforced corporate dissolution; disqualification from ability to undertake certain types of work, for example, certain public contract activities; 'stock dilution' whereby a corporation is required to meet fines by issuing new shares equivalent in value to a deterrent level of fine, these shares being vested in some form of compensation fund; corporate probation whereby corporations which have offended are required, under supervision, to investigate and amend the ways which led to the offence – this might extend to requiring a polluter not just to introduce 'state of the art' anti-pollution techniques but also to go further by developing new non-polluting technologies; adverse publicity being given to a corporate offender by order of the court; community service under which, for example, a polluter might be required to set up a charitable or public service institution related to countering pollution, as in *United States v Allied Chemical Corpn*[5] where a company was ordered to set up a charity, the Virginia Environmental Endowment. The application of the 'polluter pays' principle is by no means a straightforward and non-contentious issue, tough it does feature as part of European Union (EU) law.

Best practicable environmental option

BPEO was initially developed as an idea by the Royal Commission on Environmental Pollution in their Fifth Report (Cmnd 6371). They returned to the matter in their 10th and 11th reports (Cmnd 9149 and 9675), defining it as 'the use of different sectors of the environment to minimise damage overall' and finding 'the optimum combination of available methods ... so as to limit damage to the environment to the greatest extent achievable for a reasonable and acceptable total combined cost to industry and the public purse'. While BPEO takes account of local conditions and the current state of knowledge, it also weighs in the balance long term as well as short term issues, so as to produce, as the Royal Commission said in their 12th Report (Cm 310) 'the option that provides the best benefit or least damage to the environment as a whole, at acceptable cost, in the long term as well as in the short term.' BPEO is clearly a concept which links legal and economic thinking, and could be given wide application in environmental law.

A miscellany of principles

1   Action should be taken on the basis of the best scientific data. The exact relationship of this principle with the precautionary principle is somewhat unclear

---

5   420 F Supp 122 (ED Va 1976).

– much depends upon the formulation given to the latter. The principle is enshrined in UK policy by Cm 1200 paras 1.16–1.17.

2   The concept of the 'cradle to grave' duty/life cycle analysis. This requires that the environmental impacts of a product from its initial inception in the gathering of raw materials right through to its final disposal should always be considered. This is an application of sustainable development to which allusion has already been made.

3   The preventive principle/the requirement that harm should be rectified at source. This is encountered in both EC and UK law, see Cm 1200 at para 3.9. The concept of prevention of pollution at source underpins much of UK planning law which seeks to 'plan out' nuisances.

The exact relationship of all the foregoing principles one to another is as yet unclear. If any hierarchy exists in them it must surely be that sustainable development must be the first and greatest principle and that all others should serve that end.

There are, however, at a perhaps more mundane level principles which are relevant to the setting of individual environmental standards. Where the law imposes standards of environmental regulation there is debate over what the type of standard should be, and the parameters of any tests carried out there-under to determine whether compliance is taking place. The various types of standard include:

1   *Absolute prohibition* of a particular activity.

2   *Specification standards* which attempt to prevent harm by means of specified design, construction and use matters.

3   *Emission standards* numerically laying down fixed upper limits for emissions from relevant processes – sometimes known as 'Uniform Emission Standards' where applied to *all* relevant discharges, or 'Local Emission Standards' where they may vary from place to place.

4   *Ambient standards* requiring regulatory agencies to apply controls so that the maximum permitted concentration of a pollutant at any given place and time is not exceeded by the aggregate of emissions of relevant local processes.

5   *Receptor standards* specifying control on a process when a particular level of damage in a receiving medium is perceived.

6   *Quality standards or objectives* whereunder a particular quality (the quality objective) goal is set for an environmental medium, usually to make it suitable for a defined use, and processes must be modified or eradicated so as not to ensure diminution of that standard, while a quality standard follows and fixes, numerically, the concentration of particular allowable substances in the medium, irrespective of source, which may not be transgressed if the quality objective is to be maintained.

7   *Managerial or licensing standards* whereunder whether or not to allow a particular activity, or level of activity, in a location is left to the discretion of some authorising agency, usually acting according to published guidelines or policies; planning law is a regulator of this type.

8   *Limit values* whereby a maximum permitted limit for discharge of an emission is set numerically, a term used in EU law.

Confusion arises where 'emission standards' and 'limit values' are used as interchangeable terms. In EC law 'limit value' is a Community Maximum Standard, while states are sometimes free to fix their own stricter emission standards. Likewise 'quality objective' sometimes subsumes 'quality standard'. It is quite clear that there are 'families' of standards. Some require operators to achieve emission levels which regulators consider to be both low *and* reasonable. 'As low as reasonably achievable' (ALARA) is a standard sometimes found in UK practice. Its 'close cousin' in US practice is the requirement that operators should use 'reasonably achievable control technology' (RACT). Another 'relative' is the old standard of requiring use of 'best practicable means' (BPM). Each of these allows some debate between operators and regulators. Another 'family' of standards requires emissions to be 'as low as technically achievable' (ALATA) whose transatlantic counterpart is use of 'maximum achievable control technology' (MACT) and whose other 'relatives' include requirements to use 'best available techniques (originally technologies) not entailing excessive costs' (BATNEEC). Under these standards there is an obligation always to use 'state of the art' control technologies and to upgrade systems and performances in line with new developments.

The problem of choosing an appropriate standard is compounded where there is no consensus on the desirability of regulation. Generally speaking, to be successful an environmental measure to counter a hazard needs: agreed perception of a hazard, its nature, quality and consequences; a body of supportive scientific evidence detailing the issues; an available corrective technology, technique or substitute process or product; and a convergence of interest between 'the public' and 'the polluter' so that it makes economic and social sense to eradicate the hazard and for any enhanced costs flowing therefrom to be borne. Where these requirements are not met some element of compromise will exist in relation to the regulatory measure, very often reflected in its form. This may result in the measure being broadly managerial in character and discretionary in operation. Great use in such circumstances may be made of educative or exhortatory styles of regulation as opposed to strictly sanctioning approaches, and much will depend upon the ethical perceptions and professional codes of values of the regulators, as well as the moral perception of issues by 'polluters' and 'public' alike. This brings us to the issue of whether law and principles are underpinned by a deeper ethical or moral foundation.

THE CURRENT LEGAL AND POLICY POSITION OF THE UK

In the United Kingdom much of the present law concerning the environment reflects, as has been seen above, long development and the influence of historical forms of regulation. There is no reason to suppose that the influence of history will dissipate rapidly; see Cm 1200, p 272 on the likely continuance of 'flexible' administrative modes of regulation while the same document at p 10 broadly accepts the need for the law to reflect stewardship concepts examined above. UK law has traditionally stressed the need to reconcile conflicts between various users of the environment, with the environment itself being passive in the process; its approach has thus been one of conflict mediation and *environmental management*. Though a move towards a philosophy of *environmental protection* can be seen, UK law is still very far from regarding the environment as having inherent rights. The common law tradition vests rights in persons, not in things or animals, and certainly not in landscapes or water, etc. It may be, however, that notions of 'rights of the environment' will have to be developed, even if the vindication of such rights is entrusted to some person or body such as an environmental trustee, commissioner or ombudsman, or some form of environmental protection agency or service. Equally it is important to remember the 'Hawkins Principle' (so named after Richard Hawkins, a founder member of the United Kingdom Environmental Law Association and a tireless campaigner on the issue) that a legal evil occurs when there is 'over regulation and under enforcement'. This will arise in situations where enforcement agencies are under resourced or where the law is unclear, or where there are too many strands of regulation, or where an inapposite form of regulation has been chosen, or where regulators do not feel ethically justified in enforcing the law.

The law/economics/policy interface

The law must not only be well founded in terms of principles, however. There must be harmonisation between legal and economic means of regulation.

Governmental moves in this direction were presaged in the White Paper Cm 1200 where, at p 8, it was accepted that : 'government needs to ensure that its policies fit together in every sector, that we are not undoing in one area what we are trying to do in another; and that policies are based on an harmonious set of principles rather than a clutter of expedients.'

Certainly both legal and economic or fiscal means of environmental regulation need to be harmonised to a greater extent than is currently so, and innovatory means of regulation developed. Appendix A of Cm 1200 provided examples of such forms of regulation, for example administrative charge recovery schemes; levies on particular industries or products to finance particular pollution control measures; pollution charges directly related to the burden on the environment of a particular activity or product; the use of subsidies, grants and schemes of public compensation to induce changes in particular activities. However, such 'economic instruments' may only work well where the cost imposed on a polluting activity is clearly appreciated by all concerned, and where the incentive or penalty, as the case may be, is very accurately targeted. Where an extra charge can simply be lost amongst many cost factors, the position may be otherwise. Thus in 1992 the European Commission proposed a punitive energy tax adding 14 pence to the price of a gallon of fuel by 2000 in order to drive down fuel consumption and cut CO_2 emissions, while in 1993 the UK government achieved more than that increase in a single budget, coupled with the yearly promise of rises in fuel duties by 3% pa in real terms as part of the same strategy. Some, however, have seen that as *more* a means of raising finance for government spending and *less* a means of environmental protection, and indeed in comparison to some of our European partners our systems of direct taxation appear but little developed with regard to encouraging environmental protection.

This is not to say that the UK, along with other nations, is making no use of taxation as an environmental protection measure. As from 1999 that has been a feature of government policy, especially as represented by the Finance Act 2000. This introduced:

- an industrial energy tax (the climate change levy) which aims to encourage renewable energy production and the efficient use of energy where 'heavy' users sign up to meet particular targets by the granting of tax reliefs;
- tax relief on the use of ultra low sulphur petrol;
- lower vehicle excise duties for fuel efficient cars;
- changes to the taxation of company cars from April 2002 so taxes increase in line with CO_2 emissions;
- enhancement of the existing landfill tax system introduced in 1996 (see generally chapter 14) to encourage minimisation and recycling of waste;
- levies on aggregate extraction (see generally chapter 13) from 2002.

While it is not appropriate here to examine the pros and cons of such policies, what is important is acceptance that legal regulation by itself is an insufficient means of environmental protection. 'Command and control' strategies of regulation must be integrated with economic instruments.

Further reading

FUTURE DEVELOPMENTS

Bateman, I, 'Social discounting, monetary evaluation and practical sustainability' (1991) 60 Town and Country Planning (6) 174.

Cairncross, F, *Costing the Earth* (1991) Business Books Ltd.

Decleris, M, *The Law of Sustainable Development: General Principles* (2000) European Communities.

Fairley, R, 'Environmental Policy and Audit – What's in it for us?' [1995] 7 Environmental Law and Management 31.

Fisse, B, 'Sentencing Options against Corporations' (1990) 1 Criminal Law Forum 211.

Franklin, D, Hawke, N, and Lowe, M, *Pollution in the UK* (1995) Sweet & Maxwell, chapters 1, 2 and 8.

Kerry Turner, R, Pearce, D, and Bateman, I, *Environmental Economics* (1994) Harvester Wheatsheaf.

Kramer, L, 'The Open Society, its Lawyers and its Environment' (1989) 1 Journal of Environmental Law 1.

Lammers, JG (et al), *Environmental Protection and Sustainable Development: Legal Principles and Recommendations* (1987) Graham and Trotman.

Pearce, D, Markandya, A, and Barbier EB, *Blueprint for a Green Economy* (1989) Earth Scan Publications Ltd.

Pearce, D, and Markandya, A, *The Benefits of Environmental Policy* (1989) OECD.

Pearce, D, and Turner, RK, *Economics of Natural Resources and the Environment* (1990) Harvester Wheatsheaf.

Pearce, D, et al, *Blueprint 2: Greening the World Economy* (1991) Earthscan Publications Ltd.

Pearce, D, and Warford, J, *World Without End* (1993) OUP.

Tromans, S, (ed) *Best Practicable Environmental Option – A New Jerusalem?* (1987) United Kingdom Environmental Law Association.

Winter, G, 'Perspectives for Environmental Law – Entering the Fourth Phase' (1989) 1 Journal of Environmental Law 38.

World Commission on Environment and Development, *Our Common Future* (1987) OUP.

ENVIRONMENTAL ETHICS AND POLICY

Aakvaag, T, 'Can the Needs of Society and the Environment be reconciled?' (1995) Vol CXLIII RSA Journal p 30.

Alder, J, and Wilkinson, D, *Environmental Law and Ethics* (1999) Macmillan.

Allison, L, *Ecology & Utility* (1991) Leicester University Press.

Attfield, R, and Belsey, A, *Philosophy and the National Environment* (1994) CUP.

Boyle, A, and Anderson, M, (eds) *Human Rights Approaches to Environmental Protection* (1996) OUP.

Brown-Weiss, E, 'Agora: What Does Our Generation Owe to the Next? An Approach to Global Environmental Responsibility' (1990) 84 AJIL 190.

Carr, IM, 'Saving the Environment – does utilitarianism provide a justification?' (1992) 12 Legal Studies 92.

Dobson, A, *Green Political Thought* (1990) Harper Collins.

Eckersley, R, *Environmentalism and Political Theory* (1992) UCL Press.

Glasbergen, P, and Blowers, A, *Environmental Policy in an International Context: Perspectives*, chapters 1–4 and 6–7, (1995) Arnold.

Holdgate, M, 'How Can Development Be Sustainable?' (1995) Vol CXLIII, RSA Journal p 15.

Hughes, D, 'Environmental Protection: Underlying Concepts' Part I [1998] Vol 10, Environmental Law and Management (ELM) 41–47, Part II [1998] 10 ELM 236–240, Part III [1998] 10 ELM 276–280.
Hurrell, A, and Kingsbury, B, *The International Politics of the Environment* (1992) OUP.
McCormick, J, *British Politics and the Environment* (1991) Earthscan Publications Ltd.
Miller, C, *Environmental Rights*, (1998) Routledge.
Tromans, S, 'High Talk and Law Cunning' [1995] JPL 779.

TAXATION ISSUES
Essers, PHJ, Flutsch, PA, Ultee, MA (eds) 'Environmental Policy and Direct Taxation in Europe (2000) Kluwer.
European Environment Agency, 'Environmental taxes: recent developments in tools for integration' (2000) Office for Official Publications of the European Communities.

Chapter 3

The players: bodies responsible for the formulation and implementation of environmental policy and regulation

Any study of the effectiveness of environmental law and policy depends on a general appreciation of the institutions concerned, their role in the formulation and development of law and policy in environmental protection matters and in the policing of these rules. This chapter includes only a selection of the major players in environmental law and policy in the UK, including the sources of environmental policy in central government, organisations responsible for enforcing environmental regulation and the major institutional sources of specialist advice on policy matters. The Environment Agency is singled out for detailed discussion in this chapter due to its role as a 'one-stop shop' for pollution regulation. The separate legal systems of Northern Ireland, Scotland, Wales and England in many cases have produced separate agencies regulating environmental laws, for example, the Scottish counterpart of the Environment Agency for England and Wales, the Scottish Environmental Protection Agency. Both bodies were created by the same legislation and on the whole have common statutory powers and functions. The umbrella regulator for Northern Ireland is the Environment and Heritage Service.

A CENTRAL GOVERNMENT AND THE ENVIRONMENT

The Department for Environment, Food and Rural Affairs

Following the general election of 2001, the new Department for Environment, Food and Rural Affairs (DEFRA) was constituted by melding components of the old Department of Environment, Transport and the Regions (DETR), much of the Ministry of Agriculture, Fisheries and Food and fragments of other departments.[1] The remit of the new department reaches across environmental protection, rural issues, food, animal welfare and hunting. Its proclaimed aim is to 'enhance the quality of life through promoting: a better environment; thriving rural economies and communities; diversity and abundance of wildlife resources, a countryside for all to enjoy, sustainable and diverse farming and good industries that work together to meet the needs of consumers.'[2] This reorganisation of environmental responsibilities in central government should not pass

---

1 SI 2568/2001 effects the necessary changes.
2 *Department for Environment, Food and Rural Affairs: Aims and Key Tasks*, Department for Environment, Food and Rural Affairs, 2001.

without comment. Prior to 1997, there had been longstanding criticism of the then Department of Transport for failing to give sufficient priority to environmental considerations in transport preferences, for example, the frequent preference of road building over the strengthening of the rail network. This prompted a merger in 1997 of the Departments of Environment and of Transport into the DETR with a view to developing a more integrated approach to the policy issues in these areas. The dismantling of the transport and environment coalition and the placement of transport into the Department for Transport, Local Government and the Regions (DTLR) is a curious move and one which is hardly likely to facilitate the development of environmentally sustainable transport policies. A further source of confusion is the separation of urban and rural development in the new DEFRA despite the interdependence of these policy areas. Whilst urban regeneration resides in the DTLR and the Regional Development Agencies are placed in the Department of Trade and Industry, responsibility for rural regeneration is with the DEFRA. Planning issues have also been severed from environmental protection by being moved to the DTLR. It is hard to see how these changes can be anything other than a hindrance to the government's self-professed aim of sustainable development which requires that 'decisions throughout society are taken with proper regard to their environmental impact' (see below).

The result of these redrawn lines of responsibility has meant the dismantling of the old Ministry of Agriculture, Fisheries and Food (MAFF). MAFF had long been regarded as harbouring a conflict of interests due to its responsibility for both the promotion of public health and safeguarding the interests of agriculture and the food industry. This conflict appeared to have inhibited its effectiveness in dealing with the BSE crisis, its desire to protect the meat industry leading it to play down any reported threats to public health from infected beef.

Inevitably, the work of other government departments has implications for environmental policy, including particularly the Department of Trade and Industry (which has responsibility for ensuring sustainable supplies of energy), and as already indicated, the DTLR and the Department of Health. In this sense, the conflicts between departments on environmental issues can never be eliminated, but efforts have been made to ensure other policy developments do not continually undermine environmental strategies.

Green Ministers

The introduction in 1998 of 'Green Ministers' should, in part, be capable of offsetting the problems caused by the severance of environment and transport in the latest department re-shuffle. Each government department has its own Green Minister responsible for co-ordinating efforts within their respective departments towards the furtherance of sustainable development. Departmental policies are to be screened for their environmental costs and benefits, and where the environmental costs are regarded as being significant, a full environmental appraisal is to be performed on the proposed policy.[3] In addition, all government departments are to adopt an environmental management system and include a section in their annual departmental reports on environmental performance in their department. The aim is to ensure that efforts towards sustainable development are integrated and embedded in the public sector as a whole.[4]

3   *Policy Appraisal and the Environment* (DETR, 1998).
4   *The Work of Green Ministers* (DETR, 2000). See also *Greening Government: The First Annual Report of the Green Ministers Committee 1998/99* (DETR, 1999).

The relative success of the Green Ministers initiative is monitored by the Environmental Audit Committee.

Greening Government and the Environmental Audit Committee

The House of Commons Environmental Audit Committee ('EAC') was established in 1997 as part of the Labour Party's election manifesto to firm up the Tories' 'Greening Government Initiative.' The EAC is pivotal in ensuring the implementation of environmental protection and sustainable development at the heart of government departments.[5] The necessity for an audit function attached to the Greening Government policy is that statements of commitment to the environment from the government and the placing of Green Ministers in all departments provide no guarantee that the spirit of Green Government will be honoured. The remit of the EAC is to report to the House of Commons on the extent to which government departments and Non Departmental Public Bodies contribute to environmental protection and sustainable development and their performance against targets set by Ministers in this regard. (This last aim has thus far proved futile as Ministers have yet to set departmental targets on sustainable development.[6]) The Select Committee for Environment, Food and Rural Affairs is responsible for the scrutiny of the department of that name, and, given the clear overlap between these two mechanisms, it is unfortunate that their interrelationship was not addressed when the EAC was introduced.

The EAC has to date reported on the greening of government budgets, the Multilateral Agreement on Investment (an agreement to liberalise foreign investment), the Government's Comprehensive Spending Review, Genetically Modified Organisms, Energy Efficiency and Climate Change. As is probably self-evident, the focus of the EAC's inquiries has been largely on issues and policies which are cross-departmental and which address aspects of government expenditure. Ross observes that the EAC has adopted a very broad construction of its remit and, consequently, has yet to examine the performance of individual departments against their commitment to environmental protection and sustainable development.[7] As a mechanism for ensuring governmental accountability to parliament, the EAC has received qualified approval for its progress so far. EAC reports have offered a mix of support and criticism for the government's policies and whilst the EAC can only 'recommend' improvements to government policy, some of these recommendations have been accepted and acted upon. Even praise and support for government performance can be a valuable mechanism in assisting the government to stick to what are often difficult decisions.[8]

In addition to central government departments there are a number of central advisory bodies charged with various environmental responsibilities including the Environment Agency (the main player in the enforcement of environmental regulation), the Countryside Agency, the Royal Commission on Environmental Protection, the Commission on Sustainable Development and Parliamentary Select Committees. The following sections are ordered into 'regulators' (which might also have advisory functions) and 'advisory bodies' (with no direct regulatory functions).

---

5   A policy which was stressed in *A Better Quality of Life* (1999 Cm 4345).
6   A Ross, 'Greening Government: Tales for the New Sustainability Watchdog' (2000) JEL 12(2) 175 at 192.
7   Ross at 191.
8   Ross at 193.

B   REGULATORS AND THE ENVIRONMENT

All the bodies discussed under this section are undoubtedly 'public bodies' for the purposes of the Human Rights Act 1998 and, therefore, according to s 6 of that Act, they must act in a way which is compatible with Convention rights (see further chapter 5). They are also subject to the freedom of information provisions discussed in chapter 7.

The accumulation of research on law enforcement has repeatedly identified two distinct styles of enforcement, the 'co-operative' or 'compliance-based' approach (which has regularly been deployed in the administration of regulatory regimes in the UK[9]) and the 'sanction-based' approach. Whilst the latter relies primarily on punishing law breakers as a means of enforcing legal standards, the compliance-based approach relies predominantly on informal/non-confrontational resolution of compliance-related issues and employs prosecution as a last resort. It will be seen from the following that the Environment Agency and its predecessors conform in different degrees to this typification of enforcement.

Repeated calls were made in the 1980s and 1990s for an integrated body with responsibility for the majority of environmental issues. The government's intention to create an environmental protection agency was announced in 1991, and, finally, after the delay caused by a general election, the Environment Act 1995 was passed. The Act created the Environment Agency, to commence operations the following year and to be responsible for the majority of matters of environmental regulation.

A potted history of twentieth century environmental regulation

It might be helpful before looking at the Environment Agency to briefly outline the arrangements for environmental regulation immediately before the Agency was created. Prior to 1996, environmental regulation was largely administered by three enforcement limbs:

• Water pollution regulation – the subject of national legislation since the Rivers Pollution Prevention Act of 1876 (see Part IV);

• Waste management regulation – legislation in this area not being enacted until the Deposit of Poisonous Waste Act 1972 (chapter 14); and

• Integrated processes regulation – a composite field of regulation covering discharges to air, land and water, and having its roots in the Alkali legislation of 1863 (see chapter 17).

These three regimes of pollution control shared a broadly similar framework of regulation, each operating a licensing system[10] and relying on the criminal law to impose sanctions upon non-compliant operators. Yet, these regimes were diverse; they developed along distinct time scales, they were created on the basis of different institutional models and under discrete legislative regimes, and they appeared to endorse contrasting enforcement policies and strategies.[11]

9   The following texts explore the concept of enforcement style: B M Hutter, *The Reasonable Arm of the Law* (1988) Oxford, Clarendon Press, P Grabosky and J Braithwaite, *Of Manners Gentle – Enforcement Strategies of Australian Regulatory Agencies* (1996) OUP, D Vogel, *National Styles of Regulation* (1986) Cornell University Press, K Hawkins, *Environment and Enforcement* (1984) OUP, A Ogus et al, *Policing Pollution: A Study of Regulation and Enforcement* (1982) OUP.

10   This system is used by the regulator to authorise emissions and discharges on an individual basis.

11   D Hughes, 'Of Regulation and Regulators' (1993) 5(6) Environmental Law & Management 175.

Pre-Agency regulation of prescribed processes: Her Majesty's Inspectorate of Pollution: 1987–1996

With 148 staff and a budget of £24 million, Her Majesty's Inspectorate of Pollution (HMIP) was intended to initiate an integrated approach to difficult industrial pollution at source, whether affecting air, land or water. HMIP was, then, the first attempt at 'cross-sectoral' pollution control. The Environmental Protection Act 1990 (EPA 1990) created a regime of Integrated Pollution Control (IPC) to be regulated by HMIP. The IPC regime aimed to induce operators to both produce and dispose of waste in a way that would involve minimal impact on the environment as a whole. Regulations issued under EPA designated a number of processes as 'prescribed.' The basis of designation for IPC regulation was the potential impact of the process on the environment. Operators who conducted 'prescribed processes' or dealt with radioactive substances, tended to be large corporate entities conducting hazardous operations or handling large quantities of chemicals. Small operators under IPC were the exception rather than the rule, and many of these were owned by large holding companies that would determine the management systems within the small-scale operation. Clearly then, IPC created integrated regulation only at the 'top end' of pollution control and gave rise to fragmentation in environmental regulation. Both HMIP, and its forerunner the Alkali Inspectorate, were consistently criticised for their 'cosy relationship' with regulated industries and the secrecy associated with their operations. These criticisms stemmed, in part, from the co-operative relationship that their inspectors appeared to have developed with regulated organisations. Bugler,[12] writing in 1972, identified the Inspectorate with a very low public profile, neither appearing in the telephone directories nor operating in marked buildings. Of the three pre-Agency pollution control regimes, it is HMIP that is most closely associated with reluctance to prosecute and using co-operation and persuasion as its preferred means of securing compliance. In its last five years, HMIP prosecutions were raised from the negligible levels of the pre-1990s (ranging from nought to two) to a range of between 12 and 15 per year. This increase to double figures in 1991 coincided with the claiming of costs for the time spent preparing cases for prosecution, a practice that only began in April 1991.[13] HMIP did not have a legal department as such, but employed local solicitors to initiate prosecutions when necessary. The generally low level of court action was perhaps in part due to this lack of a legal nucleus within the regulatory body and the inhibiting effect of being unable to recoup legal costs.

Pre-Agency regulation of water pollution: the National Rivers Authority: 1989–1996

Prior to 1989, the functions of both supply of water and sewerage services and of the enforcement of water pollution controls rested with Water Authorities. Ironically, the pollution regulators in this instance were also the largest polluters, a conflict which, it was suggested, compromised their enforcement function. In 1989, the government planned to privatise the Water Authorities. This was considered to be the best way of raising the necessary capital for improving water quality in line with growing pressure from the EU, and for upgrading outdated sewage treatment works. Part of the privatisation package included the creation of a 'National Rivers Authority', a new

12   J Bugler, *Polluting Britain* (1972) Penguin, London.
13   National Audit Office (1991) *Control and Monitoring of Pollution: Review of Pollution Inspectorate* HC 637 90-91 vol XXXVIII.

independent body, to inherit the regulatory functions of the Water Authorities. The 'new agency' idea was successful in helping to subdue fears concerning the accountability of the privatised water companies.

The National Rivers Authority ('NRA') was created by the Water Act 1989 and was staffed by ten times the head count at HMIP. It was distinct from the other two limbs of pollution control because of its substantial operational functions. Its responsibilities outside pollution control included: water management;[14] navigation;[15] land drainage;[16] fisheries;[17] flood defence;[18] angling; recreation; and conservation. Of the three pre-Agency regulators, it is the NRA which was considered to employ the greatest degree of legalistic enforcement style, needing little prompting to initiate formal enforcement action, and of being 'almost robotic'[19] in their prosecution practice. The evidence on the NRA's approach to enforcement is, however, equivocal.

The NRA engaged a team of in-house specialist lawyers, which inevitably facilitated its approach to legal enforcement. From its inception, the NRA demonstrated an apparently stealthy approach to enforcement of pollution controls, with one of its first prosecutions raising a record fine of £1million.[20] The rate of polluter prosecutions soared within the first two years of NRA regulation. The sheer number of binding precedents obtained during the NRA's existence, on water pollution laws which had remained largely untested since their original enactment in 1876, is testimony to this regulator's increased emphasis on court-centred enforcement.[21] Water pollution prosecutions were brought at a rate of between four and five hundred per year, a significant increase on former prosecution rates of the Water Authorities. The NRA made an immediate impact in the courtroom. Certainly, in isolation, the increase in enforcement statistics seems to suggest a strict approach to enforcement. Yet, prosecution was generally only embarked upon when the enforcement team was very confident that the ingredients of the offence were fulfilled and there was still in fact an 'enforcement to substantiated pollution incident' ratio of only around 1%.

Pre-Agency regulation of waste: Waste Regulation Authorities: 1990–1996

Prior to 1991, waste management regulation was afflicted with the same conflict of interests as the Water Authorities had been. The concurrent responsibilities of Waste Disposal Authorities for both the disposal of municipal waste and the regulation of those very activities, struck at the heart of regulatory impartiality. This problem was addressed by the creation of Waste Regulation Authorities ('the WRAs') by the Environmental Protection Act 1990, s 33. Regulation of waste management remained with local authorities but, as had happened with water, the functions of municipal waste disposal and local regulation were separated to ensure greater regulatory independence. Waste Disposal Authorities ('the WDAs') became private companies, wholly owned

14   Water Industry Act 1991 and Water Resources Act 1991.
15   Pilotage Act 1987, Sea Fish Industry Act 1951.
16   Land Drainage Acts 1991 and 1976.
17   Salmon Act 1986, Wildlife and Countryside Act 1981, Salmon and Freshwater Fisheries Act 1975, Diseases of Fish Acts 1983 and 1937.
18   Regulated by local byelaws.
19   N Carter, and P Lowe, 'The Establishment of a Cross Sector Environment Agency' in T S Gray (Ed), *UK Environmental Policy in the 1990s* (1995) Macmillan Press, London at p50.
20   *National Rivers Authority v Shell (UK)* (1989) unreported, Liverpool Crown Court.
21   *National Rivers Authority v Yorkshire Water Services* [1995] 1 AC 444, HL; *R v CPC(UK) Ltd* [1995] Env LR 131, CA; *National Rivers Authority v Taylor Woodhouse* [1994]; *NRA v Alfred McAlpine* [1994] UKELA Journal Winter 1995, 34; *A-G's Reference (No 2 of 1994)* [1995] 2 All ER 1000; *National Rivers Authority v Wright Engineering; R v Dovermoss* [1995] Env LR 258, CA.

by the local authority. WDAs would then compete with the private sector for any waste disposal work and the Waste Regulation Authorities (WRAs) would be responsible for the regulation of waste disposal and management activities in the region.

Whilst general statements from some of the old WRAs on enforcement confirm a compliance-based approach, there were many proactive authorities who were bringing the same number of formal enforcement actions as the regions of the NRA. While certain broad themes within those policies were recurrent throughout the country, there was a significant disparity between certain elements of those policies, evident both in the annual reports and in practice. Each authority differed in size, procedures and staff grading. While some WRAs had a large number of full-time staff, others had no officers working in regulation full-time.[22] As to legal staffing, the local WRAs relied on in-house local authority lawyers for legal services (unlike the NRA) for whom environmental cases were only one of many priorities. In fact, waste offences seemed to have been fairly low on council agendas and their solicitors were often unfamiliar with the waste legislation. Local firms of solicitors were brought in when necessary. Again, as with HMIP, prosecution was often viewed by the WRAs as very much as a final option. There was a general preference for a conciliatory approach, with the use of prosecution being reserved for cases where all other methods had failed.

The development of environmental regulation prior to 1996 was highly fragmented. The growth of regulation for the separate media of land, air and water was spurred by ad hoc events, such as plans to privatise the utilities and the need to resolve conflicts of interest, rather than a concerted effort to create an integrated system of environmental protection. The first major step towards integration, the IPC regime, gave rise to further fragmentation. For whilst the environmental effects of prescribed processes were to be regulated as a whole, IPC stripped off segments of the jurisdiction of water, waste and air regulators, creating a bizarre two-tier regulatory structure. Despite this legacy of fragmentation in regulatory structure, the differences between the regulatory styles of the Agency's predecessors have often been exaggerated:

1 All three bodies used the same concepts of *serious harm* and *serious fault* in their prosecution policies.
2 There was a general feeling that the NRA's reputation was a result of careful and strategic publicity, capitalising on the 1989 Shell prosecution which attracted a £1million penalty, and the dogged pursuit of unlicensed anglers.
3 HMIP, as a body limited to the supervision of the most advanced industrial processes, could not compete with the prosecution profile of a regulator responsible for the majority of discharges to controlled waters. The scale of HMIP's jurisdiction and staffing mean that direct comparison of its enforcement statistics with those of the NRA is unfair.
4 Meanwhile, waste regulators were outstaging the NRA in prosecution statistics but, possibly due to their fragmented local structure, were less well positioned to attract national publicity.

The Environment Agency: integration and defragmentation

Section 1 of the Environment Act 1995 (EA 1995) brought these three streams of pollution control regulation, comprising 85 regulatory bodies, together within the jurisdiction of a single inspectorate for England and Wales – the Environment Agency

---

22 A Qadeer Khan, 'The Environment Agency and the Waste Regulatory Functions' National Society for Clean Air conference paper (1994).

('the Agency'). When proposals for reform of environmental regulation were being canvassed, four models for an Environment Agency were suggested:[23]

1   a body with responsibility for disposals to air and land only (water pollution regulation would remain independent);

2   a body responsible for overseeing and co-ordinating water pollution regulation and integrated processes regulation (leaving waste management activities to be regulated perhaps by a separate arm of the new body);

3   the creation of a fully integrated agency covering all the agencies (ie waste management, water quality and Integrated Pollution Control and including all the functions of the National Rivers Authority); and

4   a structure incorporating waste management and integrated pollution control functions. This fourth option would exclude from the Agency the functions of water resources management, flood defence, navigation and fisheries.

It was the fully integrated model, embracing both pollution control and water management functions (3), which was adopted for the new Agency. One difference between the Scottish Environmental Protection Agency ('SEPA') and the Environment Agency is that SEPA did not inherit the same breadth of water resources management functions and its functions in this respect are narrower. SEPA is also not subject to the EA 1995, s 4 duty to make a contribution to sustainable development (see below). Despite the government's expressed objective for the Environment Agency to be a 'one-stop shop' of pollution regulation, fragmentation still remains due to the large number of aspects of environmental regulation which fall outside the Environment Agency's remit. Examples of such continued fragmentation include: issues of nature conservation which are dealt with by the Countryside Agency and English Nature; the local authorities' role in the contaminated land regime under the Environment Act 1995 and in enforcing Part B authorisations under the Integrated Pollution Control regime; the role of the Drinking Water Inspectorate in enforcing drinking water standards; and the continued existence of the Nuclear Installations Inspectorate.

As a Non Governmental Public Body, the Agency is not its own master. It is very much shaped by the mandate and jurisdictional boundaries set out by Parliament in the Environment Act 1995. It must also comply with regulatory laws and principles which bind all enforcement bodies such as, for example, the general principles of administrative law and the principles of the Deregulation and Contracting Out Act 1994. As a creature of the state, the Agency is dependent upon the government for funding, and political necessity requires it to heed cautions from the government.

The Environment Agency's statutory duties

THE PRINCIPAL AIM

Section 4 of the EA 1995 states that it is the 'principal aim' of the Agency (subject to and in accordance with the provisions of this Act or any other enactment and taking into account any likely costs) in discharging its functions to protect or enhance the environment, *taken as a whole*, to bring about the ministerially specified objective of achieving sustainable development. Thus particular statutory duties may supersede the 'principal aim' while there will inevitably be a certain element of cost benefit anlaysis affecting the Agency's workings (see further below).

23   House of Commons Environment Committee (1991-92) *Improving Environmental Quality – The Government's Proposal for a New Independent Environment Agency*, Session 1991-92, First Report, Paper 55 (paras 35-37).

The concept of 'sustainable development' has already been considered in chapter 2 and will be returned to below. The Agency's duty to make a contribution to sustainable development is vulnerable to the charge of being vague and equivocal. 'Sustainability' as a legal term has its origins in the 'soft law' of international conventions, thus meaning it is too vague to give rise to legal sanction.[24] Uncertainties inherent in the sustainable development duty are of wider import now that local government is the subject of similar duties by virtue of the Local Government Act 2000, s 2. Much parliamentary debate on the Environment Bill focused on the lack of consensus on the meaning of the sustainable development clause and a House of Commons Select Committee the same year spent a significant proportion of its time attempting to solve essentially the same riddle.[25] The statutory guidance issued to the Agency to supplement the Environment Act 1995 adopts the 'Brundtland' definition of sustainable development, that is: '[D]evelopment that meets the needs of the present without compromising the ability of future generations to meet their own needs.'[26] The needs of the economy and those of the environment are to be pursued in harmony and to be reconciled: neither must be pursued at the expense of the other.

The Draft Management Statement for the Agency indicates that the goal of sustainable development involves reconciling: '... the dual objectives of achieving economic development and of providing effective protection and enhancing of the environment.' This guidance has lagged behind developments in sustainable development policy. At the time of writing, the guidance is based on the government's 1994 strategy and has not been updated to reflect the new strategy published in 1999, *A Better Quality of Life*.[27] The main distinction between the two strategies is one of extension rather than fundamental re-orientation. The 1999 strategy takes a broader view of sustainable development as involving the reconciliation of the competing needs of environment, economy and *community*. It is not clear as yet to what extent this reformulation will have implications for the Agency and its Draft Management Statement. In playing its part in promoting sustainable development, the Agency is to adopt across all its functions an integrated approach which addresses the 'impact of substances and activities on all environmental media and on natural resources,' and which delivers 'environmental requirements and goals without imposing excessive costs (in relation to benefits gained) on regulated organisations or society as a whole.' To assist in this role the Agency prepares an annual corporate plan which indicates the areas of work which it wishes to emphasise and the resources it intends to devote to these tasks. This plan is subject to ministerial approval and is part of a longer term corporate strategy agreed with ministers.

Ecological criteria must be taken into account in decision making, for example, the concept of 'carrying capacity' which, broadly, means the capacity of the environment to absorb pollution or waste. The environment cannot be asked to accept more than its carrying capacity, while habitats and ecosystems have to be considered in the light of their ability to sustain particular population species. These criteria may have to be taken into account on a precautionary basis where there is a risk of potential damage to the environment which is both uncertain and significant. Sustainable development further requires that natural resources are used prudently. Thus, it is officially accepted that a principal challenge for sustainable development strategy is to promote ways of

---

24   See L Kramer, *EC Treaty & Environmental Law* 2nd Edn (1995) Sweet & Maxwell London, p 64.

25   House of Lords Select Committee on the Environment, *Sustainable Development* (1995) 1994-95 HL 72.

26   Taken from the 1987 Brundtland Report, The World Commission on Environment and Development, *Our Common Future* (1987) Department of the Environment London.

27   (1999 Cm 4345).

encouraging environmentally friendly economic activity while discouraging or controlling damaging activities. At the same time, renewable resources should not be squandered while those that are non-renewable are used at a rate which considers the need for future generations, always bearing in mind the need to consider any irreversible environmental effects and their significance. In some cases environmental impacts can be reduced by the application of the 'polluter pays' principle which, by driving up the cost of operation to polluters and thus the cost of their products to society, may reduce demand for their activities.

THE AGENCY'S OTHER GENERAL DUTIES
The EA 1995, ss 5 and 6 impose further duties on the Agency: '... the Agency's pollution control powers shall be exercisable to prevent or minimise or remedy or mitigate the effects of pollution to the environment' (s 5). This mandate provides a new 'standard' against which Agency action is to be measured, but again, one so general as to be unlikely to give rise to successful legal challenge. There is no duty to prevent or minimise pollution but only its effects, which suggests that the Agency has a reactive rather than a proactive role to play in environmental protection. As it is the same Agency which, on the one hand, actively authorises pollution by the distribution of authorisations, licences and consents, and on the other must minimise the effects of pollution, this reactive role is inherent in the diverse functions of the body itself. The Agency must also:

> '... promote to the extent it considers desirable; (a) the conservation and enhancement of natural beauty and amenity of inland and coastal waters ... (b) conservation of flora and fauna ... and (c) the use of such waters and land for recreational purposes' (EA 1995, s 6).[28]

This subjective duty to 'promote' could probably be fulfilled by the publicity of the above issues and represents a lower requirement than the antecedent duty on the National Rivers Authority, 'to further' which required at least assisting the progress of conservation and enhancement.[29] Once again, this dilution of the statutory duty tends to suggest a reduced emphasis on the proactive role of the Agency.

THE COST BENEFIT DUTY
The Environment Act 1995, s 39 places the Agency under a duty to take into account the 'likely costs and benefits' when deciding whether to exercise its statutory powers. The Environment Act expressly declares that the duty does not apply where: (i) it would be unreasonable in the circumstances; and (ii) the Agency has a mandatory obligation.[30] The duty does apply when the Agency is *'deciding whether to exercise its* powers.*'*[31] Thus the obligation to take account of costs and benefits applies to situations where the Agency has the option of more than one means of achieving a given objective. Guidance on the application of the cost benefit duty (published by the Agency) suggests that enforcement is a 'duty' and that there is no requirement to conduct cost benefit assessments of enforcement decisions.[32] It is submitted that this would not be

---

28   EA 1995, s 6 relates to the Agency's pollution control functions. EA 1995, s 7 places similar duties on the Secretary of State for the Environment, but does not apply to the functions of pollution control.
29   Water Resources Act 1991, s 16.
30   Environment Act 1995, s 39.
31   Environment Act 1995, s 39.
32   Environment Agency *Taking Account of Costs and Benefits* (1996), Sustainable Development Series SD3, at 11.1.

a correct interpretation of the duty, for while there is a duty to enforce the law,[33] there is a discretion as to how enforcement should be pursued.

FUNDING

Inevitably, a primary constraint on the Agency's performance of its statutory duties is limited resources. Agency funding is largely composed of income from its government sponsors and self-generated income. Its government sponsors are DEFRA and the National Assembly for Wales. For the year 1999/00, the Agency received £104.9 million 'grant in aid' (less than 20% of the Agency's income) from the government and £31.6 million in capital grants and contributions.[34] The remainder of its income (£461.3 million) was derived from the Agency's own activities, namely levies on local authorities (particularly in connection with flood defence works), charges to holders of environmental licences and licence fees. When compared with previous years there is a clear trend of the Agency becoming increasingly self-sufficient as grants in aid decline. There are significant problems with funding of the Agency which directly compromise its independence and its ability to set its own priorities. The Agency has no less than 70 ringfenced income streams, most of which are separate only because of historical reasons, but each of which must be spent on specific priorities. If a particular environmental issue comes to the forefront one year, the Agency has little flexibility to use money from other income streams (eg water quality) where no such pressing need is present. Ringfencing also results in a distortion of the Agency's activities. Site inspections may not be a high environmental priority where the site is usually well run and poses little hazard to the environment, but it is a source of valuable funding for the Agency. If the Agency reduces such inspections to concentrate on high risk work, it loses the funding that routine site inspections produce. Thus, although the amount of funding may not be a huge problem, the way in which it is arranged is, and represents a further barrier to integration of environmental protection.

Environment Agency enforcement: policy and practice

Dictionary definitions of 'enforcement' refer to 'forcing someone to do something', for example, to obey the law. In the context of environmental regulation, however, 'enforcement' must be taken to mean the use of incentives and strategies to *encourage* obedience of the law, for the law does not, strictly speaking, provide means for 'forcing' obedience. The primary means of encouraging obedience in British environmental law is the criminal sanction, which hinges on the licence (a prior approval awarded to the person or organisation who will be responsible for the economic activity concerned) and prosecution. A licence is issued to an operator, permitting the performance of activities which would otherwise be unlawful. An offence is committed either by conducting the activity without a proper licence, or conducting those activities otherwise than according to the conditions of that licence (see, for example, chapters 12, 14, 17 and 20). In order to deter the breach of environmental legislation, regulatory officials are equipped by statute with an armoury of 'enforcement' tools, which include: the powers of revocation or modification of the licence, issuing cautions, prosecution

---

33 For example, as a necessary ingredient of the broader duty which stipulates that '...the Agency's pollution control powers shall be exercisable to prevent or minimise or remedy or mitigate the effects of pollution to the environment.' (Environment Act 1995, s 5). There is also a more precise enforcement duty in the waste management sector to ensure compliance with waste management licences and to ensure waste management activities do not cause harm to the environment (EPA 1990, s 42).

34 *Annual Reports & Accounts 1999-2000* (2001) Environment Agency 77.

and service of formal notices requiring improvements. Alongside these formal enforcement mechanisms there are non-statutory tools of formal and informal warnings and education and persuasion which can also be used to the same end of increasing compliance. To these mechanisms could be added the use of strategic publicity to encourage compliance.

The least formal enforcement response to identified non-compliance is, of course, to ignore the operator's breach. Alternatively, Agency staff could use persuasion. Here, officers might point out the long-term benefits of site improvements without actually demanding any change in practice. Such informal strategies of regulatory bargaining can involve enforcers acting 'like salesmen,' in manipulating the perceived advantages of improvements in order to make them more attractive. At the opposite end of the spectrum, formal enforcement mechanisms include, primarily, forms of court action. These are relatively expensive mechanisms which Hawkins concluded were only used as 'a last resort'.[35]

Environmental offences are hallmarked by the absence of a number of fundamental criminal law concepts. Criminal liability generally requires some form of *mens rea*, a mental condition of either reckless or deliberate causing of harm, yet most environmental offences require no *mens rea* as such, and can be committed without what most lawyers understand as fault. In addition, the identifiable 'victim' in traditional crimes, whose suffering excites moral outrage toward the criminal, is also absent. The 'victim' of environmental offences tends to be society collectively, with individuals not even realising that their interests have been compromised. Just as the victim is absent, so is the recognisable 'damage'. The majority of environmental offences are inchoate and require no proof that there was as much as an 'interference' with the environment. Although environmental prosecutions do not require that *mens rea*, damage or victims must be proved for a conviction, failure to convince the court of these things surely results in a tendency towards leniency in sentencing. It is no coincidence that most prosecutions by the Environment Agency, perhaps excepting those under the waste management provisions, are of incidents that have resulted in identifiable 'damage' in terms of polluted waters or harm to aquatic life. These cases are understandably preferred for prosecution because the courts will be more likely to impose significant penalties.

The Environment Agency's power to prosecute environmental offences is discretionary. Models of efficient enforcement acknowledge, generally, that prosecution of all identifiable offences is too costly to be feasible. A regulator must therefore make policy decisions as to which cases should be prosecuted, and how often to prosecute, in order to maximise enforcement efficiency. The style of enforcement employed in pollution control has changed substantially in the last 50 years. In the 1970s, the Chief Inspector of the Alkali Inspectorate remarked:

'... large firms, concerned for their public image, will go to almost any lengths to avoid prosecution. If we had to prosecute ICI, for example, ... heads would roll right, left and centre for the disgrace of it.'[36]

To what extent does Environment Agency enforcement fit this template of co-operative enforcement? The general 'enforcement style' of the Environment Agency (not unlike its immediate predecessors) seems to have been one of preferring on the whole to rely on informal negotiation with non-compliant operators. In 1997, the Chief Prosecutor of the Environment Agency stated:

35   K Hawkins, *Environment and Enforcement* (1984) Clarendon Press, Oxford, at p 4.
36   M Frankel, *Social Audit – A Special Report: The Alkali Inspectorate* (1974) Social Audit Ltd, London.

'The Agency is not a knee jerk prosecutor, and will not leap straight into a prosecution upon the detection of any offence. It has a variety of options "lower" than a prosecution which it can employ, depending upon such factors as the attitude of the defendant and the severity of the incident.'[37]

This statement indicates that a 'ratcheting' approach to enforcement is being adopted. The regulatory grip is gradually tightened in an effort to secure improvement at least cost. The initial response to a failure to comply with a licence/consent condition would normally be an informal or formal warning. If improvements are not forthcoming thereafter, the warning may be followed by an escalation in the formality of action by the Agency. This generally informal approach can involve seeking to induce site improvements by a process of negotiation and incentives, including educating and advising operators on how to improve their environmental performance and threatening formal enforcement action when persistent non-compliance is encountered. Broadly speaking, the enforcement function was performed, therefore, using a twin-track system, whereby very serious or flagrant violations or those accompanied by obstructive behaviour bypassed the ratcheting approach and would often result in the relatively immediate service of an enforcement notice or summons for prosecution.

The Agency's Management Statement (a document arising out of the Conservative government's deregulation initiative), clearly anticipates the predominance of the compliance/co-operative style of enforcement: 'much of (the Agency's) dealings with those on whom the law places duties (businesses and persons engaged in potentially polluting activities) are informal ...'. In dealings with regulated operators, the Agency will: 'advise and inform ... those it regulates ... offering advice and support...' and '... be sensitive to the needs of business ...,' and the Agency will seek to achieve: 'the imposition of minimum burdens ...' and finally, 'the Agency should seek *constructive relationships* with regulated bodies.'

There are a number of formal principles which currently regulate Agency officers' prosecutorial discretion. They include the Agency's statutory duty to have regard to the costs and benefits of its actions and the Enforcement Code of Practice.[38] The Agency's Enforcement Code endorses four 'standards' which are to inform the administration of both formal and informal mechanisms of enforcement.[39] These are known as the four principles of 'firm but fair regulation':

i   *proportionality* (balancing action taken to protect the environment against risks and costs);
ii   *consistency* (taking a similar approach in similar circumstances);
iii *transparency* (helping those regulated and others, to understand what is expected of them and what they should expect from the Agency); and
iv   *targeting* (ensuring that regulatory effort is directed primarily towards those sites where the environmental risk is greatest).

On the specific issue of deciding whether to prosecute, the code adopts the framework of the two-stage test used by the Crown Prosecution Service:[40]

(i) The sufficiency of evidence test A prosecution will not be commenced or continued unless the Agency is satisfied that there is sufficient, admissible and reliable evidence that the offence has been committed and that there is a realistic prospect of conviction.

---

37   Ed Gallagher, *Annual Report & Accounts 1997/98* (1998) Environment Agency.
38   *Enforcement and Prosecution Policy* (1998) Environment Agency.
39   The principles of 'fair' consistent and transparent enforcement emanate from the Deregulation and Contracting Out Act 1994, Sch 1.
40   *Code for Crown Prosecutors* (1994) HMSO.

Success rate is very important to the Agency, as publicised failures to attain conviction may result in a trend of deterioration, encouraging more defendants to plead 'not guilty', and consequently resulting in a higher rate of prosecutions failing. Once the Agency is satisfied that the evidence exists on which to prosecute, its attention turns to:

(ii) The public interest test Where there is sufficient evidence, a prosecution will not be commenced or continued by the Agency unless it is in the public interest to do so.

Assessments of the public interest side of the equation are intended to be qualitative in nature and do not involve a process of counting the factors weighing on each side. The code creates a 'presumption of prosecution' where any of the following are present:

i   significant consequences (or potential consequences) for the environment;
ii   unlicensed activities;
iii excessive or persistent breach;
iv   failure to comply with formal remedial requirements;
v   reckless disregard for management or quality standards;
vi   failure to supply information without reasonable excuse or knowingly or recklessly supplying false or misleading information; or
vii obstruction or impersonation of Agency staff.

It is also clear that where company officers can be shown to have consented to, or turned a blind eye to, the commission of an offence by their company or where the offence was attributable to their own neglect, that individual may be the subject of a prosecution. The code goes on to suggest that such cases may prompt the Agency to consider seeking a Director's disqualification order.[41] In practice, the prosecution of those individuals and the pursuit of disqualification orders is likely to be very rare.

There are numerous safeguards against regulatory inertia in the enforcement of environmental obligations; the potential for judicial review, private prosecution (on which see chapter 7) and external political pressure from Select Committees, DEFRA and pressure groups. Whilst judicial review of the power to prosecute is rare, it remains a real possibility. In *R v General Council of the Bar, ex p Percival*,[42] Lord Denning's judgment in *R v Metropolitan Police Comr, ex p Blackburn (No 3)*[43] was followed, to the effect that the decision of whether to prosecute an individual case was prima facie reviewable. This species of review was recognised as being applicable to any body with a discretionary power of prosecution.[44] On the same issue of the degree to which the courts would intrude on prosecutorial discretion, the case of *Environment Agency v Stanford*[45] provides further confirmation that the opportunities for challenge of prosecutorial judgement exist, although they are few. Lord Chief Justice Bingham stated:

'The question whether or not to prosecute is one for the prosecutor ... . If a prosecutor obtains a conviction in a case which the court feels on reasonable grounds should never have been brought, the court can reflect that conclusion in the penalty it imposes. The circumstances in which it can intervene to stop the prosecution, however, are very limited indeed.'[46]

---

41 See the *Code*, para 24. The relevant provision would be the Company Directors Disqualification Act 1986, s 2.
42 [1991] 1 QB 212, [1990] 3 All ER 137.
43 [1973] QB 241.
44 [1973] QB 241.
45 [1999] Env LR 286, QBD.
46 [1999] Env LR 286, QBD at 296-7.

This case clearly recognised a jurisdiction to challenge prosecutorial discretion and indicated further that such jurisdiction would probably have been exercised on the facts, had the defendants been able to prove a representation or assurance from the Environment Agency that criminal proceedings would not be taken.[47]

General Powers of Entry, etc

The Agency has power to do anything calculated to facilitate the carrying out of its functions including instituting criminal proceedings, under the EA 1995, s 37, while at both the local and central levels the enforcing bodies have considerable powers of entry and search, etc (see EA 1995, ss108 and 109).

Thus an enforcing body may in writing authorise a 'suitable person' to exercise certain powers: to determine whether pollution control enactments are being complied with, to exercise pollution control powers, or to determine whether and how such a function should be exercised. The various powers are:

1   To enter any premises it is reasonably believed it is necessary to enter at any reasonable time, or at *any* time in an emergency.
2   To enter premises accompanied by other persons or equipment or, where there is reasonable cause to believe obstruction will take place, a constable.
3   To carry out investigations and examinations.
4   To direct that premises which may be entered are to be left undisturbed.
5   To take measurements, photographs and samples – the latter not just from the premises but also of land, water or air in, on, or in the vicinity of, the premises.
6   To test or dismantle any article found on premises where there is cause to believe it has caused, or is likely to cause, pollution or harm to human health, and to take possession of such material for the purpose of further examination.
7   To require persons to answer questions.
8   To require information to be given, including extracts from records.
9   To require assistance and facilities from any person with respect to matters in that person's control.
10   To undertake test borings on a site or to install equipment to determine issues of compliance with pollution regulation.

It appears that the power to take samples is not limited to *either* soil *or* water, where a soil sample is taken that includes water in it. The bringing of an appeal against the refusal of a licence or authorisation, etc, also does not prevent the taking of samples from the site which is the subject of the appeal.[48]

Except in emergencies, seven days' notice of intention to enter has to be given and then entry may only take place under the authority of a warrant or with the consent of a person in occupation of the relevant premises. Similarly, except in emergencies, where it is proposed to enter premises and the use of force appears on reasonable grounds to be likely to be called for, entry shall normally be by warrant.

Where in relation to any article or substance found on any premises there is power to enter, and an authorised person has reasonable cause to believe that the article or substance is a cause of imminent danger of serious pollution to the environment or of serious harm to human health, that person may seize, and if necessary render harmless, that substance or article.

47   [1999] Env LR 286 QBD at 292.
48   *Polymeric Treatments Ltd v Walsall Metropolitan Borough Council* [1993] Env LR 427.

It is an offence under the EA 1995, s 110 intentionally to obstruct authorised persons in the performance of their powers and duties. However, before any of the foregoing powers are used the Agency needs to have a reasonable belief that they should be.[49]

Sentencing in environmental cases

The whole area of criminal litigation in environmental litigation is ripe for an overhaul, which is hardly surprising given that, in many cases, we are still using statutory tools designed in the nineteenth century to deal with twenty-first century problems. Recent suggestions for reform are geared particularly towards sentencing:

1   *Fines to be used for repairing the environment.* At present, the fines arising out of an Agency prosecution merely accrue to Treasury funds. It is difficult therefore to conceive of a prosecution as being directly beneficial to the environment, a fact which might explain in part any reluctance by regulators to prosecute offenders.

2   *Heavier sentences.* The Court of Appeal was recently invited by the Sentencing Advisory Panel to draft sentencing guidelines for environmental offences. Bingham LJ in *R v Milford Haven Port Authority,*[50] however, did not feel that he could 'usefully do more than draw attention to the factors relevant to sentence' which were enumerated in the case of *R v F Howe & Sons (Engineers) Ltd*[51] for the purposes of health and safety offences. Is it satisfactory that environmental law should be dependent on guidelines developed for another area of law?

3   *Companies to publicise the fines imposed on them in their annual reports.*

Assessment of the Environment Agency: A 'champion' for the environment?

Media comment confirms that the Agency, in common with its predecessors, has adopted the traditional non-legalistic approach to enforcement. After its first year of regulation, the Agency stood accused of being a 'Toothless Tiger ... On The Run'[52] when it refused to prosecute anyone after the Sea Empress supertanker ran aground spilling over 100,000 tonnes of oil into the sea. Evidence presented to a Select Committee in 1996-97 showed a recurrence of many of the criticisms once aimed at the regulatory approach of the Alkali Inspectorate. The Agency was attacked specifically for its regulation of the cement industry,[53] which was characterised by secrecy, non-enforcement and a close relationship with the regulated industry. These criticisms correspond precisely to the allegations of secrecy, announced inspections, policies of non-enforcement and the protection of commercial information which were levelled at the Agency's predecessors, particularly HMIP and the Alkali Inspectorate. In the same year, Michael Meacher, the environment Minister, criticised the Agency for failing to punish offenders properly and directed them to take a tougher line on enforcement.[54] Finally, the Select Committee on Environment, Transport and the Regions reprimanded the Agency over its prosecution profile: '... the Agency ... needs to reconsider the message which it is sending out to the industry, that it would really rather not prosecute

49   *JB & M Motor Haulage v London Waste Regulation Authority* [1993] Env LR 243.
50   [2000] JPL 943.
51   [1999] 2 All ER 249.
52   O Tickell, 'Toothless Tiger on the Run' (1997) *The Guardian* 23 April.
53   House of Commons Select Committee on the Environment *The Environmental Impact of Cement Manufacture* (HC 124 (1996–97)).
54   J Burke et al 'Revealed: The Chemical Giants Polluting Britain' (1997) *The Sunday Times,* 1 June, p 1.

... the Agency must ensure it remains, and is recognised as, the dominant partner.'[55] The Committee also concluded that there was a damaging shortage of waste management expertise in the Agency and the view of many was that the Agency was 'NRA dominated'.[56] It is not hard to see why this might be the case. Many of the strategic management positions were occupied by ex-NRA personnel and the legal department in particular was initially dominated by members of the NRA's legal department. The House of Commons Select Committee expressed some disappointment that the Agency had not yet achieved the role of 'one stop shop' which had been the reason for its inception. There had been a failure in the early stages to develop a vision and coherent strategy for the Agency which had resulted in a very low public profile and confusion by many as to the Agency's functions. In some parts of the Agency, the old sectoral divisions remained with suggestions being made that Agency officers did not demonstrate concern for matters which were outside their direct responsibility and there were inconsistencies of policy and practice applied to different geographical areas.

Two years later the same Select Committee in its *Inquiry into the Workings of the Environment Agency*[57] regarded the Agency as having limited success as a 'champion' for the environment. The Committee expressed disappointment with the Agency's 'contribution to sustainable development,' in particular because the Agency had been 'punching below its weight' in failing to assert itself as a contributor to public debate or to influence policy. On the high profile issue of genetically modified organisms which had dominated the headlines for much of the year of the Committee's inquiry, the Agency had refused to take a strong public line saying that it was a matter beyond its statutory remit. In the Committee's view this was: 'an abnegation of its central statutory responsibilities to protect the environment and to contribute to the promotion of sustainable development.'

One of the recurrent themes in the evidence submitted to the Committee was the allegation that the Agency's measurement of its own performance focused too heavily on process rather than outcome, with detrimental effects for the Agency's fulfilment of its duty to protect the environment and make a contribution to sustainable development.[58] The examples highlighted in the report included the use of arbitrary targets for waste management inspection targets which discouraged visits to problematic (and therefore potentially damaging) sites.[59] The Agency's performance-related pay was also implicated as attaching too much importance to the quantity of officers' work (process) rather than its quality (outcome).[60] The preference for process over outcome also featured in discussions of the Agency's enforcement activities. Allegations were made in evidence that the Agency was spending a disproportionate level of resources on enforcement at the 'bottom end' of pollution (ie that the smaller companies were far more likely to experience the full weight of the Environment Agency's enforcement powers than the large and wealthy operators). This assertion suggests not only that the pursuit of environmental protection is not being optimised, but also that the 'targeting' principle in the Agency's enforcement policy is being subverted.[61]

55 House of Commons Select Committee on Environment, Transport and Regional Affairs, 6th Report, *Sustainable Waste Management* (HC 484 (1997–98)).
56 House of Commons Select Committee on Environment, Transport and Regional Affairs, 6th Report, *Sustainable Waste Management* (HC 484 (1997–98)).
57 House of Commons Select Committee on Environment, Transport and Regional Affairs, 6th Report, *Sustainable Waste Management* (HC 484 (1997–98)).
58 Environment Act 1995, s 4.
59 Above at n 1, paras 103-5.
60 *Ibid* at 106.
61 *Enforcement and Prosecution Policy* (1998) Environment Agency.

One of the Agency's enforcement initiatives has been the 'naming and shaming' of companies which have proved to be the worst polluters in its annual *Spotlight on Business Performance* report. These league tables of the best and worst companies in terms of environmental impact have been criticised for presenting a misleading and unbalanced view.[62] Companies are entered on the table of poor performers, in part due to the number of prosecutions brought against them and the amount of fines imposed, but the tables failed to identify the improvements these same companies had made in delivering environmental benefits. Certainly, given the comments made in the House of Commons' *Inquiry into the Workings of the Environment Agency* it is questionable whether the fact of repeated appearances in court can be regarded as an accurate performance indicator.

The courts: the case for an environmental court

New South Wales, Queensland, South Australia and New Zealand all have a form of environmental court. Lord Woolf's Garner Lecture in 1991 expressed support for such an arrangement for the UK and, more recently, the Grant Report, commissioned by the then DETR, discussed the feasibility of establishing an environmental court for England and Wales. This substantial review of the need for an environmental court and the success of such courts in Australasia concluded that a two-tier environmental court with a specialist judiciary and providing the opportunity for third party rights of appeal against planning decisions might be desirable. Impetus for a revival of the debate arose from the Aarhus Convention 1998 (of which the UK is a signatory) and the Human Rights Act 1998. It was argued by some that the current regime may disclose a violation of Article 6 of the ECHR and, possibly also, the Aarhus requirement that Parties should provide: 'fair, equitable, timely and not prohibitively expensive' access to judicial/ administrative procedures to challenge acts or omissions by private persons and public authorities which breach national environmental laws.[63]

The Grant report[64] offered the following criticisms, frequently levelled at our current arrangements for administering environmental justice, as arguments 'for' an environmental court:
1   the ineffectiveness of governmental agencies;
2   an unsympathetic judiciary; and
3   the lack of public empowerment which is due (at least in part) to limited access to the courts.

It is tempting to refute such arguments supporting the creation of an environmental court on the grounds that arguments could similarly be raised for a specialist forum in almost any field of litigation. Special considerations affect the resolution of banking law matters, housing law disputes and medical malpractice cases, and yet it is clearly not practicable to create a highly fragmented court structure with a separate forum for every reasonably distinct field of litigation. The force of these objections is weakened, however, in the case of environmental law because it is so demonstrably unlike any other area of law. Its marks of distinction include the fact that environmental law affects the entire range of industrial activities, from resource extraction to production, and from consumption to disposal, and the fact that it regulates the conduct of individuals separated by thousands of miles. More importantly, the environment is far more

62   'Spotlight on Business Performance' *Water UK,* 28 September 2001.
63   *UNECE Convention on Access to Information, Public Participation in Decision Making and Access to Justice* (Aarhus, 1998) Art 9(3) (see further chapter 7).
64   Department of Environment, Transport and the Regions, *Environmental Court Project: Final Report* (2000).

deserving of a special forum for the simple fact that although its public health origins were anthropocentric, or 'people-centred', environmental law can no longer be regarded as a 'people-centred' discipline (a fact clearly demonstrated by the definition in the Environmental Protection Act 1990 of environmental harm as including potential interference with any living organism).[65]

There is a marked trend of specialisation in the court structure which might be argued to go part way in addressing the need for judicial specialism in environmental cases, for example, the fact that High Court and Court of Appeal judges are allocated to cases with regard to their experience and the needs of the case. This development is only of limited benefit, however, given that it is the lay bench which disposes of the majority of environmental prosecutions. In any case, despite the resurgence of interest in this area prompted by the Aarhus Convention, the government has shown no signs of considering the idea further. A House of Lords' Debate in October 2000 resolved that the need for an environmental court had not been established.

The Nature Conservancy Councils

A Conservation Agency was first proposed in a White Paper of 1947 (*Conservation of Nature in England and Wales* (Cm 7122)). Two years later, 'Nature Conservancy' was established with the remit of providing scientific advice on conservation and control of natural flora and fauna. It was replaced in 1973 by the Nature Conservancy Council (NCC). The NCC was divided into three by the EPA 1990, one each for England, Wales and Scotland. As a matter of convention, the NCC for England became known as 'English Nature,' a name which has been legally recognised in the Countryside and Rights of Way Act 2000 (CROWA 2000). English Nature is a government department which 'champions' the conservation of wildlife and natural features by, amongst other things, identifying and designating Sites of Special Scientific Interest ('SSSIs'). The Act has complicated the task of English Nature regarding its protection of these sites because under the Act an estimated 70% of SSSIs became land to which the public have a statutory right of access (see further chapter 10). English Nature will be working in partnership with the Countryside Agency on the implementation of this statutory access right. English Nature has been regarded by some as more ready to engage and stimulate public debate than the Environment Agency and as carving itself a role as shaping and influencing policy and legislative development.

The Countryside Agency

The Countryside Agency was created by a merger of the Countryside Commission and the Rural Development Commission using powers written into the Regional Development Agencies Act 1998, s 35. It was designed to play a central role in the government's policy of developing a sustainable countryside, whilst recognising the interdependence of urban and rural areas. The Agency aims to secure the best deal for the countryside by providing research and advice and seeking to influence government and policy makers on relevant issues. Its interests are in protecting the rural environment from pollution and traffic, policies affecting access to the countryside, protecting the rural economy and ensuring people in rural areas have access to services. When the Countryside Agency's creation was announced, it was labelled 'the champion for

65   EPA 1990, s 1(3).

the environment.'[66] Is this Agency capable of living up to this claim of being the 'rural champion'? Doubts have been raised regarding the constitution of this new body by the House of Commons Select Committee on Environment, Transport and the Regions on the Countryside Agency.[67] In this short report, views were expressed that it had been 'cobbled together for convenience' and that insufficient thinking had gone into its remit. The Agency's draft prospectus was criticised for prioritising economic interests over environmental interests, in particular, the Committee felt that the Agency should have a stronger role in protecting the countryside from 'inappropriate development,' and feared that it might be overpowered on policy issues by the urban bias from Regional Development Agencies. It also remarked that funding for the Agency was very low and might undermine its capacity to fulfil its prospectus mandate.

Food Standards Agency

The Food Standards Agency is a 'UK wide' body but has a separate Executive for Northern Ireland with a soon to be created Advisory Committee for Northern Ireland which will relay information and advice to the Food Standards Agency on matters affecting Northern Ireland. Similar arrangements exist for Scotland and Wales. The notion of a Food Standards Agency was an election pledge by the Labour Party prior to the 1997 election. The James report[68] identified three reasons for the crisis of confidence in the regulation of food standards:
(1)   a perceived conflict of interest in the Ministry of Agriculture, Fisheries and Food, the department then responsible for food standards. This department was responsible for both the promotion of public health and safeguarding the interests of the agriculture and the food industry;
(2)   fragmentation in responsibilities for food; and
(3)   disparate enforcement of food laws.
The creation of the Food Standards Agency in April 2000[69] was therefore an example of history repeating itself, as we have already seen that similar concerns had led to the creation of the National Rivers Authority and the Waste Regulation Authorities before it. The Food Standards Agency ('FSA'), a corporate body, was to have jurisdiction from end to end of the food chain, from farm to table (including the restaurant table). The overall aim of the FSA is to 'protect public health from risks which arise in connection with the consumption of food (including risks caused by the way in which it is produced or supplied) and otherwise protect the interests of consumers in relation to food.'[70] This statutory objective makes it clear that the FSA's remit extends beyond health issues to issues more generic to quality and information such as labelling, advertising and descriptions of food.[71] Despite the primary emphasis being on public health, the FSA's remit extends to 'animal feeding stuffs.'[72] This remit is not solely concerned with the impact of animal feed standards on food for human consumption as the Food Standards Act 1999, s 9(4) clarifies, the FSA is also concerned with the safety of such products for the animal itself. The FSA's board is collectively responsible

66   DETR Press notice, 248/ENV, 27 March 1998.
67   Fourth Report (HC 6 (1998–99)).
68   Professor Philip James, *A Food Standards Agency – An Interim Proposal*. (1997) Stationery Office.
69   Food Standards Act 1999, s 1.
70   Food Standards Act 1999, s 1(2).
71   See, for example, the Food Standards Act 1999, s 36(3).
72   'Animal feeding stuffs' has a broad definition which encompasses not only animal feed but nutritional supplements and similar which may not be fed through the mouth. (FSA 1999, s 36(1)).

for the Agency activities and is accountable to Parliament via the Secretary of State for Health.

The Food Standards Act 1999, ss 6–12 set out the functions of the FSA including development and assisting development of food policies, the provision of advice, information and assistance to public authorities on these matters.[73] The Act extends the advisory/informative function to the public, but this function is qualified, for whilst the FSA is under a statutory duty to comply as far as reasonably practicable with requests from public authorities,[74] no such duty exists in relation to requests from the public. It must merely inform, assist and advise the public so as to ensure that the public are 'adequately' informed and advised about such matters. The FSA 1999, s 8 requires the FSA to collect and review data relating to food including monitoring scientific development and commissioning and co-ordinating research. As regards these functions, they are specifically extended to 'animal feeding stuffs' by the FSA 1999, s 9. The qualified advisory/informative function already referred to is extended specifically to animal feed users in respect of animal feeding stuffs. Such information or advice as is provided under these sections can be published.[75] The FSA can also issue guidance on food-borne diseases[76] and authorise any person to carry out an observation of any food, agricultural, fish farming or animal feeding stuffs premises.[77] Powers of entry, inspection of records and sampling of food, articles or substances are provided in order to conduct observations. The results of an observation can also be published.[78]

When local authority food law enforcement fell under the remit of MAFF and the Department of Health, there had been very little in the way of monitoring or scrutiny of localised performance. This is one of the areas where the FSA should be able to improve current practice and strengthen the link between local and central government. As regards the enforcement of food standards laws, the Agency has a supervisory role, monitoring the enforcement performance of local authorities.[79] It is early days to comment on the effectiveness of this new regulatory body in ensuring consistent and improved enforcement standards at a local level. To date it has published a Food Law Enforcement Standard and commenced its audit function of local authority enforcement in 2001.

The FSA is under a statutory duty to publish a statement of its general objectives.[80] Although originally the Secretary of State and others were empowered to modify these objectives without Agency approval, this provision of the draft bill was amended to require Agency approval. A *Statement of General Objectives and Practices*[81] has been drawn up which states that its objectives relating to its primary aim of protecting public health will be the development of effective policies based on consultation, the provision of clear, practical advice, information and assistance to its stakeholders, the building and maintenance of a reputation of expertise in food safety and the promotion of the interests of UK consumers in EC and international forums. These objectives are to be translated into targets for the FSA to work towards. The FSA pledges to put the consumer first and to strive to gain and maintain the trust, respect and confidence of its stakeholders.

73 FSA 1999, s 6.
74 FSA 1999, s 6(3).
75 FSA 1999, s 19(1)(a).
76 FSA 1999, s 20.
77 FSA 1999, s 11.
78 FSA 1999, s 19(1)(b).
79 FSA 1999, s 12.
80 FSA 1999, s 22.
81 Food Standards Agency, *Statement of General Objectives and Practices* (2000) Food Standards Agency.

'Proof of the pudding...'

So has the FSA lived up to expectations set out in *A Force for Change*? The White Paper proposals for a Food Standards Agency stressed the importance of creating a regulator, independent from sectoral interests, which would 'strengthen arrangements for the management of food safety' and 'restore public confidence' in British food, in part by ensuring that the consumer's voice was heard.[82]

The FSA is accountable to Parliament through the Secretary of State for Health and to this end, it must make an annual report of its activities to Parliament. It is subject to the power of the Secretary of State to issue directions where he/she believes that it has seriously failed in the performance of any of its duties.[83] Failure to comply with these directions may result in members of the FSA being removed from office.[84] This raises some rather obvious concerns relating to the Agency's independence. The provisions remained intact despite the House of Commons Select Committee's concerns that the provisions imposed enormous restrictions on the FSA's powers and were open to political abuse.[85] The Committee raised similar concerns regarding the FSA's duty when considering whether and how to exercise its powers to consider the costs and benefits of so doing.[86] Clearly, this provision may compromise the FSA's pursuit of public health where costs would be experienced by the food industry. A clearer definition of 'costs' and 'benefits' would perhaps have been desirable. Reception of the new agency thus far has been mixed with some encouraging comments regarding the FSA's treatment of the BSE issue, but some disparagement regarding in particular its research into organic food and alleging a tendency to select research findings which defend the status quo.[87]

C ENVIRONMENTAL ADVISORY BODIES

The Royal Commission on Environmental Pollution

The Commission was set up in 1970 by Royal Warrant to address rising concerns regarding the environment and the lack of coherence in the government's allocation of responsibilities for environmental matters. The Commission's role is to provide 'independent, fearless and non-partisan' advice on complex environmental issues which are often scientific, technical and philosophical. Research can be initiated by the Commission itself or in response to a request from Secretaries of State or ministers. The most visible aspects of the Commission's work are its reports such as *Setting Standards* (1998 Cm 4053) and *Energy – The Changing Climate* (2001 Cm 4794) which have become increasingly wide-ranging and multidisciplinary, but the Commission also responds to consultations and submits memoranda to parliamentary committees. Although the Commission is described as 'constitutionally independent' from government departments, it is resourced by DEFRA which requires evidence from the Commission that the resources have been put to good use and that the Commission's services provide value for money. Reports from the Commission are usually intended to inform the government, Parliament and regulators, although some reports are regarded as valuable reference points for the public also. The *Financial, Policy and*

82   *The Food Standards Agency: A Force for Change* (1998) Stationery Office.
83   FSA 1999, s 24.
84   FSA 1999, s 24(8).
85   House of Commons Select Committee on Food Standards, First Report (1998-99) *Food Standards Draft Bill* (HC 276 (1999)).
86   FSA 1999, s 23(2)(b).
87   L Woodward, 'A vegetable stew' (2000) *The Guardian,* 6 September.

Management Review of the Royal Commission on Environmental Pollution reporting in 1999 was set up to comment on the performance of the Commission and its role in the future development of environmental policy. The Review concluded that the Commission's work was not widely known and did not necessarily reach its intended audience, and further that there was a lack of clarity as to the different roles of advisory bodies and their interrelationship. It was recommended that DEFRA address this by setting out a clear framework by which the delineation of the roles and responsibilities of the various advisory bodies should be made clear. The strengths of the Commission over other advisory bodies are its independence and its expertise, a combination which often results in more radical recommendations than those supplied by other bodies.

Advisory Committee on Business and the Environment (ACBE)

The ACBE was set up in 1991 to stimulate debate and provide advice on business aspects of environmental issues. Its members are appointed jointly by the Secretary of State for Trade and Industry and the Deputy Prime Minister and comprise prominent individuals from industry and the service sectors. There is no attempt to combine the interests of the industrial sector and pro-environment groups in this Committee's membership. The Committee reports to government on a diverse range of environmental issues ranging from climate change to biodiversity and water resources, and makes proposals regarding the way ahead. It sees its role as attempting to mobilise industry's efforts to improve environmental performance and liaises with many business organisations to such ends. Given that the industrial sector is pivotal in the furtherance of sustainable development, the concept of the ACBE has much to offer the development of environmental policy both in the UK and at European level in the formulation of directives, but there is a danger that it will become, or at least be seen as becoming, an institutionalised form of lobbying for industry.

Parliamentary select committees

The existing select committee system was established in 1978 for the purposes of scrutinising the performance, policies, draft Bills and expenditure of each government department and the regulators and quangos associated with those departments. Clearly, the main source of select committee scrutiny in environmental matters is the House of Commons Select Committee on Environment, Food and Rural Affairs (and its predecessor, the Committee for Environment, Transport and Local Regions), but contributions to the examination and development of environmental policy are also made in particular by the House of Commons Select Committee on Science and Technology and that for Trade and Industry. The pre-2001 election Select Committee on Environment, Transport and Local Regions concluded in its Annual Report to the Liaison Committee that government responses to its recommendations were 'variable' and sometimes 'terse and unhelpful'.[88]

The strength of committee scrutiny is that the committees select their own issues for examination and the government is expected to reply to the findings of committee reports. The force of these strengths is however diluted by criticisms directed towards the method of appointing members to the committees. In 2000, a report entitled *Shifting the Balance: Select Committees and the Executive* by the House of Commons Liaison

---

88 House of Commons Select Committee on Environment, Transport and Local Regions, *Annual Report of the Work of the Committee to the Liaison Committee* (HC 65 (2000-2001)).

Committee criticised the fact that nomination of members was under the control of the Whips. Such a mechanism was regarded as failing to secure public confidence as to the independence of the committees' work as members could be chosen because of their known views. The government's response was largely negative[89] – one of the grounds for rejecting reform to the selection of members was that it could result in more time being spent on debates as to membership than on substantive issues.

Commission on Sustainable Development

The Commission replaces the Round Table on Sustainable Development and the British Government Panel on Sustainable Development and should not be confused with the United Nations Commission on Sustainable Development. Whereas the Environment Audit Committee reviews the progress of government departments towards sustainability, the Commission on Sustainable Development conducts a similar task across all activities in the UK. Its remit is to review progress towards sustainable development 'across all relevant fields' and promote awareness and consensus on sustainability issues. In particular, it must identify policies which are currently undermining such progress and areas where unsustainable trends have developed, proposing remedial action. Its emphasis is therefore on the implementation of sustainable development policies. Funded by DEFRA, the Commission was launched in October 2000 in response to the commitment to this effect in *A Better Quality of Life.*[90] The Committee has a cross-sectoral membership (drawing from industry, government, pressure groups and academia) of 22. It is the 'advocate' of sustainable development in the UK but has only five years to prove its worth. After this time, the government will review the continuing need for such an organisation. To date it has produced one report on the *Future of Aviation* in response to the government's consultation process.

D   SUSTAINABLE DEVELOPMENT – UK POLICY

The government's first sustainable development strategy was published in January 1994, *Sustainable Development, the UK Strategy* (Cm 2426), its response to the commitments made at the 'Earth Summit' in Rio, 1992. The status of the strategy was one of guidance to assist the government in drawing up its policies. The strategy document itself begins by stating the widely quoted definition of sustainable development as 'development that meets the needs of the present without compromising the ability of future generations to meet their own needs.' It proceeds on the basis that there will not be less economic development, arguing 'a healthy economy is better able to generate the resources to meet people's needs.' It accepts that not 'every aspect of the present environment should be preserved at all costs,' and concludes that what is required is that 'decisions throughout society are taken with proper regard to their environmental impact.' Those decisions should be based on the best possible scientific information and assessment of risks, although precautionary action may be needed where there is uncertainty and potentially serious risks exist. In particular, ecological impacts must be considered, particularly with regard to non-renewable resources and irreversible effects, and the cost implications of decisions must be brought home to all those responsible for them via the application of the 'polluter pays' principle.

89   (Cm 4737).
90   (1999 Cm 4345).

In 1999, the government published *A Better Quality of Life: A Strategy for Sustainable Development for the UK* (Cm 4345), its revision of the 1994 strategy. A new strategy was considered necessary: firstly, to incorporate the social dimension of sustainable development which had previously been lacking in the 1994 document and secondly to place an emphasis on devolution. Since the 1994 strategy devolved administrations had been set up in Wales, Scotland and Northern Ireland. These administrations needed to consider their own role in delivering sustainable development to their populations. The principle of devolution (or 'think globally, act locally') is referred to in the strategy as an important part of sustainable development. The third reason for revision was to reflect changes in the scope of sustainable development in EU documentation since 1994. In his *Foreword* to the new strategy, the Prime Minister expressed the view that sustainable development is about reversing the trend of previous governments which have routinely assessed progress solely in monetary terms, thereby ignoring the impact of their policies on the people and their environment. The new strategy is based on four aims: (1) social inclusion; (2) environmental protection; (3) prudent use of natural resources; and (4) maintaining high levels of stable economic growth and employment.

The new strategy lists ten principles and approaches (constituent parts of sustainable development) which are to provide guidance for the government on developing policy and emphasises the three sides to sustainable development: social, economic and environmental. All three forms of capital (social capital, economic capital and environmental capital) are to be maximised by developing policies which pursue harmony between the three aspects rather than the dominance of economic capital to the exclusion of the other forms which are crucial to 'quality of life'.

The ten principles of the new strategy for sustainable development

1   *Putting people at the centre* – this principle confirms that sustainable development in the sense adopted by the UK's strategy is anthropocentric. The ultimate gains achieved by sustainable policies are a *better quality of life* for this generation and for future generations.
2   *Taking a long-term perspective* – the strategy advocates evaluating the implications of policies beyond the next decade. This is implicit in the traditional understanding of sustainable development that *future generations'* interests must be protected.
3   *Taking account of costs and benefits* – this principle advocates taking a broad view of the costs and benefits associated with particular policy options.
4   *Creating an open and supportive economic system* – this principle attaches importance to economic growth and competition being used as a stimulus for greater efficiency in the use of resources.
5   *Combating poverty and social exclusion* – this principle recognises the social dimension of the 'new improved' version of sustainable development. The social dimension is both national and international in requiring that in the UK 'everyone should have the opportunity to fulfil their potential' through access to decent housing, education, employment and public services and that assistance should be given to other countries in fighting poverty.
6   *Respecting environmental limits* – the limits referred to are those which represent serious or irreversible damage to the environment.
7   *The precautionary principle* – as the 'limits' referred to above (the points at which environmental damage/deterioration becomes serious or irreversible) are often difficult to identify, precautionary action is advocated. The precautionary principle

requires that 'where there are threats of serious or irreversible damage, lack of full scientific certainty shall not be used as a reason for postponing cost-effective measures to prevent environmental degradation.'

8   *Using scientific knowledge* – the importance of identifying reliable high quality scientific knowledge is emphasised.

9   *Transparency, information, participation and access to justice* – this principle emphasises the importance of access to justice and public participation in decision making, themes which were at the fore of the Rio Summit.

10   *Making the polluter pay* – this last principle requires that those responsible for pollution ought to bear the cost. This way, environmentally damaging activities and industries are discouraged and will eventually be replaced by industries/ activities which recycle and replenish the environment.

Both strategies represent not so much a decision or policy in itself but an approach to decision-making and policy formulation. They also accept that some environmental costs will have to be borne as the price of economic development, and that implies that the process is inevitably evaluative and judgmental and may be effectively political in that it will have to decide between competing claims and values. To this end, better indicators of environmental impact have to be developed and systems of natural resource accounting so that the benefits/disbenefits of growth can be properly assessed and duly informed decisions taken.

The three sides of the sustainable development 'triangle'

A sustainable economy As sustainability of the economy has traditionally occupied a place of prominence in the debate about sustainable development, it is on the whole not difficult to see the connections between economic policies and environmental issues. For the purposes of a sustainable economy, the new strategy assumes a need for wider availability of goods and services to the population, in particular decent housing, safe and nutritious food, efficient household equipment and access to leisure activities. For the economy to be sustainable the strategy requires that consumption of resources be more efficient. Changing habits of the population can counteract advances that have been made in the conservation of resources. Whilst environmental impact is increasingly a design consideration in the manufacture of cars, people are travelling further than ever before in their cars and are neglecting public transport. The point is made that whilst industry has managed to make significant energy savings in the last decade, households have not made any such savings. A sustainable economy must also maintain stability and provide a competitive environment for business. Healthy competition is hopefully to facilitate industry and business in providing better value and less impact on the environment. Sustainable development must also entail the development of a skilled workforce, retaining people in the work force and providing fair work conditions so that workers can spend time with the family. Clearly these considerations extend far beyond protection of the environment. It seems almost as if 'sustainable development' has become a byword for whatever the government's current policy preferences happen to be. Almost any policy can be justified with reference to this wider-than-ever notion of sustainable development.

A closer link with the environment is made with the concept of 'market transformation'. This involves changing the market in ways that ensure that industry/ business and consumer trends make a contribution to sustainable development. The strategy anticipates that such transformation is possible by monitoring and promoting best practice, providing consumers with detailed labelling on the environmental credentials of the products they purchase and use (enabling informed choice) and supporting research and innovation. The recent amendment to the Pensions Act 1995 which requires pension funds to publicise their policy on ethical, environmental and socially responsible investments should hopefully enhance consumers' capacity to contribute to sustainable development by investing wisely. Government-provided incentives for 'green businesses' and encouragement of environmental reporting by companies are also part of making the economy play its part in sustainable development. This section of the strategy extends into the individual's homelife with the promotion of better energy saving practices in homes across the country and safer food.

Sustainable communities the plans for improving the sustainability of communities represents the addition of the social dimension to sustainable development. The paper anticipates improvements being made in access to services, particularly health, reducing poverty and social exclusion, reducing crime and fear of crime and strengthening local and regional economies. Although the concerns expressed in this part of the report on the whole address the social environment rather than the physical, protection of the environment features in a number of ways in the pursuit of 'sustainable communities'. For instance, local authorities are encouraged in the exercise of their land use planning functions to revitalise town centres and encourage development in existing urban areas. *Planning for Sustainable Development: Towards Better Practice*[91] pursues this aim by advising local authorities on how to further sustainable development in their development plans and planning decisions. A link is also made between improving the health of the population and the environment. The strategy document comments that up to an estimated 24,000 people per year die prematurely due to air pollution. In addition therefore to increasing access to and the quality of health care, the cause is also to be addressed by investing in diverting people from their cars and thereby reducing carbon dioxide emissions and also by reducing the need for travel by improving services.

A sustainable environment An integrated approach to environmental protection is a prime concern in ensuring that solving problems arising out of, for example, water pollution from landfill sites does not give rise to problems elsewhere (eg air pollution from the use of incinerators in the place of landfill). The system of IPC mentioned earlier in this chapter and discussed in more detail in chapter 17 is identified as of great assistance in this regard. Specific policy areas identified in *A Better Quality of Life* include:

1 reducing greenhouse gas emissions to slow down climate change, to be effected by the Kyoto agreement;
2 shifting towards a target of 10% of energy consumption from renewable energy sources;
3 reduced emphasis on nuclear energy in recognition of the absence of an acceptable method of disposal for intermediate and high level radioactive waste and the huge cost of building nuclear installations;
4 reducing air pollution by developing an integrated transport system, the use of cleaner fuels and increases in fuel duty to deter unnecessary single person journeys and uneconomical vehicles;
5 redressing the lack of policy in the area of soil protection and devote equal attention to this field as to air and water;
6 improving river quality and imposing tougher penalties on water companies for wasted water through leakage whilst keeping water affordable by cutting water bills; and

91 (October 1998) Department of Environment, Transport and the Regions.

7   increasing the viability of the UK's shipping industry whilst also tightening international and environmental standards to prevent the discharge of hazardous substances into the sea and working to protect habitats and species.

Whilst there is an internal logic to many of the sustainable development strategies which now incorporate the social dimension of sustainable development, it is difficult not to feel that environmental issues have been diluted in what was originally an environmental concept.

Proposals for an EC Sixth Environmental Action Programme are currently being considered (*Communication from the Commission to the Council, the European Parliament, the Economic and Social Committee and the Committee of the Regions on the Sixth Environment Action Programme of the EC: 'Environment 2010: Our Future, Our Choice* 2001/0029 (COD)). The new action programme sets out the direction of environmental policy over the next five to ten years. Four priority areas are named: climate change, nature and biodiversity, environment and health and the sustainable use of natural resources and management of wastes. In the Commission's document on the Sixth Action Programme, the environment is definitely still central, although it does say '… sustainable development is more than a clean environment. The social and economic implications of environmental action must be taken into account when pursuing sustainable development. So whilst this Action Programme targets the environmental dimension of sustainable development, it also aims to improve the environment and quality of life of citizens in the European Union more generally.'[92]

Further reading

GENERAL BACKGROUND

Bugler, J *Polluting Britain* (1972) Penguin Books.

Hawkins, K *Environment and Enforcement* (1984) Oxford University Press.

Richardson, G, Ogus, A and Burrows, P *Policing Pollution* (1983) Oxford University Press.

Ashby, E and Anderson, M *The Politics of Clean Air* (1981) Clarendon, Oxford.

Ayres, I and Braithwaite, P *Responsive regulation. Transcending the deregulation debate* (1992) Oxford University Press 1992) Oxford.

Vogel, D *National Styles of Regulation* (1986) Cornell University Press, London.

Lofstedt, R E and Horlick-Jones, T 'Environmental Regulation in the UK: Politics, Institutional Change and Public Trust' in Cvetkovich, G and Lofstedt, R *Social Trust and Management of Risk* (1999) Earthscan, London.

Baldwin, R, Scott, C, and Hood, C *A Reader on Regulation* (1999) OUP, Oxford.

Baldwin, R, Cave, M *Understanding regulation: theory, strategy, and practice* (1999) OUP, Oxford.

JOURNAL LITERATURE

Jewell, T and Steele, J, 'UK regulatory reform and the pursuit of "sustainable development": the Environment Act 1995' (1996) JEL 8(2) 283.

Ross, A 'Greening Government: Tales for the New Sustainability Watchdog' (2000) JEL 12(2) 175.

Abbot, C, 'Controlling Environment Agency Discretion: A Public Law Perspective' (2001) 13(5) Environmental Law & Management 232.

92   *Communication from the Commission to the Council, the European Parliament, the Economic and Social Committee and the Committee of the Regions on the Sixth Environment Action Programme of the EC: 'Environment 2010: Our Future, Our Choice'* 2001/0029 (COD).

Lofton, J A 'Environmental enforcement: the impact of cultural values and attitudes on social regulation' (2001) 9(1) Environmental Liability 167.

de Prez, P 'Biased enforcement or optimal regulation? Reflections on recent Parliamentary scrutiny of the Environment Agency (2001) 13(3) Environmental Law & Management 145.

'towards a more accountable environment agency' (2001) ENDS Rep 320, 28.

OFFICIAL REPORTS

A Better Quality of Life: A Strategy for Sustainable Development for the UK (1999 Cm 4345).

House of Commons Select Committee on the Environment, Transport and Regional Affairs, 6th Report 1999-2000, *Inquiry into the Workings of the Environment Agency* (HC 34).

House of Commons Environment Committee (1991-92) *Improving Environmental Quality – The Government's Proposal for a New Independent Environment Agency*, Session 1991-92, First Report.

The Food Standards Agency: A Force for Change. (1998 Cm 3830) Stationery Office.

Statement of General Objectives & Practices (Food Standards Agency, London, 2000).

House of Commons Select Committee on Food Standards, First Report (1998-99) *Food Standards Draft Bill* (HC 276 (1999)).

Chapter 4

Environmental law: the international and European dimension

Environmental problems raise supra national issues. Reasons of space preclude this work from dealing at length with the regulation of these problems under international law, but supra national aspects of law and practice cannot be ignored. Thus a *brief* introduction to international legal environmental issues follows, coupled with rather lengthier treatment of EC obligations. Our membership of the EC has considerable implications for the future of the law, as well as bringing this country into partnerships with continental states some of whose nationals are, from the point of view of environmental problems, very *politically* advanced. There is hardly any aspect of environmental law that has no EC dimension.

A INTERNATIONAL ENVIRONMENTAL LAW

International law (by which here is meant 'public' international law as opposed to 'private' or 'conflict of laws') has been described as an 'indispensable body of rules regulating ... the relations between states without which it would be virtually impossible for them to have steady and frequent intercourse',[1] and the system governing relations between States [covering] every aspect of inter-state relations such as jurisdiction, claims to territory, use of the sea and state responsibility to name but a few.[2] From an environmental point of view it tends, sadly, to be a weak system of law lacking an effective system of sanctions. Though as Birnie and Boyle point out in *International Law and the Environment*, to which any serious student of the subject must be referred, despite problems remarkable progress has been made in developing international environmental law. Sands, in *Environmental Law, the Economy and Sustainable Development*, observes that the environment is becoming a more pressing issue in the international legal order. He cites the view of the International Court of Justice in the Request for an Examination of the Situation in Accordance with Paragraph 63 of the Court's Judgment of 20 December 1974 in the case of *New Zealand v France (Nuclear Tests)*[3] that it is an obligation of states to 'respect and protect the natural environment'.

1   Starke, *Introduction to International Law* (10th edn) p 15.
2   Lyster, *International Wildlife Law*, p 3.
3   [1995] ICJ Rep 306.

The sources of international law are custom, general principles recognised by civilised states, decisions of international arbitral and judicial bodies, the views of international public lawyers of high renown and, most importantly, treaties, both general and particular, establishing rules accepted by states; see art 38 of the Statute of the International Court of Justice. None of these sources is fully adequate as a bedrock for international environmental law, but though treaty based law is inevitably likely to be the principal pathway for future developments, customary law cannot be ignored.

Customary international law though relevant in environmental issues has been weak in its impact for it has recognised the principle state or territorial sovereignty, ie the right of states to carry on their activities and to use their resources for their own benefit, which, of course, includes the right to utilise territory and to exploit resources, to name but two issues. However, the principle of state sovereignty is not unlimited. In the *Trail Smelter* case[4] it was argued at p 1965 that: 'No State has the right to use or permit the use of territory in such a manner as to cause injury by fumes in or to the territory of another … when the case is of serious consequence and the injury is established by clear and convincing evidence'. The United Nations charter of Economic Rights and Duties of States reiterates that sovereign rights should only be used 'without causing damage to the legitimate rights of others'. The principle has received wide acceptance by most commentators on international law, and modern state practice appears to be founded on it. It has been adapted by the United Nations General Assembly in its Resolution 1629 of 1961: 'fundamental principles of international law impose a responsibility on all states concerning actions which might have harmful biological consequences … by increasing levels of radioactive fall out' and adopted in the 1972 Stockholm Declaration on the Human Environment, Principle 21: 'States have … the responsibility to ensure that activities within their jurisdiction or control do not cause damage to the environment of other states or of areas beyond the limits of national jurisdiction'.

As Birnie and Boyle[5] point out, two principles seem now to enjoy significant support: (a) to prevent, reduce and control polluting and environmental harms, (b) to co-operate in mitigating environmental emergencies and risks. Other customary principles for which arguments are put forward include concepts such as inter-generational equity, sustainable development and the 'polluter pays' principle, already examined in chapter 1, above. Furthermore many commentators now argue that concepts of sovereignty have to a considerable extent faded over the last 40 years as states have come to accept — to some extent at least — the concept of obligations to act within their jurisdictions for the benefit of humankind as a whole. This has led to recognition that states have a *common interest* in the global environment which may lead to the development of a body of international rules which apply to all states and are enforceable by all states. Similar linked emerging concepts are those of *common heritage* under which, for example, the management of natural resources may be seen to be a matter transcending state jurisdictions, and *common concern* which recognises the existence of entities such as the ozone layer and the global climate which are matters of international concern whose regulation demands that territorial jurisdictional claims must be transcended.

Both *Birnie and Boyle* chapter 3, and Brown-Weiss, *Environmental Change and International Law* point to important customary developments such as the concept of *global* international environmental law, and the interplay which takes place between custom and treaty with the former's development underpinning the growth and importance of the latter as a system of international environmental regulation and protection. The United Nations Law of the Sea (UNCLOS 1982), which contains a number

4   *United States v Canada* 3 RIAA p 1907 (1941).
5   International Law and the Environment.

of measures designed to offer some protection to the marine environment, provides a clear example of such interplay.

'Soft' international environmental law

As in the case of the EC (see below) the difficulties of securing international agreements in a diverse and plural world have led to the emergence of 'halfway houses' known collectively as 'soft law'. This includes Codes of Practice, recommendations, guidelines, resolutions, declarations, etc of or by states. Though the term may be something of a 'shorthand' expression denoting a collection of rather vague legal norms, nevertheless, as Birnie and Boyle (p 27) point out, states *expect* such soft law to be adhered to on a long term basis, and thus have a normative effect on international conduct even though it does not fit into conventional legal categories. On the other hand the degree of commitment by states to 'soft' law can vary greatly; though the fact that an obligation is 'soft' may enable a state to embrace its underlying concept and in consequence modify its activities when it would find it impossible to embrace the concept as a 'hard' rule in a treaty. 'Soft' law enables states to adopt a collective though flexible approach to an environmental problem when, for example, scientific knowledge points generally in the direction of caution but is otherwise inconclusive on an issue; see further *Birnie and Boyle*, pp 26–30 to which indebtedness is acknowledged.

General principles of international environmental law

It is now commonly accepted that the future development of the law should reflect certain principles, particularly in the drafting of treaties; see below. These principles are: the 'Polluter Pays', Precautionary Action, Intergenerational Equity, see chapter 1 above, *and* Non-Discrimination: ie that a polluter who causes transboundary pollution should be treated no less severely than if the harm was caused in the polluter's own country, and Common but Differentiated Responsibilities, ie states should divide the cost of environmental measures according to their contribution to environmental degradation. This latter point is reflected well within the provisions of the United Nations Framework Convention on Climate Change. It has also been suggested that environmental assessment should be undertaken by a state where there is the risk of transboundary damage. The ICJ in the *Gabaèikovo-Nagymaros Project (Hungary v Slovakia)* (ICJ Report (1997) 7) case went as far as to state that this concerned not only future activities, but the continuation of those previously undertaken.[6] The case is outlined further below.

Treaty based law

Despite customary law's flexibility and current resurgence, its inherent problems have led to emphasis in environmental matters being placed on treaty based law. 'A treaty may be defined … as an agreement whereby two or more states establish or seek to establish a relationship between themselves governed by international law' and 'the treaty is the main instrument which the international community possesses for the purpose of initiating or developing international co-operation'.[7] Treaties can exist in

---

6   See further D French, *A Reappraisal of Sovereignty in the light of Global Environmental Concern* (2001) 21 LS 376.
7   *Starke*, pp 436 and 437.

various forms, but in environmental terms the most commonly encountered treaties are likely to be multilateral instruments made in formal style by many states or international institutions, such as the International Civil Aviation Organisation, and known as 'Conventions', together with 'Protocols' which are less formal agreements often subsidiary or ancillary to a Convention, other nomenclatures include 'covenant', 'pact' or 'act'. Treaties may be either 'law-making' in that they lay down generally applicable rules, or 'treaty contracts' which deal with individual issues concerning only two or a very few states. From a global point of view the first type is of greater importance, but environmental treaties have been made in a variety of forms by a variety of states for many years, dating from the 1868 Mannheim Convention on, inter alia, water supply on the Rhine (between Belgium, France, Germany, The Netherlands and the UK), to the numbers of multi-party arrangements made from the 1970s onwards. The yearly rate of treaty making now exceeds that for the century's opening decades. However, a warning note needs to be sounded: 'treaties are often weaker [than national legislation] because no state can be bound without its consent. The greater the number of participants in the formulation of a treaty, the weaker or more ambiguous its provisions are likely to be since they have to make compromises making them acceptable to every state involved'.[8] Treaties are also not rapidly made, and a five year negotiating time between states is average in relation to environmental issues, though, as Birnie and Boyle (p 12) point out treaties can be made and can enter into force quite quickly as was the case with the 1985 Vienna Convention on Protection of the Ozone Layer.

Treaties may arise in a number of ways, for example because of pressure from a state, groups of states or an international organisation, and a treaty will normally be finally formulated at an international conference. State representatives at such a conference may sign such a document, though this creates *no* legal obligation to ratify or comply with the treaty's terms on the state's part, but a strong moral obligation and an expectation between signatories that none of them will frustrate treaty objectives. Ratification is the process whereby states undertake binding legal obligations under treaties. State practice as to the mode of ratification varies: in the UK, Parliamentary approval, normally in legislative form, is required for any treaty which, inter alia, affects the private rights of British subjects, or changes or modifies the law of the land, or requires a grant of new powers or financial responsibilities to the Crown, or which has been made expressly subject to Parliamentary approval. It is usually provided in treaties that they will come into force after a specified number of ratifications by states has been reached. Some treaties are restricted in that only certain specified states may be party to them, others are open to all to be original parties to them or, by accession, to become subsequent members of them; whilst others are also open to 'regional economic integration organisations' such as the EC. Treaties may also be made subject to 'reservations' whereunder a state releases itself from certain treaty obligations. Such a reservation may be made when a state becomes party to a treaty, and then to a substantive treaty provision, or, when a state declares it will not accept a particular regulation made according to a procedure existing under the treaty, though there is debate as to whether such a practice should properly be called a 'reservation'. As Lyster (p 9) points out, reservations are useful in importing flexibility to treaties so that states which accept most, but not all, treaty obligations can become parties, but they 'also provide a loophole enabling a State to defend its vested interests which conflict with the spirit of the Treaty'. In some cases making reservations is prohibited by the treaty itself, while reservations generally cannot be made which are incompatible with treaty objectives; see art 19(c) Vienna Convention on the Law of Treaties. The form and content of treaties also varies considerably. For example it is now the practice to have basic

8   Lyster, *International Wildlife Law*, p 4.

general provisions in one document — which may receive the title 'Convention' — while highly specified technical standards, say on emissions, are placed in subsidiary documents — which may be known as protocols — to allow for their amendment in the light of technical progress. This, however, has the disbenefit of allowing states to opt out of detailed control by objecting to the terms of the protocol. Other treaties are mere 'frameworks' simply creating no more than a generalised obligation on states to take some, unspecified, action — of course the obligation can be 'fleshed out' by a subsequent protocol, but the initiative to do this lies with states. A treaty can also take the form of an 'umbrella' whereunder there is a principal framework convention and a number of protocols each dealing with a specific issue. States ratifying the principal convention may also be required to ratify one or more of these accompanying protocols.

In 'dualist' states such as the UK it is generally further necessary, once a treaty has come into force, to pass national legislation giving the treaty domestic legal force. Thereafter what will be enforced within the state is the domestic legislation, though as Robin Churchill points out in *Law, Policy and the Environment*, p 156: 'it is not unknown for a treaty to have been formally implemented by legislation but for it not actually to be applied in practice ... because of defects in the implementing legislation or because the legislation is not properly given effect to'.

International organisations may also have powers under treaty to bind parties to such a treaty by their decisions, for example the International Maritime Organisation, the Oslo and Paris Commissions on countering certain pollution threats to the North Sea and North Eastern Atlantic, and the International Whaling Commission. Such organisations, as Birnie and Boyle (ch 2) point out may also adopt 'soft law' techniques by producing codes of practice which states observe in practice, while some may actually take such documents into their own legislative frameworks.

A convenient starting point for modern treaty based international environmental law is the Stockholm Conference of 1972 and its Declaration on the Human Environment. Sufficiently imprecise to leave much to the discretion of states wishing to advance their own interests, the Declaration has served as a basis for subsequent international developments and formulations of legal principle. So in 1982 at its 60th Annual Conference in Montreal, the International Law Association defined transboundary pollution in terms of the introduction by human action of material or energy into the environment so as to affect deleteriously health, living resources, ecosystems, property, amenity and legitimate use of the environment where pollution originates wholly or partly in one state and then invades another's territory. States, it was argued, should abate and control such pollution, and should limit new or increased pollution sources, and give warning of activities likely to cause significant transboundary pollution. Likewise in 1982 the United Nations set up the Intergovernmental Committee on the Development and Utilisation of New and Renewable Sources of Energy, and a gathering of 105 states at Nairobi reaffirmed the Stockhold principles. This was followed in 1983 by the creation of the World Commission on Environment and Development by the United Nations.

One current weakness of international environmental law is the problem of compliance. Disputes arising between states are initially submitted to negotiation, and only thereafter is recourse had to international arbitration and the International Court of Justice, and even then only in exceptional cases, for the remedy 'is seen as a politically unfriendly act ... and ... it is often difficult to achieve a satisfactory remedy by this means' (Lyster, p 11). Recourse may also be had to the good offices of another state acting as a mediator between disputants. To ensure more effective compliance it is important to build into treaty provisions requirements that states: establish regular meetings to review treaty implementation and revise terms as and when necessary; create administrative agencies to assist with implementation; impose regular reporting .

obligations, or create monitoring or observer systems, or provide for financial sanctions or rewards as 'carrots and sticks'. The Court has tended towards agreements parties have made themselves rather than develop a jurisprudence that sets forth justicable environmental principles. On the recognition of principles see further below. This point is illustrated in the *Gabaèikovo-Nagymaros Project (Hungary v Slovakia)* (ICJ Report (1997) 7) case where a dispute arose between Hungary and Slovakia in relation to an agreement made by a Treaty in 1977 between the two countries to build a hydro-electric dam on the river Danube, as well as ancillary works. Hungary pulled out of the project in 1989 on the basis, it claimed, of the project's likely environmental impact. Slovakia continued with the project, which ultimately had a negative effect on the flow of the Danube. In turn the countries agreed to refer the dispute that had arisen between them to the ICJ. The court found that the original 1977 Treaty was still in force and therefore governed Hungarian/Slovak relations. It was thus up to the parties to use their Treaty provisions to address their difficulties. Slovakia had argued that the rules of the Treaty could only be supplanted by agreement. Hungary on the other hand was of the view that subsequent customary and Treaty-based law became applicable to the situation. The deference to the provisions of the Treaty does not demonstrate a willingness on the part of the ICJ to adopt a creative or expansionist role in ensuring environmental protection. However, as a more potentially encouraging aside, the separate opinion of Judge Weeramantry is notable. He went as far as to say that the term sustainable development is a 'principle with normative value'. How valuable that view proves to be remains to be seen. For a compelling discussion of the issues in the case see V Lowe, *Sustainable Development and Unsustainable Argument* in Boyle and Freestone (eds) *International Law and Sustainable Development.* Supervision by means of the creation of international agencies has been found a useful means of law enforcement, though it 'also entails the negotiation and elaboration of detailed rules, standards and practices' (Birnie and Boyle, p 201). Sands, however, has been scathing about the effectiveness of some of the environmental bodies at international level (*Revesz,* op cit p 394), suggesting a duplication and in some case differing approaches to problems. He questions the sense 'for there to be separate secretariats dealing with trade in endangered species, biodiversity, migratory species and wetlands'. His solution would be to have a unified body with 'overarching competence and particular jurisdiction'.

This is not to say that international environmental law is without significance. Some principles are translated into national practice and as Lyster (op cit p 14) points out, 'there is another overriding factor which ensures that, by and large, States make every effort to enforce a treaty once they have become a Party to it: it is in the interests of almost every State that order, and not chaos, should be a governing principle of human life and if treaties were made and freely ignored chaos would soon result'. Moreover the future may see the development of a universal convention, consolidating existing and establishing new principles of legal environmental protection, and setting out the concomitant rights and duties of states. A UN Commission for Environmental Protection and Sustainable Development has been debated as a monitoring and investigative body, as has a High Commissioner or 'Environmental Ombudsman' to act as a 'trustee' for the environment and to take action on behalf of its protection. In 1989 a 24-nation conference at The Hague called for such a new authority to be known as 'Globe'. This would be an executive body, operating alongside the International Court of Justice at The Hague (the judicial compliance enforcing and arbitral body) and the UN Assembly as a legislative organ, able to lay down the framework of international environmental regulation. 'Globe', however, would be an unprecedented agency able to make decisions by majority vote, and possessing powers to enforce environmental standards. 'Globe' would also be able to pursue actions for damages against polluting states before the

ICJ. The concept of 'Globe' necessarily involves some surrender of the concept of state sovereignty.

Trends in international environmental law

Since 1972 emphasis has shifted quite definitely from attempts to create an international system to ensure that states make reparation for environmental harm inflicted on other states towards a system based much more on the 'control and prevention of environmental harm and the conservation and sustainable development of the natural resources and ecosystems of the whole bisophere ... [ie] a preventive or regulatory regime ...' (Birnie and Boyle, p 137). As Iwama points out in his contribution to *Environmental Change and International Law* there are now emerging principles of prevention and mitigation of harm. These are that: humanity has a common interest in protecting entities such as the climactic system, the ozone layer, rainforests and the biological diversity of the earth, and this is reflected in the development of measures such as those to phase out ozone depleting substances; to enter into co-operation in scientific research, systematic observation and to render mutual assistance in this connection, a very useful step on the way to later more specific agreements; to exchange information — often through the medium of an international institution; to give prior notice of activities which might entail a significant risk of transfrontier pollution, and to undertake prior environmental impact assessment of such activities and consult with other potentially affected states; where an environmental disaster occurs to have made available a prior risk assessment to other concerned states, and to provide emergency assistance to those affected. The development of a preventative regulatory framework internationally and its implementation nationally was one of the issues recognised by the 1992 Rio Conference on Environment and Development (UNCED). As is pointed out in Sand (ed), *The Effectiveness of International Environmental Agreements* (pp 24–27), the terms of Agenda 21, one of the documents to emerge from UNCED, make it clear that country specific laws and regulations are most important measures for environmental protection and regulation and the promotion of sustainable development, for it is by these that international obligations are translated into concrete action. These need, however, to conform to certain general principles. States thus need to develop and implement programmes of laws which are integrated, enforceable and effective, and which are based on sound social, ecological, economic and similar principles, and to ensure review of, and compliance with, those laws. Many states will, however, need technical assistance in achieving these objectives.

Flying on from Rio?

Rio produced a number of disparate documents: the Rio Declaration — an expansion of the 1972 Stockhold Declaration; the Framework Convention on Climate Change — a treaty providing for further negotiated protocols on issues such as greenhouse gas emissions and deforestation; the Convention on Biological Diversity — a rather hurriedly negotiated document which nevertheless aims to arrest the rate of species loss consequent on pollution and habitat destruction; a declaration on forests, and 'Agenda 21' an 800 page 'action plan' for the rest of the decade and the 21st century on the diversity of issues such as oceans, forests and industry. Though, as Professor Freestone points out in his 1993 inaugural lecture 'The Road from Rio', these treaties represent the lowest common denominator of consensus, ie what the 'most reluctant participant will accept', he also argues that Rio's main contribution to the development of international environmental law is 'through the crystallisation of principles', in particular with regard to enshrining the precautionary principle (see chapter 1 above) as a guideline for future treaty making on all environmental issues thus entailing 'a shift in decision-making in favour of a bias towards safety and caution', ie 'preventive or remedial action is to be taken if scientific evidence makes it plausible that detrimental effects to the ... environment may result'.

Sustainable development in particular lies at the heart of Agenda 21, a document which builds on the earlier 1987 Brundtland Commission's finding that world poverty and environmental degradation are closely interrelated issues, so that environmental protection and providing for the development of third world countries must go hand in hand for the future. All nations must co-operate to combat existing environmental problems, to develop and apply environmentally sound technologies and also produce that level of economic growth and development in all countries necessary to combat poverty, especially in those countries already burdened with massive foreign debts. This involves the devotion of new financial resources on a vast scale to development coupled with environmental protection, while 'advanced' nations must also be prepared to afford favourable access to science and technology for the less developed states. The basis for this has to be the recognition by states of their common interests, mutual needs and common, but differentiated, responsibilities. To achieve this Agenda 21 has a number of themes: first, the revitalisation of growth with sustainability — this policy has implications for the pattern and content of treaties on world trade for reducing the debt burdens of poorer states, for lifestyle changes in wealthy nations, changes in consumer preferences and practices, for making the overall level, pattern and distribution of consumption and production compatible with the ecological capacity of the globe; secondly, the substantial reduction and ultimate eradication of world poverty; thirdly, the creation of a habitable, healthy and sustainable living environment for all the world's people — this policy has particular implications for pollution control and waste minimisation; fourthly, the reversal of the destruction of natural resources and the implementation of strategies for the sustainable use of land, water, biological and genetic resources, biotechnology and energy — a policy having vast implications for the task of sustainably raising the productivity and incomes of the poor without irreversibly degrading systems of life support, for energy production and consumption and for protecting the biodiversity of the world; fifthly, the creation of action programmes to protect on a total and global basis the world's atmospheric and oceanic resources; sixthly, the management of chemicals and waste to create a habitable 'clean world'.

Agenda 21 recognises that governments alone cannot achieve these goals, all relevant people and groups of people must be involved, which involves fundamental change in public education, awareness and training, great transparency in public decision making processes and a greater flow of relevant information to the public, not just within but between nations.

In order to ensure institutional arrangements to bring about the integration of environment and development issues Agenda 21 also brought about the creation of a Commission on Sustainable Development (COSD). This body reports to the UN General Assembly.

Other principles given special emphasis by Rio include those of 'differentiated responsibilities', ie a recognition that developed nations bear special responsibilities in respect of pursuing sustainable development because of the pressures their societies place on the environment and the technologies and resources at their command; ensuring the effectiveness of environmental laws, and creating adequate systems of environmental impact assessment. Freestone is thus able to hail Rio as a coming of age of international environmental law, but he also points out that the framework laid down at Rio has to be developed into a truly effective system of protection.

In some ways international environmental law since Rio has developed apace. In UNCED's immediate aftermath considerable attention was given to the problem of ozone depletion already addressed by the Vienna Convention 1985, and the Montreal Protocol 1987. In 1992 in London an enhanced schedule of phasing out ozone depleting chlorofluorocarbon (CFC) gases was agreed. In 1994 the USA unilaterally decided to bring forward its CFC phase out programme to 1996. The Copenhagen agreement of 1994 committed other nations to a similar programme, made arrangements to ensure financial help for third world nations to help them comply with new requirements, and also brought within regulation for the first time hydrochloroflurocarbons (HCFC) and methyl bromide, which is used in commercial pesticides. In respect of the latter it was agreed to freeze production at 1991 levels by the end of 1995, with phasing out to be postponed for some years; in respect of the former, production curbs will come into force in 1996 with production falling to one third of that level by 2015, while a ban on production will operate from 2030. Even so these curbs disappointed environmental activists as not being sufficiently stringent.

Even more a cause for concern was the 1994 conclusion of the Intergovernmental Panel on Climate Change (IPCC) which argued that stringent cuts in emissions of the 'greenhouse' or global warming gases of 60% of current emissions are needed to stabilise the climate and achieve the Rio conference's objectives on climate change. This issue is expanded upon in chapter 16.

The World Trade Organisation (GATT)

Modern discussion of international protection of the environment would be incomplete without a mention of the impact of the World Trade Organisation (WTO). The WTO is an international trade body that seeks to promote liberalised trade throughout the world between its members. It is often demonised in the eyes of those who are of the view that it is a vehicle for the negative aspects of 'globalisation'. The WTO and its predecessor, the GATT, have had to deal with environmentally-related trade disputes and attempt a settlement when the disputes have reached its dispute settlement panels. It is impossible to do any justice to the concepts of the trade/environment dichotomy here, and readers are directed to specialist materials. What follows provides only a flavour of the issues involved. The basic question surrounds the idea of whether or not a particular state may impose its own higher standards of environmental protection, first, in order to prevent the import of goods which are unable to match those standards; and secondly, whether those higher standards can be imposed outside of that state's jurisdiction. Sands (Revesz p 391) states that the difference between the two is between the regulation of products and processes. There are obvious differences between states' standards and the issue is whether, in breach of the WTO agreement (art XI GATT 1994), such preventions are in the mould of a quantitative restriction on imports Two particular case are of relevance here the *Tuna/Dolphin* disputes and the *Shrimp/Turtle* dispute.[9] Put very simply, all the cases concerned US attempts to prevent imports of tuna and shrimps which it claimed were caught, or harvested in a way that harmed other marine life, particularly dolphins and turtles. Under the GATT 1994, art XX provides some exceptions to the rule against quantitative restrictions on imports. Paragraph (b) permits such interference if there is a necessity to protect plant animal or human life; and para (g) on the basis that the measure adopted is concerned with the conservation of exhaustible natural resources. Both of these are subject to the requirement that the measures do not arbitrarily discriminate between countries, and so long as they do not

9   *Mexico v USA, EEC and the Netherlands v USA* International Environmental Law Reports, Vol 2, pp 48, 80 (GATT Panel Report), *India Malaysia, Pakistan and Thailand v USA* International Environmental Law Reports, Vol 2, p 234 (W.TO appellate body).

represent a hidden restriction on trade. The US lost both case before the GATT and WTO panels: in the *Tuna/Dolphin case* on the basis that the US was seen to be trying to exert its influence extra-territorially, in that the US was trying to dictate a conservation measure to the Mexicans, who were fishing in a way that the US did not consider 'dolphin friendly'. In the second *Tuna /Dolphin* case the Appellate panel found against the US, but did leave the door open in the subsequent case for states to impose restrictions so as to influence environmental protection for an exhaustible natural resource pursuant to an international environmental agreement. In *Shrimp/Turtle,* the US actions in prohibiting imports of shrimp from various Asian countries on the basis that their harvesting methods threatened species of turtle, were again held to be in breach. The body found that the US's restrictions were provisionally justified under art XX(g), but that as they had failed to reach an agreement on the issue, their actions became inconsistent with the provisions of the GATT 1994. Here though the appellate body did recognise that it was permissible for one state to act to protect resources outside of its own jurisdiction. It was the manner of the application of the measure that was in conflict.

Where the WTO and environmental protection go on into the future is unclear. It may be that there needs to be a revisiting of the GATT 1994 to make the exception in art XX more explicitly 'environmentally friendly' or that specific exemptions be introduced for issues or species already regulated by international law. The WTO secretariat has considered trade and the environment and had concluded that the way forward is to 'reinvent environmental policies in an ever more integrated world economy so as to ensure we live within ecological limits'. To do this it envisages greater use of mechanisms and institutions for multilateral cooperation.

International environmental law: a summary and a vision?

A hesitant — though many would add far too slow — start has been made towards creating a discrete body of international environmental law having at its heart a precautionary and preventive approach to environmental protection. And while the speed of the world convoy is still that of its slowest ships, a number of encouraging developments have occurred:

1   The emergence of international prohibitions on the production and use of particular chemicals, eg those on ozone depleting substances.
2   The development of international regulations constraining permissible conduct on the part of nations and companies, for example requirements as to limiting emissions of SO .
3   The creation of international standards by which industry can regulate itself to ensure protection of the environment, see chapter 1 above.
4   Gradual acceptance of the need for environmental impact assessment particularly at a world regional level.
5   Emerging recognition of the need to give as much public information as possible abut the adverse consequences of activities on the environment via enhancing public access to relevant information, independent surveillance and observation of activities and monitoring programmes.
6   Continued adherence to such established principles such as the 'polluter pays'.
7   Gradual acceptance of the need to use economic and fiscal instruments to encourage clean technologies and low resource demand activities, while subsidies given to environmentally unfriendly activities are subject to increased scrutiny within the framework of international agreement on trade.
8   The emergence of international forums having jurisdiction to enforce a number of international agreements.

9   The possibility that some states may refuse to allow the import of goods not meeting international requirements — as can already happen with endangered species.

10   Acceptance of differentiated obligations by developed nations, together with an acceptance of the need to compensate, financially or otherwise, less developed nations when they take on board environmental obligations.

11   The continuing use of 'soft law' techniques.

Even so no-one should labour under any illusion that the way forward from Rio is or can be easy. We must move towards a principle of equal ecological security so that no state achieves its well being at the expense of others, towards requirements of foresight and prevention of harm, towards sharing knowledge and technology, towards, of course, sustainable development, towards acceptance that humans have the right to an acceptable environment. Much of the framework for achieving this currently exists, but how fast and far we can go depends on the will of nations and peoples. What that has been, and is, at a local world regional level is our next concern.

EC or EU — Community or Union?

The initial entity was the European Economic Community (EEC) established by the Treaty of Rome in 1957 along with the European Coal and Steel Community (ECSC) and Euratom. The EEC was enlarged in 1972 when the UK, Ireland and Denmark joined, and again in 1981 (Greece) and 1986 (Spain and Portugal). Austria, Sweden and Finland joined in 1995. Enlargement of institutional powers came with the Single European Act (SEA) 1987 and the Treaty of European Union (Maastricht Treaty) 1992. Under the latter the EEC changed its name to the European Community (EC) while the European Union (EU) was also created which subsumed the objects of the EC (such as the common internal market) and added other objectives of its own such as a single currency, common defence and foreign policies, etc. The European *Union* therefore comprises more than just the EC Treaty; EC will be used throughout this work in relation to the specific duties imposed by the Treaties and the secondary legislation, as it refers more accurately to the role imagined.

Further important institutional and other amendments have been made through the Treaties of Amsterdam and Nice, although in the case of the latter, mainly concerning enlargement, not all of it is currently in force. The Treaty of Amsterdam has consolidated and renumbered the majority of Treaty Articles and throughout this chapter the new numbers will be used with the corresponding predecessor or successor article numbers listed in parentheses where appropriate.

B EUROPEAN COMMUNITY (EC) ENVIRONMENTAL LAW

Ideally, there should be vertical integration between international, regional and national systems of environmental law. In its international aspect the EC goes some way to realising this. Before examining this it is necessary to remind ourselves what the EC is. It grew out of the post 1945 desire to: rebuild western Europe; remove the likelihood of future Franco-German conflicts; counter perceived threats of Soviet aggression, with economic reconstruction and expansion as key policies. Hence in 1957 the six original member states declared their desire to create a 'European Economic Community' to establish a 'common market' and to approximate the economic policies of the states, their harmonious economic development, continuous and balanced expansion, increased stability, accelerated rising standards of living and closer relationships. Since then the EC has grown by the accession of new states and the development of community powers. Today the EC is a special entity not easily compared 'with other political entities: it contains some of the features of an ordinary international organisation and, less prominently but nevertheless quite distinctly some features of a federation. The latter are gradually becoming more prominent' (Hartley, *Foundations of European Community Law* (3rd edn) p 9). The EC does, however, possess powers to enter into treaties either by itself or acting together with its member states. These exist in some cases under express provisions of the Treaty of Rome, the basic constituent of EC law which relates to co-operation with other international organisations. The EC also has under 'the doctrine of parallelism' implied treaty making powers that cover virtually all areas of activity covered by the EC legal system.[10]

Under its powers the EC is a party to a number of international environmental measures. It was furthermore argued by the EC Commission Task Force Report on the Environment and Common Market that a global environmental role should be developed and that external and internal environmental policy should derive from the principles.

The influence of the EC on the development of international environmental law has already been marked. EC measures serve as models for other world regions and it appears that in the coming decade the importance of this aspect of EU law will continue to increase considerably; see further Sands, 'European Community Treaty Obligations in the Field of International Environmental Law — An Overview' in Vaughan (ed), *Environment and Planning Law.*

C THE INCEPTION OF THE EC'S ENVIRONMENTAL POLICY

In October 1972 the heads of government of the then enlarged EEC meeting for the first time in Paris called for proposals for an EEC environmental policy. Just over a year later on 22 November 1973 the First Action Programme for the Environment was formally adopted.

The decision of the summit meeting in 1972 reflected a growing awareness that the degradation of the environment was a problem of great urgency and international political significance. It followed shortly after the United Nations conference on the Human Environment at Stockholm (also in 1972). The policies at both EC and international level have subsequently developed a symbiotic relationship to embrace and define principles for action, as set out in chapter 1 above, which further reflect their importance.

D THE PLACE OF THE ENVIRONMENTAL POLICY IN THE OVERALL EC SCHEME.

The aims of the original EEC were set out in the Treaty of Rome, Art 2, and were concerned with approximating the economic policies of member states to promote increases in trade, rising living standards, and economic growth.

It is original proposal for a Community environmental policy (Bull, EC Supplement 5/73), the Commission revealed that this statement must now be taken to comprehend environmental issues: 'To remain balanced, economic growth must henceforth be guided and controlled to a greater degree by quality requirements. Conversely, the protection

10   *EC Commission v EC Council* [1971] ECR 263, [1971] CMLR 335; *North-East Atlantic Fisheries Convention Case* [1976] ECR 1279; *Opinion 1/76 on the Laying-Up Fund for Inland Waterway Vessels* [1977] ECR 741.

11   See eg S Bar and RA Kraemer, *European Environmental Policy after Amsterdam* JEL 10(2) 1998) and T Schumacher: *The Environmental Integration Clause in Article 6 of the EU Treaty – Prioritising Environmental Protection* Env L Rev (2001) 3).

of the environment is both a guarantee of and a prerequisite for a harmonious development of economic activities'. Further, references to living standards had to be reinterpreted to take account of the *quality* of life.

While there is the potential for distortions within the Common Market consequent on divergent national policies, this has not been the only rationale for change. As the EC Treaty has evolved to encompass a more social agenda, the need to incorporate broader and deeper environmental protection competences has become irresistible. The most recent manifestation of this expansion can be observed through the provisions of the treaty of Amsterdam which has expanded the principle, first included by the SEA, that environmental concerns should be integrated into all other Community policies. Moving the principle from its former position in the environmental chapter of the Treaty (Art 130r – now Art 174) to the beginning of the Treaty, in Art 6 EC may only have cosmetic value: however, it has been argued that the provisions are strengthened by the increased emphasis and the requirement that integration should be 'with a view to promoting sustainable development'. Some commentators[11] have questioned whether the clause has legal force per se or is just a tool to achieve environmental law objectives, or even just a mandatory factor for consideration.

E THE ACTION PROGRAMMES

There have been a number of consecutive Action Programmes for the Environment. The first in November 1973 (OJ C112), the second in May 1977 (OJ C139), the fifth in May 1993 (OJ C138) and the sixth, proposed in January 2001 runs until 2010. The sixth Action Programme, entitled Environment 2010, Our Future, Our Choice (COM(01)0031), emphasises a strategic approach to attaining the EC's environmental objectives. In particular the Commission sees a greater role for the ECJ in the implementation of environmental law, and the further integration of environmental concerns into other policies: this particular aspect will no doubt be improved by virtue of the integration clause in Art 6 EC as outlined above. The sixth Action Programme identifies four special priority areas where the EC will take action: climate change; nature and biodiversity; environment and health; and the sustainable use of natural resources and waste management are all of particular concern. The relationship between the EC and the wider world community is also addressed in the Action Programme. A greater role on the world stage is envisaged, especially when considering the context of moves towards an enlarged European Union. The Commission is of the view that it is one of the main tasks of the candidate countries to implement EC environmental legislation, with support coming through the Community's funding programmes to help achieve this.

The first programmes laid down a number of underlying principles, still current, to which all subsequent legislation should adhere. The most important of these are that pollution should be eliminated or reduced at source and that the polluter should pay the cost of prevention, elimination or disposal measures.

In its early years, environmental policy concentrated on 'clean-up' measures: the reduction of pollution and the improvement of certain aspects of the environment. These were essentially curative measures, designed to deal with pressing problems. With the second and third programmes came a change of emphasis and an opportunity to take a longer term view. This was to lay stress on the preventive aspects of policy seeking to achieve an overall improvement in environmental quality.

Environmental policy now holds a centre stage position in EC affairs, and the integration clause in Art 6 EC will ensure that there is, theoretically at least, parity with the Community's traditional objectives. In 1972 the Community's Heads of State declared 'economic expansion is not an end in itself' and the crystallisation of environmental policy into a significant balancing factor in other policy areas reflects that sentiment. The EC proceeds on the basis that strict environmental standards are economically justifiable for they can be associated with economic growth and job creation. Economic measures have tended historically to play little part in the implementation of the environmental policy, for the EC, as it was, tended to rely on legal controls such as licensing standards, emission limits, bans and other restrictions, these often existing on a segmented basis with individual controls for the individual environmental media; see further Alexander, 'Competition, Subsidy and Environmental Protection' in Vaughan (ed), *Environment and Planning Law*. Enhanced use of economic regulation is clearly cost effective, however, and following the interim review of the fifth Action Programme in 1994 it was accepted only slow progress had been made in broadening the range of policy instruments, and integrating environment policy into other policy areas. The consideration of the use for example, of more market based mechanisms to combat climate change and air pollution are now at the heart of the EC's strategy.

F THE LEGAL BASIS OF EC ACTION

Before the SEA came into effect in 1987, environmental measures were underpinned by no specific treaty provision. This did not prevent the former EEC from making more than 100 environmental instruments relating to protection of water and air quality waste management and control, controls over chemicals, protection of flora, fauna and the countryside and noise. These were considered to be within the powers of Art 100 (now Art 94) which allowed the Council, acting unanimously on a proposal from the Commission, to issue directives to bring about approximations of the provisions of law, regulations or administrative actions in member states affecting the establishment or functioning of the common market. Reliance was also placed on Art 235 (now Art 308), a 'sweep-up' provision, which permits action by the EC institutions appropriate to securing any objectives of the Community that are otherwise unable to be achieved through other treaty powers. A driving force behind the development of the law at this stage was a collective desire by member states to harmonise away distortions of trade by setting common standards for products, motor vehicles for example. This collective desire did, however, enable the former EEC to develop a competency in environmental issues — the so called 'soft law' technique.

Since 1987 a legal firm base for environmental action has existed. The SEA inserted Title VII — 'Environment' in Part 3 of the Treaty of Rome on EC policies. This was itself considerably modified by the Maastricht Treaty of 1992 largely because under the SEA provisions, Art 130S (now 175) of the Treaty of Rome had provided for environmental provisions to be adopted only unanimously, while at the same time providing under Art 100A (now 95) that measures intended to facilitate completion of the internal market could be adopted by qualified majority voting. This led to litigation as to which was the appropriate legal base for environmental action.

The position was clarified to an extent in *EC Commission v EC Council*[12] which turned on whether the correct legal base had been used for a directive which sought to reduce pollution by titanium dioxide by harmonising national programmes in that regard. The Commission had wished to use Art 100A, the Council Art 130S. The court stated that the legal basis for a directive cannot be left to the *wish* of a community institution; an objective decision has to be made and that involves considering the purpose and content of the measure in question. In the present case the directive was directed both

12   [1991] 3 LMELR 164.

to harmonising internal market rules and to environmental protection. The court considered that simply because a directive has an environmental component, it does *not* therefore *have* to rest on Art 130S: Art 100A *may* be an appropriate basis for a programme which seeks to harmonise national rules on an industry's production conditions so that distortions of competition are eliminated. This decision was a liberal interpretation of Art 100A, but in part related to the fact that the article enabled greater involvement of the European Parliament and thus offered greater democratic legitimacy. However, in *EC Commission v EC Council*[13] the court considered that the primary objective of a Community measure should determine its legal base, and that points to use of Art 130S, see also *Mondiet v Islais*.[14] Over time, taking account of the fact that there remains little practical difference in the decision-making processes that permit either harmonisation or environmental directives, the legal base issue has become less pressing. Recent case law[15] has considered the legal basis of other areas of responsibility that have to consider the protection of the environment. The EC's ability to accede to international environmental Treaties was recently considered in *Spain v EC Council*[16] where an interpretation of 'management of water resources' in Art 175 was determinative of the correct legal basis for the EC's accession to a measure designed to offer additional protection to the river Danube. It has been argued by Schumacher that by virtue of Art 6 (see further above) measures with environmental impacts should state in their citation of reasons the purpose of the measure in question and the reasoning behind a particular legal basis.

G THE INSTITUTIONS AND LEGAL BASE OF EC ENVIRONMENTAL ACTIVITY

Article 3(1) of the Treaty of Rome specifically declares that EU activity extends to the creation of 'a policy in the sphere of the environment'. The Treaty of Amsterdam further amended the original Treaty position by the inclusion of a new Art 6. This important article, as mentioned above, states that 'environmental protection requirements must be integrated into the definition and interpretation of the Community policies and activities referred to in Art 3, in particular with a view to promoting sustainable development'. The new integration clause is an important further development arguably placing environmental concerns at the heart of all other EC actions.

The Council

Made up of ministerial representatives from each member state having power to bind their governments, the Council, whose presidency rotates amongst the states, is the EC's law-making body. A Committee of Permanent Representatives of Member States (COREPER) and the General Secretariat prepare the Council's Agenda. The Actual composition of the Council varies according to the matters under discussion; thus environment ministers will meet to discuss environmental issues.

The so called 'European Council' is not an EC institution but a body provided for by the SEA. At the end of a period of the presidency the state holding that office holds a meeting of the political leaders of member states. Important decisions can be taken at this gathering, for example on the doctrine of subsidiarity, see below.

13   [1993] ECR I-939.
14   [1993] ECR I-6133.
15   Cases C-164/97 and C-165/97 [1999] ECR I-1139.
16   (2001) unreported; see ELM 13 [2001] 2.

The Commission

The Commission is made up of members at least one of whom must come from each member state, larger nations such as France, Germany and the UK having two. The Commission is headed by a President appointed by member states' governments, who must achieve unanimity on the issue, following consultation with the Parliament. The first duty of Commissioners is to the EC, they are not there to serve the interests of their home states. The Commission is a policy making body whose task is to put proposals before the Council. It is also the enforcer of EC law against member states in breech under Art 226, by which if the Commission considers a member state has failed to fulfil an obligation under the treaty, it is to deliver a reasoned opinion on the issue, after giving the state in question the opportunity to make observations. If that state then still fails to comply within the Commission's stated period the Commission may bring the matter before the European Court of Justice.

The 'civil service' of the Commission is divided into a number of Directorates-General. The Environment Directorate General is itself split into Directorates A-E dealing with sectoral issues of environmental concern.

The Parliament

The Parliament is not a legislature in the traditional sense of being primarily a law making body, though it has the functions of advising and supervising other institutions. Its members (MEPs) having political affiliations, and from them are drawn committees to examine legislative proposals and make recommendations on which the full body can vote, eg the Environment and Social Affairs Committee. Since the Maastricht Treaty the law making powers of the Parliament have increased, and the Treaty of Amsterdam has increased those further still.

The European Court of Justice (ECJ)

The ECJ consists of judges drawn from the member states, assisted by a number of Advocates-General whose task is to assist the decision making process of the Court by presenting an opinion on a case following legal argument before the Court: *normally* the Court follows this opinion in its judgment. The Court may sit in a number of chambers or panels. The principal function of the Court is to secure the observation of the Treaty of Rome according to law.

In addition to the ability of the Commission to take action against defaulting member states, member states can themselves take action against their fellows under Art 227 in respect of purported breaches of treaty obligations.

Should the ECJ find that a member state has failed to fulfil its obligations that state is to be required to take the necessary measures to ensure compliance. Until the Maastricht Treaty that was all that could be done and the enforcement of the law then left much to be desired. However, Art 228 now provides that where the 'necessary measures' have not been taken the Commission may go through the reasoned opinion process (see above) and specify the matters in respect of which compliance is still outstanding, and set a time limit for remedial action. If the requisite steps are not taken the matter may again be brought before the ECJ who may, if satisfied that there is non compliance, impose a lump sum or penalty payment on the defaulting state. Recently the procedure has been utilised effectively against Greece.[17] In July 2000 the ECJ

---

17   Case C-387/97 *EC Commission v Greece* (2000) (not yet reported) see Env Law Mgmt (2000)12(5), Env L Rev 3(2001) 131-138.

imposed a daily fine of 20,000 Euros on Greece for its breach of its obligations under the waste framework Directive and the directive on toxic and dangerous waste in respect of fly-tipping at a site in Crete. Greece was found in breach of its obligations under EC law in an earlier case[18] and the Commission commenced Article 228 proceedings in view of its opinion that Greece had not sufficiently remedied the earlier breach. In determining the rate of fine the Commission had issued guidance that takes account of, inter alia, the duration of the breach, its seriousness and the GDP of the offending state so as to be determinative of its ability to pay.

The Economic and Social Committee (ECOSOC)

The body's tasks are described in Arts 257-262. It is solely an advisory body dealing with both the Council and the Commission.

The Court of Auditors

This body audits EU accounts.

The environmental provisions of the Treaty

The term 'environment' is not defined in the Treaty, but it extends to cover protection of humans, land use and town and country planning issues, waste, management and use of water and other natural resources, including flora and fauna, climate, and energy use; see Kramer, *EC Treaty & Environmental Law*, 4th edn.

Article 174 provides that policy on the environment shall contribute to pursuit of: protecting, preserving and improving the environment; protecting human health, prudent and rational utilisation of natural resources; promoting international measures to deal with environmental problems. Policy is: to aim at a high level of protection, considering regional diversities; to be based on the precautionary and preventive principles, and on the principle that damage should be rectified at source and that the 'polluter pays'. Environmental policy *should* be integrated into other policies. In the preparation of policy account is to be taken of available scientific and technical data, regional environmental conditions, the costs/benefits of action/inaction, and the economic and social development of the EC as a whole and the balanced development of regions. Within their spheres of competence both the EC and member states are to co-operate with third countries and competent international organisations. Article 176 provides that protective measures adopted pursuant to Art 175 do not prevent member states from maintaining or introducing more stringent protective measures of their own, provided they are compatible with the Treaty and are notified to the Commission.

The decision making procedure

The usual procedure on environmental issues under Art 175 is that the Council, under Art 252, after consulting ECOSOC may decide on action by way of a 'qualified majority' (see also Art 205). Under this system individual states have different numbers of votes, with the larges having most, eg the UK has ten while Luxembourg has two. Currently 62 out of the 87 votes from at least 10 states is the majority required (see Art 205). The Treaty of Nice will change this picture again from January 2005 as the Community is

18   Case C-45/91 *EC Commission v Greece* [1992] ECR I-2509.

expected to enlarge to 27 states and the voting numbers will change to requiring 258 of the 345 votes available. However, under Art 175 certain measures may only be adopted unanimously. These are: those primarily of a fiscal nature; or measures concerning town and country planning and land use (*except* waste management and measures of a general nature) and management of water resources; or measures significantly affecting a member state's choice between different energy sources and the general structure of energy supply. The Council may further define those matters which are to be subject to unanimous voting. Under Art 94 directives may be issued for the approximation of such laws, etc as directly affect the establishment or functioning of the common market, and here a unanimous decision is also required. However, by way of derogation from Art 94, Art 95 is available to provide for the adoption of measures having as their object the establishment and functioning of the internal market, but, in relation to environmental protection, any such measures must take as their base a high level of protection. The voting procedure under Art 95 is QMV requiring co-decision with Parliament (see below).

Thus the procedure to be adopted depends very much on the matter in hand. The normal rule is that the Council acts by qualified majority, *but* provisions of a primarily fiscal nature such as energy taxes, town and country planning and land use matters, the management of water resources and energy related issues are still subject to unanimity requirements. General environmental action programmes setting out priority objectives to be attained are to be adopted by QMV in the Council under the co-decision procedure (Art 175(3)) as are measures under Art 95 (ex 100A). General action programmes also need consultation with ECOSOC and the Committee of the Regions. Thus there are three 'law making procedures', in two of which the Parliament is involved in a decision-making capacity.

Where unanimity is required ('consultation procedure')

The procedure here is:

(i)	The Commission makes a proposal.

↓

(ii)	Which goes to the Council who may involve COREPER, and who send it to the Parliament on a consultative basis only.

↓

(iii)	Amendments may be made.

↓

(iv)	The Council adopts unanimously.

Where Art 252 (ex 189C) applies ('co-operation procedure')

(i)	The Commission makes a proposal.

↓

(ii)	The Council receives the proposal and refers it to the Parliament for the first time.

↓

(iii)	Amendments may be made by the Commission or by unanimous decision of the Council (unusual).

↓

(iv)	The Council by qualified majority voting adopts a 'common position' on the proposal.

↓

| (v) | The 'common position' is sent to the Parliament — the second time the Parliament will have seen the matter — and the Parliament will also receive the Commission's opinion on the issue. Parliament may by absolute majority approve, amend or reject the proposal within three months of reception. |

| (vi) | If Parliament approves, or, within the three month period takes no action, the Council may *adopt* by qualified majority. |

| (vii) | If Parliament *rejects* the proposal the Council may only adopt it *unanimously*. |

| (viii) | If Parliament *amends* the proposal the amendments will be sent to the Commission. If the amendments are then accepted the proposal will be sent to the Council who may *accept* it by a qualified majority, *or amend* it further only by unanimity. |

Where Art 251 (ex 189B) applies (joint legislative or co-decision procedure)

The stages here are as in (i)–(vii), above, ie the point at which Parliament *rejects* or indicates an intention to amend the proposal. At this point the stages become as follows.

| (i) | A conciliation committee may be convened by the Council. |

| (ii) | If the parties agree within the conciliation committee (Council by QMV Parliament by majority) a joint text then it may go on to the next stage, if not the Act is not adopted. |

| (iii) | Fail to agree — Act not adopted. |

| (iv) | Within six weeks Council (QMV) and Parliament (majority can either approve or fail to adopt joint text. |

| (v) | If both approve the joint text the Act is adopted if either fails to approve the joint text the Act is not adopted. |

The principle of subsidiarity

Subsidiarity was introduced into EC law by the Maastricht Treaty. In danger of being an 'all things to all persons' 'get out' clause to be used by those wishing to argue for continued national sovereignty, subsidiarity has in any case a somewhat vague core of meaning. The Maastricht Treaty itself, Art A, states that decisions are to be taken 'as closely as possible to the citizens'. Article 35 of the Treaty of Rome amplifies this by stating that, in areas which do not fall within its exclusive competence, the EC shall, in accordance with the principle of subsidiarity, take action 'only if and in so far as the objectives of the proposed action cannot be sufficiently achieved by the member states and can therefore by reason of the scale or effects of the proposed action, be better achieved' by EC action. In addition the European Council has agreed that subsidiarity is to be taken into account at every stage of the legislative process.

What effect does this have on environmental policy? At the moment policy on the environment is *not* within the EC's exclusive competence, hence subsidiarity applies. In practice, however, to mount a legal challenge to, say, a Directive on the basis that it contravened the principle, it would have to be shown that each and every one of the measures and objectives of that Directive could be better achieved at member state level. It is thus likely that Professor Hartley is right in arguing that 'the effectiveness of subsidiarity will depend, to a considerable extent, on the attitude and policy of the European Court ... it is doubtful whether the Court will want to give it any real bite'. (*The Foundations of European Community Law*, 3rd edn, pp 163–164: a title to which interested readers are commended and indebtedness acknowledged). So far as UK case law is concerned, the only comment to date in an environmental context on subsidiarity was by Smith J in *R v Secretary for Trade and Industry, ex p Duddridge*[19] who considered that Art 5 allows member states 'to take such steps as they think right in connection with environmental and health issues until such time as [the EU] acting through its institutions produces a harmonising measure ... to give effect to [the EU] policy on the environment which by that time will have been formulated'. This appears to state that where *a* specific EC policy on an environmental issue has been agreed and formulated and is incorporated in a measure[s] *designed to harmonise* the practice of member states, that will be sufficient to exclude the operation of subsidiarity.

H THE FORMS OF EC SECONDARY LEGISLATION

Article 249 lists three types of legally binding measures capable of being made by the Community institutions: regulations, directives and decisions.

Regulations are binding in their entirety and directly applicable. This means that they become law in the member states without the need for any action by national legislatures: 'they are an integral part of, and take precedence in the legal order applicable in the territory of each of the member states': *Amministrazione delle Finanze dello Stato v Simmenthal SpA*[20] The direct applicability of regulations is secured in the UK by the European Communities Act 1972, s 2(1). Regulations are mainly employed in matters relating to the establishment of the common market and have been comparatively little used in relation to environmental issues. One regulation of particular note, however, is Council Regulation 3322/88 EEC on chlorofluorocarbons (CFCs) and halons which deplete the ozone layer. This effectively translated into EC law the terms of the 1987 Montreal Protocol on taking precautions against ozone depletion. See further chapter 10 and Sands, 'European Community Policy on Ozone Depletion and Greenhouse Gases' in Vaughan (ed), *Environment and Planning Laws* (see also for eg Council Regulation 2037/00/94 on Substances that Deplete the Ozone Layer).

Directives are binding 'as to the result to be achieved ... but shall leave to the national authorities the choice of form and methods'. In other words, directives are *not* directly applicable and require implementation by national authorities within a given period, usually between one and two years, which is specified in the directive. The European Communities Act 1972, s 2(3), makes provision for the implementation of Community law in the UK by means of delegated legislation. However, the government does not always choose, or need, to exercise these powers. Sometimes the relevant legal provision is already in force in the UK, sometimes regulations are made under empowering legislation in other statutes and sometimes the government of the day chooses to enshrine the necessary rules in a new Act of Parliament. More

19   [1995] 7 JEL 224.
20   Case 106/77, [1978] ECR 629 at 643.

controversially, the UK has in the past relied upon changes in administrative and 'managerial' practice in implementing environmental directives. Even within the area of environmental regulation the objects of directives can vary. In some cases there will be clear procedural objectives to be achieved by member states, in others detailed substantive obligations will be stated which leave little effective discretion as to the mode of implementation by member states, in yet other cases a 'framework' will be provided to be expanded by more detailed future directives. The issue of highly detailed directives blurs the distinction between this form of legislation and regulations but this issue does not seem likely to attract judicial condemnation.[21]

Decisions are binding on those to whom they are addressed. A number of decisions (not discussed here) have been addressed to the member states in the course of the environmental programme. They deal primarily with either the establishment of information networks and advisory bodies or the entry by the Community into international agreements. There are also a number of non-legally binding 'recommendations'.

I DIRECT EFFECT

Whereas the direct applicability of regulations is laid down in the Treaty, the separate notion of direct effect is a creation of the European Court of Justice. In the landmark case of Case 26/62: *Algemene Transport — en Expeditie Onderneming van Gend en Loos v Nederlandse Belastingadministratie*,[22] the Court held that:

'the Community constitutes a new legal order of international law for the benefit of which the states have limited their sovereign rights, albeit within limited fields, and the subjects of which comprise not only member states but also their nationals. Independently of the legislation of member states, Community law therefore not only imposes obligations on individuals but is also intended to confer upon them rights which become part of their legal heritage.'

Thus where a provision is directly effective, it confers rights directly upon the citizen which he can invoke before national courts. Not all provisions of Community law give rise to direct effect — it is now clear from the judgments of the Court that in order to give rise to direct effect a measure must satisfy the following criteria:
1   It must be clear, precise and unambiguous.
2   It must be unconditional nor subject to qualifications making obligation contingent on some other event, etc.
3   It must not be dependent on further action being taken by either the Community or member states. These requirements are met even where directives confer discretion *how* to act on member states, provided there is an inescapable minimum *obligation* which a member state owes, in the sense of having no choice as to *whether* or not to act.
These requirements apply to each relevant part of the legislation being relied upon; it is not enough to argue that it is clear and unambiguous' etc 'overall'.[23]

21   *EC Commission v Italy* [1980] ECR 1099; *EC Commission v Italy* [1980] ECR 1115; and *EC Commission v UK* [1988] ECR 3921, [1988] 3 CMLR 437.
22   [1963] ECR 1.
23   *Enichem Base v Comune di Cinisello Balsamo* [1989] ECR 2491, [1991] 1 CMLR 313; and *Twyford Parish Council v Secretary of State for the Environment* [1992] JEL Vol 4 No 2 p 273; and contrast *Kincardine and Deeside District Council v Forestry Commission* [1992] JEL Vol 4 No 2 p 289.

In sum, the provision must be such that the judge in the national court is able to define the right claimed with sufficient precision to enable the court to enforce it. Judges are, of course, entitled to seek the assistance of the European Court by making a preliminary reference on the interpretation of the Community measure under Art 234, but if the judge cannot determine the content of the right, or of the correlative duty, it cannot be told whether or not it has been infringed and the judge will be unable to prescribe the appropriate national remedy.

For some time after the decision in *van Gend en Loos*, it was thought that although provisions of the Treaty and of regulations were susceptible to direct effect, directives were by their very nature unable to comply with the second and third conditions laid down by the Court and consequently would never give rise to direct effect. In Van Duyn,[24] however, the Court concluded that part of Directive 64/221 was capable of creating directly effective rights.

The main reason underlying the Court's decision appears to be the principle of '*effet utile*' — the effectiveness of directives would be undermined if individuals were not allowed to rely upon them in national courts.

In addition, the court appears to rely on the concept of 'equity'. In other words, directives provide member states with discretion in how to implement them but they should do so by the specified deadline/date of implementation. Should they fail to do so, or do so in a defective manner, it would be inequitable for them to deprive individuals of their community law rights by relying on their own breach of obligations. This can be witnessed in the ECJ's judgment in *Becker v Finanzamt Münster-Innenstadt*[25] where the Court stated that a member state 'may not plead … its own failure to perform the obligation that the directive entails'.

There are, though , two limitations on the scope of the direct effect that directives may be capable of. First, in order to comply with the need to be non-dependent, the deadline for implementation must have expired with the member state either failing to or inadequately/defectively implementing the directive: see *Ratti*.[26] Secondly, directives may only give rise to rights for individuals as against the 'state', ie directives have vertical direct effect but not horizontal direct effect. This was concluded in *Marshall v Southampton and South West Hampshire Area Health Authority (Teaching)*.[27] But what is 'the state'? Certainly state bodies charged with maintaining public order and safety are included, see *Johnston v Chief Constable of the Royal Ulster Constabulary*[28] and local authorities, see *R v Freight Transport Association Ltd v London Boroughs Transport Committee*.[29] Indeed any body or institution, no matter what its legal form, which is responsible under state measures for the provision of services under state supervision and has, for that purpose, special powers beyond those applicable between individuals *may* be an emanation of the state for this purpose, see *Foster v British Gas*.[30] Even a commercial understanding may be an 'emanation of the state' provided it carries out a public service which is under overall state control,[31] see further Howells, 'European Directives — the Emerging Dilemmas' (1991) 54 MLR 456. On the other hand

24   [1974] ECR 1337.
25   [1982] ECR 53.
26   Case C-148/78 *Pubblico Ministero v Ratti* [1979] ECR 1629.
27   [1986] QB 401, [1986] 2 All ER 584; *Verbond van Nederlandse Ondernemingen v Inspecteur der Invoerrechten en Accijnzen* [1977] ECR 113, [1977] 1 CMLR 413; and *Faccini Dori v Recreb Srl* [1994] 6 ELM 149.
28   [1987] QB 129, [1986] 3 All ER 135.
29   [1991] 3 All ER 915.
30   [1991] 1 QB 405, [1990] 3 All ER 897.
31   *Griffin v South West Water Services* [1995] IRLR 15.

it appears that a local authority may *not* rely on the doctrine of direct effect *against* an individual.[32]

Some relief to the lack of horizontal direct effect for directives can be found in the ECJ's creation of the indirect effect' principle following statements in *Von Colson v Land Nordrhein-Westfalen*[33] that national courts should so interpret relevant national law that directive objectives are brought about regardless of whether, according to *Marleasing SA v La Comercial*[34] the date of implementation has expired. Also known as 'sympathetic interpretation' this principle rests on Art 10 of the Treaty, which obligates member states to ensure that community objectives are attained; an obligation that extends to national courts. This is subject to requirements to preserve legal certainty and avoid retroactivity, see *Officier van Justitie v Kolpinghuis Nijmegen BV*.[35] In *R v Secretary of State for the Environment, ex p Greenpeace*[36] the *Marleasing* principle was adopted by Potts J who considered that, to interpret UK legislation consistently with EU law, he could read words into the UK statute *provided* he did not thereby alter its plain meaning. See also Fitzpatrick [1992] JEL Vol 4 No 1 p 121. Thus sympathetic interpretation may result in the obligations within the directive being imposed as against another individual, albeit in an indirect way.

It must also be remembered that it is a fundamental principle of community law that any directly-effective Community provision prevails over conflicting national legislation.[37]

Thus it is generally clear that member states and their emanations are under a duty to apply all directly effective provisions to the exclusion and setting aside of any provisions of national law to the contrary. Individuals may rely on this principle to ground a defence to criminal charges, or to resist demands for payments of illegal charges, or, in appropriate cases, to claim injunctive or declaratory relief. Directives may be relied on by parties to establish whether any relevant national measures accord with their provisions, and directives must be applied by national courts in cases where national provisions clash with directives. Where a directive imposes a direct obligation on the member states, the directive itself is the origin of rules of law on which, *provided the period for implementation has passed without necessary action being taken*, the individual may rely. Indeed where the relevant provisions of a directive are capable of direct effect, *and* an individual is thereunder given a right *and* has the necessary locus standi within the legal system, positive action against the defaulter can be taken in national courts.

In the UK, the European Communities Act 1972, s 2(1), ensures the recognition and enforcement in the UK of all directly-effective Community rights. Section 2(4) provides that 'any enactment passed or to be passed ... shall be construed and have effect subject to' inter alia s 2(1). Thus the Act purports to subordinate past *and* future national legislation to Community law. English courts will give priority to Community law in accordance with s 2(4) unless and until 'Parliament deliberately passes an Act with the intention of repudiating the Treaty or any provision in it or intentionally of acting inconsistently with it and says so in express terms', per Lord Denning in *McCarthys Ltd v Smith*.[38]

---

32   *Wychavon District Council v Secretary of State for the Environment* [1994] 6 JEL 351.
33   [1984] ECR 1891, [1986] 2 CMLR 430.
34   [1990] ECR I-4135, [1992] 1 CMLR 305.
35   [1987] ECR 3969, [1989] 2 CMLR 18.
36   [1994] 6 ELM 82.
37   *Costa v ENEL* [1964] ECR 585, [1964] CMLR 425.
38   [1979] 3 All ER 325 at p 329; see also *Factortame Ltd v Secretary of State for Transport* [1989] 2 All ER 692, [1990] ECR I-2433 and [1991] 1 All ER 70.

Many of the provisions of directives concerning the environment are sufficiently precise and detailed to qualify for direct effect (although, equally, many are not, those for example which require member states to take 'appropriate measures' or state that they should 'endeavour' to achieve certain targets). Thus, it is submitted, the direct effect of *some* provisions of *some* of the environmental directives cannot be excluded. An individual could therefore, provided he/she could establish the necessary locus standi, bring an action in the British courts founded on such a measure. However, this is not to say that a remedy would always be forthcoming. Litigation in British courts so far has been largely concerned with the direct effect of the Environment Assessment Directive 85/337/EEC and its subsequent tardy implementation in UK law by SI 1988/1199, etc, see chapter 5. UK courts have sought to dispose of such issues on procedural grounds, such as delay in bringing an action, *R v Swale Borough Council, ex p Royal Society for the Protection of Birds*,[39] or by arguing an authority has carried out the equivalent of an environmental assessment in cases where its applicability as such was not mandatory, *R v Poole Borough Council, ex p Beebee*,[40] or by finding that the court should not exercise its discretion to grant a remedy by way of judicial review because the applicant could not show any substantial prejudice suffered as a result of the breach of the EU obligation, *Twyford Parish Council v Secretary of State for the Environment*.[41] It appears that a British statutory agency specifically charged in the UK with promoting a policy largely emanating from and driven by EU policy would have the necessary locus standi to seek judicial review of UK measures considered contrary to EU obligations,[42] while a large, well organised and well informed pressure group, with a long involvement in a particular environmental issue and a number of members living in the vicinity of that issue may also be accorded standing.[43] But being granted that status is no guarantee that a remedy will follow, not least because of the highly discretionary nature of judicial review proceedings, and because of the need to show harm before a remedy is granted.[44] This is an aspect of our law that has received considerable criticism, see Ward [1993] JEL Vol 5 No 2 p 221 and Geddes [1992] JEL Vol 4 No 1 p 29. however, it is now clear that a failure to comply with the 'primary' obligation of a directive will, if it results in an adverse decision of the ECJ, result further in a 'secondary' obligation to comply with that judgment which must be achieved as soon as possible, and if it is not a party otherwise having the necessary locus standi may seek judicial review of the failure to comply with the 'secondary' obligation. Even in such a case, however, the UK courts appear to consider they retain a discretion as to whether to grant a remedy, and will order nothing in vain.[44]

It has been argued that a number of directives may well have 'direct effect':

1   Those laying down limit or maximum concentration values, eg 76/464 (protection of the aquatic environment).
2   Those prohibiting the use or discharge of certain substances, eg 78/319 on toxic and dangerous waste.
3   Those imposing clear obligations to act on member states, eg 85/337 on environmental assessment. (See further Kramer (1991) 3 Journal of Environmental Law 39, to which the author acknowledges indebtedness.) However, it is doubtful whether an individual would have locus standi to seek a remedy in relation to *all*

39   [1991] JPL 39.
40   [1991] 3 LMELR 60.
41   [1991] 3 LMELR 89, 166, 196.
42   *R v Secretary of State for Employment, ex p Equal Opportunities Commission* [1995] 1 AC 1.
43   *R v HM Inspectorate of Pollution and Ministry of Agriculture, Fisheries and Food, ex p Greenpeace Ltd* [1993] 5 ELM 183.
44   *R v Secretary of State for the Environment, ex p Friends of the Earth Ltd* [1995] 7 ELM 140.

such directives because they do not all immediately concern themselves with protection of humans, eg 76/464.

State liability

The ECJ's refusal to grant Directives horizontal direct effect limited their potential effectiveness as they were only to be complied with by member states. The problem is exacerbated by the generally weak enforcement process existing ion the hands of the Commission. When attempting to secure a remedy for any breach of EC law the ECJ originally insisted that claims had to be decided by the national courts, subject to certain minimum conditions such as the remedy being effective and adequate.[45] This position changed with the land mark case of *Francovich and Bonifaci v Italy*.[46]

In *Francovitch* the ECJ identified that there was a duty in EC law to make reparation for injury caused by a member state failing to comply with its EC obligations. The court concluded that the effectiveness of EC law would be 'impaired' if individuals were denied compensation for injury caused by the illegal actions of member states. This liability was not unlimited in that three conditions had to be met:

1   the purpose of the Community measure had to create rights that were conferred on private individuals;
2   the content of those rights had to be identifiable from the content of the measure itself; and
3   there had to exist some causal link between the injury and the failure of the member state to comply with the Community measure.

The leading case on state liability is now *Brasserie du Pêcheur SA v Federal Republic of Germany* joined with *R v Secretary of State for Transport, ex p Factortame Ltd*.[47] This case clarified the conditions and scope of the principle, whilst emphasising that member states were liable to private citizens for damage resulting from any infringement of EC law, be it the failure to implement a directive (as in the *Francovich* case) or any other breach, such as the breach of a Treaty provision.

The court clearly indicated that any organ of the state could potentially attract liability for both its acts and omissions. The court also established that liability is a route of action both alternative and additional to other courses of action, such as using direct effect. However, the court did point out that failure to use another available course of action in preference for state liability may not be appropriate in securing individual rights and that in such circumstances applicants may have difficulty in mitigating their loss.

In terms of the conditions necessary to secure such liability, the court concluded that state liability should be analogous to the liability of Community institutions themselves under art 288 EC. The three-part test provided by the court was that:

•   the EC measure infringed must have been intended to confer rights on individuals;
•   the breach must be 'sufficiently serious'; and
•   there must be a direct causal link between the breach and the damage suffered.

The court concluded that a sufficiently serious breach would be one where the member state has manifestly and gravely disregarded the limits on its discretion. The national court can ascertain this by considering factors such as the clarity/precision of the breached rule; the extent of discretion left to the authorities of the member state; whether

45   C-33/76 *Rewe-Zentralfinanz eG and Rewe-Zentral AG v Landwirtschaftskammer für das Saarland* [1976] ECR 1989 and 14/83 *Von Colson and Kamann v Land Nordhein-Wesfalen* [1984] ECR 1891.
46   Cases C-6/90 and C-9/90 [1991] ECR I-5357.
47   Joined cases C-46/93 and C-48/93 [1996] ECR I–1029.

the infringement was deliberate or unintentional; whether there existed an excusable error of law; and whether a Community institution in some manner contributed to the infringement.

Jurisprudence post *Brasserie* has unfortunately been inconsistent in the way in which the test has been used. It appears that the court may have adapted two approaches of assessing liability. The first is where the court has focused on the clarity and precision of the supposedly infringed EC measure whereas the second approach has been to establish liability on the basis of the existence of the infringement per se.

In the first approach, the court has emphasised the need for the allegedly breached EC measure to be clear and precise before liability can be incurred. This has been most clearly witnessed in cases involving liability for damage sustained as a result of incorrectly implemented directives. In *R v HM Treasury, ex p British Telecommunications plc*[48] BT claimed damages as a result of the incorrect implementation of Directive 90/351. Using the *Brasserie* test, the court concluded that the Directive had been imprecisely worded, that the UK's implementation had been consistent with that adopted by other member states, and that consequently the UK had acted in good faith. The breach was not therefore, sufficiently serious to warrant the extension of liability[49]. In contrast, in *Rechberger, Greindl and Hofmeister v Austria*[50] the court held that the incorrect implementation of Directive 90/314 was sufficiently serious. This was because the Directive was clear and precise in the level of protection it required and because Austria had only permitted claims to be made at a date after that prescribed for the implementation of the Directive.

The second approach apparently adopted by the ECJ in a number of preliminary references has been to determine liability solely on the basis of the infringement itself. In other words, that the mere existence of the infringement was a sufficiently serious enough breach of EC law to incur liability. This appears to be the case where the court determines that the national authorities had to make no legislative choices or had little discretion in how to comply with the EC measure[51]. This can be clearly seen in cases involving the failure to implement a directive by its prescribed deadline.

In *Dillenkoffer v Germany*[52] the court determined that the failure of Germany to implement Directive 90/314 by its deadline was a per se sufficiently serious breach of EC law. The court did not make any attempt to apply the *Brasserie* test. The same approach was used in *Norbrook Laboratories Ltd v Minister of Agriculture Fisheries and Food*[53] in which the court also referred to the need for the national court to determine the extent of the liability and the level of compensation with reference to the *Francovich* test.

In sum, the relatively new principle of state liability may go some considerable way to both mitigating those problems inherent in the direct effects doctrine and in reinforcing the obligation on member states to comply with their Community law obligations, whatever form they may be in. State liability though may not turn out to be the great panacea many thought it would be, particularly given the more stringent test laid down in *Brasserie*. Whilst those suffering damage where the state had limited discretion, particularly in failing to implement directives by their deadlines, may find that liability is relatively easy to secure, others will have to prove that the breach was sufficiently serious. This may prove a difficult and heavy burden given that the court appears willing

48   C-392/93 [1996] ECR I-1631.
49   See also Cases C-283, 291 and C-292/94 [1996] ECR I-5063.
50   C-140/97 [2000] 2 CMLR 1.
51   See *R v Ministry of Agriculture, Fisheries and Food, ex p Hedley Lomas (Ireland) Ltd* Case C-5/94 [1996] ECR I-2553.
52   Cases C-178, 179, 188, 189 and C-190/94 [1996] ECR I-4845.
53   C-127/95 [1998] ECR I-1531.

to accept a range of 'excuses' to mitigate the breach. The doctrine of state liability, especially as it applies to environmental directives, which by their nature do not often give direct individual rights, will no doubt require further clarification into the future.

J ENFORCEMENT ISSUES

Because the Commission is a legislative initiator it is inevitably proactive, both in the formulation of proposals, and increasingly with regard to taking action against member states under Art 226 in respect of failures to implement directives. The Commission can receive written complaints from individuals that Community obligations are not being satisfied, and the number of such complaints rose from eight in 1983 to 465 in 1989 and to 1185 in 1992, though these arose across every sector of the Commission's competence. This has given the Commission something of a role as an 'Environmental Ombudsman'. The Commission may also suspend regional development grants to those states who fail to implement environmental obligations, and so acted against Portugal in 1990.

The Commission's role as guardian of the treaties creating the Community is also crucial. The Commission is charged with ensuring the implementation of Community obligations, and it requires notification from member states that they have translated those obligations into national law, and further inquiries whether national measures comply formally and practically with the obligations. It also has wide powers under Art 211 to investigate such issues. States found to be committing infractions of obligations may, of course, be proceeded against under Art 226, and see earlier comments on the revised Art 228. Though most infractions appear to arise from oversight or inefficiency, the numbers of Art 226 proceedings, and the consequent strain on the Commission and Court, are increasing. In 1992 there were *587 suspected* infractions in the environmental sector — more than in any other, while the Commission remains heavily dependent on complaints from individuals/organisations to alert it to breaches. Some commentators argue for an even stricter compliance policy by the Commission, others, however, consider that the need for such a policy could be obviated if greater thought were to be given to issues of securing *implementation* at the *formulation* stage of directives.

The role of the Court was examined at length in 'The European Court of Justice as an Environmental Tribunal' by Jacqueline Minor (in Vaughan (ed), *Environmental and Planning Law* p 267 et seq) to which indebtedness is further acknowledged. The attitude of the ECJ appears to vary according to whether the EC has legislated or not, and, in the former case, whether harmonisation of national laws is full or partial. Where there should be harmonisation under EC legislation the ECJ considers the directives should be implemented in a manner fully consonant with EC obligations, so for example, the technical requirements of directives are considered exhaustive.[54] In cases of partial harmonisation, however, the ECJ has seemed to favour striking a balance between protecting the environment and promoting free trade in relation to the exercise by member states of residual powers. Where the Community has not legislated *EC Commission v Denmark*[55] (the 'Danish bottles' case) indicates environmental protection may be used as a justification for a national measure which applies *without distinction* between domestic and imported goods so as to restrict trade between member states, provided it is *proportional*, ie where no 'measure less restrictive of trade would be as effective in protecting the environment' (Minor op cit p 275). But a measure imposing a charge

54   Case 60/86 *EC Commission v United Kingdom* [1988] ECR 3921, [1988] 3 CMLR 437.
55   Case 302/86 [1988] ECR 4627.

equivalent to a customs duty and discriminatory internal taxation is not acceptable and cannot be justified on environmental grounds, see *EC Commission v Germany*.[56] The first case involved a national requirement that drinks containers should be reusable so as to encourage deposit and return schemes, the second concerned attempts to tax road vehicles so as to force freight from road to rail transport. Nevertheless there is a general body of opinion which views the statement in the 'Danish bottles' case that 'the protection of the environment is a mandatory requirement which may limit the application of Art 30 [now 28] of the Treaty' ('Quantitative restrictions on imports and all measures having equivalent effect shall ... be prohibited ...') as indicating the potential of the ECJ to emerge as a forum much concerned with environmental protection. This is largely supported by other decisions, thus domestic circumstances within a member state's legal system do not justify failure to meet environmental obligations,[57] and a merely changeable administrative practice is no fulfilment of a directive's obligations.[58]

Even so the ECJ is vigilant in maintaining a delicate balance between trade and environment issues. Article 28 of the Treaty forbids quantitative restrictions on imports and measures having equivalent effect, subject to Art 30 which allows prohibitions on imports, exports, or goods in transit where these can be justified on grounds of public morality, public policy or security, protection of human life and health, protection of animal and plant life, protection of national artistic treasures, or protection of industrial or commercial property. Such prohibitions, etc, must not be arbitrary discrimination between states, nor disguised restrictions on trade. In this connection the ECJ has required that a national measure must be proportionate, ie it must not place more restrictions on trade than would have been imposed by a less restrictive measure which would still have achieved the same purpose.[59] Beyond formal enforcement issues, at a wider level, IMPEL (European Union Network for the Implementation and Enforcement of Environmental Law) represents an informal network of member states' authorities with environmental responsibilities. Funded by the Commission through the Environment DG's budget its stated objective is 'to create the necessary impetus in the EC to ensure a more effective application of environmental legislation' (see *Second Annual Survey on the Implementation and Enforcement of Community Environmental Law: January 1998 – December 1999, EC Commission 2000*). IMPEL has two standing committees: one concerned with legal policy and member states implementation; and the other concerning inspection and enforcement issues. It has produced reports (accessible via the Commission) relating to inspections, and has informed legislative proposals on minimum criteria for environmental inspectors. The network is hailed as a success by the Commission in improving enforcement of Community environmental law in the member states.

The Court of First Instance

Established in 1989 following amendment of the various constituent treaties by the Single European Act, the Court of First Instance was intended to deal with cases having no political or constitutional importance and to relieve the work load of the European Court of Justice. Effectively one judge sits for each member state. The Court has a

56   [1991] 2 LMELR 210.
57   Case 30-34/81 *EC Commission v Italy* [1981] ECR 3379; Case 134/86 *EC Commission v Belgium* [1987] ECR 2415.
58   Case 96/81 *EC Commission v Netherlands* [1982] ECR 1791 at 1819.
59   Case C-131/93 *EC Commission v Germany* [1994] ECR I-3303, [1995] 2 CMLR 278.

particular jurisdiction in judicial review, concerning both annulment actions and actions in respect of remedies for failures to act, where action is being taken by a private individual or company against the EC itself. See further Hartley, *The Foundations of European Community Law*, (4th edn), chapter 2, indebtedness to which is acknowledged.

However, to seek a remedy before the Court one must have a sufficient legal interest in the matter in hand. Article 230 allows individuals (ie natural or legal persons) to challenge the legality of action taken by the Commission or other EC institution where there is '*a decision* addressed to that person' or where there is a '*decision* which, although in the form of a regulation or a *decision* addressed to another person, is of direct and individual concern' to the individual.

In effect this means that the decision must affect the individual by reason of certain attributes peculiar to him/her, or by reason of circumstances which differentiate him/her from all others. The application of this understanding makes it very hard for environmental pressure groups to challenge decisions in the Court of First Instance, for it is hard for them to demonstrate sufficient 'individual concern'. Furthermore an association which has been formed to protect the collective interests of a group of people does not have an entitlement to take action which its individual members do not have. A decision affecting a large number of people in an area may therefore not be susceptible to challenge by any one of them if all are affected in the same way and none is affected in a way distinct from others, see *Stichting Greenpeace Council v EC Commission*[60] and *Danielson v EC Commission*.[61]

On the other hand it must be pointed out that despite an obvious readiness to find member states in breach of obligations in Art 226 (ex Art 169) proceedings the ECJ has yet to find in any wholesale manner that the environmental directives have direct effect which could open up many more domestic remedies for individuals and organisations in their own state's court.[62] A notable exception to this has been the amended Directive 85/337/EEC on Environmental Assessment (see further chapter 8) where the ECJ dealt with the issue of direct effect in a most perfunctory way in the so-called 'Dutch Dykes' case.[63]

Clearly some more effective form of enforcement is required. That role could in future be discharged by the Environment Agency created under Regulation 1210/90, and which is located in Denmark — a state with an exceedingly 'clean' environmental record and thus, arguably, not the most appropriate place for the location of the agency which might be seen to be 'preaching to the converted'. Currently the Agency is primarily concerned to collect, process, analyse, and disseminate information on the environment, and publishes triennial reports on the state of the environment. The Agency has no enforcement role, but it could become involved in monitoring the implementation of EC law and obligations, promoting the use of 'clean' technology and processes, establishing criteria for environmental assessment purposes etc.

---

60 Case T-585/93 (1996) 252 ENDS Report 43.
61 Case T-219/95R (1996) 252 ENDS Report 44.
62 Case 236/92 *Difesa Dela Cara v Regione Lombardia* [1994] 6 ELM 112; *Article 177 Reference from the Bavarian Higher Regional Administrative Court* [1995] 7 ELM 6.
63 Case C-72/95 *Aannemersbedrijf PK Kraaijeveld BV v Gedeputeerde Staten van Zuid-Holland* [1996] ECR I-5403; confirmed in C-287/98 *Luxembourg v Linster* (2000) Times, 3 October Env Law Mgmt (2000) 12(6)).

K EC LAW: AN EVALUATION AND VIEW ON FUTURE PROSPECTS

Although EC policy on the environment has generated a great deal of legislation (well over 400 legislative instruments between 1967 and 1994) decision making procedures have been slow and have tended to militate against the adoption of radical proposals. There seems little doubt, however, that it has reinforced the strongly growing concern about environmental issues on the domestic political scene and has without any doubt accelerated and influenced the content of already planned domestic legislation. In some areas, notably water and air pollution, it certainly has forced a change in long established practice and approach.

The EC's attitude to environmental protection has, however, been characterised by (i) a regulatory approach, (ii) use of harmonisation of national laws (notwithstanding the subsidiarity principle) and (iii) a degree of passivity in merely upgrading environmental measures to keep pace with technology, as opposed to forcing the pace of technological change by legal requirements as is the case in the USA. As to (i) it may be commented that an over regulatory style may inhibit the use of other means of environmental protection such as fiscal or economic aid policies … although in some case, notably the adoption of a plan for a Community wide emissions trading scheme (see further chapter 16) moves are being made to adopt this sort of instrument. Here it must be remembered that Art 88 of the Treaty forbids the granting of state aids not compatible with the common market, and that Art 87 forbids aids which distort competition by favouring certain undertakings or goods. This is not to say that all environmental fiscal measures fall foul of the Treaty. There is a wide, and vague, provision in Art 87(3)(c) to allow aid to be given to facilitate the development of certain economic activities or certain economic areas, and aids granted to projects regarded as 'environmentally friendly' are generally acceptable, eg research into renewable energy resources, though aids are open to question where they effectively allow those aided to escape the operation of 'the polluter pays' principle, and the same is true where state aids are given to polluting industries; see further Alexander, 'Competition, Subsidy and Environmental Protection' in Vaughan (ed), *Environment and Planning Law*. Note also Art 87(3)(d) which allows aid to promote culture and 'heritage conservation'. As to (ii) it can be said that harmonisation techniques were appropriate before the amendments made by the SEA and still have a significance until the completion of the internal market. As to (iii) the dominance of harmonisation appears in the past to have inhibited a pace setting approach in the creation of standards. This may be predicted to change, especially allowing the Maastricht agreement and Treaty of Amsterdam amendments.

A quickening pace of change?

Despite set backs every now and again the 'curve' of EC legislative activity on the environment was definitely set upwards, with no less than 48 measures in 1994, the largest number ever. A new environment commissioner, a new Environment DG and the formal inception of the Environment Agency in October 1994 seemed to have reinvigorated the EU in relation to environmental issues. The Treaty of Amsterdam incorporated some important reforms in 1997, as previously discussed. The role of the Parliament has been strengthened with potential benefits for environmental protection: the Parliament has traditionally, at least in its thinking, been a more radical institution than the Council. Finally, while the treaty of Nice is primarily concerned with the management of the EC's enlargement, the need for the acceding states to adopt EC environmental standards and law, albeit in a transitional form for some, will bring benefits for the Community's environment as a whole.

Protection of environmental interests under the European Convention on Human Rights (ECHR)

The ECHR does not specifically mention environmental protection as a fundamental human right.[64] Since some early case law on the issue, seeking to make a link between elements of environmental degradation and infringements of a person's rights under the Convention, the law has evolved relatively quickly with some discernable rules emerging. Cases, while not many in number, have succeeded on a variety of issues as diverse as not being advised of risks from a chemical factory, to aircraft noise. The position of this human rights discourse in the UK has been brought into sharper relief since the coming into force of the Human Rights Act 1998. Human rights litigation in all areas of law has burgeoned with many challenges on 'rights' grounds decided or in the pipeline. A detailed evaluation of this increasingly important new source of law to offer some environmental protection spin-off can be found in chapter 5 below.

Further reading

EC LAW
de Búrca, G, 'Giving Effect to European Community Directives' (1992) 55 MLR 215.
Churchill, R, Warren, L and Gibson, J (eds), *Law, Policy and the Environment* (1991) Blackwell.
Craig, PP, 'Francovich, Remedies and the Scope of Damages Liability' (1993) 109 Law Quarterly Review 595.
Curtin, D, 'State Liability Under Community Law: A New Remedy for Private Parties' (1992) 21 Industrial Law Journal 74.
Geddes, AC, '*Foster v British Gas:* widening the field of direct effect' (1990) 140 NLJ 1611.
Glasbergen, P and Blowers, A, *Environmental Policy in an International Context: Perspectives* chapter 5 (Kamminga) (1995) Arnold.
Hartley, TE, *Foundations of European Community Law* (3rd edn) (1994) and (4th edn) (1998) OUP.
Howells, G, 'European Directives: The Emerging Dilemmas' (1991) 54 MLR 456.
House of Lords Select Committee on the EC, Session 1994–95 5th Report, HL Paper 29, European Environment Agency (1995) HMSO.
Johnson, S and Corcelle, G, *The Environmental Policy of the European Communities* (2nd edn 1995) Kluwer Law International.
Kramer, L, EC Treaty and Environmental Law (4th edn) (2000) Sweet and Maxwell.
Kramer, L, *EEC Treaty and Environmental Protection* (1995) Sweet and Maxwell.
Kramer, L, 'The Implementation of Community Environmental Directives within Member States: Some implications for the Direct Effect Doctrine' (1991) 3 Journal of Environmental Law 39.
Kye, C, 'Environmental Law and the Consumer in the European Union' (1995) 7 Journal of Environmental Law, Part I, 31.
Langrish, S, The Treaty of Amsterdam: Selected Highlights (1998) 23 EL Rev 3.
McEldowney, JF and McEldowney, S, *Environmental Law and Regulation* (2001) Blackstone Press.
McGrory, DP, 'Air Pollution Legislation in the United States and the Community' (1990) 15 European Law Review 298.
McRory, R, 'The Enforcement of Community Environmental Laws: Some Critical Issues' 29 Common Market Law Review 347.

64   *X and Y v Germany*, Application 7407/76, 5 DR 16.

Rehbinder, E and Stewart, R, *Environmental Protection Policy* (1985) Walter de Gruyter and Co.

Rehbinder, E and Stewart, R, 'Legal Integration in Federal Systems: European Community Environmental Law' (1985) American Journal of Comparative Law 371.

Sands, P, 'European Community Environmental Law: Legislation, the European Court of Justice and Common Interest Groups (1990) 53 Modern Law Review 685.

Scott, J, *EC Environmental Law* (1998) Longmans.

Snyder, F, 'The Effectiveness of European Community Law' (1993) 56 Modern Law Review 19.

Szyszcak, E, 'European Community Law: New Remedies, New Directions?' (1992) 55 Modern Law Review 690.

Vandermeersh, D, 'The Single European Act and the Environmental Policy of the European Economic Community' (1987) 12 European Law Review 407.

Vaughan, D (ed), *Environment and Planning Law* (1991) Butterworths.

Wils, WPJ, 'Subsidiarity and EC Environmental Policy: Taking People's Concerns Seriously' (1994) 6 Journal of Environmental Law, Part 1, 85. Wyatt, D, 'Litigating Community Environmental Law — Thoughts on the Direct Effect Doctrine' (1998) JEL 10 (1).

INTERNATIONAL LAW

Bethlehem, Crawford, Sands (eds), *International Environmental Law Reports,* volumes 1-3, (2001) Cambridge.

Birnie, PW, and Boyle, AE, *International Law and the Environment* (2nd edn, 2002) OUP.

Boyle, A, 'Saving the World? Implementation and Enforcement of International Environmental Law through International Institutions' (1991) 3 Journal of Environmental Law 229.

Boyle A, Freestone D (eds), *International Law and Sustainable Development, Past Achievements and Future Challenges*, (1999) OUP.

Brown Weiss, E, *Environmental Change and International Law* (1992) UN University Press.

Churchill, R and Freestone, D (eds), *International Law and Global Climate Change* (1991) Graham and Trotman.

Freestone, D, 'The Road from Rio' (1993) University of Hull Press, and also (1994) 6 Journal of Environmental Law, Part 2, 193.

French, DA, 'A reappraisal of sovereignty in the light of global environmental concerns' (2001) 21 Legal Studies 376.

Lammers, JG (ed), *Environmental Protection and Sustainable Development* (1987) Graham and Trotman.

Massey, SC, 'Global Warming and 1992 UNCED' 22 Georgia Journal of International and Comparative Law, 175.

Oesterle, D, 'Just say "I don't know": a recommendation for WTO panels dealing with environmental regulations' Env L Rev 3 (2001) 113-130.

Revesz, RL, Sands P, and Stewart, RB (eds), *Environmental Law, the Economy and Sustainable Development* 2000 CUP.

Sand, PH, *The Effectiveness of International Environmental Agreements* (1992) Grotius Publications.

Sands, P, *Chernobyl: Law and Communication* (1988) Grotius Publications.

Sands, P, 'Innovation in International Environmental Governance' (1990) 32 Environment 9.

Chapter 5

Human rights and the environment

There are two issues here. The first is the theoretical one of how we conceive of and articulate the notion of a 'human right' to a clean environment. The second, which will occupy us for longer, if only because we now have some 'hard' UK law on the issue, are the implications for environmental law of the European Convention on Human Rights.

A THE HUMAN RIGHTS APPROACH TO ENVIRONMENTAL ISSUES

The readiness of Western societies since 1945 to characterise matters in terms of 'rights' is understandable in the light of the 20th century's history of violence, oppression and aggression. By dignifying matters as issues of 'rights' in political and social discourse we exalt their importance, and, we hope, give them a degree of protection.

The second half of the 20th century saw much development of inter-connected notions of human and environmental rights, and both human rights and environmental activists began to pursue common goals. This was not without its tension, for reconciling the notion of decent living conditions for all people, fundamental to human rights thinking, is not immediately always compatible with protecting a limited and vulnerable natural resource base. Even so it is arguable that by protecting the environment we are pursuing a particular way of achieving human rights by, for example, stressing entitlements to health, good living conditions and a healthful working environment, or by developing entitlements to be informed about and to participate in environmental decision making, while some would go so far as to argue that a satisfactory environment in itself an inalienable human right.

Even though the relatively simple language of rights is not always suited to the complex questions raised by environmental questions (because, for example, environmental issues may involve highly precise regulatory standards), overall there are advantages to basing environmental protection on concepts of human rights. The issues become justifiable in human terms, and regulation may thus be more attractive than when it is simply seen as a bureaucratic process. For example, restrictions on the use of motor vehicles in towns may be more acceptable if they are supported by arguments that the 'right to health' of people – including motorists and their children – is at stake.

It is possible to argue that a human-rights based approach to the law is too bound up with notions of reciprocity between individuals and generations, and is altogether far too anthropocentric, leading to a failure to stress the moral status of other living and natural entities. Nevertheless the main thrust of 'rights'-based thinking on environmental issues, particularly within international law, is now well established as the basis for future development.

B FROM MORAL TO LEGAL HUMAN RIGHTS

International law, as stated, has accepted the moral argument that there should be legal rights to a clean environment. But how does that translate to national systems, in particular that of the United Kingdom?

The principal source of law here is the European Convention on Human Rights (EConHR) whose history and incorporation into our legal system we must now consider.

C HISTORY OF THE CONVENTION

In 1948 the United Nations adopted the Universal Declaration of Human Rights, which was much wider than the European Convention, and only morally binding. Following this in 1949 the Council of Europe was established, and this drew up the European Convention on Human Rights in 1950, which was *largely drafted by UK lawyers*.

The Convention came into effect in 1953, and has since been amended by a number of protocols, but not all the states who have 'signed up' to the Convention have signed up to all protocols. The UK was a 'signatory state', but did not incorporate the Convention into its legal system. This had a number of consequences.

(i)   the Convention was *not* a source of legal rights for UK citizens;
(ii) our judges would try to find a meaning for UK Acts of Parliament which was consistent with the Convention wherever possible as the UK was under an international obligation to conform with the Convention by virtue of having signed up to it;
(iii) In cases where there was a clear and inescapable conflict between the Convention and UK law our courts had to apply UK law;
(iv) Anyone wishing to challenge the government on a human rights issue had to go to Strasbourg to do so – and if the point of law there was decided against the UK our government would, as a matter of practice, amend UK domestic law to come into line with the declarations of the European Court of Human Rights (ECHR) – situated at Strasbourg and *not* to be confused with the European Court of Justice (ECJ) which is in Luxembourg and which deals with EC law.

What does the Convention say?

It is quite a short document, but it contains a *number of different kinds of rights*. Some are absolute, ie they cannot be modified by a signatory state – in lawyer's language there can be 'no derogation' from them. Some are qualified, ie, there can be exceptions. Thus by Art 2 'Everyone's right to life shall be protected by law' – *but* under the Convention itself the death penalty was allowed, so this right is not absolute, and there is no breach of Art 2 where someone is killed as a result of the 'use of force *which is no more than absolutely necessary*', in certain situations.

'The margin of appreciation'

Because some of the rights in the Convention are not absolute – a number allow for departures from rights where this is 'necessary in a democratic society', for example on the basis of national security, public safety, protection of public order, health, morality, or the protection of the rights and freedoms of other people – the Court at Strasbourg developed the idea that states should have a degree of discretion – some freedom of manoeuvre – in complying with and applying the Convention. This became known as 'the margin of appreciation'. This is because the ECHR accepted that state authorities were in day-to-day contact with events in their own countries and were thus equipped to decide on issues of law and morality within those countries, and so could be allowed some freedom of action. However, this has never given states total freedom of action – rather they have limits within which they – and subordinate public bodies such as local authorities – must act. The exact limits of the 'margin of appreciation' have also been decided on a case by case basis, and the prime obligation remains on the state to ensure that convention rights are applied and protected, and nothing must take place under the 'margin of appreciation' which goes beyond what can be demonstrated to be strictly required.

The starting point has to be that any restriction on a Convention right that is not absolute has to be justified, and nothing less than an important competing public interest will be sufficient to justify such a restriction. Initially public authorities have to make a decision on that issue, but then they may have to justify their decision to a court if a human rights challenge is made.

Will our courts develop the 'margin' notion?

There is little case law so far, but in *R v Lambert*,[1] there were some indications this might happen. The case actually arose under ss 5 and 28 of the Misuse of Drugs Act 1971, and Lambert contended that, as currently interpreted, the MDA 1971 places on a defendant a burden of disproving certain elements of drugs offences, and that this conflicts with the presumption of innocence contained in Art 6(2) of the Convention. The Court of Appeal began by stating that its task was to adopt 'a broad and purposive approach not a rigid approach to the Convention, an approach which will make the Convention a valuable protection for the protection of the fundamental rights of individual members of the public as well as society as a whole'. However, it then added: 'the court does not have to ignore the wider interests of the public in applying those provisions of the Convention which have no express limitation'. In other words in determining the application of Art 6 the nature of problems addressed by specific pieces of legislation are to be taken into account. The court then added: 'legislation is passed by a democratically elected parliament and therefore the Courts under the Convention are entitled and should, as a matter of constitutional principle, pay a degree of deference to the view of Parliament as to what is in the interests of the public generally while upholding the rights of the individual under the Convention'. Therefore, it appears where there is a pressing social problem addressed by legislation the courts may well be inclined to find that, when a balance has to be struck between the rights of an individual and those of the wider community, it is not improper to decide the issue in

1   [2000] 1 All ER 1014.

favour of a restriction on the rights of the individual as Parliament, which is democratically elected, has passed the relevant legislation. We shall return to this issue subsequently in our consideration of what has come to be known as the '*Alconbury* case'.

Bringing rights home

Following the White Paper 'Bringing Rights Home' the government introduced legislation which became the Human Rights Act 1998 (HRA 1998). This now imposes positive duties on courts and public bodies to ensure that rights under the Convention are neither breached nor otherwise interfered with. Thus: it is unlawful for any public body – including a court – to act in any way incompatible with 'Convention rights'. Courts will also in effect have powers over both new and existing legislation – even if a point arises in a case concerning only two private parties, thus giving rise to the law having a 'horizontal' effect between individuals as well as a 'vertical' effect between an individual and the state.

These principles apply to the 'Convention rights' which are to be found in Sch 1 to the 1998 Act – these are Arts 2-12 and 14 of the Convention and certain provisions which have been included in subsequent amendments or 'protocols' to the Convention.

The task of applying the new law will fall to the courts. In doing this they may take into account all the existing decisions on the Convention. They will also be free to develop further interpretations and applications of the law. In developing the law UK courts will be able to rely on the jurisprudence of case law before the ECHR. This case law is non-binding in nature, but, of course, it has to be 'taken into account'.

D A THUMBNAIL SKETCH OF THE HRA 1998

So far as possible all UK legislation (ie statutes, statutory instruments etc) will have to be interpreted and applied in a way compatible with the Convention rights – see the HRA 1998, s 3.

What if a court cannot achieve compatibility?

Under the HRA 1998, s 4 the court can only make a 'declaration of incompatibility'. It *cannot* declare the legislation invalid and note also that only the High Court, Court of Appeal or House of Lords can only make such a declaration.

Who can do anything about such an incompatibility?

Under the HRA 1998, s 10(2) it is for ministers to take action where there are 'compelling' reasons to act, and then they *may* make amendments to the incompatible legislation. The procedure for doing this is found in Sch 2 to the HRA 1998 Act, and as a general rule the approval of Parliament is required for any remedial order made by a minister, though in 'urgent cases' ministers may act without parliamentary approval, in which case an explanation has to be given to Parliament, and the subsequent approval of Parliament sought.

E DUTIES OF PUBLIC AUTHORITIES – INCLUDING LOCAL AUTHORITIES

Unless a public authority *has* to act in a particular way because of the requirements of *incompatible* legislation, it *must* otherwise act in ways which are compatible with Convention rights – HRA 1998, s 6.

What if such an authority breaks that rule?

'A person', including a 'legal person' such as a company, may proceed against such an authority which has acted or proposes to act in an incompatible fashion, but *only* if he/she is or would be the victim of the unlawful act. It must also be remembered that, as already stated, courts themselves are 'public bodies' and so must give effect to Convention rights, where relevant, in cases between private individuals.

How can action be taken?

This may be done either by initiating proceedings against the authority, or by relying on Convention rights in any other relevant legal proceedings, ie the rights can be used as a sword and as a shield. Relevant proceedings include claims and counterclaims against authorities, judicial review proceedings and proceedings initially instigated by the authority, and any appeal proceedings against the decision of a court or tribunal. Where a person actually initiates action against a public authority, he/she must do so within a year from the date of the alleged unlawful act, though a court may extend that period if it considers it just to do so in all the circumstances – but that time limit is subject in judicial review cases to the more restrictive time limits imposed in such cases, ie three months, and promptly within that period see HRA 1998, s 7.

What remedy can a court give?

If an unlawful action is found to have occurred, the court may give such a remedy, or make such an order as it considers 'just and appropriate' – provided such remedy etc is within the court's powers; see HRA 1998, s 8.

Possible remedies therefore include damages (from a court having power to award them in civil proceedings), and then only when the court considers such an award is 'necessary' to achieve full 'satisfaction' bearing in mind any other relief or remedy granted, and the consequences of the decision of the court.

F CONVENTION RIGHTS AND THE ENVIRONMENT

A number of provisions of the Convention are relevant. From a substantive point of view Art 8 of the Convention and Art 1 of the First Protocol are the most important. From a procedural point of view Art 6 has to be considered.

'*Article 8*

1   Everyone has the right to respect for his private and family life, his home and his correspondence.
2   There shall be no interference by a public authority with the exercise of this

right except such as is in accordance with the law and is necessary in a democratic society in the interests of national security, public safety or the economic well-being of the country, for the prevention of disorder or crime, for the protection of health or morals, or for the protection of the rights and freedoms of others.'

It will be noted that this does not confer any absolute rights. There is room for 'justifiable' interference.

'THE FIRST PROTOCOL

Article 1
Protection of property

Every natural or legal person is entitled to the peaceful enjoyment of his possessions. No one shall be deprived of his possessions except in the public interest and subject to the conditions provided for by the law and by the general principles of international law.

   The preceding provisions shall not, however, in any way impair the right of a State to enforce such laws as it deems necessary to control the use of property in accordance with the general interest or to secure the payment of taxes or other contributions or penalties.'

Again this is not an 'absolute' provision, but between them these provisions provide a degree of protection for a person's home and possessions.

G THE ATTITUDE OF THE ECHR TOWARDS ENVIRONMENTAL ISSUES

The ECHR's initial 'line of argument' was that there was no right to environmental protection or to a particular environmental quality in the Convention.[2] This, however, changed with the decision in *Lopez Ostra v Spain*.[3]

   Here a plant for treating liquid and solid tannery wastes was built near the applicant's home. The plant released fumes and smells and contaminants leading to nuisances and local health problems. The local authority evacuated the area for a while and closed down some operations but not all problems were solved and Mrs Lopez Ostra took action under Art 8.

   The ECR held: 'Severe environmental pollution may affect individuals' well-being and prevent them from enjoying their homes in such a way as to affect their private and family life adversely, without, however, seriously endangering their health'. That did not mean the state had an absolute obligation – there was room for discretion and manoeuvre in striking a balance between the economic advantages flowing from the plant and the disadvantages to the applicant. However, that balance had not been struck on the facts of the case. *Lopez Ostra* was followed by *Guerra v Italy*.[4] Here a factory was built which released large amounts of inflammable and toxic substances. There were several incidents leading to local evacuations. Two complaints were made:
(a) failure to reduce pollution risks and to avoid major accidents;
(b) failure to provide information about the risks.

2   *X and Y v Germany* 15 DR 161 (1976).
3   (1994) 20 EHRR 277.
4   (1998) 4 BHRC 63.

The applicants succeeded. The ECHR reiterated *Lopez Ostra* and also found there had been a failure to give adequate information leading to a breach of Art 8.

The ECHR thus established:

- interference with a person's integrity or physical wellbeing can be found to breach Art 8 irrespective of the level of severity;
- interference with 'quality of life' can be found to breach Art 8 where it is sufficiently severe but that is a question of fact in each case.

Remember in these cases the state was liable even though the pollution was caused by commercial organisations, because the state had not protected the applicants' Convention rights. But remember also that state obligations are not absolute under Art 8:

- States may act to defend national security, public safety, and economic wellbeing – though they must justify their actions.
- So far only in *extreme* cases has the ECHR found against states.
- Art 8 only protects homelife – wider lifestyle issues do not seem to be contemplated.
- Art 8 only applies to humans – not to the environment as a whole, even where the destruction of features of the environment causes distress to individuals. Art 8 is reinforced by Protocol 1, Art 1. In *Rayner v UK* [5] it was considered that noise which affects a property's value amounts to a partial 'taking' of the property and so could violate Protocol 1, Art 1. However, an interference with property may be justifiable. [6]

H TO SUM UP SO FAR

- The absence of an article guaranteeing a 'right' to a clean environment has not prevented the ECHR from developing other articles in a creative way to go some way to supplying the need.
- The ECHR has not gone too far, however, down this road – relying on the notion of 'the margin of appreciation' it has generally declined to substitute its own views of the merits of a situation for those of the government of a member state.
- The ECHR has also been quite generous in the way in which it has interpreted the articles. The obligations are not absolute and quite intrusive environmental activities – eg noise at Heathrow – were historically allowed to continue, justified by the manifest economic benefits to the state as a whole arising from the operation of the airport. [7] On this point, however, see now further below.
- The Convention exists to deal with *breaches* of human rights, not a suspicion of a possible breach, though a remedy may be available in respect of proof of a real threat of breach. [8]

I THE POSSIBLE APPLICATION OF ART 2

This provides that everyone's right to life is to be protected by law. Arguably if a public body, such as a regulatory agency, were to expose people to a real and immediate life endangering risk which materialised, it could be found liable under Art 2: see *Osman v United Kingdom*. [9] But this obligation is not to be interpreted so as to impose

5   47 DR 5 (1986), EComHR.
6   *Fredin v Sweden* (1991) 13 EHRR 784.
7   *Powell and Rayner v UK* Series A, No 172 (1990), ECtHR.
8   *Tauira v France* Application 28204/95.
9   (1998) 29 EHRR 245.

disproportionate or impossible burdens on authorities. It arises where an authority knew or ought to have known of a *real and immediate* risk to the life of an identified individual or group. In addition it is 'life' that is protected, not 'quality of life', which is what is likely to be at issue in environmental matters. There are dicta in *Guerra*[10] suggesting that in an appropriate case the withholding of information about a matter which presents a real risk to health and physical integrity would fall to be dealt with under Art 2, and while this seems to go beyond what was said in *Osman*, there were also comments in *LCB v United Kingdom*[11] to the effect that a duty to warn of dangers may exist as states are under an obligation to safeguard the lives of those within their jurisdiction. However, it is quite arguable that a regulatory body which allowed highly toxic material to enter the midst of a community in an uncontrolled fashion with resulting loss of life could face a claim based on Art 2.

J PROCEDURAL RIGHTS

'*Article 6*
1   In the determination of his civil rights and obligations or of any criminal charge against him, everyone is entitled to a fair and public hearing within a reasonable time by an independent and impartial tribunal established by law. Judgment shall be pronounced publicly but the press and the public may be excluded from all or part of the trial in the interest of morals, public order or national security in a democratic society, where the interests of juveniles or the protection of the private life of the parties so require, or to the extent strictly necessary in the opinion of the court in special circumstances where publicity would prejudice the interest of justice.
2   Everyone charged with a criminal offence shall be presumed innocent until proved guilty according to law.
3   Everyone charged with a criminal offence has the following minimum rights:
    a   to be informed promptly, in a language which he understands and in detail, of the nature and cause of the accusation against him;
    b   to have adequate time and facilities for the preparation of his defence;
    c   to defend himself in person or through legal assistance of his own choosing or, if he has not sufficient means to pay for legal assistance, to be given it free when the interests of justice so require;
    d   to examine or have examined witnesses against him and to obtain the attendance and examination of witnesses on his behalf under the same conditions as witnesses against him;
    e   to have the free assistance of an interpreter if he cannot understand or speak the language used in court.'

A wide meaning has been given by the ECHR to 'civil rights and obligations' in both civil and criminal proceedings, so as to protect property rights business and commercial undertakings. Thus in *Zander v Sweden*[12] a licensing authority allowed a company to dump waste at a tip without requiring the imposition of conditions to protect Zander's water supply, and he had no means available to challenge this decision. Art 6 was held to be breached. Similarly in *Benthem v Netherlands*,[13] Bentham applied for a licence to

10   (1998) 4 BHRC 63.
11   (1998) 27 EHRR 212.
12   Series A No 279-B (1993), ECtHR.
13   Series A No 97 (1985), ECtHR.

run a plant to deliver liquid petroleum gas to vehicles. Such a licence was needed because the plant could be a source of danger to the locality. The licence was granted by the local authority but then revoked by a central decree. Benthem's rights had not been determined by an independent tribunal, and a breach of Art 6 occurred.

Consider also *Ortenberg v Austria*.[14] An area of land was designated by a local plan as building land and later grants of permission for housing development were made to various people. The applicant's land adjoined the site. She tried to make various administrative appeals but these failed. She applied to the Austrian Administrative Court arguing that her personal rights as a neighbour had been infringed, and that she would suffer nuisance because of road works etc. The court rejected her case. She next applied to the ECHR alleging breach of Art 6. While on the merits of the case no breach was found as a *court* had exhaustively considered the case, the ECHR said Art 6 did apply: Ortenberg was seeking to protect private pecuniary rights – but that was no bar – her claim that the grant of planning permission would (i) jeopardise her enjoyment of her land; (ii) reduce its market value, should be considered by an appropriate tribunal.

Article 6 has given rise to a considerable amount of case law, but even there the ECHR has applied certain limits. Only those who have been able to show that they are 'victims' of the action complained of have been able to pursue a remedy – campaigning organisations have been denied assistance, even when they have claimed to be acting on grounds of public interest.[15] Indeed the restrictive attitude of the Court on this issue is shown by the fact that a non-governmental organisation seeking to act in the public interest has been refused 'victim' status even though it had an office close to a polluting site.[16] In the, so far unreported, decision of *Vettelein v Hampshire County Council* it was considered that objectors to a waste incineration facility did not have a sufficient connection with the issue to fall within the ambit of Art 6.

The influence of Art 6 has been felt, however, in claims concerning substantive rights, for the ECHR has appeared receptive to claims under Art 8 where there has also been some unfairness such as a procedural error, or an arbitrary action, or the deprivation of property without adequate compensation provisions.[17]

K THE IMPLICATIONS FOR, AND DEVELOPMENTS IN, UK LAW

Article 8 may affect a number of central and local government activities, for example those creating adverse effects or risks, and those which affect family life. Similarly Protocol 1, Art 1 may be relevant to activities which affect the enjoyment of possessions. Failures to act may be as open to challenge as actually actions on the basis of *Lopez Ostra*.

Thus in *Booker AquacultureLtd v Secretary of State for Scotland*[18] under Fish Health Regulations orders were made to destroy salmon stocks, for which no compensation was payable. The Court of Session dealt with the issue as a freedom of property issue and declared the failure to provide compensation was illegal, especially as the safeguarding of fish health could have been achieved by other less stringent means.

---

14 (1994) 19 EHRR 524.
15 *Ayuntamiento de M v Spain* 68 DR 209 (1991); *Greenpeace Schweiz v Switzerland* (1997) 23 EHRR CD116; *Balmer-Schafroth v Switzerland* (1997) 25 EHRR 598; *Tauira v France* Application 28204/95.
16 *Asselbourg and Greenpeace Association Luxembourg v Luxembourg*, Application 29121/95.
17 *Sporrong and Lönnroth v Sweden* (1982) 5 EHRR 35; *Hentrich v France* (1994) 18 EHHR 440; *Lithgow v UK* (1986) 8 EHRR 329; *Holy Monasteries v Greece* (1994) 20 EHRR 1.
18 (1998) Times, 24 September, Scots Law Report.

L ARTICLE 8 ETC AND PLANNING LAW

Historically the impact of Art 8 and Protocol 1, Art 1 on planning issues has not been marked, largely because of the restrictive view taken by the ECHR of who is a 'victim' for application purposes, so that pressure groups have not been assisted. But it should be remembered that:

- third parties may rely on Convention rights to argue for a particular interpretation of the law in any case where they are involved;
- a court may admit argument from a third party in a Convention case on 'friend of the court' or 'amicus curiae' basis;
- the HRA 1998 will not affect third party rights already existing in planning law.

Historically while Convention rights have had little impact on planning, some judges have relied on them as tools of interpretation when there has been ambiguity in the legislation.[19]

However, in the future planning controls (and indeed wider environmental protection powers) will fall to be considered against both Art 8 and Protocol 1, Art 1. Thus, the use of planning powers may have to be justified – the existence of a legitimate aim may have to be shown – their use must depend on a manifestly reasonable foundation, and their use must be proportionate. However, as environmental protection in general is regarded as a proper and legitimate activity for central and local authorities, overall the balance is in favour of authorities. Even so it will be necessary from time to time for authorities to show they have considered Convention rights, both as to initial decisions and appeals.

The classic case here has been *Buckley v UK*.[20] Mrs Buckley was a gypsy; she purchased land and parked her caravans there. There was no grant of planning permission and enforcement action was taken. She argued that she was prevented from living with her family in her caravans on her own land and from following her traditional lifestyle, contrary to Art 8. Despite the fact that the site had been unlawfully established the ECHR considered Art 8 could apply to such a home, but then also considered that on the facts of the case the interference with Art 8 rights was justified on public health and road safety grounds, inter alia.

Similar conclusions have been reached by our own courts. Thus in *Brazil v Secretary of State for Transport, Local Government and the Regions*,[21] applying *Chapman v United Kingdom*[22] an interference with a gypsy's 'right' to live in a mobile home in respect of which planning enforcement action had been taken was held to be justified as it could be shown to be proportionate and needed to meet a pressing social need. It was also relevant in this context to remember that Brazil had set up his home unlawfully. Note, however, the conclusion in the similar case of *Clarke v Secretary of State for Transport, Local Government and the Regions*[23]. In certain circumstances there could be a breach of the European Convention of Human Rights where an inspector considered the provision of alternative, permanent housing when refusing planning permission for a caravan site. In order for those circumstances to arise, the inspector first had to be satisfied of the applicants' status, since not all travellers could be regarded as gypsies. The relevant criteria were whether a person lived in a caravan, whether that person was Romany, or subscribed to the gypsy culture, whether the person was itinerant or nomadic for a substantial portion of the year, and whether that itinerancy was linked to the person's livelihood. It was clear that many travellers and persons of gypsy descent

---

19   *R v Dacorum District Council, ex p Cannon* [1996] 2 PLR 45.
20   (1996) 23 EHRR 101.
21   [2001] All ER (D) 192 (Oct).
22   (2001) 10 BHRC 48.
23   [2001] All ER (D) 120 (Oct).

would not subscribe to the tenets of the culture. It was for claimants to satisfy the inspector that they subscribed to those tenets, including an aversion to conventional housing. In the instant case, the inspector had accepted that it was unreasonable for the authority to expect the claimant to live in a conventional house. It had not been clear as to what the inspector would have decided had he not considered C's refusal of conventional housing. The inspector had made insufficient findings to demonstrate that he had not taken into account irrelevant considerations. It followed that the decision would be quashed and the matter returned to the inspector for a formal hearing.

The Court of Appeal followed a similar route of argument in *Porter v South Bucks District Council*,[24] a further gypsy site case. Here it was held that a local planning authority may seek injunctive relief under the Town and Country Planning Act 1990 s 187B, in respect of an unauthorised gypsy site where such relief can be shown to be proportionate, ie appropriate and necessary to attain the public interest objective in question while not imposing an excessive burden on the individual whose interests are at stake. In this context the fact that breach of an injunction may lead to imprisonment for contempt of court should be borne in mind, as also the hardship towards the individual and his/her family, including the question of whether an alternative site for the family home exists, and the health and educational needs of the family. Against this the public interest in enforcing the law has to be considered, as must the flagrancy of the breach in question, the urgency of the matter and the use of other means of enforcement. It also has to be borne in mind that the planning authority is the local democratically elected and accountable body and their decision to seek relief has to be given a degree of weight in judicial proceedings. Do we again see here a 'margin of appreciation' line of thinking in the court's arguments?

It is also necessary for anyone wishing to rely on a Convention right to ensure he/she does so at the appropriate stage – rights can be lost if relied on too late. Thus if someone wishes to raise an Art 8 issue in a planning appeal it must be done as a matter of fact before the inspector. Though Convention rights can be relied on in statutory appeals and in judicial review proceedings any facts relevant to the legal arguments must be entered into the fray at the earliest moment.[25].

Article 8 has been relied on outside the context of land planning in the analogous area of sewerage planning. In *Marcic v Thames Water Utilities* Ltd[26] a property was subject to flooding and a back flow of foul water from a sewerage system so that the dwelling became effectively unsaleable. The sewers had been initially properly constructed and had been maintained, but there was a risk of flooding for which major surface drainage works were required. The defendant company had not prioritised such works in its financial planning, and there was only a most distant prospect of funding being made available. The claimant sued in nuisance, for breach of statutory duty, and for a violation of Art 8, which is our present concern. At first instance it was held that under Art 8 a statutory undertaker may be liable for a failure to carry out works needed to prevent the repetition of a nuisance, even though they had not created or caused that nuisance. The claimant also succeeded in a claim under Protocol 1, Art 1 as he had been deprived of the enjoyment of his possessions which amounted to an expropriation of them. The salient issues were seen to be that there was no prospect of works being carried out for a very long time, that the defendant had known of the repeated flooding of the property since 1992, and that the value of the dwelling had been seriously and adversely affected. The arguments of the defendant that as specialists in sewerage they should be allowed to determine priorities for its provision did not amount to a

24 [2001] All ER (D) 184.
25 *Woolhead v Secretary of State for the Environment and Epping Forest District Council* (1995) 71 P & CR 419.
26 [2001] 3 All ER 698.

justification. Clearly their prioritisation procedures did not strike a fair balance between the needs of their customers. On appeal it was held that the inadequate system of sewers constituted a nuisance, and while the defendants' use of these sewers was passive, by utilising them there was an adoption of the nuisance for which the defendants were liable; see further chapter 6. However, in addition the Court of Appeal agreed with the finding of the High Court that what the defendants had done constituted an infringement of the claimant's Convention rights. The fact that the defendants had known about the claimant's predicament for many years, and had done nothing to factor this into their calculations for doing work so that there was no current prospect of rectification work being undertaken constituted an unjustifiable interference with Mr Marcic's rights.[27]

Article 8 was also relied on in *Hatton v United Kingdom* (Application 36022/97, unreported, judgment given 2 October 2001). This decision of the ECHR once again concerned night time flights at Heathrow. Until October 1993 night time flights at Heathrow were controlled by restrictions on take-offs and landings. Thereafter a noise quota system was introduced allowing more flights by quieter aircraft or fewer flights by more noisy ones at the choice of operators. The controls were strictly imposed between 11.30 pm and 6.00 am, but there was a degree of leniency between 11.00 pm and 11.30 pm and 6.00 am till 7.00 am. Though the scheme was variously challenged by local authorities in the area, in a modified form it went ahead, and it was accepted that overall the level of noise during the 'quota period' had increased under the new scheme. The scheme was challenged as an infringement of Art 8. The ECHR concluded that states are required to take reasonable and appropriate measures to protect Art 8 rights, and this entails striking a fair balance between the rights of individuals and those of the wider community. States should seek to minimise interference with Art 8 rights; they should seek alternative solutions where schemes can affect those rights and should in general seek ways of achieving their aims which have the least onerous impact in terms of human rights. It is not enough to argue a scheme is justified by merely referring to the economic well being of a nation where people's sleep is being severely disturbed. States should rather ensure they conduct a proper and complete investigation and study of all the issues with the aim of finding the best possible solution in advance of procedure with schemes. That involves a properly conducted appraisal of alleged economic benefits, and a similar study of the likely disruptive consequences of a scheme. In the instant case a fair balance had not been struck between the national interest and the right of the applicants to home, family and private life.

While there are immediate implications here for the operation of Heathrow, the tenor of the judgment points towards a much greater need in the future for any scheme having deleterious environmental implications for identifiable individuals to be much more carefully researched and evaluated. Reliance on overall economic benefits of an unquantified variety will clearly be insufficient in this context. Furthermore there may be a need for those who are the identifiable 'victims' of such a scheme to have a more effective remedy than judicial review which only enables the legality of a scheme to be questions. They may need an opportunity to test its justifiability – see also further below.

Protocol 1, Art 1 may also affect planning powers. This protects possessions – but the ECHR has given this word a wide meaning to cover economic interests arising out of a grant of planning permission,[28] and rights to extract gravel.[29] Under Art 1 anything amounting to a deprivation (including denials of permission) can be resisted. The state must show justification. Yet again the state/local authority must show it is pursuing a

27   [2002] EWCA Civ 65, [2002] 2 All ER 55.
28   *Pine Valley Development Ltd v Ireland* (1991) 14 EHRR 319.
29   *Fredin v Sweden* (1991) 13 EHRR 784.

legitimate aim and that its actions are proportionate, ie any burden imposed by the state on an individual must not be disproportionate to the public benefit that will result from the control of land use. It is a case of showing that a fair balance has been struck between the needs of the community and the rights of the individual.[30]

National authorities under both Arts 8 and 1 must initially satisfy themselves of the necessity of their action, both as to the legal methods they choose to use and the way in which they go about implementing their choices. What they do must be in accordance with the law, must be done for a proper purpose and must be necessary[31],[32].

When therefore may Convention rights otherwise affect planning processes?

• When adopting a development plan, if a restrictive policy is adopted that may amount potentially to a breach of Protocol, 1 Art 1,[33] and so justification and a 'fair balance' test may have to be shown.

• When a planning application is determined. One possible argument for the future is that while the current range of permitted 'material considerations' do not extend to protecting private interests of individuals *as such*, it may be that in future the Convention rights of individuals will also have to be taken into account. Provided the necessary justifications etc can be shown no major problems should arise – even so it may be advisable to ensure that a proper regard is always had to these matters to disarm criticism and forestall action!

M THE IMPACT OF ART 6

This requires, it should be remembered, that:

'1 In the determination of his civil rights and obligations or of any criminal charge against him, everyone is entitled to a fair and public hearing within a reasonable time by an independent and impartial tribunal established by law ...'

This article extends to cover commercial as well as private interests, and may be relied on by those who are seeking some licence or permission from the state, or by those who object to any grant of a licence, etc, provided they can show they are 'victims'. The article will apply wherever civil rights and obligations are at stake, in a dispute that is genuine and justiciable, and where the proceedings in question will determine those civil rights etc. The dispute could arise over a right of property, or over a grant or refusal of planning permission affecting property, or the compulsory purchase of property, for example. In all such cases Art 6 requires:

• a right of access to a court;
• a fair hearing procedure;
• a right to a public hearing and a judgment;
• a right to a prompt adjudication;
• a right to an impartial and independent tribunal established by law.

But the article does not lay down the content of these rights.

In 'Human Rights and Environmental Wrongs. Incorporating the European Convention on Human Rights: some thoughts on the consequences for UK Environmental Law' (1999) 11 JEL 35, Justine Thornton and Stephen Tromans (to whose

---

30 *Sporrong and Lönnroth v Sweden* (1982) 5 EHHR 35.
31 See also *(1) Catscratch Ltd (2) Lettuce Holdings Ltd v Glasgow City Licensing Board* [2001] Scot SC 142, 2001 SC 218 (public entertainment licence as 'property').
32 *R v Leicestershire County Council, ex p Blackfordby and Boothorpe Action Group Ltd* [2001] Env LR (2) ('justifiable' grant of planning permission for waste disposal).
33 *Katte Klitsche de la Grange v Italy* (1994) 19 EHHR 368.

work indebtedness here and throughout this chapter is acknowledged) considered possible causes of complaint could be that the tribunal in question was not independent and impartial, or that there has been some procedural unfairness to a person – for example by giving that person inadequate notice of issues, or where an unreasonable time limit has been placed on the matter, or where a decision has been made supported by inadequate reasons, or where inadequate access to information relevant to proceedings has been given to parties. These issues might, for example, arise in the context of plan making, such as the situation where members of the public have no *right* to be heard, eg at the Examination in Public of a Structure Plan (see further chapter 8 below).

In fact the issue that reached the courts first turned on allegations that the tribunal deciding a matter was not independent and impartial. The issue can be briefly stated: if the policy maker is also the adjudicator in a dispute concerning the application of the policy how can the disputants be sure that the matter will be impartially determined? Historically our courts side stepped the issue by arguments such as that Parliament had entrusted certain decision-making powers to certain individuals and judges could not question what Parliament had done.[34] But could that attitude survive the enactment of the Human Rights Act 1998? In Scotland it was initially thought not.

In *County Properties Ltd v Scottish Ministers*[35] a company made an application under Scottish planning statutes to redevelop a listed building, and an objection to this was received from Historic Scotland, an executive agency operating under Scottish ministers. The ministers decided to 'call in' the matter for their own determination and appointed an inspector to hold an inquiry and make a report to them so that they could come to a decision. The company alleged this was a breach of their Art 6 Convention rights, in that the decision deprived them of their right to have the issue determined by an independent and impartial tribunal (ie the local planning authority). The court pointed out that in some cases the existence of a right of appeal to an independent judicial body will be sufficient to provide compliance with Art 6, provided that body has itself full jurisdiction to review the determination,[36] but the company argued that did not in any case apply here as the lack of independence in the initial determining body (ie ministers) was so blatant. The court, however, replied that there could still be compliance with Art 6 provided there was available a review of the decision before a judicial body having 'full jurisdiction'.[37] There was no doubt that a challenge to the decision could be mounted in court, but the real issue was whether that court had 'full jurisdiction' to determine the matter. Case law indicated that in an area like planning it can be enough for an appellate body to be restricted, as far as matters of fact are concerned, to satisfying itself that the initial decision taker had reached a decision that is 'neither perverse nor irrational'. That is acceptable where the facts at issue have themselves been determined by an initially fair procedure complying with Art 6.

That was not quite the case here, however. The decision would not be made by an inspector but by ministers. These ministers would be deciding an issue between the company and their own Executive Agency – they would be judges in their own cause. The decision would also largely turn on issues of taste, and in such cases the ability of a court to act as an independent arbiter is very limited. Further, as the ministers had conceded that if their decision was not one that would be reached by an independent tribunal, they had to show that there would be an avenue of appeal to a court with full jurisdiction to review the substantive issues. This they had not done – no court existed able to reconsider the substantive issues of planning judgment. Accordingly there had been a breach of Art 6 and the ministerial decision to 'call in' the matter was quashed.

---

34   *Franklin v Minister of Town and Country Planning* [1948] AC 87.
35   2000 SLT 965, Times, 19 September.
36   *Findlay v UK* (1997) 24 EHHR 221.
37   *Albert and Le Compte v Belgium* (1982) 5 EHHR 533 and *Bryan v United Kingdom* (1995) 21 EHRR 342.

The issue then arose in England in what has come to be called the *Alconbury* case.[38] The exceptionally complex facts need not trouble us at length for in essence the issue was the same as in the *County Properties* case, namely the exercise of a power of 'call in' of a planning matter by the Secretary of State under section 77 of the Town and Country Planning Act 1990, s 77 so that the decision in the matter becomes his and thus the issue of the non-independent decision taker arises. In the Divisional Court it was concluded the exercise of this power contravened Art 6 and a Declaration of Incompatibility was granted under the HRA 1998, s 4.

The House of Lords, however, came to a very different conclusion. It was accepted that where a minister is dealing with a 'called-in' matter there is no question of acting as an 'independent tribunal' as the minister is both making and applying policy. However, that need not be fatal to the minister's case provided there is a degree of subsequent control by a judicial body that has full jurisdiction and which does meet the requirements of Art 6 – *and whether that is so is a question of fact in each case.* Lord Slynn, for example, considered that there were factors indicating that, overall, the procedural requirements of Art 6 are met. First there *is* an inquiry in 'call in' cases, and that is conducted by an experienced professional – and in most cases the report of that person is conclusive of the matter. All material considerations needed to reach an informed, fair, unbiased and reasonable decision as quickly as is practicable are, Lord Slynn argued, considered at that point. The minister also takes the decision and senior civil servants who assist distance themselves from others involved, though that procedure alone by itself is not enough to satisfy Art 6. Lord Slynn then argued that the ECHR has recognised that in the UK and in other European states, decisions have to be taken by elected or appointed officials who are subject only to limited judicial review. Furthermore when applying planning or other similar policies ministers are not pursuing a 'judicial function', but have to take into account policy for which they are responsible to Parliament. It is then enough (and this is what satisfies Art 6) if judicial review is available on the traditional grounds of legality, eg error of law, taking into account irrelevant matters (and vice versa) acting in a perverse fashion or making procedural errors.

Lord Hoffmann reached a similar conclusion, arguing that in a democratic society there are certain policies which can be equally applied to all by means of general rules – eg taxation – while others have to be applied on a case by case basis by those to whom Parliament entrusts that power – eg planning matters. In addition while there are certain rights which inhere in individuals simply by virtue of their humanity (where the greatest degree of legal vigilance and control is required), other matters – for example the allocation of resources – are not matters for courts: 'the only fair method of decisions is by some person or body accountable to the electorate'.

Lord Hoffmann considered the development of the jurisprudence of the ECHR on Art 6, showing how case law has developed to require that 'all administrative decisions should be subject to some form of judicial review', *but the extent of that review is limited* – and it is not necessary that there should be the possibility of the review on the merits of a policy decision.[39] Thus there will be times where it is necessary to distinguish cases concerning the application of policy and those where rights in the narrower and more traditional sense such as issues of civil liberty are determined. In the former class of cases it is 'expedient' that the decision is made by a public official, though one subject to judicial review on issues of legality, without, however, the courts having the power

---

38   *R v Secretary of State for the Environment Transport and the Regions, ex p Holding and Barnes plc, R (on the application of Alconbury Development Ltd) v Secretary of State for the Environment Transport and the Regions, Secretary of State for the Environment Transport and the Regions v Legal and General Assurance Society Ltd* [2001] UKHL 23, [2001] 2 All ER 929, Times, 10 May.

39   *Zumbotel v Austria* (1993) 17 EHRR 116.

to substitute their views on matters of planning policy.[40] Thus while the possibility of an inquiry into a planning dispute does not satisfy the requirements of Art 6, as the inspector holding it is subject to the powers of the minister and is not 'independent', the subsequent possibility of judicial review on grounds of legality, etc, is sufficient. Lord Hoffmann concluded '[an] administrative act does in theory come within Article 6 but the administrators' lack of impartiality can be cured by an adequate and impartial judicial review'.

The *Alconbury* decision, of course, cuts away the ground under the *County Properties* decision, and while at the time of writing there was the possibility of a further appeal by the disappointed parties to the ECHR – which is still possible even after the HRA 1998 – it is clear that the traditional view of English courts alluded to above has been reiterated, and that the impact of Art 6 – on planning law at least – is for the moment limited. What is a matter of concern in particular is the distinction Lord Hoffmann appeared to make between the various types of rights and procedures to which Art 6 may apply, seeming to suggest that in relation to resource allocation issues, where matters frequently concern procedure and fairness, the courts may be less willing to intervene on a human rights basis. Within the context of the most developed thinking on the sustainable development question – see chapter 2 above - this is a matter for real concern. Such thinking emphasises the paramountcy of the law with regard to resource allocation questions and emphasises that it is only where people are given clear and protected procedural rights that society can begin to move towards the goal of sustainable decisions acceptable to all affected.

Following *Alconbury* the somewhat restrictive attitude of the courts was again demonstrated in *R (on the application of Kathro) v Rhondda Cynon Taff County Borough* Council.[41] Here the issue was whether a determination by a local planning authority of its own application to develop land could be acceptable under Art 6. The case was dismissed on the basis that as no decision had yet been reached the application was premature, but there were interesting comments from Richards J. His approach was to ask first of all whether there was an initial apparent breach by virtue of the decision-making mechanism, and it was concluded there was. However, that is not in itself enough. It has then to be asked whether the availability of judicial review could mean there is compliance with Art 6. The supervisory jurisdiction of the court was sufficient to prevent an *automatic* breach of Art 6. Thereafter the question, on a case-by-case basis, is whether that jurisdiction is sufficient to prevent an actual breach. The test is *not* whether the decision taker *might* be in breach of the Convention rights; rather it is whether the decision-making procedure *must inevitably* lead to a breach, and it is for those who oppose the decision taker to prove that. Those who would seek to rely on Convention rights in this connection therefore appear forced to face a tough uphill struggle, but not an impossible one, for the mere availability of judicial review does not guarantee that there will be effective independent scrutiny of the factual basis of a decision. A similar decision was reached by Forbes J in *R (on the application of Friends Provident Life and Pensions Ltd) v Secretary of State for Transport, Local Government and the Regions.*[42] Also worthy of note in this context is the Court of Appeal's comments in *Adan v Newham London Borough Council*,[43] that a right of appeal to or review by a court may not be sufficient to guarantee a fair hearing by an independent body where there are disputes between the parties as to primary facts. This may only rarely be the case in planning where essentially appeals are about the application of policy to agreed facts, but the situation of a disputed primary fact is not

40   *Bryan v United Kingdom* (1995) 21 EHHR 342.
41   [2001] EWHC Admin 527, [2001] All ER (D) 130 (Jul).
42   [2001] All ER (D) 274 (Oct).
43   [2001] EWCA Civ 1916, [2001] All ER (D) 216 (Dec).

inconceivable. It is hard to state hard and fast rules here, however, as the courts are proceeding on a case-by-case basis.[44] Argument on this matter also took place in the *Hatton* decision considered above. The ECHR there concluded that in the present instance traditional judicial review did not afford the applicants an effective remedy as is required by Art 13 of the Convention, as all that could be considered was whether the scheme in question was irrational, unlawful or patently unreasonable. That was not enough; a proper remedy would allow consideration of whether a scheme is a justifiable restriction on Convention rights. In this context it has to be noted that Art 13 was *not* included in the Convention rights 'brought home' by the HRA 1998. The official 'line' on this is that of the HRA 1998, s 8 gives courts sufficient powers to ensure an effective remedy is given where needed. However, it has to be asked whether traditional judicial review proceedings which are highly concerned with issues of procedure and legality are appropriate to deal with situations where the justifiability of a decision is called in question. In such cases the boundary between legality and 'merits' is eroded,and judges may find themselves under pressure to become surrogate decision takers.

Perhaps one way forward in relation to the granting of an effective remedy by UK courts would be for the development of notions in both the *Marcic* and *Hatton* decisions, namely the award of damages. If it is argued that the HRA 1998 imposes a set of statutory duties on public authorities, the question is what is their nature? We have seen earlier that most of the duties imposed by the Articles of the Convention are not absolute – breaches can be accepted if they are 'justified'. If therefore a public body unjustifiably breaches a Convention right, a species of breach of statutory duty action arises. Damages can be awarded for that. The defence to such an action would be to show that justification existed. Where the breach arose because of the implementation of a policy, the defence would be to show that the policy had been arrived at following a process in which the issues of justifiability had been addressed. Such a way forward would enable the courts to develop the law along lines with which they are familiar, and would be preferable to trying to develop judicial review as a means of questioning the merits of public decision taking. Public bodies would be able to continue to take decisions without fear of needless review proceedings, but would have to live with the possible consequence that 'victims', ie those who can show definite consequential loss following on from the decision-making process and/or its implementation, would be able to recover their losses through the civil courts. No issue would then arise as to whether the merits of the policy were 'right' or 'wrong', only whether the duty to show 'justifiability' had been breached.

But are there other areas of environmental regulation where Art 6 could have an application? The issue here concerns the investigatory powers of bodies such as the Environment Agency. Where such a body has power to require persons to answer questions, could this give rise to self-incriminating statements that would offend Art 6?

N SELF INCRIMINATION

In *R v Hertfordshire City Council, ex p Green Environmental Industries Ltd*[45] the question was whether a notice issued under the Environmental Protection Act 1990 (EPA 1990), s 71(2) requiring information to be given about waste amounted to requirement to give answers leading to self-incrimination and a contravention of the

---

44   *R (On the application of Johns and McLellan) v Bracknell Forest District Council* (2000) 33 HLR 495.
45   [2000] 2 AC 412, [2000] 1 All ER 773.

Art 6.1 right to a fair and public hearing. In *Saunders v UK*[46] the ECHR held 'public interest' could not be relied on to justify the use of answers compulsorily obtained in a non-judicial investigation to incriminate an accused during his subsequent trial. Similarly in *Orkem v EC Commission*[47] a questionnaire had been sent to Orkem which in effect required Orkem to confess it had acted illegally. However, the case law indicates that a regulatory body may ask for *purely factual information* even if it may be incriminating. What it may not ask for is an admission of guilt, or of any other wrongdoing. In the instant case the EPA 1990, s 71(2) notice simply asked for factual information, and therefore did not contravene Art 6.

Now the HRA 1998 is in force in cases like *Green* not only will there need to be strict observation of *Orkem* by decision takers, but also where a case is brought to trial and an answer to an EPA 1990, s 71 question is put forward in evidence, *the judge* at that point will have to consider whether to exclude the evidence because any 'interview' with a suspect under s 71 *may* not have been subject to the same strict requirements as apply under the Police and Criminal Evidence Act 1984 (with cautions etc). So there would appear to be two matters to bear in mind:

• the need to observe a distinction between asking only for factual information as opposed to obtaining a confession of guilt;
• at the trial itself convincing the judge *any* information obtained by questions has been fairly obtained with due regard to legal process, etc, etc.

The European Commission on Human Rights in preliminary proceedings considered that the existence of compulsory questions does not per se infringe the right to a fair trial and any privilege against self-incrimination.[48] But what of the subsequent use of information obtained compulsorily in a trial? This matter has now been dealt with by the Privy Council.

In *Stott (Procurator Fiscal Dunfermline) v Brown*[49] the question arose in the context of the Road Traffic Act 1972, s 172 whether the existence of a power to administer compulsory questions would lead to a breach of Art 6 of the Convention if the answers were subsequently used at trial.

Lord Bingham began by pointing out that there is no *express* guarantee of a privilege against self-incrimination in the Convention. Such a right is implied under Art 6 but its exact scope is not laid down. Furthermore it is clear that none of the constituent rights under Art 6 – whether express or implied – is absolute. National authorities may limit those rights in the pursuit of clear and proper objectives, and provided the limitation or qualification of the right is no greater than is called for. A 'hard edged' approach to rights is not justified, nor is it contained in the jurisdiction of the ECHR. In the case of road traffic issues it had to be remembered there is a high incidence of accidents and deaths in all Convention states. There is a need to address this problem for the public good, and one way of doing this is to subject motor vehicles to a regime of regulation with provisions for identifying and punishing guilty drivers. Thus the public benefit requirement was satisfied. Was, however, RTA 1972, s 172 a disproportionate response? Long Bingham thought not.

• As phrased s 172 provides for the putting of a single simple question – evidence as to the identity of a driver – that of itself does not incriminate a suspect as it is not an offence simply to drive a car. (We may ask, however, would the result be different in cases where more complex questions can be asked?) In addition the penalty for failing to answer is moderate and non-custodial, *and there was no*

46   (1996) 23 EHRR 313.
47   Case 374/87 [1989] ECR 3283 – a case before the ECJ.
48   *JP, KR, GH v Austria* (Application 15 133/89, S/9/89).
49   [2001] 2 All ER 97, [2001] 2 WLR 817.

suggestion in this present case of coercion or pressure to answer. If such coercion had occurred at trial the evidence could then have been excluded.
• The regulatory regime applies to all drivers equally, and everyone knows that, and the regime applies because of the dangers which cars can cause. Lord Bingham concluded that RTA 1972, s 172 is not a disproportionate response to a problem.
So it appears that compulsory question powers of themselves do not automatically fall foul of the Convention, provided:
• they can be justified in the light of problems within society;
• the questions asked are simple and do not of themselves incriminate the answerer;
• there is no coercion or pressure in the questioning process.
(On this issue, however, see *Heaney and McGuinness v Ireland*,[50] and *Quinn v Ireland*[51] and *JB v Switzerland,*[52] all decided at Strasbourg post-*Stott*, and which may call that decision in doubt. In all these cases the threat of penalties in respect of failures to give information, was held to offend Art 6.)

In any case there still remains the court's decision to refuse to admit any evidence it feels has been improperly obtained.

The *Green* decision does not of itself prevent authorities from obtaining information for the purposes of mounting a prosecution – though there are implications for how they go about doing it.

This may also have implications for planning contravention notices, see chapter 8 below.

O ARTICLE 6 AND EXCLUSIONARY RULES OF CIVIL LIABILITY

Article 6 may affect certain rules of the common law which have the effect of preventing certain people from pursuing a remedy otherwise available to others – arguably an example of unfairness: similarly a rule preventing claims being made against a particular class of person. It is open to question whether the rule that a person must have an interest in land before being able to sue in nuisance (see chapter 6) survives Art 6, perhaps also the rule that a lessee of property takes a letting of a dwelling subject to all defects existing at the time of the commencement of the lease on the 'let the buyer beware' principle.[53] However, somewhat confusingly it appears that a rule preventing a cause of action from arising against anyone does not fall foul of Art 6.[54]

P REGULATION OF INVESTIGATORY POWERS

It may be that the *practice* of regulatory bodies could be the area where the HRA 1998 has a particularly noticeable impact, not just with the regard to *justifying* action taken, to which allusion has already been made, but also by virtue of compliance with the Regulation of Investigatory Powers Act 2000 (RIPA 2000). Part II of this Act has general relevance to environmental issues.

This creates a system of authorisations for a number of different types of surveillance. There is no obligation on a relevant 'public authority' to obtain an authorisation where one could be available (RIPA 2000, s 80) but one consequence of not obtaining an authorisation could be that there is an infringement of Art 8 rights and an unjustifiable,

50 [2001] Crim LR 481.
51 [2001] 5 Arch News 5.
52 [2001] 5 Arch News 5.
53 *Southwark London Borough Council v Mills* [1999] 4 All ER 449.
54 *Mowan v Wandsworth London Borough Council* [2001] EGCS 4.

and hence unlawful, interference with those rights. A number of bodies are prescribed as 'public authorities' under RIPA 2000, ss 28 and 29. These *include* local authorities, the Environment Agency and the Food Standards Agency.

There are two basic types of surveillance – 'Directed' and 'Intrusive'. The former is, under RIPA 2000, s 26, a covert process taken in relation to a specific investigation or operation, where the result is likely to be that private information is gathered about a person, otherwise than by way of immediate response to events whose nature is such that it would not be reasonably practicable to seek an authorisation. 'Covert' processes are those carried out in ways calculated to ensure the person subject to surveillance is unaware of what is happening. 'Intrusive' surveillance is similarly 'covert' but relates to activities taking place on residential premises or in private vehicles, and involves the employment of persons or devices located within such premises or vehicles, or devices outside which consistently provide data of equivalent quality to internal devices. This latter type of surveillance is what is popularly known as 'bugging'.

Surveillance is, under RIPA 2000, s 27, lawful where it is carried out in accordance with a relevant authorisation. Authorisations under RIPA 2000, ss 28, 29 and 30 have to be granted by designated persons within the relevant authority: see SI 2000/2417. Before, however, an authorisation is granted, the person granting it must believe, under RIPA 2000, ss 28 and 29, that it is needed on specified grounds (ie, inter alia, that it is necessary in the interests of national security, or to prevent or detect crime or prevent disorder, or to protect public health) *and* that the authorised activity is proportionate to what it is sought to achieve by the surveillance. The clear parallel here between the language of RIPA 2000 and that of the Convention and the cases decided under it should be noted. These provisions apply to directed surveillance; a more restrictive regime under RIPA 2000, ss 32 to 39 of the Act apply to intrusive surveillance, as this is largely an activity likely to involve the police or customs officers.

RIPA 2000, s 43 lays down certain procedural requirements in respect of authorisations. Normally an authorisation must be in writing, though one may be granted or renewed orally in urgent cases. Authorisations are generally time-limited, and will usually in the case of local authorities last for three months, subject to renewal. Where a renewal is sought (which must take place before the initial authorisation runs out) the criteria to be applied are those for the initial grant (see above). Authorisations may be cancelled by those who grant them under RIPA 2000, s 45 where they are satisfied the criteria leading to the initial grant are no longer satisfied.

It should finally be noted that under RIPA 2000, s 71 the Secretary of State must issue Codes of Practice in relation to the provisions of RIPA 2000, and these will explain in detail the Act's provisions.

Further Reading

The HRA 1998

Reid, K *A Practitioner's Guide to the European Convention of Human Rights* (1998) Sweet & Maxwell.

Baker, C *Human Rights Act 1998: A Practitioner's Guide* (1998) Sweet & Maxwell.

Alston, P (Ed) *The EU and Human Rights* (1999) OUP.

Lester, A and Pannick, D *Human Rights Law and Practice* (1999) Butterworths.

Starmer, K *European Human Rights Law* (1999) LAG.

Thornton, J and Trumans, S 'Human Rights and Environmental Wrongs. Incorporating the European Convention on Human Rights: some thoughts on the consequences for UK Environmental Law' (1999) 11 JRL 35.

Coppel, J *Human Rights Act 1998: Enforcing the European Convention in the Domestic Courts* (1999) Wiley.

GENERAL ISSUES

Boyle, A and Anderson, M (eds), *Human Rights Approaches to Environmental Protection* (1996) OUP.

Miller, C *Environmental Rights* (1998) Routledge.

Hughes, D 'Environmental Protection: Underlying Concepts – A Personal Exploration' Part I [1998] 10 Environmental Law and Management 41–46; Part II [1998] 10 Environmental Law and Management 236–240; Part III [1998] 10 Environmental Law and Management 276–278.

Chapter 6

Civil liability for environmental damage

THE LAW OF TORTS AND THE ENVIRONMENT

The law of torts and its dependence for enforcement on private litigants is not best suited to the task of protecting the environment. The majority view is one of tort as being of diminishing importance given the rise of statutory regulation[1] (not least the crucial provisions of the Environmental Protection Act 1990), although there is a less widely held view that the systems of tort and statutory regulation are mutually reinforcing.[2] The law of torts' concern with compensating the claimant for injury to the person and tangible damage to assets gives rise to a lacuna in the protection of the 'unowned environment'. Of all the torts, nuisance has to be the one which holds the greatest promise of environmental guardianship, but even this cause of action is increasingly hampered by the courts' attempts to assimilate it to fault-based forms of liability, and to return it to its 'historical home' of protecting interests in land.[3]

There is some argument that, contrary to the thrust of this chapter, environmental issues are not deserving of any special treatment and that the principles of civil liability ought not to be given a benevolent interpretation in order to provide remedies for environmental damage. Cane raises two broad arguments to this effect, positing firstly that there are no satisfactory grounds for distinguishing harm arising from pollution incidents and other conventional sources of harm.[4] For example, harm to the person arising from a road accident is just as likely to be 'irreversible' as environmental harm. To argue that special treatment is merited, according to Cane, is to focus on the source of the harm rather than the nature of the harm and to cause 'legal confusion.' Furthermore, justice would be better served by using taxation or the criminal law to penalise polluters, and compensation would be put to better use by relieving human suffering than repairing environmental damage.[5] Such an argument assumes that

1   B Pontin, 'Tort Interacting with Regulatory Law' (2001) 51(4) *Northern Ireland Legal Quarterly* 597.
2   Bartrup and Burman, *The Wounded Soldiers of Industry* (1983) Oxford, discussed in B Pontin, 'Tort Interacting with Regulatory Law' (2001) 51(4) *Northern Ireland Legal Quarterly* 597.
3   J Wightman, 'Nuisance – the Environmental Tort?: Hunter v Canary Wharf in the House of Lords' [1998] 61(6) *MLR* 870.
4   P Cane, 'Are Environmental Harms Special?' (2001) 13(1) Journal of Environmental Law 3 at 17.
5   Cane, at p 11.

compensation for environmental harms necessarily detracts from compensation for personal harms when it is far from self evident that this is the case.

A THE TORT OF PRIVATE NUISANCE

Private nuisance is defined as some 'unlawful interference with a person's use or enjoyment of land or some right over or in connection with it'.[6] To be an actionable nuisance the activity must not arise on premises in the claimant's occupation. It must arise outside the claimant's land and then proceed to affect the land or its use. Second, it must generally be a continuing wrong. Most nuisances arise because of a regular, long-standing unreasonable use of land. A single instance of 'unreasonable interference' may, however, be evidence of a continuing unreasonable use of land, or so serious and grave an occurrence in itself as to amount to an act of nuisance.[7]

Unreasonable user

The first requirement of an action in nuisance is that the interference arises out of the defendant's unreasonable use of land. The lack of clarity which has attended this concept belies its central importance. The use must produce an interference which is more than trivial.[8] In the nineteenth-century case of *St Helen's Smelting Co v Tipping*,[9] Lord Westbury was heard to say: 'the law does not regard trifling and small inconveniences, but only regards sensible inconveniences, which sensibly diminish the comfort, enjoyment or value of the property which is affected.' Lord Goff has described the requirement of 'unreasonable user' as:

> 'the principle of give and take as between neighbouring occupiers of land under which those acts necessary for the common and ordinary use and occupation of land and houses may be done, if conveniently done, without subjecting those who do them to an action.'[10]

This creates the further difficulty of predicting what will be regarded as a common and ordinary use and occupation of land. Two negative examples are helpful here. In *Blackburn v ARC*, the requirement of 'unreasonable user' was described as 'virtually equivalent to establishing negligence' with the further comment that it was quite clear that the use of land as a rubbish tip which creates smell and gas is not a reasonable use of land.[11] Similarly in *Graham & Graham v Rechem International Ltd*,[12] Forbes J regarded the incineration of chemical waste as not 'necessary for the common and ordinary use and occupation of land'. Thus it seems that the community benefits of waste deposal services are not sufficient to rescue them from the label of 'unreasonable user' and that most commercial or industrial uses, if creating interference beyond ordinary domestic use, will be classed as 'unreasonable users.'

---

6   Winfield and Jolowicz, *The Law of Tort* (13th edn, 1994) p 404.
7   *British Celanese Ltd v A H Hunt (Capacitors) Ltd* [1969] 2 All ER 1252.
8   *Walter v Selfe* (1851) 4 De G Sm 315.
9   (1865) 11 ER 1483 at 14487.
10   *Cambridge Water Co v Eastern Counties Leather plc* [1994] 2 AC 264.
11   *Blackburn v ARC* [1998] Env LR 469, QBD.
12   [1996] Env L R 158.

Types of interference

In *Sedleigh-Denfield v O'Callaghan*,[13] Lord Wright remarked that: 'the forms which nuisance may take are protean.' The *Hunter v Canary Wharf*[14] litigation, however, illustrates a number of reinstated and modern limitations which apparently confine the types of interference to which nuisance can be applied. The *Hunter* case arose out of two different complaints; the first, that the defendant's construction of the 250 m Canary Wharf tower had interfered with the residents' television reception and the second, that excessive amounts of dust, produced in the course of constructing a road from the Canary Wharf development to central London, had been deposited on their properties. In the Court of Appeal, the issue of whether the deposit of dust could give rise to an actionable nuisance was resolved in the affirmative provided there was proof of 'physical damage', described as a 'physical change which renders the article less useful or less valuable.'[15] This finding is of significant import for environmental law as it applies directly to the deposit of any airborne contaminants affecting the claimant's property. *Hunter v Canary Wharf* did not spell the end of the litigation arising out of the dust issue. A claim was heard in the European Court of Human Rights under Art 8 which guarantees the right to respect of home, private and family life. The court concluded that the dust levels did not contravene Art 8 as the development was in pursuance of a 'legitimate aim' and was 'proportionate to that aim'.[16]

The issue of whether interference with television reception gave rise to an action in nuisance was finally resolved in a further appeal to the House of Lords. Their Lordships held unanimously that such interference was not actionable on these facts, although the reasoning which led to such a conclusion did not display the same unanimity. Lord Lloyd, for example, regarded the obstruction of television signals as equivalent to the obstruction of a view, and as a line of authority confirmed that the law of nuisance conferred no right to a view,[17] there was no right to receive television signals free from the obstruction of tall buildings. Their Lordships were careful not to exclude altogether similar claims where the obstruction of the signal was other than passive, for example, where such obstruction was the result of an emanation from land or where it arose from the operation of machinery rather than the solid mass of a static building.

Lord Goff preferred to say that actions in nuisance generally require an 'emanation from the defendant's land,' whereas the defendant's monolith, in merely passively obstructing television signals, was not actionable. The requirement of an 'emanation' has received further confirmation in *Anglian Water Services Ltd v Crawshaw Robbins & Co Ltd*.[18] The court had to consider whether the interruption of gas supplies could constitute an actionable nuisance. Although a discontinuation of supply clearly gave rise to inconvenience in the form of depriving householders of their usual heating and cooking facilities, the judge, relying on *Hunter*, concluded that such was not an actionable private nuisance as it did not involve an invasion of any substance or form of energy onto the claimant's land (in fact, it involved quite the opposite – the removal of the supply of gas from the claimant's property). Additionally, householders had no property right in their gas supply, only contractual rights. Disconnection therefore gave rise to contractual remedies against the supplier. The courts' insistence on an emanation from the defendant's land in both *Hunter* and *Anglian Water* is, however, at odds with

---

13   [1940] AC 880 at 903.
14   [1996] 2 WLR 348 and [1997] AC 665.
15   Per Pill LJ [1996] 2 WLR 348.
16   *Khatun v UK* (1 July 1998, unreported), EComHR 357.
17   *A-G (ex rel Gray's Inn Society) v Doughty* (1752) 2 Ves Sen 453; *Dalton v Henry Angus & Co* (1881) 6 App Cas 740.
18   [2001] BLR 173, QBD.

the authority of *Laws v Florinplace*[19] where the court accepted that a 'sex centre and cinema club' in a residential area could constitute a nuisance notwithstanding the absence of a physical emanation from the defendant's land. Although nuisance *usually* concerns a physical emanation, it is submitted that the absence of such an emanation is a less than sound reason for denying the existence of an unreasonable interference with the claimant's use and enjoyment of land.

Although the simple questions in the *Hunter* litigation as to whether the claimants should succeed or not were answered with a largely united front by the House of Lords, the more complex question of *why* they should or should not succeed demonstrated a diversity of opinion at every turn. For the highest court in the land to express such a level of disagreement on these questions which fundamentally affect the scope of the tort raises serious questions regarding the ability of the common law to provide coherent environmental protection.

A further restriction in the law of nuisance as fashioned by the courts is that the interference suffered must not arise merely out of the defendant's ordinary use of land. In *Baxter v Camden London Borough Council*,[20] the court expressed great sympathy for a claimant who sued her local authority landlord because of the inadequate sound insulation in her flat. This defect in the property meant she could quite easily hear all the noises of day to day living from her neighbours, including snoring, television noises, creaking floorboards down to the switching on and off of lights, and of course, they could hear the same from her property. The House of Lords regarded the claim as falling outside the ambit of nuisance as the complaint arose without any suggestion that the neighbours were making an unreasonable use of land. This was in truth a complaint about defective property and not the use of the land. Such an interpretation of the law of nuisance focusing on the requirement of an unreasonable use rather than the reasonableness of the interference suited the House of Lords' concern that liability in such a case would involve a substantial financial burden on local authorities and private landlords which even Parliament had not seen fit to impose.

The relevance of locality

The prevailing quality of the environment can be crucial in determining whether or not a given interference is 'unreasonable' for the purpose of liability in nuisance. In *St Helen's Smelting Co v Tipping* the House of Lords distinguished two types of nuisance; those causing physical damage and those causing only intangible damage which Lord Westbury referred to as 'amenity damage' or 'personal discomfort'.[21] The distinction is not always easy to apply in practice, but it is clear, for example, that the vibration of heavy traffic causing structural defects in a house would constitute physical damage, whereas the noise and fumes causing disturbance of sleep would be a matter of personal discomfort. The House of Lords confirmed that only in cases of interference causing intangible damage would the character of the locality be relevant to determining its reasonableness. The distinction is essentially one which determines the burden of proof – it is almost as if there is a presumption that the interference is unreasonable in cases of actual physical damage.

In cases of intangible damage/personal discomfort, locality *is* relevant. Consequently, the actionability of these intangible interferences, such as noise and odour nuisances, will vary from place to place. Thus, the malodorous emissions from a solvents factory

19   [1981] 1 All ER 659.
20   [1999] 4 All ER 449, HL.
21   (1865) 11 HL Cas 642.

are less likely to be considered 'unreasonable' if experienced against the backdrop of an industrial estate than if the plant were situated in a largely rural/residential area. This creates obvious problems for the enforceability of nuisance in environmental 'blackspots' of the country where industry tends to congregate in one area. Residents affected but not 'damaged' by emissions from local industry must not only identify which individual company is responsible for their discomfort, but also convince the court that the level of interference is an unreasonable one as against the backdrop of a local environment which is expected to suffer from pollution. Moreover, where the defendant is a substantial local employer this often further quells residents' willingness to litigate against pollution where there is no proven tangible damage. Defendants causing pollution in already polluted areas therefore have no immunity from actions in nuisance, but are often relatively safe from such litigation.

Two cases serve to illustrate the harsh results of the locality rule in *St Helen's Smelting Co v Tipping*. In *Murdoch v Glacier Metal Co Ltd*[22] the plaintiff brought proceedings against the incessant noise and vibration from a neighbouring factory. The Court of Appeal found there to be no actionable nuisance on the grounds that the noise was not unreasonable given that the factory was situated in an area dominated by an industrial estate and the claimant also lived close to a busy main road. Thus a claimant in an already polluted neighbourhood is often, in effect, denied the protection of the law of nuisance. It is worthy of further note that another reason for the court's decision was that nobody else had complained about the level of noise. Should this be a relevant consideration given that it is only in public nuisance that a group of people must be affected? In the second and more recent case of *Baxter v Camden London Borough Council*,[23] the claimant complained about the noise caused by neighbours living upstairs in the same house which was owned by the defendants. The noise was found not to be actionable with reference to the locality, as those living in low cost, high density housing must be expected to tolerate higher levels of noise from their neighbours than others in more substantial and spacious premises. Once again, the common law appears to discriminate against those claimants who are already disadvantaged.

Who can sue?

A logical corollary of the scope of private nuisance being returned to its 'historical home' of protecting interests in land is that, generally, only those with an interest in land capable of protection can sue. This much was explicitly reasserted by the majority of the House of Lords in the now familiar case of *Hunter v Canary Wharf Ltd*.[24] The case was brought by almost 700 claimants, many of whom did not have an interest in the land but were spouses, children or lodgers of those that did. An interest in land will usually be determined by the claimant's name being on the title deeds or lease for the property. Lord Cooke's dissenting judgment on this point preferred to articulate nuisance as a right of action available to anyone with 'substantial occupation of the land' who suffers interference with their use or enjoyment of the land. 'Temporary visitors' who were 'merely present in the house' would, however, be excluded from being able to sue. Lord Cooke's position was, he felt, only consistent with the status of children in modern times as 'fully fledged beneficiaries of human rights' and spouses who are accorded special status by statute in respect of the matrimonial home.[25]

22   [1998] 07 LS Gaz R 31, CA.
23   [2001] 1 AC 1.
24   [1997] AC 655 reinstating the rule as applied in *Malone v Laskey* [1907] 2 KB 141, CA.
25   At 715-718.

The House of Lords' judgment on standing to sue in private nuisance is laudable to the extent that it is an attempt to inject clarity and clear boundaries into the common law by creating a 'bright line' obligation to an ascertainable group of people. In so doing, however, their Lordships forfeit the interests of precisely those sectors of the public who are traditionally disadvantaged; the 'propertyless'. Thus, the lodger, homeless persons in hostels and bed and breakfast accommodation, children and older relatives who have moved in with their families are all potentially excluded from the broad range of protection offered by private nuisance. Having said this, the majority judgment in *Hunter* did not exclude all persons without a proprietary interest in land from suing in nuisance. Persons who enjoy or assert *exclusive* possession of the property where the nuisance is suffered can also sue, despite the absence of a proprietary interest in the property. This exception was recently confirmed by the Court of Appeal in *Pemberton v Southwark London Borough Council.*[26] The court accepted that a 'tolerated trespasser' (in this case a local authority tenant living in a flat which had been the subject of a possession order due to her non-payment of rent arrears) had sufficient interest to bring a nuisance action. Her *exclusive* possession of the premises, which could be brought to an end by the execution of a warrant to evict her, provided her with the necessary 'interest' to bring an action in nuisance for cockroach infestation.[27]

One final point worthy of comment follows on from *Hunter's* curtailment of the scope of nuisance. If the tort of nuisance is only concerned with the effect of activities on land rather than the effect on the person or their chattels, then the relevance of locality must be increased. This is because only in cases where there is proven physical damage to the land itself will locality be disregarded under the rule in *St Helen's Smelting Co v Tipping.*

A remedy for personal injury?

The House of Lords' pronouncement that nuisance is a tort against the land has further implications than tightening the rules on standing to sue. It also proved to curtail the scope of the tort by affecting/delimiting the types of interference which could give rise to a claim. Previous authorities and academic musings seemed hopelessly divided on the issue of whether private nuisance was a proper remedy for personal injuries and damage to goods or chattels. F H Newark pointed out in 'The Boundaries of Nuisance'[28] that much confusion with regard to this issue had arisen because an action for public nuisance consequent, for example, on some use of the highway could give rise to a remedy for personal injury. In *Woolfall v Knowsley Borough Council,*[29] for example, damages were awarded for injury caused to the claimant by a fire in a pile of rubbish on the land. The local authority should have moved the rubbish which lay by the highway.

The House of Lords' judgments in *Hunter* did little to resolve this uncertainty. The judgments of Lord Lloyd and Lord Hoffmann went so far as to say that damages for personal injuries were not recoverable in private nuisance. That is not to say that a claimant who suffers a severe skin reaction as the result of noxious fumes from the local paint factory has no right to compensation, but that the appropriate measure of damages in private nuisance would be that which represents the diminution of the value or utility of the *land* caused by the interference. Where the interference takes the form

---

26   [2000] 3 All ER 924.
27   Following *Foster v Warblington UDC* [1906] 1 KB 648.
28   [1949] 65 LQR 480.
29   (1992) Times, 26 June, CA.

of amenity damage/personal discomfort it will, of course, be difficult to measure the extent to which the value or utility of the land has been affected. On this point their Lordships did say that damages were to be assessed objectively with regard to the reduction of amenity value and not subjectively with regard to the impact on the particular individuals whose enjoyment of the land is affected. Thus, the measure of damages will be the same whether the property is 'occupied by the family man or the bachelor'.[30] This restatement of the boundaries of nuisance as a tort against land and not the person has the peculiar effect of prioritising property interests over security of the person and ties the tort even more firmly to the 'owned' environment.

Who can be sued?

The person who creates the nuisance is liable for it. Occupiers of land whence nuisances come may be liable also. They will be liable for nuisances committed by servants, and may be liable for the acts of independent contractors where they lead to special dangers for neighbours such as interferences with rights of support;[31] the making of noise and dust;[32] the creation of fire hazards;[33] or where a nuisance arises on the highway.[34] *Sedleigh-Denfield v O'Callaghan* is authority for the proposition that occupiers are not generally liable for nuisances arising either from the actions of a trespasser or from the operation of nature except insofar as they adopt or continue them.[35] The nuisance of another is 'adopted' if it is made use of by the defendant and it is 'continued' if the occupier, with actual or constructive knowledge of the nuisance, fails to take reasonable steps to abate it.

In cases of 'nuisance by omission' (ie where the defendant is alleged to be responsible for the interference by failing to abate its occurrence) liability is determined in much the same way as in negligence. This is most clearly illustrated by the case of *Holbeck Hall Hotel v Scarborough Borough Council*[36] which concerned the defendant's failure to abate a nuisance caused by the force of nature. The claimants owned a hotel on a cliff top at Scarborough. The defendants, who owned the land in between the hotel and the sea, had conducted remediation works to the land after two minor landslides in 1982 and 1986. In 1993, a massive landslip occurred which necessitated part of the claimant's hotel being demolished. The claimants alleged that their loss was caused by the defendant's failure to take further steps to abate the nuisance. The Court of Appeal found that there was a duty to take steps to abate the nuisance, given that the defect in the land was known and it was reasonably foreseeable that it would affect the claimant. Such findings would equally give rise to a duty of care in negligence. Where, however, the nuisance liability could only be attributed to an omission on the defendant's part the scope of the duty was narrower. Stuart-Smith LJ held that it would not be 'just and reasonable' (again, a throw back to negligence) for liability to be imposed for damage which is 'greater in extent than anything foreseen or foreseeable', especially where the defect 'existed as much on the claimant's land as the defendant's.' The judgment went further and suggested, obiter, that in cases where the defendant did not create the danger constituting the nuisance, the duty may be fulfilled by issuing a warning to those who are at risk from the nuisance. Indeed, the

30   [1997] AC 655, per Lord Lloyd at 696.
31   *Bower v Peate* (1876) 1 QBD 321.
32   *Matania v National Provincial Bank Ltd* [1936] 2 All ER 633.
33   *Spicer v Smee* [1946] 1 All ER 489.
34   *Leakey v National Trust for Places of Historic Interest or Natural Beauty* [1978] QB 849.
35   [1940] AC 880.
36   [2000] 2 All ER 705.

law adopts a subjective approach to determining the steps that a defendant is expected to take in order to abate a nuisance which they have not created. Unlike the objective standard usually applied in the tort of negligence, the requisite standard is intrinsically linked to considerations of the resources of the defendant and their general ability to abate the nuisance.[37] Although the *Holbeck Hall* case concerned potential liability for a nuisance triggered by a natural event, the Court of Appeal drew no distinction between such cases and those where the immediate cause was a third party.

It should be clear from the above that occupiers cannot escape liability for nuisances which arise on their land merely because they were not responsible for the creation of the nuisance. Where either a third party or the forces of nature are the originating causes of the nuisance, the liability of the occupier is determined by whether the court regards there as being what could loosely be termed 'negligence' on the part of the defendant in failing to address a known risk. A recent affirmation of this general principle arose out of *Bybrook Barn Garden Centre v Kent County Council*.[38] The Court of Appeal in *Bybrook* confirmed that the defendant's liability for the flooding caused by their overflowing culvert could not be denied on the grounds that the culvert had only flooded because natural forces had caused the neighbouring stream to swell over time. As soon as the defendants became aware of the fact that, due to natural forces, the culvert was no longer adequate to prevent flooding of neighbouring properties, a duty arose to take reasonable steps, taking account of practicality and cost, to remedy the situation.

The position of landlords is slightly different, at least where they are not also occupiers of the property concerned. There are four prominent Court of Appeal decisions on the liability of local authorities for disruption caused by tenants/tolerated trespassers which create some dubious distinctions in nuisance law. The liability of a non-occupying landlord is narrower than that of an occupier and extends only to those nuisances that they create or that they expressly or impliedly authorise. A landlord can impliedly authorise a nuisance where it is certain to result from the purposes for which the property is let. The first of the Court of Appeal cases, *Page Motors Ltd v Epsom and Ewell Borough Council*,[39] concerned interference with the claimant's business caused by the acts of gypsies camping on local authority property. Although technically trespassers, the local authority were liable for the gypsies' conduct because they had encouraged their continued presence by providing water and waste disposal facilities for them. This fact led to the Court of Appeal's finding that the local authority had 'adopted' the nuisance. *Page* was distinguished in the later case of *Hussein v Lancaster City Council*.[40] The claimants owned a shop with adjoining residential accommodation on the defendant local authority's housing estate. Over several years, the claimants had been subjected to severe overt racial harassment by a gang which included a number of the tenants of the housing estate. The claimants brought proceedings in nuisance against the council on the grounds that they had not taken reasonable steps to abate the nuisance. The Court of Appeal struck out the claim as disclosing 'no reasonable cause of action' – firstly, because the claim fell outside the scope of nuisance. For the local authority to be liable, the nuisance must arise from the 'tenant's use of the land' whereas these acts of harassment had no connection with the use of land. In any case, the Court of Appeal held that landlords were only liable for the acts of their tenants which were expressly or impliedly authorised. The first reason

---

37   *Leakey v National Trust for Places of Historic Interest or Natural Beauty* [1978] QB 849.
38   [2001] Env LR 30.
39   (1982) 80 LGR 337.
40   [2000] QB 1, [1999] 4 All ER 125.

does not sit easily with the traditional focus of nuisance which is that the claimant's use of land has been interfered with – a requirement clearly fulfilled on facts such as those in *Hussain.*

The third case was heard within two weeks of the *Hussain* judgment. In *Lippiatt v South Gloucestershire Council*[41] the claimants were tenants of farmland adjacent to a strip of land owned by the defendant local authority. A large group of travellers had squatted on the land and made their presence felt by the claimants by stealing from them, assaulting them and dumping rubbish and excrement on their land. The claimants sued the local authority for failing to abate the nuisance and the defendants, using the authority of *Hussain,* argued that the claim should be struck out as disclosing 'no reasonable cause of action'. The court rejected the defendant's argument on the grounds that *Hussain* could be distinguished. The travellers had used the defendant's land as the base of their activities and, therefore, the action could not be struck out, as it was arguable that their nuisance emanated from their use of land. The line drawn between the facts of *Hussain* and those of *Lippiatt* is at best a thin one and at worst illusory. The implications of these decisions for nuisance as a vehicle for environmental protection are a matter of some concern. It seems to be easier to impose liability on the defendant for acts of a trespasser than for the activities of their tenants, and yet surely the former are often more predisposed to resist the defendant's attempts to abate the nuisance. Further, the *Hussain* judgment's emphasis of interference flowing from the use of the defendant's land detracts from the protective traditions of nuisance.

Finally, in *Mowan v Wandsworth London Borough Council,*[42] the claimant brought proceedings against her local authority landlord for interference caused by her tenant neighbour who was suffering from a mental disorder. The interference ranged from flooding the property by leaving the taps on, chanting and moaning late at night to threatening to kill the claimant. She argued that her complaints to the council meant that they were aware of the nuisance and that they were liable for failing to take any steps to abate it. The Court of Appeal disagreed stating that a landlord's knowledge is not sufficient to give rise to liability. There had been no direct participation in the nuisance and it was not certain to arise out of the purposes for which the property was let. The cases of *Page* and *Lippiatt* were distinguished on the grounds that they concerned landlords as occupiers. It is necessary, therefore, before assessing the landlords' liabilities to determine whether or not they are in occupation.

For what damage will the defendant be liable?

Although damage is not a requirement of proving the tort of nuisance, a claimant seeking compensation may refer to damage sufficient to help the court fix an appropriate sum. It is for the claimants to prove any damage that they have suffered. This can cause problems of proof for claimants who have, for example, suffered damage by multiple pollution from a variety of sources, but the law will allow them to recover the totality of the loss, from anyone with whom they can establish a sufficient causal link.[43] In such circumstances the existence of another tortfeasor whose acts by themselves could be sufficient to produce the harm complained of will not excuse the person sued who must recover what has been paid in damages from fellow wrongdoers. An asbestos case, *Holtby v Brigham & Cowan (Hull) Ltd,*[44] demonstrates a pragmatic approach to issues of cumulative damage. The claimant developed asbestosis after working for over thirty

41   [2001] QB 51, [1999] 4 All ER 149.
42   [2001] All ER (D) 2411.
43   *Clark v Newsam* (1847) 1 Exch 131.
44   [2000] 3 All ER 421.

years as a marine fitter in close proximity to asbestos. For approximately half that time, the claimant had worked for the defendants and the court accepted that both the employment with the defendants and the later employment with other companies had contributed to the condition. The court confirmed the general rule that a 'material contribution' was sufficient to give rise to liability for the full extent of the damage, unless it could be shown that other contributions were made to the damage. In this case, the Court of Appeal felt that a sensible approach would be to use the time periods as a convenient means of reducing damages. Therefore, as the claimant had worked for the defendant for approximately half his working life he should be liable for approximately 50% of the damage (although the court did not disturb the trial court's finding that 75% was a suitable figure). Where the cumulative effect of a number of acts of pollution results in an actionable wrong, the claimant may be able to bring one action against all those who can be shown to be responsible for the individual acts. See also *Pride of Derby and Derbyshire Angling Association v British Celanese Ltd*[45] where Harman J said: 'I cannot believe that the law, while holding all of a number of defendants liable if none of them individually commits an actionable wrong, will relieve the rest if the wrong of one of them is big enough by itself to be actionable.' Furthermore it is no defence to prove that the act of the defendant by itself is not a nuisance and only became so when combined with the act of others.[46] Once the claimant proves the nuisance and damage the defendant will, since the decision in *Overseas Tankship (UK) Ltd v Miller Steamship Co Pty, The Wagon Mound (No 2)*,[47] be liable for the reasonably foreseeable consequences of the nuisance.

In this context it is important to note the implications of the House of Lords' judgment in *Cambridge Water Co v Eastern Counties Leather plc.*[48] A water company found one of its wells contaminated by perchloroethene (PCE), a chemical used in tanning. It was concluded that the chemical had percolated down to the water after having been spilled over a number of years on the defendant's premises. The PCE was present in quantities rendering the well unusable because of contravention of drinking water standards under Directive 80/788/EEC, laid down *after* the chemical's escape. To pollute water percolating through to another's land *can* be an actionable nuisance where wells are contaminated (see *Ballard v Tomlinson*[49]) but not only must a causal link be demonstrated, there must be foreseeability of the broad 'type of harm' that will result from the defendant's acts. In the *Cambridge Water* case, Kennedy J sitting in the High Court would not accept 'pollution' as a broad 'type' of harm, nor that those responsible for the spillages in past years could have foreseen the creation of an environmental hazard, or a material affectation of water supplies. More importantly, one reason the well could not be used was because of the existence nowadays of stricter water quality standards. Those responsible for past spillages could not have foreseen the development of those standards, and their *past* acts could *not* be considered wrongful simply because *present* knowledge and standards show the risk involved.[50]

In the Court of Appeal, *Ballard v Tomlinson*[51] was, however, treated as completely determinative of the issue, but this was reversed by the House of Lords. The House of Lords held that foreseeability of the *type* of damage which has eventuated is a

---

45   [1952] 1 All ER 1326 at 1333.
46   *Thorpe v Brumfitt* (1873) 8 Ch App 650.
47   [1967] 1 AC 617, [1966] 2 All ER 709.
48   [1994] 2 AC 264.
49   (1885) 29 Ch D 115.
50   (1991) Times, 23 October, QBD.
51   (1885) 29 Ch D 115.

prerequisite for liability in nuisance as in negligence.[52] In the present case there could be no liability because the defendants could not possibly have foreseen that damage of the type complained of, ie that the presence of the chemical would contravene subsequent European drinking water standards, might be caused by their spillages.

The House of Lords refused to acknowledge liability for 'historic pollution' ie historical spillages of emissions of material not at the time of loss subject to regulation and so not then likely to give rise to a foreseeable type of damage. They added, significantly, that there could be no *future* liability for damage arising from such a spillage where the material in question is still in the land and is now known to be polluting another's property, where that material has passed out of the defendant's control by percolating down through strata.

It must now be asked what degree of foresight will impose liability on a defendant. It would appear that there must be foreseeability of the type of effect which gives rise to the damage complained of, and this implies a degree of specificity. So foresight of possible mere contamination, following an activity, would probably be insufficient to ground liability; rather there should be foresight of the particular type of pollution (ie a harmful or illegal condition) which ultimately eventuates. Much will thus depend upon the facts of individual cases. In *Paterson v Humberside County Council*[53] householders claimed for damages to a house caused by a tree drying out soil of medium shrinkability. The soil conditions in the area were well known and the subject of local authority advice. It was held that the damage in the circumstances was foreseeable.

Remedies

A person injured by a nuisance will wish to obtain recompense for loss and cessation of the activity. The law can award damages and an injunction, but it must be asked whether the practice of the courts with regard to these remedies produces the best possible results. As has been shown by Ogus and Richardson in 'Economics and the Environment: A Study of Private Nuisance',[54] (to whom the author acknowledges indebtedness), the results can be criticised when considerations of economic efficiency are taken into account because they do not always bring about the most good for the least cost; that is they do not always remedy the harm by the cheapest means.

Damages

Generally, the common law will grant damages only for past losses. Equitable damages can be awarded in respect of future loss, though the courts frown on such awards as they effectively enable the defendant to pay in advance for a continuation of unlawful activity. Equitable damages may be awarded in lieu of an injunction under the Supreme Court Act 1981, s 50 in exceptional circumstances: if injury to the claimant's rights: (i) is small; (ii) is capable of being estimated in monetary terms; (iii) can be adequately compensated by small monetary payments and (iv) it would be oppressive to the

52 This was followed in *Bybrook Barn Garden Centre v Kent County Council* [2001] Env LR 32, the Court of Appeal agreeing that if the defendants could not have foreseen the increased flow of water, they could not have been held liable in nuisance.
53 (1995) Times, 19 April.
54 [1977] CLJ 284.
55 *Shelfer v City of London Electric Lighting Co* [1895] 1 Ch 287 and *Kennaway v Thompson* [1981] QB 88, [1980] 3 All ER 329.
56 [2002] EWCA Civ 65, [2002] 2 All ER 55.

defendant to grant an injunction.[55] In *Marcic v Thames Water Utilities Ltd*,[56] the defendant's failure to provide the claimant with proper drainage and the subsequent flooding of the claimant's premises was regarded as a violation of the claimant's right to peaceful enjoyment of his possessions (protected by the European Convention of Human Rights, Protocol 1, Art 1). The claimant argued that as the defendants intended to allow the inadequate drainage/flooding to continue, he was entitled to damages for the inevitable future violations in lieu of an injunction. Despite the common law generally precluding the award of damages for future wrongs, the High Court awarded such damages as contrary authorities were distinguished on the grounds that it was the claimant and not the defendant requesting the damages.

The House of Lords in *Delaware Mansions Ltd v City of Westminster*[57] was asked to address the related issue of whether damages were recoverable to compensate the claimant for the cost of remedial expenditure necessitated by the encroachment of tree roots. The issue was novel because the evidence suggested that the damage to the block of flats caused by the tree roots had probably occurred before 1990, the year in which the claimants had acquired the property. Their Lordships, in a unanimous judgment, concluded that the requirement in *Hunter* of a possessory or proprietary interest in the land did not prevent recovery in this instance because the nuisance could be described as continuing into the time of the claimant's ownership. Notwithstanding the possibility that all the cracks in the structure of Delaware Mansions had occurred before 1990, the presence of the encroaching roots constituted a risk that further damage to the foundations would be caused and therefore remediation was necessary. *Delaware Mansions* demonstrates that damage can be recoverable in nuisance not only for past damage but to protect the claimant's property from future damage, provided the nuisance can be described as 'continuing'.[58]

Damages awarded by the common law will generally reflect the diminished market value of the claimant's property.[59] Where transient interference with the use and enjoyment of land only is claimed, for example, a nuisance arising from smell, only modest sums will be awarded. More substantial sums may be awarded for long-standing or more offensive interferences with the enjoyment of land.[60]

Injunctions

An injunction is an order requiring the abatement of a nuisance. The remedy is awarded at the discretion of the court. The order may be

1   *Perpetual* – an order issued at the end of proceedings.
2   *Interlocutory* – an order issued pending the outcome of proceedings but not prejudging the final result.
3   *Mandatory* – an order requiring defendants to take positive steps to remedy the wrong they have done.

An interlocutory injunction will only be granted where the claimant establishes that there is a serious issue for trial, as in *Laws v Florinplace Ltd*[61] where such an injunction was granted to restrain the operation of a sex shop in a predominantly residential area, even though no breach of the criminal law had occurred. Thereafter the court must

---

57   [2001] UKHL 55, [2002] 1 AC 321.
58   Cf the tort of negligence where the cost of remediation to prevent future damage would be regarded as a pure economic loss and not recoverable: *Murphy v Brentwood District Council* [1991] 1 AC 398, [1990] 2 All ER 908.
59   *Moss v Christchurch Rural District Council* [1925] 2 KB 750.
60   *American Cyanamid Co v Ethicon Ltd* [1975] AC 396, [1975] 1 All ER 504.
61   [1981] 1 All ER 659.

decide whether the balance of convenience lies in favour of granting interlocutory relief.[62] A mandatory injunction will generally only be awarded where the claimant can show a very strong probability that grave damage will accrue in the future, and that damages would not be an adequate remedy. Moreover the amount to be expended by the defendant in discharge of the injunction must also be taken into account. The court will be more ready to impose positive requirements on a defendant who has acted wantonly than on one who has acted reasonably and whose actions have yet to result in harm. When a mandatory injunction is issued the court must ensure that it is clear what the defendant has to do.[63] In *Tetley v Chitty*[64] local residents were awarded both damages and an injunction against a local authority which had allowed go-karts to race on its land under, first, a licence, and then a seven-year lease.

An injunction may be issued before the occurrence of actual damage *provided* the claimant can show that the defendant's conduct, if unchecked, is almost certain imminently to result in substantial damages. In such circumstances the injunction is known as *quia timet*.[65] Once granted an injunction may be suspended. This may be coupled with an award of damages in respect of loss suffered pending implementation. This practice is followed when it is desired not to impose an immediate crushing burden on the defendant. Where the immediate loss to the defendant would vastly outweigh any immediate gain to the claimant a suspension may be granted.[66] A suspension is also granted to enable a public utility to continue the supply of essential services.[67]

The courts generally fail to take into account the full economic consequences of an injunction for either the defendant or third parties. Ogus and Richardson show that in some parts of the US the courts take a much wider view of the consequences of their orders. In *Boomer v Atlantic Cement*,[68] the New York Court of Appeals dismissed an application for an injunction because the economic hardship to the defendant would have outweighed the benefit to the plaintiff. In *Madison v Ducktown Sulphur, Copper and Iron Co*,[69] an injunction was refused on the ground that the resulting loss to the community consequent on unemployment would be unacceptable. It is unlikely that such considerations will find their way into the decision-making processes of English courts. Nevertheless, as Ogus and Richardson point out, the results of a decision may have unforeseen consequences. If, for example, polluting activity is stopped by injunction, it may lead to an increase in land values in the vicinity and hence to the charging of higher rents and rates on properties in that locality; or it may lead to higher productions costs with regards to particular goods. To what extent are the courts suitable arbiters of issues such as these?

Self-help

Occupiers may take action to abate nuisances which adversely affect them. In so acting they must not commit any unnecessary damage. Furthermore it seems that notice must be given to the responsible party before action is taken, unless the abatement can be

62 *American Cyanamid Co v Ethicon Ltd* [1975] AC 396, [1975] 1 All ER 504.
63 *Redland Bricks Ltd v Morris* [1970] AC 652, [1969] 2 All ER 576.
64 [1986] 1 All ER 663.
65 *Midland Bank plc v Bardgrove Property Services Ltd* [1992] 2 EGLR 168.
66 *Stollmeyer v Petroleum Development Co Ltd* [1918] AC 498n; *Halsey v Esso Petroleum Co Ltd* [1961] 1 WLR 683 and *A-G v Gastonia Coaches Ltd* [1977] RTR 219.
67 *Prices Patent Candle Co Ltd v LCC* [1908] 2 Ch 526 and *Manchester Corpn v Farnworth* [1930] AC 171.
68 257 NE 2d 870 (1970).
69 83 SW 658 (1904).

effected without entering the party's land, or there is an emergency in that the nuisance threatens to cause immediate harm. See generally *Lemmon v Webb*.[70]

B PUBLIC NUISANCE

Public nuisance is both a crime and a tort and has been defined at common law as conduct: 'which materially affects the reasonable comfort and convenience of life of a class of Her Majesty's subjects.'[71] Spencer wonders whether the concept of public nuisance is so broad that we have no need for further torts or criminal offences.[72] The two main issues for determination in any particular case are, therefore, is there a 'material' effect on comfort and convenience? And does the group affected constitute a 'class'? Lord Denning in *A-G v PYA Quarries Ltd*[73] commented that the latter question: 'is as difficult to answer as the question when does a group of people become a crowd?' His reformulation of the requirement was that the nuisance must be so 'widespread in its effect that it would not be reasonable to expect one person to take proceedings to put a stop to it.'[74] In *R v Johnson*[75] the Court of Appeal found that harassing telephone calls made to at least thirteen women was to be regarded as a nuisance affecting a 'class'. The problem persists with smaller numbers. What if the number of women affected was six? Would this have been regarded as widespread and indiscriminate?

The law of public nuisance is enforceable at the instance of any individual suffering 'special damage' over and above that suffered by the rest of the affected class or by a relator action (an application for an injunction restraining the public nuisance made in the Attorney General's name but not with the private litigant's funds). A third option is to urge the relevant local authority to bring enforcement action under the statutory nuisance provisions of the Environmental Protection Act 1990. Statutory nuisances are defined by the EPA 1990, s 79(1) as matters which constitute a nuisance or are prejudicial to health by reason of:
(a)   the state of premises;
(b)   smoke emitted from premises;
(c)   fumes or gases emitted from premises;
(d)   any dust, steam, smell or other effluvia arising on industrial, trade or business premises;
(e)   any accumulation or deposit;
(f)   the keeping of animals;
(g)   noise emitted from premises and
(h)   any other matter declared by any enactment to be a statutory nuisance.
Where the nuisance falls into any of the above categories, the local authority is under a duty to take reasonably practicable steps to investigate the nuisance.[76] Once satisfied that a statutory nuisance exists, the authority is under a statutory duty to take enforcement action in the form of serving an abatement notice on the person responsible for the nuisance or the owner/occupier of the land from which the nuisance emanates.[77]

---

70   [1895] AC 1.
71   *A-G v PYA Quarries Ltd* [1957] 2 QB 169 at 184.
72   J R Spencer, 'Public Nuisance – A Critical Examination' (1989) CLJ 48(1) 55.
73   [1957] 2 QB 169.
74   [1957] 2 QB 169 at 191.
75   [1996] 2 Cr App Rep 434.
76   EPA 1990, s 79(1).
77   EPA 1990, s 80(1).

Failure to comply with a properly served abatement notice is a criminal offence.[78] (For more detail on statutory nuisance, see chapter 1.)

One of the most common uses of public nuisance is obstruction to the highway, free passage along the highway being a public right. Nuisance on the highway need not amount to a de facto obstruction nor what might be commonly regarded as a hazard. In *Wandsworth London Borough Council v Railtrack plc*,[79] the claimant Highway Authority brought proceedings against the defendant in connection with their failure to address an infestation of roosting pigeons on the underside of one of its bridges. The public, both in cars and on foot, who passed under the bridge suffered inconvenience by virtue of the 'obvious fallout'. The Court of Appeal refused to disturb the finding of Gibbs J that the number of complaints, the amount of cleaning necessitated by the pigeons and the fact that there was no dispute as to how the nuisance could be abated meant that the interference was sufficiently severe to constitute a nuisance.

Where public nuisance occurs on the highway, the relevant Highways Authority has the power to abate the nuisance and bring proceedings to recoup the costs of abatement from the person liable for the nuisance.[80]

Assessment of nuisance as a tool of environmental protection

1   There is a general trend of curtailment of nuisance as a remedy discernible in numerous aspects of the *Hunter v Canary Wharf Ltd*[81] judgments including: the restriction of private nuisance claims to complainants with an interest in the land, the restriction of compensation to reductions in the value or utility of the claimant's land (the owned environment) and the general insistence on an interference in the form of an emanation. All of these restrictions reduce the utility of nuisance, which although 'protean' in its capacity to extend protection against a multitude of activities is being moulded into an increasingly specific form of protection for land ownership.

2   The modern interpretation of nuisance as concerned with land value and ownership brings its own practical limitations. The pool of potential claimants is radically reduced, where protection of the environment was already dependent on the few financially equipped and sufficiently motivated to incur the time and expense of litigation.

3   In addition to the specific trends which have afflicted the common law of nuisance, the common law appears, arguably, to be plotting the demise of the strict liability protections once available in tort. The incorporation of remoteness considerations into nuisance liability by *Cambridge Water* reverses the traditional emphasis in nuisance which was on the interference/the impact of the defendant's activities on the claimant to an emphasis on the reasonableness of the defendant's activities given what could have been foreseen. Antonia Layard draws the conclusion: 'After Cambridge Water it is the victims who bear the burden of any gaps in scientific knowledge, which are not reasonably foreseen, even if the uses are "non-natural" or apparently "unreasonable".'[82]

4   Lord Goff in *Cambridge Water* gave a further reason for refusing to provide a remedy in nuisance – that as Parliament was already dealing with the issue of environmental protection by means of a number of entries on the statute books,

---

78   EPA 1990, s 80(4).
79   [2002] Env LR 9.
80   *Goodes v East Sussex County Council* [2000] 1 WLR 1356.
81   [1997] AC 655.
82   A Layard, 'Balancing Environmental Considerations,' (1997) 113 LQR 254.

'there is less need for the courts to develop a common law principle to achieve the same end, and indeed it may well be undesirable that they should do so.' It is more than a little ironic that given that Parliament's devotion of time and space on the statute book is a clear indicator of the importance attached to environmental issues, the courts should regard this as justification for refusing to intervene in the allocation of environmental liabilities.

As the process of assimilating the remaining pockets of strict liability into the fault-based tort of negligence continues, environmental lawyers must be prepared to test the boundaries of this tort to ensure its capacity to support environmental claims.

C THE RULE IN *RYLANDS v FLETCHER*

Once thought to be a stand-alone tort, the principle in *Rylands v Fletcher*[83] states that 'the person who for his own purposes brings on his lands and collects and keeps there anything likely to do mischief if it escapes, must keep it in at his peril and if he does not do so, is prima facie liable for all the damage which is the natural consequence of its escape.'[84] On appeal to the House of Lords, Lord Cairns laid emphasis on the defendant having made a 'non-natural use' of the land. This additional requirement of a non-natural use has been adopted by subsequent case law.

Given that the House of Lords in *Cambridge Water*[85] regarded the principle as an extension of the rules in nuisance, presumably the limitations on private nuisance claims apply also to actions under *Rylands v Fletcher*. It is therefore conceivable that *Rylands v Fletcher* actions will require the claimant to prove an interest in the land (this is consistent with the earlier authority of *Weller & Co v Foot and Mouth Disease Research Institute*[86]). If Lord Lloyd and Lord Hoffmann's dicta in *Hunter v Canary Wharf Ltd*[87] are to be followed then we can further assume that no remedy will be available for personal injury as nuisance is a tort against the land and will only provide compensation in so far as there is a diminution of value in the land. Such a position is clearly at odds with earlier cases such as *Hale v Jennings Bros*[88] where the plaintiff suffered personal injuries when hit by a chair-o-plane which had escaped from the defendant's fairground stall. The plaintiff in this case recovered compensation for his injuries notwithstanding the absence of any interest in the land (cf *Read v J Lyons & Co Ltd*[89] which preferred to categorise *Rylands* as an action against the land).

The escape need not originate from the defendant's own land, but may apparently be an escape from the public highway.[90] Furthermore, the escape does not have to be of the thing accumulated (*Miles v Forest Rock Granite Co*[91]) but must be a consequence of a non-natural accumulation. A very narrow definition of 'escape' was confirmed in *Read v J Lyons & Co Ltd*[92] of escape from the land rather than 'escape from the defendant's control'. The implications are that no remedy under the rule is available where workers are injured by a chemical spill which has not exceeded the factory gate.

83   (1868) LR 3 HL 330.
84   Per Blackburn J.
85   [1994] 2 AC 264.
86   [1966] 1 QB 569.
87   [1996] 2 WLR 348.
88   [1938] 1 All ER 579.
89   [1947] AC 156.
90   *Rigby v Chief Constable of Northamptonshire* [1985] 2 All ER 985.
91   (1918) 34 TLR 500.
92   [1947] AC 156.

Although comparisons have been made between 'unreasonable user' and the requirement of 'non-natural use' in *Rylands v Fletcher* actions,[93] there is precious little in the way of further guidance on the requirement of 'non-natural use.' We can say, however, that the concept has been the subject of a change in emphasis over the years, so that while former applications of non-natural use required some 'special use bringing with it increased danger to others',[94] the modern meaning is far less demanding. In *Cambridge Water*,[95] Lord Goff referred to the large scale storage of chemicals as 'an almost classic case' of a non-natural use. This is clearly good news for those considering legal action against escapes from industrial uses of land. Furthermore, Lord Goff added that the requirement of 'foreseeability' (which he regarded as being applicable to both nuisance and *Rylands v Fletcher* actions: see earlier), performed the function of controlling liability. It was, therefore, unnecessary for the non-natural use criterion to do the same – the implication being that it would henceforth be relatively easy to fulfil the requirement of non-natural use. Given this apparent relaxing of the 'non-natural use' condition, it remains unclear whether previous authorities which indicated that uses of land which served the community could not be regarded as non-natural (see, for example, *Rickards v Lothian*,[96] where a non-natural use was defined as one which would not 'merely be the ordinary use as is proper for the general benefit of the community'). It would seem that *Rickards v Lothian* could be used to exclude the provision of services to a local community to a business park or industrial estate from consideration as a non-natural use. Part of the answer is provided by *Transco plc v Stockport Metropolitan Borough Council*.[97] Here liability of the defendants under the rule in *Rylands v Fletcher* was overturned in the Court of Appeal. The Court of Appeal made some useful comments on the meaning of non-natural use. The defendant supplied water through a pipe to the basement of a tower block of flats. A crack in the pipe caused the escape of large volumes of water over time to a nearby railway embankment. The embankment collapsed exposing Transco pipes. Transco sued the Council for the cost of works necessary to make their pipeline safe. The Court of Appeal concluded that the strict liability principle under *Rylands v Fletcher* did not apply: (i) where the defendant was merely using his land for a purpose for which it might in the ordinary course of the enjoyment of land be used; (ii) to the supply of utilities by common place methods (utilities); or (iii) for acts necessary for the common and ordinary use and occupation of land and houses, provided he is acting reasonably (domestic use).

In *Ellison v Ministry of Defence*[98] the escape of flood water from the defendant's airfield was not actionable under the rule in *Rylands v Fletcher* as the accumulated water was rainwater and therefore not 'non-natural.'

As liability is (supposedly) strict, the defendant can only raise a limited number of defences:

1 Consent (express or implied).
2 Contributory negligence.
3 That the accumulation is maintained for the common benefit of both parties.[99]
4 That an act of a stranger caused the escape (provided that act was of a kind which the defendant could not reasonably have contemplated and guarded against).
5 An act or default of the claimant led to the damage.

93 Lord Goff in *Cambridge Water Co v Eastern Counties Leather plc* [1994] 2 AC 264.
94 *Rickards v Lothian* [1913] AC 263.
95 [1994] 2 AC 264.
96 [1913] AC 263 at 280.
97 [2001] All ER (D) 190 (Feb).
98 (1996) 81 BLR 101, QBD.
99 *Dunne v North Western Gas Board* [1964] 2 QB 806, [1963] 3 All ER 916.

6   An act of God, that is an escape occurring without human intervention which no human foresight could provide against, and the occurrence of which human prudence could not be expected to anticipate.
7   Statutory authority.

Assessment of *Rylands v Fletcher* as a tool of environmental protection

On the face of it, the *Rylands v Fletcher* action is well suited to the role of environmental protection. So many environmental incidents can be described as a 'non-natural' use of land involving the accumulation of something likely to cause mischief if it escapes and which does escape causing damage. This set of conditions and pattern of events characterises most instances of pollution, whether of water or the atmosphere and also contamination of the land where there is an 'escape' of polluting substances into the soil. Its greatest merit, as far as environmental claims are concerned, has historically been the strict nature of *Rylands* liability. The absence of any reference in the rule to 'foreseeability' or 'reasonableness' meant that liability could be imposed without having to prove anything equivalent to fault on the part of the defendant. The *Cambridge Water* judgment changed that by adding the requirement of foreseeability of the risk. Had the House of Lords in *Cambridge Water* decided to perceive *Rylands v Fletcher* as a 'general rule of strict liability for damage caused by ultra-hazardous operations' this would have been a major step towards fulfilling the objectives of the EC White Paper on environmental liability.[100] Arguably, however, the courts had already begun to assimilate *Rylands v Fletcher* into fault-based liability much earlier. For example, the requirement that the accumulation is likely to do mischief if it escapes, suggests a degree of hazard associated with the thing accumulated and some academics go so far as to say that the accumulation must be of something 'dangerous.' Furthermore, the requirement of a non-natural use may also imply something approximating high risk (*Mason v Levy Auto Parts of England Ltd*[101]).

The torts of nuisance (and *Rylands*) now occupy a hybrid position between fault-based liability and strict liability, for Lord Goff in *Cambridge Water* was emphatic that reasonable care was no defence to these actions:

> 'knowledge, or at least foreseeability of the risk, is a prerequisite of the recovery of damages under the principle; but ... the principle is one of strict liability in the sense that the defendant may be held liable notwithstanding that he has exercised all reasonable care and skill to prevent the escape from occurring.'[102] (*sic*)

D THE TORT OF NEGLIGENCE

Actions for negligence constitute the majority of civil claims, but the usefulness of such actions in environmental litigation is limited. An action for negligence may be the only remedy available to a person who cannot sue for nuisance because, for example, the pollution/harm does not constitute an 'emanation from the defendant's land', it

---

100 It is not undisputed that strict liability is beneficial in deterring pollution given the absence of empirical evidence in this regard; M Wilde, 'The EC Commission's White Paper on Environmental Liability: Issues and Implications' (2001) 13(1) *Journal of Environmental Law* 21 and P Cane, 'Are Environmental Harms Special?' (2001) 13(1) *Journal of Environmental Law* 3.
101 [1967] 2 QB 530.
102 [1994] 2 AC 264 at 302.

does not affect the value of the land or the claimant has no interest in the land upon which to sue.

A civil claim in negligence requires proof of: a duty of care owed to the claimant; a breach of that duty; and that the breach *caused* some damage to the claimant. Those intending to bring an action in negligence against a polluting act or activity face several obstacles including:

• the need to convince the court that damage to the environment is a recoverable head of loss in negligence;
• establishing that a duty of care is owed to the complainant not to pollute;
• proving that the defendant's activity *caused* the damage; and
• resisting defences of statutory authority when the defendant has been granted a licence to pollute.

A concept of environmental damage at common law?

The traditional forms of 'damage' in negligence are:
• physical injury to the person (including psychiatric injury);
• property damage; and
• consequential economic loss (that is, a financial loss which is consequent on some damage to the plaintiff's property).

Adoption of 'environmental damage' as a new head of loss would provide a first step towards implementing the White Paper on environmental liability, which seeks recognition of 'impairment to the environment' as a form of damage (see below). There are, however, no signs that environmental damage will become an independent head of loss at common law, although there have been a handful of recent English cases which have dealt with specific incidents of pollution within the context of property damage. The defendant in *Blue Circle Industries plc v Ministry of Defence*[103] owned an estate on which it carried out the research, development and production of nuclear weapons. During heavy rainfall, ponds on the defendant's land overflowed onto the plaintiff's estate. Surveys later showed that parts of the plaintiff's land had become contaminated and, although not harmful to health, exceeded levels prescribed under radioactive substances legislation. On discovery of the contamination, prospective purchasers of the plaintiff's estate withdrew from negotiations. In awarding damages under the Nuclear Installations Act 1965 for the consequent delay in the sale of the plaintiff's land, the Court of Appeal concluded that there had indeed been damage to property, and in so deciding, placed the emphasis on physical change:

'Damage will occur provided there is some alteration in the physical characteristics of the property, in this case the marshland, caused by radioactive properties which render it less useful or less valuable.'[104]

The conceptualisation of damage in *Blue Circle* involves a dual emphasis on physical change and a change in the usefulness or value of the property.[105] These two requirements are not always distinct, as in *Blue Circle*, the fact that radioactivity affected the market value of the plaintiff's land was a factor which convinced the court that there had been a physical change in the characteristics of the property. The proviso of

103 [1997] Env LR 341, QBD, [1998] 3 All ER 385, CA.
104 Per Aldous LJ [1998] 3 All ER 385, CA at 393b.
105 See also *McMullin v ICI Australia Operations Pty Ltd* (1998) 10(1) ELM at 5, where damage was also equated with 'physical change' in contaminated cattle.

physical alteration demonstrates that the Court of Appeal is not willing to go as far as *The Orjula*,[106] where contamination of a ship due to leakage of hydrochloric acid was treated as 'damage'. The judge arrived at this conclusion on the express assumption that there had been no alteration to the ship. The requirement of physical change means that publicised radioactivity which affects the market value of a property due to the stigma attached to it will not give rise to a claim as against the source of radiation if the radioactive material does not become intermingled with the fabric of the claimant's property.[107] It is this more liberal approach which has attracted support in later decisions. Although relied on in *Blue Circle*, *Hunter v Canary Wharf Ltd*[108] is in fact a hybrid of the approaches physical change requirement and the 'expense' emphasis of *The Orjula*. The Court of Appeal had to decide as a preliminary issue whether the deposit of dust on houses, caused by the construction of a road, could constitute property damage. Pill LJ held that for the purposes of nuisance, dust was capable of constituting damage:

> 'it follows from the effects of excessive dust on fabric that (if) professional cleaning of the fabric is reasonably required, the cost is actionable.'

This consequentialist approach to 'damage,' with its focus on expense is an implicit rejection of the objective change demanded by *Blue Circle*. Thus *Hunter*, *The Orjula* and *Blue Circle* show differing degrees of willingness by English courts to liberate the concept of property damage in order to facilitate compensation claims for the effects of contamination.

The finding of property damage in *Blue Circle* is very difficult to reconcile with the earlier decision of *Merlin v British Nuclear Fuels plc*.[109] In *Merlin*, the radioactive contamination of house dust, caused by the Sellafield nuclear power plant, was held not to constitute property damage (although again reducing the value of the plaintiff's property). Despite the obvious parallels between the two contamination claims of *Merlin* and *Blue Circle*, the distinction between the 'owned' and 'unowned' environment remains intact. While contaminated soil in *Blue Circle* was treated as part of the plaintiff's estate and therefore gave rise to a claim for property damage, on the facts of *Merlin*, only the airspace within the house was changed, and airspace did not constitute 'property'.[110] Radioactive contamination of airspace could only therefore give rise to recognised property damage where tangible items, such as livestock, were affected.[111] This creates a somewhat unfortunate distinction from the point of view of environmental claimants (particularly as the radioactivity levels in *Merlin* were higher than those in *Blue Circle*); it is a distinction which once again highlights the fact that tort is a regime protecting property rights, and offers only incidental remedies for environmental damage. Of further interest is the impact of regulatory standards in expanding the court's understanding of legally recognised 'damage.' In *Cambridge Water*, the courts accepted that the violation of the water quality standard fixed by an EC directive gave rise to damage.[112] Indeed, there was no evidence that the pollution presented a public health hazard and in the absence of the directive it would have been unlikely to have

---

106 *Losinjska Plovidba v Transco Overseas Ltd, The Orjula* [1995] 2 Lloyd's Rep 395, QBD.
107 This much is made clear by Aldous LJ in *Blue Circle Industries plc v Ministry of Defence* [1998] 3 All ER 385, CA at 393g-h.
108 [1996] 1 All ER 482, CA. Although this case has since been heard in the House of Lords, the 'dust' issue was not dealt with there.
109 [1990] 2 QB 557.
110 See Gatehouse J in *Merlin v British Nuclear Fuels plc* [1990] 2 QB 557 at 570 F-G.
111 Gatehouse J at 571 B.
112 S Tromans, 'EC Environmental Law and the Practising Lawyer' in H Somsen (Ed), *Protecting the European Environment: Enforcing EC Environmental Law* (London, Blackstone, 1996) at 271.

been treated as sufficiently serious to constitute 'damage.' In a similar vein, Carnwath J in *Blue Circle Industries plc v Ministry of Defence* commented that regulatory standards could be useful in determining whether levels of contamination could be regarded as a legally recognised form of 'damage'.[113]

Establishing a duty of care

It is a legal requirement that the situation is one in which the defendant must show care towards the claimant. The existence of a duty of care is not conclusive of the question of liability, for it only determines that the area of activity in question is one where liability is potentially capable of existing. The general approach to duty of care is to utilise a three-pronged test, all three components of which must be answered in the affirmative for a duty of care to exist:
(i)   Was harm a reasonably foreseeable consequence of the defendant's lack of care?
(ii)   Did the claimant and defendant share a relationship of proximity?
(iii)   Is it just, fair and reasonable to impose a duty of care?[114]
The recent attitude of the courts is to be wary of extending situations in which a duty of care applies. So in *Stephens v Anglian Water Authority*[115] the Court of Appeal denied the existence of a duty of care in respect of the abstraction of water flowing in undefined channels under their land by defendants, even where this led to damage to the plaintiff's land, and in *Gunn v Wallsend Slipway and Engineering Co Ltd*,[116] it was held that no duty of care existed in respect of a woman who had died of mesothelioma after inhaling asbestos dust from clothes worn by her husband while working in the defendant's shipyard. The same conclusion was reached in *Hewett v Alf Brown's Transport Ltd*[117] but it is otherwise if there is an occupational link with asbestos, or one based on living and playing amidst asbestos dust.[118] Similar reticence can be seen in Scotland where in *Landcatch Ltd v Gilbert Gillies*,[119] no duty of care was found to exist in respect of loss of profit following the death of young salmon brought about by a failure in a system to pump salt water through their tanks. Though there have been cases where supplying agencies have been held subject to a duty of care to warn, in respect of polluted material,[120] the general consensus, particularly since the generally restrictive attitude towards duty of care shown by the House of Lords in *Murphy v Brentwood District Council*,[121] is that a solely *regulatory* agency would not be liable simply because a person suffers pollution damage in consequence of activities of which a warning *could* have been given, but was not (see *Dear v Thames Water*[122] and in the context of planning, *Ryeford Homes Ltd v Sevenoaks District Council*.[123])

---

113 [1997] Env LR 341 at 347-348.
114 *Caparo Industries plc v Dickman* [1990] 2 AC 605, [1990] 1 All ER 568. See the House of Lords judgment in *Marc Rich & Co AG v Bishop Rock Marine Co Ltd* [1996] AC 211 which stated that all types of loss were to be subjected to the same test for determining when a duty of care exists.
115 [1987] 3 All ER 379, [1987] 1 WLR 1381.
116 (1989) Times, 23 January.
117 [1992] 4 LMLER 48.
118 *Margereson and Hancock v JW Roberts Ltd* [1996] Env LR 304.
119 1990 SLT 688.
120 *Barnes v Irwell Valley Water Board* [1939] 1 KB 21; *Scott-Whitehead v National Coal Board* (1987) 53 P & CR 263.
121 [1991] 1 AC 398, [1990] 2 All ER 908.
122 (1992) 4 Water Law 116.
123 (1989) 46 BLR 34.

Breach of duty – a civil duty to regulate?

A claimant may face great difficulties in proving breach of duty. The claimant must demonstrate that the defendant's conduct failed to meet the standard of care required by law. Such a standard is dependent on factors such as the magnitude of the risk of harm presented by the defendant's conduct, the utility of the defendant's actions and the ease with which the risks can be reduced or eliminated. Where the defendant's conduct conforms to common practice in that particular industry/activity, it becomes very difficult for the claimant to convince the court that the defendant was nevertheless in breach of duty. In *Hammersmith Hospitals NHS Trust v Troup Bywaters and Anders*[124] the claimants alleged that the defendant environmental consultants had been negligent in advising them as to the suitability of boilers for the disposal of clinical waste, resulting in the abandonment of the boilers. The court confirmed that the standard of care required by environmental consultants was fulfilled by reference to other responsible persons in the same profession who would have done the same. The court expressly approved Butler-Sloss LJ's judgment in *Sansom v Metcalfe Hambleton & Co*[125] that: '... a court should be slow to find a professionally qualified man guilty of a breach of his duty of skill and care towards his client without evidence from those within the same profession as to the standard expected on the facts of the case.' Where there was division of professional opinion, this will generally work in the defendant's favour.[126] It is only if the court finds the expert evidence supporting the defendant's conduct to be not 'responsible' that the court will find for the claimant.[127] Of course, as pollution abatement technology is generally a complex area of specialism, the courts will be slow to find practitioners of such technology to be 'irresponsible'.

Conformity with common practice in pollution abatement techniques is persuasive although not conclusive evidence that the standard of care has been met *(Brown v Rolls Royce Ltd*[128]). The claimant who has suffered damage due to the defendant's pollution may derive some assistance from any successful prosecution of the defendant arising from the same incident of pollution[129] although the courts might be reluctant to use conviction of a strict liability offence such as the Water Resources Act 1991, s 85 as assistance in reaching a finding of negligence.

A further problem in establishing breach of duty arises from the defendant's argument that the relevant authorities had not expressed dissatisfaction with the defendant's operations. A defendant polluter accused of negligence may convincingly argue that harm was not 'foreseeable' to him as the agencies responsible for enforcing environmental laws had not drawn the potential for harm to his attention.[130] Polluters can argue that they relied on liaison with the regulators to alert them of any dangers, given their statutory duties in this regard. There is evidence, however, that this argument may be less likely to succeed for companies falling under the 'prescribed processes' regulations, as the onus is more clearly on the companies' risk management mechanisms to identify foreseeable risks.

---

124 [2001] EWCA Civ 793, [2001] All ER (D) 341.
125 [1998] PNLR 542.
126 *Maynard v West Midlands Regional Health Authority* [1984] 1 WLR 634.
127 *Bolitho v City and Hackney Health Authority* [1998] AC 232, [1997] 4 All ER 771.
128 [1960] 1 WLR 210.
129 Civil Evidence Act 1968, s 11.
130 See *Graham v Rechem International* (1995) August ELB vol 1, p 1, where the court relied on inaction by the enforcement body to draw an inference that the dioxins being released from the defendant's incinerator weren't causing any harm, and *Hughes v Dwr Cymru* (1996) Water Law p 40, where a communication from the National Rivers Authority was treated as the first time the defendants became aware of the problem.

Would it then be feasible to make an alternative civil claim by putting environmental regulators in the frame for a 'failure to regulate'? The Environment Agency, the main environmental regulator, may have 'permitted' the emission or discharge by granting a licence, or may have 'failed to take action' to prevent the release which caused the damage. The obstacles presented in an allegation of failure to regulate are close to insurmountable. At least five obstacles stand in the way of an argument that the Environment Agency ('the Agency') owes a common law duty to the victims of pollution.

(i)　As was seen in chapter 3, the Environment Act 1995 does not compel the Agency to regulate in a particular way but merely grants regulatory powers. An allegation of failure to regulate will therefore usually take the form of an alleged negligent exercise of statutory powers. In such a case, it seems that the claimant would have to show that the action/inaction was 'so unreasonable that it falls outside the ambit of discretion' before the matter will be regarded as giving rise to a common law action. [131] There has however been a slight liberalisation in the House of Lords' treatment of cases alleging negligence in the exercise of statutory discretion, no doubt spurred by the increased interest of the European Court of Human Rights with this aspect of English law.[132] In *Barrett v Enfield London Borough Council*,[133] for example, Lord Slynn preferred to say that the ultimate question was whether the particular issue is justiciable/whether the court should accept it has no role to play. The issue of discretion was simply a guide with which to answer that question. It would be likely that decisions which are not so unreasonable as to be outside the ambit of discretion or which involve policy decisions involving the balancing of public interests would not be justiciable, but this is not an absolute rule. There would be some cases in which decisions involving discretion could give rise to a duty of care and it was preferable to simply apply the usual tests of reasonable foreseeability, proximity and justice, fairness and reasonableness to determine whether a common law duty arose. (Note, however, that such complications do not affect the liability of statutory authorities in nuisance[134].)

(ii)　Liability in negligence rarely arises out of an omission to act. Such litigation would typically rest not on the Agency's positive act but on their failure to control the wrong of another. Where liability has been imposed in the past on water authorities in negligence for a failure to warn the victim of the risk of pollution, the pollution had resulted from the defendant's own operations and not those of a third party.[135]

(iii)　There is unlikely to be sufficient proximity between regulator and victim. Cases of 'failure to control' where proximity has been established, have demonstrated a control relationship between the regulator and the agent of harm, so close as to be, for example, 'equivalent to parent and child'.[136] Environmental regulators rarely have the degree of control necessary to give rise to such proximity as their power arises from periodic inspection rather than day-to-day control.[137] There are, however, indications that liability could be fixed onto a negligent inspection which

---

131　*X v Bedfordshire County Council* [1995] 2 AC 633, HL, at 736B, per Lord Browne-Wilkinson. The courts sometimes prefer the test set out in *Anns v Merton London Borough Council* [1978] AC 728 which generally allows only operational decisions as opposed to policy decisions to give rise to a duty of care.

132　*Osman v UK* [1999] 1 FLR 193; *Z v UK* [2001] 2 FCR 246.

133　[1999] 3 WLR 79.

134　*Stovin v Wise* [1996] AC 923, per Lord Hoffmann at 958.

135　*Scott-Whitehead v National Coal Board* (1985) 53 P & CR 263 where the harm arose from the defendant's own abstraction operations and *Barnes v Irwell Valley Water Authority* [1939] 1 KB 21 where the defendant had failed to replace lead piping.

136　*Home Office v Dorset Yacht Co Ltd* [1970] AC 1004.

137　*Yuen Kun Yeu v A-G of Hong Kong* [1988] AC 175 which involved a failure to regulate, used this fact to deny the existence of proximity.

failed to prevent an incident as opposed to a complete failure to inspect.[138] See also *Sasea Finance Ltd (In Liquidation) v KPMG (No 2)*[139] for an example of the Court of Appeal refusing to strike out a claim alleging failure to warn in the analogous field of auditor's liability.

(iv) Should the duty to prevent damage be made out thus far, it may yet fall at the proviso that imposing a duty of care should be just, fair and reasonable. The shadow of potential civil liability can inhibit the exercise of sound judgement and may prompt those exercising important public functions, to perform these functions in 'a detrimentally defensive state of mind.'[140] Public policy arguments of this type are commonly used to deny a duty is owed by public bodies in their performance of public functions. In the Environment Agency's case, it might be argued for example that the threat of civil liability would involve an undesirable diversion of legal department resources from the pursuit of polluters. There is further evidence to suggest that the English courts are eager to maintain the discrete nature of the civil and environmental protection regimes, and adopt a non-interventionist position.[141]

(v) It may also have to be proved that the purposes of the regulator's statutory powers include protection of the claimant from this type of damage.[142] The Environment Agency is under a statutory duty to exercise its functions so as to prevent, minimise, remedy or mitigate 'pollution to the environment',[143] which is further defined as including harm to persons, offence to the senses and damage to property.[144] It may therefore be relatively easy to convince a court that protection of the plaintiff's interest does fall within the regulator's statutory duties.

Causation

In any civil liability claim arising out of damage to the environment, proof of causation is often the crucial hurdle in litigation. The precautionary principle is often advanced as offering a solution to the difficulties of establishing causation.[145] The principle advocates action in advance of scientific proof and could be implemented by tampering with the legal burden of proof in order to assist the victim. But the statement of the precautionary principle in the Rio Declaration relates only to action taken to prevent environmental damage, and not the laws designed to determine liability once damage has occurred. It is therefore questionable whether the principle in its original form was ever intended to apply to issues of post-incident liability.

In civil trials, there is a very thin line of authority which states that where an inference of causation has been raised and the defendant is in a better position to know the cause of the injury, it is for the defendant to disprove causation.[146] This approach addresses the inevitable imbalance of power between victim and industrial defendant. While this

---

138 *Perrett v Collins* [1998] 2 Lloyd's Rep 255 – Civil Aviation Authority owing a duty of care to a flight passenger to make adequate inspection.

139 [2000] 1 All ER 676.

140 *Hill v Chief Constable of West Yorkshire* [1989] AC 53. Although note the increased reserve with which such arguments are accepted expressed in *Barrett v Enfield London Borough Council* [2001] 2 AC 550.

141 See Lord Goff in *Cambridge Water Co v Eastern Counties Leather plc* [1994] 1 All ER 53, at 76, HL.

142 *Curran v Northern Ireland Co-ownership Housing Association Ltd* [1987] AC 718.

143 Environment Act 1995, s 5.

144 Environmental Protection Act 1990, s 1(3) and (4).

145 K Vanderkerckhove, 'The Polluter Pays Principle in the EC', *Yearbook of European Law* (1993).

146 See *Snell v Farrell* (1990) 72 DLR (4th) 289.

approach has some following in the English courts[147] it has yet to be utilised in the field of environmental litigation. In *Reay and Hope v British Nuclear Fuels plc*[148] two complainants who had developed leukaemia sought to cast the blame on radiation from the nuclear installation where their fathers had both worked. While the court showed some willingness to use epidemiological studies in legal proceedings, they would not accept anything less than scientific proof of a causal relationship.

A defence of statutory authority?

The issue of whether the grant of an environmental licence provides a defence to civil liability raises important questions of public policy. Licences and permissions granted under statutory powers could arguably attract a common law defence of 'statutory authority' to polluting acts authorised by the licence.[149] At the crux of this issue is whether the courts will respect the discrete aims of the two legal regimes of civil liability and statutory regulation, or will intervene to protect one from being undermined by the other. Preliminary indications are that the common law will not tolerate a defence based on compliance with a regulatory licence.

Planning permissions granted for a given activity do not appear to attract an automatic defence to the tort of nuisance (except to the extent that the permission changes the character of the neighbourhood and thereby renders the conduct 'reasonable').[150] Can the common law negligence standard require more from the polluter than his discharge consent or waste management licence granted by the Environment Agency?[151] The view of the House of Lords Select Committee on the matter,[152] was that the environmental licence should not provide a defence to civil liability, as the 'costs' of the damage would remain on the public, thereby directly contradicting the 'polluter pays' principle. A search of the statutory provisions is unhelpful. Although the Water Resources Act 1991 states that nothing in Part III of that Act (which provides for the grant of discharge consents authorising limited pollution of controlled waters) shall derogate from any civil *right of action*, that is not necessarily the same thing as stating that discharge consents provide no *defence* to civil liability.[153]

In *Blackburn v ARC Ltd,*[154] the plaintiffs brought proceedings in private nuisance against the defendants who were tipping domestic waste at a neighbouring quarry site. The complaints related to litter and smells emanating from the site. The defendants argued that the possession of planning permission and a waste disposal licence were a valid defence against any civil claims. The court agreed only in so far as any nuisance might be an *inevitable consequence* of the authorised activity. Where, as here, the litter and smells could be avoided and were not an inevitable product of the tipping operations, the defence was not available. The court confirmed that the law should be

147 See *Hollis v Young* [1909] 1 KB 629 and Lord Bridge's comments in *Wilsher v Essex Area Health Authority* [1988] 1 All ER 871 on the case of *McGhee v National Coal Board* [1973] 1 WLR 1.
148 [1994] Env LR 320.
149 The defence of statutory authority is illustrated in *Allen v Gulf Oil Refining Co Ltd* [1981] 1 AC 1001.
150 See *Gillingham Borough Council v Medway (Chatham) Dock Co Ltd* [1993] QB 343; *Wheeler v JJ Sanders* [1996] Ch 19; both approved in *Hunter v Canary Wharf Ltd* [1996] 1 All ER 482 (unaffected by the House of Lords decision).
151 See further, the first instance hearing of *Hughes v Dwr Cymru* (1996) Water Law p 40, where the judge concluded that a water company's operation within its discharge consent could be a defence to civil liability.
152 *Third Report of the House of Lords Select Committee on EC* (1993–94) (EC Green Paper on Civil Liability for Environmental Damage).
153 WRA 1991, s 100(b).
154 [1998] Env LR 469, QBD.

slow to allow an administrative decision to extinguish private rights. It seems then that environmental licences are to be treated similarly to planning permissions in that their existence does not necessarily bar a civil action. This does not address the slightly different issue of whether it is a defence to act under a licence but beyond what is an inevitable consequence of authorised activities where the Agency have not taken any action or expressed any dissatisfaction with the defendant's activities. A number of convincing arguments can be made to support the finding that Agency action or inaction should generally be irrelevant to civil means of enforcement. Civil and regulatory regimes represent different legal aims; the aim of the regulatory system seemingly being to deter acts of unacceptable environmental risk and so to protect precious resources, and that of the civil system to compensate those who suffer loss as a consequence of the activities of another. Quite apart from fears that one system of law should not undermine the principles of liability in another,[155] there are practical reasons for excluding consideration of regulatory action/inaction in civil cases. Bearing in mind the limited financial and manpower resources of public bodies, it is questionable whether developments in legal protection should be dependent on their regulatory activities.

Even if the defendant's interference is not an inevitable result of the licensed activities, the fact of an Agency licence or approval could still undermine a claimant's chance of success in a negligence suit. It is unlikely that a court would decide the defendant's conduct was 'unreasonable' and therefore constituted a breach of his duty of care, when his polluting activities had been sanctioned by the Agency.[156] Alternatively, the view of the court in *Graham v Rechem International*[157] was that absence of regulatory action to prohibit the defendant's emission of dioxins, supported evidence that the dioxins were not causing harm.

Assessment of the tort of negligence as a tool of environmental protection

1   There are clear indications of the courts' willingness to treat certain environmental harms as forms of recoverable property damage in order to award compensation provided they are convinced that there has been a loss of value or utility (once again echoing torts' concern only for the owned environment).

2   Fixing liability on a regulatory agency for failing to prevent pollution is fraught with difficulties such as establishing a proximate relationship with the claimant, imposing liability for omissions and policy arguments being raised against the justice of imposing a duty of care.

3   The primary emphasis in negligence is on how the harm was caused rather than the fact that it has been caused, therefore in the absence of proven fault, as defined by the law, damage will go unremedied.

4   The usual remedy in negligence is damages. Compensation does little to prevent the damage occurring at the outset.

5   The courts do, however, apparently regard regulatory regimes and civil liability as separate, at least in so far as refusing to accept a licence to pollute as a blanket defence to activities authorised by the licence. The positive resolution of this issue in *Blackburn v ARC* lessens the importance of bringing civil actions against the regulator.

155 See, for example, *Tai Hing Cotton Mill Ltd v Liu Chong Hing Bank Ltd* [1986] AC 80, PC, Lord Scarman at 107 expressing the need to keep tort and contract separate.

156 See the US case, *O'Connor v Commonwealth Edison Co* 748 F Supp 672 (CD Ill 1990), in which the standard of care was automatically fulfilled where there was evidence that the federal permissible dose limits were complied with.

157 (1995) August ELB vol 1, p 1 at n 26.

E TRESPASS TO LAND

For an action in trespass to land, the claimant must prove 'possession' of the land at the time of the trespass. The requirement of 'possession' was the subject of a strange twist in *Monsanto plc v Tilly*.[158] Monsanto brought proceedings in trespass to land and goods against protestors who had entered fields where Monsanto's crops were growing and uprooted them. Whilst it was clear that Monsanto could bring an action for trespass to goods (as soon as their crops were severed from the land they became 'goods'), it was less clear that they could maintain an action in trespass to land – the field was owned by a third party who had agreed to allow Monsanto to grow crops on it. Despite the absence of a proprietary interest in the land, the Court of Appeal regarded the right to grow crops on the land which were subsequently damaged by the trespasser gave rise to sufficient 'possession' for an action in trespass to land.[159]

The tort of trespass to land has occasionally been utilised to seek redress for the deposit of waste to land (*Gregory v Piper*[160]). In *Blake v Isle of Wight County Council*[161] such an attempt failed, but this was due to the fact that the claimant had accepted the waste onto the land as part of a contractual agreement. The real complaint was that the local authority had failed to fulfil the terms of the agreement by levelling and reinstating the land when it had completed its tipping operations. The Court of Appeal held that leaving the accepted waste uncovered was not a continuing trespass as the waste had become the property of the site owner once it was dumped. There was therefore no agent capable of constituting a trespass on the defendant's property.

The requirement of 'directness' in trespass actions serves to exclude consideration of many water pollution incidents where, for example, heavy rainfall washes pollutants onto the claimant's land or into the claimant's watercourse.

F AN ACTION FOR BREACH OF STATUTORY DUTY

An aggrieved individual may be able to bring an action in tort for breach of a statutory duty, where, for example, the defendant breached a provision of the Environmental Protection Act 1990 and this resulted in harm to the claimant. This option is particularly appealing to an environmental claimant because it offers the best of both worlds; a strict liability provision with a civil burden of proof (on the balance of probabilities). As most provisions of the Environmental Protection Act 1990 and Water Resources Act 1991 are strict liability, this would avoid the burden of having to prove negligence or the requirement that the damage was of a foreseeable type which attends actions in nuisance, *Rylands* and negligence. The first difficulty is that the claimant must show that the statute concerned was designed with a view to avoiding the particular type of harm complained of.[162] It may be possible to do this in the context of environmental protection statutes creating pollution offences if reliance is placed on dicta from *Phillips v Britannia Hygienic Laundry Co*[163] where Lord Atkin stated that the statutory duty need not designate the claimant as a specific beneficiary for an action to be available: 'The duty may be of such paramount importance that it is owed to all the public.' Surely a duty to prevent pollution is of such 'paramount importance'. In such cases, a civil action for breach of the statutory duty *may* be available if the claimant can prove they

---

158 [2000] Env LR 313.
159 Following *Black v Daniels* [1925] 1 KB 526.
160 (1829) 9 B & C 591.
161 [2000] All ER (D) 1296, CA.
162 *Gorris v Scott* (1874) LR 9 Exch 125.
163 [1923] 2 KB 832 at 841.

suffered special damage as a result of the breach over and above that suffered by the public as a whole.[164] A further difficulty is presented, however, by the fact that most statutory provisions already carry criminal sanctions for their breach. This creates problems because of the common law presumption that where a remedy is provided in the statute itself, that is the only remedy.[165] This will be particularly important when it is considered that where pollution offences are prosecuted, the prosecutor can attach a request that the court makes a compensation order if it convicts the defendant. If this prevents the claimant using breach of statutory duty proceedings, there is always the possibility of private prosecution (see chapter 7) although the burden of proof will be one of 'beyond reasonable doubt' rather than the less stringent civil standard of 'the balance of probabilities'.

G DAMAGE FROM NUCLEAR INSTALLATIONS

The liability of the United Kingdom Atomic Energy Authority or other licensed bodies is contained in the Nuclear Installations Act 1965, which lays down a comprehensive and exclusive code of liability. Without a nuclear site licence no person may use a site for the purpose of installing or operating a nuclear installation such as a nuclear reactor or plant designed or adapted for the production or use of atomic energy or associated ancillary purposes, or for the storage, processing or disposal of nuclear fuel or other bulk quantities of radioactive matter resulting from the production or use of nuclear fuel.[166] The NIA 1965, s 7 imposes strict liability in respect of certain occurrences on or in connection with the uses of licensed nuclear sites, and s 8 imposes similar liability on the Atomic Energy Authority. The regime includes certain prohibitions, such as that there must be no occurrences involving nuclear matter[167] on site, elsewhere nor in the carriage of nuclear matter, unless the occurrence is 'excepted' under the NIA 1965, s 26(1). Furthermore, there must be no ionising radiation emitted during the period of the licensee's responsibility, whether from anything caused or suffered by the licensee to be on the site which is not nuclear matter, or from any waste discharged in any form on or from the site.

Grounds of liability

Compensation provisions under the Act relate to specified types of damage. Where damage other than that set out in the Act occurs, liability will fall to be dealt with at common law. The NIA 1965, s 7 imposes strict liability on the licensee when injury to a person or damage to property arises from radiation or from a combination of radiation and the toxic, explosive or other hazardous properties of nuclear matter.[168] However, the damage must be physical, not purely economic loss, and it must relate to tangible, not incorporeal property or property rights (see *Merlin v British Nuclear Fuels plc*[169]). Another decision under the provisions of the 1965 NIA, *Blue Circle Industries plc v*

---

164 Per Lord Atkin in *Lonrho Ltd v Shell Petroleum Co Ltd (No 2)* [1982] AC 173. Doubt has been cast on the existence of actions for breach of statutory duty where there is violation of a public right with special damage given that this form of action has been untested.
165 *Lonrho Ltd v Shell Petroleum Co Ltd (No 2)* [1982] AC 173.
166 NIA 1965, s 1.
167 Defined in NIA 1965, s.26(1).
168 The NIA 1965, s 8 imposes similar liabilities on the Atomic Energy Authority.
169 [1990] 2 QB 557, [1990] 3 All ER 711.

Ministry of Defence[170] requires that loss will only be regarded as 'damage to property' for the purposes of the NIA 1965, s 7 where there is physical change so as to render the property less useful or valuable. Further losses arising out of long-term risks and as yet unascertained physical harm are not covered, such as stress caused by rational fear of ill-health.[171] Clearly within the restricted circumstances of s 7, the NIA 1965 supersedes the protections available at common law. Liability does not require proof of fault, and unlike the *Rylands v Fletcher* action, there is no requirement of an 'escape.' It is, however, perhaps a little odd that whilst the nuclear industry is the subject of strict liability in respect of many of the harms that it causes, similar provisions do not extend to other, equally hazardous industries.[172]

The Congenital Disabilities (Civil Liability) Act 1976, s 3, lays down that where a child is born disabled as the result of an injury to either of its parents caused in breach of duty imposed by any of ss 7–11 of the NIA 1965, the child's injuries are to be regarded as injuries caused on the same occasion and by the same breach of duty as was the injury to the parent. Thus where the child's disabilities are attributable to an incident under the NIA 1965 compensation can be payable. However, under the CD(CL)A 1976, s 3(5) compensation is not payable in the child's case if the injury to the parents preceded the time of the child's conception, and at that time the injury was that their child might be born disabled. The CD(CL)A 1976 also declares that any occurrence under the NIA 1965 which affects the ability of a man or a woman to have a normal healthy child, or which affects a pregnant woman so that her child is consequently disabled is an injury for the purposes of compensation under the NIA 1965.

It is a defence to claim under the CD(CL)A 1976 to show an occurrence was attributable to hostile action in the course of armed conflict, but natural disasters, even if entirely exceptional, causing occurrences give no ground for a defence.[173] Acts of the Queen's enemies may be a defence, but acts of God, for example, earthquakes, are not. Compensation may be reduced if the injury was partly caused by the claimant himself doing an act with 'the intention of causing harm to any person or property with reckless disregard for the consequences of his act' (NIA 1965, ss 12 and 13). On a voluntary basis, and without concession of liability, British Nuclear Fuels Limited (BNFL) and the United Kingdom Atomic Energy Authority (UKAEA) operate a scheme to compensate dependants of current and past employees dying from leukaemia or other forms of cancer. The scheme does not extend to other persons. The Ministry of Defence announced in 1992 a similar scheme for certain personnel and civilian employees suffering from cancer and previously exposed to radiation.

The problem lying at the heart of imposing liability for nuclear incidents is, as made clear by Christopher Miller,[174] that of causation. It *may* be comparatively easy to attribute effect to cause where a major nuclear incident occurs and those on site at the time display 'radiation sickness' symptoms thereafter. It is much harder to show causation where a person in the vicinity of a nuclear installation simply develops cancer over a period of years. In the circumstances there is much to commend Dr Miller's thesis that an alternative compensatory approach, based on enhanced social security and other pension benefits and funded by novel taxes on the activities of the nuclear industry, needs to be examined.

170 [1999] Ch 289, [1998] 3 All ER 385, CA. Note that both these decisions concern the property damage limb of the NIA 1965, s 7. There is as yet no decision concerning the personal injury aspect.
171 Although, where negligence causes stress meeting the levels of a recognisable psychiatric disorder, it might be that there would be a duty of care recognised at common law: *Re Creutzfeldt-Jakob Disease Litigation (No 3)* (1996) 54 BMLR 79.
172 M Lee, 'Civil Liability of the Nuclear Industry' (2001) 12(3) *Journal of Environmental Law* 317 at 320.
173 See CD(CL)A 1976, s 13(4).
174 Radiological Risk and Civil Liability' (1989) 1 Journal of Environmental Law 10.

The causation issue was well illustrated by *Reay v British Nuclear Fuels plc* and *Hope v British Nuclear Fuels plc.*[175] In both cases, compensation was sought for injury outside *BNFL*'s concessionary scheme. Mrs Reay claimed damages in respect of her daughter who had died of childhood leukaemia, while Miss Hope claimed for being affected by non-Hodgkin's lymphoma. Mrs Reay's husband and Miss Hope's father had worked at Sellafield for many years. It was alleged that there had been exposure to plant radiation outside the plant while the children were in their mothers' wombs, and after birth, that radiation from the plant had damaged their mothers' ova pre-conception, and, novelly, that the fathers had suffered genetic damage to their sperm pre-conception and this had been passed on to the children. Ninety days of hearings with evidence from 30 scientific witnesses led to a conclusion by French J that the plaintiffs had failed to prove on the balance of probabilities that BNFL had *caused* the injuries by breach of its statutory duties. The overall problem is twofold. First, the scientific epidemiological evidence is simply inconclusive and often contradictory as to the link between exposure or radiation and subsequent development of cancer. Secondly, in any given population a number of people will die from cancer, and it appears impossible generally to distinguish a radiation induced cancer from one otherwise occurring.

Limitation and compensation arrangements

The maximum period for bringing an action under the NIA 1965 is 30 years from the occurrence giving rise to the claim, or, where the occurrence was a continuing one, or one of a succession all attributable to a particular happening on site, 30 years from the last relevant date.[176] The 30-year period offers a balance between the need for closure for licensees and the claimants' need for flexibility given the likelihood that their injury may not be discovered immediately.[177] Where injury is caused by a breach of the duties imposed under the NIA 1965, ss 7–10, compensation in respect of the injury is payable wherever it occurred, but no other liability is incurred by any person in respect of it. Any injury or damage not actually caused by the breach but also not reasonably separable from injury so caused is deemed to have been caused by the breach.[178]

Claims arising under duties imposed by the NIA 1965 to the extent to which, though duly established, they are not payable by the persons subject to the duties, *or* which are made after the expiry of the period of the first ten years after the occurrence, *or* arise in respect of injury arising from occurrences involving nuclear material stolen from, or lost, jettisoned or abandoned by persons subject to the duties where the claim is made after the expiry of 20 years from the date of the loss etc, must be made to the appropriate authority, generally the Secretary of State for the Department of Trade and Industry. During the first ten years after an occurrence, claims are generally made to the licensed body or authority. Under the NIA 1965, s 16(1) as amended by the Energy Act 1983, s 27 liability to pay compensation is limited to £140m in the aggregate in respect of any one occurrence, or £10m in the case of certain prescribed small operators.[179] These sums are limited with a view to satisfying international obligations and to counter the effects of inflation, but may be increased by order.

175 [1992] 4 LMELR 195, [1993] 5 ELM 178.
176 NIA 1965, s 15(1).
177 M Lee, 'Civil Liability of the Nuclear Industry' (2001) 12(3) Journal of Environmental Law. 317 at 319.
178 NIA 1965, s 12.
179 SI 1994/909.

Under the NIA 1965 s 19, as amended by the Atomic Energy Act 1989, licensees must make ministerially approved arrangements to make funds available to satisfy claims made up to the amounts required under the NIA 1965, s 16. To meet claims over these limits there is an obligation under s 18, as amended by s 28 of the Energy Act 1983 and Atomic Energy Act 1989, to make available, in the case of any relevant nuclear occurrence, out of money provided by Parliament, such necessary sums as will meet in the initial ten-year period claims *up to an aggregate* amount per incident of £300m 'special drawing rights' as defined by the International Monetary Fund under the EA, s 30 (though the value of a drawing right will vary from day to day according to agreed formulae). Thus a serious nuclear incident causing damage exceeding a licensee's insurance provision would place a burden on public funds. This contribution is in the nature of a 'top-up'; the sum of £300m special drawing rights represents an aggregation of public funds with those made available by the licensee to meet his obligations. Under the NIA 1965, s 16(3) where a claim is made to the Secretary of State's satisfaction, and to the extent that it cannot be satisfied out of sums provided under NIA s 18, it must be satisfied out of funds provided by such means as Parliament may determine.

H WHITE PAPER ON ENVIRONMENTAL LIABILITY

Moves towards an EU wide scheme of environmental liability have been mooted for a number of years. The justifications offered for Europe level intervention have included harmonisation of civil liability provisions to prevent distortion of the internal market, furtherance of the Community aim of environmental protection and addressing the inevitability of transboundary pollution.[180] The European Commission published its White Paper on Environmental Liability in February 2000[181] with a view to securing approval for a framework directive on environmental damage. The proposals have been greeted with criticism, in particular that they have been weakened by pressure from industry to the extent that they could be mistaken for Green Paper proposals.[182] It is by no means a certainty that the framework directive will ever come into being. All that is needed to defeat the Commission's proposal is a minority block of the qualified majority voting procedure (see chapter 4). The opposition of France, Germany and the UK which was voiced to the Green Paper proposals would suffice to prevent the enactment of the directive.

What is 'damage'?

The White Paper proposals are underpinned by the 'polluter pays principle' and aim to establish a system of strict liability (with some defences) for both traditional forms of damage (to person and to property but excluding pure economic loss) and environmental damage. Whilst the definition of traditional forms of damage would be left to member states, 'environmental damage' is specifically defined in the proposals as damage to biodiversity and contamination of sites and therefore extends to the 'unowned environment' which the existing common law, as we have seen, is so inadequate at protecting. As to liability for contaminated sites, the White Paper discusses the design

---

180 M Wilde, 'The EC Commission's White Paper on Environmental Liability: Issues and Implications' (2001) 13(1) Journal of Environmental Law 21.
181 (Cm 66, 2000).
182 European Environmental Bureau, *Analysis of the White Paper on Environmental Liability* (Cm 66 *Final* 2000).

and implementation of Community wide standards for clean-up – a task not to be underestimated. Damage to biodiversity is however restricted to sites included in the Natura 2000 network (The Natura 2000 network encompasses species and locations designated or awaiting designation under the Wild Birds Directive 1979 and the Habitats Directive 1992).

The paper has been criticised for using such a timid/diluted definition of environmental damage and doing little to extend the ambit of existing protections.[183] The exclusion of pure economic loss is also disappointing. Many 'environmental' cases have failed in the past because of their inability to demonstrate damage other than pure economic loss.[184] The inclusion of 'traditional damage' is intended to provide coherence in liability regimes and to recognise that personal injury is also often an environmental concern.

One of the strengths of the White Paper is that compensation for environmental damage received under the putative directive would be subject to the requirement that it be used to restore the environment, an obligation not found at common law. Where restoration of the damaged resource is not directly possible, steps must be taken to provide and pay for an alternative natural resource equivalent to the one damaged or destroyed. No definition of 'equivalence' is provided in the Paper. It is proposed that the restoration obligation should be subject to a cost-benefit test meaning that the costs of restoration should not exceed the benefits of restoration. This provision will act as a ceiling protecting polluters from 'disproportionate' liability and in this sense would perform a similar function to that of 'remoteness' at common law. The regime proposed would have prospective effect, applying only to damage known after its entry into force. It is not clear how this would operate as against cumulative pollution which both predates the implementation of the directive and continues beyond its coming into force.

Who will be liable?

The standard of liability to be applied would be 'activity based,' that is, it would depend upon the type of activity which caused the 'damage'. If the said activity is classified as a 'hazardous' activity, liability would be strict, with the proviso that certain defences might be available (see below). There is no definition of hazardous activities, other than that they are those activities which are already regulated by existing EC environmental legislation. It is thought that this form of definition has been chosen in the interests of legal certainty.[185] Non-hazardous activities will attract only fault-based liability, thus, the Paper would possibly reinstate the distinction once made in English common law by *Rylands v Fletcher*. However, whereas the use of fertilisers on farmland would probably be regarded as a 'non natural use' under *Rylands v Fletcher* and therefore attract liability, it would not count as a 'dangerous activity' and would therefore attract only fault-based liability under the White Paper. Many would have liked to have seen a broader application of strict liability encompassing any damage to biodiversity from whatever source. Lenders will only be liable for environmental damage in so far as they have some control over the polluter's activities, a fact which will exclude most lending institutions from liability. Thus, it seems that a bank with knowledge of the environmental risk at the outset of their relationship with the polluting company would not be subject to liability under the proposed directive.

183 E Rehbinder, 'A Community Wide Environmental Liability Regime,' [2000] Env Liability 85.
184 *Merlin v British Nuclear Fuels plc* [1990] 2 QB 557.
185 M Wilde, 'The EC Commission's White Paper on Environmental Liability: Issues and Implications' (2001) 13(1) Journal of Environmental Law 21.

Although liability is to be strict, the Paper anticipates certain defences, most of which echo the UK's civil and criminal liability provisions in removing liability when the event is beyond the control of the defendant. Such defences would include intervention of a third party, a natural event, consent by the claimant and contribution to the damage. There is also discussion of the possibility of a 'state of the art' defence. Perhaps more controversial, however, is the section which states that compliance with licence requirements will be a defence, and that in such cases, action might be taken against the public authority responsible for setting the licence limits. The European Environmental Bureau concludes that this provision is likely to operate as a disincentive to public authorities to bringing proceedings against companies.

Who can bring an action?

The proposals endorse a two-tier approach to standing rights. The right to bring action upon breach of the directive is primarily vested in the state which is under an obligation to ensure restoration of biodiversity damage and decontamination. In the UK's case this may translate as the Environment Agency or the Secretary of State for the Environment. In cases where the state fails to bring action and in 'urgent cases', Non-Governmental Organisations would have the necessary standing to bring proceedings for an injunction or damages against those responsible.

Further reading

Cane, P, 'Are Environmental Harms Special?' (2001) 13(1) Journal of Environmental Law 3.

Lee, M, 'Civil Liability of the Nuclear Industry' (2001) 12(3) Journal of Environmental Law 317.

Lipton, JD, 'Project Financing & the Environment: Lender Liability for Environmental Damage in Australia' [1996] 1 Journal of International Banking Law 7.

McLaren, JPS, 'Nuisance Law and the Industrial Revolution – Some Lessons from Social History'Oxford Journal of Legal Studies 3(2) 155.

Michelman, 'Pollution as a Tort: A Non-Accidental Perspective on Calabresi's *Costs*' (1971) 80 Yale Law Journal 647.

Newark, FH, 'Non-natural Use and Rylands v Fletcher' (1961) 24 MLR 557.

Ogus, A and Richardson, GM, 'Economics and the Environment: A Study of Private Nuisance' [1977] CLJ 284.

O'Sullivan, J, 'Nuisance, Local Authorities & Neighbours from Hell' [2000] *CLJ* 11.

Penner, JE, 'Nuisance and the Character of the Neighbourhood' (1993) 5 JEL 1.

Pontin, B, 'Tort Interacting with Regulatory Law' (2001) 51(4) Northern Ireland Legal Quarterly 597.

Wetterstein, P, *Harm to the Environment: The Right to Compensation and the Assessment of Damages* (1997) Clarendon Press, Oxford.

Wightman, J, 'Nuisance – the Environmental Tort?: Hunter v Canary Wharf in the House of Lords' [1998] 61(6) MLR 870.

Wilde, M, 'The EC Commission's White Paper on Environmental Liability: Issues and Implications' (2001) 13(1) Journal of Environmental Law 21.

Chapter 7

Access to environmental information and environmental justice

INTRODUCTION

The Chairman of the 1984 Royal Commission on Environmental Pollution[1] announced that limited access to information was the main obstacle to better environmental protection. The road towards freedom of information is littered with attempts to legislate rights of access to environmental information in order that consumers, employees and citizens generally, can better inform themselves of the environmental consequences of industrial activity. Their motives in seeking such information may not be solely connected with litigation; they may be interested in selecting a product from the supermarket shelf which presents the least risk to the environment or in finding a place to live where the land is uncontaminated by abandoned industrial sites. This chapter focuses on the interrelated rights of *access to information* (which promote citizens' involvement in the legal process and which facilitate participation in environmental decision making, such as planning and environmental licence applications) and *access to justice* (the means by which such information can be used to challenge decisions in the courts).

Access to environmental information has fundamental importance for the mobilisation of citizens' enforcement mechanisms; the efficacy of the rights of private prosecution, judicial review and civil litigation are all contingent on the existence of established and enforceable rights to environmental data, whether it concerns identifying the source of pollution, the nature of contaminants being released or the levels of pollution sanctioned by a factory's discharge consent or authorisation. Similarly, environmental data enables the public to assess the environmental performance of operators and the regulatory performance of the authorities. It is therefore the key to the enforcement of environmental law, accountability and public confidence in environmental matters. Without rights of access to information, environmental justice collapses and environmental law becomes unenforceable, unaccountable and produces discontent from a suspicious public. Improved access to environmental information is also beneficial in terms of increasing the quality of decision making by encouraging a broader number of participants. There are also advantages for the Government, in that the perception of risks associated with activities such as incineration and large scale industry will be magnified in the eyes of the public if they are shrouded in secrecy. Restrictions on information and evasiveness have a correlative impact on levels of distrust.

1   Tenth Report, *Tackling Pollution – Experience and Prospects* (Cmnd 9149).

BEHIND CLOSED DOORS: TRADITIONS OF SECRECY

Environmental regulation has traditionally been shrouded in secrecy, due to both legally enforceable obligations of confidentiality and voluntary practices of secrecy by the regulatory authorities. The mechanisms by which secrecy was maintained included the draconian s 2 of the Official Secrets Act 1911, which created a blanket prohibition on unauthorised disclosure of 'official information', defined incredibly broadly as: 'information which a Crown servant acquired in the course of duty.' The OSA 1911 is now displaced by the more liberal provisions of the Official Secrets Act 1989.

Environmental information was once zealously guarded by government inspectors who treated pollution data as the property of the relevant company and protected it from public scrutiny.[2] For example, although since 1878 a Royal Commission had recommended the publication in annual reports of recorded emissions from named factories,[3] the Alkali Inspectorate (a predecessor of the Environment Agency) was very reluctant to engage in this type of publicity. This apparently protective attitude towards industry was undoubtedly due in part to the fact that the Public Health Act 1936 punished officers' divulgence of effluent details to the public by up to three months' imprisonment (there is still an offence of disclosure of trade secrets under the Radioactive Substances Act 1993, s 34). In contrast, the only sanction available for river pollution at that time was a financial one.[4] This provides a stark illustration of the distribution of priorities between environmental protection and commercial interests. The change in emphasis in 21st century environmental regulation is clearly made out by reference to the Environment Agency's practice of 'naming and shaming' the worst polluters on an annual basis in their *Spotlight on Business Performance* report,[5] and the conditions requiring emissions reporting which are generally found in IPPC authorisations.

MODERN REGULATION OF ACCESS TO ENVIRONMENTAL INFORMATION

The current regime is complex and fragmented and consists of separate legislative schemes of access to environmental information as they relate to, for example, Integrated Pollution Prevention and Control (IPPC), water resources and waste management. Each of these three sectors of pollution control has a statutory register which details breaches of licence conditions and enforcement action against licence holders. The main regulations currently in force (the Environmental Information Regulations 1992[6]) apply only to matters falling outside and beyond these statutory registers. Further, the new Freedom of Information Act 2000 is largely superfluous in the case of environmental information because it was decided to legislate separately on environmental information under the anticipated EC directive (see later). The following discussion details the main sources of rights of access to environmental information including: the statutory registers, the Environmental Information Regulations 1992, the Aarhus Convention, the proposed EC directive which will implement the Convention and the Green Claims Code.

---

2   J Bugler, *Polluting Britain*. (1972), Penguin, London, p 8.
3   HC 1878 (C2195 – I) XLIV.
4   Hansard HC 13 March 1972, col 204.
5   Environment Agency, *Spotlight on Business Performance* (2001).
6   SI 1992/3240.

A THE STATUTORY REGISTERS

Any member of the public is entitled to search waste management, water quality and IPPC registers,[7] thereby gaining direct access to 'compliance entries' (particularly in IPPC and IPC, where the register records all reported breaches of the relevant authorisations) and 'enforcement entries' (detailing notices, cautions and prosecutions brought by the Environment Agency).[8] The existing registers represent a form of corporate accountability, as the public, unsurprisingly, view the entries on the registers as a measure of environmental performance. (In addition to registers, the Environment Agency also publishes a 'Pollution Inventory' providing details of IPPC Part A processes, nuclear power stations and large sewage treatment works serving populations of more than 150,000 persons). The public availability of register entries is clearly a potentially valuable tool in crystallising pressures to make site and operational improvements. The usefulness and likely impact of these register entries is discussed further below.

Reliability of register entries as a measure of compliance

One major shortcoming of the registers is that they are licence-specific. Details of infringements by non-licensed operators are not represented in the register. In the case of licensed operators, are register entries a reliable mechanism of corporate accountability? The main strength of the registers is their inclusion of data relating not only to the number of enforcement actions taken, but also the number of breaches. If enforcement entries were to be used as the sole indicators of operator performance, any bias or reticence by the regulator in taking enforcement action would be disguised by the register entries. In 2000, the Environment Agency was accused of 'bottom heavy' enforcement; prosecuting the smaller companies at the expense of taking enforcement action against larger operators.[9] Enforcement entries in the register would conceal such a bias, suggesting that smaller companies were simply more likely to break the law than large, multinational operators. Clearly, the number of breaches that appear on the register is influenced by the size of the plant and by how strict authorisation limits are. The numbers of breaches could not therefore be considered as absolutes for the purposes of comparison with companies of different sizes, or with companies regulated by different regions of the Environment Agency.

By recording compliance statistics alongside enforcement action taken by the Agency, the registers provide a record of enforcement performance against the backdrop of compliance levels and are, potentially, a valuable mechanism of regulatory accountability.

Register entries and public inspection

If we can assume then that register entries offer a *reasonably* reliable measure of corporate compliance, can it be said that they are actually put to use? Registers may be used by the public to assess the legality of a site's operations with a view to private prosecution, or by the finance sector to assess the environmental risk presented by a

---

7   The provisions are as follows: EPA 1990, s 20 for IPC, EPA 1990, s 64 for waste management and for water quality, WRA 1991, s 190.
8   EPA 1990, ss 20(1)(c), (f) and 64(1)(e), (h), (i) and s 190(1)(f) respectively.
9   House of Commons Select Committee on the Environment, Transport and Regional Affairs, 6th Report 1999-2000, *Inquiry into the Workings of the Environment Agency* (HC 34).

particular company. Whilst the legal right of access to these registers has been in place for some time, there are factors which present practical hindrances to the exercise of those rights. These registers must be searched on Environment Agency premises and are not as yet available on the internet, a fact which surely inhibits the accessibility of this vital information. (There are, however, proposals to integrate the existing system of registers into a publicly accessible electronic version.[10]) Not surprisingly, it has been suggested that the members of the public are not frequent users of the registers. Certainly, a cursory glance at recorded visits to the registers indicates that only around 1,000 checks are made per year.[11] It is, however, more usual for an enquiry to be made which requires the Environment Agency to check the register and to communicate the results to the enquirer. Around 10,000 such checks are made annually. This figure suggests that register entries *are* being utilised, although it is difficult to ascertain in what way and by whom.

In addition to the pollution control registers outlined above, similar registers exist for the purposes of making information on approval of genetically modified organisms publicly accessible (see chapter 12).[12] The Environment Act 1995, s 78R also requires local authorities and the Environment Agency to keep publicly available registers of land designated as 'contaminated land'. Regulations were introduced in 2000 which state that the registers must contained details of remediation notices, declarations, appeals against remediation notices, convictions in relation to such notices and designations of land as a 'special site'.[13] See chapter 15 for further detail on the contaminated land regime.

B ENVIRONMENTAL INFORMATION REGULATIONS 1992

These regulations implement the 1990 Directive 90/313/EEC.[14] Applying within Great Britain, the regulations cover any information relating to the environment which is held by a 'relevant person' in any accessible form otherwise than for judicial or legislative function purposes, and is not either information required by statute to be provided on request to everyone who makes a request, or information contained in records which statute requires to be available for public inspection (for example, registers).

Who are 'relevant persons'?

Whilst the 1990 directive imposes obligations on 'public authorities', the 1992 regulations prefer the terminology of 'relevant persons' who are further defined as:
(a) Ministers of the Crown, government departments, local authorities and other persons carrying out functions of public administration at a national, regional or local levels have responsibilities in relation to the environment; and
(b) any body with public responsibilities for the environment which is under the control of a person falling under paragraph (a).

10 Interim Report of the Steering Group on *The Review of Legislation Relating to Integration Within the Environment Agency and the Scottish Environmental Protection Agency*, June 2000.
11 Communication with the Environment Agency's Operations Division revealed that in the first quarter of 1998, 234 direct visits had been made to pollution control registers and 237 in the second quarter.
12 EPA 1990, s 122.
13 SI 2000/227.
14 SI 1992/3240.

It is arguable, following *Griffin v South West Water Services Ltd,*[15] that as water companies were held there to be 'emanations of the state' for the purposes of a directly effective employment directive, they and other utilities should also fall within the scope of the regulations. Although they are not local or central government bodies with environmental responsibilities (these are clearly within the regulations) they are caught because they are bodies with environmental responsibilities which are regulated by agencies (such as OFWAT) which are clearly public.

What is 'environmental information'?

It is that which relates to the state of any: water, air, flora, fauna, soil, natural site or other land; any activities or measures which adversely affect, or are likely to adversely affect, any of the foregoing; and any activities or administrative or other measures designed to protect the first mentioned entities. 'Information' includes 'anything kept in any records, including registers, reports, returns and computer records.' The courts have, moreover, refused to recognise a distinction between 'primary' information (which has to be released) and 'secondary' information which enables its holder to check whether the primary information is correct.[16]

The general obligation to make information available

Relevant persons are under an obligation to make relevant information in their possession available to every person requesting it and to make arrangements to see that such requests are responded to promptly and certainly within two months. Where a request is refused they must give reasons for the refusal and such reasons can include that a request for information is 'manifestly unreasonable' or formulated too generally. Similar procedural requirements are imposed in respect of the supply of information dealt with by other statutory provisions. Charges may be made in connection with the supply of information and the obligation to make disclosure only applies in reasonable places and at reasonable times.

There are, however, exceptions to the right to information. Thus, 'confidential' information is excluded. Information is *capable* of being treated as confidential *only* if it relates to: matters subject to actual or prospective legal proceedings including disciplinary and public inquiry proceedings; the confidential deliberations of 'relevant persons', or the contents of internal communications of a body corporate or other undertaking or organisation; information still in the course of completion; matters of commercial or industrial confidentiality or affecting any intellectual property. However, the apparent width of the exemption is cut down by requirements that information *must* be treated as confidential *if and only if* the information is:

1   capable of being treated as confidential and its disclosure would otherwise amount to a breach of the law or of some agreement; or
2   personal information contained in personal records on individuals who have not consented to its disclosure; or
3   held by a 'relevant person' who has been supplied with the information by a person who was under no legal obligation to supply it, and who did not supply it in circumstances such that the relevant person is entitled apart from these regulations to disclose it, and who has not consented to disclosure;

15   [1995] IRLR 15.
16   *R v British Coal Corpn, ex p Ibstock Brick Building Products Ltd* [1995] 7 ELM 202.

4   such that its disclosure would increase the likelihood of damage to the environment affecting anything to which the information relates.

Problems with the 1992 regulations

Given the British penchant for secrecy, a number of potential problems exist with regard to the application of the regulations. There are a multitude of permissible reasons for refusing requests for information, for example, that the body concerned is not a 'relevant person', that it does not hold the information, that the request is too general or is manifestly unreasonable, or that the information is within an exempted category. Furthermore, there is no appeal mechanism to deal with a refusal. The aggrieved party can only seek judicial review, which means that the decision will not be looked at afresh and will only be quashed if it was wrong in law.

According to Jenn, the 1992 regulations leave huge discretion to the public bodies controlling the information and fall a long way short of a universal right of access to information.[17] There are very few decisions on the application of the 1992 regulations but those that do exist tend to concern the confidentiality exemption and send mixed signals about the courts' willingness to interpret the regulations liberally. In *R v Secretary of State for the Environment, ex p Alliance Against the Birmingham North Relief Road*[18] the applicants sought to challenge the decision to build a new stretch of motorway to relieve congestion on the M6. The applicant was concerned that the Secretary of State had wrongly taken into account an agreement obliging the Government to pay compensation to the developer if the road building did not proceed. Access to the details of the agreement was refused on the grounds that it came under the 'commercial confidentiality' exemption. The court accepted that the document was covered by the exemption in part, but stated that the decision as to whether information was 'environmental information', and whether it was capable of being treated as confidential, were matters for the court to decide. In other words, the courts' jurisdiction as to these matters was not confined to inquiring whether the public authority's decision was *Wednesbury* unreasonable. In *Maile v Wigan Metropolitan Borough Council*[19] access was sought to a database of potentially contaminated sites in the region which had helped the council to draft a report on pollution in Wigan. The council's refusal to disclose was upheld on the grounds of its being capable of being treated as confidential – it concerned the ongoing deliberations of the council as to how it should respond to the issue of contaminated land and the information was inchoate. The court considered that disclosure of the database would be detrimental because it would cause unnecessary alarm and despondency amongst local citizens and landowners. Comment on this case has been negative alleging that the confidentiality exemption has been construed too widely. The finding that access was not available because the information was not complete is particularly worrying because of the fact that most databases are subject to updating and might equally be described as 'incomplete'.

In 1996, member states were asked to report to the European Commission on their experience of the 1990 directive from which the 1992 regulations were born. The main problems identified in the Commission's subsequent report related to excessive charging, refusals to provide information on the grounds that information relating to public health effects of the state of the environment, nuclear energy and radiation was

---

17   H Jenn, 'Public Interest Litigation and Access to Environmental Information' (1993) WL 4(5) 163.
18   [1999] JPL 231.
19   [2001] Env LR 11.

not environmental information and that public bodies whose functions did not directly relate to the environment were not covered by the directive.[20]

C THE AARHUS CONVENTION

The UK (and the EC), along with 38 other countries, are signatories to the Aarhus Convention (the UNECE Convention on Access to Information, Public Participation in Decision Making and Access to Justice (Aarhus, 1998)). The Convention stands on 'three pillars' of 'access to information', 'public participation' and 'access to justice' and is an expression of Principle 10 of the Rio Declaration (the principle of public participation in environmental decision making).

The Scope of the Convention

The Aarhus Convention is described by its implementation guide as 'the most ambitious venture in the area of environmental democracy.'[21] The objectives set out in Art 1 clarify the fundamental relationship of access to information and justice to the possession of the right to live in a healthy environment. Beyond this initial statement, the Convention deals with the mechanisms/procedural rights which need to be in place if the human right to a clean and healthy environment is to be enforceable at the instance of the citizen. The Convention supports the existence of a 'right to a healthy environment' to the extent that its provisions are predicated/necessitated by the acknowledgement of such a right.

The Aarhus obligations are imposed on 'public authorities'. Debate as to whether an institution constitutes a 'public authority' is likely. Although water companies are privately owned, it is submitted that their public functions would render them public authorities for the purposes of the Convention.[22]

Aarhus Convention, Art 4: *passive* access to information

'Environmental information' under the Aarhus Convention[23] covers not just emissions data, but also information related to decision making affecting the environment and analyses of the environment, including any information in any form on the state of the environment. This definition is far broader than that enshrined in the 1992 regulations, in particular in extending to the state of human health and safety and factors such as energy, noise and radiation. Any natural or legal person is entitled to environmental information held by a public authority, thus there is no standing requirement in respect of the access provisions of the Convention.

The Aarhus Convention provides access to 'information' rather than documents, meaning that it applies to a complete set of data which has not yet been compiled into a finished product, a fact which possibly extends beyond the remit of the 1992 regulations as construed in *Maile v Wigan Metropolitan Borough Council.*[24] Requests for the purposes of Art 4 can be oral or written. The public authority is not required to

20   COM (2000) 400.
21   Aarhus Convention: An Implementation Guide, United Nations/Economic Commission for Europe 2000.
22   *Griffin v South West Water Services Ltd* [1995] IRLR 15.
23   Defined in Art 2(2).
24   [2001] Env LR 11.

provide information in the form requested by the applicant if (a) it is reasonable to provide it in another form and reasons are given or (b) if it is already publicly available in another form. Provision of the information must comply with a one-month time limit under the Convention, extendable to two months when the volume or complexity of the request justifies it. Refusal to fulfil the request is permitted if:

(a) the public authority does not hold the information;
(b) the request is manifestly unreasonable or too general;
(c) the material is in the course of completion or concerns an internal communication protected by national law; or
(d) if disclosure would *adversely* affect:
      (i)   confidential proceedings protected by national law;
      (ii)   international relations/national defence/public security;
      (iii) the course of justice;
      (iv)   commercial confidentiality protected by national law (this exemption does not apply to emissions data);
      (v)   intellectual property rights;
      (vi)   confidentiality of personal data protected by national law if the subject has not consented;
      (vii) interests of a third party who has disclosed the information without being under a legal obligation to disclose; or
      (viii) the environment to which the information relates (eg breeding sites of rare species).[25]

These exemptions are to be construed narrowly taking into account the 'public interest' in disclosure.

Article 5: *active* access to information

Article 5 of the Aarhus Convention creates active obligations to collect and disseminate information including product information, pollutant release and transfer information, information relating to laws, policies and strategies and information about how to get information ('metainformation'). (Clearly, the maintenance of pollution control registers would be regarded as an aspect of *active* access to information.) The inclusion of metainformation is a logical corollary of the right to information, given that unless members of the public are aware that information exists they cannot exercise their right to access it.

Article 5 requires that information contained in lists, registers or files be made accessible free of charge. It also creates a progressive obligation to make environmental information available in electronic databases. This progressive obligation applies to:

(a) reports on the state of the environment;
(b) tests of legislation on or relating to the environment;
(c) policies/plans and programmes on or relating to the environment and environmental agreements (as appropriate).

The obligation to actively disseminate information (Art 5(5)) includes legislative and policy documents, international treaties, conventions and agreements on environmental issues and other significant international documents on environmental issues as appropriate. Article 5(6) requires parties to the Convention to encourage operators whose activities have significant impact on the environment to inform the public regularly on the environmental impact of their goods/services. To this end, the government has issued guidelines for companies to report on their environmental

25   Art 4(3)–4(4).

performance, specifically, their emission of greenhouse gases, waste management and impact on the water environment (see 'Environmental Reporting' below)[26].

Articles 6–8: public participation in decision making

These three articles are closely related and set out procedural requirements for environmental decision making, in particular who should be informed/notified in advance of such decisions. Article 6 sets out detailed procedures for public participation in the granting of licences or authorisations including planning permissions and Environmental Impact Assessments. Parties to the Aarhus Convention must ensure that public participation is 'adequate, timely and effective' and that the ultimate decision with reasons is communicated to those involved in public participation. Concerns have been raised at the time of writing that Green Paper proposals to streamline the UK planning regime (by, inter alia, introducing business zones where developers will not need planning approval, faster processing of planning applications, with councils facing tough targets and a new fast-track system for large-scale projects) will severely curtail rights of local people to object to such proposals and may violate Art 6 obligations, particularly the provision of *adequate* and *effective* public participation.[27] Whilst there are no standing requirements for the purposes of the access to information provisions under Arts 4 and 5, many of the rights under Art 6 are restricted to the 'public concerned', defined as the 'public affected by the environmental decision making or having an interest in it'. (Aarhus Convention, Art 2(5)). This test does not appear to be as liberal as some developments in judicial review cases (see below) and it is unclear whether 'the public concerned' would extend, for example, to an applicant in London complaining about deforestation in her home county of Cumbria.

Article 7 creates similar obligations in relation to the preparation of plans and programmes 'relating to the environment', a phrase which is envisaged in the Implementation Guide for the Covention[28] as broader than proposals 'affecting the environment,' and as including land use strategies, tourism, water resources, health and sanitation. Again, such plans must invite public participation. Article 8 extends such rights to the preparation of executive regulations and legally binding instruments.

Article 9: access to environmental justice

The 'access to justice' provisions of the Aarhus Convention concern the mechanisms with which the rights relating to passive access to information (Art 4) and other laws relating to the environment are to be enforced. For example, parties must provide an inexpensive and expeditious review procedure when requests for information under Art 4 are ignored, inadequately answered or thought to be wrongly refused.[29] The review must be by a court of law or another independent and impartial body, established by law. The latter is satisfied by 'quasi-judicial bodies with safeguards to guarantee due process, independence of influence by any branch of government and unconnected with any private entity.'[30] This right of review is only required to be extended to those

---

26   See, for example, *Environmental Reporting: Guidelines for Company Reporting on Waste* (Department for Environment, Transport and the Regions, June 2000).
27   *Planning: Delivering a Fundamental Change* (Department of Transport, Local Government and the Regions, 2001). See further chapter 8 on reform of the planning regime.
28   At n 20.
29   Aarhus Convention, Art 9(1).
30   Aarhus Convention: An Implementation Guide at n 20.

with a 'sufficient interest' (although in countries where standing requires the 'impairment of a right' that test is preferred). Additionally, parties to the Aarhus Convention must ensure that members of the public have access to judicial or administrative procedures to challenge acts or omissions by private persons and public authorities which breach national environmental laws.[31] Compliance with this latter 'access to justice' provision can be tested by reference to the availability of private prosecution and civil liability in English law. All of the above enforcement mechanisms are required to be: 'fair, equitable, timely and not prohibitively expensive.'[32]

A power was created in the Freedom of Information Act 2000 (FOIA 2000) to bring UK law into line with the Aarhus obligations[33] and, at the time of writing, the Department for Environment, Food and Rural Affairs is working towards a revised public access to environmental information regime to replace the 1992 regulations. These proposals represent an attempt to implement the UK's commitment under the Convention and to pre-empt the further requirements under the EC's proposed directive on access to environmental information.[34]

D PROPOSED DIRECTIVE ON ENVIRONMENTAL INFORMATION

The Aarhus Convention provisions act as a 'floor not a ceiling' on access to information and therefore invite provisions which create stronger protections, an invitation which the EC has responded to with proposals of its own. As a direct result of the Aarhus Convention and the European Commission's reflections on the shortcomings of the 1990 directive, a new EC directive is proposed which will supersede the 1990 directive as implemented in the UK by the Environmental Information Regulations 1992. At the admission of the EC, these proposals extend beyond the Aarhus Convention requirements. As originally proposed, the new directive would affect a broader range of institutions than the Aarhus Convention and would cover all privatised bodies 'which affect or are likely to affect elements of the state of the environment.' Such a definition would appear to cover not only the water companies by reason of their public 'environmental' functions, but also some private sector bodies without any environmental duties or responsibilities, for example, businesses in the telecommunications, shipping, transport, construction, waste disposal and utilities sectors.[35] Proposed provisions requiring electronic dissemination of all environmental information and prohibiting charging in advance for information raised further concerns as to the financial burden imposed by the proposals. The extended reach of the new directive unsurprisingly met strong opposition from the private sector in the UK, but negotiations with the European Parliament have so far suggested that these provisions will be modified. At the time of writing, the directive is still under discussion and it is likely that it will be become law some time in 2002.

There is much to be said for the practice of some countries of maintaining a single regime for access to information, whether environmental information or otherwise. Their implementation of the 1990 directive extended to all information and avoids the fragmented and over-complex range of regimes available in the UK. Given that the

---

31   Aarhus Convention Art 9(3).
32   Aarhus Convention Art 9(4).
33   FOIA 2000, s 74.
34   *Proposal for a Directive of the European Parliament and of the Council on Public Access to Environmental Information* COM (2000) 402 Final.
35   *Supplementary Explanatory Memorandum on EC Legislation: Public Access to Environmental Information – Proposals for a Revised Regime* (DEFRA, 2001).

directive is only at the consultation stage, it is not clear when regulations implementing the Aarhus Convention will be implemented in the UK.

E FREEDOM OF INFORMATION ACT 2000

Where a request for information falls outside the definitions of 'relevant persons' or 'information relating to the environment' (or the terms which will soon replace them) an applicant may turn to the provisions of the Freedom of Information Act 2000. The Act was a result of Labour's long standing electoral manifesto commitment to freedom of information and its objectives were explored in the 1997 White Paper, *Your Right to Know*.[36] The White Paper proposed the introduction of an enforceable right of access to information across the public sector and recommended that the general test for legitimating non-disclosure of requested information would be one of 'substantial harm'. The Bill did not live up to the over-optimistic visions of the 1997 White Paper, such optimism perhaps being attributable to the Labour government's recent accession to power. The Bill was published for consultation in May 1999, but within a few months had received trenchant criticism from the House of Commons Select Committee on Public Administration[37] and an ad hoc House of Lords Select Committee on the draft Bill.[38]

The framework of the Act sets out a general right of access to recorded information held by public authorities, establishes a list of 'class exemptions' and creates enforcement mechanisms, namely the new Information Commissioner. The Commissioner's role is to determine specified disputes over disclosure and the Commissioner's decisions will ultimately be enforceable by the courts. Somewhat bizarrely, the post of Information Commissioner is filled by the same person who acts as Data Protection Commissioner under the Data Protection Act 1998. This duality of roles, involving responsibility for both data protection and disclosure, raises interesting questions about conflicts of interest.

Under the FOIA 2000, s 39, environmental information which is required to be disclosed under the regulations implementing the Aarhus Convention are specifically exempted from the provisions of the FOIA 2000. Having said that, the Information Commissioner will probably hear appeals against refusals/failures to provide information to supplement the option of judicial review which exists under the 1992 regulations. The FOIA 2000 therefore acts only as a 'backstop' in the case of environmental information as it is only relevant to information which will fall outside the anticipated regulations. Nevertheless, the Act provides a valuable reference point against which regulations applicable to environmental information can be usefully compared.

The right to information

The right of access to information is contained in the FOIA 2000, s 1 and applies only to 'recorded' information held by a 'public authority'. Where a public body has decided not to compile statistics on a specific subject, the Act creates no duty to compile them (cf the Aarhus Convention). Public authorities are defined in FOIA 2000, s 3 as specifically including publicly owed companies, in addition to bodies referred to at Sch 1 to the Act, or referred to by an order which makes an addition to the Schedule.

36 Cm 3818.
37 Public Administration Committee *Freedom of Information Draft Bill* (3rd Report Session 1998-99, HC 570).
38 House of Lords *Report from the Select Committee Appointed to Consider the Draft Freedom of Information Bill* (Session 1998-99, HL 97).

For an institution to be added to the Sch 1 list, it must be established by the Crown or by primary or secondary legislation or by a minister, and appointments to that body must be at least partially made by the Crown, a minister or government department (FOIA 2000, s 4). The party requesting information (the applicant) must identify themselves, but need not prove UK nationality or residency. Public bodies may charge fees for providing information.

Exempt information

FOIA 2000, Part II creates two types of exemptions: absolute and qualified exemptions. Absolute exemptions from the duty to disclose include information reasonably accessible by other means (FOIA 2000, s 21), information attracting parliamentary privilege (s 34), information attracting a duty of confidence (s 41) and communications prohibited by law. Qualified exemptions concern information which is exempt unless the public authority decides in favour of disclosure after weighing the need for exemption against the public interest in disclosure. Amongst the qualified exemptions are information intended for future publication (FOIA 2000, s 22), information likely to prejudice international relations or national security (ss 24 and 27), information which might prejudice the operation of the criminal justice system (s 31), trade secrets (s 43) and, perhaps the two most controversial exemptions – information relating to the formulation/development of government policy (s 35) and information which would be prejudicial to the effective conduct of public affairs! Where discretionary disclosures of exempted information are made because of the public interest in disclosure, FOIA 2000 allows the public body to require the applicant to explain their purposes in seeking the information, and to impose conditions on their use of information should it be disclosed. If information was requested to assist the initiation of prosecution, perhaps against the public body itself, how likely is it that the disclosure would be found to be in the public interest?

The applicant does not generally need to demonstrate a 'need to know' the information nor disclose the purpose for which they intend to use the data. The test for lawful non-disclosure of data covered by a qualified exemption was downscaled from 'substantial harm' in the White Paper to one of 'prejudice.' It is submitted that the prejudicial threshold is far lower than one requiring harm and that the term is so vague as to be meaningless. The House of Lords Select Committee recommended that the prejudicial test should at least be further elaborated by the qualification of 'substantial' or 'likely'. This is to be contrasted with 'adverse effect' which is the comparable phrase in the Aarhus Convention. Whenever a request for information is met with a refusal relying on one of the exemptions, the reasons for the decision must be given[39]. The House of Lords Select Committee on the Bill expressed concern that the exemption provisions departed fundamentally from the White Paper by removing a large amount of information from the general enforceable right of access and transferring it to exempted information which enabled disclosure only at the public authorities' discretion (under FOIA 2000, Part II). Of course, such provisions tend to tip the balance back towards a presumption of non-disclosure rather than towards a universal enforceable right to know.

The enforcement arrangements under the FOIA 2000 are weak and therefore a major source of criticism. No action lies under the Act for breach of the statutory duty to disclose. Furthermore, the discretion of public authorities to decide whether the public interest demands the disclosure of information which has a qualified exemption, can

39   FOIA 2000, s 17.

not be overruled by the Information Commissioner. The Commissioner may merely issue a notice which requires the discretion to be properly exercised and can specify considerations the authority should have regard to. The Commissioner's power was clearly intended to be one of review only and not one of substantive correction.

This brief review suggests that the general right of access to information secured by the FOIA 2000 is in many ways less extensive than the right to environmental information in the UK, given that the latter regime is restricted to 'recorded' information and is qualified by a far greater number of exemptions.

F THE GREEN CLAIMS CODE

The consumer's role in furthering sustainable development is to make informed choices on the products they buy on the basis of their impact on the environment. It is therefore vital that consumers should not be confused about the environmental merits or demerits of the products on offer. The Green Claims Code (launched in 1998 and revised in June 2000) is an initiative developed by the then DETR and the Department of Trade and Industry. The code is an instrument representing the voluntary regulation of 'claims' made regarding the environmental credentials of consumer products and aims to stamp out the use of meaningless and sometimes misleading verbiage which accompanies some products, such as the once prevalent 'ozone friendly', 'environmentally friendly' and 'respecting the environment'.[40] Whilst the Green Claims Code clearly does not guarantee access to environmental information, it is a mechanism designed to facilitate such access.

A 'green claim' was originally defined in the code as any information appearing on a product or its packaging, which can be taken as saying something about the environmental aspects of a product. The revision of the code in 2000 extended this to the product's literature or advertising material. According to the new code, green claims should be:

- Truthful, accurate and able to be substantiated.
- Relevant to the product in question and the environmental issues connected with it.
- Clear about what environmental issue or aspect of the product the claim refers to.
- Explicit about the meaning of any symbol used in the claim (unless the symbol is required by law, is underpinned by regulations or standards or is part of an independent certification scheme).
- In plain language and in line with standard definitions.

According to the code, a green claim should not:
- Be vague or ambiguous.
- Imply that it commands universal acceptance.
- Imply more than it actually covers.
- Make comparisons unless the comparison is relevant, clear and specific.
- Imply that a product or service is exceptional if the claim is based on what is standard practice.
- Use language that exaggerates the advantages of the feature the claim refers to.
- Imply that the product or service is endorsed or certified by another organisation when it has not been.

40   See also the Food Standards Agency's proposals for legislation in the area of misleading 'green' food claims: *Food Advisory Committee Review of the use of the terms fresh, pure, natural etc in food labelling 2001'* (July 2001).

In 1999, the National Consumer Council prepared a report on the impact of the Code.[41] It concluded that the number of green claims had declined since the code's introduction, but that the main impediment to the effectiveness of the code was the lack of a strong sanction for non-compliance. A response to the sanctions issue was introduced in the White Paper, *Modern Markets: Confident Consumers*,[42] where the government proposed the extension of the Control of Misleading Advertisement Regulations 1998 to green claims which appeared on consumer products. These regulations enable the Office of Fair Trading to obtain an injunction against misleading advertisements. Criminal proceedings might also be brought against claims regarding the green credentials of given goods or services which are factually incorrect under the Trade Descriptions Act 1968, s 1. In addition to the code is the international standard on environmental claims. ISO 14021, again a voluntary measure, was introduced in 1999 and extends to claims made in the company's annual report.

G ENVIRONMENTAL REPORTING

As with the statutory registers, environmental reporting is a means of information provision which is not triggered by a request and would be classed under the Aarhus Convention as an aspect of *active* access to information. Although reporting practice in the UK is largely voluntary, there is a discernible shift towards increasing the role of mandatory reporting on environmental matters, illustrated, for example, by:

1   amendments made in 2000 to the Pensions Act 1995 which require pension fund managers to state their policy on ethical investment in their Statement of Investment Principles;
2   the Turnbull Report on corporate governance which requires London Stock Exchange companies to monitor and review the entire range of risks created by the company (including environmental risks) as part of its responsibility for internal control;[43] and
3   the fact that IPC/IPPC authorisations generally make the reporting of certain emissions a legal requirement.

A 1998 survey of the scope of social and environmental reporting by the FTSE 350 companies revealed that 65% of the FTSE 350 companies and 89% of the FTSE 100 companies reported in some form on environmental issues.[44] The report noted drastic variations across sectors with 100% of companies involved in mineral extraction and oil production engaging in environmental reporting, but only 33% of the financial sector doing the same. Criticisms arising out of the survey include: that current arrangements are almost entirely voluntary (meaning that companies may choose to omit details they feel will be prejudicial without fear of legal sanction) and that the available guidance fails to establish a standardised 'custom' of reporting, so that those companies who do implement the guidance will inevitably produce information which cannot be meaningfully compared with other companies. Recent government guidance on environmental reporting recommends that companies should add such reporting to

41   National Consumer Council *The Green Claims Code: Is it Working?* (1999).
42   Department of Trade and Industry 1999 (Cm 4410).
43   Institute of Chartered Accountants, *Internal Control: Guidance for Directors on the Combined Code* (1999).
44   *Environmental and Social Reporting: A Survey of Current Practice at FTSE 350 Companies* (Pensions, Investment Research Consultants Ltd, London, 1998).

their annual reports and thereby make them available to the public.[45] The guidelines recommend in addition the disclosure of any prosecutions, but only those where the fine imposed was in excess of £1,000.

H GENERAL PROVISIONS

Under the Local Government (Access to Information) Act 1985, the public are entitled to view agendas and reports relating to local government meetings three days in advance of the meeting. The right of access extends to the meeting itself and meeting documents. The right is however heavily qualified by the exempted categories of information.

The provisions of the Human Rights Act 1998 may, in exceptional cases, be prayed in aid of a complaint that environmental information has not been provided, particularly where that information implicates the health of the applicant. In *McGinley and Egan v UK*,[46] a case concerning the Christmas Island nuclear weapon tests, the European Court commented that Art 8 (which protects the right to respect for private and family life) could in some cases create positive obligations, such as in this case where a government engaged in hazardous activities which may have had hidden adverse consequences on the health of those involved. Such a positive obligation would require that an effective and accessible procedure be established to enable such persons to seek relevant and appropriate information. The failure to keep the applicant's medical records from the time of the experiments was therefore a violation of this right. (See chapter 5 for the further implications of the Human Rights Act 1998 for environmental law.)

I ACCESS TO JUSTICE: LEGAL CHALLENGE OF ENVIRONMENTAL DECISION MAKING

Environmental information may be used to directly challenge the activity/inactivity of industry, government or regulatory bodies. The aim might be to challenge the grant of a planning permission or licence, to sanction a pollution incident or to overturn a government policy thought to be prejudicial to the environment. The means by which such challenges can be launched include in the main: private prosecution, judicial review and direct action or protest, each of which is explored in the remainder of this chapter.

J PRESSURE GROUPS/NON-GOVERNMENTAL ORGANISATIONS (NGOS)

Pressure groups can be defined as organisations seeking to 'influence a comparatively small range of public policy without seeking to govern.'[47] Their power in the legal framework is a secondary power. It is one of influence, usually exercised by critical appraisal and challenge of government policy and that influence might be applied to the executive, the legislature, the media or the public at large. The importance of pressure groups has soared in the last twenty years as is illustrated by the fact that the public gauge their trustworthiness as far above that of politicians[48] and that their UK

---

45 *Environmental Reporting: Guidelines for Company Reporting on Waste* (Department for Environment, Transport and the Regions, June 2000).
46 (1998) 27 EHRR 1.
47 D Simpson, *Pressure Groups* (1999), Hodder & Stoughton, Oxon, p 5.
48 P Rawcliffe, *Environmental Groups in Transition* (1998) Manchester University.

membership far outstrips membership of political parties in this country.[49] Their power is increasingly being exercised at European level, given the general recognition that lobbying of European institutions is a valuable platform for influencing policy at a domestic level. A key development in this area is the European Environmental Bureau, founded in 1974, which represents national environmental groups at European level.

Probably the oldest established environmental pressure group in the UK is the Commons, Open Spaces and Footpath Preservation Society, founded in 1865. The leading pressure groups, *Friends of the Earth* and *Greenpeace* are youngsters by comparison, dating back to the 1970s. Greenpeace evolved out of a Canadian group which united opposition against environmental destruction and nuclear weaponry (hence the name). Friends of the Earth owes its roots to a group of American environmentalists breaking away from established groups to form a more activist organisation. Ironically, it is now Greenpeace and Friends of the Earth who are criticised for becoming institutionalised and losing their activist emphasis by new groups committed to direct action.

Pressure group influence derives in the main from their attempts to lobby officials involved in policy formation. This activity is primarily focused on civil servants from Whitehall. Most major pressure groups have strong links with civil servants. Lobbying activity extends also to parliamentary lobbying, presenting evidence to select committees and obtaining media coverage. One of the best examples of pressure groups influencing legislation is the Council for the Protection of Rural England's pursuit of 48 amendments of the Planning and Compensation Bill 1991. Of particular concern to pressure groups is ensuring a legal constitution which does not leave them vulnerable to litigation by those whose activities they oppose. To this end, both Friends of the Earth and Greenpeace have developed into two separate organisations. Each has a 'limited company' arm, overcoming the obstacle of charitable status which confines the organisation to non-political activities.[50] Meanwhile, the other arm takes advantage of charitable status in order to reap the financial advantages that flow from such a status.[51]

Pressure groups in the UK are not as practised in the art of using court action to further their cause as their American counterparts. Nevertheless, there is some recognition that litigation has its place in policy formation and in further awareness and politicising crucial issues. Judicial review actions explicitly attacking the grant of planning permissions, environmental licences and government policies are the most popular usage of the court room as a stage for environmental protest. Victories have also been witnessed in the legal process at the European level with pressure groups acting as 'whistleblowers' reporting on the government's failure to comply with EC directives.[52] The legal process represents not only an opportunity for pressure groups to air their views, challenge government policy and mark up symbolic if not legal victories, it also provides the government and industry with a means for silencing the dissension of pressure groups and activists. This instrumental use of litigation by governments and industry has acquired the label of 'Strategic Lawsuits Against Public Participation' (SLAPPS).[53]

---

49   Membership of large environmental pressure groups was estimated as exceeding 4.5 million in 1995. D Toke, 'Power & Environmental Pressure Groups,' (1996) Talking Politics 9(2) 107–115.
50   *McGovern v A-G* [1982] Ch 321.
51   P Rawcliffe, *Environmental Groups in Transition* (1998) Manchester University.
52   D Simpson, *Pressure Groups* (1999) Hodder & Stoughton, Oxon.
53   FF Ridley and G Jordan (eds), *Protest Politics: Cause Groups and Campaigns* (1998) Oxford University Press, Oxford.

Judicial review and the standing of NGOs

There is no provision for the public to 'appeal' against the grant of a licence to pollute or a planning permission, therefore the availability of judicial review is crucial in securing a public voice in regulatory decisions.[54] Civil actions in the English legal system also fall short of satisfying a broad right of access to the courts, for they only provide environmental protection in so far as it is coextensive with property rights and the right to be protected from personal injury (see chapter 6).

In judicial review cases, the doctrine of 'standing' requires applicants to show that they are directly affected by the subject of their complaint. In other words, 'uninvolved' citizens are barred from influencing the enforcement of the law by the rules of standing.[55] The English courts use the test of 'sufficient interest'[56] to determine whether a person or group possesses the required standing to challenge the legality of a decision by judicial review. Obviously, as the subject of Environment Agency enforcement action, a defendant will automatically have sufficient interest to bring judicial review proceedings, as an individual may stand to be deprived of their liberty if convicted (the legislation for most environmental offences authorises the imposition of custodial sentences). However, the question of whether a concerned citizen or pressure group representing public rights has standing is far from clear.

Concerned citizens and standing

The right of the 'concerned resident' to challenge local licensing decisions (particularly planning permissions and environmental licences) has been repeatedly tested, yet, surprisingly, the issue of whether local members of the public have standing to challenge such decisions remains unsettled. The two High Court rulings in *R v North Somerset District Council, ex p Garnett*[57] and *R v Somerset District Council, ex p Dixon*[58] have only added to this uncertainty. Both cases relate to the standing of local residents to challenge the grant of planning permissions to quarry. The applicant in *Garnett* used the parkland which was the subject of proposed quarrying for leisure purposes, and had objected to the quarry, but had made no written representations to the planning authority. The High Court held that this was insufficient to establish standing in a review application. The same court in *Dixon* treated the applicant as having an interest no greater than the general public, yet the court held that this gave rise to sufficient standing.

It appears that no meaningful distinction can be made between the facts of these cases, for whilst Mr Dixon was a member of more than one environmental organisation, Ms Garnett was also a member of Friends of the Earth. In any case, Mr Dixon's involvement with environmental groups did not seem to be of any significance to the judge. The difference seems to be more in the approach taken by the court. In Dixon, Sedley J, as he then was, stated:

'Public law is not about rights ... the courts have always been alive to the fact that a person or organisation with no particular stake in the issue or the outcome may, without in any sense being a mere meddler, wish and be well placed to call the attention of the court to an apparent misuse of public power. If an arguable

54 See EPA 1990, ss 15 and 43 and WRA 1991, s 91.
55 DJ Black, 'The Mobilisation of Law' (1983) 2 Journal of Legal Studies 125.
56 Set out in Supreme Court Act 1981, s 31(3) and CPR Ord 54 (replacing RSC Ord 53).
57 [1998] Env LR 91.
58 [1998] Env LR 111.

case of such misuse can be made out on application for leave, *the court's only concern is to ensure that it is not being done for an ill motive.*' (emphasis added)[59]

Standing is here being treated as a preliminary issue, and the requirement of sufficient interest as being designed only to exclude vexatious claimants. By contrast, Popplewell J in the *Garnett* case emphasised a number of judicial statements which treated standing as a matter of statutory interpretation. The legislation under which the decision was made was to be analysed to determine whether that same legislation expressly or impliedly conferred rights or expectations on persons such as the applicant. The difference then, lies in differing constructions of 'sufficient interest' and the function of standing rules: *Dixon* – where the requirement of standing was regarded as excluding only persons with bad motives, and *Garnett* – where standing was regarded as requiring something in the form of a right or expectation. A number of criticisms can be made of the rights-based approach endorsed in *Garnett*. The use of the 'rights' terminology in issues of standing is a misguided attempt to transfer rules from private law into the realms of public law, and thereby produces arbitrary restrictions on the review mechanism. Reliance on 'rights' to give rise to standing is, in any case, inconsistent with the rejection of the legal rights test in the statutory standing rules themselves.[60]

In a further application brought by a concerned member of the public, the decision appears to represent a retreat from the liberal approach espoused in *Dixon*. In *R v North West Leicestershire District Council, ex p Moses*[61] the applicant sought judicial review of planning permission to extend an airport runway. Although she had originally lived close to the runway she had moved six miles away from the area after commencing proceedings. Miss Moses argued that despite her relocation she maintained 'sufficient interest' as the matter concerned the rights of the public at large and she was acting responsibly and not officiously. Scott Baker J disagreed. While admitting that the threshold for standing was low he did not consider that it extended to all persons who were acting in good faith. In what appears to be a departure from the *Dixon* test, he stated that the test for standing was to be applied so as to ensure that all persons who had no real justifiable concern did not take precious time from the Crown Office List and that the court and opposing parties would not be burdened with cases that were bound to fail.

Standing and NGOs

Clearly, the problem of standing is particularly acute where there are no persons who can be said to be locally or personally affected who are willing to initiate court action. The English courts in judicial review proceedings have, however, recognised some pressure groups as 'guardians of the environment', overcoming to an extent the lack of locally affected individuals willing to litigate. In *R v HM Inspectorate of Pollution, ex p Greenpeace (No 2)*,[62] the court ruled on whether Greenpeace as a pressure group had standing to challenge the grant of an intermediate authorisation to British Nuclear Fuels Ltd (BNFL) for a new thermal oxide reprocessing plant.[63] Otton J gave several reasons for the ruling that *Greenpeace* had standing. Firstly, he commented that they

---

59   At 1037.
60   The reforms which resulted in the sufficient interest test were considered to be an improvement and relaxation of the restrictive tests of 'legal rights.' See P Craig, *Administrative Law* (3rd edn 1994) Sweet & Maxwell.
61   [2000] JPL 733, QBD.
62   [1994] 4 All ER 329, QBD.
63   See M Day, 'Shifting the Environmental Balance' in D Robinson (ed), *Public Interest and Environmental Issues* (1995) Chancery Law Publishing.

were a responsible and respected body with a genuine concern in the environment. That concern led to a bona fide interest in BNFL's activities. Secondly, organisations such as Greenpeace represented the only vehicle for challenge with the resources and expertise necessary to fund such an action. Thirdly, he took into account the fact that Greenpeace had been 'treated as consultees,' and were invited to comment. These justifications for extending standing were significant in moving away from a requirement of local Greenpeace members being affected by the decision. Greenpeace was therefore represented as a third party or 'surrogate' applicant,[64] which fulfilled standing requirements. The difficulties of this decision are that it fails to establish a framework for future evaluations of standing, and it remains unclear whether reputation, invitations to participate in the decision making process or the absence of alternative challengers is alone constitute a 'sufficient interest'.[65] Further, while the *Greenpeace* case appears to recognise standing in a surrogate applicant, the position of Greenpeace is ambiguous. Although an international organisation, they had local residents who would be affected by radioactivity levels from the THORP plant. This may provide the means for distinguishing future cases.

The 'Pergau Dam case': confirmation of 'surrogate' standing[66]

The *World Development Movement*, a pressure group concerned to increase the amount and quality of overseas aid, sought judicial review of the Foreign Secretary's decision to fulfil the offer of aid for the Pergau Dam Scheme against the advice of the Overseas Development Administration. On the issue of standing, Rose LJ stated:

'Its supporters have a *direct interest* in ensuring funds furnished by the UK are used for genuine purposes ... If there is a public law error, it is difficult to see how else it could be challenged and corrected except by such an applicant.'[67]

Two things can be said about the advances made by the *Pergau Dam* case. Firstly, as distinct from the *Greenpeace* case, none of the members of this pressure group were likely to be directly affected by the decision challenged. The World Development Movement is a true 'surrogate' in this sense, representing the interests of others rather than the collective interest of their members. *Pergau Dam* provided a very liberal interpretation of standing; the emphasis was placed on the absence of alternative challengers, which, when added to the purpose of the applicant group, seemed to be sufficient in itself to constitute standing.[68] This is a somewhat bizarre definition of sufficient 'interest,' as it relies on the absence of an 'interest' in other parties. This semantic contortion shows a concern to maintain a bottom line that no decision should be excluded from review merely because of a lack of challengers.

An argument against such liberal approaches to standing is the fear of crowding the courts and of rationing judicial resources. Yet, as judicial review is attended by strict time limits, it is an option only generally available to the well-informed – a restriction which in itself serves to exclude many applicants. Any failure to recognise these 'surrogate' rights of standing would severely curtail the utility of the review mechanism

64 A term used in CJ Hilson and I Cram, 'Judicial Review & Environmental Law – Is there a Coherent View of Standing?' (1996) Legal Studies 16(1) at 1–26.
65 Cf *R v Secretary of State for Social Services, ex p Child Poverty Action Group* [1990] 2 QB 540 where a token member with standing was required.
66 *R v Secretary of State for Foreign Affairs, ex p World Development Movement* [1995] 1 All ER 611, QBD.
67 At 618.
68 At 618–619.

in environmental law. We have noted already that common law protections are confined to particular complainants who can identify something which conforms with accepted conceptualisations of 'damage' which flows from the decision or activity complained of. To deny the availability of review where no particularised impact can be identified would be to cross-pollinate public law with private law restrictions, creating particular difficulties for environmental complainants. Decisions with a diffuse impact on society may produce a greater mass of harm than those which materialise as 'damage' against an individual complainant, but would go unchecked. [69] (See chapter 6 on the difficulty of proving 'damage' at common law.) Whatever the true position of NGOs, they appear to be treated more favourably under the sufficient interest test than under the Human Rights Act 1998. Where the applicant is raising a challenge under the Human Rights Act they must fulfil the more onerous test of being able to claim 'victim' status (HRA 1998, s 7(3)). Convention jurisprudence demonstrates that the test will often exclude NGOs. [70] (See further chapter 5 on the human rights and the environment).

The *Alconbury* case: Art 6 and the right to a fair hearing

Despite the general availability of judicial review of environmental decision making, the House of Lords in 2001 heard a complaint that the planning regime for England and Wales violated the right to a fair hearing as guaranteed by Art 6(1) of the European Convention of Human Rights (further secured in English law by the Human Rights Act 1998). The challenge did not relate directly to environmental information issues but to the need for impartial decision making and safeguards in decision making processes, and to this extent, the content of the judgment may be of some general interest. The case, which is discussed in more detail in chapter 5, is the case of *R (on the application of Holding & Barnes plc) v Secretary of State for the Environment, Transport and the Regions; R (on the application of Alconbury Development Ltd) v Secretary of State for the Environment, Transport and the Regions; R v Secretary of State for the Environment, Transport and the Regions, ex p Legal and General Assurance Society Ltd*[71] (more commonly known as the *Alconbury* case). Each of these joined appeals rested on different facts but shared a common challenge of the Secretary of State's powers under the planning regime, in particular his power to determine applications for planning permissions in the cases of compulsory purchase orders, called-in applications and recovered appeals. The kernel of each complaint was that the ability of the Secretary of State to take these decisions did not constitute an 'independent and impartial tribunal' for the purposes of Art 6(1). The Secretary of State could not be impartial given that his ability to decide the outcome of these planning applications conflicted with his involvement in laying down planning policies. The Secretary of State and the House of Lords agreed that the Secretary of State was not an impartial decision maker in such cases, but their Lordships decided that this did not constitute a violation of Art 6(1). The decision-making process must be looked at as a whole rather than in its component parts, and the Secretary of State's lack of impartiality was 'cured' by the availability in all three cases of judicial review, notwithstanding the fact that such review could only be used to challenge the legality of the Secretary of State's decision and not its merits. Lord Hoffmann added that if Art 6(1) were construed as always requiring that the courts

---

69   See P Craig, *Administrative Law* (3rd edn, 1994) Sweet & Maxwell, at 506, who argues that decisions which affect the community at large but indiscriminately, should not be less deserving of reviewability than those where an individual is affected more than his fellow citizens.

70   *Greenpeace Schweiz v Switzerland* (1997) 23 EHRR CD116 and *Tauira v France* (1995) 113-A DR 83 (1995).

71   [2001] UKHL 23, [2001] 2 WLR 1389.

should be able to review the merits of a decision, that might not be impartial, but would rather be a subversion of democracy (given that the judiciary was not elected). Lord Woolf has commented extra-judicially in support of the ruling, arguing that there must remain room for the executive to interfere with personal property rights where necessary in the public interest; after all, this is the essence of environmental protection.[72]

The judgment in *Alconbury* tells us a great deal about the House of Lords' approach to the right to a fair hearing in an environmental context, but it tells us only a little about whether the apparent absence of rights for third party objectors to appeal against planning permissions and environmental licences is compatible with Convention rights. Before a violation can be identified, it must be demonstrated that Art 6(1) is engaged: that is, the decision making procedure challenged must involve the determination of the complainant's 'civil rights and obligations.' *Alconbury* confirms at least Art 6(1) is implicated by decisions concerned with the grant or refusal of planning permissions, at least as far as the person making the application is concerned. It is unlikely, however, that someone who wished to challenge a planning permission would be able to convince a court that their 'civil rights and obligations' were at stake. Apart, that is, from those exceptional cases where the complainant might be able to show that exercise of the permission would involve a violation of his right to privacy or right to respect for his family life as guaranteed by Art 8.

The right to private prosecution

To constitute an effective safeguard against regulatory inertia or partiality, the availability of private prosecution must not be unduly hindered by obstructions of a formal or practical nature. According to Lord Diplock in *Gouriet v Union of Post Office Workers*,[73] every citizen has a public right in the enforcement of criminal law, and the case of *R v Stewart*[74] confirms that every citizen may bring a private prosecution unless an Act of Parliament restricts that right. Early environmental regulation tended to nullify the right of private prosecution by the requirement of Attorney General consent, a condition which prevailed in water protection legislation up until the Control of Oil Pollution Act 1970 and the Rivers (Prevention of Pollution) Act 1951. Similarly, under the Control of Pollution Act 1974, private prosecutions for waste management offences could not be brought without the consent of the Director for Public Prosecutions.[75] This restriction has also been repealed. Restrictions remain in place for offences under the sewerage provisions of the Water Industry Act 1991 which cannot be prosecuted except by the Attorney General, an aggrieved person or a body whose function it is to enforce those provisions.[76] Prosecutions for water supplied of an unsatisfactory quality can only be brought by the Secretary of State or Director of Public Prosecutions[77] and legal action against offences relating to the Radioactive Substances Act 1993 and genetically modified organisms under the Environmental Protection Act, Part VI, still require the consent of the Director of Public Prosecutions or Secretary of State.[78]

---

72 Lord Woolf, *Environmental Risk: The Responsibilities of Law & Science* Professor David Hall Memorial Lecture for the Environmental Law Foundation (2001).
73 [1977] 3 All ER 70 at 97.
74 [1896] 1 QB 300.
75 Control of Pollution Act 1974, s 6(3).
76 Water Industry Act 1991, s 211.
77 Water Industry Act 1991, s 7(4).
78 See Radioactive Substances Act 1993, s 38 and Environmental Protection Act 1990, s 118(10).

Whilst the prima facie availability of private prosecution in environmental matters is now in place,[79] the 'right' of enforcement must of course be accompanied by provisions which ensure access to the evidence necessary to support court action. Access to the evidence required to prove an offence is dependent on availability of information on operator compliance records. Of course, the private citizen does not enjoy the extensive investigative powers possessed by Environment Agency officers, and is heavily dependent on observation and the statutory registers discussed at the outset of this chapter.

It has been suggested that the trend towards mechanical means of monitoring discharges and emissions, which are managed by the operator, and which convey monitoring data to the Environment Agency may create evidential problems in the context of prosecutions.[80] The privilege against self-incrimination permits courts to refuse to compel the defendant to produce evidence against himself.[81] Clearly it might be thought that this could effectively bar private prosecutions where the prosecutor in a pollution case would be dependent on evidence which originates from the defendant's own monitoring activities. In *R v Hertfordshire County Council, ex p Green Environmental Industries Ltd*, however, the House of Lords had to answer the question of whether a notice served under the EPA 1990, s 71(2) upon the discovery of illegal handling of clinical waste by the applicant company, and requesting further particulars of Green Industries' dealings with clinical waste, was a violation of the protections against self-incrimination. Their Lordships expressed the view that:

> 'Those powers have been conferred not merely for the purpose of enabling the authorities to obtain evidence against offenders but for the broad public purpose of protecting the public health and the environment. Such information is often required urgently and the policy of the statute would be frustrated if the persons who knew most about the extent of the health or environmental hazard were entitled to refuse to provide any information on the ground that their answers might tend to incriminate them.'[82]

Presumably this reasoning could be applied equally to the requirement of information to be disclosed on the statutory registers.

It has also been suggested that the private prosecutor may be confronted by a 19th century provision which requires certification of register entries before they will be admissible as evidence in criminal proceedings.[83] The photocopies or printouts which are the result of a search of the pollution control register (and which would form the evidential basis of a private prosecution) could possibly be classed as 'hearsay', a form of evidence which is generally inadmissible. Why has this evidential objection not as yet prompted challenges in prosecutions by the Environment Agency? The prosecution of large corporate interests appears to be based on an 'understanding.' The regulator who keeps to the bargain and prosecutes only in the exceptional case will generally not meet a very adversarial defendant, and the possible challenges of

79   See, however, Public Order Act 1986, s 24 which allows an application to the High Court where the action is alleged to be 'vexatious'.

80   W Howarth, 'Self-Monitoring, Self-Policing, Self-Incrimination and Pollution Law' (1997) MLR 60(2) 220.

81   See for example Police and Criminal Evidence Act 1984, s 78. The right of protection against self incrimination is often assumed to exist unless restricted by statute – *R v Director of Serious Fraud, ex p Smith* [1993] AC 1 at 40.

82   Per Lord Hoffmann (HL) [1998] Env LR 153, CA at 434.

83   S Jackson, 'Private Prosecutions under the Control of Pollution Act 1974' (1988) ELB, 3, at 9.

self-monitoring evidence as inadmissible or self-incriminating are likely to lie dormant. After all, the trust associated with self-monitoring serves the operator well in terms of the largely conciliatory approach to enforcement. As against the private prosecutor with whom the operator has no such understanding, evidential challenges may be more likely to arise. Alternatively, the operator who casts an eye to the future will realise there is much to gain from minimising confrontation with its regulator, such as forbearance of legal sanction in relation to other breaches. It is far less likely, however, that the operator would contemplate such an exchange with the private prosecutor.

It is unclear, given the general availability of private prosecution, why this enforcement mechanism is so little used. There is certainly no shortage of breaches to prosecute. If we consider the suggestions of low prosecution rates by public regulators detailed in chapter 3, there is plenty or scope, if not a positive invitation for private enforcement. The problem may be one of resources. Yet, whilst 'cost' is considered to be one of the major inhibitors of regulatory enforcement of the criminal law,[84] cost does not in theory stand in the way of the exercise of private prosecution. The courts' discretion to award the costs of prosecution out of central funds is to be exercised in favour of a private prosecutor, unless there is good reason for not doing so.[85] It seems, therefore, that if the prosecution was reasonably brought, the costs of private prosecution, whether or not successful, will be funded by the state. We can say then, that Diplock's 'public right' of enforcement is largely recognised in the form of a general right of private prosecution of environmental offences (although limited in some cases), which does not require proof of standing.[86] From the above it seems clear that there are, however, substantial evidential difficulties with such prosecutions which may act as disincentives to commencing proceedings.

The courts and strategic lawsuits against public participation

This final section concerns the litigation which activist groups must be prepared to defend. In 1993, the Court of Appeal heard libel proceedings against both Greenpeace and the BBC in connection with comments made about the safety of incineration on a Six o'Clock News report.[87] The *McDonalds* corporation famously brought a libel case against two unemployed protesters who had been distributing leaflets outside their restaurants alleging that the fast food merchant was in part responsible for the Third World debt. The fact that *McDonald's Corpn v Steel*[88] resulted in a 726 page judgment and the longest ever civil trial in the UK is testimony both to the corporation's considerable resources and to its determination to resist the critical voice of protesters. Libel action is a particularly effective silencer given its expense and the non-availability of legal aid. It provides corporations with big pockets a perfect tool with which to browbeat impecunious defendants into submission. Friends of the Earth allegedly downsized their activism against new road building when threatened with sequestration of their assets.[89]

New legislation in the form of Criminal Justice and Public Order Act 1994 and, to a lesser extent, the Protection from Harassment Act 1997, had marked potential to be

84   P Grabosky and J Braithwaite, *Of Manners Gentle – Enforcement Strategies of Australian Regulatory Agencies* (1986) OUP, at 45.
85   Practice Direction (Crime: Costs), s 17(1) [1991] 1 WLR 498.
86   See *R v Stewart* [1896] 1 QB 300 at n 63.
87   *Rechem International Ltd v Greenpeace* (1993) unreported.
88   (1997) unreported. See, however, J Vidal, *McLibel: Burger Culture on Trial* (1997) Macmillan.
89   FF Ridley and G Jordan (eds), *Protest Politics: Cause Groups and Campaigns* (1998) Oxford University Press, Oxford.

used in litigation to silence protesters. For example, the CJPOA 1994, s 68 creates an offence of 'aggravated trespass'. The offence is committed by an act of trespass in the open air which has the effect of 'intimidating', 'disrupting' or 'obstructing' any lawful activity which (other) persons are engaging in or about to engage in on that or adjoining land. The defendants in *DPP v Tilly*[90] were convicted of the CJPOA 1994, s 68 offence in relation to their destruction of crops on a farmer's land which was being used for government authorised trials of genetically modified maize. The conviction was overturned on appeal, given the fact that neither the landowner nor his representative was present at the time of the alleged offence. Here, the court endorsed a narrow construction of 'engaging in a lawful activity' as requiring the physical presence of persons who might be 'intimidated', 'disrupted', or 'obstructed' and thereby suffer anxiety and inconvenience. Provisions from the Protection from Harassment Act 1997 were used by a research laboratory seeking an injunction to keep anti-vivisection protesters away from its staff and premises.[91] The case concerned whether the injunction could be varied so as to exclude from its terms an activist group which the court was convinced had conducted its protest in a peaceful fashion. Judge Eady in the High Court agreed to the variation saying that the 1997 Act: '... was clearly not intended by Parliament to be used to clamp down on the discussion of matters of public interest or upon the rights of political protest and public demonstration which are so much part of our democratic tradition.'

There are a number of further cases which are of substantial importance in the determination of the action that can be taken against 'eco-warriors' who choose to protest by physical obstruction of unwanted developments on greenfield sites. In many instances, the presence of a protest camp can delay proceedings and exert pressure on developers, landowners and the government to reconsider. At its most effective, physical obstruction can discourage developers and potential purchasers from proceeding with the development at all. The cases of *Countryside Residential (North Thames) Ltd v Christiana Tugwell*[92] and *Manchester Airport Plc v Dutton*[93] are particularly instructive on the rights of developers to eject protest camps. In the former case, a protest camp had been set up in woodlands to protest against plans for a housing development. Developers, who had been granted a licence to enter the land for the purposes of performing investigatory tasks, brought proceedings to eject the 'trespassers.' The court held that such a remedy was unavailable as the limited licence did not confer 'possession' on the developers, a necessary precondition of being able to eject trespassers.

The scope of an injunction against protesters can be problematic where the group is an unincorporated association. Such groups cannot sue or be sued in their own right and therefore the court must decide how wide to cast the net of an injunction. In *United Kingdom Nirex Ltd v Barton*[94] a small group protesting against the dumping of low level radioactive waste in their locality defended an application for an injunction to stop them entering the proposed disposal site. The court considered and rejected the possibility of a representative action which would be binding against all members of the group whether or not they had trespassed. Clearly, such an injunction, by effectively stigmatising the whole group could discredit the group's activities and discourage non-members from joining the group. Only the small minority of members who had broken the law were to be subject to the injunction. Nevertheless, if anyone knowing the terms

90   [2001] EWHC Admin 821, [2002] Crim LR 128.
91   *Huntingdon Life Sciences Ltd v Curtin* (1997) Times, 11 December.
92   [2000] JPL 1251 CA.
93   [2000] 1 QB 133.
94   (1986) Times, 14 October, CA.

of the injunctions were to do what was forbidden by the injunctions, such acts would, prima facie, be liable to contempt proceedings.[95]

In *Monsanto plc v Tilly*[96] the Court of Appeal was asked to consider the defence of 'necessity' in the context of public protest. Members of the protest organisation *Genetix Snowball* used 'non-violent' action, namely the uprooting of genetically modified crops from farm land, as a means of furthering their aims of challenging public policy on genetic modification. *Monsanto*, the producers of the genetically modified seed, sought an injunction against the protesters using the law of trespass. *Monsanto* were in a strong position as they could bring an action in either trespass to goods (because the crops became goods as soon as they were 'severed' from the land) and also for trespass to land (a fact which might be surprising given that *Monsanto* did not own the land on which the crops were growing). *Monsanto* were held to have sufficient interest to maintain an action for trespass to the land because of their entitlement to the crops which was determined by the written agreements between *Monsanto* and the farmers. The defence of necessity was held not to extend to the defendant's acts and the court advised the protesters to pursue the conventional means of challenging government policy by using judicial review and 'discharging the very considerable burden' of proving the grant of licences by the then DETR was *Wednesbury* unreasonable.[97] The court clearly saw the conflict embodied by this dispute between the supporters and dissenters in the GMO debate as a matter which was outside the courts' remit: 'The court must resist the invitation to assume jurisdiction to resolve an issue of a kind which it is not its constitutional function to decide and which it is not competent and equipped to decide.' This litigation was not an appropriate vehicle for determining whether the growing of GM crops was 'in the public interest.' It came as no surprise that the defendant's allegations failed, given that they cited no statutory or common law authority for their uprooting being justified by necessity. Their defence was a thinly disguised attempt to challenge government policy in the court room and may have fared better if heard before a jury.[98] Yet most litigation is fought in legal terms which often bear little relationship to the real motivations and complaints of the parties. Such legal argument, even if unsuccessful, can nevertheless serve the aims of the protest group by providing further welcome publicity for their cause.

Further reading

House of Lords Select Committee on the Draft Freedom of Information Bill, First Report 1998-99.

House of Commons Select Committee on Public Administration *Your Right to Know* (Cm 3818) (Cabinet Office, 1997).

House of Lords Select Committee on the European Communities, First Report, *Freedom of Access to Information on the Environment* 1996-97 HL paper 9.

Birkenshaw P and Parry, N 'The end of the beginning: The freedom of information bill 1999' (1999) 26 Journal of Law & Society 538.

Dalton, RJ *The Green Rainbow* (1994) Yale University Press, London.

Grant, W *Pressure Groups, Politics and Democracy in Great Britain* (2nd edn, 1995) Harvester Wheatsheaf, Hertfordshire.

95 *Z Ltd v A-Z and AA-LL* [1982] QB 558.
96 [2000] Env LR 313.
97 Per Stuart Smith LJ.
98 See also Greenpeace press release, 13 June 2001, on the Edmonton incinerator.

Jendroska, J and Stec, S 'The Aarhus Convention: Towards a New Era in Environmental Democracy' (2001) 9(3) Environmental Liability 140.

Le Seur, A 'Taking the soft option? The duty to give reasons in the draft Freedom of Information Bill' [1999] Public Law 419.

Ridley, FF and Jordan G (eds), *Protest Politics: Cause Groups and Campaigns* (1998) Oxford University Press, Oxford.

Rowan-Robinson, J 'Public access to environmental information: a means to what end?' JEL (1996) 8(1) 19.

Rowan-Robinson, J et al 'Public Access to Environmental Information: A Means to What End?' (1996) 8(1) Journal of Environmental Law 19.

Rowell, A *Green Backlash: Global Subversion of the Environmental Movement* (1996) Routledge, London.

Simpson, D *Pressure Groups* (1999) Hodder & Staughton, Oxon.

Vick, DW and Campbell, K 'Public Protests, Private Lawsuits and the Market: The Investor Response to the McLibel Case' (2001) Journal of Law & Society 28(2) 204.

Wilson, D (ed), *The Secrets File* (1984) Heinnemann Educational Books, London.

Part II

Protection of the land

Chapter 8

The basic structure of planning control

This is *not* a book on planning law; readers must turn to standard texts such as Telling and Duxbury's *Planning Law and Procedure*, or Moore's *A Practical Approach to Planning Law* (to whose work particular indebtedness is acknowledged), or, at the practitioner level, Grant's *Urban Planning Law*, or Purdue, Young and Rowan Robinson's *Planning Law and Procedure*. Nevertheless it is impossible to understand the ways in which land is used, developed, exploited and protected without having *basic* knowledge of planning law. The variations, departures, special procedures and particular controls that make up the body of land use controls can then be viewed in context. Furthermore in relation to some issues, eg protection of visual amenity, or development of wind farms (see *The Times* 23 April 1991) to name but two disparate matters, planning law is the principle mode of regulation. Local authorities are, in addition, granted general powers to promote or improve the environmental well-being of their areas under the Local Government Act 2000, s 2 while s 4 requires authorities to develop 'Community Strategies' to facilitate this function.

However, planning has limitations as a means of environmental regulation. It is basically a reactive and managerial rather than a protective system, being primarily concerned with the orderly management of change, and fundamentally political in nature, providing a framework within which various issues and values can be weighed one against the other, with economic arguments, for example, being able to outweigh environmental concerns on occasions.

Planning and sustainability

The fact that 'sustainable' is linked with 'development' in policy thinking inevitably means that the planning system which is so closely concerned with land use issues must assume greater environmental importance in future years, though sustainable development is not, nor must not, be limited solely to planning issues. Nevertheless many planners now see a major role for planning in ensuring 'sustainability' which is often interpreted in the present context as leaving a better future for following generations. Planners may thus seek to stress the encouragement and revival of existing communities and areas rather than the establishment of new ones, the reuse and retention of existing buildings for new uses wherever possible, or the reclamation of their materials where they must be demolished, the bringing together of work and housing opportunities, and, perhaps above everything, the reduction of needs to travel either for work, shopping or leisure opportunities, with travel where necessary being encouraged by means of public transport.

However, while planning has had an environmental role for many years in relation to: elimination of nuisances by separation of residential and industrial areas; protection of 'amenity' ie the 'pleasantness' of an area; and containment of urban sprawl, there are many who argue that planning embraces change; its historic philosophy is *not* that development is bad, indeed it believes development on the whole is good. Planning is moreover a highly politicised, discretionary system of *control* over land and landbased resources which accepts a certain degree of environmental degradation and despoliation may be necessary in particular cases.

Cm 1200 'This Common Heritage' p 17 lists the following as features of the planning system:

1   Economic growth.
2   Provision of work opportunities.
3   Provision of housing.
4   Creating a safe environment against risks of flooding, subsidence, industrial hazards.
5   Protecting prime agricultural land for food production.
6   Ensuring there is adequate access to shops.
7   Using mineral resources to best advantage.
8   Sustaining the diversity and character of the countryside.
9   Defending greenbelts against urban encroachment.
10 Maintaining the character and vitality of existing town centres.
11 Revitalising older run down urban areas.
12 Safeguarding the amenity of existing residential areas.
13 Conserving historic and quality architecture.

Not all of the foregoing would *necessarily* qualify as 'sustainable development'. PPG1, however, in its 1997 edition stresses planning's role in promoting sustainable development, stressing the need for striking a balance between development and respecting environmental objectives, promoting the most efficient use of already developed areas, conserving cultural and natural resources, and shaping new developments so as to minimise the need for travel. Thus the reuse of existing developed sites is to be preferred, existing town centres should be redeveloped on a mixed use basis, incorporating housing where possible; development should also take place along established transport corridors. New development in general should be compatible with the objectives of reusing previously developed land, maintaining clean air and reducing travel needs, especially reliance on private cars.

A PLAN MAKING

Both counties and districts where they survive have planning functions as, of course, do unitary authorities. The role of counties tends to be strategic; that of districts is tactical. The functional division is laid down by the Local Government Act 1972, ss 182–84 and Sch 16, as amended by the Local Government, Planning and Land Act 1980, the Local Government Act 1992, the Local Government (Wales) Act 1994 and the Environment Act 1995. Under these Acts counties are primarily concerned with: preparation of structure plans; control of developments concerned with mineral and aggregate working and processing, and associated plants and developments; cement works, and waste disposal sites.

The Local Government Act 2000, s 6 enables the Secretary of State to repeal, revoke or disapply enactments requiring local authorities to prepare plans, while the National

Assembly for Wales has a similar power under the LGA 2000. It does not yet appear that these quite extensive powers will be applied to planning in the current context.

A note on National Parks

The Environment Act 1995, ss 63 and 64 granted power to the Secretary of State to replace the existing English authorities within National Parks with National Park Authorities (NPAs), with similar provisions to apply in Wales; see s 64(3). The NPAs under the Town and Planning Act 1990, s 4A (as inserted in 1995), have become the *sole* planning authority for the Park(s) in question. This provision, inter alia, grants mineral planning functions to the NPA. There are, however, a number of planning functions which are exercised concurrently with NPAs by district planning authorities within Park areas, these are: tree preservation, trees in Conservation Areas, and land adversely affecting the amenity of a neighbourhood. Section 67(2) of the Environment Act 1995 further enables the Secretary of State to apply the provisions relating to Unitary Development Plans to NPAs in place of those concerned with structure and local plans.

Unless the Secretary of State makes an order for an NPA under s 67(2) of the 1995 Act, each NPA has responsibility for both structure and local plans in its area.

Where an application to develop land solely within a National Park is made the NPA has exclusive jurisdiction, but where the land in question straddles a park boundary the application in so far as it relates to land outside the Park will, under the Town and Country Planning Act 1990, Sch 1, as amended, fall to the county council to determine.[1]

An emerging patchwork quilt of planning authorities

In *England* recommendations may be made under the Local Government Act 1992, s 14 and subsequently implemented under s 17, for the replacement of the existing tiers of local government with a single tier, ie either for counties to take over district functions for an area *or* for a district to take over county functions within its area.

Recommendation has to be made whether such new unitary authorities should make unitary plans for their areas under the Town and Country Planning Act 1990, Part II, Chapter I, and as to the inclusion of mineral and waste policies *or* whether the existing provisions relating to structure and local plans should continue to apply to affected areas with appropriate adjustments. *Most* of 'shire England' has not been affected by change, though some counties have found themselves denuded of their historic county towns, eg Leicestershire, while in other cases particular areas with strong local identities and economies have been given unitary status, including some former shire counties such as Herefordshire.

The Secretary of State determines whether unitary authorities should retain structure and local plans having considered whether strategic planning needs to be carried out over an area greater than that of an individual authority, and some of the Unitary Authorities have now prepared Unitary Development Plans (see below).

In Wales, however, the Local Government (Wales) Act 1994 provides that 22 'principal councils' shall be the local planning authorities. These bodies are 11 counties and 11 county boroughs, all of which are unitary authorities, see the 1994 Act, ss 1 and 18. The Town and County Planning Act 1990, Sch 1A as inserted in 1994, distributes planning functions, while s 10A of the 1990 Act provides that the new Welsh unitary

---

1   *R v Northumberland National Park Authority, ex p Secretary of State for Defence* (1998) 77 P & CR 120.

authorities shall adopt the planning system of the existing English unitary authorities, eg as to unitary plans, though s 23A provides for the Welsh authorities to make joint unitary development plans. These changes in Wales are to be brought into effect by order. DoE Circular 4/96 gives guidance on the new system.

Note also that the Broads Authority is the local plan making and development control authority for its area under the TCPA 1990, s 5, and see the Local Government, Planning and Land Act 1980, ss 148 and 149 for the power which can be conferred on urban development corporations.

B DEVELOPMENT PLANS

Statute currently knows the following kinds of plan:
1   Unitary development plans — metropolitan areas plus the Welsh and some English unitary authorities as outlined above.
2   Structure plans — 'shire' counties and districts, and some English unitary authorities.
3   Local plans — 'shire' counties and districts, and some English unitary authorities. No other plans have statutory force, which is not to say that they do not exist. Local authorities may have 'non statutory plans' and other forms of supplementary guidance either to 'fill the gap' until a statutory plan is made, or to supplement plans, such as 'planning briefs' issued in respect of particular sites in need of redevelopment, while non statutory planning is used by government. This rests on no real statutory basis, but the important point is that such guidance, for example the various issues of Regional Planning guidance (RPG) and see PPG 11 (2000), is recognised by the courts as being a matter that local authorities have at least to take into account when exercising their statutory planning functions, particularly with regard to the revision of structure plans. On the use of supplementary planning guidance (SPG) see PPG 12 para 3–15 et seq. Strictly, however, any such guidance should only be resorted to once a proper statutory plan is in force for an area. Policies that are germane to planning issues should generally and as a matter of principle be included in development plans.

Unitary Development Plans (UDPs)

UDPs replace the two tier structure and local plans for the metropolitan districts in London, the West Midlands, Greater Manchester, Merseyside, South Yorkshire, Tyne and Wear and West Yorkshire. They exist under the TCPA 1990, ss 10–28. UDPs were originally introduced under the Local Government Act 1985, and will, in time, cover the areas of *some* unitary authorities according to the Secretary of State's determination.

UDPs are the sole plans for their areas and supersede other plans. They provide the framework for development, development control and conservation, and cover the whole of a relevant authority's area, stating clear and concise policies on land use issues — but *not* on any matter which is not land use related, though economic and social criteria may have been had in regard in their formulation. The basic assumption is that reappraisal and replanning will take place after a ten-year period. Authorities should consult with the DTLR on drawing up plans, and with the Countryside Agency and the relevant nature conservancy body (in England, English Nature) where a UDP will bear upon wildlife and the countryside.

The basic scheme of the legislation is as follows:
1   The Secretary of State has issued, and in some cases has revised, strategic guidance for the areas where UDPs are to exist. This relates to land use issues going beyond individual district boundaries.

2   Commencement orders have brought the UDP provisions into force within individual MDCs and LBCs, see s 28 of the TCPA 1990.
3   Thereafter relevant authorities are required to prepare UDPs for their areas. The Secretary of State has power to direct that a particular plan must be prepared within a specific period; see the TCPA 1990, s 12.

Further guidance may now be found in PPG 12, 1999.

UDPs have two parts under the TCPA 1990, s 12(3), (4). Part I is a written statement of the local authority's general development and land use policies for its area, including conservation of the natural beauty and amenity of land, improvement of the physical environment and traffic management. Part I is the framework for Part II and should contain only major policies which *should*, according to s 12(6), be drawn up having regard to:

1   The Secretary of State's strategic or regional guidance.
2   Any other current national policies (eg those in PPGs).
3   Likely available resources for realistic plan implementation.
4   Any other matters prescribed. In this context note the Town and Country Planning (Development Plans) Regulations. SI 1999/3280, reg 20: *this relates also to local plans, minerals local plans and waste local plans*, and requires regard to be had to economic, environmental and social considerations, the national waste strategy, the objective of preventing major accidents, the need to maintain appropriate distances between establishments where a major accident could occur and residential, other public areas and areas of particular sensitivity.

Part I should generally be short, illustrated by a minimum of maps and diagrams and intelligible to lay persons.

Part II must be in general conformity with Part I, see TCPA 1990, s 12(7) and must take account of centrally prescribed issues, and will be, under s 12(4), a written statement of policies and proposals to form the basis for deciding individual applications. In addition it will contain a reasoned justification of the Part I proposals, and a statement of the regard had to the matters 1–4. Part II proposals must also be shown on a 'proposals map'. Part II will give detailed guidance on those matters which are likely to form the basis of planning decisions, and on the likely conditions which will be attached. Particular locations within a plan area may be designated, under s 12(8), as 'Action Areas' for comprehensive redevelopment in accordance with plan proposals within ten years. Under the TCPA 1990, s 12A the Secretary of State may direct that a UDP shall not be prepared or shall not operate in relation to the area of an Urban Development Corporation.

UDPs are to be made in a multi stage process. Consequently authorities must ensure, under the TCPA 1990, s 13, that adequate local publicity is given to the proposed content of the UDP in accordance with regulations made under s 26 see SI 1999/3280, and that any representations made in due form are considered. As part of an overall drive to speed up the preparation of UDPs (and local plans) under the 1999 Regulations great stress is laid on much greater consultation at an early stage to clarify the issues with which the plan is to deal. An initial period of six weeks to make objections to and representations about a plan is allowed at the draft stage. Revisions may be made at that stage and a further opportunity is allowed for objections to be made. Provision is also made for the holding of public inquiries into objections and for the speedy publication of any report from such an inquiry. Central guidance stresses the point that the two stage objection procedure enables authorities to produce an initial draft which may then be refined to produce the formal 'deposited plan'.

It is specifically provided that among the objectors to a deposited draft UDP the Secretary of State is included, see the TCPA 1990, s 13(5) as amended in 1991. A UDP may not be adopted until after any objections made have been considered in accordance with regulations, or, where there are no objections, until after the expiry of the 'prescribed period'. Such a draft may be withdrawn under the TCPA 1990, s 14 by the authority at any time before adoption by the authority or approval by the Secretary of State, and *must* be withdrawn if the latter so directs. Section 15 provides for the adoption of UDPs either as originally prepared or following modification to take account of objections or other material considerations. However, where DEFRA has objected to a plan and these objections have not been acted on the authority must explain their actions to the Secretary of State and must not adopt the plan unless authorised to do so. Furthermore where objections in due form have been received a public inquiry *must* be held to consider these, while any other objections *may* be the subject of any inquiry or hearing (see the TCPA 1990, s 16 as amended). See also PPG 12 Annex B for further details of the objection and inquiry process.

The Secretary of State has quite extensive powers concerning UDPs. Once a copy of a UDP has been sent to him/her, he/she may direct the authority to modify it as he/she directs (see the TCPA 1990, s 17 as amended) and thereafter the authority may not adopt the plan unless the Secretary of State is satisfied as to modification. Alternatively he/she may 'call in' a plan for approval, see s 18, either in whole or part. Approval is then at his/her discretion under s 19, and he/she may take into account *any* matters considered relevant, though the decision on a plan must be supported by a statement of reasons. Moreover, before deciding whether or not to approve a plan the Secretary of State must consider objections made in due form. The 'call in' power is extreme, and normally will only be used where a plan raises issues of national or regional importance; where Part I is out of conformity with strategic guidance; where Part II is out of conformity with Part I; where DEFRA presses an objection to the plan, or where the plan is publicly controversial. The giving of a 'holding direction' freezes the entire plan (TCPA 1990, s 18(2)) and transfers the matter to the Secretary of State. Where Part I (in whole or part) alone is 'called in' the Secretary of State may hold an examination in public of relevant issues. If a whole plan or any part of Part II, however, is 'called in' a public local inquiry must, under the TCPA 1990, s 20(2), be held into any objections not already considered by the local authority. If the Secretary of State decides to reject the 'called in' plan he may do so without a further inquiry. The Secretary of State's powers extend to direct modification of Part II of a 'called in' plan to make it conform to Part I (see TCPA 1990, s 19(4)). These powers are extensive and allow the Secretary of State to remove over-prescriptive plan policies, provided that power is not exercised in an unreasonable fashion.[2] Where the Secretary of State approves such a plan he/she will set a date on which the plan will come into operation (see TCPA 1990, s 19(5)).

There is the usual six-week period, under TCPA 1990, s 284(1), of challenge on a point of law after approval/adoption.

Where a UDP is drawn up, Part II *must*, according to central guidance (initially given in Circular DoE 3/88) incorporate any existing local plans for its area.

Joint UDPs may be drawn up by two or more authorities though only where they are in the same metropolitan area. The procedure is generally as outlined above (see TCPA 1990, s 23). [Remember that particular powers exist in Wales under the 1994 reforms, and that central planning powers there are exercised by the National Assembly.]

In common with *all* other plans UDPs should be subject to *environmental appraisal* in accordance with 'Planning for Sustainable Developments Towards Better Practice' (DETR 1998), to ensure compliance with the government's sustainable development objectives of: maintenance of high and stable levels of economic growth and employment; social progress for all; effective protection of the environment, and prudent use of natural resources: see further below.

---

2   *R v Secretary of State for the Environment, ex p Islington London Borough Council* [1995] JPL 121.

Structure plans

In the shires a two-fold system of plans still exists. Structure plans now cover the nation; what follows therefore relates to how such a plan is *replaced* or otherwise modified.

Before a structure plan is drawn up, the TCPA 1990, s 30 requires a review of the matters which may be expected to affect the development of its area by the planning authority. Review *must* be constant, and may involve surveys. This must include a review of physical and economic characteristics of the relevant area, and those of neighbouring areas where they are likely to be of consequence; size, composition and distribution of population; communications, transport and traffic; any other matters relevant to the foregoing, or prescribed by the Secretary of State, or subject to projected change and the likely consequences for the development of the area.

Under the TCPA 1990, s 31 of the 1990 Act, as amended, a structure plan contains a written statement formulating the authority's general land development policies which must include policies on conservation of the natural beauty and amenity of the land, improvement of the physical environment and traffic management, though regulations may be made under the TCPA 1990, s 31(4) which prescribe those matters with which a structure plan is to concern itself, see SI 1999/3280 which requires consideration of, inter alia, social, economic and environmental issues. The plan must also contain prescribed diagrams, maps, etc, and such material as is centrally directed. Plans are to be formulated in addition taking into account regional *or* strategic planning guidance given by the Secretary of State, current national policies, resources likely to be available and other matters prescribed or directed by the Secretary of State. According to PPG 12, chapter 3, the following issues are apt for inclusion in structure plans (and Part I of UDPs): housing provision, including targets for reuse of previously developed land; green belts; conservation and improvement of the natural and built environment; employment and wealth creation issues for an area; transport and land use strategies; mineral working; waste treatment; tourism and leisure issues; energy generation, including renewable energy. However, only *general* policies may be included in structure plans — detailed policies have to be included in local plans. There is no power to decide that a particular policy is detailed but is best dealt with by the structure plan.[3]

In unitary areas where structure and local plans are retained it is *expected* that authorities will work together on their structure plans, and may, in effect, be required to under s 21 of the Local Government Act 1992; see further PPG 12 Annex A Appendix 1 for the list of 'who does what'.

Under the TCPA 1990, s 32 (as substituted) an authority may at any time prepare proposals for altering its structure plan or to replace it, and must do so if directed by the Secretary of State, though they may *not* so act with regard to a plan approved by the Secretary without his/her consent. Such proposals may relate to the whole of the authority's area or a part, but must be accompanied by an explanatory memorandum explaining and justifying proposals, together with supporting information. The memorandum is not, however, part of either the structure plan nor the overall development plan for the purposes of the TCPA 1990, s 54A, see further below.[4] There will be public participation in the proposal making process under the TCPA 1990, s 33 (as substituted), though the form and content of this will be determined by regulations made centrally under the TCPA 1990, s 53, or as is otherwise centrally directed, see SI 1991/2794. Any representations then received in due form must be considered. Once the proposals are made then copies must be made publicly available and a prescribed

3   *J S Bloor Ltd v Swindon Borough Council* [2001] All ER (D) 365 (Nov).
4   *Holden v Secretary of State for the Environment* [1994] JPL B1.

time stated during which objections can be made. A copy must also be sent to the Secretary of State, who may also be an objector to the plan. Any objections made in due form — that form to be as prescribed under central regulations — must be considered by the authority, who may, under the TCPA 1990, s 34 (as substituted) withdraw their proposals at any time before formal adoption by them or approval by the Secretary of State. Structure plan alteration/replacement proposals may be modified to take account of objections received or in the light of other material considerations and may then be adopted by the authority under the TCPA 1990, s 35 (as substituted), but this is subject to the Secretary of State's power to direct them to modify their proposals before adoption, and to the TCPA 1990, s 35B, see below. Section 35A further empowers the Secretary of State to 'call in' proposals before adoption. He/she then has a wide discretion as to the fate of the proposals, though he/she must consider any objections made in due form together with *any* other matters considered relevant, and in this connection a wide power of consultation is given. Reasons must, however, be given to the authority explaining the Secretary of State's decisions on proposals, though the form and content of the reasons is left to his/her decision. The TCPA 1990, s 35B further requires that before adopting proposals the authority must, unless the Secretary of State otherwise directs, cause 'an examination in public' (EIP) to be held of such matters concerning the proposals as they consider should be examined, or which the Secretary of State directs are to be examined. Similarly where the Secretary of State calls in proposals he/she may hold an examination in public of any specified matter. An EIP is held by persons specifically appointed by the Secretary of State, but it is not a public inquiry in the full sense, even though the Tribunals and Inquiries Act 1992 applies, for no person has a *right* to be heard, while certain bodies or persons *may* take part, for example the authority and those invited to participate by the person(s) holding the examination. Regulations may be made with respect to examinations, see SI 1999/3280.

Finally note TCPA 1990, s 35C under which an authority responsible for a structure plan must, where their alteration or replacement proposals are adopted or approved, notify local plan authorities of this and supply them with statements as to whether their local plans are or are not in conformity with the new or altered plan, and the extent of any non-conformity shall be specified.

Local plans

The TCPA 1990, s 36 (as substituted) provides that 'local planning authorities' (generally districts) must, within such time as the Secretary of State directs, prepare *a* local plan for their area. Such a plan must contain a written statement of detailed policies for land use and development which must include policies on the conservation of the natural beauty and amenity of the land (a phrase which must assume that there is beauty, etc, to conserve), the improvement of the physical environment (which is apt to deal with situations where there is no beauty) and traffic management. Similar requirements have, of course, already been met in relation to UDPs and structure plans. Local plans must *not* contain policies on winning and working minerals or mineral waste deposition, nor any policies on waste or refuse deposition. But plans must contain maps, illustrating policies and such other diagrams and illustrations as are prescribed, together with other material considered appropriate by authorities, and plans must also be in general conformity with structure plans. In formulating plan policies authorities must have regard to such matters as are prescribed or directed by them by the Secretary of State. Plans may designate a part of an authority's area as an 'action area' for comprehensive development, re-development or improvement within a prescribed period. Once in force a local plan may be altered or replaced at the authority's discretion, though they must *consider* alteration or replacement if supplied with a nonconformity notice under TCPA 1990, s 35C (see above) and *must* prepare proposals for alteration, etc where the Secretary of State so directs. Such alterations, etc, may relate to the whole or part of a plan area, see TCPA 1990, s 39 (as substituted). PPG 12 counsels authorities not to produce over-detailed plans as this may lead to over many objections at the deposit stage (see below) and consequentially longer times before plans take effect. Plans should concentrate on dealing with those matters that are likely to be relevant to deciding those planning applications that are likely to be received, or to determine the type of conditions to be applied to permissions granted. More detailed guidance can then be issued as non-statutory SPG (see above).

Public participation in plan making or alteration, etc, exists under TCPA 1990, s 40 (as substituted) and is dependent on regulations made centrally, and directions given by the Secretary of State, under TCPA 1990, s 53. [See SI 1999/3280.] Representations made in due form must be considered by the authority and when their proposals are finally formulated they must make them publicly available, and send a copy to the Secretary of State. A statement of the time allowed for objecting to the proposals must also be made, and again it is specifically provided that the Secretary of State may be an objector. The procedure for adoption is the same as that for UDPs, ie a two-stage objection procedure, etc. A plan or its alterations or replacement may not be adopted until after any duly made objections have been considered, and in any case where objections have been duly made a local inquiry or other hearing must be held for consideration purposes under TCPA 1990, s 42(1) (as substituted) while an inquiry or hearing *may* be held to consider any objections not made in due form, ie in accordance with regulations. An inquiry will be held by a person appointed by the Secretary of State. Thereafter under TCPA 1990, s 43 (as amended) the plan etc, may be adopted by resolution either as originally prepared or modified to take account of objections or any other material considerations, though proposals not in general conformity with the structure plan may not be adopted. The obligations to consult and consider, however, impose no obligation to comply with views received — even if these receive the support of the person holding a local plan inquiry into them — provided the planning authority behaves reasonably.[5] However, departures from recommendations made must be reasoned and must be the result of a full and proper reconsideration of the issues.[6] The reasons must show why the authority have taken a particular line on an issue.[7]

The Secretary of State may intervene in the local plan process at a number of points. After a copy of plan proposals has been sent to him/her, he/she may under TCPA 1990, s 43(4), as amended, direct modification before adoption, or he/she may under TCPA 1990, s 44 call in proposals, or any part of them, for consideration. If such a call is made the authority cannot take any further steps to adopt the proposals, or any of them, until the Secretary of State has given a decision, and it is for him/her to approve them or not as the case may be: if he/she does approve no further adoption by the authority is required. TCPA 1990, s 45 then grants the Secretary of State a wide discretion to approve or reject the proposals or modify them, taking into account any matters considered relevant. However, if he/she does not determine to reject proposals he/she must consider any objections that have been made in due form and give objectors the chance to be heard, perhaps also holding a hearing or a public inquiry.

5   *R v Hammersmith and Fulham London Borough Council, ex p People Before Profit Ltd* [1981] JPL 869.
6   *Black Country Development Corpn v Sandwell Metropolitan Borough Council* [1996] JPL B117 and *Stirk v Bridgnorth District Council* [1996] EGCS 159.
7   *Hall Aggregates (South Coast) Ltd v New Forest District Council* [1996] EGCS 108 and *Gillenden Development Co Ltd v Surrey County Council* [1997] JPL 944.

Action to ensure conformity between structure and local plans is to be taken under TCPA 1990, s 46 (as substituted). When preparing local plan proposals the preparing authority must notify those proposals to the structure plan authority who must within a prescribed period state whether the proposals are/are not in general conformity with the structure plan, and, if not, to what extent there is nonconformity, and any such statement is to be treated as a duly made objection to the proposals. Once the local plan is finally made/altered, etc, as the case may be and is adopted/approved its provisions will apply in any case of conflict with those of the structure plan, unless the case falls within TCPA 1990, s 35C (see above) and no remedial action has been taken to deal with the lack of conformity.

PPG 12 is highly critical of the time it has taken to produce comprehensive coverage of the nation by local plans and UDPs (where appropriate). Indeed in January 1999 only 67% of such plans had proceeded to adoption. Full coverage is expected by 2003.

Recovery of inquiry costs

Under the TCPA 1990, s 303A (introduced by the Town and Country Planning (Costs of Inquiries etc) Act 1995) the Secretary of State may make local planning authorities responsible for those costs of holding inquiries into, inter alia, local plans and examinations in public which would otherwise have fallen on him/her.

Other types of plan

Two types of local plan remain to be mentioned, though their relevance is to mineral extraction and waste disposal, see chapters 13 and 14. Section 37 of the TCPA 1990 (as substituted) *requires* 'mineral planning authorities' (*generally* counties) for areas *other* than National Parks to prepare within such period (as any) directed by the Secretary of State 'a minerals local plan' (MLP) for their areas. This is a local plan which contains a written statement formulating detailed policies in respect of winning or working minerals or deposition of mineral waste. Within National Parks the obligation will fall on the NPA, see above. The TCPA 1990, s 38, as substituted, requires the making of 'waste local plans' (WLP) containing detailed policies in respect of refuse or waste deposition. It will *generally* be county authorities who will prepare such plans, while in Metropolitan and some other unitary areas such plans will be part of UDPs. The obligation may be discharged either by making a separate WLP or by including policies in the MLP. NPAs are under a separate but similar obligation.

In unitary areas where UDP functions are not conferred each unitary authority will make a MLP and a WLP, or will, as in Leicester, include policies in the local plan, see DoE Circular 4/96.

Challenges to the validity of plans may be made under the TCPA 1990, s 284 as amended, and s 287. Challenge is allowed on a point of law only, procedural or substantive, and may only take place within the six-week period of notice of adoption or approval as the case may be as required by regulations. The challenge may be made by any 'person aggrieved' which would certainly include any person whose land is affected by the terms of a plan. For this, and an excellent example of the generally beneficent attitude of the courts towards the powers of authorities concerning plan making, see *Westminster City Council v Great Portland Estates plc*.[8]

---

8   [1985] AC 661, sub nom *Great Portland Estates plc v Westminster City Council* [1984] 3 All ER 744.

It is possible to challenge an individual policy in a plan on grounds of legality, for example on the basis that its inclusion is insufficiently reasoned in the light of comments made at a local plan inquiry[9] or where there has been a change of mind over a green belt boundary during an inquiry leading to prejudice for a landowner.[10]

London

The Greater London Authority Act 1999 created a new structure of strategic local government for the metropolis with an elected mayor, and an elected assembly charged with promoting the economic and social development of London and the improvement of its environment. While local plan making and development control remain functions of the London boroughs, the Mayor of London is required to produce and keep under review a 'spatial development strategy' for Greater London. The initial public moves towards the creation of the strategy were taken in May 2001 with the publication of consultation documents, 'Towards the London Plan'. A draft of the plan should appear in 2002. Features of the proposals include provision of improved and extended public transport links, and higher density mixed-use developments at accessible locations, with an emphasis on East London as the target area for new commercial and housing developments, ie the 'Thames Gateway' area. UDPs in Greater London will be required by the TCPA 1990, s 21A as inserted, to conform with the strategy as and when replaced. In addition the Mayor of London will have to be consulted by relevant development control authorities on a number of issues where applications for planning permission raise issues of strategic importance, for example major housing or infrastructure projects. The mayor may direct the refusal of permission in such cases where this is considered to be necessary for reasons of strategic planning. For the details of relevant classes of development see the Town and Country (Mayor of London) Order SI 2000/1493.

Plans and the environment

Reference has already been made to planning and sustainability. PPG12 makes particular comment on the need to ensure that planning plays its part in achieving the sustainable development policy.

Reference has also been made to the stress placed by PPG12 on four basic principles of sustainable development, namely: maintenance of high and stable levels of economic growth and employment, social progress for all; effective environmental protection and prudent use of natural resources. All of these are undoubtedly desirable, whether they are mutually compatible is another matter, and the suspicion must be that in practice some trade offs between these principles will have to be made in practice. So far, however, as planning is concerned it is policy that a contribution has to be made to achieving the overall sustainable development strategy. To this end the environmental and social implications of policies designed to produce growth and employment have to be considered, and advice given in 'Planning for Sustainable Development: Towards Better Practice' (DETR 1998) has to be taken into account. Inter alia, this urges that new development should take place within existing urban areas, thus also helping to regenerate them. It should also utilise wherever possible existing public transport modes,

9   *Charles Church Developments plc v Hart District Council* [1994] JPL B133.
10   *Thames Water Utilities v East Hertfordshire District Council* [1995] JPL 706.

so as to reduce the pressure for increased private motoring. Planners should therefore aim for a vision of improved urban areas over a 25-year timescale so that they will be places where people wish *to both live and work.* Urban development should follow a mixed pattern of residential, employment and recreational uses, with moderately high densities and reduced parking provision to, once again, encourage use of public transport, cycling and pedestrian access over car use. A key policy in all of this has to be the reuse of previously developed land. These policies have to be built into new development plans as they are made, but also have to be grafted onto existing ones. A further new departure is central insistence on the need for monitoring of plans to check on the progress of sustainable development in practice. PPG12 adds to this guidance by arguing that: 'Development plans should be drawn up in such a way as to take environmental considerations comprehensively and consistently into account.' These considerations include: energy conservation, energy efficiency and the need to reduce global warming emissions (see also PPG22 and PPG13); air quality issues (see also PPG23 and DETR Circular I5/97); noise and light pollution (PPG23); needs to maintain the character and diversity of rural and undeveloped coastal areas (see also PPGs 7 and 20); conservation of wildlife habitats, biodiversity and environmental enhancement (see PPG9, currently under revision); preserving landscape quality (see PPG7); the need to improve the physical and natural environment or urban areas, and their revitalisation (see PPGs 3 and 6); enhancing the quality of urban design (see PPG1); policies on coastal protection, flood defence and land drainage (see PPG20 and DoE Circular 30/92); the need to protect ground water from contamination by development; avoiding development on unstable land (see PPG14) and enhancing natural beauty by tree and hedgerow protection and planning (PPG7). In addition when plans are being made account should be taken of particular natural resources such as water, land and minerals and the need to prevent their over exploitation.

At the same time, however, PPG12 points out the need to foster new types of innovative economic authority, and counsels where possible the clustering of such new activities so that, once again, the need for travel between companies and sites is reduced. Planning must additionally address the needs of disadvantaged sectors of the community, and must pay particular attention to the siting of housing, educational, recreational, religious and other social facilities, especially taking notice of the need to 'plan out' crime to the greatest possible degree.

All of these policies when included in the planning process should be subject to an appraisal process. Central guidance has been issued on the environmental appraisal of development plans – 'Planning for Sustainable Development: Towards Better Practice' (DETR 1998), and 'Environmental Appraisal of Development Plans: A Good Practice Guide' (DoE 1993). Such an appraisal policy lays particular stress on identifying, quantifying, weighing up and reporting on the environment effects of policies and proposals. From such a process a clear set of environmental criteria should emerge and these should enable choices to be made.

At this point it should be noted that the various processes outlined above are not separate and linear, rather they are cumulative and iterative. There should be a fluid interaction between the formulation of plans and the various processes of appraisal, thus enabling insights from appraisal to be acted on during the stages of plan preparation and approval. PPG12 sums this up by stating: 'The deposited version of the plan should not include the full environmental appraisal within it, but it should be clear from the reasoned justification/explanatory memorandum of the plan what elements of the appraisal have informed the policies and proposals of the plan'. Once, however, a plan is in place appraisal does not cease. Monitoring of the environmental effects of plans in practice is needed to ensure there is critical material to inform the future review and replacement of plans.

It should also be noted that chapter 5 of PPG12 gives further guidance on the need for plans to pay attention to local transport strategies.

Clearly the current revision of PPG12 is a considerable advance on its predecessor with regard to sustainable development as a feature of planning law and practice. The message is clear that while new development is needed and is desirable to a considerable extent this must take place by virtue of the reuse of previously developed land as opposed to greenfield sites. This policy should also help to regenerate and revitalise existing urban areas by restricting 'off-centre' development. Furthermore a less 'car-friendly' future pattern of development seems to be envisaged. Having said all of that, however, the question arises whether all of this is somewhat utopian in nature. There is a very real 'chicken and egg' issue here. It is all very well to argue for reuse of previously developed land for new housing, recreational and employment purposes, but none of that will work unless there is real 'joined-up-thinking' with other policy areas such as the provision of medical, dental and educational facilities. For example people with children are not going to wish to live and work in areas where there are no schools – these days one should say no *good* schools. *Who* is going to provide that facility and *when* – after the houses and work places are built or beforehand – and to what extent should the private sector be involved in such provision?

As we return to rather more obviously 'legal' issues it is important that we should remember the matters considered above. While the law should be the servant of policy, lawyers need to know that the law will not work well where policy is confused or contradictory or is attempting to achieve too many results with insufficient resources.

What is the 'development plan'?

The TCPA 1990, s 54 (as amended) provides that the 'development plan', an entity to which many other provisions of the Act refer, is to be (outside Greater London and the metropolitan areas where, of course, UDPs exist) the provisions of the structure plan for the time being in operation for any area in question, alterations to such a plan, the provisions of the local plan and any MLP and WLP in force, and alterations to such plans.

C GENERAL PLANNING CONTROL

The TCPA 1990, Part III promulgates the meaning of 'development' and the requirement of planning permission. 'Development' is defined by s 55, though many actions are either excluded from the definition, by the TCPA 1990 or orders made under it, or are given automatic planning permission by order.

The definition of development

The general rule is that development is carrying out building, engineering, mining or other operations in, on, over or under land, or making any material change in the use of land or buildings. This has two limbs, 'operational' development, and making material changes of use. With regard to operational acts the courts generally define these as matters resulting in physical alteration to land and having some degree of permanence, see *Parkes v Secretary of State for the Environment*.[11] Courts consider factors such as: the size of the operation, whether it is permanent, whether physically attached to land. These factors are not given equal weight in every case, see *Buckinghamshire County Council v Callingham*,[12] where creating a small model village was held an act of development, and *Barvis Ltd v Secretary of State for the Environment*,[13] where erection of a large tower crane running on rails, but nevertheless capable of being dismantled and moved was held to be development. It is clear that the test has a threefold nature: regard has to be had to size, physical attachment and permanence. Mere temporary dismantling of a structure will not in this context prevent it from being 'permanent'.[14] (Mining developments will be dealt with in chapter 13.) The TCPA 1990, s 55(1A), as inserted in 1991, now further provides that 'building operations' include demolition, rebuilding, structural alterations of or additions to buildings, and other operations normally undertaken by a builder. Demolition may thus (either as a 'building' or an 'engineering' operation) be an act of development requiring permission. However, TCPA 1990, s 55(2)(g), as inserted, provides that the demolition of any *description* of building specified in a direction from the Secretary of State to an authority, or authorities generally, is *not* to be an act of development. See DoE Circular 10/95 which contains the current direction, and which effectively provides that *only* the demolition of dwelling houses (and their adjoining buildings) *outside* conservation areas, and demolition of gates, walls and fences *within* conservation areas is subject to planning control. Development consisting of a 'material change of use' is more difficult to define, and is generally decided as a matter of fact and degree. It is not always necessary for a change to be one of *kind* for it to be 'material'. Indeed changes of degree made by a marked intensification of use can be *sufficient changes of character* to constitute development. This rule applies to both main and ancillary uses of a site, see *Brooks and Burton Ltd v Secretary of State for the Environment*,[15] where production of concrete blocks rose from 300,000 to 1,200,000 per annum. The *practical* problem for planning authorities in such cases lies in detecting changes constituted by intensification, and in determining a point at which a creeping intensification reaches such a point as to be reasonably recognisable as a change of character.

Whether change is 'material' must be assessed by reference to its effect on an appropriate area of land, known as 'the planning unit'. Generally this will be the whole area in a landholder's ownership or occupation, see *Trentham v Gloucestershire County Council*;[16] a question of fact in each case. Following *Burdle v Secretary of State for the Environment*,[17] there are three ways of dealing with the issue: (a) where an occupier has a single main purpose (with or without ancillary uses) the whole of his unit of occupation is the planning unit; (b) if there is a variety of uses, or 'composite use' where activities may vary and fluctuate, the whole unit is the planning unit; and (c) where, however, within a holding physically separate and distinct areas are occupied for different and unrelated purposes, each separate area is the planning unit. The basic test is whether physically *and* functionally there are separate uses. A unit having

11   [1979] 1 All ER 211, [1978] 1 WLR 1308.
12   [1952] 2 QB 515, [1952] 1 All ER 1166.
13   (1971) 22 P & CR 710. Note also *Bedfordshire County Council v Central Electricity Generating Board* [1985] JPL 43.
14   *Skerritts of Nottingham Ltd v Secretary of State for the Environment, Transport and the Regions (No 2)* [2000] 2 PLR 102.
15   [1978] 1 All ER 733, [1977] 1 WLR 1294; note also *Hilliard v Secretary of State for the Environment* (1978) 37 P & CR 129 — intensification of one ancillary use of a farm building did not mean intensification of the use of the whole farm.
16   [1966] 1 All ER 701, [1966] 1 WLR 506.
17   [1972] 3 All ER 240, [1972] 1 WLR 1207.

varying fluctuating uses may experience change without 'development', but particularly marked changes, for example major intensification of individual uses, may amount to material change of use. The main site use will generally carry with it minor and ancillary uses, minor fluctuations do not constitute changes provided they remain merely ancillary.[18] What constitutes a separate planning unit is normally a question of fact and degree. It is the factual position (not the identity of the owner) which is determinative of whether land has discrete uses, even where on a plot in single ownership there are two uses integral to the owner's overall undertaking. Two or more uses of land may be 'distantly related' by being parts of an overall business, but that does not necessarily mean that one is ancillary to the other(s).[19] It is not *just* the effect on the land where a material change of use has occurred that has to be considered. The effects of the change off-site also have to be taken into account.[20]

Under the TCPA 1990, s 55(2)(f) the Use Classes Order 1987 SI 1987/764 (as amended), lays down that where buildings or land are used for a purpose of a specified class, their use for another purpose of that same class is deemed not to be development. Four broad 'bands' of use are identified, each subdivided, so as *to provide eleven classes*.

The basic principle of the Use Classes Order (UCO) is that a change of use of a building or land *within* a class will not be an act of development, while a change of use *across* classes *may* be, provided it is 'material', see *Rann v Secretary of State for the Environment*.[21] Certain uses classified as 'sui generis' are excluded from the operation of the UCO and a change of use to or from such a use will, provided it is material, need planning permission. Such uses include theatres, fun fairs or scrap yards. From a broad environmental point of view the most important classes are: B1, business use, inter alia, for research or development of products and purposes or for any industrial process provided it can be carried out in *any* residential area without detriment to amenity by virtue of dust, grit, soot, smoke, smell, vibration or noise (ie it is irrelevant to argue the area in question is noisy or dirty, etc, see *W T Lamb Properties Ltd v Secretary of State for the Environment*),[22] and B2, general industrial, processes not falling within B1. Particular provisions relating to changes of use between somewhat environmentally unfriendly uses of land previously found in the UCO have now been abandoned, as it is thought the IPPC, IPC and LAAPC systems of control (see chapters 16 and 17) are more apt to regulate them.

It is possible (though central policy as declared in DoE Circular 11/95 is averse to the notion) to restrict these rights by conditions in a grant of planning permission, see *City of London Corpn v Secretary of State for the Environment*.[23]

D THE NEED FOR PLANNING PERMISSION

Under the TCPA 1990, s 57 planning permission is generally required for acts of development. This is subject to exceptions. Lawful use of land under a grant of planning permission or a development order generally requires no further grant of permission, nor does a use continued since and commenced before 1 July 1948.

---

18   *Wood v Secretary of State for the Environment* [1973] 2 All ER 404, [1973] 1 WLR 707.
19   *Essex Water Co v Secretary of State for the Environment* [1989] JPL 914.
20   *Devonshire County Council v Allens Caravans (Estates) Ltd* (1962) 14 P & CR 440; *Blum v Secretary of State for the Environment* [1987] JPL 278; and *Forest of Dean District Council v Secretary of State for the Environment* [1995] JPL B14.
21   [1980] JPL 109.
22   [1983] JPL 303.
23   (1971) 71 LGR 28, 23 P & CR 169.

The Crown requires no permission for its developments,[24] and no enforcement notice can be issued in respect of development carried out by or on behalf of the Crown on Crown land the TCPA 1990, s 294(1). There is a non-statutory consultation procedure under DOE Circular 18/84 whereby central departments and other Crown bodies consult local planning authorities before carrying out development. There is, of course, no need to duplicate consultations that may take place with local authorities under other legislation, for example with regard to trunk roads under the Highways Act 1980. See also DoE Circular 15/92 on publicity for development proposals by the Crown.

Departments will consult local planning authorities on proposed developments likely to be of special concern within a locality, and such consultation will be in good time, though consultation and notification procedures cannot apply in their entirety to developments involving security issues. Local authorities should give adequate publicity to proposed Crown developments generally as if permission were needed. Local authority views on proposed Crown developments should be transmitted to the relevant department, generally within eight weeks of receiving a 'Notice of Proposed Development' which is the formal notice of a firm proposal. These views should be reasoned. A proposal which departs from a development plan may be made subject to a non-statutory public inquiry, with the Secretary of State considering the issue. Strong objections to a development should be notified to relevant departments who may then refer the issue to the Secretary of State for an inquiry and a decision. Where the local planning authority objects to a proposal, and the disagreement cannot be resolved, the Secretary of State will also be involved, and a non-statutory inquiry may have to be held with the Secretary of State making a determination. Security considerations may, however, inhibit the use of procedures laid down in Circular 18/84, in which case the procedures have to be followed only up to the point of inhibition.[25]

The TCPA 1990, s 90 provides a procedure whereby need to apply for planning permission may be obviated. Where central authorisation is statutorily required in respect of development to be carried out by a local authority or statutory undertaker, the relevant department *may*, on granting authorisation, direct planning permission 'deemed to be' granted, subject to such conditions as may be imposed. Development is taken to be authorised where a department consents, authorises or approves a development under statute, or confirms a compulsory purchase order on land for development purposes, or otherwise appropriates land acquired by agreement to the purpose, or gives permission for borrowing money for the purpose, or undertakes to make a statutory grant for the purpose. Statutory undertakers are defined by the TCPA 1990, s 262 as including: railway; road and water transport; docks and harbours undertakings. Likewise where consent is given under s 36 of the Electricity Act 1989 for the construction of an electricity generating station with a capacity of over 50 MG, planning consent may be deemed granted, though where the application for consent is opposed by a local planning authority a public local inquiry must be held. Similar provisions apply under s 37 of the 1989 Act to consents for the installation of above ground power lines, see further chapter 11. In practice this procedure is used only in cases where there may be a serious local environmental impact in respect of developments by the energy undertakings. Normally under the TCPA 1990, s 266 statutory undertakers are expected to apply for planning permission in the usual way, though it may be that where planning permission is refused, or granted subject to unacceptable conditions, any appeal will have to be heard under s 266 by the Secretary of State and 'the appropriate minister' as defined in s 265, for example, in relation to an electricity undertaking, the Trade and

24   *Ministry of Agriculture, Fisheries and Food v Jenkins* [1963] 2 QB 317.
25   *R v Secretary of State for Defence, ex p Camden London Borough Council* [1994] EGCS 33.

Industry Secretary. The TCPA 1990, s 266 applies to the 'operational land' of statutory undertakers, as defined in ss 263 and 264, and land in which the undertakers hold, or propose to acquire, an interest with a view to using it for the purposes of carrying on their undertaking where permission, if granted, would be for development involving use of land for that purpose.

Permitted development (PD)

The Town and Country Planning (General Permitted Development) Order SI 1995/418 (GPDO) (as amended) gives permission for types of development in a number of categories, thus obviating the need for an application for permission. From an environmental point of view the most important of these classes are:

- Part 6, class A — carrying out on agricultural land comprised in an agricultural unit of 5 ha or more in area of works for erecting or extending a building, or excavations or engineering operations requisite for the land's use for agricultural purposes, subject to specified limitations on size, height and position. Note also classes B and C which respectively permit similar developments on agricultural units of between 0.4 and 5 ha in extent, and winning and working minerals on land held with land used for agricultural purposes of minerals for use for those purposes within the agricultural unit in question. (See further chapter 9.)
- Part 7, class A — carrying out, subject to limits, on land used for forestry (including afforestation) of requisite building, and other operations (other than providing dwellings) and laying out private ways. (See further chapter 9.)
- Part 8, class A — extending or altering industrial buildings or warehouses provided this is for the purposes of the undertaking concerned, and the building is not to be used for a purpose other than an industrial process or storage or distribution as the case may be. Height and volume limits must also be complied with. Note also classes B, C, and D which allow replacement or emplacement of plant, services, conveyors, etc, creation of hard standings and certain waste deposits on sites already in use for waste deposition purposes on 1 July 1948.
- Part 11 — development authorised under local or private Acts, or under an order approved by Parliament, or under the Harbours Act 1964, ss 14 and 16, where the nature of the development and the designated land are specified; but where development comprises a building or an access way to a highway or erecting a bridge, aquaduct, pier or dam prior approval of detailed plans and specifications must be obtained from the relevant local planning authority, though they may not withhold approval except where satisfied that either the design of the building etc, would damage amenity and could be suitably modified, or the building ought reasonably to be placed elsewhere on the land.
- Part 12 — works carried out on land by local authorities and consisting of the erection of, inter alia, lamp standards and like amenities. Note also Part 13 allowing highway authorities to undertake certain highway maintenance or improvement works.
- Parts 14, 15, 16, works carried out, inter alia, by drainage bodies, the Environment Agency and sewerage undertakers in respect of certain of their functions.
- Part 17 — development work by Statutory undertakers, for example: development on operational railway land in connection with railway traffic, *other* than the construction of railways or railway station car parks and other specified buildings; certain development by electricity and gas undertakings.
- Part 18 — certain airport developments, see chapter 11.
- Parts 19, 20, 21, 22, 23 — relate to mineral works and developments, see chapter 13.

- Parts 24 and 25 — relate to telecommunications developments, such as emplacement of equipment for the 'mobile phone' industry.

General permission is given for development of the type specified in the GPDO. Hazardous developments are generally controlled for planning purposes by the Planning (Hazardous Substances) Act 1990, see chapter 11 and SI 1995/419 Art 10 (Table) (d).

Under Art 4 of the Order if either the Secretary of State or the local planning authority (*usually* the district or unitary authority council) is satisfied that development of any specified class(es) should not be carried out in a particular area, or that any particular development of any of the classes should not be carried out, unless permission is granted, they may direct accordingly. Where the direction is given by the local authority the Secretary of State's approval is required except in matters of effectively local concern. Such directions can be useful to restrict the activities of persons wishing to avail themselves of the ability to hold temporary markets on open land — so called 'car boot sales'. Where a direction is made it is still possible to apply for permission, and the grant of permission may also expressly exclude PD rights of specified sorts on the land in question.[26]

Simplified planning zones

One other means of obviating the need for planning permission, is the Simplified Planning Zone (SPZ). This follows on from the concept of the Enterprise Zone (EZ) introduced by the Local Government, Planning and Land Act 1980 which utilised a combination of tax advantages and notions of permitted development in an attempt to revive depressed areas. The SPZ was introduced in 1987 by the Housing and Planning Act 1986, see now the TCPA 1990, ss 82–87, as amended, and for further guidance see DoE Circular 25/87 and PPG 5.

Local planning authorities (generally districts) must consider, under TCPA 1990, s 83, for which part of their areas it is desirable to have SPZ and then to keep this matter under review. Before proceeding authorities are *counselled* to consult with owners of land likely to be affected, see PPG5. Where it is *proposed* to make a scheme certain specified bodies and persons *must* be consulted, see SI 1992/2414, reg 3. In an SPZ the designation scheme identifies the land and grants planning permission for development or classes of development specified, subject or not, as the case may be, to conditions or limitations contained in the scheme. The scheme consists of a map and written statement together with appropriate diagrams the TCPA 1990, s 82 and Sch 7 as amended. If it is felt that SPZ designation or alteration at any time is desirable then the local planning authority are to prepare a scheme, TCPA 1990, s 83. They must then inform the Secretary of State, and decide a date on which they will begin to prepare the scheme see TCPA 1990, Sch 7. *Anyone* can ask an authority to make or alter an SPZ scheme, and if they refuse (except where designations or alterations were made within the previous 12 months) or do not decide to act as requested within three months, the individual or organisation involved can refer the matter to the Secretary of State see TCPA 1990, Sch 7. If the matter is referred to the Secretary of State the local authority is notified as soon as practicable and invited to comment on the idea in writing within 28 days. Any representations made to the Secretary of State and not previously sent to the Local Planning Authority are sent to them at this point. The Secretary of State *can* consult with anyone he/she chooses and then make a direction that the authority shall make or alter an SPZ scheme. He/she must notify both the authority and the applicant and give them a statement of reasons for making or refusing to make a direction. This direction can add or exclude any area of land to or from the SPZ, it need not necessarily entirely relate to the land for which the original request was made.

Whether voluntarily or under compulsion the authority are to publicise, in a way prescribed by the Secretary of State, the fact that they are to prepare (or alter) an SPZ scheme, and any representations made in due form must be considered. The Secretary of State must also be consulted with regard to highway implications before the scheme is prepared. In a *non*-metropolitan county where a *district* council decide to make an SPZ scheme, they must consult the county authority before proceeding. Where a scheme has been prepared, or where alterations to a scheme are proposed and prepared, copies of the proposals must be made publicly available and this must be advertised. Objections made in prescribed form will be received, and copies of the scheme, etc, sent to the Secretary of State, and the relevant county council.

If there are objections to a scheme normally an inquiry must be held with an inspector appointed by the Secretary of State, or in prescribed cases by the authority, or some other hearing may be held. After the inquiry or where no objections were received the proposals *may* be revised in the light of objections and the outcome of the inquiry. There is no obligation, however, to modify a proposal. Adoption may then take place, subject to the power of the Secretary of State to direct modifications to the proposal prior to adoption. He/she can also 'call in' an SPZ proposal and determine the form of the SPZ designation. Where this power is used he/she has wide discretionary powers, but must generally consider objections made. He/she may also hold an inquiry or some other form of hearing.

Under the TCPA 1990, s 84 conditions and limitations which may be imposed on planning permissions, and which may be specified in an SPZ scheme may include: conditions or limitations in respect of all or some development permitted by the scheme, and conditions or limitations requiring the consent, approval or agreement of the authority in relation to particular types of development. However, nothing in an SPZ scheme may affect a person's right to do anything that is not 'development' or to carry out development for which permission is not required or for which permission has been granted otherwise than by the scheme. Where a permission containing limitations, etc, has been granted otherwise than under the scheme, those limitations are not to affect a person's right to carry out development for which the scheme gives permission.

Schemes last ten years: see the TCPA 1990, s 85. Schemes can be modified. Modifications providing for withdrawal of permission, or to exclude land from a scheme, or to impose new conditions on development if confirmed, do not come into effect for 12 months: see the TCPA 1990, s 86.

The Secretary of State has power by order to exclude land from, or to modify permission in, an SPZ. Furthermore, land in environmentally sensitive areas such as National Parks, conservation areas, areas of outstanding natural beauty, the Broads, green belt land, or sites of special scientific interest may *not* be included in an SPZ, see the TCPA 1990, s 87. Neither can permission be granted by a scheme for development for which Environmental Impact Assessment is a necessity, see further below. SPZs should *not* be set up in areas containing hazardous installations, explosive facilities and licensed nuclear sites. Central guidance stresses that SPZs will only work properly if their creation is co-ordinated with other powers relating to land assembly and disposal and grant aid and other forms of assistance. An SPZ may be of any size, and should certainly be of significant size. The form of the SPZ may also vary considerably according to the nature and location of the land and its best possible use. Schemes may be either specific, it itemising *a* type of development permitted, or general, giving wide permission for *types* of development subject to specific exceptions which will still require grants of permission in the normal way. It was also initially envisaged that SPZs could be used to provide for the creation of new industrial parks, or the regeneration of older industrial estates, or the bringing back into use of old railway land such as marshalling yards, or even to enable new areas of housing to be built.

SPZs in the view of central government should be flexibly used to cater for the needs of large, old, depressed urban areas, disused sites suitable for new employment, and even green field sites which have been previously targeted for development by a development plan.

SPZs, however, cannot be used to grant permission for mineral and waste disposal developments (see SI 1987/1849). SPZs should also only give permission for aerodromes, caravan sites, casinos, funfairs, scrapyards and slaughterhouses after careful thought, and should not grant permission for any other hazardous development; see PPG5, Annex A.

SPZ schemes should, authorities have been advised, contain only the minimum number of conditions and limitations, and should not be concerned with too much detail, and they should ensure that health and safety are protected, and may need to regulate polluting emissions (except insofar as otherwise legally controlled), use of contaminated or unstable land, vehicular access and highway construction. Height and density controls for buildings may also need specification, as may floor space limited for particular developments and parking standards. Landscaping requirements may also be appropriate. Conditions should, wherever possible, be clearly expressed *in advance* of development so that only rarely should developers need to obtain specific consent to an act.

Sub zones within SPZs may be needed because of local needs — eg to exclude an area from the scheme because it is contaminated land or is to act as a buffer between the SPZ and some environmentally sensitive area, or to restore some normal planning controls, such as those over noise, within a particular part of an area.

Whether SPZs will become enduring features of the planning system is open to doubt. By December 1992 there were only three SPZs in England and a further three in Scotland; since then it appears five SPZs have been created in England, two in Wales and four in Scotland. They might, however, have a part to play in realising the government's sustainable development policy as a means of encouraging the reuse of urban 'brownfield' sites, ie 'previously developed land'. However, where this is also contaminated (see chapter 15) it may be that further 'carrots' in the form of grant aid may be needed to encourage developers to venture their capital.

E APPLYING FOR PLANNING PERMISSION

Applications for planning permission must, under the TCPA 1990, s 62, be in the prescribed manner. Detailed requirements are contained in the Town and Country Planning (General Development Procedure) Order SI 1995/419 (GDPO) and the Town and Country Planning (Applications) Regulations SI 1988/1812, any required details must be supplied, and the land in question must be identified. Applications may be made for outline planning permission. Where such permission is granted subsequent approval by the authority must be obtained for those 'reserved matters' (ie siting, design, external appearance, means of access and landscaping) specified by a condition in the permission. Successive applications, for the same or different development, may be made for a site, though implementing one permission may have the effect of rendering the other incapable of being used.[27] Note, however, the effect of the TCPA 1990, s 70A as inserted by the 1991 Act whereunder a local planning authority *may* decline to

27　*Pilkington v Secretary of State for the Environment* [1974] 1 All ER 283, [1973] 1 WLR 1527.

determine a planning application if in the preceding two years the Secretary of State has refused a similar application referred to him/her under s 77 (see further below) or has dismissed an appeal against the refusal of a similar application *and* the authority consider there has been no significant change since that event in the development plan or in any other material consideration. 'Significant change' is not defined by the legislation, but it would surely include a new plan or a major change in economic or demographic circumstances. 'Similar' is, however, defined by reference to the authority being of the opinion that the application in question must be the same or substantially the same. This will be a question of fact. If the determination is that the application is 'the same', etc, then an authority *may* determine not to determine; but that discretion has to be reasonably exercised and can be challenged by a judicial review application.[28] Applications are made to district councils or unitary authorities where appropriate and London borough councils. A fee is payable according to regulations made under the TCPA 1990, s 303.

[NB By virtue of the TCPA 1990, s 74(1A) and the GDPO, Art 5 applications in respect of 'country matters', effectively waste and minerals applications, are to be made to the relevant county council.]

Publicity requirements

Planning law was not historically generally over-concerned with giving third parties rights at the development control stage.[29] Nevertheless there are now considerably more publicity and notification requirements under the TCPA 1990.

The TCPA 1990, s 65, as substituted, provides that a development order may make provision requiring notice to be given of any application for planning permission, and requiring any applicant for permission to issue a certificate as to the interests in the land to which the application relates or the purpose for which it is used. Provision may also be made for publicising applications, and for 'owners' of affected land, or those who are tenants of agricultural holdings of the land, to be given notice of applications relating to the land in prescribed form. A local planning authority will not be able to entertain an application unless the requirements of the law are complied with. 'Owners' for the purposes of the provision are fee simple estate owners, those with tenancies of which not less than seven years remain unexpired, or, in prescribed cases, those entitled to mineral rights.

Under the GDPO 1995, Art 8 an obligation now lies on the Local Planning Authority to publicise applications. Basically applications are divided into three which may be denominated as: 'very major', 'major' and 'minor'.

'Very major'

Any application which is the subject of an Environmental Impact Assessment (Sch 1 or 2 applications) and is accompanied by an environmental statement (see further below); any application not in accord with provisions of relevant development plans; any application which would affect rights of way subject to Part III Wildlife and Countryside Act 1981. Here there must be a site notice display on or near the relevant land for at least 21 days *and* local advertisement.

---

28 *Noble Organisation Ltd v Falkirk District Council* 1994 SLT 100.
29 *Buxton v Minister of Housing and Local Government* [1961] 1 QB 278, [1960] 3 All ER 408.

'Major'

Mineral working; waste disposition; provision of ten or more dwelling houses; provision of dwelling houses on a site of 0.5 ha or more where it is not known whether ten or more houses are to be built; provision of building(s) with floor space to be created of 1000m² or more; development of a site of 1 ha or more. Here there must be a site notice for not less than 21 days *or* notice must be served on adjoining owners/occupiers, *and* (in either case) local advertisement. Notice served on adjoining owners, etc is appropriate where there are interested parties living in the vicinity of the proposed development and they, and only they, are likely to be interested. In addition to the legislatively specified categories, DoE Circular 15/92 lists the following as also *worthy of consideration* for local newspaper advertisement: those affecting nearby property by noise, smell or vibration; those attracting crowds, traffic and noise into quiet areas; those causing activity and noise during unusual hours; those introducing significant changes to an area; those affecting the setting of ancient monuments; those affecting trees subject to tree preservation orders.

'Minor'

In all other cases the development is classed as 'minor' in which case *either* a site notice display *or* notice to adjoining owners/occupiers is required.

Deciding the application

The basic principle with regard to deciding a planning application is enshrined in the TCPA 1990, s 70(2); 'the authority shall have regard to the provisions of the development plan, so far as material to the application, and to any other material considerations'. A planning application is generally to be decided on the basis of all relevant considerations, even though in any given case some will be more important than others.[30] The weight to be given to each 'material' or relevant consideration is entirely a matter for the decision taker, subject to the overriding requirement that decisions must be taken fairly and reasonably. In particular cases, for instance with regard to green belts, additional tests may apply, see chapter 9, below. To this basic principle has to be added now the requirement of the TCPA 1990, s 54A as introduced in 1991, that 'where in making any determination under the planning Acts, regard is to be had to the development plan, the determination shall be made in accordance with the plans unless material considerations indicate otherwise'. Clearly this section is designed to give plans an enhanced importance. Development, according to PPG12, is a 'plan led process' in that plans provide a no objective basis against which development proposals can be judged, and plans are also *guides* and *incentives* to development, setting out the main considerations on which proposals are judged. While plans are not blueprints, the TCPA 1990, s 54A provides that development control decisions should accord with the development plan unless material considerations otherwise indicate, and common sense combined with the case law indicates that:
1   Where a proposed development accords with the plan the presumption is in favour of permission, though there may be isolated instances where other considerations indicate otherwise.

30   *London Residuary Body v Lambeth London Borough Council* [1990] 2 All ER 309, [1990] 1 WLR 744.

2   Where development clearly is in major conflict with the plan the presumption is against permission being given save where the 'march of time' has overtaken the plan or some other convincing reason can be put forward for allowing the development.

3   The plan obviously governs cases where there are *no* other material considerations and there is relevant material in the plan.

4   What of cases where there is no clear conflict, however, between the plan and the proposal, or there is only minor conflict, or the plan is silent? The decision is to be made on the basis of all relevant considerations, but *there is a presumption in favour of development*. The problem then is to distinguish major and minor conflicts.

Perhaps what is needed here is to disaggregate situations (a) where the plan is silent where the 'all relevant considerations test' applies including a presumption in favour of development; and (b) where there is, however, no clear or only minor conflict. Here the presumption in favour of the plan is only a starting point and the presumption may be quite easily rebutted.[31] A similar position may be taken in relation to cases where there are conflicting policies in a plan.[32]

To sum up: in deciding a planning application the decision taker (usually, of course, the authority, but on appeal, for example, the Secretary of State) must first take into account *all* 'material' considerations including the question of whether a development will cause demonstrable harm to interests of acknowledged importance, but, secondly, should then decide the issue in accordance with the plan save where 'material' issues indicate otherwise. See further PPG1 (1997) para 40. Where there are other material considerations the development plan should be taken as a starting point, and the other material considerations should be weighed in reaching a decision.[33] Where, however, a decision taker departs from relevant plans and policies in reaching a decision, clear and soundly reasoned arguments for that decision must be given.[34] The decision maker's duty is thus to give priority to the development plan's provisions, and where a development does not accord with them, *or* some of them, to weigh against them material considerations in favour of granting permission. Where plan provisions have been superseded by subsequent government guidance, or overtaken by other factual events they will have less weight than if they were newly or recently approved. Thus, while there is a presumption in favour of the plan, in any given case the weight to accord to the plan is a matter for the decision takers.[35] The plan *has to be considered* wherever relevant,[36] and some clear indication has to be given in decisions that the implications of the TCPA 1990, s 54A have been taken into account, eg by a statement as to whether a proposal is or is not in accordance with the plan.[37] There is no similar presumption in favour of a plan which is only in course of preparation, though it is a material consideration.[38] Clearly it is also therefore necessary to identify what the other material considerations may be.

31   *St Albans District Council v Secretary of State* [1993] JPL 374; *Sainsbury plc v Secretary of State* [1993] JPL 651; *Gateshead Borough Council v Secretary of State* [1994] JPL 55; *Bylander Waddell Partnership v Secretary of State* [1994] JPL 440.

32   *Delaney v Secretary of State for the Environment* [2000] PLCR 40.

33   *Loup v Secretary of State for the Environment and Salisbury District Council* [1996] JPL 22.

34   *EC Gransden & Co Ltd v Secretary of State for the Environment* [1986] JPL 519.

35   *City of Edinburgh v Secretary of State for Scotland* (1997) 3 PLR 71 and *R v Leominster District Council, ex p Pothecary* [1998] JPL 335.

36   *R v Canterbury City Council, ex p Springimage Ltd* [1994] JPL 427.

37   *Jones v Secretary of State* [1998] 1 PLR 33.

38   *Nottinghamshire County Council and Broxtowe Borough Council v Secretary of State for the Environment, Transport and the Regions* [1999] EGCS 35.

For many years the courts appeared to engage in a process of 'listing' — 'this is relevant, that is not'. Thus the following are 'relevant': development plans; consultations with affected parties (see further below); planning circulars and other publicly available ministerial guidance and policy statements, though when given in the form of after dinner speeches this is open to some doubt.[39] Previous appeal decisions on matters closely related to the matter in hand are also 'material'[40], as is the general planning history of the site in question.[41] Clearly the physical site specific factors applying to the land in question are relevant considerations and financial considerations may be[42] (for a further exhaustive analysis of this particular issue see Purdue, Young and Rowan Robinson, *Planning Law and Procedure* pp 213–217). Other relevant considerations appear to be: amenity (a vague term but one which relates to the appearance and layout of land so as to make for a pleasant way of life); the compatibility of the proposed development with other land uses in the vicinity; safety issues, though here planning authorities must be somewhat wary of trespassing too far on the territory of other regulatory authorities and of seeking objectives attainable under other legislation; the existing use of the land and its planning history;[43] need for the development; the existence of an alternative site for the development; safeguarding land for other public developments;[44] protecting archaeological sites;[45] preventing flood risks;[46] the likelihood that a development will eventuate; [47] preventing noise nuisances to neighbours[48] On the other hand the following appear to be irrelevant considerations: rigid 'fetters on discretion', whereunder an authority binds itself never to allow, for example, some particular sort of development, though a 'normal policy' which may be subject to exceptions in a proper case is allowable, as is a party political leaning in favour of a particular type of development.[49] Similarly the issue of whether a development is economically worthwhile has been held irrelevant,[50] as are attempts to protect an authority's own use of a piece of land by means of refusing permission for development,[51] and refusals based on the absence of public gain in a proposed development,[52] or purely moral obligations to a development.[53] Consideration of the cost to an authority of otherwise modifying or revoking a grant of permission have been said to be 'irrelevant' or 'immaterial' as has the taking into account of a mere

---

39   *Sears Blok v Secretary of State* [1987] JPL 844; *Dimsdale Developments Ltd v Secretary of State for the Environment* [1986] JPL 276; *Kent County Council v Secretary of State for the Environment* (1976) 75 LGR 452, and *R v Wakefield Metropolitan District Council, ex p Pearl Assurance plc* [1997] JPL B 131.

40   *North Wiltshire District Council v Secretary of State for the Environment* (1992) 65 P & CR 137; *R v Secretary of State for the Environment, ex p David Baber* [1996] JPL 1034; *Beaulieu Property Management v Secretary of State for the Environment* [1997] EGCS 129.

41   *Postwood Developments Ltd v Secretary of State for the Environment* [1992] JPL 823; *Haven Leisure Ltd v Secretary of State for the Environment* [1994] JPL 148.

42   *R v Westminster City Council, ex p Monahan,* [1989] 2 All ER 74.

43   *RMC Management Services Ltd v Secretary of State for the Environment* (1972) 222 Estates Gazette 1593.

44   *Westminster Bank Ltd v Minister of Housing and Local Government* [1971] AC 508.

45   *Hoveringham Gravels Ltd v Secretary of State for the Environment* [1975] QB 754.

46   *Wimpey & Co Ltd v Secretary of State for the Environment* [1978] JPL 773.

47   *Sovmots Investments Ltd v Secretary of State for the Environment* [1979] AC 144.

48   *Ladbroke (Rentals) Ltd v Secretary of State for the Environment* [1981] JPL 427.

49   *Stringer v Minister of Housing and Local Government* [1971] 1 All ER 65, [1970] 1 WLR 1281; *R v Exeter City Council, ex p Thomas & Co Ltd* [1991] 1 QB 471; *R v Amber Valley District Council, ex p Jackson* [1984] 3 All ER 501.

50   *Walters v Secretary of State for Wales* [1979] JPL 171.

51   *Westminster City Council v British Waterways Board* [1985] AC 676, [1984] 3 All ER 737.

52   *Westminster Renslade Ltd v Secretary of State for the Environment* [1983] JPL 454.

53   *Finlay v Secretary of State for the Environment* [1983] JPL 802; *Ladbroke (Rentals) Ltd v Secretary of State for the Environment* [1981] JPL 427.

desire to render lawful an otherwise unlawful development where that was the sole or prime motivation of the decision as opposed to the merits of the situation.[54]

More recently an attempt to formulate a principle whereby relevance and irrelevance can be identified has been made. In *Bolton Metropolitan Borough Council v Secretary of State for the Environment*[55] Glidewell LJ pointed out some matters have to be taken into account because statute says so. However, those are not necessarily the only matters that are 'relevant', because: 'the decision maker ought to take into account a matter which might cause him to reach a different conclusion to that which he would reach if he had not taken it into account ... By the verb "might" [is] meant where there was a real possibility that he would reach a different conclusion if he had taken that consideration into account'. This excluded matters of 'trivial or small importance'.

Some matters to be taken into account are implied from the nature of the decision and of the matter in question, and in situations of this sort 'it is for the judge to decide whether it was a matter which the decision maker should have taken into account'. Here, however, the views of Cook J in *CREEDNZ Inc v Governor-General*[56] can be prayed in aid: 'it is safe to say that the more general and the more obviously important the consideration, the readier the Court must be to hold that Parliament must have meant it to be taken into account'. Further general guidance on 'material' or relevant considerations is given in PPG 1 chapter 4, particularly paras 46 et seq.

Where a judge concludes a matter is fundamental, or that it was an issue consideration of which would have made a difference to the outcome, non-consideration enables the judge to conclude the decision was invalidly made. Where a judge, however, is uncertain whether the matter would have had this effect or would have had such importance for the decision making process, he/she does not have the material necessary to conclude the decision was invalid.

Even where a decision is invalid there remains a residual discretion in the judge to refuse the reward of relief — eg in cases of no substantial prejudice to the applicant.

It may be argued on the basis of the foregoing that the following continue to be relevant considerations: representations received in respect of planning applications publicised; the effect on the land of the financial consequences of granting or not granting permission;[57] the financial implications for an area of allowing a new development elsewhere; the need to avoid creating an undesirable precedent for future development.[58] Though as stated earlier planning authorities must be wary of trespassing too far on the powers of other regulatory bodies, the desirability of 'keying in' planning controls to other forms of regulation is a relevant consideration,[59] and so are issues relating to noise, dust, smell, grit, etc, likely to emanate from a development. There is little judicial guidance as to how far an authority may go in using planning powers to control matters that could be controlled under other environmental legislation. Ministerial appeals are a little more helpful; in the *Ferro Alloys and Metals, Smelter, Glossop* decision[60] the minister indicated planning controls could be used to supplement controls under air pollution controls in that the former provided reasonably easily enforced long-term protection. It was accepted in Cm 1200 at para 6.39 that potential

---

54 *Alnwick District Council v Secretary of State for the Environment, Transport and the Regions* [1999] JPL B 190, and *R v Essex County Council, ex p Tarmac Roadstone Holdings Ltd* [1998] JPL B 23.
55 [1991] JPL 241.
56 [1981] 1 NZLR 172.
57 *Sovmots Investments Ltd v Secretary of State for the Environment* [1979] AC 144; *Sosmo Trust Ltd v Secretary of State for the Environment* [1983] JPL 806.
58 *Collis Radio Ltd v Secretary of State for the Environment* (1975) 73 LGR 211.
59 *Esdell Caravan Parks Ltd v Hemel Hempstead Rural District Council* [1966] 1 QB 895.
60 [1990] 1 LMELR 175.

pollution dangers constitute a 'relevant consideration' and that planning permission should not be given if the result is to expose people to danger. Certainly it appears that the fears of local residents about, for example, noise pollution or other forms of nuisance or annoyance can be taken into account by decision takers, though the weight given to such fears will vary according to how justified those fears are.[61] On the specific issue of the relationship between IPC and planning controls, see also chapter 16 and p 222 below. But note that an *inflexible* adherence to the principle of furthering another body's pollution control policies is an unlawful fetter on discretion.[62]

In some circumstances the planning authority must consult with other bodies before coming to a decision. Districts must consult with counties under the terms of the TCPA 1990, Sch 1, which provides for consultation: where a proposal is made which materially conflicts with or would prejudice the policies and proposals of a structure plan or its proposed replacement; where a proposal, by reason of scale or nature, would be of major importance for the implementation of a structure plan; where the proposed development is situated in an area stated in writing by the county to the district as one where development is likely to affect or be affected by mineral working (other than coal), or where (in England) it is notified by the county that they have proposed use of the relevant land for waste disposal; where the land has been stated in writing by the county as subject to their proposed development, or where the application development would prejudice their development, or a proposed use of the land for waste disposal, and so notified to the district.

In these cases the district may not determine the application until it has received and taken into account county representations, or has been notified that the county has none to make. Districts being under a duty to seek to achieve the general objectives of the structure plan also safeguards county interests to some extent.

The GDPO 1995 imposes requirements to consult, inter alia, with other planning authorities where it appears a development will affect land in their areas; with the Secretary of State where it appears a development will increase traffic on a trunk road; with the Coal Authority where a building or pipeline is to be erected in a notified area of coal working; with the Agency where, inter alia, the development consists of storage of mineral oils and derivatives, or use of the land for waste, refuse, sewage or sludge disposal; with nature conservation authorities in areas of special interest under the Wildlife and Countryside Act 1981, Sch 17, Part I and s 28; with DEFRA in respect of developments of agricultural land for non-agricultural purposes and not in accordance with a development plan involving the loss of specified amounts of land, and with the Health and Safety Executive where it appears the development will involve the manufacture or use, etc, of notifiable quantities of hazardous substances. With regard to installations handling hazardous substances, the Health and Safety Executive will inform local planning authorities of instances notified to them, see further chapter 11. Note further the consultation paper 'Policy and Practice for Groundwater' (November 1991, issued by the former National Rivers Authority) in which it is made clear that in consultations they would resist development proposals, including highways, railways, mines and boreholes, that could adversely affect groundwater; the Agency is likely to maintain this stance, see further chapter 20 below. In November 1991 it was reported that planning consent for a £20m toxic waste incinerator near Doncaster had been refused by the Secretary of State because the underlying aquifer had no impermeable clay shield.

---

61   *West Midlands Probation Committee v Secretary of State for the Environment* [1998] JPL 388; *R v Broadland and District Council St Matthew Society Ltd and Peddars Way Housing Association, ex p Dove, Harpley and Wright* [1998] JPL B84.

62   *Ynys Mon Borough Council v Secretary of State for Wales* [1993] JPL 225.

Discretionary consultation may also take place with bodies and individuals likely to be affected by a proposed development; see further DoE Circular 9/95. Views received are relevant in deciding applications. In *R v Sheffield City Council, ex p Mansfield*[63] it was held that a planning authority has wide discretion as to whom to consult; ratepayers and local residents have no right to be consulted as such. It may be *wise* to consult organised bodies where these can be identified but there is no *obligation* to do so.

The growth of third party rights

As stated earlier planning law has not been historically particularly concerned with granting rights generally to third parties. This may be changing for a variety of reasons, partly because of greater use of judicial review as a remedy in planning disputes and partly as a result of EC intervention.

The obligation to act fairly

The courts require authorities to conduct their planning functions fairly, and not to mislead applicants for permission or objectors to proposed developments by conduct or representations, or failing to give proper notice of the likely outcome of deliberations; though it is for those who challenge decisions to prove that they have been prejudiced, and that had they been given a chance to state their arguments this would have affected the outcome.

In *R v Great Yarmouth Borough Council, ex p Botton Bros Arcades Ltd*[64] an authority had a non-statutory plan identifying the need for commercial entertainment development on their sea front, though general policy was not to give permission for new amusement arcades. A developer wished to convert a hotel into an amusement arcade. At first the authority did not wish to grant permission, but after further consideration, including giving the developer's architect a hearing, the planning committee decided in favour of the application. During the course of the deliberations Botton Bros learned of the application. They did not initially object because they knew of the policy bias against permission for new arcades. On hearing rumours that permission was to be granted, they asked for the decision to be deferred so they could enter an objection. The local authority refused to defer and granted permission. Botton Bros applied for judicial review of the grant.

Otton J pointed out that there was no *duty* to give Botton Bros notice of any sort, nor did they have a right to be heard before the planning application was decided. Furthermore they had no 'legitimate expectation' of consultation in that they had no enforceable right that would be affected by the planning decision, nor could they show that such an expectation had arisen from past practice or undertakings that their views would be taken into account. However, the council was under a duty to act fairly in administering the planning system. What is 'fair' is a question of fact in each case, and on the facts of this case that duty had been broken. However, there is no general rule that potential objectors must be provided with an opportunity to object on every occasion when an application falls to be decided, or even when a decision in favour of an application will depart from normal policy. The *sort* of facts that might lead a judge to find a 'breach of fairness' in any given case are:

---

63   (1978) 37 P & CR 1.
64   [1988] JPL 18.

1   Where the authority misleads objectors as to its intentions.
2   Where special treatment is given to an applicant while potential objectors are not even informed of the application.
3   Where the authority knows leading objectors would wish to press their case at any appeal, and they fail to inform them of an appeal.[65]

The courts seem to prefer basing third party rights on a general duty of authorities to act 'fairly', rather than on the basis that any given third party has a legitimate expectation that an authority will act in a particular way, and some sort of statement or action relevant to the matter in hand on the part of the authority seems requisite, though mere past practice is not enough.[66] The notion of 'legitimate expectation', was, however, taken up in *R v Swale Borough Council, ex p Royal Society for the Protection of Birds*[67] where Simon Brown J concluded that assurances that consultation would take place before development was permitted gave rise to a legitimate expectation on the part of the would be consultee and gave it locus standi to make a challenge. No one should, however, underestimate the problems faced by third party objectors to planning applications. These include:

•   'Inequality of arms' – a major developer will be able to employ high quality planning, legal and public relations advice whose cost may be well beyond the means of private individuals;
•   lack of expertise coupled with the fact that objecting is a part time concern, not a full time job;
•   the fact that an unsuccessful developer can appeal to the Secretary of State while an unsuccessful objector cannot;
•   a determined developer may 'return to the fray' with a revised proposal after failing to gain permission, perhaps hoping that persistence will wear down opposition;
•   fear of being made liable in costs following the outcome of an appeal *may* persuade some authorities to grant permission;
•   the fact that a planning proposal once it comes to light may be highly developed and may well have been the subject of informal negotiations between the developer and the authority, while objectors will then have little time to marshal their case;
•   where a major development proposal straddles district boundaries there are problems of dealing with more than one authority.

On the other hand objectors sometimes unjustifiably seem to argue that the very fact of objection should be enough to ensure refusal of an application, while many are unaware of the duty of planning authorities to take into account all material considerations which, of course, do include public fears and concerns.

F ENVIRONMENTAL IMPACT ASSESSMENT

The introduction of Environmental Assessment (EA) *now* Environmental Impact Assessment (EIA) also gave cause to believe that planning law was broadening out to encompass a wider range of issues and interests. The product of the first major incursion of EC law into the planning system in pursuance of Directive 85/377 EEC which came into effect in July 1988, the basic principle was and is that techniques are needed to ensure that a development's likely effects on the environment will be taken into

---

65   Note also *R v Torfaen Borough Council, ex p Jones* [1986] JPL 686; and *Wilson v Secretary of State for the Environment* [1988] JPL 540.
66   *R v Secretary of State for the Environment, ex p Barratt (Guildford) Ltd* (1989) Times, 3 April.
67   [1991] JPL 39.

consideration before the development is authorised to proceed. These techniques are applicable to projects other than those needing planning permission, and there are parallel regulations applying to them.

The EC's objective in adopting EA was to prevent pollution at source by requiring environmental information to be considered as part of project authorisation procedures. The preferred method of implementing the EC requirement in the UK has been to incorporate assessment requirements almost entirely into existing planning procedures, and by ensuring that where there is a dispute as to the need for assessment there is a right of appeal for the developer to the Secretary of State and tight timetabling of questions about the need for assessment. Both EA and EIA go beyond simple land use considerations. They do this by requiring information about environmental effects to be provided by the developer for the deciding agency to consider in the decision making process, and further gives bodies with relevant environmental responsibilities an opportunity to comment before consent is given. Certain information has to be given to the public.

The development of an idea

The EC derived the notion of EA from the US National Environmental Policy Act 1969, though EC and US requirements are very different, as the US requirements applied to Federal Agency activities, while EC requirements apply to a wider range of developments. Though first proposed in the EC's Second Action Programme on the Environment in 1977, a formal proposal was not made by the Commission until 1980, and five years of debate ensued until 85/337 appeared. In the course of debate the proposal was much modified, largely because of British objections. Annex I was reduced in scope, and the information to be supplied by the developer is only such as the member state concerned considers relevant. The UK government's initial attitude was that EA should not generally add significantly to existing procedures and should be implemented wherever possible within existing legal procedures without undue recourse to extra subordinate legislation. In 1986 a Consultation Paper was issued by the DoE. This led to the first batch of regulations in the summer of 1988 to begin implementation of the Community obligation. Initially the government proposed that EA for Annex II projects should be at the discretion of the Secretary of State. This in the view of the Commission was less than the Directive required. Taken as a whole the Directive requires EA in relation to Annex II projects likely to have significant environmental effects by virtue, inter alia, of size, location, nature etc; discretion is therefore limited to deciding whether a particular project's characteristics are such that they are/are not likely to be 'significant'. DoE Circular 15/88 indicated the central view that EA would apply to the second class of projects where they were major and of more than local importance, or irrespective of size, where they affected particularly sensitive or vulnerable locations, or where they would have unusually complex and potentially adverse environmental consequences making it desirable that a detailed, expert analysis of those consequences should take place, provided that examination was relevant to the issue of deciding whether or not a development should be permitted.

The introduction of this assessment procedure had importance in the UK because of the *range* of issues to be considered in the development process. Issues of pollution control became, in relation to certain developments, relevant considerations, and planning authorities ceased to be limited to taking into account only land use considerations.

Directive 85/337/EEC was amended by Directive 97/11/EC, and the former EA regulations were superseded by the Town and Country Planning (Environmental Impact

Assessment) (England and Wales) Regulations SI 1999/293, which came into effect on 14 March 1999. See also DETR Circular 02/99.

Scope, application and form of EIA

EIA gives a chance to authorities giving 'primary consents' to adopt or modify a scheme to mitigate adverse environmental consequences, and for taking the environmental dimension into account in project decisions. This is not to say that environmental considerations will override all others, but they will have to be considered. EIA is, furthermore, *not a document but a process*, indeed it is the whole process needed to reach decision on a relevant application, involving the collection of information, the consideration thereof and the final decision.

In cases falling under Annex I of the directive EIA is *mandatory* ie crude oil refineries, large thermal power stations (300 mgwatt+) and nuclear stations; installations for reprocessing irradiated nuclear fuels, or for the production or enrichment of such fuels, radioactive waste reprocessing storage/disposal facilities; integrated plant for initial smelting of iron and steel; asbestos extraction and procession installations; installations for non-ferrous crude metal production; integrated chemical installations; construction of motorways and other new and express roads, long distance railway and airport construction where the basic runway length is 2100 m or more; trading ports and inland waterways; hazardous waste treatment, incineration or landfill installations; explosives production plants; groundwater abstraction schemes where the annual volume is equal to or more than 10 million cubic metres; waste water treatment plants with a capacity exceeding 150,000 population equivalent (see Directive 91/271/EEC); plant for transferring water between river basins; extraction of petroleum or natural gas, dams and pipelines more than 40 km long, intensive pig/poultry rearing plant for 85,000+ hens or 3,000+ production pigs or 900 sows; industrial timber pulp plants; quarries over 25 ha. There will only be a few of these each year.

In other cases, EIA will take place if the project will have 'significant' effects on the environment by virtue of size, nature, location or the 'sensitive' nature of the area for which it is proposed. In all cases falling under Annex II a determination has to be made whether the project will have a 'significant' environmental impact. If 'yes' then EIA *must* take place. NB it is *not* the size of the project that determines the issue, but its overall 'significance'. For this purpose SI 1999/293 Sch 2 lays down that a decision on 'significance' has to be taken where a development listed in the regulations, Sch 2 (a) meets one of the listed relevant criteria, *or* exceeds one of the listed relevant thresholds, *or* (b) is located in a 'sensitive area'. It is impossible within a work of this size to give the full list of developments but below are representative examples:

- use of uncultivated land for intensive agriculture where the area is more than 0.5 ha;
- water management projects for agriculture exceeding 1 ha;
- intensive fish farming which will give rise to more than 10 tonnes deadweight of fish pa;
- reclaiming land from the sea;
- quarries, open cast mining and peat extraction and underground mining;
- deep drilling for water supplies where the area of works exceeds 1 ha;
- surface industrial installations for extracting, inter alia, petroleum or natural gas where the development exceeds 0.5 ha;
- industrial installations for carrying gas, steam or hot water where the area of development exceeds 1 ha;
- installations for producing electricity not falling within SI 1999/293, Sch 1 where the size of the development exceeds 0.5 ha;

- wind farms involving more than 1 turbine *or* where the height of a turbine exceeds 15 metres;
- motor car plants, shipyards, aircraft construction facilities, railway equipment production facilities where the new floor space area exceeds 1000 square metres;
- coke ovens, cement manufacture installations, glass and glass fibre production installations, ceramic product installations where the area of new floor space exceeds 1000 square metres;
- facilities for producing pesticides and pharmaceutical products, paints and varnishes where the area of new floor space exceeds 1000 square metres;
- facilities for manufacturing vegetable and animal oils and fats and canning meat and vegetable products where the area of new floor space exceeds 1000 square metres;
- dairy product plants where the new floor space area exceeds 1000 square metres;
- paper and board making plants where the new floor areas exceeds 1000 square metres;
- shopping centres where the area is more than 0.5 ha;
- road, railway and airfield construction falling outside SI 1999/293, Sch 1 where the area exceeds 1 ha;
- coastal works to combat erosion;
- motorway service areas exceeding 0.5 ha;
- motor race and testing tracks exceeding 1 ha;
- golf courses, camp sites and caravan sites exceeding 1 ha;
- holiday villages and theme parks exceeding 0.5 ha.

NB Where a listed Sch 2 development is sited in whole or in part in a 'sensitive area' the size thresholds do not apply.

'Sensitive Areas' *include* SSSIs, National Parks, AONB, The Broads, 'European Sites' within SI 1994/2716 and World Heritage sites.

Thus a *very* simplified 'flow chart' is:

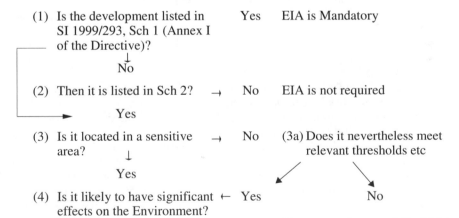

(1) Is the development listed in   Yes   EIA is Mandatory
    SI 1999/293, Sch 1 (Annex I
    of the Directive)?
                  ↓
                  No

(2) Then it is listed in Sch 2?   →   No   EIA is not required
                  Yes

(3) Is it located in a sensitive   →   No   (3a) Does it nevertheless meet
    area?   ↓   relevant thresholds etc
              Yes

(4) Is it likely to have significant ← Yes   No
    effects on the Environment?
                  ↓   The matter does not fall within
              Yes   Sch 2

The determination must be made
publicly available and EIA will
apply [Even if 'No' – the
determination and the supporting
reasons must still be publicly be
registered].

In determining whether a project will have 'significant' effects, regard must be had to the criteria contained in SI 1999/293 Sch 3. In general these relate to a project's size, its cumulative effect taken along with other developments, its use of natural resources and waste production capacity, nuisances and pollution which may arise from the development and the risk of accidents. More particularly regard has to be had to location, in terms of existing land uses, the relative abundance, quality and regenerative capacity of natural resources in the area, the absorption capacity of the natural environment (paying particular regard here to wetlands, coastal zones, mountains, forests, nature reserves and parks and areas classified and protected under the conservation provisions of Directives 79/409/EEC and 92/43/EEC, areas where EC environmental quality standards have already been exceeded, densely populated areas and landscapes of historical, cultural or archaeological significance). The characteristics of the potential impact have to be considered with regard to the matters outlined above, but also by having particular regard to the extent of the impact, in terms of its geographical size and the number of people affected, any transfrontier impacts, the magnitude and complexity of the impact and its probability, and the duration, frequency and reversibility of the impact. Thus the principal issues to be considered are the development's characteristics, the location's environmental sensitivity and the potential impact's characteristics. Circular 02/99 argued that in general EIA in SI 1999/293, Sch 2 situations will normally be confined to: major developments of more than local significance; developments proposed in locations of particular environmental sensitivity or vulnerability, and those with unusually complex and potentially hazardous effects.

Circular 02/99 gives further guidance on these proposals *likely* to be considered 'significant' as follows:

- development of uncultivated or semi-natural land for intensive agricultural purposes eg greenhouses – likely where the land area is 5 ha+;
- development for water management for agriculture – again where the area is 5 ha+;
- intensive livestock installations – there the numbers are 750 sows/2000 fattening pigs/60,000 broiler chickens/50,000 laying chickens;
- intensive fish farming – ie that is likely to produce more than 100 tonnes dead weight of fish pa;
- land reclamation from the sea – where site is 1 ha+;
- mineral working – ie where the site is 15ha+, or where production is 30,000 tonnes or more pa;
- dredging minerals – ie where production is 100,000 tonnes or more pa;
- deep drilling – ie where the site is 5 ha+;
- surface installations for extracting petroleum – ie where the site is 10 ha+ or where production is 100,000 tonnes or more pa;
- power stations – ie where power output is 50MW+;
- surface stores of fuel – ie where the capacity is 100,000 tonnes+;
- radioactive waste storage/processing – normally required for all new sites;
- hydro electricity production – ie where the capacity is 5MW+, and similarly for wind farms;
- industrial sites – likely where a scheduled process is utilised, and/or where Environment Agency consent is needed for discharges to water, and/or the process would give rise to presence of significant quantities of hazardous substances and/or process would give rise to radioactive waste;
- industrial estates – likely if the site is 20 ha+;
- urban projects (eg shopping centres) likely on new sites of 5 ha+, or where 10,000 m^2 floorspace is to be provided, or where the development would have a major urbanising effect;
- inter-modal transhipment facilities – likely where development is 5 ha+, and similarly where new motorway service areas are proposed;

- transport works – likely where construction is for a facility over 2 km in length and similarly new canals;
- flood relief works – likely where the site is 5 ha+;
- airfields – likely for all new airfields;
- harbours and ports – likely if site is 10 ha+;
- dams – likely on sites of 20 ha+;
- pipelines – likely if length is 5 km+;
- coastal works – likely on sites of 1 ha+;
- groundwater abstraction – likely on sites of 1 ha+;
- ski runs and lifts etc – likely if the length is 500 m+;
- marinas – likely if for more than 300 berths;
- holiday villages – likely if for more than 300 bed spaces;
- golf course – likely for 18 hole courses;
- race tracks – likely on sites of 20 ha+;
- non hazardous waste disposal sites – likely on sites of 10 ha+ or where the capacity is 50,000 tonnes or more pa;
- sludge lagoons – likely on sites to hold 5,000m³;
- scrapyards – likely on sites of 10 ha+;
- waste water treatment plants – likely on sites of 10 ha+.

But remember in *all* cases the local planning authority must consider:
- the *characteristics* of a development;
- the *location*;
- the *characteristics of impact*.

Additional factors relevant in particular situations may include local biodiversity action plans, air quality management areas and the presence of designated bathing waters.

What is subject to EIA is the actual project proposed, but where a project is clearly part of a greater whole that may be an indication that its effects would be 'significant' and the need for EIA of the whole development should then be considered: *R v Swale Borough Council, ex p RSPB*.[68] Such an approach is in line with the opinion of the Advocate-General of the ECJ in *Bund Naturschutz in Bayern v Freistaat Bayern*.[69] See also Circular 02/99, para 46 giving guidance on consideration of more than one application in order to determine whether EIA is required. Further case law on the concept of 'project' will be considered below under the heading 'EIA in Court'.

The problem of permitted development rights

The General Permitted Development Order, as amended, provides that any development falling within the EIA regulations, Sch 1 cannot be permitted development. Where development falls within Sch 2 it will not generally be permitted development unless the local authority has adopted a screening opinion (see below) that the development is not EIA development, or the Secretary of State has otherwise acted to exempt the development. Thus where an authority determines EIA is required there will have to be a 'normal' planning application with an accompanying environmental statement.

The decision on whether EIA is required

It will be clear from what has been considered above that in some cases it will not be initially clear whether a project will be one requiring EIA.

68 [1991] JPL 39.
69 Case C-396/92 [1994] ECR1-3717.

Determination of this issue may take place as follows.

- The developer decides EIA is needed and submits the Environmental Statement (ES) which begins the process with the application. If it is not made clear that information submitted is an ES and the authority consider the development is *not* one subject to EIA, no assessment will be needed, though the information given may still be a 'material consideration'. Developers may, however, submit a document containing the information needed but may not formally entitle the document an ES. In such a case the authority must still determine whether EIA is required, and if the determination is positive then the document submitted may be treated as an ES.
- The developer asks (under the 1999 Regulations, reg 5) for a 'screening opinion' before applying. Such a request has to be accompanied by a plan identifying the land and a brief description of the nature and purpose of the development and its possible environmental effects, together with any other information or representations the developer wishes to make. If the information supplied is not sufficient to enable the authority to come to an opinion, they may ask for further information. In general, however, screening opinions have to be adopted by authorities within three weeks of being requested, though a longer time scale may be agreed. Full reasons for the conclusions reached by the authority have to be given clearly and precisely in writing: this is also a requirement with regard to screening directions made by the Secretary of State (see below). If the developer disputes the need for EIA, an application can be made to the SoS for a 'screening direction' on the issue, see SI 1999/293 Reg 7.
- An authority may decide EIA is needed if an application is received without an ES; then the authority must proceed *as if* they had been requested to give a screening opinion. If they determine EIA applies the developer must then provide the ES within three weeks, or apply to the Secretary of State for a direction on the issue and if a positive direction is given the application cannot proceed without the statement.
- The Secretary of State may decide that EIA is needed on an application which is before him for decision – eg on an appeal, or where an application has been called in. In such cases the Secretary of State will request an ES from the developer. Failure to supply this will result in the matter being lost as the Secretary of State's jurisdiction in such circumstances is limited to refusal.
- The SoS may direct that EIA is required at *any stage* before consent is given by means of a screening direction even where one has not been requested, for example on an appealed decision or a 'called in' one.

It is always helpful if developers consult the authority informally about EIA at the earliest possible stage. The authority will make its screening decision on the basis of the factors outlined above concerning 'significance'. If a screening opinion is given that EIA is required then that determines the matter unless the Secretary of State intervenes and overrides the decision.

Where an authority deals with an application where EIA is clearly mandatory, but no such process takes place, they are behaving in an ultra vives fashion. There may, of course, be cases where it is unclear whether the project is one requiring mandatory EIA. The approach of UK courts has been to argue that where there is uncertainty the issue is a question of fact for the decision taking authority which should only be upset if it was clearly unreasonable.[70] The attitude of the ECJ, however, is to be highly critical of national rules which enable projects to slip out of regulation in this way,[71] and certainly to require that no relevant development within SI 1999/293, Sch 2 which will have a significant effect should be enabled to evade assessment.[72] Certainly our own courts have been unwilling to allow a decision on whether a development falling within Sch 2 needs EIA to be made by Authority Officers acting without formally delegated powers to take such decisions.[73] However, the overall stance of UK courts has been somewhat restrictive with regard to the doctrines of EC law, and thus, *in general* the UK has been considered to have implemented its obligations under the relevant directives, so that the doctrine of direct effect has not given rise to rights for third parties.[74]

Thus attacks by third parties have had to rely on the application of general administrative law principles. In cases where EIA is not mandatory and the authority decide a project's effects are not likely to be so 'significant' as to make EIA necessary their decision can only be challenged by third parties by way of judicial review. The courts have only granted relief in such cases where it is obvious an authority has not taken into account material it should have done, *and* where the applicant can show substantial prejudice as a result of that failure: see *R v Poole Borough Council, ex p Beebee,*[75] *Twyford Parish Council v Secretary of State for the Environment.*[76] Indeed UK courts have been loath to interfere with authorities' discretion, and have been likely to intervene only where it could be shown that had EIA taken place, the outcome would have been different on the application, see *R v Wirral Metroplitan Borough Council, ex p Gray*[77] and also *R v Secretary of State for the Environment, ex p Marson.*[78]

Recent developments

However, much of what has been said above has to be reconsidered in the light of case law from both the ECJ and UK Courts. In *World Wildlife Fund (WWF) v Autonome Provinz Bozen*[79] to which earlier allusion was made the ECJ stated that the EIA Directive confers *directly enforceable* rights upon citizens of member states and where a member state has exceeded the discretion conferred by the directive, individuals may then rely on the directive itself before a member state's courts to obtain the setting aside of the relevant incompatible national measures. In *Berkeley v Secretary of State for the Environment*[80] the House of Lords, following this case, and applying the requirements of the EC Treaty, Art 10 which obligates member states to 'take all appropriate measures … to ensure fulfilment of the obligations arising out of this Treaty', considered that member states must take all necessary steps to ensure that relevant projects which may attract the operation of the EIA Directive are examined in order to determine whether they are likely to have significant effects on the environment, and, if so, to ensure that they are subject to assessment. That decision has to be taken at some point by some competent authority, either the local planning authority, or the Secretary of State.

Furthermore where the directive applies the information that the decision taker requires in order to reach a decision must be obtained by a particular procedure, namely

72   *World Wildlife Fund (WWF) v Autonome Provinz Bozen* Case C-435/97 [2000] 1 CMLR 149 and see *EC Commission v Germany* Case C–431/92 [1995] ECR I-2189 on Sch 1.
73   *R v St Edmundsbury Borough Council ex p Walton* [1999] JPL 905.
74   *R v London Borough of Hammersmith and Fulham, ex p CPRE* [2000] JPL 847 and *Becker v Finanzamt Munster-Innenstadt* Case 8/81 [1982] ECR 53, but contrast *R v Durham County Council and Sherburn Stone Co Ltd, ex p Huddleston* unreported, CA a case on the particular issue of EIA and old mining permissions; see chapter 13.
75   [1991] JPL 643.
76   [1990] Env LR 37.
77   [1998] Env LR D13.
78   [1998] 10 ELM 161.
79   Case C-435/97 [2000] 1 CMLR 149.
80   [2001] EWCA Civ 1012, [2001] JPL 58.

EIA, and this imposes procedural requirements. In particular the 'environmental statement' (see further below) must have been made available to the public and the public must have been given an opportunity to comment.[81] In other words citizens must be given a right to be heard in such cases.[82] Thus in the current view of the House of Lords 'A court is therefore not entitled retrospectively to dispense with the requirement of an EIA on the ground that the outcome would have been the same or that the local planning authority or Secretary of State had all the information necessary to enable them to reach a proper decision on the environmental issues'. Thus where the requirements of the directive are not met, it appears to be the duty of the court to quash the planning permission which has been improperly granted. Nothing less than 'substantial compliance with the Directive' can enable a grant to permission to be upheld.

However, what in such circumstances is 'substantial compliance'? It appears that the procedure involved need not go by the name of EIA, but it *must* in substance be an EIA. In other words there must be a *simple and accessible* compilation of relevant information produced by the applicant at the very start of the application process. This must contain the relevant environmental information which must in addition be summarised in non-technical language. A disparate collection of documents that can be read together, and which have been produced by a number of parties and bodies, and which can only be brought together and read following persistent efforts by the public does not satisfy the law's requirements.

It would appear to follow from this decision that in future where there is a violation of a directive which, as in the instant case, confers directly enforceable rights on citizens, that decisions taken in consequence of that violation should be quashed unless the violation was of only a very negligible nature: Community rights must be fully and effectively enforced. It also appears to follow that the EIA process must be highly structured and formal, and that the initial statement from the applicant for permission (see further below) must be both concise and also adequate in its provision of information. As the learned commentator on this case in the JPL argues, this may open the door for future challenges to be made concerning the adequacy of Environmental Statements.

One further issue remains to be considered. The directive applies generically to 'projects', but a planning application may be made for a single act of development, or it may be made in an 'outline' form in which the exact detail of the proposal is not disclosed while certain important 'reserved' issues are left to be determined subsequently: see generally SI 1988/1812. Where such an application is received and approved in a grant of 'outline planning permission', the local planning authority will be bound by accepting the principle of the development,[83] and cannot then refuse to approve a 'reserved' matter if this would derogate from the 'in principle' commitment.[84] How is this affected by EIA requirements? In *R v Rochdale Metropolitan Borough Council, ex p Tew*[85] an 'outline' application was made to develop a large business park, and a mere illustrative plan was included of future possible activities. The siting, design and access issues were all left to be treated as 'reserved' matters. The proposal fell within EIA requirements and an Environmental Statement and a subsequent ecological survey were submitted. However, the grant of permission was successfully challenged on the basis that the

81   This applies *EC Commission v Germany* Case C–431/92, [1995] ECR I-2889, and goes further than *R v North Yorkshire County Council, ex p Brown* [2000] 1 AC 397.
82   *Aannemersbedrijf PK Kraaijeveld BV v Gedeputeerde Staten van Zuid-Holland* Case C-72/95 [1996] ECR I-5403.
83   *Thirkwell v Secretary of State for the Environment* [1978] JPL 844.
84   *R v Newbury District Council, ex p Stevens* (1992) 65 P & CR 438.
85   [1999] JPL B200, [2000] Env LR 1.

information which was truly needed had not been submitted. The statement had been made in the light of the illustrative plan only and was too generalised to comply with EIA requirements. The main environmental effects of a proposal, its size and scale, etc have to be identified in order for public scrutiny to take place, and that had not happened because of the way in which the proposal had been submitted. It is now thought that where a development falls within EIA requirements it is unwise for an application to be made in outline form, unless the reserved matters are of only minor importance. However, those who wish to challenge on the basis of the decision in *Tew* must do so promptly. The normal judicial review principles apply that challenges must be, in general, be made in time, ie within three months of the ground(s) for review arising, and promptly *within* that period. The court has a discretion under the relevant statutory and practice provisions to extend that time, but has appeared unwilling to countenance delays in late challenges to grants of outline planning permission on the basis of *Tew*.[86] Arguments that assessment *has* to take place at both the initial consideration of the outline application *and* at the approval of reserved matters stage have been rejected by the Court of Appeal. Where required EIA *has* to take place at the outline application stage.[87]

One final point to note is that it appears possible to avoid the need to undertake EIA by including steps in a development proposal whose effect is to ensure that there are no 'significant' environmental effects.[88] However, where a project will have significant environmental effects the EIA process can be applied even though the operation/activity in question has commenced, provided it is clear that such a process remains possible because the development is still at a very early stage.[89]

Procedure once it is determined EIA is required (or where it is mandatory)

The applicant must prepare an Environmental Statement (ES). This must contain the information specified by the regulations, so as to enable the authority to make a reasonable assessment of the project's effects, see SI 1999/293, Reg 2. In brief the requirements are for:
(1)   A description of the development, ie:
  –   its physical characteristics and land use requirements during construction and operation;
  –   the main characteristics of any production processes including nature and quantity of materials used;
  –   estimates of types and quantities of expected residues and emissions (including pollution of water, air and soil, and by noise, vibration, light and radiation);
(2)   an outline of the main alternative studies by the applicant together with a statement of the main reasons for choosing the project subject to the application taking into account its environmental effects;
(3)   a description of aspects of the environment likely to be significantly affected – eg flora, fauna, soil, water, climate, population, cultural heritage, etc;
(4)   a description of the likely significant effects on the environment (both direct and indirect, primary, secondary and cumulative, short and long-term, positive and

---

86   *R v Hammersmith and Fulham London Borough Council, ex p CPRE* [2000] JPL 847 (three and a half years' delay) and *R v London Borough of Bromley and London and Regional Properties Ltd, ex p Baker* [2000] JPL 1302 (over a year's delay).
87   *R (on the application of Barker) v London Borough of Bromley* [2001] All ER (D) 361 (Nov).
88   *R v St Edmundsbury Borough Council, ex p Walton* [1999] JPL 805 and *Swan v Secretary of State for Scotland (No 2)* [2000] Envr LR 60.
89   *Swan v Secretary of State for Scotland* [1998] Env LR 545.

negative) arising from the existence of the development, its use of natural resources and its emissions etc, together with a statement as to forecasting methods utilised;

(5)   a description of measures envisaged to reduce/prevent/offset significant effects;

(6)   a non-technical summary of the foregoing;

(7)   an indication of any difficulties encountered in compiling the statement (eg lack of know-how).

The foregoing are the requirements of SI 1999/293, Sch 4, Part I. Here as much of the information as is reasonably required to assess the development's environmental effects must be given, if it is reasonable to demand this of the applicant having regard to the current state of knowledge and method of assessment. As an absolute minimum, however, SI 1999/293, Sch 4, Part II lays down that there *must* always be:

•   a description of the development with site, design and size information;

•   a description of mitigating and corrective measures to deal with significant adverse effects;

•   data required to identify and assess the main likely effects of the development on the environment;

•   an outline of the alternatives considered by the applicant and an indication of the reasons for choosing the proposed development, taking into account its environmental effects;

•   a non technical summary of the foregoing.

In compiling the ES the developer should utilise the DETR Good Practice Guide of 1995, and should consult with relevant bodies/organisations about the information to be included eg the authority themselves. Under SI 1999/293 (reg 10) the developer *may*, before making a planning application, ask the authority for a 'scoping opinion' on the information to be supplied in an ES. To do this the same information as would be supplied for a screening opinion must be submitted – indeed both requests may be made simultaneously, and a draft ES may also be submitted. The authority may then ask for further information, and must consult with relevant statutory consultees and the developer before adopting its scoping opinion. The authority have, generally, five weeks to prepare and adopt such an opinion. Note that an ES will not necessarily be invalid if it fails to comply with a scoping opinion, but a deficiency in this respect may lead to calls from the authority for more information. In any case the authority can always call under the regulations for further information. Where the authority fail to respond to a request for a scoping opinion an application for one may be made to the Secretary of State.

Once the developer has given notice he intends to submit an ES, the authority must inform the statutory consultees and remind them they are under obligation by virtue of the Environmental Information Regulations, SI 1992/3240 (amended by SI 1998/1447) to make available to the developer relevant information in their possession if requested. The consultees include English Nature, the Countryside Commission, the Environment Agency, and other relevant local authorities, such as highway authorities and may include the Health and Safety Executive. The actual process of consultation on a development subject to EIA may begin before formal submission of the ES and may begin before a scoping opinion, if any, is sought. The various statutory and other consultees who should be involved (albeit in the latter case on a non-statutory basis) should be identified as early as possible.

Submitting the ES

Where the ES is submitted with the planning application the applicant must submit four copies of the ES, a note of the name of every body to which the applicant has already sent, or intends to send, a copy of the statement, further copies (as needed) to enable all the consultation bodies to receive one. A reasonable number of copies must also be made available for the public.

On receipt the authority must publicise the application and must state where copies of the ES are available for inspection or can be obtained. Copies of the ES must be sent to all the consultation bodies who have not yet received one, and the Secretary of State must be given three copies along with a copy of the application. Applicants are encouraged to publicise the non-technical summary of the ES and to make it available free of charge to facilitate public discussion.

Where the ES is submitted after the application the procedure is similar but the applicant is responsible for publicising the ES (SI 1999/293, reg 14).

It is the responsibility of the authority to ensure that the submitted ES is adequate, and should notify the applicant as early as possible of any need for further information. Authorities have powers under the regulations to compel the submission of such further information – though their powers should not be used simply to obtain clarification or non-substantial information. Any information obtained must of course be submitted to the consultation bodies, as should any information voluntarily supplied. An application is not invalid by virtue of an inadequate ES, or by virtue of failure to comply with a request for further information. However, under SI 1999/293, reg 3 a developer who fails to provide an ES which generates information to complete the application must be refused.

Once the application subject to EIA is made the authority have 16 weeks (as opposed to the usual 8) in which to determine it because of the consultative requirements – this period may be extended by the agreement of the parties (SI 1999/293, reg 32). The authority must allow at least 14 days from receipt for consideration and feedback from consultation bodies and must not make a determination before the expiry of that period.

During the consultation exercise which, of course, is intended to help generate the 'information' needed to determine the planning application, the principal issues for determination should, if not immediately obvious, become clarified. Much of the effect at this stage could, however, be obviated by earlier informal consultation on methodologies to be used, for example to quantify and determine impacts and likely adversely affected interests.

While the authority is considering the application the Secretary of State will, inter alia, be considering the ES to see if the project could have a significant transboundary effect on another EC country (SI 1999/293, regs 27 and 28). Such a phenomenon is likely to be rare, but if it happens the Secretary of State will consult with the government of the affected nation and will direct that permission may not be granted until consultation has finished. The Secretary of State is likely also to exercise his 'call in' powers (see below) so that he may make the decision on the application.

Determining the application

Where an application is subject to EIA the decision taker must consider.
- the information in the ES;
- any comments from consultation bodies;
- any representations from the public.

However, a decision does not have to be made solely on the basis of the EIA, all other relevant considerations must be taken into account, and a decision could be reached that despite environmental disbenefits a project should nevertheless be allowed to go ahead.

If in the ES the applicant has proposed measures to alleviate environmental disbenefits flowing from the project these should be secured by means of either planning conditions, see below (generally minor matters), or planning obligations, see below (generally more important matters). However, authorities should not use their planning powers to duplicate other forms of control – eg those operated by the Environment Agency.

Once the application has been determined the applicant must be notified, and also the Secretary of State, and local press announcements made stating what the decision is and informing the public of their right to inspect relevant documentation (SI 1999/293, reg 21). The documentation must include statements of the decision reached, any conditions attached, and of the main reasons and considerations for reaching the decision. Where appropriate a description of preventative and ameliorative measures to reduce impact must also be given.

EIA: an assessment

Confusion has existed as to when assessment is required, as witness the *Beebee* case supra, and some projects appear to have evaded assessment in the past. Developers may, as we have seen, submit an 'environmental document' without calling it an environmental statement while authorities themselves have interpreted central government guidance in different ways. The consultation process has been found to operate unevenly, with some potential consultees not being consulted, or not being involved in presubmission consultations on statements, while voluntary groups and the public appear to be, in some cases at least, marginalised.

Research carried out for the DoE in 1991 further revealed the following major issues:
1   It was hard to assess the effect of assessment because there was deficient monitoring of relevant projects.
2   Many involved in the process are not sufficiently trained, so procedures were not always followed, this applied to both authorities and developers.
3   It was unclear what information should go in the statement and what in the planning application.
4   Central guidance needed clarification.
5   More pre-application consultation was needed.
Since 1991 further guidance on improving the quality of ESs has been given, for example by the EC Commission in its 1996 document 'Environmental Impact Assessment: Guidance on Scoping.' In addition the DoE issued 'Evaluation of Environmental Information for Planning Projects' in 1994 and 'Preparation of Environmental Statements for Planning Projects that Require Environmental Assessment: A Good Practice Guide' in 1995. Even so there is still no centrally required 'core standard' to which an ES must conform, and this constitutes a weakness within the entire EIA system. Part of the problem is the uneven operation of the law in practice. Thus there are cases where the assessment process may go, on a voluntary basis, beyond the strict requirements of the law. This may happen, for example, where an applicant agrees to have an independent third party audit the ES at its preparatory stage. There also remain questions as to the auditing of local authorities' own statements where it is a development they wish to undertake that requires EIA. There is also no requirement for post-authorisation monitoring of projects that have been subject to EIA. Furthermore while EIA is designed to ensure that there is available to the public a great deal of relevant information in a structured form so that comment and criticism can be voiced, there are arguments that the whole exercise may become no more than a public relations exercise if the information itself is of dubious quality. In addition, of course, the current law make no provision for the EIA process to be initiated by a third party. Third parties are thus forced to rely solely on judicial review and can only mount a challenge where some point of law is

involved. Where they wish to seek review they must always act promptly, and must take action at the earliest reasonable moment within the three month period which begins to run from the date of the alleged illegality.[90]

It has also been pointed out that developers can be faced with difficulties when their projects are subject to both EIA and IPC/IPPC controls (see further chapter 16, below).

The consequential problems are:

1   While an IPC authorisation or IPPC permit application is made to a politically neutral body (the Agency) and is usually highly technical, EIA takes place under the aegis of a local democratically answerable and politically conscious body, and may be a very wide ranging, non-technical process.

2   There is some confusion in industry as to who is responsible for what as a result of the dual system.

3   Dual controls add to the length and expense of the 'pre-creation' phase of any given project.

4   Dual controls can lead to conflicts of requirements, eg where a small chimney stack is required for amenity reasons, while pollution control demands a tall one.

To meet these and other problems it has been suggested that rationalisation of the two system could bring benefits. Thus the ES could be expanded to fulfil the information requirements of both application procedures. Similarly the systems should not operate totally in isolation but wherever possible in parallel, thus encouraging even more dialogue between regulators and enabling the creation of solutions acceptable to all where problems are encountered. This is an appropriate method of proceeding where it is clear a development proposal will involve a process prescribed for IPC or IPPC purposes, see *Overlaps in the Requirement for Environmental Assessment* (United Kingdom Environmental Law Association and the Institute of Environmental Assessment, 1993), and note earlier comments on the Agency's likely policy with regard to duplication of controls.

RECENT DEVELOPMENTS AT EC LEVEL

Assessment of the effects of plans and programmes on the environment

The EC has recently adopted measures to assist in integrating environmental concerns into the preparation and adoption of plans and programmes liable to have significant effects on the environment. These are now required to undergo a form of environmental assessment.

Directive 2001/42/EC, which has a deadline for implementation into the legislation of member states of 21 July 2004, supplements the environmental impact assessment system for projects initially introduced by Directive 85/337/EEC on the assessment of the effects of certain public and private projects on the environment. The present EIA system relates to, inter alia, construction work and other installations or schemes, as well as other measures affecting the natural environment or landscape; this further directive introduces a system of *prior environmental assessment at the plan making stage*.

The directive applies to *plans and programmes liable to have significant effects on the environment* where these are prepared and adopted by a competent authority, or

90   *R (on the application of Burkett) v London Borough of Hammersmith and Fulham* [2000] All ER (D) 2257.

where prepared by a competent authority for adoption by means of a legislative act. It also further applies to amendments to such plans and programmes. Assessment is to be required for plans and programmes which are prepared for town and country planning, land use, transport, energy, waste management, water management, industry, telecommunications, agriculture, forestry, fisheries and tourism, where these provide the framework for subsequent consent for specific projects currently subject to EIA. Similar requirements apply to the adoption of plans and programmes liable to affect *sites* protected by Directive 92/43/EEC where assessment is required under that directive. Other plans and programmes setting frameworks for future consent of development projects will be subject to assessment if an examination according to the criteria laid down in Annex II to the directive indicates that they are liable to have significant effects on the environment.

The process

Prior to adopting a plan or programme etc the relevant competent authority within the member state will have to carry out an environmental assessment and, after consulting relevant competent environmental authorities, will have to prepare an environmental report setting out inter alia:
- the contents of the plan or programme and its main objectives;
- the environmental characteristics of any area likely to be significantly affected by that plan, etc;
- any existing environmental problems relevant to the plan etc;
- any national, EC, or international environmental protection objectives relevant to the plan;
- likely environmental effects of implementing the plan;
- measures envisaged to prevent, reduce and offset any significant adverse effects on the environment;
- the envisaged monitoring measures.

The report must also include a summary of this information in non-technical language.

The draft plan in question and the environmental report on it must be made available to relevant environmental authorities *and* to the public. They will be then able to express their views on the draft prior to its adoption.

The member state responsible for preparing the plan will be required to send a copy of the draft (together with a copy of the environmental report) to other member states if it considers that the plan is liable to have environmental effects on the territory of those other member states, or where they make a request for it.

These other member states may then request consultations regarding the transboundary effects of the plan, and the measures envisaged to reduce or eliminate such effects.

The environmental report, any opinions expressed by other relevant authorities and the public, and the results of any transboundary consultations (if any) must be taken into account by the competent authority during the preparation of the plan and before it is adopted.

When the plan is then adopted the member state responsible must inform all of the parties concerned who have been consulted, and make available to them: the plan as adopted; a statement summarising how environmental considerations have been integrated; the environmental report; the opinions and the results of consultations; the reasons for choosing the plan or programme as adopted; the planned monitoring measures.

H CALL IN POWERS

The TCPA 1990, s 77 empowers the Secretary of State to give directions requiring applications for planning permission to be referred to him. Before determining such an application the Secretary of State must, however, give the parties the opportunity of a hearing before a person appointed by him. This power is only selectively used, as was originally made clear in DoE Circular 2/81.

A ministerial parliamentary statement of 16 June 1999 reiterated that the power will only be used where a proposal raises conflicts with national policy on an important matter, or where it could give rise to significant effects outside its locality; or where substantial regional or national controversy could occur; or where significant issues of architectural or urban design are concerned, or where national security or the interests of foreign governments are involved. The Secretary of State's decision on whether or not to exercise his powers is, however, subject to judicial review.[91]

Reasons do not have to be given for 'calling in' an application, though they usually are.[92] Where a 'call in' direction is made the Secretary of State may withdraw or revoke it, even though this is not expressly stated in the TCPA 1990. Arguably such a withdrawal ought to be justifiable, and not merely arbitrary.[93]

I THE GRANT OF PLANNING PERMISSION, PLANNING CONDITIONS AND OBLIGATIONS

The general rule is that once permission is given for development the grant enures for the benefit of the land and all those interested in it, see s 75. Section 91, however, limits this by imposing an implied condition that the development in question must be *begun* within five years of the date on which the permission is granted. This is subject to exceptions, eg where a specific time limit is laid down in the grant. In any case for development to be *begun* very little needs to be done provided it is genuinely intended to be an inception of the work.[94]

By virtue of the GDPO 1995, s 78(2) and Art 20 authorities should give notification of their decision on an application within eight weeks. As a general rule non-determination gives rise to a right of appeal to the Secretary of State. However, many developers agree to extend the decision making period knowing that authorities have consultative obligations. In any case an out of time decision is not void.[95] The TCPA 1990, s 70A, as inserted in 1991, further empowers an authority to decline to determine an application where within the two-year period ending with receipt of the application the Secretary of State refused a similar application on 'call in' or refused on appeal to overturn a decision refusing a similar application provided the authority consider there

---

91 *R v Secretary of State for the Environment, ex p Newprop* [1983] JPL 386; *Lakin Ltd v Secretary of State for Scotland* [1989] JPL 339; *R v Secretary of State for the Environment, Transport and the Regions, ex p Carter Commercial Developments Ltd* [1999] PLCR 125.
92 *South Northamptonshire District Council v Secretary of State for the Environment* (1995) 70 P & CR 224.
93 *R v (on the application of trustees of Friends of the Lake District) v Secretary of State for the Environment, Transport and the Regions* [2001] EWHC Admin 281, [2001] All ER (D) 19 (Apr).
94 *Hillingdon London Borough Council v Secretary of State for the Environment* [1990] JPL 575; *Malvern Hills District Council v Secretary of State for the Environment* (1982) 262 Estates Gazette 1190.
95 *James v Secretary of State for Wales* [1966] 1 WLR 135.

has been no significant change in circumstances concerning the development plan or any other material consideration.[96]

The TCPA 1990, s 73 permits applications to develop land without compliance with any conditions previously attached. In such cases only the conditions may be considered. Authorities may refuse such applications if they believe the original conditions should continue to apply, or the conditions may be lifted or varied. Disappointed applicants may, of course appeal. Where a condition is lifted third parties may seek to challenge (on the basis of some illegality) by way of judicial review, though a challenger must show 'sufficient interest' in the matter to be able to pursue the case.[97] So far as the authority is concerned, however, they must when faced with a s 73 application take into account the relevant provisions of the development plan, and all other relevant considerations, and these include the consequences of imposing a different set of conditions, and the factual circumstances as they are at the time of the application.[98]

Planning authorities may under the TCPA 1990, s 70 impose 'such conditions as they think fit on a grant of permission. This is supplemented by s 72 which allows the imposition of conditions for regulating the use of any land *under the applicant's control*, whether or not comprised in the application, so far as is expedient *in connection with the authorised development* (the power under s 70 only extends to land comprised in the application,[99] but is not dependent on the applicant's control of the land),[100] and for requiring the removal of works or the discontinuance of a use at the end of a specified period: a 'permission granted for a limited period'.

DoE Circular 11/95 gives general guidance on the imposition of planning conditions. It has been central policy since the issue of Cmnd 9571 that conditions may be imposed to protect the environment against appreciable risk of harm, but that onerous conditions should not be imposed where environmental problems are less certain to occur, reliance being placed, in case of future difficulties, on public health or pollution control legislation. Furthermore conditions should only be imposed where they are necessary, relevant to planning matters, relevant to the development permitted, enforceable, precise and generally reasonable. Conditions should usually only be imposed where, if they were not, permission would have to be refused, and conditions not satisfying this criterion need special and precise justification. Conditions should thus be imposed where they are needed to meet specific problems. Conditions should not duplicate controls available under other statutes,[101] nor should they import forms of control into planning issues simply because such control is considered socially desirable,[102] nor should they seek to usurp the powers of central regulatory agencies.[103] Circular 11/95 points out that planning conditions are not appropriate to control the level of emissions from proposed developments where these are subject to pollution controls, but adds they: 'may be needed to address the impact of emissions to the extent that they might have land-use implications and are not controlled by the appropriate pollution control authority'. PPG 23 paras 3.23–3.28 gives further guidance on this issue, and points out

---

96   See generally *Noble Organisation Ltd v Falkirk District Council* 1994 SLT 100.
97   *R (on the application of Barber) v Waverley Borough Council* [2001] All ER (D) 58 (Apr).
98   *Pye v Secretary of State for the Environment* [1998] 3 PLR 72, and *R v Leicester City Council, ex p Powergen UK plc* [2000] All ER (D) 696.
99   *Peak Park Joint Planning Board v Secretary of State for the Environment and Imperial Chemical Industries* (1979) 39 P & CR 361.
100 *Atkinson v Secretary of State for the Environment* [1983] JPL 599.
101 *Fawcett Properties Ltd v Buckingham County Council* [1961] AC 636, [1960] 3 All ER 503.
102 *Chertsey UDC v Mixnam's Properties Ltd* [1965] AC 735, [1964] 2 All ER 627.
103 *British Airports Authority v Secretary of State for Scotland* [1980] JPL 260.

that conditions may be used to control the amenity issues arising from a development, eg its impact on the landscape, or its hours of operation. They may further be used to: secure the use of particular modes of transport to/from the site of development; ensure decontamination of soil so that a site can be suitable for particular afteruses after development has taken place; ensure relocation and after care of landfill sites; require provision, where appropriate, of recycling facilities. Conditions should not be used to require provision of information to enable the impact of the development to be monitored safe insofar as this relates to some definite planning objective. Conditions may, however, be used where there are parallel systems of regulation where this enables a development to proceed acceptably and to avoid the later onerous and invasive other use of other powers, eg to secure adequate sewerage provision on a site. Conditions may also be attached to a permission granted after EIA to ensure incorporation of mitigation measures proposed in the ES, provided these do not duplicate other legislative controls, and do not substitute the planning authority's views on pollution for those of the appropriate pollution control body. Planning conditions may, however, be used for noise control purposes. The use of conditions to effect general environmental improvement by requiring the tidying up of eyesores has been condemned.[104]

The power to impose conditions is, as stated above, subject to requirements of reasonableness. Conditions must be imposed only for relevant reasons, and must be such as a reasonable authority would impose.[105] The decisions of the courts, coming to and applying these rules, have resulted in planning conditions being limited to somewhat narrow land use considerations. Planning conditions may thus legally, as well as in terms of policy guidance, only serve a planning purpose and must not seek to promote an ulterior object.[106] They must not derogate from an existing permission by pursuing an aim having no necessary, essential, direct or close connection with the authorised development.[107] They must not be unreasonable, in that they are so oppressive, arbitrary or partial in their operation that no reasonable authority could have imposed them. Authorities may not seek the payment of money or money's worth, nor may they destroy private rights of property, or seek to transfer a public burden to private shoulders.[108] However, the courts will not lightly set conditions aside, interpreting them benevolently to preserve the discretion of authorities.

A bad condition dealing only with minor issues, and which does not go fundamentally to the heart of the permission, may be severed and the rest of the permission saved.[109]

Planning obligations

As an alternative to imposing a planning condition, an authority may seek to reach an agreement (now a 'planning obligation') with a developer concerning the use and development of land. Such agreements (as they were known) *have* had the character of restrictive covenants which are enforceable despite the existence of any subsequent

104 *Newbury District Council v Secretary of State for the Environment* [1981] AC 578, [1980] 1 All ER 731.
105 *Pyx Granite Co Ltd v Minister of Housing and Local Government* [1958] 1 QB 554, [1958] 1 All ER 625.
106 *R v Hillingdon London Borough Council, ex p Royco Homes Ltd* [1974] QB 720, [1974] 3 All ER 643.
107 *Allnatt London Properties Ltd v Middlesex County Council* (1964) 15 P & CR 288.
108 *Hall & Co Ltd v Shoreham-by-Sea UDC* [1964] 1 WLR 240, and *City of Bradford Metropolitan Council v Secretary of State for the Environment* [1986] JPL 598.
109 *Kent County Council v Kingsway Investments (Kent) Ltd* [1971] AC 72, [1970] 1 All ER 70.

inconsistent grants of planning permission.[110] Indeed authorities have been able to apply for injunctions to restrain breaches of agreements even where other planning enforcement procedures have not been exhausted.[111] Under the provisions of the legislation as amended in 1991 positive covenants may be imposed, and see further below.

A problem, however, relates to what it is legitimate for a planning obligation to bring about. DoE Circular 16/91 warned authorities to be generally cautious in their use of obligations, and it is clear that obtaining unreasonable returns by way of obligation could give rise to suspicion that there has been bartering of planning permission. Circular 16/91 (which developed advice given in Circular 22/83) was an attempt to make it clear that obligations are not to be used by authorities to obtain extraneous gains from developers, nor should they be used to duplicate controls imposed by condition. Further guidance was issued in the form of Circular 1/97, which again stressed that obligations *should* only be utilised where necessary and relevant, and an unacceptable development should not be allowed because a developer offers some benefit. Yet again the need for there to be a relationship between the development and any benefits gained by the authority was stressed, as was the overall need for obligations to be reasonable in all respects. However, despite policy guidance recent decisions by the courts enable what can only be called a 'highly creative' use of obligations, so that very little is required of an obligation to satisfy general public law requirements as to its *vires*. The cases appear to establish that:

1   Each situation requires careful evaluation on its own facts.
2   Much is going to depend on the 'planning background' of each obligation, ie the plans and other policy documents relevant to the development in operation which may have indicated for all to see that particular developments could not go ahead without contributions from developers towards infrastructure costs, etc, for there is nothing illegitimate in arguing that those whose proposed developments will come to fruition as a result of the provision of infrastructure by a public body should not contribute towards its cost.
3   In cases such as the former it is perfectly acceptable to use percentage formulae based on the enhanced value of land with planning permission to calculate what a developer's contribution should be, provided it is bona fide used only to transfer an appropriate percentage of costs to developers' shoulders.
4   The offer, however, of benefits by a developer where these are wholly unconnected with the development is a matter not to be taken into account by a planning authority, and its consideration technically renders an authority's decision open to challenge.
5   Conversely an authority should not seek benefits wholly unconnected with a proposed development.
6   Where there are two competing development proposals it is legitimate for a planning authority to choose that one offering the more attractive package of on site benefits, or off site benefits provided these can be seen as linked to the proposed development.

Planning obligations must be reasonable, in the general administrative law sense of that term; they must serve a planning purpose, but, provided what is offered by way of benefit or 'planning gain' is in some way *connected with* the proposed development, there is no legal requirement that a benefit has to be *necessary* to, or *proportionate* to, the development. What constitutes the necessary *connection* between an obligation

110   *Re Martin's Application* [1989] JPL 33; *Abbey Homesteads (Developments) Ltd v Northamptonshire County Council* (1986) 278 Estates Gazette 1244.
111   *Avon County Council v Millard* (1985) 50 P & CR 275.

and a proposed development remains to be worked out on a case by case basis. However, there would appear to be no reason why a developer should not offer to undertake a major environmental 'clean-up' or restoration of land provided that can be seen to be related to the proposed development by, for example, making the site more attractive to the developer's customers.[112]

Where a developer puts forward a series of unrelated proposals, or proposals that appear composite but are in fact unrelated, where some proposals offer the allure of public gain while others would bring about unacceptable detriment to an interest of acknowledged importance, benefits available by way of an agreement are not to be used as counterbalances to the disbenefits. Where however, proposals are related it appears proper to weigh benefits against disbenefits.[113]

Obligations; the technicalities

The TCPA 1990, s 106 (as substituted) allows *any* person interested *in land* in the area of a local planning authority to enter into a planning obligation (by agreement or otherwise) with the effect of:

1 Restricting the development or use of the land in a specified way.
2 Requiring specified operations/activities to be carried out in, on, under or over the land.
3 Requiring the land's use in a specified way.
4 Requiring sums to be paid to the authority on a specified date(s) — or periodically. Such an obligation may be conditional or unconditional, it may be time limited or indefinite, and may in relation to payments require them to be of a specified amount, or fixed according to a formula. Such an obligation is also enforceable against the original obligatees and those deriving title from them, and any restrictions/requirements imposed are enforceable by injunction. Furthermore the authority with whom the obligation is struck may enter on the land, on giving 21 days' notice to the obligatee, to do any operations required by the obligation and may recover their costs.

A planning obligation will have to take the form of *a deed*, stating that a planning obligation is created thereby, and identifying the land and the obligatee's interest therein and which identifies the obligatee and the relevant authority. Such an obligation then becomes a local land charge.

Obligations may be imposed either by agreement, *or* by a unilateral undertaking on the part of the obligatee.

The TCPA 1990, s 106A allows for a prescribed period (or where none such exists a period of five years) to elapse after which the obligatee may apply to the planning authority for the obligation to be modified or discharged. Thereupon the authority must determine either to continue, modify or discharge the obligation. Section 106B enables appeals to be made against decisions to continue obligations unmodified, or in cases of non-determination. The appeal will be made to the Secretary of State, and may take the form of a hearing.

---

112 *R v Plymouth City Council, ex p Plymouth and South Devon Co-operative Society Ltd* [1993] JPL 1099; *Good v Epping Forest District Council* [1994] 2 All ER 156; *R v South Northamptonshire District Council, ex p Crest Homes plc* [1995] 7 ELM 11; *Tesco Stores Ltd v Secretary of State for the Environment* [1995] 2 All ER 636.
113 *Barber v Secretary of State for the Environment* [1991] JPL 559.

Multi party obligations

Major housing and retail developments may well entail an authority entering into a number of obligations with a variety of developers. Where an obligation agreed with one developer has implications for another — for example where it relates to a formula to decide how monetary contributions are to be assessed — fairness demands that all affected parties should be able to comment on the relevant terms.[114]

Application of planning control to land of interested planning authorities and development by them

The TCPA 1990, s 316 was replaced by the 1991 Act so that in relation to land of interested planning authorities and the development, singly or jointly with others, of land by such authorities, development control, enforcement and special controls will apply subject to regulations to be made centrally.

The Town and Country Planning General Regulations, SI 1992/1492 now provide that:

1   Where a local authority wishes to carry out development itself on land in its area it must make, and may grant, the necessary planning application.
2   Where there is a proposal to carry out development on local authority owned land by other parties, the authority must seek permission from the relevant development control authority, ie the district in most cases.
3   Authorities applying for permission are in generally the same position as all other applicants.
4   The normal publicity requirements apply to authority applications.
5   Applications must, however, be determined by persons/committees not responsible for the land in question.

J CHALLENGING A PLANNING DECISION

Section 78 of the Act allows disappointed developers to appeal to the Secretary of State against, inter alia, refusals or conditional grants of planning permission. The Secretary of State has wide powers to allow or dismiss appeals, or to vary or reverse any part of the original decision, and may deal with the application as if it had been made to him/her in the first instance. Most appeals are heard and determined by ministry inspectors. This serves somewhat to distance appeals from the executive arm of government, but it remains in the eyes of many, a weakness of planning law that the appeals and inquiry system is not independent, nor sufficiently open to public participation, see McAuslan, *The Ideologies of Planning Law* pp 45–74 and see also chapter 5 above on the question of the general compatibility of the appeal system with the Human Rights Act 1998. The formal, frequently legalistic, and sometimes theatrical English inquiry does not always compare well with French practice in the Enquête Publique, see Macrory and La Fontaine *Public Inquiry and Enquête Publique.* (See further chapter 11, below on particular types of inquiry.)

Where either the applicant or the authority request it the Secretary of State must hold an inquiry *or* hearing, though they may opt for the matter to be settled by way of written representations, a procedure used in the majority of all cases. Where an inquiry

---

114   *R (on the application of Lichfield Securities Ltd) v Lichfield District Council* [2001] EWCA Civ 304, [2001] All ER (D) 78 (Mar).

is held it will usually be a local inquiry under s 320 of the Act. Procedure at the inquiry is governed by Inquiries Procedure Rules, in the case of matters determined by the Secretary of State, SI 2000/1624, and for those determined by inspectors, SI 2000/1625. Procedure is similar until the post inquiry stage. (For procedure on written representations see SI 2000/1628, and for procedure at a hearing as opposed to an inquiry see SI 2000/1626.

The overwhelming majority (99% in 1998/99) of appeals are now determined by inspectors (see SI 1997/420), but the Secretary of State has indicated he/she will 'recover' jurisdiction in relation to issues such as: major residential development proposals, ie 150 or more houses; major developments having more than local significance, or raising novel issues; developments consisting of 100,000 sq ft or more of retail space; greenbelt developments; major mineral working proposals; proposals raising major legal issues or where a government department has raised a significant objection and cases which are 'linked' to other cases where an inspector could not have jurisdiction: in 1994/95 the Secretary of State 'recovered' 188 cases, while in 1998/99 the figure was only 105, rising to 163 in 2000 (with, in the same year, 127 'called in' applications).

The procedure rules are designed to enhance the speed with which appeals are dealt, by bringing about exchanges of information between the parties, identification of the points of dispute before the inquiry begins and by setting much stricter statutory timescales within which the various stages of the appeal have to be dealt with. These changes followed the 1998 Consultation Paper 'Improving Planning Appeal Procedures'.

Once it has been determined by the Secretary of State that an inquiry is to be held the planning authority must inform him of all those who have made representations to them in consequence of being served with notice of the application because they are owners of the land or its agricultural tenants. The rules further ensure that any views expressed to a body or institution on which the planning authority intend to rely must be made known to the appellant in advance of the inquiry. In relation to major planning issues where the matter is one for the Secretary of State a pre-inquiry meeting may be held see also chapter 11 on the conduct of such 'major inquiries'. In relation to matters to be decided by an inspector, however, provision is also made for a pre-inquiry meeting to be held and for the inspector to indicate what matters he/she believes are relevant to the consideration of the appeal. At such a meeting issues such as hours of sitting, estimates of duration of the parties' cases, order of presentation, venue facilities, identification of issues, agreements on preparing and exchanging proofs of evidence, etc, will be addressed. Both authorities and appellants have to serve statements of their cases according to a timetable fixed by the rules, and other persons who wish to appear *may* be required to provide a statement of case by the Secretary of State. Those who are required to provide statements will then have the right to appear, however. Statements give the full particulars of a party's case and list relevant documents, thus identifying what the issues in dispute are and aiding the efficiency of the inquiry. Details of supporting data and methodologies should also be given. These statements will circulate between the principal parties and those third parties who have been required to give a statement. Inquiries *may* be timetabled, and *have to be* with regard to major inquiries. See SI 2000/1625, reg 8, and SI 2000/1624, reg 8. Where an assessor is appointed to assist the inquiry that person's name and address will be notified to the parties, as will the date of the opening of the inquiry which has to take place within a set period, and once that date is fixed it will only be altered in exceptional cases. Once the Secretary of State has fixed a date (and such a date will in practice only be fixed after some consultation has taken place with the parties) the decision on commencement will not easily be challengeable in court.[115] Publicity concerning the inquiry is left largely to

---

115 *R v Secretary of State for the Environment, Transport and the Regions, ex p Kirklees Borough Council* [1999] JPL 882.

the discretion of authorities, but they are counselled to ensure that all those who are known to have an interest in the issue are informed on the date of the inquiry. In any case the Secretary of State may direct publicity requirements.

Holding the inquiry

At the inquiry the following are entitled to appear: the applicant, the local planning authority, other planning authorities in whose area the land in question is situated, eg the county council, and the parish council provided they made representations in respect of the planning application, and persons who are the owners or agricultural tenants of the land and who having been made originally aware of the planning application made representations concerning it (known as 'statutory parties'). In addition the Secretary of State may in relation to inquiries to be determined by himself or an inspector require any other person who has notified him of a desire or intention to appear to serve a statement of case on the 'statutory parties' and such persons then have a right to appear. Other persons appear at the discretion of the inspector, though this limitation on third party rights is modified in practice by the willingness of inspectors to allow all genuinely interested persons the chance to appear.

The inquiry will be held largely at the inspector's discretion. He/she must observe the rules of natural justice, and conduct the inquiry fairly with regard to the rights of parties to be heard and present an adequate case,[116] as must the Secretary of State.[117] Though inspectors may have an opinion of the merits of an appeal before commencing, they must give all those appearing before them proper opportunities to state their cases.[118] Inspectors may help unrepresented parties, where appropriate, to put their cases, but are under no obligation to be advocates.[119] Parties are not permitted to be noisy and disruptive, and may lose their rights in cases of misbehaviour.[120] The inspector has discretion to proceed if a person entitled to appear fails to do so. A person permitted to appear is entitled to have his views considered.[121] Statements ('proofs') of evidence from those entitled to appear, and intending to speak or to call evidence, are to be submitted to the inspector, normally three weeks in advance of the inquiry, and provision is made for such material to be circulated to other parties by the sets of inquiries procedure rules.

Generally at an inquiry the appellant opens and has a final right of reply, other persons entitled to appear do so in the order permitted by the inspector, as do those permitted to appear. Those entitled to appear may call evidence, and the appellant, authority and owners, etc, of the land may cross-examine, otherwise the examination of evidence is at the inspector's discretion. Inspectors may refuse to permit examination or cross-examination which is irrelevant or repetitious, though inspectors must behave fairly and reasonably in the exercise of this power.[122] The rules of fairness and natural justice apply to the discretion to allow cross-examination, though an inspector must consider, before allowing cross-examination on technical issues, the nature of the evidence, the qualifications of the witness and the cross-examiner to deal with the material, and whether the cross-examination will lead to the production of a better report,

116   *Performance Cars Ltd v Secretary of State for the Environment* (1977) 34 P & CR 92; *Nicholson v Secretary of State for Energy* (1977) 76 LGR 693.
117   *R v Secretary of State for the Environment, ex p Field Estates (Canvey) Ltd* [1989] JPL 39.
118   *Halifax Building Society v Secretary of State for the Environment* [1983] JPL 816.
119   *Snow v Secretary of State for the Environment* (1976) 33 P & CR 81.
120   *Lovelock v Secretary of State for Transport* (1979) 39 P & CR 468.
121   *Turner v Secretary of State for the Environment* (1973) 28 P & CR 123.
122   *Nicholson v Secretary of State for Energy* (1977) 76 LGR 693.

or will merely unnecessarily prolong the inquiry. Government policy may not be debated at an inquiry. In *Bushell v Secretary of State for the Environment*,[123] the House of Lords commented on what may be a matter of 'government policy'. National policies, debateable in Parliament, are clearly such. At the other extreme minute details and particular issues of implementation of policy in individual cases clearly are not. In the 'grey area' between lie established departmental practices for deciding national priorities between possible implementations of policy and the 'need' for action. It seems these should not be debated at individual local inquiries. However, it appears that it can be arguable that central policy is not applicable in a given context or to a particular locality.[124] Certainly while a government representative may *not be required* (as is laid down in the sets of inquiries procedure rules) to answer questions relating to the merits of central policy, such a question may be *allowed* where the representative is *prepared* to answer it.

Evidence at planning inquiries must be given in public, though the Secretary of State may direct otherwise where satisfied it would result in the disclosure of information as to national security, or the security of any premises or property, and that this would be contrary to the public interest, see s 321 of the 1990 Act.

It must be remembered that one purpose of an inquiry is to ensure citizens closely affected by a scheme are given the opportunity to state the case for their objection to it, and thereby the minister is better informed of the facts. Inquiries should not be 'over-judicialised'. They are not like civil litigation, even though a decision is challenged. The concept of a 'burden of proof' is inappropriate, as the inquiry is into whether there are sound and clear cut reasons emerging from the facts for a refusal of permission. It is unclear how far a policy contained in a statutory plan can place a burden of proving why permission should be granted on an appellant.[125] Inspectors may make unaccompanied inspections of the site before or during inquiries without giving notice to the parties, and must inspect it if requested by the appellant or the authority, at which time the appellant, the authority and the owners, etc of the land are entitled to be present. *Accompanied* site inspections may also take place during the inquiry. Receipt of other information on this visit, for example by making inquiries of neighbours, as in *Hibernian Property Co Ltd v Secretary of State for the Environment*,[126] or coming to conclusions on observations which the parties are given no opportunity to deal with,[127] may amount to a denial of natural justice.

After the inquiry, in cases to be ministerially decided, the inspector makes his/her report to the Secretary of State, including conclusions and recommendations or reasons for not making recommendations, any assessor's report made must be appended to the inspector's report with comments thereon. The report must fairly and accurately present principal arguments; irrelevant and peripheral issues may be omitted, so that the issues are intelligible to the Secretary of State, and so that proper material is set before him/her.[128] Where the Secretary of State differs from the inspector on a matter of fact, or after the inquiry takes into account new evidence of facts (not being matters of government policy), and is consequently not disposed to agree with the inspector's recommendations, he/she must not come to a decision at variance with the recommendations without notifying the persons who were entitled to appear of his

123 [1981] AC 75.
124 *R v Secretary of State for Transport, ex p Gwent County Council* [1988] QB 429, [1987] 1 All ER 161.
125 *Federated Estates v Secretary of State for the Environment* [1983] JPL 812.
126 (1973) 27 P & CR 197.
127 *Fairmount Investments Ltd v Secretary of State for the Environment* [1976] 2 All ER 865, [1976] 1 WLR 1255.
128 *North Surrey Water Co v Secretary of State for the Environment* (1976) 34 P & CR 140.

views and reasons therefor, and afford them a chance to make representations. The Secretary of State has a discretion in any case to reopen an inquiry, and *must* reopen it if either the applicant or the local planning authority request it where he/she has taken into account new evidence or new matters of fact which are not matters of government policy. (A similar provision applies to appeals to be determined by an inspector.) These rules do not apply to disagreement by the Secretary of State with the inspector's judgements, see for example *Lord Luke of Pavenham v Minister of Housing and Local Government*,[129] where there was a disagreement whether a development would harm the countryside. An *opinion* on a matter of fact, is not itself a matter of fact.[130] The Secretary of State is also free to consider matters of government policy, and to consult other ministers, even without giving the parties an opportunity to comment.[131]

The decision on appeal

Decisions and supporting reasons must be notified to the statutory parties, and to any other person who appeared at the inquiry and asked to be notified. Reasons must be adequate, clearly intelligible, reasonably precise, and must set out the relevant issues.[132]

The law was reviewed in *Save Britain's Heritage v Secretary of State for the Environment*.[133] The question here was whether a decision letter satisfied the requirements of the Inquiries Procedure Rules that 'the Secretary of State shall notify his decision ... and his reasons for it ...' Lord Bridge reviewed the existing case law. In *Re Poyser and Mills' Arbitration*[134] Megaw J stated that a duty to give reasons is one to give proper and adequate reasons, reasons which are intelligible and deal with the substantive points that have been raised, ie reasons which enable a person to know on what grounds an issue has been decided, and which identify in sufficient detail the conclusions reached on the principal issues of controversy.[135] Reasons must also be understandable to those to whom they are addressed, though a decision letter's reasons are to be read as a whole, and not construed as a statute, ie not sentence by sentence or paragraph by paragraph.[136] Added to this, it appears from the '*Save*' case that decision letters may also be read with a degree of benevolence. However, can it also be said, as Woolf CJ argued in the Court of Appeal, that reasoning should be such as to enable the person receiving it to make a proper assessment as to whether a further challenge should be mounted?

Lord Bridge accepted Woolf CJ's contention — sufficient particularity is required in order to enable the recipient of a decision to make a proper assessment of whether or not to mount a further challenge. Nevertheless as a general principle Lord Bridge declined to move far from the basic tests laid down in *Re Poyser and Mills' Arbitration*. Lord Bridge further added that even if reasons were not found to be adequate, a remedy should not be given unless it can be shown that the applicant has been substantially prejudiced by the failure to give adequate reasons. Lord Bridge did, however, deny a

---

129   [1968] 1 QB 172, [1967] 1 All ER 351.
130   *Portsmouth Water plc v Secretary of State for the Environment* [1994] JPL 1001.
131   *Kent County Council v Secretary of State for the Environment and Burmah Total Refineries Trust* (1976) 33 P & CR 70.
132   *Givaudan & Co Ltd v Minister of Housing and Local Government* [1966] 3 All ER 696, [1967] 1 WLR 250.
133   [1991] 2 All ER 10.
134   [1964] 2 QB 467.
135   *Westminster City Council v Great Portland Estates plc* [1985] AC 661 at 673; *Hope v Secretary of State for the Environment* (1975) 31 P & CR 120 at 123.
136   *Ward v Secretary of State for the Environment* (1989) 59 P & CR 486 at 487.

contention that an inadequacy of reasoning may itself give rise to a presumption of substantial prejudice which it is then the duty of the decision maker to rebut. Thus a decision letter does not have to refer to every material consideration, no matter how insignificant, nor does it have to deal with every argument, no matter how peripheral. Indeed provided reasons are *adequately* expressed they do *not* have to be *well* expressed.[137] The basic requirement appears to be that the decision letter read as whole should leave no room for genuine doubt in the mind of a well informed, though not necessarily legally qualified, reader.[138]

Human rights issues and other matters

The impact of the Human Rights Act 1998 on planning matters has already been discussed in chapter 5. However, it is worthwhile at this point to remind ourselves of the decision in *R (on the application of Holding & Barnes plc) v Secretary of State for the Environment Transport and the Regions*,[139] which, though concerned with 'call in' procedures is clearly relevant to the determination of planning appeals, and the question of the 'fairness' of determination of such matters. It will be remembered that the overall finding of the House of Lords was that the Secretary of State's decisions in planning matters are of an administrative law nature rather than involving the determination of civil rights even though they are taken by a minister answerable to an elected body. These decisions may be challenged in the High Court and there is a sufficient judicial control to ensure a subsequent determination by an independent and impartial tribunal. There is no requirement for a rehearing of an application by way of an appeal on the merits in view of the difference of functions between (a) the minister exercising his statutory powers (for the policy of which he is answerable to the legislature and ultimately to the electorate) and (b) the court. What is required on the part of the latter is that there should be a sufficient review of the legality of the decisions and of the procedures followed. There is no necessity for a court to have full jurisdiction to review policy or the overall merits of a planning decision nor for it to conduct a complete rehearing on the merits of the decision.

Costs

Under the Local Government Act 1972, s 250 and the TCPA 1990, s 320 the Secretary of State may award costs at an inquiry, and this power now extends to proceedings determined by written representations: indeed inspectors may now exercise the cost awarding power. Principles governing exercise of the power are contained in DoE Circular 8/93. These relate to situations where the appellant has failed to follow procedural requirements, or has behaved in such a way that proceedings have been adjourned or unnecessarily prolonged, or is wilfully unco-operative, or failed to pursue the appeal or has failed to attend meetings, or has introduced new grounds of appeal

---

137 *Bolton Metropolitan District Council v Secretary of State for the Environment* [1996] 1 All ER 184.
138 *Clark Holmes Ltd v Secretary of State for the Environment* (1993) 66 P & CR 263; see also *Boulevard Land Ltd v Secretary of State for the Environment* [1998] JPL 983; *McLean Homes (Midland) Ltd v Secretary of State for the Environment* [1999] JPL B30; *Michael Shanley Group Ltd v Secretary of State for the Environment, Transport and the Regions* [1999] PLCR 188 and *Brentwood Borough Council v Secretary of State for the Environment, Transport and the Regions* [1999] JPL 528.
139 [2001] HRLR 45; [2001] 2 All ER 929.

at a late stage, or has pursued an appeal with no reasonable chance of success. Planning authorities may be subjected to costs where they fail to comply with procedural requirements, fail to provide planning evidence to substantiate their decisions or to show they have taken into account relevant laws and policies, or where they have behaved obstructively by refusing to discuss a planning application, or where they have introduced new ground for refusal at a late stage in proceedings, or have imposed unreasonable conditions of pursued unreasonable demands in connection with a grant of permission. Section 322A further empowers the Secretary of State to award costs against a party in respect of any other party where arrangements have been made for an inquiry or hearing which does not then take place. This contemplates situations where either the authority or the appellant pull out of an inquiry before it has opened leaving the other side with abortive preparation costs. Note also s 79(6A) under which if at any time during the determination of an appeal it appears to the Secretary of State that the appellant is responsible for undue delay in the progress of the appeal, he/she may warn the appellant that the appeal will be dismissed unless specified steps are taken to expedite matters, and may then dismiss the appeal if those steps are not taken in due time.

Further challenge

'Persons aggrieved' by the decision on appeal have, under the TCPA 1990, ss 284 and 288, a six-week right to apply to the High Court on a point of law to quash the decision. That period begins to run from the date of typing, signing and stamping of the Secretary of State's notification, not its date of reception.[140] The time limit is absolute.[141] Furthermore the existence of such an absolute time limit is not incompatible with civil rights under Art 6 of the European Convention on Human Rights as it pursues the legitimate objective of legal certainty and finality in the context of planning.[142] The term 'persons aggrieved' is given an extended meaning. Mere busybodies are not included, but third parties, such as neighbours, who have been allowed to appear at the inquiry are within the formula.[143] The grounds of challenge are limited to arguments that the appeal was substantively or procedurally ultra vires. Courts will intervene where there is no evidence on which the minister could have acted, or where the evidence cannot reasonably support conclusions made. Furthermore he/she must not act perversely or misinterpret the statute, or take into account irrelevant factors, or vice versa. Ministers must comply with statutory procedures, especially with regard to the holding of inquiries and should apply the principles of natural justice which involve giving a fair hearing.[144] With regard to procedural irregularities, applicants must show consequential substantial prejudice to their interests, though generally the discretion of the court not to quash will be exercised only if a point is purely technical or where there could be no possible detriment to the applicant.[145]

140   *Griffiths v Secretary of State for the Environment* [1983] 2 AC 51, [1983] 1 All ER 439.
141   *R v Secretary of State for the Environment, ex p Ostler* [1977] QB 122, [1976] 3 All ER 90.
142   *Matthew v Secretary of State for Transport, Local Government and the Regions* [2001] All ER (D) 147 (Oct).
143   *Turner v Secretary of State for the Environment* (1973) 28 P & CR 123; *Bizony v Secretary of State for the Environment* [1976] JPL 306.
144   *Seddon Properties Ltd v Secretary of State for the Environment and Macclesfield Borough Council* (1978) 248 Estates Gazette 950.
145   *Peak Park Joint Planning Board v Secretary of State for the Environment and Imperial Chemical Industries* (1979) 39 P & CR 361.

Appeals may only be on points of law, not on the merits of the planning application. This is not always an easy distinction to draw, but is illustrated by *R v Haringey London Borough Council, ex p Barrs*.[146] An attempted challenge was made on the grounds of the architectural standard of the development. The court declined to act as a forum of taste, stating it could only intervene where a development was of such a character that no one could reasonably permit it in its location. It is not enough to justify intervention for the court merely to disagree with a decision on its facts.[147] It is also possible to challenge on the basis that a relevant planning policy has been misconstrued or misapplied on appeal.[148] Where a policy has been treated as having a meaning it cannot reasonably bear challenge is also possible.[149]

A non-statutory mode of questioning planning decisions for which the TCPA 1990 makes no specific provision for challenge, *especially those of local planning authorities*, is application for judicial review under RSC Ord 53 and the Supreme Court Act 1981, s 31, and see now the Civil Procedure Rules, Ord 54. So far as the powers of planning authorities are concerned this is the method of proceeding for quashing orders (formerly certiorari) — the most commonly sought remedy, mandatory orders (formerly mandamus) and prohibiting orders (formerly prohibition). Injunctive and declaratory relief is also available, but will not often be awarded.[150] Leave must be sought to make applications. This is granted at the court's discretion. The attitude of the courts is, where there is an alternative remedy by way of appeal, a remedy by way of judicial review should only be granted where the alternative is not convenient, or where there is a real question as to the way in which the authority reached its decision.[151] Applications for leave to apply for judicial review must be made promptly, and usually within three months of the date when grounds for the application arose. In considering applications the courts may frown on delay in general and be unwilling to grant relief that would be detrimental to good administration, see the Supreme Court Act 1981, s 31(6), and *R v Swansea City Council, ex p Main*.[152] The three-month period for applications does not entitle a party to wait for almost three months before applying, prompt action is almost always needed.[153] Furthermore in an attempt to harmonise the rules on judicial review with those relating to statutory challenge the courts now normally require a judicial review action to be commenced within six weeks of the alleged illegality.[154] The court will only grant leave where it considers the applicant has a sufficient interest in the matter; for example an association of local residents likely to be affected by a development,[155] or a ratepayer living close to a development site,[156] or a neighbour whose privacy would be invaded by a development,[157] but not, it seems, an applicant who is a user of the highway adjoining the site in question but who lives

---

146 (1983) Times, 1 July.
147 *Asher v Secretary of State for the Environment* [1974] Ch 208, [1974] 2 All ER 156.
148 *South Somerset District Council and Secretary of State for the Environment v David Wilson Homes (Southern) Ltd* [1993] 1 PLR 80.
149 *Virgin Cinema Properties Ltd v Secretary of State for the Environment* [1998] 2 PLR 24.
150 *R v Secretary of State for the Environment, ex p Ward* [1984] 2 All ER 556; *R v Secretary of State for the Environment, ex p Greater London Council* [1985] JPL 543.
151 *R v Secretary of State for the Environment, ex p Ward* [1984] 2 All ER 556.
152 (1981) Times, 23 December.
153 *R v Poole Borough Council, ex p Beebee* [1991] JPL 643.
154 *R v Ceredigion County Council, ex p McKeown* [1998] 2 PLR 1; *R v Bristol City Council, ex p Moira Anderson* [2000] PLCR 104; *R v Leicester City Council and W M Morrison Supermarkets plc and Powergen UK plc, ex p Safeway Stores plc* [1999] JPL 691.
155 *Covent Garden Community Association Ltd v Greater London Council* [1981] JPL 183.
156 *Steeples v Derbyshire County Council* [1981] JPL 582.
157 *R v North Hertfordshire District Council, ex p Sullivan* [1981] JPL 752.

some miles away.[158] The courts will consider the nature of the statutory power, and the implications for the applicant of its use in deciding what is a 'sufficient interest', likewise the applicant's history of involvement with the matter. However, the law will not recognise that a group of persons has locus standi simply because they form themselves into an interest group to campaign on the issue in question. Though a person may not need a direct interest in an issue to have locus standi in relation to it, some sort of indirect interest, such as residence in an area likely to be affected by a proposal, or a close involvement with the site in question over a number of years may be needed.[159]

The position appears to be different, however, with respect to commercial undertakings, so, for example, a company may have a 'sufficient interest' where there is a real possibility that its commercial interests may be prejudiced by a grant of permission to another, so that it is likely the first company is likely to be refused permission on its application, or its development is likely otherwise to be adversely affected.[160] Likewise a very well established and reputable environmental pressure group, with a number of its members living in an area affected by a proposed development, who raise a serious and well-focused objection to that development, and who can pursue their challenge with much greater ease and efficiency than could any individual, may well be considered to have a 'sufficient interest' for judicial review purposes.[161] However, it also appears such a pressure group may also need the 'capacity' to bring an action, ie it must have legal personality, for example by way of incorporation.[162]

K   FINANCIAL CONSEQUENCES OF REVOKING OR REFUSING PERMISSION

Permission granted on an application may be revoked or modified under s 97 before an operational development has been completed or a change of use has taken place. An order revoking permission requires the Secretary of State's confirmation, save where under the TCPA 1990, s 99, the parties affected by the order have in writing stated they do not object. The Secretary of State must not confirm an order without affording affected persons and the authority a hearing or a local inquiry. Where planning permission is revoked or modified, compensation may be payable under the TCPA 1990, s 107 to persons interested in the land who have incurred expenditure in carrying out work rendered abortive by the revocation or modification, or have otherwise sustained loss or damage directly attributable thereto (including elements in respect of depreciation in value of the claimant's interest), subsequent to the grant of permission (*or* in connection with preparatory plans or matters for the work in question).

The TCPA 1990, s 102 allows planning authorities to secure by order the discontinuance of any *use* of land, for example, scrap sorting,[163] or the removal of the buildings and works, or imposition of conditions on a continued use, in the interests of the proper planning and amenity of their area, including the preservation of amenity in

---

158   *R v Bradford-on-Avon UDC, ex p Boulton* [1964] 2 All ER 492, [1964] 1 WLR 1136 and note *R v North Somerset District Council and Pioneer Aggregates (UK) Ltd, ex p Garnett* [1997] JPL 1015.

159   *R v Secretary of State for the Environment, ex p Rose Theatre Trust Co* [1990] 1 QB 504.

160   *R v Canterbury City Council, ex p Springimage* [1994] JPL 427; *Morbaine Ltd v Secretary of State for the Environment* [1994] JPL B81.

161   *R v HM Inspectorate of Pollution and Minister of Agriculture, Fisheries and Food, ex p Greenpeace* [1994] 4 All ER 329.

162   *R v Darlington Borough Council, ex p Association of Darlington Taxi Owners* [1994] COD 424.

163   *Parkes v Secretary of State for the Environment* [1979] 1 All ER 211, [1978] 1 WLR 1308.

the future.[164] The power does not apply to *continuing* building or engineering developments, but may apply to buildings or works thereby produced. Orders under this section must be confirmed by the Secretary of State. Persons affected by the order, having been served with due notice by the authority, have the right to a hearing or a local inquiry, as also do the authority. Where an order requires steps to be taken for the alteration or removal of buildings and works, and no action ensues, the authority may enter the land and take action, see the TCPA 1990, s 190. Section 102 orders can apply to land uses that have never needed planning permission. Where an order is made, compensation is payable under the TCPA 1990, s 107 in respect of depreciation of value of a person's interest in the land suffered in consequence of the order or as a result of disturbance. Where a person carries out works in compliance with an order he/she is entitled to compensation in respect of reasonable expenses. The rules for assessing compensation are under the TCPA 1990, s 117, laid down by the Land Compensation Act 1961, s 5.

In principle compensation is not payable in respect of *refusals* of permission for developments, even where this means a loss of profit to a prospective developer. More important are situations where a purchase notice can be served, particularly in relation to plots of land which the owner wishes to 'off-load'. The TCPA 1990, ss 137–148 lay down procedures whereby a purchase notice can be served by the owner of relevant land who claims, as a result of the refusal or conditional grant of permission, the land has become incapable of reasonably beneficial use in its existing state, *or* beneficial use is inconsistent with compliance with planning conditions, *and*, in either case, the land *cannot* be beneficially used by carrying out other development for which permission is available. Purchase notices are served on district councils. They may pass a notice on to another local authority or statutory undertaker who agrees to comply with it in their place. Disputed notices are referred to the Secretary of State who has certain powers, subject to holding a hearing. Where convinced that the land is incapable of reasonably beneficial use, he/she may confirm the notice unconditionally, or may confirm it with the substitution of another local authority or statutory undertaker as the acquiring body, or may grant planning permission for the development comprised in the application, revoking or amending conditions where appropriate, or may make provision for a grant of permission for other development. A successful purchase notice operates as a type of 'reverse compulsory purchase'. The relevant authority are forced to acquire the site. Purchase notices may also be served as a result of revocation or modification of planning permission, or required discontinuations where land has in consequence become incapable of reasonably beneficial use in its existing state, see the TCPA 1990, s 137.

Having to pay compensation in respect of interferences with existing land uses seems to deter authorities from taking action, or even from refusing permission in some cases.

L ENFORCEMENT

No system of control is effective unless enforced, and for many years enforcement was the 'Cinderella' of planning, bedevilled by complex and uncertain legal provisions and not highly esteemed as a function. Officers were irritated at the cumbersome legal procedures involved and the feeling that they were 'fighting with one arm tied behind their backs' as the record of magistrates' courts in punishing those prosecuted for infringing enforcement action has not been good, with a generally low level of fines imposed. Following publication of the Carnwath Report, *Enforcing Planning Control*,

---

[164] *Re Lamplugh* (1967) 19 P & CR 125.

in 1989 the legal provisions were amended by the 1991 Act. Unauthorised development is still not a criminal offence, but the new provisions are a clear advance in clarity on their predecessors, and enhanced penalties are provided for those who flout the law. Furthermore research into enforcement ('Evaluation of Planning Enforcement Provisions', DoE, 1995) concluded that the new provisions are working well.

The current law

The TCPA 1990, s 171A defines expressions; thus a *'breach of planning control'* arises where development requiring permission takes place without permission, or where any conditions in a grant or permission are not complied with; *'enforcement action'* consists of either issuing an enforcement notice, or a breach of condition notice (a *new* term). The TCPA 1990, s 171C applies where the local planning authority suspect a breach of planning control. They may serve a *'planning contravention notice'* (PCN) on 'any person' who is the owner/occupier of the land, or who is carrying out operations on, under or over it, or using it. This will require specified information to be given as to operations, uses, any conditions, etc, imposed in any grant of permission, etc. Particular questions may be asked about when an activity began. The PCN may give notice of a time and place at which the person served with it may make representations or make an offer to apply for planning permission, or undertake to refrain from activities or carry out remedial works. The PCN must also inform the person served of the likely consequences of failure to respond, and that enforcement action may be taken. Serving a PCN does not affect any other enforcement powers. However, a PCN may only be used where there is evidence upon which a reasonable authority would conclude there is an indication of a breach of control. The procedure cannot be used for mere 'fishing trips'.[165]

The TCPA 1990, s 171D makes it an offence to fail to comply with a PCN's requirements within 21 days, though defences will exist of having a reasonable excuse for failure to comply with the requirements of the PCN. It is likewise an offence intentionally or recklessly to make false or misleading statements in response to a PCN.

These provisions go some way towards meeting the often repeated criticism that planning authorities have been in a weak position when taking enforcement action because they have frequently been in no position to know exactly what has unlawfully been going on on the land in question.

TCPA 1990, substitute s 172 provides that an enforcement notice may be issued where it appears there has been a breach of planning control, and that it is expedient so to act, considering the provisions of the development plan and other material considerations. A copy of this notice is to be served on the owner/occupier of relevant land, and others having materially affected interests in the land, and service is to take place not more than 28 days after the date of issue and not less than 28 days before the specified date for the notice to take effect.

The notice must, under the TCPA 1990, new s 173, state the matters *appearing* to constitute a breach of control and whether in the authority's opinion they consist of *either* unauthorised development *or* a breach of condition. A notice will be taken to comply with this requirement if it enables the person on whom it is served to know what the matters constituting the alleged breach are. The notice will have to specify the steps to be taken, or the activities to be ended, in order to achieve, *in whole or part*:

165   *R v Teignbridge District Council, ex p Teignmouth Quay Co Ltd* [1995] JPL 828.

1   Remedying the breach by complying with the terms of any relevant planning permission or restoring land to its original condition, or by discontinuing any use.
2   Remedying any injury to amenity.

In particular a notice may require demolition of buildings, carrying out of operations, cessation of a land use, reduction of a use/activity to a specified level, contouring of refuse or waste materials. The notice will also have to state the date on which it will take effect, and the period(s) within which steps are to be taken or activities concluded. However, a notice cannot require more than is necessary to cure the breach, for example by requiring the cessation of an otherwise lawful use of land.[166]

Where the alleged breach consists of demolition of a building, the notice may require construction of a 'replacement building' generally similar to that demolished, subject, of course, inter alia, to any relevant building controls. Certain prescribed matters must be included in the notice, including rights of appeal.

TCPA 1990, s 173A provides for the withdrawal of an enforcement notice before it takes effect, and for the informing of all those served with copies of the notice. *Alternatively* the authority is able to waive or relax enforcement notice requirements, *and* this power is exercisable even after a notice has taken effect, though again notice of intention to vary will have to be served on every person originally served, and any representations made in consequence considered. This power is without prejudice to the authority's ability to issue a further notice.

TCPA 1990, s 174 (as amended) provides that appeals against enforcement notices may be brought on the following grounds, namely that:
1   In respect of any breach of control covered by the notice permission ought to be granted or the condition/limitation discharged, as the case may be.
2   The matters alleged have not occurred.
3   The matters do not amount to a breach.
4   At the date when notice was issued no enforcement action could be taken (eg because of limitation, see further below).
5   Copies of the notice were not served as required.
6   Steps required to be taken, etc, exceed what is necessary to remedy any breach of control in the circumstances.
7   Time periods specified for taking action are unreasonably short.

In respect of the specified grounds a notice may only be challenged by an appeal, not by way of judicial review, see the TCPA 1990, s 285(1), but it is still possible to seek judicial review of a notice in respect of non-specified matters — eg an allegation that the notice is a nullity because of some defect 'on its face' such as failure to specify steps required to remedy a breach.[167]

The appeal is to be made either by giving written notice to the Secretary of State, or by sending the notice to him/her by post, in the latter case before the notice would have taken effect but for delays in the post, or before it does take effect. The grounds of appeal must be specified in the notice of appeal together with such other information as is specified.

The TCPA 1990, s 175 empowers the Secretary of State to make regulations concerning appeals procedures, in particular to govern the submission of the planning authority's case and other exchanges of information (see SI 1991/2804). Note also TCPA 1990, Sch 6. Enforcement appeals are generally dealt with in a manner similar to appeals against refusal of permission. The Secretary of State's discretion concerning the outcome of an appeal under TCPA 1990, s 176 as amended is wide. He/she may correct

166   *Mansi v Elstree RDC* (1964) 16 P & CR 153.
167   *MacKay v Secretary of State for the Environment* [1996] JPL 761 and *Tandridge District Council v Verrechia* [2000] PLCR 1.

misdescriptions, defects or errors in enforcement notices or vary their terms, provided this will not cause injustice to the appellant or the authority, while s 177 permits the grant of permission for development, or part of a development, or a development on part of relevant land, or discharge conditions, or the determination of lawful land uses. However, in exercising these powers the Secretary of State must consider the development plan and any other relevant considerations.

The TCPA 1990, s 178 of the TCPA 1990 (as amended) provides that where steps required by an enforcement notice are not taken, the planning authority may enter the land and take them and may recover their reasonable expenses from the then owner of the land. Thus an authority may now take action against, for example an unauthorised *use* so that it complies with any grant of permission; the previous law only allowed the taking of action to restore land to an existing use.

The TCPA 1990, substituted s 179 provides that where at the end of a compliance period any steps required by an enforcement notice have not been taken, or where an activity has not been terminated, a breach of enforcement notice occurs. This is an offence, and a continuing one until the state of affairs constituting the breach ceases. Defences include showing that the person charged did everything in his/her power to secure compliance with the notice. Further defences include showing that the person charged has not been served with a copy of the enforcement notice, or that the notice has not been duly registered under s 188. Likewise a person who is an occupier of relevant land must not carry on or cause or permit to be carried on an activity required to end by an enforcement notice, and non-compliance after the end of the period for compliance is, again, an offence. On summary conviction a fine of up to £20,000 may be levied, on indictment the fine is unlimited, but in either case the court in calculating the fine is to take into account any financial benefit accruing to the accused from the commission of the offence. Criminal proceedings can only be defended by way of a challenge to the vires of an enforcement notice where it is defective on its face and a nullity, in all other cases where vires is in issue (for example allegations of bad faith, perversity, failure to consider the correct issues) the proper course of action is to seek an adjournment of the trial and to apply for judicial review of the enforcement notice, assuming, of course, one is in time to do this.[168]

TCPA 1990, s 180, as substituted, provides that where after service of a copy of an enforcement notice or breach of condition notice (see further below) planning permission is granted for any development carried out previously the notice shall, in so far as inconsistent with the grant, cease to have effect, though this does not exculpate persons in respect of previous criminal liabilities already incurred. TCPA 1990, s 181 then provides that compliance with an enforcement notice does not prevent it from applying to any later unauthorised act of development to which the notice applies.

With specific regard to enforcement of planning conditions, a new s 187A provides a new optional procedure so that where conditions are not complied with a 'breach of conditions notice' (BCN) may be served on the person responsible through having committed the breach of having control of the land, requiring compliance with the conditions specified in the BCN, and the steps to be taken/activities ended in order to secure compliance. A compliance period of not less than 28 days beginning with the date of service is to be allowed, though the authority may extend this. If the steps specified to be taken are still lacking, or where any activity to be ended goes on, the person responsible will be in breach of the BCN and will commit an offence, though it will be a defence to prove that all reasonable measures to secure compliance with conditions were taken.

---

168 *R v Wicks* [1998] AC 92, [1997] 2 All ER 801, and note also *Bracken v East Hertfordshire District Council* [2000] All ER (D) 579 (Apr).

A BCN *cannot* be appealed, though challenge is available on a point of law by way of judicial review.[169] It also appears possible to raise the issue of the general vires of a BCN by way of a defence to a prosecution for the breach.[170]

Enforcement: further action

In some cases enforcement action alone will be insufficient to deal with unauthorised development. In some instances an immediate cessation of the activity in question will be desirable, and here the 'stop notice' provisions of the TCPA 1990 may be resorted to (see further below). In other cases stronger remedies may be needed. The persistent unauthorised developer may regard any fines imposed as 'mere overheads' and the threat of imprisonment for contempt of court may be a more potent deterrent, hence injunctive relief is available, originally under the Local Government Act 1972, s 222. The remedy is, of course, discretionary, and will not be issued as a matter of course. Evidence of a breach of control must be clear, the breach must be deliberate and it must appear that the breach will occur or continue unless restrained.[171]

A new s 187B specifically provides that injunctive relief may be applied for in either the County or High Court where the local planning authority consider it necessary or expedient for *actual or apprehended* breaches of planning control, whether or not any other enforcement powers are to be used. It is clear, following *Croydon London Borough Council v Gladden*[172] and *Harwood v Runnymede Borough Council*[173] that the power to apply for injunctive relief is a wide and flexible one which applies *equally* to cases of apprehended breaches of planning control as well as actual ones. Injunctions generally should be precisely worded so that the injunctee knows exactly what must not be done, but it is possible to word an injunction very widely where this is clearly the only way to prevent a particular breach of planning control.[174] Furthermore it is no longer necessary for a planning authority to show that an injunction is needed because the criminal law alone is insufficient to deter a person's unlawful development activities. The decision in *Kirklees Metropolitan Borough Council v Wickes Building Supplies Ltd*[175] that a local planning authority does not have to give a cross-undertaking in damages where an interim injunction is sought against an activity (ie where its cessation is sought while its legality is being determined) may promote the popularity of seeking injunctive relief in respect of contravention of planning control. The previous rule that an authority had to undertake to indemnify the injunctee should the final decision be there was no illegal activity in the first place, which could have led to authorities facing claims for considerable losses of profit, was from a planning authority point of view most unfortunate. The power of the court to issue an injunction does not contravene the injunctee's rights under the European Convention where it can be shown the order is necessary to uphold the provisions of planning law and to protect the environment.[176]

The stop notice provisions of the TCPA 1990 were extensively modified in 1991. The TCPA 1990, s 183 is largely substituted with new provisions which provide that where a planning authority consider it expedient that a 'relevant activity' (ie any activity

169 *R v Ealing London Borough Council, ex p Zainuddin* [1995] JPL 925.
170 *Dilieto v London Borough of Ealing* [1998] PLCR 212.
171 *Westminster City Council v Jones* [1981] JPL 750; *City of London Corpn v Bovis Construction Ltd* [1989] JPL 263; *Southwark London Borough Council v Frow* [1989] JPL 645n.
172 [1994] JPL 723.
173 [1994] JPL 723.
174 *Kettering Borough Council v Perkins* [1999] JPL 166 and *Wealdon District Council v Krushandel* [1999] JPL 174.
175 [1993] AC 227.
176 *Macclesfield Borough Council v McMahon* [2001] All ER (D) 123 (May).

the authority require to cease, and any ancillary or associated activity) should cease before the date for compliance with the enforcement notice, they may, *when* they serve a copy of that notice, or afterwards, also serve a 'stop notice' prohibiting the activity on the land in question, or on any part of it. The notice may be served on any person with an interest in the land, or engaging in the prohibited activity. However, such a notice may not be served:

1   Where the enforcement notice has taken effect.
2   Where the unauthorised activity is use of a *building* as a dwelling house.
3   Where the activity has been carried out (continuously or not) for a period of *four* years ending with service of the notice, though no account is to be taken of any period during that time when the activity was permitted by planning permission, *and* this prohibition on taking action does *not* extend to prevent service of a stop notice prohibiting activity consisting of or incidental to building, engineering, mining or other operations or depositing refuse or waste.

The TCPA 1990, s 184 provides that a stop notice must refer to the enforcement notice to which it relates and have a copy of that notice annexed to it.

Under the TCPA 1990, s 184(3) a stop notice will take effect on a date specified and which must not be earlier than three days after service, *unless* the authority consider special reasons justify an earlier commencement, and a statement of those reasons is served with the stop notice. Likewise a notice must *not* commence later than 28 days after its first service on any person.

The TCPA 1990, s 187(1) and (2) as amended provides that if a person contravenes a stop notice after such a notice has been served on him/her, or a site notice (under s 184 stating stop notices have been served) has been displayed, he/she commits an offence. Contravention will include causing or permitting contravening activities.

Fines may be up to £20,000 on summary conviction or unlimited on indictment in respect of stop notice contraventions, but, as with the similar provisions relating to enforcement notices, the court is to take into account any financial benefit accruing to the accused from the breach. Stop notices may be challenged by defending on the merits of the case any criminal proceedings brought under them,[177] or by attacking their legality in an application for judicial review.[178]

Reference has been made above to time limits within which enforcement action has to be taken. Section 171B of the TCPA 1990 as inserted in 1991 provides that where there has been a breach of planning control which consists of operational development *no* enforcement action may be taken after the end of four years beginning with the date on which operations were *substantially* completed. This may introduce complexities for authorities who may find unauthorised developers arguing that the time for taking action has passed because their operations were substantially complete more than four years previously. TCPA 1990, s 171B(2) further provides that where the breach consists of a *change of use* of any building to that of a *single* dwelling house again there is a *four*-year limitation. In the case of any other breaches of control eg all other *material changes of use* the limitation period is *ten* years from the date of the breach.

Enhanced rights of entry for enforcement purposes are given by sections 196A–C. These allow any person duly authorised in writing by a local authority to enter land at any reasonable hour to ascertain whether a breach of control has taken place, and to determine how and whether enforcement powers should be used, provided reasonable grounds for entering the land exist. The Secretary of State has similar authorising powers, though only after consultation with the local planning authority. This power under TCPA 1990, s 196A exists without a warrant. TCPA 1990, s 196B will allow

177   *R v Jenner* [1983] 2 All ER 46, [1983] 1 WLR 873.
178   *R v Epping Forest District Council, ex p Strandmill Ltd* [1990] JPL 415.

application to a magistrate where an entry could be made under TCPA 1990, s 196A and where admission has been refused, or refusal is reasonably apprehended, or where the case is one of urgency. The magistrate may issue a warrant authorising entry at a reasonable hour (or at any time in urgent cases), and this entry may take place at any time up to one month from the warrant's issue. Under TCPA 1990, s 196C it will be an offence to obstruct these powers of entry.

Finally note TCPA 1990, s 289(4A), (4B) and (5A). The High Court now has power to order that, pending determination and consequential proceedings an enforcement notice shall have full or modified effect. The making of such orders is at the discretion of the court and authorities may be required to give cross undertakings in damages in the event of the final outcome being to strike down the enforcement actions. TCPA 1990, s 289(6) further provides that s 289 proceedings may only be brought by leave of the court. This is designed to deter frivolous and unmeritorious appeals.[179]

M CERTIFICATES OF LAWFUL USE/DEVELOPMENT

Sections 191–194 of the TCPA 1990 as substituted, provide that where any person wishes to ascertain the lawfulness of any *existing* use of buildings or land, or any operations, or any matter which might constitute a breach of condition, an application specifying the issues may be made to the local planning authority. Under TCPA 1990, s 191 which relates to current uses, etc, uses and operations will be lawful if:

1 no enforcement action may be taken in their regard either because they never needed planning permission or because lapse of time precludes enforcement; and
2 they do not contravene any current enforcement notice. Similar requirements apply in respect of conditions.

If, on an application, the authority are provided with information satisfying them on the lawfulness of the matter in question they must certify accordingly, otherwise they must refuse to certify. The certificate, if given, must specify the land, and the matter in question, giving reasons for the determination of lawfulness and stating the date of the application. Such a certificate also has a significance for the purposes of other legislation, eg the EPA 1990, s 36(2). TCPA 1990, s 192 makes provision (similar to that under s 191) for applications to determine whether a *proposed* use or development would be lawful.[180]

Applications for TCPA 1990, ss 191 and 192 certificates must be in prescribed form, see s 193, and specific provisions is made in this respect by the GDPO. A certificate may be given in respect of all or some relevant land, and, where uses are multiple, in respect of one, or more, or all of them. Certificates may be revoked if the local planning authority discover statements made to them in connection with certificates were false or that material information was withheld, and TCPA 1990, s 194 provides that it is an offence knowingly or recklessly to give false information or use false or misleading documentation in this connection.

---

179 *Huggett v Secretary of State for the Environment* [1995] 7 ELM 99.
180 For guidance on the application of the procedure see *Panton and Farmer v Secretary of State for the Environment, Transport and the Regions and Vale of White Horse District Council* [1999] JPL 461.

The future of planning law

In December 2001 the government issued a radical consultation paper – 'Planning Green Paper – Planning: Delivering a Fundamental Change'. (This applied to England, similar proposals may be expected for Wales.) While reiterating the need for a 'proper' planning system that: will deliver land for development in the right place at the right time; encourages urban regeneration and opposes urban sprawl; conserves greenfield sites and reuses brown field land; values the countryside and heritage; will play its part in delivering the sustainable development policy of government, this also promised the most fundamental change in the planning system in over 50 years. In particular it promised a more user friendly – *and business friendly* – system, with planning applications being dealt with *efficiently and predictably* with reduced delays and less complex bureaucracy. The current planning system is characterised in the document as: complex, remote and hard to understand, with too many layers of plans, many of which can be out of date and inconsistent with one another; having too much and unfocussed national planning guidance which mixes up general principles and good practice advice; possessing too many unclear rules, and an obscure appeals procedure. The rules, in particular, are attacked as perceived as being there to prevent development rather than ensuring the progress of 'good development'. Quite what is 'good' of course depends on one's point of view, but similar criticisms can be levelled at many other parts of the government's document which seems too often to be yet another exercise in attempting to reconcile the irreconcilable by simply including them in one document in an exercise of trying to be all things to all people.

Even so the document did make certain criticisms of the current system that have had a degree of currency in many circles for some years. Thus there have been complaints about the speed of decision taking – more than 90% of authorities fail to meet the best practice target of deciding 80% of planning applications in eight weeks. There are complaints about the lack of predictability of decision taking because the criteria that will be employed are uncertain, while the process of updating plans remains time consuming and expensive, and the appeal process is similarly long winded. At the same time the delay in the plan-making process renders it hard for communities and community groups to sustain involvement in the process. Once plans are made decisions on applications are often made without applicants or objectors having a chance to put forward their arguments, while the whole process is legalistic and is inaccessible to those lacking professional help and guidance.

To address these problems a fundamental restructuring of the planning system has been proposed. This would begin with the nature and role of plans. The government has declared its commitment to the continuation of a 'plan led' system, but the number of planning tiers, they have argued, should be reduced and the object should be to deliver shorter, better and more flexible and focussed plans at a local level which are amenable to faster revision. In addition local plans should key in with the obligations of local authorities to have proper community strategies which are developed with public, private and community sector organisations and which seek to promote the economic, social and environmental well being of an authority's area. Thus the government's proposal is *to abolish structure, local and unitary development plans* and to replace them with a single *Local Development Framework* (LDF) consisting of: a *statement of core policies* setting out the vision and strategy for development control within an area; detailed action plans for smaller local areas such as town centres, and a map showing areas for which action plans are to be prepared and conservation areas etc. The 'core policies' statement would complement the vision of the community strategy and would state clear objectives for the development and improvement of the physical environment with a proposed timetable for achieving this. The statement would also lay down arrangements for involving the community in reviewing the LDF and in 'significant' development control decisions, with 'criteria' based policies on issues such as housing, business development, planning obligations, transport, waste and the historic environment. The objective of the proposal is to create plans which take less time to prepare and amend, and which provide predictable criteria according to which businesses can plan while also allowing community involvement in decision taking. The new law on planning would lay down absolute requirements for community participation and the timetabling of plan preparation and review – with the emphasis in terms of time being upon months and not years. The core policy statement would also be required to be continuously updated to be consistent with national and regional policies. The LDF would also have to be subject to sustainability appraisal which will take account of the need to comply with the new EC Directive on Strategic Environmental Assessment (see above). The Secretary of State would also retain a reserve power to direct amendment of the LDF.

The principal planning tier of local government

The proposals clearly envisage District, Metropolitan and Unitary Authorities as the principal plan makers – though it is accepted that such authorities could cooperate together in their work. In such a 'new world' (brave or otherwise) there would be no role for county level structure plans which should be phased out – a proposal seen by some commentators as an attempt to end the opposition of county councils to major house building proposals. Counties would, however, continue to produce minerals and waste plans. At a level above the counties planning should exist at a regional and subregional level. Thus existing centrally issued Regional Planning Guidance (RPG) should be replaced with a new *statutory* system of Regional Spatial Strategies (RSS) with which LDFs would have to be consistent. RSS should concentrate on the broad location of major development proposals and set targets and indicators for development, while also reflecting regional diversity and the specific needs of regions. RSS should be integrated into the wider strategies of the Regional Development Agencies which are statutory – *though non-elected* – bodies under the Regional Development Agencies Act 1998. The bodies that will be charged with preparing RSS will have to enter into a consultation process with a 'broad range of regional stakeholders through focus groups or planning forums'. It may, however, be objected that the interposition of RSS will create a new statutory planning tier which will lack democratic accountability, and that will not satisfy those who will be opposed to the elimination of the county-based structure plan. As a sop to wounded democratic feeling the proposals indicate that 'provision should be made for directly elected regional government in regions where people decide in a referendum to support it and where predominantly unitary local government is established', and a further white paper on this issue is promised. However, one may point out that in such areas – eg the West Midlands – there used to be an effectively regional level of democratically accountable local government in the form of the metropolitan county council – a tier of local government abolished in 1985. Here, as with so many other Green Paper proposals one is left with a distinct feeling of déja vu!

The Green Paper concludes that though nationally applicable Planning Policy Guidance (PPG) has been a success, its current volume (852 pages) is too great and it needs both to be reduced and refocused, with a reduction also in its prescriptive quality. Thus 'national planning policy should concentrate on the important policy issues that need to be resolved at national level', with national policies set out clearly as principles, with good practice separated out as guidance only. This – if implemented – would be a desirable change for at the moment some PPGs are exceptionally detailed, which invites their interpretation and application almost as if they were statutes, while the initial distinction which was intended to be made between PPGs and Departmental Circulars (with the latter concentrating on advice and guidance) has never been fully achieved.

Fundamental changes in development control

The government argues that development control is not 'customer-friendly' and is not 'well understood', furthermore the speed with which applications are handled varies between authorities, with business users complaining that the 'slow pace of decision making' impacts adversely on business planning and investment. To address these issues there are proposals to:

- introduce planning checklists to assist in the production of good quality applications;
- tighten determination times, in particular dealing with delays caused by statutory consultees;
- encourage 'masterplanning' (see further below) to improve the quality of development;
- promote better community involvement by offering advice in planning to community groups;
- introduce delivery contracts for planning for major developments;
- introduce 'business zones' where no planning permission is required for certain forms of development;
- seek enhanced enforcement in respect of those who week to evade planning control.

Expanding on these proposals, the consultation paper further proposes greater pre-application discussion between would-be developers and authorities – something that has been a feature of certain planning applications, such as mineral developments, for some years. As such applications are a drain on authority resources the possibility is raised of charging for such consultation. The planning checklist notion is further expanded on to indicate that developers might have to carry out their own pre-application consultations with the wider community to conform with the requirements of a 'Statement of Community Involvement', with all correspondence with consultees being kept for record purposes. This would be in addition to consultations with other statutory and non-statutory consultees.

It may at this point be pertinent to comment that such proposals may help in cutting down the processing time *after* an application has been made, but do so at the cost of increasing the length and complexity of the pre-application phase.

The government further proposes that 'nominated officers' should be appointed to whom applicants will be able to turn for advice and information on the progress of their application. This is in addition to stressing the need for planning services to be provided 'on line' – something that is to be expected from a government which is arguably over fond of 'E' solutions to problems. It is also proposed to move towards a 'one stop shop' approach to harmonise and standardise application and consent procedures where more than one permit is needed, for example where both planning consent and listed building consent are required, or where consent is required from more than one authority, for example a planning consent and a permit or authorisation from the Environment Agency. Further consultation was promised here on how such situations can be more harmoniously and speedily dealt with.

Under the 'Best Value' provisions of the Local Government Act 1999 the government has already set new handling target dates for 2002/03 for planning applications of 60% of major commercial and industrial applications to be determined in 13 weeks, 65% of minor commercial, etc applications to be determined in eight weeks and 80% of all other applications to be determined in eight weeks. However, it is accepted that larger development proposals need longer consideration times. In return for the loss of the right to appeal against a non-determined application, 'business organisations' appear to have told the government they would accept the notion of 'delivery contracts', which would give greater predictability about *when* decisions will be made, and information on *how* applications are progressing. Thus decision making would be timetabled and made the subject of binding obligations between the parties. The consequences of 'non-delivery' would be that either party would then be able to refer the matter to the planning inspectorate for a 'fast track' decision. This, of course, could result in authorities losing their current ability to non-determine controversial applications knowing that any subsequent appeal will transfer the decision making onus onto the shoulders of central government.

One allegedly time-consuming feature of the current development control process is the emphasis on consultation – both statutory and non-statutory. The government believes such consultation can be a major source of delay, particularly as 'most planning authorities will not take a decision in the absence of advice from a statutory consultee'. (It may be pointed out they are wise to behave in this way should they wish to avoid possible judicial review action based on allegations they have either failed to comply with required procedures or have failed to take into account relevant considerations.) The government proposes a number of ways of dealing with this problem. First of all developers are to be encouraged to carry out their own pre-application consultation processes, though they might have to pay fees for receiving such a service from statutory consultees. Secondly the number of statutory consultees could be reduced so that only 'those bodies whose advice has health and safety implications or which operate another parallel consent regime … will be given statutory consultee status'. Next it is proposed that statutory consultees should have power to charge for their services, provided that advice is given within a fixed timescale, with, in addition, a statutory obligation being imposed to respond to consultation requests within set times. The 'stick' of threats to future cuts in central funding of 'slow responders' amongst consultees is also used in addition to the 'carrot' of allowing charges to be made for consultation.

Business Planning Zones would be created by local planning authorities where the need for such an area is justified by regional economic and planning strategies. No planning permission would be needed in such zones, but only certain types of industry would be able to benefit, such as 'high-tech' enterprises which would not significantly increase already high local housing demands, and which would not create large infrastructure requirements nor demand special environmental precautions. Such zones should be planned in conjunction with regional development strategies, in conjunction with the regional development agencies, universities and relevant companies – any of whom should be able to initiate proposals for such a zone. It is envisaged that each region should have at least one zone.

It may be here commented that such 'exempt' zones have been a feature of our planning system in one form or another for some 20 years or so, and there is therefore nothing really new or radical in the proposal.

The concept of 'master planning' was alluded to above. This refers back to the notion of the Local Development Framework which will make provision for particular action plans for particular areas. The proposal is that such plans *might* take the form of 'master plans' which indicate clearly the type, nature and design of development expected for particular sites or areas. In addition there would be community involvement in drawing up the 'master plan'. Furthermore under these arrangements, rather than making 'outline' planning applications, developers could instead seek certification that it is agreed they may for a defined period work up detailed schemes in accordance with parameters determined in agreement with the authority. When an actual planning application is made it would be in detailed form, and its compliance with the agreed criteria 'would weigh heavily' in the final determination of planning consent.

It may be commented that this proposal seems to be moving in the direction of something like a 'zoning system' whereby detailed land allocations for particular areas are agreed in advance with conforming applications being most likely to succeed – a plan-led system certainly, but one in which the proposals envisage a considerable amount of input from business – eg housebuilders – and from the rather more nebulous 'community'.

Further proposals

Repeat applications

It is proposed that once an application has been refused and not appealed, or has been appealed and refused, no substantially similar application for the same site should be accepted unless material circumstances change, eg a change in the Local Development Framework.

Twin tracking

The ability of developers to make 'twin' applications for the same development so that one can be made subject to appeal once the statutory period for determination has expired (which is a negotiating ploy to force the hand of authorities) will be abolished.

Time limits

The current law allows a planning permission to stand unimplemented for five years. This would be reduced to three years in order to speed up the development process, with no automatic ability to seek renewal at the end of that period; renewal applications would be treated as new applications for the development in question and would be determined as such.

Land assembly

Major changes in the law of compulsory purchase are proposed in order to allow authorities a speedier means of assembling land otherwise in diverse ownership where redevelopment is needed – eg for the purposes of urban regeneration.

Appeals

Where an appeal is made on the basis of non-determination, the inspector should assume the planning authority's jurisdiction so that he (she) may have access to all the work already done on the application.

The period of time for making an appeal should be reduced from six to three months.

Permitted development rights

It is possible that local supplementation of the current system of permitted development could be allowed in the form of 'local permitted development rights'.

Community consultation and involvement

The involvement of 'the community' is a major theme of the consultation exercise. Thus the proposal is that major developments – ie the larger and more complex proposals – should be the subject of pre-application consultation carried out by the would-be developer. There are further, somewhat vague, proposals to extend 'planning aid' to communities and individuals to ensure access to planning consultancy and advocacy. This proposal would, apparently, rely heavily on voluntary service given by planners, though there is a hint of some government funding for such a service. Under the terms of the Local Government Act 2000 which, inter alia, deals with local authority committee functions, authorities will be 'encouraged' to hold planning committee meetings in public and the public should be given the opportunity to speak. In addition it is proposed that it should become a legal requirement to give reasons when an application is consented as well as when it is refused, while access to relevant planning papers should be made easier by use of electronic means of dissemination, and the deposit of copies of certain documentation in public libraries.

Planning obligations

To meet the criticism that planning obligations lead to 'planning behind closed doors' with insufficient transparency as to how they are negotiated, a further consultation exercise is promised, but it is certainly proposed that it should be a requirement that information on planning obligations should be entered in the register of planning permissions so that such information is publicly available.

Enforcement

It is accepted that a simpler and faster development control system requires a more effective enforcement regime which currently remains complex and expensive to operate. The government's proposals here are vague – deliberately so – and are designed to seek comments. However, possible reforms include:
*   deliberate development without consent or in breach of consent could become a criminal offence;
*   levels of fines and the severity of other punishments could be increased;
*   the ability of an unauthorised developer to delay enforcement procedures by appealing could be modified;
*   where a retrospective application is made for an unauthorised development a punitive charge for handling the application could be imposed.

Other fundamental changes at national, regional and local levels

Major development projects

The government is to press ahead with producing a system whereby a series of policy statements is made on major infrastructure proposals, with such proposals then being made subject to 'in principle' parliamentary approval. These arrangements will include regional frameworks for identifying investment needs and strategies, 'robust arrangements' for prior public consultation, consideration at public inquiry level only of detailed issues. Major developments by the Crown will be subject to these new procedures, while other Crown developments will become subject to normal planning control, thus removing the Crown's immunity from development control in all cases, saving certain instances where defence or security issues are concerned – it may be commented that it is, however, the use of land for 'defence' purposes that is a particularly controversial issue, so the proposals give little away here. (See further chapter 11.)

Appeals

Some minor appeals would be referred from planning inspectors to mediators, eg where the dispute truly relates to an inter-neighbour dispute over small scale household development, or where, with regard to an enforcement appeal, scope exists for a negotiated solution, or where mediation could play a role in narrowing down areas of disagreement prior to the inquiry stage.

Called-in decision

These relate to the largest and most controversial development proposals, but it is accepted by the government that such decisions are not handled speedily. Administrative undertakings have been given to reduce the current delays and it is possible that statutory timetables should be set for making decisions – subject to exceptions when particularly difficult cases are encountered.

Third party rights of appeal

It is well known that our current law does not allow a third party to appeal against a grant of planning permission. The argument supporting this is that local planning authorities are democratically accountable bodies who take account of the views of objectors in taking their decisions and who can subsequently justify those decisions to their electorates. This line of argument is maintained by the consultation paper which steadfastly sets its face against allowing third party rights of appeal, even though they appear to work well in other jurisdictions with a similar legal tradition to our own, such as the Republic of Ireland. Whether such a stance is compatible with our obligations under the Human Rights Act 1998 remains to be seen. (See further chapter 5.)

Delegation and contracting out

This seemingly innocuous issue is 'tucked away' near the end of the consultation paper. Powers exist under the Local Government Act 1972 for authorities to delegate their decision-making powers to committees, sub-committees and officers. The proposal is that: 'To speed up decision making, authorities should delegate decisions to officers as far as practicable. To encourage this process we have set for 2002/03 a new target of delegation of 90% of decisions to Officers which will be monitored through Best Value'.

By relying on the use of existing legislation the government thus announces a major change in planning practice, for it may be argued that officers are much less likely to be swayed in their decision making than are elected members conscious of their electorate. Other legislation (eg the Deregulation and Contracting Out Act 1994) facilitates contracting out of local authority functions, and the consultation paper counsels authorities to consider the use of private sector providers to undertake planning functions, such as jurisdiction in minor planning procedures where staff resources in house are needed for major projects.

Comment

Public reaction to the proposals has been quite predictable. They were generally welcomed by groups representing industry and commerce – in particular the house building industry which points to the delays in the planning as the reason for house building in 2001 being at its lowest peacetime level since 1924 according to some sources, despite builders owning land to construct 2m dwellings. Equally condemnatory, however, were environmental groups who argued that environmental protection and local democracy were being sacrificed at the altar of corporate profits. Such reactions are to be expected where points of view are polarised. What is, nevertheless, disappointing about the consultation paper is that much of it consists of a rehash of arguments about planning that have raged for many years. The problem of delay appears to be endemic in a system which must balance out a large number of countervailing forces before a decision can be reached. Where the consultation proposals strike new lights here is the recognition that speeding up the process demands greater resources for authorities, and this is reflected in the proposals that charging regimes should be enhanced. This 'carrot' is, however, accompanied by the 'stick' of threats to impose tougher performance targets using the 'best value' provisions of the Local Government Act 1999 coupled with the threat of direct central intervention in the case of 'poorly performing' authorities. That is, perhaps, only to be expected in the current governmental climate where 'league tables' are of such importance and 'naming and shaming' is seen as a legitimate governing measure.

Another 'old favourite' resurrected in the consultation paper is public participation – this time under the title of ('Community Involvement'). There is little evidence to show that communities as a whole wish to be involved in planning issues. Individuals and groups may wish to be involved where a proposal affects them, but the history of public involvement is in general one of highly selective and uneven involvement. Whether that can be changed by the new proposals is open to question.

If, however, the government presses ahead with its proposals – and formal legislation was expected at the time of writing to go before Parliament in the autumn of 2002 – the result will be a radically altered planning system in both principle and detail.

Further reading

BOOKS
Blowers, A, *The Limits of Power: The Politics of Local Planning Policy* (1980) Pergamon Press.

Bruton, M, and Nicholson, D, *Local Planning in Practice* (1987) Hutchinson.

Carnwath, R, (ed) *Blundell and Doby's Planning Appeals and Inquiries* (4th edn) (1990) Sweet and Maxwell.

Churchill, Gibson and Warren, *Law, Policy and the Environment* (1991) Blackwell.

Cullingworth, B, and Nadin, V, *Town and Country Planning in the UK* (13th edn, 2002) Routledge.

Fortlage, CA, *Environmental Assessment* (1990) Gower.

Grant, M, *Urban Planning Law* (1982) Sweet and Maxwell.

Grove-White, R, 'Land Use, Law and the Environment' in Churchill, Gibson and Warren.

Kenyon, S, and Walton, D, *Development Plans: Laws and Practice* (1998) Sweet and Maxwell.

McAuslan, P, *The Ideologies of Planning Law* (1980) Pergamon Press.

Miller, C, and Wood, C, *Planning and Pollution* (1983) Clarendon Press.

Miller, C, (ed) *Planning and Environmental Protection* (2001) Hart Publishing.

Moore, V, *A Practical Approach to Planning Law* (7th edn, 2000) Blackstone.

Morgan, P, and Nott, S, *Development Control: Law Policy & Practice* (1995) Butterworths.

Purdue, M, *Planning Appeals: A Critique* (1991) Open University Press.

Purdue, M, Young, E, and Rowan Robinson, J, *Planning Law and Procedure* (1989) Butterworth.

JOURNALS

Alder, J, 'Environmental Impact Assessment' [1993] JEL 203.

Blowers, A, 'Planning a Sustainable Future' (1991) 60 Town & Country Planning 174.

Bruton, M, and Nicholson, D, 'A future for development plans?' [1987] JPL 687.

Carnwath, R, 'The Planning Lawyer and the Environment' [1991] 3 Journal of Environmental Law 57.

Cocks, R, 'Unreasonable Behaviour' (1988) 138 NLJ 730.

Cornford, T, 'The Control of Development Gain' [1998] JPL 731.

Elvin, D, and Robinson, J, 'Environmental Impact Assessment' [2000] JPL 876.

Healey, R, 'The Role of Development Plans in the British Planning System: An Empirical Assessment' (1986) 8 Urban Law and Policy 1.

Herbert-Young, 'Reflections on Section 54A' [1995] JPL 292.

Hinds, W, 'Third Party Objections to Planning Applications: An Expectation of Fairness' [1988] JPL 742.

Hough, 'Standing in Planning Appeals' [1992] JPL 319.

Lichfield, N, 'From Planning Gain to Community Benefit' [1989] JPL 68.

Millichip, D, 'Sustainability: A long established Concern of Planning' [1993] JPL 1111.

O'Keefe, J, 'Planning Law – Section 54A' [1993] 5 ELM 117.

Popham, J and Purdue, M, 'The Future of the Major Inquiry' [2002] JPL 137.

Purdue, M, 'The Impact of s 54A' [1994] JPL 399.

Stanley, N, 'Public Concern: the decision makers' dilemma' [1998] JPL 919.

Tromans, S, and Clarkson, M, 'The Environmental Protection Act 1990: Its relevance to planning controls' [1991] JPL 507.

Tromans, S, 'Environmental Risk and the Planning System' [1996] JEL 354.

Walton, W, Ross-Robertson, A, and Rowan-Robinson, J, 'The Precautionary Principle and the UK Planning System' [1995] 7 ELM 35.

Chapter 9

The use of land in rural areas and powers to deal with derelict land

Thinking of agriculture as 'natural' land use is far from correct. Patterns of non-urban land use have changed dramatically, often controversially (sometimes with the consequences of violence and misery) over the centuries, and still change. Agriculture is an industry. Its use of land puts pressure on the natural environment and calls in question the future of traditional landscape patterns with habitats for flora and fauna. That such use of land must be controlled and managed so that we produce food truly needed at prices realistically affordable, consistent with the protection of the natural environment is a major issue for central and local authorities — with sharp divisions of opinion in the debate. Calls to protect the rural environment *can* represent pressure from small numbers of highly articulate persons whose views, if implemented, might prejudice the long-term well being of others by opposing change and ignoring cases that can be made for changes in rural development patterns.

Pye-Smith and Rose in *Crisis and Conservation: Conflict in the British Countryside* pointed to: agriculture's traditional virtual exemption from planning control, and resistance by agricultural interests to its introduction; the subsidisation of agriculture by the British government and the EU; the influence of substantial landowners in Parliament; the impact of technological farming and the disappearance of hedgerows; increasing impact of chemicals on natural cycles of flora and fauna; bringing into agricultural use of marginal lands — wetlands and moors for example — and blanket afforestation with exotic species of overseas trees as causes for concern. To these may be added: demands for land in rural areas for expensive residential development; need to use rural areas for amenity and recreation, and concern over the vulnerability of sites supporting rare flora and fauna. Debate goes on against a background of little consensus on, and increasing politicisation of, the issues involved: the debate over the countryside is not just about urban versus rural conflicts but includes debates *between* rural interests.

The skeins in the tangled web of argument have been: growing demand for preservation of rural landscapes for amenity and access; the realisation, dating from the second world war, that 'home grown' food and timber are of major importance to the life of the nation; the desire to contain urban development within greenbelt boundaries; beliefs that farmers should be the prime custodians of the countryside and its traditional appearance and ways of employment — a belief increasingly untenable as mechanised 'agribusiness' has superseded agriculture with consequent loss of landscapes and employment; transfers of population between town and country as agricultural workers have left the land to be replaced by middle class town dwellers seeking 'country lifestyles' or second homes; the emphasis on voluntarism (ie reliance on co-operation by farmers and landowners in countryside conservation, very often aided by grant aid) evinced by central government and bodies such as the Countryside Commission, and opposed by many voluntary and campaigning bodies, and the realisation that it is impossible to separate ownership of land from its control. This last point needs elaboration. The vast majority of land in the UK is privately owned, most of it by a comparatively small body of persons and institutions. In law though the *legal* and *beneficial* ownership of land can be separated, this applies only between individuals and there is no *general* concept that land should be held in trust for all, ie that the ownership of land carries with it *obligations* to keep it in good heart and more than just cosmetically attractive so that it can provide sustenance and support — not just for humans — for generations to come. This has forced governments largely to rely on the voluntarist approach outlined above; which is not to say that change cannot be perceived. Following Cm 1200 the government undertook to integrate environmental issues more fully into the economics of the countryside, and to pursue particular policies to this end (see further below).

A THE EC DIMENSION

What is also clear is the close connection between UK and EC food and agricultural subsidy policies and the current changes in the face of Britain's countryside. Subsidies take away market forces and the controls inherent in them, and at the same time cost the taxpayer dear. It is not possible in this work to go into the full complexities of the EC's Common Agricultural Policy (CAP). Suffice it to say that the Treaty of Rome enshrined principles of *increased* agricultural productivity, technical progress, optimum utilisation of all factors of production, increased agricultural earnings, stable markets, certainty of supply and reasonable consumer prices. These were further supported by community wide marketing arrangements for particular products. Though over the years a 'producer responsibility' principle was grafted onto CAP, it was not able to assume the level of importance in policy terms as other principles such as common prices and common financing for farmers. Great use was made of regulations in this context, with particular emphasis being laid on the fixing of various prices for products. CAP was undoubtedly a victim of its own success. Living standards amongst farmers did increase, but so did food costs: production increased, but so did accumulation of unwanted surpluses.

CAP 'capped'

In May 1992 CAP was substantially reformed and the £23bn pa paid to farmers which led to food prices being artificially high *and* the creation of food 'mountains and lakes' was redistributed with, for example, farmers receiving a 29% cut in grain prices, while at the same time having to take 15% of cereal land out of production — for which, however, compensation is payable to relieve what could otherwise have been a jolting sudden drop in farm incomes. Grants of up to £88 per acre were agreed for British farmers taking 15% of their land out of production. By 1993 some £800m was earmarked — to rise to £1,000m in 1994 — to pay farmers to 'set aside' land by leaving it fallow. Arable farmers were paid £104 per acre to leave land uncropped. These schemes were introduced under EC Regulations 1765/92 and 2293/93. Criticism of the scheme was not, however, long delayed. Arguably the programme was primarily a food production reduction scheme, not one of positive countryside conservation whereunder farmland surplus to requirements could be taken out of production on a long term basis and positively managed to encourage wildlife and species diversification. Under the EC scheme farmers had to rotate the 15% of the land set aside so that a different area each year was taken out of production and left to lie fallow, the object here being to prevent farmers 'mothballing' the least productive land on a long-term basis. The requirement to leave land fallow also forced farmers to leave their set aside land in a semi-derelict condition.

The 1992 reforms did not meet all their expectation, and in 1998 the Community began a further round of reforms, driven this time not just by financial questions but by issues arising from the proposed expansion of the EC to include nations from the former Soviet bloc and from the wider context of world trade. A reform package was agreed in Berlin in 1999 which proposed to reduce price fixing for crops, beginning in 2000/2001, while direct payments are to be made to farmers whose incomes suffer in consequence. The voluntary set aside of land by farmers is also to be retained and enhanced as a policy.

CAP in the future

Despite the 1999 reforms there are continuing doubts as to the future of CAP which still remains based on increasing agricultural productivity, enhancing agricultural earnings, stabilising markets, making food supplies available, and ensuring reasonable prices for consumers. For the future new principles will need to be added such as guaranteeing food safety and quality, making food production environmentally friendly while integrating environmental goals into the instruments employed to further CAP, and seeking to diversify income and employment opportunities for rural workers. The future may be in a Common Agriculture and Rural Policy for Europe (CARPE) which has been under consideration since 1995. This would balance economic efficiency, environmental concern and rural development equally, and would involve reducing price support to farmers, enhancing payments to them for positive action taken to enhance the environment, while pursuing sustainable rural development. (For further detail see McMahon, *Law of the Common Agricultural Policy* to which indebtedness is acknowledged.)

Pesticides

The EC has also taken action on pesticides. Beginning with Directive 76/895 (as amended, and dealing with residues on fruit and vegetables) and further by 86/362, (as amended, and dealing with foodstuffs of animal origin) the EC has acted, *principally to protect consumers*, to set limits on food pesticide residues. Maximum limits for such residues were laid down.

Under Directive 90/642 provision was made for the setting of maximum residue levels, and an implementation date of December 1992 was set. However, progress on daughter directives setting levels for particular residues has been slow, and implementation has been continued for over a decade. For further detail see chapter 7.9 of Haigh, *Manual of Environmental Policy*.

In order to protect wildlife by ;protecting its natural habitats Directive 79/409 (as amended) sought to conserve wild birds by, inter alia, protecting their habitats by the creation of 'specially protected areas' (SPAs), which member states were requested to designate and notify to the Commission which was required to make an inventory of them; UK implementation has been achieved under the National Parks and Access to the Countryside Act 1949, the Countryside Act 1968 and the Wildlife and Countryside

Act 1981, see further below. Once an SPA is established by a member state that state has no general power to alter or reduce its area, and may only do so in exceptional cases where general public interest requires flood prevention or coastal protection and this justifies disturbance of the interests of wildlife, though the degree of disturbance must not exceed the minimum necessary to achieve the general public interest. Economic or recreational interests only will not justify disturbance of a designated SPA.[1]

Directive 92/43 (as amended), aiming to promote biodiversity by establishing a 'favourable conservation status' for types of habitats and species possessing an EC 'interest', extends the techniques established under 79/409 to such habitats and species. As nature conservation is generally outside the scope of this book interested readers are referred to Nigel Haugh's treatment of the issue in his *Manual of Environmental Policy: the EU and Britain* at section 9.9. The relevant UK implementing measures are to be found in SI 1994/2716 (as amended), and the effect of these on grants of planning permission will be considered below.

However, in general terms the obligation of member states is to identify to the Commission all those sites which meet the criteria for designation as a 'Special Area of Conservation' (SAC). They may not take into account economic and social interests in doing that, but may only furnish information on such issues to the Commission whose task it is to decide on the eventual designation of sites.[2]

Though international law, in the form of treaties, has concerned itself with the protection of flora and fauna, for over a hundred years, it was not until the Ramsar Convention of 1971 (protocol added 1982) that it turned specifically to the protection of habitats, more particularly wetlands of international importance as water fowl habitats. Note also the Berne Convention of 1979 on the conservation of European wildlife and natural habitats.

The UK has been a contracting party to the Ramsar Convention since 1976, and so falls within the general treaty obligation to promote conservation of relevant habitats, particularly by establishing nature reserves. There are further obligations to adapt planning policies to further the conservation of wetlands designated and listed under the treaty provisions, with each contracting state listing at least one such site. Following designation and listing sites may only be reduced on the basis of 'urgent national interests': compare and contrast the EC and ECJ approach under Directive 79/409. 'Wetlands' include marshes, fens, peatlands, and water, whether these are natural or human created, permanent or temporary, while water may be static or flowing, brackish or salt, and marine water up to six metres deep may be included. Adjacent land such as banks and islands may also be included.

Implementation in the UK of the Convention is largely by means of designating sites as of Special Scientific Interest under the Wildlife and Countryside Act 1981 (as amended).

The Countryside and Rights of Way Act 2000, s 77 imposes a duty on the Secretary of State to notify conservation agencies, ie English Nature (formerly the Nature Conservation Council for England) and the Countryside Council for Wales, of wetlands designated under the Ramsar Convention. The agencies must then notify relevant local planning authorities, owners and occupiers of relevant land, the Environment Agency and relevant water and drainage bodies of the designation. Protection will continue to be given to such sites through planning controls and SI 1994/27/6. Currently advice on planning controls is given in PPG9, which, along with the statutory instrument, is to be revised in the light of the new importance accorded to Ramsar sites.

1   *EC Commission v Germany* [1991] 3 LMELR 97.
2   *R (on the application of First Corporate Shipping Ltd) v Secretary of State for the Environment, Transport and the Regions* Case C-371/98 (ECJ) [2000] 12 ELM 215.

Biodiversity

The UK is a signatory of the Convention on Biological Diversity, Rio, 1992. Again the topic of nature conservation under international law is largely outside this work's coverage: interested readers are referred to Cm 2428 'Biodiversity: the UK Action Plan of 1994. Also relevant is the Statement of Forest Principles also adopted at Rio, though this is not a legally binding Convention. The UK is, nevertheless, committed to the forest principles and has set out its policy response in CM 2429, 'Sustainable Forestry: the UK Programme'.

Under the UK's 1994 plan there were in 2000 action plans for 172 plant and animal species and 24 habitat types, while 200 other species were being considered for plans. However, the Countryside and Rights of Way Act 2000 has given a new prominence to this matter. The CROWA 2000, s 74 makes it the duty of all ministers, government departments and the National Assembly for Wales to have regard to the 1992 Convention's biodiversity conservation requirements when carrying out their functions – so far as that is consistent with their functions. The Secretary of State and the National Assembly are required to publish a list or lists of those habitat types and species which are considered to be of principal importance for the purposes of conservation of diversity, while 'conservation' is defined to include the restoration or enhancement of a species population or habitat. Before lists are published consultation must take place with appropriate conservation bodies – English Nature and the Countryside Council for Wales – and those bodies must also be involved in the review of the lists. The Secretary of State and the National Assembly are, under the CROWA 2000, s 74(3) required to take, or to promote the taking by others, of reasonably practicable steps to further the conservation of living species and habitat types included in the published lists.

B AGRICULTURE AND PLANNING LAW

Under the Town and Country Planning Act 1990, s 55(2)(e), use of any land for the purposes of agriculture or forestry, including afforestation, and use for any of those purposes of any building occupied together with land so used does not involve an act of development. Planning permission is not required for bringing any land or building into agricultural use, nor for changing from agricultural use to another. The provision allows a change of use *from* non-agricultural *to* agricultural use.[3] The TCPA 1990, s 336(1) defines agriculture as including horticulture, fruit and seed growing, dairy farming, livestock breeding and keeping, including fur and wool farming, market gardening, and the use of woodlands ancillary to the farming of land. Within this definition fall allotments,[4] and using land for grazing, as opposed to the breeding for non-farming purposes, of horses.[5] Whether land is being used for the purposes of agriculture is a question of fact for the local planning authority whose decision can be challenged if taken on the basis of insufficient evidence.[6]

However, the width of the exemption is wide, extending to the retailing of agricultural produce provided it is grown on the land in question,[7] using an old caravan on

3   *McKellen v Minister of Housing and Local Government* (1966) 198 Estates Gazette 683.
4   *Crowborough Parish Council v Secretary of State for the Environment and Wealdon District Council* [1981] JPL 281.
5   *Belmont Farm Ltd v Minister of Housing and Local Government* (1962) 13 P & CR 417; and *South Oxfordshire District Council v Secretary of State for the Environment* [1981] 1 All ER 954, [1981] 1 WLR 1092.
6   *R v Sevenoaks District Council, ex p Palley* [1995] JPL 915.
7   *Williams v Minister of Housing and Local Government* (1967) 18 P & CR 514.

agricultural land for animal food storage and preparation,[8] using a building for agricultural purposes,[9] using land solely for the purpose of grazing horses – though not for exercising them in the course of a business,[10] and making wine from grapes grown on the land.[11] There are, however, limits so that where large numbers of animals are kept on land primarily for the purpose of producing skins for tanning, that is not within the exemption,[12] and neither is a large scale cheese-making plant that is simply situated on land where farming takes place.[13] There is thus ample room for error and disagreement.

Though some agricultural and forestry ancillary operations *may* require planning permission, considerable permitted development rights are given under the Town and Country Planning (General Permitted Development) Order SI 1995/418. Thus Part 6 Class A permits the carrying out on units of five hectares or more of works to erect, extend or alter a building, or to carry out excavation or engineering operations reasonably necessary for agricultural purposes within the unit. This wide power is, however, subject to conditions and limitations. Thus it does not apply to land which is a separate parcel of land, though part of the unit, less than one hectare in area, nor does it permit erection, etc, of dwellings. It does not extend to permit non-agricultural buildings and is subject to size, and location, limits. Nor does it allow the erection, etc, of a building, etc, to be used for accommodating livestock, or to store slurry or sewage, where the building, etc, would be within 400 m of the curtilage of a 'protected building' ie a permanent building occupied by people. Note also that the foregoing rights may be restricted in certain ways in relation to the erection or extension or alteration of buildings or the laying out of private ways, in that prior notification of the proposal must be given to the local planning authority.

The developer must apply to the planning authority for a determination whether their approval is needed as to siting, design and external appearance. A written description of the development and proposed materials must be submitted, and a plan. Development consisting of a 'significant' extension or alteration may only be carried out *once* by virtue of Class A. In this context a 'significant extension' is one where the original cubic content of the building would be exceeded by more than 10%. Following notification, the proposal may not proceed until a written statement is received from the authority that prior approval is not required, *or*, where notification is given within 28 days of receipt of the application that approval is required, following such approval — before which the applicant must give public site notice publicly to the proposal for not less than 21 days; where no notification is given within 28 days of receipt the proposal may proceed. Thereafter the development should, where prior approval is required, take place in accordance with the approval, otherwise in accordance with submitted details. Note that the limitations outlined above apply to agricultural permitted rights *everywhere*. It should further be noted that where work to erect or significantly extend or alter a building are carried out under permitted development rights, and agricultural use ceases within the agricultural unit within ten years, the general rule is that, unless planning permission is given for some other purpose within a further three years, the building is to be removed and the land restored. The Local Planning Authority may, however, agree otherwise.

Further permitted agricultural development rights include the winning and working on land held or occupied with land used for the purposes of agriculture of any minerals

---

8   *Wealdon District Council v Secretary of State for the Environment and Day* [1988] JPL 268.
9   *North Warwickshire Borough Council v Secretary of State for the Environment* [1984] JPL 434.
10   *Sykes v Secretary of State for the Environment* [1981] JPL 285.
11   *Millington v Secretary of State for the Environment* [2000] JPL 297.
12   *Gill v Secretary of State for the Environment* [1985] JPL 710.
13   *Salvatore Cumbo v Secretary of State for the Environment* [1992] JPL 366.

reasonably necessary for agricultural purposes within the unit of which it forms part. This is subject, inter alia, to use and movement restrictions.

On units of *less* than five hectares but more than 0.4 hectares, permitted development rights extend to extending or altering agricultural buildings, installing/replacing plant/ machinery, providing or replacing sewers and mains, etc, providing/rearranging private ways, providing/rearranging hard surfaces, waste deposits, carrying out certain fish farming activities such as repairing ponds, provided the development is reasonably necessary for agricultural purposes. Once again there are restrictions on such development similar to those above.

The permitted development (PD) rights given to agriculture are extensive. However, to enjoy the PD rights the land itself must not only be agricultural, it must be comprised in an agricultural unit, ie agricultural land occupied as a unit for agricultural purposes. Thus land that has been appropriated for leisure is no longer 'agricultural',[14] while a grazing site in the middle of playing fields would also not qualify as the 'unit' is not agricultural.[15]

Forestry has similar PD rights including erecting, etc, buildings other than dwellings and the formation of ways for the purposes of forestry and afforestation.

Future prospects

Historically the role of planning control with regard to agriculture has been weak, and this has been the subject of criticism, for example as long ago as the early 1980s when the House of Lords Select Committee on the European Communities 20th Report on 'Agriculture and the Environment' (Session 1983-84) criticised CAP. Many commentators argued that the former Department of the Environment too easily followed the policy line of the former Minister of Agriculture Fisheries and Food (MAFF), which was very much concerned with food *production*. Certainly the overlap of functions and responsibilities led to confusion and uncertainty in the application and conception of policy. From 1984 onwards there was some 'greening' of MAFF with the creation of an internal 'Environmental Unit'.

In 2000 there was a major reappraisal of rural policy in the White Paper 'Our Countryside: The Future' (Cm 4909) which included as a major policy objective the conservation and enhancement of rural landscapes and the diversity of wildlife by, inter alia: a vigorous countryside protection policy which would redirect house building away from greenfield sites (while allowing for the creation of sound and affordable housing in rural areas to maintain the balance and viability of communities); implementing agricultural support systems to take account of environmental benefits from farming, and taking a holistic approach to assessing landscape value. Some of these are matters to be returned to below in the context of National Parks, Areas of Outstanding Natural Beauty and greenbelts. However, in general terms the declared aims of government policy include the reduction of pressure for new house building in rural areas by stressing regeneration of existing urban sites and the more efficient use of land in towns, so that by 2008 60% of additional housing should be provided on reused land or in reused buildings. At the same time the need for some development in rural areas was accepted – for example by the reuse of redundant farm buildings where appropriate, by the creation of village design statements to supplement development

14   *Pittman v Secretary of State for the Environment* [1988] JPL 391.
15   Note also *Salvatore Cumbo v Secretary of State for the Environment* [1992] JPL 366; *Clarke v Secretary of State for the Environment* [1993] JPL 32; and *Brill v Secretary of State for the Environment* [1993] JPL 253.

plans, and that these should be the result of local initiatives to ensure that they are responsive to rural needs. It was also stressed that new buildings in the countryside need to be well thought out and designed to fit in their surroundings. Furthermore where a planning decision is taken on development in rural areas the White Paper declared that the overall value of the land should be considered, not just agricultural quality, which is only one factor to take into account. Thus weight should be given to landscape quality, wildlife and habitats, recreational amenity and historic and cultural heritage issues. A holistic approach to development issues should be pursued, with strict controls applying to developments in open countryside. It was accepted that the introduction of intensive agricultural practices, such as the ploughing up of previously uncultivated land or the draining of areas can have major impacts on landscape and wildlife. Certain such intensive practices are now subject to the requirement for Environmental Impact Assessment (see the previous chapter) though most are not. Significantly, the preferred policy approach remains one not of legal control but of pursuing agri-environment countryside stewardship scheme agreements whereby farmers are *paid subsidies* in return for taking measures to conserve and improve landscapes, historic heritage and wildlife sites.

With further regard to agriculture's impact on wildlife diversity and the natural environment, it was stated in the White Paper that mechanisation, fertiliser and pesticide use and a reduction in diverse habitat types have impacted on wildlife populations, for example farmland birds have declined by 36% between 1970 and 1998, while some 40% of sites of special scientific interest (see further below) are not in favourable condition. The White Paper promised action on wildlife sites and again stressed the importance of voluntary agreements under agri-environment schemes and the promotion of best agricultural practice to reverse impacts on wildlife populations. In this context habitat restoration is a crucial issue, and this is also of major significance to enhancing and restoring the diversity of plant and animal species to which allusion was made earlier in the context of the Ramsar and Biological Diversity Conventions. Targets were promised in the White Paper for recreating and enhancing habits at risk, and clearly these will have implications for the agricultural use of land. Yet again, however, a compulsion-based approach was shunned, and the policy is to rely on funding from sources such as the National Lottery, and prioritisation and coordination of existing programmes, special mention being made once again of the existing agri-environment schemes. Once more the policy emphasis is on shifting subsidy payments away from production towards supporting farming practices to enhance and preserve wildlife and its habitats. A major review of existing agri-environment schemes with a view to simplifying them was promised for 2003. In addition other voluntary schemes such as compliance with revised Codes of Good Agricultural Practice and the 2000 pilot study '35 Indicators of Sustainable Agriculture' are to be encouraged, as is the concept of integrated farm management. This is a 'whole farm' policy, which aims to ensure both economic viability and environmental responsibility. It combines beneficial natural processes, eg utilising natural predators to consume crop pests, traditional practices, eg crop rotation, with modern technology and the selective use of agri-chemicals in an attempt to minimise pollution and reduce the use of chemicals and energy.

A yet more radical approach?

It may be asked whether the foregoing proposals, which are essentially voluntaristic in nature and dependent on the payment of subsidies, go far enough. The nature of farming has changed – it is commonly spoken of as 'agri-business' – and so has the nature of the farming community. In many areas small family run holdings have largely disappeared, and problems with animal farming in the wake of the BSE and 2001 foot and mouth disease outbreaks have exacerbated that trend. Agriculture is increasingly a corporate business. Could it be that provision should be made for some sort of licensing system combining the current agri-environment schemes, together with the code of good practice and the dissemination of best practice mentioned above, and also taking into account any record of odour and/or water pollution or waste disposal offences (maybe infringements of certain food standards and animal welfare issues as well) – at least for the larger types of holding? Just as we have developed an increasingly integrated system of regulation with regard to manufacturing industry, is there not a case for a similar approach to 'agri- business'?

There could be the opportunity for such a development now that the Department of the Environment, Food and Rural Affairs exists. However, there must be a cause for some concern that environmental and planning responsibilities have been separated with the latter remaining under the purview of the Department of Transport, Local Government and the Regions. In this connection comments from the Chief Executive of the Environment Agency on 11 June 2001 need to be borne in mind:

> 'Sustainable development and the environment need to be integrated across the whole Department (DEFRA). We must also ensure continued close working with the new Department for Transport, Local Government and the Regions (DTLR) and with the Regional Development Agencies.
>
> The Agency will be looking to DEFRA to deliver a holistic approach to the environment – with sustainable development as its pervading theme.'

C AGRICULTURE AND COUNTRYSIDE LEGISLATION

Few environmental controls over agriculture have had, historically, the force of law. The voluntary approach, supplemented in some cases by Codes of Practice, as has been argued, has been, and continues to be, favoured by central government and farmers.

The Countryside Act 1968, s 11, imposes a vague duty on ministers, government departments and public bodies to have regard, in the exercise of their functions relating to land under statute, to the desirability of conserving the natural beauty and amenity of the countryside. The CA 1968, s 37 as amended in 1981, imposes a duty on ministers, the Environment Agency and the nature conservation authorities, and local authorities to have due regard to the needs of agriculture and forestry and the economic and social interests of rural areas. However, the former Nature Conservancy Council (NCC) admitted in *Nature Conservation in Great Britain* that the law had never been generally effective in giving adequate support to nature conservation. This was very true of the principal legislation, the Wildlife and Countryside Act 1981, an Act most severely criticised by commentators.

A troubled Act

The Wildlife and Countryside Act 1981, even though it was amended quite shortly after its enactment, was regarded as toothless legislation. In 1999 English Nature argued that Sites of Special Scientific Interest (SSSIs), the principal designation method of protecting conservation sites, were ineffective. In the previous year 8,300 acres of land in SSSIs had been actively damaged, but neglect and mismanagement had led to 28% of the natural features protected by designation being in poor condition, while some

750,000 acres of designated land had suffered from neglect and inappropriate farming practices such as allowing meadow land to become choked with grass and scrub or overgrazing of uplands. Yet other SSSIs were being damaged by excessive water extraction. Studies by the 'Sunday Times', Friends of the Earth and the Royal Society for the Protection of Birds found that a number of major companies were responsible for damage to SSSIs, either because of accidental happenings or through ignorance of designation. The World Wide Fund for Nature had the year before pointed to a rate of species extinction in Britain of three in every two years, and argued the situation would become worse without new protection measures being introduced.

The government responded to pressure from concerned groups, and also the 350 or so MPs who in 1999 signed an early-day motion requesting enhanced legislation with provisions contained in the Countryside and Rights of Way Act 2000, following undertakings given in the Rural White Paper (Cm 4909), and the 1998 DETR paper 'Sites of Special Scientific Interest – Better Protection and Management'.

The new law

The Countryside and Rights of Way Act 2000 (aptly known as 'CROWA') creates a new framework for the law. The change of nomenclature of the Nature Conservancy Council to English Nature and the duties to conserve biological diversity in CROWA 2000, ss 73 and 74 have already been encountered. The 'meat' of the new law is found in CROWA 2000, s 75 and Sch 9 which extensively amend the WCA 1981 so that the former designation provision of that Act, s 28, is replaced by ss 28 – 28R.

Designation and its consequences

WCA 1981 s 28 enables English Nature, and its Welsh counterpart, to notify land which is of 'special interest' by virtue of its flora, fauna, geological or physiographical features, to the local planning authority, the owner and occupier and the Secretary of State. Such a notification must specify the natural features making the land of special interest, and any operations likely to damage those features. It must also contain a statement of views about how the land should be managed and conserved. At least three months must also be allowed during which representations about or objections to the designation may be made and these have to be considered, and the designating body then has power within the following nine months to withdraw or confirm the notification. It should, however, be remembered that the designation is effective as from the time it is initially made. Any unconfirmed designation comes to an end automatically at the end of that nine-month period. Notifications are registrable as local land charges. WCA 1981, s 28A enables variations to be made to designations, though not as to the area of land in question, once confirmation has occurred. Notification must be given as under WCA 1981, s 28 and the same period of time given for the making of representations and objections, with similar provision also being made as to confirmation or withdrawal. Designation decisions, and it would appear, the various other decision-making powers are open to challenge by way of judicial review.[16]

The WCA 1981, s 28B allows the designation of 'extra land' to increase the area of an SSSI provided the combined area is of the requisite 'special interest' once the initial designation has been confirmed. The 'extra land' designation procedure is in all respects

---

16   *R v Nature Conservancy Council, ex p London Brick Property Ltd* [1996] JPL 227; *R v Nature Conservancy Council, ex p Bolton Metropolitan Borough Council* [1996] JPL 203.

similar to the initial one. The WCA 1981, s 28C also enables the enlargement of an SSSI to the area of land including but extending beyond a SSSI, again provided it possesses the necessary special interest features. As before there are notification provisions mirroring those outlined above under s 28. An 'enlargement notification' under the WCA 1981, s 28C – which can only occur once the initial designation is confirmed – supersedes that initial designation and so here it is possible additionally to amend those matters forming part of the original notification, eg the listing of potentially damaging operations and the expression of views on management.

'Denotification' is possible under the WCA 1981, s 28D with regard to *all or some* of the land in question which is no longer considered to be of special interest. In addition to the 'usual notifiees', denotification must be communicated to the Environment Agency and relevant water undertakers and drainage bodies whose works, operations and activities may affect the land. As before provision is made for representations and objections to be made and for the subsequent confirmation or withdrawal of notification procedure, and, also as with designation, where a denotification is neither withdrawn or not confirmed, it ceases to have effect at the end of nine months. It will be noted that this procedure allows an SSSI designation to be either brought to an end or for the area of land in question to be reduced.

Owners and occupiers of designated sites must not, under the WCA 1981, s 28E, carry out, or cause or permit the carrying out of, a specified operation, unless the designating body has been given notice of the proposed operation by either the owner or the occupier, *and* either the designating body has given written consent, or the operation is carried out under a management agreement made under the National Parks and Access to the Countryside Act 1949, s 16 or the Countryside Act 1968, s 15 or under a management scheme made under the WCA 1981, s 28J, or a management notice under s 28K. Consents may be given subject to conditions and for limited periods, or may be refused, or subsequently withdrawn or modified, and where refusal takes place or there is a withdrawal or modification or where conditions are imposed, the person serving the initial notice of a proposed operation has to be given written notice which will set out the reasons for the action taken by the designating body. It is an offence for owners or occupiers to carry out the specified operations without following the foregoing procedure – see further below.

Appeals

Owners and occupiers who have been refused consent, or who are aggrieved by the conditions of a consent, or by the length of a consent period, or by the modification or withdrawal of a consent have a right of appeal under the WCA 1981 s 28F to the Secretary of State or the National Assembly for Wales as the case may be. The same right of appeal applies where a deemed refusal arises where the designating body has neither granted nor refused consent. Such an appeal must normally be made within two months of the decision complained of, though this may be extended by agreement in writing. A hearing or local inquiry may then be held, and power is given to enable the making of appropriate procedural regulations.

Exemptions for 'public bodies'

Certain 'public bodies' also have rights of exemption from these provisions under the WCA 1981, s 28G where they are carrying out their functions and these are likely to affect an SSSI. These bodies include ministers, the National Assembly for Wales, local authorities, holders of offices under the Crown, eg the police, and statutory undertakers. These bodies are under a duty to take reasonable steps to further the special features of relevant sites insofar as this is consistent with their duties, while, under the WCA 1981, s 28H, they must also notify the designating authority of their proposed operations – and that requirement extends to work outside an SSSI which may affect it. The designating body may refuse consent for the operation, or give consent conditionally, but if they do not respond within 28 days of receiving the notice from the 'public body' they are deemed to have refused. Where assent is in any way refused (or where the 'public body' proposes to carry out the work otherwise than in accordance with the terms of the assent) the body may only proceed if:

- once the 28-day period referred to above is expired they notify the designating authority of the date on which they propose to start the operation – this must be at least a further 28 days from the date of this second notification;
- they state how – if at all – they have taken account of any written advice from the designating authority given in respect to the first notification;
- the body then carries out the operation in such a way as to give rise to as little damage as is reasonably practicable in the circumstances, and
- they restore the site to its former condition, so far as is reasonably practicable, if any damage to the features of special interest does occur.

The WCA 1981, s 28I deals with situations where 'public bodies' have power to grant *permissions, authorisations, or consents* before an operation likely to damage the special interest features of an SSSI is carried out – including situations where the land in question is outside the relevant SSSI. Before permission is given the body must give the designating authority not less than 28 days' notice, and must take into account any advice given by that authority in deciding whether or not to grant permission, and, if so, what conditions to apply. If the designating authority advise against granting permission, or advise that certain conditions should be attached, and that advice is not followed, the body must give the authority notice of the permission and of its terms, including a statement of how, if at all, account has been taken of the advice, and must not give actual permission to start before the end of 21 days from that notice. This enables discussions to take place – on a voluntary basis it should be noted – to see whether a management agreement can be reached or the ill-effect of the permission otherwise mitigated.

Management schemes and notices

Historically management schemes could be made under the National Parks and Access to the Countryside Act 1968, s 16 and these have provided for voluntary agreements, for example laying down restrictions on cultivation or other agricultural uses of land; for the detail see pp 231-234 of the 3rd edition of this title.

The WCA 1981, s 28J creates new powers for the designating agencies to formulate management schemes for all or part of an SSSI. Such a scheme is designed either to conserve the special interest features of a site, *or* to restore them, or both, and that power to restore is an innovative feature of the new law. Notice of a proposed scheme has to be served on all owners and occupiers of relevant land but before this consultation with them must have taken place, though the scheme notice may be served at the same time as, or after, the initial notice designating the SSSI. Once the notice of the proposed scheme is served there is a specified period of not less than three months, within which representations and objections may be made, and these must be taken into account. Thereafter within nine months the designating authority must confirm the scheme (with or without modifications) or withdraw it. If a scheme is confirmed, it takes effect as from the date of notice of confirmation – contrast the procedure for site designation. Once made, schemes may be cancelled or modified at any time, though again due notice has to be given. Provision is made for bringing agreements made under the 1949 and the 1968 Acts into line with those made under the new provisions.

It is envisaged that 'new style' management schemes should be 'positive' systems of management available for use by owners and occupiers. They should be greatly detailed and designed to ensure a site is kept in a favourable state, and may specify permitted activities as opposed to giving advice on how to avoid proscribed ones. A further objective for such schemes is that all parties should be aware of the recommended management regime for a site.

The WCA 1981, s 28K reinforces the new management philosophy by empowering the designating agencies to serve 'management notices' where the owner or occupier of land appears not to be giving effect to a provision of a scheme and as a result the special interest features of the site in question are being either inadequately conserved or inadequately restored – a further indication of the 'positive' nature of schemes. Such a notice is a 'long stop' for first of all voluntary agreement should be sought, and a notice should only be served where such an agreement cannot be concluded on reasonable terms. A notice may require the owner or occupier to carry out specified work on the land, and to do other specified things with respect to it within a specified time period, provided these are reasonably required to ensure management of the land in accordance with the scheme. Copies of any such notice must be served on all other owners and occupiers of the land. Non-compliance with a notice entitles the designating agency to enter the land, or any other land, to carry out the work and to recover reasonable expenses.

Management notices may be appealed to the Secretary of State or the National Assembly as the case may be, under the WCA 1981, s 28L, and an appeal suspends the operation of the notice until determination or withdrawal. An appeal may be made on the basis that some other owner or occupier of the land should be responsible for some or all of the specified measures, or should meet some or all of their cost. On appeal the notice may be quashed, varied or confirmed, either as to the steps required or the apportionment of costs. Where it is alleged some other person should take responsibility for steps or costs, that other person has to be served with notice of the appeal, and in making determinations of responsibility between persons, their relative interests in the land, relative responsibilities for the state of the land, and relative degrees of benefit to be gained from carrying out the notice's requirements have to be taken into account. Appeals may be the subject of a hearing or inquiry.

Payments

Under the WCA 1981, s 28M designating agencies may make payments – single or serial – to owners and occupiers of land subject to management schemes. This continues the 'financial carrot' approach adopted with regard to management agreements under the 1949 and 1968 Acts. Where under the WCA 1981, s 28E a consent to carry out an operation is withdrawn or modified a payment *must* be made to any owner or occupier of the land who suffers consequential loss. The level of payments will be determined in accordance with ministerial guidance.

Powers of compulsory purchase

The designating agencies have various powers of compulsory purchase where land has special interest features, for example the National Parks and Access to the Countryside Act 1949, s 17 with regard to the establishment of national nature reserves.

The Countryside Act 1968, s 15 provides for the making of management agreements with persons with interests in land included in an SSSI, and this is reinforced by the WCA 1981, s 15A inserted by the CROWA 2000 which enables compulsory purchase of such land where an agreement cannot be reached on reasonable terms, or where an agreement has been breached so that the special interest features of the land are not being satisfactorily conserved. Land so acquired may be retained and the designating agency may take conservation measures themselves, or it may be disposed of on terms designed to secure conservation. The WCA 1981, s 28N grants similar powers to those contained in s 15A, considered above, so that compulsory purchase may take place but only where an agreement cannot be reached in respect of an SSSI or where an agreement that has been made has been broken so that the land is not being satisfactorily managed. Once again the land may then be retained and managed or disposed of to ensure future satisfactory management.

Offences

Under the WCA 1981, s 28P various offences are created. It is an offence for an owner or occupier to cause or permit damaging operations contrary to the WCA 1981, s 28E unless there is a reasonable excuse, with a penalty of a fine of up to £20,000 before justices or an unlimited fine on indictment. 'Public bodies' face similar penalties if they carry out operations contravening the WCA 1981, s 28H without reasonable excuse. 'Reasonable excuse' includes acting to deal with an emergency, such as a flood, provided details were furnished to the designating agency as soon as practicable, or where the action was permitted by a grant of planning permission, or where permission or consent was given in accordance with the WCA 1981, s 28I. In the past much criticism was levelled at the ability of landholders to damage SSSIs under the protection of a grant of planning permission over which nature conservation agencies had little control. However, under the new law before any operation or change of use which could damage an SSSI is consented (even if not on the land constituting the SSSI) it has to be the subject of consultation between the designating agency and the local planning authority. Though a planning authority may decide to grant permission for development against the advice of the designating agency, the WCA 1981, s 28I allows time to enable the agency to seek a voluntary mitigation scheme with the owners and occupiers of the land. In addition judicial review could be available in a case where a local planning authority had perversely granted permission or had failed to take into account the advice given. In February 2001 a new PPG9 giving guidance to planning authorities on nature conservation and biodiversity was promised, but this was still awaited in November 2001.

Any person who intentionally or recklessly damages or destroys the special interest features of an SSSI, *or* who recklessly disturbs any fauna in respect of which the site was notified, *and* who knew that what was destroyed, damaged or disturbed was within an SSSI commits an offence under the WCA 1981, s 28(P)(6) for which the penalties are as outlined above. Once again, however, a reasonable excuse defence is provided. This provision should obviate difficulties centred on the fact that the legislation generally lays duties on owners and occupiers, and not on those who are merely transiently on the land, for example as contractors.[17] If a contractor damages an SSSI a penalty could be imposed under this provision. It is also an offence to fail to comply with a management notice.

17   *Southern Water Authority v Nature Conservancy Council* [1992] 1 WLR 775.

Note generally that the designating agencies are the prosecuting authorities under s 28P, and that in calculating fines the courts are to take into account any financial benefit accruing to a person in consequence of a s 28P offence. Note also that the WCA 1981, s 31 is also amended so that where a person has been convicted of an offence under s 28P, the court may order that person to restore the SSSI, and a similar power applies where a public body has been guilty of such an offence.

Miscellaneous and consequential issues

Under WCA 1981, s 28Q where the owner of land in an SSSI disposes of an interest in it or becomes aware of a change of occupation, notification has to be given to the designating agency within 28 days. The notice must specify the land concerned and the date of the change, etc. The provision applies in particular to sales, leases, exchanges, creation of easements and rights but not mortgages, and it is an offence not to comply.

WCA 1981, s 28R enables designating agencies to make byelaws in respect of SSSIs.

Under CROWA 2000, Sch 11 all existing SSSIs are continued under the new law, though the designating agencies have a period of five years to provide their owners and occupiers with a statement as to the management of the land, and a right to make representations in return is given. Though consents for operations on an SSSI given under the former law remain valid, such a consent may now be withdrawn under the WCA 1981, s 28E, though it should be remembered that this is subject to rights of appeal and compensation. Under the previous law where no management agreement or consent related to an SSSI and the owner or occupier gave notice to the designating agency of an intention to carry out a prescribed operation, and no response was made without four months, a right to proceed arose. This will continue in respect of sites designated under the old law, but a new power is given to designating agencies to serve stop notices preventing or modifying the operation. Once again, however, this is subject to rights of appeal and compensation.

The former powers in the WCA 1981, ss 29 and 30 to make Nature Conservation Orders on land – an additional form of protection – have been repealed under the CROWA 2000, as the new provisions are considered to make them redundant, however transitional provisions to preserve the protection already given to sites under those powers are contained in CROWA 2000, Sch 11.

Evaluation

The new law will enable designating agencies permanently to refuse consent for operations specified on designation, and also provides more flexibility in that notifications may be varied both as to the land covered and the operations in question, while 'denotification' may also take place. The agencies are *required* to provide affected landholders with a statement of views on the management of the land, and must also publicise notifications in the local press so that the general public may be better informed about SSSIs in their area. Enhanced powers are given to make management schemes and to serve management notices, while a new system of appeals has been created. Previously where disputes arose the legal modes of challenge were either the 'sledgehammer' of judicial review or the less than edifying spectacle of points of law being raised as defences to criminal charges. There are also enhanced levels of fines, and the new structure of offences clearly applies to any persons who intentionally or recklessly damage an SSSI. Perhaps even more significant are the enhanced obligations laid on 'public bodies' in respect of SSSIs; historically many of their activities have been the prime cause of site decline. There are also new provisions to control specified operations being carried out by virtue of planning permission, while permitted development rights within SSSIs will as before only be exercisable with the consent of the designating agency, though there are rights of appeal where such consent is refused. Even so the designating agencies have no total power to veto planning permission being given in respect of a damaging operation on an SSSI, though new central guidance due in late 2001 is expected to counsel against this, and the old reliance on voluntary control and compliance induced by financial agreement still underpin the law.

Commencement

Part III of the CROWA 2000 which introduced the foregoing changes in the law came into effect on 30 January 2001.

D SPECIAL PROTECTION AREAS, SPECIAL AREAS OF CONSERVATION AND ENVIRONMENTALLY SENSITIVE AREAS (ESAs)

Under EC Directives 79/409 and 92/43 the UK is bound to have particular rules for the protection of SPAs and SACs. The Conservation (Nature Habitats) Regulations SI 1994/ 2716 implement these requirements. The object here is (a) to take special measures to conserve the habitats of certain bird species; (b) to contribute to bio-diversity by conserving natural habitats and wild fauna and flora of EC importance; (c) to create a coherent EC wide network of SACs (to subsume existing SPAs) known as Natura 2000; (d) to take steps to avoid in SACs and SPAs *deterioration* of habitats and *significant* disturbance of species; and (e) to ensure that proposed developments not directly connected with site management and likely to have an effect on an SPA or SAC should be assessed for their conservation implications and should only go ahead if it is found the proposal will not adversely affect the integrity of the site. However, that degree of protection is dependent on a site being designated, and there can be room for disagreement here between central authorities and groups seeking protection for an area. The official policy is that SACs should be designated only from the ranks of SSSIs. Furthermore unless the drawing of SAC boundaries is so irrational as to fly in the face of zoological and ornithological reason the courts are unwilling to intervene.[18]

However, where designation occurs, if a development proposal is received affecting an SPA or SAC, and following *assessment* of the proposal a negative effect is found, the development may only be allowed if there is no alternative solution *and* there are imperative public interest reasons which override the conservation interest. In such a case there is an obligation on member states to compensate the loss so as to preserve the overall coherence of Natura 2000. In some cases where particular habitats or species are at risk ('priority sites') a development scheme may only be considered if there are overriding reasons of human health or public safety, or there will be beneficial consequences of primary importance for the environment, or where the EU Commission considers there are other imperative overriding public interest reasons, and these seem

18   *R v Secretary of State for Transport, ex p Berkshire, Buckinghamshire and Oxfordshire Naturalists' Trust* [1997] EnvLR 80; *World Wildlife Fund UK and Royal Society for the Protection of Birds v Secretary of State for Scotland* [1999] EnvLR 632.

able to include economic interests, and the need to build roads provided they are part of a demonstrably needed European road networks.

Not all SSSIs will be designated as SACs, but all SACs will, as has been stated, *also* be designed as SSSIs, and thus will receive now the enhanced protection given under CROWA 2000. Under reg 22 of the Habitats Regulations the Secretary of State may also, on the advice of the appropriate conservancy council, make a Special Nature Conservation Order (SNCO) specifying operations not to be carried out *at any time* without the conservancy council's consent. If then a plan or project is put forward likely to affect the site significantly it must be made subject to an 'appropriate assessment' (see reg 24), and if the conclusion of the conservancy council following this is adverse to the proposal, it cannot be consented, though the matter can be referred to the Secretary of State who may only permit it where 'there being no alternative solutions, the plan or project must be carried out for reasons of overriding public interest' (see above for the particular requirements where the land in question is also a 'priority site'). Compensation will be payable for the loss of rights consequent on the making of an SNCO, see the Habitats Regulations, reg 25.

Prior to designation of land as an SPA/SAC, ie as a 'European site', planning authorities are asked to consider unimplemented or partially implemented grants of permission affecting the area, and should indicate whether implementation would have significant effects on the ecological value of the land. The Natural Habitat Regulations (SI 1994/2716), regs 50, 51, 55–58 require a review as soon as reasonably practicable of grants of permission in relation to existing SPAs, to future SPAs as declared and SACs on the agreed designation by the government and the Commission. The appropriate conservation agency will give advice in relation to this matter. Where the integrity of the site would be adversely affected, and provided the permission in question would not satisfy the requirements which would apply to approving a new development proposal, the potential for harm must be removed unless the planning authority conclude there is no likelihood of the development being carried out or continued. The safeguarding action for the land the authority may take includes entering into planning obligations to restrict or regulate the use of the site, otherwise revocation or modification action may take place — subject to central consent — though, of course, compensation may be payable. Note that similar provisions apply to secure the review, etc of other consents/authorisations.

The 1994 regulations also make provision to ensure that permitted development (PD) rights under SI 1995/418 do not result in breaches of relevant EC obligations. Development which would be likely to significantly affect an SPA or SAC may not benefit from PD status unless the relevant planning authority decides, after consulting the appropriate conservancy council, that it would not affect the integrity of the site. The 1994 regulations are due to be amended in the light of the changes made by the Countryside and Rights of Way Act 2000.

ESAs

Under the Agriculture Act 1986, s 18 (as amended), where it appears to the minister that it is particularly desirable to conserve and enhance the beauty of an area, and its flora and fauna, geological or physiographical features, or to protect buildings or other archaeological, architectural or historic features, *and* that the maintenance or adoption of particular agricultural methods are likely to further such ends, he may designate relevant land as an 'environmentally sensitive area' (ESA). Such designation takes place after consultation with, inter alia, the Countryside Agency, English Nature, and, in Wales, the Countryside Council for Wales. Management agreements may be made with appropriate landowners in ESAs, and requirements as to agricultural practices and methods may be specified for such agreements in the order designating an ESA, together with requirements as to the length of such agreements (initially five years) requirements for agricultural practices, methods and operations, any agreed requirements as to public access, remedies for breach and rates of payment under agreements. Such agreements once made in England and Wales act as restrictive covenants over the land in question, and may contain other provisions relating to the conservation, enhancement or protection of natural beauty etc.

The origins of ESAs derive from attempts to conserve areas of the Broads grazing marshes, and allowance by the EC (Regulation EC/797/85) of state aid to farmers to encourage farming practices favourable to the environment in areas of high conservation value. After 1987 Regulation EC/1760/87 further permitted community grant aid to go to such schemes.

Commission Regulation (EC) No 746/96 currently permits aid to be given for agricultural methods of production compatible with environmental protection, and in pursuance of this the Agriculture Act 1986, s 18(4A) further enables ESA agreements to contain provisions requiring the payment of penalties where an agreement is broken, or for the withholding of payments in specified circumstances.

ESAs once designated have, under the AgA 1986, s 18(8), to be reviewed and monitored and this occurs according to environmental, economic and social criteria. It is asked whether environmental enhancement or preservation has followed designation, what interest in designation has been shown by farmers, what savings and costs have eventuated, and what effect on farm business has occurred.

The ESA concept appears to represent a concerted attempt to tie together conservation and agricultural policies within a wider context of preservation of amenity. See further SIs 2000/3050, 3051, 3052. Concern must still be voiced, however, at the lack of such coherence with regard to land outside such areas.

E LIMESTONE PAVEMENT ORDERS

Under the WCA 1981, s 34 (as amended) where the appropriate nature conservancy council or the Countryside Agency are of the opinion that any land in the countryside comprising a 'limestone pavement' (ie an area of limestone lying wholly or partly exposed on the surface and fissured by natural erosion) is of special interest by reason of its flora, fauna, geological or physiographical features, it is their duty to notify that fact to the local planning authority for the area. Where the Secretary of State (in Wales the National Assembly) or the planning authority consider that the character of any land so notified would be likely to be adversely affected by the removal or disturbance of the limestone, either the Secretary of State or the authority may make a 'limestone pavement order' designating the land and prohibiting the removal of limestone on or in it.

The procedure for making orders is laid down in the WCA 1981, Sch 11. Orders may be amended or revoked. It is an offence to remove or disturb limestone in designated land without a reasonable excuse. Such an excuse is provided by a grant of planning permission under the TCPA 1990. There are no compensation provisions, nor any excluding agricultural operations from the control such an order imposes. The weakness of designation is that while suburban dwellers continue to desire lumps of limestone in their gardens, clandestine removal will still take place. It is not a market solution that is required here, but market dissolution. However, the increase in the maximum fine for an offence to £20,000, which is in line with penalties for damaging an SSSI, may have some deterrent effect, DETR Circular 04/2001 acknowledged limestone pavements as a 'nationally important habitat'.

F PESTICIDE CONTROL

The seventh report of the Royal Commission on Environmental Pollution considered pesticide control. Pesticides have played a major role in increasing agricultural production. Ending their use would dramatically reduce cereal crop yields. However, there are risks inherent in pesticide use. Interference with biochemical processes may increase food yields, but may release into the environment substances harmful to human and animal life. The process of manufacturing some pesticides may put production workers at risk. The process of discovering new biologically active chemicals is a lengthy and expensive one with a 'trial and error' element. No matter how stringent testing and development processes are, the possibility of unforeseeable and undesirable side-effects remains.

Government policy, as declared, in Cm 1200, is that: pesticide use should be limited to the minimum necessary for pest control compatible with human health and environmental protection; in taking decisions on pesticides ministers will consider health, environmental and amount efficacy issues; approvals for use will be regularly reviewed and withdrawn if new evidence indicates harmful health or environmental effects; in general information about pesticides should be publicly available, subject to commercial scrutiny, approval procedures must be independent of sectoral interests.

The relevant UK law is to be found in the Food and Environment Protection Act 1985 (FEPA 1985). Part III, as amended by the Pesticides (Fees and Enforcement) Act 1989, the Pesticides Act 1998, and the Food Standards Act 1999, is the relevant portion.

FEPA 1985, Part III is specifically concerned with pesticide control, specifically with a view to developing means to: protect human, animal and plant health; protect the environment; secure safe, efficient and humane methods of controlling pests; make information about pesticides publicly available. Ministers have extensive powers under FEPA 1985, s 16 to impose specified prohibitions on pesticides, though this is subject to ministerial power to exempt specific pesticides from prohibition, or approve and give consent in relation to specified pesticides to an otherwise prohibited act. Ministers are required to consult the Food Standards Agency before making regulations under their powers, and may be required to consult the Health and Safety Commission where worker safety matters are relevant. The specified prohibitions include bans on importation, sale, supply, storage, use and advertisement. Ministers have powers to seize and dispose of pesticides where there has been a breach of a prohibition, and these powers extend to items treated with the pesticide. Other remedial actions may be directed. Overall, provisions governing pesticide authorisation must, under EC requirements secure a high level of protection, while pesticides posing risks to health, groundwater and the environment should not be authorised. Regulations may provide that pesticides imported in breach of a prohibition shall be removed from the UK. They may also lay down how much pesticide or pesticide residue may be left in any crop, food or feeding stuff, and that where such limits are exceeded ministers shall have power to seize and dispose of the crop, etc. Regulations are to be made in the form of statutory instruments, and ministers may set up an advisory committee to give advice on pest control issues and the purposes of FEPA 1985, Part III. This committee must be consulted, inter alia, on regulations contemplated by ministers. Information may be required by ministers of importers, exporters, manufacturers and users of pesticides for controlling pesticides in the UK and to fulfil international obligations. It is an offence to contravene regulations without reasonable excuse. The current regulations are the Pesticides (Maximum Residue Levels, etc) Regulations SI 1999/3483 as amended by SI 2001/1113 and SI 2001/2420.

In this connection pest means organisms harmful to plants, wood or plant products; pesticides are substances, preparations or organisms for destroying pests, and FEPA 1985, Part III also applies to any substance, etc, used to protect plants, etc, from harmful organisms, to regulate plant growth, to give protection against harmful creatures or to render them harmless, to control organisms with unwanted effects on other systems, buildings or products or to protect animals against ectoparasites as if it were a pesticide.

Under FEPA 1985, s 17 ministers may, after appropriate consultation, issue and keep up to date codes of practice to give practical guidance on the provisions of Part III and the regulations. FEPA 1985, s 18 (as amended) enables ministers to charge fees to applicants seeking approval of pesticides, and payments may be required in respect of the handling and evaluation of applications, the collation of relevant information and monitoring the effect of pesticide use in the UK, and the amount to be paid may be calculated by reference to either or both of the turnover in the UK within a specified period of a pesticide to which an approval relates, *or* turnover in the UK of *all* pesticides to which approvals relate held by the person who is to make the payment. FEPA 1985, s 19 (as amended) confers extensive powers of enforcement, and these may be exercised either by a ministerially authorised person or by a duly authorised officer of a local authority, and local authorities have jurisdiction over, inter alia, pesticide sale and use, etc, in wholesale and retail outlets from April 1992.

Control over aerial spraying

Spraying of potentially hazardous chemicals from aircraft has been a cause for concern for many years. Use of aerial spraying has increased, offering certain technical advantages over conventional spraying techniques. Present controls are found in the Air Navigation Order SI 2000/1562, Arts 56 and 58.

Articles, including pesticides, may not be dropped for agricultural, horticultural or arboricultural purposes from an aircraft unless the operator holds an aerial application certificate from the CAA. The operator's staff must also be properly trained and supplied with an application manual containing relevant safety information. The CAA must grant an aerial application certificate only if satisfied that an applicant is a fit person to hold such a certificate, and is competent, having regard in particular to previous conduct and experience, equipment, organisation, staffing and other arrangements, to secure the safe operation of the aircraft specified in the certificate for aerial spraying flights. The certificate may be granted subject to such conditions as the CAA thinks fit for ensuring that neither the aircraft nor any sprays endanger persons or property. A certificate may be revoked, suspended or varied by the CAA under Art 81 of the order, but otherwise remains in force for the period specified in the certificate.

G NATIONAL PARKS, ACCESS TO, AND LEISURE IN, THE COUNTRYSIDE

National Parks are defined by the National Parks and Access to the Countryside Act 1949, s 5, as amended in 1995 and 1999 (SI 1999/416). They are areas of extensive open countryside where particular measures are necessary to conserve and enhance natural beauty, and the wildlife and cultural heritage of those areas, and where opportunities for understanding and enjoying the special qualities of those areas by the public are to be promoted. These measures may not be the same in each park, and those responsible for parks need to consider how best to reflect their areas' particular characteristics in their policies. However, conservation is not preservation, and relevant authorities must co-operate with those who live and work in National Parks, and take into account their needs and aspirations. So far as promotion of the understanding of parks by the public is concerned, particular emphasis should be placed on enabling the public to savour open space, wildness and tranquillity, particularly in remote and less heavily visited areas — though the legislation as amended does not limit public appreciation of the parks — as some would have wished — to *quiet* activities only.

The National Parks are not publicly owned, but are publicly administered. This has always raised in some minds the question of whether supervision minus ownership can lead to effective control. They were initially designated by the National Parks Commission under ss 6 and 7 and Sch 1 to the 1949 Act. That jurisdiction (in England) is now vested in the Countryside Agency (see the Regional Development Agencies Act 1998, ss 35 and 37 and SI 1999/416). Designation is subject to confirmation by the Secretary of State, and the usual procedure for publicising designation proposals, receiving objections, and holding hearings applies under Sch 1 to the 1949 Act. Powers exist to vary boundaries of National Parks, see s 7 of the 1949 Act as amended.

The Environment Act 1995, s 63 enabled the Secretary of State in England to establish National Park Authorities (NPAs) for any existing or new National Park and provides for these to supersede any existing authorities: particular provision is made for the establishment of such bodies in Wales by the EA 1995, s 64.

NPAs superseded in the case of existing parks the 'existing authorities', ie under the EA 1995, s 79(1) any joint or special planning boards previously existing under Sch 17 of the 1972 Act (the Peak and the Lake District authorities) *and* any National Park Committees (the remainder of the parks). The NPAs are the local planning authority for their areas and also the hazardous substances authority in place of other local authorities any part of whose area lies within a National Park.

Under Sch 7 NPAs are corporate bodies consisting of some members appointed by relevant local authorities and some by the Secretary of State, with the former in the majority. While the Secretary of State's appointees will represent the wider national purposes of park designation, where possibly they will also have local connections with 'their' park. Provision is further made for the Secretary of State's appointees to include 'Parish members', ie persons who serve on relevant Parish Councils and meetings within park areas. Each NPA must appoint a National Parks Officer (NPO) who is responsible for co-ordinating the ways in which the NPA carries out its functions. Schedules 8 and 9 confer further powers on NPAs, including the power to acquire land compulsorily, and functions with regard to Nature Reserves and the establishment of Country Parks.

However, the prime functions of NPAs, under the EA 1995, s 65, are to conserve and enhance the natural beauty, wildlife and cultural heritage of parks and to promote opportunities for public understanding and enjoyment of the parks, including general powers to protect countryside interests and avoid pollution under the Countryside Act 1968, ss 37 and 38, and to do anything calculated to facilitate, or conducive or incidental to, the accomplishment of these purposes. In particular under s 11A of the 1949 Act NPAs in pursuing their park objectives must *seek to foster the economic and social well being of local communities but without incurring significant expenditure* in doing so, and must for those purposes, co-operate with other relevant public bodies and local authorities. However, in performing any functions with regard to land they must bear in mind their duty to conserve and enhance natural beauty, and if it appears there is a conflict between purposes they are to favour the conservation duty.

The object of the legislation is to free each park to express its character individually within a national framework. Consultation, however, is encouraged so that the NPAs can bear in mind the interests of those living and working in parks, those whose living is derived from park resources and those who visit the parks. The NPAs will work closely with the Countryside Agency and its counterpart in Wales and also with the appropriate conservancy bodies, etc.

Within the context of the NPAs' prime conservation duty it should be noted that while *no* recreational activity is excluded in principle, it is accepted that some are inappropriate in certain areas. The task of NPAs, by careful planning and management, is to accommodate as many types of leisure interest as possible. Codes of Practice should be drawn up to ensure an amicable and effective segregation of uses. Where, however, a recreational activity would cause unacceptable damage or disturbance to natural beauty, etc, and that also affects the understanding and enjoyment of that beauty, *the conservation duty is to come first*. Mediation, negotiation and co-operation will be used to try to ensure an absence of such conflicts but where reconciliation is not possible then the duty to conserve must take precedence.

The EA 1995, s 66 requires the continuation of National Park Management Plans created under the Local Government Act 1972, and also that new plans shall be made following quinquennial review. Proposals for plans must be submitted to relevant local authorities, the relevant countryside agency in England, to English Nature and in Wales, to Countryside Council for Wales.

The TCPA 1990, s 4A inserted in 1995) provides that where an NPA has been established for a park it is to be exclusively the *sole* planning authority for the whole area of the park, including mineral planning functions. The NPA will have planning authority functions under the Wildlife and Countryside Act 1981: see s 69 of the EA 1995, and s 68 for further amplification of planning powers enjoyed by NPAs.

Planning in the National Parks: further considerations

Development control exists in National Parks under the same laws as elsewhere, though there are detailed modifications in the law and variations in practice. Design features of a development and implications for nature conservation or the beauty of the countryside will loom large in considering a planning application. How far the previous authorities were successful in preserving the National Parks from intrusive development is likely to remain for some time a matter of some controversy. The issue is particularly controversial with regard to mineral extraction in the parks, see *Peak Park Joint Planning Board v Secretary of State for the Environment*,[19] but is otherwise a subject of debate. Note, however, the guidance of MPG 6 with regard to extraction within parks, namely that it should take place only in exceptional circumstances which are demonstrably in the public interest, and after strict examination of the need for the material from a national point of view, the impact of permission or refusal on the local economy, the cost and availability of alternative supplies, and detrimental environmental and landscape effects. Anne and Malcolm MacEwan in *National Parks: Conservation or Cosmetics?* Showed that the number of planning applications varies greatly each year between parks. However, there was no real evidence to suggest that the previous park planning authorities were more strict in rejecting planning applications than other authorities. In their *Greenprints for the Countryside* (1987) the MacEwans were rather more generally hopeful in regard to this issue. The parks have been largely successfully protected against urban developments, but, of course, the controversial operations of agriculture and forestry are largely beyond the control of planning law. Furthermore, there is only some evidence that planning controls over building designs have been in any way successful in preserving the use of local building styles and materials in the parks. Planning seems to have had little success with regard to the positive planning of parks, but has had to bow to pressures created by commerce, education, water supply, sewerage, transport and health and other service policies. This was historically particularly evident with regard to attempts to restrict house building to serve local

19   (1979) 39 P & CR 361.

needs only. Structure plans were modified by the Department of the Environment where they sought to promote such policies.

Note, however, that PD rights in National Parks (as also in Areas of Outstanding National Beauty and The Broads) are restricted, because on so called Art 1(5) land such rights are only exercisable to a limited degree in respect of enlargement/improvement of dwelling houses, the extension of industrial buildings and warehouses, certain developments by certain statutory undertakers and by telecommunications code system operators. Further restrictions also exist on PD rights with regard to land in a park or Area of Outstanding Natural Beauty with regard to exploratory borehole drilling and the removal of material from mineral-working deposits.

The evidence in the Countryside Commission's 1991 Report 'Landscape Change in the National Parks' was that agriculture and forestry have been primarily responsible for landscape change in the parks over the last 20 years. Some 1,000 acres per annum of heath and moorland had gone, while a similar acreage of conifers had been planted. Quarrying, house and road construction have consumed only 2% of the parks' areas, but it is the loss of grass moor, rough pasture, lowland heath, bracken, upland heath and scrub that was marked, while conifer forest, improved pasture, cultivated land, and developed land all increased, the first three markedly. Rather more positively broad leaf and mixed woodland, rocky and coastal land and water and wetlands have also somewhat increased. The Report nevertheless argued that the worst effects of intensive farming and forestry had been avoided while expressing fears for the future of traditional upland farming.

The Wildlife and Countryside Act 1981, ss 42–44 (as amended), confers extra protection on certain land in National Parks. Under s 42, ministers may apply an order in the form of a statutory instrument to any land consisting of or including moorland or heath in a National Park. Thereafter no person may, on pain of committing an offence, plough or otherwise convert into agricultural land any such moor or heath which has not been agricultural land at any time within the preceding 20 years, or carry out on such land other agricultural operations or forestry operations specified in the order as likely to affect its character or appearance. This protection does not cover operations carried out, or caused or permitted to be carried out, by the owner or occupier of the land, if notice of the proposed operation has been given to the National Park Authority *and* that authority have *given* their consent, *or* where they have *neither given nor refused* consent, three months have expired since notice was given, *or* where they have *refused* consent 12 months have expired since notice was given. Where the authority refuse consent they therefore have a period of 12 months during which they may (as the local planning authority) offer a management agreement under the WCA 1981, s 39, under which restrictions on the cultivation of land, or its use as agricultural land, or on the exercise of rights over that land may be imposed. Such an agreement may also impose positive obligations, and will be binding on successors in title to the land.

One other authority is relevant in connection with the parks. The Broads Authority exists under the Norfolk and Suffolk Broads Act 1988, and was established following growing disquiet over the fate of this area of some 111 square miles of land in the valleys of the Bure, Ant, Thurne, Yare and Waveney. Concern in particular focused on the division of responsibility for the area between disparate authorities, and there were calls for the Broads to be designated as a National Park. In the end a special regime was created whereby the Broads Authority is, by virtue of s 2 of the 1988 Act, to conserve and enhance the natural beauty of its area, to promote its enjoyment by the public and to protect the interests of navigation. However, the conservation of beauty includes conserving flora, fauna, geological and physiographical features, see s 25(2) of the 1988 Act. The authority thus has a definite environmental role, along with its other tasks of protecting its area's natural resources from damage, while remembering the needs of agriculture and forestry and the interests of Broads dwellers along with the importance of the area as a nationally popular place of beauty and recreation. Though the authority has no structure planning functions, it is generally otherwise the planning authority for its area and it must also prepare, under s 3, 'The Broads Plan', a strategic document, subject to quinquennial review, which sets out its policies with regard to its functions. Section 4 further requires the authority to prepare a map showing areas within the Broads whose natural beauty it is particularly important to conserve. Such a map must be kept under review, and must be prepared after consultation with English Nature and other representative bodies, while guidelines with regard to this task may be issued by the Countryside Commission. Ministers may further, under s 5 of the 1988 Act specify both certain types of land (grazing marsh, fen marsh, reed bed or broad leaved woodland) within the Broads, and operations appearing to them likely to affect the character or appearance of such an area. Thereafter the specified operations may only be carried out lawfully after the Broads Authority has been notified and has consented in writing *or* has allowed three months to pass from the notification without either giving or refusing consent, *or* has refused consent and 12 months have gone by. Management agreements may be made to ensure proposed activity does not take place. It is an offence without 'reasonable excuse' (not defined by the 1988 Act) to contravene a prohibition on designated activities. The foregoing procedure is clearly akin to, but different in material respects from, that in respect of SSSIs.

One final issue is whether there are enough parks. Marion Shoard's *This Land is our Land* after pointing out, pp 464–465, that there are limits to the protection afforded to land *within* parks, went on to point out that many areas of great beauty are not designated, and that there had been official resistance to further designation. London has no National Park within 150 miles; other areas such as the South Downs, Somerset Levels and the coasts of Cornwall and Devon could well have been designated as parks, while in 1972 ministers refused to hold an inquiry into the designation of parts of mid-Wales as a National Park. Some of Shoard's favoured areas were given ESA status, but that simply added one more piece to the confused patchwork of rural designations — evidence of a continuing failure to pursue a policy which integrates access, conservation, economic and social policies within an overall framework which maintains a vibrant countryside but one where the soil and its natural flora and fauna, etc, are maintained in good heart.

In April 1998 it was, however, accepted by the then Countryside Commission (now Agency) that the New Forest then classified as a 'heritage area' should become a National Park; however, it appeared this designation would not be applied to the South Downs, another area for which Park status had long been sought. Then in 1999 the government indicated a desire that both areas should be designated. The designation process began on 13 April 2000. See further http//www.cnp.org.uk/national_parks.htm.

H AREAS OF OUTSTANDING NATURAL BEAUTY (AONB)

Under the NPACA 1949 Act the former Countryside Commission (now, of course, the Countryside Agency in England and the Countryside Council in Wales) had power to designate land outside National Parks as Areas of Outstanding Natural Beauty (AONB), and in due course some 40 areas were designated. Planning powers played a great part in the protection of AONB, and there were provisions to enable planning authorities to further the conservation and enhancement of the beauty of such an area. However, the discretionary nature of the powers led to differences of approach and management between authorities, and by 1998 there were calls for a more coherent set of obligations to be emplaced. These are now found in ss 82-91 and Schs 13 and 14 to the Countryside and Rights of Way Act 2000 (CROWA 2000). The declared object of the government is introducing these provisions was to give to the 5.6 m acres of land in AONB a similar degree of protection to that of land within National Parks.

The CROWA 2000 enables the designation of AONB outside National Parks where this is desirable in order *to conserve and enhance* natural beauty. The designation procedure is contained in s 83 and requires consultation with affected local authorities, publicity in local newspapers, the reception of representations and their consideration by the designating body, and then confirmation by the Secretary of State (in Wales the National Assembly), a process which may involve further consultations if the confirming body determines to refuse to confirm or determines to make modifications to the order.

CROWA 2000, s 85 requires ministers, public bodies (which includes local authorities), statutory undertakers and persons holding public offices (including for example the police) when exercising or performing any function in relation to land in an AONB to have regard to the prime aim of conserving and enhancing natural beauty. This is a general not an overriding duty, but it mirrors similar requirements applying to National Parks.

Under CROWA 2000, s 86 either the Secretary of State or the National Assembly (as the case may be) may establish a 'Conservation Board' for any AONB, and may transfer certain powers from local authorities to such a board, though *not* planning powers under the TCPA 1990, Parts II, III, VII or XIII. Before such a board is established there must be consultation with the relevant countryside body (Agency or Council) and affected local authorities, and a majority of these authorities must consent to the establishment of the board before it can proceed. Such a board once established is subject to disbandment by revocation, or to having its area altered by a subsequent order. Though the exact functions of each board may vary according to the terms of the order under which it exists, under CROWA 2000, s 87 such a board must in the exercise of its functions have regard to the conservation and enhancement of the beauty of its area, and to increasing the understanding and enjoyment of the special qualities of the area by the public, though where there is a conflict between these objectives the former is to be given more weight. Again the parallel with National Park policy should be noted. In pursuing these duties boards must also seek to foster the economic and social well being of local communities, though without incurring significant expenditure. To this end they are to cooperate with other relevant public and local authorities. The powers of such boards under CROWA 2000, Sch 14 include the ability to acquire and dispose of land on a voluntary basis. Thus they may acquire land for the purpose of letting it to tenant farmers. The procedure for creating such a board is laid down by s 88, and this requires the establishing order to be in the form of a statutory instrument subject to the affirmative resolution procedure.

Management Plans within AONB

CROWA 2000, s 89 further requires such boards, within two years of their establishment, to prepare a management plan for their area formulating their management policies. Where such a board does not exist a similar duty lies with local authorities – acting jointly where more than one has part of its area in an AONB, though in this case the local authorities have three years from the date of the commencement of CROWA 2000, s 89 in which to draw up the plan. Such plans are to be known as 'AONB management plans', and may subsume any existing non-statutory plans which fulfil a similar purpose: see CROWA 2000, s 89(5). Such a management plan has to be reviewed at intervals of not more than five years as a general rule. Where a plan is to be made or reviewed consultation with other relevant bodies, eg English Nature, the Countryside Agency, the Council (in Wales) and affected local authorities (where a Conservation Board exists), must take place, see CROWA 2000, s 90. CROWA 2000, s 91 further empowers the Secretary of State and the National Assembly, as the case may be, to make grants to Conservation Boards.

As a result of the new provisions concerning AONB roughly one quarter of England will be subject to a similar protective regime – the 8% in National Park and the 16% (some 5.6 m acres) in AONB. It is expected that Conservation Boards will be set up for the larger AONB, such as the Chilterns and the Cotswolds. It is thought that the formal powers under the legislation will be supplemented by guidance from ministers which could indicate a willingness to 'call in' for central determination planning applications which planning authorities are minded to consent and which the Conservation Board oppose. More funding has been given to AONBs, increasing from £2.1 m in 1998-99 to £5.9 m in 1999-2000. It remains to be seen, however, whether the new legislation and funding policy will provide an effective means of conserving and enhancing AONBs – which heretofore have been the 'poor relations' of the National Parks. Even so the intent of the new policy is clear – land in AONBs should receive the same level of protection under planning law as that in the National Parks.

I COASTLINE PROTECTION

Much of the coastline is within National Parks or AONBs. Development plans may also indicate coastal sites as 'Areas of High Landscape Value' or 'Areas of Scientific Interest'. The coastline is, however, vulnerable to development, particularly where permission is sought for proposals involving the creation of major facilities handling great quantities of bulky and/or potentially harmful cargoes. In 1992 PPG 20 replaced earlier guidance on coastal planning. This, though land based, acknowledges the need for consideration to be given to the offshore impacts of an onshore development, and thus it is a step towards integrated coastal zone management. Furthermore, a pro conservation policy is favoured in that constraints on coastal zone development will be in general supported, while recognising that some exceptions have to be made for developments needing access to the sea. Authorities are encouraged to consider policies dealing with flooding, erosion and soil instability, though the emphasis is placed on pursuing such policies as will avoid putting other development at risk and obviating need for expensive engineering coast protection works.

The overall policy stance is to maintain the natural character of undeveloped coastline where it survives, thus constraining development in such areas, especially where an area has been designated as having landscape value and there is a need to limit development, particularly anything visually intrusive. Development plans should include policies for improving and enhancing the coast in any area of natural beauty and/or possessing conservation value. Policies should also be included on regenerating run down coastal towns and for restoration of despoiled areas.

The PPG was a step forward but even so it could be criticised for not addressing such issues on the cumulative effect of small developments, none of which may be visually intrusive individually but which despoil by incremental progression. Furthermore there remained a distinct lack of integration of coastal planning with other marine and nature conservation measures, see further Warren and Smith 'Planning for the Use of the Coast' [1994] 6 ELM 57, to which indebtedness is acknowledged.

Coastal policy now falls within the remit of DEFRA which has responsibility for the twice yearly meeting of the government's Inter-Departmental Group on Coastal Policy and the annual Coastal Forum which enables other interested organisations to put forward their views on coastal issues. DEFRA has also been involved with the European Commission's Demonstration Programme on Integrated Coastal Zone Management which from 1996 to 1999 considered, inter alia, the issue of sustainable management of coastal zones, and this has since led to the Commission's communication to the Council and European Parliament 'Integrated Coastal Zone Management: A Strategy for Europe'. At a more specifically 'legal' level DEFRA has responsibility for the review of coastal byelaws. These are made under a variety of parent statutes, including the Public Health Acts of 1936 and 1961, and the Local Government Act 1972. An inter-departmental working party examined the various byelaws and relevant procedures, reporting in 1998 and recommended modernisation and consolidation of the various powers to make byelaws. Thus a single statute would be enacted to enable byelaws to be made on a range of issues pertinent to today's use of the coast, including jet skiing and power boating. It was proposed that there should be power to designate areas of the coast as exclusive bathing zones, while the power to make byelaws should be extended to the regulation of activities which affect the wider environment. These proposals were made in response to concerns that currently the power of local authorities to make byelaws is inadequate to regulate modern uses of the coast. New primary legislation would be needed to implement these proposals.

As with so many other issues affecting rural land the response of the UK government to pressures on coastal areas is still largely voluntaristic in nature. Thus much of the protection of the undeveloped coast relies on the work of the National Trust's Neptune Coastline Campaign. This was commenced in 1965 after surveys revealed that of the 3,082 miles of the UK's coastline almost 33% was already developed while six miles a year of undeveloped land were being lost. Since then the National Trust has brought within its protection 600 miles of coastline; even so between 1965 and 2000 a further 250 miles of coastline had been taken up by housing and other forms of development. In 2000 at a cost of £3.5m the Trust acquired a further 12 miles of coastline.

J COUNTRY PARKS

The Countryside Act 1968, ss 6 to 10, confers powers on local authorities (that is (in England) county and district councils, in and around London, London borough councils, and the National Park and Broads authorities) to provide, maintain, and manage 'country parks' on suitable country sites, to provide for public enjoyment of the countryside, having regard to the location of the area in question in relation to urban areas, and the availability and adequacy of existing facilities for public enjoyment of the countryside. Supplementary services and facilities may be provided on such sites. Local authorities may acquire land by agreement or compulsorily to create a country park, or the park may be set up on land belonging to others by agreement with them. Such parks exist for recreational and leisure purposes, and for furthering the enjoyment of the countryside by the population. For the powers of Welsh authorities the position under the Local Government (Wales) Act 1994 should be checked.

K FORESTRY

The Forestry Act 1967, s 1 (as amended), continues the Forestry Commission (FC) constituted under the Forestry Acts 1919 to 1945 and charges it with the general duty of *promoting the interests of forestry, the development of afforestation, and the production and supply of timber, including the provision of adequate reserves of growing trees.* These duties are predominantly, but not exclusively, commercial, though the Commission is also required under the FA 1967, s 1(3A)(b) to strike a reasonable balance between timber supply and the conservation and enhancement of natural beauty and the conservation of flora, fauna, geological and physiographical features of special interest.

Forestry policy

For a number of years policy, as declared in 'Our Forests: the Way Ahead' (1994) was that forests should be sustainably managed to meet the 'social, economic, ecological, cultural and spiritual needs of present and future generations' and sought to combine sustainability with multi-purpose management — an aim of the Rio conference. Thus timber production was stressed, as was preventing woodland loss, especially ancient woodland, alongside public access to woodlands whose environment was to be maintained and improved. While planting of conifers was to continue to meet commercial demands, broadleaf and mixed woodland was to be encouraged where suitable, with planting of small woods as an alternative use of land to that of agriculture.

Current forestry policy

The Rural White Paper Cm 4909 building on the government's 1998 document 'A New Focus for England's Woodlands' declared a continuing commitment to the principles of quality, integration, partnership and public support with regard to the future of forests and woodlands. Thus against the commercial value of timber there also has to be set the value woodlands have in terms of beauty, recreation and nature conservation. The government believes that the long-term decline in wooded cover has to be reversed, not just in terms of commercial timber growth, but also for visual, environmental and recreational reasons. Thus while the Forestry Commission will continue to be the largest producer of timber in the nation, the days of unmixed conifer plantations have ended, and the objective of the Forestry Commission to earn a return on investments will sit alongside the other objectives outlined above. Forestry in future will be used to aid rural development and economic regeneration but will also be important in environmental and conservation terms. From an economic point of view existing woodlands and new planting will be managed so as to ensure the continued existence of jobs for the 19,000 people who currently work in forestry and wood processing. Economic regeneration will be assisted by tree planting on derelict land which has no other alternative use, eg pit spoil banks. Such planting will not only improve damaged environments but will also create new local jobs. Recreation will continue to be a major feature of woodland management and the Forestry Commission will encourage access to its estates. The Commission also manages 180 SSSIs, and has now agreed management plants with English Nature for these. The government will also continue to support the National Forest Company which is a public body specially created to encourage afforestation within the East Midlands from the current level, within the relevant area, of 6% to 30%.

Some of these policy initiatives build or work already undertaken. The Forestry Commission's 1983 Report 'England, Census of Woodlands and Trees; Wales, Census of Woodland and Trees' claimed that the total area of woodland in England had risen by some 14% since 1945, and in Wales by 40%. In England broad leaved woodland accounted for 57% of the total, but much of this was in southern and eastern England, while conifer plantations in Wales had by the mid 1980s grown from 42,000 ha in 1947 to 168,000 ha. The decline of natural and other broadleaf woodlands was recognised and measures to reverse it, such as the private sector's voluntary code 'The Forestry and Woodland Code' of 1985, together with other documents from the FC, were even then designed to be the basis of environmental standards for woodlands in both the public and private forestry sectors. A policy of encouraging broadleaf planting was introduced in 1985 and by 1993/94 more than 60% of new planting was of broadleaves. Furthermore since 1988 there was a move away from blanket planting of upland areas. Woodland planting of course also helps to husband the invaluable natural resource of wood and to combat the greenhouse effect by mopping up CO_2 — though the amounts which can be so dealt with are small indeed compared to the capacity of the threatened equatorial forests.

Grant aid and forestry policy

The Forestry Act 1967, s 5, empowers the FC to enter into forestry dedication agreements to provide for the afforestation of land and its long-term restriction to such use by means of restrictive covenants. Grant aid is given to agreed dedication schemes containing appropriate covenants in return for which the landowner further agrees to manage the land in accordance with an approved plan. Grant aid is given under the Forestry Act 1979, s 1, from the Forestry Fund maintained under the Forestry Act 1967, s 41, and is given on such terms as the FC thinks fit. Local planning authorities and other relevant statutory bodies are invited to comment on proposals for dedication of land to forestry use. Local and national amenity groups may be informed and consulted; they have no right to be; since 1992 there has been a public register of grant applications. Traditionally the discussion of proposals has been conducted confidentially, with no advertisement or publication. Disagreements over proposals which cannot be resolved locally and informally are referred, for their assistance, to Regional Advisory Committees maintained under the Forestry Act 1967, s 37, *and appointed by the FC*. These have representatives of forestry, agricultural, planning, environmental and trades union interests. Where disagreements cannot be resolved with the assistance of the appropriate committee, the FC has traditionally sought the views of the Minster of Agriculture who has consulted the Secretary of State for the Environment, where there are 'planning or amenity' issues. The final decision rests with the FC, which, historically, was criticised, along with the Ministry of Agriculture as not being receptive to the arguments of environmental organisations, see *National Parks: Conservation or Cosmetics?* p 229. Now, of course, forestry policy falls within the remit of DEFRA, and afforestation and the management of woodlands will fall to be considered within the wider objectives of reducing greenhouse gas emission and enhancing conservation and biodiversity under the UK's EC and international legal obligations.

The grant schemes are primarily administrative in nature apart from the basic statutory authority to pay money, though it appears the FC's decisions on grants may be open to judicial review.[20] Grant applications are examined to see whether they are acceptable in silvicultural, landscape, nature conservation and other environmental terms, and the consultations alluded to above will assist in this process. Where initial afforestation may lead to adverse ecological changes EIAs may have to take place according to Directives 85/337 and 97/11, and the Environmental Impact Assessment (Forestry) Regulations SI 1999/2228 (see the previous chapter for procedures). Not all afforestation projects are caught by this procedure, only those likely to have significant effects by virtue, inter alia, of size, nature or location. 'Relevant projects' include afforestation, deforestation, forest quarry and road works which do *not* involve acts of 'development' under planning legislation. Such projects may only be carried out with

20   *Kincardine and Deeside District Council v Forestry Comrs* 1992 SLT 1180.

consent from the FC, or (on appeal) from Ministers/the National Assembly as the case may be. Certain projects are generally excluded if they fall within particular size thresholds, but may still need EIA if the FC, etc, consider exceptional circumstances make it likely there will be substantial environmental effects. Where the EIA is required it must, of course, be taken into account by the FC in its grant aiding decision.

The present grant system was introduced in 1988 as the Woodland Grant Scheme (WGS) and was put into its current form in 1990. It takes account of both timber production and environmental issues as opposed to just the former. Hence there are requirements that there should be species diversity, watercourse protection, open spaces for wildlife, etc. Grants are paid in instalments or in arrears so the 'power of the purse' can be maintained, while grant aid is increased in respect of broadleaf planting to encourage the return of native woodlands. Note also the Farm Woodland Premium Scheme which encourages the conversion of farmland to woodland, and which was introduced under the Farm Land and Rural Development Act 1988.

Within the new National Forest a special 'Natural Forest Tender Scheme' fosters new planting by funding landowners who in return enter into binding contracts to provide public access, nature conservation and educational facilities. It is also central policy to work with The Woodland Trust, The Royal Society for the Protection of Birds, The National Trust, the National Small Woods Association and Groundwork trusts as well as private landowners to increase sustainable afforestation.

Local planning authorities can also use other planning powers. The Town and Country Planning Act 1990, s 197, requires authorities to use their powers when granting planning permission to preserve, where appropriate, trees. Some indication of local authority thinking on woodlands may be included in structure and local plans, and, of course in Indicative Forestry Strategies. Further detailed guidance is to be found in the document issued by the government in 2000 and referred to further below. Under the TCPA 1990, s 198, local planning authorities, that is *generally* district councils and London borough councils, while in National Parks the appropriate NPA, have power to make tree preservation orders on trees, groups of trees or woodlands to preserve them in the interests of amenity. Such an order may, inter alia, prevent the felling, lopping or uprooting of trees without consent, which may be given subject to conditions, of the local planning authority. Where felling, etc, is permitted by an order, the order may also require replanting. What constitutes a tree for the purposes of the law is uncertain. Larger growths with a diameter of seven inches or more would seem to be contemplated, *Kent County Council v Batchelor*[21] Smaller saplings *may* also be covered, *Bullock v Secretary of State for the Environment*,[22] but not, it seems, hedges, bushes and scrub. DoE Circular 36/78 counselled authorities only to make orders where public benefit will accrue in consequence, and where the removal of a tree or area of woodland would have significant environmental effects. This circular was effectively replaced by 'Tree Preservation Orders: A Guide to the Law and Good Practice' (2000). This adds to existing advice that the trees in question should be publicly visible as a general rule; they may be preserved because of intrinsic worth, or because of their contribution to the landscape, or because they screen eyesores. Trees providing wildlife habitats may be made subject to orders; but central guidance counsels against including trees that are dead, dying or dangerous. It is considered that trees in an old hedge that have grown to a reasonable height may be protected, while if an order applies to an area of woodland trees planted or growing there subsequently appear to be protected.[23]

21   [1978] 3 All ER 980, [1979] 1 WLR 213.
22   (1980) 40 P & CR 246.
23   *Evans v Waverley Borough Council* [1995] 3 PLR 80.

The procedure for making an order is laid down in SI 1999/1892. Such an order must be specific as to the trees and woodlands to which it applies, and should be supplemented by a map of the trees, etc. Once made a copy of the order must be served on persons interested in the relevant land, and a copy must also be made available for public inspection. A notice with the order must state the reasons why it has been made, and must invite objections or other representations, which must be made in writing by a specified date. Confirmation of an order may not take place until objections and representations have been taken into account. Once confirmation has occurred persons interested in land affected by the order must be informed, and also told of the time within which they may challenge the validity of the order under the Town and Country Planning Act 1990, s 284. Once an order is made it may be either varied or revoked, and in both cases persons interested in affected land must be informed. Once an order is in force the protected tree or woodland may not be cut down, lopped, damaged or uprooted save in particular circumstances, see below, and consequently as the mode of challenge to a tree preservation order (TPO) is limited to a six weeks right of challenge in the High Court following confirmation, great care is needed in making orders, see *Bellcross Co Ltd v Mid Bedfordshire District Council*.[24]

Under the TCPA 1990, s 199, a TPO does not take effect until it is confirmed, and can be modified before confirmation, but not to the extent that a totally different type of order is substituted for that initially made.[25] A TPO will not apply to cutting down, etc, a tree that is dying, dead or dangerous, though where this defence is raised in a prosecution the burden of proof lies on the defence,[26] while 'dangerous' in the present context appears to mean dangerous by virtue of disease, damage, size or location.[27] Exemptions do exist where a tree is felled, etc, in pursuance of obligations imposed under an Act of Parliament.

Compensation issues etc

The TCPA 1990, s 203 provides that a TPO may make provision for the payment of compensation by a planning authority in respect of loss or damage caused in consequence of the refusal of any consent required under the order, or its conditional grant. However, consequent on the decision in *Bell v Canterbury City Council*[28] the model TPO issued centrally provides that *no* compensation is payable where it is certified that the refusal was in the interests of good forestry or that the trees have an outstanding or special amenity value. See further the Town and Country Planning (Trees) Regulations SI 1999/1892.

Where a tree subject to a TPO is unlawfully removed, etc, TCPA 1990, s 206 provides that the landowner shall be under a duty to replace it with a tree of appropriate species and size. Where trees in a woodland are removed, however, the duty is to replace the same number of trees on or near the land where the previous trees stood or on such other land as the authority may agree, in both cases at points designated by the authority. The TCPA 1990, s 206 duty may be enforced by the local planning authority under s 207, as amended in 1991, by a notice which specifies a period at the end of which it will come into effect, not being less than 28 days from service of the notice. An appeal against such a notice may be made under TCPA 1990, s 208, while default powers are given to authorities by s 209 as amended and it is an offence wilfully to obstruct an

24   [1988] 1 EGLR 200.
25   *Evans v Waverley Borough Council* [1995] 3 PLR 80.
26   *R v Brightman* [1990] 1 WLR 1255.
27   *Smith v Oliver* [1989] 2 PLR 1.
28   (1988) 56 P & CR 211.

authority exercising this power. TCPA 1990, s 210 as amended provides for offences in connection with non-compliance with TPOs. Thus it is an offence to cut down, uproot or wilfully destroy a relevant tree, or to wilfully damage, lop or top a tree so as to be likely to destroy it. Liability is not dependent on knowledge of the TPO,[29] but does not extend to situations where an independent contractor with knowledge of a TPO and in breach of specific instructions *not* to touch a tree nevertheless uproots it.[30] A fine of up to £20,000, on summary conviction, may be imposed, and in all cases the court is to take into account in fixing the fine any financial benefit accruing to the accused in consequence of the offence. TCPA 1990, s 214A, as inserted in 1991, further provides that injunctive relief may be sought to prevent apprehended offences, while extensive rights of entry to relevant land are granted by TCPA 1990, s 214B–D.

The relationship between the provisions of the Forestry Act 1967, controlling felling, and of the Town and Country Planning Act 1990 relating to tree preservation is somewhat complex. Control of felling by virtue of the FA 1967, s 9 (as amended) under a Forestry Commission licence is not always the best way of protecting individual trees or small groups of trees for which a tree preservation order is appropriate. Making a tree preservation order is inappropriate where the management of large areas of woodland may require regular lopping and thinning. For such woodlands felling control under the FA 1967 is a better system of regulation. Some trees will be subject to one form of control, some to the other, some to both.

Where a tree is subject to control *only under the FA 1967* because no tree preservation orders have been made, control is in the hands of the Forestry Commission. In this connection it should be noted that under the TCPA 1990, s 200, where land is subject to a *forestry dedication covenant* entered into under s 5 of the FA 1967, a tree preservation order may only be made if there is no plan of operations in force approved under the covenant by the Forestry Commission, *and* if the Commissioners consent to the order. Furthermore where an order is made in these circumstances, it may not have effect so as to prohibit, or require the local planning authority's consent for cutting down any tree in accordance with a Forestry Commission approved plan of operation in force under a covenant, or under a woodlands scheme of covenants and agreements made under the FA 1967, s 5. Thus 'dedicated' woodlands agreed by the Commission cannot be made subject to a parallel system of control by the local planning authority.

Where, however, trees are subject to both forms of control, applications to fell must be made to the Forestry Commission, and may not be entertained by the local planning authority, see the FA 1967, ss 10 and 15. The Commission may refuse a felling licence, refer the matter to the local planning authority for it to be dealt with under the TCPA 1990, or notify the local planning authority they propose to grant the licence. Should that authority object to such a grant, they may require the application to be referred to the Secretary of State to be dealt with under the TCPA 1990. Where no such objection is made, the Commission's licence is also a grant of consent to fell under the tree preservation order.

The Forestry Act 1967, s 9, *generally* requires that growing trees may only be felled under a Forestry Commission licence, which is granted, under s 10, at the discretion of the Commissioners. In the exercise of this discretion there is a general presumption against allowing the clear felling of hardwood areas where the owner intends to put the land to another use.

It is an offence under the FA 1967, s 17 to fell relevant trees without a licence — such trees are those that are growing and meet certain size criteria, and which are *not*

---

29   *Maidstone Borough Council v Mortimer* [1980] 3 All ER 552.
30   *Groveside Homes Ltd v Elmbridge Borough Council* [1988] JPL 395.

fruit, orchard or garden trees, or which stand in churchyards or public open spaces. (Neither does the prohibition extend to the topping or lopping of trees or laying of hedges.) Where an offence is committed under the FA 1967, s 17, the Forestry Commission has power under s 17A(4) (as inserted in 1986) to require the restocking of the land, though this power does not extend to trees subject to TPOs.

L HEDGEROWS

A major countryside concern for many years has been the rate of hedgerow loss, which itself is a feature of overall species loss noted in particular in the government's *Countryside Survey* of 1990. Modern farm machinery functions best in large open spaces and this, coupled with the drive to bring more land under cultivation, led to large numbers of hedges being 'grubbed up' from 1945 onwards. What is not always realised, however, is that many of those hedges were themselves quite recent being the result of enclosure awards in the 18th and 19th centuries. Between 1984 and 1990, 9,500 km of hedgerow disappeared each year, but this subsequently declined to 3,600 km, while new planting has reversed the decline of hedgerows, with some 4,400 km being planted annually. The problem now is the expense of hedgerow maintenance. Payments under the ESA and Countryside Stewardship campaign have helped here, but farmers often find it economic to let hedges go derelict by allowing them to grow into lines of bushes or trees, to the detriment of biodiversity and amenity. See the Countryside Stewardship Regulations SI 2000/3048.

The Environment Act 1995, s 97, enables ministers to make regulations to protect what they determine to be 'important hedgerows', in particular by allowing for the prohibition of certain acts without permission on pain of criminal conviction. Note the Hedgerows Regulations SI 1997/1160. The unrestricted right to grub out hedgerows is now limited.

Any hedgerow growing in or adjacent to any common land, protected land (ie land managed as a nature reserve or SSSI), agricultural land, forestry land, or land used for breeding or keeping horses, ponies or donkeys, which has a *continuous length* of or exceeding 20 m or, though shorter, meets at each end another hedgerow, *can be* the subject of protection. Gaps of up to 20 m are to be disregarded in determining length, while hedgerows round dwellings are excluded from protection. However, protection is particularly further afforded to 'important' hedgerows, ie those which have existed for 30 years or more, *or* which satisfy at least one of the following criteria:

- The hedgerow marks the boundary of an 'historic' parish or township, ie existing before 1850;
- The hedgerow incorporates a scheduled archaeological feature;
- The hedgerow is wholly or partly on an archaeological site and is associated with monuments thereon;
- The hedgerow marks the boundary of a pre 1600 AD estate, or is visibly related to features of such an estate;
- The hedgerow is recorded as part of a field system pre-dating the Inclosure Acts;
- The hedgerow contains certain listed species of birds;
- The hedgerow contains a minimum number of certain woody species such as lime, alder, beech, birch, aspen, elm, hawthorn, holly, maple, oak, poplar, rose, rowan, ash, walnut, yew, willow – NB *not* sycamore;
- The hedgerow is adjacent to a bridleway or footpath and includes certain of the 'woody species" given in outline above.

The removal of a hedgerow (ie its uprooting or destruction) is prohibited without the following:

(a) the local planning authority must have received written notice from the owner that he/she proposes to remove the hedgerow;
(b) they must then determine whether the hedgerow is 'important' (see above);
(c) 'important' hedgerows may not be removed if the local authority then serves a 'hedgerow retention notice' on the owner, which they must do within 42 days of receiving the notice from the owner, unless they conclude there are circumstances justifying the removal.

However, certain actions are permitted and require no authorisation from the planning authority:

•   making a new entrance to land – provided the old one is within eight months planted with a hedgerow;
•   gaining emergency access to land;
•   obtaining access to land where other means of access are not available;
•   acting in pursuance of national defence;
•   carrying out development for which planning permission has been granted;
•   carrying out works of flood defence and/or land drainage;
•   preventing the spread of plant or tree pests;
•   carrying out highways or electricity wayleave works;
•   hedgerow maintenance.

It is an offence to remove a hedgerow intentionally or recklessly, or to cause or permit another to remove a hedgerow without informing the local authority as required. Similarly it is an offence to remove a hedgerow in contravention of a hedgerow retention notice.

Furthermore, where a hedgerow has been removed in contravention of the regulations, the planning authority may require the hedgerow owner to replace it, specifying the species of plants it is to contain. The hedgerow so planted is then to be treated as 'important'.

A person served with a hedgerow retention notice may within 28 days appeal to the Secretary of State, who may allow the appeal or dismiss it and given any necessary consequential directions. A local inquiry may be held in connection with such an appeal. Local planning authorities must compile and retain publicly available records of hedgerow removal and retention notices. In order to prevent offences authorities may apply to either the High Court or the county court for an injunction to restrain a potentially illegal hedgerow removal.

Section 98 reinforces these provisions, and in fact goes *much* further, by making provision for the payment of grants to persons who undertake *anything* conducive to the conservation or enhancement of the natural beauty or amenity of the countryside or the promotion of its beauty by the public. These powers are additional to any other grant aiding powers by relevant ministers; again see SI 2000/3048.

M GREEN BELTS AND DEVELOPMENT IN RURAL AREAS

There is a long-standing concern over the future of rural land control regarding loss of land to non-agricultural uses, particularly at the edge of urban areas, and where the land has only been marginally used for agriculture, perhaps in hope that it could be sold for more profitable urban uses. The issue is complicated often with disagreement as to the rate of loss of rural land. In 1992 the former DoE claimed 190 square miles pa were built on, the Council for the Preservation of Rural England claimed it was 460 square miles pa. Certainly between 1984 and 1990 the area of rural land covered by buildings and roads increased by 4%. There is frequently no 'clean break' between town and country. The 'fringe' of an urban area is often a place for a patchwork of mixed uses. Land may also be under pressure for amenity or recreational use. There may be a pattern of mixed administrative responsibility. Both DEFRA and DTLR will have an interest in such areas. More than one local planning authority may be involved. Concern is particularly voiced over loss of the best qualities (Grades 1 and 2) of agricultural land to urban development, and the gradual urbanisation of pleasant villages within commuting distance of towns as urban dwellers move out to more pleasant locations. Planning strives to restrict the erosion of rural land both on the urban fringe and in the open countryside, and to create 'clean breaks' between urban and rural land uses. Its task is far from easy.

Thus containing new development in urban areas by means of planning law has the effect of producing whole areas of the country entirely dependent on an agriculture which, in its increasing mechanisation and technology, has had job opportunities for fewer and fewer people. On the other hand attempts to introduce new economic activities in previously rural areas can meet with resistance from some planners, landed interests and environmentalists, though this remains an aim of government policy, see 'Our Countryside: The Future' (Cm 4909). Decline in the numbers *employed* in the countryside has been matched by a decline of other rural services. Furthermore, considerable numbers of urban-employed middle-class people have in fact moved out of towns to live in commuter homes set in rural areas for planning controls have not stopped housing developments in small towns and villages. But in the continuing debate over the planning of rural areas one strand in the argument remains the view that more economic activities should be encouraged in rural areas so that there may be an increase in the numbers of those who both live *and* work there.

It is against this background that the issues of the green belts must be set. Ebenezer Howard, the pioneer of planning, formulated ideas of cities whose growth would be limited by belts of green land kept permanently open. The idea of a 'green girdle' around London was proposed in 1933 by Sir Raymond Unwin, another founder of planning. The Green Belt (London and Home Counties) Act 1938 led to some 60,000 acres of land in the area of London and the home counties being subject to special constraints on development and sale requiring the consent of the Secretary of State and appropriate local authorities. Planning legislation gave planning authorities the power to restrict development in safeguarded rural areas without having to acquire the land compulsorily. Under this legislation the London green belt was incorporated in county development plans between 1954 and 1959. The idea of green belts for other major urban areas was canvassed by MOHLG Circular 42/55, especially to prevent the development of further conurbations. The circular counselled in general against new construction in green belt areas. Guidance was amplified by MOHLG Circular 50/57. Policy was not so much to protect the countryside but to shape, separate and contain urban growth by green belt land used for agriculture, recreation, cemeteries and some other institutional uses. Central policy also favoured dispersal of population from over-crowded cities into new towns developed beyond the green belt.

Green belts have now been generally established in the vicinities of, Newcastle and Sunderland, York, the North West (ie Greater Manchester, Merseyside, Cheshire and Lancashire including Lancaster and the Fylde Coast), West and South Yorkshire, the Potteries, Nottingham and Derby, the West Midlands, Burton-on-Trent, Cheltenham, Oxford, Cambridge. Greater London and its surrounding counties, including effectively also the areas around Luton and the areas of Hertfordshire and Southern Bedfordshire, Avon, South West Hampshire and South East Dorset, Gloucester and Cheltenham. The designated area in 1997 was 1,652,300 ha.

The various green belts have many diverse characteristics, but share the common aim of *urban containment rather than countryside protection*. To this end they impose strict constraints on development, stricter indeed than those on development in open countryside beyond. Current green belt policy is contained in PPG2 (January 1995).

PPG2 largely repeats the guidance of its 1988 predecessor, and previous guidance back to 1955. The five basic principles of including land in green belts are:
- to check unrestricted sprawl by large built up areas;
- to prevent the merging of neighbouring towns;
- to *assist* in protecting the countryside from urban encroachment;
- to preserve the setting and character of historic towns;
- to further urban regeneration by encouraging re-use of urban land.

Objectives for the use of land in green belts are set by PPG2 which confirms that such areas must be protected as far as is foreseeable, hence their boundaries should be carefully set in accordance with central guidance while sufficient land is also safeguarded for development needs. Thus once a green belt boundary is fixed it should only be changed in exceptional circumstances and only after all other development possibilities have been considered. Furthermore attempts should be made to ensure that green belts are some miles wide so as to create an appreciable open area around a built up core. PPG2 continues the presumption against 'inappropriate' development in green belts and refines the categories of development considered 'appropriate', including providing for the future of major existing developed sites and revising policy on the re-use of redundant buildings. New positive uses for green belt land are listed, including: provision of access to open countryside; providing opportunities for outdoor sport and recreation near urban areas; retaining attractive landscape; enhancing landscape near residential areas; improving derelict and damaged land around towns; adding security to areas with conservation interest; retaining agricultural, forestry and related uses. Even so land is not to be included within a green belt solely because of its attractiveness. Land is to be included because it needs protection, and that is the dominant purpose of designation.

On the basis that green belt boundaries once fixed should only be exceptionally altered, the Court of Appeal in *Carpets of Worth Ltd v Wyre Forest District Council*[31] considered that an extension of a green belt should be made only where this can be justified for the purposes for which the green belt was designed, though it appears that change may also be made where as a result of supervening changes in a structure plan original green belt boundaries become meaningless or anomalous. However, the courts are otherwise generally unwilling to enter into debate on the drawing of green belt boundaries, restricting themselves to situations where it is alleged that a planning authority has failed to consider the relevant factor of central guidance in a proper fashion.[32]

Turning to development control in green belts, PPG2 points out that general countryside development policies apply within green belts. these are concerned with development involving agricultural land generally, and reflect the move away from seeing agricultural land in terms of its food production capacity and towards a wider view comprising the need to diversity the rural economy and also to 'protect the countryside for its own sake'. Accordingly, development plans should contain appropriate policies on agricultural land, and the making of such plans should reflect consultation between planning authorities and DEFRA. Likewise consultation is obligatory under Art 10 of SI 1995/419 in respect of development concerning the loss of more than 20 ha of land of Grades 1, 2 and 3a quality, or the loss of less than 20 ha where this is likely to lead to future losses cumulatively leading to a +20 ha loss: non-statutory consultation may also take place in relation to other developments coming to MAFF's attention. Grades 1 and 2 land account for 17% of the agricultural land in

---

31   (1991) 89 LGR 897.
32   *Stewart v Secretary of State for the Environment* [1991] 3 LMELR 63; and *Grosvenor Developments (Avon) plc v Secretary of State for the Environment* [1991] 3 LMELR 165.

England and Wales and are the most adaptable and fertile land; such land should not be irreversibly developed unless there is no site suitable for the particular purpose proposed. Grade 3 land is subdivided into a, b and c, and together these grades account for 50% of the land in England and Wales. Grade 3a land has comparatively few agricultural limitations and may well be the best land in an area; it should normally therefore receive comparable protection to Grades 1 and 2 land. Grades 3b, 3c, 4 and 5 land are of poorer quality, and development of such land will not normally be resisted on agricultural grounds, though there will be exceptions in respect of upland areas.

To these constraints, which it is stressed apply to *all* agricultural land, green belt guidance adds the principles that within a belt planning consent should not be given, save in very special circumstances, for construction of new buildings, or the change of use of existing ones, for purposes *other* than agriculture, forestry, outdoor sports, cemeteries, institutions standing in extensive grounds or other appropriate rural uses (including mineral extraction provided high environmental standards are maintained and good restoration takes place). However, it should not be assumed that *all* land in a green belt is truly 'green' or even agricultural, and an important point of distinction between green belts and National Parks and AONB is that in green belts there are no legislative restrictions on permitted development rights. Furthermore where built up and urban areas meet there can be particular 'urban fringe' problems where farming uses of land are in decline. Here positive action is needed to promote environmental improvement, wildlife and landscape conservation, access to land and general education for town dwellers about the countryside. These objects may be achieved via the creation of Urban Fringe Management Schemes.

The principles of green belt protection have been considered in court, and again the judicial 'line' is that it is for authorities to take decisions that will affect green belts, but that legal intervention is appropriate where there is a failure to take into account relevant considerations, such as the principle that development should normally only be permitted where special circumstances justify an exception to green belt policy.[33] Furthermore the courts have laid down that the historic presumption in favour of development is superseded in green belts by the notion that where a proposed development is inappropriate, in the light of central guidance, there is an assumption that there is demonstrable harm to an interest of acknowledged importance. This will *not always* be fatal where the applicant can show the proposed development carries advantages that outweigh the disbenefits of inappropriate development. Applicants may also point to any relevant plan policies in their favour *and* to any planning permissions already given for inappropriate development in the greenbelt in question, though it may be argued such past developments should be reasonably close to the proposed development site. It is then for the planning authority to weigh the issues and decide whether that special circumstance exists that justifies an exception to normal greenbelt policy.[34] However, authorities must be able to show that there are reasons for allocating land as 'green belt', especially where this might cause or exacerbate a housing shortfall. In such cases the test *for an authority* is whether they have reason to believe the green belt merits of the land are sufficient to be given overriding weight.[35]

Nevertheless the basic position appears to be that where an application to develop land in a green belt is received the first task is to determine whether it is an 'appropriate' or 'inappropriate' development. If the latter, the presumption is against a grant of

33 *Grosvenor Development (Avon) plc v Secretary of State for the Environment* [1991] 3 LMELR 165.

34 *Vision Engineering v Secretary of State for the Environment* [1991] JPL 951; and *R v Secretary of State for the Environment, ex p Tesco* [1991] 3 LMELR 199.

35 *Peel Investments (North) Ltd v Bury Metropolitan Borough Council* [1999] JPL 74.

permission, for such development is per se 'harmful' to the green belt though the decision taker must weigh the disbenefits of allowing the development against any benefits flowing from it. The onus is on the applicant to show the balance tips in favour of the development. The courts will not interfere with this exercise unless the decision taker comes to an utterly unreasonable decision, or where the decision taker puts the wrong components into the balance.[36] PPG3 lists the following as 'inappropriate': the construction of new building *unless* for agricultural/forestry purposes, or as essential facilities for outdoor leisure, or as limited extensions/replacement of existing buildings, or as limited infilling in existing villages, or as redevelopment of a major existing developed site. Re-use of buildings, mineral extraction, community forests, higher and further education facilities are *not* per se 'inappropriate'.

Land for Housing: 'Greenfield v Brownfield'

One issue that has been particularly controversial for a number of years is that of housebuilding, not just in green belts but in rural areas generally. The problem is complicated by the need to ensure that there is a sufficient number of houses at affordable prices in rural areas for those who traditionally live and work there, and because housebuilding proposals vary from those to build just a few units to those to build whole new settlements.

There is ample room here for conflict between central and local government. The former has to take overall view of national needs – bearing in mind the overall commitment to sustainable development – while the latter may well seek to preserve what are legitimately regarded as important local amenities, including the preservation of agricultural and other open land. While strategic plans at a local level – eg structure plans in 'shire counties' – may seek to restrict the amount and location of new housing, the ability of the Secretary of State to intervene to direct modification to such plans under the Town and Country Planning Act 1990, s 33 so that more land is allocated for housing, is extensive. The courts are clearly unwilling to intervene to check the exercise of these powers.[37]

PPG3 (reissued in March 2000) is the principal source of guidance on land for house building. It marks a radical rethinking of housing and allocation policy away from the traditional 'predict and provide' notions (see further below) and followed many years of criticism and increasing pressure – especially from authorities in what many believe to be the overcrowded and over developed South East of England. PPG3 now declares an initial commitment to providing decent homes for all, maintaining economic growth through new building and the promotion of labour mobility, and sustainable development whereby economic growth has to be reconciled with social and environmental considerations. Within this framework provision is made for Regional Planning Guidance (RPG) whereby overall levels of regional housing land allocations will be fixed, and this then has to be reflected in structure and unitary development plans.

Overall policy requires that the pattern of housing development should be sustainable, by concentrating most new housing within existing urban areas, by re-using previously developed sites, by conversion and re-use of existing buildings, by reviewing the existing allocation of land for housing and carefully managing the release of land for this purpose, and by adopting a sequential approach to housing land

---

36   *Barnet Meeting Room Trust v Secretary of State for the Environment* [1993] JPL 739; and
       *Barnet London Borough Council v Secretary of State for the Environment, Cox, Archdeacon
       and Pointon York Trustees Ltd* [1993] JPL 767.
37   *R v Secretary of State, ex p West Sussex County Council* [1999] PLCR 365.

allocation. This sequential test (see further below) was adapted from a similar measure introduced with regard to restricting the growth of out of town retail developments see PPG6. The *national* target is that by 2008, 60% of additional housing will be provided by re-use of previously developed sites, or by conversion of existing units. Such previously developed sites are those previously covered by permanent structures or infrastructure, and may be found in both urban and rural areas – for example cleared urban sites, former quarries, redundant defence installations. However, the definition does not extend to agricultural and forestry sites, nor open land in urban areas such as parks, recreation grounds and allotments. Each region and local planning authority will be expected to contribute to achieving the national target. The 'sequential test' approach to identifying land appropriate for housing development, referred to above, requires plan making authorities to begin plan preparation by starting with the re-use of previously developed land and buildings within urban areas that they identify as being suitable sites, and only then to target land which is an extension of an existing urban area. Beyond that, where needed, land for housing should then be targeted around 'nodes in good public transport corridors'. Furthermore only sufficient land to meet the housing requirements set under relevant RPG should be identified. Land identified should be assessed in the light of the availability of previously developed sites, the location and accessibility of employment and service and retail facilities otherwise than by use of cars, the capacity of existing and potential infrastructure, eg water and sewerage services, the ability to build communities and the overall physical and environmental constraints on development of land, eg flood risks, contamination issues, etc. Thus it is clear that overall policy is that *normally* previously developed sites should be reused for housing before greenfield sites, save where such sites perform poorly in relation to the assessment criteria outlined above. To achieve the assembly of sufficient land under the sequential policy, local authorities may have to resort to compulsory purchase of vacant or under used sites to bring them back into use, though PPG3 counsels acquisition by agreement wherever possible.

Where housing is developed this should take place within a planning context that requires connections between new developments and public transport links so as to reduce car use wherever possible. Mixed use development should also be encouraged, for example, flats and apartments over shops in existing town centres to promote urban regeneration. Special emphasis should be laid on 'green residential developments', eg those which are efficient in their use of energy and which contribute to biodiversity by retaining existing trees and shrubs. Rather higher residential densities than have obtained in the past should be aimed for, ie 30 dwellings per hectare, as opposed to 20-25 which is current at the moment, as such a degree of 'land take' is unsustainable.

PPG3 accepts that some new development outside existing urban areas will have to take place, but stresses that any such new schemes 'should not consist exclusively of housing, but must be planned as a community with a mix of land uses, including adequate shops, employment and services'. Extensions to existing urban centres are, however, to be preferred to new freestanding settlements, and to this end in exceptional cases some relaxation of green belt boundaries may be acceptable where these have been too tightly drawn in the past. Expansion of villages by new housing is not favoured save in certain circumstances:

- where development occurs around a major node in a transport corridor;
- where the development is small scale infill of a settlement or a small peripheral extension;
- significant additional housing may be allowed where this will support existing local services which might otherwise become unviable, *and* where additional housing is required because of local needs, and where such housing can be provided in a sympathetic style.

Exceptionally, however, particular provision may be made to allocate land for affordable housing to meet the needs of local people in rural areas, eg housing for rent provided by registered social landlords such as housing associations.

Subsequent to the issue of PPG3 it was the subject of comments from the House of Commons Environment, Transport and Regional Affairs Committee. The government's response to that, Cm 1667, is illustrative. It was made clear that the majority of previously developed land to be recycled for housing development will be in urban areas, thus further underlining the policy objective of concentrating a majority of new housing within existing towns. Furthermore while the national target is 60% of housing on previously developed land it was made clear that this figure *should* be exceeded in areas where there is a 'significant amount' of such land. Also worthy of note is DETR Circular 08/00 containing the Town and Country Planning (Residential Development on Greenfield Land) (England) Direction 2000. This pointed to the need for development plans to be reviewed at an early stage and revised to take account of PPG3. It also pointed out that as an interim measure PPG3 is a material consideration in planning decision-making that may supersede plan policies. This applies even to applications in respect of sites allocated for housing development in existing plans: these have also to be considered in the light of PPG3's 'recycling' targets and the sequential test. To indicate central commitment to the new policy planning authorities are directed to notify the Secretary of State of proposals 'which in themselves or as part of a wider but contiguous allocation for housing relate to a site of 5 hectares or more of greenfield land for housing, or comprise 150 dwellings or more regardless of the size of site, and which the local planning authority resolve to approve'. This will enable central determination of whether there has been compliance with PPG3, and whether the matter should be called in for a decision by the Secretary of State.

A further ministerial statement of 7 March 2000 accompanying the release of PPG3 also reinforced the move away from the previous policy of 'predict and provide' with regard to allocation of land for housing. Under this planning authorities had been expected to predict housing growth within their areas and provide for it over a 20-year period. Demand prediction of this sort is a notoriously inexact science and had led to criticisms of too great an area of land being earmarked for housing – particularly in the South East of England. The new approach to provision is, as PPG3 states, based on the principles of *planning, monitoring and managing* housing provision whereby housing demand will be regularly reviewed, and while initial demand predictions have to be set they will be subject to review at least once in every five years. Furthermore the principles outlined above rest on the fundamental policy that 60% of new homes should be built on previously developed sites.

Overall policy has turned its face against locating new housing on greenfield sites. But even so it must be remembered that PPG3 allows for 40% of new residential provision to be made in this way, and that in some parts of the country where there is high demand – eg the so-called 'silicone valley' along the M4 from London to Bristol and the surrounding counties of the south west of England – the supply of previously developed land could be inadequate to provide sufficient sites. The 'Greenfield v Brownfield' controversy is far from over. Note also on planning and rural land issues PPG7: The Countryside – Environmental Quality and Economic and Social Development (1997) and PPG9: Nature Conservation (subject to revision).

N DERELICT LAND

Derelict land has been a problem in both urban and rural areas for many years, sometimes being compounded by problems of contamination. A further difficulty was the lack of accurate surveys of the size of the problem. However, in 1991 the DoE published 'The

Survey of Derelict Land in England 1988'. This found 40,500 ha of derelict land, with 31,600 ha justifying reclamation.

The follow up 'Survey of Derelict Land in England 1993' was published in 1995. This found 39,600 ha of derelict land on 10,400 sites with 34,600 ha considered worth reclamation. Industrial dereliction and spoil heaps account for 48% of the total, most of this percentage also being in urban areas. In rural areas derelict is often the result of past military use, or use for metaliferous spoil heaps, or the consequence of excavation and pits. Almost half the derelict land was in Northern England, with the smallest amounts being in East Anglia and London. Almost half the derelict land was in private sector ownership, local authorities owned 16% and other public sector bodies 20%. Where authorities' areas are afflicted by derelict land there tends to be quite an area of such affliction, and such authorities are usually urban.

Between 1988 and 1993 9,500 ha of derelict land was reclaimed, 55% by local authorities, nearly all of this with grant aid from the former DoE. This led to a decrease in the stock of such land by 2%, much less than the 11% decrease between 1982 and 1988. Of the reclaimed land 8,400 ha was put to beneficial use, 40% for 'hard' uses, eg industry and commerce, but 'soft' end uses, eg recreation, predominated in rural areas. The figures down to 1993 appear to be the last easily digestible official indication of the size of the problem. The present government's net-based 'Indicators of Sustainable Development' indicate that less land now is being reclaimed than used to be the case, despite enhanced expenditure. This is apparently due to the employment of higher reclamation standards than were previously in use. Further data may be obtained from the National Land Use Data website at http://www.nlud.org.uk/

Land has continued to become derelict, with 8,600 ha falling into this category between 1988 and 1993. Much of this, however, was a result of abandonment of military uses of land, but the former DoE recognised that the flow of land into dereliction is a problem which, though it cannot be eradicated, needs to be reduced — if only to reduce demands for grant aided restoration. Restoration conditions in mineral planning permissions have helped towards preventing dereliction and it has been argued such conditions should be included in development permissions, say, for major heavy industrial developments, though there could be debate as to the appropriate standard to which reclamation should take place. The alternative would be to grant authorities enhanced powers under the Town and Country Planning Act 1990, s 215 to enable them to take action in respect of serious dereliction of land where landholders have failed to initiate a programme of reclamation and where the derelict land is adversely affecting the amenity of a part of their area.

At the end of 1995 in response to the report 'Derelict Land Prevention and the Planning System' ministers indicated that it is up to both developers and planners to look beyond the expected life of a proposal and to make provision for the eventual rehabilitation and re-use of the land.

Legislation dealing with derelict land has been on the statute book for many years, and was to be found in the National Parks and Access to the Countryside Act 1949, the Local Authorities (Land) Act 1963, the Local Government Act 1966, the Countryside Act 1968, the Local Employment Act 1972 and the Local Government, Planning and Land Act 1980. The various provisions are now largely contained in or substituted by the Derelict Land Act 1982. However, the basic power of local authorities to reclaim derelict land has been the NPACA 1949, s 89. This granted local planning authorities, that is county and district authorities (county and county boroughs in Wales), powers to:

1   Plant trees on land in their area to preserve or enhance natural beauty.
2   Carry out reclamation works on land in their area appearing to be either derelict, neglected or unsightly, or likely to become so by reason of the actual or apprehended collapse of the surface resulting from underground mining

operations, *other* than coal-mining, which have ceased. This power extends to improving land, or bringing it into use, and enables work on the land in question and on other land. The powers may be exercised over an authority's own land, or over other persons' land with their consent. Land may be compulsorily acquired by authorities exercising the powers, subject to ministerial confirmation under the NPACA 1949, s 103.

The restoration powers are supplemented by the Mineral Workings Act 1985, ss 7 and 8. Section 7 gives local authorities certain powers of entry, and to search and bore, in relation to land which is being considered for reclamation in consequence of past underground mining operations, otherwise than for coal. Section 8 allows reclamation work to proceed *without* the consent of those who are interested in the land where in the relevant authority's opinion the surface of the land under which mining was carried out has collapsed, or is in danger of collapse, *and* the works are urgently necessary to protect persons, *and* consent to the work has been unreasonably withheld. Notice of intention to proceed under this power must be given to those interested in the land, and such persons may appeal to the Secretary of State who shall decide the issue.

Section 1 of the Derelict Land Act 1982 relates to grant aid in respect of derelict land in England. The Secretary of State, subject to Treasury consent, may make such grants in respect of appropriate expenditure. Similar powers exist with regard to Wales under the Derelict Land Act 1982, s 2. Grants may be made in respect of land which *is* derelict, neglected or unsightly, or which is likely to become so by virtue of actual or apprehended subsidence.

Policy on derelict land grants was revised with effect from June 1991. Until then grant aid had been concentrated on the restoration of land for urban building purposes. The new policy was broader in encompassing both restoration for development and general environmental improvement, with encouragement for local authorities to create their own programmes for derelict land. Voluntary organisations now receive more funding for restorative and reclamation projects, particularly with a view to the promotion of nature conservation and creation of new habitats on reclaimed land.

A further change occurred in 1993 with the enactment of the Leasehold Reform, Housing and Urban Development Act, under Part III of which an Urban Regeneration Agency (known as 'English Partnerships') was created. This body's functions extend to securing the regeneration of land in England which is contaminated, derelict, neglected or unsightly or which is likely to become derelict, neglected or unsightly by reason of the collapse of its surface as a result of past underground operations, and that there is a clear parallel wit the work of local authorities. However, English Partnerships is subject to ministerial direction and is concerned with securing the development and reuse of land, but also with urban regeneration generally and the creation of new jobs and investment under the LRHUDA 1993, s 160 to acquire, manage and develop land. It may also give financial assistance, for example by way of grant/ loan, advice, services and facilities to others to promote its statutory functions.

Derelict land grant has been integrated into a unified system of financial support *operated* by English Partnerships, though of course, funding still comes from central government. The implications of this for reclamation activity must now be considered.

Derelict land grant reclamation activity has been generally considered a success in value for money terms, at least with regard to reclamation for further development. The 1994 'Assessment of the Effectiveness of Derelict Land Grant in Reclaiming Land for Development' found that, over the years, a wide range of derelict sites had been reclaimed with a high (66%) rate of development after reclamation. Programme objectives have been largely met at a reasonable cost (on average £54,000/ha) and local authorities have carried out their tasks well.

O CONCLUSION

The laws regulating land use in rural areas and open and derelict land in urban areas continue to be a microcosm of the confused state of environmental law and policy. They illustrate the fragmented nature of environmental control, with responsibility being divided, unnecessarily perhaps in many cases, between central government, local authorities and a range of statutory ad hoc agencies or 'quangos'. The number of involved bodies could be reduced: the answerability of those remaining could be increased. Rural land use policy also reflects a general lack of consensus on environmental issues. One's stand on a land use issue may be eccentricity to another, and elitist politics to a third. Debate becomes confused. It is hard to distinguish 'friends' from 'foes' in relation to particular issues: various groups use similar words with different meanings. Nevertheless there remains concern for the future of the countryside and over the future of CAP, while there is increasing realisation that much more sophisticated land management is required if the countryside is to continue to give us the food we need, the employment many seek, the amenities and recreation we require, and a habitat for the other species with whom we share our land.

The future

In January 2002 the government published the report of the Policy Commission on 'The Future of Farming'. This is likely to provide the basis for much of future regional policy. The emphasis is likely to move away from the notion that has lain at the root of policy for over 50 years, namely ever more food produced ever more cheaply, and with emphasis on grant aid being given in response to environmental needs. This will entail phasing out general subsidies for food production.

The principal relevant recommendations of the report are:
- the UK government should press for the earliest possible reform of CAP according to a fixed timetable, while supporting farming while it has to adapt to change, in particular EC funding should refocus on 'public good' (as opposed to subsidising over-production of food) such as rural development and environmental benefits and programmes not otherwise likely to be achieved by market measures;
- price support and production control systems should disappear;
- direct payments in respect of food should be phased out as soon as possible and while they exist they should be 'decoupled' from food production and be subject to 'environmental conditions';
- UK funding should be switched to rural development and environmental protection schemes, in particular the various 'suites' of stewardship schemes should be rationalised as 'tiers' with one overall scheme, with the lowest tier being given to areas of land and land managers not currently 'caught' by stewardship, and in due course woodland and flood protection schemes should in due course become part of the 'tiered; stewardship scheme;
- a network of demonstration farms should be set up to disseminate good practice in food production;
- planning authorities should be proactive in giving advice on rural business diversification;
- more emphasis should be placed on the growing of renewable raw material and energy crops, with planning guidance supporting the creation of localised heat and power projects to utilise 'bio-fuels';

- strict farm standards with regard to food production practices should be required with the 'back-up' threat of requiring farmers to be licensed before they may practise agriculture;
- farming would be given support as a sustainer of the rural environment, with farmers being rewarded for good countryside management;
- with further EC directives expected on nitrates, water and waste there should be a clear environmental strategy in place for their implementation;
- continuing public support for organic farming remains justified, but it should be funded as a 'tier' in the overall stewardship scheme outlined above, and to this end an organic food production strategy is needed;
- capital allowances should be made available to farmers who adopt environmentally beneficial technologies and pollution control equipment;
- while current controls, including voluntary ones, on pesticide use should be maintained, the case for a tax on pesticide use should continue to be investigated;
- farmers should 'embrace' the notion of public access to land as part of a 'new contract with taxpayers' who are the funders of environmental management payments.

The clear message of the document is that a major shift in policy on the countryside is needed, away from general food production as such and towards recreation and environmental enhancement. However, there are questions over the proposals. First of all the reduction in food subsidies may lead to an increase in the already quite high number of farmers quitting agriculture. That would result in land ownership being concentrated in a smaller number of largely corporate 'hands'. Secondly even farmers who currently farm in an organic fashion are concerned that their practices will not be economically sustainable without a continuing high level of subsidy. They point to the fact that there is no clear monetary return to them if they dig new ponds for wildlife or allow their hedges to thrive or diversify.

Further reading

BOOKS

Curry, N, *Countryside Recreation, Access and Land Use Planning* (1994) E & F Spon.
Elson, MJ, *Green Belts* (1986) Heinemann.
Garner, JF, and Jones, BL, *Countryside Law* 3rd edn (1997) Shaw and Sons.
Hawke, N, and Kovaleva, N, *Agri-Environmental Law and Policy* (1998) Cavendish.
Howarth, W and Rodgers, C, *Agriculture, Conservation & Land Use* (1992) University of Wales Press.
Lowe, P, Cox G, MacEwen M, O'Riodan T, and Winter M, *Countryside Conflicts* (1986) Temple Smith/Gower.
MacEwen, A, and M, *National Parks: Conservation or Cosmetics* (1982) George Allen and Unwin.
MacEwen A, and M, *Greenprints for the Countryside* (1987) George Allen and Unwin.
McMahon, J, *Law of the Common Agricultural Policy* (2000) Longman.
Pye Smith, C, and Rose, C, *Crisis and Conservation* (1984) Penguin Books.
Reid, C, *Nature Conservation Law* (1994) W Green/Sweet & Maxwell.
Rowan-Robinson, J, and McKenzie Skene, D (eds), *Countryside Law in Scotland* (2000) T & T Clark.
Shoard, M, *This Land is Our Land* (1987) Paladin.
Winter, M, 'Agriculture and the Environment' in Churchill, R, Warren, L, and Gibson, J, *Law Policy and the Environment* (1991) Basil Blackwell.

JOURNALS, OCCASIONAL AND CONFERENCE PAPERS
Basden, A, 'Cramping Our Style' (1991) 60 Town and Country Planning 294.
Chesman, GR, 'Local Authorities and the Review of the Definitive Map under the Wildlife and Countryside Act 1981' [1991] JPL 611.
Corbett, 'Protecting the Human Resources of the Countryside — affordable housing initiatives' [1994] 6 ELM 64.
Forster, M, 'The Countryside and the Law: making the new rights of Way Act work' [1990] 2 LMELR 126.
Robinson, PC, 'Tree Preservation Orders: Felling a Dangerous Tree' [1990] JPL 720.
Scrase, AJ, 'Agriculture — 1980s Industry and 1947 Definition' [1988] JPL 447.

OFFICIAL REPORTS AND CONFERENCE PAPERS
House of Commons Agricultural Committee: '2nd Special Report on The Effects of Pesticides on Human Health', Session 1986–87, HC 379–1.
House of Lords Select Committee on the European Communities: '20th Report on Agriculture and the Environment', Session 1983–84, HL 247.
'Access to the Countryside for Recreation and Sport', CCP 217 (1986) Countryside Commission.
'New Opportunities for the Countryside', CCP 224 (1987) Countryside Commission.
'Planning for Countryside in Metropolitan Areas', CCP 244 (1987) Countryside Commission.
'Environmentally Sensitive Areas' (1989) HMSO.
'A Farmer's Guide to the Planning System' (1993) HMSO.
'Permitted Development Rights for Agriculture and Forestry' (1991) HMSO.
'The Effectiveness of Green Belts' (1993) HMSO.
'Our Forests: the Way Ahead' (1994) Cm 2644 HMSO.
House of Commons Environment Committee; 3rd Special Report Session 1994–1995, 'The Environmental Impact of Leisure Activities', HC 761.
'Derelict Land Prevention and the Planning System' (1995) HMSO.
Land Use Consultants: 'Planning Controls Over Agricultural and Forestry Development and Rural Building Conversions' (1995) HMSO.
Elson et al: 'Planning for Rural Diversification' (1995) HMSO.
Royal Commission on Environmental Pollution, Nineteenth Report: 'Sustainable Use of Soil', Cm 3165 (1996) HMSO.
'Our Countryside: The Future. A fair deal for rural England' (2000) HMSO.

Chapter 10

Access to the countryside and public rights of way

The National Parks and Access to the Countryside Act 1949, provides the basic legal structure for public access to the countryside, based on the principle of access for recreation in the 'open country', defined by s 59(2) as areas consisting wholly or predominantly of mountain, moor, heath, down, cliff or foreshore, to which the Countryside Act 1968, s 16, added *certain* woodlands, rivers, canals and their banks, etc. However, no *right* to wander through such countryside was given by the NPACA 1949 save where land is acquired compulsorily for such a purpose, or made subject to an access order or access agreement.

Under the NPACA 1949, local planning authorities were put under a duty to review their areas for the purpose of considering open country and access arrangements thereto. This has now been rendered unnecessary and is repealed by the Countryside and Rights of Way Act 2000, see further below. The NPACA 1949, s 64 empowers authorities to make *access agreements* with persons who have interests in land in open country in their areas. This power continues under CROWA 2000, s 68 with regard to land *other* than 'access land', see further below. Agreements may provide for payments to be made by authorities. In respect of land situated in a National Park before an access agreement is made the relevant authority must consult with the Countryside Commission in England, the Countryside Council in Wales. Where an access agreement (or order) is in force under the NPACA 1949, s 60, the public entering and being on the land for open air recreational purposes, without doing any damage, are not to be treated as trespassing. Open air recreation does not include *organised* games, see the NPACA 1949, s 114(1). Agreements (and orders) may impose restrictions on access. The right of access does not extend to certain categories of excepted land, *including:* agricultural land, other than land which is agricultural land solely because it is used to rough graze livestock; land covered by buildings; parks, gardens and pleasure grounds; surface mines and quarries; railway land; golf courses, race courses and aerodromes and other operational land of statutory undertakers; and Nature Reserves, see the NPACA 1949, s 60(5). Agreements (and orders) must also exclude from access all land expedient for the purpose of avoiding danger to the public, or to persons employed on such land, see the NPACA 1949, s 80. The Countryside Act 1968, s 18 further empowered authorities who make access agreements to agree restrictions in such agreements on the rights of other parties and thus provide for agreements not to convert land into excepted land under the NPACA 1949, s 60(5).

Once an agreement (or order) is in force persons interested in affected land, not being excepted and, may not carry out any works thereon having the effect of substantially reducing the area to which the public have access: see the NPACA 1949, s 66. Local planning authorities have power under s 68 to enforce this provision. Agreements (and orders) may, under the NPACA 1949, s 67, make provision for securing sufficient means of access to affected land. Section 69, however, allows suspension of access rights where, on the application of a person interested in affected land, the relevant authority decide that, in view of exceptional weather conditions, there is a risk of fire.

Access *orders* may be made, under the NPACA 1949, s 65, by local planning authorities, subject to ministerial confirmation, where it appears to an authority that making an access agreement to secure public access for open air recreation is impracticable. The NPACA 1949, ss 70 to 73 enshrine the right to, and lay down procedures for obtaining, compensation in respect of access orders. Where the value of a person's interest in land is depreciated in consequence of the making of an access order compensation is payable by the local planning authority in whose area the affected land is. Such compensation, however, cannot be claimed or be payable before the end of five years from the coming into force of the order so that compensation may be assessed in the light of experience gained of the effect of the order on the land. The NPACA 1949, s 73 allows payments on account during the initial five-year period in a case of special hardship.

The NPACA 1949, s 76 confers powers of compulsory purchase, subject to ministerial confirmation, on planning authorities in respect of land, other than excepted land, where the acquiring authority consider it expedient and requisite for the purpose of public access that acquisition should take place. The NPACA 1949, s 77 confers a supplementary compulsory purchase power for access purposes on the Secretary of State in respect of open country in National Parks, other than excepted land. For the meaning of 'excepted land' see above and NPACA 1949, s 60(5).

The powers to create access to the countryside were attacked as ineffective, largely because of the general presumption of the law that entry upon another's land is a trespass save in narrowly defined exempted circumstances. In *This Land is Our Land*, for instance, Marion Shoard called for adoption of the system in Sweden. 'The Right of Common Access', whereby all have the *right* to cross the land of others on foot, provided no damage is done, and subject to exceptions to ensure privacy and the safety of crops. In 1986 the Countryside Commission and the Sports Council considered in *Access to the Countryside for Recreation and Sport* that followed reform of CAP public access as a land use should be a major component of future rural land policy. The Countryside Access Regulations SI 1994/2349 went some way in meeting calls for an open access policy in that farmers could be paid grant aid for a period of five years from 15 January following the date of acceptance of their applications for aid where they permitted members of the public to have free access to areas of set aside land known as 'access areas' for quiet recreational purposes.

A 'THE RIGHT TO ROAM'

Though under the NPACA 1949 access to 50,000 ha of open countryside had been secured, by the late 1990s it was calculated by central government that 500,000 ha were closed to access, while there were 600,000 with informal access tolerated. This led to the 1998 consultation paper 'Access to the Open Countryside in England and Wales' in which it was further calculated that mountains, moor, heath, down and registered common land amounted to some 1.2 – 1.8 m ha, about 10% of the land surface of England and Wales. Most consultees favoured a right of access to such land, and the government announced a decision to proceed in 'The Government's Framework for

Action: Access to the Countryside in England and Wales' in February 1999, while the Countryside Agency further recommended in October 1999 that a right of access should extend to beaches and cliffs. This led to the Countryside and Rights of Way Act 2000 (CROWA 2000). Under Part I of this Act there is provision for a new statutory right of access for the purposes of open-air recreation on mountain, moor, heath, down and registered common land, with a power given to extend this to coastal lands (see the Countryside and Rights of Way Act 2000, s 3) while landowners may voluntarily give public access over any land provided they do so irrevocably.

The scheme of the Act

Under CROWA 2000, s 1 the right of access applies to 'access land', ie that which is shown as open country on maps issued by the relevant countryside bodies (the Countryside Agency in England, the Countryside Council for Wales in Wales) and which consists predominantly of mountain, heath, moor or down land, *or* which is registered common land, *or* which is situated more than 600 m above sea level in any area, irrespective of whether a map has yet been issued. Certain land is, however, 'excepted' under CROWA 2000, Sch 1 of the Act, ie land ploughed during the preceding twelve months for crop or tree planting, land covered by buildings or within their curtilage, land with 20 m of a dwelling, pool or garden land, land used for quarrying or railway purposes, golf course, racecourse or aerodrome land, land used by statutory undertakers or telecommunications code system works, land which will fall within any of the foregoing classes as a result of development which is in the course of being carried out, land within 20 m of buildings used for housing livestock, land covered by livestock pens, racehorse training grounds, military land. Furthermore, mountain, moor, heath or down land does *not* include land consisting of improved or semi-improved grassland. It can thus be seen that there are quite extensive exceptions to the category of 'access land', and these extend to lands in respect of which there are other existing statutory rights of access for recreational purposes, eg land already subject to an access order or agreement under the NPACA 1949. Land may, however, become 'access land' by dedication under CROWA 2000, s 16: see further below.

CROWA 2000, s 2 enshrines the right of access to 'access land', though this must be exercised without breaking any wall, fence, hedge, stile or gate, and is subject to restrictions imposed under the Act. These restrictions under CROWA 2000, Sch 2 include the use of vehicles and bicycles, watercraft and horse riding. Neither is access permitted where entry is otherwise forbidden under other legislation, or for the commission of crimes, including breaches of byelaws. There are additional restrictions relating to the control of dogs, particularly at designated periods (eg keeping dogs on leads in the period March to July). Breach of these restrictions leads to those concerned losing their right of access to land in the same ownership as that on which the breach occurred – perhaps rather more importantly from the point of view of sanctions, they may be treated as trespassing, and sued see CROWA 2000, s 2(4). It is possible for the restrictions to be amended by order, and certain restrictions may be relaxed where a landowner consents to allow the exercise of wider rights, eg riding horses. See also further below on exclusion and restriction of access.

Mapping

The Countryside bodies under CROWA 2000, ss 4–11, and Sch 3 to the Act have duties with regard to mapping 'access land'. CROWA 2000, s 4 creates the duty of preparing maps of open country and registered common lands. Such maps under s 5 must be prepared in draft form and opened to public consultation, with any representations made being taken into account. They must then confirm the map, with or without modifications, and if confirmed without modifications maps are to be issued in 'provisional form'; this is also the case with a modified map, though here it must be provisionally issued in its modified form. Any person having an interest in any land shown in a provisional map as either open country or registered common land may appeal – in England to the Secretary of State, in Wales to the National Assembly. 'Interest' in this context under CROWA 2000, s 45 extends to interests under licence or agreement such as sporting rights. Following such an appeal the appellate body may confirm the map with or without further modifications, or the preparation of a new map – which will be subject to the consultation procedure – may be directed: see CROWA 2000, s 6. CROWA 2000, ss 7 to 8 and Sch 3 lay down procedural requirements for determining appeals. There is a discretion to hold a hearing or a public local inquiry, and if a party requests either a hearing or an inquiry one must be held. The appellate bodies may delegate their determinative powers under CROWA 2000, s 8.

Once all appeals, if any, have been dealt with, CROWA 2000, s 9 provides for the confirmation of the map as a 'conclusive map'. The appellate body may direct the issue as a conclusive map of any part of a provisional map where there is no outstanding appeal. These maps must, under CROWA 2000, s 10, be reviewed within 10 years, and at not less than 10-year periods thereafter to determine whether land shown as 'access land' should retain that designation, and whether other land should be included. CROWA 2000, s 11 enables regulations to be made to lay down procedures, inter alia, for reviews and the manner and form of plans – eg their scales.

The rights and liabilities of landholders

Under CROWA 2000, s 12 the operation of the right of access is not to increase any liabilities owed by landholders in respect of the land or what is done on it, nor will it give rise to any breach of a restrictive covenant on the land. Similarly under CROWA 2000, s 13 a person entering by way of the right of access is not a 'visitor' for the purposes of the Occupiers Liability Act 1957, and under the Occupiers' Liability Act 1984 (liability to non-visitors) at any time when the right of access is exercisable no duty is owed to those using it in respects of risks arising from natural features of the landscape, such as plants and trees, nor from any river, stream, ditch or pond (natural or otherwise) nor from the passage of any person under or through any wall, fence or gate except by proper use of a gate or stile. Liability will arise in such circumstances where the occupier has behaved intentionally or recklessly with regard to the creation of a risk. In any case in determining liabilities under the OLA 1984 courts are to take into account: the fact that the existence of the right of access ought not to place undue burdens on occupiers; the importance of maintaining the character of the countryside and its features, and any guidance issued under CROWA 2000, s 20 (see below).

It is an offence under CROWA 2000, s 14 to display notices containing false or misleading information on or near 'access land' likely to deter exercise of the right of access – eg a notice forbidding access.

Dedication

A person who holds the fee simple absolute in possession of land, or who holds a legal term of years absolute with at least 90 unexpired may, under CROWA 2000, s 16, dedicate land as 'access land'. Such a dedication is irrevocable (in the case of leaseholder dedication only for the remainder of the term of years) and can, inter alia, be used to ensure that land is made freely available for access free of the normal restrictions set out in CROWA 2000, Sch 2– eg to allow access on horseback. Dedication has to be made in due form, and notified to the appropriate countryside body.

Exclusion and restriction of access

We have already seen that there are limits generally to the right of access under CROWA 2000, s 2, further provision to exclude or restrict access may be made under CROWA 2000, ss 21 to 33. An 'exclusion' occurs when a person excludes the application of CROWA 2000, s 2 to relevant land; a 'restriction' on the other hand is where the right of access is exercisable along only specified routes or ways, or only after entering the land at a specified place, or is exercisable only without dogs, or is exercisable only subject to particular conditions.

Under CROWA 2000, s 22 an 'entitled person', ie the owner and other prescribed persons such as tenants under a farm tenancy, are able to *exclude or restrict* access for up to 28 days in any calendar year, not more than four of these days to fall on a Saturday or Sunday, but not on *any* Saturday between 1 June and 11 August, nor any Sunday between 1 June and 30 September, nor on Christmas Day or Good Friday, nor on any Bank Holiday. The exclusion is effected by the entitled person serving notice to the relevant authority, ie the appropriate countryside body, or, in a National Park, the National Park Authority, or, in cases of woodland dedicated under CROWA 2000, s 16, the Forestry Commission. Regulations may be made to require that this power is exercised only with regard to land whose boundaries have been determined in accordance with the regulations.

Owners of grouse breeding moors may under CROWA 2000, s 23 restrict access on a 'no dogs' basis for specified periods, while a similar restriction for up to six weeks may be imposed with regard to fields of up to 15 ha in connection with lambing. Such restrictions do not apply to guide dogs or trained hearing dogs.

Access may also be restricted by the 'relevant authorities' see above, under CROWA 2000, ss 24 to 27. Under s 24 a person interested in relevant land may apply for a direction excluding or restricting access from such an authority for a specified period, and they may grant it if satisfied it is necessary in the interests of land management. In deciding whether or not to exercise this power the authority must consider the extent to which use has been made of CROWA 2000, s 22. By direction the authority may under s 25 exclude or restrict access for a specified period, either on application from a person interested in the land, or on their initiative (again having taken into account the use made, if any, of s 22) for the avoidance of fire risks or dangers to the public. Similarly access may be excluded or restricted by the relevant authority for a specified period in the interests of nature conservation and heritage protection: see CROWA 2000, s 26.

Before any action is taken by an authority under the foregoing provisions which could lead to an indefinite restriction, or one which would exceed six months in duration, they are to consult the 'local access forum' created under CROWA 2000, ss 94-95 as an advisory body. Directions given may be revoked or varied, and must be subject to review after five years where they are of indefinite duration, or are to last for more than five years, or where they apply for a part of every year of each of six or more consecutive calendar years. Before revoking or varying a direction the authority must also consult the original applicant for the direction. It is clear from the wording of CROWA 2000, s 27 that restrictions, etc on access may last for a considerable period of time, eg to protect a SSSI or other sensitive sites.

The Secretary of State has a similar power under CROWA 2000, s 28 to exclude or restrict access for defence or national security purposes, again subject to review after five years in relevant cases.

Under CROWA 2000, s 29 proposals for directions under s 26 by a relevant authority may be referred to ministers by 'relevant advisory bodies', where the relevant authority has sought advice from the advisory body and has decided either not to direct the exclusion or restriction, or has otherwise decided not to act in accordance with the advice. The 'relevant advisory bodies' are, for the purposes of nature conservation, English Nature and the Countryside Council for Wales, and for the purposes of heritage conservation, the Historic Buildings and Monuments Commission for England, and the National Assembly for Wales (acting via Cadw).

Disappointed applicants for directions under CROWA 2000, ss 24 or 25, may, under s 30, appeal to ministers (or, as appropriate, the National Assembly for Wales). CROWA 2000, ss 7 and 8 and Sch 3 (Appeal provisions) have effect here as they do with regard to the mapping provisions (see above). CROWA 2000, s 31 makes provisions for regulations to be made enabling 'relevant authorities' to exclude or restrict access in an emergency for any of the purposes specified in ss 24 to 26, for a period of up to three months – for example because of the outbreak of a disease where public health has to be protected.

CROWA 2000, ss 32 and 33 are supplementary provisions. The former enables the making of regulations relating to exclusion and restriction of access issues, eg with regard to procedures and the form of requisite notices etc. The latter provision empowers the Countryside Agency and the Countryside Council for Wales as the prime administering bodies for the legislation to issue guidance to National Parks Authorities and the Forestry Commission in relation to these matters where, for example, by virtue of location or dedication, they are 'relevant authorities'.

Means of access

Under CROWA 2000, ss 34–39 provisions exist to enable access to 'access land' to be secured or improved. These relate to matters such as openings in fences, walls, hedges, or gates, or the construction of stiles and bridges etc which enable the public to have access: see CROWA 2000, s 34. These powers belong to 'access authorities' under CROWA 2000, s 35, who are, under s 1(2)(a) and (b) the National Park Authority (where appropriate) or the local highway authority, but their powers do not apply to land where particular exclusions are in place with at least six months unexpired. Where an access authority considers access ways could be improved, repaired or opened up, or a new means needs construction, or an existing one maintained, or impedances to access ways need to be restricted in order to give the public reasonable access to 'access land', they may enter agreements with the owner or occupier of the land for such purposes. They may do the work themselves and may contribute to the cost of works done by the landholder. Failure on the part of the landholder to honour such an agreement enables the access authority after giving at least 21 days' notice to do any agreed work themselves and to recover their costs see CROWA 2000, s 36.

CROWA 2000, s 37 reinforces s 35 by making provision for cases where no agreement for the purposes of access is achievable on reasonable terms. Here the authority on giving not less than 21 days' notice of their intention may take all the necessary steps themselves – for example clearing an access way blocked by obstacles and overgrown with weeds. This notice has to be served on either the owner or occupier of the land, and copies served on all other owners and occupiers. Where such powers are exercised the authority must consider the requirements of efficient land management in deciding where means of access are to be provided.

There is a right of appeal for owners and occupiers against a CROWA 2000, s 37 notice, or one under s 36(3) (failure to honour an agreement that impedances to access (eg removal of access ways) will be restricted). The grounds of appeal are:
* the notice requires the carrying out of unnecessary works;
* where means of access are required, that they should be differently provided, or provided elsewhere – this enables arguments based on effective land management to be adduced.

The appellate authority (the Secretary of State or the National Assembly for Wales) may confirm the notice with or without modification or may cancel it. While an appeal is pending no action to carry out works by the access authority under CROWA 2000, ss 36 or 37 can take place. The procedural requirements for appeals are those laid down in ss 7 and 8 and Sch 3.

Under CROWA 2000, s 39 where two or more notices relating to a means of access have been given to a person within the preceding 36 months and there is non-compliance, the access authority may apply to the justices for an order that the person is to take specified steps to remove impedances to access, and shall not obstruct it while the right of access is exercisable. Failure to comply with such an order is an offence, and also entitles the authority to remove the obstruction and recover their reasonable costs from the person responsible.

General and Miscellaneous provisions

CROWA 2000, s 40 empowers the various responsible bodies – countryside bodies, local highways authorities, national park authorities and the Forestry Commission – to authorise persons to enter on land so that they may discharge their functions. Where land on which entry is needed is not access land, 24 hours' notice of intention to enter must be given to the occupier, unless it is not reasonably practicable to do so, or where an offence under CROWA 2000, ss 14 or 39 is being committed. It is also an offence to obstruct authorised entry. Under CROWA 2000, s 41 compensation is payable to a person suffering damage in consequence of an entry.

CROWA 2000, s 42 enables regulations to be made to provide that the status of land as 'access land' is to be disregarded in determining whether that land is a 'public place' for the purposes of various enactments – eg those on public order offences. The legislation will bind the Crown, see CROWA 2000, s 43, while orders and regulations made centrally under s 44 are to be made in the form of statutory instruments.

CROWA 2000, s 17 enables access authorities to make byelaws for relevant land in their areas to preserve order, prevent damage and to prevent undue interference by those exercising the right of access by others also exercising that right. Such byelaws are subject to consultative requirements with the appropriate countryside body and the local access forum, and do not affect public rights of way.

CROWA 2000, s 18 empowers access authorities and district councils to appoint wardens for access land. These wardens will advise the public and landowners, and will secure compliance with byelaws etc. Access authorities may also under CROWA 2000, s 19 erect notices indicating the boundaries of both access and excepted land, and informing the public of the effect of general access restrictions, and of any particular exclusions or restrictions in place. Before such notices are erected there should be consultation with the owner or occupier of the land. Authorities may defray the costs of such notices provided by other persons.

Under CROWA 2000, s 20 the countryside bodies are to issue codes of conduct with regard to exercising the right of access, and must also take steps to inform the public of the existence and extent of that right, and of their rights and obligations when exercising the right of access.

Commencement and guidance

At the time of writing (August 2001) many of the provisions considered above were in force, but the right of access itself under CROWA 2000, s 2 remained to be commenced, along with CROWA 2000, ss 12-14, 18 and 20. Further guidance can be found in the Explanatory Notes to the Countryside and Rights of Way Act 2000, to which indebtedness is acknowledged, and DETR Circular 04/2001.

B PUBLIC RIGHTS OF WAY AND LONG-DISTANCE ROUTES

The National Parks and Access to the Countryside Act 1949, Part IV, laid down provisions relating to and requiring the ascertaining, surveying and definitive mapping of public footpaths, bridleways and other public highways in the countryside. Provision was made for regular reviews of 'the definitive' map'. The law was unsatisfactory in practice. Earlier provisions were generally replaced by the Wildlife and Countryside Act 1981, ss 53–58. These provisions have themselves been considerably extended and amended by the Countryside and Rights of Way Act 2000. Under the NPACA 1949, s 53 'surveying authorities' (generally county councils) are required, on the happening of certain specified events, to modify the definitive map and statement of public rights of way, and to keep the map and statement continuously under review. The specified events 'triggering' modification of the map and statement are: (a) the stopping up, diversion, widening or extension of a public highway required to be shown on the map; (b) the ceasing of any highway shown on the map to be a highway of the type shown; (c) the creation of a new right of way over land in the area of the map; (d) the passage of 20 years without interruption during which the public has used a way so as to raise the presumption of dedication as a public path (even where at the time of that use the way was not included in the definitive map, it appears); and (e) the discovery of evidence showing omissions or mis-descriptions in the map. Any person may apply to the surveying authority for an order to make modifications requisite in consequence of events falling within heads (d) and (e) above. Under the NPACA 1949, s 53B, introduced in 2000, such applications have to be registered and kept by authorities. Such applications are to be made and determined in accordance with Sch 14 to the WCA 1981. There is a right of appeal to the Secretary of State in the event of a refused application. The WCA 1981, Sch 15, as amended by CROWA 2000, also applies to modifications made to maps and statements, following reviews, and/or the occurrence of specified events, *other* than the events specified in heads (a), (b) and (c) above, in which case the order making the modification comes into effect on its being made. WCA 1981, Sch 15 provides for: consultation in relation to the making of orders; publicity on making orders; opportunities for making objections to orders; holders of hearings and local inquiries into objections; appointment of inspectors; confirmation by the Secretary of State with or without modification; and appeals, on points of law, to the court following the coming into effect of an order.

The court is precluded from entertaining an application to quash a decision to make a modification order until after it is confirmed,[1] but where a variation is sought *and refused* judicial review of that decision may be possible.[2]

---

1   *R v Cornwall County Council, ex p Huntingdon* [1994] 1 All ER 694.
2   *R v Secretary of State for the Environment, ex p Bagshaw and Norton* [1994] 6 ELM 117, (1994) 68 P & CR 402. See also *O'Keefe v Secretary of State for the Environment and Isle of Wight County Council* [1996] JPL 42.

C A CONTINUING DUTY

Litigation has made it clear that the duty to maintain a 'definitive map' is a continuing one, and that the map though stated in WCA 1981, s 56 (see further below) to be 'conclusive evidence' is actually of an interim nature because of the ongoing obligation to keep the map under review, and revision is to occur not just on the happening of particular acts, such as a stopping up order, but on the discovery of evidence that a way is shown incorrectly, or is not shown at all. Accordingly rights shown on such a map can be both down and upgraded in status where evidence comes to light that the record of the map is incorrect, see *R v Secretary of State for the Environment, ex p Simms and Burrows*[3] and *R v Devon County Council, ex p Fowler.*[4] The evidence in question is in formation *not known* to the authority at the time the map was made; it need not be 'new' or 'fresh'.[5] However, a definitive map should only be altered after careful consideration of all the evidence and observance of all procedural requirements, see *R v Isle of Wight County Council, ex p O'Keefe*[6] though if there is some credible evidence of the existence of a right of way, it appears reasonable to subject the matter to the order making and consequent inquiry procedure.[7] Note that a right of way can exist even if it is used only for recreational walking, see *Dyfed County Council v Secretary of State.*[8]

D REFORM UNDER CROW A 2000

Under CROW A 2000, which, inter alia, fulfils the government's pledge to legislate on rights of way in 'The Government's framework for Action: Access to the Countryside in England and Wales' and 'Improving Rights of Way in England and Wales' (both 1999) action has been taken on the somewhat confusing classification into which such rights of way could fall. Historically these are:
- footpaths where there was a right of way on foot only;
- bridleways over which those on foot, horse or bicycle could pass;
- byways open to all traffic (BOATs), which are largely used in the same way as bridleways but over which all traffic can pass;
- roads used as public paths (RUPPs), which was an old classification which under the WCA 1981, s 54 was to be phased out and the ways in question shown as either of the three above.

The CROW A 2000 repeals WCA 1981, s 54 and states in s 47 that every RUPP is to be shown as a 'restricted byway', and under s 48 the public are to have 'restricted byway rights' over such RUPPs, and under WCA 1981, s 49 every such way becomes maintainable as a highways at the public expense, even where only used on foot or on horseback.

A new s 54A of the WCA 1981 introduced in 2000 sets a cut off date of 1 January 2026 for the making of orders recording a BOAT on a definitive map (save in place of one already recorded). On the other hand CROW A 2000, s 52 enables the Secretary of State to make regulations to apply, *or to exclude from applying,* legislation relating to

---

3   [1990] JPL 746.
4   [1991] 3 LMELR 133 and *Fowler v Secretary of State for the Environment* (1991) 64 P & CR 16.
5   *Mayhew v Secretary of State for the Environment* [1993] COD 45.
6   [1989] JPL 934, and see *Marriot v Secretary of State for the Environment, Transport and the Regions* [2000] All ER (D) 1346.
7   *R v Secretary of State for Wales, ex p Emery* [1998] 4 All ER 367.
8   [1990] 1 LMELR 209.

highways or restricted byeways or ways shown on definitive maps as restricted byeways. This power, as the explanatory notes to CROWA 2000, point out, could be used to enable the creation of new restricted byeways. CROWA 2000, ss 53–56 reinforce the WCA 1981, s 54A by setting cut off dates for recording certain rights of way on definitive maps and the extinguishments of any not so recorded, that date being 1 January 2026.

Thus under CROWA 2000, s 53 any public rights of way such as footpaths or bridleways which were created before 1 January 1949 but which are not shown on definitive maps on the cut-off date are to be extinguished, though there are certain exceptions to this under s 54, for example in respect of ways diverted after 1 January 1949 which connect with other recorded ways, and footpaths or bridleways any part of which is in inner London, or ways falling within classes prescribed by regulations made by the Secretary of State or the National Assembly for Wales. Under CROWA 2000, s 55 where a way was before 1949 either a footpath or a bridleway and is in fact on the cut-off date only a footpath, but is incorrectly recorded as a bridleway on the cut-off date, that way is to be subject to bridleway rights, and it will not thereafter be possible for it to be downgraded to a footpath. Some latitude with regard to the cut-off date may be allowed under regulations to be made under CROWA 2000, s 56 by either the Secretary of State or the National Assembly for Wales. In areas where ways have been recorded on definitive maps since the National Parks and Access to the Countryside Act 1949 commenced, the last date for postponement of 'cut-off' is 1 January 2031. There is no limit set to postponement for certain other areas; these are largely, however, urban as opposed to rural areas.

By virtue of the WCA 1981, s 56 the map and statement are conclusive evidence (until revised) of: (a) where the map shows a footpath, that the public had the right to pass on foot, without prejudice to any greater right for the public; (b) where the map shows a bridleway, that the public had the right to pass with horses, without prejudice to any grater right for the public; (c) where the map shows a byway open to all traffic (a BOAT), that the public had rights for vehicular and all other kinds of traffic; and (d) where the map shows a road used as a public path (a RUPP) (now a 'restricted byway — see above), that the public had a right to pass on foot or with horses, but without prejudice to any other greater right for the public. In deciding what rights the public has a crucial provision is the Highways Act 1980, s 31 under which the presumed dedication of a way of a particular type may arise by the conduct and intention of parties. The important questions here are whether on the part of the public there has been use of the way in the manner claimed, as of right, for a full period of 20 years and whether on the part of the landowner this can be rebutted by sufficient evidence of a lack of intention to dedicate.[9] However, the procedure under the WCA 1981 is not to be used for the purpose of closing the whole length of a public right of way — the procedure for doing that lies in ss 116, 118 and 119 of the Highways Act 1980. These provide that, subject to ministerial approval, a way may be stopped if it is expedient on the basis it is no longer needed for public use.[10]

In relation to the question of whether a way has been enjoyed 'as of right', the test is to ask whether there has been an honest belief that there is a public right of passage on the part of those who use the way. Use of a way knowing that this can occur only because of the landowner's toleration is not, however, enough.[11]

9   *R v Secretary of State for the Environment, ex p Cowell* [1993] JPL 851; and *Jacques Amand Ltd v Secretary of State for the Environment* [1994] 6 ELM 117.
10 *R v Secretary of State for the Environment, ex p Cheshire County Council* [1991] 2 LMELR 206.
11 *O'Keefe v Secretary of State for the Environment and Isle of Wight County Council* [1996] JPL 42.

E FURTHER REFORM UNDER CROWA 2000

Under CROWA 2000, s 57 and Sch 6 a means is provided for negation in advance, or pre-negation of the presumed dedication of a way to public highway use. Landowners may deposit with their local authorities maps and statements of admitted dedicated highways, and may then within six years of that deposit lodge a declaration that there has been no additional dedication. Further declarations maybe made every six years thereafter.

A number of other changes are also made to the Highways Act 1980 to revise the law on rights of way so as to: allow landholders to apply to their local authority for extinguishing or diverting a public path where land is used for agriculture, forestry or breeding or keeping horses; to enable the stopping up of footpaths or bridleways by local authorities in order to prevent crime, or where they cross school premises and the action is needed to protect pupils and staff, or where this is needed to protect a SSSI; to enable occupiers of land to divert footpaths or bridleways temporarily for up to 14 days a year where dangerous works are being carried out. For further detail see the Explanatory Notes on the Countryside and Rights of Way Act 2000, ss 22-28 to which indebtedness is acknowledged.

Under CROWA 2000, ss 60-62 outside Inner London local highways authorities have five years from the commencement of s 60 to prepare and publish a 'rights of way improvement plan'. This will assess, inter alia, the extent to which local rights of way meet current and future public needs and the opportunities they provide for exercise and open air recreation. It will also state the management action proposed for rights of way and for an improved network of local rights of way. Thereafter there should be a ten-yearly review cycle of the plan. CROWA 2000, s 61 requires consultation before a plan is made, inter alia, with adjoining authorities, district councils, National Park Authorities (where appropriate), countryside bodies, local access forums and others prescribed under regulations or who appear to be appropriate. Plans will be made in draft and publicised and any representations made have to be considered, while relevant authorities must also have regard to guidance issued by the Secretary of State or the National Assembly for Wales as the case may be. Inner London boroughs may under CROWA 2000, s 62 choose to adopt ss 60 and 61 by resolution.

One major problem with access and the exercise of rights over rights of way has been the blocking, either by deliberate action or by neglect, of paths, etc, by landholders. CROWA 2000, attempts to deal with this issue by inserting new provisions into the Highways Act 1980. HA 1980, s 130 enables members of the public to serve notice on local highway authorities requesting the removal of obstructions to footpaths, bridleways, restricted byeways, or ways shown on definitive maps as restricted byeways or BOATs. The provision applies to unlawful obstructions, e.g. vegetation, save, inter alia, buildings or building works or structures for human habitation, or where it is the presence of a person which constitute the obstruction. The notice must include the name and address, if known, of any person responsible for the obstruction. Thereafter the authority has one month to serve notice on the person responsible and on the person who served them with notice, with a notice stating what action, if any, they propose to take. HA 1980, s 130B reinforces s 130A by enabling the person who served the initial notice, if not satisfied that the obstruction has been removed, to apply to the justices who may order the local highways authority to remove the obstruction. Before making such an application the applicant must serve notice of the intention to apply on the authority, see the HA 1980, s 130C, and that notice cannot be served until after a period of two months from service of the initial notice under s 130A, and thereafter there is in effect a period of six months for proceedings before the justices. The applicant must give the court the same names as those given to the authority under the HA 1980, s 130A, and the person allegedly responsible for the obstruction has the right to be heard on relevant issues at any hearing.

Under the HA 1980, s 130B(2) and (4) the court *may* make an order requiring the authority to take reasonable steps within a fixed period to remove the obstruction if satisfied the obstruction falls within s 130A, that the way obstructed is a highway within s 130A (eg it is a footpath or bridleway) and that the obstruction significantly interferes with the exercise of public rights over the way. However, no order may be made under the HA 1980, s 130B(5) if the authority satisfy the court, inter alia, that there is a serious dispute as to whether the way is a relevant highway, or that under wider arrangements made by the authority removal of the obstruction will be secured in a reasonable time having regard to the number and seriousness of the obstructions in respect of which they owe duties. Where an order is made the authority must publicise it in prescribed form, together with the right of appeal to the Crown Court against it, which exists under the Highways Act 1980, s 317 as amended by CROWA 2000.

Wilful obstructions of the highway already constitute offences under the Highways Act 1980, s 137, CROWA 2000, s 64 amends the law by inserting s 137ZA into the HA 1980 under which a person convicted of an offence under s 137 may be ordered to remove the obstruction, failure to comply being itself a continuing offence. CROWA 2000, s 65 also amends HA 1980, s 154 so that where trees, shrubs or hedges overhang highways and this causes danger or inconvenience to horse riders, local authorities may require the owners or occupiers of the land in question to cut back the vegetation to a suitable height or to remove it altogether.

The creation of new ways and the recording of old ones is only a partial answer to the access issue: ways must be kept open and usable, something that the new legislation attempts to address. The Rights of Way Act 1990 was also passed in an attempt to deal with this problem. The Act amends the Highways Act 1980 to provide that under s 131A of that Act it is an offence for anyone without lawful authority or excuse to disturb the surface of a bridleway, footpath or any other highway (other than a made up carriage way) so as to render it inconvenient to exercise the public right of way, though taking proceedings is limited to local authorities, including highway and parish councils. A substituted HA 1980, s 134 then provides that where a footpath or bridleway (other than a field edge path) passes over agricultural land and the occupier wishes, in accordance with principles of good husbandry, to plough, etc, the land and it is not reasonably convenient to avoid disturbing the path, the public right of way is subject to a condition that the land may be ploughed and the way disturbed. However the surface so disturbed must be *made good* to not less than its minimum width (1 m, for example, in the case of a footpath) and the line of the path must be indicated. This duty must be discharged within 14 days where a path has been disturbed for crop sowing, otherwise within 24 hours of disturbance, and it is an offence not to comply, though the compliance period may be extended on application to the highway authority. Further obligations are laid on occupiers under HA 1980, s 137A to prevent encroachment of crops on rights of way, while HA 1980, Sch 12A empowers highway authorities, inter alia, to take default action where a way has been disturbed, and to recover their costs from relevant occupiers. HA 1980, s 135 further empowers authorities to authorise works for agricultural purposes which may disturb paths, and they may also authorise a temporary diversion.

Note, however, that HA 1980, s 134 may remain subject to the old common law rule that it is possible for a footpath to be dedicated subject to a right for the landholder to plough it up.[12]

12   *Mercer v Woodgate* (1869) LR 5 QB 26.

F MISCELLANEOUS AND COMMENCEMENT

The Road Traffic Regulation Act 1984, s 22 (as amended in 2000) enables traffic authorities (generally county councils) to regulate traffic so as to conserve or enhance the natural beauty of certain areas, or to enable the public the better to enjoy the amenities of those areas. The powers are exercisable over roads in, or forming part of or adjacent to or contiguous with National Parks, AONB, country parks, nature reserves, long distance routes (see below), National Trust land and SSSIs. A new s 22A in the RTRA 1984 enables authorities to make orders controlling vehicular traffic on unclassified road and byways throughout England and Wales for the purpose of conserving or enhancing the natural beauty of an area, including its flora, fauna and geological and physiographical features. CROWA 2000, s 67 and Sch 7 also amend and enhance the Road Traffic Act 1988, s 34 – the prohibition on driving motor vehicles without lawful authority elsewhere than on roads. The prohibition now extends to mechanically propelled vehicles which previously escaped the prohibition because they were not intended or adapted for road use. It is likewise already an offence under the RTA 1988, s 34 to drive mechanically powered vehicles on footpaths or bridleways, and under the new law this prohibition extends also to restricted byways.

Part II CROWA 2000, under which the changes outlined above is only partly in force at the time of writing (August 2001), in particular ss 47-50, 53-56 and 60-63, along with ss 69 and part of s 70 remained to be commenced. Regular perusal of a service such as Halsbury's '*Is it in Force*?' is recommended.

Section 57 of the WCA 1981 requires the surveying authority to keep the map and statement and its modifications available for inspection by the public, free of charge at all reasonable hours in one or more places in each district comprised in the area to which the map and statement relate.

G THE FORM OF THE DEFINITIVE MAP AND STATEMENT

The definitive map and statement originally required under the 1949 legislation and now maintained under the 1981 Act does not have to be a particular form of document. What is required is that there should be provision of substantial information about public paths sufficient to meet the requirements of the legislation. The statement must supplement the map as appropriate and must be reasonably related to it, but need not be physically annexed to it.[13]

H LONG DISTANCE ROUTES

The National Parks and Access to the Countryside Act 1949, ss 51–55 and 57, relate to the creation of long-distance routes for walking, riding and cycling. Such routes, which must not pass for the whole or greater part of their length along roads mainly used by vehicles, are proposed in reports by the Countryside Commission (in England, but similar powers exist for the Countryside Council in Wales) and are subject to ministerial confirmation. A proposed route map must show existing rights of way over which the long-distance route will pass, and for providing and maintenance of such new public paths as may be required to enable the public to journey along the route. Proposals for providing ferries where needed, and for accommodation, means and refreshment along the route must also be shown on the maps, together with recommendations for restriction of traffic on existing highways along which the route will pass. The proposals must also be costed out on an estimated capital and annual recurrent cost basis.

13   *O'Keefe v Secretary of State for the Environment and Isle of Wight County Council* [1996] JPL 42.

Ministerial approval of a report does not mean that the long-distance route will *immediately* be available for public use. One reason has been that the *implementation* of approved proposals has been in the hands of local authorities who have to use their powers under the Highways Act 1980 to create new footpaths and bridleways, by agreement, or by compulsion. The Countryside Commission has no executive power to bring about implementation. Even so under Cm 1200 it was policy that the entire network of rights of way should be in good order by 2000, and by 1995 within National Parks.

I ASSESSMENT OF ACCESS

The government from 1997 onwards has pursued a policy of widening access to the countryside, despite opposition from many rural landholders. The CROWA 2000, should put beyond question a number of long-running disputes over rights to roam across moors, fells and downland, for example the Forest of Borland in Lancashire, the Brontë moors in Lancashire and Yorkshire, the Peak District, the Berwyn mountains in North Wales, Shirburn and Pyrton Hills in Oxfordshire and Ranmore Common in Dorking. However, the new legislation is subject to many exceptions, particularly, and quite properly, where nature conservation interests should triumph over access. However, there are many technical exceptions also, and there is no right to roam over agricultural land where voluntary access only will still apply, and many ramblers were unhappy that the first head of the Countryside Agency, the enforcement body of the right to roam, was also president of the Country Landowners Association. Individual disputes over blocked or restricted rights of way will no doubt continue, and though the new legislation gives enhanced powers to various bodies to deal with obstructive activities it will remain to be seen how forcefully and effectively these are pursued by bodies whose personnel resources are already limited.

Further reading

Books

Shoard, M, *This Land is Our Land* (1981) Paladin.

Articles

Cheshman, G R, 'Local Authorities and the Review of the Definitive Map under the Wildlife and Countryside Act' [1991] JPL 611.
Forster, M, 'The Countryside and the Law: Making the new Rights of Way Act work' [1990] 2 LMELR 126.
Reid, D, 'Access to the Countryside – The New Law in Scotland and England' [2001] 13 ELM 138.

Official Reports

'New Opportunities for the Countryside' CCP 224 (1987) Countryside Commission.
'Countryside and Rights of Way Act 2000: Explanatory Notes' (2001) HMSO.
'Countryside and Rights of Way Act 2000' DETR Circular 04/2001 HMSO.

Chapter 11

Controversial uses of land

A TRUNK AND SPECIAL ROADS

The Highways Act 1980 provides for creation, improvement and maintenance of roads, and for acquisition of land. The Act creates highway authorities. In England central government functions with regard to highways are exercised by the Secretary of State for Transport, Local Government and the Regions who is responsible, inter alia, for 'trunk roads' and 'special roads', see the HA 1980, s 1(1)(a) and (aa). Otherwise the normal highway authority outside Greater London in England is the county council or metropolitan district where appropriate, to whom the 'Secretary of State may delegate powers of maintenance, improvement and dealing with' in respect of trunk roads under the HA 1980, s 6. Agreements may also be made with county authorities for construction of trunk roads: see HA 1980, s 6(5). It should be noted that, under HA 1980, s 337, nothing in the Act authorises carrying out of development without planning permission of operations for which permission is required. Engineering operations in connection with trunk road building would generally require planning permission from the appropriate authority, but for the rule that planning legislation does not bind the Crown,[1] see also the Town and Country Planning Act 1990, s 294. *Non-statutory* consultation procedures in respect of Crown developments are not generally applied to trunk road proposals; it is considered that procedures under the highways and compulsory purchase legislation should not be duplicated. Maintenance and improvement work carried out by *local* highway authorities within the boundaries of a road is excluded from the definition of development under the TCPA 1990, s 55(2)(b).

Trunk roads and special roads, which expressions include motorways, are provided for under the Highways Act 1980, Part II. A 'special road' is one reserved for use by traffic of particular classes, see ss 10 and 16 of that Act. The various classes of traffic for special roads are prescribed under the HA 1980, s 17 by reference to those set out in Sch 4. The minister is under a duty under HA 1980, s 10(2) to keep under review the national system of routes for through traffic. After considering the requirements of national or local planning, including the requirements of agriculture, the minister may conclude it is expedient to extend, improve or reorganise that system, and may accordingly by order direct that any highway, or any highway he/she proposes to construct should be a trunk road. It should be noted that roads principally used for

---

1   *Ministry of Agriculture, Fisheries and Food v Jenkins* [1963] 2 QB 317, [1963] 2 All ER 147.

local traffic may still be classified as trunk roads provided that is expedient for the *through* system of traffic nationally.[2]

Special roads are provided under the authorisation of schemes prescribing their routes, but before making or confirming such a scheme the Minister must consider the requirements of national and local planning and those of agriculture. Such roads in due course become trunk roads, see HA 1980, s 19. HA 1980, s 18 further allows the transfer to the minister as 'the special road authority' of existing highways comprised in the route prescribed in the scheme authorising the special road and the appropriation of existing highways already under the minister's jurisdiction for this purpose. HA 1980, s 24 actually empowers the minister, with the approval of the Treasury, to construct new highways.

Procedure

Before a trunk or special road is constructed there is a lengthy process of preparation of which public inquiry procedures are but part. This procedure was summarised in the National Audit Office Report, Department of Transport: 'Environmental Factors in Road Planning and Design' (1994). The procedure (see further below) should take some 10 years, but there are some commentators who argue this ten-year scenario is wrong, and that reality is closer to 15 years — a period many consider unduly protracted. However, equally the 'procedure' provides little opportunity for public involvement while the Department of Transport Local Government and the Regions (DTLR) historically may well have become committed to promoting roads proposed, partly because of the traditional commitment of the Department to extensive road building programmes, see 'National Road Traffic Forecasts (Great Britain)' 1989 and 'Roads for Prosperity' (Cm 693), and partly because of 'administrative momentum' which builds up behind proposals as they are processed. Frequent criticism of governmental claims to be 'environmentally conscious' have been made by those who point to major spending on road building programmes, when the majority of the transport department's allocation of public finance has been earmarked for road building.

Traditionally road building plans were based on a cost benefit analysis (COBA) whereby the cost of building the road, which includes land acquisition and engineering costs, was balanced against 'benefits' to be derived from its construction, for example shortened journey times and accident prevention.

COBA took into account shortened journey times, reduced accident rates and lower operating costs and extrapolated them over a 30-year period, comparing such costs against the schemes' construction costs. A value was placed on shortened journey times by considering how much people would pay to have reduced journey to work times. COBA was supplemented by QUADRO which estimated traffic costs caused by lane maintenance closures. COBA *did not* 'monetise' environmental considerations, however, though environmental factors did lead to *modifications* of some schemes, even where this led to their having *negative* cost benefit assessments. As from March 1992, however, monetisation techniques were introduced to set a notional 'price' on countryside features at the start of the road planning process for COBA evaluation.

This was the first step in changes in road planning policy and procedure whose exact outcome remains uncertain. Much of this stemmed from public opposition to, and official concern over, the cost of widening the M25 around London. In June 1992 it was announced that sections of the M25 were to be widened to 14 lanes, at a cost of £144m. By July the proposal was for two 14-lane sections at a cost of £250m. In 1993 a

2   *Walters v Secretary of State for the Environment* [1979] JPL 171.

leaked report from the Department of the Environment indicated that the roads programme in general was costed at £236m over 15 years, that 243 road projects were potentially controversial, with 103 likely to engender high controversy with 118 in all also likely to have a particularly damaging effect on the environment as they would affect SSSIs and other land of high conservation interest, etc. At this time direct protest against road building became regular, with, for example, those opposed to the building of the M11 link road setting up tree houses in the path of the development. At the same time the total cost of widening existing motorways was found to be 78% above initial estimates; this led in March 1994 to the scrapping of 49 road projects, one third of the 1989 programme, some of them on environmental grounds. Even so concern over the rest of the programme continued especially as some proposals were only 'postponed'.

By that point, however, certain changes had occurred in road planning policy. The National Audit Office's report on road planning revealed that as from July 1993 central government had introduced environmental assessment techniques into the road planning programme at a number of points. The stages in road planning thus became:

1	Identification for the need for a scheme and its entry into the road programme — subject to an assessment of environmental constraints and, where possible, costed proposals to mitigate undesirable effects.

2	Broad assessment of the environmental impact of a scheme (which is *not* necessarily, nor even usually, an examination of a *whole* road) takes place.

3	Consultation with the public on the initial options for road schemes, followed by an analysis of the results of this exercise.

4	The preferred route is announced.

5	There is then a detailed environmental appraisal of the preferred route. This will follow the pattern required by Directive 85/337, but will certainly draw together material on the effects of the scheme on air quality, cultural heritage disruption, nature conservation, the landscape, existing communities, agriculture, traffic noise and vibration, road users, views, water, underlying soils and geology, other policies and plans for roads — *where possible* combined and cumulative assessments will be undertaken where schemes are linked.

6	The draft statutory orders and environmental statement are published and views and objections sought.

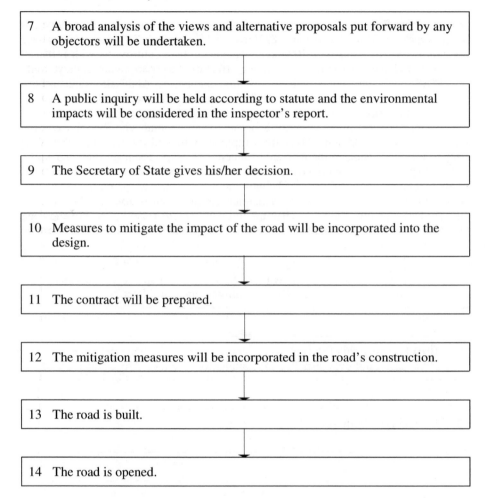

7   A broad analysis of the views and alternative proposals put forward by any objectors will be undertaken.

8   A public inquiry will be held according to statute and the environmental impacts will be considered in the inspector's report.

9   The Secretary of State gives his/her decision.

10   Measures to mitigate the impact of the road will be incorporated into the design.

11   The contract will be prepared.

12   The mitigation measures will be incorporated in the road's construction.

13   The road is built.

14   The road is opened.

It should be noted, however, as the National Audit Office pointed out, that this procedure did not deal with the global and cumulative effect of schemes, though this short coming had been pointed out and it had been agreed to examine the possibility of extending the overall procedure.

The road to hell is paved with good intentions

In September 1994 came two major policy critiques. The Standing Committee on Trunk Road Assessment (SACTRA) delivered its report 'Trunk Roads and the Generation of Traffic' which concluded that: extra traffic (known as 'induced traffic') does occur simply because of improvements in the road system; the amount and significance of this traffic will vary considerably from place to place, but is likely to be most significant on roads in and around urban areas, on estuary crossings and on 'strategic capacity-enhancing interurban schemes', including motorway widening; that the current COBA system fails to take adequate account of induced traffic and so may overestimate the benefits of road schemes. SACTRA concluded: 'scheme appraisal must be carried out within the context of economic and environmental appraisals at the strategic area-wide level which take account of induced traffic … Much more emphasis needs to be placed on the strategic assessment of trunk routes …' Then in its 18th Report, 'Transport and the Environment' Cm 2674 the Royal Commission on Environmental Pollution recommended, inter alia, that a sustainable transport system needs to ensure that traffic is moved from roads to less damaging modes of transport, and accordingly 'a fundamental review of the definition and purpose of a separate system of trunk roads' was recommended, *together with* the subjugation of the road development programme to the development control system, and changes in highways inquiry procedures so that government representatives should be capable of being required to answer questions on the merits of roads policy, and so that an inspector at such an inquiry (see further below) should be able 'to take account of the interactions of the proposal with other government policies in his recommendation'. The Royal Commission went on to argue that insofar as a central government road programme survives, the construction or widening of trunk and special roads should only be undertaken where that is the *best practicable environmental option* for meeting access needs. Furthermore road schemes not yet subject to contractual arrangements should be reassessed in the light of changes in policy and road assessment methodology, and planned motorway expenditure reduced by a half. By April 1996, however, ministers had declined to set specific targets for decreasing car journeys and increasing journeys by cycle and public transport.

At a time (mid-1994) when responsibility for the operation of the roads programme was being transferred from a central Department of State to a 'nextsteps' body — the Highways Agency — it thus appeared that cost considerations, expert external advice, and public opposition might combine with Treasury doubts as to the veracity of the argument that road schemes stimulate economic growth to bring about a major change in transport policy. Ministers were certainly changing road building funding policy in favour of privately built toll motorways and the introduction of charge metering schemes for other major public roads, while ad the same time reducing road spending by £400 m over the years 1994–96. By December 1994 ministers had agreed to implement the SACTRA recommendation that all future road schemes should be assessed on the basis of gauging their 'induced traffic' impact, though this would not apply to schemes which had already gone through a public inquiry process.

In April 1995 the government decided to scrap the 14 lane proposals for the M25 and a number of other associated motorway schemes — not least because it was realised the proposal was deeply unpopular in many constituencies in Surrey which have traditionally voted Conservative. Further evidence of a shift away from traditional road policy came in the November 1995 budget. Five per cent of the road budget was cut, but significantly this related to projected schemes and no major new road starts were expected for 1996/97, save the continuingly controversial Newbury by-pass and a handful of other schemes. 77 motorway and trunk road schemes were withdrawn, while new privately financed road schemes were not expected to start until 1997/98.

A New Deal for Transport?

Following the 1997 election the Blair government published in 1998 'A New Deal for Transport: Better for Everyone' (Cm 3950). This stated that 'simply building more and more roads is not the answer to traffic growth', while accepting that the demand for transport is likely to grow – possibly by 33% over the year to 2021 for cars, and even more for vans and lorries. The government proposed an integrated transport policy for dealing with this growth – integration between different types of transport, integration with environmental protection, with land use planning so as to reduce the need to travel to work, integration with other policies such as those on health. A key element in such a strategy is the need to reduce the rate of road traffic growth, and to achieve an absolute reduction in those areas where traffic is causing the worst environmental damage. So far as road transport was concerned, the key elements of the new policy included:

- prioritising the maintenance and management of existing roads over building new ones, while improving capacity on existing roads where this is needed to address existing congestion;
- considering all possible alternatives before building new trunk routes – eg improvements to existing roads and creation of bypasses – it being accepted that new roads can lead to the creation of yet more traffic demand;
- integrating the 'core' trunk network with other forms of transport to allow interchange between routes and traffic management;
- accepting that there should be a strong presumption against any new transport infrastructure affecting any environmentally sensitive areas and sites;
- creating a Commission for Integrated Transport to advise on promoting the integrated transport policy;
- considering the possibility of introducing road charging on motor and trunk roads.

There was already on the statute book the Road Traffic Reduction Act 1997 under which local authorities (generally county and metropolitan councils) are to prepare reports on the traffic levels within their areas, while under RTRA 1997, s 2 the Secretary of State may require the submission of reports containing reduction targets. However, this legislation is somewhat vague and weak and an authority may decline under RTRA 1997, s 2(5) to set a specified reduction target where they are able to give reasons why they consider this inappropriate. Further this Act does not apply to trunk and special roads. The RTRA 1997 was effectively superseded by the Road Traffic Reduction (National Targets) Act 1998 passed under the Blair administration. This relates to all mechanically propelled road vehicles, but effectively excludes buses and coaches. The Secretary of State is placed by RTR(NT)A 1998, s 2 under a duty to publish road traffic reduction targets with the aim of reducing the adverse environmental, social and economic impacts of road traffic, though this duty need not be discharged where the Secretary of State considers that other targets or measures are more appropriate for dealing with such problems. Where this is the case a report reasoning the conclusion and assessing the impact of the other measures etc has to be published. In discharging the above duties the Secretary of State is to take into account the emissions of climate change gases, effects of emissions on air quality and health, congestion, effects of road traffic on land and biodiversity, the dangers to other road users, social impacts of road traffic, the mobility needs of the disabled and adequate provision of taxi services. The Secretary of State may publish further 'target' reports from time to time.

The first report under the RTR(NT)A 1998 was 'Road Traffic Reduction (National Targets) Act 1998: Tackling Congestion and Pollution – The Government's First Report' (DETR 1998). This declined to set a national traffic reduction target and concluded that a reduction in traffic to below 1996 levels would be unachievable. Instead the report referred to the 1998 White Paper and concluded that the important task is to produce certain outcomes rather than to set targets, and argued that these can be achieved by pursuing the proposals on reducing pollution and congestion.

However, the government in a 1998 Roads Review undertook to reconsider a number of bypasses and other road schemes planned by the previous administration, and in particular undertook a 'multi modal' reappraisal to see whether alternatives to new roads were feasible – eg improvements in local rail and bus services. A number of such studies were commissioned for the period 2001 to 2003, and cover a wide variety of schemes from dualling some roads, through widening existing roads, to new motorway construction, eg in Cambridgeshire. These schemes could all have adverse social and environmental consequences. The outcome of the first of these studies was announced on 12 July 2001 when the DTLR announced a package in which two bypasses for Hastings which would have had severe implications for two SSSIs and one AONB were rejected, while other public transport improvements were announced. The Secretary of State, however, stressed that as part of the ten-year Transport policy following the 1998 White Paper, that this decision should not be seen as a precedent. In each case it was emphasised the impact of a new road on the environment would be assessed but in some cases the benefits of a particular road or rail link could be considered to outweigh that impact, but in all cases matters will be decided not just on the basis of regional issues; determinations will reflect national policy objectives.

Overall, policy on road building appears to have entered a restrictive phase, but individual sections of roads could still give rise to controversy. To the law relating to their possible construction we must now return.

Under HA 1980, s 10(5), Sch 1, Parts I and III and Sch 2 apply to trunk road orders, and, under s 16(7), Sch 1, Parts II and III and Sch 2 apply to special road schemes. Where the minister proposes to make a *trunk road order* he/she must prepare a draft and publish a notice in at least one local newspaper circulating in the affected area, and in the *London Gazette*. This must state the general effect of the proposal, name a place in the locality where a copy of the draft, and any maps or plans referred to in the draft, may be inspected, free of charge at reasonable hours, during a specified period of not less than six weeks from the date of publication, and must state the right of any person to object to the order. Additional publicity steps may be taken within the affected area. Environmental Impact Assessment will already be under way on the preferred route for the road as shown in the draft. Not later than the day on which the notice is published the minister must serve on certain persons a copy of the notice, a copy of the draft order and a copy of any map or plan referred to in the draft order relating to a matter which in the opinion of the minister is likely to affect the persons served. The persons to be served are: (a) every council (including counties and districts) in whose area the highway or proposed highway is situated; and (b) where the order provides for bridges and tunnels or the diversion of navigable watercourses, relevant navigation authorities and the Environment Agency.

If any objection to the proposed order is received by the minister from any person *statutorily* listed to receive a copy of the notice or from *any other person* appearing to the minister to be affected, and that objection is not withdrawn, then he/she must hold a public inquiry. There is a discretion to dispense with this inquiry where it is considered unnecessary in the circumstances, *except* where the objection is made by a person statutorily required to be served with notice. A court will inquire only as to whether there is material on which the minister could reasonably conclude an inquiry is unnecessary.[3] The minister has no general discretion to dispense with an inquiry, nor may he do so on grounds of mere expediency. In *Binney v Secretary of State for the Environment*,[4] it was held that a minister may not refuse to hold an inquiry simply because of a belief that enough about the matter in question is already known. The minister must be satisfied that the objects to be attained by an inquiry, which include evaluating various conflicting public points of view and interests, and ensuring that those having rights to make representations have such representations considered, can be achieved without an inquiry. Where there are substantial groups holding conflicting views on a major road proposal a reasonable minister should hold an inquiry, thus ensuring proper argument on an examination of the various points of view. Even where he/she decides an inquiry need not be held and that decision is proper in the circumstances, it may be he/she should at least allow both those supporting the proposal and those objecting to it to see each other's representations.

Where an inquiry is held the report of the person holding it must be considered. Thereafter the minister may make the order with or without modifications as he/she

---

3   *Shorman v Secretary of State for the Environment* [1977] JPL 98.
4   [1984] JPL 871.

thinks fit. Where any modifications proposed will, in the minister's opinion, make a substantial change in the order, he/she must notify persons likely to be affected, give them an opportunity of making representations to him/her within a reasonable period, and must consider representations made (see below on the role of environmental assessment with regard to the decision making process).

Under HA 1980, s 257(3) proceedings under the power to acquire land compulsorily (part of the general land acquisition powers in connection with highway construction and improvement granted by HA 1980, Part XII may be undertaken concurrently, in respect of trunk and special road schemes. The line order, side road orders (see HA 1980, s 14) and compulsory purchase orders are not, in fact, generally taken together, because most public involvement in the road planning process will have been concentrated at the line order stage. When inquiries are held to hear objections to side road orders made in consequence of a major road proposal, the inspector holding the inquiry may refuse to receive objections attempting to re-open the question of the line of the principal road already determined after an inquiry.[5]

Where the minister proposes to make a *special road scheme* he/she must publish in local newspapers and in the *London Gazette* a notice which: states the general effect of the proposed scheme; names a place in the affected area where a copy of the draft scheme, and any map or plan referred to in it may be inspected by the public, free of charge at reasonable times, during a specified period of not less than six weeks from the date of the notice; and states the right of any person to object to the making of the scheme. Contemporaneously the minister must serve a copy of the notice, together with a copy of the draft scheme and supporting maps, etc, on every council in whose area part of the route of the special road is situated, and, where bridges or tunnels are to be constructed over or under navigable waters, on relevant navigation authorities and the Environment Agency. Where objections are received from the specified authorities or from any other person appearing to the minister to be affected, and these are not withdrawn, there is a general obligation to hold an inquiry similar to that imposed in respect of trunk road orders. After the inquiry is held, and the report thereof considered, the scheme may be confirmed with or without modifications. Modifications substantially altering a scheme must be notified to those likely to be affected and they must be given a chance to make representations, which must be considered.

Environmental impact (EIA) assessment of roads

In order to implement Directive 85/337 and Directive 97/11 on environmental impact assessment (see further chapter 8) s 105A of the 1980 Act as amended and SI 1991/369 provide that in any case where the Secretary of State has under consideration the construction or improvement of a highway he/she shall initially determine whether it falls within Annex I or II of the Directive. The Secretary of State must determine whether the road will fall within Annex I, or whether it is within Annex II (according to the criteria within Annex III) and should therefore be subject to EIA.

Where EIA is required the Secretary of State must publish, *not later* than the date of publication of the details of the road project, ie the draft orders concerning the preferred route, an environmental statement.

This statement must contain the information required by the 1997 Directive, Annex IV where the Secretary of State considers that it is relevant to the specific characteristics of the 'relevant project' and those features of the environment likely to be affected by

---

5   *Mayes v Minister of Transport* [1982] LS Gaz R 448.

it, where that information may reasonably be gathered. As a minimum that information must include:

- a description of the project, its size, site and design;
- a description of the measures envisaged to avoid, reduce and where possible remedy significant adverse effects;
- data required to identify and assess the main environmental effects;
- an outline of main alternatives studied in relation to the project and an indication of the reasons for choosing the project selected;
- a non-technical summary of the above.

'Relevant projects' for present purposes are those for constructing or improving a highway where the area of the completed works together with the land occupied during the construction phase exceeds one hectare, or where *any* such area is situated in a 'sensitive area', ie in general, SSSIs, land subject to Nature Conservation orders, land in National Parks, in an AONB, in the Broads, property on a World Heritage List, a scheduled ancient monument, or a European site under SI 1994/2716.

Under HA 1980, s 105B the Secretary of State must publish the determination of whether EIA should take place. Where the determination is positive the Environmental Statement has to be published within a reasonable time so that concerned members of the public have a reasonable opportunity to express their views before a decision to proceed is made. Furthermore the 'consultation bodies' have to be given an opportunity to express their views on the project and the environmental statement. These bodies include: the local authority for the affected area; in England, the Countryside Agency, English Heritage and the Nature Conservancy Council (English Nature); in Wales, Cadw and the Countryside Council for Wales; the Environment Agency.

Before proceeding with the project the Secretary of State must then take into consideration the environmental statement and any opinion expressed on it by a member of the public and the consultation bodies. In addition under HA 1980, s 105C where it appears to the Secretary of State that a relevant project is likely to have a significant effect on the environment of another EC member state, or where such a state asks for information about the project, that state must be supplied with a description of the project and information about its likely impact, about the EIA procedure, and about the nature of the decision which may be taken on the project. The affected state must then be given a reasonable period within which to indicate if it wishes to participate in the EIA procedure, and if it does it must be given a copy of the environmental statement and other relevant information – which must also be notified to, amongst others, members of the public in the affected state who are likely to be concerned. Those informed must then be given a reasonable opportunity to make their views known and there must be consultation with the affected state on the potential significant effects of the project and on measures to reduce or eliminate those effects. Opinions obtained from the affected state must also be taken into account by the Secretary of State in the decision-making process.

If after the EIA has taken place the Secretary of State decides to proceed, the decision must be published in the London Gazette and in the local press, and information must be made public about the content of the decision, the main reasons for the decision and the considerations on which it is based, and a description of the main measures to avoid, reduce or offset major adverse effects.

The Line Inquiry Stage

Much of the litigation over roads has arisen out of issues relating to the line inquiry stage. Procedure here is governed by the Highways (Inquiries Procedure) Rules SI 1994/

3263. Certain general requirements relate to all types of highway inquiry. These rules, replacing earlier ones from 1976, are designed to establish a clear timetable for the procedural steps connected with an inquiry, and now specifically provide, inter alia, for the submission of written proofs of evidence in advance from those proposing to give, or call others to give, evidence, all with the object of streamlining inquiry procedure.

Where the Secretary of State proposes to hold an inquiry he/she must give notice within four weeks of the period within which objections to the road scheme should have been made. This must be given to each 'statutory objector', ie a person who has made and maintained an objection, *and* who is an owner, lessee or occupier of any land likely to be required for highway works, *or* is a person likely to be able to claim compensation in respect of the use of the highway works, *or* is a person likely to be able to claim compensation in respect of the use of the highway works, *or* one of the persons/bodies falling within HA 1980, Sch 1. The Secretary of State's outline statement of case must be further served on these persons within a further eight weeks.

Particular provision is made with regard to pre-inquiry meetings. Such a meeting may be held if the Secretary of State considers it 'desirable', and he/she must then give notice of the meeting in local newspapers within three weeks of the notice of intention to hold a meeting — the inquiry inspector also has power to call a further meeting once the initial one has been held, and may also convene a meeting even where the Secretary of State has not done so. Outline statements of other parties' cases must be served, if the Secretary of State so decides, within eight weeks of the local newspaper notice, and the actual meeting itself held within 16 weeks. The pre-inquiry meeting will be conducted in accordance with the inspector's total discretion, and he/she will determine the order and agenda and may eject and exclude disruptive persons — even to the extent, it appears, of forbidding them to attend the subsequent inquiry itself. More than one such meeting may be held at the inspector's discretion.

Not less than six weeks after notice of intention to hold an inquiry (or within four weeks following a pre-inquiry meeting) the Secretary of State must serve his/her statement of case on statutory objectors, and other persons may be required to serve notice of their case on the Secretary of State. Anyone who has submitted a statement of case may be required by either the inspector or the Secretary of State to amplify it.

Where a pre-inquiry meeting is held the inquiry thereafter *must* be timetabled by the inspector, and normally the inquiry must begin within 22 weeks of notice of intention to hold it and not less than eight weeks of the end of any pre-inquiry meeting.

All statutory objectors are entitled to appear at the inquiry, and other persons may be allowed to appear — such permission is not to be unreasonably withheld. Where government witnesses are called — and the Secretary of State *must* provide a representative to elucidate the official statement of case — they may be cross examined in just the same way as other persons, but they may *not* be required to answer any question which, in the opinion of the inspector, is 'directed at the merits of government policy' (see further below).

The regulations also make provision for summarised reading of proofs of evidence at inquiries, and for inquiry procedure — including giving powers to inspectors to exclude material they consider is irrelevant or repetitious.

One other feature worthy of note in the regulations which is a departure from historic practice is the ability for the Secretary of State to appoint an assessor to advise the inquiry inspector. Where that assessor makes a report to the inspector, the report must be considered by the inspector in making the inquiry report. It would appear that, as was the position under the previous rules, at the inquiry, the Inspector has no power to *require* the DTLR to carry out surveys on the soil and topography of alternative routes so that it may be put before the inquiry. All an inspector *can* do is *invite* the Department so to act, and even then he acts at discretion.[6]

The rules of natural justice generally apply, though these may not apply to a disruptive objector, and, of course, the 1994 rules specifically provide for the exclusion of disruptive persons.[7] However, objectors should normally be given an adequate opportunity to present their views, particularly as the inquiry may be the only opportunity they have to state a formal view in public.[8] Site inspections may be made. After the inquiry is over the inspector makes the report, including conclusions and recommendations, which *must* be considered, and the Secretary of State makes and notifies the decision. The Secretary of State may not take into account new evidence or facts, nor differ from the inspector on a finding of fact, so as to be disposed to disagree with the inquiry recommendations, and so come to a decision at variance with them, without notifying the statutory objectors, and allowing them to make representations or ask for the inquiry to be re-opened. The Secretary of State may, however, consult his departmental staff on the issue. Where major new evidence comes to light from an outside source after an inquiry radically changing the whole basis for a proposed road, or where a major issue has not been taken into account at the inquiry, the rules of natural justice *may* require it to be re-opened.[9] The test *appears* to be whether the new evidence is of such importance that reopening the matter may lead to the whole issue being determined in an altered way. If that is so then the court appears to have no choice but to quash the decision and require the inquiry to be reopened. However, apart from situations such as this the courts are generally unwilling to interfere with decisions taken in consequence of inquiries. Their task is to see that the procedures are operated fairly and reasonably, not to try to attempt to answer questions to which there can be no objectively 'right' answer.[10] Indeed the courts have had little sympathy with cases brought by objectors with little merit, pointing to the disbenefits caused by delays to schemes that have been accepted as necessary.[11]

Under HA 1980, Sch 2 as soon as may be after a scheme or order has been made by the minister, he/she must public notice of that fact in the *London Gazette*, and take such other steps as he/she thinks best to inform affected persons of the notice. He/she must state that the order has been made, and name a place where a copy of it may be inspected, free of charge at reasonable hours. Persons aggrieved by a scheme or order who wish to question its validity on the grounds that it is not within the powers granted by the HA 1980, or that there has been an irregularity in the procedures required by law, have six weeks from publication of notice to apply to the High Court. The High Court may suspend orders and schemes until final determination of issues, and, if satisfied that the scheme or order goes beyond the powers conferred by the Act, *or* that the interests of an applicant have been *substantially prejudiced* by a procedural irregularity, may quash the scheme or order either generally, or insofar as it applies to the applicant's property. Otherwise schemes and orders may not be questioned in legal proceedings, and become operative o the date on which notice of making is published, or on such later date as is specified in the scheme or order. The provisions of HA 1980, Sch 2 are a preclusive system of appeal. Challenge by way of judicial review *once an order or scheme has been made* is not possible, nor is any challenge out of time possible,

6   *R v Vincent, ex p Turner* [1987] JPL 511.
7   *Lovelock v Secretary of State for Transport* [1979] RTR 250.
8   *R v Secretary of State for Transport, ex p Gwent County Council* [1987] 1 All ER 161.
9   *Rea v Minister of Transport* [1984] JPL 876.
10 *Lewin v Secretary of State for the Environment* [1989] 1 LMELR 30.
11 *Burton v Secretary of State for Transport* [1988] 2 EGLR 35; and *R v Tickell, ex p London Borough of Greenwich* [1988] JPL 280 (summary).

even where an applicant has acted under misapprehension as to the effect of a scheme or order.[12] (The procedures in respect of their highway proposals are similar to those above, see *Encyclopaedia of Highway Law and Practice*).

Criticisms of highway procedure

Many criticisms of highway procedures have been made. Large numbers of people are opposed for a variety of environmental reasons to particular road schemes, or roads policy in general. There are those who wish to use inquiries as a forum in which to debate roads policy. There is also feeling that the odds at an inquiry are 'stacked' against objectors who face the might of a government department often though of *not* as a department of overall co-ordinated transport policy, *rather* as a department of road building. But at an inquiry many competing voices will be heard. The Department will promote its proposals, and will be supported by organisations representing road users. There will be those seeking to argue a case for an alternative route; others will seek to argue a case for particular route changes. There will be those who oppose the road totally. Many objectors feel frustration because the inquiry is into a small scale scheme which they know is truly part of a much longer project yet they will be unable to question the wider scheme. Equally there will be those who support the proposal and who *may* have little time for arguments based on environmental considerations.

It is the frustration felt by many with road policy coupled with growing environmental consciousness that led to the growth of direct confrontation between road builders and protesters, particularly, for example, at Twyford Down over the building of the M3. This led central government to seek a number of ways of preventing protest and otherwise stopping direct action against road building. Thus in *Department of Transport v Williams*[13] the Court of Appeal concluded that there is a tort of wrongful interference with business — a wrong which extends to unlawfully preventing a central Department of State going about its lawful business of authorised road building. Those who wilfully obstruct road building may also commit an offence under the HA 1980, s 303, and commission of this offence is also enough to constitute an unlawful interference with the Department's 'business' *which can be restrained by injunction*. Similarly in *DPP v Todd*[14] the Divisional Court concluded that the Trade Union and Labour Relations (Consolidation) Act 1992, s 241 which relates to those who wrongfully and without lawful authority hinder persons in their work with a view to compelling them to abstain from work, applies not just to trade disputes but is wide enough to allow prosecution of those who prevent road constructors from going about their work by non-violent protests such as positioning themselves in cranes.

Public inquiries do not stop roads being built, though they may result in particular re-routeings, simply because their function is to inform the minister of the issues, not to debate or formulate policy. The decision on the road is for the minister. Following *Bushell v Secretary of State for the Environment*,[15] and *Lovelock v Secretary of State for Transport*,[16] objectors to a road must be given a fair chance to put forward their arguments, and supporting factors. Equally they must be given sufficient information about the Department's case for the proposal. Nevertheless an inquiry is called to consider the *line (ie the choice of route) of a proposed road*, and may not be used to debate overall road policy. Neither may it be used to debate techniques used to decide

---

12   *R v Secretary of State for the Environment, ex p Ostler* [1977] QB 122, [1976] 3 All ER 90.
13   [1994] 6 ELM 12.
14   [1995] 7 ELM 127.
15   [1981] AC 75, [1980] 2 All ER 608.
16   [1979] JPL 456.

whether there is a need for a road within the context of national policy. However, in view of the changes in roads policy outlined above, this latter point may now be less fixed than was once thought. It certainly appears possible to argue the need for a *particular* local link in the road system, on the basis that existing roads can adequately take traffic. It may also be possible to attack the methods used in scheme assessment in relation to *special* local factors or conditions which raise doubts as to the applicability of normal assessment techniques, though such local issues are normally considered by the project assessment system.

Future reform?

For the future, comments made by the Law Society in response to the government's Road Review consultation exercise referred to earlier should be borne in mind:
- where a new road has to be built as the 'least worst' solution to a problem of traffic, this should take place only after a 'sequential test' has been utilised to identify and eliminate all the alternatives;
- weighting could then be given to environmental issues to ensure new roads are built only where absolutely necessary;
- whatever criteria are adopted, however, they need to be clear and consistent;
- however there is an argument to the effect that the current road decision-making process is too attenuated and suffers too much from alterations of policy, which leads to unnecessary worry for those who may be affected between the initial proposal being made and the holding of the line inquiry.

See further below on the Secretary of State's July 2001 reform proposals.

Compulsory purchase powers

HA 1980, Part XII confers powers to acquire land, by agreement or compulsion, on highway authorities. Land may be acquired for road construction, or improvement, and for ancillary purposes such as the provision of service areas and public conveniences, under HA 1980, ss 239 and 240. Land may also be acquired for mitigating any adverse effect on surrounding areas arising from the existence of a road constructed or improved, or proposed for construction or improvement, by a highway authority: see HA 1980, s 246. Under HA 1980, s 248 land may generally be acquired for highway purposes notwithstanding that it is not immediately required. So far as compulsory purchases are concerned this is not a '*carte blanche*' power. Where there is power to acquire land for an 'initial stage', adjacent land for a 'subsequent stage' may also be acquired compulsorily, even though not immediately required, *provided* the stages are linked as laid down in HA 1980, Sch 17, *and* it is intended to incorporate the 'subsequent stage' land forthwith upon acquisition within the boundaries of the highway or proposed highway, *and/or* the proposed use of the 'initial stage' land involves working on, under or over 'subsequent stage' land, *and/or* plans for use of the 'subsequent stage' land have been made by the minister. Thus, for example, under HA 1980, s 239(1) the 'initial stage' may be concerned with acquiring land for the construction of a highway, the 'subsequent stage' for which, the above conditions being fulfilled, land could be acquired in advance of requirements is the improvement of that highway.

Compulsory purchase power is subject to limits on distance from the highway under HA 1980, s 249 and Sch 18. For example the power to acquire land under HA 1980, s 239(1) (land for road construction) is limited to 220 yards from the middle of the highway or proposed highway. HA 1980, s 253 empowers the making of agreements with persons interested in land adjoining or in the vicinity of the highway for regulating the use of the land, permanently or temporarily, for the purpose of mitigating any adverse effect which the construction, improvement or existence or use of the highway has on its surroundings. As already stated, HA 1980, s 257 allows proceedings in respect of compulsory acquisitions to be concurrent, so far as is practicable, with making other related schemes and orders under highway powers. Compulsory purchase orders made in the exercise of powers to acquire land for specified highway purposes may come into operation on the same day as related schemes or orders: see HA 1980, s 257(3) and Sch 20. HA 1980, s 258 lays down that where proceedings are required to be taken in respect of a compulsory purchase order made in the exercise of highway powers *after* the making of an order or scheme, the minister may disregard in compulsory purchase proceedings any objection which, in his opinion, amounts in substance to an objection taken in earlier proceedings in the order or scheme.

Under HA 1980, s 247 the procedure applicable to the compulsory acquisition of land for highway purposes is, in general, that provided by the Acquisition of Land Act 1981. In *R v Secretary of State for Transport, ex p de Rothschild*[17] a compulsory purchase order was made under the HA 1980, on land for a by-pass, and at the public inquiry into the order the appellants put forward four alternative routes over land they owned and were prepared to sell. The inspector found the advantages of these routes would be outweighed by extra cost and delays, and in due course the Secretary of State confirmed the order. The appellants sought to contend that confirmation of the CPO was wrong because such an order can only be confirmed if it can be shown to be in the public interest. The court rejected such a contention, but pointed out that because a CPO is a draconian measure it may be more vulnerable to challenge for failure to comply with the '*Wednesbury*' rules unless sufficient grounds can be adduced to justify it on its own merits. It is up to the Secretary of State to consider all relevant factors before confirming an order, including landscape issues, matters of feasibility, potential delays and costs. Provided he/she does that the courts are unwilling to intervene.

B AERODROMES

Under the Civil Aviation Act 1982, s 105(1), an aerodrome is an area of land or water designed, equipped, set apart, or commonly used for aircraft to land and depart, including facilities for helicopters and vertical take off and landing fixed-wing aeroplanes. Aerodromes may be provided by various bodies including the Secretary of State, local authorities, the Civil Aviation Authority and private persons and companies.

In the management and administration of his aerodromes the Secretary of State must undertake adequate consultation with local authorities in the vicinity and other organisations representing the interests of those concerned with the locality, see the CAA 1982, s 26. The Civil Aviation Authority has a duty under CAA 1982, s 5 to consider environmental factors in relation to licensing of any aerodrome which may be designated by the Secretary of State, *other than* those regulated in respect of noise and vibration from aircraft under CAA 1982, s 78, ie Heathrow, Gatwick and Stansted airports.

The functions of the Secretary of State with regard to all civil aviation matters remain entrusted to the DTLR. Development by the Secretaries of State for Transport and Defence requires no planning permission, otherwise the construction of aerodromes and ancillary buildings and works does generally require permission.

17   [1989] 1 All ER 933.

Note, however, that the General Permitted Development Order 1995, Sch 2, Part 18 allows airport operators of sites falling within the Airports Act 1986, s 57 to carry out on their operational land developments including erecting or altering operational buildings in connection with the provision of services and facilities, but *excluding* the building/extending of runways, terminal construction of over 500 m^2 and similar major terminal extensions, and in any case development is permitted subject to a condition requiring consultation with the local planning authority before commencement. Further permitted development rights are given to operators in respect of the provision at or near (ie within 8 km) airports of air traffic control services, and similar rights are given to the Civil Aviation Authority in respect of air traffic control services, air navigation and monitoring services. Note further that 'airport' as the popular term is used in the AA 1986 in preference to aerodrome, and is defined therein (AA 1986, s 82(1)) as the aggregate of land, building and works in an aerodrome.

Guidance on permitted development rights was initially to be found in DoE Circular 22/88 pointed to the restrictions on terminal development, see para 70, and stressed the need for consultation even before permitted development is carried out. With regard to non-permitted development Environmental Impact Assessment (see chapter 8) is mandatory under SI 1999/293, Sch 1 in respect of aerodromes with basic runway lengths of 2,100 m or more, and so will also be subject to publicity and public consultation requirements. On EIA and permitted development see SI 1999/293, reg 33. In exceptional cases authorities or the Secretary of State may revoke permitted development rights under Art 4 of the 1995 Order. Because of permitted development rights which were more extensive than is now the case, examination of proposals to develop a third London airport largely took place on a non-statutory basis. In respect of the 1980 proposals to develop Stansted airport the then British Airports Authority included some non-operational land in their planning application and opted to have the whole area treated as a single entity subject to planning control.

The airports for London controversy

Principal controversy concerning development by airport authorities has arisen in relation to airports for London; especially the Stansted site, a heated debate that continued for over 30 years. Readers wishing to pursue the factual history of the issue are referred to Hall *Great Planning Disasters* chapter 2, and Eyre *The Airport Inquiries 1981–1983* part II (inspector's report).

'Airports Policy' (Cmnd 9542) declared the intention of government to allow development of Stansted on grounds that Heathrow, Gatwick and regional airports could not meet projected traffic demands for the 1990s. the development of a second runway at Gatwick was considered to be environmentally unacceptable, and there is also an agreement under planning legislation between the British Airports Authority and West Sussex County Council dating from 1979 whereby a second runway at Gatwick would not be built until 2019, see *The Times* letters, 5 June 1985. The proposal formed part of a 'package' dealing, inter alia, with further growth at Luton, encouragement for the use of Manchester for international services, and measures to increase use of regional airports, and to postpone a fifth terminal at Heathrow.

New powers to control numbers of aircraft, particularly those using Stansted were given under the Airports Act 1986, Part III. The AA 1986, s 31 gives the Secretary of State power to make traffic distribution rules providing for apportionment of traffic between two or more airports serving the *same area* in the UK, and in this context traffic distribution rules have been made which relate to the airports serving the London area, in particular Heathrow and Gatwick. The AA 1986, s 32 further empowers the

Secretary of State to impose, by order, limits, overall or partial, on aircraft movements at particular airports where he considers the existing runway capacity of the airport is *not* fully utilised for a substantial proportion of the time when the runway(s) is/are available for take off or landing; such orders may not limit movements to numbers lower than the highest level of any corresponding movements at the airport occurring at equivalent periods within the three years before the order, or the level permitted under a previous order. See, for example, SI 1999/212. AA 1986, s 33 allows the Secretary of State, where a s 32 order is in force in relation to an airport, *or* where he/she considers that demand for an airport's use exceeds or will exceed in the near future its operational capacity, to direct the CAA to make a scheme to restrict access to the airport. Such schemes can prevent certain aircraft from using relevant airports, and can provide for charges in respect of take off and landing times or 'slots'. Use of this power appears so far to have been avoided but may prove necessary if congestion builds up at individual airports.

The London STOLPORT

Along with the development of Stansted, a short take off and landing (STOL) airport to be known as London City Airport, was given ministerial approval on 23 May 1985. This is in the old London docklands and was built by private developers, with most flights being provided by a private airline. The Secretary of State for the Environment approved a single runway with associated terminal and hotel buildings, subject to conditions banning helicopters, club and recreational flying, limiting the number of flights and the times of operation of the airport, limiting the types of aircraft permitted to use the facility and the length of runway to be built, and requiring that noise barriers be provided. The Secretary of State's decision was challenged, inter alia on grounds of fairness, in *R v Secretary of State for the Environment, ex p Greater London Council*.[18] At the inquiry into the 'Stolport' application the inspector recommended that permission be granted subject to certain conditions as to numbers of aircraft movements and types of aircraft permitted to use the airport. The Secretary of State sought advice from the Department of Transport on the technical drafting of these conditions, though he gave the objectors a real opportunity to comment on the technical advice received. It was held that on the evidence no need to reopen the inquiry had arisen and that the Secretary of State had acted reasonably and fairly.

Continuing airport controversy

The debate on London's airports still continues: the official belief remains that a policy combining minimum environmental damage with the ability to protect jobs, attract foreign earnings, and so encourage economic growth, has been developed. Even in 1986, following the Stansted decision, the air transport industry began to call for further airport expansion such as a further runway at a south eastern airport.

In May 1992 BAA proposed a fifth terminal, though no new runway, for Heathrow, doubling its capacity to 80 million passengers pa, the new terminal itself to have a capacity of 600,000 passengers per week. The justification for the new development was the need to deal with a forecasted 3.25 million passengers per week by 2016 as opposed to 1.2 million per week in 1993, with the usual argument that Heathrow's expansion is vital to ensure the UK does not 'miss out' in the growth of air traffic. There was no argument

18   [1986] JPL 32.

for a further runway because the theory was that larger aircraft coming on stream would be able to deal with demand for flights.

However, by 1993 the Department of Transport's 'Runway Capacity to Serve the South East', basing its findings on total passenger demand up to 2025, with up to 170 million passengers a year then expected, with 195 million at the main London airports by 2015, recommended the provision of further runways at Heathrow or Gatwick by 2010, or at Stansted by 2015. It was, however, accepted that this could not happen without great environmental cost, either by affecting open landscape or, at Heathrow, entailing the demolition of 3,300 homes. It was further expected that there would be an aircraft noise problem, though the report believed that with improved technology the numbers of those affected by noise in 2025 would not be greater than in 1993. Opposition to the proposals from affected local authorities and residents' groups was immediate and considerable, and BAA dropped its support for a further runway at Heathrow, preferring to rely on the proposed fifth terminal. In February 1995 the government rejected the proposals for new runways at Heathrow and Gatwick, arguing that more work needed to be done on the environmental impact of the proposals before any decision could be taken.

BAA's formal planning application for T5 having been received, the matter went to a public inquiry which began in May 1995.

The report of the inquiry was not expected until 1997, but the matter was into its 162nd day before the proposed T5 plans were unveiled, and by mid-1996 it was predicted that the inquiry could the longest, costliest (£10 m at 1996 levels) and most contentious ever held in the UK. The arguments, however, were sharply divided along established lines. The proponents of the developments argued T5 was essential if Britain is to continue to be the 'hub' of world travel by air into Europe, and that the terminal was essential to preserve London's financial and commercial position in the world. Opponents claimed the development would create unacceptable noise levels and overcrowded roads without compensating environmental despoliation with new job creation. The four-year inquiry finished in December 2000, but ministers delayed a decision until after the general election. In the meantime there was evidence that Charles de Gaulle Airport (Paris), Schipol (Amsterdam) and Frankfurt were rapidly overtaking Heathrow in terms of passengers handled, development of facilities and new runways.

The decision on T5 was announced on 20 November 2001, and was in favour of the terminal. The Secretary of State and the inquiry had had to take into account the enormous economic important of Heathrow: it generates wage payments of over £5 bn pa, and supports over 250,000 jobs in all, 68,000 actually at the airport. On the other hand the airport generates over 5,000 complaints about noise each year, though in 2000/2001 it appears 45% of these came from only 20 people.

In announcing the go-ahead for the terminal which will open in 2007, the Secretary of State argued the permission was in the national interest, and would enable Heathrow to remain a world class airport. However, a 'precautionary' cap of 480,000 flights pa was imposed – still an increase, however, on the 460,000 flights handled in 2000, and with no guarantee that the cap will not be lifted following further research into the impact of engine noise. Further conditions were imposed to limit noise, though these will not come into effect for 15 years, by which time the noisiest current jets will have been phased out. By 2016 the area within which noise is permitted to exceed the 'serious disturbance' level of 57 Dba will be reduced to 145 sq km; even so in 2000 the area affected by that level of noise was 136 km, and 275,000 people were affected.

The Secretary of State's decision was in line with the inquiry recommendations where environmental impacts of noise, extra road traffic, diminution of air quality, intrusion into green belt land and disturbance from construction were weighed against the economic benefits of the proposal to the nation as a whole. The inquiry had, however, also found that there is considerable concern over night flights and early morning noise. The Secretary of State undertook to commence a consultation exercise on the night noise regime for all London's BAA airports by 2003. It will be remembered that the European Court of Human Rights found against the British government on whether the current noise regime contravenes the European Convention on Human Rights see chapter 5. However, the government has already announced that there will be changes to the management of flights into Heathrow so that the number of night flights over the built up area of West London will be reduced. Furthermore the Secretary of State accepted the recommendation of the inquiry that there should only be 42,000 extra car parking spaces as opposed to the 46,000 applied for, and *no* widening of the M4 in the vicinity, and the Secretary of State added generally in announcing his decision: 'I will, of course, wish to ensure that the night noise regime at Heathrow complies with the European Convention on Human Rights'.

There is likely to be pressure from the Air Industry for two more runways by 2015 in south east England – one at Stansted and, more controversially, one at Heathrow. In 1997 ministers approved a new runway for Manchester Airport, and a further new airport on the site of the former RAF Finningley (Doncaster) went to a planning inquiry in 2001. The T5 Inquiry recommended that no further runway should be constructed at Heathrow, but the Secretary of State conspicuously did not endorse that, and it thus remains possible that a further runway will be constructed.

Compulsory purchase powers

The Secretary of State has power to acquire land and rights over land by agreement or compulsorily for civil aviation purposes, see the Civil Aviation Act 1982, ss 41 and 44. Where *land* is acquired the procedure is that under the Acquisition of Land Act 1981. This provides the standard procedure for land acquisition whereby land is taken under a compulsory purchase order made in draft departmentally, in the case of a ministerial acquisition, then advertised in local newspapers, and notified to owners, lessees and occupiers. The information required for this purpose is a description of relevant land, a statement of why it is required, a statement of the place where the draft order can be inspected, and a time period, at least 21 days from the date of first publication, within which objections can be made. Owners and lessees, etc, must also be informed of the effect of the order. Where objections are made and not withdrawn a public local inquiry or other hearing must be held. Thereafter, following consideration of the inquiry report, the order may be made, and due notice of this fact published, and notified to owners, lessees, etc. There is a limited right of challenge for 'persons aggrieved' on a point of law in the High Court for a period of six weeks from first publication of notice of the making of the order.

The power to acquire *rights over land* is exercisable where the Secretary of State considers it expedient to secure the safety and efficiency of navigation of civil aircraft, the safe and efficient use of land vested in a 'relevant authority', or proposed for acquisition by them, or to provide services required in relation to such land. 'Relevant authorities' include the Secretary of State and the Civil Aviation Authority. The rights acquired or created by the Secretary of State's order may include easements, rights to enter, subject generally to giving notice to the occupier, to carry out and maintain works, and to install structures and apparatus, etc, see CAA 1982, s 44. Under CAA 1982, s 43 where rights (to enter land, or to install and maintain apparatus, or to do works, or to restrict the use of the land) are granted to the Secretary of State or to the Civil Aviation Authority the grantor's successors in title are also bound by the grant. CAA 1982,

Sch 7 contains the procedure for making orders obtaining *rights over land*, and for other connected civil aviation purposes.

CAA 1982, s 48 confers power on the Secretary of State, where satisfied such action is necessary for the safe and efficient use for civil aviation of any land vested in him/ her or the Civil Aviation Authority, or proposed for acquisition by him or them, to authorise by order the stopping up or diversion of highways. Consequential action may also be taken, for example to secure the provision or improvement of highways so far as the Secretary of State thinks necessary or desirable in consequence of a diversion or stopping up. CAA 1982, s 49 empowers the Secretary of State to acquire land compulsorily to provide or improve highways under s 48.

Where, under CAA 1982, s 52, land has been acquired for aviation purposes and the use of the land by the person who acquired it, or executing the direction, will involve the displacement of residential occupiers, *and* there is no other residential accommodation available on reasonable terms to those persons, suitable to their reasonable requirements, a duty to provide such accommodation arises. This will generally fall to be discharged by either the Secretary of State or the Civil Aviation Authority as the case may be. Home loss, farm loss and disturbance payments may also be payable in such circumstances, see the Land Compensation Act 1973, ss 29–38 as amended. Section 9 of that Act also makes compensation payable for depreciation in the value of land caused by alterations at an aerodrome where these take the form of new runway construction, runway re-alignment, extension or strengthening of existing runways, or increased provision of taxiways or aprons in order to accommodate more aircraft. Merely to *intensify* the use of an existing runway, without more, gives rise to no claim for compensation.

The Civil Aviation Authority has power to acquire land compulsorily, subject to ministerial consent, in connection with the performance of its functions. The procedure is that under the Acquisition of Land Act 1981: see CAA 1982, s 42. Note that under the Transport Act 2000 provision is made for 'licence holders' to take on air traffic control functions from the Civil Aviation Authority. The land and rights acquisition powers of such licence holders are generally equated with those of the authority.

C ELECTRICITY UNDERTAKINGS

Certain works connected with electricity undertakings are given automatic planning permission under the General Permitted Development Order 1995: (i) installation of electric lines on, over or under land, and the construction of ancillary shafts and tunnels; (ii) installing an electric line feeder or service pillars, transforming and switching stations not exceeding 29 cubic metres in capacity, (iii) installing telecommunications lines connecting electrical lines to plant or buildings; (iv) extending or altering buildings on operational land, subject to height and size limits; (v) temporary borehole sinking; (vi) erecting buildings on operational land, solely for protection of plant or machinery, subject to limits on height; and (vii) carrying out other development on, in or under operational land *except*: (a) erections or reconstructions materially affecting the design or external appearance of buildings; (b) installing or erecting, by way of addition or replacement, plant or machinery, etc, exceeding 15 m in height, or the height of the plant or machinery so replaced, whichever is greater. Carrying out works for inspecting, repairing or renewing cables and other apparatus does not constitute 'development', see the Town and Country Planning Act 1990, s 55(2)(c). However, if a tree preservation order is made under the TCPA 1990, s 198 preventing the wilful destruction of trees save with the consent of the local authority, and in the course of laying underground cables an electricity undertaking severs the roots of trees and so reduces their life expectancy, the undertaking may be liable, provided injury is so radical that a competent forester would decide in the circumstances, and considering safety issues, that the tree ought to be felled.[19]

The construction of power stations and installation of power lines

Under the Electricity Act 1989, s 36(1) a 'generating station' (which in the case of one driven wholly or mainly by water includes all the ancillary works and structures for holding or channelling water, see the EA 1989, s 64) cannot be *constructed*, extended or operated save in accordance with consents granted by the Secretary of State, though this prohibition does *not* extend to stations not exceeding a capacity of 50 megawatts or less, or in the case of a station to be constructed or extended which will not exceed that capacity once constructed or extended. The 50 megawatt figure may be varied by the Secretary of State, and he/she may by order further direct that the restrictions on construction, etc, are not to apply to stations of particular classes or descriptions. Consents given under the EA 1989, s 36 may include such conditions as the Secretary of State thinks fit, including conditions as to ownership and operation, and consents may be subject to time limitations. It is an offence to contravene the EA 1989, s 36 prohibition. The provisions outlined above, however, do *not* replace the need to obtain planning permission, though it appears clear that planning consent and generating stations consent procedures will be channelled together through a common public inquiry. Where the application is to build a nuclear station or a conventional one of 300 megawatts or more capacity EIA will be mandatory, and may be required for other stations, for example where an industrial installation for electricity production, other than one falling in the mandatory class, has an area of development exceeding 0.5 ha, see SI 1999/293, Sch 2. The Electricity Works (Environmental Impact Assessment) (England and Wales) Regulations, SI 2000/1927 more generally apply EIA procedures to EA 1989, s 36 applications.

The procedure for obtaining consent is laid down in the EA 1989, Sch 8. Applications must be in writing and must refer to maps showing the land on which the station is to be built, extended, etc, and must be supplemented by such other information as is ministerially directed. Fees may be charged in connection with applications. A copy of the application must be served on relevant local planning authorities, and where such an authority objects and so informs the Secretary of State he/she must hold a public inquiry and must consider objections and the inquiry report before reach a decision. Time limits for the making of objections may be laid down. Regulations may further be made for securing that consent applications are publicised in prescribed fashion and that copies are served on prescribed persons. Such publicity must state a time and manner for persons *other* than local planning authorities to make objections. Where third party objections only are received there is no obligation to hold a public inquiry, instead the Secretary of State must consider the objections along with all other material considerations to determine whether in any case an inquiry should be held. The clear assumption in case law is, however, that in such circumstances an inquiry should be held unless the minister is properly satisfied he/she can weigh the conflicting issues without an inquiry and that the objectors' representations will be in any case properly taken into account.[20]

---

19   *Barnet London Borough Council v Eastern Electricity Board* [1973] 2 All ER 319, [1973] 1 WLR 430.
20   *Binney v Secretary of State for the Environment* [1984] JPL 871.

Where a public inquiry is held the Secretary of State must inform the applicant and the applicant must then in two successive weeks: publicise in the local press the application and its purpose and describe the relevant land; state a local place where a copy of the application and supporting maps can be inspected; and announce the date and time of the public inquiry. The Secretary of State may direct the applicant to undertake further publicity measures. The public inquiry may subsume any inquiries for consents needed because multiple permissions are a prerequisite for a particular activity, eg compulsory acquisition of land by relevant generators — which may be authorised under EA 1989, Sch 3: see also s 61.

On the grant of EA 1989, s 36 consent in respect of any matter amounting to 'development' the Secretary of State *may* direct that planning permission for the development and any ancillary matters is deemed granted, subject to such conditions as he may impose. Likewise where a EA 1989, s 36 consent relates to operations or changes of use involving the need for a hazardous substances consent the Secretary of State may direct such consent deemed granted, but only after consultation with the Health and Safety Commission.

Overhead power lines may not be installed or kept installed save with the consent of the Secretary of State: see EA 1989, s 37. However, this prohibition does not apply to lines having a normal voltage of not more than 20 KV *and* used by a single consumer nor in relation to that portion of a line as is within premises occupied or controlled by the person responsible for installation. Other exemptions may be made. Consent may be given subject to conditions and may be varied or revoked by the Secretary of State at any time after the end of a specified period, and may in any case be made subject to time limits. It is an offence to contravene this provision though, just as with contraventions of EA 1989, s 36, proceedings for infraction can only be brought by or on behalf of the Secretary of State. See SI 2000/1927 for the EIA requirements in respect of EA 1989, s 37 applications.

EA 1989, Sch 8 once again provides the procedure for obtaining consent. This replicates that for generating station consents with appropriate modifications, eg the necessary map must show the land across which the line is to be installed and applications must state whether all necessary wayleaves have been agreed with the owners of relevant land. However, where an application states that the necessary wayleaves have *not* been agreed the Secretary of State may give notice to the applicant that he does not intend to proceed until satisfied that in relation to all affected land an application has been made under EA 1989, Sch 4, para 6. This latter provision applies where attempts to negotiate wayleaves have foundered (or where a land owner is attempting to bring an existing wayleave to an end). In such cases an application to the Secretary of State can be made and he may grant the necessary wayleave subject to such conditions as he thinks fit. However, a wayleave application cannot be entertained in respect of land covered by dwellings, and before granting wayleaves he must give occupiers and owners of the land in question the right to be heard. Compensation is payable in respect of wayleaves granted, and further compensation in respect of any damage caused by the exercise of the wayleave right. Where an overhead line is thus 'held up' pending resolution of wayleaves the Secretary of State *may*, however, give consent to the line on the condition that the work of installation may not be begun without his permission. Obtaining a wayleave for a line carries with it the power to support it on pylons, and the affected landowner may not specify the form of such pylons.[21]

The foregoing provisions are subject to the requirements of EA 1989, Sch 9 which provides that in formulating proposals, eg for generating stations, relevant persons

21   *Central Electricity Generating Board v Jennaway* [1959] 3 All ER 409, [1959] 1 WLR 937.

must have regard to the desirability of: preserving natural beauty, conserving flora, fauna and geological or physiographical features of special interest and of protecting sites and buildings, etc, of historic architectural or archaeological interest. They must further do what they reasonably can to mitigate the effects of their proposals on the countryside, flora, fauna, etc. Such considerations are also to be taken into account by the Secretary of State in considering applications for consents. These requirements apply to proposals to construct/extend generating stations of not less than 10 megawatts capacity, to install lines above *or below* ground or for the exemption of other electricity supply or transmission works. Regular statements are required from operators as to how they intend to comply with the foregoing requirements. Such statements must be published and must be based on consultations with the Countryside Agency and relevant nature conservatory (eg English Nature) and historic buildings bodies.

Relevant electricity operators (ie those licensed to supply electricity) have further important ancillary powers under EA 1989, Sch 4. Where a tree is in close proximity to an electric line or plant so that it obstructs or interferes with the installation, maintenance or working of the line or plant, or otherwise constitutes an unacceptable source of danger, notice may be given to the occupier of the land on which the tree is growing requiring him/her to fell or lop the tree or cut back its roots so as to abate the problem. If such a request is not complied with within 21 days the operator may cause the work to be done provided he acts in accordance with good arboricultural practice, doing as little damage as possible to trees, and making good damage to the land. Should any dispute arise as to the necessity for the work the matter is to be referred to the Secretary of State who, after giving the parties an opportunity to be heard may make such order as he thinks fit.

Special provisions for nuclear installations

The consent provisions are additional to nuclear site licensing in the case of nuclear powered generating stations. The Nuclear Installations Act 1965, s 1, requires a nuclear site licence for a nuclear powered generating station, and before such a licence is granted there must be consultation with the Environment Agency: see NIA 1965, s 3(1A) inserted in 1995. Licences are issued by the Health and Safety Executive (HSE). The HSE must, under NIA 1965, ss 3(6A) and 4(3A), consult the Environment Agency before such a licence is granted or varied, or is made subject to a condition relating to the creation, accumulation or disposal of radioactive waste. Licences are granted subject to safety conditions, which may be varied in the future or during construction. A licence is only granted after the NII has conducted exhaustive assessments, a process that can run parallel to other public inquiry procedures. Licences may only be granted to bodies corporate, and cannot be transferred: see NIA 1965, s 3. Before a licence can be granted applicants may be directed to inform (by serving notice on them containing specified *particulars*) local authorities of licence applications, giving them specified information and informing them of their right (within three months of the date of service) to make representations to the HSE, though this requirement is lifted where the application is in respect of a site where a consent under EA 1989, s 36 is being sought, for otherwise there would be a duplication of effort. The conditions attached will vary from site to site and may cover matters as diverse as the provision of design information, quality approvals, the inspection of components, the authorisation of workers, protective measures in respect of radiation, storage of waste fuel and other wastes. Conditions under NIA 1965, s 4 (which may only be imposed, varied or resolved following consultation with the Agency, see NIA 1965, s 4(3A)) will also regulate the working life of a commissioned plant, requiring detailed regulation inspections and other safety checks. Conditions may relate to: the efficiency of radiation emission monitoring devices; the design, siting, construction, installation, operation, modification and maintenance of plant; dealing with accidents and emergencies, and discharges; handling, treating and disposing of nuclear material. To ensure safety, plants should be shut down once in two years, and may not then recommence operation until consent is given. An emergency plan will also be required by the licence conditions to deal with incidents involving escaping radioactive matter. Further conditions will relate to recording radioactivity, design, siting, construction and maintenance of plant. Conditions may be added at any time in respect of the handling, treatment and disposal of nuclear material, and conditions may be varied or revoked at any time. Site licences may be revoked by the HSE (following consultation with the Environment Agency) at any time (see NIA 1965, s 5) or surrendered by the licensee, though such revocation or surrender does not free the licensee of responsibility for the site, for licensees have a 'period of responsibility' from the date of grant of their licences until they are informed by the HSE that there has ceased to be any danger from ionising radiations from anything on site, *or* until a new licence supervenes the old one. During this period the original licensee remains subject to the HSE's supervision powers. The duty of licensees is, under NIA 1965, s 7, to see that 'no' prohibited occurrence involving nuclear matter causes injury to any person or damage to any property where that injury arises from radioactive properties of matter, or these in combination with toxic, explosive or other hazardous properties of the matter, *and* that no ionising radiations emitted in the 'period of responsibility' from anything caused or allowed by the licensee to be on site even though not nuclear matter, or from any waste discharged from the site cause personal or property damage. Where there is an occurrence it must be reported under NIA 1965, s 22 to the HSE, and an inspector's report may be required and published, or even a court of inquiry. The prohibited occurrences are: on site occurrences involving nuclear matter and certain off site occurrences involving material in carriage. The duty is not, however, *absolute*, despite NIA 1965, s 7's use of the word 'no', for there can be no guarantee that a nuclear site will be free from natural but unforeseen events, or improbable failures of equipment, nor proof against human error (as seems to have been the case at Chernobyl) or acts of malice.[22]

A 'culture of safety' should, however, be the dominant feature of the operation of nuclear power stations so that there should be no hesitation on the part of staff in shutting down a power plant should even a minor incident occur. Operators of such plant may expect to incur hefty fines should they breach site licensing conditions and other health and safety provisions.[23]

Central planning policy is generally averse to other developments in the neighbourhood of a nuclear powered generator. A planning authority may also be involved where there is an application for development involving nuclear installations *other* than generating stations. Planning permission is needed, but the issue is likely to be 'called in' by the Secretary of State, and may be made subject to special development procedure, as with the Sellafield (Windscale) plant, see Ian Breach *Windscale Fall-out*.

22   *Re Friends of the Earth* [1988] JPL 93.
23   *Health and Safety Executive v Nuclear Electric* [1995] 7 ELM 203.

Inquiries and nuclear installations: further controversies

The most controversial inquiry so far held in relation to the building of an electricity power station was into the proposal to erect a pressurised water nuclear reactor (PWR) at Sizewell in Suffolk. This was an inquiry of monumental complexity and questions arose whether the inquiry could be full, fair and thorough because of the complexity of the issues involved; the tension between the interests of local people and national policy on nuclear power (see chapter 3 above), and the disparity in resources between the various parties, those objecting to the proposal being largely dependent on fund raising efforts of local and national pressure groups. It is, however, debatable how far the concepts of 'fairness' and 'thoroughness' are compatible. The more 'thorough' an inquiry, the greater the weight of evidence and the more daunting its bulk to objectors. However, an inquiry has to be as fair as possible to all parties because of the need to ensure that its recommendations are reached in a way acceptable to all.

The inquiry saw unusual combinations of allies, such as the National Coal Board, the National Union of Miners, the South of Scotland Electricity Board, the Town and Country Planning Association and the Council for the Protection of Rural England, to mention a few. The deceptively simple single issue of whether permission should be given for the erection of the first British PWR on a site next door to an already functioning nuclear power station, expanded as the inquiry progressed into consideration of disposal of nuclear waste, and decommissioning or 'entombing' nuclear stations whose economic life has ended. The inquiry could not concentrate on the safety issue, a major part of the inquiry in view of the incident involving a pressurised water reactor at Three Mile Island in the USA. It had also to consider and investigate the means whereby the Central Electricity Generating Board (CEGB) and the Department of Energy estimated national energy needs, bearing in mind prices of alternative fuels, variations in fuel supply and demand.

The inquiry had additionally to consider the views of objectors alleging, variously, that: demand forecasts had overestimated national generating capacity needs; better electricity generating options existed in the form of combined heat and power schemes; massive investment in nuclear capacity could starve other projects of much needed capital, for example, the development of solar, wind and wave power; the CEGB was wrong to believe a PWR could be quickly and cheaply built; preference could be given to another British type of reactor, the Advanced Gas Cooled system; on safety grounds the PWR was unacceptable, and that fuel from the reactor would form the basis for nuclear weapons. The inquiry thus became a complex multi-faceted entity in which the issue of nuclear energy policy, indeed energy policy overall, was never far from anyone's mind as the various issues were discussed.

Even though overall policy on nuclear power could not, as such, be questioned by the inquiry, it examined policy closely. To examine the issues the 'inquiry team' consisted of the person appointed to hear the inquiry, Sir Frank Layfield, with assisting technical experts in mechanical and nuclear engineering, economics and radio biology. Before the inquiry appeared a variety of legally qualified and lay advocates. Additionally Sir Frank Layfield appointed, following representations from the Town and Country Planning Association, a full time 'counsel to the inquiry'. His task was to help inexperienced objectors and to pursue lines of inquiry they were unable to.

The inquiry had to direct itself to key issues including: the '*need*' for the particular generator; its *economics*, and its *safety*. Each of these was a highly technical issue involving argument on many matters.

1   Likely future demand for generating capacity, which in turn depended on forecasts of economic activity, consideration of energy saving measures, provision for sudden demands for electricity, predictions of the future useful life of existing generating plant, and considerations of energy source diversification.

2   Cost savings alleged to flow from building a PWR constituted an issue involving complex economic modelling, argument over likely commissioning dates for the new reactor, and the likely future cost of alternative fuel sources; higher fossil fuel costs might justify the large initial capital cost of a PWR.

3   Safety issues involved consideration of highly technical matters such as fracture mechanics, 'problematic risk assessments' and other issues of 'engineering judgment'. Of course, the larger the number of safety restrictions placed on such a PWR the more its initial and operating costs become. British nuclear reactors have a long history of safe operation, but the near-disaster at Three Mile Island in the USA in 1979 involved a PWR. Issues of the safety of the proposal were raised and considered at the inquiry, though responsibility for approving the design of the proposed reactor lay with the NII (see above).

4   A final issue was whether the American PWR should be preferred to the British Advanced Gas Cooled Reactor. This was an issue less than appropriate for a 'planning type' inquiry as it involved questions of sustainable capacity in the *international* reactor construction industry.

NB The issue of the *cost of decommissioning* the PWR at the end of its working life was not a central topic, and was dealt with in much less detail in official evidence than was the matter of safe operation. Indeed it has only been in recent years that much official attention has been given to this problematic subject.

It is impossible for the law to supply a 'right' answer in such circumstances. The Law's task is to provide a framework within which matters can be fairly and fully discussed so that *the most informed recommendations* can be made. The Sizewell inquiry was undoubtedly fair in the way it allowed the presentation of issues and afforded those interested a chance to present their case. In this respect it represented an important development in the handling of major public inquiries. The Sizewell inquiry lasted over two years with 340 days of hearings and in its conduct moved away from the traditional concept of an inquiry being a fact finding, administrative mechanism, albeit one conducted in adversarial fashion. This concept had been less than effective in explaining the nature of major inquiries for some time; it could not disguise ministerial involvement in promoting the very projects over which inquiries were being held, supposedly the 'better to inform' those same ministers. Nor could it account for the 'salami' technique whereby a major project could be authorised after a *series* of inquiries each separated from the others, nor yet the inability of the inquiry system to inquire into the statistical and other techniques underlying policy formulation. A further weakness in the traditional conception of a 'public' inquiry is the vast discrepancy in resources between promoting agencies and objectors making it hard for the latter to present their arguments fully. To meet the last objection the Sizewell inquiry introduced the major innovation of 'counsel to the inquiry', and this led to the inquiry adopting a much more inquisitorial role with the inspector, the assessors and counsel to the inquiry taking over functions from objectors. Though fair and thorough examination of the issues involved may dictate a more inquisitorial style of inquiry, it could result in objectors being marginalised, their lack of resources being even more emphasised by those of the inquiry mechanism itself.

D CONCERN OVER AND REFORM OF INQUIRY PROCEDURE

National projects to implement policies, themselves the subject of fierce debate and concern are not, however, easily fairly investigated by public inquiries. The well-rehearsed argument remains that such proceedings can never be truly legitimate. Projects may be too closely identified with their ultimate ministerial arbiters, who may be, without total justification, *assumed* to represent 'public interest', and the resources of proponents and opponents continue to be greatly unequal. Inquiries are thought by some to be merely cosmetic, giving a semblance of legitimacy to conclusions already reached. Controversy over trunk road proposals, the Vale of Belvoir Coalfield, the siting of, and need for, a third London airport, and the nuclear fuel reprocessing plant at Windscale led to major public inquiries becoming longer and more expensive as attempts to ensure fairness for all concerned. The Sizewell inquiry did not resolve any of these issues, even though it marked a major development in inquiry *procedure*. At the end of the day the inquiry still had to rely on expert evidence given, not always in a coherent fashion, by various bodies and agencies identified in the public mind as part of the structure of government. To that extent the inquiry could not bring about legitimation of the proposed PWR, even less legitimation of nuclear policy overall, policy formulation techniques, or public inquiry procedures in general.

The following fundamental flaws in major inquiry procedures must always be borne in mind:

1   An inquiry is not a means of formulating policy nor yet a means of policy critique: it lies midway between a decision made by an administrator and one made by a court.

2   Any inquiry must accept official policy and much of the techniques used to assess the factual basis of policy, even when they are not put forward in the most coherent style, and even where they alter during the course of events.

3   The resources of the various participants remain uneven, major 'players' may be able to afford the very considerable fees charged by leading counsel and their juniors, but many voluntary organisations have to depend solely on their own staff, and private citizens must look to their own resources, perhaps having to launch fighting funds to meet costs for not only are lawyers' fees considerable, there is also the high cost of expert witnesses.

4   Inquiries still consume much time, and ways of shortening them (by excluding *all* consideration of policy issues, by empowering inspectors specifically to exclude evidence or questions on grounds of repetition or irrelevance, by more vigorously awarding costs against the long winded and by concentrating more on the pre-inquiry preparation stage) may further reinforce the argument that inquiry procedure cannot be fair.

The form of the future inquiries continues to be a matter of debate. Historically there has been little consensus on a number of major issues.

1   Should inquiry procedure be so very adversarial, as traditional, with probing examination and cross-examination, or much more investigatory and inquisitorial, with the inquiry itself opening up questions and identifying issues it wishes to have studied and researched? Indeed, should inquiries be given powers to question the need for projects and policies in the broadest economic, social and environmental terms, with the ability to examine alternatives? This could raise constitutional issues over the conventional responsibility of ministers to Parliament for the formulation of policy. Such inquiries could become *non-elected* forums for debate.

2   Should inquiries be held by single inspectors who, no matter how eminent, and no matter how well assisted by assessors, cannot possibly be expert in all relevant fields of knowledge? It is questionable whether lawyers are the best equipped people to hold inquiries. Lawyers are 'at home' with very formal inquiry procedures, but many objectors find these inhibiting. Lawyers also use adversarial cross-examination techniques, but some descriptive and evaluative evidence, for example, the social consequences of similar projects elsewhere, is not susceptible of such

examination. Lawyers are, by training, well equipped to identify *what the issue for debate* is, and to present arguments for and against a particular point of view; they are not, traditionally, trained to see how the *issue for decision* relates to its social, political, economic and environmental setting, though is any profession able to claim that its members could comprehend all these complex matters? Other critics direct their attention to the argument that there is insufficient public scrutiny of the process of appointing inspectors for major inquiries.

3   Do inspectors have sufficient powers to order the disclosure of all relevant documentation before an inquiry so that parties may know well in advance the various arguments? Indeed, is it even possible to know the arguments when policy is unclear?

4   Do objectors to a proposal have a fair chance to state their case? Legal aid is not available. The technical and financial resources of those proposing a project are greatly out of proportion to those of objectors, even considered collectively.

   Furthermore would it be 'fairer' to hold major inquiries only in the evening so that those at work may be able to attend more easily, and also should child minding facilities be provided at inquiries to enable those with small children to participate more?

5   Assuming that 'pressure groups' opposed to a project can muster sufficient resources to enable them to present their cases, is more help needed for individuals to enable them to join in the debate effectively?

6   Are inquiries becoming too long, and expensive so that much needed projects are being delayed for unacceptable periods?

7   What is the proper limit of an inquiry, and who is to set it? When in 1994 planning permission was refused for the construction of an underground laboratory at Sellafield, at the subsequent inquiry it was argued the government had set its terms of reference too narrowly. The inspector stated only the courts can determine an inquiry's limits, but the scope and effectiveness of an inquiry may depend on the practice of the inspector holding it.

8   Would it be preferable for major projects to be subject, so far as policy issues are concerned, solely to parliamentary debate? 'Site specific' inquiries would be limited then solely to local planning considerations, and to 'yes' and 'no' recommendations on such matters, with no wider debate; assuming it is possible to devise rules to prevent objectors raising policy issues under the guise of local considerations. Site specific inquiries raising no possibility of debating, albeit in limited ways, policy might be politically acceptable if they took place against a background of consensus on policies already well debated in Parliament, though such policies generally are rare. This is an issue we shall return to below.

These matters raise the fundamental issue of what form of government is acceptably legitimate. In an increasingly articulate and informed society decisions on projects having major environmental implications will not be let simply to ministers, civil servants and public authorities. Many people want to participate in decisions that will shape their lives, and are no longer prepared to leave matters to their parliamentary representatives. Many seriously question how it is that a whole mass of planning and conservation legislation can be seemingly set aside in the name of roads policy — and the easy legal answer that no Act of Parliament has a special sanctity which makes it immune from the operation of other Acts is not an acceptance response. At least some people will reject the framework of society if confronted by decisions to which they strongly and bitterly object, taken by procedures which seem to give them no effective means of debating the issues or of influencing the final outcome. Not all of these who protest can be dismissed as simply 'drop outs' and extremists.

Muted responses to concern over inquiry procedure

Governmental responses to the foregoing concerns have traditionally been muted. In 1988, in DoE Circular 10/88, the Code of Practice for major inquiries under the *Planning Acts*, was issued with the purpose of ensuring more smoothly running and better structured inquiries. This was replaced by DETR Circular 15/96, and that in turn was replaced by DETR Circular 05/00 Annex 4. The Code applies to inquiries where major public interest is aroused because of national or regional implications, or where extensive and complex environmental, safety, technical or scientific issues are involved, and where there are numbers of third parties involved. The Code does not apply to orders proposed by ministers, or to inquiries held other than under planning legislation, but it has elements that could be applicable to such inquiries, and see Highway Inquiries above. However, it is for the DTLR to decide whether or not in any given case the code will apply. It is considered that only a few inquiries will have the code applied to them ie those falling within the scope of SI 2000/1624 (the inquiry procedure rules), ie where pre-inquiry meetings have to be held.

Once the Code is applied to an inquiry copies of it will be sent to the applicant and the planning authority together with an indication of the matters about which the Secretary of State particularly wishes to be informed. The authority will also be sent a form for use by those who wish to register as inquiry participants. This will indicate, inter alia, whether participants have affected land, whether they will be formally represented, and whether they wish to play a major role by calling witnesses, etc. All those having the *right* to appear will also be notified by the DTLR to the authority. The application of the code has to be publicised in the local press and registration forms will further give the address of the Secretariat which will be set up in the DTLR to handle the inquiry and liaise with the authority.

The next task is the creation of a register of participants. Part 1 will be 'major participants' who will be allowed to speak irrespective of the strict legalities. Part 2 will be those indicating a desire to give oral evidence only; they will normally be allowed to appear provided what they have to say is relevant and not repetitious. Part 3 will consist of those making written representations only, they may be allowed to appear at the inspector's discretion. This register will be circulated to the parties and the major participants, copies will also be publicly available. Major participants will thereafter be expected to comply with the Code, eg as to exchange of documents.

There follows the announcement of the name of the inspector, the assessors (if any) arrangements for pre-inquiry meetings and a target inquiry commencement date. This will be publicised locally by the authority. Not later than eight weeks after notification that an inquiry is to be held the applicant and the authority will be asked to provide outline statements of case and arguments. Other major participants may be asked to provide statements within four weeks of receipt of a request. The statement should indicate the likely time presentation of the case will take and information about witnesses, special studies undertaken, etc. This information will normally be circulated to the parties, and made publicly available. These statements will outline lines of argument thus enabling issues for the inquiry to be identified, and allowing the inspector to structure the inquiry, perhaps enabling the inspector to invite some participants to submit joint arguments, and showing whether any issues have been missed so that the deficiency may be remedied. Statements may also enable agreed *facts* to be identified thus enabling such matters to be settled before the inquiry commences.

At the following pre-inquiry public meeting(s) chaired by the inspector clarification of issues is to be sought, eg on agreed facts, timetabling of any further pre-inquiry issues, identifying relevant issues, the role of the assessors, etc. Procedural issues will also be considered, eg times and places of sitting, programming, the facilities needed by the inquiry, opening and closing procedures, document exchange systems. No discussion of the merits of the issue is allowed. The conclusions of the meeting will be circulated to parties and major participants by the secretariat, and the date, time and place of the inquiry will be circulated to all relevant persons and bodies. Further meetings may be held to establish statements of agreed facts, and these will be reported and circulated. Informal meetings on particular issues, eg statistical methodology, *may* be held. The parties will, and the major participants may, then be required to write a statement giving full particulars of their proposed submissions and listing documents intended to be placed in evidence. These statements, where required, will have to be made within four weeks of the final pre-inquiry meeting. Statements (or 'proofs') of evidence to be read at the inquiry must under the statutory rules be given beforehand to the inspector, and summaries of such evidence may be required under the Code. Where a participant who gives oral evidence at an inquiry wishes to introduce an argument outside his pre-inquiry statement, an adjournment *may* be allowed for others to consider the issues raised. Unreasonable conduct leading to such an adjournment may result in an order for costs being made against the guilty person.

E THE TRANSPORT AND WORKS ACT 1992

Disquiet over inquiry procedure is a long standing issue, a matter of rather more recent controversy was the use of private/hybrid bill procedure in Parliament to give particular powers to persons/companies to proceed with major projects, eg the Channel Tunnel Bill 1986.

To calm this anxious opposition the Transport and Works Act 1992 was passed whereunder an improved procedure is introduced to deal with such matters. Concerned with transport projects — railways, tramways and inland waterways — and ensuring that they can be constructed with their promoters being given appropriate planning consents and compulsory acquisition powers and freedom from liability in nuisance arising from their operation (such projects inevitably interfere with private rights), the Act nevertheless also addresses relevant environmental concerns.

Thus under TWA 1992, s 1 the Secretary of State may make orders as to railways and tramways (and under TWA 1992, s 3 with regard to inland waterways) where, under TWA 1992, s 6, an application is made to him/her in due form: authorising their construction, alteration, repair, maintenance, etc; creating or extinguishing rights over land, etc; see also TWA 1992, s 5 and Sch 1. In particular approval may be given for: the compulsory acquisition of land; planning consent under the Town and Country Planning Act 1990, s 90(2A) and hazardous substances consent under the Planning (Hazardous Substances) Act 1990, s 12(2A). Where, however, under TWA 1992, s 9 an application relates to matters considered by the Secretary of State to be of national significance, an order may *not* be made without the prior approval of both Houses of Parliament. Where an application for an order authorising the construction/operation of a railway, tramway, or canal, etc, provision is made under TWA 1992, s 1 for holding a public local inquiry, and the procedure follows the 'normal' pattern for such events.

Rules made under TWA 1992, s 6 ensure that EIA of projects falling within the terms of the Act takes place: see SI 2000/2190.

F FOR THE FUTURE ... ?

On 20 July 2001 the Secretary of State for Transport, Local Government and the Regions announced a policy review on major infrastructure projects such as new airports and rail links, following on from the 1999 Consultation Paper 'Streamlining the processing of major projects through the planning system'. This pointed to the prevalence of delays and cumbersome decision taking in the current processes. It was accepted that major new projects are essential in economic terms, but they are controversial and affect the lives of people living near proposed development sites. It is essential, it was argued, to streamline produce, reduce delay while at the same time increasing public consultation and involvement.

The new proposals are:

- up-to-date statements of government policy should be in place before major projects are considered, thus helping to reduce unnecessary delay at the inquiry stage;
- normally there should be a prior consultation stage before a policy statement is released so that people have the chance to comment, though the nature and approach of statements may vary from case to case;
- enhanced Regional Planning Guidance (RPG) will be issued to guide the broad location of new developments and infrastructure at a regional level;
- multi-modal studies of transport issues will continue and these will also inform the RPG process;
- *approval in principle for major infrastructure projects should be a matter for Parliament*;
- procedures will be developed for allowing objections to proposals before Parliamentary debate;
- once Parliament has approved a project the task of any subsequent inquiry will be to examine detailed issues only;
- these proposals will, however, require new legislation, coupled with a review of the operation of the Transport and Works Act 1992;
- where inquiries take place further measures will be introduced to ensure stricter timetabling and more clearly focussed terms of reference;
- there will be enhanced powers for those who conduct inquiries to deal with more issues at the pre-inquiry stage;
- there will be no abolition of the right of cross-examination at Inquiries.

A number of issues arise from these proposals:

- The announcement referred to infrastructure projects such as airports, rail links and roads, but should similar changes extend to other controversial developments such as power stations, nuclear and other major waste disposal sites and major mineral extraction sites of national significance?
- What criteria are to be used for determining what a 'major project' is? A 'major' road could be built as a series of 'minor' sections.
- Will the proposals achieve the desired balance between speed and efficiency and effective public involvement? Is it not likely that government would use its majority in Parliament to plush through proposals despite objections?
- Once agreed 'in principle' will the role of objectors at any subsequent inquiry be limited to 'damage limitation', ie seeking to minimise disruption, but being unable to prevent it? Though it is arguable that that is no different from what happens under the present system.
- Will the 'in principle' approval of Parliament be directed not just to the desirability of a project but also to its location? In some cases this would have to be so. A major new road scheme for, say, the West Midlands could only be built there, though the 'line issue' could be a matter which could be left to an inquiry as at the moment.

Comparisons can be drawn with the French attitude to major infrastructure developments. In France it is possible for a presidential decree to state that a project is of national importance, and this effectively bars challenge in court. Furthermore the French attitude is that while there may be local strong environmental feeling about a project this has to be balanced against the wider national interest and the interests of the consumers of services. France has in this way developed many exciting infrastructure projects, including its TGV railways and Charles de Gaulle airport – but it must be remembered that France is roughly twice the size of England with much lower population densities.

Real reform?

A thoroughgoing reform of major inquiry procedure could be based on a development of the sequential test notion already mentioned above with regard to road inquiries. 'Sequentialism', which may be regarded as an application of the sustainable development arguments considered in chapter 2, would operate as follows:

- there would be a requirement for the sponsors of the major project to show initially *a real need* for it;
- there would then follow a sequential procedure in which there would be debated before Parliament or a parliamentary Select Committee, not only the alternative physical sites for the proposal, but also alternative policy options, eg in the case of a road scheme traffic management and demand reduction and diversification options;
- the test the project would have to pass would be to have demonstrated that all other viable options have been considered, and that the project in question has emerged as the best practicable option in environmental, economic and social terms.

The elements of such a system, for example Environmental Impact Assessment, are already in place, but they need bringing together with a new publicly acceptable – and accessible – framework. It should be remembered that as long ago as 1979 the Outer Circle Policy Unit argued the case for 'project inquiries' able to examine issues of 'need', and comprising two stages. The first would be inquisitorial and would determine issues to be researched and information to be made available. The second would then determine arguments over the inferences to be drawn from the facts. Only then would the Commission make a report on its recommendations for debate in Parliament. That proposal retains merit today.

G PIPELINES: UNCONTROVERSIAL LAWS?

Pipelines, that is systems for transporting materials, other than air, water, steam or water vapour from one locality to another, not being drains or sewers, may not be constructed across country without ministerial authorisation, see the Pipe-lines Act 1962, ss 1 and 65. Procedure for deciding applications for pipeline authorisation is laid down in PA 1962, Sch 1, Part I, as amended. Applications must, inter alia, specify the points between which a proposed pipeline is to run, and what is proposed for conveyance in the pipeline. The minister (the Secretary of State) has discretion whether or not to grant authorisation. Where he/she proposes to grant authorisation he/she must inform the applicant, who must take specified steps to inform persons inhabiting land in the vicinity of the proposed route of the proposal, stating the time for making objections. Relevant local planning authorities must also be served with notice of the proposal. Where objections are received, objectors must be given a hearing. This may take the form of a public inquiry where the objection is made by a local planning authority, though the minister has a discretion to enable the matter to be dealt with by way of written representation. After considering the report of the person who heard objectors, the minister makes his decision. If he refuses the application he must give the applicant a written statement of his reasons. Under the PA 1962, s 5 upon granting authorisation the minister may direct that planning permission is deemed to be granted for any work of development involved, subject to such conditions as he may lawfully impose. The procedure for inquiries is contained in the Pipe-lines (Inquiries Procedure) Rules SI 1995/1239 and follows the by now familiar modern pattern enabling the holding of pre-inquiry meetings, the timetabling of the inquiry service of witness statements, proofs of evidence, appointment of assessors, appearances and procedures at the inquiry, etc.

The statutory scheme only applies to 'cross country' pipelines, that is, *generally* under the PA 1962, s 66(1), a pipeline whose intended length will exceed ten miles. Other pipelines, being *generally* designated 'local', fall within development control powers of local planning authorities. In formulating pipeline proposals and in ministerial consideration of such proposals, regard must be had to the effect they will have on natural beauty, flora, fauna, geological and physiographical features of special interest and historic buildings and objects. The minister must also consider the need to protect water against pollution from pipelines. A person executing pipeline works in agricultural land is under an obligation to secure, so far as practicable, that, on completion of the works, the land is restored so as to be fit for that use to which it was put immediately before the works began, see PA 1962, ss 43, 44 and 45. the PA 1962 also does not apply to pipes and associated works for waste collection purposes, see the Environmental Protection Act 1990, s 45.

Compulsory purchase powers in connection with pipeline construction are conferred by PA 1962, s 11, alternatively compulsory acquisition of rights over land for construction purposes is allowed by PA 1962, s 12. These powers are subject to ministerial authorisation. Under PA 1962, s 13 the minister may impose conditions on a compulsory rights *order*, and compensation in respect of such orders may be payable under PA 1962, s 14. Even though there is now a network of oil and gas pipelines nationwide this legislation seems to have been generally uncontroversial in practice, despite the fact that pipelines run through many scenic areas.

H CONTROLS OVER HAZARDOUS DEVELOPMENTS AND INSTALLATIONS ON LAND, AND MAJOR INDUSTRIAL HAZARD SITES, ETC

With regard to developments on land involving hazardous substances special regimes are needed. Planning law exists to control development on land, but not necessarily specific activities taking place after development. Nor is planning law an obviously appropriate medium for dealing with health and safety issues, for it has to deal with other matters such as social and economic factors such as the need to attract or preserve jobs, as well as safety matters in relation to a proposed development. Accordingly a dual system of control over hazardous developments has grown up with planning law running in parallel with, and sometimes connected to, various health and safety and other environmental controls.

Major accident hazards

For many years control here existed under the Control of Industrial Major Accident Hazards Regulations ('CIMAH'), which were made to comply with the 'Seveso' Directive, 82/501 on the control of major chemical accidents. In 1996 the 'Seveso II' Directive (92/82) was adopted and so new regulations were needed. These are the

Control of Major Accident Hazards Regulations ('COMAH') SI 1999/743.
Under Seveso II there are two principal aims:
- to prevent major accidents arising from particular industrial activities;
- to limit the consequences of any such accident for humans and for the environment.

The 1999 regulations therefore have a wider extent than their CIMAH predecessors, applying to 'establishments' at which 'dangerous substances' are used or stored where these substances reach or exceed specified threshold levels. No distinction exists between processing and storing the substances. The operators of relevant establishments are required to identify major accident hazards and to implement preventive measures and accident limitation measures, and there should be for this purpose a major accident prevention policy (MAPP) for the relevant establishments, with, inter alia, a high level of environmental protection. For these purposes under the directive an 'establishment' is the 'whole area under the control of an operator where dangerous substances are present in one or more installation, including common or related infrastructures or activities'. A 'dangerous substance' is a substance, mixture or preparation listed in the directive Annex 1, Part 1 and fulfilling certain listed criteria, and present on site as a raw material, product, by-product, residue, or as a substance which it is reasonable to assume will be generated should there be an accident. A 'major accident' is 'an occurrence such as a major emission, fire or explosion resulting from uncontrolled developments in the course of the operation of any [relevant] establishment ... and leading to serious danger to human health and/or the environment, immediate or delayed, inside or outside the establishment, and involving one or more dangerous substances'. Under the regulations relevant substances are listed in Schedule 1, and there are 63 substances named individually or generically, from ammonium nitrate through to sulphur trioxide. There are in addition further generic classifications of substances and preparations not specifically listed but which have the quality of being very toxic, toxic, oxidising, explosive, flammable, highly flammable, extremely flammable or dangerous for the environment, to which control applies where they are held in particular specified quantities. The regulations (reg 2) further define relevant 'establishments' as the whole area under the control of the operator where dangerous substances are present in one or more 'installations', which are themselves defined as units in which the substances are present or where they are intended to be produced, used, handled or stored, including, equipment, structures, pipework, machinery, tools, ancillary railway sidings, docks and quays, jetties and warehouses.

Under the regulations the HSE and the Environment Agency are the competent authority for England and Wales. However, the prime duty (1999 regulations, reg 4) lies on the operators of relevant establishments to take the necessary preventive measures with regard to accidents and damage limitation measures where an accident does occur. To do this such operators must (under reg 5 and Schedule 2), prepare the major accident hazard policy document (MAPP). In addition operators must send specified information and regular safety reports to the competent authority, and must review and revise it in specified circumstances. The specified information to be supplied to the competent authority *includes* statements on: features of the landscape that might give rise to an accident, eg flooding, and environmental features whose presence might make an accident's consequences more severe – eg the presence of an SSSI, or where a high-quality water source or aquifer is near at hand. Information on local land uses should also be supplied. The safety report must include:
- an identification of all major hazards, and the potential consequences of potential accidents, whether caused by internal or external events, with particular regard to the extent in time and area of an accident, and its severity;
- provision of maps of local land uses and sensitive environmental areas in the locality;
- a description of the environment and surroundings of the establishment, including

areas where an accident may occur, at a level of detail that is proportionate to the hazard in question, ie where a resource of high environmental value could be under threat a higher degree of detail will be required;

- evidence that the exotoxicology of substances that might be released in an accident has been identified, including the synergetic or additive effects of releases;
- a description of the protective and interventionist measures proposed to limit the consequences of an accident, eg measures to limit the exposure of relevant environmental resources to during and following an accident;
- provision of post-accident mitigation proposals including those designed to aid environmental recovery.

Such reports have to be reviewed whenever circumstances change in important ways – including environmental changes. The competent authority is empowered to ask for information additional to that which is initially supplied, see generally also the 1999 regulations, reg 8.

Regulation 9 and Sch 5 further require the preparation of on-site and off-site emergency plans whose purpose is to contain and control incidents with a view to minimising their effects, so as to limit damage to humans, to the environment and to property. Such plans must make provision for cleaning up the environment after an accident. The operator's task is to prepare the on-site plan, while the off-site plan is prepared by the local authority (see the 1999 regulations, reg 10), and to assist them in this task the operator is required to provide specified information to the authority, who may also under reg 13 charge the operator for the preparation of the off-site plan. 'Local authority' for this purpose generally means the district council in England and in Wales the county council or county borough council as the case may be. Under the 1999 Regulations, regs 11 and 12 these emergency plans have to be reviewed, tested and implemented. In addition operators have to make certain information available to specified persons and to the general public at particular times, ie persons who are likely to be in the area who are likely to be affected by a major accident at the establishment. Such people must be supplied with information about the safety measures at the establishment, and what they should do should a major accident occur. The information must include details of the dangerous substances at the establishment that would give rise to an accident, and their principal dangerous characteristics. General information on the nature of the major accident hazards must also be given, including their potential effects on local populations and the environment. Furthermore details of the on-site emergency plan must be supplied, and references to the off-site plan also: see the 1999 regulations, reg 14 and Sch 6.

Should a major accident occur the site operator in addition to implementing the emergency plan has to inform the competent authority and has to supply them with information, including information needed to assess environmental effects and to enable alleviation of medium- and long-term effects. In certain cases falling within the 1999 Regulations, Sch 7 the competent authority is under a duty to report matters to the Commission of the EC. Such accidents are those which, inter alia, involve death or the rendering uninhabitable of dwellings or the evacuation of people from the area for a specified period of time, or where particular environmental damage is caused such as significant or long-term damage to specified areas of freshwater and marine habitats, or where trans-boundary effects arise.

Duties of the competent authority

The 1999 Regulations, Part 6 contains the duties of the competent authority. These include:

- receiving safety reports from operators and examining them;
- to prohibit the operation or bringing into operation of any establishment or installation where the preventive and mitigatory measures taken by the operator are seriously deficient;
- to prohibit the operation of an establishment, etc where the operator fails to submit any of the notifications, reports or other classes of information requirement under the regulations (such prohibitory action requires the prior issue of a notice giving reasons for the action and specifying the date when it is to come into effect, and it may further specify measures which, if taken, would lead to the withdrawal of the notice – an appeal against such action may be mounted under the Health & Safety at Work Act 1974, s 24);
- to inspect relevant establishments according to a regular programme, generally involving an on-site inspection every 12 months, such inspections lead to reports and, where needed, action to be pursued with the operator;
- to receive major accident reports from operators and to ensure that urgent, medium and long-term measures needed in consequence are taken, including analysing the accident and its causes and taking action to ensure that the operator takes any necessary remedial measures, and making recommendations as to future preventive measures;
- to enforce the legislation, including issuing codes of practice and prosecuting offences which fall to be dealt with under the Health & Safety at Work Act 1974, ss 23–32;
- to receive fees payable by operators in respect of the discharge of the functions of the competitive authority.

Planning and hazardous substance controls

With the implementation of the Planning (Hazardous Substances) Act 1990) (PHSA 1990) a further link in the chain of hazardous activity controls was forged. The powers exist to meet a deficiency in planning control, namely that a hazardous use can commence on land and not necessarily constitute development so that no planning permission is required.

The Act commences by defining 'hazardous substances authorities' (HSA) see ss 1 and 3. These are: in Greater London, London borough councils; elsewhere, district councils (in Wales, the county borough council as the case may be), save that in shire counties the county council is the HSA in respect of land subject to mineral working or waste deposition. Certain other bodies may have HSA functions, eg the Broads Authority, Urban Development Corporations, Urban Regeneration Agencies and Housing Action Trusts.

The PHSA 1990 (as amended), lays down the basic requirement that the presence of a hazardous substance (above a specified quantity for the substance in question) on, over or under land requires the consent of the HSA. Regulations under PHSA 1990, s 5 specify what are 'hazardous substances'. The Planning (Control of Major Accident Hazards) Regulations SI 1999/981 amending SI 1992/656 lay down the material, and the 'controlled' quantities of such material, subject to control. The list basically mirrors that found in the COMAH regulations above. The presence of a hazardous substance will require consent (see below) where it is present on, over or under land in a quantity equal to or greater than the 'controlled quantity' for the material in question. This is calculated by aggregating the quantity of the substance in question on, over or under the land with that on, etc, certain other land or structures which together from 'the control zone' – effectively land controlled by the same person and which, in all the circumstances, forms together a single establishment. The temporary presence on land of a hazardous substance is not, however, to be taken into account while it is being transported from one place to another, unless it is unloaded, or it is on, over or under land, where there is or ought to be a hazardous substances consent. There are further exemptions in SI 1992/656 as amended by SI 1999/981 inter alia in respect of hazardous materials in certain pipelines, or which have been off loaded from vessels in certain specified emergencies – in this latter case for 14 days only – or where the material is at a waste land fill site, or where the material falls within the controls over nuclear sites under the Nuclear Installations Act 1965.

A hazardous substance consent (HSCo) may be *granted* on an application, or *deemed to exist* under PHSA 1990, ss 11 and 12 (see below), but in any case enures for the benefit of the land in question: see s 6. PHSA 1990, s 7 lays down a framework for applications for HSCos, and regulations (SI 1999/981 amending SI 1992/656) make provision for the way in which applications are to be made, information is to be supplied and publicity undertaken, and time limits for consideration of applications. 21 days' local press notice and site notice publicity for applications must be given. Provision is made under PHSA 1990, s 10 for consultation to take place on applications and these are with the Health and Safety Executive and other prescribed persons such as other relevant environmental regulation and protection agencies etc eg the Environment Agency and, in relation to land of special scientific interest or of particular natural sensitivity, English Nature or, in Wales, the Countryside Council for Wales.

PHSA 1990, s 9 empowers HSAs to decide consent applications conditionally or unconditionally or to refuse them. In coming to a decision a HSA must take into account only material considerations, especially: current and contemplated uses of the land in question; the way in which land in the vicinity is, or is likely to be, used; planning permissions granted for land in the vicinity; development plans, advice given by the HSE, etc, in consultations. The procedure is clearly derived from planning law, and thus decisions have, normally, to be made within eight weeks of applications, and where refused, rights of appeal exist, see below, while reasons must be given for refusals or any conditions imposed, see ss 9–11.

Where an application relates to more than one hazardous substance, PHSA 1990, s 9(3) allows different determinations to be made in relation to each, while s 9(4) requires that where consent is given it must contain a description of the land in question, the hazardous substance(s) and a maximum quantity to be on site in respect of each substance.

There are no specific requirements that an applicant should be a 'fit and proper person' but an applicant's history of abuse of hazardous substances would presumably justify a refusal, for the PHSA 1990 though a 'planning statute' is concerned with uses of land in a sense apparently wider than land use matters under the TCPA 1990. HSE statements on consultation would be relevant here also. What could be a little more problematic is whether an applicant has to have *sufficient experience* to handle a particular substance. It is, however, worthy of note that PHSA 1990, s 29 provides that *nothing* in any HSCo is to require or allow anything to be done in contravention of 'relevant statutory provisions', ie the Health and Safety at Work etc Act 1974 and health and safety regulations.

Conditional consent

Consents may be granted subject to conditions, and this power is supplemented by PHSA 1990, s 10 which allows grants to be conditional on the commencement or partial or complete execution of development on the land in question under a grant of planning permission. Further conditions may relate to: how and where relevant hazardous substances are to be kept or used; the times at which substances may be present; the permanent removal of substances at the end of specified periods; but in these cases such conditions can only be imposed on the advice of the HSE.

Reference has been made to deemed consents for hazardous substances; PHSA 1990, ss 11 and 12 relate to such consents. A HSCo is, under PHSA 1990, s 11, a matter of right where a hazardous substance was present on, over or under land at any time within the 12 months preceding the 'relevant date', ie 1 June 1992. If a valid claim to such a consent is made, it is deemed to be granted, and the relevant HSA need only take action in cases where they consider the claim is not validly made. Such consents are subject, however, to conditions restricting the quantities of hazardous substances to 'the established quantity'. This latter figure is: where before commencement there was a notification under SI 1982/1357, the quantity notified or last notified before commencement, *or* a quantity equal to twice the quantity so notified or last notified before the start of the period of 12 months before commencement, whichever is the greater. Where no such notification was required the established quantity is that which exceeds by 50% the maximum quantity which was present on, over or under the land at any one time within the period of 12 months before commencement. Further conditions are prescribed by the regulations, and these relate to issues of storage temperatures and pressures. Claims for deemed consent had to be made within the period of six months following commencement.

Further deemed consents may exist under the PHSA 1990, s 12. Where the authorisation of a government department is required under a statute in respect of development to be carried out by a local authority or a statutory undertaker and that development would involve the presence of a hazardous substance in such a way as to necessitate a consent, on the grant of authorisation consent may also be directed to be deemed granted, though conditions may be imposed, and prior consultation must take place with the Health and Safety Commission (HSC). A similar provision, PHSA 1990, s 12(2), applies to consents given under s 36 of the Electricity Act 1989.

Variation and revocation of consents

Conditions imposed on consents may be, in effect, lifted or varied under PHSA 1990, s 13 in whole or in part, or by the substitution of other conditions. Alternatively the initial conditions may be allowed to stand. This is brought about by means of an application for consent without the initial condition(s) which the HSA must then consider. Normally it will be the consent holder who applies, but it appears that a third party may make the application. PHSA 1990, s 14(1) grants to authorities a *general* power by order to revoke or modify a HSCo where, on consideration of material circumstances, they consider it expedient so to act. In *particular* under PHSA 1990, s 14(2) they may revoke or modify consents where there has been a material change of use of the relevant land, or where planning permission has been granted for development involving such a material change and implementation of the permission has begun, or where the HSCo relates only to one substance and that substance has not for at least five years been present in controlled quantities on, over or under the land, or, in the case of a consent for many substances, none of them has been present for five years. Any order made, however, must specify the grounds on which it is made. However, orders under PHSA 1990, s 14 do not, under s 15, take effect unless ministerially confirmed, and the Secretary of State has a wide discretion in relation to such matters. Thus to revoke a consent the HSA must submit their order to the Secretary of State and must serve notice of the order on owners of the relevant land, persons having control over relevant land and any other persons likely to be affected by the order, and such persons must be given notice of their right to be heard by a ministerially appointed person. After confirmation of the order copies of it must be served on owners and controllers of relevant land and other affected persons. Compensation will then be payable under PHSA 1990, s 16 in respect of orders made under s 14(1), ie the *general* power of revocation, etc. *Any* person who has suffered damage in consequence of the order by virtue of depreciation of the value of his interest in the land, or by disturbance of his enjoyment of the land is entitled to compensation which is calculated according to the principles of the TCPA 1990, ss 117 and 118.

Revocation, appeals and enforcement

The PHSA 1990, s 17 provides for the automatic revocation of consents where there is a change of the person in control of *part* of relevant land, save where a previous application for continuation of the consent is made. Note the revocation only occurs on a *partial* change of control, though the revocation will extend to the *whole* consent. The provision, it appears, is directed towards preventing the piecemeal disposal of sites having HSCos. Where in such a case of partial disposition a continuation application is made, the HSA may under PHSA 1990, s 18 modify the consent as they consider appropriate or may revoke it, and in coming to a decision they must consider all relevant factors, but in particular they shall consider the current and contemplated use of the land, the use of neighbouring land, any planning permissions granted on neighbouring land, the provisions of the development plan and any advice received on consultation with the HSE consequent on regulations made under PHSA 1990, s 17(2). A fixed period is prescribed within which continuation applications must be determined, otherwise the general rule is that they are deemed granted. PHSA 1990, s 19 further provides that where on a s 17 continuation application, modification or revocation of the HSCo takes place compensation will be payable to the person in control of all the land before the application was made.

The Secretary of State has 'call in' powers with regard to the consent or continuation applications, see PHSA 1990, s 20, though use of this power is likely to be rare. Under PHSA 1990, s 21 there are powers to hear appeals against refusals of consents or continuation applications, and similarly in respect of non-determined applications and conditions imposed on consents. There is a wide discretion in relation to such matters, though the parties must be given an opportunity of being heard. The procedure on appeal is contained in the PHSA 1990, Schedule, and in regulations made under s 21(3), so, for example, a public local inquiry may, and normally will, take the place of a hearing. Where a person is aggrieved by a decision of the Secretary of State under PHSA 1990, ss 20 and 21, a further appeal on a point of law only may be made within six weeks of the decision in question being made, otherwise the validity of such decisions cannot be questioned: see PHSA 1990, s 22.

The normal procedure is for the Secretary of State to make the decision on appeal having received advice from the inspector who heard the appeal. The appeal will be conducted in accordance with the spirit of the Inquiries Procedure Rules.

Contravention of hazardous substances control by virtue of the presence of a quantity of a hazardous substance when there is no consent or above consent limits, or as a consequence of a breach of consent conditions is an offence on the part of 'the appropriate person'. Such a person can be a person who *knowingly* causes a substance to be on (etc) the land, or one who *allows* it to be present, or the person in control of the land: see PHSA 1990, s 23. It is provided by PHSA 1990, s 23(5) that it is a defence to prove one took all reasonable precautions and exercised all due diligence to avoid committing the offence, *or* that the offence could be avoided only by taking action amounting to a breach of statutory duty. Other defences effectively amounting to showing 'no knowledge' are also available. In determining fine levels for offences committed under PHSA 1990, s 23(4A), financial benefits accruing to the accused in consequence of the offence are to be taken into account.

PHSA 1990, s 24 empowers HSAs who consider there is or has been a contravention of hazardous substance control to issue notices specifying the alleged contravention and requiring specified remedial action. Copies of such 'hazardous substance contravention notices' must be served on the owner of relevant land, on the person in control of the land, and on such other persons as may be prescribed. Such a notice must also specify a date, at least 28 days after date of service, on which it will take effect and the time periods for the taking of requisite steps. One requisite step may be the removal of the hazardous substance in question, and in such a case a direction may also be given that any HSCo for the substance in question shall, at the end of a specified period, cease to have effect. The terms of such contravention notices may be waived or relaxed under PHSA 1990, s 24A. Note that such enforcement action may not take place: where the Secretary of State has issued a temporary exemption direction under PHSA 1990, s 27 (see below); in respect of Crown Land, s 31; where contravention of control can only be avoided by acting in breach of statutory duty, s 24(3), and nothing in a contravention notice may allow or require anything in contravention of health and safety requirements under the HSWA 1974, s 29.

There are a number of miscellaneous provisions of interest. PHSA 1990, s 26A, inserted by the Environmental Protection Act 1990, provides for regulations to be made concerning the charging of fees for consent applications, while s 26AA allows HSAs to seek injunctive relief to restrain actual or apprehended breaches of control, irrespective of the use of other powers of enforcement. PHSA 1990, s 27 empowers the Secretary of State on a temporary basis (*generally* three months at a time) to exempt specified contraventions from criminal liability where he considers either that the community is, or is likely to be, deprived of an essential service or commodity, *or* that there is or is likely to be a shortage of such a service or commodity affecting the community, *and* that the presence of a specified hazardous substance is necessary for the effective provision of the service or commodity.

The PHSA 1990, s 28 imposes obligations on HSAs to maintain public registers containing prescribed information on applications, consents, deemed consents, revocations, modifications, and directions issued under s 27. PHSA 1990, s 29 as already stated provides that no HSCo is to require or allow anything to be done in contravention of the Health and Safety at Work etc Act 1974, and avoids any consent which offends this prohibition, thus securing the primacy of that legislation and the leading role of the health and safety authorities. PHSA 1990, s 30 applies the provisions of the Act generally to any consents needed by HSAs themselves while s 31 applies the Act to land where there is *a* Crown interest but *only* in relation to other interests in that land held otherwise than by or on behalf of the Crown. The Crown itself is not subject to control under the Act, though PHSA 1990, s 32 empowers the Crown to apply for HSCos so as to allow its land to have the benefit of consent for disposal purposes.

Finally, PHSA 1990, s 36–36B should be noted. Section 36 allows any person authorised in writing by the Secretary of State or a HSA to enter any land at any reasonable time to survey it (including power to search and bore to check subsoil) in connection with any application for a HSCo, or any proposal to issue a contravention notice. Furthermore such duly authorised person may enter any land at reasonable hours to ascertain whether any offence under the Act has been committed. Where a contravention notice has been issued similar rights of entry exist with regard to checking whether there has been compliance. PHSA 1990, s 36A empowers justices to issue warrants to allow any person duly authorised in writing by a HSA to enter land for s 36 purposes, while it is an offence under s 36B to obstruct such a right of entry.

Further reading

ROADS
Bryant, B, *Twyford Down: Roads, Campaigning & Environmental Law* (1996) E & F
    N Spon.
Hall, P, *Great Planning Disasters* (1980) Penguin, chapter 3.
Joseph, S, 'Traffic Growth: The Problems and the Solutions' in Churchill, Gibson and
    Warren, *Law, Policy and the Environment* (1991) Blackwell.
McAuslan, P, *Land Law and Planning* (1975) Wiedenfeld and Nicolson, chapter 2.
Plowden, S, *Towns against Traffic* (1972) Andrew Deutsch.

AIRPORTS
Eyre, G, *The Airport Inquiries 1981–1983* (1984) DOE.
Hall, P, *Great Planning Disasters* (1980) Penguin, chapter 2.

POWER STATIONS
Breach, I, *Windscale Fallout* (1978) Penguin.
Cameron, P, Hancher, L, and Kuhn, W, *Nuclear Energy Law After Chernobyl* (1988)
    Graham and Trotman.
Ince, M, *Sizewell Report* (1984) Pluto Press.
O'Riordan, T, Kemp, R, and Purdue, HM, *Sizewell B, An Anatomy of an Enquiry* (1988)
    MacMillan.

ARTICLES
Hart, G, 'The value of the Inquiries System' 1997 JPEL Occasional Papers 8.
Price, A, 'Pipelines and the Public' (1989) 40 Mineral Planning 8.
Purdue, M, and Kemp, R, 'A Case for Funding Objectors at Public Inquiries?' [1985]
    JPL 675.
Purdue, M, Kemp, R, and O'Riordan, T, 'The Layfield Report on the Sizewell B Inquiry'
    [1987] Public Law 162.
Tromans, S, 'Roads to Prosperity or Roads to Ruin' (1991) 3 Journal of Environmental
    Law 1.

OFFICIAL REPORTS
'Policy for Roads in England': 1987 Cm 125, HMSO.
'The Cost of Decommissioning Nuclear Facilities' (1993) National Audit Office HMSO.
'Runway Capacity to Serve the South East' (1993) Department of Transport.
Department of Transport: 'Environmental Factors in Road Planning and Design' (1994)
    National Audit Office, HMSO.
Royal Commission on Environmental Pollution, 18th Report: 'Transport and the
    Environment' (1994) Cm 2674, HMSO.
Standing Advisory Committee on Trunk Road Assessment: 'Trunk Roads and The
    Generation of Traffic' (1994) HMSO.
House of Commons Transport Committee, 3rd Report, Session 1994/95: 'Urban Road
    Pricing' (1995) HMSO.
'A New Deal for Transport: Better for Everyone' : 1998 Cm 3950, HMSO.
'Guidance on the Interpretation of Major Accident to the Environment for the purposes
    of the COMAH Regulations': 1999, DETR.

Chapter 12

Genetic modification technology and the environment

INTRODUCTION

The regulatory and policy issues surrounding the cultivation of genetically modified crops is a relatively new facet of environmental law, although the subject of a report from the Royal Commission on Environmental Pollution as long ago as 1989.[1] Despite the recency with which genetic modification has stimulated nationwide controversy, the debates provoked by this new technology resonate strongly with issues which have pervaded environmental law since its inception. Who should bear the brunt of liability for the foreseen and unforeseeable damage caused by genetic modification ('polluter pays')? What balance should be struck between pursuing the promises of this technology and awaiting further information regarding the risks to health and environment ('precautionary principle')? How much should unsubstantiated public concern be allowed to influence regulatory policy ('public participation')?

A NEWFANGLED OR 'OLD HAT'?

Genetic modification describes the new technology of deliberately altering the characteristics of an organism by inserting genes from another organism. It is a misconception that cloning experiments such as those which resulted in 'Dolly the sheep' involve genetic modification. In fact, no gene was altered or inserted into Dolly and the process therefore falls outside the genetic modification regulations.[2] For the purposes of the Environmental Protection Act (EPA) 1990, Part VI an organism is 'genetically modified' if:

'any of the genes or other genetic material in the organism (a) have been modified by means of an artificial technique prescribed in regulations by the Secretary of State; or (b) are inherited or otherwise derived, through any number of replications, from genes or other genetic material which were so modified.'[3]

1   Royal Commission on Environmental Pollution, *The Release of Genetically Engineered Organisms into the Environment* (Cm 720, 1989).
2   House of Lords Select Committee on the European Community, Second Report, *EC Regulation of Genetic Modification in Agriculture* (1998-99) at n 3.
3   EPA 1990, s 106(4). GMOs created by mutagenesis, cell of protoplast fusion or cloning are excluded from the regime.

Clearly, such a definition includes not only those organisms modified in the laboratory, but also their many potential 'descendants.'

Biotechnology is not a recent phenomenon and can be traced back to fermentation and cheese-making processes developed by the Egyptians over four thousand years ago.[4] Moreover, supporters of genetic modification technology have been heard to argue that genetic modification ('GM') is not a 'new' development, but has been practised relatively uncontroversially for hundreds of years in the form of selective breeding, the products of which include prize-winning roses and pedigree pooches. The important distinction, however, between selective breeding practices and GM technology is that natural barriers, which would normally prevent gene transfer between unrelated species, no longer confine the possibilities. Now animal can be spliced with fruit, a process which is arguably more than a continuation of selective breeding. 'Tomatoes can be mated with oak trees, fish with asses, butterflies with worms [and] orchids with snakes.'[5] Significantly, the EPA 1990 makes a distinction between genetic modification and selective breeding by excluding 'techniques which involve no more than, or no more than the assistance of, naturally occurring processes or reproduction (including selective breeding techniques or *in vitro* fertilisation).'[6] Similarly, the (now superseded) Deliberate Release Directive 90/220 defined a genetically modified organism as one which is altered in a way that 'does not occur naturally by mating and/or natural recombination.'[7] The Nuffield Council's Report, 'GM Crops: The Ethical and Social Issues,'[8] prefers however not to focus on the distinctions between selective breeding and genetic modification, which: 'differ in the methods used and the extent and speed of the changes that can be produced. But, to date, they do not differ fundamentally in their broad objectives.'[9]

The United States Supreme Court case of *Diamond v Chakrabarty*[10] is widely regarded by some as creating the legal conditions which enabled genetic modification to reach its present heights. Chakrabarty was a microbiologist who launched a legal challenge to the Patent and Trademark Office (PTO) decision to refuse a patent for his genetically modified bacteria. The PTO's refusal was on the grounds that living things were unpatentable. There were two strong arguments against plants and other living organisms from being patented: (i) the belief that they were products of nature for the purposes of patent law; and (ii) that they were not thought to be amenable to being given the 'written description' requirement of patent law. The Supreme Court ruled by a slim majority of 5:4 that living things were patentable. The relevant distinction for the purposes of patent law was whether the subject matter was a 'product of human ingenuity' in which case it was patentable, or 'nature's handiwork' and therefore unpatentable.[11] So, whilst a new mineral or a new plant found in the wild could not be the subject of a patent, a 'new bacterium with markedly different characteristics from any found in nature' could. The dissenting judgment preferred to leave its resolution to Congress which was better suited to the weighing of public policy arguments. The

4   House of Lords Select Committee on the European Community, Second Report, 1998–99, n 1. at para 7.
5   N Batalion, '50 Harmful Effects of Genetically Modified Foods' (Oneonta, Americans for Safe Food, 2000).
6   EPA 1990, s 106(5).
7   Directive 90/220, Art 2.
8   Nuffield Council on Bioethics *GM Crops: The Ethical and Social Issues* (1999, London).
9   *Nuffield Council on Bioethics* at p 122.
10   Supreme Court, 447 US 303 (1980).
11   *Funk Brothers Seed Co v Kalo Innoculant Co* 333 US 127 (1948).

majority decision however meant that with legal safeguards in place, the commercial exploitation of biotechnology could gather speed.[12]

B ARGUMENTS FOR AND AGAINST GM TECHNOLOGIES

Views on the benefits offered by genetically modified organisms (GMOs), and the extent to which those benefits might be cancelled out by attendant risks to human health and the environment, are polarised. At one extreme, the pro-GM camp, including, predictably, the immensely powerful biotech industries, focuses on the infinite potential applications for such revolutionary techniques. Emphasis is laid on the costs and energy savings that can be reaped by the agricultural sector and the flavour, aesthetic and nutritional enhancements to be enjoyed by their consumers. Amongst the more captivating innovations which GM technology has to offer are apples which protect against tooth decay, rice crops with increased vitamin 'A' to combat sight problems in the developing world, fruit and vegetables with increased shelf life, insecticide and herbicide resistant crops, bouncier bread, tomatoes which fight cancer and calorie-free chocolate. Supporters of GM crops also raise concerns that reluctance to foster GMO technologies will have a detrimental impact on domestic farming and biotech industries which will quickly become unable to compete with their counterparts in the less wary food culture of the United States. More important than all these claims, however, has been the assertion that GM technology holds the answer to famine and starvation. The promise of genetic modification is that it could be used to overcome the difficulties of poor arable land and drought. [13]

Opposers of GMO technologies argue that the temptation of the non-fattening chocolate eclair ought to be resisted for a variety of social, ethical and environmental reasons. In a surprising reversal of traditional political priorities, the force of concerns related to human health risks have been at the very least equalled by pressure arising out of environmental concerns. 'People-centred' objections have stressed consumers' rights to be fully informed about the food they eat and the possibility that within these new technologies may lie hidden risks to human health. An example of such a risk is said to be the possibility that genes which resist commonly prescribed antibiotics ('antibiotic resistant marker genes') will be passed to bacteria creating a wave of uncontrollable human epidemics.[14] The closest to proof of such risk has been the results of research by Arpad Pusztai which suggested that his laboratory rats' diet of genetically modified potatoes caused organ damage and damage to the rats' immune systems. (Although discredited by the Royal Society, the research was controversially published in the *Lancet* in 1999.)[15] Of further concern is the extent to which GM technology has the capacity to enslave agricultural producers to biotech companies. This latter concern derives from the development of the 'terminator technology', which involves a further genetic modification of a GM crop in order to prevent it from pollinating. Such a

---

12 The developments in patentability of genetically material is outside the scope of this chapter, but more detail can be found in, for example, T Hart & L Fazzani, *Intellectual Property Law* (1997, Macmillan) Basingstoke, WR Cornish, *Intellectual Property : Patents, Copyright, Trade Marks and Allied Rights* (1999, Sweet & Maxwell) London, or P J Groves, *Sourcebook on Intellectual PropertyLaw* (1997, Cavendish) London.

13 Although see the contradictory evidence in A Simms, *Selling Suicide* (2000, Christian Aid) London.

14 These GMOs are to be phased out under the new Deliberate Release Directive (2001/18/EC).

15 S W Ewen and A Puzstai, 'Effect of diets containing genetically modified potatoes expressing Galanthus Rivalis lectin on rat small intestine' *Lancet* (1999) 354:1353.

characteristic forces farmers to purchase new seed from biotech companies year after year, with a significant loss of autonomy in the farming community.

Environmental objections emphasise the lack of detailed knowledge as to the ecological impact of GM plants and argue that the precautionary principle should inform all GM policy and regulation. The main identified ecological risks include: herbicide resistant crops which facilitate the use of more powerful 'broad spectrum' weed killers, causing the obliteration of weeds now classified as endangered species. Such loss of plant life would impact on the survival of insects and the wildlife dependent on them as a food source, such as ladybirds and skylarks, with obvious knock-on effects for their main predators. There are also fears of 'genetic pollution' caused by GM crops cross-breeding with wild plant varieties. The possible outcome of GMOs crossed with wild plants may be that the original variety disappears and is replaced by a new virulent, unstoppable GM 'weed'. Cross-pollination from GM varieties also threatens the livelihood of organic farmers who may no longer be able to convince certification bodies that their crops are 'GM free'. Evidence suggests that no matter what the separation distance between GM crops and traditional crops, cross-pollination can never be ruled out as pollen can be carried long distances by the wind and by bees.[16]

Quite apart from these risk-based environmental and 'people-centred' arguments are the ethical objections to GM technology. The main thrust of these arguments is that genetic modification is 'unnatural', an unwarranted tampering with nature which ought to be avoided: 'for all the decline in formal religion, there remains a deep-rooted belief that we tinker with nature at our peril.'[17] It is these latter objections, which are not concerned with a premise of risk, which add to the complexity of regulating GMOs. Opinion is divided on the extent to which such public feeling should be allowed to influence government policy and regulation. In 1999, the Nuffield Council commented: 'In short, it is the deleterious consequences of our farming techniques to our environment and human health, not their "unnatural" character that should preoccupy us.'[18] In the same year, however, the House of Commons Select Committee on Science and Technology criticised the government's advisory system on GMOs on the grounds that no mechanism existed for incorporating such values into government policy.[19] A change at EU level in the detail of the new Deliberate Release Directive (see below) seems to reflect a shift in thinking on the relevance of such ethical arguments in policy development.

C REGULATION OF GMOS

On the issue of regulation, there are equally divided views. Those who focus on the unknown quantity of risks produced by GMO technology favour detailed, rigorous and precautionary regulation. Those who stand to profit financially from the exploitation of GMO technology argue that strict regulation is an undue restriction on competition and is damaging to the nation's economy. Ironically, it can be argued that strict regulation is in the interests of the biotech industries – for unless the regulatory framework is seen to be demanding and rigorous, advocates of the GMO technology will need to battle even harder to win over public opinion. A rigid legal framework on the other hand is likely to legitimise the regulated activity in the eyes of the public.

16   J Emberlin, *The Dispersal of Maize Pollen* (1999) Soil Association.
17   Nuffield Council on Bioethics *GM Crops: The Ethical and Social Issues*, (1999) Nuffield Council, para 1.7.
18   Nuffield Council on Bioethics, para 1.7.
19   House of Commons Select Committee on Science and Technology, First Report: *Scientific Advisory System – Genetically Modified Foods* (HC 286) (1998-99).

The regulation of GMOs raises issues of great complexity, some of which are unique to GMOs and cannot be easily compared with the control of more conventional emissions to the environment. Most perplexing of all is the fact that, once unleashed, GMO technology has the capacity for self-perpetuation in the environment. GMOs are living organisms and, unlike chemical discharges, their flow cannot be turned off by the flick of a switch. It is this capacity to replicate which, perhaps more than any other feature of GMO technology, justifies a precautionary approach to regulation.[20] EC regulation of GMOs falls largely under two headings: the Deliberate Release Directive (2001/18/EC)[21] and the Contained Use Directive (98/81/EC),[22] both directives being attempts to harmonise the law relating to GMOs across member states. EC intervention arises out of the specific concern that release of GMOs for either commercial or experimental purposes may result in their reproduction in the environment and their crossing national frontiers, the effects of which may be irreversible.

1 Contained use of GMOs[23]

A 'contained use' of GMOs refers to activities carried out in, for example, laboratories, industrial production plants or greenhouses. In 1999, *Gene Watch UK* conducted research into the contained use of genetically modified micro-organisms (GMMs) used to manufacture enzymes, food additives and drugs.[24] They concluded that the regulations facilitated the unmonitored release of GMMs from laboratories and factories in the UK as there was no legal requirement for all micro-organisms to be killed or *inactivated* before disposal. While the micro-organisms are usually given heat treatment before disposal, this does not necessarily kill all the micro-organisms. The risk is that the few which could survive for a few days outside their laboratory environment might be ingested by animals and be absorbed into the food chain or indeed replicate outside the confines of the laboratory. The Health and Safety Executive was criticised for practising only very limited monitoring of the containment of GMMs. The regime is largely responsive in nature, acting mainly on the basis of information submitted by industry rather than gathered by unannounced inspections. The limitations of a responsive regulatory system which relies largely on regulated organisations to be forthcoming is highlighted by the tale of a university laboratory which failed to notify the HSE of its research with a genetically modified version of HIV![25]

The arrangements for contained use of GMOs were revised by the new Contained Use Directive 98/81/EC which amends 90/219/EEC. The main driver behind the new directive was pressure from industry to deregulate 'contained use' of GMOs where the risks involved were low and to speed up the application process. The definition of contained use for the purposes of the directive is: '… any activity in which micro-organisms are genetically modified and for which specific containment measures are

20 J Hill, 'The Precautionary Principle and Release of GMOs to the Environment,' in T O'Riordan and J Cameron (eds) *Interpreting the Precautionary Principle* (1994) Cameron May, London, at 175.
21 Replacing Directive 90/220.
22 Replacing Directive 90/219.
23 The directives and regulations discussed in this section do not provide an exhaustive list of the provisions which deal with the contained use of GMOs. Reference should also be made to the Genetically Modified Organism (Risk Assessment) (Records and Exemptions) Regulations 1996 (SI 1996/1106) and EPA 1990 both of which concern the obligation of containment.
24 *Leaking from the Lab? The Contained Use of Genetically Modified Micro-organisms in the UK* (1999) Gene Watch UK.
25 *Leaking from the Lab? The Contained Use of Genetically Modified Micro-organisms in the UK* (1999) Gene Watch UK.

used to limit their contact with the general population and the environment.' The implementing regulations (the Genetically Modified Organisms (Contained Use) Regulations 2000[26]) replace the 1992 regulations and they cover not only genetically modified micro-organisms but also the contained use of GM plants and animals. These regulations therefore go further than the directive provisions, which only regulate contained use of plants or animals where their genetic modification poses an increased likelihood of damage to human health. The 1998 directive also removes the equation of containment with physical barriers. Under the 2000 regulations 'limiting' can be achieved by physical, biological or chemical barriers.[27] The UK's provisions under EPA 1990 did not require altering in this respect as the 'control' of GMOs is already defined as: 'contained by any system of physical, chemical or biological barriers or a combination of such barriers.'[28] According to the new regulations, activities with GMOs fall into one of four risk-dependent categories. All activities across all categories must be the subject of a risk assessment and notification to the HSE as to the premises where the activity is to take place. Where the activities fall within Class 1 or 2 (low risk), activities must first be approved by the HSE. Once such approval is given, subsequent activities within Class 1 or 2 at the same premises must be notified to the HSE, but the activities can commence as soon as an acknowledgement is received. There is no requirement of HSE approval. The users of the GMOs remain responsible for deciding which classification their use falls into. The HSE is under a duty to keep a register of notifications made under the regulations and to make this register accessible to the public. The enforcement provisions of the Health & Safety at Work Act 1974 are to be available for the enforcement of the regulations.

The regulations require that exposure of these GMOs to people and the environment is to be reduced to the lowest levels reasonably practicable.[29] Although the term 'reasonably' requires that exposure must be commensurate with risk it will also take into account the costs of preventing exposure. Unintended releases of significance, even within the confines of the approved premises, are to be notified to the HSE.

2 Deliberate release of GMOs: marketing and release of GMOs

Although imported foodstuffs can lawfully contain GM products, in 1998 the government announced a *de facto* moratorium on the cultivation of GM crops, meaning that they could not be grown commercially in the UK until spring 2000 (on the legality of the moratorium, see below in this chapter at 'H'). In November 1999, the agreement was extended until such time as the current trials of GM crops was completed in 2003 and the government was convinced that they presented no appreciable risk to the environment. Under the moratorium, Farm Scale Evaluations (FSEs), or crop trials as they are sometimes known, are the only form of permissible cultivation of genetically modified crops. This restriction of cultivation to FSEs is the cornerstone of the government's precautionary policy on GMOs. It is evidence from the FSEs which will assist the government in deciding whether to accept commercial growing of these crops in the future. These trial crops have been the focus of anti-GM protestors' attentions, with a number of sites being damaged or destroyed by activists (on which see chapter 7). The small-scale and short-term nature of FSEs (they are to end in harvest 2003) means that they cannot be hoped to disclose *all* the environmental and health risks posed by GM crops. Given the announcement in January 2002 that a further 50 trial sites are to be

26   SI 2000/2831.
27   Genetically Modified Organisms (Contained Use) Regulations 2000, reg 1.
28   EPA 1990, s 107(9).
29   Genetically Modified Organisms (Contained Use) Regulations 2000, reg 17(1).

introduced, it seems that the government is some way from being convinced as to the safety of these controversial crops.

The EPA 1990, Part VI establishes a regulatory regime for dealing with GMOs in the UK which will be subject to amendment by way of regulations implementing the new directive. The stated purpose of the EPA regime which represents the current regime is: 'preventing or minimising any damage to the environment which may arise from the escape or release from human control of GMOs'.[30] It therefore governs the movement and transfer of GMOs as opposed to their contained use in a laboratory or a greenhouse. Its provisions were a response to the Royal Commission on Environmental Pollution, Thirteenth Report, *The Release of Genetically Engineered Organisms into the Environment.*[31] The Commission concluded that although there were a number of statutes which could in principle be used to control release of GMOs, they made no mention of GMOs specifically (for example, the Health & Safety at Work Act 1974 was concerned solely with human health and safety and could not be used to regulate GMOs which only posed risks to the environment). The report recommended the implementation of a 'precautionary but realistic system of regulation.'

EPA controls of deliberate releases

The EPA regime covers genetically modified organisms in all forms excepting humans or human embryos.[32] The relevant provisions regulate what might be called the five 'controlled activities' with GMOs, namely the keeping, import, acquisition, marketing and release of such organisms. Where all these activities are implicated in this chapter, the term 'controlled activities' will be used. The provisions of EPA 1990 relating to GMOs were decided before even the old Deliberate Release Directive and so any adjustments required by the Directive have been achieved by way of regulations (see particularly, the Genetically Modified Organism (Deliberate Release) Regulations 1992[33]). EPA 1990, s 111 prohibits controlled activities with GMOs unless they are authorised by a consent granted by the Secretary of State. Whilst the meaning of 'marketing', 'acquisition' and 'import' are fairly uncomplicated, the meaning of 'release' should be explained. 'Release' is defined broadly to encompass active and passive release, that is, where a party deliberately causes or permits it to cease to be under his control or the control of any other person and to enter the environment' (s 107(10)). The term thus covers: 'everything from a few plants being put in a field as part of an experiment to tomatoes being sold in the supermarket.'[34] 'Marketing' includes the marketing of products consisting of or containing 'live' GMOs (eg a fruit containing seeds which, of course, have the potential to produce descendants).[35]

At the heart of these provisions are the general duties imposed on anyone keeping or proposing to import, acquire, release or market GMOs imposed by EPA 1990, s 109. These duties require 'all reasonable steps' to be taken to prevent damage to the environment and to identify the risks of such damage associated with such activities.[36] They come into play prior to the granting of a consent and therefore are designed to

---

30   EPA 1990, s 106(1).
31   1989, Cm 720.
32   EPA 1990, s 106(2).
33   SI 1992/3280 as amended by SI 1995/304 and SI 1997/332.
34   J Hill, 'The Precautionary Principle and Release of GMOs to the Environment,' in T O'Riordan and J Cameron (eds) *Interpreting the Precautionary Principle* (1994) Cameron May, London, p174.
35   EPA 1990, s 107(11).
36   EPA 1990, ss 109(2)-(4).

ensure that persons involved with GMOs fall under the regulatory regime as early as possible. It is an offence to breach the EPA 1990, s 109 duties which rest heavily on the requirement that steps be taken to prevent/identify risks of 'damage to the environment.' Given that the prevention of such damage is also stated as the overall aim of the regime in EPA 1990, s 106(1), it is important to understand the meaning of this phrase. The definition of 'damage to the environment' requires merely the presence of GMOs in the environment with the potential to cause harm to living organisms supported in the environment.[37] Proof of actual harm is not necessary – a feature which closely resembles the offences in water pollution and waste management regimes.[38] The inchoate nature of these offences is especially important in the regulation of GMOs, given the difficulty of controlling or tracking their movement in the environment. In requiring potential for harm, however, it is not clear what level of scientific certainty will be required to convince a court of such potentiality. 'Harm' is given the same extended meaning as in the rest of EPA as including 'offence' to a person's senses or damage to their property.[39]

In *R v Secretary of State for the Environment and Ministry of Agriculture Fisheries and Food, ex p Watson,*[40] the Court of Appeal was invited to rule on the issue of whether the activities authorised by a GMO release consent could only be performed by the consent holder, or whether such powers could be transferred to other persons/bodies. The Court of Appeal decided that, although the consent holder remained responsible for the authorised activities, the holder could delegate their powers to others. It seems somewhat of an anomaly that the powers (although not the obligations) under the consent should be so freely transferable given the height of concern over these organisms, and the risks which could flow from mismanagement of a GMO trial. Contrast the grant of a waste management licence[41] which hinges on the Environment Agency being satisfied of the licence holder's competence to handle waste.[42] Presuming the *Watson* judgment is a correct interpretation of the EPA provisions, it appears to have exposed a weakness in the regulation of GMOs whereby the suitability of the releaser of the GMOs is not under any scrutiny.

Once a consent has been granted, the Secretary of State may revoke or vary the conditions of that consent by notice to the consent holder.[43] No specific details are set out defining in which circumstances such power is exercisable, but it has been assumed by the Court of Appeal in *R v Secretary of State for the Environment and Ministry of Agriculture Fisheries and Food, ex p Watson*[44] that such power must be exercised for the stated purposes of EPA 1990, Part VI generally, that is, for the purpose of 'preventing or minimising damage to the environment'.[45] Parties who are required to obtain consents for their dealings with GMOs are automatically subject to monitoring and notification conditions implied into those consents by virtue of EPA 1990, s 112.

Consent conditions rarely require monitoring of GMOs for longer than three years, a fact which has been criticised for being short-sighted, as the possibility of GM plants evolving into superweeds has been estimated as taking up to 50 years.[46] Consent

37   EPA 1990, s 107(3).
38   See chapters 14 and 20.
39   EPA 1990, s 107(6).
40   [1999] Env LR 310. For another attempt to pre-empt the damage which might be caused by GM trials in the UK, see *Monsanto plc v Tilly* [2000] Env LR 313 discussed in chapter 7.
41   See chapter 14.
42   EPA 1990, s 74.
43   EPA 1990, s 111(10).
44   [1999] Env LR 310 discussed further below.
45   EPA 1990, s 106(1).
46   J Hill, 'The Precautionary Principle and Release of GMOs to the Environment,' in T O'Riordan and J Cameron (eds) *Interpreting the Precautionary Principle.* (1994) Cameron May, London, p 180.

holders must keep GMOs under control and use the 'best available technique not entailing excessive cost' to stay informed of any risks of damage to the environment posed by the activities authorised by the consent. Where any new information as to such risks comes to the consent holder's attention, the Secretary of State must be notified. Additionally, where the consent authorises the 'keeping' of GMOs or their release or marketing, the consent holder must also use the 'best available technology not entailing excessive cost' to prevent damage to the environment as a consequence of the authorised activities. [47]

Enforcement and publicity provisions

The Secretary of State may appoint inspectors to discharge the Secretary of State's functions under the Act. Such inspectors are armed with extensive powers including the prosecution of offences under the Act. They are also empowered to enter premises in which the inspector has reason to believe (objective test) GMOs are kept, or were being kept or from which GMOs have escaped or been released.[48] Having entered such premises, inspectors may exercise a host of statutory powers including the performance of tests and inspections as may be necessary, to take samples, to require the production of records required to be kept under the EPA 1990 and to cause any item which contains or once contained GMOs to be tested, dismantled or subjected to a process. Had the proceedings in *Watson*[49] resulted in the conviction of the consent holder for an offence under EPA 1990, Part VI, the court would have had the power to order the offence to be remedied (see EPA 1990, s 120). In the case of unlawful cultivation of GMOs which may cause damage to the environment, it is submitted that this power may enable the court to order the grower to destroy the crop in as safe a manner as possible.

EPA 1990, s 122 imposes a duty on the Secretary of State to maintain a publicly available register to include details of prohibition notices, applications for consents, consents granted, information furnished in pursuance of consent conditions or required under EPA 1990, s 108 and convictions for offences under Part VI of the Act. As always, the public interest in freedom of information is tempered by exceptions in the name of other competing public interests. Certain information is excluded from the register, namely that which in the Secretary of State's opinion would adversely affect national security,[50] that which might cause damage to the environment[51] or that which is commercially confidential and disclosure of which the individual or business to which it relates has not consented.[52] In order for information to be excluded from the register on this last ground of 'commercial confidentiality', the process of exclusion must be initiated by an application from the individual or business concerned (although the Secretary of State may alert the applicants to the potential for an application). The 'commercial confidentiality' exception cannot be used to exclude information as to the identity of the person furnishing the information, a description of the GMOs concerned and their location or the results of any risk assessments as to the activities which are the subject of the information. The protection of commercial confidentiality ceases after four years' exclusion from the register, after which time a fresh application as to its continued exclusion can be made.

---

47   EPA 1990, s 112(3)-(4).
48   EPA 1990, s 115.
49   [1999] Env LR 310.
50   EPA 1990, s 123(1).
51   EPA 1990, s 123(3).
52   EPA 1990, s 123.

EPA 1990, Part VI creates a myriad of regulatory offences in s 118 including: failing to conduct a risk assessment prior to the import, acquisition, release or marketing of GMOs, failing to keep records of such risk assessments, failing to comply with notices served or prohibition notices, conducting any of the controlled activities without a consent (unless the exemptions made by regulations under EPA 1990, s 111(7) apply) or otherwise than in accordance with the conditions of such a consent. In 1999, Monsanto were prosecuted for failing to provide adequate safety barriers to prevent their GM crops escaping into the environment. They were fined £17,000 with £6,150 costs a significant penalty given the absence of proven damage, although probably a 'drop in the ocean' for a company the size of Monsanto.[53]

Marketing GMOs in the EU: the Deliberate Release Directive

The marketing and deliberate release of GMOs is now subject to the provisions of the Deliberate Release Directive 2001/18/EC replacing the earlier Directive 90/220 of the same name.[54] The directive is based on the precautionary principle, and is designed to effect protective measures for the benefit of human health and the environment. Aspects of its precautionary emphasis include the fact that under the directive, risk assessment is to include long-term effects of GMOs before an approval will be granted. Further, product approvals will only be valid for ten years. Directive 2001/18/EC fine-tunes the consent scheme for the authorisation of marketing GMOs throughout the EU which was created by the earlier Directive. The new Directive's definition of GMOs includes genetically modified plants, micro-organisms and animals, the latter of which had previously been excluded from the old directive on the grounds that genetically modified livestock would generally be used in containment and would not be released into the environment.[55] Again, this change required no amendment of English law which only excludes humans and human embryos from its definition of GMOs.[56] 'Deliberate release' is defined in the Directive 2001/18/EC as 'any intentional introduction into the environment of a GMO or a combination of GMOs for which no specific containment measures are used to limit their contact with and to provide a high level of safety for the general population and the environment.' It includes 'placing on the market' but excludes carriage of GMOs by road, rail, sea or air. 'Placing on the market' is further defined as 'making available to third parties, whether in return for payment or free of charge.'

Both old and new directives set out the means by which a deliberate release is to be approved and identify two broad types of release: Part B releases (small scale research trials) and Part C releases (releases for commercial purposes). Consents for Part B releases are granted by the national competent authority. In England's case this is the Secretary of State for the Environment, Food and Rural Affairs (after consultation with the Advisory Committee on Releases to the Environment and if the application concerns food or animal feed, the Advisory Committee for Novel Foods and Processes). In Wales it is the National Assembly that exercises the powers of the Secretary of State.

The procedures for securing a Part C release authorising the product to be placed on the European market are more complex. Under the new Directive 2001/18/EC the 'competent authority' is to be notified of any proposed deliberate release and must

53   *The Independent* (1999) 18 February.
54   Implemented by the Genetically Modified Organisms (Deliberate Release) Regulations 1992, SI 1992/3280 and 1995, SI 1995/304.
55   House of Lords Select Committee on the European Community, Second Report, *EC Regulation of Genetic Modification in Agriculture* (1998-99) at para 3.
56   EPA 1990, s 106(2).

acknowledge receipt followed by a response in writing within 90 days. A proposal to market a GMO/product containing a GMO must be forwarded to the competent authority of the member state where it will be first marketed. In the UK's case, the competent authority is the Health and Safety Executive. The competent authority must forward the summary of the dossier to the competent authorities of other member states and the Commission. The aim here is to enable the differences in environment between member states to be taken into account in the risk appraisal process. If one member state objects to the application, the European Commission must consider the application and reach a decision by qualified majority voting. If either the Commission or a competent authority raises an objection, a decision is to be adopted within 120 days. Once a consent is granted via unanimous approval of member states or qualified majority vote of the Commission the consent is effective throughout all the member states. It is therefore possible for a GM crop to be marketed in the UK despite the UK's competent authority having objected to it – a fact which has implications for UK sovereignty regarding the food we eat. Notwithstanding the grant of an EU-wide marketing consent, individual member states can provisionally prohibit the use or sale of GMOs which are found to present a risk to health or the environment. In the case of such action the Commission and member states should be informed. One of the major changes in EC regulation of GMOs brought about by Directive 2001/18/EC, is that for the first time ethical considerations may be taken into account when deciding whether GMOs should be placed on the market. In addition to satisfying directive requirements for placing on the market, new crop varieties must comply with conditions of entry on the National List of Seeds or the European Common Catalogue.

Directive 2001/18/EC places an emphasis on public access to information, sharing of experience between member states and linking regulation with the Cartagena Protocol on Biodiversity. The public must also be provided with information on all releases by the competent authority. Under the provisions of the new Directive 2001/18/EC, member states must provide penalties where release or placing on the market is contrary to the directive, particularly when the breach is the result of negligence. Disappointment has been expressed that the Directive did not make use of the opportunity to protect organic farms from the risks of contamination from GM crops or to create a specific liability regime for damages caused by GMOs. At the time of writing, regulations implementing Directive 2001/18/EC are being drafted and are to be in force by 17 October 2002.

D GMOS IN FOOD AND FOOD LABELLING: 'FROM ETHICAL COFFEE TO ENVIRONMENTAL TEA'[57]

The labelling of products derived from GMOs is not unconnected with environmental issues. For consumers to be able to differentiate environmentally sound products from those which they might regard as 'on probation' because of their GM origins, all products derived from GMOs must be clearly labelled. This is not just an issue of pandering to the consumers' whim for product information, it is one of enabling consumers to make lifestyle choices which accord with their environmental and ethical beliefs. The potential power of the 'green pound' is perhaps one of the environmentalist lobby's best chances of influencing sustainable development, for if industry can be persuaded that increased profit lies in the pursuit of environmentally compatible products and processes, their production patterns will shift towards them.

---

57   House of Commons Environmental Audit Committee, 5th Report, *Inquiry into Genetically Modified Organisms and the Environment* (1998-99) HC 384.

The House of Commons Environmental Audit Committee[58] suggested that labelling might be extended to GM processes involving non-food products such as GM cotton, enabling consumers to avoid *all* GM goods. EU law requires only that foodstuffs derived from GM soya and maize are to be labelled (Council Regulations (EC) 1139/98[59]), but there are a number of loopholes which have been accused of excluding more products than they cover. Particular concerns were voiced over the difficulty of labelling soya and maize imported from the US because their producers do not segregate GM and non-GM crops, meaning that it is impossible for importers to accurately label their goods. The difficulty of labelling soya and soya products perversely has the greatest impact on vegetarian/vegan consumers, as soya is often used as a meat substitute. Yet, it is this sector of the population which is most likely to have ethical and/or environmental objections to GMOs.

The Regulation for Novel Foods and Novel Food Ingredients (EC 258/97) requires that all new foods, new ingredients or foods subjected to new processes comply with certain safety and environmental assessments and labelling requirements. 'Novel' in this context means those foods, processes or ingredients which have not been consumed in the EC before, and will therefore by definition often apply to genetically modified foodstuffs. These provisions establish a similar licensing procedure to that for the marketing and release of GMOs, but anyone intending to plant a new GM variety to be used in human food will need to obtain a consent under both regimes. The Novel Foods Regulations only require GM foods which are chemically distinct from their non-GM equivalents to be labelled. This does not satisfy those who believe consumers should be made aware of the fact of genetic modification.

Novel foods, ingredients and processes must not be marketed without approval of the competent authority (which in the UK was MAFF and is now the Advisory Committee on Novel Foods and Products, a committee of the Food Standards Agency (see below)). Regulation EC 258/97 requires that such novel food and ingredients:

1   are safe for the consumer when eaten in the foreseeable manner;
2   are not presented in a way which would mislead the consumer; and
3   do not differ from the food/ingredient they replace in such a way that their foreseeable consumption is nutritionally disadvantageous.

The Food Labelling (Amendment) Regulations 1999 (SI 1999/747) (implementing the amended EC Labelling Regulation (EC 1139/98)) now require that maize and soya-derived products be labelled for genetic modification. These regulations apply to loose food, pre-packed food, food cooked and sold on the same premises and food sold from catering establishments. Failure to comply with the regulations is a criminal offence. The exemptions from the labelling requirement include:

• food additives;
• food flavourings;
• food produced and labelled before 1 September 1998; and
• items packaged in small glass bottles or packaging with less than 10 cm² surface area.

Catering establishments are required to indicate on their menu that some of their dishes may include GM foods and state that more information is available from their staff. The regulations are enforced by Trading Standards Officers, although it is not clear how effective such enforcement can be given that officers are unlikely to be provided with the necessary equipment for testing the presence of GM material.

58   House of Commons Environmental Audit Committee, 5th Report, *Inquiry into Genetically Modified Organisms and the Environment* (1998-99) HC 384.
59   OJ L159 (3 June 1998), pp 4-7.

The 1997 Regulation (EC 258/97) was criticised for failing to state how foods should be labelled (for example, it was unclear whether the label *'may* contain genetically modified starch' would suffice) and have since been amended. This uncertainty caused variations in supermarket labelling, with some supermarkets over-labelling their products, representing that they contained GM soya on the suspicion that they might. The 1999 Regulations specify that the wording to be used should be: 'produced from genetically modified [soya or maize]'.

The regulation has since been further amended to extend to foods sold to mass caterers[60] and additives and flavourings containing genetically modified material which are *included in food or food ingredients.*[61] With regard to all the above, labelling requirements are only triggered by the presence of genetically modified or novel DNA or protein in food. There are limits to the labelling requirements; for example, where foodstuffs include parts of crops, which have been genetically modified but not including the genetically modified DNA itself, the labelling rules treat the substance as conventional food. Further, there is a 1% de minimis threshold for novel foods, ingredients and processes, but not as yet extended to the presence of additives and flavourings containing GM material. Where the 1% threshold applies, only food or ingredients containing 1% or more of genetically modified material need to be labelled.

Two additional Regulations proposed by the European Commission in July 2001 will address a number of the shortcomings noted in the labelling of GM foods. The first proposed regulation would establish arrangements for ensuring traceability of GM products. The aim of new rules on traceability would be to facilitate monitoring of GM products and possibly withdrawal of GM products from the market, should any evidence of an unforeseen hazard arise. These provisions would require information on the presence of GMOs placed on the market to be transmitted by industry through the commercial chain and for such information to be retained for five years. The second regulation concerns GM food and feed labelling and authorisation. Labelling requirements are to be extended to highly refined soya and maize oil, previously excluded from EU regulation. A further extension of the regulations will bring animal feed containing GMOs within the regulatory regime. Prior to these proposals, animal feed was not subjected to any GM labelling requirements. Where GM products are to be used for either food *or* feed, the new regulation requires that authorisation for both uses be obtained. This particular fortification of the regime was prompted by the controversy surrounding 'Starlink', a form of GM maize in the US which was approved only as GM animal feed but which found its way into food for human consumption.

Again, there are loopholes in the proposals. The usual 1% exemption applies, although operators wishing to avoid the labelling requirement on this ground must be prepared to demonstrate to the competent authority that they have taken steps to avoid the presence of GM material. Furthermore, the proposed regulations will not require labelling of food from animals fed on GM feed or food production with the help of a GM enzyme.

E RELEVANT BODIES IN THE REGULATION OF GMOS

The role of the Food Standards Agency

Genetically modified crops have provided a test case for the Food Standards Agency's (FSA) credentials in managing public concern. The FSA recently provoked adverse

60   EC Regulation (49/2000).
61   EC Regulation (50/2000).

comment from the National Consumer Council ('NCC') for its stance on the labelling of GM derivatives. Research by the NCC showed that 79% of those surveyed wanted meat produced from animals fed genetically modified feed to be labelled as such. When the European Commission proposed the two regulations discussed above to extend GM labelling to animal feed derivatives, the FSA refused to support these reforms.

If organic farmers were looking to the FSA to support their cause, they were to be disappointed. The FSA has been at the centre of a row over organic foods. The FSA denied that there was any scientific evidence that organic produce was 'nutritionally different' from non-organic foods.[62] Organic food is a curious choice of hobby horse for the FSA. It is somewhat ironic that one of its early reports should take organic food as its subject, given that this is a food type that is increasingly trusted when genetically modified foods are increasingly treated with suspicion. (For further detail on the FSA, see chapter 3.)

The role of the Advisory Committee on Releases to the Environment (ACRE)

ACRE is an independent body which reviews applications for GMO trials and acts as an adviser to DEFRA. Before approval is granted the Secretary of State for the Department of Environment, Food and Rural Affairs must be satisfied that proposed controlled activities with GMOs will not harm animals, humans or the environment. ACRE has developed operating practices which reflect the principles set out in the Phillips Report on BSE, namely, openness requiring recognition of uncertainty where it exists and transparency in the scientific investigation of risk. Despite these efforts, criticism has been levied at the composition of ACRE.[63] The need to maintain actual and apparent independence creates a 'catch 22' situation, as in order to perform reliable risk assessments, ACRE requires a membership of experts and yet, inevitably, most high calibre experts in the field will be or will have been employed in the biotechnology industry itself. The consequent accusations of partiality have damaged public confidence in ACRE. The independence of ACRE has been questioned further on the grounds that in its role of approving controlled activities it acts as an examiner, reviewing the risk assessments conducted by the applicant company themselves rather than producing its own risk assessments. Whilst ACRE approval usually takes 90 days, a 'fast-track' procedure was introduced for repeat trials and low risk trials, taking only 30 days and not requiring ACRE's review of the applicants' environmental risk assessment.

The role of the Advisory Committee on Novel Foods and Processes (ACNFP)

The assessment of novel foods is carried out by ACNFP which comprises a body of experts. Its safety assessments use the concept of 'substantial equivalence' (a test endorsed by the WHO and OECD) which compares novel/GM foods with their conventional counterparts. Since the Novel Foods and Novel Foods Ingredients (Amendment) (England) Regulations 1999,[64] all information submitted to ACFNP as part of a market approval for novel foods is to be disclosed to anyone who asks for it and is to be published on the internet, unless ACFNP agrees that it is confidential because it would harm the competitive position or intellectual property rights of the

---

62   N Hawkes, 'Report proves organic food is healthier' *The Times*, 7 August 2001.
63   See House of Commons Select Committee on Science and Technology, *First Report 1998-99: Scientific Advisory System – Genetically Modified Foods* (HC 286).
64   SI 1999/3182.

applicant. The remit of the ACNFP is to 'advise central authorities responsible in England, Scotland, Wales and Northern Ireland respectively on any matters relating to novel foods and novel food processes including food irradiation, having regard where appropriate to the views of relevant expert bodies.' Before the product is approved, the ACNFP must be convinced that controlled activities will not damage human health and it acts as adviser to the Department of Health on the risks associated with novel foods and foods produced by novel processes.

The public are understandably wary of new developments in food technology given the UK's experience of the BSE scandal and several E-coli outbreaks. A new independent body was set up to give advice to ministers on GM technology: the Agriculture and Environment Biotechnology Commission, launched in 2000.

F WORLD TRADE ORGANISATION RULES

Further complicating the multi-layered provisions already described are international trade agreements creating general prohibitions on trade restrictions and which may therefore indirectly impinge on the regulation of GMOs. The World Trade Organisation has produced a number of international agreements with the potential to restrict the regulation of GMOs at national level. These include the General Agreement on Tariffs and Trade (GATT), the Agreement on Technical Barriers to Trade (TBT Agreement) and the Agreement on the Application of Sanitary and Phytosanitary Measures (SPS Agreement). The SPS Agreement is probably the most likely to be implicated in the context of GMO regulation. To fall within the agreement, the regulatory measure concerned must be a 'sanitary or phytosanitary measure,' that is, broadly speaking, it must be designed merely to protect the life or health of humans, animals or plants. The SPS Agreement would not therefore apply to labelling regulations designed to provide better information for consumers.[65] The SPS Agreement requires that such sanitary or phytosanitary measures must be '*necessary* to protect human, animal or plant life or health' and be based on 'sufficient scientific evidence.'[66] It is envisaged that these provisions will present difficulties in that states seeking to act on the precautionary principle by regulating GMOs in a risk averse fashion might be accused of violating World Trade Organisation rules under the SPS Agreement. In further support of these provisions, the SPS Agreement requires that regulatory measures be based on risk assessments disclosing 'ascertainable risks' as opposed to 'theoretical uncertainties'.[67]

Labelling requirements at national or international level are also liable to come into conflict with World Trade Organisation rules. Those opposed to labelling of GM products often argue that mandatory labelling would be a 'disguised restriction on trade'.[68] This issue is most likely to be affected by the TBT Agreement. The TBT Agreement, Art 2.1 provides that products imported from other member states are to be treated no less favourably than [the treatment] accorded to *like products* of national origin and to *like products* originating in any other country. The problem arises out of varying interpretations of *like products*. To those who are wary of GM products, they cannot be likened to non-GM goods, as the modification process makes them fundamentally less acceptable. To supporters of GM technology, GM maize and non-

---

65 D French, 'International Regulation of GMOs' (2000) Environmental Liability 9(3) 127, pp 129-30.
66 SPS Agreement, Art 2.2.
67 See *EC – Measures Concerning Meat and Meat Products (Hormones) 1998*, WT/DS26/AB/R and WT/DS48/AB/R for discussion of the relationship between the precautionary principle and the SPS Agreement.
68 D French, at n 60.

GM maize are like products (because they are basically of the same composition), therefore to require one to be labelled and the other not would be potentially discriminatory to countries producing GM maize and a violation of the TBT Agreement. Once again, the lack of scientific evidence that GM organisms present real risk to health or to the environment is likely to reduce the possibility that GM and non-GM tomatoes will be regarded as anything other than 'like products.'

G THE CARTAGENA BIOSAFETY PROTOCOL 2000

The Cartagena Protocol to the Convention on Biological Diversity[69] was signed on 29 January 2000 in Montreal and aims to set up a mechanism of global governance of cross-boundary transfer of living modified organisms (LMOs) in order to minimise the risks to human health and the environment. There are two central mechanisms in the protocol which further these aims. The first is that the Protocol establishes an internet based 'Biosafety Clearing House' which will facilitate the exchange of information relating to LMOs.[70] Secondly, it creates a system of informed consent for importing countries of LMOs. All bulk shipments of LMOs are subject to an 'Advance Informed Agreement' (AIA) which means that they must seek the consent of the imported country before bringing the LMOs into the country. Information regarding the dates of the proposed transfer, quantities of LMOs, scientific information, origins and intended use of the LMOs are to be supplied to the importing country. This information will then be used to conduct the risk assessment which will form the basis of the importer's decision. The AIA does not apply to the transboundary movement of LMOs intended for contained use, but only to LMOs which are intended for introduction into the environment, for example, GM seeds to be planted (and therefore released) in the imported country. This does not include organisms intended for direct use as food or feed or for processing (FFPs).[71] Pharmaceuticals for human use which contain LMOs are also excluded, as are GMOs in transit and those intentional transboundary movements considered unlikely to have adverse effects on biodiversity.[72]

A source of considerable controversy during the negotiation of the Cartagena Protocol was whether the AIA mechanism should be founded on decision making according to sound science or whether it should allow importing countries to take a precautionary approach to its decision. Despite the initial opposition of the 'Miami Group' (Canada, Australia, the US, Argentina, Chile and Uruguay) to precautionary decision making, they finally agreed to the inclusion of the precautionary principle in the Cartagena Protocol's objectives[73] and also to importing countries being able to restrict import on precautionary grounds: 'Lack of scientific certainty due to insufficient relevant scientific information and knowledge regarding the extent of the potential adverse effects of LMOs shall not prevent that party from taking a decision ... to avoid or potentially minimise adverse effects'.[74] It is questionable whether this double homage to precautionary decision making will have any legal force, however, as the Cartagena Protocol contains a 'savings clause' which states that the parties intend that the agreement should not alter the rights and obligations of governments under the World Trade Organisation rules or other international agreements already in place when the Cartagena Protocol was signed. This failure to anticipate and resolve conflicts between

---

69 29 January 2000, Montreal.
70 Cartagena Biosafety Protocol 2000, Art 20.
71 Cartagena Biosafety Protocol 2000, Art 8.
72 Cartagena Biosafety Protocol 2000, Art 7.
73 Cartagena Biosafety Protocol 2000, Art 1.
74 Cartagena Biosafety Protocol 2000, Art 11(8).

the Cartagena Protocol and the WTO framework gives rise to some uncertainty as to the effect of the Cartagena Protocol.[75] By subordinating the Protocol's effects to the trade rules of the WTO discussed above, particularly to the extent that these rules prohibit precautionary measures which restrict trade, the precautionary objectives mentioned in the Cartagena Protocol are unlikely to have more than symbolic effect.

H THE LEGALITY OF A UK MORATORIUM

As public concern swelled over the rising tide of GMO products appearing on supermarket shelves, English Nature, amongst others, called for the government to impose a moratorium on the import, growing, patenting or marketing of GMOs. The campaign, known as the 'Five Year Freeze', was rejected by the government on the grounds that a ban on imports would be unlawful, contravening EU law and World Trade Organisation rules (see above). In October 1998, the government opted instead to form a non-enforceable voluntary agreement with UK industries that GMOs would not be grown commercially until the existing trials produced satisfactory results that no significant or lasting damage to the environment was entailed. This arrangement is in effect a de facto moratorium which was originally intended to last for at least three years. The government's trials end in 2002, but the moratorium has been extended until 2003.

Clearly, the voluntary nature of the current arrangement gives rise to concern as to its stability. While industry may comply now in order to pre-empt stricter regulation, when current research produces results, there are likely to be differing views held by industry and others as to whether the results are 'satisfactory'. No legal sanction would attach to companies that breached the agreement by commencing commercial growing of GMO crops on the grounds that *they* viewed the research as proving to their satisfaction the safety of GMOs. Moreover, trial crops which are not granted the necessary licences for marketing must be destroyed. It was admitted, however, in 1999 that trial crops which did succeed in obtaining marketing consents from the European Commission could enter the food chain and the government would be powerless to stop them.

Phillipe Sands was asked by Friends of the Earth to provide an opinion on the legality of a moratorium. Sands pointed to Art 100a(4) of the EC Treaty which permits member states to create national provisions which address major needs relating to, inter alia, protection of the environment. Such provisions must however be approved by the Commission, provided it is satisfied that the measures do not constitute a disguised restriction on trade between member states or a means of arbitrary discrimination.

I CIVIL LIABILITY FOR RELEASES OF GMOS

It has been argued that, given the unknown risks which manipulation of genetic materials may give rise to, before GMOs are grown commercially, the framework of liability ought to be clarified. Such a strategy would perhaps encourage acceptance of GMOs, because mechanisms for compensating those adversely affected financially by GM technology would already be in place, thus reducing some of the uncertainty which surrounds their use. By creating certainty in terms of liability mechanisms it would be possible to

---

75 See A Quereshi, 'The Cartagena Protocol on Biosafety and the World Trade Organisation' (2000) ICLQ 49(4) 835.

offset some of the public hostility due to the current uncertainties regarding the effects of GM technology. The Royal Commission on Environmental Pollution reporting in 1989[76] recommended a strict liability mechanism for harm caused by GMOs along the lines of the *Rylands v Fletcher* action[77] – see chapter 6. (Of course, in 1989, actions under *Rylands* were still strict liability). The opportunity to create such a remedy was however rejected by Parliament on the grounds that it needed to be considered on an international scale and that the government was awaiting proposals for a directive from Europe on environmental liability.[78] Given that we are still awaiting the outcome of Europe's ruminations on such a directive, it is questionable whether such a deferral was justified. In any event, until a directive is forthcoming, those who suffer damage as the result of deliberate or accidental releases of GMOs must rely on the common law.

The House of Commons Environmental Audit Committee[79] listed some of the possible forms of harm which might result from GMOs. The potential for civil liability arising from two of these 'harms' will be considered: cross-pollination of organic crops and the development of new allergies.

Cross-pollination of organic crops

Organic farming constitutes around 2.5% of arable land in the UK. The use of GMOs in the production of organic crops is prohibited by EU law. This prohibition does not however directly prohibit the marketing of organic produce which has been contaminated by GM crops.[80] The United Kingdom Register of Organic Food Standards (the body that sets national standards for organic farming) has determined that 'organic' produce means not only farming which does not make use of synthetic chemicals but also non-genetically modified crops. Difficulties then arise where organic farmers' fields are in close proximity to fields of genetically modified produce as there can be no guarantees that organic seeds will not be contaminated with non-organic seed transfer.[81] If contamination does occur, organic farmers may lose their 'organic' certification. The potential for pollen from genetically modified crops to contaminate organic crops has, of course, already been litigated in the guise of *R v Secretary of State for the Environment and Ministry of Agriculture Fisheries and Food, ex p Watson*.[82] Watson was an organic farmer concerned that the trial of genetically modified maize on an adjacent farm could contaminate his crop of sweetcorn. The respondents refused to vary or revoke the EPA 1990, s 111 consent granted for the trial on the grounds that the current distance between the GM and the non-GM crops was two kilometres, a distance which ACRE advised presented a likely zero risk of cross-pollination. The aim of this litigation was therefore to halt the GM trial before the maize pollinated and, therefore, the action was one of judicial review of the refusal to reconsider the consent, rather than one seeking to impose civil liability. Suppose that the worst happened, and Mr Watson's crop of sweetcorn had been contaminated with GM pollen from the

76   Royal Commission on Environmental Pollution, 13th Report, *The Release of Genetically Engineered Organisms to the Environment* (1989).
77   (1868) LR 3 HL 330.
78   Hansard, HL, vol 522, cols 704-706. See chap 6.
79   House of Commons Environmental Audit Committee, 5th Report, *Inquiry into Genetically Modified Organisms and the Environment*. HC 384, (1998-99).
80   *Crops on Trial* (2001) AEBC, London.
81   C Moyes and P Dale, 'Organic Farming and Gene Transfer from Genetically Modified Crops: MAFF Research Project' (1999) John Innes Centre.
82   [1999] Env LR 310. For another attempt to pre-empt the damage which might be caused by GM trials in the UK, see *Monsanto plc v Tilly* [2000] Env LR 313 discussed in chap 7.

neighbouring GM trial, with the result that the Soil Association had withdrawn their accreditation of Mr Watson's produce. In *Watson* itself, Simon Brown LJ commented on the potential for an action in nuisance, should such cross-pollination occur. Such a claim, he suspected, would face the obstacle that the cultivation of organic crops would be regarded as an 'abnormally sensitive' use of land (this is perhaps very likely when we consider that organic farming makes up only approximately 1.5% of agricultural activity in the UK). The consequence of such a finding is that cross-pollination would fall outside the protection of the law of nuisance unless it could be said that the GM crops would have caused interference with non-sensitive uses.[83] The Nuffield Council's report treated consumers' desire for organic/non-GM food products as anomalous, which would tend to add force to this argument. Of course, litigants using the rule under *Rylands v Fletcher*[84] may face the additional problem of convincing the court that the cultivation of GM crops constituted a 'non-natural use.'

Actions in negligence would raise the difficulties of proving that contamination of the crops constituted 'damage'. The mere presence of GMOs in the environment, constitutes 'damage' for the purposes of the EPA 1990 (see s 107(3)) and it might be that provided the defendant has violated EPA 1990's regulatory provisions (for example, by not installing sufficient buffer zones between the GM crops and neighbouring plants), that this will constitute damage at common law.[85] Given the prior action for judicial review in *Watson,* it seems unlikely that a court could conclude that damage was of a type that was not 'foreseeable'.

A further problem arises where *Rylands v Fletcher* is being considered, and that is that it has been traditionally regarded as applying only to non-deliberate releases.[86] If this is the case, then only accidental releases of GMOs might give rise to liability under *Rylands.* It has been pointed out, however, that a more lenient approach was taken by Potter J in *Crown River v Kimbolton*[87] who, in the context of deliberately released fireworks, professed that he could see no reason why the rule should be restricted to non-deliberate releases.[88] Further support for a liberal application of *Rylands* can be taken from Lord Goff's judgment in *Cambridge Water*[89] discussed in chapter 6. Lord Goff is of the view that the addition of the requirement of remoteness to *Rylands* actions lessens the need for insisting on other restrictive features such as the 'non-natural use' requirement. By the same token, arbitrarily restricting *Rylands* liability to accidental releases is surely unnecessary given the limiting function of remoteness.

Allergies and other personal injury

In the event of harm to human health as a result of consuming GMOs, by, for example, the development of an allergy, further problematic issues would arise. Although the use of markets might help in identifying a particular variety of GMO as the cause of the illness, there would still be the difficulty of proving the causal link between a specific

---

83 *Robinson v Kilvert* (1889) 41 Ch D 88, CA.
84 (1868) LR 3 HL 330.
85 M Wilde in 'The Law of Tort and the Precautionary Principle: Civil Liability Issues Arising from Trial Planting of Genetically Modified Crops.' (1998) 6(6) Environmental Liability. 163 puts forward this argument and uses *Blue Circle v Ministry of Defence* [1998] 3 All ER 385 as support, citing Carnwath J: 'although the existence of a statutory regulatory system cannot alter the requirement that there should be some physical change, it may be relevant in considering whether the physical change is of any practical significance.'
86 *Rigby v Chief Constable of Northamptonshire* [1985] 1 WLR 1242.
87 [1996] 2 Lloyd's Rep 533.
88 A Waldron, 'Transgenic Torts' [1999] JBL 395.
89 [1994] 2 AC 264.

food source and the injury. If the food source was a staple ingredient such as soya, how could a specific producer be identified as responsible as above all the other GM soya producers? Where a risk emerges for the first time, producers may be able to argue that the risk was not foreseeable and therefore no breach of duty can be proved.[90]

The Consumer Protection Act 1987 would offer no comfort to those such as *Watson* as compensation extends only to damages for personal injury or damage to personal property and not to commercial property such as a farmer's crops. Its provisions may, however, offer some protection to those made physically ill by consuming GMOs. While GM crops are not specifically mentioned in the Act, it is possible to predict whether such a case might succeed under the Act if harm to the person were proved. Crops can constitute products provided they have been the subject of an 'industrial process'.[91] Deliberate genetic manipulation for the purposes of profit is quite likely to be regarded as such a process. Waldron agrees saying: 'it is difficult to imagine a more fundamental interference with an agricultural product than that involved in deliberate mutagenesis, aptly described by molecular biologists as "transformation". In addition to being a "product", the crop or foodstuff must also be "defective" which means that its safety is not such as people are entitled to expect.'[92] It is probable that the greatest obstacle to a claim under the Act would be what is known widely as the 'development risks defence'. This defence precludes the imposition of liability if: 'scientific and technical knowledge at the relevant time was not such that a producer of products of the same descriptions as the product in question might be expected to have discovered the defect if it had existed in his products while they were under his control.'[93]

The pitfalls faced by such litigants are many and varied and it would surely be preferable to set out a compensation scheme which ensures that the biotech industries absorb the risks of their technological enterprises.

J CRITICISMS OF GMO REGULATION

To what extent are current regulatory arrangements truly precautionary in nature? The following outlines the main criticisms which have been levied at the regulation of GMOs. The 'deliberate release' provisions emanating from Europe have been applauded for being the first example of international legislation which truly represents the precautionary principle.[94] Nevertheless, there are a number of risks which the present framework fails to deal with:

1   The Nuffield Council's report[95] recognised a number of inadequacies in current regulation. The Advisory Committee on Releases to the Environment ('ACRE') was not under any duty to monitor impacts of GMOs on the environment, neither were they under a duty to safeguard vulnerable interests such as the environment or non-GM agriculture. It is, of course, a frequent failing of environmental law, that while isolated activities appear not to cause significant harm and are tolerated, the accumulation of these small risks pose real and substantial threats to the environment. The regulation of GMOs is no exception. The approach to regulation is currently fragmented; licence applications are dealt with on a 'case by case' basis which focuses on the risk posed by this particular proposal. Such

90   *Roe v Ministry of Health* [1954] 2 QB 66, CA.
91   Consumer Protection Act 1987, s 2(4).
92   CPA 1987, s 3. See Waldron, n 88.
93   CPA 1987, s 4(1)(e).
94   Dr Von Schomberg as cited in House of Lords Select Committee on the European Community, Second Report *EC Regulation of Genetic Modification in Agriculture*. (1998-99) at para 42.
95   *GM Crops: The Ethical and Social Issues*, (1999) Nuffield Council.

assessments do not take into account the cumulative effects which may arise from this GM trial in conjunction with all the other authorised GM releases.

2   There is at present no mechanism in English law for addressing the value-based judgements (eg that genetic modification is somehow unethical or unnatural and ought to be avoided (see above at 'B')) and incorporating them into ministerial decisions on GMO policy.[96]

3   Guidelines as to the distance to be maintained between GM crops and non-GM crops remain voluntary, notwithstanding the concerns shared by many that harm to organic farmers' livelihoods and the wild plant population will result.

4   It has been argued that although the provisions of EPA 1990 relating to GMOs are precautionary in the sense that they regulate GMOs in the absence of any evidence that they will cause harm, enforcement of these provisions has not reflected this precautionary spirit. For example, in *Watson*, the regulations had been applied in a 'half-hearted manner' and the respondents were not even aware that their neighbour was an organic farmer.[97]

5   The Advisory Committee on Releases to the Environment (ACRE) has been criticised for the number of its members who have links with the biotechnology industry and are therefore likely to be committed to the pro-GM arguments.[98] In autumn 2000, ACRE had yet to decline any of the applications made to it.

6   In some circumstances the need for risk assessment to be communicated to a competent authority can in theory be avoided by the applicant defining her use of GMOs as a 'contained' use rather than one which would involve 'release' to the environment.

7   Under the Deliberate Release Directive, GM foods which have been processed to an extent whereby they pose no risk to the environment, do not require consent for release to be imported. This exception covers, for example, tomato paste, soya flour and soya oil, as such substances even if released present no threat of seeding or pollination.

8   The current regulatory system has also been criticised for its emphasis on the regulation of 'means' (ie the technique of genetic modification) rather than the 'ends' (ie the use to which GMOs are put).[99]

9   The lack of clarity with which the interrelationship between WTO rules and the Cartagena Protocol have been expressed.

Further reading

Campbell, D 'Of Coase and Corn: A (sort of) Defence of Private Nuisance.' [2000] 63 Modern Law Review.

Eggers B & Mackenzie, R 'The Cartagena Protocol on Biosafety.' (2000) Journal of International Economic Law 3(3) 525.

French, D 'International Regulation of GMOs' (2001) Environmental Liability 9(3) 127.

---

96   House of Commons Select Committee on Science and Technology, First Report 1998-99: *Scientific Advisory System – Genetically Modified Foods* (HC 286).

97   M Wilde in 'The Law of Tort and the Precautionary Principle: Civil Liability Issues Arising from Trial Planting of Genetically Modified Crops' (1998) 6(6) Environmental Liability. 163 at 166.

98   D Campbell, 'Of Coase and Corn: A (sort of) Defence of Private Nuisance' [2000] 63 Modern Law Review 1997.

99   Campbell, [2000] 63 Modern Law Review 1997, para 40.

Hill, J 'The Precautionary Principle and Release of GMOs to the Environment', in T O'Riordan and J Cameron (eds) *Interpreting the Precautionary Principle* (1994, Cameron May, London).

Hutchison, C 'An Overview of the Risk Analysis Provisions in the Cartagena Protocol on Biodiversity' [2001] 2 Environmental Liability 65.

'International Trade in Living Modified Organisms: The New Regimes' (2000) 49(4) ICLQ 856.

Leaking from the Lab? The Contained Use of Genetically Modified Micro-organisms in the UK. (1999, Gene Watch UK).

Quereshi, A 'The Cartagena Protocol on Biosafety and the World Trade Organisation' (2000) 49(4) ICLQ 835.

Waldron, A 'Transgenic Torts' [1999] Journal of Business Law 395.

Wilde, 'M The Law of Tort and the Precautionary Principle: Civil Liability Issues Arising from Trial Planting of Genetically Modified Crops' (1998) 6(6) Environmental Liability 163.

OFFICIAL PUBLICATIONS

Royal Commission on Environmental Pollution, Thirteenth Report, *The Release of Genetically Engineered Organisms to the Environment* (Cm 720, 1989).

Parliamentary Office of Science & Technology. *GM Foods: Benefits and Risks, Regulation and Public Acceptance.* (1998).

House of Commons Environmental Audit Committee, 5th Report, *Inquiry into Genetically Modified Organisms and the Environment* (HC 384) (1998-99).

House of Commons Select Committee on Science and Technology, *First Report 1998-99: Scientific Advisory System – Genetically Modified Foods* (HC 286).

House of Lords Select Committee on the European Community, Second Report *EC Regulation of Genetic Modification in Agriculture* (1998-99).

GM Crops: The Ethical and Social Issues (1999) Nuffield Council.

A Guide to the Genetically Modified Organisms (Contained Use) Regulations 2000 SI 2000/2831 (2000, Health & Safety Executive).

Crops on Trial (2001, AEBC, London).

A further invaluable source is the National Centre for Biotechnology Education located on the University of Reading's website.

Chapter 13

Mineral extraction

The extraction of minerals is an indispensable contributor to and consequence of economic development. Fuel minerals (such as oil, coal and natural gas) and construction and industrial minerals (for example, limestone, metal ores and bulk aggregates such as sand and gravel) not only constitute the raw materials for physical development itself, but also make an important contribution to the national economy. Conversely, some degree of environmental harm is an inevitable result of mineral extraction: not only might land be 'removed' by surface working, but some nuisance from extractive operations and ancillary works caused by dust, noise, vibration, traffic and visual intrusion is almost inevitable. This intrusion is compounded by the incidence in the UK of a wide range of minerals (often in environmentally sensitive areas), the potential duration of mineral workings and high (if fluctuating) demand. The results are widespread environmental effects in many varied local environments.

Recognition of the need to regulate mineral extraction in the public interest is long-standing, but certainly not static. And whilst having their roots in the general planning system, controls over mineral extraction have been influenced by the individual characteristics of minerals and their exploitation. In particular, unlike other uses of land, there is little choice in the location of mineral workings: minerals can only be worked where they are found, although minerals need not be worked everywhere they are found.

The result is a system of control largely within mainstream planning, but with its own rules. Some circumstances have proved beyond the flexibility of planning, such as onshore hydrocarbon exploitation and marine extraction, and so alternative systems have emerged for their control. Yet both planning and other specialised controls have also been modernised to meet contemporary environmental expectations – a modernisation process which is a key feature of minerals policy in the last 15 years, and which is increasingly reflected both in statute and in the decisions of the courts. More recently still, a general recognition of the need to diversify the regulatory tools used to pursue environmental policy has led to initiatives using economic incentives or sanctions to affect extraction practices. The example of the landfill tax has laid the foundations for direct taxation of the extraction of primary mineral resources.

A EXTRACTION AND THE ENVIRONMENT

As Mineral Planning Guidance Note 1 (MPG 1) reiterates, workable mineral deposits often encroach upon areas of great beauty or environmental worth, and whilst dereliction is largely avoidable, the use of such land for extraction is not. It is not possible to employ alternative sites as minerals can only be worked where they are found. Economic demands may also lead to a concentration of ancillary operations, including processing and manufacturing. The expense of extraction in terms of plant and machinery, in relation to the low value by volume of extracted material, is another reason for operations being locally extensive. Production of minerals and the consequent use of land also varies over time: some minerals, such as iron ore and now offshore petroleum, are in decline whilst others have remained stable or increased. There has, for example, been a substantial growth in consumption of primary aggregates over the past 30 years, a trend exacerbated by projections of demand which anticipate that by 2011 annual demand for primary aggregates could be between 410 and 490 million tonnes: an increase of between 40 and 60% on 1989 consumption levels. Energy minerals (considered below) add to these figures, although the demand for bulk minerals ensures that aggregates account for the majority of mineral extraction permissions granted each year.

Problems consequent upon extraction are not amenable to easy solutions. The public wants minerals for construction but does not want extraction on its doorstep. The cause of this contention is the nature of mineral workings themselves: they are visually intrusive; working can go on for many years — up to 70 depending upon the mineral in question; noise and vibration from blasting can cause damage and distress; as can dust emissions and the use of land for post extraction waste disposal. Different types of mine have different environmental implications, from opencast coal, through sand and gravel pits to deep-mined coal sites, whilst marine extraction presents its own problem. What all mines share, however, is the ability to affect all environmental media, and both local and national interests (such as world heritage sites as in *Coal Contractors Ltd v Secretary of State for the Environment and Northumberland County Council*,[1] where an application was refused because of the possible effects on the setting of Hadrian's Wall).

But there is a broader environmental policy context too. The protection of the landscape for its own sake is increasingly advocated. This is now complemented by a deepening policy commitment on the part of central government to the notion of 'sustainable development', both generally and in its particular application to minerals, a good example of a non-renewable resource. Consistent with planning policy more generally, minerals planning policy now places increasing emphasis on sustainable development as a policy keystone[2]. However, against this background must be set the rights of landowners to develop and exploit land consistent with the presumption in favour of development in accordance with the development plan; the national need for minerals; and the economic benefits, locally and nationally, of allowing development. The most marked step towards these general objective can be found in greater reliance on secondary rather than primary sources, and on moderating traditional policy which has been driven more by commercially defined demand for minerals than environmentally acceptable supply.

B BASIC STRUCTURES OF CONTROL

No single legal code embraces extraction and infilling: controls exist under planning, public health, transport and environmental protection legislation. Detailed control is principally the responsibility of county and district local authorities, although a number of central departments, including the DTI, DTLR and DEFRA are also involved. Other

1   [1995] JPL 421.
2   MPG 1, *General Considerations and the Development Plan System*, June 1996.

public authorities and related organisations, eg the Coal Authority, National Power and PowerGen, also have specific responsibilities.

Control over mineral extraction as a use of land is exercised within the general planning system. Those general controls have been adapted, both in law and through practice, for specialist application to minerals. This is despite the principal recommendation of the landmark DoE report, 'Planning Control Over Mineral Working' (the 'Stevens Report') in 1976 that a 'special regime' should apply. Direct regulation through planning licensing is therefore the predominant method of regulating the environmental harm deriving from mineral extraction, although hybrid controls have been developed in relation to onshore energy minerals, including oil and gas. This places the responsibility on planners to impose appropriate environmental standards, although there remains some overlap in the case of, eg discharges to water from extraction sites. Whilst the law thus provides a basic (and disparate) structure, the peculiarities of minerals and their incidence are such that both central and local authorities must exercise very flexible control.

Central supervision of minerals policy is unevenly divided between the Department of Trade and Industry (over industrial minerals, coal, oil and natural gas) and the Department for Environment, Food and Rural Affairs and the Department for Local Government, Transport and the Regions (concerned with land use issues). In terms of regulatory planning the DTLR has central responsibility, although subject to wide consultation. Government policy favours market forces as the main determinants of extraction programmes. This is anathema to environmental interests which advocate the principal importance of, eg National Parks and other areas of great natural beauty or interest, whether statutorily designated or not. Guidance on minerals (now contained in a series of Mineral Planning Guidance Notes (MPGs) which have replaced the 1960 *Memorandum on the Control of Mineral Working* — the 'Green Book') emphasises this conflict between economics and the environment. MPG 1 recognises that the long term national need for minerals must compete with growing demands for environmental protection, yet reiterates that the many unique characteristics of mineral development inevitably result in environmental harm. For example, minerals can only be worked where they are found, often beneath high grade agricultural land or land of conservation or scientific importance; authorities should make a contribution to meeting local, regional and national demand for minerals; investment in mineral exploitation also has positive local and national economic effects. The historic approach to substantive minerals planning policy has therefore been that authorities should have a predisposition to grant permission unless there are very strong environmental objections or there is no real economic need (eg *Mid-Essex Gravel Pits v Secretary of State for the Environment and Essex County Council*).[3] In practice this is a difficult balance to achieve, as was recognised by both the Stevens Report and the report of the Verney Committee, 'Aggregates: The Way Ahead' (1976), in stressing the importance of long-term planning. This is now also subject to the emergence of sustainable development as a central strand of planning policy.

Mineral planning authorities

Under the Town and Country Planning Act 1990, s 1(4) authorities responsible for mineral development control and plan making are county councils, London borough councils and, where they exist, metropolitan district councils — known as mineral planning authorities (MPAs). This sub-category of planning authorities includes county and county borough councils in Wales[4] and unitary authorities in England (which, where they exist, are generally treated as both a county and a district: Local Government Changes for England Regulations 1994, SI 1994/867, reg 5(6)). All applications for planning permission for minerals matters must be made directly to the MPA, rather than via the district as was the case before 1991 (TCPA 1990, Sch 1, as amended). This change is controversial. Under the TCPA 1990, Sch 1, the following fall within MPAs' jurisdiction: winning and working minerals and erecting any building or plant ancillary thereto, for the purpose, eg, of treatment, disposal or processing; using land or erecting buildings or plant for mineral processing, or manufacturing mineral products where the site in question adjoins or is part of a mineral-working area, or where the mineral is transported to the land by conveyor, pipeline or via a private road, rail or waterway; mineral exploration (but see further below); disposal of mineral waste; use of land in connection with the rail or water transportation of aggregates (ie, sand, gravel, crushed rock or similar manufactured or reclaimed material) or the erection of buildings or plant intended to be used in connection with aggregates; erection of buildings or plant for road-stone coating, or artificial aggregate or concrete production or processing, on land on or adjoining a mineral working area; development of land used or previously used for winning or working minerals where such development would prejudice restoration; and the development of land relating to the deposit of refuse or waste. In rare cases an application may include both county and district matters: it may be a 'hybrid' application. In such cases the legal test is unclear: the Court of Appeal has concluded that if the application is 'in substance' an application for permission to develop land in a county matter, then the fact that it is also related to other matters is immaterial[5]. A more complex test based on predominant and ancillary purposes was expressly rejected. In such cases the whole application will be determined by the MPA.

As the Stevens Report heavily stressed, control over mineral extraction is dependent upon adequate numbers of well-trained staff. They must be able to advise on the feasibility of proposals and carry out continuing supervision of individual sites to ensure compliance with the terms of planning permissions. The recommendations of the Stevens Committee were that, in the absence of sufficient resources at county level, regional teams should be formed, or staff-sharing arrangements entered into. Although considered in the Stevens Report to be the mainstay of effective continuing control over mineral development, the availability of staff is still a problem. Indeed, in many counties it precluded beginning the review of mineral working sites which until the Environment Act 1995 was not required within a specified timetable (see below). The role of local residents in supplementing the responsibilities of MPA staff as 'quasi-enforcement officers' should, however, not be discounted: their detailed knowledge and interest in local development can be a very effective method of overseeing extraction operations. Some development plans even provide for the formation of local 'liaison committees' to maximise this contribution. As a means of communication and negotiation between developers, authorities and local communities, both before and after the granting of planning permission, they provide perhaps the best existing example of *true* public participation in planning. This approach receives express endorsement in proposals for radically modified policy on community involvement in minerals planning (*Controlling and Mitigating the Environment Effects of Minerals Extraction in England*, Consultation Paper on Revised MPG 11, May 2000, paras 49-52). Those proposals place considerable emphasis on the need for operators to be good

4   TCPA 1990, s 1(4B); Local Government (Wales) Act 1994, s 18.
5   *R v Berkshire County Council, ex p Wokingham District Council* [1997] Env LR 545. Potter LJ added the words 'a substantial element' in referring to that part of the application required to relate to a county matter, but these were not adopted by the remainder of the court.

neighbours, for example, it is made plain that 'minerals operators have the primary responsibility for ensuring that local communities are given accurate information about their proposals, and in trying to accommodate their legitimate concerns. A progressive company will try to establish a good working relationship with the people it has to work with. It will try to be a good neighbour and it will contribute to the community in which it operates' (para 50). This principle is developed through a series of good practice points on community consultation, which include advice on the formation and operation of liaison committees, publicity, and complaint handling.

Policy preparation and content

The policy context for determining applications for mineral extraction is provided by structure plans (or unitary development plans) and specialised minerals local plans, the preparation of which is the responsibility of MPAs. Mineral development is a 'key topic' under PPG 12, and strategic plans must contain authorities' 'general policies' for extraction. Minerals local plans must include a written statement setting out an authority's detailed policies in respect of development consisting of the winning and working of minerals or involving the depositing of mineral waste, and translate strategic policies to identifiable areas of land. MPAs should consider the interactions between minerals proposals and other matters. In formulating local plans authorities must take many views into account, including: central guidance (from MPGs and specific consultation with individual departments); the findings of Regional Aggregates Working Parties (RAWPs), as representative bodies of industry and central and local government concerned with matters of supply and demand; structure plan policies; those of other affected authorities, including the relevant district councils and, eg, the Agency on such things as hydrology and flood plain implications; as well as opinions expressed by the general public. Detailed provisions concerning consultation and comment on proposals for structure plan amendments and for local plan proposals are set out in TCPA 1990, ss 33 and 40. Public involvement in plan making is of great importance in view of the controversy of many mineral development proposals. Effective participation at an early stage may even make the question of individual applications, decided from the basis of plans, less contentious. In addition to making written representations, members of the public may appear at local inquiries held into plans.

MPG 1, 'General Considerations and the Development Plan System' (June 1996), sets out the aims of planning control in relation to mineral development. In particular, it emphasises what are described as the objectives for sustainable development for minerals planning: to conserve minerals as far as possible, whilst ensuring an adequate supply to meet needs; to ensure that the environmental impacts caused by mineral operations and the transport of minerals are kept, as far as possible, to an acceptable minimum; to minimise production of waste and to encourage efficient use of materials, including appropriate use of high quality materials, and recycling of wastes; to encourage sensitive working, restoration and aftercare practices so as to preserve or enhance the overall quality of the environment; to protect areas of designated landscape or nature conservation value from development, other than in exceptional circumstances and where it has been demonstrated that development is in the public interest; and to prevent the unnecessary sterilisation of mineral resources.

With this in mind, plans should contain policies on: safeguarding deposits which are, or may become, of economic importance from unnecessary sterilisation by surface development; making appropriate provision for the supply of minerals and provide an effective framework within which the industry may make applications – as minerals can be worked only where they occur, MPAs should make an appropriate contribution to meeting local, regional and national needs which reflects the nature and extent of minerals in its area; ensuring continuity of production for mineral extraction, through maintenance of a 'landbank', that is a stock of planning permissions which relates to non-energy minerals and which provides for continuity of production; areas for possible future working. The appropriateness of defining 'preferred areas' will be dependent upon factors which include: the authority's knowledge of the extent of viable mineral resources; the precision of demand forecasts; the urgency with which consents to meet demand will be needed (itself dependent upon the existence of a satisfactory land-bank); the nature of the mineral; and pressure from competing land uses. The practical importance of minerals local plans' role in identifying areas within which extraction would normally be permitted (or not) is shown by recent experience of challenges to the adoption of plans. For example, the developer in *Western Aggregates v Hereford and Worcester County Council*[6] sought to promote its own land for extraction, and thus challenged the adopted plan, which omitted that land from its 'preferred areas'. Whilst the challenge failed, the decision of the High Court does emphasise both the scope of MPAs' discretion to determine the scale and location of such preferred areas, and also the consequential influence of those determinations in deciding individual applications.

Other policies relating to specific factors to be taken into account in deciding individual applications should also be included, and these will include criteria that will be applied to minerals proposals to ensure that they do not have an unacceptably adverse impact on the environment (MPG 1, para 59). These might incorporate: consideration of the impact of extraction, processing or distribution on, eg the landscape, the local economy (including employment) and residential areas by way of visual intrusion or noise; the quality and extent of the deposit; traffic volume and consequent environmental disturbance; impact on agriculture, forestry or environmentally important areas; the protection of agricultural land and environmentally sensitive areas; the need to ensure protection of the flow and quality of surface and groundwater supplies and that changes in the water table as a result of mineral extraction do not cause unacceptable changes to the water environment, particularly water resources; working programmes; ancillary development, including plants for recycling building and construction wastes; and any reclamation requirements (detailed further in MPG 7).

Plans may contain specific policies on individual minerals or groups of minerals such as: sand, gravel, crushed rock, high specification aggregates for road construction, pulverised fuel ash ('PFA') and other similar waste materials ('aggregates'); non-aggregate minerals such as industrial limestone (a major constituent of the flue gas desulphurisation process intended to reduce atmospheric emission of sulphur dioxide), gypsum (used in plaster manufacture), silica sand, slate, and china and ball-clay (of which the UK is a leading world producer and exporter); and energy minerals such as coal (including opencast coal), oil and natural gas. Each type may have appropriate constraint policies depending upon, eg its availability or the extreme difficulties which its extraction causes (as in the case of opencast coal). Unless specific statutory controls exist in relation to certain types of minerals, the impact of legal constraints on the extraction of this range of minerals will therefore be determined not by different legal rules but by variations in policy.

Minerals can have dramatic environmental implications, and this is reflected in the policy provision that should be made, and the site-specific controls which ultimately may be applied. More explicit policy guidance has now been proposed to complement that in, for example, MPG 1 and this is also more comprehensive than any guidance that has preceded it (Draft MPG 11, *Controlling and Mitigating the Environment Effects of Minerals Extraction in England*, May 2000). The types of considerations that may arise include: maintaining buffer zones between workings and residential or environmentally sensitive areas; minimising subsidence which might result in surface damage; protecting water resources, particularly groundwater; controlling noise, blasting and dust; the provision of screens of vegetation; the location and design of stockpiles and soil storage, perhaps for the provision of protective 'bunds'; regulating the construction and location of ancillary development; maximising the use of less disruptive forms of transportation, such as canals or railways; requiring phased working and restoration; and guidance on suitable or preferred after-uses.

Plans must allow for flexibility in the application of their policies; real discussion of the merits of a case must not be pre-empted. Presumptions and predispositions are permissible in plans, predeterminations are not. For example, where a plan is too precise in restricting future extraction to certain areas, making it clear that applications outside those areas will be opposed, its legality is questionable: see *Buckinghamshire County Council v Hall Aggregates (Thames Valley) Ltd and Sand and Gravel Association Ltd.*[7] Similarly, whilst TCPA 1990, s 54A, which requires that planning decisions be made in accordance with the development plan unless material considerations indicate otherwise, has apparently introduced a period of plan-led planning, as indicated in chapter 8, this is not absolute. Plans cannot be prescriptive, central policy provides local authorities with considerable latitude in the formulation and interpretation of plans, whilst their wide content suggests considerable potential for conflict in their application. Given this intrinsic flexibility, local influences on local decision-making are, in practice, very important. Equally, other relevant factors not to be found in plans may include: sudden unforeseen demand; advances in extractive and processing technology making previously uneconomic development feasible; and the discovery of previously unknown mineral resources or finding lower actual reserves than expected. Changes in attitude towards some policies may also necessitate reconsideration, as witness the increasing weight given to environmental factors. In evaluating the extent to which a plan will be relied upon, its age is therefore of crucial importance: a plan is always a consideration, the question for the authority in determining an application is the weight that it should be given.

Minerals applications, appeals and 'call-in' applications are always particularly contentious in areas of high scenic, environmental or amenity value — 'sensitive areas'. National Parks and Areas of Outstanding Natural Beauty currently amount to some 23% of the land area of England and Wales. Government policy in such areas is more restrictive than outside, hence policy dictates that proposals for mineral development in sensitive areas should, by virtue of the very serious effects which mineral development can have on them, be subject to 'the most rigorous examination'. Policy is set out in PPG 9, *Nature Conservation.*

C 'MINING' AND 'MINERALS'

'Mining operations in, on, under or over land' constitute an act of development under TCPA 1990, s 55. Whilst not otherwise defined, this includes: the removal of material of any description from a mineral working deposit; from a deposit of PFA or clinker; or from a deposit of iron, steel or other metallic slag; and the extraction of minerals from a disused railway embankment. TCPA 1990, s 336(1) further provides that a 'mineral working deposit' is any deposit of material remaining after minerals have been extracted from land, or otherwise deriving from development for the winning and working of minerals. The essential meaning of 'the winning and working of minerals' was

7   [1985] JPL 634.

considered in the Court of Appeal in *English Clays Lovering Pochin & Co Ltd v Plymouth Corpn*[8] to be the 'separation of raw materials from the solid earth in which it occurs'. If the treatment of china clay after extraction was within this definition, then the claimant company would have been able to take advantage of (then) extant permitted development rights. It was held not to be (see also *South Glamorgan County Council v Hobbs (Quarries) Ltd* [1980] JPL 35). In relation to mining, every shovelful is a separate act of development, a conclusion also significant for enforcement purposes when limitation periods on enforcement action run from the alleged breach of planning control, including the act of unauthorised development: *Thomas David (Porthcawl) Ltd v Penybont RDC*.[9] This rule may be applied quite creatively. For example, it has been held that removal of topsoil prior to mineral extraction was not capable of amounting to the winning and working of minerals, and therefore did not lawfully commence a permission for the extraction of those minerals[10], although the context was a rather clear attempt simply to resurrect an old planning permission. Sample boring which is of short duration, unlikely to have a permanent effect and undertaken as preparatory to investigatory drilling is not development: *Bedfordshire County Council v Central Electricity Generating Board*.[11] Investigatory drilling of deep boreholes for the purpose, eg of oil or gas exploration, *is* development requiring permission.

'Minerals' are defined by TCPA 1990, s 336(1) to include 'all substances of a kind ordinarily worked for removal by underground or surface working, except that it does not include peat cut for purposes other than sale'. TCPA 1990, s 315 provides a power to modify the effect of various provisions of the Act in relation to development consisting of the winning and working of minerals or involving the depositing of mineral waste. By virtue of sub-s (4), regulations so made shall not apply to development consisting of the winning and working of minerals: on land held or occupied with land used for agriculture, of any minerals reasonably required for that purpose; Coal Authority minerals; or gold or silver, which are vested in the Crown. Under this power, regulations have provided further relevant definitions and development rights. The Town and Country Planning (General Permitted Development) Order 1995, SI 1995/418 grants certain rights (see below) and, with the Town and Country Planning (Minerals) Regulations 1995, SI 1995/2863, further defines 'mining operations' as 'the winning and working of minerals in, on or under land, whether by surface or underground working'. This extensive definition of 'mining' has been necessary historically and has emerged by a process of evolution. The most notable amendments were made by the Town and Country Planning (Minerals) Act 1981, enacted to implement some of the recommendations of the Stevens Committee.

Development must normally commence within five years of consent (s 91 of the 1990 Act), and whilst in the case of mineral development this period was previously 10 years (Town and Country Planning (Minerals) Regulations 1971, SI 1971/756, reg 6) these regulations were repealed by the 1995 Regulations, SI 1995/2863, reg 4. Authorities have discretion to relax this constraint and have been urged, by, inter alia, the Stevens Report to do so where justified by a developer's real needs. Under TCPA 1990, s 91 it is further provided that the time limit does not apply to any permission for development by the winning and working of minerals or involving the depositing of mineral waste which is granted (or deemed to be granted) subject to a condition that the development to which it relates must begin within a specified period from the completion of other mineral development being carried out by that applicant, or after the cessation of the

8   [1974] 2 All ER 239.
9   [1972] 3 All ER 1092, CA.
10   *Staffordshire County Council v Riley* [2001] EWCA Civ 257, [2002] PLCR 75.
11   [1985] JPL 43.

depositing of mineral waste already being carried out by that applicant. Although necessarily of longer duration than most developments, the permitted life of an extraction site is not unlimited. TCPA 1990, Sch 5 provides that every permission granted after 22 February 1982 is subject to a condition restricting its life to 60 years from the date of the consent, although this may be extended or reduced by the planning authority. The same schedule also imposes a condition on permissions granted before February 1982 that they must cease after 60 years, ie 22 February 2042. Applicants may appeal to the Secretary of State against the imposition of a time limit. As well as accommodating the particular physical demand of mineral development, these time limit provisions (particularly the power to modify time limits) enable a mineral planning authority to limit the environmental effects of extraction in time. They have now been complemented by new powers introduced by the Environment Act 1995, s 96 and Schs 13 and 14 which set out authorities' powers and duties in respect of reviewing *existing* minerals permissions. The relatively crude method of limiting the duration of extraction is therefore refined by this new review (considered in detail below).

Environmental Impact Assessment (EIA)

There is a common perception that environmental assessment for minerals development under the 1988 Regulations (Town and Country Planning (Assessment of Environmental Effects) Regulations 1988, SI 1988/1199) was not undertaken as frequently as for other projects with similarly significant impacts. This perception derives, at least in part, from the expectation that mineral development will be accompanied by an unusually detailed process of pre-application consultation and discussion, which is coupled to detailed working and restoration programmes. It is true that the number of environmental assessments undertaken by the extractive industry has remained constant at around 60 a year (certainly up to 1994), but they are also amongst the most frequent categories of 'Schedule 2 projects' (see below) for which EA has been required[12]. The environmental assessment process has recently been substantially revised, however, and, when taken with other minerals-specific developments, this can be expected to lead to an increase in the number of minerals projects for which EA is required.

The general reforms to EIA law are considered elsewhere (chapter 8), and came into force for planning applications received after, or permitted development not begun by, 14 March 1999 (Town and Country Planning (Environmental Impact Assessment) (England and Wales) Regulations 1999, SI 1999/293). The most pertinent aspects for minerals are twofold. The first relates to the criteria which must be applied in determining whether EIA is (or may be) required for minerals development. The basic obligation to undertake EIA remains as before: EIA must be undertaken for Schedule 1 development; but must only be undertaken for Schedule 2 development where it is 'likely to have significant effects on the environment by virtue of factors such as its nature, size or location'. However, in deciding whether a project is Schedule 2 development, and then whether it is 'EIA development', complex new conditions apply. First, development will only be Schedule 2 development if it falls within the familiar categories set out in the Schedule *and* it is *either* in a 'sensitive area' (essentially, defined statutory and extra-statutory designations: reg 2(1)), or the development meets or exceeds certain thresholds or criteria set out in the Schedule itself. Having applied this definition, it

---

12   Generally see Jones & Bull, 'Analysis of Changing Trends in UK Environmental Statements, 1988-94' [1997] JPL 1091.

should be clear whether or not development is, in fact, 'Schedule 2' development. In the case of the extractive industry, the relevant thresholds are:

(a) for quarries, open-cast mining and peat extraction (unless included in Schedule 1), and underground mining: all development except the construction of buildings or other ancillary structures where the new floor space does not exceed 1,000 square metres;

(b) for extraction of minerals by fluvial development: all development; and

(c) for deep drillings, with the exception of drillings for investigating the stability of soil: in relation to any type of drilling, the area of the work exceeds 1 hectare, or in relation to geothermal drilling and drilling for the storage of nuclear waste material, the drilling is within 100 metres of any controlled waters.

The second relevant aspect of EIA reforms is the additional complication that has been lent to minerals development by application of EIA to cases of the compulsory review of minerals consents under other statutory powers. The particular point in issue in *R v North Yorkshire District Council, ex p Brown and Cartwright*[13] was a narrow but significant one: whether EA (as it then was) was required in respect of the compulsory statutory review of 'interim development order' (IDO) permissions under the Planning and Compensation Act 1991, Sch 2. IDO permissions are old mining permissions granted before the general application of planning controls by the Town and Country Planning Act 1947[14]. The two main reasons for the introduction of the 1991 provisions were the lack of registration of IDO permissions and the fact of their environmental inadequacy, by modern standards. The general effect of Schedule 2 was therefore to require IDO permissions to be registered, and to update (within limits) the conditions to which they are subject. The key planning issue – the desirability of the development itself – was not open to challenge, other than in the normal way (see below).

In *Brown*, the House of Lords concluded that although the principle of the development was not open to challenge through the statutory review, that review was nonetheless a precondition to the exercise of rights to continue mining operations. This confirmed the decision of the Court of Appeal[15], after which the DETR issued interim guidance to MPAs[16]. The House of Lords' decision therefore means that the registration and updating of the IDO is a 'development consent' within the meaning of the EIA Directive, to which the obligation to consider the need for EIA under the 1999 Regulations attaches. As Lord Hoffmann put it: '... although the determination [of the terms of the IDO registration] does not decide whether the developer may proceed but only the manner in which he may proceed, it is nevertheless a necessary condition for his being entitled to proceed at all'. Since old mining permissions granted after 1947 are also now subject to a similar statutory review[17], the effect of *Brown* is that the review of all old mining permissions, IDO consents or otherwise, must be subjected to the new regime (Town and Country Planning (Environmental Impact Assessment) (England and Wales) (Amendment) Regulations 2000, SI 2000/2867). This does not mean the automatic requirement for an EIA, but will require the application of the ordinary rules, slightly modified.

13   [2000] 1 AC 397.
14   See Jewell, 'Paying for Environmental Improvement: The Potential Example of Minerals' (1992) 4 LMELR 81.
15   Reported at [1998] Env LR 385.
16   *Review of Mineral Permissions and Environmental Impact Assessment*, 20 October 1998
17   Environment Act 1995, Schs 13 and 14; MPG 14, *Environment Act 1995: Review of Mineral Planning Permissions*, September 1995.

Permitted development

Whilst planning permission is generally required for all mining development, the consolidated general development orders made in 1995 (the Town and Country Planning (General Permitted Development) Order 1995, the 'GPDO' and the Town and Country Planning (General Development Procedure) Order 1995, the 'GPDO' (SIs 1995/418 and 419)), provide for extensive permitted development rights and other modifications of general planning rules in respect of minerals. Classes of development permitted by the GPDO include: development ancillary to mining operations (Part 19); coal mining development by the Coal Authority and licensed operators (Part 20); waste tipping at a mine (Part 21); mineral exploration (Part 22); removal of material from a mineral working deposit (Part 23); and mineral working for agricultural purposes (Part 6, Class C).

Permitted development rights in respect of development ancillary to mining operations are granted by the order. In the case of underground workings, these are restricted to 'approved sites', ie the site with planning permission for the winning and working of minerals or land immediately adjoining an active access to an underground mine which is used as such (these rights are not available to the Coal Authority or coal operators, whose particular permitted development rights are examined below). Under Part 19, Class A, the carrying out of operations for, inter alia, the erection, rearrangement or other alteration of any plant, machinery, buildings, private railways or pipes, cables, etc, on land used as a mine is permitted. These rights do not apply where: the principal purpose of the development would be other than a purpose connected with the mineral development or the treatment, storage or removal of site-derived minerals or waste; the external appearance of the mine would be materially affected; if works carried out would exceed a height of 15 m from the level of the excavation, the level of any immediately adjacent unexcavated land or the height of the replaced, etc, building, plant or works (whichever is the greater) — if on the floor of the excavation; if works carried out would exceed a height of 15 m from ground level or the height of the replaced, etc, buildings, plant or work (whichever is the greater) — if not in the excavation; if a building erected would have floor space exceeding 1000 sq m; or if the cubic content of the alteration would exceed that of the original building by 25%, or the floor space by 1000 sq m. Development permitted under this Part is conditional upon the removal of such buildings, plant or works and satisfactory restoration of the site within 24 months (extendable by the MPA) of the permanent cessation of mining operations. Where the prior consent of the MPA has been given, the carrying out, on land used as a mine or ancillary mining land, of operations for, inter alia, the erection, rearrangement or other alteration of any plant, machinery, buildings, structures or erections is also permitted by Part 19, Class B. Thus, Class B allows for a wider range of development, and the requirement of prior approval means that fewer limitations are imposed by the GPDO itself. Such development is not subject to the height restrictions of Class A but must still be for a principle purpose: in connection with the operation of the mine; the treatment or utilisation, etc, of site-derived minerals; or the storage or removal from the mine of site-derived minerals or waste. The MPA may only refuse consent if it is satisfied that the proposed development would injure the amenity of the neighbourhood, and such injury cannot be avoided by the imposition of conditions, or the development ought, and could reasonably, be sited elsewhere. The restoration conditions applicable to Class A also cover Class B. Class C of Part 19 grants permission for works to repair or make safe a mine or land at or adjacent to a mine, subject to the authority's prior consent. Similar conditions to those restricting Class A permitted development apply.

The GPDO also gives certain permitted development rights in respect of mineral exploration. Thus, development of land for a period not exceeding 28 days consisting of drilling boreholes, carrying out seismic surveys or other excavations for the purpose of mineral exploration, and the construction of connected structures does not require consent (Part 22). However, such operations may not: be for petroleum exploration; be within 50 m of a school, hospital or occupied residential building; be within a National Park, an Area of Outstanding Natural Beauty or a site of archaeological or special scientific interest and result in more than 10 excavations in any 1 ha of land in the course of 24 months; use explosive charges of greater than 1 kg; exceed 10 m in depth or 12 sq m in surface area; exceed 12 m in height (or 3 m if within 3 km of an aerodrome). There are also requirements regarding hours of working, the protection of trees and soil, and post-operative remedial treatment. If the MPA has been informed and not, within 28 days, issued an order restricting or revoking permitted development rights at the proposed site, such operations can continue under Part 22, Class B for up to four months — subject to similar environmental protection conditions as apply to Class A permitted development.

Removal of material from a mineral-working deposit also requires planning permission unless it falls within Part 23. Two situations are covered: removal of material from a stockpile (Class A); and removal of material from a deposit other than a stockpile (Class B) where notification has been given to the MPA of the developer's intention to remove the material, and the deposit is smaller than 2 ha (unless it was deposited more than five years previously), and the deposit is not derived from permitted development rights allowing operations reasonably connected with agriculture (under Part 6). Interestingly, quite sophisticated conditions can now be placed on the exercise of Class B rights requiring not only compliance with a scheme of working submitted to the MPA but also, if the authority requires, submission of a scheme providing for the restoration and aftercare of the site. In this way the authority can bring up-to-date environmental protection conditions to bear on existing areas of minerals-related dereliction without reliance on either an existing consent or a new application.

The final generally applicable mineral related development under the GPDO is the tipping of waste connected with the extraction, treatment, processing, etc, of minerals, on land used as a mine or on ancillary mining land, where that waste is a product of working at that site. Such development is permitted under Part 21, Class A provided that excavations are not filled higher than adjoining land, nor the size or height of sites existing on 21 October 1988 are enlarged by more than 10%, unless the terms of an approved waste management scheme so allow. In any case, a waste management scheme must be submitted to, and approved by, the MPA if that authority requires it, and all tipping must be in conformity with it.

Publicity requirements relating to applications for planning permission for mineral development are set out in the GDPO. With TCPA 1990, s 65, art 8 of the order defines development involving the winning and working of minerals or the use of land for mineral working deposits as 'major development'. This must be publicised either by display of a site notice for 21 days on or near the land to which the application relates, or by serving notice on any adjoining owner or occupier, and by local advertisement. This is a change from the pre-1991 provisions which required display of a site notice in every case. Applications not conforming with the s 65 requirements 'shall not be entertained'[18]. This is supplemented by art 6 of the order which requires separate notification to be given to the owner or tenant of the land to which the application relates by individual notice, by local advertisement or by site notice left in place for at least seven days in the 21 immediately preceding the date of the application. Further, under art 16, where notice has been given to a MPA by the Coal Authority (in respect of coal), the Secretary of State for Trade and Industry (in respect of gas or oil), or the Crown Estates Commissioners (in respect of silver or gold), an authority shall not

18   TCPA 1990, s 65(5).

determine applications for mineral development in the area to which that notice relates without first informing the body giving notice.

Permitted development rights are extensive, and allow for a high degree of sophistication in controlling the environmental and other impacts of development associated with mineral extraction. Clearly, however, it may not be appropriate for such rights to be exercised in all cases. Article 4 of the GPDO therefore expressly enables MPAs to restrict permitted development rights. Article 7 further provides that rights under Part 22, Class B (mineral exploration for up to four months) or Part 23, Class C (removal of material from a stockpile) may be restricted where an authority considers that a planning application ought to be submitted because: the site is within a National Park, an Area of Outstanding Natural Beauty, a site of archaeological or special scientific interest, or the Broads; it would cause serious detriment to amenity or adversely affect the setting of a Grade I listed building; it would constitute a serious nuisance to the inhabitants of a 'nearby' residential building, hospital or school; or the development would endanger aircraft. Finally, it seems to be accepted that permitted development rights can be removed by a planning condition (eg *Dunoon Developments v Secretary of State for the Environment and Poole Borough Council*[19]), although this should be limited to cases where there are compelling planning reasons to do so[20]. This may be particularly the case where conservation interests may be affected, or the protection of a National Park or green belt it considered to take priority.

Continuing control I: conditions and obligations

The many unique characteristics of mineral development have been considered, their full implications have not. The potential duration of extraction is one feature of significance, as is the fact that, unlike other development, mineral extraction is not a 'one-off' operation: the development itself is the aim and not merely, eg conversion of land to another purpose. Planning law, which has as its root the notion of 'once-and-for-all' permission, has been historically weak in extending control beyond the initial grant of permission. Little thought has been given to restoration and 'aftercare' — the establishment and maintenance of a specified standard in the condition of land. Current mineral planning practice is very different, with comprehensive control by the imposition of numerous conditions, under s 70 of the 1990 Act, now being the norm. Those conditions can be usefully compared with the sorts of conditions imposed on other environmental licences in that they may provide not only for detailed regulation of the process of mineral extraction, but also the ultimate impact of the development on the environment[21]. Thus, matters commonly provided for in conditions include: methods of working, including the progressive working of a site with a rolling programme of restoration; commencement and duration of mining operations; hours of working and other limitations on noise emissions from extraction sites; soil movement, storage (including screening), treatment and replacement; transport access and regulation (although conditions cannot normally be used to control off-site routes to be taken by works traffic); limitation on the depth of working, and of production volumes (where increased production would have planning impacts); buildings fixed plant and machinery; the importation of waste; surface water, drainage and pollution control (where other statutory powers are not applicable); environmental protection and nuisance abatement; and the provision of vegetation to mitigate visual intrusion. As

19   [1992] JPL 936.
20   MPG2, *Applications, Permissions and Conditions*, July 1998, para B42.
21   See MPG 2, 'Applications, Permissions and Conditions' paras 40–60, and Annexes C and D.

MPAs have become more conscious of the full environmental implications of mineral extraction, so conditions have become more sophisticated, both in scope and drafting. And so conditions have emerged in practice in relation to such matters as hydrogeological surveys of proposed sites, safeguarding groundwater resources, and the exploration and protection of archaeological interests revealed in the course of extraction.

The drafting of conditions can now also be very complex, sometimes including detailed provision for the protection of water courses and other environmental media (often at the suggestion of other environmental agencies), the separate treatment of different soil types, for notice to be given to the MPA in advance of environmentally sensitive operations to facilitate supervision, and for extensive record-keeping. Many of these details, and in particular the details of steps to be taken to restore a site for post-extraction use (see MPG 7, 'The Reclamation of Mineral Workings' November 1996), may be reserved for definition of 'schemes' of working or restoration. These will be subject to post-planning permission approval, frequently by local authority officers under delegated powers. The legality of these sorts of 'permissions within permissions' has been recognised by the Court of Appeal in *Cadogan v Secretary of State for the Environment*,[22] although it makes it more difficult for third parties to discover the detailed implications of planning controls in any given case. The incorporation of details in consents by reference to documents other than the consent itself (eg correspondence in connection with an application) whilst also lawful, has been described as a 'very unfortunate practice' because of the relative inaccessibility of those documents: Wilmer J in *Wilson v West Sussex County Council*.[23] Two cautionary notes must be mentioned. First, despite the complexity of the conditions imposed on minerals consents, there are limits (albeit they are ill-defined). Revised policy guidance emphasises the core principle underpinning imposition of planning conditions: that this may enable development to be permitted which would otherwise be refused planning permission (MPG 2, July 1998, para 43). Equally, further advice is that conditions 'should deal with points of major importance, including issues which are likely to arise during the lifetime of the permission', but what they should not do is impose a multitude of minor obligations to cover every conceivable contingency (para 46). The second cautionary point relates to the relationship between planning and pollution controls. This is a complex issue, which is considered in chapter 8. It should be noted as a matter of principle, that minerals planning advice suggests that a condition which duplicates the effect of other enforceable controls will be unnecessary, and one whose requirements conflict with those of other controls will be ultra vires because it is unreasonable (MPG 2, para 56).

Planning obligations under TCPA 1990, s 106 are a common supplement to conditions as a means of reducing the environmental impact of mining operations. They are used to control, eg off-site screening, vehicle routing, and less frequently, to provide for the establishment of liaison committees of representatives of planning authorities, developers and local residents to enable on-going consultation and monitoring of long-term workings. National policy (MPG 7) suggests that the situations in which planning obligations may be appropriate include: retention of the after-use, to guarantee its implementation and retention in the longer-term; long-term maintenance and management, beyond the aftercare period; maintenance of water levels, including provision for drainage and water pumping; and provision of facilities for sport, recreation, nature conservation and other amenity uses.

22   [1993] JPL 664.
23   [1963] 2 QB 764 at 777.

Continuing control II: aftercare

The environmental effects of extraction are not confined to the period of extraction itself, but extend to the risk of post-extraction dereliction and, eg continuing pollution from materials deposited in extracted sites. To ensure that controls imposed on an active site, including restoration, are of lasting effect MPAs have unusual powers in relation to mineral development to extend their supervision of a site beyond the end of extraction operations and restoration. Following the recommendations of the Stevens Committee, TCPA 1990, s 72(5) and Sch 5 (originally to be found in the Town and Country Planning (Minerals) Act 1981) now provide that where permission for development involving the winning and working of minerals is granted subject to a 'restoration condition' (one involving reclamation with subsoil, topsoil or soil-making material) it may also be made subject to an 'aftercare condition'. Since 1991 this power may also be exercised over development involving the depositing of refuse or waste materials. This may require such steps as necessary to be taken to bring the land to the required standard for use in: agriculture (when its physical characteristics have been restored to as they were when the land was last used for agriculture as specified by DEFRA or, if the land has not previously been used for agriculture, when it is reasonably fit for that use); forestry (reasonably fit for growing a utilisable crop of timber) or amenity (reasonably fit for sustaining trees, shrubs or other plants). The aftercare condition may either specify the required steps or provide that steps be taken in accordance with an 'aftercare scheme' approved by the MPA. Compulsory steps may include planting, cultivating, fertilising, watering, draining, or otherwise treating land. However, measures may only be required during the 'aftercare period': five years (or such other period as may be prescribed) from compliance with the restoration condition for the whole, or part, of the site.

Before imposing an aftercare condition, MPAs are required to carry out certain consultations. Where the proposed after-use is agriculture or forestry, DEFRA and the Forestry Commission respectively must be consulted as to: whether the proposed use is appropriate; if so, whether control should involve an aftercare scheme; and the terms of any proposed scheme. Further consultation regarding the implementation of aftercare should be undertaken from time to time. On completion of aftercare to the satisfaction of the MPA, it shall issue a certificate to that effect on the application of any person with an interest in the land in question.

An aftercare condition may be the subject of an appeal to the Secretary of State under TCPA 1990, s 78; judicial review would also be available to question its validity. Both of these possibilities are reduced by the modern practice of negotiating site management over a long period *prior* to the submission of the application (see MPG 2, paras 10–13). Detailed and time consuming discussions often take place between developers, authorities and affected third parties with a view to minimising a proposal's short- and long-term environmental effects. The concerns of local people and authorities can be assuaged by the establishment of a positive and continuing relationship with a potential developer, similarly, a developer who is willing to conduct such discussions can often reduce the potential for time wasting conflict. There is no requirement to conduct pre-application negotiation which, for large projects, can take as long as three years. Nor are local authorities empowered to levy charges for those negotiations (*McCarthy & Stone (Developments) Ltd v Richmond-upon-Thames London Borough Council*[24]), although the Secretary of State has an enabling power under the Local Government and Housing Act 1989, s 150. If consultations are carried out after submission of an application, they could very easily force an application 'out of time'

24 [1992] 2 AC 48, [1992] JPL 467, HL.

according to the eight-week period for decision given by art 20 of the GDPO. Frustrated applicants always have the final resort of submitting their application and then appealing, after eight weeks, under TCPA 1990, s 78 against deemed refusal.

Continuing control III: review of planning permissions

The most controversial aspect of continuing control over mineral planning permissions — in fact an approach applying uniquely to them — is the compulsory review and modification of existing consents. Given that in the case of mineral extraction it is the development itself which is sought and not the conversion to some other or renewed purpose, the planning system is in fact licensing a continuing use of land which may last for many years. Given also the environmental effects of extraction, it is no wonder that a consent granted at the beginning of mineral extraction might soon lag behind emerging environmental standards. As has been explained, through the use of planning conditions and obligations and the availability after 1981 of aftercare, the planning system has adapted to accommodate the special needs of minerals. However, since 1991 more dramatic changes have been introduced which for the first time in any planning context allow for the widespread review and modernisation of existing planning consents, often without compensation liability falling on planning authorities.

Old mining permissions

Before the introduction of the modern planning system and the uniform requirement for planning control under the TCPA 1947, development could still be regulated by way of 'planning schemes'. These could be adopted by local authorities with a view to securing proper sanitary and amenity standards, and the convenient lay out and use of land. Schemes were voluntary unless an area had a population, after 1919, of 20,000 or more; they only became mandatory in 1943, under the Town and Country Planning (Interim Development) Act of that year. From 1932, their scope was extended to the general object of controlling the development of land and the preservation of buildings and objects of architectural, historic or artistic interest. The significance of planning schemes resulted originally from compensation. Whilst no restriction was placed upon the right to develop, once a scheme came into operation (sometime after an authority's resolution to prepare one) the authority had the right to remove, pull down or alter buildings or works not in conformity with it. Where a developer had begun works between the authority's resolution to adopt a scheme and its actual adoption — the 'interim development period' — and was injuriously affected by the coming into operation of the scheme, compensation was only payable where permission to build had been secured. Such permission was granted under the terms of an 'interim development order' (IDO) issued by central government.

IDO permissions were different from planning permissions in significant respects: they were not recorded in planning registers; they were subject to few, if any, planning conditions and those conditions which are imposed were, by modern standards, inadequate; and they were rarely of limited duration. These characteristics led to the recent significance of IDO permissions, as until 1991 it was still possible to develop under their terms. A survey by the Chief Planning Officers' Society in November 1990 found 980 largely unworked, 'ideal sites' with IDO permission for mineral extraction, whilst a survey of county councils also revealed more than 300 valuable wildlife habitats similarly affected, including 19 sites of special scientific interest. The fact that restrictive and expensive restoration and aftercare conditions are imposed on new permissions led to significant concern that these old and largely unrestrained (hence, cheap to work) sites would be 'resurrected' — the uncertainty of their existence and the potential for large-scale and unexpected mineral development in previously unspoilt rural areas led to the introduction of controversial provisions in the Planning and Compensation Act 1991 to eliminate them. Those provisions have now provided the basis for an extensive review of all minerals consents granted before 22 February 1982 under the terms of s 96 and Schs 13 and 14 of the Environment Act 1995 (which have effect as insertions into TCPA 1990, Part II).

Under the Planning and Compensation Act 1991, s 22 and Sch 2 (inserted into TCPA 1990, Part III) all IDO permissions not worked 'to any substantial extent' in the two years before 1 May 1991 ceased to have effect on 1 March 1992 unless an application for their registration was made and approved by the relevant MPA. That application was required to include details of what the developer claimed to be an IDO permission's terms, including the land it covers and any conditions to which it is subject. If satisfied that the developer's interpretation was correct, the MPA must have registered the IDO permission. Having been registered and placed on the planning register kept under the TCPA 1990, IDO permissions are now being made subject to modern conditions. These may include any conditions which may be imposed on a permission for the winning and working of minerals under the TCPA 1990 and must include one that all developments cease not later than 21 February 2042. Again, developers have had the onus of proposing the conditions to which permissions may become subject, although the MPA can substitute its own. Having been registered and made subject to modern conditions, IDO permissions become the same in all respects as any other mineral permission (see also MPGs 8 and 9).

Other minerals permissions

The very complex provisions of the Environment Act 1995 adapt the specific IDO provisions for a review of all minerals consents granted between 1948 and 1982. They also make some concessions to the existing powers available to all planning authorities to revoke, modify and discontinue existing planning consents in that compensation *may* still be available to operators for the effects of modifications required under the review. The distinctive feature is the fact of a mandatory review, which supersedes the review previously 'required' under TCPA 1990, s 105. That review, although ostensibly mandatory, was not set within any prescribed time frame, nor did it provide for significant alterations to the compensation regime which had in practice proved to be a total bar on effective use of planning authorities' review powers. TCPA 1990, s 105 has been repealed.

EA 1995, s 96 and Schs 13 and 15 comprise four principal elements: an initial review of sites where the predominant minerals permission was granted before 22 February 1982; two reviews of active mineral sites in successive three year periods for the purposes of updating old conditions, the first relating to 'Phase I' sites where the permissions in question were granted after 30 June 1948 but before 1 April 1969, and 'Phase II' sites relating to permissions granted after 31 March 1969 and before 22 February 1982; and thereafter periodic reviews of all consents at 15-year intervals. Older consents were therefore reviewed first under Phase I, although this category also includes sites which are wholly or partly within National Parks, Areas of Outstanding Natural Beauty or Sites of Special Scientific Interest. With the exception of the 15-year periodic reviews, these provisions do not apply to remaining IDO permissions already subject to review under the 1991 Act. The potential effects of this review are severe. The lists of active and dormant sites prepared under the review become exhaustive lists of those sites with planning permission for mineral extraction; permissions not included on those lists 'cease to have effect' except insofar as they impose restoration or aftercare requirements (Sch 13, para 12).

By 31 January 1996 MPAs were required to prepare a list of all dormant or active sites in their area, known as 'the first list'. That list distinguishes between dormant sites, active Phase I sites and active Phase II sites. Following the example of the IDO provisions, the first list specified for *active Phase I* sites a date by which an application for approval of conditions was required to be submitted to the MPA. If sites were omitted from those lists, a land or relevant mineral owner had the right to apply to the MPA within three months for its inclusion, followed by a further right of appeal to the Secretary of State against the MPAs determination of that application. This statutory appeal was and is the sole means of challenging non-inclusion of a site on the list[25]. Equally, inclusion of a site on the list is not conclusive of the validity of that permission: an important conclusion, in that otherwise the MPA could inadvertently resurrect permissions that have in fact lapsed[26]. A site is 'dormant' if no minerals development had been carried out to any substantial extent in, on or under the site at any time in the period beginning 22 February 1982 and ending with 6 June 1995. In such cases, it is not lawful to carry out development until full modern planning conditions have been approved for that site by the MPA. There was no right of appeal against an MPA's decision to classify a site as dormant. By 31 October 1998, MPAs were under a further obligation to draw up a 'second list' of *active Phase II* sites, specifying in respect of each site a date by which it too must be the subject of an application for the determination of new conditions. The second list is therefore an update of the first list in respect of Phase II sites, that enables MPAs to concentrate their attention for the first three years of the review on the oldest sites and those in the most environmentally sensitive areas. Although the time limits for the preparation of the lists and the submission of applications for the determination of new conditions are set out in the Act (and, in the latter case, generally allow a year for the submission of revised conditions), there is provision for the review to be postponed in individual cases on the grounds that the existing conditions on the permission are satisfactory, and that a review would be unnecessary. as postponements may be for up to 15 years, these provisions are of continuing relevance.

The central feature of the review is the determination of new conditions for existing minerals consents. Conditions imposed in response to land or mineral owners' applications may include any conditions which may be imposed on the grant of planning permission for minerals development and may be in addition to, or in substitution for, any existing conditions. An MPA need not apply the conditions proposed for a site, but may alter them or substitute its own. The provisions in general serve to highlight the significance of changing policy for the scope and detail of conditions imposed on minerals consents, rather than any change in the law. The legal framework for controlling mineral-related environmental harm is not substantively changed by the new Act, rather, it allows the existing once-and-for-all system to be applied again.

But the power to apply new conditions is not unlimited: mineral operators with existing consents have been operating under what are effectively statutory licenses to develop, and their curtailment has traditionally given rise to liability to pay compensation. However, compensation is only provided for in a limited number of cases, namely, when the effect of restrictions on workings imposed by an MPA would be such as to prejudice adversely to an unreasonable degree either the economic

25   *R v North Lincolnshire Council, ex p Horticultural and Garden Product Sales (Humberside) Ltd* [1998] Env LR 295.
26   *R v Oldham Metropolitan Borough Council and Pugmanor Properties Ltd, ex p Foster* [2000] JPL 711.

viability of the site or the asset value of the site. EA 1995, Sch 13, para 1(6) provides that working rights are restricted or reduced if specified characteristics of the site are modified. These include: the size of the area which may be used for development; the depth to which operations may extend; the height of any deposit of mineral waste; the rate of extraction; the expiry date of the development previously permitted; or the total quantity of minerals to be extracted from a site or mineral waste to be deposited there. If new limitations on any of these characteristics have been imposed, then the MPA must consider whether the operator is prejudiced adversely by it. If this is the case, then TCPA 1990, Parts IV and IX in relation to modification orders will have effect (see below). The effect of these limitations on the review (without compensation) is that a distinction is applied between conditions that deal with the environmental and amenity aspects of the working of a site, which should not affect asset value, and conditions that would fundamentally affect the economic structure of an operation. No compensation is payable for any new environmental, amenity or restoration conditions imposed (see generally MPG 14, 'Environment Act 1995: Review of Mineral Planning Permissions' (1995)). The operation of these provisions was also considered in *Earthline Ltd v Secretary of State for Transport, Local Government and the Regions and West Berkshire County Council*[27], which considered the application of the review provisions as to the duration of old mineral permissions.

Continuing control IV: other powers of intervention

Notwithstanding the 1995 powers of review and modification of existing consents, MPAs retain their pre-existing powers to make orders revoking, modifying, discontinuing, prohibiting or suspending development involving the winning and working of minerals or the disposal of mineral waste (see MPG 4, *Revocation, Modification, Discontinuation, Prohibition and Suspension Orders*, August 1997).

Revocation, modification and discontinuation

By an order under TCPA 1990, s 97, and where it appears expedient, a local planning authority may revoke or modify a planning permission. In doing so it must have regard to all material considerations, and may affect only so much of a permission for operational development as has yet to be carried out, or a use which has yet to be materially changed. Such an order must be submitted for the approval of the Secretary of State (unless agreed) and, if subject to the opposition of people who may be affected and who have been notified as required by TCPA 1990, ss 98 and 99, may be the subject of an appeal inquiry. Alternatively, the Secretary of State himself may, having consulted with the local planning authority, issue a revocation order. Orders under TCPA 1990, s 97 in relation to mineral extraction may only include an aftercare condition if a restoration condition is either already attached to the permission or if one has been imposed by the order itself: TCPA 1990, Sch 5, Part II. The inability of this provision to affect operations already carried out, coupled with the compensation liability normally incurred by its use, restricts its application in terms of mineral permissions.

Where a permission is modified or revoked by an order under s 97, any person interested in the affected land or minerals who can show either that expenditure incurred in carrying works has been rendered abortive by the order, or that they have otherwise suffered loss or damage directly attributable to the order, can claim compensation under

TCPA 1990, s 107. However, in respect of development consisting of the winning and working of minerals or depositing mineral waste, that compensation may be varied. TCPA 1990, s 116 and Sch 11 previously set out the circumstances in which compensation for modification of planning permission might be varied in the case of mineral extraction. However, that Schedule was repealed by the PCA 1991 and a new TCPA 1990, s 116 provides the Secretary of State with a power to make regulations to modify the basis for such compensation. This has been done through the Town and Country Planning (Compensation for Restrictions on Mineral Working and Mineral Waste Depositing) Regulations 1997, SI 1997/1111 which revoked and replaced the Regulations of the same name made in 1985 (SI 1985/698, themselves amended in 1988 and 1990). The Regulations are broadly consistent with the reforms made to mineral planning by both the 1991 and 1995 Acts, in that they place a more onerous (and thus expensive) burden on minerals operators to ensure that planning conditions applying to minerals sites meet contemporary environmental standards. In particular, they will operate in many cases to reduce the levels of compensation payable under the 1985 Regulations. Regulations 3 and 4, for example, provide that *no* compensation shall be payable in some circumstances following the making of a modification or discontinuance order. Here, the familiar pattern of defining certain basic and fundamental features of minerals sites is adopted: where compulsory modifications do not affect defined working rights or other principal features of site operation, the consent was issued before 1982 and it has not been compulsorily modified recently, then no compensation will be payable. In this way, important, but less central features of a site than those affecting its essential economic viability, can be upgraded to modern standards without minerals planning authorities incurring liability to pay compensation. Conditions relating to localised environmental disturbance (for example, noise or dust) or restoration and aftercare may therefore be modernised in this way at site operators' expense. However, this will not always be the case. For example, where suspension of workings is required, then works carried out for the purposes of removing or alleviating any 'injury to amenity' shall still be compensable (TCPA 1990, s 115(3A), as amended by reg 6 of the present Regulations).

The effect is that compensation will generally be payable at a reduced level only where 'fundamental planning issues' over the general acceptability of the site and its economic working are not interfered with. This reflects the opinion of the Stevens Committee that mineral developers ought not to bear the full cost of bringing old mineral permissions up to modern standards, and is mirrored in the provisions of the EA 1995. Thus, where conditions governing the commencement of the development, the size of the working area, the depth of working, the rate or period of extraction, the duration of the permission or any other condition restricting the total quantity of minerals to be extracted are altered by a s 97 order, full compensation will be payable.

Where it appears to an MPA expedient in the interests of proper planning, and subject to the payment of compensation, they may, under TCPA 1990, s 102 and Sch 9, para 1, require the discontinuance of a *use* of land (see the Town and Country Planning (Minerals) Regulations 1995, reg 2). For the purposes of this provision, 'use' includes development consisting of the winning and working of minerals and the depositing of refuse or waste materials. Discontinuance is not the only option; the authority may alternatively impose conditions upon the continuance of the use of land for mineral development or the depositing of waste, or require the alteration or removal of buildings, plant or machinery on land so used. Conditions imposed may relate to restoration and aftercare and must include, under PCA 1991, Sch 1, a condition restricting the duration of the development. Orders under this provision must be approved by the Secretary of State (who may modify them) and advertised in accordance with TCPA 1990, s 103. They may also grant planning permission for buildings or works constructed or carried out, or a use instituted, before the order was submitted for approval. The power under

TCPA 1990, s 97 to revoke or modify permissions applies to any permission given under TCPA 1990, Sch 9. Schedule 9, para 1 may be used in relation to the discontinuance of development permitted under the GPDO (to which TCPA 1990, s 97 does not apply as no application need be made for permitted development — a requirement of the use of s 97); although it is also appropriate where an authority wishes to impose restoration and aftercare conditions on exhausted portions of a site upon other parts of which extraction is still continuing.

Prohibition and suspension

Supplementing MPAs' powers to revoke, modify or discontinue mineral development is TCPA 1990, Sch 9, para 3 which empowers them to prohibit the resumption of mineral development where it appears to them that such working has permanently ceased. Such an assumption may be made where no development has been carried out to any substantial extent anywhere on the site for two years, and it appears to the authority at the time it makes the order that resumption of working is unlikely. Subject to ministerial approval, an authority may require: the alteration or removal of any buildings used for, or ancillary to, the winning and working of minerals at the site; specified steps to be taken within a specified time to remove or alleviate damage to amenity resulting from the mineral development (except subsidence caused by underground working); compliance with any conditions to which the original permission was subject; and restoration and aftercare.

Conversely, where working has only temporarily ceased, the powers provided by TCPA 1990, Sch 9, para 5 to make a suspension order may be employed. Where it appears to an authority that no development has been carried out to any substantial extent anywhere on a site for 12 months and resumption appears unlikely, they may require steps to be taken for the protection of the environment. These are steps required during the period of the suspension for the purpose of preserving the amenity of the area in which the site is situated, protecting the area from damage or preventing a deterioration in the condition of the land. At any time after making a suspension order an authority may alter its terms by virtue of a supplementary suspension order (under TCPA 1990, Sch 9, para 6). Under paras 7 and 8, both types of order are subject to the approval of the Secretary of State and are registrable as local land charges. Paragraph 9 provides that MPAs are under a duty to review suspension and supplementary suspension orders, and whether they should make additional orders, at intervals of no more than five years. Whilst suspension orders do not prevent the resumption of development, under para 10 notice of the intended date of recommencement must first be given to the authority. Where development recommences to a substantial extent, an authority must revoke a suspension order; where there is a dispute as to whether development has actually recommenced, an appeal lies to the Secretary of State. If the Secretary of State is satisfied of recommencement, he must revoke the order himself.

As with revocation orders under TCPA 1990, s 97, action under TCPA 1990, Sch 9, paras 1, 3 or 5 and 6 will result in the payment of compensation to land and mineral owners. Similar principles apply to calculation of that compensation as in the case of compulsory revocation or modification. However, unlike revocation or modification, where resumption of working is prohibited under para 3 of that Schedule or suspended under para 5, then compensation may instead be reduced rather than any entitlement removed withdrawn completely. In such cases, the maximum reduction of the level of compensation will be £7,800, or part thereof, depending on the affected persons' interest in the land or minerals as a proportion of the gross value of the land or minerals affected by the order in question (SI 1997/1111, regs 5 and 6). These provisions do not apply to orders made in respect of mineral development carried out by the Coal Authority or licensees.

TCPA 1990, s 189 provides that it is an offence to cause or permit the breach of any orders issued under TCPA 1990, s 102. It is a defence to prove that all reasonable measures were taken and all due diligence exercised to avoid the commission of an offence. In the event of non-compliance with any order under TCPA 1990, s 102, the MPA can enter upon land, take the steps required in the order and recover from the owner of the land expenses reasonably incurred in so doing. Revocation and modification orders under TCPA 1990, s 97 remain to be enforced under normal planning procedures. The modification and compensation regime is therefore complex and, for any authorities proposing its widespread use, expensive.

Taxation of aggregates extraction

Shortly after it was first elected in 1997, the Government announced that it had commissioned research into the environmental costs of quarrying, particularly of aggregates. This is part of a wider trend in environmental law and policy towards more active use of economic instruments to complement traditional, regulatory approaches to controlling the environmental impacts of industrial activity. This research resulted in the proposal of an aggregates tax (*Consultation on a Potential Aggregates Tax*, HM Customs & Excise, 15 June 1998) to ensure that the environmental impacts of aggregates production, not already addressed by regulation (mainly the land use planning system), are more fully reflected in the price paid for their use. The tax would also, Customs suggested, encourage recycling, and thus complement both MPG 6 and the exemption from the landfill tax of material produced as a by-product of mining and quarrying (Finance Act 1996, s 45; see chapter 15). The proposal in respect of aggregates was for a simple volume-based tax, applied to the point of first sale, use or transfer of the material away from the site of extraction, with associated exemptions for recycled materials. This reflects the general shape of the landfill tax.

Whilst Customs & Excise published draft provisions for the introduction of such a tax (*Potential Aggregates Tax: Draft Legislation and Summary of Consultation*, 30 April 1999), the consultation process revealed some additional complexities. The Quarry Products Association (QPA) in particular, although perhaps not surprisingly, criticised the rationale for the tax, pointing to the limited prospects it presents for lessening the environmental impacts of extraction by encouraging reduced demand for aggregates. Unlike waste minimisation, re-use and alternative disposal methods vis-à-vis the landfill tax, the QPA suggested that recycled material is only ever likely to provide a relatively small proportion of the aggregates needed for economic development, with a consequential ceiling on the environmental advantages securable by taxation (Memorandum from the Quarry Products Association to the House of Commons Select Committee on Environmental Audit, November 1998, published as Annex 7 to the Committee's Fourth Report, Session 1998-99, *The Pre-Budget Report 1998*, HC 93, 23 February 1999). The tax's failure to distinguish between operations with different environmental standards would also rid it (it was suggested) of any incentive effect on operators to improve site-specific environmental performance.

What has since been developed is a 'package' of both voluntary measures to be adopted throughout the industry to generate environmental improvements, and a new aggregates levy. The new emphasis on voluntary mechanisms, including the adoption of codes of good environmental practice and environmental management systems, appears in revised planning guidance (Draft MPG 11, paras 43, 60-67). Separate provision has been made for the aggregates levy itself (Finance Act 2001, ss 16-49 and Schs 4-

10). The levy applies to the commercial exploitation of 'taxable aggregates', that is, any rock, gravel or sand together with any substances incorporated in that, including those which occur naturally (FA 2001, ss 16, 17). The starting rate of the levy is £1.60 per tonne, and the levy itself has effect from 1 April 2002. As with the landfill tax, certain exemptions apply. These include materials removed during the course of ordinary building, dredging for the purposes of river or harbour maintenance, highway construction and maintenance and pipe-laying, and china clay spoil. Also exempt are aggregates which arise as a by-product of related activities, such as off-cuts from dimension stone production, and material produced as result of processing specialist minerals such as ball clay, flint, fluorspar or fuller's earth. The Finance Act provisions, whilst themselves elaborate, are also complemented by regulations (Aggregates Levy (General) Regulations 2002, SI 2002/761; Aggregates Levy (Registration and Miscellaneous Provisions) Regulations 2001, SI 2001/4027). These include details of the necessary registration, accounting and record-keeping obligations, payment of the tax, and provision for tax credits.

E EXTRACTION OF MARINE AGGREGATES

As the environmental pressures of onshore extraction have increased, and local communities have become more sensitive to proposals for land-based mineral extraction, so the consideration of alternative sources of supply has developed. Those alternatives include not just the use of extraction related wastes, such as china clay, sand, colliery minestone, slate wastes and recycled materials such as demolition arisings and asphalt road planings, but alternative sources of supply. One obvious source is marine resources, which provide an important supplement to land-won material. In 1994 marine aggregates accounted for 19% of national consumption, and a further 6 million tonnes was exported or directly used for coast protection works. Their percentage contribution is even greater in the south east of England and London, where 21% and 40% respectively of aggregates are from marine sources. The annual rate of extraction increased markedly in the 1970s and 1980s, reaching a peak of 28 million tonnes in 1989. The figure has subsequently been in the region of 24 million tonnes per year. That extraction is centred on six main areas: the east and south coasts, Thames Estuary, Bristol Channel, Humber and Liverpool Bay. The total area in 1999 where licences permit dredging is 1467km² (around 0.8% of the UK continental shelf), although actual dredging does not take place in this whole area every year.

The benefits of marine extraction include a reduction in gross production costs through the relative proximity of wharfage to areas of high use; removal of the inevitable environmental disruption associated with onshore sites; and the ability to supply the demands of the south east of England with building materials. Whilst therefore preferable in many respects to onshore extraction, the exploitation of marine reserves does create a whole different range of environmental consequences. These include possible fisheries and habitat destruction, coastal erosion problems, deleterious water quality effects and the more mundane hazard to marine navigation and questions over the siting of wharfage and onshore processing facilities. It is unfortunate that the increasing significance of marine extraction in terms of volume is not balanced by a full understanding of these long term environmental consequences.

The control of marine extraction is radically different from land based controls exercised by MPAs. The basic legal problem is that the marine extraction of aggregates does not fall within terrestrial planning control. Ownership of sea-bed minerals resources in UK territorial waters vests in the Crown (Crown Estate Act 1961; Continental Shelf Act 1964) and its development falls outside the jurisdiction of planning authorities. Consequently, until very recently, merely an 'informal' process had become established by which the Crown Estates Commissioners (CEC) exercised controls over marine dredging, in conjunction with (then) DETR, MAFF and the DTI. The CEC's ownership extends to 2,735 kilometres (1,700 miles) of foreshore, 55% of the beds of tidal rivers and estuaries, and almost all of the seabed out to the 12 nautical mile territorial limit, and resulted (in 1997) in an annual revenue for the CEC of £22.1 million. However, this non-statutory system was the subject of considerable criticism, not least by the House of Commons Environment Select Committee (*Coastal Zone Protection and Planning,* HC 17, Session 1991-92). Particular criticisms have been made of the lack of transparency in the CEC process, the delays it creates for business, and its inadequate consideration of environmental issues. As a result, June 1998 saw the introduction of a new non-statutory process to meet some of these criticisms, pending the preparation of a statutory scheme to regulate marine aggregates extraction.

The current position is that new policy and legal frameworks are being developed to impose more modern controls on marine aggregates extraction. At a policy level, a new series of 'marine minerals guidance' (MMGs) is in preparation to articulate a clearer policy framework. The proposed general aim of that guidance is to provide the dredging industry with sufficient access to suitable long-term resources to meet its varied and fluctuating markets, so as to provide the industry with sufficient confidence to invest in new ships and wharves, while ensuring that the extraction of the mineral does not have an unacceptable impact on the marine or coastal environment, or on other legitimate uses of the sea (*Draft MMG 2: Guidance on the Extraction by Dredging of Sand, Gravel and other Minerals from the English Seabed,* February 2001). It is proposed that these objectives can be achieved by:

(a) the careful location of new dredging areas;
(b) considering new applications for 'Dredging Permissions' in relation to the findings of an EIA;
(c) minimising the overall impact of dredging;
(d) controlling dredging operations through the use of legally enforceable conditions attached to dredging permissions; and
(e) requiring operators to monitor, as appropriate, the environmental impacts of their activities during, and on the completion of, dredging.

It is the legal context which has contributed to provoke this modernisation process and, in particular, the need to assess environmental impacts more formally and comprehensively. As we shall see, this is to lead to the introduction of a statutory system of permitting which will supersede the informal arrangements currently in place.

The old system

The system in place between 1968 and 1998 provided for the CEC to issue prospecting and production licences on the Crown's behalf. The licences place a ceiling tonnage on the material which may be extracted and had a normal duration of four years. Applications for licences were not subject to any binding requirement to undertake consultation. However, outline proposals were submitted to CEC who would consult, for example, local coastal protection authorities, the Environment Agency, local fisheries interests, local off-shore operators, the (then) Department of Transport or (its then successor) the DETR, the Ministry of Defence, the relevant conservation authorities, Trinity House and the relevant MPA. Consultants would also be commissioned to assess whether the proposal presented an unavoidable risk of coastal erosion, in which case it would be rejected. After 1989, proposals were also required to be accompanied by an environmental assessment, although this to operated on a non-statutory basis.

An application for a production licence could only be made after completion of this pre-application informal consultation. That application was required by the CEC to include a response to the outcome of the consultation and any measures proposed to alleviate or mitigate objections. The application was then put through the so-called 'government view procedure', by which the co-ordinating department (generally the DETR) initiated wide-ranging inter-departmental discussion. If agreement that a proposal was in the public interest could be reached, then a favourable (usually conditional) 'government view' would result. If an department had an overriding objection, an unfavourable view would result. On average, 50% of applications received a favourable response, 25% did so when initial objections had been overcome, while 25% were rejected. In addition, an extractor might have required the separate consent of the Department of Transport (then DETR) or local coast protection authority (Coast Protection Act 1949, ss 18 and 34), MAFF (Food and Environment Protection Act 1985, Pt II) or an adjoining MPA (where extraction would extend below low water in an estuary).

The revised non-statutory system

In June 1998 the DETR published a short guidance booklet on marine dredging, which sets out a revised process for obtaining a government view on applications for the extraction of marine aggregates. The purpose of the revised process was to incorporate the principles of land use planning controls into the consideration of seabed applications. Compared to the land use planning system, however, the revised procedures are very slight. There are five stages: application (12 weeks), consultation (10 weeks), confirmation (2 weeks), assessment and determination (6 weeks), and decision. Applications must be made to DTLR (previously DETR), supported by plans and others details of the proposal. DTLR and the applicant thereafter share responsibility for initiating consultation with relevant bodies, although it falls to the applicant to consider the scope of a formal environmental impact assessment. If the applicant wishes to proceed, having considered initial the views of respondents to the consultation, then they will be required to commission a 'coastal impact study' (CIS) and an environmental statement (ES).

The consultation stage hinges on the CIS and ES. Advertisement of the application is required, with copies of the reports to be lodged with the closest LPAs. The applicant must consult various bodies, providing them with copies of all the relevant papers. The applicant must also prepare a summary of the responses to the consultation process, indicating how consultee's concerns 'have been resolved' (*Minerals Dredging Guidance Booklet*, p 5, paragraph (g)). That summary is re-circulated by DTLR to all the consultees as part of the confirmation stage, the purpose of which is to secure the consultee's agreement that their concerns have been resolved. The guidance booklet makes no provision at this stage for cases in which those concerns are *not* resolved. Following this, the DTLR certainly does have more developed and thorough information on which to form a government view – the next stage – than under the old procedure. Unless a favourable or unfavourable government view is formed at this 'assessment and determination stage', the guidance makes new provision for an informal hearing to be held before a Planning Inspector, the first time the Inspectorate has been formally involved in marine extraction applications. Indeed, if there are major unresolved issues affecting several parties a public inquiry on the land use planning model may be held. Eight weeks after the outcome of any hearing, or the end of the required consultation, a government view will be formed and communicated to the applicant.

Towards a statutory system

Whilst an improvement on the old system, there are clearly major gaps in the new procedures. These relate to many matters of essential detail in respect of the process, as well as the substance of the various reports. It can be observed, for example, that some of the most controversial features of the statutory environmental assessment process on land have been the ambiguity of required environmental information, and the lack of consistency in the quality of environmental statements. It seems unlikely, that applications under the revised government view process should be much better, when the 'informal' guidelines are much more sparse even than the applicable land use rules. It is partly to meet objections such as this that further reform is now underway.

In 1998 the DETR issued a consultation draft of *Guidance on Marine Dredging Procedures*, to accompany draft Environmental Assessment and Habitats (Extraction of Minerals by Marine Dredging) Regulations (28 September 1998). The aim is to ensure compliance in respect of marine dredging with the relevant EC Directives on environmental assessment. Although the draft suggested that the new Regulations would come into force on 14 March 1999 (in conjunction with the Town and Country Planning (Environmental Impact Assessment) (England and Wales) Regulations 1999, SI 1999/293), a proposed MMG 1 is still in preparation (*Regulatory Procedures for the Extraction of Minerals by Dredging from the English Seabed*).

The system proposed by the draft Regulations is stated expressly to be 'separate from commercial and land ownership considerations', a veiled confirmation that EIA under any new Regulations would form part of the revised government view procedure itself. This is confirmed by the curious statement that 'the Government intends ... that there should be continuity between the existing informal procedures for the control of marine dredging... and the practical arrangements to give effect to the new Regulations so that the statutory control of marine dredging is carried out as effectively and efficiently as possible in the public interest'. The new Regulations will therefore introduce the main elements of EIA into the government view procedure, in the same way that the principal regulations introduce EIA into the land use planning system. The policy aim of the new regime is proposed as being to: conserve minerals as far as possible whilst ensuring adequate supply; ensure that environmental impacts are kept to a minimum; minimise the production of waste and encourage the efficient use of materials; encourage responsible working; protect coastal and marine areas designated for their national and international nature conservation value; and to prevent the unnecessary sterilisation of mineral resources (draft MMG2, para 13). In legal terms far more elaborate provision will also be made in respect of the considerations that must be taken into account in considering applications for dredging permissions, and the conditions that can be imposed on them (draft MMG2, paras 49-50 and Annex B respectively). However, the new system will not apply retrospectively – to areas licensed before the new regulations come into effect – unless this is necessary to comply with European conservation legislation. To this extent a review will have to be undertaken of existing operations, in a similar manner required in the case of extant planning permissions on land (Conservation (Natural Habitats &c) Regulations 1994).

F COAL

Few areas of industrial, and by extension minerals, policy are as controversial as coal mining. Not only has a growing reliance on opencast coal production increased awareness of the environmental implications of energy use, but major structural changes in the coal industry have increased the number of operators likely to be involved in extraction. Before 31 October 1994 the British Coal Corporation had exclusive rights to search for, bore for, work and get coal in Great Britain. However, the Corporation's interests are now vested in the Coal Authority established by the Coal Industry Act 1994, s 1 and Sch 1 (SIs 1994/2189, 2552 and 3063), and much of the Coal Industry Nationalisation Act 1946 has been repealed (see CIA 1994, s 67(8)). Whereas the Corporation was previously responsible for the largest part of coal extracted in the UK (97%, or 95.4 million tonnes, in 1989), that responsibility, having passed to the Coal Authority, is now progressively falling to private contractors and licensees. Controls over coal extraction are therefore becoming subsumed by the general framework of planning controls over mineral extraction.

Notwithstanding this general position there remain certain variations in law, but more particularly policy, that alter the effect of general planning controls in the case of coal. For example, the British Coal Corporation had extensive permitted development rights in addition to those available to extractors of other minerals. Consistent with the general trend towards privatisation those rights were significantly reduced by the Town and Country Planning General Development (Amendment) Order 1992, SI 1992/2450, but certain rights in connection with coal mining development by the Coal Authority and licensed operators remain under the GPDO 1995. Part 20, Classes A and B of the GPDO permit the winning and working underground by a licensee of the Coal Authority of coal or coal-related minerals in a mine started before 1 July 1948. Classes C and D permit development required for the purposes of a mine to be carried out on an authorised site at that mine by a licensed operator in connection with coal mining operations. 'Authorised sites' are either those sites identified in planning consents as being subject to Part 20 or land immediately adjoining an access which, on 5 December 1988, was in use for the purposes of that mine in connection with coal mining operations. Land used for the permanent deposit of waste or on which there is a conveyor, railway, pipeline, etc, not surrounded by other land used for that purpose is excluded. Class C covers less intrusive development than Class D, which needs the prior approval of the MPA. That approval may only be refused if injury to amenity could not be removed by the imposition of conditions or if the development ought, and could reasonably, be sited elsewhere. Class C development is subject to conditions restricting, eg its height, volume and external appearance, whilst the creation of a new surface access to underground working is not permitted. Neither is such an access permitted by Class D, but the same conditions are not imposed upon Class D development in terms of height, appearance and volume. Both classes of development are subject to conditions requiring its removal, and the restoration of the site, within 24 months of working finally concluding (unless the MPA agrees otherwise). Rights in connection with prospecting for opencast deposits were revoked in 1992. Finally, Class E allows development for the purposes of maintaining or making safe mines or land adjacent to mines, whether active or disused. The prior approval of the MPA must be obtained (which may only be refused on the same grounds as under Class D), and any development is subject to, eg height and volume restrictions. As with other permitted development rights, the above may be removed by the MPA by an art 4 direction.

Coal mining and planning policy

The policy differences between coal and other minerals are of two broad types. First, the role of coal as an energy mineral, and the national interest in its production that results have historically been reflected in extensive exploration and then consultation in connection with both individual applications to extract coal, and regional or national planning for future production. Before applications are submitted, extensive investigations will include: examining potential prospects, ie, areas where coal is believed to lie; preliminary exploration of areas where coal is known to lie but where its boundaries are indeterminate; intensive exploration of areas where boundaries are known, and where tests are justified to discover the coal's physical characteristics; and the feasibility of a site, including issues of access, production levels and the economics of extraction. The broad environmental impact of proposals will also be considered. Only then, as a matter of practice, will the formal planning application be prepared and submitted.

Other interests will also be involved in the process of preparing the formal application, including National Power, PowerGen and other coal users, affected trades unions, and local residents and environmental groups, this is consistent with advice on pre-application consultation and liaison in MPG 3, 'Coal Mining and Colliery Spoil Disposal' (1999). Local and national interests may be in conflict, and decisions of MPAs may be subject to appeal, or pre-empted by the Secretary of State's call-in powers.

The second policy difference between coal and other minerals lies in the distinctive approach taken to determining the appropriate level of coal development. The new MPG 3 is strongly-phrased in this respect:

'It is not … for the planning system to seek to set limits on or targets for any particular source or level of energy supply; nor to predetermine the appropriate levels of coal to be produced by underground or opencast mining. It is for individual operators to determine the level of output they wish to aim for in the light of market conditions' (para 4).

The role of the MPA remains, of course, to have regard to the acceptability of individual proposals in light of normal principles, and by reference to broader policy objectives. These include the sustainable development criteria for minerals set out in MPG 1, and re-emphasised in MPG 3 (para 6). Yet, as that guidance points out, coal working – and opencast working in particular – has some notable differences from other types of mineral working. For example, much larger volumes of overburden must be removed in opencast pits, there is a need for access to large engineering plant and machinery, and coal must often be transported over larger distances for use.

The implications of this policy are most pronounced in the case of opencast mining, which in the last 25 years has provided an increasing share of total coal production. For example, in 1989 opencast coal constituted 19% of all coal production, compared with 10.7% in 1979 and 4.2% in 1969. In the five years to 1991, production rose from 14 to 19 million tonnes pa, and in 1994 stood at 17 million tonnes. At the same time, deep mined coal production is in decline. In the five years to March 1992, production fell from 82.4 million tonnes to 71 million tonnes pa, whilst the number of working collieries fell from 94 to 50.

Since 1986, opencast coal mining has been controlled within the planning system, the special regime applying under the Opencast Coal Act 1958 having been repealed in that year. Opencasting has a number of advantages over deep mining: opencast coal is considerably cheaper to produce than deep mined coal; many millions of tonnes of high-quality coal reserves lie at depths unsuitable for deep mining; modern opencast extraction techniques enable economic extraction of some reserves previously ignored; coal reserves from areas of industrial dereliction can be reclaimed as part of an opencasting scheme, providing a nett environmental improvement in the long term; valuable deposits which would otherwise be sterilised by, eg housing and industrial development, can be exploited by opencast means; the chemical composition of shallow deposits can be such that, by a process of blending, it can make deep mined coal acceptable for sensitive industrial uses when it would otherwise not find a market;

similarly, the quality of opencast coal in itself makes it a valuable resource; finally, opencasting, as with any mineral development, can make a valuable contribution to employment and the economy.

It follows that there are distinctive policy difficulties in balancing the need for coal as an energy mineral with heightened environmental awareness in general, and the demands of sustainable development in particular. MPG 3 seeks to set a framework within which such decisions are to be made – a framework which creates hurdles in addition to those faced for other minerals operators. Most notable in this respect is that in applying the principles of sustainable development to coal extraction (both opencast and deep-mine), and to the disposal of colliery spoil, MPG 3 provides that there shall be a presumption against development unless certain pre-conditions are met (para 8). A number of tests therefore apply:

(a) is the proposal environmentally acceptable, or can it be made so by planning conditions or obligations?

(b) if not, does it provide local or community benefits which clearly outweigh the likely impacts to justify the grant of planning permission?

(c) in National Parks and Areas of Outstanding Natural Beauty, the New Forest and the Broads, major developments should not take place except in exceptional circumstances. Even then, proposals will be subject to the most rigorous examination, and must be demonstrated to be in the public interest. Proposals must also include an assessment of: the need for the development; the impact on the local economy of permitting or refusing permission; whether alternative supplies can be made available at reasonable cost; detrimental environmental effects that can be moderated; and in the case of extensions to existing mines, the extent to which proposals can enhance the local landscape.

(d) proposals within or likely to affect SSSIs or national nature reserves will also be subjected to the most rigorous examination. Consultation must be undertaken with English Nature, and other binding legal rules may apply under conservation law.

(e) in the greenbelt, proposals will be tested against the 'highest environmental standards' as required by PPG 2, and if permission is granted then it will be subject to stringent conditions.

Decisions on individual applications should be made on the basis that the greater the benefits of an opencast site, the stronger the environmental objections would need to be to deny permission, and in particular it is notable that cross-subsidisation of more expensive deep mined coal may provide justification for cheaper opencast working: *Northumberland County Council v Secretary of State for the Environment.*[28] Environmental impact assessment may be required where a proposal is likely to have significant effects on the environment, consistent with normal rules. A distinctive addition, however, is that the coal industry is under an additional environmental duty, by virtue of the Coal Industry Act 1994, s 53. This requires operators, in formulating coal mining proposals requiring planning permission, to have regard to the desirability of the preservation of natural beauty, the conservation of flora and fauna and geological or physiographical features of special interest, and the protection of sites, buildings, structures and objects of architectural, historic or archaeological interest. They must also formulate proposals for the adoption of measures to mitigate any adverse effect of proposals on such matters. The government has made clear that it places 'great importance to the effective discharge of this duty' (MPG 3, para 46), and in particular that it considers that proposals which are not prepared in accordance with it are 'most unlikely' to be consistent with policy.

28 [1989] JPL 700.

The ability of MPAs to deal adequately with any mineral application has been questioned in the past (most notably by the Report of the Stevens Committee, 'Planning Control over Mineral Working'), the question of opencasting is even more contentious. The lack of policy governing need (except in sensitive areas) and the environment effects of both extraction and the use of fossil fuels, complicate an authority's decision. In light of the growing contribution of opencast coal as a proportion of national production, controversy can only increase.

G ONSHORE OIL AND GAS

Onshore oil was first commercially discovered in 1895 in East Sussex, but real interest in onshore fields is a feature of the last 15 years. Between 1986 and 1990 onshore crude oil production increased by some 237% (to 1,752 thousand tonnes in 1990) and gas by 220% (to 48 billion cubic metres). Since then, oil production has declined, but gas production has increased to 52 billion cubic metres a year. Despite their relative insignificance in terms of total production (oil accounted for 2% of 1990 home-based supply), onshore reserves are a valuable resource. Many potential onshore sites, possibly with recoverable reserves similar to North Sea mid-range fields, lie in the South and East of England, where strong and articulate middle class opposition to environmentally intrusive works can be expected. Factors in support of the case for exploitation include: the relative security of home-based reserves compared with imports; the desirability of to ensure maximum economic exploitation over time to boost tax revenue (whilst not jeopardising an operation's economic viability), to aid the national and local economy and create employment; onshore resources are ten times cheaper to exploit than North Sea reserves; free competition in the overall energy market is healthy, onshore oil and gas have their part to play and should be allowed to do so, although as oilfield development is costly and a long-term issue, commercial companies must be allowed time to explore and appraise sites. However, exploitation must be consistent with the protection of the environment; in some cases environmental considerations will preclude development. Special policies will apply in National Parks, Areas of Outstanding Natural Beauty, Sites of Special Scientific Interest, National Nature Reserves, etc, with rigorous examination of any proposed working, and a burden of proof on the developer to show that need for development outweighs environmental objections (MPG 1). Similarly, the Countryside Commission has stated the conservation and exploitation are not necessarily in conflict provided that exploiters are prepared to 'pay the price' in terms of, eg, restoration costs. The feasibility of restoration must be considered before development begins. Water supplies must also be safeguarded.

Regulation of the extraction of on-shore oil and gas has two elements. First, the control of hydrocarbons as an energy mineral, in the context of rules governing hydrocarbon exploitation generally. Secondly, planning rules about the regulation of the environmental impacts of on-shore oil and gas. It is clearly the latter which is of most relevance here. By way of introduction to hydrocarbon regulation generally, however, a few introductory points can be made. Ownership of the petroleum resources of Great Britain and the United Kingdom territorial sea is vested in the Crown by the Petroleum Act 1998, s 2. That Act also allows the Secretary of State for Trade and Industry to grant licences to persons to 'search and bore for and get' those resources. This relatively new statutory basis for licensing, under consolidated provisions, complements and, to an extent, supersedes general controls over the exploitation of on-shore oil and gas by means of exploration and production licences under the Petroleum (Production) Act 1934, as amended. The framework of regulations which provide the detail of controls in respect of on-shore resources remains largely unaffected by the substitution of this new statutory basis (*On-Shore Oil, Gas and Coalbed Methane Development*, Consultation on a new MPG, 1999).

Since 1995 the licensing system has been based on a single licence, the Petroleum Exploration and Development Licence, (PEDL), which grants exclusive rights in relation to a particular area to cover the three main stages of petroleum activity (exploration, appraisal and development: Draft MPG, Annex C). The licence enables the holder to undertake seismic investigations (subject to notifying the DTI and to consulting the local planning authority), drill wells (subject to the permission of the landowner or occupier and the granting of planning consent) and develop any discoveries. Drilling and development consents will not be granted by the DTI unless the necessary land use planning permission has been granted. The legal framework is provided by the Petroleum (Production) (Landward Areas) Regulations 1995, the Petroleum (Production) (Seaward Areas) Regulations 1995 and the Hydrocarbons Licensing Directive Regulations 1995 (SIs 1995/1436, 1435 and 1434 respectively). The 1995 Regulations, and the model clauses for licences which they introduced; apply to all applications made after 30 June 1995. Applications for the new exploration and development licences must relate to specified geographical blocks identified by the Secretary of State and published in the Official Journal of the European Communities (in accordance with the requirements of Council Directive 94/22 on the conditions for granting and using authorisations for the prospecting, exploration and production of hydrocarbons). That publication must include the latest date by which applications are to be made, and the period within which licences are to be granted. As well as technical information in respect of an area's geology and its petroleum prospects and a work programme for evaluating the potential petroleum production from the area which the applicant would be prepared to undertake, applicants are required to provide evidence that they have sufficient resources available to them to undertake the work programme. This is intended, in part, to minimise the risk of activities commencing and then stopping prematurely through financial default, with only incomplete site remediation.

The Hydrocarbons Licensing Directive Regulations restrict the criteria which the Secretary of State may take into account when considering an application for a licence made under the principal regulations. Regulation 4 dictates that no licence shall be granted upon terms or conditions other than those justified exclusively for the purpose of: ensuring the proper performance of the activities permitted by the licence; providing for the payment of fees; or any of a limited number of considerations relating to health and safety, environmental or resources issues. These include national security, public safety, protection of the environment, protection of biological resources and of national treasures possessing artistic or archaeological significance, and planned management of hydrocarbon resources, including the rate at which hydrocarbons are depleted and the optimisation of their recovery. This is a more extensive list of relevant criteria than under the previous system and expressly introduces longer term, 'sustainable development' type considerations into individual decisions. Exploration and development licences have an initial term of six years (corresponding to the term of old-style exploration licences) which may be continued for a further five years (as with old-style appraisal licences) and then extended for a further 20 years (as with old-style development licences).

The licensing of exploration and development by the Secretary of State is in addition to, rather than in substitution for, planning controls. Local control over onshore oil and gas or coalbed methane development remains the function of MPAs, although the Secretary of State may exercise 'call-in' powers in exceptional cases. Authorities should have adequate policies in structure and local plans to provide a policy background against which proposals can be assessed. Policies should deal with issues of exploration, appraisal and development. As with other energy minerals, government energy policy is to ensure secure, diverse and sustainable supplies of energy at competitive prices (Draft MPG, para 6). Consequently, and as with coal, it is not the function of the planning system to set national limits on targets for any particular source or level of energy supply. However, planning controls will be employed to ensure that industry demonstrates how the adverse environmental effects of oil and gas development can be removed or reduced, and MPAs to determine any proposals on their merits. There may be cases where a proposal would have such an adverse effect on other natural resources, the environment and the quality of life for a locality that planning permission should not be granted (para 15). In appropriate cases, EIA may be required. Part 22 of the GPDO specifically excludes the drilling of boreholes for petroleum exploration from permitted mineral exploration development rights.

As with all planning consents, conditions may be attached to grants of permission for hydrocarbon exploitation. While these should not duplicate specific pollution controls under other legislation, conditions may be used to secure the environmental acceptability of a project. There may therefore be something of an uneasy relationship between planning controls and pollution controls, as well as the limitations on exploration and development licences themselves, although this may in practice be mitigated in the negotiations encouraged by policy guidance and typically pursued as good industrial practice. Conditions might relate to siting, screening, landscaping and design of works and plant, timing and method of gas flaring, noise minimisation, and transporting petroleum products. Details of such matters will be included in development programmes submitted to the Secretary of State (DTI) under licensing procedures, and may be referred to in planning applications. Aftercare requirements may also be imposed, and should be settled at the time permission is granted for exploration and development licences.

Further reading

Cope, DR, Hills, P, and James, P (eds), *Energy Policy and Land Use Planning* (1984) Pergamon Press.

Department of the Environment, 'Environmental Effects of Surface Mineral Working' (1992) HMSO.

Department of the Environment, 'Mineral Policies in Development Plans' (1991) HMSO.

Department of the Environment, 'Planning Control over Mineral Working' (1969), Report of the Committee under the Chairmanship of Sir Roger Stevens GCMG, HMSO.

Eggert, RG (ed), *Mining and the Environment: International Perspectives on Public Policy* (1994) Resources for the Future.

Hammersley, R, 'Minerals Planning and Sustainability' (1993) 63 Town Planning Review xiii.

House of Commons Select Committee on the Environment, 2nd Report, Session 1991–1992, 'Coastal Zone Protection and Planning', HC Paper 17, 1992, HMSO.

Jewell, T, 'Paying for Environmental Improvement: The Potential Example of Minerals' (1992) 4 Land Management and Environmental Law Report 81.

Jewell, T, 'Planning Regulation and Environmental Consciousness: Some Lessons from Minerals?' [1995] Journal of Planning and Environment Law 482.

Rutherford, L, 'The Environmental Costs of Opencast Coal Mining: Issues of Liability' (1990) 2 Journal of Environmental Law 161.

Chapter 14

Waste management

A THE BACKGROUND

Waste is ubiquitous, its creation is universal, it is in fact created on a massive scale, and it has hardly ever received the attention it deserves. An understanding of the practical problem is informed by incomplete estimates which suggest that over 400 million tonnes of waste are created in England and Wales every year.[1] This currently comprises 106 million tonnes of commercial, industrial and household waste – 30, 48 and 28 million tonnes respectively – with the remaining 300 million tonnes being construction and demolition waste, agricultural waste, mining waste, sewage sludge and dredging spoils. Even these startling statistics are underestimates, however, as there is considerable variation in how waste is classified and measured. For example, these figures exclude radioactive wastes, 'special' wastes with particularly dangerous or harmful characteristics, along with waste that is imported for treatment or disposal. Indeed, part of the background to policy and legal problems in addressing waste is that reliable statistics are remarkably hard to find: a very significant problem if effective policy goals are to be set, or legal controls to be put in place. This absence is not of recent origin: in the most recent Report of the House of Commons Environment, Transport and Regional Affairs Committee – which is robust even by that Committee's standards – the longstanding shortcomings in the quantity and quality of information are described as having reached 'extraordinary proportions', with the waste management industry itself expressing 'no confidence' in even the figures upon which the new national waste strategies have been based.[2]

Other practical reasons contribute to explain an historic paucity of effective policy and legal responses to the waste problem. First is the universality of waste production. Unlike other aspects of environmental concern, controls over waste focus not on polluting plant but on every human activity which gives rise to waste, whether individual or organised. The scale and variety of these can be imagined, but the practical complexity or effecting any sort of control is staggering. It is no surprise that, until remarkably recently (probably 1994, as we shall see), legal mechanisms relating to waste had the most 'end-of-pipe' orientation of any environmental rules.

1   *Waste Strategy 2000: England and Wales*, May 2000 (Cm 3040) ('*Waste Strategy: E&W*').
2   *Delivering Sustainable Waste Management*, HC Paper 36 (Session 2000-2001); Pontin (2001) 13 ELM 69.

This is compounded by two further characteristics of the human relationship with waste. The first is that individual producers or transporters of waste are invariably insulated from the aggregated effects of waste production. At an individual level, 22 kg per household per week of purely domestic waste may seem little, yet an aggregated 24.6 million tonnes a year is more alarming.[3] 83% of that waste – over 20 million tonnes – is 'disposed of' to landfill (ie, expensively buried). In Scotland, 11.9 million tonnes of all waste is landfilled each year.[4] The second characteristic is the understandable controversy associated with waste disposal facilities, for example, landfill sites, waste recovery or recycling centres, and incinerators.[5] Proposals for the construction of such facilities certainly feature very prominently in environmental litigation,[6] one consequence of their wide and potentially insidious environmental impacts. In the case of landfill, these include: pressures on land use, often in rural or semi-rural areas, where space is already at a premium; the noise, odour and general disturbance resulting from landfill itself, including from the importation of large volumes of waste, by road, for long periods; infestation by vermin; the prospect of migration to watercourses or (worse) water-sources of contaminated leachate, the liquid chemical cocktail arising from the degradation and dilution of wastes; or the potentially explosive escape of methane, one particularly volatile by-product of landfilled biodegradable organic wastes. Not without reason have old landfill sites been referred to as environmental 'ticking time-bombs'.[7] Incineration brings additional anxieties, relating to known or suspected atmospheric pollution, despite the advantages in waste reduction and the potential for energy-from-waste facilities that modern schemes may offer,[8] and the pressures to increase incineration capacity that may arise from implementation of the Landfill Directive (which are considered below).

A second practical reason for the difficulty in establishing effective legal controls is the commercialisation of the waste chain. The transport, treatment and disposal of waste comprise a major industry: it employs around 77,000 people, and costs £3.5 billion every year.[9] The industry also has an important role to play in the pursuit of environmental goals. The balance between environment and economy therefore has a particularly direct impact in matters of waste regulation. At a very practical level, for example, the definition of recoverable or recyclable material as 'waste' has everyday implications for the regulation and economics of the waste minimisation schemes the encouragement of which is increasingly central to waste policy.[10] A balance must therefore be struck between the need to encourage the recovery of resources from waste, and the avoidance of doing so in environmentally careless ways. At a more abstract level, the clichéd observation that one person's waste is another's raw material gives rise to profound complications in the regulation of intra-Community trade – from early attempts to forge a European free market in the transport of waste, to more recent emphasis on the environmental desirability of disposing of waste as near as possible to its point of creation.[11] But it remains unsurprising that, almost thirty years after the

3   *Waste Strategy: E&W*, para 2.15.
4   *National Waste Strategy: Scotland*, SEPA, 1999 ('*Waste Strategy: Scotland*').
5   Tromans, 'EC Waste Law – A Complete Mess?' (2001) 13 JEL 133.
6   Eg, *Gateshead Metropolitan Borough Council v Secretary of State for the Environment* [1995] JPL 432, on planning and incineration controls; *Lopez Ostra v Spain* (1994) 20 EHRR 277, unlicensed waste treatment and human rights; and *R v Hampshire County Council, ex p Vetterlein* [2002] Env LR 8 on human rights.
7   House of Lords Select Committee on the European Communities, *Sustainable Landfill*, HL Paper 73 (Session 1997-98), para 278.
8   Eg, Royal Commission on Environmental Pollution, *Incineration of Waste* (1993, Cm 2181).
9   DTI, *The Competitiveness of the Waste Management Industry* 1997.
10   Eg, *Mayer Parry Recycling Ltd v Environment Agency* [1999] Env LR 489.
11   The 'proximity principle' that featured first in *A Community Strategy for Waste Management*, SEC(89)934 Final; Laurence, *Waste Regulation Law*, chapter 1.

introduction of the first European Community waste measures (eg Directive 75/442), the European Court of Justice remains taxed with many variations on the question of what 'waste' actually is.[12]

From this brief introduction, an impression begins to form of the scale of the policy and legal difficulties inherent in effective waste management. The policy background is complex and now fast-moving, and it has been observed that it has given rise to 'a body of EC and national law that is notoriously difficult, even for specialist lawyers and which – even for such lawyers – makes little sense in terms of some points of detail'.[13] But the evolution of that policy, and the development and current shape of that law, can be introduced in outline.

Waste management law in outline

The development of waste controls

The development of waste management law in the UK has been sporadic. Local authorities were given powers, then duties, in relation to accumulations of noxious wastes as long ago as 1848, by the Public Health Act of that year, enhanced by the Sanitary Act 1866. Those provisions provided the basis for what is now statutory nuisance control, and their public health – rather than explicitly environmental – orientation is very evident. They were complemented in practice from 1947 by planning controls, through which prospective regulation of, for example, location, and aspects of landfill design and implementation could be guided. Here too, however, the limitations of planning control are well known (see chapter 8) despite their evolution in both breadth and depth since 1947. A land use focus and an inability to distinguish between successive operators of waste sites intrinsically limited the potential of planning to impose competence-linked, longer-term waste controls. Yet planning does have an important, if re-focussed, continuing role, which is considered below.

The real innovation in waste control derived from a series of government and parliamentary reports on waste, the waste industry, and the implementation of European waste obligations. The early 1970s saw the first of these,[14] followed unfortunately fortuitously by the Deposit of Poisonous Wastes Act 1972, an emergency response to the highly-publicised discovery of dumped cyanide residues. There has also been a crucial two-way flow in the development of both law and policy between national and European levels. The domestic statutory revolution began in a notable, if limited, way with the enactment of the Control of Pollution Act 1974, which for the first time imposed national controls over the deposit of a wide class of 'controlled wastes', including municipal waste to landfill. The first European Waste Framework Directive appeared shortly afterwards.[15] The momentum for change continued to develop, in the UK this was thanks in part to parliamentary committees and the Royal Commission on Environmental Pollution.[16] Yet, as recently as 1989, the House of Commons Environment Committee noted that:

12 Eg, *ARCO Chemie Nederland Ltd v Minister van Volkshuisvesting* and *EPON* (joined cases C-418 and 419/97) [2000] ECR I-4475.
13 Tromans, above.
14 *Disposal of Solid Toxic Waste*; *Refuse Disposal*, DoE (1971).
15 Directive 75/442/EC.
16 House of Lords Select Committee on Science and Technology, *Hazardous Waste Disposal*, HL Paper 273 (Session 1980-81) and HL Paper 40 (Session 1988-89); House of Commons Environment Committee, *Contaminated Land*, HC Paper 170 (Session 1989-90); RCEP, *Managing Waste: The Duty of Care* 1985.

'Never in any of our enquiries into environmental problems have we experienced such a consistent and universal criticism of existing legislation and of central and local government as we have during the course of this enquiry... [Department of the Environment] inaction on waste management has been a catalogue of neglect since 1974... there has been a vacuum of central guidance, legislative change and leadership on waste management issues.'[17]

The committee's criticisms of waste controls generally, and of the scheme of COPA 1974 in particular, retain their importance. They relate to almost every aspect of the waste disposal regime: the inadequate legislative basis, not least its focus on disposal rather than management; the lack of priority given to waste by different authorities, partly because of a tension within local authorities between their dual functions as collectors of waste and regulators of its disposal; the absence of sufficiently qualified and respected staff; the deficiencies of the waste disposal industry; and the absence of effective planning for waste minimisation, recycling, and disposal plans, despite obligations that they be produced.

Some reform initiatives did follow: a compulsory scheme of registration of waste carriers was introduced by the Control of Pollution (Amendment) Act 1989; and a sharp response to the Committee's Report (Cm 679) was complemented by, for example, a commitment to develop waste minimisation strategies.[18] Significant legal reform did not take place until the implementation in 1994 of the provisions of the Environmental Protection Act 1990, Part II, however. EPA 1990, Part II introduced for the first time a waste management licensing regime, the essence of which is an extension of regulation to embrace every aspect of the waste chain – production, transport, storage and ultimate disposal. This remains the key regulatory tool in the UK, but it cannot be considered in isolation, for two main reasons. First, to some extent it owes its origins to international and European measures: an important function of EC law in this area is to regulate the movement of and trade in waste; and, as we shall see, there is an extremely close relationship between EPA 1990, Part II and European waste law. Equally, as European measures have multiplied, so too has waste management licensing been complemented and adapted to enable the UK to comply with its increasing European obligations. An important current example is the difficulty being experienced in implementing the Landfill Directive (1999/31), to which we shall return.

Secondly, despite the reach and relative novelty of waste management licensing, and the fact that its scope continues to expand, it operates alongside pre-existing prospective controls provided by planning law, and by a range of measures that have been introduced subsequently. These include waste minimisation initiatives such as the notion of 'producer responsibility', and a variety of new regulatory mechanisms including the controversial use of economic instruments, notably the landfill tax and proposals for tradable landfill permits. This begins – but only begins – to explain the complexity of waste law already referred to. Despite that growing complexity, and the considerable changes that continue to be made, criticisms remain. Indeed, it is perhaps appropriate that this outline should end with more recent comments of the House of Commons Environment Committee:

'It is important to stress ... our profound disappointment, on the basis of the evidence we have received, that waste management in this country is still characterised by inertia, careless administration and ad hoc, rather than science-based, decisions. Lip-service alone, in far too many instances, has been paid to

17   *Toxic Waste,* HC Paper 22 (Session 1988-89), para 190.
18   *This Common Inheritance,* 1990 Cm 1200.

the principles of reducing waste and diverting it from disposal. Central government has lacked the commitment, and local government the resources, to put a sustainable waste management strategy into practice'.[19]

International measures

The important continuing role of international waste law in the development of both EC and domestic policy and law should also be noted at this stage, although this is the subject of more elaborate discussion by international environmental lawyers. Three points can be made in passing, however. First, an international regime is in place in respect of the transfrontier movement of wastes, and this is closely reflected in EC law. Secondly, international measures have been important in regulating the disposal of waste, particularly at sea. Thirdly, international law has contributed to addressing the definition of waste itself.

In 1972 the Stockholm Declaration on the Human Environment stated that toxic substances should not be discharged, in order to protect ecosystems from harm. The United Nations Environment Programme (UNEP) has built on that formulation with regard to waste, and has been accompanied in doing so by the Organisation for Economic Co-operation and Development (OECD). The latter has had a particular influence through its decisions on, for example, the transfrontier movement of both hazardous wastes and wastes destined for recovery operations.[20] These provided the initiative for the most well-known international measure in this area, the Basel Convention on the Control of Transboundary Movement of Hazardous Wastes and their Disposal (1989), which entered into force on 5 May 1992. This is a framework treaty which makes provision for additional agreements to deal with waste issues bilaterally or multilaterally, and for matters such as liability and funding. At its heart lie a number of principles:

1 International trade in hazardous waste is to be cut to a minimum.
2 Information is to pass between states on their decisions limiting/banning export/ import of hazardous wastes.
3 Hazardous wastes must be managed in an environmentally sound fashion and should be disposed of as close as possible to their place of origin, thus interstate transfer is exceptional.
4 Such exceptional transfer may take place in the interests of environmental protection and human health *from* a nation without appropriate storage or treatment facilities *to* one with the necessary technology.
5 Any such transfers must be subject to stringent control.
6 Nations must co-operate to ensure application of these principles, and it is a feature of the Convention that an international secretariat is established to further this end, also that developing nations should receive assistance to enable them to manage waste safely.

Certain other features of the Basel Convention are noteworthy. For example, it seeks to ensure that party states only export waste to, or import waste from, other party states. Subsequently, every member state of the EU has been required to ratify the Convention (Council Decision 93/98/EC), and European exports of waste to 69 countries in the

19 *Sustainable Waste Management* (Session 1997-98), para 17.
20 C(88)90 Final and C(92)39 Final; Kummer, *International Management of Hazardous Wastes* 1995.

Caribbean, Africa and the Pacific have been prohibited.[21] The Convention also requires that states from which an export is to be made must prohibit that export if the receiving state does not consent to it in writing: a notion of prior notification and consent. At a general level, states retain under the Basel Convention the sovereign right to prohibit in general the import of waste for disposal, although such prohibitions are required to be notified to other party states through the Convention Secretariat. An implied power also remains for a state to prohibit a particular shipment of waste. Indeed, the general tenor of the Basel Convention is that inter-state transfers of waste are to be exceptional: there is to be no global free movement of waste. The need for appropriate disposal technology to be in place is designed to ensure a base level of environmentally sound and efficient disposal.

The second notable feature of international waste law is the regulation of the disposal of wastes – a complex topic in itself. However, by way of illustration, one particular concern has been contamination of the marine environment by wastes. Whilst the detail of some of these controls is considered in chapter 19, certain important general principles have also been identified. Not least amongst these is to be found in the United Nations Convention on the Law of the Sea, which imposes an obligation on states to 'take all measures ... necessary to prevent, reduce and control pollution of the marine environment' using the 'best practicable means' at their disposal.[22] This general duty is enhanced by Agenda 21, *Earth's Action Plan*, a product of the Rio Summit that recognises the necessity of adopting 'preventative, precautionary and anticipatory approaches to avoid degradation of the marine environment'. Particular examples of the influence of such measures include prohibitions on the disposal to the sea of certain wastes, restrictions on others, and a complete moratorium in place since 1983 on the disposal of radioactive wastes at sea. An important side effect for present purposes is the additional pressure on landward disposal options which results, hence the very concerns which gave rise to the Basel Convention in the first place.

The third contribution of international waste law of note here is its contribution to the definition of waste. There is a close correlation between international, European and domestic law in this context.[23] Not only did an OECD Decision provide the framework for the Basel Convention,[24] but direct connections are evident (for example) between further work of the OECD and other international and European waste classification schemes, including the European Waste Catalogue. One consequence is that the interpretation of domestic law must draw heavily on its European and international roots.[25]

B EUROPEAN MEASURES

It is difficult to segregate the development and substance of waste policy from the legal measures that have been introduced to give it effect. However, those legal measures do have a basis in a series of policy developments at both European and national levels, which provide a framework for waste law proper. The influence of that policy framework is pervasive, as will be evident from the remainder of this chapter. My purpose in this section is more specific: it is to provide an explanation of the

21 EC Regulation 259/93 on the Supervision and Control of Shipments of Waste within, into and out of the European Community, as amended by Regulation 2557/2001 from 1 January 2002 – the main measure through which implementation of the Convention within the EC is secured.
22 United Nations Convention on the Law of the Sea, Part XII, Arts 192-194.
23 Tromans (2001) 13 JEL 133.
24 *Kummer*, Ch 4.
25 Eg, *Mayer Parry Recycling Ltd v Environment Agency* [1999] Env LR 489.

development of waste policy at both European and national levels within which the detailed legal regulation of waste can be better understood.

European waste policy

European action on waste can be traced back to provisions in the Community's 1973 Action Programme which were concerned with eliminating toxic, non-biodegradable or bulky wastes that crossed national borders for treatment or disposal.[26] Subsequent Action programmes have become much broader. For example, the Fifth Action Programme, *Towards Sustainability*, expressly emphasised the dual objectives of Community waste policy as being resource conservation and environmentally sustainable disposal.[27] The most helpful early statement of Community policy is to be found in the 1989 Commission Communication *A Community Strategy for Waste Management*.[28] This set out a number of principles:
(a) waste arisings are to be prevented wherever possible, and otherwise reduced;
(b) where possible, waste is to be recycled or recovered and re-used;
(c) where non-recoverable waste arises, it is to be properly managed and disposed of harmlessly, with landfill being the last resort;
(d) waste is to be disposed of as near as possible to place in which it arises – the 'proximity principle';
(e) waste transportation should be properly regulated; and
(f) remedial action should be taken in respect of contaminated disposal sites.
An updated version of the Community Strategy was adopted in 1997[29] to cover the period up to 2002. Both versions illustrate the extent to which the so-called 'waste hierarchy' has been imbedded in Community policy from its earliest days, namely (in order of preference) prevention, recycling and final disposal. That hierarchy has also featured as a central part of early UK guidance on the operation of the waste management licensing system,[30] has been accepted by successive governments,[31] and has reached greater prominence still in related land use planning guidance.[32] This is likely to develop more quickly still in the next eight years, with the preparation by the Community of its Sixth Environmental Action Programme, *Environment 2010: Our Future, Our Choice*.[33] The management of wastes takes a new place in that strategy as one of four 'priority areas for action', expressly coupled more explicitly than ever before with sustainable resource use. Thus, waste prevention and increased efficiency in resource use are to be key features of a new thematic strategy on waste, which will also be combined with a particular emphasis on improving the implementation of existing legal mechanisms. As this latter objective itself suggests, however, the aspirations represented by European policy, including the waste hierarchy, have been slow to emerge in legal form and, even when they have, their legal status has been controversial and their implementation patchy.

26   OJ C112/1, 20 December 1973.
27   Laurence, *Waste Regulation Law*, para 1.17.
28   (1990) OJ L122.
29   Council Resolution 97/C76/01.
30   DoE Circular 11/94.
31   *Making Waste Work* 1995, Cm 3040; *Less Waste More Value* June 1998.
32   PPG 10, *Planning and Waste Management*, 1999, para 7.
33   COM (2001) 31 Final.

European waste law

In terms of implementing provisions – the legal tools adopted to give effect to the policy framework – the most significant early European legislative measure was the 1995 Waste Framework Directive.[34] This was substantially amended in 1991, and continues to provide a strategic framework for waste management obligations in EC law. The original Framework Directive established a number of key principles. In particular:

1   There must be 'competent authorities' with responsibilities for organising, authorising and supervising waste disposal.
2   Waste disposal plans are required dealing with types and quantities of waste, technical requirements, site details and such like.
3   Waste is to be disposed of according to a permit system, and permits may impose restrictions or conditions on types or quantities of waste to be disposed of, technical issues, precautionary measures and information to be given by licensees.
4   The polluter pays principle is to apply.
5   Recycling is to be encouraged.
6   Regular three yearly reports are to be made by member states to the Commission on their waste disposal situation.
7   Certain wastes are excluded from the Framework Directive's scope, eg radioactive and mining waste, and agricultural and animal carcasses.

The amendments to the 1975 Framework Directive made in 1991[35] effected its substantial modernisation. In an attempt to shift from purely end-of-pipe controls, the modernised Framework Directive emphasises the development of clean technologies as a means of preventing or minimising waste arisings and reducing initial resource demands, coupled with improvements in final disposal techniques. This includes shifting the cost of waste disposal to the originator of waste. The pursuit of the proximity principle, at least at European level, is also enhanced, through obligations on member states to establish a network of disposal installations, taking account of the best available technology not entailing excessive cost, to make the EU self-sufficient in waste disposal, while moving member states individually closer towards that goal. Strategic planning at national level – previously something of an afterthought – also received a boost, through an obligation to establish waste management plans. In the UK, land use waste disposal plans had served a default function, in the absence of waste-specific legislation. These have now been replaced with the first national waste strategies, but the overall position remains (as we shall see) in its formative stages. The Framework Directive also provided for a general tightening of procedural and information requirements, including: the need for collectors and carriers of waste to be registered and inspected; procedural changes to ensure that only technically qualified people are able to hold a licence; and more onerous obligations to keep and make available records of the nature of waste, its movement, and its treatment.

Two final features of the revised Framework Directive have been particularly controversial, and have given rise to particular complexity. They relate, first, to the definition of waste and, second, to the creation of new 'objectives' for waste management policy. Both the definition and the objectives find new legal form in the revised Framework Directive and, perhaps because of their transplantation into an already complex framework of UK law,[36] they have given rise to considerable legal confusion. Each is returned to below in the context of their implementation in the UK.

34   75/442.
35   91/156.
36   EPA 1990, Part II was of course enacted before the adoption of Directive 91/156.

European waste law is not confined to the Framework Directive, however. Other measures include a reviewable system of waste categories,[37] provided as the basis for the 'European Waste Catalogue', a common classification system which is increasingly central in describing waste for regulatory purposes. Also, a series of measures has been introduced to address particular waste streams, and more general provision has been made by directives on hazardous wastes, waste shipments and landfill. The consequential hazardous wastes regime, the particular problems of transboundary waste movements, and now the Landfill Directive have given rise to substantial legal reform. On the other hand, proposals first made in 1989 for a directive imposing strict civil liability for damage caused by waste have taken something of a back seat to these general measures, partly because of successful steps by the European Parliament to require in addition the establishment of funds to meet contingent liabilities under this regime. This was a step too far for the European Council, which rejected the proposal outright. It is much more recently that substantially truncated proposals for a directive on civil liability for environmental damage in general have emerged.[38]

Stream-specific waste measures

The generality of early EC waste law was compensated for, in part, through detailed elaboration of controls over particularly toxic, prevalent or large waste streams. A good illustration is Directive 76/403 on polychlorinated biphenyls (PCBs) and terphenyls (PCTs), which requires prohibition of the uncontrolled discharge, dumping or tipping of PCBs, collection of PCBs for disposal or regeneration; and disposal in a manner which does not cause harm to human health or the environment. A further general duty is in place on member states to ensure that waste or used oils are collected and disposed of without causing avoidable harm to humans and the environment.[39] Specific duties under Directive 75/439 also require the prohibition of oil discharges into water and drains, deposits of oil which may cause harm to soil, the uncontrolled discharge of process residues, and processing of waste oil causing air pollution above prescribed limits. In an important illustration of the potential for recycling and re-use (despite what is otherwise an obvious emphasis on disposal), Directive 75/439 also prefers disposal of waste oils by recycling, regeneration or combustion for a purpose other than simple destruction. The administrative arrangements required, which are generally given effect through mainstream waste management licensing, include prior inspection and approval of collection and disposal undertakings, and record-keeping by such undertakings which collect or keep more than 500 litres of waste a year.

Other specific measures include those seeking reduction in the heavy metal content of waste batteries and accumulators,[40] the reduction and ultimate elimination of pollution from the titanium dioxide industry,[41] and controls over sewage sludge.[42] Sewage sludge has been a recognised problem for decades: as early as 1976, around a third of all sewage produced in the EC was used in agriculture. Although rich in organic matter, sludge also presents environmental threats, the most problematic of which has been heavy metals. Directive 86/278 therefore imposes controls on sludge with a prescribed heavy metal content, provides for pre-treatment of sewage sludge before its agricultural use,

37   Decision 94/741.
38   *White Paper on Environmental Liability,* COM (2000) 66 Final, 9 February 2000.
39   Directive 75/439.
40   Directive 91/157.
41   Directive 92/112.
42   Directive 86/278.

and allows for limits to be imposed on the amount of sludge used every year on particular areas of land. A revised directive is now promised under the Sixth Action Programme.[43]

Packaging and related waste

The packaging commonly encountered with many modern goods and commodities has been a frequent target for environmentalists' campaigns. Not only are valuable resources consumed in the manufacture of packaging, which is intended by definition for early disposal, but it contributes to both litter and waste disposal problems. Different member states have exhibited different levels of concern, however. Germany, for example, has had strict packaging and packaging waste targets in place since 1991, which lay responsibility for recovery, re-use and recycling on manufacturers, distributors and retailers. In France, manufacturers and importers have been required to make contributions towards packaging waste disposal since 1993. Denmark's introduction of a mandatory scheme for the return and re-use of plastic drinks containers even resulted in a limited directive as early as the 1980s (85/339) and a measure of support from the European Court of Justice, which recognised a domestic qualification on the free movement of goods for the same purpose.[44]

Community action has also become more intense, with the adoption in 1994 of a wide-ranging Directive[45] to replace Directive 85/339. The directive aims to reduce the environmental impact of packaging, harmonise national packaging measures, and ensure free movement of packaged goods. Environmental improvements are to be secured through deterring the manufacture of unnecessary packaging, placing limitations on the disposal of packaging, and promoting its re-use and recovery. Three principal means are adopted. First, each member state must establish a system for return, collection and recovery of packaging from the consumer, final user of waste stream in order to channel it to the most appropriate form of waste management. In so doing, there must be no discrimination against imported goods and barriers to trade or competition must also be avoided. Secondly, national recycling and recovery targets must be set. Thirdly, there must be guarantees as to the free circulation in the EU of qualifying types of packaging. 'Packaging' itself is defined very broadly, to include all products used to contain, protect, handle, deliver and present goods, whether it is primary packaging (normally acquired by the ultimate purchaser), secondary or 'grouping' packaging (generally removed by distributors or retailers near the point of sale) or tertiary packaging (designed to help bulk handling or transport).

Determination of the precise targets for return, collection and recovery require Directive 94/62, Art 6 to be read with the relevant implementing rules in each member state. Although there are variations between states, the Art 6 targets are threefold:
(a) no later than 30 June 2001 between 50% and 65% by weight of packaging waste was to have been recovered;
(b) within this general target, and with the same time limit, between 25% and 45% by weight of the totality of packaging materials contained in packaging waste was to have been recycled, with a minimum of 15% for each packaging material; and
(c) no later than 15 June 2006, a percentage of packaging waste to be determined by the European Council will be recovered and recycled, with a view to 'substantially increasing' the above targets.

---

43   COM (2001) 31 Final, p 56.
44   *EC Commission v Denmark* Case 302/86 [1988] ECR 4607.
45   Directive 94/62.

Implementation of the notion of 'producer responsibility' introduced by Directive 94/62, and the articulation of precise targets, required legislative change in the UK. This was effected by the Environment Act 1995, ss 93 and 94 taken with the Producer Responsibility Obligations (Packaging Waste) Regulations 1997 (as amended). The regulation-making power is unusually restricted in that preconditions apply to its exercise – one indication of commercial sensitivity to introduction of packaging waste controls. Those preconditions include a requirement that environmental or other benefits will stem from an increase in the re-use, recovery or recovery of waste; that those benefits are significant as against likely costs resulting from the creation of an obligation (essentially a self-contained cost-benefit test similar to that applying more generally to, for example, the Environment Agency);[46] that burdens imposed on businesses by regulations are the minimum necessary to secure those benefits;[47] and that the burdens are placed only on the persons most able to make a contribution to the targets.[48] There has been no legal challenge to the making of the regulations.

The scheme of the regulations is complex, and its application more so. The regulations impose obligations to recover and recycle 'packaging waste' on 'producers' of such waste who both have a specified financial turnover and who handle specified amounts of waste by weight. 'Packaging' bears almost precisely the definition found in the English version of Directive 94/62,[49] but this has not been free from controversy. In particular, retailers have sought to escape liability for recovering plant pots – potentially a form of 'sales packaging' – on the basis that the pots were not conceived as sales packaging (as the definition requires), but were provided at an earlier point than sale to enable plants to grow and be handled.[50] This creative argument was rejected, however, establishing that packaging can have a number of purposes – a conclusion which sensibly broadens the definition consistent with the general purposes of Directive 94/62.

The recovery obligation itself is in three parts (regs 3-11). First, relevant producers must register with the Environment Agency, and pay the appropriate fee. Secondly, in registering, producers are required to notify the Agency of the amount of packaging waste actually produced in the previous year. This provides the baseline by which their recovery and recycling obligations are calculated, as every producer is required to take reasonable steps to recover and recycle a defined percentage of their previous year's production of packaging waste. A complex formula determines quite what that percentage is in each case, taking into account both the producer's particular place in the waste chain (whether they are, eg a manufacturer, packer, or seller)[51] and the overall national targets set for that year. Thirdly, every producer is subsequently required to certify that they have complied with their obligations. In a variation on this 'individualised' liability, the regulations also allow waste producers to join schemes through which their obligations may be met collectively: they essentially sub-contract the physical recovery of waste to a collective scheme.[52] The operation of such schemes has been encouraged through a voluntary accreditation system operated by the Agency and SEPA, under which schemes issue a standard form 'packaging waste recovery notice' to their members to enable those members to demonstrate their own compliance with their producer responsibility obligations (see (1998) 10/4 ELM 269).

---

46 Environment Act 1995, s 39.
47 A statutory 'proportionality' test.
48 EPA 1990, s 93(3).
49 Directive 94/62, reg 2(1); Art 3(1).
50 *Davies v Hillier Nurseries Ltd* [2001] Env LR 42.
51 Regulations, Sch 2.
52 Regulations, reg 4.

There has been some concern that UK businesses would be unlikely to meet the targets set for them by Directive 94/62, let alone bear any additional burdens created by setting national targets higher than the directive minima (50% recovery, 25% recycling, the latter including 15% of each type of packaging). The full directive targets were therefore introduced in the UK progressively up to 2001: the 1999 recovery target was 43%, the 2000 target 45%, and the 2001 target 56% (with 18% recycling).[53] Proposals for 2002 targets have been considered in the context of the Commission's targets to 2006, which seem likely to comprise no recovery target but a general recycling target of 60%.[54] Actual performance in 2000 was 42% recovery and 36% recycling. What also emerges from the consultation paper is a picture of a general increase in the amount of packaging waste being produced in the last two years, despite a drop after the introduction of the regulations.

Hazardous wastes

Specific attention to toxic wastes was promised by the 1973 and 1977 action programmes and Directive 78/319 dealt with that issue, by laying down stricter controls than those contained in 75/442 with regard to precise lists of 'toxic and dangerous' waste, or material contaminated by such substances. Proposals for replacement of this directive by a 'hazardous waste' Directive to draw on the work of the OECD and which would reflect the growth in the amount of such waste since 1978 — and better management techniques that have emerged — were under discussion from 1988.

Directive 91/689 (amended by 94/31) which had effect from 27 June 1995 replaced Directive 78/319, and lays down stricter requirements for controlling hazardous wastes within the overall framework initially created by Directive 75/442 of competent authorities, plans and authorisations. Domestic waste is excluded, while other types of hazardous waste are generally stipulated, together with the constituents and properties of wastes rendering them hazardous. The Commission has the task of specifically identifying and listing hazardous wastes — a task not made easier by the contention that some waste is only hazardous in particular circumstances, and the chosen way out of this problem is to list wastes considered as hazardous beyond specified threshold concentrations.

Directive 91/689 lays down particular requirements for: hazardous waste producers and transporters to keep detailed records which have to be retained (for at least three and one years respectively); documentary evidence of waste management operations to be supplied to competent authorities or previous waste holders on request; waste to be recorded and identified on every hazardous waste tipping site; relevant waste to be packaged and labelled according to international and EU requirements while being collected, transported and stored; consignment documentation to accompany transfers; creation by member states of publicly available hazardous waste management plans; reports from member states to the Commission on implementation, and information to be sent on establishments undertaking disposal or recovery of hazardous waste primarily for third parties and likely to be part of a proposed network of disposal facilities throughout the EU, including information as to types and quantities of waste to be treated and treatment methods; triennial reports from the Commission to the Parliament and Council. Implementation of Directive 91/689 has been through regulations which impose an additional layer of controls to those applicable under waste management

53   SI 2000/3375.
54   *Consultation Paper on Recovery and Recycling Targets for Packaging Waste in 2002*, September 2001.

licensing:[55] a system of hazardous waste consignment noting (which is considered below).

Transboundary movement of waste

Even before implementation of the Basel Convention in EC law, there had been growing disquiet about the transportation of hazardous wastes within Europe, and between member states and third countries. Particularly controversial was the 'misplacing' of 41 drums of waste contaminated with dioxin from an industrial accident in Seveso, Italy, which were later found in a railway siding. The report of a commission of inquiry of the European Parliament added impetus to the European Commission's own proposals, and resulted in Directive 84/631 on interstate waste transfers within the Community, and between member and non-member states. It was Regulation 93/259 which, from 9 February 1993, coordinated this European scheme with the requirements of the Basel Convention. The regulation is directly applicable in the UK, but aspects of the regime do receive attention in complementary UK regulations and policy. [56]

The nature of the obligations arising depends on: whether the exporting and importing countries are member states, the purpose of the shipment (for example, whether it is for disposal or treatment), and the type of waste being transported (using three lists – of green, amber and red waste – in order of the relative burden of the controls). The general intention is make controls proportionate to the severity of the environmental or health threat presented by particular waste, the ability of exporters and importers to deal with it, and the nature of the handling the waste will receive, whether in transport, treatment or ultimate disposal. In effect, the regulation sets out a series of 'sub-schemes', from waste shipments between member states for disposal (type '1A'), to transit from outside and through the EU for disposal outside it (type '5A'). The basic form of the controls is familiar and, like the Basel Convention itself, is based on the notion of prior notification (although some absolute prohibitions are applied). Persons intending to export waste must therefore notify the recipient or transit state of their shipment by means of a consignment note. Acknowledgement obligations follow, and the notified state may seek further information, object or impose conditions on the shipment. This necessarily means that a transit or recipient state can refuse permission for a shipment to be made. This is an important restriction upon normal principles of free movement of goods within the EU, and is a shift away from the position under the 1984 Directive and towards the proximity principle, prompted by implementation of the Basel Convention.[57]

If consent is given, then further notice must be given of the shipment itself, and its ultimate arrival at its destination. Should a shipment not in fact take place, the state from which the export was to be made falls under obligations to ensure that the waste is returned to its place of origin, unless other environmentally satisfactory means of disposal or treatment are arranged. Financial provisions must be in place prior to shipment to ensure that all of the costs arising will be met, whilst unlawful shipments are required to be prohibited. Detailed requirements in respect of consignment notes are set out in the regulation itself, and they must include: the source of waste, its composition and quantity, the identity of the producer and consignee, the route of the shipment, the relevant insurance details, and the measures taken to ensure safe transport. In practice, non-radioactive waste is not generally imported into the UK for

55 Special Waste Regulations 1996, as amended.
56 Transfrontier Shipment of Waste Regulations 1994; *United Kingdom Management Plan for Exports and Imports of Waste,* July 1996, DoE.
57 *Laurence*, para 1.33.

final disposal, save where a recovery operation is intended (including energy recovery). The 1996 *United Kingdom Management Plan for Exports and Imports of Waste* also makes clear that exports of waste from the UK for disposal are to be banned, as are exports of hazardous waste to non-OECD countries for recovery.

Landfill

The Landfill Directive (1999/31) is not the first Community measure to address the means of waste disposal. For example, Directive 89/369 sought to prevent air pollution from new municipal waste plants, and Directive 89/429 to reduce it from old ones. Equally, these early measures are themselves to be replaced on 28 December 2002 by Directive 2000/76 on the incineration of waste, which is much wider in scope, covers both incineration and co-incineration, and has a modernised environmental purpose. Yet the Landfill Directive remains the most far-reaching waste disposal measure. It also cuts in an unprecedented way across the combination of controls that apply in the UK to landfill, including waste management licensing, land use planning, and (in some cases) other pollution control regimes (particularly the new pollution prevention and control regime: see Part III). Implementation of the directive is therefore a complex administrative task for regulators, and a complex legal and practical task for operators.[58] The Directive seeks to harmonise landfill standards across the EU, and in doing so to help give effect to the waste hierarchy: the intention is to discourage reliance on landfill as a waste management option and to ensure, where landfill does take place, both that its environmental impacts are minimised and that adequate monitoring takes place.[59] That monitoring will now extend up to 30 years after closure of a particular landfill site. A conspicuous contribution towards the 'polluter pays' principle also appears in the requirement that member states ensure that all the costs involved in the setting up and operation of a landfill site, including financial security for the estimated cost of closure and after-care of the site for those 30 years, shall be covered by the price to be charged by the operator for the disposal of any type of waste at that site.

Whilst Directive 1999/31 will also require improvements in the standards applied to landfill sites (including mandatory pre-treatment of waste to be landfilled – not an established UK practice – along with tightened procedures for the acceptance of waste, and closure and aftercare procedures), its most controversial feature is the reduction it requires in the total amount of biodegradable waste going to landfill.[60] The ambitious (and reviewable) target set for the UK is a 35% reduction on 1995 levels by 2020. The implications of this are difficult to discern. On one hand, it does provide a positive incentive towards waste minimisation, recycling and re-use. However, on the other, its effect may be to shift waste disposal to other options, not least incineration. Indeed, a putative 'rush to incineration' has been discussed, with a potential capital outlay of between £3 billion and £7 billion[61] to deal with an additional 8-26 million tonnes a year.[62]

Directive 1999/31 imposes two other core substantive obligations. First, it prohibits disposal to landfill of certain types of waste, including liquid, corrosive, infectious clinical wastes and (progressively) most used vehicle tyres. Secondly, and controversially for the UK, Directive 1999/31 requires the separate landfilling of three

---

58 A series of consultation papers has been issued, eg *Limiting Landfill*, October 1999; *Implementation of Council Directive 1999/31/EC on the Landfill of Waste: Second Consultation Paper*, August 2001.
59 Parpworth [1999] JPL 4.
60 Directive 1999/31, Art 5.
61 *Sustainable Landfill*, HL Paper 83 (Session 1997-98).
62 *A Way with Waste*, DETR, June 1999.

core categories of waste: hazardous, non-hazardous and inert wastes. This will bring an end to the well-established UK practice of landfilling different types of waste together, or 'co-disposal', by which industrial wastes (including liquid wastes) are deposited with household wastes so that the interaction between the two results in physical and chemical changes to the former that render it les harmful to the environment than it would otherwise be.

The date for implementation of the Landfill Directive was 16 July 2001, after which all new landfills must comply with its requirements. The application of those requirements to established sites is more problematic, particularly as the new regulations were not in place in time. A preliminary general requirement is that a 'site conditioning plan' had to be prepared by 16 April 2002 for all landfill sites considering its compliance with the directive. Beyond this, landfill sites that are subject to the Landfill Directive are currently regulated through waste management licensing. However, with the introduction of the new pollution prevention and control ('PPC') regime, a number of these sites will fall under more integrated controls. This division of responsibility will take some years to become established, however, as implementation of PPC is itself being staged, with landfill sites not to be included until 2007. Were substantial legal changes not to be made to implement the Landfill Directive, then it has been estimated that around 1,070 landfill sites currently in operation would be regulated under PPC, leaving 930 to be regulated by waste management licensing.[63] This is clearly a less than satisfactory arrangement: there are significant differences between the two systems, yet a key shared purpose in this case would be to ensure compliance with a single set of European obligations – those set out in the Landfill Directive.

Consequently, it is now intended that all existing landfill sites will be made subject to a modified PPC regime.[64] This leaves a need for complex transitional provisions, however, not least because the Landfill Directive may have directly effective features which require compliance by operators despite late formal implementation in the UK. Operators have been advised that late implementation must not delay their preparations for implementation of the Landfill Directive.[65] Variations on 'simple' waste management licensing and PPC will therefore apply to proposals for new sites (where a PPC application will be necessary), substantial variations to old sites, sites which are currently used for co-disposal, and to all hazardous waste landfills in particular. This will include the prospect of compulsory closure of existing sites if the Agency takes the view that compliance with the Landfill Directive is not possible. In all cases, new technical guidance will apply.

An additional device is yet to come into play to assist the implementation of the Landfill Directive: tradable landfill permits for biodegradable municipal wastes.[66] It is proposed that local authorities will be issued with permits allowing them to dispose of a defined volume of such waste over a defined period. Should they fail to divert the remainder of their waste to alternative means of disposal, then they will need to purchase additional permits from other, more successful authorities. This will create a financial incentive for local authorities to shift away from landfill – a particular need given the fact that implementation of Landfill Directive targets in effect will require local authorities to reduce the amount of biodegradable waste they landfill by over 60% by 2020 from their 1998/9 levels.[67]

---

63   *First Consultation Paper* 19 October 2000 para 2.3.
64   *Second Consultation Paper*, para 1.2; Part 3, Draft Regulations.
65   *Second Consultation Paper*, para 1.5.
66   *Tradable Landfill Permits*, DETR, 2001.
67   Second Consultation Paper, para 2.6.

C NATIONAL WASTE POLICY

European waste policy and law clearly has a long pedigree. What is also clear is that a general shift from waste disposal controls for the protection of public health, to more anticipatory controls which emphasise broader environmental objectives (including the waste hierarchy, and the proximity and 'polluter pays' principles) is only a recent feature. The parallel, but connected, development of UK policy and law shows the same characteristics: UK legal responses are associated with a developing governmental understanding of the problems of waste, but any attempt to imbed in any formal way a strategic process of planning for waste minimisation, treatment and disposal is much more recent; site-specific regulatory controls have therefore pre-dated formalised policy-making by decades. Indeed, it was not until the early 1990s that proposals to develop explicit national waste policy emerged. Even then, initial progress was slow. For example, an undertaking was given in 1993 to produce a non-statutory waste strategy, in response to the report of the Royal Commission on Environmental Pollution on incineration,[68] and a White Paper on recycling was published in 1994.[69] The non-statutory policy did not itself emerge until 1995, however.[70] The preparation of national waste strategies for England, Wales and Scotland had to await the amendment of EPA 1990 by the Environment Act 1995. A second important development in respect of national waste policy is the inclusion in the waste management licensing regime of strategic 'objectives' deriving from the revised Waste Framework Directive. As strategic obligations on local authorities, these also demand consideration as a policy device.

The national waste strategies

The requirement imposed on both the Secretary of State (in England and Wales) and SEPA (in Scotland) each to prepare a national waste strategy owes it origins to the amended Waste Framework Directive.[71] The development of non-statutory initiatives is an important part of the background, however, not least as an illustration of the rapidity with which the substance of policy was developing in the 1990s, despite the absence of any statutory framework. The national strategies also supersede their more limited forebears: local waste disposal plans.[72] The national strategies for England and Wales and for Scotland were published in 2000 and 1999 respectively,[73] and with that publication waste disposal plans have lapsed.[74]

In the same period that these policy *mechanisms* have been developed, so too has the substance of waste policy itself been transformed. Objectives of the broadest sort are prescribed for the national strategies.[75] These boil down to four core ideas: proximity and self-sufficiency; the adoption of a precautionary approach; the 'polluter pays' principle; and the waste hierarchy, including an emphasis on the development of new technologies, to reduce, recycle and recover waste. The articulation of these objectives is an explicit attempt to place waste policy more securely within the over-arching principle of sustainable development. It is a marked evolution from earlier policy, which

68   Cm 2181, 1993.
69   Cm 2696.
70   *Making Waste Work: A Strategy for Sustainable Waste Management in England and Wales*, Cm 3040 (1996) 8 ELM 55.
71   Waste Framework Directive, 91/156, Art 7; EPA 1990, ss 44A, 44B.
72   EPA 1990, s 50.
73   *Waste Strategy 2000: England and Wales*, May 2000, Cm 3040; *Waste Strategy: Scotland*, December 1999.
74   EA 1995, s 92.
75   EPA 1990, Sch 2A.

has been heavily criticised for its failure to appreciate the scale of change necessary to meet recycling and recovery targets, along with its minimalist attempts to shift the costs of waste management and disposal to waste producers.[76]

The sorts of substantive targets set by the strategies are illustrated by waste disposal and reduction rates for England and Wales. It is intended, for example, to reduce by 15% the amount of industrial and commercial waste going to landfill by 2005, and to 'recover value' from 40% of municipal waste by the same year, and 67% by 2015. The strategy suggests that by 2005 25% of annual arisings of household waste should be recycled or composted. Less ambitious goals are set for recycling by local authorities, which would amount to just a 17% recycling rate by 2003. The parallels between these national obligations and the requirements of the Waste Framework Directive, both in substance and form, are not coincidental. Equally, achievement of these goals will require a complex interplay between waste minimisation, recycling and disposal options, by a host of different authorities, under a range of legal and other mechanisms. And it is here that the *Waste Strategy: England and Wales* has itself been criticised. The House of Commons Environment, Transport and Regional Affairs Select Committee has strongly condemned that Strategy's over-concentration on municipal waste, to the exclusion of industrial and commercial wastes, its over-reliance on the Waste Framework Directive, and the absence of clear connections between targets and specific means for their achievement. It notes in particular that: 'The most serious criticism of the Strategy is that it is a misnomer: that there is no strategy, or vision, rather a list of aspirations and some relatively weak levers to achieve those aims'.[77] In making these observations, the Committee reflected earlier criticism of the lack of bite given to waste reduction policy, notably from the House of Lords Committee which observed in 1998 that 'waste reduction is not just an option: it is an imperative. We need to create, through education and example, a new social spirit in which Government, industry and citizens positively want to see waste reduced at all stages'.[78] Waste policy may have evolved, but according to such views it still has a long way to go.

National waste policy: 'the European objectives'

It is no surprise to discover that the legal mechanisms intended to give bite to the emerging policy framework have come under increasing scrutiny. Nowhere is this more true than in the case of certain specific duties placed on member states by the Waste Framework Directive (Arts 3-7, especially Art 4) that have been directly transposed into UK law. Authorities with responsibilities for waste management are accordingly placed under a legal duty to exercise their functions 'with the relevant objectives'[79] – in essence, the objectives of the Waste Framework Directive itself. Given that origin, the objectives are phrased more in the manner of policy goals than any more familiar type of legal obligation. Their reach is also broad, in that the functions to which the objectives apply include not just the licensing of waste management, but also the planning functions of local authorities as they relate to waste.[80] This combination of characteristics has lead to a particular legal question, namely: what is the legal status of the objectives? If this is not known, then the practical steps that must be taken to comply will be obscure, as will any chance of achieving the objectives.

76   *Less Waste: More Value* DETR June 1998; Pontin (1998) 10 ELM 180.
77   *Delivering Sustainable Waste Management*, para 18.
78   *Sustainable Landfill*, para 278.
79   Waste Management Licensing Regulations 1994, Sch 4, Part I.
80   Waste Management Licensing Regulations 1994, Sch 4, paras 2(1), 3.

The starting point is the wording of the relevant objectives themselves. In respect of both the disposal and recovery of waste they are:

(a) ensuring that waste is recovered or disposed of without endangering human health and without using processes or methods which could harm the environment and in particular without:
  (i)   risk to water, air, soil, plants or animals; or
  (ii) causing nuisance through noise or odours; or
  (iii) adversely affecting the countryside or places of special interest; and
(b) implementing the relevant National Strategy.

This corresponds to Directive 91/156, Art 4 and has been described as the 'key objective' underpinning the directive and implementation of the relevant National Strategy.[81] In respect of the disposal of waste only, additional objectives are:

(a) establishing an integrated and adequate network of waste disposal installations, taking account of the best available technology not involving excessive costs; and
(b) ensuring that that network enables:
  (i) the Community as a whole to become self-sufficient in waste disposal, and the UK to move towards that aim, taking into account geographical circumstances or the need for specialized installations for certain types of waste; and
  (ii) waste to be disposed of in one of the nearest appropriate installations, by means of the most appropriate methods and technologies in order to ensure a high level of protection for the environment and public health.

The question of the legal status of the relevant objectives is complex, partly because their phrasing is uneven. For example, the objective of 'ensuring' that waste is disposed of or recovered without endangering human health is, on its face, absolute; later objectives are not. It is clear that the Directive 91/156, Art 4 objective is not directly effective despite this phrasing, however.[82] There is authority in the Court of Appeal to suggest that the objectives look like a freestanding obligation: in exercising any of the relevant functions, a regulator may have to expressly demonstrate that it has 'cast its mind' to them.[83] As that case was a judicial review of a planning decision, there was no obligation on the local planning authority to give reasons, and so there was no evidence to show that it had failed to discharge the duty, even if it did exist.

If the objective is an additional obligation, then there are important implications: it suggests a more protective approach than that intrinsic to other controls, and thus when regulators consider other controls with a waste aspect, that more protective approach may have to be applied.[84] Indeed, this point seems to have been recognised in the High Court, where the duty to consider the relevant objectives was not considered to be co-extensive with duties under the integrated pollution control regime.[85] In a procedural sense, then, regulators would seem to be under an obligation at least to 'cast their mind' to the relevant objectives.

Neither *Kirkman* nor *Gibson* really engaged with the content of the objectives, however. In particular, those cases did not consider whether an authority casting its mind to the apparently absolute objectives is required to *ensure* that waste is recovered or disposed of without endangering human health. There are a number of options. For

81 PPG 23, Annex 6, para 3.
82 *Comitato Di Coordinamento per la Difesa della Cava v Regione Lombardia* Case C-236/92 [1994] ECR I-483.
83 *R v Bolton Metropolitan Council, ex p Kirkman* [1998] JPL 787.
84 Purdue, 'The Relationship between Development Control and Specialist Pollution Controls' [1999] JPL 585.
85 *R v Environment Agency, ex p Gibson (No 2)* [1999] Env LR 73.

example, it might be suggested that it requires all the risks of different recovery and disposal options to be considered, and – recognising that no option can be risk-free – the lowest risk scheme to be preferred. However, so strong an approach was expressly rejected in *R v Leicestershire County Council, ex p Blackfordby and Boothorpe Action Group Ltd*:[86] to interpret the relevant objectives as requiring lowest risk solutions would be to accord to them an indeterminate status, higher than that of material considerations but not so high that they must be achieved. However, these cautionary words were qualified by the Court of Appeal in *R v Daventry District Council, ex p Thornby Farms Ltd; R (on the application of Murray) v Derbyshire County Council*,[87] by reference to further decisions of the ECJ. Although resisting the invitation to create a hierarchy of importance of different factors, the Court nonetheless concluded that the objectives are something more than a material consideration: 'an objective which is obligatory must always be kept in mind when making a decision even while the decision maker has regard to other material considerations'.[88] This is rather confusing. It does create some scope to argue that the weight given to other considerations may produce a result that involves so flagrant a disregard for the objectives that there is a breach of the obligation. What is not clear, however, is what defines such a case. It also certainly implies that the court may re-engage with the substantive judgments made by an authority in order to ensure compliance with the objectives. Although this is not unique, it is certainly an extension of the approach adopted in the early cases: it lends some greater weight to the objectives, although its extent remains obscure.

D UK WASTE MANAGEMENT LAW

Control under planning law

Prospective controls over planned waste installations have long existed under the planning regime, controls which extend to site restoration and aftercare. The fact that they must operate in tandem with waste management licensing serves to reinforce the continuing relevance of local land use controls, despite the now centralised management licensing functions of the Environment Agency. The dividing line between planning and pollution controls is not clear cut, however, as PPG 10 emphasises.[89] Much clearer is the starting point: that the deposit of waste or refuse on land will normally amount to development requiring planning permission on the basis that it is a material change of use,[90] and may amount to operational development on normal principles. This is so whether or not land is comprised in a site already used for that purpose, if the area of the deposit is extended or the height increased beyond that of surrounding land.[91] It has also been held that a change in the type of disposal activity being undertaken can amount to a material change for planning purposes,[92] although a certain amount of tipping may be ancillary to a principal building or engineering project and therefore might not require permission.[93] These authorities do not, of course, resolve all practical cases, which must be considered on their own facts.

---

86   [2001] Env LR 35.
87   [2002] EWCA Civ 58, [2002] All ER (D) 149 (Jan).
88   Para 53.
89   *Planning and Waste Management*, 1999.
90   TCPA 1990, s 55(1); *Alexandra Transport Co v Secretary of State for Scotland* (1973) 27 P & CR 352.
91   TCPA 1990, s 55(3)(a).
92   *Roberts v Vale District Council* (1997) 78 LGR 368.
93   *Northavon District Council v Secretary of State for the Environment* (1980) 40 P & CR 332.

These basic rules must also be read subject to the General Permitted Development Order 1995, which grants extensive permitted development rights for waste-related development. For example, Part 20, Class C of the Order grants conditional rights to licensed coal operators to carry on development at authorised mine sites in connection with mining operations. Equally, all mineral operators are granted permission by the GPDO 1995, Part 21 to deposit waste that is operationally derived from a site at that site or on ancillary land – again, subject to conditions including height of any final deposit and the possible need for a waste management scheme to be prepared. As these illustrations suggest, the GPDO 1995 applies to development which is largely ancillary to a dominant use, albeit on a large scale. The principal reason for the waste development is the dominant activity, mining. It should be noted (although not strictly a matter of waste regulation) that further legal controls do apply to ensure the stability and safety of wastes deposited in such situations. Under the Mines and Quarries (Tips) Act 1969 (which has been superseded in part by the Quarries Regulations 1999[94] insofar as it applies to health and safety matters): certain 'tips' must be made and kept secure; notification of the beginning and end of tipping must be given to inspectors appointed by the Health and Safety Executive; and regulations have been made to ensure that rules are applied to tipping operations to ensure safety and stability. Local authorities are also empowered by the MQTA 1969 to ensure that disused tips do not constitute a public danger through instability, by seeking information, entering land to carry out testing, or requiring landowners to carry out specified remedial works.

Waste planning is among those matters designated as a 'county matter', and so the administration of waste planning powers in England and Wales falls generally to county councils, metropolitan district councils and unitary authorities. The same applies to waste-related development which is a county matter 'in substance', even if it does not fall completely within the complex definition of that term.[95] By this means, a strategic approach is implicit in the structure of planning controls, in anticipation of their substance, which may be of more than local importance. It will be remembered that waste planning functions are also subject to the European objectives set out in the Waste Management Licensing Regulations 1994, considered above.

Strategic planning

Planning has a very significant contribution to make by influencing the location of waste facilities. Regional guidance may indicate the scale of medium- or long-term demands for land for waste management facilities, and any constraints arising from cumulative impacts of existing or proposed uses.[96] National planning policy does not operate to favour particular waste management solutions, however, which remain a matter for individual planning authorities, informed by the National Waste Strategies and consideration of the best practicable environmental option for each waste stream.[97] The first vehicle for implementation is the development plan which, of course, has two aspects. First, 'waste treatment and disposal, land reclamation and reuse' is one of the key subjects for inclusion in structure plans and Part I of unitary development plans.[98] Policies in such plans should set out the planning authority's overall planning strategy for waste management, within the regional context (on which see PPG 10, Annex B,

---

94   SI 1999/2024.
95   *R v Berkshire County Council, ex p Wokingham District Council* [1997] JPL 461, which considered a waste transfer and recycling facility.
96   PPG 23, para 2.1.
97   PPG 10, para 3.
98   PPG 12, *Development Plans*, 1999.

'Developing regional strategies for waste management and the role of regional technical advisory bodies'). That regional context of waste planning is increasingly important, both practically, as a means of contributing to implementation of national waste policy, and politically, to set the scene for local consideration of frequently controversial proposals for new waste facilities. Revised planning guidance therefore requires planning authorities to ensure that an adequate planning framework is in place for the provision by the waste management industry of waste facilities, and in particular to:

(a) carefully consider the environmental implications of all waste management proposals;
(b) be guided by the national waste strategy and the need to maximise, so far as is practicable, regional self-sufficiency;
(c) be 'challenging but realistic'[99] about the scope which options for waste management may provide for reducing the amount of waste which requires final disposal;
(d) identify sites for waste management and disposal facilities, where possible;
(e) 'take care' that a lack of adequate facilities for management in one plan area should not lead to waste being transported long distances to management facilities in other areas;
(f) seek not to inhibit the ability of the waste management industry from adapting to trends in the waste market, or to legislative change; and
(g) indicate in the explanatory memorandum to, or written justification of, a strategic plan how waste policies and proposals relate to national and regional policy, the plans of neighbouring areas, four key principles (the need to consider the best practicable environmental option, the need for regional self-sufficiency, the proximity principle and the waste hierarchy), municipal waste management strategies and the relevant local plan.

Planning authorities responsible for waste are generally also required to prepare a waste local plan, or to include waste policies in their minerals local plan: an obligation in place only since 1991.[100] The strategic policy-making role of unitary authorities in this respect is exercised jointly with the authorities of the county areas of which they were formerly part.[101] As with local plans in general, waste local plans give detailed expression to the waste policies in the relevant strategic plan, with which they must generally conform. Local plan policies should identify preferred locations for new or replacement facilities, or broad 'areas of search' in which they may be acceptable. The very least that should be included is a set of comprehensive criteria against which applications can be considered.[102] This framework of plans is still new: local waste disposal plans under environment protection legislation have only been replaced by the national strategies recently (see above), and so the practical relationship between national waste policy and each level of land use plans is still in a relatively early stage of development. It is clear, however, that planning has an important role in identifying sites for waste-related development, which extends far beyond merely responding to planning applications. There is, in effect, a positive duty on planning authorities to identify and encourage the safe development of appropriate sites. Conversely, they must not seek to prohibit the development of particular types of waste facility unless they are confident that adequate alternative facilities will be in available in their area.[103]

99   PPG 10, para 29(e).
100 TCPA 1990, s 38, as amended.
101 DoE Circular 4/96.
102 PPG 10, paras 33-4.
103 PPG 10, para 34.

Development control

The relationship between planning and pollution controls is difficult, and rarely more controversial than in relation to waste facilities. For example, should permission be granted, then policy dictates that planning conditions should not be used to duplicate controls possible under dedicated statutory regimes.[104] In practice, however, planning conditions will be numerous, and extend to post-development restoration and aftercare. Core policy considerations should be set out in the relevant development plan. Other material considerations might include impacts on adjoining sites, transport, geology and hydrogeology, and potential prejudice to future long-term uses of land in the area. Planning conditions should focus on the acceptability of development in terms of the use of land, and not on the operational control of processes themselves. However, the effects of waste management facilities on other land may be material, including the proximity of other development, transportation (both traffic and access) and land instability. Also potentially relevant are local environmental impacts, such as visual intrusion, noise, dust, odour, vermin and birds, litter, hours of operation, and protection of surface and underground water. An important consideration will be monitoring and controlling landfill gas, and conditions may provide for venting, measures to exclude gas generating matter, or steps to prevent gas migration. An assessment may also be required of the risk of incidents occurring at a site, and their potential impacts.[105] PPG 10 concedes that these sorts of environmental impacts may be considered both by planning authorities in development control and the Environment Agency in waste management licensing.[106] Restoration and aftercare conditions may relate to landforms, preservation of topsoil, minimum standards and depths of soil restoration, and post-development monitoring, for example, of landfill gas or leachate. Such conditions can apply for up to five years are restoration is complete, and an extended period of monitoring and site assessment can be anticipated.[107]

Two other points can be made about development control. First, statutory provision has been made for the relationship between waste management licensing and development control. In particular, a waste management licence may not be granted unless a necessary planning permission or established used certificate is in force.[108] To this extent, 'double' controls are rigorously applied. Equally, Parliament has implied its own view of the scope of planning controls by providing that 'serious detriment to the amenities of a locality' – essentially a planning judgment – may only provide grounds for refusing an application for a waste management licence where there has been no express grant of planning permission.[109] Thus, the modern planning judgement of a local planning authority is given statutory precedence over any waste regulator's view. Secondly, as a general rule, planning permission enures for the benefit of the land and all persons interested in it, and likewise they take the burden of any planning conditions.[110] This is an important distinction between planning permissions and waste management licences, which are personal and may only be transferred with the Agency's consent.[111]

104 PPG 23, para 1.3.
105 *Envirocor Waste Holdings Ltd v Secretary of State for the Environment* [1995] EGCS 60.
106 Sch 5, para 2(7).
107 PPG 10, Annex A.
108 EPA 1990, s 36.
109 EPA 1990, s 36(3).
110 TCPA 1990, s 75(1).
111 EPA 1990, s 40.

Waste management licensing

The general inadequacy of waste law is part of the background to the contemporary development of waste policy. A number of specific criticisms have been made of the regulatory approach previously adopted in the UK, and these shed important light on the current, modernised approach. The now-repealed system of waste disposal licensing under the Control of Pollution Act 1974 was deeply limited from conception. Its focus on licensing sites used for waste disposal – the very end of the waste chain – created a huge regulatory gap between waste producers and any responsibility for safe disposal, and so a massive variety of waste-related activity went uncontrolled. Some stop-gap measures had been introduced, not least through mandatory registration of carriers of waste under the Control of Pollution (Amendment) Act 1989. Despite the importance of the COP(A)A 1989, which remains in force (see below), it was nonetheless simply bolstering a deeply limited predecessor. That system also placed waste planning, collection and disposal licensing in the hands of the same authorities – the very same authorities that had substantial responsibilities for disposing of municipal wastes. Such basic problems were also compounded by an array of technical failings: there were few grounds on which licence applications could be refused, and so there was no easily discernible base level of operator competence; licences could be surrendered at the will of the holder, at the price of the long-term control necessary even for those disposal sites which were in fact licensed; enforcement was limited to disposal itself, rather than extending to breaches of operational controls;[112] conditions could not precede disposal nor extend to aftercare beyond it, even conditions requiring that no nuisance was to be created by a licensed site were impermissible;[113] and strategic and national planning were woefully under-prioritised. Dramatic reform was therefore needed, and was finally made by EPA 1990, Part II the licensing part of which came into force on 1 May 1994.

Part II introduced a licensing regime which applies to all persons who treat, keep or dispose of waste: a cradle-to-grave regime which is far wider than merely disposal. In addition, the obligations, when they bite, are broader still. Not only is prevention of environmental harm given a higher priority (eg in more numerous, and wider, offences), but every member of the 'waste chain' must consider both their own compliance with direct obligations, and compliance by others. The starting point is one of the most controversial features, however: the definition of 'waste' itself.

Defining 'waste': the statutory position

The obligation on the UK to implement the Waste Framework Directive has ensured that 'waste' is a European legal concept. In considering its domestic interpretation, the views of the ECJ are therefore unusually important: in no other environmental regime has that which is at the very core of control been subject to such protracted dispute. This has not been assisted in the UK by a matter of timing: the waste management licensing regime may only have come into force in 1994, but it rests on provisions enacted in EPA 1990, a year before the Waste Framework Directive was itself substantially amended. Consequently, the legal meaning of waste in the UK is derived from a complex combination of the 1990 Act, the amended Framework Directive and the Waste Management Licensing Regulations 1994.[114] The Environment Act 1995 promised to bring some technical, if not substantive, clarification but the relevant parts

---

112 *Leigh Land Reclamation Ltd v Walsall Metropolitan Borough Council* [1991] JEL 281.
113 *A-G's Reference (No 2 of 1988)* [1990] 1 QB 77.
114 SI 1994/1056 – 'the WML Regulations'.

have not been brought into force.[115] Two particular policy reasons also help to explain the complexity of the definition. The first is that the definition of waste underpins the criminal controls imposed by the waste management licensing regime. Important issues of clarity and consistency therefore arise in transposing a concept which, through its supra-national origins, is perhaps not ideally suited to this purpose. Secondly, increasing emphasis on waste re-use, recovery and recycling makes it desirable in policy terms to avoid imposing the burdens of regulation on such activities wherever possible or, if controls are applied initially, then to remove them as quickly as possible. An important challenge in defining waste is therefore to identify the point at which waste that is re-used, recovered or recycled stops being waste and becomes a raw material.

Part II applies to 'controlled waste', that is household, industrial and commercial waste 'or any such waste' (depending on the nature of the premises on which the waste originates: EPA 1990, s 75(4)-(7)), a deceptively simple starting point complemented by regulations.[116] As we shall see, the scope of waste management licensing depends on the category of controlled waste into which a particular substance falls. For example, household waste (which includes waste from buildings used as living accommodation, caravans, residential homes, and universities and schools) is subject to lesser controls than industrial waste (which includes clinical waste and waste from factories, public transport facilities, and premises used by public utility companies or in connection with the provision of telecommunications or postal services). These categories are obviously not closed – hence the phrase 'any such waste' – but this is limited to wastes that are cognate with the three categories.[117]

The definition of 'waste' itself is more important, and much more elaborate. It has four cumulative stages. First, the substance in question must be included in the list set out in the WML Regulations, a list that is derived directly from the Framework Directive (Sch 4, Part II and Annex I respectively). This is not difficult, however, as the final category in that list is 'any materials, substances or products which are not contained in the [other] categories'. The second stage is almost as broad: waste includes any substance which constitutes a scrap material or effluent or other unwanted surplus substance arising from the application of any process *and* any substance or article which requires to be disposed or as being broken, worn out, contaminated or otherwise spoiled.[118] But this list is not exhaustive, and so it cannot define the outer limits of 'waste; if a substance does fall within this partial definition then it is waste, but if a substance does not then it cannot be said that it is *not* waste. If the answer is not yet clear, we must move on to stage three.

The third stage in the definition of waste derives from the WML Regulations, which seek to ensure consistency between the EPA definition and the definition provided by the Framework Directive.[119] The regulations therefore introduce a new concept, 'directive waste', which is:

> 'Any substance or object in the categories set out in Part II of Schedule 4 [our stage one: see above] which the producer or the person in possession of it discards or intends or is required to discard but with the exception of anything excluded from the scope of the Directive by Article 2 of the Directive, and "discard" has the same meaning as in the Directive, and "producer" means anyone whose activities produce directive waste or who carries out pre-processing, mixing or other operations resulting in a change in its nature or composition.'

115 EPA 1990, s 120, Sch 22, para 88; new EPA 1990, s 75(2).
116 Controlled Waste Regulations 1992, SI 1992/588, as amended.
117 *Thanet District Council v Kent County Council* [1993] Env LR 391.
118 EPA 1990, s 75(3).
119 Framework Directive, Art 1(a).

If a substance is directive waste, then it falls within the definition of controlled waste for the purposes of EPA 1990, and if a substance is not directive waste then it cannot be controlled waste.[120] The real importance of this stage is twofold. First, it introduces the key concept of 'discarding'. Not only is this a problematic concept in itself, but it also sets the scene for arguments as to the legal effect of recovery operations: if a substance is to be recovered, does it ever become waste? These issues are at the heart of the case law, and we return to them shortly. Secondly, directive waste provides us with stage four, the statutory exclusions. On the face of it, these can be dealt with quite simply as they are set out in full in Article 2 of the Framework Directive. The following are therefore excluded from the scope of the Framework Directive:

(a) gaseous effluents emitted into the atmosphere;
(b) where they are already covered by other legislation:
    (i) radioactive waste;
    (ii) waste resulting from prospecting, extraction, treatment and storage of mineral resources and the working of quarries;
    (iii) animal carcasses and the following agricultural waste: faecal matter and other natural, non-dangerous substances, used in farming;
    (iv) waste waters, with the exception of waste in liquid form; and
    (v) decommissioned explosives.

The first exception speaks for itself. The second is more difficult: in each case the legal issue is whether these wastes are in fact already covered by other legislation. The UK government view is that this means that controls were in place on 18 March 1991 which provide as effective a means of pursuing Framework Directive obligations as waste management licensing.[121] Each case is different: radioactive wastes are covered by the Radioactive Substances Act 1993; mineral waste is regulated by planning controls and the Mines and Quarries (Tips) Act 1969, whilst non-mineral waste from mines and quarries remains directive waste (although it would otherwise not be controlled waste proper: s 75(7)); certain animal wastes are subject to the Animal Waste Directive 90/667, whilst others are made subject to waste management licensing; waste waters are regulated under water legislation, although this is not the case for liquid wastes deposited in landfill (a practice now prohibited in any event by the Landfill Directive); explosives are subject to the Explosives Act 1875. Similarly, the obligations under the directive have been modernised, and detailed questions may arise as to whether the same can be said of each set of specific controls.

Defining 'waste': the case law

Whether a substance is discarded, or is intended or required to be discarded, is central to defining that substance as waste. The proper question is not whether a substance has a commercial value or (in principle) whether it is capable of re-use, recycling or recovery but instead focuses on the actions, intentions or obligations of the current holder. Yet there is an intimate connection between the meaning of 'discard' and acts of disposal or recovery. First, in legal terms because the Framework Directive lists certain disposal and recovery operations which are required to be licensed,[122] although this too is not an exhaustive list. Secondly, in practical terms because the distinction between recovery operations and 'ordinary' industrial processes which create a useable product

---

120 WML Regulations, regs 1(3), 19; Controlled Waste Regulations, reg 7A.
121 DoE Circular 11/94.
122 Annex IIA, disposal operations, and Annex IIB, recovery operations: replicated in Annexes III and IV of the WML Regulations.

is a very fine one, and so a substance which is sent for recovery may be more akin to a raw material than a waste material. The question is therefore whether a substance sent for recovery is waste at all – has it been discarded? does subjecting a substance to an operation listed in the Framework Directive conclusively resolve the issue of whether it is waste? – and it if it is, at what point (if any) it ceases to be so. The other practical difficulty, of course, is that different holders of waste can have very different intentions. Such assistance as is provided by the cases is neither comprehensive, nor straightforward.

It was clear before the new regime was enacted that the fact that material was capable of being recycled did not mean that it could not be waste.[123] The same conclusion was reached by the ECJ on the wording of the Framework Directive before it was amended: the mere fact that a substance is capable of economic re-utilisation does not mean that it cannot be waste.[124] This conclusion remains a good one after the amendments made to the Framework Directive in 1991.[125] The *Tombesi* case was something of a landmark, albeit by default. The explanation for this is that the Advocate General's detailed reasoning, particularly that relating to the relationship between 'discard' and the Annex IIB recovery operations, is not replicated by the court. That reasoning avoided the need to decide precisely when a substance is discarded: it suggested that the act of consignment to a recovery operation was sufficient to indicate that a substance had been discarded and, consequently, that it was waste. Three problems follow. First, the list of recovery operations is not exhaustive, and it can also include operations which have nothing to do with waste at all (eg treatment of land, or oil refining). This reasoning may avoid the need precisely to define 'discard' – ie consignment to recovery can amount to discarding – but it does create problems with the meaning of 'recovery': what it is, when it starts, and when it stops. Secondly, there is a certain circularity in defining waste by reference to consignment of a substance to recovery, which is then itself defined by reference to whether a substance is waste. Thirdly, the court did not employ this detailed reasoning in any event. It simply concluded that the Framework Directive was intended to cover all substances or objects discarded by their owner, even if they have a commercial value and are collected on a commercial basis for recycling, reclamation or re-use. Consignment of a substance to a recovery operation therefore can amount to discarding it, and that substance therefore can be waste.

The Advocate General's approach in *Tombesi* is reflected in UK guidance. Indeed, the UK government intervened in *Tombesi* arguing that a distinction should be made between goods that form part of the normal commercial cycle or 'chain of utility' and goods consigned to a 'special recovery operation' (such as those in Annex IIB). Goods transferred to another person and used in their existing form would therefore not fall out of the chain of utility, and would not become waste.[126] Circular 11/94 also suggests that a substance or object which is worn but functioning as originally intended or usable after repair for its original purpose is not generally waste, as neither is material which can be put to immediate use other than via *specialist* waste recoverers. On the other hand material which has degenerated and can only be put to use by waste recoverers is waste even if it has value or is transferred for value. Where, however, there is material which is simply unwanted, and for whose removal a charge has to be paid, much will depend on the facts of individual cases. If the recipient of the material can use it without special processes (as, for example would be the case of a secondhand furniture dealer) the material would not normally be waste.

123 *R v Rotherham Metropolitan Borough Council, ex p Rankin* [1990] JPL 503.
124 *Vessoso* and *Zanetti* (joined cases C-206/88 and C-207/88) [1990] ECR I-1461.
125 *Tombesi* [1997] All ER (EC) 639.
126 DoE Circular 11/94.

Subsequent decision of the ECJ are more equivocal than the UK government would wish, however. In particular, in *Inter-Environnement Wallonie ASBL v Régione Wallonie*[127] the court accepted that a distinction can be drawn between recovery operations under the Framework Directive and the normal industrial treatment of raw materials. The court did conclude that subjecting a substance to an Annex IIB recovery operation would probably indicate that it has been discarded, and that the directive could still apply to a waste recovery operation which is integral to a larger industrial process, but it provided no guidance as to how the distinction between waste recovery operations and 'ordinary' industrial processes is to be drawn. The absence of a principled distinction is undoubtedly consistent with a purposive reading of the Framework Directive – the court is erring on the side of inclusion – but this has created problems in the UK. The most potent recent illustration is the important decision of the High Court in *Mayer Parry Recycling Ltd v Environment Agency*,[128] which considered scrap metals that were to be smelted and reused. Adopting the approach of the Advocate General in *Tombesi*, Carnwath J concluded that 'discard' is used in a sense that is broadly equivalent to 'get rid of', and is concerned generally with materials which have ceased to be required for their original purpose, normally because they are unsuitable, unwanted or surplus to requirements.[129] Consequently, materials that are to be reused without any recovery operation are not to be treated as waste. Further, if a recovery operation is applied, then a substance only ceases to be waste at the conclusion of that operation. This is certainly more elaborate guidance than the ECJ had at that point provided, but even this must now be viewed with caution.

The reason for that caution is the subsequent decision of the ECJ in *ARCO Chemie Nederland Ltd v Minister van Volkshuisvesting* and *EPON*,[130] which concerned use of the by-products of a manufacturing process as a fuel in cement manufacture. The court concluded that it would be too narrow simply to say that because a substance was consigned to an Annex IIB operation then it was waste – the converse of the decision in *Wallonie*. Annex IIB is therefore not a 'shortcut' to identifying waste,[131] rather, the key issue remains whether the by-product has been discarded. Equally, the fact that such secondary fuels could be used in an environmentally sound way did not mean that they were not waste. The court concluded that all of the circumstances have to be taken into account in deciding if a substance has been discarded, and therefore implicitly provided some guidance for future cases. Indicators of a discard therefore included: the fact that the material was a by-product, or production residue; that it is commonly regarded as waste, and that its use as fuel is considered to be a recovery operation; that no other use than disposal could be envisaged; and that special precautions had to be taken when the substance was used as a fuel. One consequence of *ARCO* and *EPON* is that it can no longer be said that materials that are to be reused without a recovery operation are not waste,[132] nor that carrying out a 'complete' recovery operation necessarily results in a substance ceasing to be waste.[133] A gloss is also added by express provision which currently dictates that anything which is discarded or 'otherwise dealt with as if it were waste' is presumed to be waste unless the contrary is proved.[134] At present his gives unusual evidential weight to one of the

127 [1998] Env LR 623.
128 [1999] Env LR 489.
129 [1999] Env LR 489, at 505.
130 [2000] ECR I-4475.
131 *Tromans*, (2001) 13 JEL 133, 145.
132 *A-G's Reference (No 5 of 2000)* [2001] EWCA Crim 1077, [2001] 2 CMLR 1025.
133 *Castle Cement v Environment Agency* [2002] JPL 43.
134 EPA 1990, s 75(3).

factors identified by the ECJ in *ARCO* and *EPON*, although provision has been made to repeal this presumption.[135]

What is illuminating is that the 1994 UK guidance, set out in DoE Cicular 11/94 remains fairly sound: it is pragmatic, emphasises the importance of the circumstance of individual cases, and focuses on what has re-emerged as the key concept, namely 'discarding'. The test suggested there is to ask whether the material can be used in its present form (albeit after repair) or in the same way as any other raw material without being subjected to specialised recovery operations, and is it likely to be so used? Where the answer is 'yes' it is suggested the material has not been discarded and so is not waste. Where, however, the answer is 'no' *or* where material can only be used after subjection to specialised recovery operations, the material is normally to be regarded as discarded and hence is waste. The remaining question of the point at which waste ceases to be waste has now also been referred to the ECJ.[136]

Institutional framework

One of the major problems of the law before 1990 was the 'poacher cum gamekeeper' syndrome in that 'waste disposal authorities' (primarily counties) were responsible for both licensing the disposal of waste and disposing of it themselves. EPA 1990 partially remedied this by dividing overall waste responsibilities between Waste Collection Authorities (WCAs) who are primarily District Councils and London Boroughs in England, Waste Disposal Authorities (WDAs) primarily in England the 'shire' counties and certain other specially created statutory bodies for London, Greater Manchester and Merseyside, and Waste Regulation Authorities, again the 'shire' counties and special authorities for London, Greater Manchester and Merseyside. Clearly this still resulted in some authorities wearing more than one hat — for example in the areas of some unitary metropolitan districts — a continuing issue with the emergence of more unitary authorities in England and Wales under the 1992 and 1994 local government legislation. However, there was at least a degree of separation between the waste regulation and waste disposal arms of authorities. With the Environment Act 1995, national authorities have been established for England and Wales (the Environment Agency), and Scotland (SEPA).

The waste regulation functions of the Agency therefore include: waste licensing (both management licensing and exemption registration), including monitoring and enforcement; requiring the removal of unlawfully deposited waste; registration of waste carriers; supervision of waste disposal sites; and supervision of the statutory 'duty of care' as to waste. In exercising these functions the Agency is equipped with a wide range of investigatory and other powers. Most of these are generic, in that they may be exercised irrespective of which statutory regime is concerned (eg Environment Act 1995, ss 108, 109), although there are some exceptions (eg EPA 1990, s 71). In practice it will be important to identify precisely which powers are being exercised, not least because of the legal consequences of non-compliance. These may include human rights considerations, for example, particularly where mandatory powers to furnish information may conflict with qualified rights against self-incrimination.[137] Although that case confirmed the Agency's powers to require the provision of information to assist the exercise of waste regulation functions, the House did not conclusively resolve the matter

---

135   EA 1995, s 120, Sch 22, para 88(3).
136   *R v Environment Agency, ex p Mayer Parry Recycling Ltd* [2001] Env LR 31.
137   *R v Hertfordshire County Council, ex p Green Environmental Industries* [2000] Env LR 426, HL.

of the subsequent admissibility of such information in criminal proceedings against the person who supplied it. This question will often raise human rights concerns, although the robust approach subsequently taken by the Privy Council in *Stott (Procurator Fiscal, Dunfermline) v Brown*[138] may lessen regulators' unease.

The impetus for the exercise of these powers of investigation, and thereafter the Agency's specific regulatory powers, may be provided by the Agency's general duty to supervise licensed activities.[139] Their overriding task is to ensure that authorised activities do not pollute the environment, harm human health or become a detriment to local amenity, and to ensure licence conditions are complied with. In emergencies authorised officers of the Agency may carry out work on relevant land or plant to ensure performance of supervision, and may recover their expenditure in this connection from the licensee. The Agency may also require compliance with licence conditions. The power to require compliance arises where it appears to the Agency that a condition is either not being complied with or is likely not to be complied with. In such circumstances they may serve notice on the licence holder stating their opinion, specifying the matters constituting the non-compliance or anticipated non-compliance, and specifying remedial or preventive action and the time within which action is to be taken. If the required steps are not taken the Agency may revoke the licence in whole or in part, or suspend it, while if this would afford an ineffectual remedy they may seek injunctive relief in the High Court. In the exercise of EPA 1990, s 42 powers the Agency is subject to direction by the Secretary of State.

Waste collection functions

Under EPA 1990, s 45, WCAs are to collect all household waste in their areas, unless it is so isolated as to be unreasonably expensive to collect, and other adequate disposal arrangements have been made. They are to collect commercial waste where requested by the occupier of the premises, and a reasonable charge for this service may be made. They may collect, if requested by the occupier, industrial waste from premises, subject, in England and Wales, to the consent of the relevant waste disposal authority, and again a reasonable charge may be made. They may clear privies and cesspools and may provide facilities for waste collection and may also make arrangements for the provision of waste receptacles for household, commercial or industrial waste. Any waste collected by the WCA belongs to that authority, not to its employees or agents. Under EPA 1990, s 48 they are to deliver waste to such places as the WDA directs, subject, in the case of household or commercial waste, to where the WCA has recycling arrangements; though the WDA may override such recycling by the WCA where it has its own arrangements with a waste disposal contractor to recycle all or part of the waste.

The local application of waste policy should be assisted by what was a major departure in 1990: a new obligation on WCAs to prepare waste recycling plans in respect of household and commercial waste.[140] The obligations are, on their face, broad: authorities are to investigate waste with a view of deciding what arrangements are appropriate for separating, baling or packaging it for recycling, and then to decide on arrangements for those purposes. They must prepare a statement ('the plan') of proposed and actual arrangements showing how they and others will deal with waste. The plan must be kept under review, and must be made, and modified, in the light of the

138 [2001] 2 WLR 817.
139 EPA 1990, s 42.
140 EPA 1990, s 49.

effects of the plan on the amenities of any locality and the likely costs/savings to the authority attributable to it. The plan must state: the kinds and quantities of controlled waste the WCA expects to collect or purchase in the plan period; the kinds and quantities of such waste to be prepared for recycling; arrangements to be made with waste disposal contractors for them to deal with waste; plant and equipment to be provided, and the estimated costs/savings attributable to operations under the plan.

Plans must be publicised in relevant areas, and copies sent to the relevant WDA, the Agency and the Secretary of State so that he/she may ensure that the plan contains the requisite provisions. Plans must also be available for public inspection, but there is little public involvement formally in their creation.

EPA 1990, s 55 confers powers on WCAs *and* WDAs to further the recycling of waste. Thus WCAs may buy or otherwise acquire waste with a view to its recycling and may use, sell or otherwise dispose of waste they own or anything produced from it. WDAs may also buy or acquire waste for recycling, they may also make arrangements with waste disposal contractors for them to recycle waste, or for those contractors to produce heat or light from waste, or use or sell waste as the authority itself might otherwise do.

The obligation to make plans is now well-established, and greater coordination with national waste strategies can now be anticipated. Such plans have been less high-profile than the complementary waste recycling credits scheme, however. This initiative operates between WCAs and WDAs to ensure that either authority is not penalised for recycling. For example, if by recycling a WCA reduces the amount of waste going for disposal, then the relevant WDA's savings in disposal costs deriving from that recycling are to be passed back to the WCA.[141] If this scheme had not been established then WDAs would have received the financial benefits of WCAs' recycling initiatives, and vice versa. The general level of payments is periodically modified, but much depends on the actual costs incurred in disposal: the level of credits is based on the costliest disposal method employed, as this too provides an incentive to recycle.[142]

Waste disposal functions

WDAs are under a *duty* to dispose of all controlled waste collected in their area by WCAs and to provide deposition places for residents to place their household rubbish.[143] These places are to be reasonably accessible to residents, free of charge and generally open, and such sites may accept household waste from persons other than residents, for a fee.

However, the 'meat' of EPA 1990, s 51 is that WDAs are to discharge their duties in respect of waste disposal by means of 'arrangements' with waste disposal contractors.[144] These provisions effectively privatise waste disposal functions: exposing the appointment of WDCs to contractual competition. Initially this was through the system of local government compulsory competitive tendering, but this has since been replaced by a 'best value' system. The Secretary of State played a key transitional role through directions to WDAs to form or to participate in forming local authority WDCs.[145] Through LAWDCs, WDAs themselves can operate 'arm's length' companies to discharge waste disposal functions: the companies are therefore distanced

---

141 EPA 1990, s 52; Environmental Protection (Waste Recycling Payments) Regulations 1992, as amended.
142 *R v North Yorkshire County Council, ex p Scarborough Borough Council* [1999] JPL 1087.
143 EPA 1990, s 51.
144 WDCs. EPA 1990, s 32, Sch 2.
145 LAWDCs. Directions were given in 1991: see DoE Circular 8/91, Annex C.

from WDAs, and are intended to operate on a commercial basis with them. Such companies must operate in a commercial market, however, as private companies also compete with LAWDCs to make arrangements with a WDA for the discharge of its EPA 1990, s 51 obligations. There is therefore no guarantee that the formation of a LAWDC will lead to its appointment by a WDA, indeed, such decisions can be controversial. For example, in *R v Avon County Council, ex p Terry Adams Ltd*[146] a private contractor sought judicial review of a WDA's decision to award a disposal contract to its own LAWDC. The Court of Appeal observed that the EPA 1990 imposes three duties on WDAs: to have regard to environmental considerations in the disposal of waste, to dispose of their own waste disposal undertakings (ie to form LAWDCs), and to open up waste disposal to market forces. These duties are not easily compatible, and as no statutory indication is given of their relative importance, a number of general principles must be applied. For example, all relevant factors must be taken into account in awarding contracts, and whilst the cost of disposal services is one such factor so too is the need to ensure that disposal does not cause environmental harm. Whilst competition must be a fair process, the court did conclude that the WDA was not obliged to choose the cheapest option, as preferences may well be affected by environmental preferences. An authority's preferred disposal strategy is therefore relevant in deciding upon the award of a contract.[147]

The connection between privatised waste disposal services and discharge by WCAs of their functions is made by giving WDAs elaborate powers to direct WCAs as to the persons and places to whom and to which waste is to be delivered, and to arrange for the provision of places by WDCs at which waste may be treated or kept prior to disposal or treatment. EPA 1990, Sch 2, Part II then further regulates the contracts WDAs are to make with WDCs. Contracts are to be put out to public competitive tender by advertisement in publications circulating generally amongst WDCs, and wherever possible, at least four tenders for the work are to be invited.

Waste management licensing: key offences

Waste management licensing follows – at least initially – the familiar pattern of basic prohibitions on certain behaviour, coupled with a licensing defence. However, waste offences relate to a wider range of activities than many other environmental regimes, and a far larger group of people is potentially affected by them. There are also some innovative features, not least the statutory duty of care (to which we return below). An important insight into the operation of waste controls is provided by policy guidance, which suggests that, where regulation is necessary, then it:
(a) should be proportionate to the risks involved and the benefits to be obtained;
(b) should be goal-based, that is, it should have an objective and a means of ensuring the fulfilment of the objective;
(c) should not serve as an end in itself;
(d) should not be over-prescriptive; and
(e) should not impose an unjustifiable or disproportionate burden on those regulated, especially small business.[148]

These are important limitations in practice, not least through their potential to affect the conditions imposed on licences. The principal (but not only) offences are set out in EPA 1990, s 33(1). While the statutory phrasing embraces a wide range of activities,

146 [1994] Env LR 442.
147 *R v Cardiff City Council, ex p Gooding Investments Ltd* (1995) 7 ELM 134.
148 DoE 11/94, para 10.

each limb creates a single offence that can be committed in a number of ways, and each can therefore be alleged in the alternative.[149] Consequently, a person shall not:

(a) deposit controlled waste or knowingly cause or knowingly permit the deposit of controlled waste in or on land without, or otherwise than in accordance with, a waste management licence;

(b) treat, keep or dispose of controlled waste, or knowingly cause or knowingly permit controlled waste to be treated, kept or disposed of in or on land or by means of mobile plant other than in accordance with a waste management licence; or

(c) treat, keep or dispose of controlled waste in a manner likely to cause pollution of the environment or harm to human health.

The accompanying definitions make broad offences broader still – far beyond the predecessor offences under COPA 1974. The 'environment' thus consists of land, water and air, while its 'pollution' in the context of controlled waste means pollution by the escape or release into land, air or water from land on which controlled waste is treated or kept or deposited or from fixed or mobile plant for treating, keeping or disposing of controlled waste, of substances which are waste or result from it and which are capable of causing harm to human kind or living organisms. 'Harm' in this context means harm to health, or to ecological systems, or offence to human senses or harm to property. 'Disposal' of waste includes landward deposit, while 'treatment' means subjecting waste to any process including making it reusable or reclaiming matter from waste, and 'recycle' is to be interpreted accordingly.

The key term 'deposit' has also been judicially considered, to complement the statutory definitions. Early cases took a narrow approach, and considered a 'deposit' to be the dumping site with 'no realistic prospect of further examination'[150] and that appeared to mean physical incorporation into the site and burial under later material. However, in *R v Metropolitan Stipendiary Magistrate, ex p London Waste Regulation Authority* and *Berkshire County Council v Scott*[151] the *Leigh Land* decision was doubted, and, by adopting a purposive interpretation of the legislation, it was held that 'deposit' did not mean only 'final deposit', similarly 'disposal' means only to get rid of something, it does not mean finding a final resting place for it. Thus a temporary deposit, as at a waste transfer station, can be enough to attract the attention of the law.[152] An equally broad approach was taken subsequently in *Thames Waste Management Ltd v Surrey County Council*,[153] when a continuing state of affairs was found to be capable of amounting to a deposit contrary to EPA 1990, s 33 (in that case, failure to cover deposited waste with soil, as required by a condition). The pre-EPA 1990 inability to prosecute for breaches of condition, noted in the *Leigh Land Reclamation* case and removed by the new regime,[154] has been interpreted similarly purposively. Not only is it unnecessary to show that the defendant knew that a condition has been broken, rather than that the prohibited deposit has in fact been made,[155] but contractors have also been convicted under section 33(6) even though not themselves a licence holder.[156] It seems that 'knowing permission' may be inferred

---

149 *R v Leighton and Town and Country Refuse Collections Ltd* [1997] Env LR 411.
150 *Leigh Land Reclamation Ltd v Walsall Metropolitan Borough Council* [1991] 3 JEL 281.
151 [1993] 3 All ER 113.
152 A view confirmed by DoE Circular 11/94, Annex 1.
153 [1997] Env LR 148.
154 EPA 1990, s 33(6).
155 *Shanks & McEwan (Teeside) Ltd v Environment Agency* [1997] 2 All ER 332, applying the COPA case of *Ashcroft v Cambro Waste Products* [1981] 1 WLR 1349.
156 *Shanks & McEwan (Midlands) Ltd v Wrexham Maelor Borough Council* (1996) 8 ELM 122.

when it is clear that the defendant must have known what was going on,[157] although evidential questions will be crucial in determining the precise charge. That evidence will often be complex, not least because the burden will be on the Agency to prove the precise charge brought, for example, that controlled waste having certain specific characteristics was deposited without or in breach of a licence.[158] It may be preferable to rely on the EPA 1990, s 33(1)(c) general offence, not least because this applies whether or not a licence is needed, or in force. A person who commits any of these offences is liable on summary conviction to six months' imprisonment or a £20,000 fine or both, or two years' imprisonment or a fine or both on conviction on indictment.[159] In the latter case, up to five years' imprisonment may be imposed if the waste is special waste.[160]

It is not only depositing controlled waste that requires a licence, of course, as EPA embraces treatment, keeping and disposal of such waste. 'Treatment' includes subjecting waste to any of the disposal or recovery operations in the WML Regulations.[161] In terms of 'disposal' this includes surface impoundment, land treatment of waste, releasing wastes into seas or oceans, permanent storage, repackaging and storage pending other disposal; whilst 'recovery' adds activities such as reclaiming or regenerating solvents, recycling or reclaiming organic materials, and use of waste as fuel. 'Keeping' brings under control the retention of waste on the land of the holder whether or not that waste can be said to have been deposited.[162]

Important supplementary offences complement the extended range of activities that is subject to licensing. So, for example, EPA 1990, s 60 makes it an offence for any person to sort over or disturb anything deposited at a place provided for such a purpose by a WCA or WDC, or anything deposited in a waste receptacle provided by a WCA or WDC, unless he/she has the consent of the relevant authority. Also, where an offence is committed by a corporate body and it is proved to have been committed with the connivance, or because of the neglect of any director, manager or secretary of the company that person is criminally liable along with the corporation. Determining who are directors and secretaries of companies is not difficult as these are legal terms: determining who is a 'manager' is a question of fact in each case. The approach of the courts appears to be to ask whether any given individual was part of the 'controlling mind' of the organisation, someone with 'real authority' with 'power and responsibility to decide corporate policy and 'strategy'.[163] Where *employees* commit a wrongful act, of course, their employers *may* be liable.[164] However, in cases where a due diligence defence operates (which must be contrasted with the position under the Water Resources Act 1991), not every act of every employee will be attributed to an employer who operates sound supervisory practices. Liability will be imposed, however, in respect of those who direct and exercise the powers of the company.[165]

157 *Kent County Council v Beaney* [1991] 5 Env Law 89.
158 *Environment Agency v M E Foley (Contractors) Ltd* (2002) Times, 4 March.
159 EPA 1990, s 33(8).
160 EPA 1990, s 33(9).
161 WML Regulations, reg 1(3), Sch 4, Parts III and IV.
162 Circular 11/94, Annex 1, para 1.5.
163 *R v Boal* [1992] QB 591, [1992] 3 All ER 177; *Woodhouse v Walsall Metropolitan Borough Council* [1994] Env LR 30.
164 *National Rivers Authority v Alfred McAlpine Homes (East) Ltd* [1994] Env LR 198, a case under the Water Resources Act 1991.
165 *Tesco Supermarkets Ltd v Nattrass* [1972] AC 153.

Exclusions and exemptions from licensing

Certain activities are excluded from the scope of section 33(1) because they are already subject to legal control.[166] These include the deposit in or on land, recovery or disposal of waste other than involving the final disposal of waste by deposit in or on land under an IPC or APC authorisation; disposal of liquid wastes to controlled waters under a discharge consent; and the recovery or disposal of waste under a Food and Environment Protection 1985 licence. A far more extensive list of exemptions from licensing has also been set out, which generally cater for small, temporary or innocuous activities.[167] These differ from exclusions in two key respects. First, even when an activity is exempt from licensing, it continues to be subject to the EPA 1990, s 33(1)(c) general pollution of the environment offence. Secondly, those wishing to take advantage of an exemption must register with the Agency (which is bureaucratic but not difficult, although carrying on an exempt activity without registering is an offence, subject to a small fine: WML Regulations, reg 18(1)), and exemptions will only apply where that is consistent with the need to attain the objectives imposed by the Waste Framework Directive.[168] Neither of these conditions seems to be onerous. Both excluded and exempted activities remain subject to the statutory duty of care (see below). Registration obligations also apply to transporters and brokers of waste, although these supplement the licensing regime rather than provide an exemption from it, and each is considered below.

The exemptions themselves extend to 45 elaborate categories (subject to certain restrictions on quantities of waste and the use of defined disposal and recovery methods), and their application in a particular case is a question of fact.[169] Every case will turn on its peculiarities, but examples do include: using waste glass in glass making and storage of such glass pending use; small scale iron and steel processes where scrap is smelted in a scrap metal furnace, and storage of scrap pending smelting; burning straw, polluting litter, wood, waste oil, waste derived solid fuel and tyres where this is part of an LAPC regulated process, and storage associated with such a use; burning waste as fuel in certain small appliances; spreading specified wastes such as blood and guts from abattoirs or septic tank contents on certain types of land, eg agricultural land, again subject to weight and time limits; storage and spreading of certain types of sewage and septic tank sludge; spreading of, inter alia, rock, ash or demolition waste in connection with reclamation or improvement of land; sludge and septic tank sludge recovery operations in sewage works; certain preliminary actions such as baling and sorting particular materials such as glass, steel cans, waste paper, again subject to weight and cubic capacity limits; composting waste which is biogradable, manufacturing certain construction products from waste resulting from, inter alia, demolition or construction activities; storage in secure places of specified wastes to be used for particular defined purposes; storage on a site of that site's demolition, construction or tunnelling waste for use on that site; burning as waste on open land where it is produced of wood, bark or plant matter by its producer, eg a garden bonfire; discharge of railway lavatory waste to the trackbed; burial of dead pets at their former homes; and temporary storage of certain waste pending collection on its site of production.

166 EPA 1990, s 33(3); WML Regulations, reg 16(1).
167 WML Regulations, reg 17; Sch 3.
168 WML Regulations, regs 18, 17(4).
169 *North Yorkshire County Council v Boyne* [1997] Env LR 91.

Other registration obligations: waste brokers

The Waste Framework Directive requires member states to maintain a registration system for brokers of controlled waste – essentially a legal emphasis on those most likely to deal with waste in large volumes.[170] This obligation is transposed into UK law by the WML Regulations,[171] and applies to establishments or undertaking which arrange for the disposal or recovery of waste on behalf of others. However, brokers are only required to register if not already subject to, or exempted from, a licensing obligation (for example, they might hold a waste management licence or discharge consent). To this extent, broker registration is very much a residual obligation. Examples of those liable to registration might include environmental consultants who contract for the disposal of controlled waste from a producer.[172] The process of registration is based closely on that applying to applications for a waste management licence.[173]

Other registration obligations: waste carriers

The link between creation, storage and disposal of waste is complemented by provisions which require the registration with the Agency (or SEPA) of persons who, in the course of any business or otherwise with a view to a profit, transport controlled waste to or from any place in Great Britain[174] – provisions intended to target fly-tippers. Transport of such waste unless registered is an offence, punishable by a fine of £5,000 on summary conviction.[175] Some defences are provided, for example, that the waste was moved in an emergency and the WRA was notified, or the transporter neither knew nor had reasonable grounds to suspect that he was carrying controlled waste and either took steps to discover quite what was being carried or was acting under an employer's instructions. Certain exceptions to the registration requirements are also provided, in respect both of the nature of transport, and the persons doing it. In particular, a person shall not be guilty of an offence in respect of transport of controlled waste within the same premises between different places in those premises, to its first point of arrival in Great Britain when imported, or when it is exported from Great Britain.

The Secretary of State has further provided by Regulations that, amongst other things, certain persons or classes of persons shall not be required to be registered as carriers of controlled waste.[176] These include waste regulation, collection and disposal authorities, the producer of controlled waste except where the waste is building or demolition waste (contrast this with the exemption from waste management licensing of similar wastes) and charities and voluntary organisations.[177] The applications procedure is also set out in the regulations, including grounds on which applications for registration might be refused. These are confined to contravention of procedural requirements, and situations where the applicant or another relevant person (which, as with waste management licensing, includes employees of an applicant, companies of which the applicant was or is an officer, or officers if the applicant is a body corporate)

---

170 Waste Framework Directive, Art 12.
171 WML Regulations, reg 20.
172 DoE Circular 11/94, Annex 8.
173 WML Regulations, Sch 5.
174 Control of Pollution (Amendment) Act 1989, as amended, also implementing Art 12 of the Framework Directive.
175 COP(A)A 1989, s 1(1) and (5).
176 COP(A)A 1989, s 1(3); Controlled Waste (Registration of Carriers and Seizure of Vehicles) Regulations 1991, SI 1991/1624, as amended.
177 1991 Regulations, reg 2.

has been convicted of a prescribed offence[178] and the regulation authority considers that it would be 'undesirable' that the applicant be authorised.[179] This is not as stringent a requirement as applies under the fit and proper person test applying to the issue of waste management licences (considered below), in that it leaves the relevant authority with more limited scope to refuse an application. Indeed, all of the surrounding circumstances should be taken into account when considering an application for registration, including (it seems) the circumstances surrounding the commission of prescribed offences themselves.[180] Those circumstances may suggest the prospect of greater leniency than if the fact of a conviction were considered to be conclusive. Periodic re-registration may be required (registration generally expires after three years), and detailed provision is also made for appeals against refusals of registration.

Whilst an important addition to controls under EPA 1990, Part II the 1989 Act can be contrasted with waste management in that it is 'simply' a registration system rather than a system of licensing operational matters. The regulation authority is under a duty periodically to inspect establishments and undertakings which collect or transfer waste on a professional basis,[181] stop-checks may be made by officers of the WRA (off road) or uniformed police constables (on or off road) on vehicles transporting waste,[182] searches may be executed and samples taken, and ultimately vehicles used in unlawful waste operations may in some circumstances be seized.[183] However, when it comes to standards of packaging or ultimate disposal, the powers work only in combination with waste management licensing powers.

Defences to EPA 1990, s 33 offences

Three statutory defences are provided for persons charged under EPA 1990, s 33,[184] that: the accused took all reasonable precautions and exercised all due diligence to avoid the commission of an offence; the accused acted under an employer's instructions and did not know nor had reason to suppose the acts constituted a contravention of the prohibition; the acts were done in an emergency in order to avoid danger to the public and that, as soon as reasonably practicable thereafter, the Agency was informed, and all reasonably practicable steps were taken in addition to minimise pollution and harm to human health. The 'due diligence' defence requires a real degree of vigilance on the part of those who seek to rely on it, so (for example) the contents of skips and containers filled by other persons should always be checked by a person wishing to use the defence.[185] Similarly where a person seeks to rely on the defence of acting in an emergency, the defendant must show there was an emergency, and what constitutes an emergency is a matter for the court to determine.[186]

178 1991 Regulations, reg 1(2), Sch 1.
179 1991 Regulations, reg 5(1).
180 *Scott v Berkshire County Council* (APP/WAC/96/32/P5) [1998] JPL 94.
181 WML Regulations 1994, regs 1(3) and 9, Sch 4, para 13.
182 COP(A)A 1989, s 5.
183 COP(A)A 1989, s 6; 1991 Regulations, regs 20-25.
184 EPA 1990, s 33(7).
185 *Durham County Council v Peter Connors Industrial Services Ltd* [1993] Env LR 197.
186 *Waste Incineration Services Ltd v Dudley Metropolitan Borough Council* [1992] Env LR 29.

The statutory duty of care

One of the hallmarks of EPA 1990 is the extension of responsibility for proper handling of waste to all persons associated with it, from production, through storage and transport, to ultimate disposal. But that extension of liability does not end there, as the broad offences established by section 33 are combined with a statutory 'duty of care'.[187] Not to be confused with concepts from the law of negligence, the waste duty of care places a threefold obligation on any person who imports, produces, carries, keeps, treats or disposes of controlled waste or, as a broker, has control of such waste (other than the occupier of domestic property as respects household waste produced at that property). Failure to comply with the duty of care is an offence.[188] The obligation itself is to take all such measures applicable to him as are reasonable in the circumstances: to prevent contravention of EPA 1990, s 33 by any other person (although breach of the duty of care is not dependent on another offence actually having been committed: *Shanks & McEwan (Southern Water Services) Ltd v Environment Agency*[189]); to prevent the escape of waste from his control or that of any other person; and on the transfer of the waste, to secure that the transfer is only to an authorised person or to a person for authorised transport purposes (for example, WCAs, registered carriers of waste, or the holder of a waste management licence); and that a written description of transferred waste is provided to enable other persons to avoid contravention of EPA 1990, ss 33 and 34.

The duty of care is distinctive. In particular, it has the important effect of introducing an element of self-monitoring and enforcement into the waste chain, as each person in that chain has a responsibility to ensure, as far as is reasonable, that those preceding and following them also discharge their obligations. For example, failure to ensure that a person to whom waste is transferred is authorised to receive it may result in prosecution,[190] as might failure to inform a waste disposer of the nature of waste.[191] Given the practical complexities of enforcing waste controls this is not an unimportant feature, which also serves to provide a foretaste of other innovations in legal technique which are becoming more rooted in waste control than other areas of environmental law. Although much, of course, depends on the actions of individual holders of waste, this self-monitoring element continues to lead to reports to regulators of breach of the duty, and subsequent prosecutions (eg *Shanks & McEwan (Southern Water Services) Ltd v Environment Agency*,[192] where a consignor's incomplete description of waste was reported by a consignee to the WRA, leading to prosecution of the producer). Practical compliance with the duty of care will be a more everyday concern, however, and this is assisted through a Code of Practice issued by the Secretary of State.[193] Although failure to comply with the Code is not an offence, such failure is admissible as evidence of a breach of the duty of care itself.[194] An almost infinite range of practical factors will affect whether an individual in fact took all reasonable steps in the particular circumstances, particularly as the Code advises that this is assessed by reference to that person's capacity to discharge the duty of care, that is, their degree of control over and connection with the waste in question.

---

187 EPA 1990, s 34; Environmental Protection (Duty of Care) Regulations 1991, SI 1991/2839.
188 EPA 1990, s 34(6).
189 [1998] JPL 1125.
190 Eg, *Greater Manchester Waste Regulation Authority v T J Stafford (Contractors) Ltd* (1993) 5 ELM 189.
191 See, eg (1996) 8 ELM 204.
192 [1998] JPL 1125.
193 EPA 1990, s 34(7); *Waste Management – The Duty of Care – A Code of Practice*, March 1996.
194 EPA 1990, s 34(10).

The Code first suggests that holders of waste should establish what the waste is, for example what is its legal status, what are the particular problems it presents (such as does it need special containers), can it be mixed with other waste, what can it not be mixed with, can it be crushed, can it be incinerated, if so at what temperature and for how long, and can it be landfilled? It then proceeds to counsel waste holders to ensure that waste must be kept so that they are on guard for corrosion or wear of containers, accidental spills and leaks, accidents or breakages or weather conditions allowing waste to escape or blow away while in transit. They must also guard against thieves, scavengers and vandals. Particular advice is also given on ensuring transfers only take place to 'the right person'. Thus a carrier's registration should always be checked save in cases of repeated transfers by the same concern. Similarly the qualification of the next holder of the waste to receive the waste should be checked, eg by checking the terms and restrictions of a WML. Those who *receive* waste should always check its source and that it is being handed over in containers suitable for subsequent handling.

On particular issues the Code draws attention to the need to be wary of waste that is wrongly or inadequately described on delivery, waste being taken away with incorrect packaging so it may escape, failure of consignees/consignors to complete the required notes, or apparent falsehoods on notes, unsupported claims of exemption from registration, and failure of waste to arrive at its consigned destination.

Particular requirements apply to transfer notes.[195] Notes must identify waste, and say how much there is, what its containment is, times and place of transfer, names and addresses of transferor and transferee. These records then have to be kept for two years from the date of transfer and may be inspected by the Agency. Where, however, multiple consignments of waste take place within a year one transfer note may cover all provided the description of the waste and the identity of relevant parties remains the same.

Waste management licences

The translation of general rules to specific sites – the individualisation of controls – is achieved through the consideration of applications for waste management licences. These are licences issued by the WRA (the Agency) authorising the treatment, keeping or disposal of any specified description of controlled waste in or on specified land, or the treatment or disposal of controlled waste by means of specified mobile plant.[196]

Licences are granted on such terms and conditions as the Agency thinks appropriate and these may relate to the licensed activity and precautions to be taken and work to be done in connection with that activity, and they may relate to times before and after the activity is being carried out. Conditions may require a licensee to carry out works or do things despite his/her being unentitled to do them, and any person whose consent would be required shall grant the licensee such rights in relation to the land as will enable compliance with licence requirements; thus third parties can be compelled to assist in the process of obtaining and operating a WML.

This obligation on third parties is not unusual in environmental terms: similar provisions apply to works notices under water rules.[197] It is quite recent, however, having only come into force on 1 April 1999 and it is also accompanied by an entitlement

---

195 SI 1991/2839.
196 EPA 1990, s 35.
197 WRA 1991, ss 161A-161C.

to compensation, detailed consultation obligations, and a dispute resolution mechanism.[198]

The Agency's power to impose conditions is very wide. There are some legal limits: the Waste Framework Directive, for example, requires that technical requirements must be covered, and although this is a broad obligation a licence may nonetheless be set aside if it is not discharged.[199] As a matter of domestic law, the overall emphasis of the EPA 1990 on protection of the environment against pollution and the need to protect human health, including protection of the senses, and to protect property, seems to envisage the imposition of conditions going further than under the 1974 Act's provisions where there was a limitation to public health and water pollution issues.[200] However, the Secretary of State may make regulations as to conditions, and issue mandatory directions to the Agency in respect of a licence application as to its terms and conditions.[201] The Agency is also under a general duty under EPA 1990, s 35(8) to have regard to the Secretary of State's guidance with regard to licences. Policy guidance on conditions has been issued by the Secretary of State,[202] and the Agency has also published a 'library' of licence conditions and working plan specifications, prepared after consultation with industry, to provide some national consistency and a common starting point for consideration of applications. Reference should also be had to the policy framework provided by Circular 11/94, which emphasises the need to ensure that controls, including conditions, are both proportionate to the risks involved and cost effective (see above). An obligation to maintain records is a common feature of licences, and a failure to make appropriate entries in records is evidence of breach of such conditions. Equally, any person who intentionally makes a false entry in any required records, or who forges a licence or possesses a document so closely resembling a licence it is likely to deceive commits an offence.[203]

Applying for a waste management licence

EPA 1990 makes detailed procedural provision for licence applications, for example, that they should be made to the Agency, using a prescribed form, accompanied by a fee, and accompanied by such information as the Agency requires.[204] Failure to supply required information entitles the Agency to refuse to proceed with an application. Consultations must also be undertaken (for example, with the appropriate planning authority, the HSE and, in appropriate cases, nature conservation authorities). Unlike other forms of environmental licence, the grounds upon which an application may be refused are confined fairly closely be statute. For example, two mandatory grounds for refusal are set out: that any necessary planning permission or established use certificate is not in force; and that direct or indirect discharges of certain substances to groundwater may result from the proposed activities which will interfere with exploitation of groundwater resources.[205] The latter restriction is part of the UK implementation of the Groundwater Directive (80/68), which requires technical precautions to be taken to prevent discharges of certain substances to groundwater. Wider controls also apply for this purpose, which may extend to tipping or disposal which falls outside waste

198 EPA 1990, s 35A; Waste Management Licensing (Consultation and Compensation) Regulations 1999, SI 1999/481.
199 *Guthrie v Scottish Environmental Protection Authority* [1998] Env LR 128.
200 *A-G's Reference (No 2 of 1988)* [1990] 1 QB 77, [1989] 3 WLR 397.
201 EPA 1990, s 35(6), (7).
202 Eg, Waste Management paper No 4, *The Licensing of Waste Facilities.*
203 EPA 1990, s 35(7A)–(7C).
204 EPA 1990, s 36.
205 EPA 1990, s 36(2) and WML Regulations, reg 15 respectively.

management licensing proper.[206] There are, in addition, some important general grounds which provide the Agency with a discretion to refuse an application. The most important of these is that the Agency must normally satisfy itself that the applicant is a 'fit and proper person' to be granted a licence (see below). If so, then an application may only be refused if that is necessary for EPA the purpose of preventing either pollution of the environment or (where an established use certificate rather than a planning permission is in force) serious detriment to the amenities of the locality.[207] If not, the Agency retains a discretion to grant a licence anyway.[208]

Where the Agency fails within four months from the date of application to grant or refuse a licence the application is deemed rejected (other than where the agency is entitled to refuse to proceed under EPA 1990, s 36(1A)). Under EPA 1990, s 44 it is an offence in an application for a licence (or its modification, surrender or transfer) to knowingly or recklessly make a false or misleading statement. The period allowed for consultation under EPA 1990, s 36 is 28 days, though this may be extended. EPA 1990, s 36A, however, lays down particular consultation requirements in certain cases. The most elaborate of these relates to cases where third party consent is needed, in which case full particulars of the proposed works must be provided to each person with an interest in any of the land to be affected.[209] Consistent with general principles, any representations made in response to consultations must be taken into account. It is notable, of course, that the consultation required on an application for a waste management licence stands in poor contrast to (for example) a planning application, not least through the absence of any obligation to advertise the former.

'Fit and proper person'

In the granting of a WML much will depend on whether the applicant is a 'fit and proper person'. This is a significant feature of the 1994 regime, in that it imposes an operator competence requirement on those licensed to handle waste that is tied firmly to activities to be authorised by a licence and the fulfilment of its requirements.[210] Indeed, the meaning of 'fit and proper person' is wider than may be supposed, and has three elements. Consequently, a person shall not be treated as a fit and proper person if it appears to the Agency that:
(a) he or another relevant person has been convicted of a 'relevant offence';
(b) the authorised activities will not be in the hands of a technically competent person;
(c) the person who is to hold the licence has not made and either has no intention of making or is in no position to make financial provision to discharge the licence obligations.

The taint of an offence extends beyond simply applicants themselves, as 'relevant persons' include employees acting in the course of their employment, business partners, companies of which the applicant was an officer and officers of any applicant company. The offences which qualify are equally broad, although they have a distinctive environmental character. They include, for example, offences under the Control of Pollution (Amendment) Act 1989, EPA 1990 (both waste and non-waste offences), the Water Resources Act 1991, the Clean Air Act 1993, and offences in relation to the landfill tax.[211] Notable exclusions, however, are general dishonesty offences and offences under planning law.

---

206 Groundwater Regulations 1998, SI 1998/2746.
207 EPA 1990, s 36(3).
208 EPA 1990, s 74(4).
209 See SI 1999/481.
210 EPA 1990, s 74(2).
211 WML Regulations, reg 3.

The second limb of the fit and proper person test is technical competence. This requirement is also complemented by the WML Regulations, which links it to formal qualifications issued by the Waste Management Industry Training and Advisory Board (WAMITAB). Under regs 4 and 5 and Table 1 of the 1994 Regulations the technical competence requirements are met by those holding relevant WAMITAB certificates. Complex transitional provisions were put in place to allow for those with experience of site management to be exempted from the need to demonstrate their qualifications immediately. For example, managers in post at any time during the year before implementation of management licensing were exempted from the need to prove competence until 1999. Also, those aged 55 of over in August 1994 with five years experience in the previous ten years of a COPA licensed site are still not required to show WAMITAB certification, and will not have to until 1 October 2006 – by which time they probably will have retired.

The third and final test of being a fit and proper person is that the applicant has made or will make appropriate financial provision. This is potentially a large financial burden, as it applies in relation to all requirements imposed by a licence and thus extends to both pre- and post-operational matters. Policy guidance indicates, for example, that operators should obtain insurance or show they can be their own insurers. Financial provision issues are particularly relevant at the stages of site acquisition and preparation, site operation, site restoration and landscaping or aftercare, and in relation to post closure controls and monitoring. While specific financial provisions may appear in a licence in order to meet particular obligations, in general an applicant's financial provision is to be considered by reference to licence obligations. The Agency will also consider an applicant's business plan in relation to the life of facilities such as landfill sites — though the existence of such a plan is never a guarantee of business success.

Variation of licences

The net of controls spread by EPA 1990, Part II is tightened further by additional distinctive powers given to the Agency to revisit licensed activities even after a licence has been granted. The first illustration of this is that in certain circumstances, either of its own volition of at the licence holder's request, the Agency may vary the conditions on a waste management licence.[212] It may only do so, however, to the extent that variation is both desirable and unlikely to impose unreasonable expense on the licensee, and on the licensee's application to the extent requested, in which case a fee is payable. The Agency *must* also modify licence conditions to the extent they consider it necessary to ensure that licensed activities do not cause pollution of the environment, harm to human health or serious detriment to local amenity, or to comply with any regulations issued under EPA 1990, s 35(6), see above. The Secretary of State may also direct modifications of conditions. Modifications are effected by notice served on the licensee, but are generally subject to a consultation procedure similar to that for licence applications, with the addition of mandatory consultation with any third party land owners, lessees or occupiers who may be directly affected by the proposed variation.[213] A deemed refusal of a modification application takes place if the Agency fails either to grant or refuse an application within two months of its date of receipt. It seems that there is no statutory restriction on the extent of any modification which may be required, however dramatic,[214] although reservations have been expressed where an extension of a site is proposed.[215]

212 EPA 1990, s 37.
213 EPA 1990, s 37A.
214 *Guthrie v Scottish Environmental Protection Agency* [1998] Env LR 128.
215 Per Lord Johnston at 135.

Revocation and suspension of licences

The second illustration of the Agency's continuing ability to intervene in licensed activities is its power to revoke a licence, either in part or completely.[216] A licence may be revoked in part or entirely where variation cannot secure the avoidance of pollution of the environment, harm to human health or serious detriment to local amenities which would be caused by continuing the licensed activities, or the holder has ceased to be a fit and proper person on conviction for a relevant offence.[217] The Agency may also revoke a licence, this time only in part, if the holder has ceased to be a fit and proper person by reason of lack of technical competence.[218] Where a licence is revoked in part it ceases to have effect to authorise the activities specified in the licence, or, as the case may be, the activities specified by the Agency on revocation, but revocation does *not* affect any requirements imposed by the licence which the Agency on revocation specifies as continuing to bind the licensee. In practice, of course, partial revocation will almost invariably be preferable to complete revocation: otherwise the Agency would give up the chance of ever enforcing continuing obligations against the holder.

The revocation power is complemented by temporary suspension of a licence. A licence may be suspended where it appears to the Agency that the licence holder has ceased to be 'fit and proper' by virtue of lack of technical competence, or that serious pollution of the environment, etc, has resulted, or is about to result, from licensed activities, or the happening or threatened happening of an event affecting those activities, and that the continuation of those activities or any of them will continue to cause or may cause serous pollution of the environment or serious harm to human health. Authorisation of activities specified in the licence or such of them as are specified may be suspended. The Secretary of State may give directions as to the exercise of these powers.

Immediate suspension may cause its own environmental problems, as conditions to mitigate continuing environmental harms may be suspended along with those activities which are the reason for the suspension in the first place. Consequently, interim measures may be put in place as part of the suspension itself. For example, during a suspension the Agency may require the licence holder to take steps to deal with or avert the pollution, etc, and it is an offence to fail to comply with such requirements, with enhanced penalties applying where there is a failure to comply with any requirements relating to any special waste. Where criminal proceedings would be an inadequate remedy the Agency may take proceedings in the High Court for injunctive relief (s 38(10)–(13)). Requirements imposed may require the licence holder to carry out works he is not entitled to do — a situation already encountered above. The EPA 1990 as amended in 1995 here follows the usual pattern of requiring consultation with other affected landholders and the taking into account of any representations received from them, though EPA 1990, s 38(9C) specifically allows the postponement of service of any notice or the consideration of any representations received where by reason of an emergency it is appropriate to do so. As before, a compensation liability may arise for the licence holder.

Surrender of licences

An important feature of the new regime is the set of continuing obligations a licence holder takes on with the licence. Prominent amongst these are limitations on the

216   EPA 1990, s 38(3) and (4) respectively.
217   EPA 1990, s 38(1).
218   EPA 1990, s 38(2).

surrender of licences, in particular, that a licence may not be surrendered unless the Agency accepts surrender, for which an application must be made.[219] In order to surrender the licensee must apply on a form provided by the Agency giving such information as is required and such other information as is reasonably required, and pay the appropriate fee. The Agency must inspect the land in question and may require the furnishing of further information and evidence. The Agency shall only accept surrender if it is satisfied that the condition of the land resulting from its use – whether that use is permitted or not – is such as to be unlikely to cause pollution of the environment or harm to human health.[220] In all other cases surrender must be refused. Where the Agency proposes to accept a surrender it must first refer the matter to the appropriate planning authority, and consider any representations made, generally within a period of 28 days beginning with the day on which the proposed surrender is received by the Agency. On the accepted surrender the Agency must issue the applicant with a notice of its determination and a 'certificate of completion' stating its satisfaction as to the lack of likelihood of pollution, etc, and thereupon the licence ceases to have effect. The Agency has three months in which to determine applications for surrender, failing which the application is deemed to have been refused.

The purpose of requiring the holder of a licence to seek consent before surrender is to avoid conditions going unmet. This is particularly significant under the scheme established by the EPA 1990, as the conditions on licences are far more extensive in both time and substance than their precursors. Yet whilst the statutory scheme looks comprehensive, it does not in fact address what happens to a waste management licence should the holder die or, perhaps more significant, a holding company become insolvent. The Court of Appeal has now concluded that if a company holding a licence becomes insolvent, then the licence (depending on its terms) may be onerous property within the meaning of the Insolvency Act 1986 and may thus be disclaimed by the receiver.[221] The court reached this conclusion despite earlier, albeit problematic, contrary authority in the High Court.[222] The Court of Appeal concluded that the clearest possible words were required to exclude the effect of the IA 1986 and, unlike other statutes (such as the Coal Industry Act 1994, s 36) these were not to be found in EPA 1990. Despite the desirable environmental objectives of the EPA 1990 (which had heavily influenced Neuberger J in the earlier cases), the court was also influenced here by the Agency's concession that a waste management licence would in any event expire on the death or dissolution of the holder. This concession therefore had a more dramatic consequence than the Agency may have initially anticipated.

The practical consequences are complex. The Agency takes the view that its own investigatory powers would be available only when a licence remains in force. Sites in respect of which a licence has been disclaimed may therefore fall to be dealt with by local authorities, for example, where a statutory nuisance exists. However, as nothing may constitute a statutory nuisance if it consists of, is caused by, land being in a contaminated state,[223] a local authority's freedom of action may be limited. It may

---

219 EPA 1990, s 39.
220 EPA 1990, s 39(6), (5).
221 *Official Receiver v Environment Agency, Re Celtic Extraction Ltd* [2000] Env LR 86; *Shelbourn* [2000] JPL 134.
222 *Henry v Environment Agency (sub nom Re Wilmott Trading Ltd)* [2000] Env LR 42; *Re Wilmott Trading Ltd (No 2)* [2000] Env LR 42; *Environment Agency v Stout, Re Mineral Resources Ltd* [1999] 1 All ER 746; all decisions of Neuberger J, also the judge at first instance in *Re Celtic Extraction.*
223 EPA 1990, s 79(1A).

therefore be that in such cases reliance must be placed on the contaminated land regime: as presumably once a waste management licence has been disclaimed it is no longer 'for the time being in force'.[224] Finally, where a company holding a waste management licence is in administration but the licence has *not* been disclaimed, then the Agency requires permission from the Court before bringing any prosecution in respect of that licence.[225] In such cases, the fact that any fine imposed on conviction would be at the expense of the creditors will not 'trump' other considerations pointing towards the desirability of prosecution.

Transfer of licences

In the same way that surrender of a licence requires the Agency's consent, so too does transfer to another person.[226] Licences may be transferred under EPA 1990, s 40, even where partly revoked or suspended. The procedure is that the licensee and proposed transferee must make a joint transfer application to the Agency. The usual requirements as to information and fees apply. The Agency, if satisfied the transferee is 'fit and proper' must effect the transfer. A transfer not effected within two months of the date of receipt of the request is deemed refused.

Appeals and public registers

Appeals against refusal of an application for a waste management licence, permission to surrender, or other decision of the Agency are catered for by a generic appeals procedure.[227] No appeal can be made where a decision has been taken by direction of the Secretary of State. Judicial review would be the appropriate – if very different – remedy in such cases, and in cases involving third party challenges.[228] Appeals from Agency decisions lie to the Secretary of State, whose power to determine has, in all but the most major or difficult of cases, been delegated to the Planning Inspectorate. A longstop period of six months from the date of the decision or deemed decision is available in which to appeal. Unlike certain other regimes (eg statutory nuisance or contaminated land), no express grounds of appeal are provided, however further guidance on procedure has been issued.[229]

If a party to it so requests, or if the Secretary of State so decides, the appeal shall take the form of a hearing, which may be held in private. In general while an appeal is pending a modification or revocation of a licence has no effect, though the Agency may circumvent this by stating in the relevant notice that the action is necessary to prevent, or minimise if prevention is not practicable, pollution of the environment.[230] A suspension, however, is not affected by an appeal.[231]

Where a decision under appeal is one to modify or revoke a licence the licence holder may apply to the Secretary of State for a determination that the Agency acted

224 EPA 1990, s 78YB(2).
225 *Environment Agency v Clarke, Re Rhondda Waste Disposal Co Ltd* [2000] Env LR 600.
226 EPA 1990, s 40.
227 EPA 1990, s 43.
228 *R v Vale of Glamorgan Borough Council and Associated British Ports, ex p James* (1996) 8 ELM 12.
229 Circular 11/94, Annex 10.
230 EPA 1990, s 43(6).
231 EPA 1990, s 43(5).

unreasonably in excluding the operation of EPA 1990, s 43(4), and in the case of a suspension an application may be made for a determination that this was unreasonable. If the appeal is still pending when a decision is made that the exclusion of EPA 1990, s 43(4) or the suspension, as the case may be, was unreasonable, then EPA 1990, s 43(4) will apply *and* compensation may be payable to the licensee in respect of loss suffered.

There is a statutory obligation on the agency as WRA to maintain a register of applications and related information,[232] similar to the model provided by the Water Resources Act 1991. Waste management registers must include: all licences and reasonably current licences and applications (and associated working plans); notices issued in respect of modification, revocation and suspension; any convictions of a licence holder under EPA 1990, Part II; and any monitoring information obtained by the authority, whether obtained by itself or from a licence holder in pursuance of a condition on a licence.[233] This regulation lists 14 types of information to be included. Registers must be kept open for inspection by members of the public, and facilities made available for making copies.[234] As in the case of other registers, the Secretary of State has a wide discretion to exclude from registers any information, or information of a prescribed description, in the interests of national security.[235] Commercial confidentiality is a further ground on which information may be excluded from registers for a limited period (normally four years). In such cases, an application for exclusion must be made, refusal of which may be appealed within 21 days.[236]

The disposal of 'special waste'

In addition to the general waste management provisions, additional controls apply in the case of certain dangerous or intractable wastes, or 'special wastes'.[237] Although the additional problems associated with special waste generally speak for themselves, the UK is under a particular European obligation to regulate hazardous wastes[238] and provision has therefore been made in respect of the generation, transport, storage and disposal of hazardous wastes in the UK.[239] The Environment Agency (in England and Wales) and SEPA (in Scotland) are responsible for supervising the persons and activities subject to special waste controls.[240] An extensive range of offences support their provisions, commission of which may result on summary conviction in a fine of £5,000 or on conviction on indictment to a fine and/or two years imprisonment.

'Special waste' is any waste from the extensive list of controlled wastes which is included in the 1996 Regulations[241] and which displays defined 'hazardous properties', including being explosive, flammable, toxic, carcinogenic, infectious or ecotoxic (subject to certain thresholds).[242] This includes all those substances on the European Hazardous Wastes list,[243] medicinal products, but not household waste. Once a substance is defined

---

232 EPA 1990, s 64.
233 WML Regulations, reg 10.
234 EPA 1990, 64(6).
235 EPA 1990, 65.
236 EPA 1990, s 66(5); WML Regulations, reg 7(1)(b).
237 EPA 1990, s 62, as amended; DoE Circular 6/96.
238 Directive 91/689 on Hazardous Waste.
239 Special Waste Regulations 1996, SI 1996/972, as amended.
240 1996 Regulations, reg 19.
241 1996 Regulations, reg 2, Sch 2, Part I.
242 1996 Regulations, Sch 2, Parts II and III.
243 Decision 94/904.

as special waste, the Regulations require that a record-keeping and consignment note system shall apply. This normally requires pre-notification to the Agency of the movement of special waste, and additional information to be carried by the waste transporter and delivered to the consignee (1996 Regulations, regs 4-13). Not least amongst the additional information to be prepared is the consignment notice itself, which is in five parts and of which there must be no fewer than six copies: Parts A and B are detailed descriptions of the waste, its collection point and destination and are completed by the producer; Part C is completed by the carrier before movement of the waste; Part D is completed by the consignor to signify that he has been advised of the precautions to be taken in handling the waste; Part E is completed by the consignee on receipt of the waste. One copy of Parts A and B must be sent to the Agency between 72 hours and one month before the waste is moved and a fully completed note is then sent by the consignee on receipt: there should therefore be a closed information loop confirming to the Agency that the intended movement and disposal has been properly completed. Detailed site records must be maintained at sites where special waste is disposed of, and registers must also be kept for a minimum of three years by those despatching such waste.[244] The consignment note system normally only applies to consignments of special waste which are removed from the premises at which the waste is being held,[245] but the other provisions of the EPA 1990 apply to special waste as they would to all other controlled wastes. Equally, exemption or exclusion from waste management licensing does not bring automatic exemption from the requirements of the Special Waste Regulations 1996.

The 1996 Regulations have been under a number of parallel reviews, particularly in light of the Landfill Directive, the IPPC Directive, the National Waste Strategies and the Environment Agency's operational experience of the special waste regime.[246] Some amendments have been made in light of the latter,[247] but others can be anticipated – not least the redesignation of 'special' waste as the more understandable 'hazardous waste'. At the European level, greater coordination will also follow revisions to the hazardous waste list[248] which, from 2 January 2002, harmonised hazardous waste classifications.[249]

Removal of unlawfully deposited waste

Clean-up powers are increasingly common in environmental law, including works notices (water) and remediation notices (contaminated land). Waste is no exception, indeed, the relevant powers have a rather longer pedigree. Where any controlled waste is deposited on land in contravention of EPA 1990, s 33(1) (the general waste offence) then either the WRA or the waste collection authority (the Agency or the local authority) may issue a 'waste removal notice' requiring an occupier of land to remove waste from land, and to take specified steps to eliminate or reduce the consequences of the deposit.[250] A person served may appeal to a magistrates' court within 21 days, and the court must quash the notice if there is a material defect in the notice, or if the court is satisfied that the appellant neither deposited nor knowingly caused or knowingly permitted the deposit of the waste: essentially an 'innocent occupier' defence. The

244 1996 Regulations, regs 14 and 15.
245 1996 Regulations, reg 5(1).
246 Eg, *Review of the Special Waste Regulations*, DETR, March 2001.
247 See SIs 2001/3148 (England) and 3545 (Wales).
248 Decision 94/904.
249 Decision 2000/532, as amended by Decisions 2001/119 and 2001/573.
250 EPA 1990, s 59(1).

same phraseology is used as in the case of deposit-related offences under EPA 1990, s 33. It is an offence to fail to comply with a waste removal notice, without reasonable excuse, punishable by a fine of up to £5,000, and an additional fine of one-tenth of that for each day the failure to comply continues.[251]

The relevant authority may carry out necessary works if the land has no occupier (or none who made or knowingly permitted the deposit), in default of the recipient of a notice failing to comply, or immediately to remove or prevent pollution or harm to human health.[252] This seems to exclude authority action where an occupier 'knowingly caused' the deposit, unless there is a need to act immediately. An authority's necessary costs are recoverable from the occupier (subject to the same 'defence' as to service of a notice) and/or from any person who deposited or knowingly caused or knowingly permitted the deposit of any of the waste.[253] It is interesting to note that there is no provision for the apportionment of costs where two or more persons are both responsible for an unlawful deposit. The use of the phrase 'any person' would suggest a deliberate intention to make unlawful depositors severally liable, although this is presumably subject to an overarching duty on authorities to act reasonably and fairly.[254]

Whether this potentially wide-ranging power – which was introduced to control fly-tipping, but is not confined to it – is extensively used in practice is unclear. Some odd case law might suggest not. In the first case, *Cheshire County Council v Secretary of State for the Environment and Rathbone*[255] the Secretary of State, on considering a planning appeal, concluded that temporary planning permission should have been granted in respect of unlawful tipping; tipping which the planning authority had sought to stop using planning powers. The authority's High Court challenge failed. Whilst having rather particular facts, this may suggest that s 59 is under-utilised. Conversely, *Devonshire Waste Regulation Authority v Roberts, Warren and Snow*[256] did concern a removal notice. In that case, a bank repossessed a residential property on which waste tyres had been unlawfully deposited. The bank was subsequently the recipient of a waste removal notice, and complied with it at a cost in excess of £30,000. Whilst illustrating the breadth of lenders' potential liability as occupiers ('ownership' is not sufficient to ground liability under EPA 1990, s 59), commentators have expressed surprise that the bank did not rely on the 'innocent occupier' defence.[257]

Economic instruments: the landfill tax

Since 1990, successive UK governments have made clear that they intend to complement 'traditional' forms of environmental control with so-called 'economic instruments' for environmental protection or improvement. In that year the (then) government expressed a 'presumption in favour' of economic instruments[258] and the present government takes a similar view. Whilst at a theoretical level financial incentives look more economically efficient than relatively crude 'command-and-control' regulatory interventions, their implementation has been more complex than originally anticipated. Waste has proved

251 EPA 1990, s 59(5).
252 EPA 1990, s 59(6)-(7).
253 EPA 1990, s 59(8).
254 *Berridge Incinerators v Nottinghamshire County Council* (14 April 1987, unreported). Nottingham Crown Court noted at *Encyclopedia of Environmental Law* D21-190, a notice under predecessor legislation was (effectively) quashed as unreasonable and unfair.
255 [1996] JPL 410.
256 (1995) 7 ELM 105.
257 Cf. *Surrey County Council v McAlpine* (1995) 240 *ENDS Report* 41, a case having similar facts, but s 59 was not in issue.
258 *This Common Inheritance*, Cm 2068, p 35.

a fruitful proving ground however, with the introduction of two examples of economic instruments. The first is the waste recycling credit scheme, discussed above. The second example is the higher-profile landfill tax, although the initial impulse here was economic in that the transfer of tax burdens onto waste served to reduce employers' national insurance contributions. Even so, the environmental benefits have been much lauded despite real problems with the implementation of the tax. For example, a report of the House of Commons Environment Select Committee has considered the operation of the tax after its first few years.[259] That report has revealed that the tax has raised in the region of £361 million per annum, that 1,879 landfill sites are receiving 'taxable deposits', and that just over 1,100 operators are registered and accounting for the tax. Although broadly supportive of the operation of the tax, the Committee highlighted a number of concerns, not least of which is an increase in fly-tipping which has arisen as a consequence of the tax's introduction.[260]

Application of the landfill tax

The Finance Act 1996 established a tax, payable by landfill site operators, to be charged on the disposal of materials as waste by way of landfill at landfill sites made on or after 1 October 1996 ('taxable deposits').[261] As with general tax, the landfill tax is the responsibility of HM Customs & Excise and not the Agency. The level of the tax began at £7 per tonne for most forms of waste, and £2 per tonne of 'qualifying material', that is inert or inactive waste, but is currently £12 and £2 respectively, the former increasing by £1 a year until 2004. Descriptions of qualifying materials have been provided by regulations.[262] Although primary liability to pay the tax falls on the operators of landfill sites, in some circumstances, actual control of all or part of a site may be in the hands of that person because they control the site as an employee or agent of another person. In such cases, complex amendments made to the FA 1996 in 2000 provide a mechanism for determining who is liable to pay the tax, and in what proportion, on a site-by-site basis.[263]

A number of aspects of this primary obligation have been subject to litigation. In particular, in determining whether material is disposed of as 'waste' the VAT and Duties Tribunal has concluded that there is no necessity to have recourse to definitions of 'waste' outside the 1996 Act itself, most obviously that applying to EPA 1990, Part II.[264] The tribunal simply held that making a disposal of material with the intention of discarding it was a 'disposal' of it 'as waste' even though the material might have economic value in the hands of another person. This does have some resonance with the technical definition of waste found in EPA 1990, but the Tribunal is clearly trying – at this early point in the life of the tax – to keep things simple. A similarly broad approach has been adopted by the High Court, on appeal from the Tribunal. In that case a company passed waste to a subsidiary for final disposal. Overturning the decision of the Tribunal, it was held that it was necessary to look at the intention of each company in deciding which was in fact making the disposal.[265] The same principle applies where material is disposed of to recycling or recovery operations.[266] Accordingly, a disposal

259 *The Operation of the Landfill Tax*, HC Paper 150 (Session 1998-99).
260 Jewell, 'The Operation of the Landfill Tax' (1999) 11 ELM 213; Pocklington and Pocklington, [1998] JPL 529.
261 Finance Act 1996, ss 39-41.
262 SI 1996/1528.
263 Finance Act 1996, s 60, Sch 5, as amended.
264 *NSR Ltd v Customs and Excise Comrs* (30 July 1999, unreported).
265 *Customs and Excise Comrs v Darfish Ltd* [2001] Env LR 3.
266 *Customs and Excise Comrs v Parkwood Landfill Ltd* [2002] EWHC 47 (Ch) [2002] STC 417.

of material for the purposes of the tax is not limited to the eventual deposit at a landfill site, but may include the processes of removal and transport from its point of origin. Creative further attempts to escape liability to the tax by arguing that the terms of a waste management licence have been broken, and thus the disposal was not at a 'landfill site', have been met by a sound – and equally pragmatic – rejection.[267]

Procedure in respect of registration of persons liable to pay the landfill tax, the information which may be required by Customs and Excise, accounting for tax and Customs' power to assess is provided for by the FA 1996, itself (in general)[268] and by the Landfill Tax Regulations 1996 (in particular: SI 1996/1527, as amended). The basic administrative structure is set out in FA 1996, s 47, and this also provides that Customs and Excise will keep a register of persons carrying out taxable activities.[269]

Exemptions from the landfill tax

Both the Finance Act 1996 as originally drafted and subsequent amendments have provided for exemptions from landfill tax liability. For example, FA 1996, ss 43 to 46 exempt: material produced by dredging or similar activities in fresh or sea water; material produced as a by-product of mining and quarrying; and pet cemeteries. In addition, FA 1996, s 46 enables the Treasury to vary the tax, by extending or reducing exemptions, by order. Some important amendments have been made in this way. The first amendments made by order relate to contaminated land. New sections 43A and 43B to the FA 1996 provide that in certain circumstances a disposal is not a taxable disposal if: it is of material removed from land in relation to which the Commissioners of Customs and Excise have issued a certificate; development or reclamation work has not commenced; removal is required to enable development to proceed or to avoid the potential for harm; and the removal was not required by certain statutory notices.[270] The relevant statutory notices include works notices under the Water Resources Act 1991[271] and remediation notices[272] unless the removal was carried out by a prescribed statutory body, such as the Agency or a local authority.

The effect of this section is to exempt from landfill tax liability these deposits from reclamation work voluntarily done (including work done in accordance with planning permission) when that work is done with the objective of facilitating development, conservation, the provision of a public park or other amenity, or agricultural or forestry use of land; or reducing or removing the potential of pollutants in the land to cause harm.[273] This is confined to cases where potentially harmful pollutants which would otherwise prevent the achievement of these objectives are in fact being removed. The emphasis is thus on developers voluntarily to undertake such work, an emphasis which is broadly consistent with policy towards the reclamation of contaminated land more generally. Customs have clearly asserted that only waste arising from reclamation qualifies for this exemption, not waste merely arising from construction activity,[274] although the dividing line will not always be clear cut. If they are satisfied that what is taking place is in fact reclamation, then the waste arising from that work will be exempt

267 *R v Harris* [2001] Env LR 9.
268 FA 1996, ss 47-50.
269 FA 1996, s 69.
270 Landfill Tax (Contaminated Land) Order 1996.
271 WRA 1991, s 161.
272 WRA 1991, s 78E; see chapter 15.
273 FA 1996, s 43B(7).
274 Information Note 1/97, *Reclamation of Contaminated Land.*

even though it would have been removed in any case as part of later construction. [275]
Subsequently, the VAT and Duties Tribunal has also concluded that material actually
used to engineer a landfill is similarly exempt, as such work is not disposing of that
material as useless, or disgarding it.[276]

The second set of exemptions came into effect on 1 October 1999[277] and provide for
two particular exemptions for inert waste used either for the purposes of restoring a
landfill site, or for filling an existing or former quarry.[278] As with the contaminated land
exemption, preconditions apply. In the case of restoring a landfill site, prior notification
must be given to the Commissioners of Customs and Excise, and the restoration must
be required by a planning permission, waste management licence or resolution
authorising disposal of waste to land. In the case of a quarry, a planning consent
requiring infilling must be in place, and the waste management licence in question must
also restrict the waste to be disposed of to 'qualifying material'.

Landfill tax credits

A further intended incentive effect of the new tax is the encouragement of payments to
environmental trusts.[279] If contributions are made by landfill site operators to approved
environmental trusts, and the trust spends that money on 'approved environmental
purposes', then the operator is entitled to claim a credit on landfill tax of 90% of their
contribution up to a maximum of 20% of their total landfill tax bill in a 12-month period.[280]
Trusts are private, not-for-profit bodies independent of site operators and local
authorities. The main test in establishing whether a trader can obtain a deduction is
that the payment must be made wholly and exclusively for the purposes of the trade.
That is a question of fact, to be determined from all the circumstances of a particular
case. However, the Inland Revenue does take the view that a payment may be made for
trade purposes even though there may be no direct and immediate benefit to trade.[281]
A number of strong criticisms have been made of the operation of the landfill tax credit
scheme (eg *Operation of the Landfill Tax,* HC Paper 150),[282] in particular, that it is
unduly complex and open to abuse, and that it is more often used to secure public
relations benefits for the contributing operator than environmental improvements that
are proportionate to the tax credit gained. These criticisms have yet to prompt any
meaningful reform.

Litter

Litter continues to be a depressingly obvious manifestation of the problem of waste in
a society over-devoted to disposability, over-packaging and not sufficiently concerned
with health and amenity. Legislation was passed in 1958 and 1971, consolidated in 1983
as the Litter Act, but to little avail. In 1989 a consultation paper on litter was issued and
EPA 1990, Part IV accordingly addressed itself to the problem.

275 *Taylor Woodrow Construction Northern Ltd v Customs and Excise Comrs,* unreported, noted at
    (1999) 11 ELM 76, VAT and Duties Tribunal.
276 *ICI Chemicals and Polymers Ltd v Customs and Excise Comrs* (1998), unreported, noted at
    (1999) 11 ELM 76.
277 Landfill Tax (Site Restoration and Quarries) Order 1999, SI 1999/2075.
278 FA 1996, new ss 43C, 44A respectively.
279 FA 1996, s 51.
280 Landfill Tax Regulations, Part VII.
281 *Tax Bulletin,* June 1996.
282 Session 1998-99.

EPA 1990, Part IV has three principal features. First, it creates a duty on 'litter authorities' — usually local authorities — to keep specified land clear of litter. Secondly, it creates criminal controls over littering itself. Thirdly, it applies controls to abandoned shopping trolleys. As for the litter authority duty, EPA 1990, s 86 designates principal litter authorities, which in England and Wales are generally counties, districts and London boroughs. It proceeds to define 'relevant land' of such authorities as that which is open to the air and is land (other than a highway) under the direct control of an authority to which the public are entitled or permitted to have access with or without payment. It seems authorities need not *own* the land, but they must superintend it.[283] Other land may be 'relevant land' of bodies such as the Crown, statutory undertakers, educational institutions, though sometimes ministerial designation is required. Likewise responsibility for litter on highways is initially placed in England and Wales on districts and London boroughs, though s 86(11) permits ministerial transfer of responsibility for cleaning functions to highway authorities.

Under EPA 1990, s 89 it is the duty of principal litter authorities as respects their relevant land, and other bodies as respects theirs, together with the occupiers of relevant land within a litter control area as designated (by principal litter authorities acting in accordance with regulations made under EPA 1990, s 90 and see SIs 1991/1325 and 1997/633) to ensure that land is, so far as is practicable, kept clear of refuse and litter. Commensurate duties are placed on local authorities and the Secretary of State in respect of highways, trunk roads and motorways, and their duty extends to keeping roads, so far as practicable, clean. In setting a standard of freedom from litter and cleanliness regard is to be had to the character and use of the land as well as the practicality of measures, while litter and refuse may be defined by regulations and may extend to animal faeces (see SI 1991/961). A Code of Practice has been issued to add further substance to litter authorities' EPA 1990, s 89 duty.[284] The Code provides guidance both on standards of cleanliness themselves, and on good practice for authorities in pursuing cleanliness. It is a revised version of the Code originally issued in 1991, the application of which was considered as part of a review of the operation of Part IV by the Advisory Group on Litter in 1994.

The Code of Practice stresses the need for land to be kept clean, though it does not lay down minimum cleaning frequencies. It also stresses practicability pointing out that litter clearance from motorways, for example, may entail traffic restrictions and these may take time to plan, while bad weather may also hold up cleaning. Four standards of cleanliness are illustrated in the code, A-D — from no litter to heavily littered. A is the 'ideal' grade which 'a thorough conventional sweeping/litter picking should achieve in most circumstances — although ... it may not last for very long'. The code further divides land into five types of 'zone' to which litter authorities must allocate land in their area, from beaches, through educational land, to railway land, canal towpaths and land used for specific special events. Each category of zone is then further subdivided, and different cleanliness standards are applied taking into account he seriousness of littering and the practicability of cleaning land.

Where a member of the public (which would certainly include a resident in the area or a regular visitor) is 'aggrieved' because the EPA 1990, s 89 duties have been breached, complaint may be made to the justices (in England and Wales) on five days' notice against the person who has the duty to keep the land clear or clean.[285] If the justices are satisfied that the land in question is defaced by litter and that the defendant has not complied with his/her duties, they make a litter abatement order requiring remedial

---

283   *Johnston Fear and Kingham v Commonwealth* (1943) 67 CLR 314; *Pardoe v Pardoe* (1900) 82 LT 547.

284   *Code of Practice on Litter and Refuse*, DETR 1999.

285   EPA 1990, s 91.

action; failure to comply with this constitutes an offence, and compensation may be payable. In coming to their decision the justices will consider the Code of Practice. Note, however, that though the Crown has duties with regard to litter, it may not be prosecuted for their breach.[286] Principal litter authorities may not take action under s 91 but under s 92 certain authorities (principally districts and London boroughs) are to be actors in respect of certain land, eg that of a statutory undertaker, or land within a litter control area, though highways are excluded from the ambit of this power. The procedure is similar to that under EPA 1990, s 91.

EPA 1990, s 93 empowers certain authorities (effectively districts and London boroughs) to issue 'street litter control notices' with a view to preventing accumulations of litter in and around streets or adjacent open land. Such notices impose obligations on occupiers of premises in relation to litter. Relevant premises are those which fall within descriptions of commercial or retail premises prescribed by the Secretary of State under EPA 1990, s 94 (see SI 1991/1324) and which have a frontage to a street where there is recurrent defacement by litter or refuse of the street in the vicinity of the premises, or where the premises include open land in the vicinity of the frontage whose condition is, and is likely to continue to be, detrimental to amenity by the presence of litter, etc, or there is produced as a result of activities on the premises quantities of litter, etc, of such an amount and nature as likely to cause defacement of the street in the vicinity. Notices must identify the premises and the grounds on which they are served, and the requirements they may impose may relate to provision or emptying of litter receptacles, carrying out specified works or activities either once and for all or periodically. Before notice is served the person to be served must be informed and given 21 days in which to make representations which must be taken into account before the authority decide the issue. A person served may appeal to the justices and the court may uphold, vary, quash or add to the notice. Where there is failure to comply with such a notice the authority may apply to the court for an order requiring compliance, and it is an offence to fail to comply with such an order. Relevant authorities are to keep public registers of street litter control notices, and also of litter control areas, see EPA 1990, s 95.

The second feature of EPA 1990, Part IV, the key littering offence, follows the pattern of the remainder of Part IV in not actually defining litter itself, but instead prohibiting the acts of throwing down, dropping or otherwise depositing and leaving any thing whatsoever in such circumstances as to cause or contribute to or tend to lead to the defacement by litter of any public open space or any covered place open to the air on at least one side.[287] This is clearly extremely wide, and so can include varieties of material which would also constitute 'waste' for the purposes of EPA 1990, Part II. Commercial waste deposited in the street for collection, for example, has been found to be capable of being litter for this purpose.[288] Less protective, however, was the decision of the High Court which concluded that public telephone boxes were not places to which the principal offence applied.[289] Placing prostitutes' calling cards in phone boxes is therefore not a littering offence. Specific provisions have instead had to be introduced, which include a power of arrest.[290] The more usual penalty for littering is prosecution in the magistrates' court or (for less serious cases) payment of a fixed penalty of £50[291] – which remains a long way short of the £1,000 maximum fixed penalty suggested by the 1994 review.

286 EPA 1990, s 159(2).
287 EPA 1990, s 87(1), (4).
288 *Westminster City Council v Riding* (1995) 7 ELM 208.
289 *Felix v DPP* (1998) 10 ELM 162.
290 Criminal Justice and Police Act 2001, ss 46, 47.
291 SI 1999/424.

The third feature of EPA 1990, Part IV is power to deal with abandoned shopping trolleys. EPA 1990, s 99 allows local authorities to apply, after consultation with affected persons and due advertisement in the local press, the provisions of Sch 4 of EPA 1990. This applies to abandoned shopping or luggage trolleys and allows their seizure, removal, or retention subject to notice to their owners, disposal or return to their owners, subject to a power in authorities to charge in respect of the activities. Authorities may also agree schemes of collection with trolley owners. Although certain technical changes have been made by many shops in response to these provisions – deposit schemes or proximity locking mechanisms – the effectiveness of these controls remains in question. They may be complemented by other mechanisms, however, including in one remarkable case the prosecution of a supermarket for causing the pollution of water where it failed to take measures to prevent the abandonment of 197 trolleys in a river.[292] The company was fined £30,000 plus costs – amounting to £190 per trolley.

E RADIOACTIVE WASTE

Much waste disposal is controversial, but rarely as controversial as proposals to dispose of radioactive material. Seaward disposal took place from 1949 onwards, but became subject to a degree of international regulation following the 1972 London Dumping Convention's inception in 1975, and then ceased following industrial action by ships' crews in 1983. Dumping at sea is also subject to the 1992 Convention for the Protection of the Marine Environment of the North-East Atlantic (OSPAR) on 25 March 1998. This replaced the 1972 Oslo Convention for the Prevention of Marine Pollution by Dumping from Ships and Aircraft (Oslo Convention and Oslo Commission) and the 1974 Paris Convention for the Prevention of Marine Pollution from Land-Based Sources (Paris Convention and Paris Commission). The purpose of the OSPAR Convention is the creation of a comprehensive regime for the protection of the marine environment of the north-east Atlantic and Arctic oceans, and it places tighter obligations than its forebears. For example, the UK and France previously enjoyed an exemption allowing for the possibility of disposing of low level solid radioactive waste at sea (albeit not for 15-25 years) after implementation of the 1972 and 1974 Conventions. However, the new Convention prohibits the disposal of all radioactive wastes at sea.[293] More problematic, however, are marine emissions from land based sources, a particular concern to Norway and Ireland. Here too OSPAR can be expected to lead to reductions of emissions, with the ultimate aim of eliminating radioactive discharges to the Atlantic by 2020.[294] The consequence is that landward disposal of waste remains the only option.

International guidelines and regulations

Various bodies lay down standards for the management of radioactive waste. The International Commission on Radiological Protection (ICRP) in 1990 produced revised guidelines, while the International Atomic Energy Agency (IAEA) established by the UN in 1957 has created a Radioactive Waste Safety Standards Programme (RADWASS) and has issued 'The Principles of Radioactive Waste Management' and 'Establishing a National System for Radioactive Waste Management'. The IAEA's fundamental safety guidelines are:

292 *R v Tesco Stores plc* (2001) 320 ENDS Report 52.
293 See de la Fayette, 'The OSPAR Convention Comes into Force: Continuity and Progress' (1999) 14 *International Journal of Marine and Coastal Law* 247.
294 See *UK Strategy for Radioactive Discharges 2001-2020*, DETR, June 2000.

1   Waste must be managed so as to secure an acceptable level of human health
     protection.
2   Waste must be managed so as to provide an acceptable level of environmental
     protection.
3   In managing waste its possible effects on human health and the environment
     beyond national borders must be taken into account.
4   Waste management must proceed on the basis that predicted impacts on the health
     of future generations will not be greater than relevant levels of impact acceptable
     today.
5   Waste management today must not place unacceptable burdens on future
     generations.
6   National legal frameworks must allocate clear responsibilities with an independent
     regulatory framework.
7   Generation of waste shall be minimised.
8   Interdependencies in waste generation and management must always be taken
     into account.
9   The safety of management facilities must be appropriately assured during their
     lifetime.

These principles were largely echoed at the Earth Summit in Rio, 1992, and were reflected
in Agenda 21. The UK's policy response in 'Sustainable Development — The UK
Strategy' (1994) Cm 2426 was that radioactive waste should be managed safely so that
the present generation may meet its responsibilities to future generations.

The types of radiactive waste

Waste is of four sorts: 'low-level' (not exceeding 4 GBq/te (gigabecquerels) alpha or 12
GBq/te beta gamma levels); 'intermediate level' (above low level radiation limits, but
not requiring heating to be considered in designing storage or disposal facilities); 'high
level' or 'heat generating' wastes (wastes in which temperatures may rise significantly
in consequence of radioactivity so as to require consideration of this fact in designing
storage and disposal facilities); 'very low level waste' with the very lowest levels of
activity may be disposed of with household refuse, eg the single item with less than 40
kBq (Kilobecquerels) beta gamma activity. High level waste comes in the form of a
concentrated liquid and, although it represents some 90% of the radioactive content of
the total volume of stored radioactive waste, it also comprises just 2% of the volume of
that waste. Intermediate level waste comes in both solid and liquid forms from power
stations, fuel reprocessing, used reactor parts, nuclear fuel cladding, and effluent
treatment sludge. Between 1949 and 1982, 73,530 tonnes of low and intermediate level
waste was disposed of by the UK to the North-East Atlantic. Low level waste can be
solid, liquid or gaseous, and includes matter such as used clothing and laboratory
equipment from the nuclear industry, research institutions and hospitals. By the late
1980s/early 1990s some 30 cubic metres of high level waste was being produced annually
in the UK, 3,000 cubic metres of intermediate level waste and 45,000 cubic metres of low
level waste. In addition, facilities that have run on nuclear power have to be disposed
of. Nuclear submarines may have to be stored on land for 50–100 years before their
reactor compartments can be removed, even following fuel removal, for international
agreement has placed a moratorium on their sinking in the deep ocean, along with other
forms of nuclear waste. Redundant nuclear power stations after removal of fuel *may* be
left in 'deferred safe store' for 30 years, subject to constant security and regular
inspection; then they would be encased in structures for a further 100 years and
mounded over. It is estimated that a total of 250,000 tonnes of radioactive waste will

have been created by the time that all nuclear material in use is converted into solid waste. This figure will be doubled by the waste produced from cleaning up nuclear sites in the next century.

Current practice on nuclear waste is that high level waste is currently stored and cooled, and from 1990 onwards is increasingly being vitrified at Sellafield by BNFL. This process reduces the waste's volume by two thirds, but it can still produce heat for 50 years, and so the current policy is that it should be kept in an above ground secure store for at least 90 years, but thereafter some final disposal decision will have to be made. Most of this high level waste is the 3% of unusable waste left after BNFL has reprocessed spent nuclear fuel, 96% of which can be used again, and 1% of which becomes plutonium. Intermediate level waste is also dealt with by BNFL and as from 1991 is sealed in a £249m encapsulation plant ('the Cell') at Sellafield into concrete filled steel drums which are then stored, but again a long-term disposal route will have to be found. 1998 figures showed that there was then 71,000 cubic metres of intermediate level radioactive waste in storage, 8,500 cubic metres of which had been encapsulated. Low level waste has been landfilled at Drigg, near Sellafield, by BNFL (a total volume of around 1,000,000 cubic metres since the 1950s) but is now placed at their site into specially constructed concrete vaults. Liquid low level waste, mainly cooling pond water from fuel rod cooling processes is 'cleaned' in the Site Ion Exchange Effluent Plant (SIXEP) before discharge to the sea, the extracted waste being encapsulated, once again, in concrete.

It is clear that a distinction has to be made between 'disposal' and 'storage'. The latter is an interim practice designed to hold waste (currently high and intermediate level) in a facility until long-term action, ie disposal, with no intention to take further action save some monitoring, is undertaken. Currently only low-level waste is disposed of, but policy is to dispose of all waste, despite much expert opinion that the search for an acceptable disposal site for high- and intermediate-level waste is unnecessary and that the waste could be stored for a long period.

Disposal: the regulatory framework

Disposal sites have to be found. But how should they be selected and monitored, and is existing legal control over waste in general sufficient? A number of bodies and institutions have responsibilities here.

Responsibility for radioactive waste management is shared between the government (maker of overall policy), the regulators (who implement policy) and waste producers (who manage it in accordance with regulatory requirements, and who, in accordance with the polluter pays principle, must have adequate financial provision to meet present and future liabilities).

The Secretary of State for the Environment (along with the devolved administrations) is the prime policy maker though there are inputs from the DTI and the Ministry of Defence (MoD) and the HSE. The government is advised by: the Radioactive Waste Management Advisory Committee (RWMAC) an independent body of experts established in 1978, consisting of persons with expertise from nuclear, academic and medical backgrounds as well as lay persons; the Advisory Committee on the Safety of Nuclear Installations (ACSNI) set up in 1977 to advise on major safety issues affecting installations, and appointed partly by the Health and Safety Commission (HSC) and partly by the Confederation of British Industry (CBI) and the Trades Union Congress (TUC); the Ionising Radiation Advisory Committee (IRAC) created in 1995 by the HSC to consider all matters relating to protection against exposure to ionising radiation, eg worker protection standards, and whose membership is drawn from the CBI, TUC, local authorities, government departments and relevant professional bodies; the National Radiological Protection Board (NRPB) set up in 1970 to give advice, conduct research and provide technical services in the area of protection against ionising and non-ionising radiation; the Committee on Medical Aspects of Radiation in the Environment (COMARE) created in 1985 to advise on the health effects of natural and human created radioactivity and appointed by the Chief Medical Officer of the Department of Health.

The regulatory body in England and Wales under the Radioactive Substances Act 1993, and the Environment Act 1995, s 2 is the Environment Agency, which inherited the powers to authorise disposal of radioactive waste from nuclear sites such as power stations previously jointly enjoyed by Her Majesty's Inspectorate of Pollution and MAFF/the Welsh Office. The management of waste on a nuclear site remains subject to regulation by the Nuclear Installations Inspectorate (NII — part of the HSE), and statutory consultation arrangements are in place under the EA 1995 between the Agency and NII on applications to dispose of radioactive waste, just as the Agency is a statutory consultee of NII for nuclear site licences under the Nuclear Installations Act 1965. The HSE remains responsible for controlling exposure to ionising radiation at non-nuclear sites (such as hospitals) under the Health and Safety at Work Act 1974 and the Ionising Radiation Regulations 1985. BNFL is the operating body that currently disposes of most nuclear waste, though currently high level waste is primarily stored. The Nuclear Industry Radioactive Waste Executive (NIREX) set up in 1982 by BNFL, the former CEGB, UKAEA, and the former South of Scotland Electricity Board is a managerial body charged with responsibility for disposing of most solid low and intermediate level waste. It has a share structure with the shareholders being BNFL, Nuclear Electric and Scottish Nuclear Ltd the UKAEA and the President of the Board of Trade to ensure governmental oversight. NIREX is a commercial service-providing body that exists to ensure a common approach to nuclear waste disposed amongst nuclear operators, for legal responsibility for disposal still lies with them. However, NIREX's services extend to keeping comprehensive nuclear waste records, planning, transport and waste disposal facilities and modes of transportation, managing waste disposal, identifying potential disposal sites, conducting appropriate research and development.

The development of radioactive waste policy

Central policy on waste management was originally set out in a response to the Sixth Report of the Royal Commission on Environmental Pollution.[295] It has been policy: to ensure the minimum creation of nuclear waste and to deal with waste management issues before large nuclear programmes are begun; to pay regard to environmental considerations in handling waste; to dispose of water in a programmed fashion; to undertake research into disposal methods; to dispose of waste only in appropriate ways; and to ensure that waste management issues have been considered in the design of nuclear installations. The 1994 *National Strategy on Radioactive Waste Management* developed earlier policy, giving it an emphasis more soundly based in (for example) national environment policy, and placed particular emphasis on the need to improve the quality of the information held on nuclear waste and its creation. This included preparation of an inventory of past authorised discharges. Other aspects of the 1994 Strategy included: waste had to be stored safely for as long as necessary pending final disposal decisions; disposals had to provide at least a degree of safety equal to that of supervised storage; decisions on disposal had to be made, case by case, on the basis of what represented the best practicable environmental option; and new disposal facilities for low and intermediate level wastes were to be developed.

295 Cmnd 6820 and 8607.

This strategy was based on the polluter pays principle, with waste management costs being met by relevant industries. The co-ordinating body was NIREX. This was part of a system of management, with central government ensuring, under the now repealed and replaced Radioactive Substances Act 1960 and the Nuclear Installations Act 1965, that high standards of waste management were applied, hazards being kept as low as reasonably achievable (ALARA). Co-ordinated implementation of waste strategy was left to NIREX, though it was expected to liaise with the private sector in its operations.

In all cases the objectives of the strategy were that:

1   Practices resulting in radioactive waste had to be justified by need.
2   Exposure of persons to radiation had to be kept to levels as low as reasonably achievable, taking into account economic and social factors, while radioactivity coming from a site should be as low as reasonably practicable.
3   The average effective dose equivalent from radiation sources for representative persons should not exceed 5m Sv (0.5 rem) pa.
4   Where waste is stored, storage facilities had to contain associated radioactivity, but the waste remain retrievable, while other waste generated by storage should be minimised.
5   Storage could only be justified where there were specific technical and radiological reasons for it, as in the case of high level waste.

More recently, a wide-ranging review of policy has been launched. The first stage in this review was in 1995, with the *Review of Radioactive Waste Management Policy.*[296] This sought to connect radioactive waste policy with sustainable development ideas, and thus emphasised the need to base decisions on the best scientific information, a precautionary approach, and the 'polluter pays' principle. The aims of this policy were:

1   Prevention of the creation of unnecessary radioactive waste.
2   Safe and appropriate management and treatment of such waste as is created.
3   Safe disposal of waste at appropriate times and in appropriate ways.
4   To place all these principles in the context of protecting both existing and future generations and the wider environment in such a way as to command public confidence while taking due account of costs involved.

Particular policy controversy emerged in the 1990s, with a proposal from NIREX to establish a deep depository for radioactive waste at Sellafield, and as a precursor to this, to establish an underground laboratory (or 'rock characterisation facility') at Sellafield to undertake detailed investigation of geological and groundwater conditions. However, the proposed laboratory was refused planning permission by the Secretary of State in 1997, a decision which called into question whether deep disposal would ever be scientifically or politically acceptable. Therefore, a further policy review has been initiated subsequently, first by the House of Lords Select Committee on Science and Technology[297] along with the Government's response (October 1999), and then through a series of consultation papers.[298] The House of Lords was particularly critical of the absence of detailed policy. It recommended that

'... the Government should develop a fully comprehensive policy for the long-term management of all United Kingdom nuclear waste. This proposed policy should be put to Parliament for debate and decision, in the form of a Bill, so that

296   Cm 2919.
297   *The Management of Nuclear Waste*, Third Report, HL Paper 26 (Session 1998-99)
298   Eg, *Managing Radioactive Waste Safely: Proposals for Developing a Policy for Managing Solid Radioactive Waste in the UK*, September 2001; *UK Strategy for Radioactive Discharges 2001-2020*, DETR, June 2000.

the adopted policy has explicit parliamentary endorsement and statutory authority... It is essential that, before the policy is put to Parliament for approval, there is substantial public consultation... The Government should approach this consultation with the objectives of: (1) informing the public of the problem of nuclear waste and of the imperative need to deal with it; (2) discussing with the public the solutions open to the Government; (3) seeking views on the institutional framework proposed to handle the processes of decision-taking and implementation including, in the case of deep repositories, the process of site selection.'

The September 2001 consultation paper is intended to start this process.

The consultation paper initiates an extremely wide-ranging review. With a basis in the practical task to be faced – there is no alternative than to establish a new policy of some sort – the paper considers a variety of largely procedural measures by which a debate may be initiated to develop policy. This includes a review of the role and composition of many of the consultative bodies concerned with radioactive waste (including RWMAC and NIREX), the functions of regulators, and the substance of waste policy. A particular issue is also whether these bodies should now be complemented by a new 'liabilities management authority' to be responsible for the management of all publicly funded civil nuclear liabilities. Taking into account the need to decommission existing facilities, those liabilities are estimated at around £40 billion. As for the substance of policy, the House of Lords Select Committee recommended a phased programme of geological disposal – a more measured development than that considered, and rejected, in 1997. What the government's consultation papers does not do, however, is favour one option over any other or, indeed, rule any option out. Those options include above ground storage, sealed underground disposal, underground storage, chemical treatment to reduce waste volumes and the more remarkable (although generally ruled out) possibilities of disposal to ice sheets, and sub-seabed disposal. This fundamental review is intended to enable the identification of management options by 2004, with further consultation to follow on the options identified.

Implementation of policy through law

The Radioactive Substances Act 1993 (as amended in 1995) provides that no person may keep or use radioactive material on premises used by that person for carrying on an undertaking without a registration (see RSA 1993, ss 6 and 7), unless exempted from registration, or the material is mobile radioactive apparatus otherwise registered or exempt. Exemptions are provided for by RSA 1993, s 8 and in general exist in relation to sites currently licensed under the Nuclear Installations Act 1965, eg power stations. The Secretary of State also has power in respect of luminous articles and other low activity substances. Mobile radioactive apparatus is generally registered, but again exemptions may be given under RSA 1993, s 11. It is a criminal offence under RSA 1993, s 32 to fail to be registered.

Radioactive substances are defined as anything which, not being waste, is a substance falling with Sch 1 of the Act, and/or a substance possessing radioactivity which is wholly/partly attributable to a process of nuclear fusion, or some other process of bombardment by neutrons or ionising radiation, not being a process occurring in nature or in consequence of the disposal of radioactive wastes. RSA 1993, Sch 1 of the Act specifically refers to a number of elements which in their solid, liquid or gaseous form may be subject to control by virtue of reaching a specified limit of radioactivity, eg polonium, radium, thorium and uranium.

The Agency is the registration body under RSA 1993, s 7, and registration applications must contain specified information as to premises and substances, and must be accompanied by an appropriate fee. Applications may be refused, granted, or granted subject to conditions which may relate to premises, apparatus, operating practices, and (save in relation to conditions concerning the furnishing of information or the sale or supply of radioactive material) the Agency is only to have regard to the amount of character of radioactive waste likely to arise in consequence of the keeping or use of radioactive material on premises when imposing conditions. Registrations may be cancelled or varied, and conditions may be varied at any time.[299] In addition the Agency may take enforcement action under RSA 1993, s 21 if it is of the opinion that there is an actual or potential failure to comply with any condition or limitation of a registration. Where the Agency considers that the continuation of an activity involves an imminent risk of pollution of the environment they may take prohibitive action under RSA 1993, s 22 which may suspend a registration to the extent specified by the prohibition notice. Appeals against Agency decisions lie to the Secretary of State. However, it should be noted that RSA 1993, s 23 empowers the Secretary of State to give directions to the Agency in relation to registration applications in relation to the refusal, grant, variation, cancellation or revocation of a registration, while RSA 1993, s 24 enables the Secretary of State to require certain applications to be determined by him, and no appeal lies against such a direction or decision.

Authorisation of disposal and accumulation of radioactive waste

Radioactive waste may only be accumulated with a view to subsequent disposal or disposed of according to the terms of an authorisation.[300] The same prohibition applies to any person causing or knowingly permitting the accumulation/disposal of radioactive waste. Furthermore the prohibition on unauthorised disposal extends to the disposal of radioactive waste from premises which are situated on a nuclear site but which have ceased to be used for the purposes of the licensee's undertaking.

'Radioactive waste' is defined by RSA 1993, s 2 to be waste which consists wholly or partly of a substance or article which, if it were not waste, would be radioactive material within the meaning of RSA 1993, s 1 or a substance or article contaminated in the course of production, keeping or use of radioactive material, or by contact or proximity to radioactive waste, eg spent nuclear fuel rods, and see above for the categorisation of such waste.

Authorisations are granted by the Agency but before the grant consultation must take place with DEFRA, the Health and Safety Executive, relevant local authorities, and other relevant water bodies and public authorities.[301] Authorisations may be refused or granted subject to conditions or limitations, and may apply to radioactive waste generally, or to such descriptions of waste as are stated in the authorisation. Under EA 1995, s 17 authorisations may be revoked or varied though, again, consultation with the Minister is required. RSA 1993, s 18 provides that where radioactive waste disposal is likely to require the need for special precautions to be taken by a local authority, a relevant water body (eg a sewage undertaker) or other public authority, the Agency must consult with that authority or body before granting the authorisation. Furthermore where special precautions are taken by such a body and these precautions are either in compliance with conditions subject to which the authorisation in question

299 RSA 1993, s 12.
300 RSA 1993, ss 13, 14.
301 RSA 1993, s 16; EA 1995, Sch 22, para 205.

was granted, or they are taken with prior Agency approval, the body may charge in respect of taking precautions. Under RSA 1993, s 20 obligations may be imposed on authorisees in relation to the retention and production of site or disposal records in relation to keeping or using radioactive material or accumulating or disposing of radioactive waste.

The powers relating to enforcement and prohibition action under RSA 1993, ss 21 and 22, and the powers of the Secretary of State under ss 23 and 24 to give directions and 'call in' applications referred to above in connection with registrations also apply with regard to authorisations, similarly the provisions of RSA 1993, ss 26 and 27 with regard to appeals.

It should further be noted that under RSA 1993, s 25 the Secretary of State has power to direct the Agency that knowledge of any particular application for a registration or an authorisation, or of applications of any specified description, should be restricted. In such cases the Agency may not send a copy of the application or any subsequent registration or authorisation to public or local authorities. This power may only be exercised on grounds of national security.

Further powers of the Secretary of State and offences

RSA 1993, s 29 empowers the Secretary of State to arrange provision of facilities for the safe disposal or accumulation of radioactive waste if it appears to him/her that such facilities are not available, though prior consultation with the local authority of any area where such facilities are to be provided must take place, as must consultation with other appropriate public or local authorities. Similarly under RSA 1993, s 30 where the Agency is satisfied that there is radioactive waste on any premises, and that it ought to be disposed of, but that for any reason it is unlikely it will be lawfully disposed of unless they exercise their powers, they may dispose of it as they think fit and recover their reasonable expenses from the owner/occupier of the premises.

To enforce its various powers under the RSA 1993 the Agency has general powers along with its authorised officers under EA 1995, ss 108–110 inter alia to: enter premises at any reasonable time or at any time in an emergency — in the latter case by force if need be; enter premises it is reasonably believed it is necessary to enter along with other authorised persons and equipment; examine and investigate the premises; take measurements and photographs and other recordings; take samples; take possession of and retain for so long as is necessary (for the purposes of examination or to ensure it is available as evidence) any substance or article found on the premises which appears to have caused or to be likely to cause pollution of the environment or harm to human health; require information and records to be produced (see EA 1995, s 108). Particular powers to deal with causes of imminent danger of serious pollution of the environment or serious harm to human health by way of seizure and rendering the cause harmless, whether by destruction or otherwise, are granted by EA 1995, s 109, while s 110 provides where obstruction of persons exercising the foregoing powers occurs, or there is a failure to comply with requirements made under s 108, an offence is committed.

It is an offence under RSA 1993, s 32 to contravene the provisions relating to prohibition of unauthorised use of radioactive material, or its accumulation or disposal, or to fail to comply with the terms of registrations/authorisations. A fine of up to £20,000 and/or a term of imprisonment for up to six months is capable of being imposed on summary trial, while on indictment an unlimited fine and/or imprisonment for up to five years may be imposed. RSA 1993, s 32(3), added in 1995, allows the Agency to seek an injunction from the High Court to secure compliance where it is felt proceedings for an offence in respect of an enforcement notice or prohibition notice would not provide an effectual remedy. RSA 1993, s 34A (as inserted in 1995) creates the specific offences of making false or misleading statements so as to obtain a registration or authorisation, and of falsifying requisite records.

The application of the law in practice

There have been few major cases on the waste disposal provisions of the RSA 1993 and its predecessor. Most prosecutions have been at the level of the magistrates' court and have related to comparatively minor infractions of the law. This is not to say there have been no nuclear incidents: operators have been prosecuted in respect of breaches of site licences (which result in action under the Health and Safety at Work etc Act 1974), see *Health and Safety Executive v Nuclear Electric*[302] and for infraction of authorisations, see *HMP v Nuclear Electric.*[303] However, there has been little guidance from the courts on how regulators are to use their discretion in granting authorisations and registrations.

However, the major decision of Potts J in *R v Secretary of State for the Environment, ex p Greenpeace*[304] has to be noted. This case arose out of an authorisation granted to BNFL to allow the start up of the Thermal Oxide Reprocessing Plant (THORP) at Sellafield. During the course of judgment Potts J accepted that EU law requires that national law should be read consistently with EU provisions. On this basis he construed the 1993 legislation in the light of the Euratom Basic Safety Standards Directive, Arts 6A and 13. Thus while the RSA 1993 alone does not require *justification* to be shown before an authorisation can be granted, in the light of the Directive such an exercise is required. Effectively, regulators must be convinced that the advantages of the nuclear activity in question justify exposure to ionising radiation.

As Cm 2919 points out, this means that in deciding an application for an authorisation regulators must consider maximum discharges and limits of exposure, together with justification and optimisation, ie that exposures shall be kept as low as reasonably achievable with all relevant economic and social factors being taken into account. Such applications may be submitted at the same time as an application for full planning permission for the development of a nuclear facility is made, though the two procedures will progress separately.

Cm 2919 further declares the principles that will be applied with regard to radioactive waste discharges.
1   In relation to discharges of air borne and liquid waste the dose to members of the public from *all* man-made sources of radiactivity (other than medical exposures) should be limited to one millisievert a year (1 mSv/y — a sievert being the international unit for measuring doses of exposure). In determining applications for authorisations a maximum dose constraint of 0.3 mSv/y will be applied to new nuclear installations, while existing facilities should also be operated within this limit, and where this cannot be done the operator must demonstrate that doses resulting from the operation are as low as is reasonably achievable and within dose limits. Where there are a number of nuclear sources with contiguous boundaries at a single location there will be an overall 'site constraint' of 0.5 mSv/y irrespective of whether different sources on the site are owned or operated by the same or different organisations. Where, however, exposures are below 0.02 mSv/y regulators should not seek further reductions in exposures to the public provided they are satisfied the best practicable means to limit releases are being used.

302   [1995] 7 ELM 203.
303   [1994] 6 ELM 83.
304   [1994] 6 ELM 82.

The current policy is the result of a long process of reduction of discharges of radioactive waste to water. The Black Committee's 'Investigation of the Possible Increased Incidence of Cancer in West Cumbria' (1984) criticised discharge authorisation procedures as ill co-ordinated and unfocused and lacking in 'health input'. Even before this there had been attempts to reduce dose levels to local residents, and these had declined from 1.95 mSv/y to 0.49 mSv/y between 1980 and 1985, with authorised discharges to the sea of material being particularly reduced. It does not, however, appear possible to impose a zero limit on discharges and the relevant legislation will not be interpreted and applied so as to impose such a requirement.[305]

Unauthorised or 'accidental' discharges may also take place, with some 672 such incidents having occurred for instance between January 1979 and March 1986 according to BNFL figures, though none was 'dangerous' within the meaning of the Nuclear Installations (Dangerous Occurrences) Regulations SI 1965/1824. There are four grades of incident:

(A) Those falling within the 1965 regulations in that radiation has been emitted likely to cause death or serious injury, or there has been a fire or explosion *likely* to affect the safe operation of an installation.

(B) Those involving major leaks/escapes of radioactive material or a radiation dose uptake of twice the maximum permitted annual rate.

(C) Minor ground leaks of material, radiation uptake greater than annual or quarterly limits, or fire/explosions which *may* affect an installation's safe condition.

(D) Leakages of radioactivity leading to widespread contamination levels more than 10 times the specification for on-site working areas, or radiation uptake greater than a third of quarterly dose limits or minor fires or explosions unlikely to affect safety.

Where radioactive waste is to be discharged to the sea via a pipeline its construction will be an act of development for which planning permission is required.

2   With regard to solid waste disposal, estimates of risk have to be considered in determining the safety of a proposed disposal facility. Other technical factors also have to be considered, such as whether a facility has to be designed according to principles of good engineering and good science. There should be no prescribed cut off of the period over which risk is to be assessed. In each instance a site specific safety case will have to be made out. Much will depend on the nature of the waste to be disposed of.

The government has also conducted a consultation exercise on proposed statutory guidance to the Environment Agency on the exercise of its powers in relation to discharges of radioactive material.[306] The principles proposed in that document include some that are familiar, such as waste minimisation, consideration of the best practicable environmental option, application of best practicable means, and progressive reduction. Some, however, are novel: for example, a proposed preference for concentration and containment of radioactive wastes rather than dilution and dispersal through licensed releases. Equally, potential exposure of both workers and the general public to discharged radioactive material should be calculated, and defined dose limits should be set. Conditions on authorisations should also be applied to those radionuclides which: are of significance in terms of radiological impact for humans and non-human

305 *Re Friends of the Earth* [1988] JPL 93.
306 *Statutory Guidance on the Regulation of Radioactive Discharges into the Environment from Nuclear Licensed Sites*, 2000.

species, including those which may be taken up in food; are of significance in terms of the quantity of radioactivity discharged, which may or may not be of radiological significance; have long half-lives and which may persist and/or accumulate in the environment; are significant indicators of plant performance and process control; and which provide for effective regulatory control and enforcement.

Two other issues also arise in respect of radioactive waste: imports and exports; and the radioactive contamination of land. As to imports and exports, as a matter of general policy, radioactive waste should be neither imported into nor exported from the UK save in specific situations:

1   For the prime purpose of recovering re-usable materials.
2   For treatment to make the subsequent storage and disposal of waste more manageable where *either* the relevant processes are at a development stage *or* the quantity of waste involved is too small for treatment processes to be practicable in its country of origin (in the foregoing cases there is, however, a presumption that the activities in question must not add materially to the amount of waste needing disposal in the UK).
3   Waste may be imported for treatment and disposal if it is in the form of a spent source which was manufactured in the UK.
4   Waste may be imported if it comes from small users such as hospitals in EU member states producing such small quantities of radioactive waste that provision of specialised facilities would be impractical, or from developing nations which cannot reasonably be expected to have their own facilities.

As for land contamination, the new regime under EPA 1990, Part IIA was not developed specifically to apply to radioactively contaminated land. However, the Act does give powers to the Secretary of State to make regulations applying EPA 1990, Part IIA with any necessary modifications to radioactively contaminated land. A consultation paper was published in 1998, the *Control and Remediation of Radioactively Contaminated Land*, along with research into criteria for the designation of radioactively contaminated land. These emphasised that the policy and priorities for radioactively contaminated land are the same as those for non-radioactively contaminated land. It is envisaged that regulations will be made to provide for the provisions of EPA 1990, Part IIA to have effect for the purpose of dealing with harm so far as attributable to any radioactivity possessed by any substances, in cases where the radionuclides involved have been artificially produced or are naturally-occurring radionuclides that have been artificially concentrated as part of an industrial process, whether they are a by-product of the process or a product that is subsequently discarded.

Transporting nuclear waste

In 1973 the International Atomic Energy Agency (IAEA) issued 'Regulations for the Safe Transport of Radioactive Materials'. These formed the basis for British regulations, whose philosophy was to ensure that all transported nuclear waste must be appropriately and safely packaged in a manner sufficient to withstand a severe accident. The legislative position is now governed by the Radioactive Material (Road Transport) Act 1991. The Secretary of State is empowered by s 2 of this Act to make regulations to prevent any injury to health or property damage or damage to the environment being caused by the transport of radioactive material, and to give effect to the IAEA's regulations as issued from time to time. Such regulations may in particular make provision as to packaging of material and the manufacture and maintenance of packaging components; preparing, labelling, consigning, handling, transporting, storing in transit and delivery of radioactive packages, placarding of delivery vehicles, and keeping of records. Regulations may also provide for requisite approvals to be obtained. Failure to comply with regulations is an offence.

RMRTA 1991, s 3 gives ministerially appointed inspectors powers to prohibit the driving of vehicles in contravention of regulations, or where relevant vehicles or radioactive packages have been involved in accidents, or where such material has been lost or stolen. Likewise the transport of packages may be prohibited if they do not comply with regulations. Notices of prohibitions must be given to the person in charge of the vehicle, specifying the infraction in question and stating the effect of the prohibition. Prohibitions have immediate effect on notice being given. Extensive powers of entry are given to inspectors under RMRTA 1991, s 5 in order to enforce the regulations, both to enter land and vehicles. Entry under warrant is provided for where admission to a vehicle or premises has been refused.

Under RMRTA 1991, s 4 enforcement action may be taken against manufacturers or maintainers of packaging who are failing or who are likely to fail to meet the requirements of regulations. Where offences under the regulations have been committed by corporations with the consent, connivance or through the neglect of directors, managers, secretaries, etc, the individual(s) in question are liable with the company, see RMRTA 1991, s 6.

Further reading

Burholt, GD, and Martin, A, *The Regulatory Framework for Storage and Disposal of Radioactive Wastes in Member States of the European Community* (1988) Graham and Trotman.
Cheyne, I, and Purdue, M, 'Fitting Definition to Purpose: The Search for a Satisfactory Definition of Waste' (1995) 7 JEL 149.
Commission of the European Communities, *Environment 2010: Our Future, Our Choice*, Sixth Environmental Action Programme, COM (2001) 31 Final.
de la Fayette, L, 'The OSPAR Convention Comes into Force: Continuity and Progress' (1999) 14 International Journal of Marine and Coastal Law 247.
Department of the Environment: 'Licensing of Waste Management Facilities', Waste Management Paper No 4 (1994).
Department of the Environment: 'Licensing of Metal Recycling Sites', Waste Management Paper No 4A (1995).
Department of the Environment: 'Polychlorinated Biphenyls', Waste Management Paper No 6 (1994).
Department of the Environment: 'Landfill Completion', Waste Management Paper No 26A (1993).
Department of the Environment: 'Landfill Design, Construction and Operational Practice', Waste Management Paper No 26B (1995).
Department of the Environment, Transport and the Regions, *Code of Practice on Litter and Refuse*, 1999.
Department of the Environment, Transport and the Regions, *Managing Radioactive Waste Safely: Proposals for Developing a Policy for Managing Solid Radioactive Waste in the UK*, September 2001.
Department of the Environment, Transport and the Regions, *UK Strategy for Radioactive Discharges 2001-2020*, June 2000.
Department of the Environment, Transport and the Regions, *Waste Strategy 2000: England and Wales*, Cm 3040, May 2000.
Environment Agency, *Statutory Guidance on the Regulation of Radioactive Discharges into the Environment from Nuclear Licensed Sites*, 2000.

Her Majesty's Inspectorate of Pollution: 'Disposal Facilities on Land for Low and Intermediate Level Radioactive Wastes: Guidance on Requirements for Authorisation', (1994).

House of Commons Select Committee on the Environment, Session 1985–86 'Radioactive Waste' (1986), and Response to the Report Cmnd 9852 (1986).

House of Commons Select Committee on the Environment: Session 1988–89 'Hazardous Waste Disposal' (1989) and Response to the Report Cm 679 (1989).

House of Commons Select Committee on the Environment, Session 1997-98, *Sustainable Waste Management*.

House of Commons Select Committee on the Environment, Transport and the Regions, Session 2000-2001, *Delivering Sustainable Waste Management*, HC Paper 36.

House of Commons Select Committee on the Environment, Transport and the Regions, Session 1998-99, *Operation of the Landfill Tax*, HC Paper 150.

House of Lords Select Committee on the European Communities 25th Report Session 1989–90 'Paying for Pollution' (1990).

House of Lords Select Committee on the European Communities, Session 1997-98, *Sustainable Landfill*, HL Paper 73.

House of Lords Select Committee on Science and Technology Session 1988–89 4th Report 'Hazardous Waste Disposal'.

Jewell, T, 'The Operation of the Landfill Tax' (1999) 11 ELM 213.

Laurence, D, *Waste Regulation Law*, Butterworths, 2000.

Openshaw, S, Carver, S, and Fernie, J, *Britain's Nuclear Waste: Safety and Siting* (1989) Belhaven.

Parpworth, N, 'The Draft EC Landfill Directive' [1999] JPL 4.

Pocklington, DN, 'Waste Holder Liability' (1996) 8 ELM 101.

Pocklington, D and Pocklington, 'The United Kingdom Landfill Tax – Externalities and External Influences' [1998] JPL 529.

Royal Commission on Environmental Pollution, 17th Report: 'Incineration of Waste', Cm 2181 (1993).

Tromans, S, 'EC Waste Law – A Complete Mess?' (2001) 13 JEL 133.

Tromans, S, 'The difficulties of enforcing Waste Disposal Licence Conditions' (1991) 3 JEL 281.

Vaughan, D, (ed) *Environment and Planning Law* (1991) Butterworths (chapter 9 [Bryce], 10 [Farha], 11 [Hawkins], 12 [Bos], 13 [Freeman]).

Chapter 15

Contaminated land

The contamination of land has long been a consequence – intended or not – of land use. When contamination was on a small scale or transient, its impacts could be ignored or avoided; when contamination began to cause more appreciable environmental problems, then it became the subject of indirect controls, of waste disposal or water pollution for example; and when contamination presented hurdles to effective land use, then planning and related powers were put in place to anticipate future problems.[1] But the historic contamination of land has, until recently, not itself been the subject of effective, formalised legal attention.

There are three, interconnected sets of reasons for this: practical, political, and legal. On a practical level, historic contamination of land has often been concealed by established, subsequent uses. For example, old tar pits have been built over, old power stations have been subsumed into their replacements, and the operational land of utilities is often still used for contemporary operational purposes. Similarly, when pressures on urban space have been less intense, suspicions of gross contamination have resulted in the avoidance of known contaminated 'hot spots'. This has been coupled with limitations in our scientific understanding of the impacts of land contamination, particularly those which are long-term or indirect.

Controls over historic contamination are also politically controversial. As a further state intervention affecting property, any liability regime would have important implications for land use in general, and the property market in particular. This explains in large part the abandonment of attempts in the early 1990s to introduce registers of potentially contaminative uses of land under what was section 143 of the Environmental Protection Act 1990. The introduction of this provision followed a number of parliamentary reports, and a policy statement by the then government.[2] In an effort to avoid the costs of intrusive or intensive site investigation, EPA 1990, s 143 provided for the compilation by local authorities of registers, not of contaminated land as such, but of potentially contaminating uses of land. Although intended to create an information base to inform the property market, which could then account for contamination through the setting of property prices, the system was heavily criticised.

1 As in the case of derelict or disused land: eg, DoE Circular 21/87.
2 'Toxic Waste', HC Paper 22 (Session 1988-89); *Contaminated Land,* HC Paper 170 (Session 1989-90); *Paying for Pollution*, HL Paper 84 (Session 1989-90); *Contaminated Land* Cm 1161.

Those criticisms included: putative limitations on local authority resources to inspect, record or monitor records of uses or sites themselves; inconsistencies and inadequacies in information that was actually available about historic uses of land; the blighting effect of inclusion of land within a register even though it may not be contaminated as a matter of fact; the absence of provisions allowing for the removal of sites from the register; and the lack of any provision for action to be required as a result of inclusion of land on the register. As a consequence of these criticisms, EPA 1990, s 143 was repealed having never being brought into force.[3]

The political controversy surrounding contaminated land liabilities was compounded after the abortive enactment of EPA 1990, s 143 by further parliamentary studies, in combination with developments at European level and a growing awareness of international experience. Of particular significance was the European Commission's Green Paper *Remedying Environmental Damage*.[4] The Commission's paper was broad. Not only did it assess the need for Community action, but it also made a preliminary assessment of the relative merits of different liability models: from joint compensation schemes, to fault-based and strict liability possibilities. Despite the UK government's rejection of the need for any Community intervention at all, the concerns of the property market in this country were not alleviated and legislative reform became simply a matter of time. The Commission's own proposals have emerged in substantially truncated form[5] but the UK's own agenda has continued independently.

The third set of reasons for slow legal change relates to the legal complexity of addressing land contamination. This has two aspects. First, although systematic controls are of recent origin, land contamination has been susceptible to some legal control for years. Prospective controls over pollution and land use clearly have implications for creating new contamination (waste disposal and management powers, industrial pollution control, town and country planning), and this remains the case.[6] The duties and powers of local authorities under the statutory nuisance regime have also had the potential to apply to land contamination giving rise to harm (or potential harm) to the environment or to human health, whilst civil liabilities for damage caused by past contamination may also arise at common law. This makes the background legal framework unusually complex.

Secondly, legal complexity is inherent in a systematic liability regime. Liabilities for the consequences of land contamination are essentially retrospective in effect: they impose liabilities for the present or future impacts of past activities. Such liabilities can therefore be contrasted with other pollution controls, which are essentially prospective. This is a key part of the background to legal controls over contaminated land, and affects a series of other questions. For example: what in fact should amount to 'contamination' in the first place? How are cases of 'disappeared polluters' to be dealt with? Should contamination arising from activities that were lawful at the time they were carried on give rise to current liability? Should the purposes of liability be environmental clean-up, compensation for actual damage, or some other measure? How is liability to be apportioned, if at all, between successive polluters, land owners or occupiers? Should liabilities fall on public authorities in any situations, and if so, which?[7]

3   Environment Act 1995, Sch 24.
4   Com (1993) 47 final; see the Report of the House of Lords Select Committee on the European Communities, HL Paper 10 (Session 1993-94), and the government's response (8 October 1993: Appendix IV of HL Paper 10.
5   European Commission White Paper, *Environmental Liability*, Com (2000) 66 final, 9 February 2000.
6   For example, the new pollution prevention and control system expressly extends to emissions to land; Pollution Prevention and Control (England and Wales) Regulations 2000, reg 2(1).
7   See generally Lewis, 'Contaminated Land: The New Regime of the Environment Act 1995' [1995] JPL 1007.

A THE CURRENT POSITION IN OUTLINE

The most recent culmination of these debates is the introduction of a new liability regime for the compulsory clean-up – or 'remediation' – of contaminated land, where the extent of liability is the cost of environmental remediation itself. The controls are set out in the Environmental Protection Act 1990, Part IIA inserted by the Environment Act 1995, s 57. Those controls, with accompanying regulations and both statutory and non-statutory guidance, came into force in England on 1 April 2000, in Scotland on 14 July 2000, and in Wales on 1 July 2001. The new liabilities are 'retrospective' in form, although in a qualified sense, as their key trigger is either current 'harm' or the likelihood of such harm. But this characteristic, coupled with the long gestation of the regime itself, has not lessened the controversy with which they have been received.

Despite that controversy and (ironically) the corresponding emphasis in this chapter on the new controls, it is crucially important to keep them in perspective, for two main reasons. First, both EPA 1990, Part IIA itself and international experience with land liability regimes suggest that only a small proportion of potentially contaminated sites pose an immediate threat to human health and the environment. Equally, the formal guidance issued under EPA 1990, Part IIA[8] exhibit a policy preference for reliance on voluntary clean-up measures, or steps other than formal reliance on EPA 1990, Part IIA[9] – a preference compounded by features of the new regime itself.[10] For example, in the case of a site that it to be redeveloped, the key concern will be to negotiate planning mechanisms which incorporate satisfactory site quality in a completed scheme. It has long been the case that actual or threatened contamination can be a material planning consideration that should be taken into account both in the preparation of development plans and in the determination of individual planning applications.[11] Practical issues will therefore arise as to the relationship between EPA 1990, Part IIA and other controls.

The second reason for keeping the new regime in perspective is that it is underpinned by three core principles which will profoundly affect the circumstances in which mandatory remediation can be required, and the extent of that remediation when it does take place.

Core principles

The first principle on which the new regime is based is that of 'suitability for use': remedial action is only warranted where contamination poses unacceptable actual or perceived risks to health or the environment, and there is a cost-effective means to remediate it, taking into account the actual or intended use of the site.[12] Consequently, even where land is remediated, it will be made fit only for uses actually or likely to be affected by it. This can be contrasted with approaches formerly adopted in, for example, the Netherlands or the United States, whose 'multi-functionality' standard required land to be remediated sufficiently to safely accommodate any use at all. One purpose of the UK approach is to minimise regulatory intervention and mandatory clean-up, and the consequential harmful impacts of liabilities on the property market as a whole.

Secondly, the 'polluter pays' principle applies to contaminated land just as elsewhere in environmental policy, albeit in rather general terms.[13] The normal rule under

8   Annex 3 to DETR Circular 02/2000: 'the Guidance'.
9   Eg Annex I, paras 16-19 and 27.
10   Eg EPA 1990, s 78H: see further below.
11   PPG 23, *Planning and Pollution Control*, 1994, para 15.4; *Cheshire County Council v Secretary of State for the Environment and Rathbone* [1996] JPL 410.
12   The Guidance, Annex 1, paras 9-15.
13   'Remedying Environmental Damage', HL Paper 10 (Session 1993-94).

EPA 1990, Part IIA is that the original polluter remains liable, where they can be found, unless the statute, taken with the relevant regulations and guidance, provides otherwise.

The third principle is that, wherever possible, the property market can and should be relied upon to address contamination problems, and to resolve them. Not only should development proposals entail remediation where necessary – thus incorporating environmental costs as a normal part of the financial calculations accompanying development activity – but the terms on which property has changed hands may also be relevant in determining who is liable for remediating a contaminated site, and to what extent. The effective pursuit of this principle clearly depends on a range of factors, such as the date of transfer, the extent of information known, available or sought, and the discoverability of contamination. Thus, a compromise has had to be struck: where the price paid for contaminated land reflects any residual post-transfer liability, then it has been concluded that, generally speaking, liability based on current ownership is consistent with the 'polluter pays' principle.[14] The practical implications of this – not least for conveyancers – have been acknowledged in the circulation by the Law Society of a 'warning card' to all solicitors drawing their attention to the new regime, and the need to take it into account in making enquiries in property transactions, and negotiating terms.[15] That advice suggests that solicitors should consider whether contamination is in fact an issue in every property transaction.

Part IIA and planning controls

The first stage in appreciating the role of the new regime is to consider it in context, and this logically starts with land use planning. Planning policy favours the re-use of previously-developed urban areas – 'brownfield sites' – in preference to 'greenfield' sites,[16] and this will tend to make the development of urban contaminated land a policy priority.[17] The net effects are threefold, in that the planning system seeks: to deal with actual or perceived threats from land contamination to health, safety and the environment; to bring such land back into beneficial use; and to minimise avoidable pressure on greenfield sites.[18]

Development plans have two roles in this respect, deriving from the basic requirement that they include policies on the improvement of the physical environment.[19] The first is preventive: they should seek to avoid future contamination by identifying locations for potentially polluting development, and keeping inconsistent uses of land separate. The second function of development plans is more obviously curative, as they should also include policies for the reclamation and possible use of contaminated land.[20] Local plans (and Part II of UDPs) should include detailed criteria which will be applied in determining planning applications for the development of land which is known to be, or may be contaminated. This clearly places a premium on information, the collection of which falls mainly to the developer. Where the nature and extent of contamination is known, or a site's history suggests a risk of contamination, then LPAs are advised by central guidance to set out-site-specific proposals for use of that land so that it may

---

14   Eg Government Response to the Commission Green Paper, *Remedying Environmental Damage*, para 3.14; EPA 1990, s 78F(6).
15   Law Society, 2001.
16   PPG 12, paras 4.7-4.15; PPG 1, *General Policy and Principles* (1997), paras 7 and 21-2.
17   PPG 12, *Development Plans* (1999), para 4.5.
18   PPG 23, para 4.3.
19   TCPA 1990, ss 12(3A), 31(3) and 36(3).
20   PPG 23, Annex 10.

be readily identifiable to landowners and prospective purchasers or developers.[21] If planning permission is subsequently granted, responsibility for safe development and secure occupancy of the site remains with the developer – a fact of which they will normally be notified. Where information is less complete, LPAs may require detailed site surveys to be submitted with any proposals, with remediation plans to address contamination should it be discovered. The potential disincentive effect of this – contrary to policy – is an obvious countervailing consideration, both in plans and in respect of individual applications.

When it comes to development control – the consideration of individual planning applications – the underlying policy and legal principle is that planning controls should not be operated so as to duplicate controls which are the statutory responsibility of other bodies.[22] Close coordination between LPAs and other regulators, particularly the Environment Agency, is therefore required. The existence of other controls may be a material planning consideration,[23] and LPAs must assume that those controls will be applied and enforced properly. The particular relationship between planning control and EPA 1990, Part IIA is more uncomfortable than this, however. For example, mandatory remediation cannot be required under the new regime where a local authority is satisfied that appropriate things are being, or will be, done by way of remediation without service of a notice.[24] There may be an issue as to whether a planning permission will actually be implemented, but the preference for planning *before* EPA 1990, Part IIA is clearly apparent. The preferred policy phraseology is therefore that planning controls should complement and not substitute for pollution control arrangements.[25]

At a practical level, the need to gather information will also affect the economics of development proposals. Detailed site inspection requirements will be costly: one option may therefore be to grant an outline permission for the purposes of investigation, with reserved matters being conditional on any consequential remediation being completed satisfactorily.[26] However, where it is known or strongly suspected that a site is contaminated to an extent which would adversely effect the proposed development or statutory requirements, then an investigation of the hazards and proposals for remedial measures will normally be required before an application is determined.[27] Either way, helpful 'triggers' for appropriate action are provided in technical guidance, such as: *Guidance on the Assessment and Redevelopment of Contaminated Land*;[28] *Remedial Treatment for Contaminated Land*;[29] *The Investigation of Potentially Contaminated Sites – A Code of Practice*;[30] and *Model Procedures for the Management of Contaminated Land*.[31] Each of these documents places particular emphasis on the need for the most rigorous measures to be taken where residential development is proposed.

Site-specific control will be elaborate. If remedial action is required to safeguard future users or occupiers of a site or neighbouring land, or to protect any buildings or services, then planning conditions should be imposed specifying the measures to be carried out. These will clearly have to take account of what could be required under EPA 1990,

21 PPG 23.
22 PPG 23, para 1.3.
23 *Gateshead Metropolitan Borough Council v Secretary of State for the Environment* [1995] JPL 432.
24 EPA 1990, s 79H(5)(b).
25 PPG 23, para 4.4.
26 Graham, *Contaminated Land*, p 14.
27 PPG 23, Annex 10, paras 6-8.
28 Inter-Departmental Committee on the Redevelopment of Contaminated Land ('ICRCL'), Guidance Note 59/83 (2nd edn).
29 Construction Industry Research and Information Association.
30 July 1999, British Standards Institution.
31 DETR.

Part IIA, otherwise they may be insufficient to remove the land from the application of the new regime. In cases of slight contamination, conditions may require postponement of development until completion of full investigation and assessment, and also the incorporation of appropriate remedial measures. In many case, conditions will require notification of the planning authority in the event that any, or different, contamination is discovered in the course of development.[32]

Planning obligations may complement conditions in appropriate cases, for example, to provide further safeguards to site remediation works by way of monitoring, insurance, or bond or warranty arrangements continuing beyond the completion of the development itself. The normal rule is that conditions cannot be used in this way.[33] It is also likely that remediation under EPA 1990, Part IIA will only infrequently extend to the sort of monitoring possible under generic planning controls.[34] Obligations may also be used where alternative powers could only apply after future environmental harm has been caused, rather than to prevent such harm arising.[35] Where this may not be sufficient, planning permission should be refused.

Part IIA and waste management controls

The practical connection between EPA 1990, Part IIA and waste management controls (see chapter 14) is obvious: the disposal of waste to land involves direct pollution of land itself, and that pollution can arise from activities whether or not they are subject to waste management licensing under EPA 1990, Part II. The legal relationship between the contaminated land regime and waste controls is not in principle dependent on the distinction between licensed and unlicensed activities: it is not as simple as saying that licensed activities fall under waste controls, and unlicensed activities fall under EPA 1990, Part IIA. The starting point is that EPA 1990, Part IIA does not apply in relation to any land in respect of which there is for the time being in force a site licence under EPA 1990, except where the reason for the land being classified as 'contaminated land' under EPA 1990, Part IIA is attributable to something *other* than a breach of conditions of that licence or the carrying on of activities that are licensed.[36] The effect of this complex section is that contamination that results from either a breach of a waste management licence, or licensed activity itself, is subject to waste controls and not to EPA 1990, Part IIA.

It follows that land which is contaminated by reason of activities carried on before a waste management licence took effect would normally be subject to EPA 1990, Part IIA. However, it is important to note that waste management controls do apply in some situations where certain waste-related activities have been carried on, whether or not a licence was in force. For example, certain waste authorities are empowered in certain circumstances to require the removal from land of waste that has been unlawfully deposited.[37] The phrase 'unlawfully deposited' includes deposits made in the absence of a licence, as well as those made in breach of a waste management licence condition. Any such deposit could have given rise to the land becoming 'contaminated' for the purposes of the new regime. However, if this is the case, then EPA 1990, Part IIA will not apply if and to the extent that the powers of the relevant waste authority 'may be exercised'.[38] This is another example of a preference for specific controls to the exclusion of EPA 1990, Part IIA, which thereby becomes the mechanism of last resort.

32   'Contaminated Land', HC Paper 22 (Session 1996-97).
33   Eg [1995] JPL 1075.
34   The Guidance, paras C.61-63 and C.68-69.
35   Eg [1994] JPL 1124.
36   EPA 1990, s 78YB(2).
37   EPA 1990, s 59 – a 'waste removal notice'.
38   EPA 1990, s 78YB(3).

Three points should be made, however. First, the deposits of waste to which EPA 1990, s 59 applies only became 'unlawful' on 1 April 1992. Deposits made before that date therefore cannot be subject to EPA 1990, s 59, and so Part IIA will apply. Secondly, those deposits must actually have been of 'waste' in a technical sense (although given the breadth of the definition of waste, this may not be too high a hurdle). If this is not so then, even if the deposit was made after 1 April 1992, EPA 1990, s 59 cannot apply and Part IIA will. Thirdly, the exclusion of EPA 1990, Part IIA does not follow from the actual exercise of EPA 1990, s 59 powers, but merely from the legal possibility that they *may* be exercised. In the absence of any decided case, the extent of this important ambiguity remains unclear.

EPA 1990, Part IIA and statutory nuisance controls

One political justification for the new regime was that it is merely a 'clarification' of liabilities which would otherwise exist in any event under statutory nuisance controls.[39] Despite this gross over-simplification, there does remain the possibility of an overlap between EPA 1990, Part IIA and cases of statutory nuisance.[40] By way of resolution, the commencement of the new regime was accompanied by a truncation of statutory nuisance to avoid the possibility of any duplication. EPA 1990 was amended to declare that no matter shall constitute a statutory nuisance to the extent that it consists of, or is caused by, land being in a 'contaminated state'.[41]

The key point to note is that this exclusion is rather wider than the application of EPA 1990, Part IIA itself. Land is only in a 'contaminated state' if it is in such condition by reason of substances in, on or under the land that harm is being caused or there is a possibility of harm being caused, or pollution of controlled waters is being, or is likely to be, caused.[42] EPA 1990, Part IIA, by comparison, applies only where relevant harm, or the possibility of such harm, is 'significant'. Conversely, however, the 'harm' threshold is quite high, and so there may be situations where (for example) offence to the senses still constitutes a statutory nuisance because it does not amount to 'harm'.[43] On the face of EPA 1990, however, a gap has been created between the two systems. The practical significance of this cautious drafting must remain to be seen.

B THE NEW REGIME

The new regime is set out in a combination of EPA 1990, Part IIA itself, regulations made for England, Scotland and Wales,[44] and both binding and advisory guidance (depending on context) issued by the Secretary of State.[45] References hereafter are to the English regime, the principal features of the which are:
(a) Definition of 'contaminated land', including a category of 'special sites' which because of their greater polluting potential are the responsibility of the Environment Agency rather than local authorities (EPA 1990, s 78A).
(b) Creation of a 'duty of inspection' on local authorities to identify contaminated land and special sites, and to designate the latter (EPA 1990, ss 78B-78D).

39 HL Debates, 20 March 1995, col 1054.
40 See above.
41 EPA 1990, s 79(1A).
42 EPA 1990, s 79(1B).
43 The Guidance, Annex 1, para 63.
44 The almost identical SIs 2000/227, 2000/178 and SI 2001/2197, respectively.
45 For England, in DETR Circular 02/2000.

(c)   Creation of duties on the Agency and local authorities to require the remediation of contaminated land in certain cases and to certain extents, including provision for the service of 'remediation notices' (EPA 1990, ss 78E, 78H, 78J and 78K).

(d)   Determination of the 'appropriate person' to bear responsibility for remediation and for the allocation of liabilities between different persons (EPA 1990, ss 78F and 78K).

(f)   Consultation between authorities and the Agency, and with persons who may be 'appropriate persons' in respect of potential remediation requirements (EPA 1990, ss 78H and 78YA).

(g)   Offences for contravening Part IIA and procedural matters, including appeals and authorities' powers to undertake remediation, including in default (EPA 1990, ss 78L-78P).

(h)   Compilation of a register in respect of functions carried out under Part IIA (EPA 1990, ss 78S-78V).

C   WHAT IS 'CONTAMINATED' LAND?

It is important to distinguish 'derelict' from 'contaminated' or 'polluted' land. Derelict land is that which is 'derelict, neglected or unsightly', ie damaged by industrial or other development so as to be incapable of beneficial use without treatment. Such land falls within the terms of the Derelict Land Act 1982, and may not necessarily be contaminated.

The 1995 definition of 'contaminated' land centres on the presence in land of substances in, on or under it which may be likely to cause, or are causing *significant* harm or the pollution of controlled waters (see chapter 20 for 'controlled waters'). 'Harm' means 'harm to the health of living organisms or other interference with the ecological systems of which they form part' or 'harm to human property', while 'substance' means 'any natural or artificial substance whether in solid or liquid form or in the form of a gas or vapour'.[46] These apparently very broad definitions are substantially truncated by the Guidance. Further, the key determinations of whether harm is 'significant', or there is a 'significant possibility' of such harm, or that water pollution is 'likely' are all to be made in accordance with the Guidance,[47] thereby 'delegating' the definition to the Secretary of State.

This is a definition closer in concept to 'polluted' than to the previously accepted definition of 'contamination' which had simply centred on the presence in the environment of particular substances without any judgment as to their harmfulness. The EPA 1990 is thus confined to land which is actually causing or which poses a threat of harm.

What does not feature in EPA 1990, nor the regulations or guidance, is any precise numerical basis upon which either 'harm' or 'significance' is to be assessed. Rather, a process of risk assessment is provided which will enable judgments to be made in individual cases.[48] 'Risk' in this case is defined as a combination of the probability or frequency of occurrence of a defined hazard (eg, exposure to a property of a substance with the potential to cause harm) and the magnitude (including the seriousness) of the consequences.[49] In this way, the dangers associated with particular contaminants are assessed against the current use of land, thereby embedding the principle of suitability for use into the definition of contaminated land itself.

46   EPA 1990, s 78A(2), (4), (9).
47   EPA 1990, s 78A(2), (5).
48   The Guidance, Ch A, Pt 2.
49   The Guidance, para A.9.

The risk assessment process hinges upon individual 'pollution linkages': key physical properties whose presence may identify land as being contaminated, and on which remediation activity will subsequently focus. Identifying a pollution linkage is the first stage in determining whether a particular piece of land is actually 'contaminated' under the regime. That identification requires the presence of three elements: a *contaminant*, a substance which is in, on or under the land and which has the potential to cause harm or to cause pollution of controlled waters; a *receptor*, either a living organism, or group of living organisms, an ecological system or piece of property which is in a defined category and which is being or could be harmed by a contaminant, or controlled waters which are being or could be polluted by a contaminant; and a *pathway*, one or more routes or means by or through which a receptor is being, or could be, exposed to or affected by a contaminant.[50] The provision in the Guidance of an exclusive list of receptors is the most striking truncation of the regime's otherwise broad reach. Receptors are: human beings; any ecological system, or living organism forming part of such a system, which is within a location subject to any of eight statutory or non-statutory conservation designations (including sites of special scientific interest, actual and proposed sites under European conservation legislation, and nature reserves); property in the form of crops, produce grown domestically or on allotments for consumption, livestock, other owned or domesticated animals, and wild animals which are the subject of shooting or fishing rights; and property in the form of buildings.[51] If none of these receptors is present, then land cannot be 'contaminated' and therefore cannot be made subject to compulsory remediation.

The second stage in defining contaminated land is determining whether 'harm' to the relevant receptor is 'significant', if there is a 'significant possibility' of such harm, or if pollution of controlled waters is being caused or is likely.[52] A further – and, again, exclusive – list is provided in the Guidance of the harm to each receptor that is to be regarded as significant. For example, 'significant harm' includes: for people, death, disease, serious injury, genetic mutation, birth defects or the impairment of reproductive functions ('human health effects'); for ecological systems in designated areas, and living organisms forming part of them, harm with results in irreversible or other substantial adverse change in its functioning within any substantial part of that location, or harm affecting any species of special interest to the extent that it endangers the long-term maintenance of its population at that location ('ecological system effects'); for property in the form of livestock or such like, death, disease or other serious physical damage, or a substantial diminution in yield (minimum 20%) from such causes ('animal or crop effects'); and for property in the form of buildings, structural failure, substantial damage or substantial interference with any rights of occupation ('building effects').

The third stage arises in those cases where actual significant harm is not shown, but where there may be a 'significant possibility' of such harm arising. This requires an assessment to be made of the probability or frequency of the occurrence of circumstances which would lead to significant harm being caused.[53] A range of factors must therefore be considered, including the nature and degree of harm, the susceptibility of receptors to which the harm might be caused, and the timescale within which the harm might occur. This is a very subjective approach, and (once again) not a numerical one. The professional judgement of the person making the assessment is therefore an important factor in both the process of determination, and the outcome. As before, the

---

50   The Guidance, paras A.9-21.
51   The Guidance, para A.24 and Table A.
52   EPA 1990, s 78A(2).
53   The Guidance, paras A.27-32.

test remains the current use of the land in question. However, in an important policy elaboration, this includes any use which is 'likely' to be made of it, or the use which is consistent with any existing planning permission or which is otherwise lawful in planning terms.[54]

The fourth, and final, stage in defining contaminated land is subject to very little guidance: where substances are causing, or likely to cause, water pollution. Indeed, the DETR took the view that EPA 1990 does not permit it to provide guidance on what constitutes 'pollution of controlled waters'[55] and so there is none. Although statutory amendment is now envisaged, the Guidance suffices with the observation that 'likely' means more likely than not,[56] hence the test is the balance of probabilities.

In some case there will be a further classification step, as local authorities are also required to consider whether contaminated land constitutes a 'special site'.[57] The remediation of special sites falls under the supervision of the Environment Agency rather than the local authority, and so a delicate institutional relationship can come into play, particularly in controversial cases (the relevant body is the 'enforcing authority'). This is particularly so because of the features which distinguish special sites from other contaminated land. A special site may only actually be notified if it falls into a class prescribed in regulations. In preparing those regulations, the Secretary of State must have (had) regard to two factors: whether the harm or pollution arising from a special site will be 'serious' (as opposed to 'significant' in other cases); and whether the Agency is likely to have expertise in dealing with the type of harm in question.[58] Special sites will therefore often be the most contaminated sites, or those whose remediation requires particular, specialist skills. The regulations actually made prescribe three categories of special sites: certain serious water pollution cases, seeking to ensure a consistency of approach between contaminated land and water pollution, where the Agency is also the principal regulator;[59] industrial cases, where land is or has been used for industrial activities that either pose special remediation problems, or which are subject to defined regulatory controls;[60] and defence cases, where contamination involves either the Ministry of Defence or visiting forces.[61] Although closed landfills are not directly required to be designated as special sites, many of them are likely to fall within one of these classes in practice.

What these matters of definition do not address is the *process* by which designation of contaminated land, or notification of special sites, is actually to come about.

D IDENTIFYING CONTAMINATED LAND

Local authorities (ie London boroughs, district and unitary authorities in England and Wales) are, under EPA 1990, s 78B, to cause their areas to be inspected from time to time for the purpose of identifying contaminated land and identifying possible special sites. In carrying out these tasks, authorities are to act in accordance with ministerial guidance. On identifying land they conclude is contaminated authorities must inform (a) the Agency; (b) the landowner; (c) any person appearing to be in whole/part occupation of the land; (d) each person who is an 'appropriate person', ie a person

---

54   The Circular, Annex 1, para 11: notable because this is not guidance under the Act.
55   The Circular, Annex 1, para 2.9.
56   The Guidance, para A.36.
57   EPA 1990, s 78C.
58   EPA 1990, s 78C(10).
59   See chapter 20.
60   Eg, IPC/IPPC.
61   Contaminated Land (England) Regulations 2000, SI 2000/227 ('the Regulations'), regs 2, 3.

determined to bear responsibility for remediation (see further below). Service of notice on an 'appropriate person' does not prevent later service on others who subsequently appear 'appropriate'.

The duty to inspect is pro-active, and must follow a 'strategic approach', details of which are set out in the Guidance.[62] Written strategies were required to be in place (in England) by 20 June 2001, and in general terms these seek out the worst potential problems first. This does not mean that those strategies will yet have been given complete effect, of course, but it does mean that inspection will focus on the most likely problems first, and that inspection resources will be proportionate to the seriousness of any actual or potential risks.

There may also be an uneasy relationship between local authorities and the Agency. Primary responsibility for notifying the identification of contaminated land lies with local authorities, and this extends to the identification of special sites. At first blush, then, local authorities are the gatekeepers to the exercise by the Agency of its responsibilities over special sites. A range of scenarios can be envisaged where disputes could emerge. For example, a local authority may be reluctant to cede detailed regulation of a site in its area to the Agency. Conversely, an authority may be all too keen to shift responsibility to the Agency of a marginal site, particularly if there is a risk of default by a person primarily responsible for remediation. Anticipating these inter-authority disputes, the regime provides for a collaborative approach to be adopted by local authorities and the Agency. For example, where identification of a special site is anticipated, then the Agency's advice must be sought.[63] Equally, the Agency will have been consulted by authorities on their inspection strategy,[64] and should receive notification of the designation of all contaminated land. If nothing else, this equips the Agency to raise cases of particular concern with a local authority. More formally, default powers are also in place. So, if a site is designated as a special site, the Agency may formally disagree;[65] if a site is not so designated then the Agency itself may take the initiative.[66] In either case, if there is a continuing disagreement, then the matter will be referred to the Secretary of State for resolution.

The notification of a contaminated site will be highly technical: a scientific and technical assessment is required in every case, and very precise details of the basis for notification must be given, treating each pollutant linkage separately, and element-by-element. It seems very likely that established numerical guidelines on pollution concentrations will feature in notifications,[67] although this does jar somewhat with the qualitative, risk assessment process intrinsic to the regime.[68] Further, there is no formal appeal mechanism against notification. This notable absence is mitigated in two ways. First, normal indirect means of challenge remain available, such as judicial review or complaints to the local government ombudsman. In cases likely to involve substantial remediation costs, there must be a high probability of applications for judicial review, which at least in the early days could include general challenges to the regime itself, perhaps on human rights grounds. Secondly, the grounds of appeal against formal remediation requirements (see below) are very broad. In particular, they include failure by a local authority to comply with the Guidance in determining that land appears to be

62 The Guidance, chapter B.
63 EPA 1990, s 78C(3).
64 The Guidance, para B.11.
65 EPA 1990, s 78D(1).
66 EPA 1990, s 78C(4).
67 Eg, ICRCL trigger values.
68 Tromans & Turrell-Clarke, *Contaminated Land: The New Regime* 2000.

contaminated land, and unreasonably identifying all or any of the land as being contaminated land.[69]

E THE REMEDIATION PROCEDURE

Where contaminated land has been identified or a special site designated then the enforcing authority is normally required to serve a 'remediation notice' on each 'appropriate' person' specifying what that person is to do by way of remediation, and within what period.[70] Different requirements may be imposed on different people, in which case the proportion of the costs of remediation that each person is to bear must also be stated.[71] However, only such measures may be included in a remediation notice as the authority considers reasonable, having regard to the likely cost and the seriousness of the harm (or pollution of controlled waters) in question.[72] This, once again, qualifies the otherwise very broad definitions found (this time) elsewhere in EPA 1990, Part IIA. Of particular note is the definition of 'remediation', which is extremely wide. It means: doing anything for assessing the condition of relevant land, adjacent land, affected controlled waters, doing works or carrying out operations *or* taking steps in relation to such land or waters to prevent, minimise, remedy or mitigate the effects of any relevant significant harm or pollution of controlled waters, *or* restoring such land or waters to their previous state, *or* inspecting such land or water subsequently to keep their condition under review.[73] This definition therefore encompasses every stage from inspection, through active site treatment, to post-treatment monitoring. What a remediation notice may *not* do, however, is impede or prevent the making of a consented discharge under the Water Resources Act 1991, or (generally) relate to contamination attributable to radiation.[74]

It is important to bear in mind that the physical process of remediation will not be static. For example, the information available at each stage will by supplemented by work in progress, and will therefore invariably change. For example, it can be envisaged that detailed inspection under a remediation notice may render proposed site treatment unnecessary, or insufficient. In such cases, there is no express limitation on the duty of a local authority to serve consecutive notices, relating to successive stages in the 'remediation' of a particular site.[75] This is endorsed by the Circular, albeit only by implication.[76] The difficulty, of course, is that this gives rise to an on-going, perhaps indeterminate, period within which an 'appropriate person' may be exposed to liability under successive notices. On the other hand, a notice which requires site treatment, where that treatment is revealed by preparatory investigation to be unnecessary, would also be legally questionable. The assumption remains, however, that consecutive notices may be applied to the same appropriate persons in respect of the same site.

The regulations and Guidance complement EPA 1990's circumscription of potential remediation requirements,[77] although this does not include any real substance in terms of remediation standards. Details of each pollution linkage must be included, along with the enforcing authority's reasoning in key respects, including: why the recipient

69   The regulations, reg 7(1).
70   EPA 1990, s 78E(1).
71   EPA 1990, s 78E(2).
72   EPA 1990, s 78E(4), (5).
73   EPA 1990, s 78A(7).
74   EPA 1990, ss 78YB(4), 78YC.
75   Tromans, *The Environment Acts 1990-1995*, 1996.
76   The Circular, paras 6.4-6.5.
77   Eg, reg 4.

is an appropriate person and why those remediation requirements have been imposed. The Guidance on remediation requirements is advisory, rather than binding,[78] and describes a range of methods by which pollution linkages might be broken, and how the reasonableness of remediation can be assessed. The aim will be to ensure that land in its current use is no longer contaminated land, and that the effects of any significant harm or pollution of controlled waters are also remedied. It has been observed elsewhere that remediation requirements may go beyond that which is strictly necessary to remove land from the definition of contaminated land, as 'remediation' includes 'restoring land to its former state',[79] but this does not sit well with the Guidance, which focuses on practicality, effectiveness and durability. The 'reasonableness' of remediation requirements must also be subject to a cost-benefit analysis,[80] which extends beyond 'simple' financial costs.

It is also possible for a remediation notice to require its recipient to do things that (s)he is not entitled to do,[81] such as enter onto a third party's land to carry out remediation. If this is the case, then that third party is required to grant consent, if (other than in an emergency) they have been consulted and (always) subject to a statutory entitlement to compensation.[82]

When a remediation notice may not be served

There are three sets of limitations on the duty of an enforcing authority to serve a remediation notice. The first is procedural. Once contaminated land has been identified or a special site designated, and except in urgent cases, three months must elapse before a notice may be served, during which time the enforcing authority is obliged to 'reasonably endeavour' to consult its intended recipient.[83] This built-in delay was introduced over objections that it would create an opportunity to evade liability, on the basis that such negotiation may obviate the need to serve a notice at all.[84]

The remaining limitations on the duty to require remediation are more permanent. The second is straightforward, and precludes service where other controls apply, or powers could be used, such as waste management powers.[85] The third set of limitations is complex. They give effect to the suitability for use standard and the policy preference for other controls over Part IIA, and also allow for the exercise by enforcing authorities of their own powers in certain cases.[86] Consequently, a remediation notice may not be served where:

(a) the authority is satisfied that nothing could be specified in a notice as being reasonable, having regard to the likely cost and the seriousness of the harm (or pollution of controlled waters) in question;[87]

(b) appropriate things are being, or will be, done without service of a remediation notice;

(c) the enforcing authority would itself be the recipient of the notice; or

(d) the authority is satisfied that its own powers of remediation are exercisable.[88]

---

78   EPA 1990, s 78E(5); the Guidance, chapter C.
79   Lewis [1995] JPL 1007.
80   The Guidance, chapter C, Part 5.
81   EPA 1990, s 78G.
82   EPA 1990, s 78G; the regulations, reg 6, Sch 2.
83   EPA 1990, s 78H(3), (4), (1).
84   *Official Report*, SC B, 23 May 1995, col 328; s 78H(5)(b).
85   EPA 1990, s 78YB: see above.
86   EPA 1990, s 78H(5).
87   EPA 1990, s 78E(4), (5).
88   EPA 1990, ss 78H(5), 78N.

At first glance, these provisions do not preclude the service of a remediation notice simply because the costs of remediation would cause financial hardship to the potential recipient of the notice. Indeed, the identity or financial standing of any person who may be required to pay for any remediation are not relevant in the determination of whether the costs of the action are, or are not, reasonable for the purposes of EPA 1990, s 78E(4).[89] However, the powers of the enforcing authority under s 78N to carry out remediation may become exercisable if it concludes that an appropriate person would suffer 'hardship' if forced to bear remediation costs.[90] Once this conclusion has been reached, an enforcing authority is precluded from serving a remediation notice. Through this indirect means, the potential hardship of an appropriate person may preclude the service of a notice, although it will not affect the remediation requirements ultimately to be applied to a particular site.

The above limitations also potentially create an information gap: an important function of remediation notices is to record the condition of contaminated land, and remediation steps, in a publicly-accessible form; if no remediation notice is served, then this information will not be recorded. This gap is filled by the 'remediation declaration' which must be published if any of the above limitations apply.[91] Generally, this will set out the details that would have been included in a remediation notice, coupled with the reasons why no notice was served, but it will not create any obligations actually to remediate. Finally, and to give ultimate coercive bite to cases of voluntary remediation, or remediation by an enforcing authority itself, a 'remediation statement' must also be issued (in cases (b)-(d) above). This will set out the remediation measures that have been, are being or are expected to be undertaken, by whom, and within what timeframe. The person or body undertaking the remediation is responsible for issuing the statement, and should voluntary measures not in fact take place, the duty to serve a remediation notice is effectively reactivated.[92]

The recipient(s) of a remediation notice

This is one of the most controversial aspects of the new regime. International experience of contaminated land clean-up[93] caused concern in the UK that liability would be directed mainly to those with the most resources: the 'deepest pockets'. The concern was that current landowners and financial institutions might bear the full cost of past activities, largely because of the complexity of tracing former polluters or operators with a more obvious 'moral' responsibility. The potentially dramatic impacts of such an approach on property prices, investment and lending, and development activity were important reasons for commercial and government resistance to the proposed European liability regime. They form just as important a backdrop to the final form of EPA 1990, Part IIA, as they explain the complexity now inherent in identifying the 'appropriate persons' to bear liability for remediation, and how that liability is to be apportioned where there is more than one appropriate person. Indeed, the regime is designed to allow for that identification and apportionment without the need to ask the courts to make liability or apportionment decisions. This is in marked contrast to the United States experience, for example, where litigation on these issues has been extensive: CERCLA initially imposed liability on any and every site 'owner or operator'

89   The Guidance, para C.33.
90   The Guidance, chapter E.
91   EPA 1990, s 78H(6).
92   EPA 1990, s 78H(10).
93   Especially the United State's Comprehensive Environmental Response, Compensation and Liability Act ('CERCLA') and its best-known feature, the 'Superfund'.

who contributed to contamination, leaving different contributors to resolve between themselves disputes over how that liability should be shared.

The UK approach is the creation of a hierarchy of appropriate persons that tempers the 'polluter pays' principle with a policy commitment actually to clean-up the most contaminated sites. It seeks to balance the problems of identifying historic polluters against the mechanics of the property market, and the potentially high cost of clean-up against equitability in making individuals liable, taking into account their ability to pay. That hierarchy comprises two, modified, classes which extend from those who caused pollution at the top, to current occupiers of contaminated land at the bottom.

Attention will focus first on any person who caused or knowingly permitted the substances, or any of the substances, by reason of which the land in question is defined as contaminated land to be in, on or under that land: a 'Class A' appropriate person.[94] A Class A appropriate person is liable to undertake so much of the remediation as is referable to the substance(s) (s)he caused or knowingly permitted to be on the land, but this does include the full costs of remediation in relation to that substance (including its biological or chemical reactions with other things), even if others are partly responsible for the presence of that substance.[95] As we shall see, sharing liabilities in such cases is expressly provided for by detailed guidance,[96] in which case multiple appropriate persons will constitute a 'liability group'. It is the adoption of the phrasing 'cause or knowingly permit' – familiar from other environmental contexts[97] which is the highwater mark within the regime of the polluter plays principle, and it is applied to each separate pollution linkage in turn.

Where, after reasonable inquiry, no person can be found who caused or knowingly permitted a substance to be present, the owner or occupier for the time being of the land is the 'appropriate person' to be served with a remediation notice. Thus an 'innocent' landowner may be made residually liable for remediation costs where the original polluter cannot be found. A person attracting residual liability in this way is a Class B appropriate person.[98] The rationale is straightforward: owners and occupiers only become liable should an original 'polluter' not be located, and even then the regime is likely to operate to impose lesser liabilities the further down the hierarchy an appropriate person is. One example is that the Guidance distinguishes between different types of property interest in elaborating upon what remediation might reasonably be expected of a Class B person: the less significant or permanent a person's property interest, the smaller their contribution to any required remediation is likely to be.[99] Little of assistance is to be found in the definition of 'owner',[100] although mortgagees not in possession are expressly excluded, and 'occupier' is not defined at all.

The relatively simple formal distinction between Class A and Class B persons conceals a more complex reality, as both EPA 1990, Part IIA and the Guidance provide exclusions from, and qualifications to, inclusion within a liability group. The statutory exclusions are threefold. First, a Class B appropriate person cannot be made liable to remediate land which is contaminated by reason of actual or threatened water pollution, or to remediate controlled waters in such cases.[101] In this way the potential liability of Class B appropriate persons is *always* more limited in scope than the potential liability of Class A persons. Secondly, people acting in certain professional capacities are

---

94 EPA 1990, s 78F(2); the Guidance, para D.5(a).
95 EPA 1990, s 78F(3), (9).
96 The Guidance, chapter D.
97 See chapter 20.
98 EPA 1990, s 78F(4); para D.5(b).
99 EPA 1990, paras E.37-49.
100 EPA 1990, s 78A(9).
101 EPA 1990, s 78J(2).

entirely excluded from personal liability under EPA 1990, Part IIA – both Class A and Class B – in certain circumstances.[102] This includes insolvency practitioners, official receivers and accountants in bankruptcy.

Thirdly, in some cases liability is limited in respect of contaminating substances that escape to other land. The starting point here is that a Class A person shall be taken to have caused or knowingly permitted the substances for which (s)he is liable to be in, on or under *other* land to which those substances appear to have escaped.[103] Conversely, the owner or occupier of that other land can only be liable to remediate his own land and not any further land or waters affected by it, *unless* he is also a Class A appropriate person in respect of that land.[104] If, as will often be the case, the original Class A person has sold their interest in the originating land, the liability of their successor in title for escapes will only extend to *escapes* which they themselves have caused or knowingly permitted.[105] This is an important limitation, as the 'knowing permitting' relates to the escape and not to the original contamination. It can be contrasted with the case of a Class A person who knowingly permitted the original contamination, where liability to clean-up escapes is *not* dependent on that person also having knowingly permitted the escape. The general effect of these complex provisions is that where 'knock-on' contamination occurs the original polluter is liable for all consequential remediation, while the owners or occupiers of the knock-on sites are liable only for remediation of their own sites where the original Class A person cannot be found.

It is quite possible that no appropriate person may exist for a particular pollution linkage, either for want of their initial identification or through the application of the statutory exclusions. Such cases give rise to an 'orphan linkage', for which the enforcing authority will normally be responsible.[106] If more than one appropriate person remains after application of the statutory exclusions, then the Guidance provides both further potential exclusions, and (finally) for apportionment of the cost of remediation between two or more remaining appropriate persons.

Multiple liability: non-statutory exclusions, and apportionment

The statutory exclusions from liability are important, but are just part of the picture as the Guidance provides elaborate additional, and determinative exclusions.[107] But there is an important distinction between them. Whereas the statutory exclusions can exclude all appropriate persons (and thus result in an orphan linkage), the non-statutory exclusions cannot: the Guidance can 'pare down' a large liability group, but it will never empty it.[108] It is also possible for two or more appropriate persons to reach an agreement between themselves as to how liability for remediation will be shared, and this will take precedence over the non-statutory exclusions. Such agreements should normally be respected by the enforcing authority in deciding how the costs of remediation will be shared, although an apportionment agreement will be less helpful where a contribution is also to be made to remediation costs by a person who is not a party to it.[109]

102 EPA 1990, s 78X(3).
103 EPA 1990, s 78K(1).
104 EPA 1990, s 78K(3), (4).
105 EPA 1990, s 78K(5).
106 EPA 1990, s 78N; the Guidance, paras D.103-109.
107 EPA 1990, s 78F(6).
108 The Guidance, para D.41(c).
109 The Guidance, paras D.38-9.

The non-statutory exclusions emphasise exclusion from Class A rather than Class B and comprise six 'tests', to be applied sequentially to each separate significant pollution linkage.[110] Exclusion of a person from liability for one linkage does not presuppose their exclusion from any further linkage. The general effect of the tests is to remove from liability persons who fall into Class A through having carried out defined types of action, or whose actions have been affected by others. Their intended purpose is to allocate liability only to those who really are directly responsible for contamination, and who have not yet made any contribution to the costs of its remediation. The exclusions are applied, and responsibility is therefore allocated, according to a hierarchy, with those judged to be least responsible being excluded first. Briefly, the tests are:

1   Excluded activities: persons are excluded if they have, for example, provided loans or insurance, consigned waste, created a tenancy, or provided legal, financial or other defined types of professional advice. It should not be assumed, however, that this list is conclusive of whether someone is, as a matter of law, a Class A person in the first place.

2   Payments made for remediation: those who have met their responsibilities by making payments to another member of the liability group, which would have been sufficient to pay for adequate remediation, are excluded by this test. This includes vendors of land who have reduced its sale price (subject to conditions).

3   Sold with information: a test which provides for the exclusion of a vendor if it would be 'reasonable' for a purchaser who is also a member of the liability group to bear the costs of remediation. Four onerous conditions must be satisfied for this exclusion to apply, and so it is far from automatic in the many cases where contaminated land has been sold at some point.

4   Changes to substances: this test provides for the exclusion of a Class A person when a substance introduced by them results in a significant pollution linkage only because of its interaction with another substance which was later introduced to the land by another person.

5   Escaped substances: where a Class A person would otherwise be liable for the remediation of land which has become contaminated as a result of the escape of substances from other land, that person can be excluded where it can be shown that another member of the liability group was actually responsible for that escape.

6   Introduction of pathways or receptors: in the same way that Test 5 excludes from liability those who are responsible solely because of the introduction by another member of the liability group of a substance, this test excludes liability where that other Class A person introduced other pathways or receptors in the significant pollution linkage in question.

Exclusions of Class B persons are much more brief. Their intention is to exclude from liability those who do not have an interest in the capital value of the land in question, for example, if their interest cannot be assigned or has no market value.[111]

Having applied the non-statutory exclusions, two or more members of a liability group may remain, or particular remediation requirements may involve two or more liability groups (for example, where more than one pollution linkage has been identified in relation to one site, and a particular physical clean-up operation will resolve, or contribute to the resolution, of both linkages). In the case of orphan linkages, there may also be issues about apportionment between a liability group and an enforcing authority. In each of these cases, the actual costs of remediation must be apportioned between a number of appropriate persons. As with exclusion, the Guidance is determinative of

110 The Guidance, paras D.47-72.
111 The Guidance, para D.87.

how liability is to be apportioned[112] – a dramatic contrast with other liability regimes (particular the United States'), although it will certainly not rid apportionment decisions of controversy, as disputes over the interpretation and application of the Guidance are highly likely to arise in practice.

The principle informing the Guidance on apportionment between Class A persons is that their relative responsibility for the presence of a significant pollution linkage should be reflected in their share of remediation costs.[113] That assessment of 'relative responsibility' may be assisted by considering if the circumstances set out in the tests for exclusion might apply, but not so much as actually to justify exclusion. Apportionment between Class B persons should be done either on the basis of discrete areas of the land in question owned or occupied, or in proportion to capital value of their interest in the land in question.[114] Where liability is shared between Class A and Class B persons, then members of the Class A liability group will bear most, if not all, of the remediation costs.[115]

F SUPPLEMENTARY PROVISIONS

Appealing against a remediation notice

EPA 1990, s 78L provides 21 days to appeal against service of a remediation notice to the Magistrates' Court where the notice was served by the local authority and to the Secretary of State where served by the Agency. An extensive list of grounds of appeal is set out in the regulations,[116] which includes both familiar 'procedural' grounds (eg incorrect service or non-compliance with binding guidance) and more complex and unusual matters. These include that the enforcing authority 'unreasonably failed to be satisfied' that appropriate things were being done by way of remediation without service of a notice, and that the authority 'could not reasonably have taken' certain views.[117] Remediation notices are suspended pending final determination or abandonment of an appeal.[118] On appeal a notice *must* be quashed if there is a material defect in it, otherwise the appellate authority may confirm the notice, with or without modification, or may quash it. The existence of the statutory appeal procedure will limit the availability of judicial review to challenge remediation notices, although the types of 'reasonableness' grounds open on appeal bear a certain similarity to aspects of judicial review itself. The opportunity to take human rights points – whether on appeal or by way of judicial review – is not explicit in the regulations, but is clearly open in accordance with general principles.

Offences

Liabilities under the new regime are, as with similar systems, enforceable in two principal ways. First, the regime is underpinned by a series of criminal offences. Secondly, enforcing authorities may themselves carry out works in some cases, and recover their costs from those who would otherwise have been responsible for it. This is invariably

112 EPA 1990, s 78F(6), (7).
113 The Guidance, para D.75.
114 The Guidance, paras D.91-97.
115 The Guidance, para D.99.
116 The regulations, reg 7.
117 The regulations, reg 7(1)(i), (h).
118 The regulations, reg 14(1).

going to be more costly than if an appropriate person does the work for him or herself. A more distant possibility is for an enforcing authority to take proceedings in the High Court, should it conclude that criminal proceedings are inadequate, but this is even less likely given the existence of authorities' default powers. The key provision is that it is under EPA 1990, s 78M an offence to fail without reasonable excuse to comply with any of the requirements of a remediation notice. However, where the cost of remediation has been apportioned under EPA 1990, s 78E(3) it is a defence for one contributor to show that the sole reason why he/she has not complied with requirements is that another contributor has refused or is unable to comply. Failure to comply is a continuing offence. The usual penalty is a fine of level 5 fine for each day of the continuing offence, but where the land is used for industrial, trade or business purposes the maximum level of fine is increased to £20,000 with £2,000 per day for the continuing offence.

Powers of enforcing authorities to carry out remediation

Enforcing authorities' own powers may be used in a number of situations. These include cases of imminent danger of escape and default by the recipient of a remediation notice,[119] but extend to cases: where a written agreement has been made with the authority to carry out remediation on behalf, and at the cost, of an appropriate person; where the authority is precluded from requiring an appropriate person to do something by way of remediation;[120] where the authority would decide not to recover (all of) the costs of remediation; and where no appropriate person has been found after reasonable inquiry, that is, the site is an orphan site.

The power of an enforcing authority to recover the costs it has incurred in exercising its powers of intervention[121] is a powerful incentive on those potentially affected to cooperate with an authority before it does so. That intervention is, of course, the very last resort: it amounts to a gamble by the authority that it will be able to recover its full costs. This is doubly-so, as the enforcing authorities' cost-recovery powers are limited. In particular, an authority must have regard both to the Guidance, and to any hardship that cost recovery may cause.[122] This is very different from determining the reasonableness of remediation itself having regard to cost, where the Guidance makes clear that the financial standing of any person who may be required to pay for remedial action is not relevant.[123] Clean-up standards are therefore set without regard to the ability of an appropriate person to meet them.

In making any decision on costs recovery, the enforcing authority must have regard to two general principles: that the overall result should be as fair and equitable as possible to all who may have to meet the costs of remediation, including taxpayers; and the 'polluter pays' principle, by which the authority should consider the degree and nature of responsibility of the appropriate person for the creation, and continued existence, of the land being identified as contaminated.[124] In general, this will mean that the enforcing authority should seek to recover in full its reasonable costs.[125] Class B appropriate persons receive a measure of special protection against costs recovery from the Guidance, which advises on the reduction of costs in situations where an

119 EPA 1990, s 78N(3)(a), (c).
120 Eg, the limiting provisions concerning escapes or water pollution apply: EPA 1990, ss 78J, 78K.
121 EPA 1990, s 78P.
122 EPA 1990, s 78P(2).
123 The Guidance, para C.33.
124 The Guidance, para E.11.
125 The Guidance, para E.12.

'innocent' owner or occupier took steps to enquire of the state of property which were reasonable at the time of their acquisition, and was unaware of the pollutant ultimately giving rise to contamination.[126]

Registers

As with other environmental regimes, public registers must be maintained by every enforcing authority under EPA 1990, Part IIA, which must be open for free inspection, with the facility to make copies of entries in it.[127] Registers must include details of, inter alia: remediation notices (and appeals), statements and declarations; designations of land as a special site; notification by recipients of remediation notices of 'what they claim has been done' by them by way of remediation;[128] and prescribed matters including details of convictions under EPA 1990, Part IIA, and details of where service of a remediation notice has been precluded. The Agency, as enforcing authority, must also copy entries made on its register to the relevant local authority. What is notably lacking is a process by which a site may be 'signed off' as having been adequately remediated – an absence which has been controversial since the enactment of EPA 1990, Part IIA.[129]

Information shall be excluded from inclusion in registers if, in the opinion of the Secretary of State, its inclusion, or the inclusion of information of that description, would be contrary to the interests of national security.[130] The Secretary of State has very wide powers to direct enforcing authorities as to what information shall be excluded – powers identical to those applying in respect of water registers.[131]

Under EPA 1990, s 78T where information relates to the affairs of an individual or business it cannot be registered without that individual or business's consent provided it is commercially confidential. Information falls into this class if publication would prejudice to an unreasonable degree the individual or business's commercial interests[132]; though information relating only to the ownership/occupation of relevant land or to its value is not confidential.[133] The decision on whether or not information is confidential is for the enforcing authority, subject to an appeal to the Secretary of State. Where the authority consider information might be commercially confidential they must, before registration, give the affected person the opportunity to object to its inclusion. Once information is excluded it remains excluded for four years, after which a further application for its continued exclusion may be made. The Secretary of State may by direction override the confidentiality exception in relation to specific information or descriptions of information where it is considered publication is in the public interest.

Agency reports and guidance

The final public record provision of EPA 1990, Part IIA is that which requires the Agency, from time to time (or as directed), to prepare and publish a report on the state

126 The Guidance, chapter E, Part 6.
127 EPA 1990, ss 78R-78T; the regulations, reg 15 and Sch 3.
128 EPA 1990, s 78R(h), (j).
129 'Contaminated Land', HC Paper 22 (Session 1996-97).
130 EPA 1990, s 78S(1).
131 EPA 1990, s 78S(2); Water Resources Act 1991, s 191A(2) – see chapter ?
132 EPA 1990, s 78T(1).
133 EPA 1990, s 78T(11).

of contaminated land.[134] Local authorities are required to cooperate in the supply of information acquired in the exercise of their functions under EPA 1990, Part IIA.[135] Properly speaking, this is a relatively narrow obligation, as authorities may well acquire relevant information other than in the exercise of powers under this part of the Act. The Agency may also issue guidance to local authorities with respect to the exercise of their powers in relation to *specific* contaminated sites, and authorities are to have regard to such guidance in exercising their functions, save where the guidance is inconsistent with any guidance issued by the Secretary of State. The Secretary of State has a corresponding power to issue site-specific guidance to the Agency in respect of the latter's contaminated land powers.[136]

Further reading

Atkinson, S, 'The Regulatory Lacuna: Waste Disposal and the Clean up of Contaminated Sites' (1991) 3 JEL 265.
Department of the Environment, Transport and the Regions, *Environmental Protection Act 1990: Part IIA – Contaminated Land,* DETR Circular 02/2000, 20 March 2000.
Department of the Environment, Transport and the Regions, Environment Agency, Institute for Environment & Health, *Guidelines for Environmental Risk Assessment and Management,* 2000.
Hellawell, T, *Blackstone's Guide to Contaminated Land*, Blackstone Press, 2000.
House of Commons Select Committee on the Environment, Session 1989-90, *Contaminated Land*, HC Paper 170.
Rossi, H, 'Paying for Our Past – Will We?' (1995) 7 JEL 1.
Steele, J, 'Remedies and Remediation: Foundational Issues in Environmental Liability' (1995) 58 MLR 615.
Tromans, S and Turrell-Clarke, R, *Contaminated Land: The New Regime,* Sweet & Maxwell, 2000.
Waite, A and Jewell, T, *Environmental Law in Property Transactions*, Second Edition, Butterworths, 2001.

---

134 EPA 1990, s 78U.
135 EPA 1990, s 78U(2)-(3).
136 EPA 1990, s 78W.

Legal protection for the atmosphere and integrated controls over major polluting activities

Chapter 16

IPC and IPPC

In this chapter we will be concerned with the regimes which exist to achieve an integrated approach to the control of pollution to *all* environmental media. At the domestic level, a key event in the background to the introduction of a system of integrated pollution control (IPC) was the publication in 1976 of a report by the Royal Commission on Environmental Pollution entitled *Air Pollution Control: An Integrated Approach.*[1] Although the remit of the Royal Commission had originally been limited to a review of the efficacy of the system of air pollution control which existed at the time, in carrying out the review the Royal Commission actually cast its gaze somewhat more widely on the basis that the 'pollution of air cannot be looked at in isolation from pollution of land or water'.[2] In its opinion, by seeking to achieve a reduction in emissions to one environmental medium there was a real possibility that emissions would be increased to other environmental media. In other words, media-specific pollution control did not solve the problem of environmental pollution; it merely pushed it in a different direction. Accordingly, the Royal Commission recommended that to achieve effective pollution control it was necessary to take an integrated approach. It further recommended that the task of acting as regulator for a system of IPC ought to be undertaken by a unified pollution inspectorate rather than the collection of bodies which exercised various pollution control functions at the time.[3]

The government's response to the Royal Commission's recommendations was only published some six years after the original report.[4] When it did finally appear, it was apparent that the government's acceptance of IPC was qualified. Although the logic of the approach was regarded as being 'unassailable', the government was not entirely convinced that introducing IPC would result in clearly identifiable benefits. By 1988, however, the government's position had changed. The publication of a DoE consultation paper on IPC in that year indicated that during the interim, the government had become convinced of the need to introduce IPC. In its opinion such a system would, inter alia: introduce an effective cross-media approach to pollution control leading to a real and lasting overall reduction in pollution; build upon the existing UK approach to pollution control in terms of recognising the need to balance the application and

---

1   Fifth Report of the Royal Commission on Environmental Pollution, (1976, Cmnd 6731).
2   Fifth Report, para 13.
3   These included the Alkali and Clean Air Inspectorate which became Her Majesty's Inspectorate of Pollution (HMIP) on 1 April 1987.
4   *Air Pollution Control*, (1982) Pollution Paper No 18.

cost of technology with effective protection of the environment; be clear and transparent in operation; not impose excessive costs or delays on industry; be practicable and cost-effective to implement; and, be adaptable to future developments in science and technology. These objectives were largely reflected in the Environmental Protection Act 1990 (EPA 1990), Part I (see below).

The discussion thus far has been concerned with the background to the establishment of the IPC regime in this country. It should be noted, however, that the EPA 1990, Part I also provides for Local Authority Air Pollution Control (LAAPC). Whereas IPC is concerned with emissions from the more complex industrial processes to *all* environmental media (land, air and water) and is regulated by the Environment Agency, LAAPC on the other hand is concerned with emissions from the less complex industrial processes to the *atmosphere only*. Emissions to land and water from such processes are therefore dealt with by the Agency.

If domestic integrated pollution control could simply be explained in terms of IPC and LAAPC the task would be relatively straightforward given the overlap between those two regimes (see below). However, the position has become more complicated in the light of developments at the European level which have required legislative action at the domestic level. The advent of the Integrated Pollution Prevention and Control Directive 96/61/EC (the IPC Directive) (see below) and its national implementing measures, the Pollution Prevention and Control Act 1999 (see below) and the Pollution Prevention and Control (England and Wales) Regulations 2000 (see below) has meant that for some years at least, IPC and IPPC will co-exist. In the discussion which follows, therefore, it will be necessary to examine the features of both regimes since although IPPC was based on IPC, in a number of important respects the new regime goes beyond the old regime.

A   THE IPC AND LAAPC SYSTEMS

The EPA 1990 is a wide-ranging measure which deals with a number of important issues which fall under the heading of 'environmental protection'. Although the rag-bag nature of its provisions provoked criticism in some quarters,[5] EPA 1990, Part I, which established the IPC and LAAPC regimes, achieved broad parliamentary approval. Indeed, the then Chairman of the House of Commons Environment Select Committee, Sir Hugh Rossi MP, opined during the course of the debate on the second reading of the Bill that Part I would 'introduce the most stringent form of pollution control to be found in Europe'.[6]

The Environmental Protection Act 1990, Part I

The provisions of the EPA 1990 relating to IPC and LAAPC principally came into force on 1 January 1991.

Emission limits and quality objectives

The EPA 1990, s 3 empowers the Secretary of State to make regulations to establish 'standards, objectives or requirements in relation to particular prescribed processes or

---

5   See the words of the then 'Shadow' Environment Secretary, Bryan Gould MP, during the course of debate on the Bill's second reading: HC Deb, Vol 165, col 50 (15 January 1990).

6   HC Deb, vol 165 at col 59. The correctness of this view is reflected in the fact that IPPC is largely based on IPC.

particular substances'. In particular these regulations may prescribe standard limits for the concentration or amount, generally or in a particular time period, of a substance released from a prescribed process into any environmental medium (air, land, water). The characteristics of releases of substances, measuring and analysis techniques, standards and requirements of prescribed processes may also be set by regulations. Further regulations may establish quality objectives or standards for environmental media in relation to any substances which may be released, mediately or immediately, from any process.

EPA 1990, s 3(5) further empowers the Secretary of State to make and keep under review plans for establishing limits on any substance which may be released into the environment in the UK, to bring about progressive reduction of environmental pollution by limiting releases of substances from prescribed processes, and to improve progressively quality objectives and standards.

Discharge and scope of functions

EPA 1990, s 4, as amended, proceeds to determine the allocation of functions under Part I. As already stated the principal distinction is between more and less complex processes which are divided between the Agency and local authorities, though all are enjoined to exercise their powers to minimise pollution, in the case of local authorities this being further limited to pollution of the atmosphere. The Secretary of State may, under EPA 1990, s 4(4) and (5), direct that an atmospheric pollution regulation function under Part I normally exercisable by a local authority shall be transferred to the Agency.

Prescribed processes and prescribed substances

EPA 1990, s 2 empowers the Secretary of State to prescribe *processes* for the purpose of regulation, and to identify them as being subject to control either by the Agency or local authorities: EPA 1990, s 2(4). Under EPA 1990, s 2(5) the Secretary of State may also prescribe *substances* whose release into the environment may be regulated, again providing for either central or local control. These substances are prescribed by the Environmental Protection (Prescribed Processes and Substances) Regulations 1991,[7] as amended.[8]

Schedule 4 to the Regulations relates to substances whose release to *air* is subject to control. It includes sulphur dioxide, nitrogen oxide and the oxides of carbon, as well as asbestos, halogens and smoke. Schedule 5 relates to substances released to *water* and includes mercury, cadmium, isomers of DDT, aldrin, dieldrin, polychlorinated biphenyls (PCB), and atrazine.[9] Schedule 6 relating to *landward* releases includes organic solvents, halogens, oxidising agents, phosphorous, and chemical pesticides. Some such *substances* may be released, of course, from a prescribed *process*, but where particular provision is made for a substance it must be complied with.

---

7   SI 1991/472.
8   See SIs 1991/836, 1992/614, 1993/1749. 1993/2405, 1994/1271, 1994/1329, 1995/3247, 1996/2678 and 1998/767.
9   See further chapter 20.

The 'A' and 'B' lists

Central to understanding the IPC/LAAPC system is the realisation that there are two lists, 'A' and 'B', of prescribed processes. The 'A' list is subject to IPC and is within the jurisdiction of the Agency, while the 'B' list is subject to local authority regulation with regard to atmospheric pollution only. Pollutants entering, for example, water from 'B' list processes would still therefore fall within the powers of the Agency under water legislation.[10] The 'A' and 'B' (which fall into six groups) lists are prescribed by the Environmental Protection (Prescribed Processes and Substances) Regulations 1991,[11] Sch 1, as amended. 'A' processes are:

1   *Fuel production and combustion*, eg gasification and associated processes, such as refining natural gas or producing gas from coal; carbonisation and associated processes, eg pyrolysis or distillation of coal or lignite; combustion processes carried on primarily for energy production, eg burning any fuel in a boiler or furnace with a net rated thermal input of 50 MW or more, or in gas turbine or compression engines of like capacity; petroleum processes, eg physical, chemical or the thermal treatment of crude oil.

2   *Metal production and processing*, eg iron and steel production such as making, melting or refining iron, steel or ferro alloys, or desulphurising iron or steel, heating iron or steel so as to remove grease, oil or other contaminants, eg burning plastic off scrap cable, where this is related to other Part A iron and steel processes; non-ferrous metal processes such as zinc or tin mining where cadmium may be released into water, refining non-ferrous metals, or processes for producing, melting or recovering by chemical means any lead or lead alloy which may result in lead tainted smoke being released.

3   *Mineral industries*, eg cement and lime manufacture such as blending cement or heating calcium carbonate so as to make lime; asbestos processes such as producing raw asbestos or making asbestos products or stripping asbestos from scrap railway vehicles; mineral fibre processes such as glass fibre making; glass manufacture and production such as making glass frit; ceramic production such as firing heavy clay goods.

4   *Chemical industries*, eg petrochemical processes such as production of unsaturated hydrocarbons; manufacture and use of organic chemicals such as manufacture of styrene or vinyl chloride or of acetylene or any aldehyde, amine, isocyanate, or organic sulphur compounds where the process may result in the release of such substances into air; acid processes, eg making sulphuric acid or oxides of sulphur or nitric or phosphoric acid; processes involving halogens such as making hydrogen fluoride/chloride/bromide/iodide or any other acids; inorganic chemical processes such as making hydrogen cyanide or processes involving its release to the air or the production of compounds containing, inter alia, arsenic, gallium, indium, lead, tellurium, thallium; chemical fertiliser production; pesticide production likely to release into water, inter alia, mercury, cadmium, isomers of DDT, aldrin, dieldrin, PCBs, atrazine; pharmaceutical production, again where it is likely to result in the release to water of any of the immediately foregoing substances which are particularly listed in the Regulations, Sch 5.

5   *Waste disposal and recycling*, eg incineration processes, for instance of waste chemicals or certain compounds listed substances, or of animal remains; processes for recovery by distillation of, inter alia, oil or organic solvents; fuel production from waste by utilising heat to make a solid fuel from waste.

10   See chapter 20.
11   SI 1991/472.

6   *'Other industries'*, eg paper making processes above certain specified levels; processes for making di-isocyanates; tar and bitumen processes; certain coating and printing processes; manufacture of dyestuffs in the process involves use of hexachlorobenzene; timber processes such as chemical treatment of timber using any 'Schedule 5' substance; treatment and processing of animal or vegetable matter, eg storing or drying dead animals or plants or plant products where a 'Schedule 5' substance may be released into water.

'B' processes are: combustion processes such as burning fuel in a boiler or furnace for energy production where the plant has a net rated thermal input of not less than 20 MW but less than 50 MW; iron and steel processes such as small scale smelting, eg in an electric arc furnace with a designed holding capacity of less than seven tonnes; non-ferrous metal processes, again such as small scale production in furnaces with designed holding capacities of less than five tonnes; cement processes such as blending cement in bulk other than at a construction site, or batching ready mixed concrete; asbestos processes such as minor finishing of certain asbestos products; certain other mineral processes such as crushing or grinding designated minerals such as clay, sand, gypsum, boiler or furnace ash, etc; most glass manufacture and production processes, including those involving the use of lead, or where glass is polished or etched by hydrofluoric acid; certain types of ceramic production; some incineration processes such as crematoria; certain small scale di-isocyanate processes; certain medium scale coating and printing processes and likewise certain medium scale dyestuff, printing ink or coating material manufacturers; timber processes involving manufacture of wood products by, inter alia, sawing, drilling or sanding, where certain specified amounts of timber are used each year; processes involving rubber such as mixing, milling, or bleaching of natural rubber if carbon black is used; certain animal or vegetable matter processes such as maggot breeding.

It will be noted that the range and complexity of 'A' processes is greater than that of 'B'. However, the *numbers* of places subject to local authority regulation are much greater than those within the jurisdiction of the Agency.[12]

Because of the existence of complex processes made up of many component parts not always immediately recognisable as either 'A' or 'B', and because of the existence of complex sites with more than one process 'in situ', the Environmental Protection (Prescribed Processes and Substances) Regulations 1991, as amended, in general terms, provide:

1   Where *in one location* there are numbers of processes all *operated by the same person* and those processes fall into the same class under the Regulations, Sch 1 only *one authorisation* is needed.
2   Where a Part A process overlaps with a Part B process as one of a number of processes in operation, only one authorisation will be required and that will be *centrally* issued, ie by the Agency.
3   Where there are many processes each within a separate Sch 1 category separate authorisations will be required.
4   Processes not fitting neatly into a Sch 1 definition are to be treated as falling within that definition which is most apt.

Note that control is primarily exercised over *processes*, and that most releases of *substances* are regulated consequentially as part of the process authorisation, but where a substance is prescribed the operators of certain prescribed processes have to deal in particular ways with the substance in question.

12   See further below.

Authorisations

Under the EPA 1990, s 6, no person is able to carry on a relevant process without an authorisation from the appropriate authority. Those requiring such authorisations need to apply, paying, under the EPA 1990, s 8 in the case of LAAPC, and the Environment Act 1995, s 41 in the case of IPC, a prescribed fee.

EPA 1990, Sch 1 lays down the authorisation process, providing for applications to be made in prescribed form, for their advertisement, for consultations with specified persons, for representations to be received from others, eg in consequence of advertisements, for directions to be given to enforcing authorities by the Secretary of State, and for the Secretary of State to have 'call in' powers in respect of applications or classes thereof.

The Environmental Protection (Applications, Appeals and Registers) Regulations 1991,[13] provide, inter alia, for the following particulars to be required: the address of relevant premises and a map of their location; a description of relevant processes and substances; a description of relevant techniques to be used to reduce or mitigate releases; details of proposed releases and an assessment of environmental consequences; proposals for monitoring releases; and, indications of how the BATNEEC condition (see further below) will be achieved. Consultation is also required by the Regulations with the Health and Safety Executive in all cases, and with certain other bodies or persons, eg sewerage undertakers, in specified circumstances.

EPA 1990, Sch 1 also makes provision for a determination period, in general four months, and non-determination may be deemed a refusal. In particular instances, the determination period may be varied.[14] Enforcing authorities have, under s 6(3) power either to refuse applications, or grant them subject to conditions, though they may not grant an authorisation unless they consider the applicant will be able to carry out the process in accordance with conditions. Under EPA 1990, s 6(5), the Secretary of State may direct an authority as to whether or not to grant a particular authorisation. Authorisations granted under EPA 1990, Part I are subject to a periodic review at least every *four years*.[15] Such a review is not required to take place, however, where the prescribed process is carried on: in a *new* Part A installation/mobile plant; in an *existing* Part A installation/mobile plant and the review would be carried out within two years of the beginning of the period for making an application for an IPPC permit (see below); in an *existing* Part B installation/mobile plant and the review would be carried out in the same circumstances as described above.[16]

Conditions of authorisation

EPA 1990, s 7 lies at the heart of the IPC/LAAPC system of regulation. It obligates the inclusion in authorisations of such conditions as are specified by the Secretary of State, such other conditions as appear appropriate to the relevant authority, together with an *implied condition* relating to the use of the *best available techniques not entailing excessive cost* (BATNEEC) to prevent or reduce pollution. In the case of 'A' processes,

13   SI 1991/507.
14   See the Environmental Protection (Authorisation of Processes) (Determination Periods) Order 1991, SI 1991/513.
15   EPA 1990, s 6(6). The Secretary of State may substitute for this period such other period as he thinks fit: s 6(7).
16   EPA 1990, s 6(6A). This provision was inserted by the Pollution Prevention and Control (England and Wales) Regulations 2000 to take account of the phased introduction of the IPPC system.

an authorisee must use BATNEEC to prevent the release of substances prescribed for any environmental medium into that medium, or where such is not practicable to reduce such releases to a minimum and for rendering them harmless, and also to render harmless any other substance which might cause harm if released into an environmental medium. In the case of 'B' processes, the references to release relate only to those to the air.

BATNEEC

The implementation of the BATNEEC[17] requirement has reflected attempts to pursue a UK environment policy which is based, avowedly, on the principles of stewardship and sustainable development. Accordingly, the IPC system is operated on the basis that a process should be looked at in the round, with the need to protect the environment acknowledged and balanced against the cost of doing so, which should lead to a search for the best solution for the environment as a whole. This search requires adopting a holistic approach, ie one should search for releases of material to be to that medium where they will have the least impact, a philosophy that prevention is better than cure, and an approach that requires unavoidable emissions to be minimised and rendered harmless.

The UK approach to the implementation of BATNEEC is that though operators conceive, design, build and operate their plants so as to meet legal requirements, these are not all legally pre-set. There is, however, a dialogue with operators as to how best the object of environmental protection can be achieved — preferably with operators finding more economical ways to operate in the process. This results in a concentration of effort on individual processes and a consideration of each process's effect on the environment as a whole, which further entails identification and qualification of releases from the plant in question, a determination of which are significant and what are the environmentally acceptable outcomes. This is clearly a very evaluative process which demands the active co-operation of processors if it is to succeed. It is against this background that official guidance on the meaning of BATNEEC has to be set.

The 1997 DoE publication, *Integrated Pollution Control: A Practical Guide*, suggested that in determining BATNEEC, each process should be looked at in an individual and holistic manner, with significant emissions being determined along with what would be an acceptable environmental outcome. Thus the determination of BATNEEC is inevitably an evaluative and judgmental process. The 'BAT' part of BATNEEC was defined as follows:

Best
: The techniques which are most effective in preventing, minimising or rendering emissions harmless, but there may be more than one 'best' technique.

Available
: The technique must be procurable by the process operator. In other words, the technique must be generally accessible though not necessarily in general use, and availability includes availability outside the UK. 'Available' also implies, however, that a technique has been *developed* (ie not just theoretical) and can be applied with business confidence. A technique does not cease to be available if its source is outside the UK, nor does the fact that only one person can supply it.

Techniques
: This terms embraces both the plant in which the process is carried on and how the process is operated in practice. The

17   This concept first appeared in the framework directive on combating industrial air pollution, 84/366/EC, and required *preventative* measures and the use of 'best available *technology*' not entailing excessive cost.

concept and components of the plant are thus considered along with the numbers and qualifications of the staff, working methods, training and supervision of the workforce and the design, construction, maintenance and layout of the relevant buildings.

The NEEC part of the concept means that the best available techniques can be modified by economic considerations where the costs of applying BAT would be *excessive* in relation to the nature of the industry and the degree of protection to be achieved. This is essentially a balancing exercise — where greater environmental harm can result from a process, more can be required from an operator in terms of expenditure. 'NEEC' has different meanings depending upon whether it is applied to new or existing processes:

New processes — Fixing the BAT requires harm to be weighed against cost – the greater the harm the more that is required by way of regulation. Costs can be taken into account where the costs of BAT would be excessive with regard to the industry in question and the degree of protection to be achieved, ie marginal costs will be considered. If a process could have its emissions reduced by 95% for £20,000, and by 96% for £100,000, it is likely that the first option will be justified on 'NEEC' criteria. If, however, even after the BATNEEC requirements have been met serious harm could still result, then the authorisation must be refused. In other words the greater the likely harm, the more that can be required by way of expenditure to achieve BAT. Moreover the test is to be applied on an industry-wide basis — it is not the unprofitability of a particular operator that is to determine the issue.

Existing processes — 'NEEC' justifies requiring the replacement of plant over time periods to be established, ie there is no requirement for 'state of the art — now'. NEEC will also entail consideration of the technical characteristics of existing plant, its rate of use and predicted life, the nature and volume of emissions, the economic condition of *processors in the category in question*, and further developments in techniques. However, as was the case with new processes, the profitability of an individual operator will not be a reason for BATNEEC standards to be relaxed.

BPEO

Where IPC applies, the EPA 1990, s 7(7) requires that the operator must endeavour to ensure that BATNEEC will be used for minimising the pollution which may be caused to the environment as a whole from such releases having regard to the best practicable environmental option (BPEO)[18] available in respect of the substances which may be released. In other words, BATNEEC must be applied in order to achieve BPEO.

Although BPEO clearly has an important role to play in the operation of the IPC system, it is not actually defined by the EPA 1990. In its Twelfth Report, *Best Practicable*

---

18   The term BPEO first appeared in the Royal Commission on Environmental Pollution's fifth report, *Air Pollution Control: An Integrated Approach*, (1975 Cmnd 6371).

Environmental Option,[19] the Royal Commission on Environmental Pollution defined the concept thus:

'A BPEO is the outcome of a systematic consultative and decision-making procedure which emphasises the protection and conservation of the environment across land, air and water. The BPEO procedure establishes, for a given set of objectives, the option that provides the most benefit or least damage to the environment as a whole, at acceptable cost, in the long term as well as in the short term.'[20]

This definition is broadly the same as that which the Environment Agency has subsequently adopted for the purposes of IPC. In Technical Guidance Note E1 *Best Practicable Environmental Option Assessments for Integrated Pollution Control,*[21] the Agency defines BPEO as:

'The option which in the context of releases from a prescribed process, provides the most benefit or least damage to the environment as a whole, at acceptable cost, in the long term as well as the short term.'[22]

The key distinction, however, between the Royal Commission's definition of BPEO and that formulated by the Agency is that the latter is confined to 'releases from prescribed processes'. In other words, it is not concerned with the other environmental effects which may arise from the carrying on of the process, such as the production and consumption of raw materials, the use of water by the process, the generation of transport movements etc.[23]

In seeking to justify a chosen method as the BATNEEC having regard to the BPEO for a process, the Agency will follow an 'audit trail'[24] which provides a framework for the detailed and rigorous assessment of options in each case. In particular, the methodology adopted by the Agency reflects the route which was recommended by the Royal Commission on Environmental Pollution in its Twelfth Report. Essentially this consists of six stages: (1) define the objective; (2) generate options; (3) evaluate those options; (4) summarise and present the evaluation; (5) select the BPEO; (6) review the BPEO.

Technical Guidance Note E1[25] is, however, confined to selection of the BPEO. It does not deal with the implementation and monitoring of requirements. Thus the document is primarily methodological, designed to be usable by a whole range of IPC processes, being also designed to strike a balance between a justifiable process option and ensuring that over-heavy burdens are not placed on the administrative and financial capabilities of operators. Though a number of authorisations have followed the model of the Guidance, its use is not compulsory and it should not therefore be mechanically applied.

---

19   (1988, Cmnd 310).
20   See the Royal Commission's Report, para 2.1.
21   Published by the Agency in 1997.
22   See the Guidance, para 3.5.1.
23   This may be contrasted with the position under the IPPC regime: see further below.
24   The value of producing an audit trail was highlighted by the Royal Commission on Environmental Pollution in its Twelfth Report, *Best Practicable Environmental Option.*
25   This Guidance consists of Volume 1 (Principles and Methodology) and Volume 2 (Consultation documents).

It must also be appreciated that the methodology does *not* require the prior determination of BPEO which is then taken into account in determining BATNEEC. Rather, the procedure is a *single stage* and the Guidance relates to selecting the BATNEEC having regard to the BPEO. Thus (a) initially the task *for the operator* is to produce a product or service which meets IPC requirements including the use of BATNEEC. The operator will then (b) guarantee options whereby that initial object may be achieved. These options must then (c) be assessed economically and environmentally. That assessment will be (d) summarised and presented setting out all the evaluative factors. From the options the BATNEEC, having regard to the BPEO, will (e) be selected by the operator who will have to justify the choice, and that will (f) then have to be reviewed, ie tested, to determine the correctness of assumptions and conditions made by reference to the 'audit trail' undertaken. Stages (b), (c) and (e) are the core stages, and (b) in particular represents the bedrock of the whole system.

The generation of options at stage (b) will take into account many factors, including: the harmfulness of emissions; the magnitude of releases; ambient pollution concentrations to which releases will be added, eg in a heavily polluted area any release will add to already significant problems; the features of the receiving environments. Where there is a statutory Environmental Quality Standard (EQS) it would be intolerable if an anticipated release were to contribute to its breach. Accordingly, such a standard would have to be absolutely complied with in relation to a receiving medium, although it is worth noting that few such standards exist.

Where there is no EQS the Agency suggest the use of Environmental Assessment Levels (EALs), which are provisionally contained in Volume 2 of the Guidance. These are 'reference levels' which express for listed substances their relative potential for harm in air, land or water. In determining whether any release would be 'significant' and thus a 'priority for control', the initial rules of thumb would be to consider whether *either* the maximum contribution from the process in question alone to the levels of a given substance in air or water or on land is *more* than 2% of the EAL, *or* whether the environmental concentration of a substance, including emissions from the process in question is likely to exceed 80% of the EAL for the substance in the given medium to which release would take place. Where a release is thereafter considered 'insignificant' there will be in general no need for further detailed assessment of a range of disposal options. All the operator will be required to provide is a summary of the screening process used to identify the preferred disposal/control option. *Alternatively*, the 'significance' of an emission may be assessed according to given tabular definitions of threshold mass release rules for a variety of pollutants for different stack heights or according to aquatic dispersion characteristics.

The EALs will be the key indicators for assessing the overall environmental impact of the release of substances into the environment. There are current quality standards for some substances, as already stated, but to work out in detail a complete list will be a long and complex process in itself. The task will be made even more difficult by the need to ensure that both short term and long term EALs are developed on a detailed basis.

There are a number of evaluative techniques that can be used, once again applying the 'rules of thumb' referred to above. Thus each process will have an 'Environmental Quotient' (EQ) for its emissions of any given substance to any given medium. That quotient is the process's emissions as a fraction of a given EAL. In relation to any given receiving medium the various EQs from a process can then be added to produce an Integrated Environmental Index of that process's total emissions to that given medium for evaluative purposes. Another evaluative technique is to use a 'Final Hazard Score' which considers what the potential hazard emissions represent if they consist of waste arising from a process. Global Warming Potential (GWP) of emissions can also be considered, as can Photochemical Ozone Creation Potential (POCP) with regard to atmospheric emissions. Values for GWP and POCP are given in Volume 2, as also are values for Odour Detection Thresholds[26] and Odour Recognition Thresholds (ODT/ ORT). All these techniques are to be used in the evaluative assessment process.

Where it is claimed by an operator that an option which is environmentally superior will in fact entail excessive costs as compared with the proposed process option, it will be necessary to carry out a cost comparison. For each component of the option this will involve estimating the capital costs of purchase and installation, the annual operating and maintenance costs, and the operating life (in years). Such information will enable the calculation of a net present value (NPV) for each option, together with an annual cost. Thus it will be possible to compare the respective costs of each option.

Following the assessment, summary and presentation of the options, it will be necessary for the operators and inspectors to identify BATNEEC having regard to BPEO for a particular site. In reaching a conclusion on this issue it will be necessary to consider the trade-off between the respective costs of options and the additional benefits that they will afford in terms of pollution reduction and prevention. Once again there is a choice of techniques. It will be possible, for example, to compare annual running costs of any given option against an index of its environmental effects such as GWP. Alternatively, a comparison may be made between the incremental costs of choosing one process option as opposed to another with the incremental change in environmental effects. In many cases there will be a 'break point' above which the cost of choosing a particular BATNEEC, having regard to BPEO, rises steeply, and that is the point at which to consider whether it is appropriate to advance further with that option.

BATNEEC, BPEO and the courts

In *R v Environment Agency and Redland Aggregates, ex p Gibson (No 2), R v Environment Agency and Redland Aggregates, ex p Leam (No 2)* and *R v Environment Agency, ex p Sellers (No 2),*[27] the High Court was required to consider, inter alia, whether the Agency had complied with its statutory duty under the EPA 1990, s 7 to ensure that the BATNEEC were being used having regard to the BPEO when granting variations of the respondents' IPC authorisations to operate plants concerned with the manufacture of lime and cement respectively. The impugned decisions related to the use of substitute liquid fuels (SLFs)[28] to fire the respondent's kilns. It was argued on behalf of the applicants that prior to varying the authorisations to allow the use of SLFs, the Agency ought to have carried out an assessment of all the practicable options and techniques relating to the process as a whole, rather than seeing the matter as a straight choice between the existing and the proposed new fuel regime. It was further submitted that the failure to carry out a BATNEEC/BPEO exercise of this nature rendered the Agency's decisions unlawful.

In finding in favour of the respondents, Harrison J concluded that the EPA 1990, s 7 did not impose a duty on the Agency to carry out an exhaustive examination of all practical options and techniques regardless of the circumstances. Rather, fulfilment of the EPA 1990, s 7 duty was a matter of fact and degree depending upon the particular circumstances of the case. In some instances, a full-scale examination of the process may be necessary before a decision could be reached. However, on the facts of all

---

26 That is to say the concentration of an odorous compound at which the human nose detects the presence of an odour.
27 [1999] Env LR 73.
28 A mixture of waste solvents.

three applications before the court, it was apparent that no such examination was necessary. The Agency had been entitled to treat the proposed new fuel regime as a continuation of the existing BATNEEC/BPEO position.

From a practical point of view the decision in *ex p Gibson* is important in that had Harrison J found in favour of the applicants, it would have meant that the Agency would have been required to carry out an extensive BATNEEC/BPEO exercise in respect of every application which it received to vary a process authorisation. This would have placed a not inconsiderable burden on the already stretched resources of the Agency. In the light of the present ruling, however, whether or not an EPA 1990, s 11 application (see further below) requires a BATNEEC/BPEO assessment will be a matter for the Agency to decide, subject to the supervisory jurisdiction of the Administrative Court.

More recently in *R v Daventry District Council, ex p Thornby Farms Ltd*,[29] the Court of Appeal was required to consider whether Collins J had been right to refuse to quash an authorisation granted by the council to a company concerned with the disposal by incineration of domestic pet animal carcasses. The level of emission authorised was that stated in Process Guidance Note (PGN) 5/3 (95), para 17. This referred to certain pollutants and stated that specified concentrations should not be *exceeded* in any emission to air. However, the measuring of emissions from the incinerators revealed that in some cases, the level of pollutants being emitted were considerably lower than the levels specified in para 17 of the PGN. The applicant thus contended, inter alia, that a condition to ensure that BATNEEC would be used had not been imposed on the authorisation and that the authorisation should therefore be quashed.

Although in the circumstances of the case the Court of Appeal was not prepared to quash the authorisation (or to make a formal declaration that the council had acted unlawfully), it unequivocally rejected the submission that the PGN, para 17 levels represented BATNEEC. In the opinion of the court, such a submission was inconsistent with the opening words of PGN, para 17. The requirement that the specified concentrations 'should not be exceeded' was not the same as providing that they were inevitably the best which could be achieved. It was, therefore, inconsistent with the obligation in EPA 1990, s 7(2) and the continuing obligation under s 4(9) of the same Act to follow developments in techniques for reducing pollution.

A final point which emerges from the decision in *ex p Thornby Farms* is worth noting since it concerns the transparency of the decision-making process where an application for a process authorisation has been made. Though no complaint was made about it by the appellants, in giving the leading judgment of the court, Pill LJ found it surprising that the council had not set out in writing, prior to taking its decision, the considerations on which it had relied. In his opinion, the case 'reinforces the need for a properly documented process to be undertaken at the time of the decision and not only when litigation arises'.

Guidance

To assist in the achievement of IPC requirements, the Environment Agency issues guidance in several forms: Industry Sector Guidance Notes (IPR); Process Guidance Notes (PGN); and Technical Guidance Notes (TGN). Although such notes are non-statutory in nature,[30] they nevertheless provide an important reference point for those who determine applications for process authorisations (or for variations of existing processes). They also help applicants and others to understand the criteria against

29   [2002] EWCA Civ 58, [2002] All ER (D) 149 (Jan).
30   In other words, they have not been issued under the EPA 1990, s 7(11).

which applications and variations will be determined. The process specific nature of PGNs ensures that they represent the current view[31] on what represents the BATNEEC for that particular process. Accordingly, if the Agency departs from a PGN when determining an application, it is required to give its reasons for so doing. For new processes the PGN represents a design standard to be achieved. For older processes, the PGN represents a standard to be achieved over a time scale to be individually set by Agency inspectors for each individual case. TGNs provide inspectors with technical guidance on specific issues such as stack heights, monitoring pollution, abatement equipment in respect of vapour emissions, etc.

Unlike IPC guidance, LAAPC guidance is issued by the Secretary of State and as such *may* amount to statutory guidance where it is issued under the EPA 1990, s 7(11). LAAPC guidance takes four forms: Process Guidance (PG) Notes; General Guidance (GG) Notes; Upgrading Guidance (UG) Notes; and Additional Guidance (AQ) Notes. Whilst the first three types of guidance are essentially self-explanatory, it should be noted that AQ Notes may be issued in respect of particular problems or difficulties which have arisen whilst administering the LAAPC regime.

Transfers and variations

Once an authorisation has been given, EPA 1990, s 9 allows its transfer to a person who is to carry on the original authorisee's undertaking. Notification of the transfer must be given to the enforcing authority by the *transferee* within 21 days of the transfer.

The legislation allows both the Agency and the relevant operator to begin *variation* procedures when a process change is contemplated. The procedure differs, however, according to whether the change is 'substantial' or 'relevant'. EPA 1990, s 10 empowers *authorities* to serve 'variation notices' specifying changes to be made in authorisations and their operative dates. Such notices require authorisees to inform the authority of action to be taken to meet the varied requirements. EPA 1990, Sch 1, Part II applies where a variation has taken place and the authorisee's action in response proposes a 'substantial change' in the manner of carrying on the process, ie a substantial change in substances released or the amount or characteristics of releases. A process of advertisement and consultation is required similar to that for an initial application for authorisation. These provisions enable authorisation requirements to be kept up to date, as the Agency is under a duty to do.

Applications for variations *by authorisees* may, under EPA 1990, s 11, generally be made at any time. An initial procedure is for the authorisee to inform the relevant enforcing authority, according to the form specified in regulations, of the proposed change requesting them to make a determination as to whether:

1   The proposal would involve any breach of authorisation conditions.
2   If not, whether they would be likely to vary authorisation conditions in consequence of the change.
3   If it would, whether they would consider altering conditions so that the change may be made.
4   Whether the proposal would lead to 'substantial change' (see above) in the manner of carrying on the process.

---

31   PGNs are reviewed on a four yearly basis in order to ensure that they properly reflect any developments in technology that may have occurred since they were last reviewed. The process of review involves consultation with industry and relevant trade associations, local authorities and environmental groups.

Where *no* 'substantial change' would be involved, but where some *'relevant'* change under either 2 or 3 above would be needed, the authority must notify the authorisee of likely changes and he may then proceed to apply for variation. Where 'substantial change' is involved that would necessitate variation of conditions then the authorisee must be informed of likely changes and he may then proceed to apply, but, of course, the advertisement and consultation procedure outlined above will apply. A 'relevant change' is a change in the manner of carrying on the process which is capable of altering emissions or their characteristics/amounts.[32] Effectively nearly all changes if *not* 'substantial' will be 'relevant' and so will require variation procedures to be followed.

In any case, however, where an application for variation is made, the relevant enforcing authority must decide whether the requirements of EPA 1990, Sch 1 Part II apply, and comply with them if they do. They have in all cases, however, discretion to refuse variation or allow it, in which case they must serve a variation notice on the authorisee.

It should be noted that to avoid the need for over-many variation applications and their attendant costs and delays, a system has been devised of 'envelope authorisations' which lay down outer parameters within which changes may be made without further action. This is particularly relevant to certain chemical industries where production quantities and qualities are subject to fairly regular change.

Revocation and enforcement

EPA 1990, s 12 empowers enforcing authorities to revoke authorisations at any time, and in particular where a relevant process has not been carried on, or not for a period of 12 months.

They may further, under EPA 1990, s 13, serve 'enforcement notices' on authorisees likely to contravene, or actually contravening, authorisation conditions. This notice must state the authority's opinion on the issue, and must specify, first, matters constituting the actual or apprehended breach, and the steps necessary to remedy or avoid it, and the time for taking action. Amendments made in 1995 allow enforcing authorities to withdraw enforcement notices.[33] According to Agency figures, 48 enforcement notices were issued in 1999/2000.

Before enforcement action is taken, however, the requirements of the Deregulation (Model Appeal Provisions) Order[34] must be complied with. 'Enforcement action' means 'any action taken with a view to or in connection with imposing any sanction (whether criminal or otherwise) for failure to observe or comply with'[35] restrictions, requirements or conditions imposed on the carrying on of any trade, business or profession, etc. It also includes refusals to grant, review or vary a licence or authorisation, or imposing conditions on grants or renewals and variations and revocation of licences.

Under the 1996 Order before enforcement action is taken an enforcing officer is required to give a notice (a 'minded to' notice) to the person against whom he proposes to take enforcement action. The notice must state that enforcement action is being considered and why, as well as informing the recipient that he may make written/oral representations. Any such representations which are made must be taken into account, and if an enforcing officer nevertheless decides to take action, he must issue a further written notice stating the reasons for that decision. Despite these requirements, immediate enforcement action may take place where the officer believes that it is

32   See EPA 1990, s 11(11).
33   EPA 1990, s 13(4), inserted by the Environment Act 1995, Sch 22, para 53.
34   SI 1996/1678.
35   See the Deregulation & Contracting Out Act 1994, s 5(6).

necessary. If this is the case, the officer must explain in writing why he believed it to be necessary.

Where enforcement action has been taken and there is a right of appeal (see EPA 1990, s 15 below), the enforcing officer must as soon as is reasonably practicable give written notice explaining how, where, within what period and on what grounds an appeal may be brought. Furthermore, where an enforcing officer takes or considers taking enforcement action, he must take reasonable steps to identify the person who may be required to pay all or part of the costs of compliance. That person must also be informed in writing of his right of appeal. If he then makes any representations, these must be taken into account, unless they are withdrawn.

An example of a polluting event leading to the service of an enforcement notice occurred in September 2001 when 1,500 cubic metres of water containing hydrochloric acid was released into the Severn Estuary from the site of a steel rolling mill. Contractors had drained a tank containing water and a low concentration of the acid into a bunded area, but the bund had a hole in its wall. The water and acid therefore escaped into a drain and thence into the estuary. The release took place over a period of two and a half hours and had a pH value of 2.6 as opposed to a minimum of 6 permitted under the authorisation. The enforcement notice required the operator of the plant to review its systems for handling acid, make any necessary repairs and to improve maintenance and training. The notice set a number of deadlines, with all the prescribed work to be completed by 10 February 2002.[36]

Prohibition

Where an imminent risk of serious pollution is a consequence of carrying on an authorised process, either generally or in a particular manner, an authority may serve a 'prohibition notice' under EPA 1990, s 14 again specifying the issues and remedial measures *and* directing that the authorisation, wholly or in part, shall have no effect to authorise carrying on the process in question. An example of circumstances leading to the service of a prohibition notice occurred in February 2001, where a company operating a clinical waste incinerator in Wrexham was observed by Agency officers to be making what were believed to be illegal discharges. The notice prohibited the disposal of liquid waste effluent except by on-site incineration or by removal from the site by a registered waste company. It did not, however, prevent the disposal of clinical waste under the terms of the authorisation. Service of the notice allowed the Agency to carry out further investigations into the incident, including examining the nature of the discharges and their potential effects on the environment.[37]

In relation to EPA 1990, ss 12, 13 and 14 the Secretary of State has wide powers to issue directions as to the exercise of their powers by relevant authorities.

Appeals

EPA 1990, s 15 provides for rights of appeal for those refused authorisations, or aggrieved by conditions imposed, or refused variations requested, or whose authorisations have been revoked, from the enforcing authority to the Secretary of State, as also is the case for those served with variation, enforcement or prohibition

---

36 Details published in the News section of the Environment Agency's website (www.environment-agency.gov.uk) on 10 October 2001.
37 See the 'News' section of the Agency's website, 19 February 2001.

notices. It will be noted that the structure of this part of the legislation closely mirrors that of the relevant portions of the planning legislation.

The Secretary of State may determine appeals himself, or refer an appeal to a person appointed by him, or refer any matter involved in an appeal to such a person, in either case with/without payment. Before determining an appeal the Secretary of State has a discretion to cause the appeal to take, or to continue in, the form of a hearing, which may, at the discretion of the person holding the hearing, then be held in full or part in private. Alternatively the Secretary of State may cause a public local inquiry to be held. An inquiry or hearing must be held if either party to the appeal requests to be heard.

The Secretary of State has on appeal various powers:

1   To affirm the original decision.
2   To grant refused authorisations.
3   To grant a varied authorisation.
4   To quash all/any conditions in an authorisation (save of course those required by law).
5   To quash a revocation.
6   To quash/affirm (with/without modification) variation, enforcement and prohibition notices.

The detailed rules on appeal are set out in the Environmental Protection (Applications, Appeals and Registers) Regulations 1991,[38] as amended,[39] particularly as to procedures and time limits to be observed. Inter alia the regulations provide that where an appeal is to be held in the form of a hearing and it is decided that it shall be wholly or partly in public, notices of the hearing are to be published in the locality of the process, and that all those who have particular interest in the subject matter of the appeal are informed, as well as those who have rights of consultation under the regulations. At the appeal the appellant and the enforcing authority have the right to be heard together with the statutory consultees. Others are heard at the discretion of the person holding the hearing, such a privilege not to be unreasonably withheld. After the appeal is heard the person holding it makes a report on conclusions and recommendations to the Secretary of State who then makes his decision and informs the parties.

Public registers of information

Under EPA 1990, s 20 each enforcing authority must maintain a register of applications and authorisations (together with details of relevant variations, revocations, convictions, directions, information, appeals, and other prescribed matters). Local authority registers must also contain prescribed particulars of processes situated in their areas but subject to the powers of the Agency, and the Agency must supply relevant particulars. Such registers must be freely available for public inspection at reasonable times, and for this purpose the Secretary of State may prescribe places where these facilities are to be made publicly available. Registers may be kept in any form, so a computerised register is possible, but they must contain the prescribed information.[40]

Certain information may be excluded from registers under EPA 1990, ss 21 and 22, for example information whose registration would be, in the opinion of the Secretary of State, contrary to *national security*. No information relating to the affairs of an individual or business may be included without permission where it is *commercially confidential*,

38   SI 1991/507.
39   See the Environmental Protection (Applications, Appeals and Registers) (Amendment) Regulations 1996, SI 1996/667.
40   See further the Environmental Protection (Applications, Appeals and Registers) Regulations 1991, regs 15 and 16, as amended by SI 1996/667.

though the Secretary of State is empowered under EPA 1990, s 22(7) to give directions under which certain information has to be registered irrespective of confidentiality. A mere claim of confidentiality is, moreover, not of itself enough to secure exclusion; it is for the enforcing authorities to determine the issue, subject to a right of appeal to the Secretary of State.[41] Information is, moreover, only commercially confidential if its registration would prejudice commercial interests to an unreasonable degree, and generally looses that status after a period four years.[42] Where such information is, however, excluded, a statement to that effect must appear on the register.[43]

The issue of 'confidentiality' was tested in 1992 by appeals to the Secretary of State by PowerGen and National Power in respect of requirements that those companies should register information about future fuel consumption in the case of National Power and future emissions in the case of PowerGen. The Secretary of State allowed the former appeal on the basis that information about future power supplies was not 'directly relevant' to the application made, but rejected the latter. This points to a distinction being made, at least in the case of power generators, between registration of information as to what *enters* a place where a prescribed process takes place and what *leaves* it in the form of emissions. It would be unwise, however, to extrapolate too much from these instances; overall there have been few appeals under s 22.

Offences

EPA 1990, s 23, as amended by the Environment Act 1995, provides for offences committed, inter alia, by those who: operate processes without authorisation, or in contravention thereof; fail to comply with enforcement or prohibition notices; knowingly or recklessly make false or misleading statements, for example so as to obtain the grant or variation of an authorisation; or make false entries in any required records. Fines of up to £20,000 or terms of imprisonment for up to three months, or both, may in general be imposed on summary conviction for offences. Where the conviction is on indictment, unlimited fines and/or up to two years' imprisonment can be imposed.

In the present context, it would seem that where emissions arise as a consequence of faulty equipment, a defendant is unable to claim therefore that he was not operating a prescribed process at the material time. The malfunction of equipment falls within the scope of 'prescribed process' and indeed is the mischief which EPA 1990, ss 6(1) and 23(1) are directed at.[44] Moreover, where a defendant is not responsible for the malfunctioning of the equipment, it is also not a defence to claim that the emissions were caused as a consequence of an emergency and in the prevention of further serious harm. In other words, no statutory defence comparable to EPA 1990, s 33(7) exists in Part I of the same Act, and it is not open to a court to infer that it does.[45]

EPA 1990, s 157 further provides that where an offence committed by a body corporate is proved to have been committed with the consent or connivance of, or is attributable to any neglect on the part of, any director, manager, secretary or similar officer of the company, etc, the individual shall be liable along with the company and may be proceeded against accordingly. Although this is a most useful provision 'tearing the corporate veil' and enabling authorities to tackle corporate crime by pursuing guilty

---

41 See EPA 1990, s 22(2) and (5) as amended, and the Environmental Protection (Applications, Appeals and Registers) Regulations 1991, reg 7.
42 See EPA 1990, s 22(8) and (11).
43 See EPA 1990, s 20(5).
44 *Dudley Metropolitan Borough Council v Henley Foundries Ltd* [1999] Env LR 895.
45 *Dudley Metropolitan Borough Council v Henley Foundries Ltd* [1999] Env LR 895.

individuals,[46] it should be noted that in the context of IPC, it has only been successfully invoked on two occasions. On the first such occasion, the director of a company which operated a drum incinerator was ordered to do 60 hours' community service by the Bradford Crown Court on the basis that he had no assets (the company having gone into liquidation) and because a custodial sentence was considered to be inappropriate.[47] The second occasion concerned a managing director of a chemical company who had issued instructions that mercuric nitrate solution was to be produced by reacting mercury with concentrated nitric acid, despite the protests of two chemists who argued that there would be a violent reaction between the chemicals giving off large quantities of nitrogen dioxide. When such a reaction did take place, the gas was discharged via the ventilation system to a car park outside the building. The managing director was fined £2,500 under EPA 1990, s 157 and disqualified from acting as a director of a company for four years under the Company Directors Disqualification Act 1986.[48]

In any proceedings concerning a failure to comply with the general BATNEEC obligation, EPA 1990, s 25(1) provides that it is for the accused to prove that there was no better available technique not entailing excessive cost than that which was used. Moreover, where there is a failure to comply with the requirements of authorisation, or failure to comply with enforcement or prohibition notices and a conviction follows, the court may under EPA 1990, s 26, in addition to any penalties imposed, specifically order the offender to take remedial action. Additionally in such circumstances the Agency may in England and Wales take remedial action and may recover the consequential costs from the party convicted of the offence, provided the Secretary of State has given written approval.[49]

It should also be noted that where an enforcing authority conclude that prosecution for failure to comply with an enforcement or prohibition notice would be an ineffectual remedy they may, under EPA 1990, s 24, take proceedings in the High Court to ensure compliance. This raises the possibility of injunctive relief.

Injunctive relief

Where an injunction is sought under EPA 1990, s 24, a court will be wary of granting relief unless it can be shown that nothing short of an injunction will restrain the defendant's unlawful activity. Furthermore, the claimant must show that there is a serious case to answer *and* that on the basis of the 'balance of convenience' an injunction should be granted. The balance of convenience test is an exercise in balancing whether the claimant could gain an ultimately satisfactory remedy, even in the absence of an injunction, against the loss to the defendant if an injunction is granted but no other remedy because the claimant's case fails when it comes to trial. In the context of pollution, issues relevant to this exercise are: the nature of the harm alleged to be emanating from the defendant's land and activities; the number of persons affected; the likely consequences (in economic and employment terms) of an injunction for the defendant; whether there is an alternative criminal remedy with an up-to-date level of fines; and whether powers exist elsewhere to require the defendant to remedy the situation.[50]

---

46   See also chapter 1.
47   See (1998) 281 ENDS Report, 50.
48   See (1999) 299 ENDS Report, 53.
49   See EPA 1990, s 27.
50   *Tameside Metropolitan Borough Council v Smith Bros (Hyde) Ltd* [1996] Env LR D4.

IPC/LAAPC and the courts

When the IPC system was introduced in 1990 it was believed that it could give rise to a number of major legal challenges to decisions made by the regulator. In practice, however, though there have been a number of IPC prosecutions over the years, there have been very few major court cases at a superior court level on appeal and authorisation issues. LAAPC though has given rise to issues which, because of the nature of the appeal provisions in the EPA 1990, have had to be dealt with by way of judicial review.

Particular problems have arisen in connection with the animal carcass rendering and vegetable oil industries. The offensive odours given off by these industries have frequently been the subject of complaints to local authorities. In some instances the relevant local authorities have taken the view that the only effective way to deal with the problem has been to refuse the process operator an authorisation. However, a right of appeal lies in respect of such a decision and it has not been uncommon for the Secretary of State to take a rather different view of the matter at the appeal stage. Thus in addition to aggrieved applicants seeking to challenge the Secretary of State's decisions, there are a number of cases where the applicant for judicial review has been the local authority.[51]

Two cases will serve to illustrate the point. In the first of these, *R v Secretary of State for the Environment, ex p West Wiltshire District Council*,[52] the District Council had refused to grant R J Compton and Sons an authorisation to operate a piggery and animal by-product rendering business on the basis of perceived inadequacies in the way in which the respondents managed, operated and maintained their business both before and at the time of the application. The views of the council were upheld by the inspector who heard the appeal under the EPA 1990, s 15. In his opinion, the general level of maintenance at the site was unsatisfactory, as was the treatment of liquid effluent and the storage of waste products. He therefore concluded in a report which accompanied his decision that the company was unlikely to be able to carry on the process so as to comply with the requirements of the Act. The Secretary of State, however, allowed the appeal on the basis that the respondents would be able to operate their process under an authorisation with conditions. In his opinion, the test under EPA 1990, s 6(4) was not whether it was *likely* that an operator would be able to comply with authorisation conditions (the test applied by both the council and the inspector) but rather, whether it was *possible* for the operator to comply. In the High Court, however, this decision was quashed and the matter was remitted to the Secretary of State for reconsideration. In the judgment of the deputy judge, the test adopted by the Secretary of State in relation to EPA 1990, s 6(4) meant that he had failed to apply the section properly. Such a wide interpretation robbed the provision of any real significance. It meant in practice that virtually every application for an authorisation would be granted if the regulator need only be satisfied that it was possible that the applicant would carry on the process in accordance with the conditions attached to the authorisation.

The decision in *ex p West Wiltshire District Council* was followed in *R v Secretary of State for the Environment and Peninsular Proteins, ex p Torridge District Council*.[53] Here the council had decided that it had no other option other than to reject an application from Peninsular Proteins to carry on its animal by-product rendering process because it was not satisfied that the renderer could prevent emissions migrating

51 See, for example, *North Kesteven District Council v A Hughes and Son* (1996) 259 ENDS Report 10 and *Walker v Seed Crushers (Scotland) Ltd* [1998] Env LR 586.
52 [1996] Env LR 312.
53 [1997] Env LR 557.

beyond the plant boundary. On appeal, however, the Secretary of State directed that the renderers be granted an authorisation under the EPA 1990, Part I, subject to conditions. One of the conditions which had previously been agreed by the council and the renderer was that all emissions to air would be free of odour outside the plant boundary. Such a condition mirrored guidance originally given by the DoE in Guidance Note PG6/1(91). However, the Secretary of State struck the condition down on the basis that it was inappropriate and unenforceable.[54] In the judicial review proceedings which followed, the council argued that the Secretary of State had failed to consider the general appropriateness of the previously agreed conditions and that he had failed to consider other relevant factors, such as the height of the emissions, the prevailing wind, the lie of the land, the density and distribution of the affected population, and the offensiveness of the smell.

In giving judgment, the High Court noted that there was nothing in EPA 1990, s 7(1)(c) to limit the range of matters an authority may take into account when deciding what conditions to attach to an authorisation. The test was whether a condition was necessary and appropriate. The Secretary of State had, however, concentrated solely on the issue of enforceability. He had given no reasons why he considered the condition unnecessary, and he had applied a general rule that it was inappropriate because such a condition was only exceptionally appropriate, without further explanation. In the opinion of the court, the Secretary of State had acted *unlawfully* by confining his considerations to the proximity of the plant to nearby residents when determining whether or not there were exceptional circumstances justifying the imposition of the condition. His failure to allow the authority to make representations to him as to why it considered that there were exceptional circumstances justifying the imposition of the condition also invoked the censure of the court.[55]

How is the IPC/LAAPC system working?

Research on how the IPC system has worked in practice has been limited but that which has been undertaken has provided some important and interesting insights into how the system has operated in practice. Thus *IPC in Practice — a Review*[56] revealed a number of things which included, inter alia:

1   Application preparation was time consuming and costly, taking 100-500 man hours and costing £29,000-£150,000, though some application costs far exceeded these figures.
2   Few applications were made for exclusion from registration on the basis of commercial confidentiality — though some claims were made by the combustion, organic chemicals and mineral industries.
3   Operators were still ignorant of some of the basic requirements of IPC, and failed to comply with clear official guidance.

---

54   In a later case, *United Kingdom Renderers Association Ltd and John Pointon & Sons Ltd v Secretary of State for the Environment* [2001] EWHC Admin 675, [2001] 34 LS Gaz R 44, it was held, inter alia, that an odour boundary condition could be imposed under either EPA 1990, s 7(1)(a) or (c) and that para 13 of Process Guidance Note 6/1(00), as amended, was not therefore unlawful for recommending the general imposition of such a condition in an authorisation for a rendering process.
55   For further cases which have raised difficulties in respect of LAAPC authorisations, see *R v Secretary of State for the Environment and Tameside Borough Council, ex p Smith Bros (Hyde) Ltd* (1996) 253 ENDS Report 8, *North Kesteven District Council v A Hughes and Son* (1996) 259 ENDS Report 10 and *Walker v Seed Crushers (Scotland) Ltd* [1998] Env LR 586.
56   Published by Environmental Data Services (January 1994).

4   It was on upgrading of equipment/plant that improvement in practices were most likely to take place.

5   There appeared to be evidence that the variation procedure was not being properly applied, with some variations being granted 'off the record' without written justification or entry on registers, while some 'substantial' alterations had been nodded through without being subjected to the appropriate statutory procedure.

6   The number of appeals was increasing, and more appeals related to fundamental issues such as setting annual mass emission limits.

7   Industry's compliance costs had increased to some extent — IPC was then likely to double environmental expenditure on prescribed processes.

8   Public registers were not as effective as they should have been because a number of decisions had been made in an 'off the record' fashion.

9   Many companies were concerned only to use technology to stop emissions 'at the pipe's end' rather than to have efficient, waste free, processes in the first place.

10   Overall the system had brought about some real improvement in investment in environmental protection but this was largely amongst companies who were environmentally committed before 1990.

The other noteworthy study into the operation of the IPC system has been undertaken by Mehta and Hawkins.[57] The fieldwork on which the study is based took place between 1993-1997. It was undertaken for two geographical areas[58] and was based on a combination of computer databases, published statistics, official documents and interviews. Twenty five firms subject to the IPC regime were chosen at random for each of the two areas and their representatives were interviewed in a semi-structured way. The interviews focused on the costs of IPC and the impact that the regime had had upon the day-to-day running of the business. Interviews were also conducted with officials from HMIP (the predecessor of the Environment Agency), the Civil Service, environmental consultants and members of the legal profession in order to provide different perspectives on the IPC regime. The following broad findings emerged from the study:

1   Firms subject to IPC were something of a 'mixed bag' ranging from the small (less than 500 employees) to the large (in excess of 10,000 employees). The size of a firm had an impact upon its awareness and understanding of the legislative regime. Small firms tended to fear the financial costs of a prosecution while big firms were more concerned about the bad publicity which may result from a prosecution and its effect upon their corporate image.

2   A small firm's comparative ignorance of the legal requirements of IPC compounded by their lack of resources meant that they often relied upon the advice of the regulator and could be bullied into compliance. However, big firms could not be bullied in such a way. Their resources meant that they could employ environmental managers and have access to expert scientific and legal advice which would enable them to mount effective legal challenges to enforcement action. For such firms, therefore, the regulator increasingly recognised the power inherent in the threat of bad publicity.

3   The costs imposed by IPC (proportional to company size) were not inversely proportional to company size as common sense might suggest. Rather, a U-shaped curve was produced demonstrating that the smallest and the largest firms incurred the greatest expenditures in complying with the requirements of IPC while the

57   See 'Integrated Pollution Control and its Impact: Perspectives from Industry' (1998) 10 JEL 61.

58   The authors assert, quite rightly it is submitted, that it is not possible to claim that a study of IPC confined to one particular geographical region is representative of the experience of the regime throughout the country: (1998) 10 JEL 61 at 63.

medium size firms faced proportionately less onerous financial burdens. For small firms, the high expenditure was attributed to their marginal turnovers and their ignorance about pollution control and their legal obligations which resulted in substantial amounts of money and time having to be devoted to 'learning the ropes'. For big firms, pushing regulatory standards as high as possible gave rise to greater expense, but it was also regarded as a means of driving less efficient competitors out of business and raised the possibility of being able to sell environmental technology to others. Thus, as the authors note, as long as the BATNEEC standard applies, it is likely that such a practice will continue.

The picture which thus emerges from the Mehta and Hawkins' study is of a regulatory regime which affects those which it regulates in different ways, depending upon the size of the industrial concern in question. What the authors term 'structural bias' exists in the system in favour of the big firms whose 'greater skill, knowledge, and talented personnel cause regulatory burdens to fall unevenly'.[59] It remains to be seen whether the uneven nature of the experience of IPC to date will also be evident when (and if) the operation of the IPPC regime is subject to empirical analysis.[60]

In order to assess how the LAAPC system has been working regard should be had to the *Local Air Pollution Control Statistical Survey*, an annual survey of local enforcing authorities in England and Wales carried out jointly by DEFRA and the National Assembly for Wales. The 2000/2001 survey is based on 326 responses out of a possible 392 respondents.[61] On the basis of the responses actually received, the estimated total number of authorised processes falling under local authority control is 18,142. During the relevant period the following occurred:

1   497 decisions were made on authorisations for new processes or substantial changes and 105 decisions were made on new authorisations for existing processes.
2   62% of the decisions on new processes/substantial changes were made within the four-month period set down in EPA 1990, Sch 1.
3   41% of the decisions on new applications for existing processes were made within six months.
4   The number of inspections per process declined from 1.62 in 1999/2000 to 1.51 in 2000/2001.
5   84 local authorities completed two or more inspections per process and 89 completed one or fewer (five authorities reported that they had not inspected any of the processes which they regulated - 38 in total).
6   85% of required first four-year reviews and 56% of required second four-year reviews were completed.
7   973 revocations took place.
8   749 enforcement, prohibition or revocations notices were served.
9   19 cautions were issued.
10 27 prosecutions were in progress, of which seven were still pending at the end of the year, seven were withdrawn, nine were successful and two were unsuccessful.[62]
11 254 of the authorities which responded had either a specific LAAPC enforcement policy, or a general enforcement policy, or both.
12 31% of local authorities had cost accounting in place ie to show how they spend the income received from charges.

Although these figures represent a general (if slight) improvement on the figures for 1999/2000, it is worth noting that on being published, the Environment Minister, Michael

59   (1998) 10 JEL 61 at 75.
60   For an empirical review of the process of applying for an IPPC permit, see further below.
61   The response rate of 83% was 1% up on 1999/2000.
62   No information was provided on the other two prosecutions.

Meacher MP, was reported to have expressed his disappointment at the fact that they show that 'a significant proportion of local authorities are letting down those they represent by failing to inspect processes sufficiently'. Moreover, he was 'dismayed' at the cost accounting figures. In his view the failure of 69% of local authorities to adopt cost accounting practices 'runs counter to the principles of transparency and accountability' that he would expect all local authorities to subscribe to.[63]

B THE IPPC DIRECTIVE 96/61/EC

On 30 October 1996 the Integrated Pollution Prevention and Control Directive 96/61/EC came into force. Under this provision certain industrial activities must be authorised in particular ways in order to achieve an integrated prevention and control of pollution in all the environmental media, ie land, air and water. The move towards an integrated approach marks a development away from previous EC requirements which were largely medium specific. It will require industry and regulators alike to consider emissions and their impacts at the design stage of a plant and not merely as an add-on 'end of pipe' solution applied later. The directive is designed to *prevent, reduce* and *eliminate* pollution *at source*, and to secure the prudent use of natural resources, thus promoting sustainability. As such it applies to energy production, metal processing, mineral production, chemicals, waste management and, what the directive terms, 'other activities'. These include plants concerned with the production of pulp and paper, textiles, tanning, food production and intensive pig and poultry rearing. From October 1999 onwards, all such activities may only be carried out at a *new plant* where the operator of that plant is in possession of a 'permit' granted by a competent authority. For *existing plant*, the directive's provisions will have taken effect by 2007.

What is a permit?

For the purposes of the IPPC system, a permit will be a part or the whole of a written decision, or series of them together, which grants authorisation to operate all or any part of an installation subject to conditions which ensure that the plant complies with the requirements of the directive. The basic requirement in the directive is that the relevant installation will operate in accordance with the 'best available techniques' (BAT), a term which bears a similar meaning to its current image in UK law. However, in determining BAT, specific regard is to be paid to utilising low waste technology, using less hazardous substances, promoting the recovery and recycling of substances generated by the processes, reducing raw materials, and the need to promote energy efficiency. Permitted installations are required by the Directive, Art 3 to: take appropriate preventive measures against pollution; ensure that no significant pollution is caused; avoid waste production; use energy efficiently; prevent accidents; and protect and clean up sites once industrial activity has ceased.

Obtaining a permit

To obtain a permit an application must be made to the competent authority. The application must include information describing, inter alia: the installation and its

---

63   See 'Meacher announces Local Authority Air Regulation statistics', News Release, 23 November 2001, on the DEFRA website: www.defra.gov.uk.

activities; the materials used; the energy used or generated; the sources of emissions; the site conditions; the nature and quantities of foreseeable emissions and the identification of their significant environmental effects; the abatement technology and prevention techniques to be used; the measures for waste prevention and recovery; and, the measures planned to monitor emissions into the environment. Since much of this information will be of a technical nature, the directive further requires that an application for a permit must be accompanied by a non-technical summary of the information.

Permits may only be granted to those plants which meet the requirements of the directive. Where more than one competent authority is involved in the process of determining an application, they are required to perform their respective functions in an integrated and fully co-ordinated manner. All permits which are granted must contain details of the arrangements made in respect of the environmental media. The Directive, Art 9 further requires that the conditions of the permit must include emission limit values for pollutants likely to be emitted from the installation in significant quantities. In the case of the environmental media of air and water, the substances which must be taken into account are listed in the Directive, Annex III. Substances common to both include cyanides, arsenic and its compounds and substances and preparations which have been proved to possess carcinogenic or mutagenic properties or properties which may affect reproduction in or via the air or aquatic environment.

In setting an emission limit, a permit is not to specify particular equipment, and BAT requirements are to take account of the technical nature of the installation, its siting and local conditions, and new EC-wide emission limits which are likely to appear after 2002. In the meantime, existing EC directives on matters such as waste and asbestos are to serve as minimum emission requirements.

The IPPC Directive further provides that arrangements must be specified in permits for dealing with waste and for protecting soil and groundwater. Long distance and transboundary pollution must be minimised by conditions in permits, and a high level of environmental protection must be sought. Monitoring requirements must also be imposed by permit conditions. The results of such monitoring must be supplied to the competent authority by the operator for the purposes of determining compliance with the permit. Although the directive requires that permit conditions be reviewed, unlike EPA 1990, Part I,[64] there is no stipulation as to the frequency with which such reviews are to take place.

The implications for UK systems

Although the IPPC regime is based on the UK's system of IPC, in a number of important respects it has gone beyond the earlier regime. Thus before we consider how the new regime has been implemented in UK law, it is appropriate to identify the key differences between IPC and IPPC, and to consider the extent of the directive's application.

1   IPC is concerned with the control of pollution from *processes* whereas IPPC is concerned with the control of *activities*.
2   IPPC therefore applies to *installations* rather than just processes.
3   IPPC seeks to prevent or reduce *emissions* whereas IPC is concerned with preventing *harm* to the environment which occurs as a consequence of releases.
4   The IPPC definition of 'pollution' is wider than that used for IPC. It also includes *vibrations* and *noise*.

64   See EPA 1990, s 6(6) which provides for a four-year review period.

5   BAT (see below) will be determined in part by issues not relevant to BATNEEC, eg use of less hazardous substances, furthering waste recovery and recycling, consumption of raw materials and water, energy efficiency and the need to prevent accidents. IPPC will look at the pollution impact of plants and will strive for the best environmental way of doing a job.

6   In determining BAT, 'costs' have a wider meaning than under BATNEEC (see further below).

7   IPPC will impose obligations to minimise waste production, to use energy efficiently, to restore sites on closure; IPC does none of these.

8   Environmental Impact Assessment undertaken at the planning permission stage will be taken into account in IPPC permitting; there was no formal link between planning permission and IPC authorisation.

9   IPPC sets fixed emission limit values or other equivalents for certain listed pollutants, while IPC makes a distinction between prescribed and non-prescribed substances.

10   Emission monitoring requirements *must* be included in IPPC permits; under IPC, though they often formed part of an authorisation, they did not have to be included.

Given the differences between the two regimes, it is apparent that IPPC will apply to a much wider range of installations than have been regulated under IPC. While the number of installations regulated under the latter has stood at approximately 2,000, the number of installations falling under the IPPC regime is estimated to be 8,000. The new raft of processes which will be regulated under IPPC include landfill sites, intensive pig and poultry units and installations concerned with the production of food and drink. There was a possibility that if the IPPC Directive had been implemented on the basis of a narrow interpretation of its wording, certain types of installation would have fallen outside the scope of the regime and would, therefore, have formed an IPC 'rump'. The confusion which such a state of affairs might have caused both for the regulators and the regulated thus prompted the Environment Agency to make the case for including all existing IPC processes within the IPPC regime, which is what has happened.

As will become apparent in the discussion which follows, the thrust of the new law is much more holistic than it has been previously. It is intended to encourage cost effective environmental performance by permit holders and is also in line with current thinking on sustainable development in terms of requiring the consideration of energy efficiency and the use of resources and water.

Inevitably the task of regulation has and will continue to become more rigorous and testing. However, it must also endeavour to remain both pragmatic and workable. It is particularly important that the various regulatory bodies in respect of IPPC, eg the Agency, local authorities and local planning authorities, properly coordinate their work so as to ensure that duplication and a blurring of responsibilities does not occur. This is especially so where, for example, an application is received to build a major new factory and the authorisation for that process will consist of a grant of planning permission from the local authority and an IPPC permit from either the Agency or from the environmental health department of the local authority. There is also a need for coordination between the work of the Agency and that of the Health and Safety Executive with regard to the need to ensure minimisation of accidents[65] in permitting.[66]

IPPC will result in fundamental changes for those who are regulated and those who regulate. It will not work, however, unless an appropriate level of resources are allocated to it. Neither will it work unless its basic philosophy is accepted; that damage to the

---

65   In this context, 'accidents' includes any abnormal operation of an installation which may increase emissions: see the IPPC General Sector Guidance (IPPC S0.01), April 2001, para 2.8.

66   It should be noted that some installations will be subject to the Control of Major Accident Hazards Regulations 1999, SI 1999/743.

environment as a whole is to be minimised and not just with regard to emissions, taking into account the issues of energy efficiency, the conservation of raw material resources and the prevention of accidents.

C DOMESTIC IMPLEMENTATION OF THE IPPC DIRECTIVE

Implementation of the IPPC Directive in domestic law[67] has been achieved by a combination of primary and secondary legislation. The two main provisions are the Pollution Prevention and Control Act 1999 (see below) and the Pollution Prevention and Control (England and Wales) Regulations 2000[68] (see below).

The Pollution Prevention and Control Act 1999

The purpose of the PPCA 1999 is to enable a single, coherent pollution control system to be set up by regulations which will apply to all of the installations to which the IPPC Directive applies *and* to installations currently regulated under EPA 1990, Part I to which the directive does not apply. The Act also provides for regulations to be made to cover various ancillary matters connected with the prevention or control of pollution, eg the collection of information about emissions for inclusion in a polluting emissions register. Thus the PPCA 1999 represents a framework within which detailed provision will be made by secondary legislation.[69]

Definitions

The PPCA 1999, s 1 defines three key terms which appear in the Act: 'activities'; 'environmental pollution'; and, 'harm'. For the purposes of the Act, 'activities' means industrial, commercial or 'other' activities which are carried on at particular premises or otherwise, including depositing, keeping or disposing of substances.

'Environmental pollution' is defined to mean pollution of the air, water or land which may give rise to any *harm*. For the purposes of this definition (but without prejudice to its generality), 'pollution' is defined to include pollution caused by noise, heat or vibrations or any other kind of release of energy. Moreover, 'air' is defined to include air within buildings and air within other natural or man-made structures above or below ground.

It will have been noted that a key feature of the definition of 'environmental pollution' is the concept of *harm*. The PPCA 1999 provides that for the purposes of that definition, harm means any of the following: harm to the health of human beings or other living organisms; harm to the quality of the environment, including harm to the quality of the environment taken as a whole, harm to the quality of the air, water or land, and other impairment of, or interference with, the ecological systems of which any living organisms

---

67   That is to say in England and Wales. In Scotland the relevant secondary legislation is the Pollution Prevention and Control (Scotland) Regulations 2000, SSI 2000/323. There have, however, been serious delays in implementing the IPPC Directive in Northern Ireland with the result that the UK faces legal proceedings in the European Court of Justice: see (2001) 312 ENDS Report, 39.

68   SI 2000/1973.

69   The central role to be played by regulations was the subject of strong criticism from the House of Lords Select Committee on Delegated Powers and Deregulation when the primary legislation was still at the Bill stage: see (1999) 288 ENDS Report, 28.

form part; offence to the senses of human beings; damage to property; or, impairment of, or interference with, amenities or other legitimate uses of the environment.

Regulating polluting activities

PPCA 1999, s 2 sets out the general purposes for which regulations may be made, including implementing the IPPC Directive. The new system will need to incorporate the principles and concepts employed in the directive, eg Best Available Techniques and the general principles concerning energy efficiency, the control of waste production and site restoration, in so far as the installations covered by the directive are concerned.

PPCA 1999, Sch 1 lists the specific purposes for which the power in s 2 may be exercised. Such purposes reveal that the procedural requirements of the new pollution control system will be very similar to those in EPA 1990, Part I. Thus the regulation power may be exercised to establish a system of pollution control requiring operators of specified installations or plants to hold permits (para 4); for those permits to contain conditions (para 7); for publicity to be given to, for example, permit applications and for information to be supplied inter alia for inclusion in public registers (para 12); for regulators to take enforcement action or to require remedial action (para 15); for the creation of offences, eg a failure to comply with permit conditions (para 17); and for rights of appeal (para 19).

PPCA 1999, s 2 and Sch 1 also enable the new pollution control system to include requirements which are similar to those in Part II of the EPA 1990. Thus, provision may be made restricting the grant of permits to those who are fit and proper persons, a test which is applied under the Waste Management Licensing system[70] (para 5). The power to make regulations in this area is necessary in order that the 'fit and proper persons' provisions may continue to apply to those waste management installations currently regulated under EPA 1990, Part II to which the directive applies and which, in future, will be regulated under the new regime.[71] Similarly, Sch 1, para 8 allows provisions to be made regulating the transfer or surrender of permits, matters which are also currently dealt with under the Waste Management Licensing system.[72] Regulations will apply such requirements to *all* installations covered by the directive to allow the implementation of the directive's requirement that appropriate preventive or remedial activity takes place (either by the permit holder *or* some other person) following closure of an installation.

Prior to making any regulations under PPCA 1999, s 2, the Secretary of State is under a duty to consult certain specified bodies, eg the Environment Agency.[73] He must also consult such bodies or persons which appear to him to be representative of the interests of local government, industry, agriculture and small businesses, and such other bodies or persons as he may consider appropriate (PPCA 1999, s 2(4)). In short, therefore, the Secretary of State is required to consult both the regulators and the regulated.

Finally it should be noted that the PPCA 1999 provides not only for the ultimate repeal of EPA 1990, Part I, which will be superseded by the IPPC regime, but for a number of consequential amendments and repeals to other legislation to take account of the replacement of the EPA 1990, Part I regimes by the new regime.[74]

70 See chapter 14.
71 The detail of the regulations is discussed below.
72 See chapter 14.
73 Where the regulations will apply in Scotland, he must consult the Scottish Environment Protection Agency (SEPA).
74 See PPCA 1999, s 6 and Schs 2 and 3.

The Pollution Prevention and Control (England and Wales) Regulations 2000

The power under PPCA 1999, s 2 was used to make the Pollution Prevention and Control (England and Wales) Regulations 2000[75] which, as the reference in parenthesis indicates, apply only in England and Wales.[76] Since these regulations set down the detail of the IPPC regime, it will be necessary to examine them in detail. However, prior to so doing, it is appropriate to consider who will act as regulator under this new regime.

The regulators

One of the many issues which the government consulted upon regarding the implementation of the IPPC Directive was the identity of the regulator for the new regime. As we have already noted, under the IPC regime the role of regulator is principally performed by the Environment Agency in England and Wales, with local authorities having responsibility for atmospheric emissions by the less polluting plants. Under the IPPC Directive (as we have also noted), it is clearly envisaged that there may be more than one regulator although there is no requirement that this must be the case. Accordingly, member states have a discretion in the matter. In the Second Consultation Paper on implementing the IPPC Directive,[77] the government considered that there were four options available: the Environment Agency as sole regulator with local authorities acting as statutory consultees; local authorities as subcontractors to the Environment Agency; the Environment Agency and local authorities as sole regulators for different installations; and coordinated pollution control which would be applied to some sectors according to appropriate criteria.[78] All but the first option therefore envisaged local authority involvement in the setting of some or all of the permit conditions for some IPPC installations.

The majority of the respondents to this consultation were in favour of the third option, ie the division of regulatory responsibilities between the Environment Agency and local authorities. This option was especially favoured by the local authorities themselves and those industries regulated by them under the LAAPC regime.[79] In response, the government noted that the local authorities had operated the LAAPC regime 'capably' and that a regulatory role under IPPC would complement their new responsibilities for local air quality management.[80] However, the government also noted that the need for an integrated authorisation of *all* emissions from installations under the directive meant that local authorities would also have to regulate discharges to *water*, a function which they had not previously performed. It therefore proposed a solution to this dilemma which is now reflected in the 2000 Regulations.

Under the 2000 Regulations, Sch 1, activities, installations and mobile plant are classified as either Part A(1), Part A(2) or Part B. Responsibility for regulating the most polluting activities etc (Part A(1)) lies with the Environment Agency. The less polluting activities etc (Part A(2) and Part B) are regulated by the local authorities. In the case of Part A(2) activities etc, local authorities act as the regulator in respect of *all* emissions. In the case of Part B activities etc, however, they act as the regulator in respect of

75   SI 2000/1973.
76   The commencement date of these regulations was 1 August 2000.
77   Published jointly by the DETR, and the Scottish and Welsh Offices, January 1998.
78   See paras 12-17.
79   See the *Third Consultation Paper on the Implementation of the IPPC Directive* (18 January 1999), paras 6 and 7.
80   See chapter 17 below.

atmospheric emissions only.[81] The Environment Agency will thus act as the regulator for discharges to *water* from Part B activities etc.

Thus the regulatory arrangements under the 2000 Regulations represent an enhanced pollution control role for local authorities. This does not mean, however, that they have a completely free hand as regards the regulation of emissions into water from Part A(2) installations or mobile plant. Under the 2000 Regulations, reg 13, the Environment Agency may in respect of any such installation or plant give notice to the local authority regulator specifying the emission limit values or conditions which it considers are appropriate in relation to preventing or reducing emissions into water. Where such notice is given, any emission limit values or conditions specified in that notice must be reflected in the permit. It should also be noted that the Secretary of State has the power to direct that local authority functions under the regulations are instead to be exercised by the Environment Agency for such period as is specified in the direction (the 2000 Regulations, reg 8(6)). Such a direction may apply *generally* to all installations/mobile plant of a certain description, or *specifically* to a particular plant or installation. A similar power entitles the Secretary of State to transfer Agency functions to local authorities, although such directions can only be made in relation to a *specific* installation/mobile plant.

Definitions

In view of the fact that IPPC is concerned with the regulation of activities at *installations/ mobile plants* rather than just with processes, it is important to define what is meant by 'installation' and 'mobile plant'.

Installations and mobile plants

The 2000 Regulations, reg 2(1) provides that 'installation' means:

'(i) a stationary technical unit where one or more activities listed in Part 1 of Sch 1 are carried out; and
(ii) any other location on the same site where any other directly associated activities are carried out with a technical connection with the activities carried out in the stationary technical unit and which could have an effect on pollution, and, other than in Schedule 3,[82] references to an installation include references to part of an installation.'

The regulation further provides that 'mobile plant' means:

'plant which is designed to move or to be moved whether on roads or otherwise and which is used to carry out one or more activities listed in Part 1 of Schedule 1.'

---

81 Under the 2000 Regulations, therefore, some installations will be regulated on the basis of IPPC/LAAPC just as some installations under the EPA 1990, Part I have been regulated on the basis of IPC/LAAPC.
82 This Schedule specifies the prescribed dates by which installations carrying out particular activities must have an IPPC permit under the Regulations. It also makes provision for transitional arrangements.

With regard to an 'installation' therefore, it follows that it may well fall short of being an entire factory. In order to assist regulators and operators (and others) in applying the definition, DEFRA has provided further explanation and some examples.[83] In order to be an 'installation' for the purposes of (i) above, therefore, it is necessary that the plant is: a technical unit where one or more relevant activities is carried out; and, that the technical unit is stationary. 'Technical unit' is to be taken to mean something which is functionally self-contained, ie the unit consisting of one or more components functioning together can carry out the relevant Sch 1 activity/activities on its own. In the case of two or more units on the same site, the Guidance states that they should be treated as a *single technical unit* if: they carry out successive steps in one integrated industrial activity; or one of the listed activities is a directly associated activity of the other; or both units are served by the same directly associated activity.

Turning to limb (ii) of the definition, the Guidance notes that there are three criteria for determining whether an activity satisfies this limb: the activity must be directly associated with the stationary technical unit; the activity must have a technical connection with the listed activities carried out in or by the stationary technical unit; and, the activity must be capable of having an effect on emissions. In the case of the first criterion, therefore, it is clear that there must be an 'asymmetrical relationship' whereby the activity serves the technical stationary unit. To take the example of the operation of a landfill, the Guidance notes that where such an activity serves a stationary technical unit carrying out a listed activity and some other industrial units on different sites carrying out non-listed activities, the activity will only be directly associated with the stationary technical unit if that unit is the *principal user* of the activity. With regard to the second criterion, the Guidance suggests that it gives rise to four types of *directly associated* activities which may be said to have a technical connection with a stationary technical unit. The four activities are: input activities concerned with the storage and treatment of inputs into the stationary technical unit; intermediate activities concerned with the storage and treatment of intermediate products during the carrying on of listed activities; output activities concerned with the treatment of waste from the stationary technical unit; or output activities concerned with the finishing, packaging and storage of the product from the stationary technical unit. In short, each of the four activities has a *technical connection* in the sense that it is an integral part of the listed activity. The third criterion, that the activity must have an effect on emissions, covers activities which have such an effect either due to their association with the listed activity or in their own right.

A number of examples are given in the Guidance to illustrate the above. Thus in the case of three combustion plants discharging through a common stack, the Guidance states that this constitutes *one unit*. None of the individual plants is a unit in its own right because none of them are functionally self-contained; the stack is an essential component of each and therefore the three combustion plants represent three components of one stationary technical unit. Where, however, three combustion plants discharge through a common stack and one combustion plant discharges through its own stack, this would constitute *two units* even if all the plants were on the same site and operated by the same operator. They might, however, be regarded as a *single installation* if they were served by the same *directly associated* activity, eg fuel handling.

Two further examples given in the Guidance are worthy of note. In the case of a power station where coal is stored on site, the power station will be the stationary technical unit and the storage of coal *will* amount to a directly associated activity. The storage area will thus be part of the installation along with the stationary technical

---

83   *Integrated Pollution Prevention and Control: a Practical Guide*, Annex II.

unit. The position will be different, however, in the case of a cement clinker manufacturing plant with an on site chalk quarry. Here the cement plant is the stationary technical unit but the chalk quarry *will not* have a technical connection with that unit; quarrying chalk is regarded as being one step further removed than the input activities that may be directly associated activities.

Permits

Under the 2000 Regulations, reg 9, no person may operate an installation or mobile plant after the 'prescribed date' for that installation/mobile plant without a permit granted by the regulator. The prescribed dates are set out in the 2000 Regulations, Sch 3. Thus, for example, in the case of a *new* Part A installation/mobile plant where an application has been made before 1 January 2001, the 'prescribed date' is the determination date for the installation/mobile plant. If, however, no such application has been made, the determination date is 1 January 2001. In effect, therefore, any new installation/mobile plant, ie one put into effect on or after 31 October 1999, could not be operated lawfully after 1 January 2001 if its operator had not applied for a permit under the 2000 Regulations. It was reported by the Environment Agency that the first IPPC permit in the UK was issued on 12 March 2001 to TXU, the operators of a new combined heat and power plant supplying energy (electrical power and steam) to a paper company plant in North Wales.[84]

In the case of an *existing* Part A installation/mobile plant, the prescribed date is determined by reference to a specified 'relevant period'.[85] Thus in the case of the burning of any fuel in an appliance with a rated thermal input of 50 megawatts or more,[86] for example, the 'relevant period' is 1 January–31 March 2006. Where the operator of such an appliance applies for a permit within that period, the prescribed date is the determination date. Where, however, no such application is made, the prescribed date is the day after the date on which the relevant period has expired. In short, therefore, an appliance as described above would be operating unlawfully if, on 1 April 2006, no application had been made for a permit under the Regulations. The 2000 Regulations, Sch 3, Part 2, makes provision with regard to Part B installations/mobile plants.

It should be noted that in October 2001, DEFRA published a consultation paper in which it sought opinions on a proposal to defer the relevant period for certain Part A(2) and Part B installations/mobile plants by 12 months. The justification for such a proposal was that work to produce tailor-made guidance for Part A(2) installations/ mobile plants and to revise existing general and additional guidance for the LAAPC regime was under way but not yet complete. It was felt important that such guidance should be available in good time before local authorities and industry begin the transition to the new IPPC regime.

Transitional arrangements

Given that the IPPC regime is now up and running in respect of *new* plant and that it will be phased in with regard to *existing* plant, IPC applications under EPA 1990, s 6 (see above) will eventually become a thing of the past. However, in the meantime, it

84 See the 'News' section of the Environment Agency's website for 12 March 2001. For details of the permit's requirements, see (2001) 314 ENDS Report, 9-10.
85 Set out in tabular form in the 2000 Regulations, Sch 3, para 2(2).
86 See the 2000 Regulations, Sch 1, section 1.1.

has been necessary to make transitional arrangements.[87] In one particular case,[88] where an application for an IPC *authorisation* for a new installation had been made before the 2000 Regulations came into force but which had not been determined until after the prescribed date ie after 1 January 2001, it was claimed, inter alia, that the Agency's granting of the authorisation amounted to a futile exercise of executive power since the installation could not be operated without a *permit* under the IPPC regime. In rejecting this argument, Turner J accepted the Agency's submission that EPA 1990, s 6(3) meant that it had no option but to do as it had done, even though the effect of the authorisation was not, and could not have been, to authorise the operation of the installation to which the application related. In the opinion of Turner J, nothing that the Agency had done could be said to have impeded or imperilled the implementation of the IPPC Directive. Indeed, the reverse was true.

Applications for permits

Under the 2000 Regulations, reg 10, applications for permits have to be made to the regulator in the prescribed form and accompanied by a fee. The requirements are set out in Sch 4, Part 1, paras 1-3. Thus, *all* applications must include (in addition to matters such as the name, address and telephone number of the applicant), inter alia: the nature, quantities and sources of foreseeable emissions from the installation/mobile plant into each environmental medium, and a description of any foreseeable significant effects of the emissions on the environment; the proposed technology and other techniques for preventing or, where that is not practicable, reducing emissions from the installation/ mobile plant; the proposed measures to be taken to monitor emissions; any additional information which the applicant wants the regulator to take into account in considering the application; and, a non-technical summary of the information contained in the application.

Specific provision is also made in relation to applications for permits to operate certain types of installation/plant. Thus in the case of an application for a permit to operate a Part B mobile plant, the application must contain either: the name of the local authority in which the applicant has his principal place of business; *or* where that principal place of business is outside England and Wales, the name of the local authority in whose area the plant was first operated; *or* where the plant has not been operated in England and Wales, the local authority in whose area the operator intends to first operate the plant.[89]

Determining an application   ·

An application which has been duly made may be either *granted* subject to the required/ authorised conditions (see below), or *refused*.[90] As is the case under IPC, therefore, a regulator under the IPPC regime is *not* able to grant an unconditional permit. A regulator's discretion when determining an application for a permit is further

---

87   See the Environmental Protection (Prescribed Processes and Substances) Regulations 1991, reg 3A as inserted by the Pollution Prevention and Control (England and Wales) Regulations 2000, Sch 10, para 24.

88   See *Furness v Environment Agency* [2001] EWHC Admin 1058, [2001] All ER (D) 242 (Dec).

89   2000 Regulations, Sch 4, Part 1, para 1(1)(c).

90   The Scottish Environment Protection Agency (SEPA) rejected its first application for an IPPC permit on the basis that the installation did not meet the BAT requirement: see (2001) 314 ENDS Report, 10.

circumscribed by the 2000 Regulations, para 10(3). This provides that an application shall be *refused* where: the regulator considers that the applicant will not be the person having control over the installation/mobile plant; or where it is considered that the person will not ensure compliance with the conditions to which the permit is subject. Where the application is for the carrying out of a specified waste management activity, further grounds for refusal apply. Thus such an application must be refused: if the regulator is satisfied that the applicant is not a fit and proper person to carry out the activity;[91] or if there has been no grant of planning permission for the activity under the Town and Country Planning Act 1990.[92]

A regulator should normally determine an application within four months from the date of its submission.[93] However, this period may be extended by agreement with the applicant. In calculating the four month period, no account is to be taken of matters such as a request made to the operator by the regulator for further information for the purposes of determining the application.[94] Where a regulator fails to give a determination within the prescribed period, an operator may inform the regulator in writing that he is treating such failure as a deemed refusal of the application.[95] The operator will then be in a position to appeal against that refusal (see below).

Practical Guidance on IPPC issued by DEFRA[96] states that it is the department's view that a proportionate approach should be taken to the determination of permit applications. In other words, 'the regulatory effort needed to determine an application and any permit conditions should be appropriate for the complexity of an installation and its environmental effects'.[97]

The Secretary of State has the power to direct that a particular application or class of applications be referred to him for determination.[98] Where this power is exercised, he may afford the applicant and the regulator the opportunity of appearing before and being heard by an appointed person, and he must do so where either party requests to be heard. On determining an application,[99] the Secretary of State must direct the regulator as to whether or not to grant the permit and if so, as to the conditions to which it is subject.

Conditions of a permit

When determining the conditions of a permit, the regulator must take into account the general principle that installations etc are to be operated in such a way that all appropriate measures are taken against pollution and that BAT is applied, and that no significant pollution should result from the operation of the installation (the 2000 Regulations, reg 11(1) and (2)). In relation to a Part A installation/mobile plant, the regulator should additionally take into account the need to: prevent waste production,[100] or where waste is produced, it is received or, where that is technically and economically impossible, it

---

91 This is to be determined in accordance with reg 4 of the 2000 Regulations.
92 See chapter 8 above.
93 2000 Regulations, Sch 4, Part 2, para 15(1).
94 2000 Regulations, Sch 4, Part 2, paras 4 and 15(2).
95 2000 Regulations, Sch 4, Part 2, para 16.
96 *Integrated Pollution Prevention and Control: a Practical Guide,* published 25 July 2000 and updated 15 March 2001.
97 Para 7.1.
98 Sch 4, Part 2, para 14(1).
99 Unlike the position for the regulators, there is no time limit on the Secretary of State's determination of an application. However, DEFRA Guidance notes that an effort will be made to deal with cases promptly: see para 7.7.
100 In accordance with Directive 75/442.

is disposed of while avoiding/reducing any impact on the environment; ensure that energy is used efficiently; take measures to prevent accidents and limit their consequences; and, ensure that on the definitive cessation of activities, measures are taken to avoid any pollution risk and return the site to a satisfactory state (reg 11(3)).

Specific provision with regard to permit conditions is made by the 2000 Regulations, reg 12. This provides, inter alia, that permits are to contain such conditions as the regulator considers appropriate, such as conditions relating to emission limit values for pollutants, especially those listed in the 2000 Regulations, Sch 5 to the Regulations, eg sulphur dioxide, nitrogen oxide and carbon monoxide, where these are likely to be emitted in significant quantities. In the case of a Part A installation/mobile plant, conditions must be imposed by reference to their potential to transfer pollution from one environmental medium to another. The emission limits apply generally at the point of emission. In other words, no allowance is to be made for subsequent dilution. In determining the emission limit values the BAT rule must be applied and account must be taken of the technical characteristics of the installation/mobile plant being permitted. However, the process must not be allowed to authorise emission levels that would infringe any specific EC Environmental Quality Standard for a particular medium.

A permit for a Part A installation/mobile plant, *must* also include conditions:
— to minimise long distance and transboundary pollution;
— to ensure protection of the soil and groundwater and appropriate management of waste generated by the installation/mobile plant;
— relating to periods when the installation/mobile plant is not operating normally, eg start up, leaks, malfunctions and momentary stoppages;
— requiring pre-operation and post-operative measures;
— setting out emission monitoring requirements;
— requiring operators to supply the regulator with the results of monitoring.

A permit *may* also include conditions imposing limits on the amount or composition of substances produced or utilised or supplementing other conditions in the permit. The Secretary of State has the power to direct regulators as to the specific conditions which are/are not to be included in all permits, in certain specified permits or permits of a particular description (the 2000 Regulations, reg 12(15)). Moreover, he may direct regulators as to the objectives which are to be achieved by conditions.

The BAT condition

Thus far no mention has been made of a condition that is *implied* in *every* permit; that in operating the installation/mobile plant, the operator shall use the BAT for preventing or reducing emissions (the 2000 Regulations, reg 12(10)). This requirement is therefore similar to the requirement under the IPC regime that all authorisations are subject to the BATNEEC condition.[101] For the purposes of the IPPC regime, BAT is defined by reg 3 to mean:

'the most effective and advanced stage in the development of activities and their methods of operation which indicates the practical suitability of particular techniques for providing in principle the basis for emission limit values designed to prevent and, where that is not practicable, generally to reduce emissions and the impact on the environment as a whole.'

101 EPA 1990, s 7(4), discussed above.

Each of the three components of BAT, ie 'available techniques', 'best' and 'techniques' is accorded a definition in reg 3. Thus 'available techniques' means:

'those techniques which have been developed on a scale which allows implementation in the relevant industrial sector, under economically and technically viable conditions, taking into consideration the cost and advantages, whether or not the techniques are used or produced inside the United Kingdom, as long as they are reasonably accessible to the operator.'

'Best' means:

'in relation to techniques, the most effective in achieving a high general level of protection of the environment as a whole.'

And 'techniques' includes:

'both the technology used and the way in which the installation is designed, built, maintained, operated and decommissioned.'

Although BAT and BATNEEC have much in common, the requirements of BAT seem to be stricter.[102] Thus there is a greater apparent emphasis on 'state of the art design' in BAT than there is in BATNEEC. Moreover, although *costs* have an important role to play in both pollution control regimes, as the government's Second Consultation Paper noted,[103] there appears to be a significant difference between BATNEEC and BAT as to which costs are relevant. In the case of the former, the costs which are weighed against environmental benefits are the costs to the process operator. For BAT, however, cost appears to have a wider meaning. To borrow the example set out in the Second Consultation Paper, it may mean that in addition to the cost to an operator of being required to use a particular type of fuel, regard should also be had to the wider energy source implications of such a measure if the result would be to cause an industrial sector to become exclusively reliant on a particular type or source of fuel.

In determining BAT, the 2000 Regulations, Sch 2 further provides that consideration should be given to certain matters, bearing in mind the likely costs and benefits of a measure and the principles of precaution and prevention. These matters relate to: the use of low-waste technology; the use of less hazardous substances; the furthering of recovery and recycling of substances generated and used in the process, and of waste; comparable processes, etc, tried with success on an industrial scale; advances in technological and scientific knowledge; the nature, effect and volume of emissions; the commissioning dates for new and existing plant; the length of time needed to introduce BAT; the consumption of energy and raw materials used in the process and the energy efficiency of the process; the need to prevent/reduce the overall impact of emissions on the environment; and the need to prevent accidents and the environmental consequences thereof.

Of these matters, the first and the last three do not apply for the purposes of determining BAT in relation to Part B installations/mobile plant. Nevertheless, it is clear

---

102 It is worth noting that during the Parliamentary debates on the Pollution Prevention and Control Bill, the government faced strong opposition from Conservative peers who wanted to amend the Bill so as to retain BATNEEC. However, it was pointed out by the government that to reject BAT would be to fail to properly implement the IPPC Directive: see (1999) 292 ENDS Report, 38.
103 At para 21.

from this list that a much wider range of considerations are relevant to BAT than were relevant to determining its predecessor, BATNEEC.

Guidance

With the advent of IPPC it has been necessary for the Environment Agency to draw up new guidance to assist both regulators and regulated alike. A number of the sector-specific guidance notes are, at the time of writing, the subject of consultation with industry, government and non-governmental organisations.[104] However, the Agency has in collaboration with the Scottish Environment Protection Agency (SEPA) and the Northern Ireland Environment and Heritage Service (EHS) drawn up the IPPC General Sector Guidance Note[105] which will apply throughout the UK where there is no IPPC sector-specific guidance. The purpose of this guidance is to supplement existing IPC guidance and to deal specifically with issues not formerly dealt with under that regime, eg energy, accidents, noise, site restoration[106] etc. The General Sector Guidance aims to:

1   Provide a clear structure and methodology that operators making applications should follow in order to ensure that they comply with all the requirements of the IPPC Regulations (and any other relevant provisions).
2   Minimise the effort by both the operator and regulator in the permitting of an installation by using clear indicative standards and material from previous applications as well as from accredited Environmental Management Systems.
3   Improve the consistency of applications by ensuring that all relevant issues are addressed.
4   Increase the transparency of the permitting process by having a structure in which the operator's responses and any departures from the standards can be clearly seen.
5   Improve the consistency of regulation across installations and sectors by facilitating the comparison of applications.
6   Provide a summary of some BATs for pollution control that are common to all sectors and which are expressed, where possible, as clear indicative standards that need to be addressed by applicants.

It should also be noted in the present context that guidance on BAT has been and will continue to be provided at the European level. The IPPC Directive, Art 16(2) requires the European Commission to organise an exchange of information between member states and the industries concerned relating to BAT. In practice, this exchange has been organised by the European IPPC Bureau which draws up BAT reference documents (BREFs). These documents must be taken into account by member states when determining BAT generally or in relation to specific cases.

BREFs contain a number of elements leading up to the conclusions as to what are considered to be the best available techniques for the relevant sector. They are thus seen as the catalyst for improved environmental performance across the Community. However, BREFs do not constitute interpretations of the IPPC Directive. Neither do they remove the obligations on operators and member states under the Directive to make decisions at national, regional or local levels. Furthermore, BREFs do not prescribe

104   For example, the consultation periods for technical guidance for the tanneries and textile sectors do not expire until 29 March 2002. Technical Guidance Notes have become available, however, for Food and Drink Installations, Hazardous Wastes and Intensive Livestock Units, reflecting the fact that these areas of activity had not generally been subject to IPC coverage in the past.
105   S0.01 (April 2001).
106   The IPPC General Sector Guidance, paras 2.7, 2.8, 2.9 and 2.11 respectively.

techniques or emission limit values. At the time of writing, BREFs have been produced for industrial sectors which include: pulp and paper manufacture; iron and steel production; cement and lime production; cooling systems; ferrous metal processes; non-ferrous metal processes; glass manufacture; and the tanning of hides and skins.

Off-site conditions

Under the 2000 Regulations, reg 12(12), a permit authorising the operation of an installation (ie Part A(1), Part A(2) or Part B) or a Part A mobile plant may include an off-site condition. In other words, a permit may contain a condition requiring an operator to carry out works etc in relation to land which is not part of the installation/mobile plant site, notwithstanding that he has no rights over such land. Any person whose consent would be required *shall* grant such rights in relation to that land as will enable the operator to comply with any requirements imposed on him by the permit. A grantor is entitled to be compensated by the operator in accordance with the Regulations, Sch 6.

The DEFRA Guidance notes that these provisions are broadly the same as measures introduced under the EPA 1990, Part II. It is intended that they will be used where it is necessary to monitor the effects of an activity in another person's land, although the Guidance does not rule out the possibility of their use for other purposes. As a general rule, however, the Guidance notes that 'most non-waste activities should be capable of being operated so that regulators do not need to set any off-site conditions'.[107]

General binding rules

Although permit conditions are generally site specific, the 2000 Regulations, reg 14 enables the Secretary of State to make generally binding rules (GBRs) containing requirements which will be applied to certain types of installation/mobile plant. The power to make such rules is, however, limited. It applies only to Part A installations/mobile plant. Moreover, the power may only be exercised where the Secretary of State is satisfied that the same high level of integrated environmental protection can be achieved as could be under conditions made pursuant to the 2000 Regulations, reg 12. Where GBRs have been made, a regulator may include them as a condition of the permit at the request of an operator. The Secretary of State has the power to vary or revoke GBRs, subject to giving notice to all affected parties.

Given that IPPC is concerned with the regulation of complex activities, the scope for GBRs is thought to be limited. However, sectoral GBRs may have some utility in respect of less complex activities which are carried out in the same way throughout the industrial sector. Potential candidates for GBRs have been reported to include: pig and poultry installations; brewing; soft drink manufacturing; flour milling; milk treatment and processing; and petrol stations.[108]

Review of conditions

Regulators are required by the 2000 Regulations, reg 15 to conduct a periodic review of permit conditions, and they may do so at any time. A review must be carried out where:

---

107 DEFRA Guidance, para 7.14.
108 See (2000) 305 ENDS Report, 43.

pollution emitted by an installation/mobile plant is of such significance that existing limit values need to be revised or new limit values included; substantial changes in BAT make it possible to significantly reduce pollutants from the installation/mobile plant without imposing excessive costs; or where operational safety requires a change.

Although the 2000 Regulations do not specify the frequency with which reviews of permit conditions are to be conducted, the government suggested in its Third Consultation Paper on the implementation of the IPPC Directive that new sector-specific IPPC Sector Guidance Notes would indicate appropriate review periods. In fact, the review periods are set out in the General Sector Guidance.[109] For an activity not formerly regulated under the IPC or Waste Management Licensing Regimes, the review period will normally be within *four years* of the issue of the IPC permit (and *six years* thereafter). For activities previously subject to IPC or Waste Management Licensing, the review period will normally be within *six years* of the issue of the permit.[110]

Change in the operation of an installation

Subject to an exception where an operator of an installation/mobile plant has applied for the variation of the conditions of his permit (see below), the 2000 Regulations, reg 16 provides that an operator who proposes to make a change in the operation of his installation must give the regulator at least 14 days written notice before making the change. Such notice must set out the nature of the proposed change. Receipt of the notice must be acknowledged by the regulator.

Variation of conditions

Under the 2000 Regulations, reg 17, a regulator may at any time vary the conditions of a permit. Variation *must* take place, however, if it appears to the regulator as a result of a review or notification of a proposed change in the operation of the installation that conditions ought to be included in the permit which are different to those currently subsisting.

An operator may apply to the regulator for the variation of the conditions of his permit. Any such application must be made in the prescribed form[111] and must be accompanied by the appropriate fee. On receipt of the application, the regulator (or the Secretary of State[112]) shall determine whether or not to vary the conditions of the permit. If it is decided to vary the conditions, a notice specifying the variations and the date(s) on which they are to take effect shall be served on the operator. An operator shall also be notified where it has been decided not to vary the conditions of his permit.[113]

Transferring a permit

Where an operator of an installation/mobile plant wishes to transfer the whole or part of his permit to another person, both he and the proposed transferee may apply jointly

---

109 S0.01.
110 See the IPPC General Sector Guidance (April 2001), para 1.4.
111 See 2000 Regulations, Sch 7, Part 1, para 1.
112 See 2000 Regulations, Sch 7, Part 2, para 6.
113 For more detailed provision with regard to the determination of variation applications and variation notices, see 2000 Regulations, Sch 7, Part 2.

to the regulator to effect the transfer (the 2000 Regulations, reg 18). Such a course of action is of course both necessary and desirable where an IPPC installation (or part thereof) has been sold by one company to another. Any application made under the 2000 Regulations, reg 18 must be made in due form, and must be accompanied by the permit and the prescribed fee. In the case of a partial transfer, the application must identify the installation/mobile unit to which the transfer applies, and where the transfer applies to the operation of an installation or Part A mobile plant, the application must also contain a map identifying the part of the site used for the operation of that installation/mobile plant. The regulator may also require further specified information to be furnished by either the operator or proposed transferee for the purposes of determining the application.

Under the 2000 Regulations, reg 18(4), a transfer must be effected unless the regulator considers that the proposed transferee will not be the person having control of the installation/mobile plant or will not ensure compliance with the conditions of the transferred permit. In the case of a permit which relates to a specified waste management activity, the transfer shall only be effected if the regulator is satisfied that the proposed transferee is a 'fit and proper person'. A transfer request must be effected within two months of the date on which the regulator received the application, or within such longer period as has been agreed by the parties. If the application has not been determined by the end of either such period, the applicants may notify the regulator that they will treat the failure to decide as a deemed refusal. They may accordingly appeal in respect of the refusal (see below).

Surrendering a permit

Where the operator of a Part A installation/mobile plant ceases or intends to cease operating the installation (in whole or in part) or the mobile plant, he may apply to the regulator to surrender the whole permit or, in the case of a partial surrender, that part of it which authorises the operation of the relevant installation/mobile plant. As with the other types of application under the 2000 Regulations, an application to surrender must be made in the prescribed form and must be accompanied by the appropriate fee.

If the regulator is satisfied that such steps (if any) as are appropriate to avoid any pollution risk arising from the installation/mobile plant, and to return the site to a satisfactory state, have been taken by the operator, surrender must be allowed. Notice of such a determination must be given to the operator and the permit shall cease to have effect. In the case of a partial surrender, the permit shall cease to have effect to the extent surrendered from the date specified in the determination. It may also be necessary for the regulator to vary the conditions of the remaining part of the permit.

Where the regulator is not satisfied as to the matters referred to above, he must refuse the application. In either case, the regulator has three months to give notice of his determination beginning with the day on which the application was received or such longer period as has been agreed by the parties. A failure to give notice of a determination entitles the operator to treat the failure as a deemed refusal, in respect of which there is a right of appeal (see below).

An operator of a Part B installation/mobile plant is similarly able to surrender the whole or part of a permit (the 2000 Regulations, reg 20). However, unlike the position described above in relation to Part A installations/mobile plants, the validity of a surrender under reg 20 is not dependent upon a determination by the regulator. It takes effect on the date specified by the operator in the notification to the regulator. The regulator's role in this type of case is thus confined to varying the conditions of a permit which has been partially surrendered.

Revoking a permit

By virtue of the 2000 Regulations, reg 21, a regulator may at any time serve a 'revocation notice' on an operator which has the effect of revoking his permit either wholly or in part. In particular, this may happen in respect of waste management activities where the regulator is of the opinion that the operator has ceased to be a 'fit and proper' person to carry out the activity by reason of his having been convicted of a relevant offence,[114] or by reason of the management of the activity having ceased to be in the hands of a technically competent person. Alternatively, revocation may take place where the holder of the permit has ceased to be the operator of the installation/mobile plant to which the permit relates.

A revocation notice may revoke a permit entirely, or in relation to specified installations/mobile plants, or in relation to specified activities at an installation/mobile plant. The notice must make it clear in the case of a partial revocation precisely what it is that is being revoked, and in all cases, the date (at least 28 days after the notice) on which revocation shall take effect. If it so wishes, a regulator who has served a revocation notice may withdraw that notice prior to the date on which it takes effect (the 2000 Regulations, reg 21(9)). With regard to a Part A installation/mobile plant, the regulator may require the operator to take steps to avoid pollution risks and to return the site to a satisfactory state.

Although the service of a revocation notice may take place at any time (see above), in practice it may be considered particularly appropriate where the use of other enforcement provisions within the 2000 Regulations (see below) has failed to achieve the proper protection of the environment.[115]

Enforcement

The 2000 Regulations, Part III is concerned with the enforcement of the foregoing provisions. It imposes a duty on the regulators to take such action as is necessary to ensure that the conditions of a permit are complied with (the 2000 Regulations, reg 23). It also makes provision for, inter alia, the service of an enforcement or suspension notice.

Enforcement notices

Where the regulator is of the opinion that an operator has contravened, is contravening or is likely to contravene any condition of a permit, it may serve an enforcement notice on the operator (the 2000 Regulations, reg 24). Where such a notice is served, it must state: that the regulator is of that opinion; the matters constituting the contravention or making it likely that a contravention will arise; the necessary remedial measures; and the period within which such measures are to be taken. With regard to remedial steps, these may include steps relating to the operation of the installation/mobile plant such as to enable it to comply with the conditions of the permit and steps that must be taken to remedy the effects of any pollution caused by the contravention. An enforcement notice may be withdrawn by the regulator at any time.

114 As defined by the 2000 Regulations, reg 4(5)(a).
115 See 'Integrated Pollution Prevention and Control: A Practical Guide', para 16.7.

Suspension notices

The 2000 Regulations, reg 25 requires a regulator to serve a suspension notice on an operator where it is of the opinion that the operation of the installation/mobile plant generally, or in a particular manner, involves an *imminent risk of serious pollution*. With regard to the operation of the installation/mobile plant in a particular manner, the power to serve a suspension notice applies irrespective of whether the manner of operating is regulated by or contravenes a permit condition. In the case of a waste management activity, a suspension notice may also be served on the operator where the regulator is of the opinion that he has ceased to be a 'fit and proper person' by reason of the management of the activity having ceased to be in the hands of a technically competent person.

A suspension notice must state: the regulator's opinion; the imminent risk involved in the operation of the installation/mobile plant; the steps that must be taken to remove it and the period within which they must be taken; that the permit shall cease to authorise the operation of the installation/mobile plant for as long as the suspension notice is in force; and, that where the permit is to continue to have effect to authorise the carrying out of activities, state any steps (in addition to those already required by the conditions of the permit) that are to be taken in carrying out those activities.

The regulator may withdraw a suspension notice at any time. Such a notice must be withdrawn, however, where the regulator is satisfied that the steps specified to remove the imminent risk of serious pollution have been taken, or in the case of a waste management activity, the management of such an activity is in the hands of a technically competent person.

Power of the regulator to prevent or remedy pollution

As an alternative to requiring an operator to carry out remedial steps under the 2000 Regulations, reg 25, reg 26 enables the regulator to arrange for steps to be taken to remove the risk of imminent serious pollution. This power is also exercisable where an offence has been committed under the 2000 Regulations (see below).

The regulator may recover from the operator the cost of any steps taken under reg 26. However, no such costs will be recoverable if the operator is able to show that there was no imminent risk of serious pollution justifying the taking of remedial steps. Moreover, even where some steps were justified, the operator will not have to pay for those which he can show were unnecessarily incurred by the regulator.

Appeals

Regulation 27 of the 2000 Regulations provides for the circumstances in which an appeal may be made to the Secretary of State against a determination made by the regulator under the Regulations. Thus an appeal may occur: where a permit has been refused; where there has been a refusal to vary permit conditions; where an operator is aggrieved by permit conditions; where an application to transfer a permit has been refused or where the applicant is aggrieved at conditions attached on transfer; where a request to surrender a permit has been refused or where the applicant is aggrieved at conditions attached to take account of the surrender; or where a variation notice, revocation notice, enforcement notice or suspension notice has been served. No appeal may be brought against a decision or notice, however, which implements a direction of the Secretary of State.

In determining an appeal, the Secretary of State has a wide measure of discretion available to him. He may affirm the initial decision. Where the decision was to refuse a permit or to vary its conditions, he may grant the permit or vary the conditions attached to it. Where the decision related to the conditions attached to a permit, the Secretary of State may quash all or any of those conditions. In the case of a decision to refuse to transfer or accept the surrender of a permit, he may direct the regulator to do either. Where an appeal relates to a variation, revocation, enforcement or suspension notice, the Secretary of State may either quash or affirm the notice. If he affirms the relevant notice, he may do so either in its original form or with such modifications as he thinks fit.

From a practical point of view it is important to note what effect bringing an appeal has upon an impugned decision. Is the decision thereby suspended pending the determination or withdrawal of the appeal, or does it remain in force? Where conditions have been attached to a permit following an application under the 2000 Regulations, reg 10, or to take account of the transfer or surrender of the permit, an appeal does *not* suspend the operation of those conditions (the 2000 Regulations, reg 27(7)). Neither does the bringing of an appeal against a variation, enforcement or suspension notice suspend the operation of the relevant notice (the 2000 Regulations, reg 27(8)). The position is different, however, where the appeal relates to a revocation notice. In these circumstances, the revocation notice will not take effect pending the determination or withdrawal of the appeal.

The 2000 Regulations, Sch 8 lays down procedural requirements with regard to the making and determination of appeals. Thus, for example, the Schedule specifies time limits within which the various rights of appeal must be exercised. Where the impugned decision relates to the refusal to grant a permit or to any of the conditions attached to it, the time limit for bringing an appeal is six months from the date of the decision. In the case of an appeal against a variation, enforcement or suspension notice, the time limit is two months from the date of the notice. Appeals against revocation notices must be brought before the date on which the notice takes effect.

Although the right to appeal against a decision made under the 2000 Regulations is, as we have seen, limited to an aggrieved applicant or operator, third party involvement in the appeal itself is provided for under Sch 8. Thus the regulator has quite a wide measure of discretion to give notice of the appeal to any persons who have made representations about the subject matter of the appeal or who appear to have a particular interest in the outcome of the issue. Such notices will invite further representations to be made by their recipients.

The Secretary of State may allow the appellant and the regulator to appear before and be heard by a person appointed by him prior to the determination of the appeal, and he must do so if either party so requests. Such a hearing may be in public or private. If a public hearing is involved and the matter relates to a Part A installation/mobile plant, local publicity must be accorded to the appeal and all those on whom notice of the appeal was served must also be informed. At the appeal itself, the appellant and the regulator have a right to speak, as do certain statutory consultees such as the Local Health Authority, the Food Standards Agency, the local authority etc.[116] Other persons may speak at the discretion of the person hearing the appeal.

Following the conclusion of the hearing, the person holding it has to make a detailed written report to the Secretary of State in which he sets down his conclusions and recommendations (or his reasons for not making any recommendations). Thereafter the Secretary of State will inform the parties of his decision. An appeal against the Secretary of State's determination may be made to a court on a *point of law*.

116 See Sch 4, Part 2, para 9.

Information and publicity

The 2000 Regulations, Part V is largely concerned with making environmental information available to the public at large, principally through the establishment of public registers of information. However, it should be noted that in order to enable him to discharge his functions under the 2000 Regulations, the Secretary of State may require a regulator or any other person (most obviously an operator) to supply him with such information as he may by notice request (reg 28).

Public registers of information

The 2000 Regulaitons, reg 29 imposes a duty on each regulator to maintain a register containing the particulars of each installation/mobile plant for which it is the regulator. The prescribed information is set out in the 2000 Regulations, Sch 9, para 1. It includes:

1 all particulars of permit applications;
2 all particulars of advertisements placed by applicants as part of the application process;
3 all particulars of permits granted;
4 all particulars of applications for the transfer, variation or surrender of a permit;
5 all particulars of permits which have been transferred, varied or surrendered;
6 all particulars of any permit which has been revoked;
7 all particulars of any enforcement or suspension notice which has been issued;
8 all particulars of any notice issued by the regulator withdrawing an enforcement or suspension notice;
9 all particulars of any notice of appeal;
10 details of any conviction or formal caution for an offence committed under the 2000 Regulations, reg 32 relating to the operation of an installation/mobile plant (see below);
11 all particulars of any monitoring information obtained by the regulator as a result of its own monitoring or supplied by the operator in accordance with a condition of a permit;
12 all particulars of any report published by a regulator of an assessment of the environmental consequences of the operation of an installation in the locality of premises where the installation is operated under a permit granted by the regulator;
13 all particulars of any direction given by the Secretary of State.

It is thus apparent that the public registers contain a considerable amount of information relating to IPPC installations/mobile plant which must be capable of being inspected (and copied at a reasonable cost) by members of the public at all reasonable hours. There are, however, exceptions to the general principle of open access to information. Thus in the case of an application which is withdrawn by the applicant before it is determined, all particulars of that application must be removed from the register not less than two months nor more than three months from the date of the withdrawal.[117] Similarly, nothing requires the keeping of monitoring information relating to an installation/mobile plant *four years* after that information was entered on the register, nor information relating to an installation/mobile plant which has been superseded by later information relating to that same installation/mobile plant four years after its entry onto the register.[118] Further exceptions exist in respect of information affecting national security or information which is commercially confidential.

117 2000 Regulations, Sch 9, para 2.
118 2000 Regulations, Sch 9, para 4.

Information affecting national security

Where the Secretary of State is of the opinion that including information in a register would be contrary to the interests of national security, such information (or information of that description) shall not be included in the register (2000 Regulations, reg 30). The Secretary of State may give the regulators directions specifying the information or descriptions of information which are to be excluded from the register, or which are to be referred to him for his determination. Information in this latter category must not be included in the register until the Secretary of State has determined that it should be included.

A person who thinks that information should be excluded from the register on the grounds of national security may give notice to the Secretary of State specifying the information and indicating its apparent nature. The regulator must be informed of any such notice the effect of which is to exclude the relevant information from the register until the Secretary of State has determined that it should be included.

Commercially confidential information

2000 Regulations reg 31 permits the exclusion of commercially confidential information from the register following an application from the person supplying the information. Whether or not information is of a commercially confidential nature is a matter to be determined by the regulator or on appeal, by the Secretary of State. Essentially it amounts to information whose inclusion on the register would prejudice to an unreasonable degree the commercial interest of the applicant or another person (2000 Regulations, reg 31(12)). It is clear that an operator must explain how such commercial prejudice might arise; it will not be enough to express concern about public opposition, or to assert commercial prejudice without supporting evidence.[119]

Notice of the regulator's determination as to whether or not information is commercially confidential must be given to the applicant. If the regulator fails to give such notice, the applicant is entitled to treat the failure as a determination that the information is *not* commercially confidential and he may appeal to the Secretary of State (see below).

Where it appears to the regulator that information *might* be commercially confidential, it must notify the relevant person of the requirement that the information shall be included in the register unless excluded under the 2000 Regulations, reg 31. The operator must give that person a reasonable opportunity to object to the inclusion of the information and to make representations on the issue. Any representations which are made must be taken into account in making a determination. If the regulator determines that the information is *not* commercially confidential, it must inform the applicant who may then appeal to the Secretary of State. Appeals relating to the issue of commercial confidentiality may take the form of a hearing and must do so if either the appellant or regulator so requests.

Despite the general thrust of the 2000 Regulations, reg 31, it does not completely exclude commercially confidential information from the public register. The Secretary of State may give directions that certain information has to be registered in the public interest, even though it is commercially confidential. Moreover, excluded information only remains in that category for *four years* after the date on which its status was determined. After this period has expired, the information will cease to be excluded unless the person who supplied it applies for it to remain excluded on the ground that it is still commercially confidential.

Provision as to offences

The key regulation in the 2000 Regulations, Part VI, reg 32, specifies the various offences that may be committed under the regulations (see below). Where the offence is that of failing to comply with the requirements of an enforcement or suspension notice, however, the regulator may be of the opinion that proceedings for such an offence will afford an ineffectual remedy. If this is the case, the regulator may take proceedings in the High Court to secure compliance with the notice (the 2000 Regulations, reg 33).

Offences

Under the 2000 Regulations, reg 32, it is an offence to do any of the following:
1   operate an installation/mobile plant without a permit;
2   contravene/fail to comply with permit conditions;
3   fail to notify the regulator of any proposed changes in the operation of the installation;
4   fail to comply with the requirements of an enforcement/suspension notice;
5   fail to furnish information when requested to do so by the regulator or Secretary of State;
6   to make a statement which he knows to be false or misleading, or to do so recklessly, in relation to the purported compliance with a request to furnish information, or for the purpose of obtaining a permit;
7   to intentionally make a false entry in connection with any record required to be kept as a condition of a permit;
8   to forge documents issued under permit conditions with intent to deceive.
Offences under this regulation may be committed by a person or a body corporate. In the case of the latter, if it can be shown that the offence was committed with the consent or connivance of, or to have been attributable to any neglect on the part of any director, manager, secretary etc of that body corporate, he shall also be guilty of the offence.[120] Where the commission by any person of an offence under the 2000 Regulations, reg 32 is due to the act or default of some other person, that other person may be charged with and convicted of the offence irrespective of whether proceedings for the offence are taken against the first-mentioned person.[121]

Power of court to order cause of offence to be remedied

Where a person has been convicted of the offence of operating an installation/mobile plant without a licence, or of contravening or failing to comply with a permit condition, or of failing to comply with the requirements of an enforcement or suspension notice, the 2000 Regulations, reg 35 empowers a court to order that person to take specified steps to remedy those matters which he is able to remedy. This power may be exercised instead of or in addition to any punishment which is imposed for the commission of the

---

120 This is a not uncommon provision in environmental legislation: see, for example, the EPA 1990, s 157 and the Water Resources Act 1991, s 217.
121 The 2000 Regulations, reg 32(6).

relevant offence. Any remedial steps must be carried out within the time limit stated in the order, although this may be extended or further extended by order of the court.

Powers of the Secretary of State

The 2000 Regulations, Part VII is concerned with the various powers which the Secretary of State has to influence the way in which the IPPC regime will be regulated. He may give *directions* of a general or specific nature to regulators as to the way in which they are to carry out any of their functions under the regulations (the 2000 Regulations, reg 36(1)). Specific directions may require the exercise of certain powers or their non-exercise in the circumstances set out in the direction. The Secretary of State may also issue *guidance* to regulators with respect to the carrying out of any of their functions (the 2000 Regulations, reg 37). Where guidance has been issued, a regulator must have regard to it. Finally, the 2000 Regulations, reg 38 empowers the Secretary of State to make plans for limiting the total amounts of particular emissions and the allocations of quotas relating to such emissions, and to make schemes for the trading or other transfer of such quotas.

Applying for IPPC permits: the experience to date

The IPPC regime is of course very new and it will not apply, as we have already seen, to a number of existing industrial activities for some years to come. It will therefore be some time before firm conclusions can be drawn as to its effectiveness in preventing and controlling pollution to the environment as a whole. Nevertheless, some early research has been carried out on an important feature of the new regime: the process of applying for an IPPC permit.

The research, which was carried out by a firm of Environmental Management Consultants[122] and jointly sponsored by DEFRA and the Environment Agency, involved reviewing a random selection of IPPC applications from the Environment Agency's public registers[123] and a follow-up questionnaire. Eight public registers were visited at various Agency regional and area offices in July 2001 and a total of 41 applications were selected for review. Although the sample was relatively small, the newness of the regime meant that some of the registers hardly contained any applications at all. The questionnaire which the applicants were sent sought information on a variety of issues, such as whether the application had been prepared with the help of a consultant, the length of time taken on the application process, the cost of making an application, the usefulness of DEFRA/Agency guidance, and how the process compared with making an IPC application.

The results of the review which were published in September 2001 make interesting reading. For example, it is noted that there appears to be a view amongst applicants that 'bigger is better'. In other words, an application should contain as much information as possible, even where this is glossy advertising material. The overall average across the sectors was 452 pages per application, although the range was 29-1700 pages. In general it was found that the applications in the shorter to mid size range were of a better quality in terms of the inclusion of relevant detail. It was also found that applications that had been produced by consultants were generally better than those which had been produced by the applicant alone. As far as the costs of making an

122 CTC Environmental.
123 Kept in accordance with the 2000 Regulations, reg 29: see above.

application are concerned, the review reveals a range across all sectors of £5,000 - £133,000, with the average being a little over £32,000.[124] Clearly, therefore, making an IPPC application may be a costly process, although there does seem to be a strong correlation between the complexity of the activity and the cost of the application.

Given the importance of BAT to the new regime, it is worth noting that the number of applicants who had fully justified their techniques as meeting BAT was found to be in the minority. In some cases, the review notes that an application made no reference whatsoever to BAT and in other cases, the applicant merely described in some detail the techniques that they used as if they must therefore amount to BAT. Accordingly, the review states that: 'BAT appears to be an area where there is a lack of understanding as to its meaning and how it should be presented in an application'. The remedy that it proposes, therefore, is that the BAT concept and how it should be presented in an application ought to be more clearly explained in the guidance given to the various industrial sectors.

A final point to note about the review concerns its findings as to how making an IPPC application compared with making an application under the IPC regime. Although only 12 responses were received on account of the fact that the question could only be answered by those with experience of both regulatory systems, these reveal that *none* of the respondents felt that the IPPC application process was less onerous than the IPC process. The majority felt that it was more onerous and more expensive and the other respondents considered that it was far more onerous and far more expensive than IPC. However, as the review notes, such responses were to be expected given the 'more comprehensive style' of IPPC.

Further reading

BOOKS

Backes, C (ed), *Integrated Pollution Prevention and Control: the EC Directive from a Comparative Legal and Economic Perspective* (1999) Kluwer.

Castle, P, and Harrison, H, *Integrated Pollution Control* (1996) Cameron May.

Hughes, D, Parpworth, N, and Upson, J, *Air Pollution: Law and Regulation* (1998) Jordans.

ARTICLES: IPC

Allot, K, 'Integrated Pollution Control: The First Three Years' (1994) Environmental Data Services Ltd.

Haigh, N, Irwin, F, 'Integrated Pollution Control in Europe and North America' (1990) The Conservation Foundation.

Harris, R, 'The Environmental Protection Act 1990 — Penalising the Polluter' [1992] JPL 515.

Harty, R, 'Integrated Pollution Control in Practice' [1992] JPL 611.

Hawkins, K, and Mehta, A, 'Integrated Pollution Control and its Impact: Perspectives from Industry' (1998) 10 JEL 61.

Layfield, Sir F, 'The Environmental Protection Act 1990: The System of Integrated Pollution Control' [1992] JPL 3.

Purdue, M, 'Integrated Pollution Control in the Environmental Protection Act 1990: A Coming of Age of Environmental Law?' (1991) 54 MLR 534.

---

124 These figures exclude the application fee which is payable to the Environment Agency.

ARTICLES: IPPC

Doppelhammer, M, 'More difficult than finding the way round Chinatown? The IPPC Directive and its Implementation: Part 1' (2000) 9 EELR 199.

Doppelhammer, M, 'More difficult than finding the way round Chinatown? The IPPC Directive and its Implementation: Part 2' (2000) 9 EELR 246.

Emmott, N, and Haigh, N, 'Integrated Pollution Prevention and Control: UK and EC Approaches and Possible Next Steps' (1996) 8 JEL 301.

Henshaw, L, 'Implementation of the EC Directive on Integrated Pollution Prevention and Control (96/61): A Comparative Study' [1998] 6 Env Liability 39.

Long, A, 'Integrated Pollution Prevention and Control: The Implementation of Directive 96/61' (1999) 8 EELR 180.

OFFICIAL REPORTS

'Integrated Pollution Control: A Practical Guide' (1993) DoE, HMSO.

'Integrated Pollution Prevention and Control: A Practical Guide' (2000) DEFRA.

'Integrated Pollution Prevention and Control: General Sector Guidance' (IPPC S0.01), (2000) Environment Agency.

'Review of the PPC Application Process' (2001) CTC Environmental.

Royal Commission on Environmental Pollution, Fifth Report, *Air Pollution Control: An Integrated Approach*, ((1976) Cmnd 6371).

Royal Commission on Environmental Pollution, Twelfth Report, *Best Practicable Environmental Option,* ((1988), Cmnd 310).

'UK Implementation of EC Directive 96/61 on Integrated Pollution Prevention and Control: Consultation Paper' (1997) DETR, Scottish and Welsh Offices.

'UK Implementation of EC Directive 96/61 on Integrated Pollution Prevention and Control: Second Consultation Paper' (1998) DETR, Scottish and Welsh Offices.

'UK Implementation of EC Directive 96/61 on Integrated Pollution Prevention and Control: Third Consultation Paper' (1999) DEFRA.

'UK Implementation of EC Directive 96/61 on Integrated Pollution Prevention and Control: Fourth Consultation Paper' (1999) DEFRA.

Chapter 17

Atmospheric pollution

A THE OVERALL PROBLEM

Air is intangible, ignored and easily damaged by pollution. The issue was fearsomely highlighted by the Bhopal disaster in India in 1984 when toxic substances escaped into the atmosphere near a major population centre. Atmospheric emissions could upset earth's fundamental ecological basis. Scientific debate on the so-called 'greenhouse effect' is based on concern over increasing atmospheric levels of carbon dioxide resulting from combustion of fossil fuels and emissions of other 'greenhouse gases' such as methane from decomposing waste, chlorofluorocarbons (CFCs) and nitrous oxides (NOx). Between 1978 and 1982 the concentration of carbon dioxide in the atmosphere increased from 315 parts per million to 340 parts per million. The Intergovernmental Panel on Climate Change (IPCC) reported in 1990 that up to one third of world grain production would be lost, the homes and livelihoods of 300m people set at risk from rising sea levels, and widespread desertification could flow from such an ecological imbalance which would result from global warming consequent on the greenhouse gases trapping heat within earth's atmosphere. Weather patterns will also become more unpredictable. The IPCC recommended an *immediate* cut in greenhouse gas emissions of 60%, but effective international action is still awaited despite the pronouncements of the Rio 'Earth Summit' in 1992. If, however, 'business as usual' emissions continue, by 2030 mean global surface air temperatures are likely to be 1.4°C higher than currently, carbon dioxide concentrations will have further increased from 350 parts per million by volume to 450, and global mean sea levels could be 20 cm higher than today, with consequences for agriculture, coastal areas, animal species, and indeed all sectors of human existence and activity. A most worrying aspect of the problem is the climatic uncertainty consequent on global warming, and this has led many to call for the application of precautionary principles nationally and internationally in the formulation of laws and policies designed, inter alia, to: promote greater energy economy; drive down the use of fossil fuels; promote the use of natural gas and renewable energy sources such as solar energy, wind, biomass and wave power; develop better public transportation and reduce consumption of fossil fuels by private vehicles.

  Though 'global warming' is the most serious atmospheric pollution problem, public concern also exists, inter alia, in relation to 'acid rain', depletion of the ozone layer, levels of ambient lead, the low level ozone problem, benzene, straw and stubble burning and volatile organic compounds (VOCs).

B PARTICULAR PROBLEMS AND SOME SOLUTIONS

Atmospheric pollution is no respecter of international boundaries. Nor is it the province of any one discipline: to reduce atmospheric pollutants requires action on a wide variety of fronts — technological, planning, social, economic, as well as legislative.

Good industrial management and improved technologies are important in reducing airborne pollution. See Coal and Energy Quarterly (1984) No 41, pp 24–29. Coal burning furnaces using 'fluidised bed' technology can reduce emissions of sulphur dioxide by over 90% by trapping the gas in beds of red hot limestone, and can be 80% thermally efficient, compared with 37% for conventional power station coal furnaces, see *The Times*, 28 April 1989, p 26. Efficiently designed furnaces can easily prevent the discharge of smokey volatile material. Incinerators can be prevented from discharging smoke into the air by the provision of afterburners. Emissions of grit and dust are controllable by use of settling chambers, bag filters, water scrubbers and electrostatic precipitators. The wise location of industry, taking into account prevailing weather patterns, topography and the incidence of population can reduce the potential for harm of emissions. Technology is, however, not so efficient in relation to polluting emissions caused by accidental leaks and spillages, evaporation from stored chemicals, and escapes arising from accidents during the course of transport. Furthermore unintended mixture of pollutants in air may produce secondary compounds.

Particular problems

'Acid rain'

There are certain emissions which are particularly difficult to control without further undesirable consequences. Sulphur dioxide (SO_2) is a major pollutant produced by chemical plants, oil refineries and power stations, yet not effectively controlled under the Clean Air legislation largely because in the 1950s no practical means of reducing SO_2 emissions was known, short of reducing fuel consumption. The method of control over SO_2 emissions was to disperse gas by discharging it at high velocity through tall chimneys, ideally, at least, two-and-a-half times the height of the nearest physical features. Discharged gas rises to a height of about 2,000 ft, dispersing over a wide area. This disposal method produced a 40% reduction in SO_2 concentrations at ground level in urban areas between 1956 and 1973, despite a 17% increase in gross energy consumption. Dispersal of SO_2 was widely accepted as the best means of control, see Scorer 'Technical Aspects of Air Pollution' chapter 3 of *Environmental Pollution Control* pp 54–56 and 58–61.

The growing body of evidence of the ill effects of SO_2 combined with water and other chemical agents to produce acid deposition, however, refocused attention on this issue. Voices were raised internationally arguing that the UK's disposal methods have resulted in British SO_2 polluting much of the rest of Europe. The 10th Report of the Royal Commission on Environmental Pollution accepted that emissions of sulphur and nitrogen oxides cause damage to fresh water and terrestrial ecosystems, but also considered the economic cost of reducing such emissions. The Royal Commission recommended, inter alia, that the electricity supply industry should investigate in the short term the various methods to abate SO_2 emissions, so that the industry would be ready and able to introduce remedial action should this prove necessary in the face of international pressure, note also the findings of the House of Commons Environment Committee in *Acid Rain* (4th Report, Session 1983–84). 'Acid Rain' (Cmnd 9397) doubted whether ozone concentration (produced by sunlight acting on hydrocarbons and NOx)

Acidification (a simplified model)

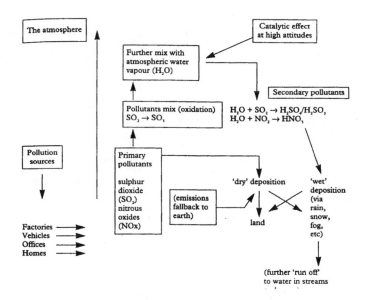

In North Western Europe the direction of prevailing winds is South West to North East, hence the most affected areas of this part of the globe are Norway, Sweden and Finland, though 'fluxes' from the UK and France also affect Germany and Poland. France is affected by 'fluxes' from Spain and Portugal.

now thought to be a possible contributor to forest damage, was principally due to transnational pollution. It also pointed out the high cost of reducing SO_2 emissions, though declaring policy to be: further reductions of SO_2 by 30% of 1980 levels by the end of the 1990s; similar reductions in NOx; stricter emission standards for motor cars; further research into atmospheric pollution and control technologies.

Caution also officially prevailed in relation to British NOx emissions, 45% of which were then produced by the electricity supply industry. It was policy not to set targets and timetables controlling emissions from existing plants and setting limits for new plant. Policy was, however, to reduce NOx emissions from motor vehicles.

Depletion of the ozone layer

Chlorofluorocarbon (CFC) gases and ozone. As a result of a complex process by which CFC compounds rise into the atmosphere reaching the stratosphere, the become 'dissociated' as a result of solar radiation and yield chlorine atoms, which destroy the ozone layer, which acts as a shield to filter out much harmful radiation from the sun.

1   CFCs are not the only 'culprits', but they are the main ones. Other 'depleters' include supersonic aircraft emissions, NOx emissions resulting from the application of nitrogen-based fertilisers, or from atmospheric nuclear weapon tests (now banned by international law) — but all of these are minor compared to the impact of CFCs.

2   CFCs are only slowly removed from the atmosphere by natural processes, and in

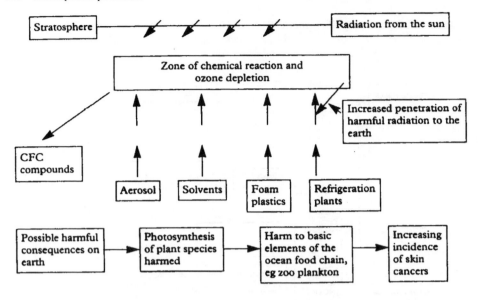

65–90 years' time virtually all CFCs ever produced with still be 'resident' in the atmosphere if released.

3　But remember CFCs have been seen in the past as very beneficial: easily made, cheap, non-toxic, non-flammable. To replace them is not easy. A range of substances can be used, the most popular were originally the HCFCs and HFCs. However, even these have various damaging effects and so they too have had to be brought under control. (See below.)

4　Similarly now subject to control are carbon tetrachloride (the 'classic' cleaning solvent) 1.1.1 trichloroethane, methyl bromide, hydrobromofluorocarbons (HBFC), and hydrochlorofluorocarbons (HCFC) as HCFCs are powerful greenhouse gases. This is 'the problem of technical bind', ie the solution to one problem creates another.

5　The hydrofluorocarbons (HFCs) are potent 'greenhouse' gases, and since January 1996 *voluntary* agreements between the UK government and the aerosol, air conditioning, refrigeration, fire protection and foam industries provide that where HFCs are used emissions will be minimised, and that they will not be used where emissions are unavoidable *and* safe, practical and more environmentally acceptable alternatives exist. However, the air conditioning and refrigeration 'agreement' is only a declaration of intent, as this industry is highly dispersed, and those who signed the document could not make a commitment on the part of those they did not represent.

The greenhouse effect

The earth receives its heat from the sun in the form of radiated energy. The atmosphere prevents most of this energy reaching the earth's surface, *only* 47% 'gets through' and that would not be enough for the planet to be habitable; its surface temperature would be some 20°C to 40°C. What keeps the planet habitable is *a* greenhouse effect — carbon dioxide (CO_2) and water (H_2O) in the atmosphere reflect back to the earth energy which is given off from the earth's surface after it has been received from the sun —

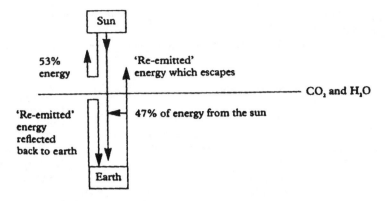

this maintains an average surface temperature of 14°C. But a change of only 2°–3°C in temperature range would have a very marked effect on the earth's climate.

What is now called *the* greenhouse effect is that certain gases, principally CO_2, if emitted from earth so that they accumulate in the atmosphere, will reflect back to the earth's surface more of the 're-emitted' energy, thus raising its surface temperature.

1 The principal 'greenhouse' gas is CO_2 emitted consequent on the use of 'fossil fuels' such as coal and oil.

2 Other gases, though present in smaller quantities, are more potent as 'greenhouse' gases, eg methane — 'marsh gas' or 'fire damp', etc.

3 CO_2 can be locked inside natural 'safes' such as trees as they breathe in CO_2 and breathe out oxygen. Thus the destruction of such natural 'sinks' exacerbates the problem.

4 Much scientific uncertainty still surrounds the greenhouse effect — indeed many still deny that it is a phenomenon that *can* occur — and its consequences.

5 Life could exist with higher earth surface temperatures — it did 4,500–8,000 years ago — but it appears the result would be wetter conditions in most of Europe, Africa, Southern Asia, Southern North America and South America, and drier conditions in most of the USA and Russia — the world's principal wheat growing areas. Thus crop yields could change dramatically.

6 Other effects of the 'greenhouse' could be (a) melting of the polar ice caps leading to massive flooding of low lying areas of the earth; (b) loss of plant/animal and fish species intolerant to higher temperatures; (c) increased global weather uncertainty with more storms.

It is, however, impossible to end using fossil fuels 'overnight', nationally or internationally, nor is a mass changeover to nuclear fission a viable alternative. Nuclear power is 'clean' from an atmospheric point of view, but disposal of nuclear waste is a great problem. It is clear, however, that the closest connection exists between environmental change and energy production and use. The current generation of laws on the issue concentrate — where they do so at all — on controlling the effects of energy production. In the future attention will have to be given to regulation of the effects of energy use. The promotion of more energy efficient appliances and buildings, coupled with positive rewards for energy saving will be of much more importance than currently. This will be in addition to the development of energy sources of a renewable nature.

The Royal Commission on Environmental Pollution's 22nd report, *Energy the Changing Climate* (Cm 4749), set out a visionary agenda involving a radical overhaul of the UK's current energy policy. Large-scale renewable energy projects will be required, in order to exceed the 2010 requirement that 10% of energy generation be from renewables, as will the need to improve energy efficiency, so as to lessen demand.

Further issues in atmospheric pollution

Consideration of 'global' atmospheric issues such as ozone depletion and the greenhouse effect should not detract attention from other problems which, though their incidence may be localised, are nevertheless capable of causing loss, injury and death. Environmental groups have argued that 10 million Britons are at risk from polluted air, and point to an alarming rate in the incidence of asthma, with 10% of children and 4–6% of adults affected, and which causes some 2,000 deaths in the UK each year (a doubling in 25 years), seven million lost working days, £400 m losses to industry and commerce and £520 m in costs to the national health and benefits budget with 200,000 people disabled by the disease. Particular pollutants causing concern include carbon monoxide, NOx and ozone, which is particularly implicated in the onset of asthma and bronchitis.

In addition fine particles in vehicle emissions, each less than 10 micrometers across and known as PM10, can be drawn into the lungs by respiration, carrying chemicals, some of them acidic. This further puts at risk the old, and those already suffering from chronic lung or heart diseases: some 2,000 to 10,000 deaths pa may be ultimately attributable to PM10. Diesel powered vehicles, heating systems and industrial systems are particularly implicated in the emission of solid particulate material, which now exceeds a realistic level of 50 micrograms per cubic metre of air on about 36 days pa in Britain, and which can reach 200 micrograms. Action on PM10 in the UK is likely to be initiated under the air quality strategy provisions of the Environment Act 1995, under new vehicle emission limits and EU measures.

Ozone, so essential at stratospheric levels, is, at ground or tropospheric levels, a highly corrosive pollutant which is formed by a complex chemical process based on reaction between sunlight, NOx and volatile organic compounds (VOCs). VOCs occur naturally, but 95% of those found in the atmosphere result from human activity. Some are highly toxic and can cause cancer, others are implicated in the formation of photochemical smog. VOCs are emitted in vehicle exhaust gases, and evaporation from petrol, paint and glue, and solvents. VOCs are gaseous pollutants containing carbon, and include hydrocarbons, and their oxygenated and chlorinated derivatives. Their common characteristic is the propensity to evaporate at normal outdoor (ie 'ambient') temperatures. A vast number of organic chemicals can be classed as VOCs, but examples include iso-octane, benzene, toluene, ethene and butane.

A regular summer problem in many cities is photochemical smog. Unlike the old 'pea souper' fogs of the 1950s (which were caused by large particles of soot and SO_2 emitted from coal burning power stations and which were common in winter when cold, dirty air can be trapped at ground level by warmer air above it) modern smog is made up of micro particles of VOCs and NOx. In summer, when anticyclonic weather over Britain induces an easterly air stream, bringing in polluted air from industrial areas on the continental mainland, the strong sunlight reacts with the 'chemical cocktail' to create ozone. To combat the problem international action, and certainly action on a world regional level, is needed. The UK's favoured approach is to press for action within the framework of the United Nations Economic Commission for Europe (UNECE). The current UNECE VOC protocol ratified by the UK in 1994, requires nations to achieve VOC reductions by 30% on 1988 levels by 1999. The UK aims to meet this target by applying the BATNEEC requirements of Part I of the Environmental Protection Act

1990 to solvent using industries and enhanced car emission controls. Actions will also be taken under the UK's national air quality strategy (see below) and will include giving public warning of high ozone risks and pleas to motorists to limit vehicle use on days when such risks would occur because of atmospheric conditions.

These problems have, however, to be kept in perspective. Atmospheric pollution risks today are less than they were 40 years ago. We are right to be concerned about the incidence of asthma; we need more research into the problems associated with PM10 and benzene; we may well have to curb the use of petrol and diesel powered vehicles which are the source of many pollutants, but the harmful effects of pollution are still much less marked or clearly observable than those of smoking.

Once again, however, we face a problem caused by a degree of uncertainty in the scientific evidence. The official Committee on the Medical Effects of Air Pollutants in October 1995 concluded that atmospheric pollution may certainly *aggravate* asthma, but it appears not to be a major *cause* of it. The problem is one of an unexplained increase in allergies, and the presence of 'biological pollutants' such as pollen and fungal spores, and styles of living (ie cramped living space and poor ventilation, deficient diets, mothers who smoke while pregnant and use of foam bedding mattresses). On the other hand traffic fumes may be much more implicated in the incidence of bronchitis and heart attacks. The lack of certain medical conclusions renders it more difficult to argue for stringent preventive controls over polluting emissions.

A report commissioned by DEFRA detailing research into several atmospheric pollution issues by the National Expert Group on Transboundary Air Pollution (NEGTAP) spanning a two-year period from 1999-2001 was recently published. The report, *(Transboundary Air Pollution: Acidification, Eutrophication and Ground Level Ozone in the UK)* considered data relating to, inter alia, acid rain, ground-level ozone pollution, emissions and atmospheric concentrations of the major pollutants. The report, rather encouragingly, shows a general reduction in emissions over time, although it remains the case that detectable deposits of certain pollutants are not directly proportionate to the level at which their emission has been reduced. Some of this difference will therefore reflect 'imported' pollution as well as the geographical spread of industry throughout the country. Also worth noting was that the acidity of rainfall in the UK had halved in the 14 years since 1985, and consequently the acidification of freshwaters was beginning to show signs of reversal. Against these positive findings, which could possibly be claimed as a victory for regulation, is the finding that critical loads for acidification were exceeded in 71% of UK ecosystems, although that figure is likely to drop below 50% by 2010. Perhaps slightly more encouraging was the finding that there had been a 30% drop in the peak concentrations of ground level ozone between 1986 and 1999, however the thresholds for impact on human health and vegetation were regularly exceeded. The reductions are identified with the progress of the law as a response to pollution difficulties: the fact that the UK is committed to a variety of international and domestic initiatives should lead to further qualitative improvements up until the end of the decade and, hopefully, beyond.

C THE LEGAL RESPONSE

There are a number of international treaties relating to atmospheric pollution ranging from the Geneva Agreement of 1958, various portions of which relate to emissions from vehicle engines, through the 1979 Geneva Convention on long range transboundary pollution, and the Vienna and Montreal Conventions of 1985 and 1987 on the protection of the ozone layer, to the 1992 framework Convention on Climate Change, part of the 'Rio package'.

International law is, however, increasingly concerned with the issues of transboundary pollution, of which the 'acid rain' issue is the classic instance, and general protection for the medium of the atmosphere, as witness agreements on protecting the ozone layer and moves towards attempts to limit emissions of 'greenhouse gases'.

Customary international law (see further chapter 4) has also some role to play in this connection. The customary recognition of the territorial sovereignty principle carries with it the notion that states may use their resources for their own benefit — for example the burning of fossil fuels. Against this it is generally argued that states should not allow transboundary pollution from activities carried out on their territory to affect other states, and the United Nations Charter of Economic Rights adds that sovereign rights are only to be used 'without causing damage to the legitimate interests of others'. See also dicta in *The Corfu Channel Case (UK v Albania)*[1] that a state is under an obligation 'not to allow its territory to be used for acts contrary to the rights of other states': *The Trail Smelter Arbitration*[2] and *The Nuclear Tests Case (Australia v France)*.[3] The concept was also recognised by Principle 21 of the (non-legally binding) 1972 Stockholm Declaration on the Environment. Whether all this amounts to a firmly settled rule of international law, however, is still a matter for some debate. (See, for example, Sands, *Chernobyl: Law and Communication* p 13 et seq.) Assuming, however, that there is a rule of customary international law relating to transboundary atmospheric pollution, how is it to be expressed? The Montreal Rules (ILA Draft Rules on Transboundary Pollution) formulate a requirement that states must prevent transfrontier air pollution to the extent that no substantial injury is caused to other states' territory, and that states 'shall refrain from causing transfrontier pollution by discharging into the environment substances generally considered as being highly dangerous to human health'. Problems arise, however, with regard to defining what constitutes 'substantial injury', as to what the requisite standard of care is, and to which injuries it applies.

Furthermore if the formulation of the customary rule in *The Trail Smelter* arbitration is followed 'clear and convincing evidence' of the injury in question must be brought forward. In that instance, however, the pollutants in question travelled only ten miles, and liability was admitted. Not all cases of transboundary pollution are so clear, and it has been a major weakness of international law that it has experienced difficulty — indeed often impossibility — in attributing responsibility for particular incidents of pollution damage in one state to particular polluting emissions from another — especially where several states emit emissions of the same type, as is the case with, for example, SO_2 It is, however, becoming easier to produce 'balance sheets' for pollution 'imports and exports' using enhanced monitoring techniques and more sophisticated mathematical models, and it is thus becoming more feasible to produce evidence that a given nation is receiving, for example, specified proportions of acidifying agents from another state, see the 1984 EMEP Report (see below) as abstracted in the Report of the 1986 62nd Conference of the International Law Association. However, it remains to be generally accepted that these new techniques enable the attribution of particular incidents of pollution damage to emissions from particular states. Indeed in the NEGTAP report referred to above , attention was focussed on the improvement and use of numerical models that 'represent current understanding of the underlying processes, *with all of their uncertainties*' (emphasis added).

1   (1948) ICJ Reps 15 at 22.
2   [1941] AJIL 684.
3   (1974) ICJ Reps 253.

Atmospheric treaties

As a consequence of the less than satisfactory condition of customary law increasing emphasis comes to be laid on treaties, both those dealing with individual issues and concerning only two, or a very few, states and, more especially, those which lay down generally applicable rules on a multi-state basis. The modern treaty based international law on atmospheric pollution dates from the Stockholm Conference of June 1972 on the Human Environment. Various non-legally binding principles were declared at the Conference. Principle 21, already referred to, provided that: 'states have ... the sovereign right to exploit their own resources and the responsibility to ensure that activities within their jurisdiction ... do not cause damage to the environment of other states ...'. Principle 22 further provided for international collaboration to develop laws concerning compensation for the victims of transboundary pollution. Following the Stockholm Conference the Organisation for Economic Co-operation and Development (OECD) undertook a study of transboundary sulphur pollution. This led to further work by the Co-operative Programme for Monitoring and Evaluation of Long Range Transmission of Air Pollutants in Europe (EMEP), the United Nations Economic Commission for Europe (ECE), and the United Nations Environment Programme (UNEP). Following this came the 1979 Geneva Convention on Long Range Transboundary Air Pollution which came into force on 16 March 1983 and which was ratified by 30 nations between 1980 and 1985, as well as by the European Community. A protocol was added to the Convention in 1984 providing for long term financial support for air pollution monitoring programmes. The 1979 Convention is a general law making framework under which signatory states commit themselves to develop strategies and policies to reduce, and eliminate where possible, atmospheric pollution, including transboundary pollution, and undertake to adopt the best available technology that is economically feasible to achieve such an end (see further below on the BATNEEC principle in the UK). The Helsinki Protocol added to the Convention in 1985 requires those states who sign it to achieve a 30% reduction from 1980 levels in the national emissions, or cross boundary flow, of sulphur by 2003 — the so called '30% Club'. Twenty one states have signed that Protocol, some promising more significant reductions than 30% by particular dates. The UK did *not* originally sign the Helsinki Protocol arguing that it had reduced its SO_2 emissions by 42% compared with 1970 levels by the mid 1980s and that it would achieve a further 30% reduction on 1980 levels by the late 1990s. However, on 14 June 1994 in Oslo the UK agreed to reduce SO_2 emissions to one fifth of 1980 levels by 2010; this follows the voluntary 37% reduction since 1980 and a projected 70% reduction by 2005. The reductions will benefit the UK as well as other nations for by the early 1990s up to 50% of our land area was receiving greater acidification than it could cope with: by 2010 there will only be 5% of land so affected. The reduction is possible because of the phasing out of coal fired power stations and their replacement by gas fired plant. It is likely that a few (currently there are two) modern coal fired power stations will be fitted with flue gas desulphurisation (FGD) equipment; but at some £0.5 bn per station this is an expensive option. FGD fitted stations will continue to burn coal at a rate of about 15m tonnes pa. Further Protocols, on heavy metals (1998), persistent organic pollutants (1998), and 'multi-effects' (1999) have all been signed, but not yet ratified. (See further below on UK compliance with EU requirements on SO_2 emissions.)

The 1979 Convention also established machinery to review its own implementation and development and it imposes quite strict requirements on signatory states to carry out research into, and exchange information on, emission problems, with co-operative monitoring and evaluation programmes. Where a dispute arises between signatory states under the Convention the primary means of mediation is to be negotiation rather than punitive or compensatory sanctions. Interestingly, in the 19th session of the executive body of the UNECE Secretariat Report serious concern was expressed that parties, including the EC, remained in non-compliance with their reporting obligations despite a request to do so.

Turning from acidification to the problems of ozone depletion and global warming, it is once more treaty based provisions of international law that are encountered. The Vienna Convention and Montreal Protocol (1985 and 1987) represent excellent examples of a 'framework' treaty and a subsequent 'fleshing out' protocol. The Vienna Convention furthered the use of a technique now common in international treaties, namely the 'conference of the parties' to keep the treaty under continuous review and a permanent secretariat.

The Montreal Protocol was subsequently amended to provide for the total elimination of use of CFCs and other ozone depleting chemicals. In Helsinki in 1989 the participating states declared the need for, inter alia, propagation of essential information between states, with all nations being committed to a concerted plan of action to counter the issue. Three conditions were identified as essential prerequisites to this: speedy development of alternative chemical substitutes for CFCs, transfer of appropriate technology to developing nations to enable them to eliminate the use and production of CFCs and an international funding mechanism to assist in meeting the costs of the developing nations in making the necessary technological changes.

Such a global environmental fund was created following the London amendments to the Montreal Protocol Convention in 1990, when a fund of $160–240m came into being so that developing nations can be assisted to adopt the use of CFC substitutes. This 'Ozone Fund' represents 'new money' set aside by the developed nations over and above their existing overseas aid budgets.

Principal features of the Montreal Protocol

A key clause is Art 6. This provides that the parties to the Protocol, beginning in 1990 and *at least* every four years thereafter, must assess, in the light of expert scientific evidence, the actual control measures which are found in the Montreal Protocol, Art 2. The parties can then decide whether further adjustments and reductions of production or consumption of the controlled substances from 1986 levels should be undertaken. The timing, scope and amount of any such changes are to be agreed by consensus; however, as a last resort, decisions can be adopted by a two-thirds majority vote of parties present and voting provided they represent at least 50% of the parties' total consumption of the substances in question.

Article 4 complements the undertakings in the Montreal Protocol, Art 2 by imposing trade restrictions between parties and states not party to the Protocol. Initially there was an import ban of controlled substances from any non-party state, and from 1 January 1993, developing country parties were not to export such substances to any non-party state. The Montreal Protocol, Art 5 is titled 'special situation of developing countries'. In essence, this gives any such country a 'limited grace' period of freedom from the operation of the control measures in Art 2, provided consumption of the controlled substances is less than 0.3 kilograms per capita on the date the Protocol enters into force or any time ten years thereafter. Parties also undertake to facilitate access to environmentally safe alternative substances and technologies for developing country parties and also to facilitate provision of financial assistance for this purpose.

Article 8 deals with 'non-compliance'. The parties, at their first meeting, were required to consider and approve procedures and institutional mechanisms for determining non-compliance with Protocol provisions and for treatment of parties found to be in non-compliance.

Following the Montreal Protocol came the Helsinki declaration on protection of the ozone layer, the London meeting of the parties in 1990, and the Copenhagen meeting of 1992. Meetings have been held more frequently than the minimum provided for.

The general pattern of adjustments, etc, has been to bring forward dates for phasing out production and use *in response to* scientific evidence of ozone thinning, not just over the Antarctic but in the Northern hemisphere. The USA has been a major force for pushing for the phase out, while the international process has been aided by the nations of the EC who have allowed the EC to act as an internationally recognised body whose politics supersede those of its constituents; hence Western Europe has effectively been one 'block' on this issue. By itself the UK might well have dragged its feet as the government was for a while much influenced by ICI, the major UK CFC maker. The current position for the EC is found in Regulation 3093/94 (see further below).

In 1995 further deleterious affectation of Antarctic ozone was noted, with the yearly 'hole' in the ozone layer, which has been noted for the past ten years, covering an area the size of Europe. The 'thinning' process which leads to the 'hole' had by mid-1995 reached its most rapidly recorded rate, 1% per day, and the 1995 'hole' was at this time twice the size it was at the corresponding period in 1993 and 1994. Ministers of participating states met in Vienna in December 1995, and agreed to bring about an even faster phasing out of ozone depleting substances. Methyl bromide use in developed countries will be cut in 2001 and 2005 and phased out in 2010, apart from certain agricultural uses. HCFC consumption is to be reduced and phased out by 2020, with some exemptions. Developing countries agreed to freeze methyl bromide production and consumption in 2002, HCFC consumption in 2016, and HCFCs are to be phased out by 2040. Acceleration of these targets will be considered before 2000. December 1999 saw the Beijing Amendments, resulting in new controls on the production of HCFCs. Developed countries are to freeze production of HCFCs in 2004 at 1989 levels. Developing countries get slightly more leeway, in that they have to freeze production in 2016 at 2015 levels. Trade in HCFCs is banned with nations who have not signed up to the Copenhagen Amendments, and provision has been made for the phasing out of bromochloromethane, another ozone depleting chemical.

However, further evidence of the weakness of international regulation appeared in The Independent, 19 September 1995. It must be remembered that no nation can be forced to agree to a particular international treaty. Russia did not agree to key portions of the Montreal Protocol, and has publicly declared it was not able to honour its earlier commitments to phase out CFC production by the beginning of 1996, pleading poverty as the reason for being unable to meet the cost of replacing CFCs — some hundreds of millions of pounds. CFC *production* in the EC was banned as from 1 January 1995, but not *use* nor, in certain cases, *export* and it appears that users of CFCs may be smuggling in supplies from Russia. The evidence is that CFC prices in general have not risen — yet one would expect such a rise as users seek to purchase the dwindling stocks of a product no longer made. CFCs may be legally imported into the UK from Russia for recycling (and re-export) or destruction, up to a limit of 500 tonnes, yet trade statistics show six monthly imports in 1995 of 3,800 tonnes — these are almost certainly unlicensed, ie effectively smuggled imports. Yet, and here there is a weakness in UK law, we lack regulations to impose penalties on unlicensed offenders, for while the EC regulation is directly applicable and requires no further action on the part of the UK government, penalties for failure to comply with EU rules are left to member states and the relevant UK regulations (SI 1994/199) were deficient on this issue. As from 29 March 1996 SI 1996/506 supplements EC law by prohibiting and restricting import, landing and unloading of relevant substances. Customs officers may detain material imported, etc, in contravention of the regulations and provision is made for offences and penalties. Unlawfully imported substances are to be harmlessly disposed of.

With respect to global warming, suggestions were made at the Toronto Conference of 1988 for reductions of 20% in CO_2 emissions by 2005, and 50% reductions in other 'greenhouse' emissions by 2020. Thirty nations subsequently attended the UN World Climate Conference at Geneva in 1990 which agreed to develop an International Convention on global warming by 1992. The UK then undertook to reduce emissions to 1990 levels by 2005, and there was an overall EC commitment to reduce them to 1990 levels by 2000 'in general' with some nations meeting the target before then. However the International Panel on Climate Change (IPCC) argued that to *stabilise* 'greenhouse gas' emissions at 1990 levels would require immediate reductions globally of over 60%.

The United Nations framework Convention on Climate Change, which technically pre-dated the 1992 Rio 'Earth Summit', entered into force in 1994. It begins with an acknowledgements that:

1   'Change in the earth's climate and its adverse effects are a common concern of mankind'.
2   'The global nature of climate change calls for the widest possible co-operation by all countries and their participation in an effective and appropriate international response ...'.
3   'States should enact effective environmental legislation, that environmental standards, management objectives and priorities should reflect the environmental and developmental context to which they apply ...'.

It also recognises the principle of state sovereignty but also enshrines recognition of differentiated responsibility for global emissions of greenhouse gases, and the need for developed nations 'to take immediate action in a flexible manner on the basis of clear priorities'. The convention further recognises the need of developing nations to have access to that advanced technology which they will need consequently on the energy growth they will experience as part of their development.

The Convention then lays down a number of important definitions, including:

1   'Climate change' — 'a change of climate which is attributed directly or indirectly to human activity that alters the composition of the global atmosphere and which is in addition to natural climate variability observed over comparable time periods'.
2   'Adverse effects of climate change' — 'changes in the physical environment of biota resulting in climate change which have significant deleterious effects on the composition, resilience or productivity of natural and managed ecosystems or on the operation of socio-economic systems or on human health and welfare'.
3   'Greenhouse gases' — 'those gaseous constituents of the atmosphere, both natural and anthropogenic, that absorb and re-emit infrared radiation'.
4   'Sink' — 'any process, activity or mechanism which removes a greenhouse gas, an aerosol or a precursor of a greenhouse gas from the atmosphere'.

The objectives and principles of the Convention follow in Arts 2 and 3.

The objective is:

'... to achieve ... stabilisation of greenhouse gas concentrations in the atmosphere at a level that would prevent dangerous anthropogenic interference with the climate system. Such a level should be achieved within a time-frame sufficient to allow ecosystems to adapt naturally to climate change, to ensure that food production is not threatened and to enable economic development to proceed in a sustainable manner.'

While the guiding principles to achieve this objective are to:

1   Protect the climate system for 'benefit of present and future generations of humankind, on a basis of equity and in accordance with their common but differentiated responsibilities and capabilities'.

2   Adopt 'precautionary measures to anticipate, prevent or minimise the causes of climate change and mitigate its adverse effects'. Where the threat is of serious or irreversible damage, lack of full scientific certainty 'should not be used as reason for postponing such measures, taking into account that … (such) measures … should be cost effective so as to ensure global benefits at the lowest possible cost'.
3   Promote sustainable development.

Article 4 proceeds to impose a variety of commitments on all participating parties to:
1   Make available to the Conference of the Parties (COP) national inventories of anthropogenic emissions by sources and removals by sinks of all greenhouse gases not controlled by the Montreal Protocol, using comparable methodologies to be agreed by the COP.
2   Formulate and implement national or regional programmes to mitigate climate change.
3   Promote and co-operate in the development and transfer of technologies, practices and processes that control, reduce or prevent anthropogenic emissions of greenhouse gases in all relevant sectors including energy, agriculture, forestry and waste management.
4   Promote sustainable development including co-operation in the conservation and enhancement of sinks and reservoirs for greenhouse gases including biomass, forests and oceans.
5   Co-operate in preparing for adaptation to the impacts of climate change.
6   Take climate change considerations into account to the extent feasible in their relevant social, economic and environmental policies.
7   Promote and co-operate in research related to the climate system and all facets of climate change; and to exchange relevant information related thereto.

There are additional obligations placed on 36 listed developed nations, largely those of Europe and North America together with Japan, Australia and New Zealand to:
1   Adopt national (or regional) policies and take corresponding measures on the mitigation of change by limiting anthropogenic emissions of greenhouse gases and protecting and enhancing greenhouse gas sinks and reservoirs.
2   Communicate regularly detailed information on the above policies and measures with the aim of returning individually or jointly to 1990 levels emissions of carbon dioxide and other greenhouse gases.

Twenty five developed nations further undertook to provide financial resources and to transfer technology needed by developing countries to meet the cost of implementing the treaty obligations and to promote and facilitate environmentally sound technology transfer. These were those listed before minus the former Communist states of Eastern Europe.

The Climate Change Convention in practice

It is beyond any reasonable doubt that the phenomenon of global warming is taking place and it seems the process is accelerating. The Third Assessment Report of the Intergovernmental Panel on Climate Change reports that the 1990s was the warmest decade since 1861 and that the increase in temperature in the 20th century has been the largest and most rapid of any century in the last thousand years.

   Since the first review of the Convention by the COP in Berlin, 1995, there have been a series of important developments as the COP have sought to build on the framework of the basic convention. Perhaps the most important, in terms of the decisions taken, was at COP3 in Kyoto, Japan, in 1997 resulting in the Kyoto Protocol. Although not yet in force the Protocol has been widely adopted. As at the end of October 2001 there were 186 parties to the Convention, one regional economic integration organisation and 42 parties having ratified it. To become effective it requires ratification by 55 state parties, with these states representing at least 55% of the 1990 level of carbon dioxide emissions emitted by the parties listed in Annex 1 to the UNFCCC. At present the Protocol is hamstrung by the failure, with the exception of Romania and the Czech Republic, of industrialised states, to ratify.

The Kyoto Protocol is notable for the range of measures agreed in order to tackle the global warming issue. The initial vision of significant reductions in greenhouse gasses by the year 2000 has been reformulated with industrialised states agreeing, under Art 3(1) to a minimum legally binding cut of 5% below 1990 levels in their CO_2 emissions between the years of 2008-12. Annex B of the Protocol sets specific and different reduction targets for the Annex 1 countries. The UK, for example has an 8% target imposed which will be achieved not least due to a switch of fuels in the generation of power. In fact the UK has adopted a voluntary target of a 12.5% reduction of greenhouse gasses, and a 20% reduction of CO_2, currently standing at 14%. Emissions reduction targets are facilitated by the inclusion of the so-called 'Kyoto Mechanisms'. First, there is provision for the possible trading of joint-implementation emissions reduction units under Art 6, which would permit the transfer of these units from Annex 1 countries with a surplus to Annex 1 countries with a greater need on the basis of joint projects to reduce emissions. It does however mean that countries with large economies, such as the USA, would be able to maintain its own emissions while claiming a reduction from units purchased elsewhere. Secondly, there is the clean development mechanism (CDM) in Art 12, which Chichilinisky (*Equity and Efficiency in Global Emissions Markets, in Revesz et al*) notes is the only mechanism that incorporates both the developing and industrialised nations. Industrial nations in Annex 1 are able to offset by way of credit a proportion of their emissions reduction targets by investment in or transfer of technology to projects in developing (non-Annex 1) countries which result in a net reduction in greenhouse gasses. Finally, Art 17 provides for emissions trading among the industrialised nations. The scheme provides for the sale and purchase of credits achieved by a country being able to reduce its emissions below the Protocol requirements. There are several issues unresolved in relation to the scheme, including the true detail of it and the protection methods built in to ensure that compliance takes place. The EC and the UK have both considered schemes to set up such a scheme and these will be examined further below.

There have been four further COPs since Kyoto which have been concerned with agreeing the necessary measures to implement the agreed reductions. COP4 in Buenos Aires (1998) and COP5 in Bonn (1999) agreed a timetable for the implementation of some of the measures and a methodology for reporting on implementing measures from the Annex 1 parties respectively. A major difference of opinion between the USA and other parties, notably the EC, on how precisely to implement the targets has resulted in some uncertainty on the future of the climate change regime. The USA, as the largest producer of greenhouse gasses, put forward the argument that it should be allowed to make the majority of its cuts through the joint implementation measures and the planting of forests to create carbon 'sinks' as opposed to cutting its own emissions. The EC in particular took exception to this, resulting in a lack of agreement at COP6 in the Hague (2000). The presidency of George W Bush has resulted in a volte-face in the planned reduction in US emissions targets, indeed, declared US policy is to not ratify the Protocol, instead pursuing its own climate change agenda (Report #:DOE/EIA-0383(2002) December 2001 –*www.eia.doe.gov/oiaf/aeoleg_reg.htm*). The Kyoto Protocol targets are still able to be met without US participation, however, the scheme would be less effective. US Department of Energy figures show a 13.6% increase in greenhouse gas emissions in the decade 1990-2000, with a 2.5% increase from 1999-2000 alone (*Greenhouse Gas Emissions in the USA US Dept of Energy November 2001*). The failure of COP6 resulted in a further meeting in Bonn in 2001, which despite the continuing intransigence from the USA, was able to agree a broad consensus on how the Kyoto Protocol should be implemented. There has been a slight watering down of some of the provisions with concessions granted to some of the larger non-EC carbon producers on aspects such as aforrestation projects and the establishment of a climate change fund to help developed countries improve their performance.

Finally, COP7 in Marrakech (2001) resulted in the finalisation of the detail for the operation of the Kyoto Protocol, with the declared aim of its coming into force by the September 2002 World Summit on Sustainable Development in South Africa. The conference formalised the rules for the operation of the Kyoto mechanisms and established rules for ensuring compliance: an executive board was also elected to manage the coming into use of the CDM.

EC and UK policy responses to the 'greenhouse' issue

The Commission has lamented the failure of the Council to progress on the proposed energy tax and proposed the initiation of the European Climate Change programme (ECCP) (see COM(2000) 88 final) . The overall objective of the ECCP, established in June 2000, is a co-ordinating role to enable all of the stakeholders to put forward policy proposals to identify 'the most environmentally friendly and cost effective additional measures enabling the EU to meet its target under the Kyoto Protocol'.

While the Kyoto Protocol has not yet been ratified by either the EC or the UK, there has been much consideration at both levels of means to implement the measures agreed. In both systems policy and to a lesser extent law have evolved to ensure conformity with the aims of the UNFCCC. A recent indication of the inevitability of its ratification occurred in October 2001 however, when the Commission proposed a Council Decision on the issue of ratification by the EC and the member states of the Kyoto Protocol (COM (2001) 579 final). The proposal states that the legal base should be Arts 174(4) and 300 of the Treaty that permit the EC's conclusion of international environmental agreements; and the enabling procedure respectively. Due to the 'burden sharing' aspect, examined further below, it is anticipated that the EC and the member states should deposit instruments of ratification simultaneously. Article 5 of the proposed decision sets out the requirement, first for member states to inform the Commission of their decision to ratify the Protocol by 2002 and, secondly to permit the simultaneous deposit of the ratification instruments by 14 June 2002.

The EC has also considered a system of greenhouse gas emission allowance trading and is currently preparing law on the issue. A Green Paper in March 2000 on greenhouse gas emissions trading (COM(2000)87) was adopted by the Commission and resulted in the publication of a proposed Directive (COM(2001) 581 final) on the issue in October 2001. The Green Paper, and subsequent meetings convened within the auspices of the 'multi-stakeholder ECCP, on the issue elicited positive responses from the member states, Accession Countries and other stakeholders. The proposal does not apply legally binding emission reduction targets for the member states within the preliminary period 2005 to 2007. A further consideration here is that there will be no charge for the initial allocations of allowances, and lesser penalties for non-compliance.

It is envisaged that the proposed system should link in with existing EC environmental legislation (in line with Art 6 EC), and the Commission gives the example that the scheme would apply to most significant greenhouse gas emitting activities that are already covered by the IPPC Directive, and that member states should be able to combine permitting procedures. In principle the scheme will cover all of the gasses in Annex II of the Kyoto Protocol, but in the first instance it will only cover carbon dioxide. It would appear that the Commission is not convinced that monitoring and verification procedures for the other gasses are currently as robust as they might be. The EC's preferred regime is somewhat different to the UK's own approach, which is outlined below. However, they share the fact that both will precede the Kyoto Protocol's commitment period and thus gain an advantage in terms of the experience of emissions trading before the commencement of the international scheme due in 2008. This perhaps also permits the coming together of the two schemes in order that the Kyoto start date is attained.

At domestic level there has been a thorough examination over time of means of reducing greenhouse gas emissions. Indeed, control of these emissions was considered explicitly in *Climate Change: The UK Programme* (2000 Cm 4748) DETR which discussed a variety of means by which emissions reductions could be delivered. It builds upon its predecessor, considering different sectoral responses to combat the problems caused by greenhouse gasses. Renewable energy sources for example are emphasised as one method of reducing reliance on carbon based fuels. Also considered are a broad range of regulatory instruments to target the problem.

Economic instruments have been a feature of measures to combat air pollution for considerably longer than in other media. Fuel duties, even discounting the now abandoned fuel escalator, have increased and a differential tax level imposed on first, on leaded/unleaded petrol and more recently use of this method in relation to the promotion of ultra low sulphur diesel. Businesses are being required to address their energy use following a 1998 report by Lord Marshall (*Economic instruments and the Business Use of Energy* HM Treasury, November 1998) which proposed that there was a role for the taxation of business energy use. As a result the government introduced legislation to establish a Climate Change Levy (CCL) by virtue of the Finance Act 2000, Part II and Sch 6. The levy applies to the industrial and commercial use of energy. There is currently no plan to extend this to domestic use of energy, however: it would not be politically or socially expedient to do so. A series of regulations, effective from 1 April 2001, have the ultimate intention of reducing energy consumption. The levy itself is payable by energy suppliers of primary and secondary fuels. Akin to the scheme established via the landfill tax (see further chapter 13), the energy suppliers will recover the levy from customers in the way a landfill operator would recover the landfill tax from those disposing of waste at landfills: the scheme is likewise operated by Her Majesty's Customs and Excise. The levy is not without controversy however, with certain energy intensive sectors, such as the steel, food and drink and cement[4] production sectors gaining significant (up to 80%) reductions. To more fully reflect the environmental credentials of the tax, renewable sources of energy generation and certain combined heat and power (CHP) generators are exempt (see SI 2001/1140).

A further legislative development, again not without controversy, is the planned emissions trading scheme. While the EC is still finalising its proposals on the issue, and law perhaps some time away, the UK will launch its own scheme in April 2002. The emissions trading scheme (the Scheme) will be one of the world's first country-wide Schemes, which in the words of DETR (now DEFRA) 'will allow UK businesses and other organisations to get early experience of emissions trading'. There are currently voluntary schemes operating within the 'closed loop' of individual companies in order that they familiarise themselves with the concept. A draft framework document was published in May 2001 (UKETS 01(01) DEFRA) with the declared objective of assisting in the reduction of greenhouse gasses: the government is looking to the Scheme to

4   Pocklington, D, *The Climate Change Levy, The End of the Beginning* ELM 13 [2001] 2 at 81.

deliver a two million tonne per annum carbon reduction by the year 2010. The Scheme as conceived is voluntary, and to participate in the scheme organisations will accept a specific reduction target that is determined by their use of energy. Three options arise for participants on the setting of their standard. They may either: meet their target by reducing their own emissions; reduce their emissions below their target and sell or bank the excess emissions 'allowances'; or, in the case of a failure to meet their targets, have to buy in emissions allowances from other participants. The detail of the scheme is complex and it is only possible to offer an overview of it within the constraints of this book.

Those who opt to participate in the scheme have four identified means of entry with the main two, discussed further below, being classed as either 'direct entrants', or 'agreed entrants'. The lesser forms of involvement with the scheme are open to organisations undertaking emissions-reduction projects with the ability to sell any resulting credits back to the Scheme; and the other envisages a trading only basis whereby a party who does not enter the Scheme on the basis of an emissions target or reduction project can open an account with the registry to buy and sell allowances.

Otherwise, organisations who adopt the principal categories of involvement will seek to gain emission allowances which will be initially supported by government funding or a reduction in the amount of climate change levy that is payable. The former, direct entrants, will be guaranteed a share of a £30 million per annum fund made available for the first five years of the Scheme. In order to qualify, companies will have to bid a quantity of emission reductions against a price set per tonne of carbon dioxide. The target will then be set and performance measured against a baseline calculated on companies' emission baselines based on the years from 1998-2000 inclusive. The calculation of these baselines will be calculated by first, quantifying all sources of emissions that the company has control of; second, identifying which sources (a company must include all emissions sources for whichever sector it wishes to include in the scheme) and which gasses (a company may choose all greenhouse gasses, or just carbon dioxide) it wishes to include; and finally by verifying the baseline data independently. Subject to the development of the compliance mechanisms, see further below, companies failing to meet their targets, or those who withdraw from the Scheme will have to pay back any earlier incentive payments. A company missing its target will have the next year's emission allowance reduced proportionate to the amount it had previously exceeded.

Those who choose to become agreed entrants will receive allowances at the end of each compliance year proportionate to their over achievement. In both cases those missing their targets will have to purchase allowances to ensure compliance.

Compliance with the Scheme is obviously crucial to its success. At the present time there is no legislative underpinning, but it will be operated by the Emissions Trading Authority (ETA) which will initially be part of DEFRA. The primary function of the authority will be to record transactions of emission allowances and the approval of emission-reduction projects. It will also need to be in a position to police the Scheme and in that regard it will need to be able to take action against any non-compliant participants. Actual sanctions for breaches of the Scheme are not yet finalised, but would possibly involve such steps as removal from the Scheme and as noted in *ENDS* (ENDS Report 316, May 2001) the 'naming and shaming' of non-compliant companies. Draft rules issued in December 2001 (UKETS 01 (06) Edition 1, DEFRA) have specified that the scheme will not impose penalties for the first two or three years of the Scheme and that a penalty factor will be applied (in line with the Kyoto formula – basic formula = 1:1.3 per tonne of carbon in excess of the agreed limit) in terms of calculating a future year's reduction in allowance. A further concern relating to a company merely cutting back production, or halting a particular process and then claiming the credit, has been addressed in the framework document. In the case of the former, credits will remain able to be claimed; in the case of the latter however, firms' baseline emission targets will be adjusted, proportionate to their new capacity. Similar adjustments are envisaged in the case of changes in company structure, such as with mergers or demergers, or even where a company outsources a particular process.

There is the opportunity to 'bank' emission allowances for future use, or as a safeguard against future failure to meet a target. The Scheme allows for unlimited banking to take place up until the end of 2007; however, beyond that date the position is unclear as it will depend on the extent to which the UK is on course to satisfy its Kyoto targets. The Scheme is clear in that it does not permit the borrowing of allowances.

European Union law: 'non-greenhouse' issues

EC law on atmospheric pollution was something of a 'late developer' growing rapidly only from the 1980s when a number of member states, Germany in particular, began to suffer from acidification. A number of techniques of regulation are used: air quality standards, sometimes known as Air Quality Limit Values (AQLVs) (either limit values for particular types of industrial plant, or limits for individual substances), vehicle emission standards, fuel composition standards and 'bubble' standards with upper limits on total emissions from all sources.

AQLVs prescribe legal maxima for the presence of pollutants in ambient air for particular time periods. A number of parameters can be used in specifying such a standard: absolute concentrations integrated over a chosen period of time, or average or percentile values. Furthermore an evaluative or subjective element enters into the creation of standards for once the physical, chemical and toxic properties of pollutants are determined, estimates of likely lethal or damaging levels of exposure have to be made, and these must then be divided by a safety factor to set a lower 'limit value' for exposure. The safety factor is determined subjectively taking into account issues such as varieties of sensitivity to exposure, the range of human pathological conditions, the possible consequences of pollutant recombinations and the quality of the data relied on. Indeed other factors of an ethical, economic, political, social and philosophical nature may well play a part in standard setting alongside purely physio-chemical, biological and mathematical issues.

The EC's reliance on AQLVs has caused difficulties for member states who have traditionally utilised emission standards to control individual stationary polluting sources. The EC also relies on the 'standstill' principle to ensure that significant deterioration in air quality set by relevant standards does not take place. AQLVs exist for SO_2 and airborne particulates and for NO_2. In respect of the former, Directive 80/779 set limits for their *ground level* presence, these to be met, where possible, by 1 April 1983, and a mandatory compliance data of 1 April 1993, together with a general duty to implement more stringent limits contained in 80/779 Annex II. The limit values are 80 microgrammes per cubic metre (pcm) for smoke over a year, with a winter limit of 130 and a year peak limit of 250. SO_2 limits vary according to the measure of smoke: where smoke is low SO_2 may increase. 85/203 (as amended by 99/30/EC) sets No_2 standards for ambient air, with a compliance date of 1 July 1987, and a general limit of 200 microgrammes pcm, though member states remain free to set stricter limits. The implementation of AQLVs has met with resistance from member states and both France and Germany have been threatened with legal proceedings under Art 226; difficulties with monitoring compliance have also been experienced.

The EC introduced vehicle emission standards in 1970 which specified limits for carbon monoxide, hydrocarbons and NOx, though also allowing block or 'type approval' for vehicle models conforming to specified design and construction standards. Where competent authorities give block approval for a model on the basis that it complies with standards, manufacturers may commence to produce in series and no member state may thereafter refuse national type approval to vehicles of that type.

Emission limits have gradually become more stringent for vehicles, particularly since 1985 as the EC has moved towards 'cleaner cars', and Directives 88/76 and 89/458 set stricter limits to reduce emissions for cars of 2,000cc or more. Directive 91/441 extended the small car emission limit of 89/458 to new models from 1 July 1992 and to new registrations from 1 December 1992. These changes resulted in further emission reductions in carbon monoxide, hydrocarbons and NOx. Yet further reductions were introduced by Directive 94/12. Other Directives have applied increasingly stricter limits to diesel engined and commercial vehicles.

Directive 75/716 introduced fuel composition standards for 'gas oil' (ie fuel used primarily for domestic heating) with a view to reduce SO_2 emissions. Stricter standards as from 1 January 1989 were introduced by 87/219. Further restrictions were introduced by 93/12 which introduced a limit of 0.2% by weight of sulphur, with a limit of 0.05% for diesel fuel as from 1 October 1996.

Directive 84/360 was a general framework Directive enabling the EU to draw up a system of limit values for a whole range of emissions, and also requiring member states to ensure that, as from 30 June 1987, certain industrial plants, including, for example, combustion plants of more than 50 MW heat output and oil power stations, should only be constructed after prior authorisation including: requirements as to appropriate preventative measures concerning pollution; use of the *best available technology not entailing excessive costs*; no exceeding of emission limits, taking into account AQLVs and on the basis that significant air pollution may not be caused by emissions, especially SO_2 and NOx. Substantial alterations of existing plants are regarded under the Directive as new plant needing authorisation, and provision is also made for existing plant over time to be adapted to the best available technology, etc, principle. The daughter Directive 88/609 on large combustion plants (LCP) was introduced to further the above programme by reducing SO_2 and NOx emissions. SO_2 emissions from existing plant are to be reduced from 1980 levels in three stages, 25% by 1993, 43% by 1998 and 60% by 2003. NOx emissions from relevant plant are to be reduced by 20% by 1993 and 36% by 1998, and for new plant emission standards are reduced by 80% (SO_2) and 50% (NOx) compared with emissions from existing plant. The implementation of this programme is allowed to vary from state to state as some have coal supplies disproportionately rich in sulphur; some states will have met target reductions faster than others. However, the overall aim is to reduce SO_2 emissions from power and refinery plant by 6m tonnes pa by 1998 and halving them, compared to 1980, by 2003.

As part of its response to the LCP Directive the UK drew up in 1990 a large combustion plant national plan which sets reduction targets for SO_2 (60% by 2003 on 1980 levels) and NOx (30% by 1998) emissions from existing plants. This plan is kept under regular review by the Secretary of State, who consults on revision with relevant industries and official environmental regulation and countryside conservation bodies. The plan effectively allows various power station operators, principally PowerGen and National Power, gradually reducing emissions quotas per annum, while similar quotas are set for refineries and other relevant industries. Each relevant site has, for example, an annual SO_2 quota fixed by the relevant environmental agency. The national plan is, of course, reinforced legally by the IPC system, under the Environmental Protection Act 1990 (see further below) and formally exists under s 3(5) of that Act.

Directive 94/63 applies to volatile organic compounds (VOCs) arising from the storage and distribution of petrol, and is one of a number of VOC proposals to enable the EU to meet international obligations under protocols to the 1979 Geneva Convention on Long Range Transboundary Air Pollution (see above). Various dates between 31 December 1995 and 31 December 2004 are laid down for compliance by new plant with VOC emission limits. Further Directives on VOCs are to follow, though the UK government is anxious that EU action should compliment national initiatives reached within the context of the UNECE framework (see above). Even within the context of EU provisions, member states have freedom to meet targets in the most practicable and effective way, but the UK government wishes to ensure that the principle is not eroded. Directive 96/62/EC (OJ 296/55) on ambient air quality and assessment was introduced as a basis for a common EC policy on air quality. The Directive, Art 4, sets out a timescale for the enactment of daughter directives in order to set limit values and alert thresholds for various pollutants and when this is done; Art 6 requires common criteria to be adopted in order to monitor and assess ambient air quality. Decision 97/101/EC establishes a data exchange network in order to facilitate these aims. In the UK the Directive is implemented in terms of limit values, assessment and classification of air quality by the Air Quality Limit Values Regulations 2001 (SI 2001/2315).

A miscellany of further EU measures

Directives 89/369 and 89/429 lay down emission limit values for both new and existing 'municipal' waste incineration plants', ie plants handling only domestic, commercial or trade waste; sewage sludge, chemical, toxic/dangerous waste and hospital waste incinerators are *not* covered. These two Directives are due for replacement by Directive 2000/76/EC on the incineration of waste in December 2005. The new Directive imposes stricter operational measures and emission limit values. So far as new plants are concerned, their authorisations, eg as required under Directive 84/360, must contain emission limit values, operating and monitoring requirements in respect of specific matter (dust, heavy metals, acidic gases) according to capacity categories. For existing plants there is a timetable for compliance with the limits for new plants, again according to capacity category, with various dates applying between 1 December 1995 and 1 December 2000. Hazardous waste incineration is further regulated by Directive 94/67. Once again the authorisation for such an incinerator must impose emission limits, operating and monitoring requirements. Relevant incinerators are those burning solid/liquid hazardous waste as defined by Directive 91/689 excluding certain combustible liquid wastes, offshore oil and gas industry hazardous waste, non-hazardous sewage sludge, while animal carcass and non-hazardous clinical waste incinerators are further excluded, while not only are hazardous waste treatment incinerators generally included, but also those co-incinerators which use waste as a fuel component. This directive again, is due for repeal in 2005 by Directive 2000/76/EC.

So far as ozone depletion is concerned the EC acted on behalf of its member states. Originally governed by Regulation 3093/94 relating to the production, import, export, supply, use and recovery of a number of listed substances, the Regulation has been replaced, from 1 October 2000, by Regulation 2037/00/EC. The Regulation incorporates the Montreal (1997) and Beijing (1999) Amendments to the Montreal Protocol (see above). The regulation applies in much the same way as its predecessor, but covers more chemicals and imposes time limits on the phasing out of, for example, certain halons in firefighting equipment by 2003. This has caused some controversy in the EC due to the fact that the majority of domestic refrigerators will have to be recycled by specialists and treated as hazardous waste as a result of their HCFC containing foam insulation. In the UK DEFRA has issued guidance in respect of the storing and disposal of old fridges and had to make extra funds available to local authorities to deal with the problem caused by the sheer volume (see ENDS Report 323, December 2001).

Note, however, Regulation 2047/93 which permits trading in relevant substances with certain states who have not adhered to the Montreal Protocol until January 2004. However, exports to states that are party to the Montreal Protocol are permitted until 31 December 2009. [For further exhaustive information on EU atmospheric policy see chapter 6 of Haigh's *Manual of Environmental Policy* to which indebtedness is acknowledged.]

Domestic law

UK domestic law has attempted to combat atmospheric pollution for centuries. The pattern that has emerged is one of divided responsibility between central and local authorities. Planning law has a very limited role to play in this context, but the common law may have a contribution to make.

Atmospheric pollution may amount to an actionable nuisance (see chapter 2) though its existence may be difficult to establish. The creation of stenches, *Walter v Selfe*;[5] causing smoke or noxious fumes to pass over the plaintiff's land, *Crump v Lambert*;[6] raising clouds of coal dust, *Pwllbach Colliery Co Ltd v Woodman*;[7] and the emission of large black smuts, *Halsey v Esso Petroleum Co Ltd*,[8] have all been held actionable. Where the nuisance causes *only* personal discomfort the nature of locality has to be considered to see if an action should lie, *Sturges v Bridgman*,[9] but generally a landowner is entitled to have air untainted and unpolluted by the acts of his neighbours. By this is meant, at least, air not incompatible with physical comfortable human existence, though such air may not be as pure and fresh as when the plaintiff's home was built. Atmospheric pollution which is a substantial interference with the use and enjoyment of land, as with stench from a sewage farm in *Bainbridge v Chertsey Urban Council*,[10] or which actually causes physical damage to the land, as with noxious fumes in *St Helens Smelting Co v Tipping*,[11] and *Manchester Corpn v Farnworth*,[12] can be remedied in nuisance. An action in public nuisance may also be available. Note also the Highways Act 1980, ss 161 and 161A (as amended) which create criminal liability in respect of the lighting of fires on or over highways, or off a highway, with the consequence that users of the highway are injured, interrupted or endangered.

The concept of waste incineration and Directives on municipal waste incineration – especially in the context of the increased role for incineration as part of the UKs waste strategy, take into account the landfill directive as well.

D STATUTORY CONTROL OF SMOKE AND OTHER ATMOSPHERIC POLLUTANTS

Perhaps the greatest tier of all encompassing regulation targeting atmospheric pollution is set out in the integrated pollution (prevention and) control and local authority air pollution control provisions in the Environmental Protection Act 1990, Part I as amended,

5   (1851) 4 De G & Sm 315.
6   (1867) LR 3 Eq 409.
7   [1915] AC 634.
8   [1961] 2 All ER 145, [1961] 1 WLR 683.
9   (1879) 11 Ch D 852.
10   (1914) 84 LJ Ch 626.
11   (1865) 11 HL Cas 642.
12   [1930] AC 171.

which are dealt with in chapter 17 below. These provisions however are directed more towards industry. Parallel to them are stand-alone legislative provisions, including an increasing amount of secondary legislation in the form of regulations, that impose further obligations to a wider base to promote the improvement of atmospheric quality.

Of these other provisions perhaps the most obvious is the statutory controls that place controls over smoke.

Control of smoke

Industry is often said to be a major air polluter, but much smoke in the atmosphere this century came from domestic coal burning. Attempts to control domestic smoke were made by the Public Health (Smoke Abatement) Act 1926. This proved ineffective. The consequences of the great London smog of 1952 showed effective legislation was needed. The Clean Air Act 1956 introduced the now familiar system of domestic smoke control. That Act, coupled with changing habits as to choice of domestic heating, reduced the emission of domestic smoke, in million tonnes, from almost 1.50 to about 0.50 between 1953 and 1974. the CAA 1956, as amended in 1968, was consolidated in the Clean Air Act 1993.

The legislation controls emission of smoke; also grit and dust. 'Smoke' is defined by the 1993 Act, s 564(1) as including soot, ash, grit and gritty particles emitted in smoke. Visible non-carbonaceous vapours, for example water vapour, may also be classified as 'smoke', but not, it seems, invisible material such as carbon monoxide or free sulphur dioxide; see Garner and Crow *Clean Air Law and Practice* (4th edn), see also Hughes, Parpworth and Upson *Air Pollution Law and Regulation*, chapter 8. Grit and dust are differentiated from smoke by particle size, but all emissions of solid particles fall within the statutory definition. Visible fumes will be a constituent of smoke. These are defined as 'any airborne solid matter smaller than dust'.

The Clean Air Act 1993

Enforcing authorities are local authorities, that is district councils and London borough councils, see the CAA 1993, ss 55 and 64(1). They have various powers and obligations.

CONTROL OF DARK SMOKE

The CAA 1993, s 1 prohibits the emission of 'dark smoke' from a chimney of 'any building'. This prohibition extends, with appropriate modifications as to the identity of persons liable for the commission of offences, to railway locomotives, s 43, vessels within specified coastal waters, s 44, and chimneys serving furnaces of boilers or industrial plants attached to or installed on land, s 1(2). 'Dark smoke' is defined by CAA 1993, s 3(1) as 'as dark as or darker than shade 2' on a Ringelmann Chart, though it seems in practice environmental health officers of long-standing do not use the Ringelmann Chart mechanically, but rely rather on their own experience. 'Chimney' includes structures and openings of any kind from or through which smoke, grit, dust or fumes may be emitted, and flues, whether forming part of a building or structurally separate. The prohibition extends to emissions from trade/industrial premises, see further below. Where dark smoke is emitted the occupier of the building with the offending chimney is guilty of an offence. The guilty occupier will be that person in control of that portion of the building where the relevant fireplace is found. Liability under the Act seems to be absolute, though there are statutory defences that the contravention:

1   Was due solely to lighting up a cold furnace and that all practicable steps had been taken to prevent or minimise emissions.
2   Was due solely to some furnace or furnace apparatus failure that could not reasonably have been foreseen or otherwise reasonably provided against, and that it could not reasonably have been prevented by action taken after the failure occurred.
3   Was due solely to use of unsuitable fuel, suitable fuel being unobtainable, that the least unsuitable available fuel was used, and that all practicable steps had been taken to prevent or minimise emissions.
4   Was due to a combination of the foregoing circumstances, and that requisite preventive, remedial and mitigating steps were taken.

CAA 1993, s 63(1) defines 'practicable' as meaning reasonably practicable in the light of local conditions and circumstances, financial implications, and the current state of technical knowledge. Also, under CAA 1993, s 1(3) emissions of smoke lasting for no longer than as specified by regulations are to be left out of account for the purposes of the section. See SI 1958/498 which provides that dark smoke emissions from chimneys for not longer than any aggregate of ten minutes in any eight hour period or, where soot blowing is carried out during such a period, for not longer than an aggregate of 14 minutes in that period, are to be left out of account. Suitable increases in the length of time of emission are made for chimneys serving more than one furnace. Nothing in the regulations authorises either the continuous emission of dark smoke, caused otherwise than by soot blowing, for a period exceeding four minutes, or the emission of *black smoke* (that is smoke as dark or darker than Ringelmann Shade 4) for more than two minutes in aggregate in any period of 30 minutes.

EMISSIONS FROM TRADE PREMISES

Emissions of dark smoke from industrial and trade premises other than via chimneys are generally controlled by the Clean Air Act 1993, s 2. 'Industrial or trade premises' are those used for industrial or trade purposes, or other premises on which matter is burnt in connection with such purposes and processes. In *Sheffield City Council v ADH Demolition Ltd*,[13] a bonfire was lit on a demolition site to burn rubbish resulting from demolition and dark smoke was emitted. It was held that demolition was a trade process, so burning this material in connection with it did come within control under the CAA 1993. Not all 'clearing-up' bonfires would be caught by the law; a reasonably close connection between the operation releasing the smoke and the industrial or trade process undertaken on site seems necessary. In proceedings under the provision it is a defence to prove contravention was inadvertent, and that all practicable steps had been taken to prevent or minimise emissions. The Secretary of State may, by regulations, exempt certain emissions from control under this section. See SI 1969/1263 which, inter alia, exempts matters such as the burning of: certain waste resulting from demolition or site clearances; tar, pitch, asphalt, etc, in connection with surfacing; and carcasses of diseased animals, or certain contaminated containers. These exemptions exist subject to conditions on supervision and minimisation of emissions. See also CAA 1993, s 2(3) extending liability to persons causing or permitting dark smoke to be emitted from industrial or trade premises where there is taken to have been an emission of such smoke because material is burned on relevant premises and the circumstances are such that the burning would be *likely* to give rise to such emissions. In such cases it is for the occupier, or the person causing or permitting the burning to show no dark smoke was emitted. The provision is aimed, inter alia, at the problem of night time burning. It should

13   (1983) 82 LGR 177.

be noted that an emission of dark smoke can take place without smoke moving beyond the boundaries of the site where the burning is taking place.[14]

CONTROLS OVER NEW FURNACES

Under CAA 1993, s 4 new furnaces, save those used solely or mainly domestically and having a maximum heating capacity of less than 6–12 kilowatts, must be, so far as practicable, capable of continuous operation without emitting smoke when used with design fuel. A boiler may be used domestically even where no residence is involved.[15] The courts have held where the purpose of which water is being used is one for which, according to ordinary usage, people require water in their homes, it is a domestic purpose. Central heating of water in a commercial building can thus be 'domestic'. Those furnaces that are subject to control may not be installed unless notice of proposed installation has been given to the local authority. Any furnace installed in accordance with plans and specifications submitted to and approved by the local authority is deemed to comply with the section. Approval under the Building Regulations would not be sufficient, nor would an approval under CAA 1993, s 4 constitute a defence to charges of emitting dark smoke under s 1. It seems resiting of an existing furnace counts as installation for the purposes of CAAQ 1993, s 4. Failure to comply with a requirement of the section constitutes an offence. CAA 1993, s 5 gives power to the Secretary of State to make regulations prescribing limits for the rates of emission of quantities of grit and dust from chimneys of furnaces in which solid, liquid or gaseous material is burns, *not* being furnaces designed solely or mainly for domestic purposes and used for heating boilers with maximum heating capacities of less than 16.12 kilowatts. See SI 1971/162 for detailed regulations and specific limits, which, subject to the standard defence of 'best practicable means', it is an offence to contravene.

CAA 1993, s 6 requires new furnaces in buildings burning pulverised fuel or solid waste or fuel at a rate of 45.4 kilograms or more an hour to be fitted with grit and dust arresting plant approved by the local authority. These obligations are modified by CAA 1993, s 7.

CAA 1993, s 7 enables the Secretary of State to make regulations exempting classes of furnace from the operation of s 6, see SI 1969/1262. Furthermore under CAA 1993, s 7(2) where, on the application of a building's owner, a local authority are satisfied that the emission of grit, etc from any chimney serving a furnace in the building will not be prejudicial to health or a nuisance where that furnace is used for a particular purpose without complying with s 6, they may grant exemption from control to that furnace while it is used for that purpose, and a failure to notify a contrary decision within a period of eight weeks of receiving the application results in the furnace being deemed exempt. Where, however, the authority decide not to grant exemption they must give reasons for their decision, and an appeal to the Secretary of State against their decision is open to the applicant.

Under CAA 1993, s 8 *domestic* furnaces are not to be used in buildings to burn pulverised fuel or solid fuel or waste at a rate of 1.02 tonnes an hour unless grit or dust arresting plant has been provided in accordance with the local authority's approval — again there is a right of appeal to the Secretary of State under CAA 1993, s 9.

Various powers exist to measure grit and dust emitted from furnaces. Under CAA 1993, s 10, where a furnace in a building is used to burn pulverised fuel, or (at a rate of 45.4 kg per hour) any other solid matter, or (at a rate equivalent to 366.4 kilowatts) liquid or gases, the local authority may, by notice in writing served on the occupier of the

14   *O'Fee v Copeland Borough Council* [1995] 7 ELM 129.
15   *Smith v Müller* [1894] 1 QB 192; *Re Willesden Borough Council and Municipal Mutual Insurance* [1944] 2 All ER 600.

building, direct that the occupier shall comply with ministerial requirements as to making and recording periodic measurements of grit, dust and fumes emitted from the furnace; see also SI 1971/161. Where a notice under CAA 1993, s 10 is in force, s 11 allows, in the case of furnaces burning solid matter, other than pulverised fuel, at a rate of less than 1.02 tonnes an hour or burning liquids or gases at a rate of less than 8.21 megawatts, the occupier of the relevant building to request the local authority to make and record measurements of grit, dust and fumes. It then becomes the duty of the authority to make such recordings. Under s 12, to enable them to perform their functions more effectively, local authorities have powers to require occupiers of buildings to furnish reasonable details of furnaces in their buildings and fuel or waste burned. Under CAA 1993, s 13, ss 5–12 apply in relation to any outdoor fixed boilers or industrial plant as they apply in relation to furnaces in buildings.

CONTROL OF CHIMNEYS

CAA 1993, s 14 applies to any furnace served by a chimney. Furnaces must not be used by, or with the permission of, the occupier of a building where they burn pulverised fuel, or solid matter of a rate of 45.4 kg or more per hour or burn liquid or gaseous matter at a rate of 366.4 kilowatts or more unless the height of the ancillary chimney has been approved, and the conditions of any approval have been complied with. A similar prohibition lies on those who have possession of fixed boilers and industrial plant, save where these have been exempted by regulations made by the Secretary of State, see SI 1969/411. Applications for such approval have to be made to the local authority in accordance with s 15, and such approval cannot be granted unless the authority is satisfied that smoke, grit, dust, gases or fumes emitted are prevented by the height of the chimney from being prejudicial to health or a nuisance having regard to the chimney's purpose, the position of neighbouring buildings and levels of neighbouring ground and other relevant circumstances. Conditions may be imposed on approvals, eg as to the rate and/or quality of emissions. Approvals not given within four weeks of applications are deemed granted; but if a refusal is given it must be reasoned, including an indication of minimum permissible height, and there is a right of appeal to the Secretary of State.

Modern high chimneys are designed to *disperse* pollutants produced by combustion, and to carry them away from the area of production. Chimney heights must be set at levels sufficient to prevent any increase in pollution at ground level beyond acceptable limits, bearing in mind geographical factors such as hills and valleys, and whether the relevant area is already highly developed with severe existing pollution levels, see DoE Circular 25/81 'Memorandum on Chimney Heights', replacing the earlier edition of 1967. This, however, has been insufficient to prevent pollution, either nationally or internationally, hence the further controls introduced the EPA 1990; see above.

SMOKE CONTROL AREAS

Under s 18 any local authority may, by order, declare all or part of their district a 'smoke control area'. The procedure for making an order is contained in CAA 1993, Sch 1. Before making the order advertisements must be placed in the London Gazette and the local press stating the proposal, its effect, a place where the proposed order can be inspected and the right of affected persons to object. Copies of the proposal must also be posted up within the affected area. Any objections made must be considered, but thereafter authorities may bring orders into effect within six months of their being made, though this is subject to a power to postpone coming into operation. Orders may be revoked or varied by subsequent orders, and may further limit prohibitions on the emission of smoke to certain buildings only, or may exempt specified buildings or classes of buildings from control, subject to conditions. CAA 1993, s 19 empowers the Secretary of State to require authorities to create smoke control areas where it is considered expedient to abate smoke pollution in a particular area and it is further considered the relevant authorities have not made use of their powers under CAA 1993, s 18.

Once an order is in force under CAA 1993, s 20 the occupier of any building in the area commits an offence if smoke is emitted from a chimney of that building, and similarly if smoke is emitted from the chimney of a furnace, fixed boiler or industrial plant. However, there may be exemptions for particular buildings under CAA 1993, s 18, or in respect of particular fireplaces under s 21, or under particular provisions in specific areas made by the Secretary of State under s 23. Furthermore it is a defence in any criminal proceedings to show that the commission of the offence was not brought to the occupier's attention by an authorised local authority officer as required by s 51. (A similar defence exists in relation to charges concerning the emission of dark smoke under CAA 1993, ss 1 and 2.) It is furthermore a defence to prove that an alleged emission was not caused by the use of any fuel other than an authorised fuel as specified in regulations. Under CAA 1993, s 23 the acquisition and use of unauthorised solid fuels in a smoke control area is itself an offence, subject to any exemptions, for example under CAA 1993, s 22, and also to the defence that the accused may prove reasonable grounds for believing that the building for which the fuel was sold was an exempt building.

Once a smoke control order is in operation in an area the local authority has power under CAA 1993, s 24 to require owners and occupiers of private dwellings to adapt their fireplaces so as to avoid contraventions of s 20. Grants are, however, payable under CAA 1993, Sch 2 towards the cost of such work. These are mandatory in respect of dwellings erected before 15 August 1964 to the extent of 70% of relevant expenditure, with authorities having a discretion to pay the remaining 30%. There is also a discretion to make payments in respect of adaptations of fireplaces in churches, chapels and buildings used by charities: see CAA 1993, s 26.

Special cases

The provisions of CAA 1993, Parts I to II considered above do *not* apply to prescribed processes under the Environmental Protection Act 1990, see CAA 1993, s 41, but the s 1 prohibition on the emission of dark smoke applies to railway locomotives whose owners must therefore use *any* practicable means available for minimising the emission of smoke if they are to avoid committing an offence, see CAA 1993, s 43. A similar prohibition applies in respect of vessels within specified waters such as ports, harbours, rivers, estuaries, docks and canals under CAA 1993, s 4. Under CAA 1993, s 42 the owners of mines or quarries from which coal has been, or is being, or is to be, obtained must employ *all* practicable means for preventing combustion of refuse deposited from their mines/quarries and for preventing or minimising the emission of smoke and fumes from such refuse, though CAA 1993, Parts I to II, and EPA 1990, Part III (statutory nuisances), otherwise do not apply to smoke, grit or dust from the combustion of refuse deposited on such tips.

The successes of clean air legislation are catalogued in *The Royal Commission on Environmental Pollution* 10th Report (Cmnd 9149). The average urban concentration of smoke index fell from 260 in 1960 to under 40 in 1980. Total industrial and domestic smoke emission from coal combustion declined from almost 2 m tonnes in 1960 to less than 0.5m tonnes in 1980. This was not, however, entirely due to legislation, and was partly due to changes in fuel usage, technological advance, dispersion techniques, conservation measures and decline in certain industries.

Are the Clean Air Act's provisions needed?

It is arguable that the CAA 1993 is partly redundant in view of the LAAPC and statutory nuisance powers, particularly with regard to powers concerned with new furnace approval, dust and grit emission rates approval and approval of chimney heights. The government accordingly proposed partial repeal of the legislation in 1993, and has power to do so under the Deregulation and Contracting Out Act 1994. The proposal has, however, been resisted by local authorities who point to the *preventive* nature of the powers in question, while statutory nuisance controls are essentially reactive. Even so it has to be remembered that the clear air legislation essentially reflects concerns current some 30–40 years ago and that it takes scant account of the problems of traffic pollution, hence the next major development in the law.

E THE NATIONAL AIR QUALITY STRATEGY

This new initiative, founded on Part IV of the Environment Act 1995, is designed in particular to ensure cleaner air in towns and cities *with a view to protecting human health* and is a national strategic plan for maintaining and improving air quality. It follows on from the government's proposals 'Air Quality: Meeting the Challenge' (January 1995). The Secretary of State is under an obligation by virtue of the EA 1995 to prepare a national air quality strategy (NAQS) which will enable the UK to meet international and EU obligations. NAQS is to be periodically reviewed and modified throughout the life time of the current sustainable development policy. In particular NAQS contains standards on air quality with reduction targets for all main pollutants; restrictions on the levels at which particular substances are present in the air; measures to be taken by local authorities and other bodies. (An air quality standard (AQS) for sulphur dioxide was thus recommended in September 1995 of 100 parts per billion measured over a 15-minute period, a standard stricter than under current EC requirements. NAQS is drawn up and reviewed following wide consultation, including consultation with the Agency (which is required under s 81 to take NAQS into account in discharging its functions) and representatives of industry, and before it is finally promulgated it has to appear in a draft form for public comment which has to be taken into account in the final revision. In drawing up NAQS the government will be advised by the expert panel on air quality standards (EPAQS) set up in 1990.

Under NAQS it will be a central government duty to identify a target or *base standard* towards which air quality should move, and *alert thresholds* which will trigger remedial action (probably the creation of an air quality management area, see below) if they are exceeded by particular pollutants. The object is to achieve the base standard by 2005, and some standards have been set, and some targets and associated policies have already been reached in respect of benzene, 1,3-butadiene, carbon monoxide, sulphur dioxide, ozone and particles. The first strategy was produced in 1997 and is subject to periodical review and modification in line with the requirements of Part IV of the Environment Act 1995. A revised draft strategy was published in 1999 with an agenda to strengthen the standards. Following consultation, the resulting *Air Quality Strategy for England, Scotland, Wales and Northern Ireland* (Cm 4548) was published early in 2000 and makes few changes to its predecessor. Ozone and sulphur dioxide objectives have not been changed, reflecting, in the case of the latter, the transboundary nature of the issue. Perhaps surprisingly, objectives in relation to particulates (PM10) have been slightly relaxed, reflecting the currently lesser, EC limit. In this connection DEFRA have issued draft regulations to transpose two EC Directives: Directive 96/62/EC on ambient air quality assessment and management and Directive 99/30/EC relating to limit values for a range of pollutants.

The most recent proposals for local air quality management propose updated standards for moist of the identified pollutants and, for the first time, include standards for polycyclic aromatic hydrocarbons (PAHs) for the first time. New objectives have been set with a timescale taking the period of control to the end of the decade.

The current regulations in force, made under the Secretary of State by virtue of powers in EA 1995, s 87, the Air Quality (England) Regulations 2000 (SI 2000/928) place the key role for implementing the statutory objectives on the local authorities.

Local authorities have long argued they are best placed to protect local air quality and who, under the EA 1995, s 82 are now under a duty to cause air quality reviews (AQR) of current and future air quality to be made in their areas, and to assess whether they are reaching or will reach air quality standards in their areas, with any parts of their areas where standards are not being/will not be achieved being identified.

This is the *appraisal* duty which all authorities must undertake. The appraisal is intended to follow the pattern of appraisal of development plans (see chapter 5, above) and should be regularly and systematically carried out.

Where the AQR shows standards are not being achieved, etc the area of failure in question must, under EA 1995, s 83, be designated as an air quality management or 'designated' area (AQMA). This is the *action* duty. To assist authorities on these tasks central funding will be available, as will the involvement of the Agency. AQMAs will be similar in concept to smoke control zones (see above).

Where a AQMA comes into operation, EA 1995, s 84 requires the relevant local authority (which will be either the unitary authority or the district council if it is not a unitary authority) to obtain information and to cause a detailed assessment to be made of current and future air quality in the AQMA with particular reference to failures to meet air quality standards and objectives. A report on the results of the assessment has to be drawn up within 12 months of the coming into operation of the AQMA, and an 'action plan' (an air quality plan) prepared to bring about the achievement of standards and objectives, with a statement of timescales within which proposed measures are to be implemented. In preparing the plan the authority will be required to consult with central government, other local authorities, industry and the public, and the plan and the assessment which precedes it must be kept under periodic review. Central government will assist this process by granting authorities improved access to air quality databases, the publication of guidelines and the promotion of research and good practice. Funding may also be available for assessing air quality. The quality standards proposed in September 2001 sparked debate and controversy as different, rather than blanket, objectives were set: London has a less stringent set of objectives for example. It has been argued by the Secretary of State, Michael Meacher, that London is a special case given the comparatively high air pollution levels in the city.

In drawing up plans authorities will be required to appraise their development, transport and pollution control policies, and will have to ensure that the relative contributions of industry, transport and other sectors to achieving plan objectives are cost effective and proportionate. The philosophy of plans should be to seek improvements by the most cost effective route; to balance out controls over various emission sources, ie domestic, industrial and transport; to avoid unnecessary regulation and to seek clarity and consistency, and certainly to draw on public, private and voluntary effort. Day to day information on air quality in an AQMA will be given to relevant sections of the public, while authorities will also be under a duty to prepare contingency plans for dealing with high pollution incidents.

Where the Secretary of State has cause to believe a local authority is not undertaking its duties, reserve powers exist under EA 1995, s 85, while in any case the Secretary has power under s 85(5) to give directions to local authorities to take specified steps for achieving UK obligations under EU or international law. Authorities are under a duty under EA 1995, s 85(7) to comply with any directions given. Furthermore where air quality problems extend beyond individual authorities, regional offices of central government will promote appropriate joint arrangements. The Secretary of State has extensive powers under EA 1995, s 87 to make regulations for the purposes of Part IV, and, under s 88, to issue guidance to authorities which they have to take into account in carrying out any functions under the Act.

As stated above the principal authorities for the purpose of the law are (a) unitary authorities (that is councils of counties in which there are *no* district councils, councils of districts in an area for which there is no county council, the councils of London boroughs and of county boroughs in Wales); (b) district councils in so far as they are not unitary authorities. However, county councils for areas in which there are districts have some functions under EA 1995, s 86, in that they may make recommendations to their districts with regard to carrying out reviews and assessments and the preparation/revision of plans, and these have to be taken into account by districts. Where an action plan is being prepared by a district the county must submit its proposals for exercising its powers to help achieve air quality standards and objectives within the area in question. Counties are furthermore subject to default action and central powers of direction with regard to the foregoing functions under EA 1995, s 86(6)–(7) and (8)–(9) respectively. Counties are relevant because of their strategic road traffic and highway powers, see further below on the use of Road Traffic Regulation Act 1984 power.

One of the principal concerns of NAQS will be with transport where it is officially accepted progress is needed in order to reduce pollution and improve air quality. To this end the government has adopted five 'key themes' on transport and air quality.

1   Continued action to encourage improvements in vehicle standards, fuel and technology, which entails: full participation at both the EU and domestic levels in promoting progressive improvements in vehicle emission standards; enhanced research into fuel and remote sensing of vehicle emissions; examination of retro fitting particulate traps to certain diesel powered vehicles.

2   Development of land and transport planning policies to achieve air quality improvements — this entails increasing emphasis on air quality issues when setting objectives for local authority transport expenditure; development of best practice guides; undertaking further research into traffic management and its impact on air quality; consultation with London authorities on developing a common approach to transport plans and programmes across the metropolis; consideration of establishing air quality monitoring subsequent to road development.

3   Ensuring that passenger transport, road haulage and taxi services play a full part in bringing about air quality improvement, which entails: consultation with relevant undertakings on improving their environmental performance, with performance targets being set for, eg London Transport; greater consideration by the Traffic Commissioners of emission performance when considering disciplinary and other action against transport operators; enhanced inspection of taxi exhausts by local authorities with a view to appropriate action; consideration of extending the statutory nuisance regime specifically to cover emissions from vehicle depots.

4   Tighter enforcement of vehicle emission standards — it is a small minority of offenders who emit the largest amount of pollution.

5   More effective guidance for industry, commerce and the public.

Implicit in the NAQS is recognition — grudging perhaps — that the consequences of what Baroness Thatcher called 'the great car economy' are, at very best, mixed. Motor vehicles contribute 36% of hydrocarbon pollution, 51% of NOx, 89% of CO, 70% of lead, 42% of black smoke and 19% of CO_2. With 24 million road vehicles already and a predicted 115% increase to 51 million by 2025 it is clear, both in the UK and throughout the EU generally, that merely to control vehicle emissions further will not be enough to prevent environmental degradation. It may well be that NAQS will have to contemplate what to many remains almost unthinkable: legal restrictions on the use of vehicular transport coupled with financial disincentives for car use and incentives to use revived and extended public transport systems. Air quality plans may: advocate setting up more pedestrian only areas; impose speed restrictions; encourage companies to restrict free parking and replace company cars with free public transport passes. As a 'last resort' measure plans could provide for vehicles to be banned from particular roads at particular times, see further below, though it appears that only the police will have the power, as they presently do, to stop vehicles and check emissions, and that power will not be given to local authorities.

Although the transport sector, and particularly the motor vehicle. is recognised as a major contribution to air pollution, specific traffic reduction targets that were once a feature of policy, have been ruled out by the government, in recognition perhaps that they would not be able to be met. Further pressure from the transport lobby was seen in one report commissioned by the London NHS Executive claiming that the health effects of traffic pollution in London were 'greatly overstated' (see 300 ENDS Report 5), which would appear to be at odds with the official line adopted by DEFRA on the issue.

Note that under the Ozone Monitoring and Information Regulations (SI 1994/440) implementing Directive 92/72, the Secretary of State is already required where appropriate to designate or establish measuring stations for ozone concentration and to take the necessary steps to inform the public in the event of particular ozone concentration thresholds being exceeded.

F PLANNING LAW AND ATMOSPHERIC POLLUTION

Planning law has had a somewhat limited role in controlling atmospheric pollution. Planning control is suited to preventing new forms of air pollution, rather than remedying existing pollution sources. Planners are not normally conversant with the technologies of pollution control and have to rely on advice from Environmental Health Departments and the Agency, which is willing to comment on proposals for potentially air polluting developments and the proposed siting of developments near existing works subject to that oversight. In 'Industrial Air Pollution' (1976) the Health and Safety Commission supported the Royal Commission on Environmental Pollution's call for mandatory consultation by local planning authorities with the inspectorate on such developments. Under NAQS, however, planning authorities will be expected to take heed of national air quality standards in formulating development plans and this will be reflected in revised planning policy guidance.

At various points planning law may help to control atmospheric pollution. First at the stage of plan making; some local authorities have included air quality objectives in local plans. There have been historic limits to the effectiveness of such policies. Attempts to include strict and rigorous air pollution standards in structure plans resulted in ministerial intervention to prevent *land use* regulatory powers being used to impose controls over other parts of the environment, see Miller and Wood *Planning and Pollution*, chapters 2 and 3. A small change in this policy was signalled by PPG 12, para 6.8 in February 1992, but, of course, the changes consequent on implementing NAQS outlined above will go much further than this.

Second, planning control exists over proposals involving development of works utilising processes falling within the powers of the Agency under the Environmental Protection Act 1990, Part I. HMIP, the Agency's predecessor, the Department of the

Environment and the Royal Commission on Environmental Pollution consistently argued against the restrictive use of planning powers, especially the imposition of planning conditions under the Town and Country Planning Act 1990; certainly where this would trespass on, or go beyond, the functions of the central authority. The Secretary of State will be disinclined to support a local planning authority in their use of planning powers to control atmospheric pollution where the Agency is happy that the development in question will satisfy the BATNEEC requirements under its statutory powers. However, some developments arouse such local hostility that the only course for the local planning authority themselves is to refuse planning permission, though they may be reversed on appeal. See further Miller and Wood, *Planning and Pollution,* p 27, and Blowers, *Something in the Air,* pp 309–11. The issue was examined in *Gateshead Metropolitan Borough Council v Secretary of State for the Environment and Northumbrian Water*[16] where there was a proposal to build a clinical waste incinerator for which the local planning authority had refused permission on the basis that insufficient attention had been given to pollution control issues. They argued that once planning permission was given it was unlikely an IPC authorisation would be refused and that would entail imposition of BATNEEC requirements, which, they considered, would not ensure any local environmental damage. In the Court of Appeal it was accepted there is an overlap between planning and pollution control powers, and that it is perfectly proper to identify pollution issues and to take them into account in reaching a planning decision. Furthermore where it is clear at the planning application stage that pollution from a plant is such as would lead the Agency to refuse an authorisation, it is proper on that basis to refuse permission. Where, however, the issue is not so clear cut and demands the exercise of particular skills and judgment, the pollution control matters must be left to the Agency. Furthermore a grant of planning permission does not obligate the Agency to grant an authorisation, and an authorisation will not be granted if the BATNEEC scheme cannot achieve a sufficient standard of environmental protection — though it should be noted the former HMIP refused only one authorisation on that basis. Planning authorities will be generally mindful of planning's managerial role, needing to achieve the best interests of their inhabitants by weighing environmental against social and economic considerations. Furthermore members of an authority will represent a wide spectrum of views within a local community on the merits of a proposed development, so it cannot be *assumed* they will wish to restrict the development.

Over processes not falling within the ambit of the Agency's powers, planning controls may be effective alternatives to some other forms of regulation. Planning conditions and planning 'obligations' have been used to secure atmospheric pollution control objectives, particularly with regard to what Miller and Wood (p 29) call: 'anticipatory controls over odour pollution'.

G MISCELLANEOUS POWERS

The Secretary of State has power under the CAA 1993, s 30, for purposes of limiting or reducing air pollution, by regulation to impose requirements as to composition and content of any motor vehicle fuel, and, where such requirements are in force, to prevent or restrict production, treatment, distribution, import, sale or use of fuels intended for use in the UK and failing to comply. Before making regulations consultation must take place with representatives of motor vehicle manufacturers and users, motor vehicle fuel producers and air pollution experts. Regulations may apply standards and tests,

16   (1993) 67 P & CR 179; affd (1994) 71 P & CR 350, CA.

etc, laid down in documents not forming part of the regulations, and may authorise the Secretary of State to grant exemptions. Regulations may also require that information as to composition and content of regulated fuel is displayed in prescribed ways. Enforcement of regulations is in the hands of weights and measures authorities, that is (in general) county and London borough councils, see the Local Government Act 1972, s 201. Under these provisions EC fuel composition standards are implemented in the UK. The current regulations are the Motor Fuel (Composition and Content) Regulations 1999 (SI 1999/3107).

The 1999 regulations implement Directive 98/70/EC relating to the quality of petrol (based on BS EN ISO 3830:1996) and diesel, and amending Directive 93/12/EEC. Regulation 18 revokes the previous regulations (SI 1994/2295). Part II of the Regulations sets out the requirements relating to the composition and content of motor fuel by reference to the directive's Annexes. Certain types of fuel are prohibited form sale, ie those not conforming to the directive requirements. The regulations do, with particular exceptions for which the Secretary of State may issue permits, ban the sale of leaded petrol. To distribute a non-complying motor fuel from a refinery or import terminal is an offence, as is the retail sale of such fuel at a retail filling station, subject to certain minor exemptions, for example with regard to experiments in connection with the composition or content of fuel.

Under the CAA 1993, s 31 regulations may be made, after appropriate consultations, to impose limits on fuel (that is any liquefied petroleum product of a refinery) used in furnaces or engines. Regulations may prescribe fuels, furnaces and engines to which they will apply, may apply standards and tests, etc, laid down in documents not forming part of the regulations, may allow the Secretary of State to confer exemptions, and may make different provisions for different areas. SI 1994/2249 has been made under this provision, also to implement Directive 93/12. It is an offence to market gas oil with a sulphur content of more than 0.2% by weight. But the prohibition does not apply to gas oil in the fuel tanks of vessels, gas intended for processing before combustion or aviation kerosene. Local authorities (districts and London boroughs) enforce these regulations.

The CAA 1993, s 33 makes it an offence for a person to burn insulation from a cable with a view to metal recovery unless the burning is a process falling under EPA 1990, Part I.

The CAA 1993 also makes provision relating to research into and publicity concerning atmospheric pollution. Under CAA 1993, s 34 local authorities may undertake, or contribute towards, costs of investigatory research into air pollution, and may arrange for publication of information on the problems. They must act in conformity with regulations made under CAA 1993, s 38, see SI 1997/19. In particular they may obtain information about polluting emissions. First, they may issue notices under CAA 1993, s 36, allowing them to require occupiers of premises, other than private dwellings, to furnish specified returns concerning polluting emissions from the premises, subject to rights of appeal to the Secretary of State under s 37. Second, they may measure and record emissions under CAA 1993, s 35(1)(b), for that purpose entering premises, other than private dwellings, whether by agreement, or under CAA 1993, s 56 giving general powers of entry to duly authorised persons. The power of entry under CAA 1993, s 35(1)(b) may only be exercised after notice in writing has been given to the occupier specifying the emissions in question, and 21 days must elapse from the date of the notice. They may not exercise powers under the notice where the occupier requests them to proceed under CAA 1993, s 36. Third, they may enter into arrangements with occupiers of premises, other than private dwellings, under which they measure and record emissions on behalf of the local authority. While exercising these powers the authority must from time to time consult appropriate persons carrying on any trade or business within their area, their representative organisations, and such others as are conversant with problems of air pollution, or have interests in local amenity, about the way in which the authority exercise their powers, and the extent and manner of release of any collected information to the public. Consultations must take place at least twice in each financial year. Nothing in CAA 1993, s 35 authorises an authority to investigate emissions from processes subject to the Environmental Protection Act 1990, Part I, otherwise than by issuing a notice under s 36, or by exercising their investigatory powers without entering the work. Under CAA 1993, s 36, which gives authorities power to require occupiers to furnish information about pollution emissions from their premises, where a notice relates to a process subject to EPA 1990, Part I the person on whom it is served is not obliged to supply any information which, as certified by an inspector, is not of a kind which is being supplied to the inspector for the purposes of that Act. CAA 1993, s 36 applies to premises used for Crown purposes, but in relation to such premises local authorities may not use powers of entry, inspection and to obtain information under ss 56 to 58. Premises may also be exempted from control under CAA 1993, s 36(6), see SI 1977/18, principally relating to defence establishments, including, inter alia, the Atomic Weapons Research Establishment at Aldermaston.

Under CAA 1993, s 39 the Secretary of State may, for the purposes of obtaining information about air pollution, direct a local authority to make specified arrangements for providing and operating air pollution recording apparatus and for transmitting information so obtained to him. Such directions may only be given after consultation with affected authorities, though it is their duty to comply with a direction once given.

Under CAA 1993, s 40 controls under the legislation cover 'emissions' into the atmosphere. These are construed as applying to substances in a gaseous, liquid or solid state, or any combination of those states.

H CONTROL OF VEHICLE EMISSIONS

Apart from lead, exhaust emissions contain substances such as NOx, carbon monoxide and hydrocarbons which may, in sufficient concentrations, be damaging to health. Emissions can be controlled by regulating fuel composition, or by vehicle design and construction regulations. UK standards have followed the tortuous development of EU Directives, while, sadly, there has not always been agreement between the EU, the USA and Japan, the world's major vehicle producers, as to the style and content of emission standards and their test parameters. Emission requirements for carbon monoxide, hydrocarbons and NOx generally depend upon the year of a model's introduction to the road and the limits in force for that year, generally those fixed under EU Directives. The Road Vehicle (Construction and Use) Regulations SI 1986/1078 (as amended), continued in force under s 41 of the Road Traffic Act 1988, provide in tabular form the minimum standards, so that from 1 October 1982 the standards of Directive 78/665 applied to motor cars while from 1 April 1991 Directive 83/351 was the basic standard for new vehicles. Directive 88/76 was the standard for new vehicles from 1993–94 depending on engine size, while provision was made for compliance with Directive 89/458 for vehicles of less than 1,400 cc capacity from the end of 1992. Further provision was made by Directives 91/441 which came into force as from 1992, applying new limits from 1996, 94/12 (cars and light vans) setting out new limits for all registrations from 1997, and from 1996 for new models, 93/59 and 91/542 which apply to larger and heavier commercial vehicles. Similar provision is made by the regulations in respect of particulate emissions, and emissions from diesel engined vehicles. The UK operates a type approval scheme as provided for by EU Directives, see SI 1994/981. It is an offence under the Road Traffic Act 1988, s 42 to fail to comply with relevant requirements of the Construction and Use Regulations.

The Road Traffic Regulation Act 1984 contains powers to regulate traffic in order to preserve the amenities of areas through which roads run: these are more generally considered below. However, RTRA 1984, ss 1, 6 and 122 (1) were amended by the Environment Act 1995, Sch 22 to provide that relevant authorities (shire counties, unitary and metropolitan district authorities and London borough councils) may make an order to achieve the purposes of the national air quality strategy (see further above), and indeed such authorities are to take the strategy into account in exercising road traffic regulation functions. The Act itself has been supplemented by the Road Traffic (Vehicle Emissions) (Fixed Penalty) Regulations 1997 (SI 1997/3058). The regulations allow certain specified local authorities (mainly metropolitan areas) to issue fixed penalty notices to vehicle users who fail to comply with regs 61 and 98, concerning respectively the emission of smoke and other substances, and the requirement that stationary vehicles should cut their engines in certain circumstances.

The official view is that use of 1984 Act powers should not take place on a temporary or ad hoc basis, or on the basis of giving little or no notice of restrictions, lest more congestion and pollution is caused by drivers seeking ways round restricted areas.[17] Such temporary bans could in any case be difficult to enforce. However, the new powers could be used on environmental grounds to allow the creation of contingency orders which regulate traffic on a planned basis and which come into effect, with restriction signs unveiled, when pollution reaches particular levels. This follows the precedent of closing certain moorland roads in times of high fire risk, but it is something of a 'weapon of last resort'.

Furthermore the Transport Act 2000 enables local authorities to make use of a variety of measures including congestion charging and work-place parking levies as a means by which to dissuade people from car use. Some controversy was generated by the dedication of a bus lane on the M4 motorway into London, and the current Mayor, Ken Livingstone, is a supporter of congestion charging. The thinking is that any revenues raised in this way should be ring-fenced to provide extra funds for transport policies. The long-awaited integration of the transport policy remains unfulfilled however.

I   STUBBLE BURNING

An issue that caused much controversy was stubble burning in fields after harvesting of crops. In the early 1980s some 14 m tonnes of straw were produced annually, half being burnt on site. In 1984 the Home Office produced model byelaws on straw and stubble burning for local authorities to adopt. These provisions were supplemented by the National Farmers Union Code which counselled that straw should be burnt against the wind, only when the wind speed was low, and only after neighbours had been informed. Though it was questionable whether police and fire authorities had resources sufficient to ensure compliance with byelaws, the summer of 1984 did see an abatement of the problem as byelaws and the NFU Code were generally observed. In 1985 the government introduced media advertisements urging precautions on farmers burning straw and stubble.

The problem did not, however, disappear and a growing body of opinion forced legislative action on the issue in the form of the Environmental Protection Act 1990,

17   See also *R v Greenwich London Borough, ex p Jack Williams* (1995) 255 ENDS Report 49.

s 152 which empowers ministers to make regulations banning farmers from stubble and crop residue burning, either generally or specifically. An interim scheme was introduced by SI 1991/1590 as from July 1991.

The Crop Residues (Burning) Regulations SI 1993/1366 now prohibit the burning on agricultural land of listed crop residues (cereal straw, cereal stubble, residues of oil seed rape, field beans and peas) subject to certain minor exemptions, such as for educational or research purposes. There are also restrictions and requirements imposed in relation to burning linseed residues, for example as to the timing and extent of burning. Burning residues in contravention of the regulations is an offence punishable on summary conviction with a fine up to level 5 on the standard scale.

Further reading

GENERAL WORKS

Aldous, T, *Battle for the Environment* (1972) Fontana, Parts II and V.

Arvil, R, *Man and Environment* (1967) Penguin, chapters 6 and 7.

Bennett, G (ed), *Air Pollution Control in the European Community* (1991) Graham and Trotman.

Blowers, A, *Something in the Air* (1984) Harper and Row.

Churchill, R, Warren, L and Gibson, J, *Law, Policy and the Environment* (1991) Blackwell.

Churchill, R and Freestone, D (eds), *International Law and Global Climate Change* (1991) Graham and Trotman.

French, D, 1997 'Kyoto Protocol to the 1992 Framework Convention on Climate Change' [1998] 10(2) JEL 227.

Hobley, A, 'Greenhouse Gas Emissions Trading in the United Kingdom' ELM 13 [2001] 2.

Hughes, Parpworth and Upson, *Air Pollution Law and Regulation*, (1998) Jordans.

Johnson, SP, *The Earth Summit: The United Nations Conference on Environment and Development (UNCED)* (1993) Graham and Trotman, chapter 5.

Okawa, P, State Responsibility for Transboundary Air Pollution in International Law (2000) OUP.

Sunkin, M, Ong, DM and Wight, R, *Sourcebook on Environmental Law* (2nd edn 2001) Cavendish.

ENERGY

Central Electricity Generating Board, 'Acid Rain' (1985) CEGB.

Everest, D, 'The Greenhouse Effect' (1988) Policy Studies Institute.

Grubb, M, 'The Greenhouse Effect' (1990) Royal Institute of International Affairs.

UK Climate Change Impacts Review Group, 'The Potential Effects of Climate Change in the UK' (1991) DoE.

PLANNING CONTROL

Miller, C, and Wood, C, *Planning and Pollution*, OUP, chapters 2, 3 and 4.

TRANSPORT

Hughes, P, 'Exhausting the Atmosphere' (1991) 60 Town and Country Planning 267.

Quality of Urban Air Review Group, 'Diesel Vehicle Emissions and Urban Air Quality' (1993) University of Birmingham.

Sharp, C, and Jennings, T, 'Transport and the Environment' (1976) Leicester University Press.

Watkins, LH, 'Air Pollution from Road Vehicles' (1991) HMSO.

ODOURS
Artis, D, 'Control of Odour Pollution' [1982] JPL 481.
Artis, D, and Silvester, S, 'Odour Nuisance: Legal Controls' [1986] JPL 565.

OFFICIAL REPORTS
'Acid Rain' (1984 Cmnd 9397).
'Acid Rain' (House of Commons Environment Committee 4th Report Session 1983–84, 446–1.
'CFC's and Halons' (1990) HMSO.
'The Effects of Acid Deposition' (1989) HMSO.
'Energy Paper No 58' (1990) HMSO.
Royal Commission on Environmental Pollution, 5th Report (1976, Cmnd 6371), 9th Report (1983, Cmnd 8852), 10th Report (1984, Cmnd 9149), 15th Report (1991, Cm 1631), 18th Report (1994, Cm 2674).
'Climate Change: Our National Programme for CO_2 Emissions' (1992) DOE.
'Climate Change: the UK Programme' (1994, Cm 2427) HMSO.
'Volatile Organic Compounds' House of Commons Environment Committee Session 1994/95, 1st Report, HC 39–1 (1995) HMSO (and the government's response of 27 June 1995).
DETR, *The Environmental Impacts of Road Vehicles in use: Air Quality, Climate Change and Noise pollution* (1999), HMSO.
European Commission, Green Paper on Greenhouse Gas Emissions Trading within the European Union (COM(2000)87).

Chapter 18

Noise

Humankind's capacity to *create* noise increases dramatically. Noise surrounds us: the roar of traffic, the irritating buzz of personal stereos, the bustle of crowds, the passage of trains and aeroplanes, and the working of industry and public utilities. The home can also be invaded by noise. The Wilson Committee on the Problem of Noise[1] found that surveys carried out in 1948 and 1961 showed that whereas only some 23% of those surveyed at the earlier date claimed to have been disturbed at home by external noises, by the later date the figure had risen to 50%. This trend has continued right up to the present day. The National Society for Clean Air and Environmental Protection (NSCA)[2] carries out an annual National Noise Survey which is sent to all Chief Environmental Health Officers in the UK asking their opinions on matters such as levels of complaint, current and proposed legislation and future policies for managing noise. The 2001 survey reveals that for 79% of the respondents in England, neighbour noise from amplified music is the main source of complaint followed by barking dogs (52%). In Northern Ireland it is the reverse (79% and 64% respectively) and in Wales, complaints about music are slightly more common than for dogs.

With regard to ambient noise,[3] the survey reveals that pubs and clubs remain by far the largest source of complaint in England. In Wales and Northern Ireland this is also the case, although the majority is smaller. Complaints about noise from industry and construction are common in all three countries, but the authors of the survey express some surprise at the fact that complaints to local authorities about traffic noise appear to be decreasing in England and are negligible in Wales and Northern Ireland despite the prevalence of traffic noise. Indeed, it is the view of the NSCA that traffic noise is eroding the few remaining areas of tranquillity in the UK. It is clearly a cause for concern that the survey's findings suggest that for the majority of local authorities there has been no improvement in the noise climate and that for a large proportion, it continues to deteriorate.

Noise is undoubtedly psychologically and physiologically harmful and an invisible but insidious form of pollution: once hearing has been damaged by noise it can scarcely ever be restored to wholeness. In addition to hearing loss, there are a number of other

1   (1963 Cmnd 2056).
2   An independent multidisciplinary non-governmental organisation which works on noise policy in the UK.
3   See the discussion of the government's commitment to produce a national ambient noise strategy (below).

actual or potential effects of noise on health: annoyance; interference with speech communication; interference with general levels of performance, especially the ability to concentrate and to carry out tasks; mental health; noise induced stress related effects eg changes in blood pressure, heart disease and other cardiovascular effects, changes in the immune system, and changes in the unborn child such as birthweight effects and incidence rates for congenital disorders; and sleep disturbance.

A WHAT IS NOISE? THE PROBLEM AND THE INTERNATIONAL RESPONSE

The Wilson Committee in its 1963 report 'Noise'[4] defined noise as 'sound which is undesired by the recipient'. This subjective definition is alien to a scientist's description of noise in terms of *frequency and intensity*. The law has failed to produce an objective definition of noise, coupled with measurement and assessment techniques. The law cannot take account of every unwanted noise, but legal regulation cannot be restricted only to those noises that are objectively 'loud' in terms of decibels, sones and phons — a continuous low pitched 'quiet' buzz may be as annoying as the occasional 'loud' bang. The law is pragmatic regarding noise as a fit subject for action only if, in its context, sound becomes excessive, unnecessary or unreasonable. Scientific methods are, of course, useful in determining situations where noise 'steps out from its background' and becomes actionable.[5] Of course the 'louder', in scientific terms, a noise is, the more likely it is that legal action will have to be taken to shield the public against it or bring about its cessation.

The following is a table of commonly occurring noise levels in decibels.[6]

Peak sound level in dB(A)

(decibels)	Environmental conditions
140	Threshold of pain
130	Jet aircraft on ground, pneumatic road breaker
125	Noise under supersonic flight path within 5 miles of take-off
120	Jet take-off at 100 m, loud motor horn at 3 ft
110–125	Pop group
115	Noise under jet flight path within 5 miles of take-off, riveting machine in sheet metal works
100	House near airport, inside an underground train
90–92	Train, inside a bus
88–92	Heavy lorry
81–91	Sports car
77–83	Cars
80	Average street corner noise
75	Major road with heavy traffic (peak level)
70	Conversational speech
65	Residential road with local traffic
60	Business office
50	Living room in a suburban area with distant traffic noise

4   (Cmnd 2056).
5   *R v Fenny Stratford Justices, ex p Watney Mann (Midlands) Ltd* [1976] 2 All ER 888, [1976] 1 WLR 1101.
6   See Keese *The Law Relating to Noise*, p 10 and Sharp and Jennings *Transport and the Environment*, pp 53-54.

40	Library
30	Quiet bedroom at night
25	Rustling leaves
20	Broadcasting studio
10	Threshold of hearing

International and European Community law lay down certain norms in respect of noise. International law has been much concerned in particular with aircraft issues (see further below on UK implementation of treaty provisions), and the principal standards-setting body is the International Civil Aviation Organisation (ICAO) set up under the Chicago Convention of 1944, Art 9 of which also acts as the international legal basis for regulation of aircraft noise. This has been supplemented a number of times, and the provisions are known collectively as Annex 16 of the Chicago Convention, which since 1981, has borne the title 'environmental protection', while a Committee on Aviation Environmental Protection (CAEP) was set up in 1983 with the object of keeping Annex 16 under regular review so that signatory states can consider amending its terms to take account, for example, of enhanced noise abatement technologies.

Noise and the EC

Despite the fact that action to reduce environmental noise has generally been accorded a lower priority in European countries than action in respect of other environmental problems such as air and water pollution, noise remains a significant problem. It has been estimated that approximately 20% of the EC's population (80 million people) suffer from noise levels that are scientifically unacceptable and that an additional 170 million people live in 'grey areas' where the noise levels cause serious annoyance during the daytime.[7]

The EC formally took action on noise for the first time in its Second Environmental Action Programme of 1977 though there had been antecedent measures. The EC has tended to rely on noise standards set by other international bodies such as ICAO, and has, historically, followed the paths of harmonising national standards, so that measures were mixed, partly directed towards the free circulation of goods and partly towards the imposition of noise limits.

The EC has, in the past, set noise standards for a number of products. These include: the permissible sound levels and exhaust systems for motor vehicles;[8] motorcycles;[9] tractors;[10] construction plant;[11] aircraft;[12] lawnmowers;[13] and household appliances.[14] Action has also been taken on workplace noise. The directive on aircraft noise is particularly interesting as an example of vertical integration between various systems of law. Directive 80/51 makes it an obligation for member states to implement the ICAO's annex 16 noise emission standards for subsonic aircraft which otherwise would not have legal force within the legal systems of all member states. Moreover, the directive

7   See the EC Green Paper, *Future Noise Policy* COM (96) 540.
8   Directive 70/157, as amended by 73/350, 77/212, 81/334, 84/372, 84/424, 87/354, 89/491, 92/97, 96/20, 99/101.
9   Directive 78/1015, as amended by 87/56, 89/235.
10 Directive 74/151 as amended by 82/890, 77/311.
11 Directive 84/532, 79/113 as amended by 81/1051, 85/405, 84/533 to 84/537, 86/662, 89/392.
12 Directive 80/51 as amended by 83/206, 89/629, 92/14.
13 Directive 84/538 as amended by 87/252, 88/180, 88/181.
14 Directive 86/594.

is an example of a mixed measure (see above) in that it is also concerned with the free movement of goods.[15]

The Fifth Environmental Action Programme of 1993 identified noise as one of the most pressing environmental problems in urban areas and stressed the need to take action with regard to various noise sources. In 1996, the EC produced a Green Paper, *Future Noise Policy*[16] the aim of which is to stimulate public discussion on the future approach to noise policy. In the Paper it is noted that although significant advances have been made in, for example, the reduction of noise from individual cars (85% reduction since 1970), the Commission nevertheless feels that changes in the overall approach are necessary if a noise abatement policy is to be successful. As part of the new noise framework the Green Paper proposed, amongst other things, a directive providing for the harmonisation of methods of assessment of noise exposure and, the simplification of EC legislation which sets noise emission limits for outdoor equipment. This latter proposal was given effect by Directive 2000/14, which has been implemented in the UK by the Noise Emission in the Environment by Equipment for use Outdoors Regulations 2001[17] (see below). The directive brings together in one legislative provision nine directives on construction plant and lawnmowers[18] in an effort to create a framework for the reduction of noise emission by equipment for use outdoors.

It seems likely that, in the future, the main area of EC activity will continue to be the reduction of noise from products. However, the Green Paper does express the view that although noise problems tend to have a local nature to them, this does not mean that all action is best taken at the local level. It is not inconceivable, therefore, that the EC will become the focus for initiatives such as the greater use of economic instruments for noise abatement. If this does happen, the EC will have to ensure that any such application of the 'polluter pays' principle is also consistent with a further principle, subsidiarity.

B   NOISE AND THE COMMON LAW

Noise can be either a public or private nuisance. The assessment of whether noise constitutes an actionable nuisance will depend on considering factors such as the: nature of the locality; duration of the noise; nature and desirability of the defendant's actions; nature of the harm suffered by the plaintiff, and the defendant's state of mind, though not all of these will be equally relevant in any given case. The following have been held to be noise nuisances: operating very noisy machinery during the night so as to disturb the plaintiff's sleep;[19] use of a circular saw for 12 hours a day;[20] playing fairground organs for eight hours a day;[21] operating a dairy with much clanging of churns, coming and going, loading of carts and noisy machinery;[22] though *not* simply supplying milk, even in large quantities;[23] *deliberately* making loud noises and shrieks so as to disrupt a music teacher's lessons;[24] using a steam hammer so noisy that it disturbed public worship and prevented schools from functioning;[25] broadcasting radio

15   See Case C-389/96 *Aher-Waggon GmbH v Germany* [1998] ECR I-4473.
16   COM (96) 540.
17   SI 2001/1701.
18   The relevant directives are: 79/113, 84/532 to 84/538 and 86/662.
19   *Rushmer v Polsue and Alfieri Ltd* [1906] 1 Ch 234, CA; affd sub nom *Polsue and Alfieri Ltd v Rushmer* [1907] AC 121, HL.
20   *Husey v Bailey* (1895) 11 TLR 221.
21   *Lambton v Mellish* [1894] 3 Ch 163.
22   *Tinkler v Aylesbury Dairy Co Ltd* (1888) 5 TLR 52.
23   *Fanshawe v London and Provincial Dairy Co* (1888) 4 TLR 694.
24   *Christie v Davey* [1893] 1 Ch 316.
25   *Roskell v Whitworth* (1871) 19 WR 804.

programmes loudly in the defendant's factory;[26] noisy testing of aero engines;[27] noisy operation of fish and chip shops or all night cafes;[28] using land as a speedway track, or for 'go-karts';[29] using a lake for organised motor boat racing and water-skiing;[30] keeping particularly noisy animals;[31] the ringing of church bells;[32] allowing the use by night of a children's playground on a council estate by noisy children.[33]

The courts are particularly concerned with the nature, quality and duration of noise, and the time of day of its occurrence; night time noise being more likely to be actionable. Each case turns on its own facts: a given outcome is not always easy to predict. Thus in *Murdoch and Murdoch v Glacier Metal Co Ltd*,[34] for example, the Court of Appeal dismissed an appeal against the finding of the trial judge that night time noise from the defendant's factory did not amount to an actionable nuisance even though the level of noise (36.7 dB(A)) was just above that at which, according to a World Health Organisation report, sleep could be affected (35 DB(A)). Although sleep disturbance was an important consideration in determining whether there was a common law nuisance in a mixed use area, a court should take account of the overall situation. Accordingly, the Court of Appeal held that the trial judge had been right to take into account other factors such as the lack of complaints by other residents, the proximity of a bypass to the claimant's home and evidence from the local environmental health officer in reaching the conclusion that the operation of the factory did not amount to an actionable nuisance.

The uncertainty of a nuisance action, coupled with the complexity and expense of litigation, renders it an unpopular method of dealing with noise. Between neighbours nuisance is an unpopular type of proceeding: actions, even in the county court, are drawn out and time consuming, frequently productive of bitterness, costly, and generally need a deal of proof from plaintiffs, such as listing and describing the quality and duration of noise in diaries. Such deficiencies justify the existence of public law controls over noise. Furthermore, planned strategies to control and reduce noise can only be implemented by public bodies: where noise afflicts a whole area or section of the community it is wrong to expect remedial action to be taken solely by individuals. However, the existence of public law controls does not inhibit the power of the court to grant a remedy stricter than that available under statute.[35] Furthermore a grant of planning permission may so change the character of an area that noise that would have amounted to a noise before a development took place may no longer do so afterwards.[36]

C PUBLIC LAW CONTROLS OVER NOISE

The development of the law

There was for many years reluctance to introduce statutory noise controls. Some local Acts dealt with noise nuisances, as did some byelaws, but it was generally left to private

---

26 *Gilbert v Marks & Co* (1949) 150 Estates Gazette 81.
27 *Bosworth-Smith v Gwynnes Ltd* (1919) 89 LJ Ch 368.
28 *Caradog-Jones v Rose* (1961) Times, 14 March; and *Charlton v Old Manor Cars* (1960) Times, 12 October.
29 *Tarry v Chandler* (1934) 79 Sol Jo 11; and *Manners v Chester* (1963) Times, 12 February.
30 *Kennaway v Thompson* [1981] QB 88, [1980] 3 All ER 329.
31 *Leeman v Montagu* [1936] 2 All ER 1677; and *Broder v Saillard* (1876) 2 Ch D 692.
32 *Soltau v De Held* (1851) 2 Sim NS 133.
33 *Dunton v Dover District Council* (1977) 76 LGR 87.
34 [1998] Env LR 732.
35 *Lloyds Bank plc v Guardian Assurance plc* (1986) 35 BLR 34.
36 *Gillingham Borough Council v Medway (Chatham) Dock Co Ltd* [1993] QB 343, [1992] 3 All ER 923.

citizens to take nuisance actions in respect of noise. However, nuisance actions are effective only in cases involving single, stationary continuous sources of noise, as opposed to combinations of noise of short and intermittent duration. Additionally a common law action is punitive and compensatory rather than preventive. It is better to plan and design the location and practices of industry so as to prevent noise, rather than imposing expensive remedial steps by means of injunctions.

Accordingly the Noise Abatement Act 1960 was passed, the first general Act devoted to controlling noise. However, it merely declared noise to be a statutory nuisance, and did little more than centralising and codifying existing byelaws of local authorities. Following the report of the Scott Committee, 'Neighbourhood Noise', in 1971 further controls on noise were included in the Control of Pollution Act 1974, Part III. Certain controls are now to be found in the Environmental Protection Act 1990, as amended, while other statutes control 'raves' and noise at night. The common law is also relevant.

Common law powers

Noise can amount to a public nuisance provided a class of Her Majesty's subjects is affected,[37] and it is established that a perpetrator may be liable where he/she knew or ought to have known of the nuisance.

The current statute law

Noise nuisances

Local authorities, eg district, metropolitan district and London borough councils, are under a duty to inspect their areas from time to time to detect noise nuisances and must take reasonable steps to investigate complaints of noise nuisances. This duty applies in respect of noise emitted *from premises* (EPA 1990, s 79(1)(g)) or noise from vehicles, machinery or equipment (including musical instruments) in streets, but excluding traffic noise and noise from protest marches (EPA 1990, s 79(1)(ga)). Where, under EPA 1990, s 80, the local authority conclude that noise amounting to a nuisance exists or is likely to recur in their area, they *must* serve a notice on the person responsible for the noise. For the purposes of the statutory nuisance regime, the 'person responsible' is the person by whose act, default or sufferance the noise arises or, with regard to vehicles, the registered owner[38] *and* the driver, or with regard to equipment etc, its operator (EPA 1990, s 79(7)) or if he cannot be found or if the nuisance is only anticipated, on the owner[39] or occupier of the premises from which the noise is, or may be, emitted. The notice may be served *either* on the person, or by being left at the person's proper address, *or* sent by post thereto: see the Local Government Act 1972, s 233(2).[40]

Although a local authority is under a duty to serve an abatement notice where the statutory circumstances apply, it is *not* under a duty to consult the person responsible prior to serving the notice.[41] In many cases it may be both sensible and appropriate for a local authority to engage in consultation. However, the Court of Appeal has warned

37   *R v Shorrock* [1994] QB 279, [1993] 3 All ER 917.
38   *Gribler v Harrow London Borough Council* [2000] EHLR 188.
39   This also includes the managing agent of a property: see *Camden London Borough Council v Gunby* [2000] EHLR 33.
40   *Lambeth London Borough Council v Mullings* [1990] RVR 259.
41   *R v Falmouth and Truro Port Health Authority, ex p South West Water Services* [2000] 3 All ER 306, [2000] EHLR 306.

that a local authority 'should be wary of being drawn too deeply and too lengthily into scientific or technical debate, and warier still of unintentionally finding itself fixed with all the obligations of a formal consultation process'.[42]

Where a notice is served, it may require the abatement of the nuisance, or prohibit or restrict its recurrence,[43] and may require the execution of such works, and the taking of such other steps, as may be necessary or specified. There is no obligation on a local authority, however, to specify works to be done or other steps to be taken.[44] It may simply serve a notice requiring the recipient to abate a noise nuisance eg the barking of dogs, without specifying how this is to be achieved.[45] Such an approach will be most appropriate where there are a number of ways in which a nuisance can be abated. Even where an abatement notice does use the word 'steps' and then fails to specify in its schedule what those steps are, it does not necessarily follow that the notice is thereby invalid. Provided that it is obvious from the notice what is required and that no unfairness has been suffered by the recipient, a court will not adopt a mechanistic approach and condemn the notice for its failure to specify.[46] An abatement notice must, however, specify the time or times within which compliance is required eg two years,[47] although a statement that compliance shall be 'forthwith' does not necessarily render the notice invalid, provided that the step or steps to be taken can be achieved so quickly.[48] Where a nuisance is likely to recur a permanent prohibition of recurrence may be imposed.[49]

Although it may be helpful, it is not mandatory for an authority seeking to prevent the occurrence of a noise nuisance to set a decibel level which shall not be exceeded. In some circumstances, it may not be necessary to provide noise data given that the effect of noise may depend upon factors other than volume, such as pitch and the nature of the noise.[50] However, where a decibel level is set, the notice must also say where that level is to be measured and stipulate the average period of time over which the readings are to be taken ie the LeqT.[51]

An abatement notice should be practicable and easily understood, not least because of the criminal sanctions that might follow a breach.[52] It should not require unnecessary repetition of works simply to reduce noise to a stated decibel level.[53] However, a nuisance may still arise for reasons other than noise decibel levels being exceeded.[54] An authority may base its actions on the expert evidence of its own officers, and does not have to prove nuisance to a particular occupier, and may require cessation of nuisance to the occupier of any residential property, though the authority's notice should make it clear which requirements are imposed under what provisions.[55]

42   Per Simon Brown LJ in *Falmouth and Truro Port Health Authority* (above) 321 of the former report.
43   Prohibition of recurrence can be stated either expressly or by implication: see *Barry Stanley v London Borough of Ealing* [2000] EHLR 172.
44   *Greenline Carriers (Tayside) Ltd v City of Dundee* 1991 SLT 673; and *Sterling Homes (Midlands) Ltd v Birmingham City Council* [1995] Env LR 121.
45   *Budd v Colchester Borough Council* [1999] EHLR 347.
46   *Sevenoaks District Council v Brands Hatch Leisure Group Ltd* [2001] EHLR 7.
47   *R (on the application of Aircraft Research Association Ltd) v Bedford Borough Council* [2001] EHLR 17.
48   *Brighton and Hove Council v Ocean Coachworks (Brighton) Ltd* [2000] EHLR 279.
49   *R v Birmingham Justices, ex p Guppy* (1987) 152 JP 159.
50   *Cambridge City Council v Douglas* [2001] EHLR 9.
51   For an example of a case where the decibel level was not in dispute but the LeqT was, see *R (on the application of Aircraft Research Association Ltd) v Bedford Borough Council* [2001] EHLR 17.
52   See, for example, *Brighton and Hove Council v Ocean Coachworks (Brighton) Ltd* [2000] EHLR 279.
53   *Newark Housing Association v Westminster City Council* [1995] Env LR 176.
54   *East Northamptonshire District Council v Fossett* [1994] Env LR 388.
55   *Cooke v Adatia* (1988) 153 JP 129.

A person served with an abatement notice has, under EPA 1990, s 80(3), 21 days to appeal to the magistrates. The grounds of appeal are set out in the Statutory Nuisance (Appeals) Regulations.[56] However, before considering the particular defences under the regulations, it should be noted that there are two general defences under EPA 1990, s 80, namely that the defendant had a 'reasonable excuse', and, where the noise was caused in the course of trade or business, that the 'best practicable means' was used to prevent, or to counteract it.[57] The court may quash or vary the notice or dismiss the appeal, and has a wide discretion as to whom to order to execute, or pay for, any necessary work. In deciding whether or not to vary an abatement notice, a court is required to have in mind the extent of any defects which it may be asked to cure and whether the substance of what the notice requires remains valid and appropriate after variation.[58] At one time it was considered that justices should decide an appeal on the basis of the facts at the time of the *hearing*.[59] However, the Court of Appeal has subsequently held that in considering the validity of a notice, a court should consider the facts at the time of the *service* of the notice.[60]

The Statutory Nuisance (Appeals) Regulations make particular provision for appeals against EPA 1990, s 80 notices issued in respect of noise nuisance. There are additions to the general grounds of appeal (ie the notice is not justified, or is subject to some informality, defect or error, or the authority have refused unreasonably to accept compliance with alternative requirements, or the notice's requirements are unreasonable or unnecessary, or the time specified for taking action is not reasonably sufficient, etc).[61] In the case of alleged nuisances under EPA 1990, s 79(1)(g) or (ga) which relate to noise emitted from premises, it can be a ground of appeal that the requirements of the notice are more serious than the requirements for time being in force in relation to the noise in question of any notice served under the Control of Pollution Act 1974, ss 60 or 66 (control of construction site noise), or any consent given under CPA 1974, ss 61 or 65 (consent for work or construction sites and for noise to exceed a registered level) or any determination made under CPA 1974, s 67 (noise control for new buildings). In the case of a nuisance under EPA 1974, s 79(1)(ga) where noise is emitted or is caused by vehicles, machinery or equipment, it is a ground of appeal that the requirements of the notice are more serious than the requirements for the time being in force in relation to the noise in question under any condition of a consent given under the Noise and Statutory Nuisance Act 1993, Sch 3, para 1, which relates to loudspeakers in streets or roads.

Where an appeal is made and the nuisance is one arising under EPA 1990, s 79(1)(g) or (ga) *and* the noise in question was necessarily caused in the performance of some duty imposed by law on the appellant, the notice is suspended until the appeal has been abandoned or decided *save* for cases where the nuisance is injurious to health or is of such limited duration that suspension of the notice would render the notice nugatory, and the notice includes a statement to that effect and which gives a statement of the basis for non-suspension on which the authority rely. In such cases suspension does not take place.

It should, of course, be remembered that all the other grounds of appeal are available, just as with other statutory nuisance allegations.

56   SI 1995/2644.
57   See further p 588 below.
58   *Lambie and Minter v Thanet District Council* [2001] EHLR 3.
59   *Johnsons News of London Ltd v Ealing London Borough Council* (1989) 154 JP 33.
60   *SFI Group plc v Gosport Borough Council* [2000] EHLR 137.
61   See chapter 1 above.

Authorities may also apply for an injunction to restrain a noise nuisance pending the outcome of an appeal.[62]

EPA 1990, s 80(4) provides that if a person served with a notice under the section contravenes, without reasonable excuse, a requirement of the notice he commits an offence. Noise nuisance allegations are criminal in nature and hence the criminal burden of proof applies. Thus in *Lewisham London Borough v Fenner*[63] (admittedly only a Crown Court decision) it was found that in relation to an alleged nuisance arising from the operation of equipment, the fact that noise emitted was below the recommended limit of BS 8233 pointed to the burden of proof not being discharged, and the case failed.

Irrespective of whether or not a local authority has instituted proceedings under EPA 1990, s 80(4), it may take action to abate a nuisance itself where the terms of an abatement notice have not been complied with: see EPA 1990, s 81(3). In the case of noise nuisance, it is now clear that abatement action includes the power to seize and remove any equipment which it appears to the authority is being or has been used in the emission of the noise in question: see the Noise Act 1996, s 10(7).

Street noise

In *Southwark London Borough Council v Ince*,[64] it was held that an identical provision to s 79(1)(a) in the Public Health Act 1936 was sufficiently wide to embrace external traffic noise. Thus it was the case following the enactment of the Environmental Protection Act 1990 that where noise from a highway penetrated or vibrated premises and made them prejudicial to health or a nuisance, action could be taken by the local authority under s 79(1)(a). However, in 1993 Parliament enacted the Noise and Statutory Nuisance Act. NSNA 1993, inserted two new provisions into EPA 1990, s 79: s 79(1)(ga) and s 79(6A). The former provision stipulates that noise that is prejudicial to health or a nuisance is a statutory nuisance where it has been emitted from or caused by a vehicle, machinery or equipment in a street. The effect of this provision is limited, however, by EPA 1990, s 79(6A) which states that s 79(1)(ga) does not apply to: traffic noise; military noise; or, noise from a demonstration eg a political march. It is clear, therefore, that in the light of the 1993 amendments to EPA 1990, s 79, the ambit of s 79(1)(a) is now more restricted than it was held to be when *Ince* was decided. Accordingly in *Haringey London Borough Council v Jowett*,[65] the Divisional Court upheld an appeal against a decision made by magistrates to the effect that external traffic noise could be within the ambit of EPA 1990, s 79(1)(a). In its judgment, since 1994 (when the new provisions in s 79 came into force) the ambit of EPA 1990, s 79(1)(a) must be regarded as restricted so as to exclude traffic noise from vehicles, machinery and equipment in the street.

EPA 1990, s 80A provides in relation to street noise nuisance that where the nuisance has not yet occurred, *or* where it consists of noise from an unattended vehicle, which includes loud hailers and, presumably, even radios, machines or pieces of equipment, the abatement notice is to be served on the person responsible for the vehicle or equipment if that person can be found. If the person cannot be found, or where the authority determine to follow this procedure, they may affix the abatement notice to the vehicle or equipment, etc. Where affixation takes place *only* because of the authority's resolution and the person responsible can be found, a copy of the notice

62 *Hammersmith London Borough Council v Magnum Automated Forecourts Ltd* [1978] 1 WLR 50 and s 81(5).
63 (1995) 248 ENDS Report 44.
64 (1989) 153 JP 597.
65 [1999] LGR 667.

must also be served on that person within one hour of the affixation of the vehicle. The person served may appeal as under EPA 1990, s 80.

Failure to comply with a street noise nuisance abatement notice entitles the local authority to take action under EPA 1990, s 81(3) — as with any statutory nuisance — to enter the source of the noise and remove it to a safe place if that is what is requisite to abate the nuisance. Penn points to an instance of vehicle alarms going off at night and being disarmed by the local authority's environmental health officers.[66] However, in such cases care must be taken not to cause more damage than is necessary, see EPA 1990, Sch 3, para 2A(4), while a vehicle that has been entered to abate a nuisance should be resecured as effectively as possible. The local authority may recover their reasonable expenses under EPA 1990, s 81(4), while ss 81A and 81B allow for such expenses to be charged on relevant premises and paid by instalments.

General defences to noise nuisance allegations

'Reasonable excuse' already mentioned above seems to mean an excuse that a reasonable person would think consistent with a reasonable standard of conduct: mere lack of finance would not amount to such an excuse.[67] In *A Lambert Flat Management Ltd v Lomas*[68] the court considered the defence of 'reasonable excuse' is designed to cover cases where there is some special difficulty in relation to complying with the notice, for example severe illness. Holding a birthday party is not a 'reasonable excuse' for noise, nor is reducing noise levels on request though this may be relevant as an issue in mitigation, or in deciding whether there was a noise nuisance in the first place.[69]

A further defence is use of the 'best practicable means' to prevent or counteract the nuisance, see EPA 1990, s 80(8). Some guidance on 'best practicable means' is found in EPA 1990, s 79(9) which defines 'practicable' as 'reasonably practicable having regard among other things to local conditions and circumstances ... the current state of technical knowledge and to the financial implications'. 'Means' is defined to include design, installation, maintenance, manner and periods of operation of plant and machinery and the design and construction of buildings and acoustic structures. The test is applied only in so far as compatible with legal duties, any exigencies of emergencies, and safe working conditions. It is, however, for the accused to establish the defence (on the balance of probabilities), and mere increased costs of operation do not automatically render a 'means' impracticable.[70]

In *Manley and Manley v New Forest District Council*,[71] which concerned a noise nuisance caused by the barking of dogs housed in kennels in the appellant's back garden, Newman J noted that an important feature of 'best practicable means' as a basis for environmental pollution control is that it allows 'for flexibility to cater for local and individual circumstances'.[72] In allowing an appeal against the decision of the Crown Court, the High Court stressed that 'best practicable means' is concerned with what can be done on the premises which are the subject of an abatement notice. The Crown Court had therefore erred in law by concluding that 'best practicable means' included moving the kennels to a non-residential location.

66   See *Noise Control*, at p 103.
67   *Saddleworth UDC v Aggregate and Sand Ltd* (1970) 69 LGR 103.
68   [1981] 2 All ER 280, [1981] 1 WLR 898.
69   *Wellingborough Borough Council v Gordon* (1990) 155 JP 494.
70   *Wivenhoe Port Ltd v Colchester Borough Council* [1985] JPL 175 and [1985] JPL 396, CA; and *Chapman v Gosberton Farm Produce Co Ltd* [1993] 5 ELM 38.
71   [2000] EHLR 113.
72   At 118.

High Court proceedings and injunctive relief

Where the local authority are of the opinion that a prosecution would not be an adequate remedy, they may under EPA 1990, s 81(5) take proceedings in the High Court to secure the abatement, prohibition or restriction of the nuisance, irrespective of whether they have or have not suffered damage.[73] In *City of London Corpn v Bovis Construction Ltd*[74] a local authority sought an injunction under the Local Government Act 1972, s 222 in respect of repeated contraventions of a notice issued under CPA 1974, s 60. The court considered injunctive relief was appropriate where necessary to prevent damage not preventable by proceedings before justices, or: where criminal sanctions are otherwise insufficient or technically deficient; where unlawful activity will continue unless restrained by an injunction. See also *Camden London Borough Council v Alpenoak Ltd*[75] where an injunction was granted after repeated noise complaints, and then breached 22 times before contempt proceedings resulted in a £50,000 fine with £5,000 costs. Authorities must be able to show, however, that the activity in question is a threat to the proper exercise of statutory responsibilities, for the court will act with discretion and caution, and not to restrain mere infractions of criminal law. Resort to injunctive relief for reasons of convenience rather than because of the inadequacy of alternative remedies is therefore clearly beyond the intention of the statute.[76]

Summary proceedings by person aggrieved

Where *any* person is aggrieved by noise amounting to a nuisance he/she may make a complaint to the magistrates under EPA 1990, s 82. If the magistrates are satisfied that the nuisance exists or, though abated, is likely to recur on the same premises they must make an order requiring the defendant either to abate the nuisance within a specified time, and to execute any works necessary for that purpose, or prohibiting recurrence and requiring the doing of necessary works. Alternatively *both* these requirements can be imposed. The procedure is available against the creator of the noise, or if that person cannot be found, the owner or occupier of the premises from which the noise emanates. Where the noise nuisance emanates from unattended vehicles or equipment, proceedings lie against the person responsible for the vehicle/equipment. Where more than one person is responsible for noise each person responsible can be proceeded against. Making the order has similar consequences as to offences and defences under EPA 1990, s 80, but where a person is convicted of an offence under EPA 1990, s 82(11), the magistrates may, after giving him an opportunity of being heard, direct the local authority to do anything the convicted person was required to do by the order. The local authority may recover their expenditure from the person in default under EPA 1990, s 81. See also EPA 1990, s 81A on expenses being charged on relevant premises and s 81B on payment by instalments. EPA 1990, s 82 proceedings are available in respect of *existing* nuisances (or those likely to recur). Additionally the complainant must be a person whose enjoyment of property in his occupation has been materially affected by the noise.

---

73 *Hammersmith London Borough Council v Magnum Automated Forecourts Ltd* [1978] 1 WLR 50.
74 (1988) 86 LGR 660.
75 (1985) Surveyor, 5 December 17.
76 *Vale of the White Horse District Council v Allen & Partners* [1997] Env LR 212.

Notices served under previous legislation

Noise abatement notices served under the predecessor legislation to the EPA 1990, ie the Control of Pollution Act 1974, remain effective to control noise even after 1990.[77]

Night noise

The Noise Act 1996 was enacted to provide local authorities with a specific means of controlling noise emitted from dwellings at night. As such, it is additional to and complements the statutory nuisance controls on noise under the Environmental Protection Act 1990, s 79. Where a local authority receives a complaint (which may be made by any means) from an individual present in a dwelling during night hours (11 pm – 7 am) that excessive noise is being emitted from another dwelling, it is under an obligation by virtue of NA 1996, s 2 to ensure that one of its officers takes reasonable steps to investigate the complaint. Where the officer is satisfied that the noise being emitted from the offending premises would or might exceed the permitted level, he may serve a warning notice on the person responsible for the noise under NA 1996, s 3. The 'permitted level' for the purposes of the Act is determined by the Secretary of State. Where the underlying level of noise does not exceed 25dB, the permitted level is 35dB. Where the underlying level is in excess of 25dB, the permitted level is 10dB in excess of the underlying level of noise: see the Annex to Circular 8/97.

Where a warning notice has been served, it takes effect not earlier than 10 minutes after the time of service. It ceases to have effect the following 7 am. NA 1996, s 4 provides that where a warning notice has been served, the person responsible for noise which exceeds the permitted level commits an offence. It is a defence, however, to show that there was a reasonable excuse for the act, default or sufferance in question. What is a 'reasonable excuse' will depend upon the particular circumstances of the case. However, the defence will not be available to a person who deliberately contravenes a warning notice in circumstances which are wholly under his control.[78]

A person who is found guilty of a NA 1996, s 4 offence is liable on summary conviction to a fine not exceeding level 3 on the standard scale. However, there is an alternative to going to court; the payment of a fixed penalty notice in accordance with NA 1996, s 8. Provided that the recipient of a fixed penalty notice pays the sum of £100 within 14 days following the date of the notice, that person cannot be convicted of the NA 1996, s 4 offence.

Since a person who commits an offence under the Noise Act 1996 has the potential to commit further offences under the Act if they remain in possession of equipment which has been used in the emission of the noise, NA 1996, s 10 confers powers of entry and seizure on officers of the local authority. Essentially these arise where a warning notice has been served and, during the time that it is extant, noise has been emitted from the dwelling which exceeds the permitted level. If, however, entry has been refused to a dwelling, or refusal is apprehended or a request by a local authority officer would defeat the purpose of the entry, the local authority can seek a warrant from a magistrate to enter and seize equipment. In any event, it is unlikely that the statutory powers will be exercised without a police presence. It is an offence to wilfully obstruct, ie to knowingly obstruct or obstruct without lawful excuse, any person who is exercising the NA 1996, s 19(2) power of entry.

77   *Aitken v South Hams District Council* [1995] 1 AC 262, [1994] 3 All ER 400.
78   *Wellingborough District Council v Gordon* (1990) 155 JP 494.

Where equipment has been seized and the defendant has subsequently been convicted of a noise offence, the NA 1996, Schedule permits a court to make a forfeiture order. Such an order may be made in addition to the imposition of a penalty for the offence. In deciding whether or not to make a forfeiture order, a court must have regard to the value of the equipment and the likely financial and other effects on the offender of the making of the order.

The Noise Act 1996 is an adoptive Act. In other words, its provisions do not take effect in an area unless or until a local authority has passed a resolution adopting its provisions or the Secretary of State has ordered that it shall have effect. In October 1999 the University of Birmingham was commissioned by the DETR to carry out a review of the take up and workings of the Noise Act 1996.[79] This review had several objectives: to establish the effectiveness of the Act; to establish how far a common approach was developing by local authorities; and to identify good practice in dealing with night noise whether or not a local authority had chosen to adopt the NA 1996. Of the 262 authorities which returned completed questionnaires (a 65% response rate for all local authorities in England, Wales and Northern Ireland), only 13 reported that they had adopted the Act. The main reasons given for adoption were the increased powers that the Act affords a local authority, that adopting was desired by the management or council or in order to secure funding for the existing service. Clearly, the vast majority of the respondents had not adopted the Act by the time of the review. The most frequently cited reasons for not having done so were: there was no local demand; the local authority had insufficient resources to fund the full requirements of the Act; the legislation was too prescriptive; or the current service was adequate.

Interestingly, the review reveals that even where the Act had been adopted, only 2% of eligible noise complaints were dealt with under it. Other provisions, most notably the statutory nuisance provisions in the Environmental Protection Act 1990, are still, therefore, the favoured means of local authorities for dealing with night noise. Nevertheless, despite the small take up, the authors of the review are firmly of the opinion that the Noise Act 1996 has had a positive effect upon the way that local authorities deal with night noise. To support this view they point to the fact that in 1994, only 52% of the respondents had a form of 'out of hours' service in place. By 1997, when the noise offence provisions were in force, this had risen to 79%. This figure had risen again to 90% of the 262 respondents by 1999.[80]

Construction site noise

Erecting, constructing, altering, repairing or maintaining buildings, structures or roads, or breaking up, opening or boring under any road or adjacent land in connection with construction, inspection, maintenance or removal works, or any demolition or dredging work, or other work of engineering construction falls within CPA 1974, s 60. Where the local authority conclude that such works are, or are going to be, carried out on any premises, they *may* serve notice imposing requirements as to the manner of doing the works.[81] Notice has to be served on the person who appears to be carrying out, or going to carry out, the works, together with such others appearing to the authority to be responsible for, or having control over, the works. Requirements may include provision as to, inter alia: specifications of plant or machinery prescribed or proscribed; permitted hours of working; permitted noise levels generally, or in specified places or

79 *Review of Implementation of the Noise Act 1996* (DETR) 28 December 2000.
80 For the government's response to the findings of the review, see below.
81 *Strathclyde Regional Council v Tudhope* [1983] JPL 536.

at specified times, and may provide for changes of circumstances. The authority must have regard to relevant provisions of any code of practice issued under CPA 1974, Part III,[82] together with the need to ensure that the best practicable means are employed to minimise noise. Before specifying particular methods or plant they must consider alternatives similarly effective to minimise noise and more acceptable to the persons to be served with the notice. General regard must be had to protecting persons in the area against noise. The notice may specify requisite steps and periods for compliance. Following service there is a 21 day period in which to appeal to the magistrates.[83] It is an offence to contravene a notice without reasonable excuse.[84] However, a notice may only apply to works actually in progress or in contemplation at the time of its issue.[85]

Noise from construction equipment is further controlled under the Noise Emission in the Environment by Equipment for Use Outdoors Regulations 2001.[86] These regulations, which came into force on the 4 June and 3 July 2001 respectively, implement EC Directive 2000/14. They have the effect, inter alia, of revoking a number of regulations, including the Construction Plant and Equipment (Harmonization of Noise Emission Standards) Regulations 1985[87] and the Lawnmowers (Harmonization of Noise Emission Standards) Regulations 1992,[88] such revocation taking effect from 3 January 2002. The regulations do not apply to equipment placed on the market before 3 July 2001. In respect of equipment placed on the market after this date, however, the person responsible, ie the manufacturer, his representative in the EC or where neither is established in the EC, the person placing the equipment on the market in the EC, is under a duty to ensure that: the equipment satisfies the specified sound power level requirements; the appropriate conformity assessment procedure has been complied with in relation to the equipment; the equipment bears the CE marking and the indication of the guaranteed sound power level; *and* that it is accompanied by an EC declaration of conformity. It is an offence to place on the market equipment for use outdoors which contravenes or fails to comply with these requirements. A defence of due diligence is available, however, where a defendant can show that he took all reasonable steps and exercised all due diligence to avoid committing the offence.

The regulations make a distinction between Sch 1 and Sch 2 equipment. Construction equipment which falls within Sch 1, eg concrete-breakers, combustion-engine driven construction winches and mobile cranes, is subject to specified noise limits. Sch 2 equipment, eg concrete or mortar mixers, construction winches with an electric motor and hydraulic hammers, is subject to noise marking only.

Because the provision to control site noise is discretionary, practice varies widely. Local authorities tend to prefer informal arrangements and agreements with builders and other similar contractors to notices. Liaison between environmental health and planning departments can be useful in alerting relevant officers to sites where planning permission for relevant work is sought. Officers then decide whether or not to implement noise control powers; much depends on whether the authority has the resources to take action.

CPA 1974, s 61 allows a person intending to carry out works to which s 60 applies to apply to the local authority for consent. Where approval under building regulations is required in respect of the works, any application for consent must be made at the

---

82 See SI 1984/1992 and SI 1987/1730.
83 See CPA 1974, s 60(7) and the Control of Noise (Appeals) Regulations, SI 1975/2116, reg 5.
84 On the issue of the service of notices, see *Wiltshire Construction (London) Ltd v Westminster City Council* [1997] Env LR 321.
85 *Walter Lily & Co Ltd v Westminster City Council* [1994] 6 ELM 44.
86 SI 2001/1701.
87 SI 1985/1968.
88 SI 1992/168.

same time as, or later than, the request for building regulation approval. A CPA 1974, s 61 application must contain particulars of the works in question, methods to be used in carrying them out and steps proposed to minimise noise. Where these satisfy the authority that they would not need to serve a CPA 1974, s 60 notice, consent must be given. Before issuing consent they must have regard to any relevant code of guidance, need to ensure the use of the best practicable means to minimise noise, suitable alternative methods similarly able to minimise noise, and the need to protect persons in the locality against noise.

Consent may be given subject to conditions, particularly with regard to limiting consent following changes of circumstances and as to duration. It is an offence knowingly to infringe or to fail to comply with such a condition.

Decisions on applications must be given within 28 days from receipt. If the authority fail to give consent within that period, or if they do consent but attach conditions or limit or qualify the consent in any way, the applicant has 21 days in which to appeal to the magistrates.[89]

Where proceedings are brought for contravening a CPA 1974, s 60 notice it is a defence to prove that the alleged contravention amounted to carrying out works in accordance with a s 61 consent. Such a consent constitutes, however, *no* defence of itself to proceedings under EPA 1990, s 82. Where consent has been given and the works themselves are carried out by a person other than the applicant, the applicant's duty is to take all reasonable steps to bring the consent to the notice of the person doing the works: to fail is to commit an offence.

Loudspeaker noise

CPA 1974, s 62 generally makes it criminal to operate a loudspeaker in a street between the hours of nine in the evening and eight the following morning *for any purpose*, and at any other time for the purpose of advertising *any entertainment, trade or business* though exceptions exist for vendors such as those of ice cream: see CPA 1974, s 62(3). 'Street' means any highway or other road, footway, square[90] or court for the time being open to the public. Exceptions exist where loudspeakers are used by, in connection with, or form part of, as the case may be:

1   The police, fire brigade, ambulance service, water undertakers or sewerage undertakers in the discharge of their functions or a local authority within their area.
2   Persons communicating with others on a vessel for the purpose of directing the movement of that or other vessels.
3   A public telephone system.
4   Persons employed in connection with a transport undertaking used by the public, where the loudspeaker is operated otherwise than on the highway for the sole purpose of making announcements to passengers or employees of the undertaking.
5   Travelling showmen on land used temporarily for a pleasure fair.
6   Emergencies (for example immediate risks to life and health). And
7   Where the loudspeaker is in or fixed to a vehicle, *and* is operated solely for the entertainment of, or for communicating with, the driver or passengers, or forms part of a traffic warning device, *and* is reasonably operated so as not to give annoyance to persons in the vicinity.

89   See CPA 1974, s 61(7) and SI 1975/2116, reg 6.
90   An open space beneath a building can, in appropriate circumstances, be described as a 'square': see *Tower Hamlets London Borough Council v Creitzman* (1984) 83 LGR 72.

The prohibition does not apply to any loudspeaker operated under local authority consent under the Noise and Statutory Nuisance Act 1993, Sch 2. Such consent may be conditional, and may not authorise use for election, trade, business or entertainment advertisement purposes. NSNA 1993, Sch 2 applies where an authority resolves it shall apply in its area.

Noise abatement zones

CPA 1974, s 63 allows a local authority to designate all or any part of its area as a noise abatement zone, though all authorities are required by s 57 to inspect their areas with a view to declaring zones. Such an order must specify the classes of premises to which it applies. 'Premises' includes land under CPA 1974, s 105(1). The classes of premises suitable for control, include commercial industrial and agricultural premises, places of entertainment, transport and public utility installations. Once an order is in force the CPA 1974, ss 64 (registers of noise levels), 65 (noise exceeding registered levels) 66 (reduction of noise levels) and 67 (powers to deal with new buildings) apply. Authorities should not designate noise abatement zones unless they have the resources to undertake functions under these provisions. Designation of a noise abatement zone should be considered whenever a planning application for a new industrial development is made, especially where this could lead to mixed industrial and residential uses. A noise abatement zone will apply to existing as well as proposed land uses, and will cover noisy developments which, as a result of statutory permissions and exemptions, would otherwise escape planning control.

Procedure for designating zones

This is laid down in CPA 1974, Sch 1 (as substituted by the Local Government, Planning and Land Act 1980, s 1(2)). Before making the order the authority must serve notice on every owner, lessee and occupier (other than tenants for a month or less) of affected premises, and also publish the notice in the London Gazette and, for two successive weeks, in a local newspaper. The notice must state the intention to make the order and its general effect; a place where the order can be inspected (free of charge and at reasonable hours) during a period of not less than six weeks from the last date of publication, and must state the right of affected persons to object in writing to the authority. If objections are made they must be considered before the order is made. Objections can be ignored where the authority conclude consideration is unnecessary having regard either to the nature of the premises to which the order will relate or to the nature of the objectors' interests. The order once made generally comes into force *not less* than one month from the date of making. There is nothing in CPA 1974, s 63 to *oblige* authorities to carry out inspections before making orders under that provision,[91] though such an inspection is desirable.

Every local authority which has designated a noise abatement zone must, under s 64, measure and record in a public register ('the noise level register') the level of noise emanating from premises of any relevant class within the zone. Methods to be used in measuring noise levels and keeping records are laid down in the Control of Noise (Measurement and Registers) Regulations 1976, SI 1976/37. The regulations include a memorandum giving guidance on where and how to measure noise, how to determine

---

91   *Morganite Special Carbons v Secretary of State for the Environment* (1980) 256 Estates Gazette 1105.

measurement points and their heights, the time of measurements and how to take into account meteorological conditions.[92] The registers must contain the noise level which has been ascertained, and the Regulations require that the methods of measurement or calculation employed, details of all relevant measurements and calculations, including locations and heights of each point at which computations were made, details of equipment used, dates and times of computations, and prevailing weather conditions must be included. Clear identification of affected premises must be made, relevant dates stated, and other appropriate details recorded. Detailed guidance is also given on when and where to take measurements, the number of measurement points, the times of measurements and compensations to be made for background noise.

A copy of the recorded measurement must be served on the owner and occupier of the premises in question, thereafter there is a 28-day right of appeal to the Secretary of State, otherwise the validity of the registered entry may not be questioned in any proceedings under CPA 1974, Part III, and see SI 1975/2116, reg 9. The Secretary of State may allow or dismiss the appeal or reverse or vary any part of the record. He may also give to the local authority such directions as he thinks fit for giving effect to his determination.

By CPA 1974, s 65 the level of noise recorded in the register in respect of any premises may not be exceeded except with the written consent of the local authority, which may be given subject to conditions as to permitted levels of excess noise, and the duration and timing of such excess. Details of any consent must be recorded in the noise level register. A decision on an application for consent for noise to exceed registered levels must *generally* be notified to the applicant within two months of date of receipt, otherwise consent is deemed to be refused. Disappointed applicants may appeal to the Secretary of State within three months, beginning with the date of notification, or, in the case of a deemed refusal, within three months of the expiry of the two-month period following the lodging of the application. The Secretary of State has a wide discretion on appeal, see SI 1975/2116, reg 9, and the local authority must act in accordance with his decision on appeal. Under CPA 1974, s 65(8) a consent must contain a statement that it does not of itself constitute any ground of defence against proceedings instituted by an aggrieved occupier under EPA 1990, s 82.

Offences

Where noise is emitted from any premises in contravention of either the registered recorded level, or a condition attached to a consent to exceed that level, the person responsible commits an offence under CPA 1974, s 65(5). On convicting for such an offence magistrates may, if satisfied the offence is likely to continue or recur, make an order requiring the execution of necessary preventive works. Contravention of any requirement of such an order without reasonable excuse[93] is itself an offence. The magistrates may, after giving the local authority an opportunity of being heard, direct them to do any works that would be required of the convicted person, either instead of, or in addition to, imposing requirements on that person. Where the local authority are ordered to execute works they may recover their expenses from the convicted person under CPA 1974, s 69.

Where, under CPA 1974, s 66, it appears to the local authority that the level of noise from any premises subject to a noise abatement order is unacceptable, having regard to the purposes for which the order was made, *and* that a reduction in that level is

---

92 See Leeson *Environmental Law*, pp 291–293 and Penn *Noise Control* (2nd edn), pp 123–130.
93 *Wellingborough District Council v Gordon* (1990) 155 JP 494.

practicable at reasonable cost and would afford a public benefit, they may serve a noise reduction notice on the person responsible. The notice must require reduction of noise emitted to specified levels, to prevent any subsequent increase in the level of noise emitted, unless the local authority consent, and to take such steps as may be specified to achieve the purpose. The notice must give at least six months from the date of service for compliance, and its particulars must be recorded in the noise level register. The notice may make specific requirements as to noise reductions for particular dates and times, *and takes effect irrespective of any CPA 1974, s 65 consent authorising a higher level of noise.*

A person served with such a notice has three months to appeal to the magistrates.[94] It is an offence to contravene a notice without reasonable excuse, though in any proceedings for an offence arising out of carrying on any trade or business it is a defence to prove that the best practicable means has been used for preventing or counteracting the noise.

Where it appears to a local authority that a building is going to be constructed to which a noise abatement order will apply once erected, or that any premises will, as a result of any works, become premises to which an order applies, they may, under CPA 1974, s 67, on *either* the application of the owner or occupier (prospective or actual) of the building *or* on their own initiative, determine an acceptable level of noise for emission from that building. This level must then be registered. Notice of intention to make a determination must be given to the relevant person(s) who may appeal to the Secretary of State within three months.[95] Where an owner or occupier makes an application to the local authority in respect of a building falling within s 67, they have two months to notify him of their decision. Failure to do so is deemed to be notice that they have decided not to make a determination, and the applicant may then appeal to the Secretary of State. Where at any time after the coming into force of a noise abatement order, any premises become, as a result of building or other works, premises to which the order applies, and no noise level has been determined under CPA 1974, s 67, the noise reduction provisions of s 66 generally apply.

Noise abatement zones — the practice

These noise abatement provisions were designed to enable authorities to introduce gradual reductions in noise in selected localities. In reality they are used to hold ambient noise levels steady if not actually to reduce them.[96] A significant comment on the provisions was the conduct of the Darlington 'Quiet Town' experiment. Following the report of the Noise Advisory Commission 'Noise in the Next Ten Years', Darlington participated in an experiment between 1976 and 1978 aimed at reducing noise levels throughout the town. The results of that experiment were published in 'Darlington Quiet Town Experiment' in 1981. All sections of the local community were involved in the project, with a strong lead given by the local environmental health department. Use was made of the powers in CPA 1974, Part III, together with voluntary agreements, forms of encouragement and education (especially for children), traffic management schemes and vehicle noise testing. No systematic study was made, however, of the usefulness of the CPA 1974, Part III powers. Only one noise abatement zone was designated, and that not until the end of the study period. The experiment was considered a success. Other local authorities have been urged to implement similar

94   See SI 1975/2116, reg 7.
95   See SI 1975/2116, reg 9.
96   See Penn, *Noise Control* (2nd edn), p 122.

projects. Success in Darlington seems attributable to a broad approach of *co-operation, education* and *exhortation* as opposed to compulsion — a very British way of achieving results! Some authorities have introduced zones to abate noise on an area basis, for example on industrial estates; others have 'mini-zones' relating to single noisy industrial locations.

Noise from plant and machinery

Wide ranging powers exist under CPA 1974, s 68 for the Secretary of State to make regulations for limiting noise levels caused by any relevant plant or machinery, or for requiring the use of noise suppression devices on such plant or machinery, and to provide that contravention of the regulations shall be offences. Before such regulations are made the Secretary of State has to hold consultations with representative producers and users of plant and machinery with a view to ensuring that no requirements are imposed which would be impracticable or would involve unreasonable expense. No regulations have yet been made under this section.

Supplemental provisions

Under CPA 1974, s 69 the local authority *may*, in respect of noise reduction notices and s 65(6) notices respectively, execute works in respect of noise, and may be *directed* to under CPA 1974, s 65(7). In such cases they may recover their necessary expenses.

Persons guilty of the various offences existing under the noise provisions are liable inter alia, under CPA 1974, s 74 as amended, on summary conviction, to fines.

To aid noise minimisation the Secretary of State has power, under CPA 1974, s 71, to prepare issue and approve codes of practice containing guidance, and a duty to approve a code of practice for the carrying out of construction works falling within CPA 1974, s 60. These codes may be relevant in determining whether the defence of 'best practicable means' should be available. For the purposes of CPA 1974, s 60, the approved code is the British Standards Institution Code of Practice relating to noise control on construction and demolition sites, BS 5228, 31 May 1984, SI 1984/1992. Other codes include Codes of Practice on: Noise from Ice-Cream Van Chimes;[97] Noise from Audible Intruder Alarms;[98] Noise from Model Aircraft;[99] Noise from Construction and Open Sites.[100]

A miscellany of codes

Codes of practice have been developed by the Noise Council in relation to noise arising from some motorcycling events, by the Midlands Joint Advisory Committee for Environmental Protection on clay pigeon shooting, and by the National Farmers Union on bird scaring devices. A code on concert noise has also been produced by the Noise Council.[101] A draft code to be issued under the CPA 1974 has been drawn up in relation to powerboat racing and water-skiing, and the Institute of Acoustics has drawn up a draft code on the control of noise from pubs and clubs. The CPA 1974, s 71 statutory

97 SI 1981/1828.
98 SI 1981/1829.
99 SI 1981/1830.
100 SI 1987/1730.
101 *Environmental Noise Control at Concerts* (1994).

codes may be taken into account in relevant legal proceedings, and compliance with their terms is evidence that the 'best practicable means' have been used, where such a defence is relevant. A voluntary code *might* be given a similar status by a court but the point is undecided.

D OTHER SOURCES OF NOISE AND MODES OF NOISE CONTROL

Audible intruder alarms

The Code of Practice on audible intruder alarms suggests measures to reduce the possibility of misfiring alarms, and, more particularly, suggests that cut-out devices should be fitted to de-activate alarms after 20 minutes, while the police should be notified of the names and addresses of key holders who can obtain access to end an alarm signal. Intruder alarms do not fall within CPA 1974, s 62(1) as loudspeakers in streets, but a continually sounding alarm could fall within EPA 1990, s 81(3) and Sch 3 so an authority could take appropriate remedial action against it. In London special powers apply under the London Local Authorities Act 1991, s 23 to enable deactivation of an alarm causing annoyance to local residents and workers where it has been ringing for more than an hour. Similar powers will exist on an adoptive basis in the rest of the country on the coming into force of the Noise and Statutory Nuisance Act 1993, s 9 and Sch 3.

Motor sports

Though holy scripture records that 'the roar of David's triumph was heard throughout the land', today motor sport competitions on public roads are prohibited under the Road Traffic Act 1988, s 13 unless carried out in accordance with the Motor Vehicles (Competitions and Trials) Regulations, SI 1969/414, which, in particular, limit the amount of night time driving. Off road racing is subject to voluntary controls operated on a contractual basis by the Royal Automobile Club Motor Sports Association over its members. Outside of these controls sanctions lie in the ordinary law of noise.[102]

Entertainment

A variety of controls exist over entertainment noise which, though defined by statute for certain purposes to include noise from boxing and similar contests, increasingly means musical noise. Such noise can be controlled if it is organised, inter alia, by way of an injunction and amounts to a nuisance.[103]

But as prevention is undoubtedly better than cure in this context a number of licensing provisions exist. The Licensing Act 1964, s 4 enables licensing justices to impose conditions on the grant of liquor on-licences in the public interest, and this could be used to control live music and other sources of noise in public houses.[104] The Local Government (Miscellaneous Provisions) Act 1982, Sch 1 enables local authorities outside London to exercise controls over public entertainments. (For 'music and dancing licences' in London see the London Government Act 1963, s 52 and Sch 12.) An

102 *A-G v Southport Corpn* [1934] 1 KB 226.
103 *New Imperial and Windsor Hotel Co Ltd v Johnson* [1912] 1 IR 327.
104 See the Report of the Departmental Committee on Liquor Licensing (Cmnd 5154).

'entertainments licence' from the district council is thus required for public music or dancing or similar entertainments and sporting events at any place. Music at religious events and pleasure fairs is exempted, but an all night dance party for 7,000 people organised on the fictitious basis they formed a club is caught.[105] Public musical entertainments in the open air on private land may also be similarly regulated should the local authority so resolve. Licences may contain provisions to prevent unreasonable disturbance of people in the neighbourhood by noise. Constables, fire officers and other duly authorised local authority officers have powers of entry to ensure that licence conditions are being complied with; penalties of up to a £20,000 fine and/or imprisonment for six months may be imposed in cases of non-compliance,[106] while confiscation of proceeds of unlicensed entertainments may occur under the Criminal Justice Act 1988, s 71.[107]

Authorities may also adopt the provisions of the Private Places of Entertainment (Licensing) Act 1967 where they already have other powers to licence public music and dancing. These powers enable control to be exercised over places which are not open to the general public but which operate for private gain, though bona fide clubs and other places where intoxicating liquor is sold and which are controlled under other legislation are excluded from the 1967 Act's operation. Where adopted, the powers apply a similar pattern of control to that under the LGMPA 1982. This enables authorities to control that range of events known popularly as 'warehouse', 'acid house', and 'dance' parties — also 'pay' parties where a number of people (usually up to 100) pay to attend a gathering in a house/flat. Where a noisy party is held/is going to be held *otherwise* than for gain the means of control is under the normal noise nuisance powers.

EPA 1990, s 81(5) and the Local Government Act 1972, s 222 enable authorities to seek injunctive relief, and this can be used to *prevent* noisy incidents such as major parties.[108] In an emergency an injunction may be obtained very rapidly. The procedure, as pointed out by Penn in *Noise Control*, is expensive and technical and is available only in respect of unlicensed events, where the location is known, also the names of the landowner and/or the organisers. The authority also has to show a nuisance will occur unless the event is restrained. It is, however, possible to obtain an open ended injunction against named persons to prevent an event taking place anywhere in an authority's area at *any* time where it is clear there is a proposal to hold a series of events.[109]

Raves

The Criminal Justice and Public Order Act 1994 grants particular powers *to the police* in relation to 'raves' provided they are unlicensed. A 'rave' is a gathering on land open, or partly open, to air of 100 or more people, whether or not trespassers, at which during the night amplified music is played, including sounds 'wholly or predominantly characterised by the emission of a succession of repetitive beats'.

Such 'music' must be such by reason of its loudness *and* duration *and* the time at which it is played as is likely to cause serious distress to local inhabitants. Such 'raves'

105 *Lunn v Colston-Hayter* (1991) 155 JP 384.
106 LGMPA 1982, Sch 1, para 12(2A) as inserted by the Entertainments (Increased Penalties) Act 1990, s 1.
107 See SI 1990/1570.
108 The relationship between these two powers was considered in *Vale of the White Horse District Council v Allen & Partners* [1997] Env LR 212.
109 *East Hampshire and Waverley District Councils v Scott and Bailie* [1993] 5 ELM 131; and *Langbaurgh on Tees Borough Council v Jowsey and Munroe* [1994] 6 ELM 44.

had become a feature of a variety of gatherings during the 1980s. A police officer of the rank of Superintendent or above having reasonable belief that two or more persons are making preparations for a 'rave' on land, or that ten or more persons are waiting for a 'rave' to begin or are actually attending such a gathering which is in progress, may direct those persons, and any others preparing or waiting for or attending the gathering, to leave the site; see CJPOA 1994, s 63. Constables in uniform may, under CJPOA 1994, s 65, prevent persons from proceeding in the direction of such an event, though only at places within five miles of the boundary of the site of the gathering. It is an offence to fail to comply with directions given under these provisions. CJPOA 1994, ss 64 and 66 contain powers to seize and forfeit relevant sound equipment.

Home Office research[110] suggests that the police have not been required to make extensive use of the rave provisions. A common theme which emerged from interviews conducted with officers with a background in public order policing was that by the time that the Act's provisions were available, illegal raves had become a rare phenomenon compared with their zenith in the late 1980s. Official figures show that in 1995, there were no cautions or court proceedings for the CJPOA 1994, s 63 offence. In 1996, one caution was issued and seven people were prosecuted for failing to leave the site of a rave under CJPOA 1994, s 63. Of these seven prosecutions, four resulted in a conviction. Two of the defendants who were convicted were required to pay a fine of approximately £250 each, whereas the other two were given conditional discharges. Of course, it might be argued that such figures demonstrate that 'ravers' are inclined to obey directions issued under the CJPOA 1994 rather than face the consequences of non-compliance. Whatever the extent of their exercise, the research places emphasis upon the police view which is that these provisions have allowed them to police raves from a stronger legal position than in the past, when they were dealt with using a variety of powers, most notably in respect of breach of the peace.

Anti-social behaviour

Under the Crime and Disorder Act 1998, s 1 a local authority or Chief Constable may apply to the magistrates' court for an anti-social behaviour order (ASBO) to be made in respect of a particular person (over the age of 10) within their area. On the basis that these proceedings are begun by complaint (which is the method for commencing civil proceedings in the magistrates' court[111]), that offensive conduct is not the only prerequisite for bringing proceedings, and that ASBOs are not about crime and punishment but are about the protection of an identified section of the community, the Court of Appeal has held that CDA 1998, s 1 proceedings are civil rather than criminal in nature.[112] This is despite the potential criminal consequences of a breach of an order. For the magistrates' court to make an ASBO, it must be satisfied that two conditions have been fulfilled: that the person has acted in an anti-social manner, ie in a manner that caused or was likely to cause harassment, alarm or distress to one or more persons not of the same household as himself; *and,* that such an order is necessary to protect persons in the local government area in which the harassment etc was caused or was likely to be caused from further anti-social acts by him. For the purpose of determining whether the first of these conditions has been fulfilled, the magistrates' court must disregard any act of the defendant which he shows was reasonable in the circumstances.

110 See Home Office Research Study 190, *Trespass and protest: policing under the Criminal Justice and Public Order Act 1994* (1998).
111 See the Magistrates' Courts Act 1980, s 51.
112 *R (McCann) v Manchester Crown Court* [2001] EWCA Civ 281, [2001] 1 WLR 1084.

Where an anti-social behaviour order has been made, it will prohibit the defendant from doing anything described in the order, eg threatening or abusing residents or passers-by. It will remain in force for at least two years, although either the applicant or the defendant can apply to the magistrates' court to have the order varied or discharged, and the defendant has a right of appeal to the Crown Court under CDA 1998, s 4. It is an offence, triable either summarily or on indictment, for a person to do anything which he is prohibited from doing by an ASBO.

Home Office Guidance suggests that the intention is that such orders will be targeted at criminal or sub-criminal behaviour rather than minor disputes between neighbours. It is possible, therefore, that persistent noisy behaviour, eg shouting or playing music excessively loudly, might be such as to cause harassment, alarm or distress and hence bring a person within the scope of CDA 1998, s 1. Manchester City Council, for example, has succeeded in obtaining ASBOs against a mother and son which prohibit, inter alia, behaviour of this nature.[113]

Some future developments

A National Ambient Noise Strategy

In November 2000, the government published *Our Countryside: the Future — A Fair Deal for Rural England* (the Rural White Paper),[114] in which it proposed, inter alia, to develop a national ambient noise strategy in England. To this end, the Air and Environmental Quality Division of DEFRA has published a consultation paper, *Towards a National Ambient Noise Strategy*,[115] in which proposals for developing the strategy are set out. The proposals envisage a three-phase approach. In Phase I (2002–2005) the aim is to establish three key sets of information. These are information on: the ambient noise[116] climate in England, ie the number of people affected by different levels of noise, the source of that noise (road, rail, airports and industry) and the location of the people affected; the adverse effects of ambient noise, particularly in respect of people's quality of life; the techniques available to take action to improve the situation where it is bad or to preserve it where it is good; and the methodology to be used to undertake economic analysis.

During Phase 2 of the strategy (2004–2006), the aim is to evaluate and identify options for prioritising the various alternatives identified in Phase 1 in terms of time-scales and synergies and conflicts with other government priorities as well as costs and benefits. Phase 3 (2007) will require the government to agree on the necessary policies to achieve the desired outcome, ie the completion of the National Ambient Noise Strategy.

With regard to the collection of data on the ambient noise climate (Phase 1), it is worth noting that noise mapping[117] has taken place in the UK in various different ways for a number of years.[118] However, it is evident that as a prerequisite of the development of a noise strategy for England, a rather more systematic approach must be taken to noise mapping in the future. The consultation paper considers that there are three options available: local authorities produce noise maps; some or all of those responsible

---

113 See www.manchester.gov.uk/news/2001/aug01/asbo.htm.
114 Cmnd 4909.
115 November 2001.
116 Defined in the consultation paper to mean noise from transportation and industry.
117 *Towards a National Ambient Noise Strategy* notes, inter alia, that it is more correctly entitled Sound Immission Contour Mapping (SICM): see para 6.2.2.
118 Basic aircraft noise contours were produced for Heathrow airport as early as 1961: see para 6.2.5 of the consultation paper.

for noise sources (road, rail, airports and industry) map those sources and the local authorities map the remaining noise sources in their areas; or central government continues to co-ordinate mapping through technical consultants who work with local authorities and the transport and industry sectors. The potential strengths and weaknesses of each option are noted, but there is no indication in the consultation paper as to which (if any) of the options DEFRA prefers. Views on this and the other matters covered by the consultation were sought by 15 March 2002.

Neighbour and neighbourhood noise

Although neighbour and neighbourhood noise[119] was, strictly speaking, beyond the scope of *Towards a National Ambient Noise Strategy*, the consultation paper does devote a chapter to considering the various means, both formal and informal, for dealing with what it describes as 'a major source of disturbance to many people'.[120] It also seeks consultees' views on how the problem might be tackled more effectively. DEFRA plans for the future in this area include: further research; a more effective publicity campaign to raise awareness about noise issues and encourage considerate behaviour; encouragement of initiatives so that those government departments who have policy responsibility for noise and anti-social behaviour work more closely together; and, work with the Chartered Institute of Environmental Health to further improve the collection of noise complaint and related statistics from local authorities in order to help inform policy development.

The second of these initiatives ties in with the recently published research on the take up and workings of the Noise Act 1996.[121] In response to the findings of that review, DEFRA has announced that it intends to make the provisions of the Act more accessible to local authorities by seeking to amend the Act so that it need not be formally adopted before it can be used.[122] By being able to utilise the night noise offence (NA 1996, s 4) in this way, local authorities will have 'another weapon in their armour to combat the problem'.[123]

IPPC

The Integrated Pollution Prevention and Control (IPPC) regime has already been discussed in chapter 16. For present purposes, therefore, it need only be noted that the definition of 'pollution' for the purposes of IPPC is such as to include 'noise' and 'vibrations'. Accordingly, an application for an IPPC permit must include an assessment of noise emissions from the installation being considered. Such an assessment will also need to identify all the noise sensitive properties likely to be affected by the installation and include an assessment of the current noise climate where a new development is proposed. Where noise issues are identified, operators will be expected to deal with them through the use of BAT. In practice it is highly likely that the

---

119 That is noise from 'household appliances, TV, music systems, noisy pets, DIY activities, construction sites, intruder alarms, parties or similar gatherings'.
120 See para 3.1.2.
121 See *Review of Implementation of the Noise Act 1996* (DETR) 28 December 2000, discussed above.
122 See the DEFRA New Release, 'Making it easier to prosecute noisy neighbours', 20 December 2001.
123 Per the Environment Minister, Michael Meacher MP.

Environment Agency and local authorities will liaise closely in respect of the noise issues generated by IPPC applications.

Byelaws

Local authorities (ie district and London borough councils) have power, subject to confirmation by the Secretary of State, to make byelaws, under the Local Government Act 1972, s 235, for the good rule and government of their areas; also for the prevention and suppression of nuisances. Byelaws have been made to cover diverse matters such as barking dogs, model aircraft, bird scaring devices, musical instruments played in streets, wirelesses, loudspeakers, gramophones and amplifiers. Breach of a byelaw is a criminal offence, though available defences include: that the byelaw was incorrectly made; that it exceeds the powers given by the statute under which it was made;[124] that it is uncertain; that it is unreasonable in that it is partial and unequal in its operation as between citizens, or is manifestly unjust, or discloses bad faith, or constitutes such a gratuitous or oppressive interference with the rights of those subject to it that no reasonable person could accept that Parliament intended the power to make byelaws to be used in that way.[125] Byelaws must also be consistent with the common law and statute.

But byelaws must not be made if provision for that purpose in hand has already been made by, or is or may be made under any other enactment. Officially byelaws still have a part to play in controlling particular instances of noise; see 'The Code of Practice on Noise from Model Aircraft' (1982) which refers to the byelaw powers of local authorities in respect of municipally owned land and certain land subject to countryside legislation.[126]

Planning controls

Noise may be a planning issue. General guidance was for many years given in DoE Circular No 10/73 'Planning and Noise'. This was concerned primarily with noise at the development control stage. However, noise can be an important consideration taken into account in drawing up statutory plans. Some authorities have, for example, included policies on noise in local plans, though practice seems to favour the control of noise at the planning application stage. Imposition of planning conditions on a grant of planning permission or coming to a 'planning obligation' under, for example, the Town and Country Planning Act 1990, s 106, may obviate the need for use of the stricter noise control powers in the Environmental Protection Act 1990. Furthermore planning powers can be used even when the actual noise level in question would not constitute a nuisance under this Act.

So far as development control is concerned close liaison between planning, highway and environmental health authorities, collation of information between them, sharing services of experts in noise reduction, and use of objective standards of noise measurement in the discharge of functions is clearly desirable. Practice again, however, varies in this respect. Planning Policy Guidance Note (PPG) 24 currently gives central guidance on the use of planning powers with regard to noise.

---

124 This argument failed on the facts in *Boddington v British Transport Police* [1999] 2 AC 143.
125 *Kruse v Johnson* [1898] 2 QB 91.
126 See further Penn, *Noise Control* (2nd edn), pp 78–84 on model noise byelaws.

General principles

These include: separating noise sensitive developments such as hospitals and schools from major noise sources such as roads; siting new noisy developments away from noise sensitive land uses; using planning conditions/obligations where such separation is not possible to minimise noise; considering where intensification or changes of use will result in intrusive noise; considering not just the level of noise but also its qualities, incidence and duration; accepting that people may expect reasonable peace in their homes and gardens in residential development areas; normally refusing permission for noise sensitive developments in areas which are, or will be, places with unacceptable noise levels, particularly at night; taking into account predicted noise levels from roads over a period of 15 years in respect of new developments; using design and layout features to minimise noise from roads and other noisy developments, eg the use of belts of trees or limiting hours of operation.

PPG 24 counsels that noise policies should be set down in development plans, with area specific policies where appropriate, and that regard may be had to safeguarding areas currently largely undisturbed by noise and which are accordingly valued for their recreational and amenity value. Particular guidance is given on a number of issues.

Noise exposure for residential developments

The guidance introduces the concept of Noise Exposure Categories (NECs) from A-D. Where a residential development proposal is received it should be 'banded' in an appropriate category. In A noise need not be considered as a determining factor; in B noise should be take into account and appropriate noise protection conditions imposed; in C permission should normally be refused save where for example no alternative quieter site exists and then noise protection conditions should be imposed; in D permission should normally be refused. This approach is to be used where residential development is to be introduced into areas with existing noise sources, not when the reverse is true, in which case normal planning rules apply. Similarly the NEC levels are *not* to be used for assessing the impact of industrial noise on proposed new housing, though the contribution of industrial noise to other more dominant noise sources can be taken into consideration. The NEC concept thus relates to noise coming from road, rail and air traffic or from 'mixed sources', ie transport noise plus industrial noise, a categorisation only to be used where no individual noise source is dominant.

The NEC categories have been drawn up largely but *not* exclusively on the basis of research findings or existing regulatory norms, for example World Health Organisation standards. *Generally* to fall in category A the noise sources affecting land should generate outdoor noise levels of *less* than 55 dB(A) from 7.00 to 23.00, and less than 45 dB(A) from 23.00 to 7.00. The outer parameters for category B are less than 55–63 dB(A) daytime and less than 45–57 dB(A) night time noise, for category C the figures are 63–72 and 57–66 respectively, while figures over 72 dB(A)/66 dB(A) place the land in category D.

Noise from road and rail traffic

Where development is proposed near a major new or improved road the planning authority should ascertain forecast noise levels for the next 15 years with help from the Highways Authority who should be consulted so that the necessary predictions for using the Department of Transport's 1988 scheme of 'calculation of road traffic noise' can be used. Co-operation with Highway Authorities can be helpful so that they may use their powers of traffic management under the Road Traffic Regulation Act 1984. Similar consultation is needed with railway operators before development near railways is contemplated. Vibration may be more of a problem from rail than from road traffic and PPG 24 counsels use of British Standard 6472: 1992 on advising on acceptable vibration levels for new developments.

Industrial and commercial development noise

Again British Standards can be used to check on acceptable limits for noise from such developments, BS 4142: 1990 being the appropriate one. Where an increase in noise of 10 dB(A) or more over the existing background noise is likely as a result of a new development, complaints about noise may be expected. Particular provision may have to be made in respect of installations operating at night or over weekends. This is particularly relevant to commercial food outlets such as takeaways, and also to discos, night clubs and public houses.

Noise from construction sites

This is already specifically dealt with under the terms of the 1974 Act, but see also BS 5288: 1984.

Sporting and recreation noise

Recreation, etc, activities will normally be controlled under the licensing provisions discussed above, but in relation to some activities planning controls may be appropriate as they involve a material change of use of land and so require planning permission. Alternatively some activities may take place by virtue of permitted development rights (see chapter 8 above). Such 'pd' rights may, of course, be withdrawn.

Waste disposal site noise

Controls over disposal practices in waste management licences will have an indirect effect on noise, and conditions in the licence may be used to control noise in the interests of local amenity protection. In addition where a planning application for a new waste disposal facility is received specific noise controls can be imposed as conditions of the grant. Consultation here with the appropriate waste regulator is essential. Conditions may relate to hours of operation, the numbers and capacity of vehicles using the site, entrances and exists from the site and provision of screening to reduce noise.

Planning conditions clearly have a generally important part to play in noise control, but any conditions imposed should be necessary, relevant to planning in general and to the development proposed in particular, enforceable, reasonable and precise. Applications for minor development should not, according to PPG 24, be used as opportunities to impose conditions on activities already having permission. Where ambient noise levels are already high conditions can be used to mitigate the effects of that noise, eg to require layout of a site so that noise barriers are erected. Where it is desirable to allow a noisy development near a noise sensitive development, conditions may again be used to mitigate the effects of noise, eg to keep the noisiest activities as far as possible from neighbours. The sort of conditions considered generally acceptable include ones: requiring that work on a more sensitive development shall not begin until a noise protection scheme has been approved and the relevant parts have been completed; to require a building style which provides a stated level of sound attenuation against external noise; to restrict the total number of movements at an airport, or the times at which they occur, or to restrict the sort and weight of or the total number of movements by aircraft using an airport; or to restrict noise emitted from industrial or commercial buildings or sites, to require the creation of a noise minimisation scheme for a site, to limit certain activities to certain parts of the site, to require plant and machinery to be enclosed in sound insulating material, limiting specified machinery to operations only within specifications.

Where planning conditions are used they may either set an absolute limit of noise not to be exceeded over a specified time period, or a relative limit derived from permitted increases in noise levels with respect to background levels. The latter are *not* appropriate where a substantial — say 15 dB(A) or more — permitted increase in noise over background levels is allowed. Authorities must also remember to have fixed monitoring points from which to measure compliance with conditions. Such points must be carefully selected to ensure that the level of noise recorded is a reliable indicator of noise levels concerning particular noise sensitive premises.

E THE CONTROL OF AIRCRAFT NOISE

Most earlier enactments on aircraft noise were repealed and replaced by the Civil Aviation Act 1982, which contains important measures, some deriving from international law. CAA 1982 enables the Crown, by Order in Council, to give effect to the Chicago Convention on International Civil Aviation[127] with respect to the operation of aerodromes and the safety of aircraft. An 'Air Navigation Order' made under s 60 may, in particular, provide for the: licensing, inspection and regulation of aerodromes; conditions under which, and in particular the aerodromes to or from which, aircraft entering, leaving or flying within the UK may fly; securing the general safety, efficiency and regularity of air navigation; safety of aircraft, their passengers and contents, preventing aircraft endangering other persons and property; prohibiting aircraft from flying over specified areas of the UK, and for regulating or prohibiting the flight of aircraft over the UK at speeds in excess of Flight Mach 1.

These provisions, with other Acts and delegated legislation, provide a general framework for the public control of aircraft noise. This will be examined below. First it is necessary to consider tortious aspects of aircraft noise.

Civil liability for aircraft noise

Under CAA 1982, s 76 no action lies in respect of trespass or nuisance by reason only of the flight of an aircraft over any property at a height above the ground which, having regard to wind, weather and all the circumstances, is *reasonable*, or the ordinary incidents of such flight, provided the aircraft is not being flown in a dangerous manner contrary to CAA 1982, s 81, and provided the provisions of any Air Navigation Order are complied with. *Unreasonable* flight over a particular property, eg frequent low level flights, appear *not* to be exempted.[128]

---

127 Cmnd 8742 (16th edn 1980), International Civil Aviation Organisation, Doc 73006.
128 *Roedean School Ltd v Cornwall Aviation Co Ltd* (1926) Times, 3 July.

Furthermore CAA 1982, s 77 states that an Air Navigation Order may provide for regulating the conditions under which noise and vibration may be caused by aircraft *on* aerodromes and may also prevent any action lying in respect of aircraft noise and vibration nuisances caused *on* aerodromes covered by the order provided the provisions of any such order are complied with. The Air Navigation Order SI 2000/ 1562, provides that the Secretary of State may prescribe conditions under which noise and vibration may be caused by aircraft (including military aircraft) at government aerodromes, aerodromes owned or managed by the Civil Aviation Authority, licensed aerodromes or aerodromes used in the course of the business of manufacturing or repairing aircraft. Such aerodromes are exempted from liability in nuisance for aircraft noise on the ground. Further detailed conditions are laid down in the Air Navigation (General) Regulations SI 1993/1622. Noise and vibration are permissible where aircraft are taking off or landing, or moving on the ground or on water, or where engines are being operated (while *in* aircraft) for the purpose of either ensuring satisfactory operation, or bringing them to a correct flight, or end of flight, temperature, or ensuring that instrumentation is in satisfactory condition. Noise *outside* statutory exceptions may be actionable;[129] where an injunction was granted to restrain certain work on the testing of aeroplane engines. A claim that CAA 1982, s 76(1) violated Arts 6, 8 and 13 of the European Convention on Human Rights was heard in *Powell and Rayner v United Kingdom.*[130] It was argued that the statute prevented the claimants from having a fair public hearing of what would otherwise be their nuisance claims, and that the noise permitted by the statute interfered with the claimants' homes and private lives contrary to the convention. The claim was rejected. Art 13 of the convention guarantees no right that signatory states will provide modes of challenge to the legality of their legislation. A right to sue exists where aircraft noise occurs *outside* the terms of the statute, and that satisfies Art 6. There was no breach of Art 8 as the UK government had struck a proper balance between individual and community interests in respect of airport operation.

Under CAA 1982, s 76(2) where material loss is caused *to* any person or property on land or water *by*, or by a person in, or an article, animal or person falling from, an aircraft *while in flight, taking off or landing*, then, unless the loss was caused or contributed to by the negligence of the person suffering it, damages may be recovered *without proof of negligence or intention or other cause of action*, as if the loss had been caused by the wilful act, neglect or default of the owner of the aircraft. This *statutory* right of action could be used in respect of damage caused by sonic boom or reverberation caused by aircraft 'breaking' the sound barrier, or arising from the spraying of chemicals.[131] The provision only applies to 'material' damage, which seems probably to mean damage measurable in monetary terms, though it may mean only 'physical' damage, in which case other damage could only be recovered on proof of negligence and loss. The better view is that material damage is any damage capable of monetary measurement. Even so, certain forms of strain and anxiety, not leading to loss of income but arising from aircraft noise, are outside such a definition.

The future of the exemption from liability has been the subject of some controversy. The Noise Review Working Group's 1990 report concluded the exemption was 'no longer appropriate'. In particular they concluded the exemption should not apply to non-commercial aircraft, ie those of a certain weight who fly beyond airspace customarily used in the zone of an aerodrome. They also considered ground running, taxiing and other static aircraft source noise should no longer be exempt from control under COPA

129 *Bosworth-Smith v Gwynnes Ltd* (1919) 89 LJ Ch 368.
130 Case No 3/1989/163/219, (1990) 12 EHRR 355.
131 *Weedair (NZ) Ltd v Walker* [1961] NZLR 153.

1974. In its response, 'Control of Aircraft Noise', 1991, the government rejected these contentions.

Public regulation of aircraft noise

Engine noise

In order to give effect to international agreements and EC requirements[132] the Air Navigation Order SI 1990/1514 and the Aeroplane Noise Regulations 1999[133] have been made. The 1990 Order applies to: all propeller driven aeroplanes having a maximum total weight authorised of 9,000 kg or less; supersonic civil aeroplanes first obtaining certificates of airworthiness on or after 26 November 1981, and conforming to prototypes, airworthiness certification of which was requested before 1 January 1975, or derivatives of such prototypes; microlight aeroplanes; all other subsonic aircraft with certified take-off distances of more than 610 metres; and, helicopters for which the 1990 Order contains applicable standards. The 1990 Order does not apply, however, to any aeroplane to which the Aeroplane Noise Regulations applies.

The order prohibits an aeroplane to which it applies from landing or taking off in the UK unless it has a noise certificate issued by the Civil Aviation Authority, or by the competent authority of such countries as are considered by the Secretary of State to operate standards substantially equivalent to the CAA's, or issued in pursuance of the Chicago Convention of 1944. *Military aircraft and the naval, military and airforce authorities and members of any visiting forces and any international headquarters are exempted from control.*[134] Likewise under the 1990 Order, Art 6 the Civil Aviation Authority may, after consultation with the Secretary of State, exempt any aeroplane or person, or any class of aeroplanes or persons, from control either absolutely or subject to conditions.

The Civil Aviation Authority are under a duty to issue a noise certificate in respect of any aeroplane covered by the 1990 Order if they are satisfied that it complies with the relevant noise standards in the 1990 Order, see Art 6 and Sch 1, Parts I, V, VII–IX. For this purpose applicants for certificates must furnish such evidence and submit aeroplanes to such flying trials and other tests as the authority may require. The authority must issue noise certificates subject to conditions as to the maximum total take-off and landing weights, and may impose such other conditions as they think fit. An aeroplane may not take off or land in the UK unless it carries any noise certificate required under the law of its country of registration, and UK registered aeroplanes must when in flight, whether in the UK or elsewhere, carry the requisite noise certificate.

Under the 1990 Order, Art 9 the authority may provisionally suspend a noise certificate pending investigations, and may, following them, revoke, suspend or vary a certificate. Breach of a condition in a noise certificate renders the certificate invalid during its continuance. It is an offence under Art 10 for a person, with intent to deceive: to use any noise certificate which has been forged, altered, revoked or suspended or to which he is not entitled; to lend any such certificate to, or allow its use by, any other person; or to make false representations for the purpose of obtaining the issue, renewal or variation of a certificate. Contravention of the 1990 Order renders a person liable to penalties contained in Art 14. Under Art 11 if it appears to the authority that any aeroplane is intended or likely to be flown in such a way as to contravene noise certification requirements, they may direct the operator or commander not to permit the

132 Directives 80/51, 83/206, 89/629, 92/14 and 98/20.
133 SI 1999/1452.
134 See the Air Navigation Order 1990, Art 15(2) and (3).

aeroplane to fly. Under Art 12 they may take such steps as are necessary to detain the craft. They have rights of access to aeroplanes, aerodromes and other places to see that the order is being complied with and to enforce their duties.

The Aeroplane Noise Regulations amended the Air Navigation Order by disapplying it to aeroplanes which now come under the terms of the 1999 Regulations. Essentially, these regulations require certain propeller driven aeroplanes registered in the UK and being used within the EC member states or states which are a party to the European Economic Agreement (EEA) or, being registered outside the member states or EEA, landing in or taking off from the UK, to be noise certified to standards at least equal to the standards specified in certain chapters of Volume I of Annex 16 to the Chicago Convention. In respect of UK registered aeroplanes, the Civil Aviation Authority has the power to grant the noise certificate. Such a certificate is not to be granted unless the Authority is satisfied that the aeroplane complies with the standard specified for it in the certificate. The 1999 Regulations create a number of offences. Thus it is an offence to operate an aeroplane without a noise certificate where that aeroplane falls within the scope of the regulations. Moreover, it is an offence to fail to carry or to produce the relevant noise certificate or to fail to comply with a direction not to take-off.

Control of airport noise

Various bodies have powers to provide and/or operate and manage airports and aerodromes. (An aerodrome is any area of land or water designed, equipped, set apart or commonly used for the landing or departure of aircraft, including sites for the take-off and landing of vertical take-off craft, see the Civil Aviation Act 1982, s 105(1)). The Secretary of State may establish and maintain aerodromes under the CAA 1982, s 25. The Civil Aviation Authority may not establish or acquire aerodromes (other than those vested in it under the Civil Aviation Act 1971, Sch 2) but may, with the Secretary of State's consent, undertake to *manage* any aerodrome (CAA 1982, s 28). Local authorities may, subject to consent by the Secretary of State, establish and maintain aerodromes (CAA 1982, s 30), though he also has power to direct authorities to transfer their airports to companies which they own, see the Airports Act 1986, s 13. Powers to make airport byelaws are conferred by the Airports Act 1986, s 63 including, inter alia, a power to control aircraft operation in, or directly above, airports in order to limit or mitigate noise, vibration and atmospheric pollution.

The Secretary of State has a general duty under s 36 of the 1982 Act to prevent danger to public health from aircraft arriving at any aerodrome which is vested in or under his control, or at any UK aerodrome which is owned or managed by the Civil Aviation Authority. That authority has certain licensing functions in respect of aerodromes used for public transport or instruction in flying under the Air Navigation Order SI 2000/1562, Art 103, and, under the Civil Aviation Act 1982, s 5, *specified* aerodromes subject to such licensing control may be made subject to further requirements that the Civil Aviation Authority must have regard to the need to minimise, so far as is reasonably practicable, any adverse effects on the environment, and any disturbance to the public arising from noise, vibration, atmospheric pollution or other cause attributable to use of aircraft for civil aviation purposes. This power, which has in fact never been used, does *not* apply to aerodromes designated by the Secretary of State under the CAA 1982, s 78 (see below).

CAA 1982, s 38 allows any aerodrome authority owning or managing a licensed aerodrome to encourage the use of quieter aircraft and the diminution of interference from aircraft noise by fixing airport use charges by reference to either the amount of noise caused by aircraft in question or the extent or nature of any inconvenience resulting from such noise. The same provision enables the Secretary of State to direct specified aerodrome authorities so to fix their charges. BAA plc aerodromes charge differential rates favouring quieter aircraft, and penalising noisy night time departures.

Certain major airports (Heathrow, Gatwick, Stansted, Prestwick, Edinburgh, Glasgow, Aberdeen and Southampton) are controlled by BAA plc under the Airports Act 1986, Part I. The Civil Aviation Act 1982, s 78, enables the Secretary of State to prescribe by notice that it shall be the duty of the *person who is the operator* of an aircraft which is to take off or land at a designated aerodrome to secure that it complies with the Secretary of State's requirements for limiting or mitigating the effect of noise and vibration arising from take-off or touch-down. He may, inter alia, prohibit aircraft of specified types from taking off or landing during specified periods, or specify a maximum number of take-offs and landings for specified types of aircraft during specified periods (see further below). An attempted contravention of take-off limitations may lead to the aircraft in question being detained. There is general power under CAA 1982, s 78(2) to withhold aerodrome facilities at the designated site from operators whose aircraft do not comply with the Secretary of State's notices. Heathrow, Gatwick and Stansted Airports are 'designated' for the above purposes: see CAA 1982, s 80 and SI 1981/651.[135]

Control of noise by means of air transport licences

Air transport licences are generally required for air transport of passengers or cargo for reward by UK registered aircraft under the Civil Aviation Act 1982, s 64. Administration of the scheme is entrusted to the Civil Aviation Authority under CAA 1982, s 65. The authority has a wide discretion, subject to holding hearings, as to granting, revocation, suspension, variation, duration and other terms of licences, though much of the 'meat' of the scheme is in regulations made by the Secretary of State. Note the Civil Aviation Authority Regulations SI 1991/1672 and the Air Navigation (Aeroplane and Aeroplane Engine Emissions of Unburned Hydrocarbons) Order SI 1988/1994. One general duty in administering the licensing system is, under CAA 1982, s 68(3), to have regard to the need to minimise, so far as reasonably practicable, any adverse effects on the environment and disturbance to the public from noise, vibration, atmospheric pollution or other cause attributable to the civil aviation use of aircraft.

This duty may not, however, conflict with the authority's duty to ensure that British airlines are able to compete effectively in aviation markets, and that they provide services to satisfy the substantial categories of public demand: see CAA 1982, ss 4 and 68(1).

A miscellany of other controls

In 1974 the Noise Advisory Council identified the concept of 'noise preferential routes' (NPR) which, on safety *and* amenity grounds, are designed to ensure that aircraft climb away safely from aerodromes over open ground and away from densely populated residential areas wherever possible. NPRs now exist for aerodromes next to developed residential areas, but they are not, and cannot be, mandatory for all wind and weather conditions and the need to maintain safety dictates departures from NPRs on occasions. Similar *operational* procedures exist to ensure that take-offs and landings take place over areas least likely to be subject to noise affectations. At Heathrow, for example, take-off and landing is normally to/from the west to avoid the built up area of London to the east.

135 See further Penn, *Noise Control* (2nd edn), pp 215–222, for technical details.

Night flying is a particularly contentious issue with regard to noise. Using powers under CAA 1982, s 78, ministers have introduced two schemes trying to establish quotas for night time flights with the loudest classes of aircraft being prohibited from flights into/from Heathrow, Gatwick and Stansted. Both schemes were quashed in court.[136] The total number of night aircraft movements for an aggregate of periods, without any maximum number for each of those periods was subsequently fixed.[137] However, those affected by the noise of aircraft flying at night have pursued other legal avenues in an attempt to put a stop to the sleep disturbance and sleep prevention which they have endured. Thus in *Hatton v United Kingdom*[138] eight individuals who lived (or had lived) in properties in the area surrounding Heathrow airport went to the European Court of Human Rights at Strasbourg and contended that increases in the level of night time noise at their homes caused by aircraft using the airport after the introduction of the noise quota scheme in 1993 amounted to a violation of the Convention, Art 8 ie the right to respect for their private and family life and their home. In addition, it was argued that there had been a violation of Art 13 in that judicial review proceedings did not amount to an effective domestic remedy for the protection of their Convention, Art 8 rights. The court upheld both complaints.

With regard to Art 8, the court noted that when determining whether a breach of that Article was justified (under Art 8(2)), regard had to be had to striking a fair balance between the competing interests of the individual and the community as a whole. Although the court accepted the government's argument that night flights contribute to a certain extent to the national economy as a whole, it noted that the extent of that contribution had never been critically examined either by the government or by independent research. Moreover, it further noted that in determining the impact of increased night flights on the applicants, only what it termed 'limited research' had been conducted into the nature of sleep disturbance and sleep prevention (ie not being able to go to sleep or difficulties associated with getting to sleep after being woken up) prior to the 1993 scheme being put into place. In the court's judgment, where 'the particularly sensitive field of environmental protection' was concerned, mere reference to the economic well-being of the country did not by itself outweigh the rights of others. A state should, as far as possible, seek to minimise the interference with these rights by trying to find alternative solutions and by generally seeking to achieve their aims in the least onerous way as regards human rights. In its judgment, in implementing the 1993 scheme, the UK had failed to strike a fair balance between the nation's economic well-being and the applicants' enjoyment of their Convention, Art 8 rights.

The alleged violation of Art 13 was dealt with more briefly by the court. In its judgment, judicial review of the 1993 scheme based on the English public law concepts of illegality, irrationality and patent unreasonableness did not allow for a consideration of whether the increase in night flights under the 1993 scheme represented a justifiable limitation on the applicants' Art 8 rights. The Convention, Art 13 had also therefore been violated.

Quite what the effect of the judgment will be on night flights at Heathrow (and possibly other airports) remains to be seen. At the time of writing, there is no indication that the government plans to appeal against the court's decision.[139] It has been reported,

136 *R v Secretary of State for Transport, ex p Richmond-upon-Thames London Borough* [1994] 1 WLR 74; (No 2) [1995] 7 ELM 52; (No 3) [1995] 7 ELM 127.
137 *R v Secretary of State for Transport, ex p Richmond upon Thames London Borough (No 4)* [1996] 8 ELM 77.
138 Application 36022/97, [2002] 1 FCR 732.
139 Under the Convention, Art 43, a decision of a Chamber of the Court can be referred to the Grand Chamber within three months of the date of the decision if one of the parties so requests.

however, that the Secretary of State for Transport may begin a process of consultation on whether night flights should be further limited or even banned.[140]

Planning controls may also be used to ameliorate aircraft noise problems. PPG 24 annex 3 points to the existence of Department of Transport measures known as 'noise exposure contours'. The general noise exposure categories considered above apply to new residential developments affected by aircraft noise, but any new major noise sensitive development, such as a school, should not normally be built where its exposure to noise would place it in NEC category B. In some cases new or replacement community facilities will be needed in areas subject to high aircraft noise. In such cases consideration should be given to requiring noise insulation measures, and account taken in deciding siting of patterns of aircraft movement. Where land is, or is likely to become, subject to significant aircraft noise it should be determined within which NEC it is likely to fall, and authorities should accordingly develop clear and consistent constraint policies in development plans. See further PPG 24 annex 3, paras 10–12, on military aerodromes, paras 13 and 14, and, on helicopter noise, paras 15–18.

The future

In the Transport White Paper, *New Deal for Transport: Better for Everyone*,[141] the government announced its intention to produce a new UK airports policy that would look 30 years ahead and would bring forward new policies on civil aviation. These new policies are to be set out in an Air Transport White Paper. As part of the process of producing the White Paper the government published a consultative document, *The Future of Aviation*,[142] which covers the main issues relevant to the establishment of an integrated air transport policy. In addition to issues such as safety and security regulation at airports and the economic and social effects of air transport, the consultative document invited views upon the environmental impacts of aviation and airports.

In the present context, it should be noted that the government expressed its willingness to ensure that noise improvement measures continue to be pursued at all airports at all times of the day. Moreover, there is a willingness that the control of noise at airports should, as far as possible, be agreed locally. In addition to local agreements to reduce noise, the government is pursuing complementary regulatory options. These include continuing attempts in the International Civil Aviation Organisation (ICAO) to negotiate a new noise certification standard which would require the industry to meet a standard which is technically feasible and economically reasonable. At a domestic level, there is government support for changing the statutory framework aimed at controlling noise at all types of airport. In a consultation paper published in July 2000,[143] the government made a number of proposals, which included repealing the Civil Aviation Act 1982, s 5 and replacing it with new powers which would enable airports to enforce noise amelioration measures on aircraft operators and adding to the powers of local authorities and the Secretary of State to make noise rules and agreements binding. In the government's opinion, the repeal of CAA 1982, s 5 would be justified on the basis that aerodrome licensing is not necessarily the best way of tackling environmental problems.

---

140 See *The Times*, 3 October, 2001.
141 Cm 3950 DETR, Jul 1998.
142 Published 12 December 2000.
143 *Control of noise from civil aircraft* (DETR).

The consultation document also raises the possibility of the greater use of economic instruments. These could take several forms: introducing mandatory noise-related levies at airports which would either be a tax paid to the government or a charge levied by the airport; imposing a specific levy on night movements. Either form of levy would act as an incentive to use quieter aircraft. The government is committed to carrying out further work in this area in producing the White Paper which, it considers, will inform thinking on possible charging strategies.

Clearly reform of the air transport sector is very much on the agenda. The scope and detail of that reform will not be known, however, until the publication of the White Paper.

F THE CONTROL OF TRAFFIC NOISE

Control under traffic regulation powers

Traffic noise, identified by the 1990 Noise Review Working Party as 'the most serious of all transportation noise problems' is also virtually intractable. The nation has become excessively dependent on road transport for goods haulage, and what remains of the rail freight transport network is ill-located in relation to commerce and industry to take much freight from the roads without a massive investment and redevelopment policy. Simply moving traffic away from settlements by building bypasses can encourage the growth of more traffic on the new roads which have their own inherent environmental disbenefits, such as land take. There is no short, easy, obvious answer to this problem, hence such legal responses as exist inevitably fall into the class of ameliorative 'controls' rather than full remedial measures.

Powers exist under the Road Traffic Regulations Act 1984 to regulate traffic, particularly for preserving or improving the amenities of areas through which regulated roads run: 'amenities' meaning the pleasantness and enjoyability of an area.[144] On trunk roads these powers are entrusted to the Secretary of State, and on other roads the appropriate traffic authority is generally the county council: see ss 1 and 121A. Similar powers exist within the Greater London area under RTRA 1984, s 2.[145] Under RTRA 1984, s 2 a traffic regulation order may provide for the prohibition, restriction or other regulation of vehicular traffic, either generally or specifically on a road. In exercising their functions under the RTRA 1984, s 122 requires local authorities generally to secure expeditious, convenient and safe movement of vehicles, having had regard to the need to secure reasonable access to premises, the effect on the amenities of affected localities, the need to facilitate passage by public service vehicles, etc. In *London Boroughs Transport Committee v Freight Transport Association Ltd*[146] the House of Lords held that the road traffic regulation powers could be used to *supplement* controls existing under national and EC legislation on vehicle construction on the basis that relevant EC legislation (Directives 70/157 and 71/320) was not, on full examination, totally exhaustive in relation to the issue in hand, the control of noise emitted from lorry braking systems. Furthermore, it was considered that *local* traffic regulation should be primarily the preserve of *local* authorities, for the EC only takes powers to itself when a particular objective can be obtained better at Community level than at any other — the 'subsidiarity' principle. The House of Lords concluded that the traffic regulation powers of local authorities may be exercised after environmental considerations have been taken

---

144 *Cartwright v Post Office* [1968] 2 QB 439, [1968] 2 All ER 646.
145 See the Local Authorities Traffic Orders, etc Regulations, SI 1996/2489.
146 [1991] 1 WLR 828.

into account, and that the powers may be used to regulate where *particular* vehicles may go at *particular* times. Their Lordships also concluded that the powers may be used to require the modification of such vehicles if they are to be allowed into particular places, *provided* restrictions do not amount to across the board prohibitions or restrictions on vehicles' use. The powers do not allow restrictions in respect of vehicle emissions.[147]

'The roaring traffic's boom'

Particular powers exist under the RTRA 1984, s 2(4) for local authorities to make regulatory provision specifying through routes for heavy commercial vehicles or prohibiting or restricting heavy commercial vehicle use in specified areas or on specified roads, subject to any exemptions contained in the order. This is to be exercised to improve the amenities of localities. Heavy commercial vehicles are defined by the RTRA 1984, s 138(1). Under the RTRA 1984, Sch 9, Part I the Secretary of State has a reserve power to give authorities directions, after due consultation with them, in respect of regulatory orders, either to make an order, or prohibit the making of an order. RTRA 1984, Sch 9, Part III lays down the procedure for making a regulatory order. Initial consultation must take place with relevant chief officers of police. The Schedule makes provision for the Secretary of State to make regulations providing detailed procedures for the making of orders. In particular these regulations may provide for publicity for proposed orders, the reception and consideration of objections to proposals, the holding of inquiries into proposals, the submission of proposals for ministerial consent, and publication of notices about the making and effects of orders. Under the RTRA 1984, Sch 9, Part VI, challenges in court to regulatory orders on the basis that they are substantively or procedurally ultra vires may be made by any person within six weeks of the making of an order.

The Highways Act 1980, s 90G as inserted in 1992,[148] gives powers to highway authorities to 'calm' traffic by reducing vehicle speeds and hence traffic noise by creating particular features such as traffic islands or constrictions of the carriageway.[149] However, the introduction of traffic calming in some areas may simply have the effect of encouraging drivers to use other 'uncalmed' roads thus merely shifting the incidence of noise.

Control of vehicle noise

Current standards are provided for under the Road Traffic Act 1988, and detailed rules are to be found in the Road Vehicles (Construction and Use) Regulations SI 1986/1078, as amended. It is an offence under the Road Traffic Act 1988, s 42, to contravene the regulations, though as CS Kerse pointed out in *The Law Relating to Noise*, comparatively few offences are detected and prosecuted, and fines are generally low. Under the Road Traffic (Consequential Provisions) Act 1988, s 7 nothing in the Road Traffic Acts authorises a person to use on a road a vehicle so constructed or used as to cause a public or private nuisance, so preserving general common law liability.

The 1986 Regulations, reg 54 requires every vehicle propelled by an internal combustion engine to be fitted with silencing equipment through which engine exhaust gases must pass, and this silencer must not be altered or replaced in any way so that

---

147 *R v Greenwich London Borough Council, ex p W (a minor)* (1996) 255 ENDS Report 49.
148 See the Traffic Calming Act 1992, s 1(2) and Sch 1.
149 See further the Highways (Traffic Calming) Regulations, SI 1999/1026.

the noise of the exhaust is increased by the alteration or replacement and must be maintained in good and efficient order. The actual noise emission standards for vehicles are contained in the 1986 Regulations, reg 55 which introduces new standards of noise emission control pursuant to European obligations, designed to supersede the previous system of regulation from 1983. In effect vehicles may comply with the specific requirements of the 1986 Regulations, reg 55 or they may comply with the noise regulation requirements for vehicles sold in the EC of the relevant Directive[150] or Regulation (51.02) in force at the time of their first use. Over a period of years directives have reduced permissible vehicle noise considerably. In 1970 the permitted 'noise value' for cars was 82 dB(A), reducing to 80 in 1977, 77 in 1984 and 74 in 1992, the last limit applying to new vehicles sold within the EC from 1 October 1994. Similar reductions in noise values have been brought about in respect of buses and goods vehicles. (For the details of the Regulations it is best to refer to *The Encyclopaedia of Road Traffic Law and Practice*, which contains the 1986 Regulations, as amended, together with the necessary references to the European Community legislation relating to noise emission controls.)

Provision exists under the Road Traffic Act 1988, s 57 and the Motor Vehicles (Type Approval) Regulations SI 1980/1182, and the Motor Vehicles (Type Approval) (Great Britain) Regulations SI 1984/981, as amended, for the issue of type approval certificates in respect of motor vehicles.[151] 'Type approval' means that the vehicle in question is of a type conforming to specified requirements of design, construction and equipment, etc, including requirements on noise and silencers, see the 1984 Regulations, Sch 1. It is an offence for any person to use, or cause or permit to be used, any vehicle subject to type approval requirements unless there is the necessary certification to show compliance with relevant type approval requirements; see generally the Road Traffic Act 1988, ss 54–65, and especially s 63. The successive type approval requirements are those laid down in EC Directives.

Although it is arguable that more of the social and environmental costs of road freight, such as noise, should be borne by the relevant operators having to pay enhanced vehicle taxes, regulation by construction and use standards remains the preferred means of control. Thus the 1986 Regulations, reg 97 states that no motor vehicle shall be used on a road in such a manner as to cause any excessive noise which could have been avoided by the reasonable care of the driver. The 1986 Regulations, 54–59 lay down noise emission limits for a wide variety of vehicles, including motor cars, goods and agricultural vehicles and motor cycles. The *basic* limits are those laid down from time to time by relevant EC Directives. The 1986 Regulations, reg 98 requires the drivers of motor vehicles to switch off machinery attached to or part of such vehicles when stationary, otherwise than when this is an enforced stoppage because of the necessities of traffic, or where the machinery has to be run as part of a necessary examination following some breakdown.

Motorcycles

Motor cycle noise is also controlled under construction and use regulations, and, as from 1 January 1996, motor cycles first used on or after that day are subject to enhanced silencer requirements by virtue of SI 1994/14. To assist in ensuring compliance with motor cycle noise requirements — a never easy task — power exists for the Secretary of State to appoint that it shall be an offence to supply in the course of business exhaust

150 The Directives are 70/157, 73/350, 77/212, 81/334, 84/372, 84/424, 92/97.
151 See also the Motor Vehicles (EC Type Approval) Regulations, SI 1998/2051, and SI 1982/ 1271 with regard to goods vehicles.

systems for motor cycles, silencers and other relevant parts not complying with prescribed requirements. Trading standards authorities enforce their requirements at the point of sale. These powers exist under the Motor Cycle Noise Act 1987 which was brought into force by SI 1995/2367 on 1 August 1996. Note also SI 1995/2370 which lays down requirements for silencers, etc, supplied in the course of carrying on a business.

G THE CONTROL OF RAIL NOISE

Noise and vibration from railways can be a problem in residential areas, especially where structures such as bridges have the effect of amplifying the noise. This problem can be further compounded in some areas by the introduction of high-speed trains such as in respect of the Channel Tunnel Rail Link. Despite this, however, little if any direct provision has been made for controlling noise emanating from our railways. Indeed, in two important pieces of railway legislation, the Railways Act 1993 and the Channel Tunnel Rail Link Act 1996, provision is made for the defence of statutory authority to proceedings in nuisance. Thus, for example, the CTRLA 1996, s 30 provides a defence to proceedings under the Environmental Protection Act 1990, s 82(1) in respect of a s 79(1)(g) nuisance where a defendant is able to show that: the nuisance relates to premises used by a nominated undertaker for the purposes of or in connection with the exercise of powers conferred by the CTRLA 1996, Part I; *and*, that the nuisance is attributable to the carrying out of works in accordance with a notice served under the Control of Pollution Act 1974, s 60 or a consent given under s 61 or s 65 of that Act. In short, therefore, the defence is limited to noise emanating from construction work in respect of the Channel Tunnel Rail Link.

H NOISE INSULATION SCHEMES

People can be protected against the worst effects of noise if they can afford the necessary insulation. Limited help in the form of grants is available for some adversely affected by certain aircraft and traffic noise.

Grants in respect of aircraft noise

Assistance in respect of insulation against aircraft noise has been uneven. In respect of certain local authority owned airports there *may* be provision for a scheme in local legislation. On a national basis certain grants have been payable since 1965. The current legislation is the Civil Aviation Act 1982, s 79. The Secretary of State has power, following consultations with affected managers, to make schemes to require such managers of designated aerodromes to make grants towards the cost of insulating such buildings or parts of buildings as he thinks fit, and which, being near to the aerodrome, appear to him to need protection against noise. The buildings must be within specified areas. Local authorities, other than county councils, may be authorised to act as agents for airport managers in the administration of the grant system. To date, two schemes have been made under this section in respect of Heathrow and Gatwick airports.[152]

---

152 See SI 1989/247 and SI 1989/248 respectively.

A number of airports are not covered by noise insulation schemes, nor are any military airbases. It is a frequent complaint that low flying military aircraft are a major noise nuisance, yet they are subject to hardly any legal regulation. According to the MOD's own statistics, military low flying training can take place in 19 areas within England, Scotland and Wales which collectively comprise 191,618 square km of the total land mass (229,961 square km). Within these areas, the MOD endeavours to distribute low flying as equitably as possible, although an even spread can never be achieved in practice. Factors which affect distribution include: the location of bases, Air Weapons Ranges and training areas; the prevailing weather conditions; and the incidence of towns, airspace restrictions and avoidance areas.

In order to minimise noise disturbance, the MOD has adopted a number of measures. These include: limiting the amount of low flying training to that strictly necessary for aircrew to achieve and maintain operational effectiveness; carrying out the vast majority of low flying during daylight hours on weekdays; only rarely permitting military jet aircraft to fly after 11 pm; and limiting the altitude and speeds of low flying aircraft. MOD statistics suggest that there has been a significant reduction in the number of hours booked for fixed wing and helicopter low flying since 1995: 66,569 hours for 1995 as compared with 42,209 hours for 2000/2001. However, where low flying does take place, noise remains a problem. Where a link can be established, on the balance of probabilities, between Crown or visiting forces aircraft activity and loss or damage suffered, ex gratia payments are made by the MOD to compensate those affected. Most claims are settled, according to the MOD, within three months. More complex claims will inevitably take longer to settle.

Grants in respect of traffic noise

Under the Land Compensation Act 1973, s 20, and the Noise Insulation Regulations 1975, SI 1975/1763 as amended by SI 1988/2000, grants are available towards insulating certain buildings against traffic noise where this has increased following alterations to, or construction of new roads, but *not* following the making of a traffic management scheme, including specification of lorry routes, or ordinary road repairs. Where a new highway or additional carriageway is opened to the public after 16 October 1972, and its use causes or is expected to cause noise not less than a specified level to a dwelling or other building used for residential purposes, the appropriate highway authority must carry out sound insulation works or make a grant in respect of carrying out such works. The specified level of noise is 68 dB(A) during an 18 hour normal working day from 6.00 to 24.00, and the use of a highway is taken to cause noise at a level not less than this if, first, the relevant highway traffic noise level as measured 1 m in front of the most exposed of any windows or doors in a building's facade, is greater by at least 1 dB(A) than the noise level before the road in question was built, and is not actually less than 68 dB(A), *and*, second, the noise caused by traffic using, or expected to use, the road in question makes an effective contribution to the relevant noise level of at least 1 dB(A). Certain buildings are ineligible for grant aid, for example buildings subject to compulsory purchase orders, clearance area procedures, demolition or closure orders, buildings *first* occupied after the date on which the highway or additional carriageway in question was first open to public traffic, any part of a building in respect of which a grant for insulation has been paid, or is payable, under other legislation, buildings *more* than 300 m from the nearest point on the road in question. A grant will basically cover the *reasonable* cost of double glazing and associated ventilation work.

Powers to make insulation grants in respect of, for example, highways opened to the public after 16 October 1969 and before 17 October 1972, altered highways, and in respect of highway construction noise also exist under the 1975 Regulations. These are at the discretion of the local highway authority.

The Land Compensation Act 1973, s 20A as inserted by the Planning and Compensation Act 1991, empowers the Secretary of State to make regulations to provide for compensation to be paid in respect of dwellings which are not buildings and which are affected or likely to be affected by noise carried by the construction or use of public works. This will enable mobile home owners whose units are on permanent sites to receive compensation.

Grants in respect of railway noise

The power to make regulations under the Land Compensation Act 1973, s 20 has also been exercised to establish a noise insulation scheme for railways and other guided transport systems.[153] The regulations are couched in broadly similar terms to those relating to grants for traffic noise. The duty to carry out insulation work or to make grants is placed upon the person responsible for the movement of vehicles using, or expected to use, initial or additional works which causes or is expected to cause noise which exceeds the specified day-time or night time level (68 dB(A) and 63 dB(A) respectively). The categories of buildings which are ineligible for grant aid are virtually the same as those in respect of traffic noise. The one additional category to be found in SI 1996/428, any part of a building in respect of which a grant has been paid or is payable under the Noise Insulation Regulations, thus precludes the possibility of receiving more than one grant for a part of a building which is adversely affected by traffic and railway noise.

I MISCELLANEOUS FORMS OF COMPENSATION

Under the Land Compensation Act 1973, ss 1 and 2, compensation is payable to certain landowners, that is 'owners' (being either freeholders or tenants with at least three years to run of their leases) of dwelling houses, occupied as residences by such owners where their interest so qualifies them, or such owner occupiers of land other than dwelling houses, being land which is, or forms part of, an agricultural holding or other hereditament of a prescribed annual value. This compensation is payable where land is depreciated in value by certain physical factors such as noise, vibration, smell, fumes, smoke, artificial lighting, and discharges onto land, caused by the *use*, but *not construction*, of a new or altered highway, aerodrome or other public works. The physical factor causing depreciation must have its source on or in the relevant works. This includes aircraft arriving or departing from aerodromes. Furthermore if an action for nuisance is available, in other words if there is no statutory immunity, no claim will arise under these provisions, and a claim must be pursued in nuisance. This does *not* apply to depreciation caused by the use of a highway. The claim must be in respect of depreciation caused after 17 October 1969 by the opening of a new highway or the first use of other new public works. No compensation is payable in consequence of depreciation arising merely from intensification of use of existing works or highways. Furthermore, the claimant must have acquired his interest in the affected land before the new highway or public works came into use for the first time. By virtue of s 3(2) of the 1973 Act, claims must generally be made within the period from one to three years of the first coming into use of the relevant new development.

153 See SI 1996/428 as amended by SI 1998/1701.

Under LCA 1973, s 28 where the enjoyment of a dwelling is affected by construction or improvement works on an adjacent highway or other public works, so that its continued occupation is not reasonably practicable, the relevant authority may pay the additional expenses of the occupier in providing himself with temporary alternative accommodation while the works are carried out.

Highway authorities have powers under the Highways Act 1980 to do works to mitigate the adverse effects of constructing or improving highways, including power to plant trees and shrubs, etc: see HA 1980, s 282. The Highways Act 1980, s 246(2A) provides that where a highway authority proposes to carry out work on 'blighted land' to construct or improve a highway, they may acquire by agreement land whose enjoyment they consider will be seriously affected by those works *or* the use of the highway. 'Blighted land' is that which is immediately affected by the line of a proposed road, and effectively means land which is unsaleable in consequence of the proposal.

Guidance on how this new subsection should be interpreted by highway authorities was supplied in Circular 15/91. Where a highway authority refuses to purchase a house under the terms of HA 1980, s 246(2A), it may be possible to seek to challenge that decision by way of judicial review or to complain that the house owner has suffered injustice as a consequence of maladministration. Such a complaint will bring the matter within the jurisdiction of the Commissioner for Local Administration, or, if the complaint relates to central government confirmation of a decision taken locally, the Parliamentary Commissioner for Administration (PCA). A complainant who is not satisfied with the conclusions reached by the PCA following an investigation may seek judicial review of his decision.[154] Thus in *R v Parliamentary Commissioner for Administration, ex p Balchin*,[155] it was held that in declining to consider a highway authority's negative attitude to its compensatory powers and its amenability to correction by the Department of Transport, the PCA had omitted a potentially decisive element from his consideration of whether the department had caused the applicants injustice by maladministration in its dealings with the highway authority.

Before the amendment of HA 1980, s 246 in 1991 the only power of acquisition related solely to properties already seriously affected by highway construction. The extent of this provision was tested in *R v Secretary of State for Transport, ex p Owen* (reported as *Owen v Secretary of State for Transport*).[156] The Secretary of State had issued guidelines as to how the statutory discretion should be used. These *included* criteria indicating purchase of a property should occur if it was considered to be likely to be affected by an unacceptable level of noise — 78 dB(A) averaged over a 12 hour period for six months, or where a property had proved incapable of sale save at a price substantially lower than what could have been sought but for the proposed road.

The section, however, requires a two-stage approach, first to ask whether the land in question will be *seriously affected* by the proposed works, and secondly, if the answer is 'yes', whether acquisition should take place, ie whether a purchase by the public purse is warranted. In the subsequent case of *R v Minister for Roads and Traffic, ex p McCreery* (15 September 1994, unreported, CA) it was considered that *Owen* had established that in cases of proposed roads the acquiring authority must always, when considering the issue of whether the enjoyment of the land will be seriously affected, take into account any likely diminution in its value. It has since been established that it is legitimate for the Secretary of State to refuse to purchase where the applicant acquired the property with knowledge of proposed roadworks. The Secretary of State may take into account the prior foreseeability of the affectation of property values.[157]

154 See *R v Parliamentary Commissioner for Administration, ex p Dyer* [1994] 1 All ER 375.
155 [1997] JPL 917.
156 [1995] 7 ELM 52.
157 *R v Secretary of State for Transport, ex p Owen (No 2)* [1996] ELM 9.

Under HA 1980, s 253, for the purpose of mitigating an adverse effect which the construction or improvement, existence or use of a highway has or will have on its surroundings, the authority may enter into agreements with persons interested in land adjoining, or in the vicinity of, the highway for restricting or regulating the use of such land. Agreements may make provision for the planting and maintenance of trees and shrubs as shelter belts.

Further reading

GENERAL

Adams, MS, and McManus, FM, *Noise and Noise Law: A Practical Approach*, Wiley Chancery.
Bettle, J, 'Noise, The Problem of Overlapping Controls' [1988] JPL 79.
Hawke, N, and Himan, J, 'Noise Pollution Law Enforcement' [1988] JPL 84.
McKnight, A, Marstrand, PK, and Sinclair, PC (eds), *Environmental Pollution Control* (1974) George Allen and Unwin, chapters 10 and 11.
McManus, FM, 'Noise Law in the United Kingdom — a very British Solution?' [2000] 20 Legal Studies 264.
Macrory, R, 'Street Noise — The Problem of Control' [1984] JPL 388.
Penn, CN, *Noise Control* (2nd edn, 1995) Shaw and Sons.
UKELA, 'Report of The United Kingdom Environmental Law Association working group on noise on the statutory nuisance provisions of the Environmental Protection Bill' [1990] 2 LMELR 9.

OFFICIAL REPORTS

'Darlington Quiet Town Experiment' Noise Advisory Committee (1981) HMSO.
'Department of Transport: Regulation of Heavy Lorries', National Audit Office (1987) HMSO.
'Lorries, People and the Environment' Armitage Committee Report (1980) HMSO.
'Lorries, People and the Environment' White Paper (1981, Cmnd 8439) HMSO.
'Neighbourhood Noise' Scott Committee (1971) HMSO.
'Noise Final Report' Wilson Committee on the Problem of Noise (1963, Cmnd 2056) HMSO.
'Noise in Public Places' Archer Committee (1974) HMSO.
'Noise Review Working Group', DoE (1990) HMSO.
'Control of Noisy Parties' (1992) Home Office and DoE.
'Neighbour Noise Working Party', (1995) DoE.
'Review of Implementation of the Noise Act 1996' (2000) DETR.

EC REQUIREMENTS

Haigh, N, *Manual of Environmental Policy: The EC and Britain* Longman, chapter 10.
EC Green Paper, *Future Noise Policy* COM (96) 540.
McManus, F, 'The EC Green Paper on future noise policy and its impact on the United Kingdom' (1999) European Public Law 125.

MOTOR VEHICLES

Plowden, W, *The Motor Car and Politics in Britain* (1973) Penguin Books.
Sharp, C, and Jennings, T, *Transport and the Environment* (1976) Leicester University Press.

AIRCRAFT
'Report of a Field Study of Aircraft Noise and Sleep Disturbance' (1992) DoT.

PLANNING POWERS
Miller, C, and Wood, C, *Planning and Pollution* (1983) Clarendon Press, chapter 9.

THE ECONOMICS OF NOISE
Flowerdew, ADJ, *The Statistician* (1972) vol 21, no 1, pp 31–46, reprinted in Porteous, A, Attenborough, K, and Pollitt, C (eds), *Pollution: The Professionals and the Public* (1977) Open University Press, pp 167–83.

Part IV

Protection of the aqueous environment

Chapter 19

Marine pollution

The oceans and seas of the world are abused as repositories for unwanted, and often dangerous, matter. Such material can move from its place of deposition, causing damage, even on an international basis. Anti-pollution measures must be internationally agreed, co-ordinated and enforced to be effective. Both international and EC law have provisions relating to water, the former being largely concerned with the protection of the world's oceans, while the latter, along with UK law, is concerned with the protection of the water medium, and the provision of water for consumption and recreation.[1] In the discussion which follows, the focus of attention will be upon marine pollution. However, given that the international law of the sea is an enormous body of principle and regulation which, for reasons of space, can only be briefly touched on here, those requiring more detail should consult the standard texts.[2]

A CUSTOMARY INTERNATIONAL LAW ON MARINE POLLUTION

Customary international law of the sea has developed for hundreds of years, but treaty-based law (see below), as usual, is now of more importance. Nevertheless, as the decision of the International Court of Justice in *Nicaragua v United States (Merits)*[3] serves to indicate, customary international law continues to exist and apply even where it is identical in content to international treaty law.

When speaking of customary law, we are essentially concerned with law that has developed as a consequence of custom or practice rather than from the process of formal legislative enactment. Obligations arise between those states which have consistently followed a particular practice. However, for rules to be correctly described as customary law, it is not enough that there is evidence of state practice. It must also be established that a state has acted in a particular way because it considers that it is obliged to do so by law.[4] Although customary law can thus be defined with relative

1 See chapter 20.
2 See, for example, Birnie and Boyle, *International Law and the Environment* and their more recent companion volume of relevant documents, *Basic Documents in International Law and the Environment*.
3 [1986] ICJ 14.
4 This second element of customary law is commonly referred to as *opinio juris sive necessitatis*.

ease, in practice it is a far more difficult task to prove that a custom has acquired the force of law.

In the context of environmental protection, a number of cases are commonly referred to in the texts to illustrate the role of customary international law. Chief amongst these is the decision in the *Trail Smelter*[5] case where a dispute arose between the United States and Canada over damage that had been done to trees and agriculture in the former country as a consequence of the emission of sulphur dioxide over a number of years from a smelting plant at Trail, British Columbia. In finding that Canada should indemnify the United States for the damage that it had suffered, the arbitral tribunal held that:

> 'Under the principles of international law ... no state has the right to use or permit the use of territory in such a manner as to cause injury by fumes in or to the territory of another or the properties or persons therein, when the case is of serious consequence and the injury is established by clear and convincing evidence'.[6]

Although this passage relates specifically to atmospheric emissions, it is clear that it may be applied equally to other forms of polluting activity. Thus in the present context, a state may well be under an obligation arising from customary law to ensure that its activities are not such as will cause water pollution to adversely affect another state.[7]

B INTERNATIONAL TREATY LAW ON MARINE POLLUTION

The 1868 Mannheim Treaty was in part concerned with protecting water supplies, and that has been followed by many others, some of which serve to create a framework for the protection of the oceans' flora and fauna (a topic which cannot be explored here), while others have been concerned with international marine pollution, particularly as a result of oil spillages.

United Nations Convention on the Law of the Sea

Of the treaties relating to marine pollution, the United Nations Convention on the Law of the Sea (UNCLOS) is generally considered to be potentially the most important. As is often the case with international treaties, however, the final text of the Convention was only adopted after many years of negotiations between the various states. Thus although the Third United Nations Conference on the Law of the Sea was convened in 1973, the final text of the Convention was not adopted until 1982. A further 12 years passed before the Convention entered into force.[8]

UNCLOS is a substantial treaty running to some 320 articles and 2 annexes. It is divided up into 16 Parts which make provision for, inter alia, the establishment of the Law of the Sea Tribunal for the determination of disputes and the International Seabed Authority, which is concerned with regulating mineral exploitation. However for present

---

5   (1940) 3 RIAA 1905.
6   (1940) 3 RIAA 1905 at 1965.
7   See the *Lake Lanoux Arbitration* (1957) ILR 101.
8   16 November 1994. For a fuller chronology of the events leading to the entering into force of the Convention, see Birnie and Boyle, *Basic Documents on International Law and the Environment*, pp 153-154.

purposes, Part XII of UNCLOS is of interest since its 46 articles are concerned with marine environmental protection and preservation. The treaty declares the general obligation of states to protect the marine environment (Art 192), though it does not abrogate sovereign rights to exploit natural resources (Art 193). More specific measures follow on pollution control, etc, while particular provision is made with regard to scientific and technical co-operation and assistance between states, and for monitoring pollution and publishing information. Special rules apply to deal with land based marine pollution (Art 207), or that which arises from states' seabed activities (Art 208), or from dumping (Art 210). Particular provision is made for enforcement of treaty obligations (Arts 213-222), and for the responsibility of states to fulfil the same, for example by affording remedies under their laws against persons under their jurisdiction who damage the marine environment by pollution. Provision is also made to preserve state obligations under other conventions (Art 237).

The weakness of UNCLOS was originally that although many states were involved in the negotiations which preceded the drafting of the treaty and although many such states signed the final text, these did *not* include major nations such as the USA, the UK and Germany. Initial ratifications were thus almost exclusively undertaken by developing nations.[9] However, the position is now somewhat different. In the UK, for example, the Merchant Shipping (Prevention of Pollution) (Law of the Sea Convention) Order 1996[10] empowered the Secretary of State to make regulations to implement UNCLOS. UK accession to the treaty accordingly took place on 25 July 1997. Furthermore, although a number of European states originally abstained from adopting the text of the Treaty, ratification has now taken place in many of them. It should also be noted that the EC has ratified UNCLOS.

Treaties relating to oil pollution

Other treaties are particularly concerned with oil pollution of the sea and dumping (see below). Those concerned with oil include: the International Convention for the Prevention of Pollution of the Sea by Oil (OILPOL) (London 1954, amended in 1962, 1969 and 1971); the International Convention relating to Intervention on the High Seas in cases of Oil Pollution Casualties (Brussels 1969, Protocol added 1973); the International Convention on Civil Liability for Oil Pollution Damage (Brussels 1969, Protocol added 1976, amended 1984); the International Convention for the Establishment of an International Fund for Compensation for Oil Pollution Damage (Brussels 1971, Protocols 1976 and 1984); the International Convention for the Prevention of Pollution from Ships (MARPOL) (London 1973, Protocol 1978); the International Convention on Oil Pollution, Preparedness, Response and Co-operation (1990); and the International Convention on Civil Liability for Bunker Oil Pollution Damage (2001).

Since MARPOL is the principal international convention covering prevention of pollution of the marine environment by ships from operational or accidental causes, it is necessary to briefly consider the background to the Convention and its main provisions.

---

9   See Birnie and Boyle, *Basic Documents on International Law and the Environment*, p 153.
10   SI 1996/282. This order was made under the authority of powers conferred by the Merchant Shipping Act 1995, s 129.

The International Convention for the Prevention of Pollution from Ships (MARPOL 1973/78)

As with the other Conventions referred to above (except for OILPOL[11]), MARPOL is a Convention drawn up by the International Maritime Organization[12] (IMO), a United Nations agency responsible for the safety of shipping and the prevention of marine pollution. The Convention is a direct consequence of the recognition that oil pollution of the seas had become something of a problem during the course of the latter half of the 20th century. Despite the OILPOL Convention (referred to above) oil pollution incidents still occurred, such as when the *Torrey Canyon* ran aground in 1967 while entering the English Channel, spilling its entire cargo of 120,000 tons of crude oil in the process. Incidents such as this raised questions about the adequacy of measures then in place to prevent oil pollution from ships and about the mechanisms for compensating those affected by the resultant environmental damage. Accordingly in 1973, an international conference adopted the International Convention for the Prevention of Pollution from Ships. However, states were slow to ratify the Convention despite the fact that only two of its original five annexes[13] (see below) had to be agreed to. Further pollution incidents involving tankers were the catalyst for an IMO Conference on Tanker Safety and Pollution Prevention in 1978. This conference adopted, inter alia, a protocol to the 1973 Convention which was still not in force at the time. The resultant MARPOL Convention is therefore a combination of the 1973 Convention and the 1978 protocol. By virtue of Art 9, it supersedes the OILPOL Convention.

The parties[14] to MARPOL desire to achieve the complete elimination of international pollution of the marine environment by oil and other harmful substances and the minimisation of accidental discharge of these substances. They have therefore agreed to give effect to the provisions of MARPOL and those annexes to which they are bound. Annexes I and II are binding on all the parties to the Convention. They came into force on 2 October 1983 and 6 April 1987, respectively, and relate to the prevention of pollution by oil[15] and the control of pollution by noxious liquid substances. The other four annexes to the Convention are *optional*. They are concerned with: the prevention of pollution by harmful substances in packaged form; the prevention of pollution by sewage from ships; the prevention of pollution by garbage from ships; and the prevention of air pollution from ships.[16] As with many other international Conventions, MARPOL has been the subject of numerous amendments since it entered into force.[17]

Treaties relating to dumping

Several treaties reflect the consensus that international action is required to protect the marine environment from the harmful effects of *dumping* polluting matter. The two key provisions are the Convention on the Prevention of Marine Pollution by Dumping

---

11   This Convention was adopted in 1954 whereas the International Maritime Organization was established in 1958. After that date, however, the IMO took over from the UK government the depository and secretariat functions in relation to the Convention.
12   Formerly known as the Inter-Governmental Maritime Consultative Organization.
13   Annex VI was adopted on 26 September 1997.
14   As at 31 October 2001, there were 118 Contracting States to the compulsory annexes to MARPOL (Annexes I and II) representing 95.9% of world tonnage.
15   Annex I is given effect in UK law by the Merchant Shipping (Prevention of Oil Pollution) Regulations 1996, SI 1996/2154, the detail of which is considered below.
16   As at 31 October 2001, Annexes III, IV, V and VI had been ratified by 99, 82, 102 and 3 contracting states, respectively.
17   Since 1983, amendments to the Convention have more or less been made on an annual basis.

of Wastes and Other Matter (London, 1972), and the Convention for the Protection of the Marine Environment of the North East Atlantic (1992).

The Convention on the Prevention of Marine Pollution by Dumping of Wastes and Other Matter (the London Convention)

This Convention, which was adopted on 13 November 1972 and which came into force on 30 August 1975,[18] has a global character. It binds its 78 contracting parties (Art I): to 'individually and collectively promote the effective control of all sources of pollution of the marine environment', and 'to take all practicable steps to prevent the pollution of the sea by the dumping of waste and other matter that is likely to create hazards to human health, to harm living resources and marine life, to damage amenities or to interfere with other legitimate uses of the sea.' Article II further binds the parties, according to scientific, technical and economic capabilities, to prevent pollution by dumping and to harmonise their policies in this respect.

The treaty provides that certain Annex I wastes are not to be dumped at sea at all, eg mercury, cadmium, radioactive wastes or other radioactive matter and industrial waste.[19] Certain Annex II substances may only be dumped with a prior *special* permit,[20] and all other waste dumping requires a *general* permit.[21] Both types of permit are to be issued by an appropriate authority or authorities designated by the contracting party (Art VI). In addition to this function, such authorities are required to keep records of the nature and quantities of all matter permitted to be dumped and the location, time and method of dumping, and to monitor, either individually or in collaboration with the appropriate authorities of other contracting parties, the condition of the sea. Parties to the treaty further bind themselves (Art VIII) to make regional agreements to counter marine pollution, to develop dispute resolution procedures (Art X) and to promote measures to protect the marine environment against listed forms of pollution, eg hydrocarbons and radioactive pollutants (Art XII).

The 1996 Protocol

On 7 November 1996, a Protocol was adopted which will eventually replace the London Convention.[22] When it comes into force,[23] it will bring about a significant change in the approach taken to the regulation of waste dumping at sea. The first point to note is that in implementing the Protocol, the contracting parties are required to apply a *precautionary approach* to environmental protection from the dumping of wastes or other matter (Art 3). In other words, the parties are required to take appropriate preventative measures when there is reason to believe that introducing wastes or other matter into the marine environment is likely to cause harm even where there is no conclusive scientific evidence to this effect. The 1996 Protocol also requires the contracting parties to take account of the 'polluter pays principle' and to ensure that implementation of the Protocol does not result in either damage being transferred from

---

18 The Convention was amended in 1978, 1980, 1989 and 1993, respectively. In 1996 a Protocol was adopted which will eventually replace the 1972 Convention.
19 See further (1972) 11 ILM 1310.
20 See further (1972) 11 ILM 1311.
21 See below for relevant UK law.
22 See Cm 4078.
23 It will come into force 30 days after it has been ratified by 26 states, 15 of which must be contracting parties to the London Convention.

one part of the environment to another or the transformation of one type of pollution into another. Perhaps the most significant change, however, to the approach to be taken to the regulation of waste dumping at sea is to be found in Art 4 of the Protocol. Unlike the London Convention which *prohibits* the dumping of Annex I wastes (see above), the wastes listed in the Protocol, Annex I *may be considered* for dumping, subject to the objectives and general obligations of the Protocol and a permit requirement. The relevant wastes are: dredged material; sewage sludge; fish waste, or material resulting from industrial fish processing operations; vessels and platforms or other man-made structures at sea; inert, inorganic geological material; organic material of natural origin; and bulky items comprising iron, steel, concrete and similarly unharmful materials for which the concern is physical impact. This latter category is limited to those circumstances where such wastes are generated at locations, eg small islands, which have no practicable access to disposal options other than dumping. By implication, therefore, the dumping of all other wastes at sea is *prohibited* by the Protocol.

The Convention for the Protection of the Marine Environment of the North East Atlantic (the OSPAR Convention)

The OSPAR Convention,[24] which was opened for signature in September 1992 and which entered into force on 25 March 1998, is the direct descendant of the Convention for the Prevention of Marine Pollution by the Dumping (etc) (the Oslo Convention)[25] and the Convention for the Prevention of Marine Pollution from Land Based Sources (the Paris Convention).[26] It has been signed and ratified by all the parties to these earlier Conventions which include France, Germany, Spain the UK and the EC.

Unlike the London Convention (see above), the OSPAR Convention is a good example of a regional international treaty. In other words, its ambit is confined to the marine environment of the North-East Atlantic which is defined as extending westwards to the east coast of Greenland, eastwards to the continental North Sea coast, south to the Straits of Gibraltar and northwards to the North Pole.[27] The Convention (and its predecessors) recognises the inherent worth of this particular marine environment and that it is necessary to coordinate its protection. Since the OSPAR Convention replaces the Oslo and Paris Conventions, it might be regarded as being something of a consolidating measure. However, this is not strictly correct. Although these earlier Conventions have been replaced, Decisions, Recommendations and all other agreements adopted under them continue to be applicable unless they are brought to an end by measures adopted under the OSPAR Convention. There is, however, a more fundamental objection to the consolidation tag; the OSPAR Convention is in part a consequence of the recognition that the Oslo and Paris Conventions did not adequately control some of the many sources of pollution of the marine environment. It therefore seeks to address all sources (eg land-based and off-shore sources) of pollution of the marine environment and takes account of the precautionary principle and the need to strengthen regional cooperation. The contrast between the earlier Conventions and the OSPAR Convention is perhaps best illustrated by briefly examining their respective approaches to marine pollution.

24   For a more detailed discussion of the provisions of this Convention, see Howarth and McGillivray, *Water Pollution and Water Quality Law*, paras 18.8-18.8.5.
25   Signed in Oslo on 15 February 1972 and amended by Protocols of 2 March 1983 and 5 December 1989.
26   Signed in Paris 4 June 1974 and amended by Protocol of 26 March 1986.
27   This area does not include the Baltic or Mediterranean seas.

The Paris Convention adopted an approach whereby harmful substances were classified into various 'lists'. Those on the 'black list' were the most harmful, eg cadmium, mercury, oil, organohalogen compounds, and persistent synthetic materials. Pollution by these was to be eradicated, though a staged approach was allowed. Those on the 'grey list' were less harmful and included arsenic, heavy metals, non-persistent oils, and organic compounds of phosphorous. Pollution by these was to be limited, and discharge authorisation was required in respect of them. The third 'list' contained all other pollutants save for radioactive substances which formed the fourth 'list'. With regard to the third list states were exhorted to reduce pollution, while with regard to the fourth they were required to undertake to forestall/eliminate pollution.

This 'list' approach has not been followed in the OSPAR Convention. Instead, the contracting parties have agreed to take all possible steps to prevent and eliminate marine pollution from all substances. For the purposes of the Convention, 'pollution' is defined to mean the introduction by man, directly or indirectly, of substances or energy into the maritime area which results, or is likely to result, in hazards to human health, harm to living resources and marine ecosystems, damage to amenities or interference with other legitimate uses of the sea. In order to achieve the Convention's objective, the contracting parties have further agreed to individually and jointly adopt programmes and measures (which take full account of the latest technological developments and practices designed to prevent and eliminate pollution) and to apply the precautionary principle and the polluter pays principle.

The institutional arrangements under the OSPAR Convention reflect those which prevailed under the Oslo and Paris Conventions. Thus Art 10 of the Convention establishes a Commission made up of representatives of each of the contracting parties which is required to meet at regular intervals and at such other times as is decided in accordance with its own rules of procedure. The Commission is the subject of a number of duties under the Convention. These include supervising the implementation of the Convention and generally reviewing the condition of the relevant maritime area, the effectiveness of the measures being adopted, the priorities and the need for any additional or different measures. There is also a Secretariat and the Commission may, by unanimous vote, admit a non-contracting party State or any international governmental or non-governmental organisation as an observer at its meetings.

C POLLUTION OF THE SEA IN UK LAW

The UK's international and EC obligations as regards the pollution of the sea by oil have been given effect in domestic law by both primary and secondary legislation. With regard to the latter type of legislation, the principal provisions are the Merchant Shipping (Prevention of Oil Pollution) Order 1983[28] and the Merchant Shipping (Prevention of Oil Pollution) Regulations 1996,[29] as amended,[30] which give effect to Annex I of the MARPOL Convention (see above).

28 SI 1983/1106.
29 SI 1996/2154. These regulations revoke and replace the Merchant Shipping (Prevention of Oil Pollution) Regulations, SI 1983/1398.
30 See the Merchant Shipping (Prevention of Oil Pollution) (Amendment) Regulations, SI 2000/483.

The Merchant Shipping (Prevention of Oil Pollution) Regulations

UK ships under the 1996 Regulations, reg 12 (including oil tankers where discharges are form *machinery space* bilges) anywhere and other ships, similarly defined, within UK territorial waters must not discharge oil or oily mixtures into any part of the sea. For the purposes of the 1996 Regulations, 'oil' means petroleum in any form including crude oil, fuel oil, sludge, oil refuse and refined products and 'oily mixture' means a mixture with any oil content. 'Discharge' means any release, however caused, from a ship and includes any escape, disposal, leaking pumping, emitting or emptying. However, it does not include dumping, or the release of harmful substances arising from either the exploration, exploitation and associated off-shore processing of sea-bed mineral resources or for the purposes of legitimate scientific research into pollution abatement or control.

The prohibition on the discharge of oil does not apply, however, where all the following conditions are satisfied: the ship is proceeding on a voyage; *and* is not within a special area eg the Mediterranean or Baltic Sea areas (1996 Regulations, reg 16); *and* the oil content of the effluent does not exceed 15 parts per million (ppm) of the mixtures; *and* the ship has in operation the filtering equipment and the oil discharge monitoring and control systems (1996 Regulations, reg 12(2)). No discharge may contain chemicals or other substances in concentrations likely to harm the marine environment (1996 Regulations, reg 12(4)). 'Ships' are vessels of any type operating in a marine environment, including submersible craft and fixed or floating structures but *not* hovercraft.

UK tankers and other tankers in British territorial waters are further regulated by the 1996 Regulations, reg 13. They may not discharge oil, etc (other than reg 12 discharges) into the sea unless they are: proceeding on a voyage; not within special areas; more than 50 miles from the nearest land; the rate of discharge does not exceed 30 litres per mile; the total quantity discharged does not exceed specified percentages of the cargo; *and* monitoring and control systems are operating. Regulation 11 provides for certain general exceptions in respect of discharges. Thus the provisions of either reg 12 or reg 13 do not apply where the discharge: was necessary for securing the safety of a ship or of saving life at sea; where it resulted from damage to a ship or its equipment; or, where it was in connection with combating other specific pollution incidents. The second of these three exceptions is, however, subject to two provisos. All reasonable precautions must have been taken after the damage to prevent or minimise the discharge *and* the owner or master must not have acted either intentionally or recklessly with regard to probable damage.

Construction requirements relating to oil discharge monitoring and control systems are contained in the 1996 Regulations, reg 14. Regulation 15 requires appropriate means of cleaning oil cargo tanks to control discharges. The 1996 Regulations, Part V imposed constructional requirements to minimise pollution from tankers due to side and bottom damage. It is an offence to fail to comply with these requirements. If any ship fails to comply with any requirement of the 1996 Regulations (save for regs 12, 13 and 16), the owner and master shall each be guilty of an offence (reg 36(1)). Where the offence involves a failure to comply with any requirement of reg 12, 13 or 16, the owner and master shall be liable on summary conviction to a fine not exceeding £250,000 or on conviction on indictment to a fine (the 1996 Regulations, reg 36(2)). High fines can therefore constitute a real deterrent to polluting behaviour, and may cover the costs of any 'clean-up' operations. Cases must not, however, be so hurried that the accused is denied the opportunity to prepare properly.[31] Prosecutions under the legislation have

31   *R v Thames Magistrate's Court, ex p Polemis* [1974] 2 All ER 1219.

in any case been limited in number, although the maximum fine of £250,000 was imposed by Southampton magistrates in *Maritime and Coastguard Agency v Bent Emanuel Christiansen*.[32]

UK oil tankers of 150 gross registered tonnage (GRT) and above, and other UK ships of above 400 GRT are subject to five yearly surveys under the 1996 Regulations, reg 4(1) to ensure compliance with the requirements of the 1996 Regulations relating to structure, equipment, systems, fittings, arrangement and material. In addition, provision is made for annual and intermediate surveys of ships in respect of which an International Oil Pollution Prevention (IOPP) certificate has been issued (the 1996 Regulations, regs 5 and 6). Defects in, or accidents to, UK ships affecting their integrity or the efficiency of their equipment must be reported to the appropriate UK authority in case surveys are necessary (reg 8(2)). Similar requirements apply to non-UK ships (reg 8(3)). After any survey of a UK ship under the Regulations no material change may be made in its structure, equipment or arrangement without the approval of the Secretary of State (reg 8(1)(b)).

The 1996 Regulations, reg 10 requires an oil record book which lists specified operations concerned with movements of oil and tank cleaning, etc. The oil record book must be in the form prescribed and must be kept in such a place (generally on board) as to be readily available for inspection and copying by appropriate authorities.

A master of a ship was formerly obliged to report the actual or likely discharge of oil or an oily mixture to an appropriate body, eg a coastguard, under the Merchant Shipping (Prevention of Oil Pollution) Regulations 1983.[33] This obligation is now to be found in the Merchant Shipping (Reporting Requirements for Ships Carrying Dangerous or Polluting Goods) Regulations 1995.[34] Under the 1995 Regulations, reg 8 the master of the ship must report to the competent authority the particulars of the incident without delay and to the fullest extent possible together with certain specified information.[35] The need for speed in making the report is further emphasised by the 1995 Regulations, reg 11 which provides that the fastest telecommunications channels available shall be used. Provision is also made for the making of supplementary reports which may be made as a consequence of a request for additional information by or on behalf of the government whose interests may be affected by the incident (1995 Regulations, reg 10).

Where the Secretary of State is satisfied that, in consequence of non-compliance with the requirements of the 1996 Regulations, a ship represents an unreasonable threat of harm to the marine environment, he may deny that ship entry to UK ports or offshore terminals (reg 35(1)). Regulation 35(2) permits the detention of ships where contravention of the Regulations is suspected. The Regulations, Part VII applies their requirements with appropriate modifications to 'offshore installations', eg any mobile or fixed oil drilling or production platform.

The Merchant Shipping Act 1995

The Merchant Shipping Act is a substantial piece of legislation which consolidates a number of enactments relating to merchant shipping. With regard to oil pollution, the MSA 1995, s 131 provides generally that discharges of any oil (ie crude oil, fuel oil and lubricating oil and specified heavy diesel oils) or any mixture containing oil from ships into waters, including inland waters, which are landward of the baseline for measuring

32 [1999] Water Law 14.
33 SI 1983/1398.
34 SI 1995/2498.
35 The specified information is set out in the Merchant Shipping Notice, Sch 1, No M 1630.

the breadth of UK territorial waters and are navigable by sea-going ships constitute offences. It is a defence to a prosecution under the MSA 1995, s 131 to prove that neither the escape nor any delay in its discovery was due to want of reasonable care and that remedial steps were taken as soon as practicable after discovery. Where a harbour master has reason to believe that the owner/master of a ship has committed an offence contrary to MSA 1995, s 131, he may detain the ship by virtue of s 144. Where this power is exercised in respect of a non-UK registered ship, the harbour master must immediately notify the Secretary of State who will then inform the consul of the state whose flag the ship is entitled to fly or the appropriate maritime authorities of that state.

Under MSA 1995, s 136, if any oil/oily mixture is discharged from a ship into a UK harbour or is found escaped there from a ship, the owner or master of the vessel must report to the relevant harbour authorities. A failure to make a report as required by the section constitutes an offence. Reception facilities at UK harbours and terminals may be provided by harbour authorities and operators (who may be directed to act by the Secretary of State), for residues, oil mixtures and noxious liquids.[36] It should be noted, however, that by virtue of MSA 1995, s 136A, the provisions of ss 131 and 136 do not apply where the discharge or escape of oil (in the case of s 136) has been authorised by an authorisation granted under the Environmental Protection Act 1990, Part I or by a permit granted under regulations made under the Pollution Prevention and Control Act 1999, s 2.[37]

Powers to intervene

MSA 1995, s 137 applies where an accident *has* occurred to a ship, and the Secretary of State believes that use of his powers is urgently needed because oil from the ship will or may cause *significant pollution* in the UK or its territorial waters.[38] The Secretary of State may give directions to prevent or reduce pollution as respects ship or cargo to the ship-owner, its master, to any pilot of the ship[39] or any person or salvor in possession of the ship. Directions may, inter alia, be given that the ship shall/shall not be moved, or that oil or other cargo shall/shall not be removed, or specified salvage operations shall/shall not be taken. Where the Secretary of State concludes that these powers are inadequate he may, to prevent or reduce oil pollution, take any action with regard to ship or cargo, including sinking or destroying it or taking over control. It is an offence under MSA 1995, s 139 not to comply with a s 137 direction. However, it is a defence for an accused to prove that he used all due diligence to ensure compliance with the direction or that he had reasonable cause for believing that compliance with the direction would have involved a serious risk to human life. Under MSA 1995, s 141 an order in council may provide that s 137, inter alia, may apply to ships not registered in the UK and which are for the time being neither within UK waters nor within a part of the sea specified by virtue of MSA 1995, s 129(2)(b), ie the UK pollution zone.[40] No directions under MSA 1995, s 137 can, however, apply to any Royal Navy vessel (s 141(4)).

36   See the Merchant Shipping (Port Waste Reception Facilities) Regulations 1997, SI 1997/3018.
37   Inserted by the Pollution Prevention and Control Act 1999, s 6(1), Sch 2, para 13.
38   As originally enacted, MSA 1995, s 137 referred to *large scale* rather than significant pollution. However it was amended by the Merchant Shipping and Maritime Security Act 1997, s 2(2) with the result that the Secretary of State's powers may now be exercised under this section even where the pollution does not cover a wide geographical area.
39   Inserted by the Merchant Shipping and Maritime Safety Act 1997, s 2(3)(a).
40   See further the Merchant Shipping (Prevention of Pollution) (Intervention) (Foreign Ships) Order 1997, SI 1997/2568 and the Dangerous Vessels Act 1985. The DVA 1985, ss 1 and 3 give harbour masters the power, subject to the directions of the Secretary of State, to give directions concerning dangerous vessels in respect of their harbour areas.

Given that significant pollution of the sea may be caused by substances other than oil, MSA 1995, s 138A[41] provides, inter alia, that any reference to 'oil pollution' in s 137 (and s 138) shall include a reference to any other substance which has been prescribed by the Secretary of State for the purposes of the section; or if not so prescribed, is liable to create hazards to human health, to harm living resources and marine life, to damage amenities or to interfere with other legitimate uses of the sea. Although the use of the word 'liable' suggests that there must be an objective connection between the relevant substance and the consequence that it produces, it should be noted that there is no requirement that the hazard, harm or damage caused must be grave.[42]

Temporary exclusion zones

By virtue of MSA 1995, s 100A,[43] the Secretary of State has the power to establish a temporary exclusion zone around a ship, structure or other thing which is wrecked, damaged or in distress in UK waters or the UK pollution zone. Such a power is only exercisable, however, where it appears to the Secretary of State that significant harm will or may occur as the direct or indirect result of the relevant casualty being wrecked, damaged or in distress and that the establishment of an exclusion zone is necessary to prevent or reduce the actual or potential harm. Where a temporary exclusion zone has been established under MSA 1995, s 100A, the extent of that zone may be subsequently reduced by the Secretary of State. In the event that a zone is no longer needed for the purpose of preventing or reducing significant harm or the risk of such harm, the direction which established it may be revoked by the Secretary of State.

The owner and master of a ship shall each be guilty of an offence where a ship enters or remains in a temporary exclusion zone contrary to the terms of the direction which established the zone.[44] It is a defence, however, to prove that the existence or area of the zone was not and would not on reasonable enquiry have become known to the master.[45]

Power to require ships to be removed

Where it is necessary for the purpose of securing the safety of a ship or of other ships, or persons on the ship or other ships, or of any other persons or property, or of preventing or reducing any risk to such safety, and for the purpose of preventing or reducing pollution or the risk of such pollution in the UK, UK waters or the UK pollution zone, the Secretary of State may direct that: a ship is to be moved or is to be removed from a specified area or locality or from UK waters; or that a ship is not to be moved to a specified place or area within UK waters, or over a specified route within UK waters. MSA 1995, s 100C[46] further provides that such directions are to be issued to the owner or master of the ship and that such persons must use their best endeavours to ensure

41 Inserted by the Merchant Shipping and Maritime Security Act 1997, s 3.
42 For a fuller discussion of the meaning and extent of s 138A, see the annotations to the Merchant Shipping and Maritime Safety Act 1997, s 3 by N Gaskell in *Current Law Statutes*.
43 Inserted by the Merchant Shipping and Maritime Safety Act 1997, s 1.
44 MSA 1995, s 100B as inserted by the Merchant Shipping and Maritime Safety Act 1997, s 1.
45 MSA 1995, s 100B(7). It should be noted, however, that where the Secretary of State issues a direction under s 100A establishing a temporary exclusion zone he is under a duty to publish the direction as soon as practicable in order to bring it to the attention of persons likely to be affected by it. He is also under a duty to send a copy of the direction to the International Maritime Organization within 24 hours of it being issued: see MSA 1995, s 100A(8)(a) and (b).
46 Inserted by the Merchant Shipping and Maritime Safety Act 1997, s 10.

that any risk to human life is avoided when complying with or taking action in respect of the directions. A failure to comply with or contravene any of the requirements of a direction constitutes an offence as does the intentional obstruction of any person who is, inter alia, acting in compliance with a MSA 1995, s 100C direction: see s 100D(1) and (2).[47] In the case of a person charged with the former offence, however, it is a defence to prove that all due diligence was used to ensure compliance with the direction *or* that the person had reasonable cause to believe that compliance with the direction would have involved serious risk to human life.[48]

Oil Pollution Compensation Fund

Two of the enactments consolidated in the Merchant Shipping Act 1995, the Merchant Shipping (Oil Pollution) Act 1971 and the Merchant Shipping Act 1974, implemented international agreements of 1969 and 1971 on the civil liability of shipowners.[49] Importers of oil (ie crude oil and fuel oil as defined by MSA 1995, s 173(10)) into the UK or persons receiving the oil are liable to pay contributions to the International Oil Pollution Compensation Fund in respect of oil carried by sea to ports or terminal installations in the UK. No liability to make contributions arises where the amount of oil imported or received in the year does not exceed 150,000 tonnes (MSA 1995, s 173(5)).

The fund, which is based on the 'polluter pays' principle so that those who derive benefits from potentially polluting activities must help bear the costs of pollution, exists to ensure that pollution victims may obtain compensation. The fund is therefore liable for pollution damage caused outside the ship in question by contamination resulting from escapes or discharges of oil and including the cost of measures taken after the occurrence to prevent or minimise damage. Ships covered are sea-going vessels and other seaborne craft provided they carry *oil in bulk as cargo*. Liability is dependent upon the person suffering damage being unable to obtain full compensation under MSA 1995, s 153 because one of the following applies:

1 The discharge or escape resulted from an exceptional, inevitable and irresistible phenomenon, or was due wholly to the malicious act or omission of a third party,[50] or was due wholly to the negligence or fault of a government or navigation authority in relation to navigation aid duties, because liability is accordingly wholly displaced by MSA 1995, s 155.
2 The owner or guarantor liable for the damage cannot meet his obligations in full.
3 The damage exceeds the limit of liability under MSA 1995.[51]

The fund incurs no obligations: if it can prove the damage resulted from an act of war, or insurrection; or resulted from oil discharged by a warship or by a ship state-owned or operated and used at relevant times only on government non-commercial service; or where the claimant cannot prove that the damage resulted from an occurrence involving a ship identified by him.[52] MSA 1995 s 178 lays down time limits in respect of claims against the fund. UK courts may not entertain claims unless action is commenced, or appropriate third party notice of an action to enforce a claim is given, within three years of the claim arising.

47 Inserted by the Merchant Shipping and Maritime Security Act 1997, s 10.
48 See MSA 1995, s 100D(3).
49 These are the International Convention on Civil Liability for Oil Pollution Damage (Brussels, 1969) and the International Convention for the Establishment of an International Fund for Compensation for Oil Pollution Damage (Brussels, 1971), referred to above.
50 For the effect of the actions of third parties upon liability for the offence of causing water pollution contrary to the Water Resources Act 1991, s 85 see chapter 20.
51 The Merchant Shipping Act 1995, s 175(1)(a)-(c).
52 MSA 1995, s 175(7)(a) and (b).

In the Scottish case of *Landcatch Ltd v International Oil Pollution Compensation Fund*,[53] the pursuers brought actions against the Oil Pollution Compensation Fund and the Braer Corporation, the owners and insurers of the tanker *Braer* which had run aground off Shetland on 5 January 1993, spilling 84,700 tonnes of crude oil and 1,600 tonnes of bulk fuel oil into the sea in the process. Their business, which was to rear salmon from eggs to smolt in freshwater conditions and then to sell them for further rearing to maturity in seawater conditions, was principally conducted at a place in Argyll some 500 km from Shetland. However, approximately 65% of their stock was sold to on-growers in Shetland. Landcatch claimed that as a result of the oil pollution and emergency exclusion orders made by the Secretary of State for Scotland under the Food and Environment Protection Act 1985, they had suffered losses which included, inter alia, the culling of smolt because of the lack of sales and the reduced selling prices of smolt in 1993 and 1994. In short, therefore, they claimed damages for economic loss. The Court of Session (Inner House) held, inter alia, that although economic loss caused *directly* by oil pollution did come within the scope of the fund, the circumstances of the case were such that Landcatch had only suffered *relational* economic loss. In other words, its loss was too remote from the causal factor ie the pollution for it to amount to a recoverable claim under the fund.

Improvement notices

The Merchant Shipping Act 1995 makes provision for improvement and prohibition notices in connection with, inter alia, ss 131-151 of the Act. MSA 1995, s 261 enables a ministerially appointed inspector who considers there has been a contravention of a relevant statutory provision to serve an 'improvement notice' on the person responsible specifying the issues and remedial measures required. MSA 1995, s 262 enables an inspector, who is of the opinion that activities falling within the ambit of the relevant statutory provisions are being, or are about to be, carried on ship by, or under the control of, any person in such a way as to involve risk of serious pollution of any navigable waters, to serve a notice prohibiting the activities. Contravention of such notices constitutes an offence under MSA 1995, s 266.

Prevention of Oil Pollution Act 1971

This Act is a more modest consolidating measure than the Merchant Shipping Act 1995 in that it is concerned only with the consolidation of the Oil in Navigable Waters Acts 1955 to 1971 and the Continental Shelf Act 1964, s 5.

Under POPA 1971, s 3, if any oil or oil mixture is discharged into *any* part of the sea from a pipeline or (otherwise than from a ship) as a result of operations for exploration or exploitation of the sea bed, in a designated area,[54] the owner of the pipeline or the person carrying on the operation are guilty of an offence, unless the discharge was from a place in his occupation, and was due to the act of a person who, without his permission, was there, ie a trespasser. Under POPA 1971, s 2(1)(c)-(e) within UK territorial waters' seaward limits and all other waters (including inland waters) within those limits and navigable by sea-going ships, if any oil or oily mixture is discharged from a place on land (including anything resting on the sea bed or shore) the occupier of that place commits an offence unless he can show the discharge was caused by a person there

---

53 [1999] 2 Lloyd's Rep 316.
54 Designated by Order under the Continental Shelf Act 1964, s 1.

without his permission. A further defence exists where it can be shown that the oil was in an effluent produced by oil refining operations, that it was not reasonably practicable to dispose of the effluent otherwise than by discharge into the water, and that all reasonably practicable steps had been taken for eliminating oil from the effluent.[55]

Dumping at sea

The Food and Environment Protection Act 1985, Part II as amended, which replaces the much criticised Dumping at Sea Act 1974, generally gives effect to the UK's obligations under the London and OSPAR Conventions (see above). Under FEPA 1985, s 5 licences are required for depositing substances in UK waters from vehicles, vessels, aircraft, marine structures and other constructions for marine deposition. Licences are also required: for deposits *anywhere* from British vessels, etc; for scuttling vessels; for loading vessels in the UK or its waters, etc, with substances for deposition. Under FEPA 1985, s 6, licences are required for incinerating substances on vessels or marine structures in UK waters, or anywhere at sea on a British vessel, and for loading vessels with material for incineration. Exemption from these requirements, subject or not to conditions, may be made by ministers in the form of a statutory instrument.[56]

Under FEPA 1985, s 8, licensing authorities, that is under s 24(1), ministers responsible for fisheries (in England or Wales), in determining whether to issue licences must have regard, inter alia, to the need to protect the marine ecosystem (ie the marine environment itself and the living resources it supports), human health, and other legitimate uses of the sea. Conditions may be inserted in licences, generally those designed to protect the marine ecosystems, etc, but also including measures to give the licensing authority a degree of detailed oversight over operations, or to require provision of recording equipment. Licensees may under Sch 3 request a statement of the reasons for inclusion of any provision in a licence. In considering licence applications authorities are to have regard to the practical availability of alternative disposal methods. Reasonable fees may be charged for licences to cover administrative costs and the costs of the authorities' investigative and inspection activities in respect of applicants and operations. A licensing authority may require applicants for licences to supply information and undergo examinations for the purposes of deciding applications, and further fees may be charged in this connection by the authority. Licences may be refused, but reasons for refusal must be given.[57] Licences may be varied or revoked where there is a breach of licence provisions, or where such action is necessary because of changes in circumstances relating to the marine ecosystems or human health, or increases in scientific knowledge relating to such matters, or for any other relevant reason.

FEPA 1985, Sch 3 lays down rights of representation for *licensees and disappointed applicants* with regard to the terms of licences, refusals, revocations or variations of licences. Representations which have been made must be considered by an expert committee, who must afford a hearing if requested, and report their findings and recommendations to the licensing authority. The authority must reconsider the initial decision in the light of that report, and inform the representer of the result of the reconsideration.

It is an offence under FEPA 1985, s 9 to do anything for which a licence is required except in pursuance of a licence and in accordance with its terms, though it is a defence to prove that the acts were done to secure the safety of a vessel, etc, or to save life, *and*

---

55   POPA 1971, s 6(2)(a)-(c) of the 1971 Act.
56   See FEPA 1985, s 7 and the Deposits in the Sea (Exemptions) Order 1985, SI 1985/1699.
57   FEPA 1985, Sch 3.

that ministers were given relevant details within a reasonable time. Under FEPA 1985, s 22 it is a defence to a charge to show the accused took all reasonable precautions and exercised all due diligence to avoid the commission of the offence. In particular this may be done by showing that the accused acted under his employer's instructions or in reliance on information supplied by another, and in both cases took reasonable steps to ensure no offence was committed.

FEPA 1985, s 10 allows ministers to carry out necessary operations to protect the marine ecosystem, human life or other legitimate uses of the sea in any case where operations requiring a licence have been done otherwise than in pursuance of a licence and/or licence conditions. Such a power is not restricted as to the means by which unlicensed work may be remedied, though the decision to exercise the FEPA 1985, s 10 power may be subject to judicial review.[58] Under FEPA 1985, s 14, licensing authorities must compile and keep available, for free public inspection, registers containing specified particulars.[59] These are set out in the Deposits in the Sea (Public Registers of Information) Regulations 1996.[60] They include, inter alia, particulars in relation to *applications* for a licence to deposit, scuttle or incinerate, and the particulars of any such licence which has been granted. Where a licence has been refused, varied or revoked, the particulars which must appear on the register include the reason for any such decision. Moreover, where a person has been convicted of an offence contrary to FEPA 1985, s 9, the register must contain the following information: the licence number; the name and address of the convicted person; the date of the offence; the reason for the prosecution; the court where the case was heard; the date of the court hearing; and, any penalty imposed by the court.[61]

A MAFF[62] report published in 1989[63] detailed how applications for licences under the FEPA 1985 are assessed according to issues such as chemistry and toxicity. Licences may be issued on an annual basis for specific dumping sites, and conditions are imposed to avoid creation of hazards, with maximum flow and load limits as appropriate. Enforcement under the Act has largely been concerned with ensuring that only licensed waste has been dumped. Infractions of a minor nature tend to have resulted in formal warning letters; more serious matters, taking into account the nature and gravity of the offence and the persons involved, may result in revocation of licences and/or prosecution.

Offshore installations

The question of the abandonment/decommissioning of the Brent Spar oil platform became something of a *cause célèbre* in the summer of 1995 when it was accepted by the government that the deep sea disposal of the 65,000 metric ton structure would satisfy UK international obligations as well as according with domestic legislation on dumping at sea.[64] Shell UK maintained that the dumping of the Brent Spar in this manner represented the safest and the most environmentally satisfactory option. However, following a concerted campaign against Shell by Greenpeace which included a consumer

---

58   *R v Ministry of Agriculture, Fisheries and Food, ex p Tracy* 19 January 1998, unreported, QBD.
59   This section was substituted by the Environmental Protection Act 1990, s 147.
60   SI 1996/1427.
61   The 1996 Regulations, reg 10.
62   Now the Department of the Environment, Food and Rural Affairs (DEFRA).
63   'Report on the Disposal of Waste at Sea 1986 and 1987'.
64   See for example, The Times, 20 June 1995, 6 September 1995, 12 September 1995 and 19 October 1995.

boycott of the company's products, it was announced that plans to sink the oil platform would be abandoned.

The abandonment of offshore installations provides a useful illustration of the complex relationships which may exist between international laws which have a global or regional application and domestic law. Thus although offshore disposal is allowed under the global London Convention and the 1996 Protocol[65] (see above), it is subject to restriction under the regional OSPAR Convention. OSPAR Decision 98/3 on the Disposal of Disused Offshore Installations affirms that the disposal of such installations in the North-East Atlantic should be governed by the *precautionary principle*. For the purposes of the Decision, a 'disused offshore installation' means an offshore installation which is neither serving the purposes of offshore activities nor another legitimate purpose in the maritime area. It does not include, however, any part of an offshore installation which is located below the surface of the seabed or any concrete anchor-base associated with a floating installation which does not and is not likely to interfere with other legitimate uses of the sea.

While the Decision generally *prohibits* dumping of offshore installations, it does provide that dumping may be *permitted* by a competent authority where it is satisfied, following an assessment in accordance with Annex 2 to the Decision, that there are significant reasons why this is preferable to reuse, recycling or final disposal on land. Permits may be issued for: all or part of the footings of a steel installation weighing more than 10,000 tonnes in air, placed in the maritime area before 9 February 1999; a gravity-based concrete installation; a floating concrete installation; a concrete anchor-base; or any other disused offshore installation when exceptional and unforeseen circumstances resulting from structural damage or deterioration, or from some other cause, can be demonstrated.

At the domestic level, the abandonment of offshore installations is governed by the Petroleum Act 1998, Part IV.[66] Under PA 1998, s 29, the Secretary of State may require a specified person,[67] eg the manager of the installation, to submit to him a programme setting out the measures proposed to be taken in connection with the abandonment of an offshore installation or submarine pipeline, ie an 'abandonment programme'. The programme must: contain an estimate of the cost of the measures proposed in it; specify the times within which the measures are to be taken, or make provision as to how the times are to be determined; and, where it is proposed that the installation/pipeline is to be left in position or not wholly removed, provision as to any necessary continuing maintenance.

A failure to submit an abandonment programme is not in itself an offence. However, various offences may be committed under PA 1998, Part IV, such as where a person who has submitted an abandonment programme fails to take remedial action specified by the Secretary of State by written notice (PA 1998, s 37(2)). A defendant charged with this offence shall not be guilty, however, if he is able to prove that he exercised all due diligence to avoid the failure.

Where an abandonment programme has *not* been submitted, or where the Secretary of State has rejected a programme which has been submitted, he may himself prepare an abandonment programme (PA 1998, s 33(1)). In order to enable him to do so, the Secretary of State may require from the person on whom he originally served a PA 1998, s 29 notice such records, drawings and other information as may be specified. A failure to provide the records etc constitutes an offence. Where the Secretary of State has exercised his PA 1998, s 33 powers, he may recover from the person originally served

---

65   Annex 1, art 1(4).
66   Other aspects of this Act are discussed below.
67   See PA 1998, s 30.

with the s 29 notice any expenditure (and any interest on that sum) which has been incurred in the production of the abandonment programme.

Under PA 1998, s 39, the Secretary of State may make regulations relating to the abandonment of offshore installations and submarine pipelines. At the time of writing, however, this power has not been exercised.

Other provisions controlling exploitation of the sea

Several other Acts on the statute book are concerned with controlling the exploitation of the sea, in particular with the mining of hard mineral resources and the production of petroleum.

The Deep Sea Mining (Temporary Provisions) Act 1981

This Act regulates exploration for and exploitation of the hard mineral resources of the deep sea bed (manganese, nickel, cobalt, copper, phosphorous and molybdenum). DSMTPA 1981, s 1 prohibits unlicensed exploration or exploitation of the bed of the high seas not subject to the sovereign rights of states, by citizens of, or bodies incorporated in, and who are resident of, the UK. Licences are granted under DSMTPA 1981, s 2, by the Secretary of State on payment of a prescribed fee, for such period as he thinks fit, and on such terms and conditions as he thinks fit. In determining licence applications all relevant factors must be considered, including the desirability of keeping areas free of mining operations to provide comparisons with areas exploited.

Under DSMTPA 1981, s 5, in determining a licence application the Secretary of State must have regard to the need to protect, so far as reasonably practicable, marine flora, fauna and other organisms and their habitat from the harmful effects of authorised activities. He must consider any representations made to him concerning such effects. Conditions in a licence under DSMTPA 1981, ss 2 and 5 may relate to inter alia: processing minerals on board ships; disposal of waste resulting from processing and action to avoid or minimise harmful effects on the marine environment. Licences may be revoked or varied where necessary, inter alia, to protect marine flora, fauna and their environment. The details of implementation are to be found in the Deep Sea Mining (Exploration Licences) (Applications) Regulations 1982.[68] These provide, inter alia, that an application for an exploration licence shall be made in writing to the Secretary of State in the form specified in the Schedule to the Regulations. They also provide that the fee for an exploration licence is £10,000.[69]

Petroleum Act 1998

This Act consolidates various enactments about petroleum, offshore installations and submarine pipelines such as the Petroleum (Production) Act 1934 and the Petroleum and Submarine Pipe-lines Act 1975.

PA 1998, Part I deals with petroleum. For the purposes of this Part, 'petroleum' is defined to include any mineral oil or relative hydrocarbon and natural gas existing in its natural condition in strata. It does not include, however, coal or bituminous shales or other stratified deposits from which oil can be extracted by destructive distillation.[70]

68   SI 1982/58.
69   See also the Deep Sea Mining (Exploration Licences) Regulations 1984, SI 1984/1230.
70   PA 1998, s 1.

The Secretary of State has powers to grant licences to persons to search and bore for and get petroleum in seaward or landward areas. The detail relating to applications for licences is set out in delegated legislation.[71] Any person may apply in writing for a licence and applications may be invited or non-invited. Fees are required to be paid in respect of applications for production or exploration licences. Where a licence is granted, it will normally contain prescribed model clauses. A person may make multiple applications for licences or hold more than one licence at the same time.

Submarine pipelines are dealt with in PA 1998, Part III. By virtue of s 14, no person shall execute in, under or over any controlled waters[72] any works for the construction of a pipeline, or use pipelines in such controlled waters, unless authorised by the Secretary of State. For the purposes of PA 1998, Part III, 'pipeline' is defined by s 26 of the Act as a pipe or system of pipes, excluding drains or sewers, for the conveyance of any thing, together with associated ancillary works and apparatus. The authorisation procedure is found in PA 1998, s 15 and Schedule. Authorisation may only be granted to bodies corporate. The procedure allows the Secretary of Sate to further consider authorisation applications or to reject them, in each case after giving reasons for the decision to the applicant. Applications to be considered further must be advertised, and representations in connection with them may be made. During authorisation periods the Secretary of State may notify the applicant, and other persons likely to be affected, that the proposed route of the pipeline ought to be altered for the purposes of, inter alia, avoiding or reducing danger to navigation or to marine flora or fauna or avoiding or reducing interference with fishing or the exploitation of mineral resources. An opportunity must be given to make representations in response.

When consideration is concluded, the Secretary of State may decide to issue an authorisation. This may contain such terms as the Secretary of State considers appropriate. It may, for example, contain terms relating to routing, design, capacity, steps to be taken to avoid or reduce interference with fishing, etc, material to be conveyed, meeting contingent liabilities for damage attributable to releases or escapes, mode of operation, etc. Under PA 1998, s 18, an authorisation may be terminated in accordance with its own terms, by agreement, or by the Secretary of State serving notice on its holder that, inter alia, a term of the authorisation has been contravened. Before terminating for breach, however, the Secretary of State must give the holder an opportunity of making written representations and must take them into account. A termination notice is not to be served where the Secretary of State considers, having regard to the nature and consequences of the contravention, that it would be unreasonable to terminate and that the holder has taken adequate preventative steps for the future.

It is an offence to contravene any provision of PA 1998, s 14 and the Secretary of State may require the removal of any works executed in contravention of any such provision.[73]

Sand and gravel extraction

Sand and gravel are regularly extracted from UK coastal waters, as is marl for fertiliser. Such dredging is licensed by the Crown Estates Commissioners. The Crown, prima

---

71   See the Petroleum (Production) (Seaward Areas) Regulations 1988, SI 1988/1213 (as amended by SI 1992/2378, SI 1995/1435 and SI 1996/2946) and the Petroleum (Production) (Landward Areas) Regulations 1995, SI 1995/1436.

72   Defined to mean the territorial sea adjacent to the UK and the sea in any area designated under the Continental Shelf Act 1964, s 1(7).

73   See PA 1998, ss 21 and 22.

facie, has prerogative rights over arms of the sea, publicly navigable rivers, and the foreshores (land between high and low water marks). Foreshore management, etc is generally vested in the Crown Estates Commissioners under the Crown Estate Act 1961, s 1. Under CEA 1961, s 3 they may not sell, lease or otherwise dispose of any land of the Crown Estate, or any right or privilege over or in relation to such land, except for the best consideration reasonably obtainable. In practice, before the Commissioners licence sand and gravel dredging they consult appropriate bodies such as English Nature and the Department of the Environment, Food and Rural Affairs to obtain a 'government view'. Removal of shingle and sand from the area between high and low water marks can only, as a general rule, take place under licence.[74]

Planning permission is not generally required for removing sand and gravel from the seabed *below* low water mark in an area *outside* the jurisdiction of the local planning authority. Most current extraction sites are between seven to twenty miles offshore. Restrictions on rights to remove materials from the sea may, however, be imposed under the Coast Protection Act 1949.[75]

D MARINE NATURE RESERVES

Under the Wildlife and Countryside Act 1981, ss 36 and 37 English Nature, etc, have power to make applications to the Secretary of State concerning land covered by tidal or sea waters in or adjacent to the UK or its territorial waters. If it appears expedient to the Secretary of State that such land should be managed by the appropriate Council so as to conserve marine flora, fauna, geological or physiological features of special interest, or to provide special opportunities for studying and researching such matters, he may, by order, designate the land and its waters as a marine nature reserve. Before making such an order he must under WCA 1981, Sch 12: consult with appropriate persons; prepare a draft order, giving notice that he proposes to make it and stating its general effect, naming a place in the relevant locality where it may be inspected, and specifying a period of at least 28 days during which representations or objections may be made.

The Secretary of State's proposal must be published in the London Gazette and in at least one local newspaper, and must be served on persons having interests in affected land, relevant authorities for the area and other prescribed or appropriate bodies including the Agency and relevant water and sewerage undertakers. His proposal must also be displayed locally. An unopposed order may be confirmed with or without modification. Opposed orders must be made subject to a hearing or local inquiry, at which representations heard must be considered before the order is made, with or without modification.

After making the order the Secretary of State must, as soon as practicable, give further notice describing its effect and stating its date of commencement, naming a place in the locality where the order can be inspected freely, and where copies may be obtained at reasonable cost. Notice must be served on those who were served with notice of the initial proposal, etc. Proceedings over the legality of orders must be commenced within 42 days of publication of notice of the effect and commencement of the order.

74   See further chapter 13 above.
75   For disposal of radioactive material at sea, see chapter 14 above.

Byelaws

English Nature may, under WCA 1981, s 37, with the consent of the Secretary of State, make byelaws to protect marine nature reserves and their contents against entry, disturbance, destruction, molestation, removal or pollution by rubbish deposition. Applications by English Nature under WCA 1981, s 36 must be accompanied by a copy of byelaws proposed for the reserve. An order made under s 36 authorises the making of the proposed byelaws without need for further central consent. Byelaws may provide for permits to enter reserves, but may not prohibit or restrict rights of passage of vessels other than pleasure boats, nor prohibit exercise of such rights by pleasure boats except with respect to particular parts of the reserve at particular times of the year. Nothing in the byelaws may make unlawful: anything done for securing vessel safety, or to prevent damage to any vessel or cargo, or to save life; discharging any substance from a vessel; or anything done more than 30m below the seabed. Under WCA 1981, s 36(6) nothing under s 36 or byelaws made under s 37, is to interfere with the function of a relevant authority (which includes local authorities, water authorities, harbour authorities, etc), nor any functions conferred by an enactment or any right of any person. The marine nature reserve powers are seriously limited by these exceptions.

Further reading

BOOKS

Bates, JH, *United Kingdom Marine Pollution Law* (1985) Lloyd's of London Press Ltd.
Birnie, P, and Boyle, A, *International Law and the Environment* (1992) OUP.
Birnie, P, and Boyle, A, *Basic Documents on International Law and the Environment* (1995) OUP.
Howarth, W, and McGillivray, D, *Water Pollution and Water Quality Law* (2001) Shaw and Sons.
Saetevik, S, *Environmental Co-operation Between The North Sea States* (1988) Belhaven.

JOURNALS

Birnie, P, 'Are twentieth century marine conservation Conventions adaptable to twentieth century goals and principles?' (1997) 12 IJMCL 488.
Coenen, R, 'Dumping of waste at sea: adoption of the 1996 Protocol to the London Covention 1972' (1997) 6 RECIEL 54.
De La Fayette, L, 'The London Convention 1972: preparing for the future' (1998) 13 IJMCL 515.
De La Fayette, L, 'The Marine Environment Protection Committee: the conjunction of the law of the sea and international environmental law' (2001) 16 IJMCL 155.
Dzidzornu, DM, 'Four principles in marine environment protection — a comparative analysis' (1998) 29 OD and IL 91.
Forster, M, 'The Third International Conference on the North Sea: International Concerns and Domestic Solutions' [1990] LMELR 12.
Gaskell, N, 'Oil pollution and the IOPC Funds 1971 and 1992' (1999) 6 Int ML 177.
Kirk, EA, 'OSPAR decision 98/3 and the dumping of offshore installations' (1999) 48 ICLQ 458.
Lomas, O, 'The Prosecution of Marine Oil Pollution Offences and the Practice of Insuring against Fines' [1989] 1 JEL 48.

OFFICIAL REPORTS
'Safer Ships Cleaner Seas', Cm 2560 and the government's response, (CM 2766), HMSO.
'Third International Conference on the Protection of the North Sea, UK Guidance Note on the Ministerial Declaration', DoE 1990.

Chapter 20

Riverine pollution

The pollution of inland and coastal waters can have a catastrophic effect on the aquatic environment which includes the flora and fauna which are dependent upon an unpolluted water source. Given the central role that water plays in sustaining human, animal and plant life and that the pollution of water is a widespread phenomenon,[1] it is imperative that every possible step is taken to ensure a high level of water quality for both the present and future generations. In this chapter, therefore, we will consider the existing legal controls in respect of water pollution and water quality both at the national and the EC level. There is, of course, a marked contrast between the ancestry of such controls. It has been stated by one leading commentator that 'Community water policy and law is about 25 years old'[2] whereas other distinguished commentators have noted that 'England and Wales have a remarkably long history of water pollution legislation'.[3] Nevertheless the comparative youth of EC water law and policy ought not to be allowed to cloud the fact that it has had and will continue to have[4] a profound effect upon the formulation and development of policy and legislation at the national level. Accordingly it is to the EC Water Directives that we must first turn our attention.

A EC WATER DIRECTIVES

Mention of the EC prompts discussion of the 'European' aspect of water protection. The chosen vehicle, historically, for action has been the directive (see also chapter 4), but there is evidence that both the Commission, through failure to monitor implementation, and the member states, through tardy action, have not 'pushed' the aquatic protection measures adequately, even though water protection is the oldest sector of EC environmental policies.[5] The list of failures include: not applying the

---

1   In 1999, 14,374 reports of environmental pollution were substantiated as having an impact on the water environment by the Environment Agency: see *Water Pollution Incidents in England and Wales 1999*, p 2. It should be noted, however, that this figure represents a decrease of approximately 20% on the previous year.
2   See Kramer, *EC Environmental Law* 4th edn para 7–01.
3   See Howarth and McGillivray, *Water Pollution and Water Quality Law*, para 2.1.
4   See, for example, the Water Framework Directive 2000/60 discussed further below.
5   See further Kramer *EC Environmental Law*, chapter 7.

Surface Water for Abstraction of Drinking Water Directive (75/440) in full, likewise the Drinking Water Quality Directive (80/778); not applying the Bathing Water Directive (76/160) to a sufficient number of beaches; not designating waters for the purposes of the Water Supporting Fish Life and Shellfish Waters Directives (78/659 and 79/923); and failing to fully implement the Nitrate Directive (91/676). The problem is compounded by differences of opinion as to the form of certain water protection standards, whether water quality objectives should be the chosen form as opposed to maximum limits for discharges.

The Water Directives are a package of measures having the *general* aim of preventing polluting discharges into water and *specific* objectives of providing quality standards or objectives for particular types of water, though it may be that the distinction between quality objectives and fixed limit standards may disappear over time with attempts made to apply the best features of both systems.[6] There are certain features which the directives tend, however, to share:

1   The use of 'I' (imperative) and 'G' (guide) lists whereby member states may not set water standards less strict than 'I' and should aim to observe 'G'.
2   There is sometimes discretion vested in states as to which waters shall be designated for the purposes of directives — this is a weakness for it enables states to evade responsibilities.
3   Compliance with directives is not to lead to any degradation in the quality of relevant waters, ie a 'standstill' rule applies, though derogations may exceptionally be allowed.
4   Competent authorities' in each state are required for the purposes of sampling, analysing and inspecting waters.
5   Provision is made to adapt directives to technical progress (see further below).

The Dangerous Substances Directive

Directive 76/464 'The Dangerous Substances Directive', is a *framework* to bring about the *elimination* of certain types of pollution and the *reduction* of other types, with daughter directives setting the standards for individual substances. It relates to virtually *all* the EC's aquatic environment. The directive was designed to further, inter alia, the provisions of the 1974 Paris Convention on the prevention of marine pollution from land based sources (see above) and hence it has two 'lists' (I and II) of substances, those from which pollution is to be eliminated and those from which it is to be reduced; unfortunately the Directive's lists are not absolutely identical with those of the Convention.

List I (the 'black' list) is of individual substances which belong to certain families and groups of substances whose toxicity, persistence and bio-accumulation make it desirable that they should be eliminated; they are organohalogen, organophosphorus and organotin compounds, proved carcinogens, mercury and cadmium and their compounds, persistent mineral oils and hydrocarbons and persistent synthetic substances. The elimination of pollution by List I substances is to be brought about primarily by the setting of limit values by daughter directives.[7] List II (the 'grey' list) contains families and groups of substances which have a deleterious effect on the aquatic environment, but which can be confined to a given area and which depend on the characterisation and location of the receiving water, such as metals, metalloids and their compounds, *including* zinc, chromium, lead, arsenic, antimony, beryllium, uranium,

6   See further Howarth and McGillivray, *Water Pollution and Water Quality Law*, chapter 5.
7   See further below.

cobalt, thallium and tellurium, biocides not appearing in List I, substances having a deleterious effect on the taste/smell of products derived for human consumption from the aquatic environment, toxic/persistent organic compounds of silicon, inorganic compounds of phosphorous, non-persistent mineral oils, cyanides and fluorides and substances having an adverse effect on oxygen balance. Also included in List II are all List I substances for which limit values have not yet been set.

It took some years for work to begin to produce such results in the setting of the specific standards for List I substances by daughter directives, but note the following: 82/176 and 84/156 — mercury and its compounds; 83/513 — cadmium and its compounds; 84/49 — hexachlorocyclohexane, 86/280 — carbon tetrachloride, DDT and pentachlorophenol, 88/347 — aldrin, dieldrin, endrin, isodrin, hexachlorobenzene, hexachlorobutadiene and chloroform. Note also the further amendments by Directive 90/415 relating to 1,2 — dichloroethane, trichloroethylene, perchlorethylene and trichlorobenzene.

Discharges[8] liable to contain List I substances require prior authorisation by a 'competent authority' within a state. Such an authorisation must be time limited and must generally lay down emission standards concerning quantities and concentrations of material. The individual standards, which are *minimum* Community wide limit values, are contained in daughter Directives and are set taking account of toxicity, persistence and bioaccumability, and the best technical means available to eliminate/reduce pollution. However, as a 'parallel' quality objectives may be set, and a member state may follow this latter system of regulation *provided* the Commission can be convinced by monitoring procedures that the quality objectives are met and maintained. The UK prefers the quality objective approach, other member states prefer limit values.

List II substances also require prior authorisation before discharge, and are subject to programmes whereby member states reduce pollution according to timetables whereunder emission standards for List II substances will be applied based on *quality objectives* for relevant waters drawn up in accordance with national standards or, where appropriate, other existing relevant Directives.

The Groundwater Directive

Paralleling the Dangerous Substances Directive is the Groundwater Directive, 80/68, which is designed to prevent, reduce or eliminate pollution of groundwater arising from 'families and groups of substances'. 'Groundwater' is defined as that below the ground surface in the saturation zone and in direct contact with the ground or subsoil. 'Pollution' of such water is defined in terms of the discharge into it directly or indirectly of substances resulting in dangers to human health, water supplies, or harm to living resources or aquatic ecosystems, or interferences with legitimate uses of water. The directive's pattern is similar to that on dangerous substances, with List I (black) and List II (grey), but the lists are not identical as between the directives, though they are very similar. For example cyanides are List I in the Groundwater Directive and List II in that on Dangerous Substances. The directive exempts from cover discharges of domestic effluent from isolated dwellings, also those where relevant substances are in innocuous quantities and those with radioactive substances.

Black list substances are to be prohibited from 'direct' discharge into ground water, while 'indirect' discharge (ie by percolation) must be subject to investigation before

8 As to the meaning of 'discharge', see the Directive, Art 1(2)(d) and the Court of Justice decisions in Case C-232/97 *L Nederhoff & Zn v Dijkgraaf en Hoohheemraden van het Hoogheemraadschap Rijnland* [1999] ECR I-6385 and Case C-231/97 *AML van Rooij v Dagelijks bestuur van het Waterschap de Dommel* [1999] ECR I-6355.

authorisation. Grey list substances must also undergo prior investigation before either direct or indirect discharge can be authorised. Authorisations are to be granted for limited periods and must be subject to four yearly review, and must specify place and method of discharge, maximum permissible quantities, precautionary and monitoring measures. For the purposes of implementing Directive 80/68, the Waste Management Licensing Regulations SI 1994/1056, reg 15 provides that the investigation process involves the consideration of a number of factors including an examination of the hydrogeological conditions of the relevant area, and, a determination of whether the discharge of List I or II Substances into groundwater is a satisfactory solution for the environment. The regulation further provides that authorities, ie the Agency are required to review all current waste management licences in the light of the Groundwater Directive and vary or revoke them where necessary.

On 20 February 1995, the Council passed a resolution[9] expressing concern at the fact that groundwater resources in certain areas 'remain endangered, both qualitatively and quantitatively'. An earlier resolution (25 February 1992) had called upon the Commission to submit a detailed action programme for groundwater protection and to draft a proposal for the revision of the Groundwater Directive. The resultant Groundwater Action Programme, with its emphasis upon action at member state level, would have necessitated the revision of the Groundwater Directive. However, such changes have now been superseded by the adoption of the Water Framework Directive which will, in due course, repeal the Groundwater Directive and make provision itself for the protection of groundwater.[10]

Other EC directives concern themselves with particular aquatic environmental issues, eg the quality of particular waters for stated purposes, and certain substances that find their way into water.

The Surface Water Directive

Directive 75/440 is concerned with the quality of surface water whence drinking water may be abstracted and is intended to ensure that standards are met and appropriate treatment given before the water in question is supplied to the public. The directive, however, goes beyond simple public health requirements and is designed to secure the progressive improvement of relevant surface waters, see Art 4. These waters are required to be classified (A1, A2, A3) by quality, which is determined according to the complexity and type of measures needed to produce drinking water from the surface water. Member states are bound to ensure that such relevant waters do not fall below the standards set in the directive, some of which are mandatory ('I' values) while others — the 'G' values — are *guidelines* which *should* be respected. Further requirements on sampling surface water for drinking were laid down in 79/869.

The Bathing Water Directive

Directive 76/160 is concerned also with public health and environmental quality in its application to bathing waters, ie those fresh or sea waters in 'which bathing is either explicitly authorised ... or is not prohibited and is traditionally practised by large numbers of bathers', and the object is to protect the quality of such waters by laying down micro-biological (particularly with regard to sewage) and physio-chemical characteristics

9   1995 OJ, C49/1.
10   See further below.

to which they should conform. Member states are required to set standards for their bathing waters — the date for implementation was 1985 — and must send regular reports on such waters to the Commission. Again a set of 'I' and 'G' values is utilised by the directive to lay down minimum requirements and desirable targets. Regular and frequent sampling is also required of bathing waters and they are generally deemed to satisfy requirements if samples meet test parameters for the quality of the water in 95% of samples ('I' values) and 90% of samples ('G' values).

In *EC Commission v United Kingdom*: C-56/90,[11] the European Commission brought an Art 169 (now Art 226) action against the UK for its failure to take all the necessary measures to ensure that the quality of bathing waters at Blackpool, Southport and Formby conformed with the limit values set out in Directive 76/160. On 31 December 1985, the date for implementation of the directive, the UK had designated only 27 resorts as bathing waters within the meaning of the directive. This figure, which did not include Blackpool, Southport or Formby, was later revised so that from 2 February 1987, 389 bathing waters were identified for the purposes of the directive, this time including the three resorts. In response to the Commission's application, the UK advanced a number of grounds in its defence, including the argument that the definition of bathing water in the Directive, Art 1(2)(a) was too imprecise to identify adequately those bathing waters that fell within the scope of the directive. The relevant article defined 'bathing water' to include waters in which 'bathing is not prohibited and is traditionally practised by a large number of bathers'. In what was claimed to be an attempt to clarify matters, the UK had decided to adopt additional criteria to help identify the relevant bathing waters. Such criteria took account of, inter alia, the number of bathers using the bathing waters. The UK's arguments, including that relating to the vague nature of the definition of 'bathing water' were ultimately rejected by the European Court of Justice. The court declared, inter alia, that it would frustrate the underlying objectives of the directive if bathing waters could be excluded from the scope of the provision solely on the basis that the number of bathers was below a specified numerical threshold. Accordingly, the UK was held to have failed to fulfil its obligation under the EC Treaty by not taking all the necessary measures to implement the Bathing Water Directive.

Further doubts were cast on the UK's proper implementation of the Bathing Water Directive during the course of judicial review proceedings relating to a decision made by the NRA to grant a consent to Welsh Water for the discharge of sewage from the Tenby Headworks, see *R v National Rivers Authority, ex p Moreton*.[12] Whilst the application was ultimately dismissed, in relation to the submission that the UK government and the NRA had decided not to apply the 'I' standard in the directive relating to entero-viruses because of their belief that there were scientific doubts as to its validity, Harrison J observed that: 'All I can say on the evidence before me is that it would appear that they [the government] are not implementing the mandatory virus standard as required by the Directive'. Moreover, although the available evidence was not sufficient to lead to the conclusion that the NRA had decided not to comply with the mandatory virus standard, Harrison J felt that such a possibility could not be discounted.

The Freshwater Fish Waters Directive

Directive 78/659 as amended by Directive 91/692 lays down requirements for setting quality objectives in respect of designated portions of rivers and other fresh waters to

---

11 [1993] Env LR 472.
12 [1996] Env LR 234.

support freshwater fish life. Member states are to designate waters to which the directive applies, and waters may be designated either as 'salmonid' (suitable for salmon and trout) or 'cyprinid' (coarse fish). The directive lays down both 'I' and 'G' values and member states are to create programmes of pollution reduction so that any designated water will comply with the values within a period of five years. At intervals of three years, member states are required to send the Commission a sectoral report informing the Commission of the record of the implementation of this directive and of other pertinent directives. Moreover, the directive further lays down sampling requirements.

The Shellfish Waters Directive

Directive 79/923 makes provision for quality of waters suitable for shellfish growth, ie bivalve and gastropod molluscs. Member states may designate coastal and brackish waters in need of protection or improvement so as to support shellfish. As with the foregoing directive 'I' and 'G' values are specified, together with sampling techniques and frequencies. Programmes of pollution reduction must also be introduced in respect of designated waters.

The Drinking Water Directive

Directive 80/778 is the Drinking Water Directive laying down requirements for water to be drunk or used in cooking, with the exception of natural mineral waters, provision for which is made in Directive 80/777. Though a public health measure it is also concerned with environmental protection, for inexpensive water treatment predicates water sources free of contaminants. Extensive provision is made in the directive, Annexes II and III as to water monitoring and analysis techniques, but it is Annex I which lists the water quality standards. As with many directives both mandatory and guide level standards are provided. In relation to matters subject only to guide level standards member states have discretion as to how to act, but in relation to the other standards, ie Maximum Admissible Concentration, and Minimum Required Concentration, member states must set their own drinking water standards, no less stringent than those of the directive. Provision is, however, made for derogations by directive, Arts 9 and 10 and for delays by Art 20. Article 9 allows for derogations in connection with exceptional meteorological conditions *or* the structure and nature of the ground whence the water supply comes, and in this latter case a long-term derogation can apply. Article 10 allows for short-term derogations in cases of emergency or where there is a constant need to use substandard water while it is not possible to treat it adequately. The Commission may under Art 20 permit a delay to a member state experiencing compliance difficulties. The failure of the water extracted from the Sawston Mill bore hole to comply with the standards laid down in the Drinking Water Directive was the reason why litigation ensured in *Cambridge Water Co v Eastern Counties Leather plc*.[13]

In *EC Commission v United Kingdom*,[14] the European Court of Justice held that the UK had failed, inter alia, properly to implement the Drinking Water Directive within the prescribed time limit and to meet the directive's maximum admissible concentrations for nitrates in 28 supply zones in England. In its defence, the UK had advanced various arguments of a procedural and a substantive nature, but with one exception, the fact that the Commission had failed to prove its case concerning excessive lead levels for

13   [1994] 1 All ER 53.
14   Case C-837/89 [1993] Env LR 299.

17 supply zones in Scotland, all such arguments were rejected by the court. Indeed, the outcome of the case was never really in doubt, particularly since the UK's belated introduction of the directive implementing Water Supply (Water Quality) Regulations 1989 had occurred nearly two years after the first stage of the enforcement procedure required by Art 169 of the EC Treaty — the letter of formal notice — had been completed.

The approach taken by the UK in relation to Directive 80/778 was further at issue in *R v Secretary of State for the Environment, ex p Friends of the Earth Ltd*,[15] where the applicants sought judicial review of a decision by the Secretary of State to accept undertakings, in accordance with the Water Industry Act 1991, s 19(1)(b) from Thames Water and Anglian Water that they would respectively take steps to ensure compliance with Directive 80/778. Friends of the Earth advanced three main arguments. First, that the acceptance of the undertakings did not amount to a sufficient compliance with the primary obligations, to comply with the directive, and the secondary obligations, to comply with the judgment of the European Court of Justice in *EC Commission v United Kingdom*.[16] Secondly, it was argued that the Secretary of State had not approached his duty under Directive 80/778 in the correct manner because instead of using his best endeavours to achieve compliance with directive obligations by taking all practicable steps, he should have been aware that what his duty actually entailed was to achieve a particular result as soon as possible. Thirdly, it was contended that the undertakings were so vague and imprecise that they could not be effectively monitored to ensure compliance or to issue an enforcement notice under the Water Industry Act 1991, s 18 in the event of a breach. These arguments were rejected both at first instance[17] and on appeal.

The Court of Appeal felt that it was clear that considerations of practicability formed part of the equation of what was possible, and there was no principle of either European or domestic law that required a court to ignore practicalities. The Secretary of State's acceptance of the undertakings constituted compliance with the secondary obligation (the ECJ ruling) to remedy the breach of the primary obligation (the failure to comply with the directive) as soon as possible. Moreover, it was apparent in the opinion of the Court of Appeal that the Secretary of State's acceptance of the water companies undertakings by no means precluded a subsequent service of an enforcement notice under WIA 1991, s 18 where it was felt appropriate to do so.

In subsequent infringement proceedings brought by the Commission against the UK government, the European Court of Justice held that the undertakings were incompatible with European law.[18] In seeking to comply with this ruling, the UK government made the Drinking Water (Undertakings) (England and Wales) Regulations 2000[19] which set out the limited circumstances in which an undertaking may be accepted by an enforcement authority. These include, inter alia, being satisfied that the specified remedial steps are being and will be taken as quickly as possible and that there is no potential danger to human health. However, as Howarth and McGillivray have noted, it is questionable whether the government's action has in fact brought about full compliance with the Directive.[20]

A final point to note is that the Drinking Water Directive will be repealed and replaced by Directive 98/83 when the latter measure comes into practical effect on 25 December 2003. Interestingly, the new measure reduces the total number of water quality standards in the original directive, although it does introduce ten new mandatory standards.

---

15 [1996] 1 CMLR 117, CA.
16 Case C-337/89 [1993] Env LR 299.
17 [1995] 7 Admin LR 26.
18 *EC Commission v United Kingdom*: C-340/96 [1999] ECR I-2023.
19 SI 2000/1297.
20 See *Water Pollution and Water Quality Law*, para 4.15.1.

Transposition of the measure into national law had to take place by 25 December 2000. In the UK, this has been achieved by the Water Supply (Water Quality) Regulations 2000.[21]

Detergents Directive

Directives 73/404 and 73/405 as amended by Directives 82/242, 82/243 and 86/94 are concerned, inter alia, with the composition of detergents so as to protect water against impairment of photosynthesis and oxygenation, and to prevent interferences with sewage treatment. To this end detergents must meet a specified standard of biodegradability in their principal constituents, the 'surfactants'.

The Titanium Dioxide Directive

Directives 78/176, 83/29 and 82/883 relate to titanium dioxide. T_1O_2 is used in paint making and waste by-products of its manufacture can pollute water if dumped — the 'red mud' phenomenon. Directive 78/176 (as amended by 83/29) provides for prior authorisation by a 'competent authority' to be required for acts of discharge, dumping storage or injection of T_1O_2 waste products; such authorisation only to be given if the material cannot be more appropriately dealt with, and only after it has been determined by assessment that there will be no deleterious consequences. Further authorisation is required for new T_1O_2 plants and then only after a survey of environmental impact and undertakings being given that the least damaging environmental techniques and materials generally available will be employed. Programmes of reduction of T_1O_2 waste pollution are required and must be notified to the Commission by member states, and regular reports on these and on monitoring of waste pollution must be made. The monitoring requirements themselves are amplified by Directive 82/883. It is a further requirement that the various national T_1O_2 waste reduction programmes should be harmonised and in 1989 the Commission adopted Directive 89/428. Inter alia this prohibited dumping into inland or marine waters of solid waste and certain strong acid waste, and waste from the treatment of such strong acid waste, etc, as from the end of 1989, together with landward discharges of such waste. The legal base chosen for the directive by the Council, Art 130S (now Art 175) became the subject of proceedings before the European Court of Justice in *EC Commission v EC Council*: C-300/89,[22] where it was argued by the Commission that the directive should have been based on Art 100A (now Art 95). It was apparent that the purpose and content of Directive 89/428 demonstrated that it pursued the dual objectives of protection of the environment and the improvement of conditions of competition. Nevertheless since Arts 130S and 100A required different legislative procedures to be followed, 89/428 Directive could not have a dual legal basis. Accordingly, the court held that the appropriate legal basis for Directive 89/429 was Art 100A since the directive was an environmental measure contributing to the establishment of the internal market. The practical consequence of this decision was the adoption of a reissued measure, Directive 92/112 which has Art 100A as its legal base. Under this new harmonising directive, the time limit for prohibiting dumping of the most polluting forms of waste arising from the manufacture of titanium dioxide was extended to 15 June 1993.

21   SI 2000/3184.
22   [1992] JEL 109.

One commentator has suggested that it is difficult to assess the contribution made by Directive 78/176 to the progressive reduction of the discharge of T_1O_2 waste into sea and coastal waters. In Krämer's opinion, this is because such a development is more attributable to other factors, such as international conventions and the possibility of recycling T_1O_2 waste in the light of technological developments.[23]

The Urban Waste Water Treatment Directive

Directive 91/271 makes requirements in respect of treatment of urban waste water. Where agglomerations of population are high enough for waste water to be collected for treatment, collection systems must be generally in place, according to population size, between 2000 and 2005. Directive 91/271 also lays down treatment standards for such water, and these are strict for areas to be defined as 'sensitive' by member states, according to criteria in Directive 91/271 *including* freshwater estuaries or coastal waters in danger of eutrophication, and surface freshwaters intended for drinking water abstraction in danger of exceeding permitted nitrate levels under Directive 75/440 though they may be relaxed elsewhere. Treated waste water is to be reused wherever possible. Provision was also made for sludge disposal to be allowed only by permit and for sludge disposal to surface waters by pipeline or by dumping from ships to be phased out by the end of 1998. Within 'sensitive areas' locations with populations of over 10,000 were to be subject to strict regulation by 1998. (This was also agreed by the Third North Sea Conference, see above.)

The Water Framework Directive

As is evident from the preamble to the directive, the background to the Water Framework Directive involved the exchange of various communications between the EC institutions. The key event, however, as Howarth and McGillivray have noted, appears to have been a call by the Council and the Environment Committee of the European Parliament in June 1995 for a review of Community water policy and the Commission's subsequent publication of a Communication on Water Policy.[24] The Commission's proposal for a Water Framework Directive was modified on several occasions and it subsequently became apparent that the Council and the Parliament could not agree on a number of issues, such as the mechanisms for controlling hazardous substances under the directive. However, a final text was eventually agreed and the directive entered into force on 22 December 2000.

Directive 2000/60 establishes a framework for the protection of inland surface waters, transitional waters,[25] coastal waters and groundwater. It seeks to prevent the further deterioration of such waters and to enhance the status of aquatic ecosystems, terrestrial ecosystems dependent on water and wetlands directly dependent on aquatic ecosystems. Directive 2000/60 promotes sustainable water use, based on the long-term protection of available water resources. It also seeks to ensure the progressive reduction of the pollution of groundwater, and focuses on mitigating the effects of floods and droughts. The ultimate aim of Directive 2000/60 is to achieve the elimination of priority

---

23 *EC Environmental Law*, para 4–06.
24 COM (96) 59 final. See *Water Pollution and Water Quality Law*, paras 5.7.1 and 5.7.2 for an extended discussion of the background to the directive.
25 These are defined as bodies of surface water in the vicinity of river mouths which are partly saline due to their proximity to coastal waters but which are also influenced by freshwater flows: Directive 2000/60, Art 2(6).

hazardous substances and contribute to achieving concentrations in the marine environment near background values for naturally occurring substances.

The foregoing summary gives some indication of the scope of Directive 2000/60. That scope is such that a practical consequence of the directive will ultimately be the repeal of a number of the EC Water Directives previously considered in this chapter. Those repeals will, however, take place in two stages. With effect from 22 December 2007, the following measures relating to surface waters will be repealed: the Surface Water Directive;[26] Decision 77/795 establishing a common procedure for the exchange of information on the quality of surface freshwater in the Community; and Directive 79/869 concerning the methods of measurement and frequencies of sampling and analysis of surface water intended for the abstraction of drinking water in member states. Thirteen years after the coming into force of Directive 2000/60, the following will be repealed: the Freshwater Fish Waters Directive;[27] the Shellfish Waters Directive;[28] the Groundwater Directive;[29] and, with the exception of Art 6, the Dangerous Substances Directive.[30]

Although the Water Framework Directive may have the outward appearance of a consolidating measure, it does include features which have not previously been part of EC water policy. Thus, for example, the directive adopts the concept of river basin management. 'River basin' is defined to mean the area of land from which all surface run-off flows through a series of streams, rivers and, possibly, lakes into the sea at a single river mouth, estuary or delta. In effect, therefore, Directive 2000/60 seeks to extend the system of river basin management which is currently operated in some EC countries to all the member states. The advantage of such an approach lies in the fact that like pollution, watercourses do not respect national boundaries. By managing such resources on the basis of river basins, therefore, a more appropriate and consistent approach will be applied throughout the EC.

In order to give effect to this new feature of EC water policy, Directive 2000/60, Art 3 places a duty on member states to identify the individual river basins lying within their national territory and assign them to an individual river basin district. Small river basins may be combined with larger river basins or joined with neighbouring small basins to form individual river basin districts where appropriate. Member states are under a further duty to ensure that the appropriate administrative arrangements, including the identification of the competent authority, have been put in place so that the rules of the Directive can be properly applied within each individual river basin district. Where a river basin covers the territory of more than one member state, such member states are under a duty to assign it to an international river basin district. Commission assistance may be sought in this regard. Given the point made previously, that watercourses do not respect national boundaries, it follows that in some cases, a watercourse will flow from an EC member state into a non-member state, or vice versa. Where this happens, Directive 2000/60 imposes a duty on the member state to endeavour to establish appropriate coordination with the relevant non-member state with the aim of achieving the objectives of the Directive throughout the river basin district. The effects of the EC's water policy may therefore be felt beyond the geographical boundaries of the Community.

Directive 2000/60 places further duties on member states in respect of each river basin district or the portion of an international river basin district which is within its territory. Thus a member state is required to undertake: an analysis of its characteristics;

26   Directive 75/440.
27   Directive 78/659.
28   Directive 79/923.
29   Directive 80/68.
30   Directive 76/464.

a review of the impact of human activity on the status of surface waters and on groundwater; and, an economic analysis of water use. All such analyses and reviews are to be carried out in accordance with the technical specifications set out in the Directive Annexes II and III within a period of four years from the date of entry into force of the directive. Thereafter, the analyses and reviews must be updated periodically: see Directive 2000/60, Art 5. Moreover, a member state is under a further duty to produce a river basin management plan for each river basin district within its territory. Any such plan must include the information specified in Directive 2000/60, Annex VII. In the case of an international river basin district extending beyond the boundaries of the Community, member states shall endeavour to produce a single river basin management plan. Where this is not possible, the plan shall at least cover the portion of the international river basin district which lies within the territory of the member state concerned: see Directive 2000/60, Art 13.

In addition to the foregoing, two further innovations in the Water Framework Directive are worthy of note: the recovery of costs for water services; and, the identification of 'priority' substances for further action. The directive Art 9 provides in respect of the former that member states shall take account of the principle of recovery of the costs (including environmental and resource costs) of water services. In so doing, they must have regard to the economic analysis conducted in accordance with Directive 2000/60, Annex III and the 'polluter pays' principle. By 2010, member states are required to ensure that: water-pricing policies provide adequate incentive for users to use water resources efficiently; and that industry, households and agriculture all make adequate contributions to the recovery of costs of water services.

With regard to the identification of 'priority' substances, the directive, Art 16 requires the Commission to produce a list of those substances which present a significant risk to or via the aquatic environment. There is a further requirement to identify priority hazardous substances having regard to those hazardous substances identified in EC legislation. 'Priority' substances shall be identified on the basis of risk assessment or targeted risk-based assessment carried out in accordance with EC legislation.[31] The Commission is required to submit proposals for the control of priority substances which will involve the reduction of discharges, emissions and losses of such substances. In particular, such action will involve the cessation or phasing-out of discharges, emissions and losses of priority substances within a timetable of 20 years or less. Thus the Water Framework Directive will provide the basis for long-term Community action against such substances.

Given some of the time-scales in Directive 2000/60 which have been referred to above, it is apparent that complete implementation of its provisions will take a long time. Quite what this will mean for UK water legislation remains to be seen. Certainly it will be necessary to modify and amend domestic law, where appropriate.[32]

B DOMESTIC CONTROLS OVER FRESH WATER

Common law controls over fresh water are almost exclusively concerned with individual rights.[33] Various statutory provisions have for many years governed the regulation of water. A major restructuring of the law was undertaken in the Water Act 1989 on the privatisation of the water industry but this did not entirely replace all pre-existing

31   See Regulation 793/93, and Directives 91/41 and 98/8 respectively.
32   See the 'First Consultation Paper on the Implementation of the EC Water Framework Directive 2000/60/EC' (March 2001) DEFRA and the National Assembly for Wales discussed further below.
33   See chapter 16 above.

legislation. Furthermore important changes were wrought by the Environmental Protection Act 1990 and it must be stressed that *for those processes and substances regulated by the IPC and IPPC systems the relevant law is now to be found in chapter 16.* The process of consolidation of the water legislation in 1991 has effected yet more change in at least the form of much of the law, whilst the Environment Act 1995 has introduced important substantive changes to this legislative framework.

The Environment Agency is the principal regulatory body with respect to the protection of water and exists under the Environment Act 1995, Part I, Chapter 1, though the Director General of Water Services has general environmental and recreational duties with regard to water under the Water Industry Act 1991, s 3. The Agency has functions with regard to water pollution under the Water Resources Act 1991, Part III, and consideration of these will form the bulk of what is to follow. However the Agency also has functions concerning water resources, droughts, flood defence and land drainage, fisheries and navigation, and a brief mention of some of these is essential as all relate to protection of the aqueous environment.

Water resource management

The Environment Act 1995, s 6 which in part replicates the terms of the Water Resources Act 1991 (WRA 1991), s 19 imposes two general duties on the Environment Agency in respect of their water resource management functions. Under the first such duty, the Agency is required to promote: the conservation and enhancement of the natural beauty and amenity of inland and coastal waters; the conservation of flora and fauna which are dependent on an aquatic environment; and the use of such waters and land for recreational purposes, taking into account the needs of chronically sick or disabled persons. In addition, the Agency has a general duty to conserve, redistribute, augment and secure the proper use of water resources in England and Wales. It should be noted that any discharge of a water resource management function is subject to the principal aim and objectives of the Agency.[34]

Under the WRA 1991, s 20 the Agency has duties to make water resource management schemes with water undertakers for the purpose of conserving, redistributing, augmenting and securing the proper use of water resources in England and Wales. WRA 1991, s 21 further empowers the Agency to submit draft statements to the Secretary of State concerning the minimum acceptable flow of inland waters (ie rivers, streams and water courses both natural and artificial, lakes, ponds or docks, channels, creeks, bays, estuaries and arms of the sea) which are *not* discrete waters (ie lakes, ponds or reservoirs not discharging to other inland waters). Such statements can only follow a publicity exercise under WRA 1991, Sch 5 and a consultation process with relevant water undertakers, drainage boards, harbour and conservancy authorities. The Agency in drawing up the statement must have regard to water flow, to its general environmental duties under the Environment Act 1995, and to any relevant water quality objectives. The minimum flow established must both safeguard public health and meet the requirements of existing lawful uses of the water in question for agriculture, industry, water supply or other purposes. WRA 1991, s 21(7) and Sch 5 empower the Secretary of State to approve statements while WRA 1991, s 22 empowers him to direct the Agency to consider the minimum acceptable flow of an inland water, and s 23 further empowers the Agency to consider the level or volume of inland waters in addition to or in substitution for the flow of inland waters in cases where they are taking action.

---

34   See the Environment Act 1995, s 4 and generally chapter 3 above.

The procedure for dealing with minimum acceptable flow statements is found in WRA 1991, Sch 5. Provision is made for publicity to be given to draft statements, and for relevant bodies and institutions to be served with copies, objections may then be made to the Secretary of State who may approve the draft or amend it as he thinks fit following which it comes into force. Calls for increased use of water conservation powers have become more urgent of late in the light of evidence of low — even no — flows in streams and rivers in some parts of the country — many famed for beauty or fishing. The problem has been compounded by low rainfall rates in some parts of England since 1988 — 20% below average in some cases. This has depleted aquifers. Rivers and bore holes for water have suffered from depleted resources. By the early years of the next century, despite new reservoirs and new wells, demand may outstrip supply, particularly in the south-east, though figures supplied by the old NRA indicate that, nationally, by 2011 supply will, narrowly, exceed demand. This has led bodies such as the Council for the Protection of Rural England, to call for 'demand management' with some form of metering, the introduction of which *could* lead to 10–15% decreases in demand. In addition some abstraction licences may have to be revoked to protect some rivers in danger of drying up.

Licences to abstract water

The WRA 1991, Part II, Chapter II deals with licences to abstract water. Thus WRA 1991, s 24 generally prohibits the abstraction of water from any source of supply save in pursuance of a licence, though, under s 28, this prohibition does not extend to abstraction in the course of land drainage. Licence applications are made, advertised and dealt with according to regulations made under WRA 1991, s 34 and can only be made by qualifying persons, effectively those occupiers who are contiguous to the source of supply. Further provision as to publicity for licence applications are contained in WRA 1991, s 37 of which requires newspaper advertisements and notifications to, inter alia, relevant drainage boards and water undertakers. It is the Agency which determines licence applications according to WRA 1991, s 38; they must take into account any representations received as a result of the publicity process, and must also in exercising their wide discretionary powers consider both existing rights of other persons to abstract water, the need to maintain river flows, whether or not a minimum acceptable flow has been determined (see WRA 1991, ss 39 and 40) and the reasonable requirements of the applicant for water. A licence, if granted, may contain such provisions as the Agency thinks fit. Licence applications may also be called in by the Secretary of State for his determination, see WRA 1991, ss 41 and 42, and appeals to him against Agency decisions may be made under ss 43–45. WRA 1991, ss 46 and 47 make provision as to the form and content of licences in particular specifying the person who has the licence to abstract, for such licences confer a *right* under s 48 to which rights of succession exist under ss 49 and 50, as amended. Licences may be modified or revoked, see WRA 1991, ss 51 to 53. If the Agency proposes such action due notice must be given to the licensee who may object to the Secretary of State who must determine the matter under WRA 1991, ss 54 and 55 taking into account representations made in writing by the Agency and licensee, and, if he so determines, after the holding of a local inquiry. Compensation may be payable by the Agency to a licensee under WRA 1991, s 61 where a licence is modified or revoked and, inter alia, this leads directly to the licensee suffering loss or damage. Decisions of the Secretary of State under the foregoing provisions may only be challenged on a point of law within six weeks of the decision in question being made, see WRA 1991, s 69. It should finally be noted that the Agency has powers under the Environment Act 1995, s 41 to make a scheme providing for charges to be levied in respect of the abstraction of water under licence.

Droughts

The WRA 1991, Part II, Chapter III, makes provision for dealing with droughts by way of: ordinary drought orders; emergency drought orders; and, drought permits.

Ordinary drought orders

WRA 1991, s 73(1) as amended, empowers the Secretary of State to make 'ordinary drought orders' where an exceptional shortage of rain has brought about or threatens a serious deficiency of supplies of water in any area, or, such a deficiency in the flow or level of inland waters that a serious threat is posed to the flora or fauna which are dependent on those waters.

The power to make an ordinary drought order is only exercisable on receipt of an application from the Environment Agency or a water undertaker. Where such an order is made, it may authorise, inter alia, the taking of water, prohibitions on taking water or its use for any purpose and may modify restrictions or obligations concerning the taking or discharge of water.

Emergency drought orders

WRA 1991, s 73(2) empowers the making of 'emergency drought orders' where there is a serious deficiency of supply because of a shortage of rain and the economic or social well being of persons in the affected area is likely to be impaired in consequence. Like ordinary drought orders, the power to make an emergency drought order can only be exercised where an application has been received from the Agency or a water undertaker.

Emergency drought orders may contain any of the provisions to be found in an ordinary drought order. Additionally, they may authorise the supply of water via stand pipes and water tanks.

Making drought orders

Drought orders (ordinary or emergency) are made as statutory instruments. The procedural requirements in connection with their making, eg as to publicity and the making, reception and consideration of objections, are contained in the WRA 1991, Sch 8.

Works, compensation and offences

WRA 1991, s 78 provides that a drought order may authorise the Agency or a water undertaker to carry out any works required in the performance of a duty or the exercise of a power under the order. Where it is necessary to enter and occupy land to carry out the relevant works, authorisation will be contained in the drought order. Compensation is payable by the Agency or a water undertaker to the owners and occupiers of the land, and to all other persons interested or injuriously affected by the entry upon, occupation or use of the land: WRA 1991, s 79 and Sch 9.

WRA 1991, s 80 provides for various offences in respect of drought orders. Thus, for example, it is an offence to take or use water in contravention of a prohibition or limitation imposed by a drought order. It is also an offence to discharge water otherwise than in accordance with a restriction or condition imposed under such an order.

Drought permits

WRA 1991, s 79A[35] provides for a system of drought permits. As with a drought order, a drought permit may be issued where a serious deficiency of water supplies either exists or is threatened due to an exceptional shortage of rain. However, unlike drought orders, the decision whether or not to issue a permit is for the Agency to make following an application from a water undertaker which supplies water to premises in the area concerned. A drought permit may, inter alia, authorise the water undertaker to take water from any source specified in the permit and suspend or modify restrictions or obligations to which the undertaker is subject as respects the taking of water from any source. The permit itself remains extant for a period of up to six months from the date on which it came into force, although the Agency may, by giving notice to the water undertaker, extend the life of the permit for a further specified period provided that the total life span of the permit is no longer than one year from the date on which it first came into force.

The procedural and financial arrangements in respect of drought orders (WRA 1991, Sch 8, s 79 and Sch 9) apply, with appropriate modifications, to drought permits: WRA 1991, s 79A(7) and (9).

Control of pollution

The WRA 1991, s 82 enables the Secretary of State to lay down a scheme of classification of water quality for 'controlled waters' — ie under s 104:
1   Relevant territorial waters, those extending seaward for three miles from specified baselines for England and Wales.
2   Coastal waters, those extending landward from the specified baselines to high tide/freshwater limits.
3   Inland freshwaters, lakes and ponds (natural or artificial and above or below ground) which discharge into rivers and watercourses mediately or immediately together with such rivers and watercourses which are not public sewers nor drains or sewers into a public sewer.
4   Groundwaters, those in underground strata.
The quality criteria may be general requirements as to the purposes for which the waters in question are suitable for application, or may be specific as to substances to be present in/absent from the waters, their concentrations, etc, or as to other characteristics of the water. WRA 1991, s 83 further empowers the Secretary of State to maintain and improve water quality by serving notice on the Environment Agency specifying water quality objectives for waters, and thereafter keeping objectives under five yearly review. Notice of the setting of quality objectives must be given by serving notice on the Agency and giving such other publicity — not less than three months in duration — of the notice as the Secretary of State deems appropriate to ensure those likely to be affected are aware of the proposal. Any representations received in response to the publicity must be taken into account before objectives are fixed/varied as the case may be.

---

35   As inserted by the Environment Act 1995, Sch 22, para 140.

It is WRA 1991, s 83 which provides 'teeth' for maintaining or improving the quality of waters while s 82 simply provides for their classification, hence the difference in administrative procedures. The powers given by WRA 1991, s 82, coupled with the general power under s 102 to make regulations to give effect to EC and international legal obligations, enable compliance with, inter alia, EC requirements as to the quality of surface water intended for drinking water abstraction: see Directive 75/440 above, and see the Surface Waters (Abstraction for Drinking Water) (Classification) Regulations SI 1996/3001) which classifies waters into three bands, DWI, DW2, DW3, according to the presence of specified quantities of named substances in accordance with mandatory directive requirements.[36] See also the Surface Waters (Dangerous Substances) (Classification) Regulations SI 1989/2286 and the Surface Waters (Dangerous Substances) (Classification) Regulations SI 1992/337 which supplement the foregoing 'bands' by three further classifications, DSI, DS2 and DS3 whereby inland and coastal waters are classified as not exceeding stated concentrations of specified substances. Further classifications (DS4 and DS5) have been added by the Surface Waters (Dangerous Substances) (Classification) Regulations SI 1997/2560 and by the Surface Waters (Dangerous Substances) (Classification) Regulations SI 1998/389 (DS6 and DS7).

The power to classify waters by way of regulation under s 82 has been further exercised to make the Surface Waters (River Ecosystem) (Classification) Regulations SI 1994/1057. These regulations classify waters into five bands RE1–RE5 on the basis of sampling results relating to the water's dissolved oxygen saturation, biochemical oxygen demand, ammonia concentration, un-ionised ammonia concentration, ph value, dissolved copper concentration and zinc concentration.

The WRA 1991, s 84 imposes a duty on the Secretary of State and the Agency to use their general water pollution powers so as to achieve water quality objectives set under s 83. The Agency is further required to monitor the extent of pollution in controlled waters and to consult as appropriate with river purification authorities in Scotland.

The 'causing' and 'knowingly permit' offences

The WRA 1991, s 85 is a key provision in the context of the protection of the aqueous environment since it creates a number of offences of causing or knowingly permitting various pollutants to enter waters of various types. Accordingly, it is an offence:

1   To cause or knowingly permit any poisonous, noxious or polluting matter or any solid waste to enter any controlled waters.
2   To cause or knowingly permit any matter, other than trade/sewage effluent, to enter controlled waters by discharge from a drain/sewer where a prohibition has been imposed under WRA 1991, s 86 (see further below).
3   To cause or knowingly permit any trade/sewage effluent to be discharged into any controlled waters or from land in England and Wales through a pipe into the sea beyond the seaward limit of controlled waters.
4   To cause or knowingly permit any trade/sewage effluent in contravention of a s 86 prohibition from a building or fixed plant onto or into any land or into any waters of a lake or pond which are not 'inland' freshwaters.
5   To cause or knowingly permit *any* matter whatever to enter inland freshwaters so as to tend (either alone or in combination with any material) to impede the proper flow of waters so as to lead, or be likely to lead, to a substantial aggravation of pollution otherwise caused or its consequences.

36   This classification was formerly found in the Surface Waters (Classification) Regulations SI 1989/1148, which were revoked by SI 1996/3001.

In the event that one of the above offences has been committed or a person contravenes the conditions of any discharge consent which has been granted, a guilty party may, on summary conviction, be subject to a fine of up to £20,000 and/or three months' imprisonment. Where, however, the conviction is on indictment, the punishment may be an unlimited fine and/or two years' imprisonment.

Words and phrases

Many of the words and phrases used in the statute have no statutory definition, and these have had to be supplied either by the practice of water authorities or from litigation. Thus in the case of *R v Dovermoss Ltd*[37] where the defendant company had been convicted of causing polluting matter, namely slurry, to enter controlled waters contrary to s 85(1), the Court of Appeal was required to consider, inter alia, the meaning of words such as 'noxious' and 'pollute'. 'Noxious' evidently means 'harmful', whilst the Court of Appeal favoured the *Oxford English Dictionary* definition of 'pollute', ie 'to make physically impure, foul or filthy; to dirty, stain, taint, befoul'. Thus it would seem that in the light of *Dovermoss* and the decision of the Crown Court in *National Rivers Authority v Egger (UK) Ltd*,[38] 'polluting matter' denotes material that has the potential for causing harm to organisms rather than material that has actually caused harm. Other 'matter', however, could cover inert material such as cans or bottles whose ability to pollute is primarily visual. Whether or not the matter has in fact polluted controlled waters will of course be a question of fact and degree for the jury. Trade and sewage effluent are, however, defined by WRA 1991, s 221 to mean any effluent discharged from premises used for trade/industry (other than surface water and domestic sewage), and this includes premises wholly or mainly used for agriculture, fish farming or scientific research, while sewage effluent means effluent from the sewage disposal or sewerage works of a sewerage undertaker.

The fact that a phrase has been defined by the statute does not of course preclude judicial consideration of what is actually meant by the phrase. For example, in *Dovermoss*, it was necessary for the Court of Appeal to determine what was meant by 'controlled waters' and 'watercourse' despite the fact that they are defined by WRA 1991, ss 104 and 221 respectively. It was argued on behalf of the appellant company that water is only controlled water while it is flowing in the watercourse; once it is diverted from its normal course as would be the case where it overflowed, it is no longer controlled water. The Court of Appeal rejected this submission. A watercourse such as a ditch does not cease to be a watercourse simply because it is dry at a particular time of the year. Moreover, where water overflowed from a river, stream or ditch, that water remains water of the watercourse.

In *Environment Agency v Brock plc*,[39] the Divisional Court rejected a finding by magistrates that a ditch was not a watercourse because it was man-made rather than naturally occurring. In the opinion of the court, WRA 1991, s 104(3) made it clear that a man-made or artificial watercourse could come within the definition of 'controlled waters'. What mattered, following *Dovermoss*, was whether water flowed through the ditch from time to time.

Whether or not a river bed was part of 'controlled waters' was an issue which the Divisional Court was required to consider in *National Rivers Authority v Biffa Waste Services Ltd*.[40] Here the company had undertaken work on a river which involved the driving of tracked vehicles along the river bed. This operation stirred up mud and silt

37   (1995) 159 JP 448.
38   (1992) Water Law 169.
39   [1998] Env LR 607.
40   [1996] Env LR 227.

from the river bed and thus caused severe discolouration of the water. In the opinion
of the Divisional Court, magistrates had been right to acquit the company where they
had been charged with an offence contrary to WRA 1991, s 85. It was clearly the case
that the draftsman of the WRA 1991 had intended that a river bed was part of controlled
waters, and thus the respondents had not caused anything to enter the watercourse
that was not there already; their actions had merely stirred up matter that was already
present. Whilst there appears to be much sense in the finding that a river bed is part of
the controlled waters, it is a moot point whether the court would have reached the same
conclusion had the river bed contained foreign matter in addition to the natural mud
and silt.[41] Moreover, it is not entirely clear why the defendant company was not charged
with an offence contrary to WRA 1991, s 90 which provides for activities that, inter
alia, disturb the bottom, channel or bed of an island freshwater.

'Cause or knowingly permit'

This phrase is by no means uncommon in environmental statutory provisions. It was
found in the predecessors to WRA 1991, s 85, such as the Rivers (Prevention of
Pollution) Act 1951, s 2(1) and currently is to be found in, inter alia, the Salmon and
Freshwater Fisheries Act 1975, s 4(1) and the Environmental Protection Act 1990, s 33.[42]
In the latter case, however, it should be noted that the phrasing is not exactly the same
since the word 'knowingly' appears prior to the word 'cause'.

'Cause or knowingly permit' has been the subject of interpretation by the courts on
a number of occasions. In *McLeod v Buchanan*,[43] the phrase was interpreted
disjunctively so as to constitute two separate offences. In the context of the water
pollution offences, the House of Lords has heard appeals on three occasions which
suggests, at first glance, that the apparent simplicity of the statutory language has
given rise to greater difficulties than might have been expected.

The causing offence

The leading authority on what the law requires to 'cause' water pollution is the House
of Lords decision in *Alphacell Ltd v Woodward*.[44] The facts of the case need not detain
us greatly; suffice it to say that the appellants were paper manufacturers who operated
a plant on the bank of a river. The process of manufacture gave rise to a polluting effluent
which was to be run into settling tanks and then recycled. Pumps had been installed in
order to prevent the lower tank from overflowing into the river. However, due to a
blockage caused by vegetative material, the pumps failed and a polluting effluent
escaped into the river. The appellants were convicted of causing polluting matter to
enter the river contrary to the Rivers (Prevention of Pollution) Act 1951, s 2(1). On appeal,
the appellants submitted that: they had not caused the pollution; and that they could
not be convicted of the offence in the absence of knowledge or negligence on their
part. The five Law Lords who heard the appeal all agreed that the appeal should be
dismissed. However, since they each delivered a speech in which they set out their

41 For instance, it is alleged that part of the river bed of the Fosse in Yorkshire contains different
    coloured layers that are the result of the production of a popular brand of chocolate
    confectionery. It would be a bold court which held that such a river bed was part of the controlled
    water.
42 See chapter 14.
43 [1940] 2 All ER 179.
44 [1972] AC 824, [1972] 2 All ER 475.

reasons for so holding, it is convenient for present purposes to adopt a summary of their judgment which is taken from the Scottish case of *Lockhart v National Coal Board*.[45] In that case, which concerned an appeal in respect of the Scottish equivalent of the causing offence,[46] the High Court of Justiciary noted that in respect of the causing offence:

1   the prosecution must prove that the accused carried out some active operation or chain of operations the natural consequence of which is that polluted matter entered a stream;
2   knowledge and foreseeability are not matters which require to be proved;
3   a common sense meaning must be given to 'causing';
4   neither negligence nor *mens rea* need be established; and
5   consideration has to be given to such things as natural forces, the act of a third party or an act of God, if the evidence justifies the bringing of such matters into consideration.

In English law, there is a general presumption that *mens rea* is a necessary ingredient of statutory offences. In other words, it is presumed that the prosecution will have to prove that a defendant either intended or was reckless as to the consequences of his actions before he can be found guilty of the offence. However, it is a presumption which may be rebutted 'by the words of the statute creating the offence or by the subject-matter with which it deals'.[47] The absence of words such as 'knowingly' or 'intentionally' before the word 'cause' in WRA 1991, s 85, together with the perception that the offence is quasi-criminal in nature,[48] thus serves to indicate that *mens rea* is not an ingredient of the offence. In other words, as *Alphacell* clearly establishes, causing water pollution is a *strict liability* offence.

The approach adopted by the House of Lords in *Alphacell* has been followed both domestically[49] and in other jurisdictions.[50] However, some confusion in this area arose as a consequence of the Divisional Court decisions in *Price v Cromack*[51] and *Wychavon District Council v National Rivers Authority*.[52]

In the latter case, the council held the sewage agency for the Severn Trent Water Authority, the statutory sewerage undertaker. The effect of this arrangement was that the council undertook, on behalf of the undertaker, the operation, maintenance and repair of sewers, ie they had day-to-day responsibility for the sewage system. The council were charged with an offence under the Water Act 1989, s 107[53] where sewage effluent entered controlled waters as a consequence of an initially undetected blockage in a sewage pipe. At first instance, the council had been convicted by magistrates of the offence. The issue for the Divisional Court was therefore whether it could be said in law that the council had 'caused' the pollution by their failure promptly to discover the source of the polluting discharge and, when once the source had been discovered, their failure to take action to clear the blockage as soon as possible. In purported compliance with the *Alphacell* approach, the Divisional Court found the council not

45   1981 SLT 161.
46   The Rivers (Prevention of Pollution) Act 1951, s 22(1).
47   Per Wright J in *Sherras v De Rutzen* [1895] 1 QB 918.
48   In *Alphacell*, Viscount Dilhorne was of the view that the 1951 legislation dealt with acts which were, to borrow from the words of Wright J in *Sherras v De Rutzen*, 'not criminal in any real sense, but are acts which in the public interest are prohibited under a penalty'.
49   See, for example, *FJH Wrothwell Ltd v Yorkshire Water Authority* [1984] Crim LR 43, and *Southern Water Authority v Pegrum* [1989] Crim LR 442.
50   See, for example, the New South Wales case of *Marjury v Sunbeam Corpn Ltd* (1974) 1 NSWLR 659.
51   [1975] 2 All ER 113, [1975] 1 WLR 988.
52   [1993] 2 All ER 440, [1993] 1 WLR 125.
53   Now WRA 1991, s 85.

guilty of the causing offence on account of the passive nature of its actions. The delay in the detection of the pipe blockage may have been such as to amount to negligence,[54] but it did not constitute a positive act that could be said to have caused the pollution.

The decision in *Wychavon* thus reflected a rather restricted view of what constituted 'causing' with the emphasis placed upon the need for a positive act on the part of a defendant. The same point could also be made in respect of the decision in *National Rivers Authority v Welsh Development Agency*,[55] where the defendants were also held not to have caused pollution despite the fact that they had designed, constructed and maintained a drainage system which carried effluent into a stream.

An opportunity to overrule *Wychavon* arose in *National Rivers Authority v Yorkshire Water Services Ltd*[56] where it was argued, inter alia, that 'the law had taken a wrong turning by insisting on a positive act by the accused as an essential prerequisite for a successful prosecution'. The House of Lords did not take full advantage of the opportunity. Lord Mackay, who gave the judgment of the court, preferred instead to observe that *Wychavon* was a case that turned on its own particular facts. His Lordship did, however, follow these remarks with the observation that in accordance with *Alphacell*, 'the word "cause" is to be used in its ordinary sense in these provisions and it is not right as a matter of law to add further requirements'.[57] It was later suggested by Lord Taylor CJ in *A-G's Reference (No 1 of 1994)*[58] that the 'further requirement' to which Lord Mackay had been alluding was the elevation of a positive act into an essential prerequisite of the offence.

In *A-G's Reference (No 1 of 1994)* itself, the Court of Appeal was faced with three points of law relating to the causing offence which had been referred to it by the Attorney General under the Criminal Justice Act 1972, s 36. Dealing with the first point, the court was of the view that the offence could be committed by *more than one person* where a number of persons performed different and separate acts, all of which either contributed to the polluting matter entering the waters, or without which the matter would not have entered the waters. With regard to the second question, their Lordships felt that a sewage company's acceptance and disposal of polluting water into a watercourse as a consequence of a defective pumping system *did* amount to a chain of operations sufficient to constitute 'causing' for the purposes of the offence. Thirdly and finally, the Court of Appeal held that a failure to properly maintain a sewerage system where a party had undertaken the day-to-day running and maintenance of that system was sufficient to entitle a jury to find a defendant guilty of the causing offence.

It is clear, therefore, that the decisions in *Yorkshire Water* and *A-G's Reference (No 1 of 1994)* do not sit very well with the restricted interpretation given to 'causing' by the Divisional Court in *Wychavon*. Further doubt has been cast upon the correctness of the earlier decision in the most recent WRA 1991, s 85 appeal heard by the House of Lords: *Empress Car Co (Abertillery) Ltd v National Rivers Authority*.[59]

Empress

The appellant company had installed or adopted a large diesel tank in their yard which contained red diesel. The tank was surrounded by a bund to contain any spillages that might occur. Diesel from the tank could be obtained via a tap which was not locked. In

54   [1993] 2 All ER 440 at 448.
55   [1993] Env LR 407.
56   [1995] 1 All ER 225.
57   Ibid at 232.
58   [1995] 2 All ER 1007.
59   [1998] 1 All ER 481.

order to gain easy access to small quantities of diesel, the appellants had affixed a pipe to the tap which then ran into a smaller drum outside the bund. Any spillages from the drum would therefore make their way into the storm drain and thence into a nearby river. On the relevant date, an unknown third party had opened the tap with the result that all the diesel had escaped from the tank. The appellants were tried and convicted by magistrates of the WRA 1991, s 85(1) offence. An appeal to the Divisional Court was unsuccessful, although that court did grant leave to appeal to the House of Lords on the basis that some of the statements in the case law as to what amounts to 'causing' were not easy to reconcile.

In giving the leading judgment, Lord Hoffmann noted that despite the exhortation in *Alphacell* to give the word 'causing' a common sense meaning, magistrates who had adopted such an approach had often found themselves reversed by the Divisional Court for error of law. For Lord Hoffmann, the central question for the purposes of WRA 1991, s 85 is 'Did the defendant cause the pollution'? The answer to this question will determine guilt or innocence. In order to assist magistrates in the future, Lord Hoffmann stated a number of propositions. For present purposes, only the first three need be noted:

1   The prosecution must at an initial stage identify what it is that the defendant is said to have done to cause the pollution. If they are unable to do so, the prosecution must fail: the defendant may have 'knowingly permitted' pollution (see below) but cannot have caused it.

2   The prosecution need not prove that the defendant did something which was the *immediate* cause of the pollution: maintaining tanks etc is doing something, even if the immediate cause of the pollution was lack of maintenance, a natural event or the act of a third party.

3   Once it has been shown that the defendant did so something, magistrates must decide whether it caused the pollution. To say that something else caused the pollution eg like brambles clogging pumps[60] or vandalism by third parties is not inconsistent with the defendant having caused it as well.

As will become apparent (see below), the appeal in *Empress* failed because the vandalism by a third party was not considered sufficient to break the chain of causation between the appellant's acts and the pollution of the river. For present purposes, it is worth noting that in reaching such a conclusion, Lord Hoffmann cast further doubt upon the decisions in *Price v Cromack* and *Wychavon*. In his opinion, both cases took 'far too restrictive a view of the requirement that the defendant must have done something'. Moreover, assuming the necessary causal connection between the defendant's acts and the respective escapes, Lord Hoffmann could not see why the magistrates had not been entitled to hold that the pollution was caused by something which the defendants had done.

Intervening acts of third parties

Given that causation is required to be established under this offence, the intervening act of a third party may amount to a defence for the accused. Thus in *Impress (Worcester) Ltd v Rees*[61] where an unknown third person entered the appellant's unguarded premises at night and opened the gate valve on a fuel oil storage tank with the result that oil escaped into a river, the Divisional Court quashed the appellant's conviction. In its judgment, the intervening act of the unauthorised third party was of so powerful a

60   As in *Alphacell*.
61   [1971] 2 All ER 357.

nature that the conduct of the appellant was not a cause at all, but rather merely part of the surrounding circumstances. Further instances of acts of third parties which have been held to have broken the chain of causation are to be found in *Welsh Water Authority v Williams Motors (Cymdu) Ltd*[62] and *National Rivers Authority v Wright Engineering Co Ltd*.[63] In the latter case, the Divisional Court rejected the NRA's appeal against the magistrates' decision to dismiss an information against the defendant company where a sight gauge on a tank used for storing heating oil had been vandalised with the result that the oil polluted a nearby brook. The defendants thus avoided conviction despite the fact that vandalism had previously taken place at their engineering works because in the opinion of the Divisional Court, the earlier vandalism was 'on a smaller scale and of a different type'. In other words, the vandalism in question had not been foreseeable and therefore could not be said to have been the cause of the pollution.

The decision in *Impress* has, however, now been overruled by the House of Lords in *Empress* and it is highly unlikely that if the facts of *Wright Engineering* arose once again, the case would be decided in the same way. Why is this so? The simple answer lies in the judgment of Lord Hoffmann in *Empress*. In that case, his Lordship sought to dispense with the language of foreseeability, which had been borrowed from the law of tort, and instead advocated a distinction between acts and events which are *normal* or *ordinary* and those which are *abnormal* or *extraordinary*. In his opinion, it was only the latter type of acts or events which could be said to have broken the chain of causation. Thus natural forces which are abnormal and extraordinary will be sufficient to break the chain of causation between a defendant's act and the pollution of water. Similarly a terrorist bomb (an example given by Lord Hoffmann) is likely to be an extraordinary event for the purposes of determining liability for the causing offence. In practice, whether or not an act or event is abnormal or extraordinary will be a question of fact to be determined by magistrates using their common sense and having regard to their own particular area. Applying his distinction to the facts of *Wright Engineering*, Lord Hoffmann was of the opinion that the defendant should have been convicted because although the vandalism in question might not have been foreseeable, it was nevertheless ordinary rather than extraordinary vandalism.

Lord Hoffmann's distinction between ordinary and extraordinary acts or events was central to the determination of the appeal in *Environment Agency v Brock plc*.[64] Here a defective seal on a hose at the respondent's landfill site meant that tip leachate escaped into a ditch whilst it was being emptied from a chimney. Before the magistrates, the respondents were acquitted of having committed the WRA 1991, s 85 offence. However, on appeal, the Divisional Court held that had the magistrates applied Lord Hoffmann's distinction, they would have concluded that the failure of the seal amounted to an ordinary fact of life. Although a defective seal was a rare occurrence, it was also an ordinary occurrence and hence was not sufficient to break the chain of causation between the respondent's acts and the pollution of the ditch.

Vicarious liability

An important issue in the present context is whether a company may be vicariously liable for those acts or omissions of its employees which result in the pollution of controlled waters contrary to WRA 1991, s 85. In *National Rivers Authority v Alfred McAlpine Homes East Ltd*,[65] the Divisional Court held that a company could be

62   (1988) Times, 5 December.
63   [1994] 4 All ER 281.
64   [1998] Env LR 607.
65   [1994] 4 All ER 286.

criminally liable in such circumstances. For such liability to arise, it is not necessary for those in the company's head office to play a direct part in the events that give rise to the polluting incident. It is enough that those with immediate responsibility on the site were employees of the company and that they were acting within the course and scope of their employment at the relevant time.

The knowingly permit offence

This offence has rarely been considered by the courts in the context of water pollution. It involves a failure to prevent pollution occurring together with actual knowledge of that failure.[66] Accordingly, where a defendant stands by and allows effluent or some other polluting matter to pass over his land into a watercourse and he does nothing to prevent it happening, it would seem that he is guilty of the 'knowingly permit' offence.[67] However, convictions for this offence are not numerous, perhaps in part because the prosecuting authorities have sometimes charged a defendant with the causing offence when a knowingly permit charge would have been more appropriate. This view has been cautiously expressed by the judiciary on several occasions[68] and it serves to highlight the care that needs to be taken when framing the charge.

In the leading case on the 'knowingly permit' offence, *Schulman's Inc v National Rivers Authority,*[69] the Divisional Court directed that the appellants should be acquitted of both charges of 'knowingly permitting' contrary to the Water Act 1989, s 107(1)(a) and the Salmon and Freshwater Fisheries Act 1975, s 4(1). The acquittal was on the basis that there was no finding, and for that matter no evidence that the appellants could have prevented the escape of fuel oil from a tank on their premises into a nearby brook sooner than they did, or that there was an escape at any time that they could have prevented but failed to prevent. This latter point emphasises an important feature of the knowingly permit offence, that there is a defence to such a charge where it was not within the defendant's power to prevent polluting matter from entering controlled waters. It would seem that for the defendant to have been found guilty of either of the knowingly permit offences in the instant case, it would have been necessary for the prosecution to prove that the company knew that: a substantial spillage of fuel oil had occurred on their premises; fuel oil from the spillage had entered their drainage system; the drainage system discharged into the brook; and, unless the drainage system was attended to, fuel oil would soon enter the brook from the drain. Furthermore, for a successful conviction on a charge under the Salmon and Freshwater Fisheries Act, s 4(1) it would also have been necessary to establish that the defendant knew the extent of the contamination that had taken place.

A final point of interest to arise from the *Schulmans* case relates to the issue of constructive knowledge. Where a defendant refrains from giving evidence of the absence of knowledge, the decision in *Schulmans* confirms that a court is entitled to infer that they had the required knowledge.[70] It remains to be seen to what extent this principle will be applied in practice since, in theory at least, it may be sufficient for all or any of the elements of knowledge that the prosecution are required to establish as outlined above.

---

66 See *Alphacell Ltd v Woodward* [1972] 2 All ER 475 at 479.
67 Ibid at 491.
68 See, for example, *Price v Cromack* [1975] 2 All ER 113 at 119; and *Wychavon District Council v National Rivers Authority* [1993] 2 All ER 440 at 448.
69 [1993] Env LR D1.
70 See *Westminster City Council v Croyalgrange Ltd* [1986] 2 All ER 353.

Prohibition of discharge

Much can depend upon whether a discharge of effluent, etc, has been prohibited. WRA 1991, s 86 provides that discharge is prohibited if:

1   The Agency has given the discharger notice prohibiting the making or continuing of the discharge.
2   The Agency has given notice prohibiting the discharge save where specific conditions are observed and they are not.
3   The effluent, etc, discharged contains a prescribed substance or prescribed concentration of a substance.
4   The effluent, etc, derives from a prescribed process or from a process which uses prescribed substances, or such substances in prescribed amounts. Regulations may be made to 'flesh out' 'prescribed' substances and concentrations.

In general terms three months' notice, at least, is required for a s 86 prohibition, save that it may be brought into force earlier where the Agency is satisfied there is an emergency justifying early commencement. General exemption from the prohibition provisions of s 86 is given to discharges from vessels.

Discharges into and from public sewers

The WRA 1991, s 87 as amended, applies for the purpose of determining liability under s 85 where a person has discharged *sewage effluent*: into any controlled waters; or into the sea via a pipe. It also applies in respect of a discharge from a sewer or works: on to or into land; or into a lake etc which is not an inland freshwater.

Even where the discharging undertaker did not cause or knowingly permit the discharge from his sewer etc, he shall nevertheless be *deemed* to have caused it if he was *bound* (conditionally or unconditionally) to receive into the sewer etc the matter in the discharge. No offence under WRA 1991, s 85 is committed, however, where the discharge from an undertaker's sewer etc contravenes discharge consent conditions if: the contravention is attributable to a discharge caused or permitted to be made into the sewer by another; and the undertaker either was not bound to receive the discharge, or was so bound but subject to conditions which were broken; and, the undertaker could not reasonably have been expected to prevent the discharge: WRA 1991, s 87(2).

In the event that the discharging undertaker has an agreement with a 'sending undertaker' under WRA 1991, s 110A, and the sewage effluent was, before being discharged from the discharging sewer, discharged into that sewer by the sending undertaker then it is the sending undertaker who is deemed to have caused the discharge: WRA 1991, s 87(1B) and (1C).

The scope of the defence afforded by what is now WRA 1991, s 87(2) was considered by the House of Lords in *National Rivers Authority v Yorkshire Water Services Ltd*[71] (see above). It was argued on behalf of the NRA that the defence only applied where it had been alleged by the prosecution that there had been a contravention of a consent relating to the relevant discharge. This argument had been accepted by the Divisional Court,[72] but in the opinion of their Lordships, the defence did not have such a restricted application. The words used in WRA 1991, s 87(2) were such as to constitute a defence in respect of any allegation of an offence under what is now WRA 1991, s 85. Accordingly, although Yorkshire Water could be said to have caused pollution where iso-octanol was discharged into a river, the fact that the initial discharge of the chemical

71   [1995] 1 All ER 225.
72   [1994] 4 All ER 274.

into a sewer for which they were responsible was by an unknown person meant that they could rely on the statutory defence.

Sampling evidence

Under WRA 1991, s 209 a tripartite sampling regime was established whereby any sample that was taken by the NRA was 'there and then' divided into three parts with each part being placed in a separate container and marked accordingly. One part was then given to the occupier of the land or the owner or master of the vessel, one part was retained by the NRA, and the other sample was submitted for analysis. This procedure inevitably became a matter for the consideration of the courts[73] since if the sampling procedure that was adopted contravened the terms of the statute, it followed that any resultant analyses became inadmissible and the prosecution case consequently became that much harder to prove. In the case of a private prosecution, however, WRA 1991, s 209 did not need to be complied with since the tripartite procedure related only to the analysis of samples taken 'on behalf of the Authority'.

The new regime

WRA 1991, s 209 was almost entirely repealed by the Environment Act 1995, s 111. In its place, s 111 has provided that information obtained pursuant to or by virtue of a condition in a relevant licence is admissible in evidence in legal proceedings against the person subject to the condition or any other person. The information in question includes information which has been provided, obtained or recorded by means of any apparatus. Where apparatus has been used, it will be presumed in any legal proceedings that it is capable of registering or recording accurately, unless the contrary is shown. For the purposes of the EA 1995, s 111, a relevant licence includes an environmental licence (defined in the EA 1995, s 56(1)). Given that waste management licences and discharge consents fall within the definition of 'environmental licence', it is clear that the reform effected by the EA 1995, s 111 has sought to introduce a more consistent approach to the admissibility of scientific evidence in pollution cases. In practice, it means that a defendant may be convicted on the basis of evidence which they have themselves supplied to the Agency in accordance with a licence condition. A defendant who thinks that the way to avoid such an eventuality is to simply fail to record whether a licence condition has been observed will be defeated by the EA 1995, s 111(4). This provides that such a failure is admissible as evidence that the condition has not been observed.

Statutory defences

Defences to the foregoing offences are contained in WRA 1991, ss 88 and 89. Thus no WRA 1991, s 85 offence occurs where the discharging entry occurs or the discharge is made under and in accordance with:
1   Consents given under the Water Resources Act 1991 and its predecessor the Water Act 1989; but note that where consent conditions are breached a separate offence

---

73   See, for example, *R v Rechem Industrial Ltd* (1993) unreported, *Polymeric Treatment Ltd v Walsall Metropolitan Borough Council* [1993] Env LR 427, *R v CPC (UK) Ltd* [1995] Env LR 131 and *A-G's Reference (No 2 of 1994)* [1995] 2 All ER 1000.

occurs each time a discharge in breach occurs: see *Severn-Trent Water Authority v Express Foods Group Ltd*.[74]

2   Permits granted under the Pollution Prevention and Control Act 1999 for the purposes of IPPC.

3   Authorisation given in connection with IPC under Part 1 of the Environmental Protection Act 1990 (see chapter 16).

4   Waste management/disposal licences.

5   Licences granted under the Food and Environment Protection Act 1985 (see above).

6   WRA 1991, s 163 (discharges by the Agency itself in connection with works on reservoirs, wells, boreholes, etc).

7   The Water Industry Act 1991, s 165 (discharges by water undertakers in connection with works on reservoirs, etc).

8   Local statutory provisions.

9   Other prescribed enactments.

Likewise no offence is committed where the discharge is caused, etc, in an emergency in order to avoid danger to life or health, *and* all reasonably mitigating measures are taken, *and* the Agency is furnished with particulars as soon as reasonably practical. In order for the 'emergency' defence to be available, it would seem that the emergency itself must amount to circumstances which are beyond the defendant's control. Accordingly in one particular case where a factory explosion resulted in the escape of chemicals, the court was not prepared to accept that such circumstances fell within the ambit of the defence.[75]

Specific exemptions from liability are given to those who: cause or permit trade/sewage effluent to be discharged from a vessel (WRA 1991, s 89(2); permit water from abandoned mines to enter controlled waters (WRA 1991, s 89(3), see below); or, deposit solid mine/quarry waste on any land so that it falls into inland freshwaters (WRA 1991, s 89(4)). The latter defence is, however, subject to the following provisos: the Agency must have consented to the deposit (see below); no other deposit site was reasonably practicable; and all reasonably practicable steps were taken to prevent the ingress of the material. It should also be noted that the WRA 1991, s 89(4) defence does not apply where the matter is poisonous, noxious or polluting.

Collateral challenge

In *R v Ettrick Trout Co Ltd and Baxter*,[76] the appellants had been charged with contravening the conditions of a trade effluent consent contrary to the Water Act 1989, s 107(6) (now WRA 1991, s 85) where a discharge of fish farm effluent during a 24 hour period greatly exceeded a 10 million gallons condition imposed by the NRA. In their defence, the appellants argued before the Crown Court that the condition as to volume was invalid because it had not been imposed for the permitted purpose of pollution control, but rather, it had been imposed for another purpose, to limit the volume of water which the appellants were permitted to extract. In effect, the appellants were suggesting that since the condition imposed upon them was legally invalid, any breach of such a condition could not amount to an offence. However, in dismissing the appeal, the Court of Appeal held that such a *collateral challenge* represented an attempt to by-pass both judicial review procedures and the statutory appeals procedure, and as

74   (1988) 153 JP 126.

75   *National Rivers Authority v ICI Chemicals and Polymers* (1992) 204 ENDS Report 37; 4 LMELR 131. See also *National Rivers Authority v North West Water* (1992) 208 ENDS Report 40; 4 LMELR 131.

76   [1994] Env LR 165.

such represented an abuse of the process of the court. In part the appellant's case failed on the basis that the evidence which they sought to adduce in support of their arguments was deemed to be inadmissible by the court, but interestingly, the Court of Appeal 'felt unable to say that in no case could the validity of a condition by challenged by way of a defence to a criminal prosecution'.

In reaching its decision in *Ettrick Trout*, the Court of Appeal was influenced by an earlier Divisional Court decision, *Bugg v DPP*[77] in which Woolf LJ (as he then was), had sought to draw a distinction between substantive invalidity and procedural invalidity. The practical importance of the distinction lay in the fact that whilst a criminal court could consider an allegation of substantive invalidity, it could not consider an allegation of procedural invalidity (as in *Ettrick Trout*) which required, inter alia, an investigation into how the impugned decision was reached. Woolf LJ's distinction has, however, since been doubted by the House of Lords in *R v Wicks*[78] and then overruled by the same court in *Boddington v British Transport Police*.[79] In the light of their Lordships' ruling, therefore, there may be circumstances where it is permissible to raise the alleged unlawfulness of a discharge consent condition as a defence to proceedings for its alleged violation. Whether or not such a challenge succeeds will, of course, depend upon the particular facts of the case.

Abandoned mines

As a consequence of an amendment made to WRA 1991, s 89 by the Environment Act 1995, s 60 the defence in relation to an abandoned mine is no longer available to the owner or operator of such a mine where the abandonment of the mine or part of the mine occurs after 31 December 1999. In the event that a mine or part of a mine has become abandoned on two or more occasions, and at least one falls on or before the relevant date and at least one falls after that date, the amended s 89 provides that the mine or part is to be regarded as becoming abandoned after that date.

Further changes to the law relating to abandoned mines were made by the Environment Act 1995. As a consequence of a number of recommendations made by the NRA in its report 'Abandoned Mines and the Water Environment',[80] the Environment Act, s 59 inserted Chapter IIA into the WRA 1991 consisting of ss 91A and 91B. Accordingly, what was considered to be the most unsatisfactory aspect of the law, the absence of a statutory definition of the concept of 'abandonment' in relation to a mine, has been rectified by s 91A where it is stated that the abandonment of a mine includes:

1   The discontinuance of any or all of the operations for the removal of water from the mine.
2   The cessation of working of any relevant seam, vein or vein-system.
3   The cessation of use of any shaft or outlet of the mine.
4   In the case of a mine where activities other than mining activities are carried on, whether or not mining activities are also carried on, abandonment will occur where some or all of those other activities are discontinued and there is a substantial change in the operations for the removal of water from the mine.

This definition of 'abandonment' has limited application. It is for the purposes of Chapter IIA and the notification requirement for those intending to abandon a mine that the term is defined. Therefore, the definition does not apply in relation to the

77   [1993] QB 473.
78   [1998] 2 AC 92.
79   [1999] 2 AC 143.
80   Water Quality Series No 14.

statutory defence under WRA 1991, s 89(3). The phrase 'activities other than mining' has been included in order to ensure that mines which are now used for educational and recreational purposes will fall within the scope of the provisions. In response to another NRA suggestion, where it is proposed to abandon a mine, WRA 1991, s 91B imposes a duty on the operator of the mine to notify the Agency at least six months before the abandonment takes effect. It is an offence to fail to give the required notice. However, by virtue of WRA 1991, s 91B(4), an operator will have a defence if he is able to show that the abandonment happened in an emergency in order to avoid danger to life or health and that notice of the abandonment was given as soon as reasonably practicable after the abandonment happened. The notice itself shall contain such information as is prescribed for the purpose, and it may include information about the operator's opinion as to any consequences of the abandonment. In addition, prescribed particulars of or relating to the notice are required to be published in one or more local newspapers circulating in the locality where the mine is situated. Thus whilst a number of the NRA's recommendations have found their way onto the statute book, WRA 1991, s 91B stops short of giving effect to what was one of its principal recommendations, the imposition of a statutory duty on a mine operator to prepare a complete mine abandonment programme.

Discharge consents

In relation to the water pollution offences much depends upon whether a particular discharge is/is not consented. WRA 1991, Sch 10 as inserted by Sch 22 of the Environment Act 1995, provides for discharge applications and their handling. However, nothing in a *disposal licence* can be treated for discharge offence purposes as authorising: any discharge consisting of matter (other than trade/sewage effluent) entering controlled waters from a drain/sewer in contravention of a s 86 prohibition; *or* any discharge of trade/sewage effluent into any controlled waters or the sea; *or* any discharge on to land or into a lake, etc, which is not an inland freshwater, of trade or sewage effluent in contravention of a s 86 prohibition.

Applications for discharge consents must be made on the form provided for the purpose and must be advertised by or on behalf of the applicant in such manner as may be required by regulations made by the Secretary of State, unless it appears to the Agency that it is appropriate to dispense with the advertising requirement. Furthermore, the Agency may give the applicant notice requiring him to provide it with such information as the Agency may require for the purposes of determining the application.

Where an application has been made for a discharge consent, the Agency is required to give notice of the application, together with a copy of the application, to all those persons prescribed or directed to be consulted in regulations or directions issued by the Secretary of State. Any representations received from consultees within six weeks of the date on which notice of the application was given must be considered by the Agency, as must any representations made by any other persons which also relate to the application. The Agency may decide to grant (conditionally or unconditionally) or refuse the application, and they have in general, four months from the day of the application to make the determination; otherwise it is deemed refused. There is a general discretion as to the imposition of conditions but in particular they may relate to:

1   Times and places of discharge and design of discharge outlets.
2   Nature, origin, composition, temperature, volume, rate, timing of discharges.
3   Steps to be taken to minimise polluting effects.
4   Sampling facilities.
5   Metering facilities.
6   Keeping of records and making returns, etc.

In consequence of representations made to him or of his own motion, the Secretary of State may 'call-in' the application. In such cases the Secretary of State may cause a local inquiry or hearing to be held to consider the issue and must do so if so requested by either the applicant or the Agency. Thereafter the power to determine the application and to impose conditions, etc, belongs to the Secretary of State.

In certain cases where unconsented discharges have taken place the Agency may, where future unconsented discharges are likely, serve notice on the discharger giving consent, subject to any conditions they specify. Such consents must, however, be publicised and any representations received in consequence considered.

The Agency is further under a duty to review consents and conditions, and thereafter they may, by notice, revoke or modify a consent. The Secretary of State may direct the Agency in the exercise of this power either to enable the UK to meet EC or international obligations, or to protect public health or flora and fauna dependent on the aquatic environment. In addition, the Secretary of State may at any time direct the Agency to conduct a general review of consents and conditions that have been granted. The Agency has a particular power to revoke a consent where it appears on review that no relevant discharge has been made at any time during the preceding 12 months. However, the variation and revocation powers are subject to restrictions in that there is, generally, a period of four years from the date of a consent/modification during which changes may not be imposed. It should also be noted that revocation or modification of a consent may involve the Agency in the payment of compensation. The holder of a consent may apply to the Agency, on a form provided for the purpose, for the variation of the consent. Furthermore, the substituted Sch 10 provides for the possibility of the transfer of a consent by a holder to a person who proposes to carry on the discharges in place of the holder, provided that the Agency is notified by the transferor within 21 days of the date of transfer. In the event of the death of a consent holder, the consent is regarded as part of the deceased's personal estate and is thus vested in his personal representatives.

Discharge consents are not free. The EA 1995, ss 41 and 42 enable the Agency to make, subject to publicity, consultation exercises and ministerial approval, schemes of charges. These schemes, which cover initial application fees and ongoing monitoring charges, reflect the Agency's *administrative* costs and are based on costings which reflect the type of pollutants whose discharge is consented, the nature and location of the receiving water, etc. The charges do *not* represent a pollution tax.

Appeals in respect of consents

Under WRA 1991, s 91, where the Agency (otherwise than at the Secretary of State's direction) refuses, inter alia, a discharge consent application, or grants it subject to conditions, or revokes or modifies a consent, the disappointed applicant may appeal to the Secretary of State. An appeal under WRA 1991, s 91 may take the form of a hearing at the request of either party or if the Secretary of State so decides. The person hearing the appeal may decide the extent to which the proceedings will take place in private.

The Secretary of State (or a person acting under EA 1995, s 114) has a wide discretion when determining an WRA 1991, s 91 appeal. He may, of course, affirm the Agency's decision. Where the decision was a refusal to grant a consent or a variation of a consent, he may direct the Agency to grant or vary the consent, as the case may be. Where the decision relates to the conditions attached to a consent, he may quash all or any of them. He also has the power to quash a decision to revoke a consent.

An important practical point to note is the status of any decision made in respect of a consent which is the subject of an appeal under WRA 1991, s 91. Where that decision was to revoke a consent, *or* to modify the conditions of a consent, *or* to impose conditions on a previously unconditional consent, the decision is suspended pending the appeal's final determination or withdrawal (WRA 1991, s 91(2F)). A suspension will not take effect, however, if the Agency is of the view that the decision is necessary to prevent or minimise the entry into controlled waters of any poisonous, noxious or polluting matter or any solid waste matter, *or* harm to human health (WRA 1991, s 91(2G)). The holder or former holder of a consent can challenge the Agency's view and if it is found that that body has acted unreasonably, the suspension of the decision will take effect and the Agency will be liable to compensate the holder of the consent for any loss suffered whilst the decision was in force (WRA 1991, s 91(2H)).

It follows from the above that the suspension of a decision in respect of a discharge consent is only of importance where the consent actually exists. Thus if the Agency has decided not to grant a consent, lodging an appeal against that decision does not mean that the applicant will be entitled to discharge pollutants into a watercourse in the interim.

Deposits and vegetation in rivers

WRA 1991, s 90 creates particular offences in connection with deposits and vegetation in rivers. It is an offence to remove from the bed or channel of an inland freshwater any deposit accumulated by a dam, weir or sluice by causing the deposit to be carried away in suspension by the waters. Likewise to cause or permit a substantial amount of vegetation to be cut or uprooted in inland waters or so near to them that it falls in followed by failure to remove the vegetation is also an offence. Neither offence is committed, however, where the Agency has *consented* to the relevant act.

WRA 1991, s 90A[81] makes provision for applications for consent for the purposes of the defence to a s 85 offence under s 89(4) and the s 90 offences. Any such application must be made on a form provided by the Agency and must be advertised in the prescribed manner. To enable the Agency to determine the application, the applicant must provide it with all such information as it reasonably requires, with such information as is prescribed and, with such further information as the Agency may by notice require. A failure to provide the further information which it has requested entitles the Agency to refuse to proceed with the application.

If the Agency is of the opinion that the holder of a consent for the purposes of WRA 1991, s 89(4) or s 90(1) or (2) or of a *discharge consent* is contravening or is likely to contravene any condition of the consent, it may serve him with an enforcement notice (WRA 1991, s 90B(1)). An enforcement notice must specify the matters constituting the contravention or likely contravention together with the remedial steps to be taken and the period within which such steps are to be completed. Failure to comply with any requirement of an enforcement notice constitutes an offence which may be tried summarily or on indictment. If the Agency is of the opinion that proceedings for an offence under WRA 1991, s 90B(3) would afford an ineffectual remedy, it may seek an injunction in the High Court to ensure compliance with the notice.

Supplementary provisions

There are a number of important supplementary provisions concerning discharge consents. Under WRA 1991, s 99 the Secretary of State has power to make regulations modifying the pollution control provisions with regard to discharge consents required

81   Inserted by the EA 1995, s 120 and Sch 22.

by the Agency itself.[82] Pollution control information together with other information about its functions must be included in the Agency's annual report required under EA 1995, s 52, and s 51 further requires the Agency to supply the Secretary of State with such relevant information as he may reasonably require. More important are the pollution control registers required under WRA 1991, s 190 as amended by the Environment Act 1995, Sch 22, para 169. These registers must be maintained in accordance with regulations made by the Secretary of State,[83] and must contain prescribed particulars of:

1   WRA 1991, s 83 notices of water quality objectives.
2   Applications for consents.
3   Consents given and conditions imposed.
4   Samples, information derived therefrom, and any consequential steps taken.
5   Applications made to the Agency for the variation of discharge consents.
6   Enforcement notices served under WRA 1991, s 90B.
7   Revocations of discharge consents under Sch 10, para 7.
8   Appeals under WRA 1991, s 91.
9   Directions given by the Secretary of State in relation to the Agency's functions under the water pollution provisions of the WRA 1991.
10 Convictions, for offences under the WRA 1991, Part III, of persons who have the benefit of discharge consents.
11 Information obtained/furnished in pursuance of conditions of discharge consents.
12 Works notices, appeals and convictions under ss 161A, 161C and 161D respectively (see below).
13 Such other matters relating to the quality of water or the pollution of water as may be prescribed by the Secretary of State.

In addition to the considerable expansion in matters to be included in the pollution control register effected by the EA 1995, that Act has inserted new ss 191A and 191B which make provision for the exclusion from registers of information affecting national security or information which is of a commercially confidential nature.

These registers must be kept publicly available at reasonable times and copies must be available at reasonable charges. The Agency is under a specific duty in WRA 1991, s 202 to furnish ministers with relevant advice and assistance in connection with their water pollution control functions and ministers and the Agency may serve notice on any person requiring specified information to be given in connection with water pollution control functions, it being an offence not to comply. The Agency and water undertakers are under mutual obligations by virtue of WRA 1991, s 203 to provide information on the quality of any controlled or other waters and concerning any incident in which poisonous, noxious or polluting matter or any solid matter has entered any such waters. However, there is a general restriction on the disclosure of information, under WRA 1991, s 204, obtained under any provision of the 1991 Act which relates to the affairs of any individual or business, though exceptions to this restriction exist, inter alia, in respect of the carrying on of their functions by relevant authorities, or in connection with criminal investigations and proceedings or in pursuance of EC obligations.

The Environment Agency has a general discretion to enforce the provisions of the WRA 1991 relating to water pollution, but note that, under WRA 1991, s 217 where a body corporate is guilty of an offence and it can be proved it was committed with the consent or connivance of, or is attributable to the neglect of, any director, manager, secretary or other similar officer then that person is guilty of the offence along with the

---

82   See also the Control of Pollution (Applications, Appeals and Registers) Regulations 1996, SI 1996/2971, reg 14.
83   See the Control of Pollution (Registers) Regulations 1989, SI 1989/1160.

body corporate. Agency designated officers may be given extensive rights of entry to premises in connection with enforcement of pollution control functions and related matters under the general power of entry which the Agency possesses by virtue of EA 1995, s 108,[84] but note also residual powers under WRA 1991, ss 169 and 172.

Anti-pollution works and operations

WRA 1991, s 161, as amended, gives the Agency a general power to carry out anti-pollution works and operations where it appears that noxious, poisonous or polluting matter or any solid material is likely to enter, or has been present in, any controlled waters. This power is obviously subject to the discharge consent provisions and, as a consequence of new s 161(1A) inserted by EA 1995, Sch 22, para 161 is only exercisable where the Agency considers it necessary to carry out any works or operations forthwith, and, where the Agency has not been able to find, after reasonable inquiry, a person on whom to serve a works notice under WRA 1991, s 161A (see below). The costs of any works which the Agency does undertake may be recovered from the polluter: see WRA 1991, s 161(3).

In *Bruton and National Rivers Authority v Clarke*,[85] the NRA initiated civil proceedings against a farmer in order to recover the costs involved in remedying or mitigating the polluting effects of the discharge of three million gallons of ammonia-saturated slurry into the River Sappiston. The NRA's claim involved the recovery of the costs of various surveys which were undertaken following the polluting incident, the scientific costs that had been incurred in terms of the investigation of the incident by scientists, and, the costs of restocking the river with mature fish and fry. In making an award of some £90,000 to the NRA, Mellor J demonstrated that any claim for costs under WRA 1991, s 161(3) will be closely scrutinised by the courts so that only those costs which can properly be attributed to polluting incidents will be recoverable. The fact that not all the surveys which had been undertaken by the NRA were as a direct result of the polluting incident ensured that not all their costs could be recovered under this head of their claim.

Works notices

The Environment Act 1995 has inserted four new sections into Part VII of the WRA 1991, all of which relate to notices requiring persons to carry out anti-pollution works and operations. The advantage of this new regime to the Agency is that it transfers the burden of carrying out anti-pollution works and operations from the Agency (as it is under WRA 1991, s 161) to the recipient of a works notice. Thus the Agency may avoid the possibility of incurring substantial clean-up costs which it is not subsequently able to recover from the polluter. WRA 1991, s 161A entitles the Agency to serve a works notice on any person who either caused/knowingly permitted any poisonous, noxious or polluting matter or any solid waste matter to be present at a place from which it is likely to enter controlled waters, or caused/knowingly permitted the matter in question to be present in any controlled waters. The 'works notice' may require the person on whom it is served to remove/dispose of the polluting matter, or remedy/mitigate any pollution caused by its presence in the waters, or, so far as is reasonably practicable, to restore the waters and such flora and fauna which is dependent on the aquatic environment of the waters to their state immediately before the polluting matter

84   See chapter 3 above.
85   (1993) unreported, see [1995] Env Liability CS13–14.

became present in the water. Prior to serving a notice on any person, the Agency is required reasonably to endeavour to consult that person concerning the relevant works or operations to be undertaken. Any works notice which is served must specify a time limit for achieving the requirements which it specifies. Continuing the special provision made in respect of an abandoned mine or an abandoned part of a mine which is a feature of the WRA 1991, no works notice is to be served on an owner or former operator who permitted water from such a source to enter controlled waters, provided that the mine or part of a mine became abandoned prior to 31 December 1999.

The Anti-Pollution Works Regulations 1999[86] make further provision with regard to works notices. They stipulate that in the case of a potential pollution incident, a works notice must describe the nature of the risk to controlled waters, identify the controlled waters which may be affected and the place from which the matter in question is likely to enter those waters. Where pollution has already occurred, a works notice must describe the nature and extent of the pollution and identify the controlled waters which have been affected. A works notice must also: specify the works/operations that are required to be carried out by the person on whom the notice is served; give the Agency's reasons for serving the notice on that person and for requiring the works/ operations; inform the recipient of his right of appeal under WRA 1991, s 161C (see below); state that the Agency is entitled to recover the costs that it has reasonably incurred in investigating the matter; and, inform the recipient of the consequences of not complying with a works notice (see WRA 1991, s 161D, below).

WRA 1991, s 161B provides that a works notice may require a person to carry out works or operations in respect of land despite the fact that he is not entitled to carry them out. In order to enable the person on whom the notice has been served to comply with it, any person whose consent is required before such works, etc, may be carried out shall grant those rights in relation to any land or waters and such a person shall be entitled on application to be compensated by the person carrying out the works, etc.

An application for compensation must be made in writing within 12 months of the date of the grant of rights in respect of which the compensation is claimed or, where there is an appeal in respect of the works notice, the date on which the appeal is determined or withdrawn, whichever is the later date.[87] The application itself must contain: a copy of the grant of rights in respect of which the compensation claim is being made; a description of the exact nature of any interest in land in respect of which compensation is being applied for; and, a statement of the amount of compensation applied for. The Anti-Pollution Works Regulations provide that compensation is payable for various forms of loss and damage, such as any depreciation in any relevant interest to which the grantor is entitled which results from the grant of the right.[88]

Appeals against works notices

WRA 1991, s 161C confers a 21-day right of appeal against a works notice on the person to whom it was served. On appeal, the Secretary of State may confirm the notice, with or without modification, or quash it.

Where a notice of appeal is given to the Secretary of State, it must state: the name and address of the appellant (and of all persons to be served with a copy of the notice of appeal); the grounds of the appeal; and whether the appellant wishes the appeal to be determined on the basis of written representations or at a hearing. An appellant must also send a copy of the notice of appeal to the Environment Agency and, where

86   SI 1999/1006.
87   See the Anti-Pollution Works Regulations, SI 1999/1006, Schedule.
88   See the 1999 Regulations, Schedule, para 4.

it is a ground of appeal that the notice ought to have been served on another, to that person. Where the appeal is conducted by way of written representations, the Agency and any party to the appeal other than the appellant have 14 days from the date of the receipt of the notice of appeal to submit their representations. The appellant has a further 14 days to reply to these representations.

Where an appeal is to be determined on the basis of a hearing, the parties must be given 28 days' notice of the date, time and place fixed for the hearing. The appeal may, at the discretion of the person hearing it, be held in public or private. Each party to the hearing is entitled to be heard and the person hearing the appeal may permit other persons to be heard. At the conclusion of the hearing, the person appointed to hear the appeal shall, unless he has the authority to determine the appeal for himself under EA 1995, s 114, make a written report to the Secretary of State setting out his views. A copy of this report will accompany the written notification of the Secretary of State's determination which will be sent to the appellant, the Agency and to every other party to the appeal.

Consequences of not complying with a works order

WRA 1991, s 161D makes it an offence to fail to comply with any of the requirements of a works notice. A summary conviction may result in the imposition of a prison sentence of up to three months or to a fine not exceeding £20,000, or to both. Where a defendant is tried in the Crown Court, he may be liable on conviction to a term of imprisonment not exceeding two years or to a fine, or to both. As was noted earlier, any conviction for a WRA 1991, s 161D(1) offence (or any works notice or appeal against such a notice) will be entered on a pollution control register maintained by the Agency in accordance with the Control of Pollution (Applications, Appeals and Registers) Regulations 1996.[89] On 23 March 2000 the first conviction for an offence contrary to WRA 1991, s 161D occurred when Okehampton Magistrates fined the owner of a residential home £2,000 for failing to carry out any works to prevent the future pollution of a stream which he had previously polluted with an illegal sewage discharge from a septic tank.[90]

Where a person on whom a works notice has been served has failed to comply with any of its requirements, the Agency may do the work required and recover from that person any costs or expenses which it has reasonably incurred. WRA 1991, s 161D(4), which is broadly the same as the EPA 1990, s 81(5) (save that the discretion in that case is conferred upon a local authority), entitles the Agency to take proceedings in the High Court for an injunction to ensure compliance with a works notice where it considers that proceedings for an offence under WRA 1991, s 161D(1) would provide an ineffectual remedy. Such a course of action may be appropriate where, for example, a previous conviction for a WRA 1991, s 161D(1) offence has not deterred a defendant from failing to comply with a works notice.

Environment Agency Policy and Guidance on the use of Anti-Pollution Works Notices

In 1999, the Environment Agency published a policy statement on the use of works notices for the benefit both of Agency staff and those on whom a works notice may be

---

89   SI 1996/2971: see reg 15(p) as inserted by reg 8(2) of the Anti-Pollution Works Regulations 1999.
90   See (2000) 302 ENDS Report 302 at p 48.

served. Its purpose is to provide a clear understanding of the way in which the Agency will proceed and of the sorts of cases of actual or potential pollution for which the Agency considers works notices to be the appropriate enforcement mechanism. The policy statement makes it clear that the use of works notices will reflect the principles which underlie its *Enforcement and Prosecution Policy Statement*,[91] namely proportionality, consistency, transparency and targeting. Moreover, in determining whether or not to serve a works notice in respect of likely or ongoing pollution, the Agency will adopt a risk-based approach and will have regard to its duty under the EA 1995, s 39 to take into account the likely costs and benefits of the exercise or non-exercise of its powers.

Extensive powers to protect water in waterworks from pollution or contamination, including powers to break up and open streets, sewers, drains and tunnels, are also granted to the Agency by the WRA 1991, s 162. The Agency also has power under WRA 1991, s 210 and Sch 25 to make byelaws in connection with its functions under the Act and these it may enforce under s 211.

Enforcement

The Agency's general policy on the prosecution of environmental offenders has already been considered.[92] Accordingly, the discussion in this chapter will be confined to comments upon the Agency's enforcement record in the water sector.

Although, as we have already seen, the various water pollution offences are of the 'strict liability' variety with no *mens rea* required, the Agency possesses 'institutional discretion' both as to the decision to prosecute in any given case and as to the standard of compliance with pollution control provisions which will be sought in the bringing of prosecutions, for it is quite clear that not all incidents of pollution result in prosecution: in 1999 there were 90 Category 1 and 863 Category 2 (see below) related pollution incidents[93] but these only resulted in 230 prosecutions. Since 1989, the Agency (or the NRA as it then was) has adopted an approach whereby pollution incidents are 'banded'. Major incidents are classified as Category 1 and involve one or more of the following: actual or potential persistent effect on the quality of water or aquatic life; closure of a source of potable water; extensive fish kill; major or frequent breach of consent conditions; extensive remedial action needed; significant adverse effect on amenity value; significant adverse effect on site of conservation importance.

Category 1 incidents normally result in prosecution. Category 2 comprises 'significant' polluting incidents and covers situations where: notification to abstractors was needed; there was a significant fish kill; there was a readily observable effect on invertebrate life; water became unfit for stock watering; the bed of a watercourse was contaminated; or the amenity value to downstream owners was reduced by odours or the appearance of the water. Here either a warning will be issued or a prosecution will be undertaken. Category 3 comprises 'minor' incidents resulting in a localised environmental impact only. These are normally dealt with by a warning. The final category, Category 4, is reserved for reported pollution incidents which prove to be unsubstantiated upon investigation.

The pragmatic approach to the question of whether or not to initiate proceedings against a polluter which was formerly adopted by the NRA has also been the hallmark of the Agency's enforcement policy. As is apparent from the figures quoted above,

91   See chapter 3.
92   See chapter 3.
93   See *Water Pollution Incidents in England and Wales 1998,* Table 19, p 33.

there is a wide discrepancy between the number of major or significant pollution incidents and the frequency with which the Agency prosecutes offenders. A number of factors will clearly need to be taken into account when deciding whether or not to bring a prosecution. These may include: the severity of the pollution incident; the past environmental record of the offender; the extent to which the offender has co-operated with the Agency; and the financial resources of the Agency. With regard to the latter, it should not be forgotten that the Agency operates within budgetary constraints and is subject to a cost/benefit duty imposed by the Environment Act 1995, s 39. Accordingly, in practice, the Agency is only likely to bring a prosecution where it considers that there is a good chance of securing a conviction. The available figures suggest that the Agency generally makes the right decision. In 1999, of the 230 prosecutions which were brought in respect of Category 1 and 2 pollution incidents, 227 resulted in a conviction.

Although the burden of enforcing water pollution law generally falls on the Agency, it should be noted that private prosecutions may be brought by individuals, pressure groups or other interested parties such as the Anglers' Conservation Association (formerly the Anglers' Co-operative Association).[94] In practice, however, such prosecutions tend to be rare, even if they are occasionally threatened.[95]

Sentencing

For some time the view has prevailed that those who pollute the aqueous environment have not always been subject to an appropriate level of punishment for their wrongdoing. Despite several high profile cases such as the prosecution of Shell following the pollution of the Mersey by massive oil leaks in 1989 and the imposition of a £1 m fine, the general level of fines imposed on polluters has been relatively low. It will be remembered that the maximum level of fine available to a magistrates' court where a defendant has been found guilty of an offence contrary to the WRA 1991, s 85(6) is £20,000. In practice, however, this statutory maximum was imposed for the first time as recently as 1998.[96] The figures for 1999 show that for all the Agency's eight regions,[97] the range of fines was 0 – £120,000.[98] Since in six of the eight regions the range did not exceed 0 – £15,000, it is not surprising that at the Agency's AGM in September 1998, its Chief Executive condemned fines of a few thousand pounds as no deterrent to multi-million pound companies and made the case for fines to properly reflect the seriousness of the crime.[99]

The maximum fine of £20,000 does not of course apply where a WRA 1991, s 85 prosecution is brought in the Crown Court.[100] This court has the power to impose an unlimited fine in the event of a conviction, hence the £1 m fine imposed on Shell. In another high profile case, *Environment Agency v Milford Haven Port Authority and*

94 See, for example: *Wales v Thames Water Authority* (1987) unreported (Aylesbury JJ); *Greenpeace v Allbright and Wilson* [1991] 3 LMELR 132, 170 and 202; and *R v British Coal Corpn* (1993) unreported.
95 Prior to the prosecution of the Milford Haven Port Authority for the *Sea Empress* oil spillage (see below), Friends of the Earth put the Agency on notice that if it did not prosecute the authority, then Friends of the Earth would.
96 *Water Pollution Incidents in England and Wales 1998*, at para 7.6, p 33.
97 Anglian, Midlands, North East, North West, Southern, South West, Thames and Wales.
98 *Water Pollution Incidents in England and Wales 1999*, Table 19, p 37.
99 *Water Pollution Incidents in England and Wales 1998*, at para 8.4, p 36.
100 The scope for imposing an unlimited fine is reflected in the range of fines awarded in the North West and Southern regions which in 1999, stood at £250 – £120,000 and 0 – £70,000 respectively: see *Water Pollution Incidents in England and Wales 1999*, Table 19, p 37.

Andrews,[101] Steel J imposed the largest ever fine for a pollution incident, £4 m, in respect of the running aground of the *Sea Empress* outside the Port of Milford Haven. In the six days between running aground and being refloated and berthed, the *Sea Empress* lost more than 70,000 tons of crude oil and 500 tones of fuel oil into the sea. A large scale clean-up operation followed and due to this and other factors, such as the type of oil and the prevailing weather conditions, the environmental impact of the spillage proved to be less dire than originally forecast. Nevertheless, the incident had a significant impact upon fishing in the area and upon the sea bird population. Although the Port Authority had pleaded guilty to the WRA 1991, s 85 offence in the Cardiff Crown Court, it subsequently appealed against the level of fine imposed. It argued, inter alia, that Steel J had given inadequate recognition to its relative lack of culpability for a strict liability offence, that it had not been given full credit for its guilty plea, and that the judge had misunderstood the financial position of the Port Authority.

In hearing the appeal, the Court of Appeal was afforded the opportunity to comment upon sentencing proposals for environmental offences drawn up by the Sentencing Advisory Panel. The Panel, which was established under the Crime and Disorder Act 1998, s 81, had published an Advice to the Court of Appeal on 1 March 2000. Although the Advice acknowledged that the imposition of a fine should be the starting point for the sentencing of both *persons* and *companies* for environmental offences, it also considered alternative sentencing options, such as community or custodial sentences and the power of the courts to make compensation and deprivation orders under what is now the Powers of Criminal Courts (Sentencing) Act 2000.[102]

The Court of Appeal had regard to the Advice, as it is obliged to do under statute, but chose not to follow it. Instead, it held that it could not usefully do more than draw attention to the factors relevant to sentence which were identified in *R v F Howe & Son (Engineers) Ltd*,[103] a health and safety case. Thus when imposing a sentence for an environmental offence such as WRA 1991, s 85, a court should have regard to aggravating factors such as: the degree of risk and extent of the danger created by the offence; whether the offence was an isolated incident or continued over a period of time; whether the motivation for breaching the relevant legislation was financial profit; and whether the defendant had failed to heed warnings. Mitigating factors included: a prompt admission of responsibility and a timely plea of guilty; taking remedial steps after they had been drawn to the defendant's attention; and, a good safety record. With these factors in mind, the Court of Appeal concluded that the fine imposed on the Port Authority had been 'manifestly excessive' and therefore substituted a fine of £750,000 for the original figure of £4 m.[104]

Ministerial regulations/directions

Under the WRA 1991, s 92 the Secretary of State has power to make regulations which may prohibit a person from having custody or control of any noxious, poisonous or polluting matter unless prescribed steps are carried out to prevent or control the entry of such material into controlled waters, or for requiring persons having custody or control of such matter to take precautionary and other relevant steps. The detailed application of such regulations may be entrusted to the Agency. Under this power the Control of Pollution (Silage, Slurry and Agricultural Fuel) Regulations SI 1991/324 have

---

101 [1999] 1 Lloyd's Rep 673.
102 See ss 130 and 143, respectively.
103 [1999] 2 All ER 249.
104 See *R v Milford Haven Port Authority* [2000] Env LR 632.

been made.[105] These require persons with custody or control over crops being made into silage, etc, or over certain fuel oils to ensure that controlled waters are not polluted, for example by taking certain steps as to storage and construction of relevant emplacements. The Agency is empowered to require action in certain circumstances, but an appeal against their decision can be made to the Secretary of State. The regulations also require compliance with certain British Standards, eg BS 5502 on buildings and structures for agriculture. Ministers may also, under WRA 1991, s 97 issue and approve codes of good agricultural practice on activities that may affect controlled waters and promote good practices to avoid or minimise pollution. Contravention of such a code is not a criminal offence in itself but the Agency must consider contraventions in relation to, inter alia, the issuing of prohibitions under WRA 1991, s 86.[106]

Ministers also have extensive powers to enable the Agency in the performance of its functions to acquire land compulsorily (WRA 1991, s 154) or to carry out compulsory works (WRA 1991, s 168). In cases of civil emergency, ie situations where in the opinion of the Secretary of State there is such disruption of water or sewerage services in an area, or such destruction of or damage to life or property as to seriously and adversely affect the area's inhabitants, he may, under WRA 1991, s 207 give such directions to the Agency as he considers requisite to mitigate the effects of the emergency. Such a power is exercisable after consultation with the Agency.

Implementing EC obligations

It is also, of course, for the Secretary of State to use his powers under WRA 1991, s 102 and the European Communities Act 1972, s 2 to make regulations to give effect to EC Directives. Thus Directives 73/404, 73/405, 82/242 and 82/243 on the biodegradability and composition of detergents are implemented by the Detergents (Composition) Regulations SI 1978/564 (amended SI 1984/1369 and SI 1986/560). Directive 75/440 on surface waters has been, as already stated, implemented by SI 1996/3001. The Trade Effluents (Prescribed Processes and Substances) Regulations SI 1989/1156 as amended by SI 1990/1629, and the Trade Effluents (Prescribed Substances and Processes) Regulations SI 1992/339 implement the Dangerous Substances Directive 76/464, etc, by listing (the 'Red List') certain prescribed substances (*including* mercury, cadmium, DDT, aldrin, dieldrin, atrazine) and certain prescribed processes whose discharge as trade effluent into sewers is subject to review and prohibition by the Secretary of State, see further below on the Water Industry Act 1991 Part IV. See also SI 1989/2286 further implementing Directive 76/464 by classifying surface waters according to the presence of the substances prescribed under the Directive and its daughters. Note further the Sludge (Use in Agriculture) Regulations SI 1989/1263 implementing the Sewage Sludge Directive 86/278 which are designed, inter alia, to protect the environment against the harmful effects of uncontrolled spreading of sewage sludge.

The Bathing Waters (Classification) Regulations SI 1991/1597 are designed to fulfil the requirements of Directive 76/160 on the quality of bathing waters. Criteria are laid down for BW1 classification which reflect the mandatory requirements of the Directive with regard to designated bathing waters, though the Secretary of State is empowered

---

105 As amended by the Control of Pollution (Silage, Slurry and Agricultural Fuel Oil) (Amendment) Regulations 1997, SI 1997/547.

106 See the Water (Prevention of Pollution) (Code of Practice) Order SI 1998/3084, which approved the 1998 Code of Good Agricultural Practice for the Protection of Water.

to allow certain derogations as contemplated by the Directive. BW1 will be used for the setting of quality objectives for bathing waters under the terms of WRA 1991, s 83. However, there was some doubt between 1989 and 1991 as to whether the UK was fully complying with the requirements of Directive 76/160, for example, in respect of the presences of viruses on certain beaches and in 1990 the EC Commission successfully commenced action against the UK in respect of 140 beaches which failed, it was claimed, to meet cleanliness standards.[107]

Directive 76/160 stipulates that in each member state, there shall be a 'competent authority' to sample and analyse bathing waters in accordance with the requirements of the directive. The NRA in the past served as the competent authority for the purposes of Directive 76/160 in England and Wales, although this is yet another task which the Environment Agency inherited. Currently there are 481 designated bathing waters in England and Wales for the purposes of Directive 76/160 (472 coastal bathing waters and nine inland bathing waters). The most recent figures published by the Agency reveal that 97% of all beaches monitored meet the mandatory coliform standard ('I' values) during the 2001 bathing season (15 May–30 September). Thus the quality of bathing waters in England and Wales has improved for the fifth consecutive year and the current compliance rate represents a significant improvement on the figure of 66.5% for 1988, when monitoring first began.

The Urban Waste Water Treatment (England and Wales) Regulations SI 1994/2841 have been made by the Secretary of State in order to give effect to Directive 91/271 on the treatment of urban waste water. These regulations are expressed in broadly similar terms to Directive 91/271 save for the fact that they prefer the term 'high natural dispersion areas' to the 'less sensitive areas' referred to in the directive. Controversy surrounding the determination of estuarine limits for the purposes of Art 2(12) of the directive culminated in a ruling that the Secretary of State acted unlawfully by classifying the Humber and Severn estuaries as 'coastal waters'.

In *R v Secretary of State for the Environment, ex p Kingston upon Hull City Council* and *R v Secretary of State for the Environment, ex p Bristol City Council*,[108] the issue between the parties related to whether primary or a more thorough, and therefore more expensive, secondary treatment level of household and industrial sewage was necessary for the purposes of the legislation. The High Court held that whilst member states have a discretion in establishing outer estuarine limits under Directive 91/271, by classifying the Humber and Severn estuaries as 'coastal waters' so as to avoid the need for more costly secondary treatment, the Secretary of State had taken account of an irrelevant consideration. In exercising his discretion, he ought to have had regard to the characteristics of the area of water in question since such water either was or was not an estuary regardless of the costs involved in treating waste water discharged into it.

The UK has also made considerable use of circulars and other forms of guidance on the implementation of EC obligations and other legislative requirements: see, for example, DoE Circulars 4/82, on the implementation of Directive 80/68 on the protection of groundwater where it was considered prior to its cancellation for England, by PPG 23, that it was not necessary to introduce any new legislation because existing legislative powers were adequate; 13/85 on public registers of discharges to the water environment; 18/85 on the implementation of Directive 76/464 and its daughters, as supplemented by 7/89 which gives specific guidance on mercury, cadmium, hexachlorcyclohexane, carbon tetrachloride, DDT, pentachlorophenol, the drins, HCB, HCBD, chloroform, and 20/90 which gives further guidance relating to the Protection of Groundwater Directive 80/68, in particular by requiring revision of waste disposal practices to ensure waste sites do not lead to prescribed substances and families of substances entering groundwater.

107 *EC Commission v United Kingdom:* C-56/90 [1993] ECR I-4109.
108 [1996] Env LR 248.

The WRA 1991, s 98 empowers the Secretary of State to make regulations to apply the Act's provisions to dealing with radioactive waste, otherwise the pollution control provisions of WRA 1991 do not apply to such waste within the meaning of the Radioactive Substances Act 1993.[109] These regulations subject radioactive waste to the provisions of the 1991 legislation relating to classification of waters, water quality objectives, pollution, offences, pollution precautions, Agency consents, anti-pollution works, registers, information collection and exchange, but in such a way that no account is to be taken of the radioactive properties of such waste; this remains subject to the RSA 1993.

Water protection zones, nitrate sensitive areas and nitrate vulnerable zones

The WRA 1991, Chapter III makes provision for various powers to prevent and control water pollution. In addition to conferring a power upon the Secretary of State to make regulations requiring precautions to be taken against pollution (WRA 1991, s 92, see above), the chapter provides for the designation of water protection zones and nitrate sensitive areas.

Water protection zones

Subject to receiving an application from the Agency in accordance with WRA 1991, Sch 11, s 93 empowers the Secretary of State (after consultation) to designate an area as a water protection zone (WPZ). This power is exercisable where it is considered appropriate with a view to preventing or controlling the entry of any poisonous, noxious or polluting matter into any controlled waters, or to prohibit or restrict activities within the area considered likely to result in such pollution. The result of designation is that specified activities within the area may be prohibited or restricted. This does not extend, however, to the entry of *nitrate* into controlled waters as a result of agricultural land use, for which special regimes may be established (see further below). A WPZ designation may empower the Agency, inter alia, to determine the circumstances in which the carrying on of an activity is prohibited, and to determine the activities to which any prohibition or restriction applies.

To date, the only designated WPZ is the River Dee Catchment.[110] The river, which is a vitally important source of drinking water for some two million people in north-east Wales and north-west England, has a number of industries within its catchment. Designation was therefore regarded as a means of protecting the river against further pollution incidents. The designation order makes it an offence to cause or knowingly permit a contravention of protection zone control. Such a contravention occurs where a controlled activity is or has been carried on within the WPZ either without consent or in breach of a consent. For the purposes of the order, a 'controlled activity' means the keeping or use of a controlled substance within a catchment control site. A number of substances fall within the meaning of 'controlled substance'. They include: a dangerous substance; a fuel, lubricant or industrial spirit or solvent which is kept in liquid form or which is a liquid under normal conditions; food or feeding stuff which is liquid under normal conditions; and, inorganic fertiliser.

109 See SI 1989/1158.
110 See the Water Protection Zone (River Dee Catchment) Designation Order SI 1999/915.

The process of applying for a protection zone consent is set out in regulations.[111] An application must be made on the form provided by the Agency and must incorporate or be accompanied by various information and documentation specified in Sch 1 to the regulations. Such information includes: a site map; a substance location plan; a substance specification statement; and a safety and emergency statement. The substance specification statement must contain details of the controlled substance, its density and solubility in water, the maximum quantity of it that is proposed to be kept or used, the manner in which it is to be kept or used and details (including its cubic capacity) of any vessel to be used for its storage.

On receipt of the application, the Agency must send a copy to relevant local authorities and to downstream abstractors. Following a process of consultation, the Agency may grant the consent either conditionally or unconditionally, or refuse the consent. Where the Secretary of State has 'called in' an application for a consent, he shall determine it by directing the Agency to respond in any of the three ways indicated. A protection zone consent ceases to have effect if there is a change in the person in control of the whole or any part of the site to which it relates, unless an application has been made for its continuation. Where this has happened, the Agency may modify the consent or revoke it.

In the case of an extant consent, the person in control of the site to which it relates may apply to have any of the conditions to which it is subject varied or revoked. The Agency has the discretion to modify the consent in the manner which has been requested or refuse the application. If it appears to the Agency that it is expedient to do so, it may serve a notice on the relevant person which either revokes the consent, *or* makes modifications to the conditions of the consent, *or* imposes conditions on a previously unconditional consent. A right of appeal exists in respect of any of these decisions as well as in respect of the refusal to grant a consent or a decision to grant a consent subject to conditions.

Nitrate sensitive areas

Provided that he has received an application from the Agency in accordance with WRA 1991, Sch 12 and provided that he has the consent of the Treasury, the relevant minister is empowered by WRA 1991, s 94 to designate land as a nitrate sensitive area (NSA) where he considers that it is appropriate to do so for the purpose of preventing or controlling the entry of nitrate into controlled waters as a result of the agricultural use of land. Orders made under this power may consequentially require, prohibit or restrict the carrying on of specified activities, and may provide for sums of money to be paid by ministers to designated persons in respect of obligations imposed (hence the need for Treasury consent). The key distinction between a WPZ and a NSA is that in the former only prohibitions or restrictions can be imposed on the carrying on of specified activities whereas in the latter, certain activities may be *required*. In short, in NSAs, *positive* as well as negative obligations may be imposed.

NSAs fall into three categories: areas where *mandatory* controls apply; areas where *mandatory* controls apply but compensation is payable; and areas where controls are *voluntary*. In relation to the latter, WRA 1991, s 95 empowers ministers to enter into agreements with relevant land owners, etc, whereby, in return for payments made by ministers, obligations are accepted with regard to the management of land, eg with regard

---

111 See the Water Protection Zone (River Dee Catchment) (Procedural and Other Provisions) Regulations SI 1999/916.

to nitrate application. These agreements amount to restrictive covenants 'running with' the land.

Originally ten areas were designated as NSAs under the Nitrate Sensitive Areas (Designation) Order 1990.[112] The order provided for two types of agreement between the minister and a farmer. The first, the *basic scheme* agreement, imposed various restrictions on the use of inorganic nitrogen fertiliser on crops, whereas the *premium scheme* agreement, with its higher rates of payment, demanded the cessation of arable production and the establishment and maintenance of grassland on the land to which the agreement related. Whilst the basic scheme proved to be quite popular with farmers, the lack of enthusiasm for the premium scheme became clear when in 1993, the government introduced an amendment order,[113] which increased the rates of payment for agricultural land in this scheme.

In 1994 the Nitrate Sensitive Areas Regulations[114] were made in order to comply with EC Regulation 2078/92, the so-called 'Agri-environmental Regulation'. Like their predecessors, they extended only to England. The regulations expanded the number of NSAs from the original ten to 22. In addition, they provided for three different types of scheme to apply in such areas: a basic scheme; a premium arable scheme; and a premium grass scheme. The undertakings given under each scheme lasted for a period of five consecutive years, but, at the request of the farmer, the minister had the power to vary the terms of any undertakings given in accordance with the regulations.

The 1994 Regulations have been amended on a number of occasions. In 1995, two amending regulations[115] had the combined effect of increasing the number of designated NSAs to 32. Moreover, the 1995 Regulations created two new options, an arable woodland scheme option and a set-aside option, both of which were available to a farmer who wished to comply with the premium arable scheme in a NSA. In 1998, regulations made under the authority of the European Communities Act 1972, s 2(2) provided that no new applications in respect of the 1994 Regulations were to be made after 30 September 1998.[116] Thus the current obligations under the scheme will cease to have effect in 2003.

Given the time that it takes for nitrate applied to land to actually reach groundwater supplies, it is not easy to assess the impact of the scheme upon nitrate concentrations in water in the designated areas. However, as Howarth and McGillivray suggest, initial monitoring results indicate that there has been a reduction in nitrate leaching in these areas.[117]

Procedural matters

The WRA 1991, s 96 supplements the foregoing provisions by empowering the Secretary of State and ministers to make regulations relating to, inter alia, applications for any consents requisite under any order, conditions which may be imposed, revocations and variations of consents, appeal[118] and dispute resolution mechanisms,

---

112 SI 1990/1013.
113 SI 1993/3198.
114 SI 1994/1729.
115 SI 1995/1708 and SI 1995/2095.
116 See the Nitrate Sensitive Areas (Amendment) (No 2) Regulations SI 1998/2138.
117 See *Water Pollution and Water Quality Law*, para 13.5.3.
118 In performing the function of determining an appeal under WRA 1991, s 96, the Secretary of State may delegate the task to an appointed person in accordance with the Environment Act 1995, s 114.

charging and registration schemes. As has already been noted, it is for the Agency to initiate the designation of WPZs and NSAs by applying to ministers for orders.

The Nitrate Directive and nitrate vulnerable zones

Directive 91/676, the Nitrate Directive, has two principal aims: to reduce the level of nitrate from agricultural sources in those areas where water is being polluted as defined by the Nitrate Directive; and to prevent the new pollution of water from arising. Accordingly, member states are required to identify water catchment areas which have nitrate levels in surface or underground waters of more than 50 parts per million. Areas with high nitrate levels are required by the Nitrate Directive to be designated as a 'nitrate vulnerable zone' (NVZ).

Implementation of the Nitrate Directive was sought to be achieved in national law by the Protection of Water Against Agricultural Nitrate Pollution (England and Wales) Regulations.[119] By virtue of these regulations, 68 NVZs have been designated (see Sch 1) in the light of recommendations made by an Independent Review Panel. Prior to considering the obligations which arise under the Nitrate Directive in respect of NVZs, several points about the designation process ought to be mentioned. First, it should be noted that all 32 NSAs are covered by the establishment of the 68 NVZs. Secondly, the UK government's approach to the implementation of the directive can be contrasted with that of other member states, such as Denmark, Germany and the Netherlands, where it was decided to designate the whole of their territory as a NVZ. Thirdly, despite the involvement of an Independent Review Panel, the designation of NVZs was not without controversy. The main source of contention appears to have been that for some of the designated areas, agriculture was not the only source of nitrate pollution. The matter reached a head in *R v Secretary of State for the Environment and the Ministry of Agriculture, Fisheries and Food, ex p Standley and Metson*,[120] where two farmers sought judicial review of the designation of two NVZs. In making such a designation, the government had adopted a three phase approach: it had identified the waters to which the Nitrate Directive applied; it had identified the land comprising the NVZs which drained into those waters; and it had assessed whether agriculture was a significant source of nitrate pollution in the identified zones. It was contended on behalf of the applicants, however, that this was the wrong approach. In their opinion, the correct approach required the government to consider first the sources of nitrate pollution and identify only those waters where the directive's nitrate limit was exceeded by virtue of agricultural inputs only.

The matter was referred to the European Court of Justice by Potts J under Art 177 (now Art 234). That Court was asked whether it was correct to interpret the Directive as requiring identification of waters and establishment of zones where member states were satisfied; that nitrates from agricultural sources made a 'significant contribution' to the overall concentration of nitrates', only where the threshold levels in the Directive were exceeded by nitrates from agricultural sources alone; or, on some other basis, and if so what? In finding that the UK government's approach to the implementation of the Nitrate Directive was not at odds with the directive itself, the Court noted, inter alia, that the wording of the measure was such that member states were not required to determine precisely the proportion of pollution attributable to agricultural origin or that the cause of such pollution had to be exclusively agricultural. In other words, the Nitrate Directive could apply where agriculture made a 'significant' as opposed to an exclusive

119 SI 1996/888. For the unsuccessful nature of this implementation, see further below.
120 [1997] Env LR 589.

contribution to the levels of nitrate in water in the relevant zone. However, the Court noted that EC law could not provide precise criteria for establishing whether there was a 'significant contribution' in a given case.

Under the terms of the Nitrate Directive, member states are required to establish an action programme detailing the measures which farmers in the NVZs should follow in order to reduce the levels of nitrate. Specific reference is made to the application of fertiliser, manure storage capacity and fertiliser application rates.[121] For organic manures, the directive states that the application rates should not exceed a nitrogen content of 170 kg per hectare assessed over the farm as a whole.[122] The Action Programme for England and Wales was established in 1998.[123] The basic requirements which are to apply in NVZs are set out in the 1998 Regulations, Schedule. These include, inter alia, the requirement that inorganic and organic fertilisers should not be applied to fields during particular times of the year, nor should they be applied to steeply sloping fields or when the soil is waterlogged, flooded, frozen hard or snow covered. Moreover, records are required to be made sufficient to allow any person inspecting them to readily ascertain, inter alia, the area of the farm, the quantities of inorganic and organic fertilisers applied to each field and the date of application, and, where livestock is kept on the farm, the quantity of each type of livestock manure moved off the farm, the date of that movement and the name and address of the consignee. Such records must be kept for at least five years after the latest event to which they refer.

In the light of the foregoing, it seems that the Code of Good Agricultural Practice for the Protection of Water (also known as 'The Water Code Revised'), which was reissued in 1998,[124] will operate on a voluntary basis in non-NVZ areas.

The Water Industry Act 1991

The relevant provisions of the WRA 1991 were, prior to their repeal by the Environment Act 1995, concerned with the structure and functioning of the Environment Agency's predecessor, the NRA, but the privatisation of the water industry created other bodies with aquatic environmental responsibilities. The water, etc, undertakers have responsibilities with regard to sewers, drains, discharges and drinking water, as in certain cases, do local authorities. These are now principally to be found in the Water Industry Act 1991 (WIA 1991). This deals with the Director General of Water Services, Ofwat and the appointment and regulation of water and sewerage undertakers. It is also concerned with the quality and provision of drinking water and the use and abuse of sewers.

It is important to appreciate both the distinctions and overlaps between the functions of the Agency and the water and sewerage undertakers. The old 'poacher cum gamekeeper' problem that troubled the former water authorities has largely disappeared as a consequence of the creation of the NRA and its successor, the Environment Agency. The Agency is the principal pollution regulatory body while the undertakers are primarily commercial organisations subject to supervision from both the Agency and the Director General and Ofwat. However, the undertakers do have regulatory powers of their own and these can result in a polluting activity being subject to prosecution by both the regulator and an undertaker: see *National Rivers Authority v*

---

121 See also the 1996 Regulations, reg 7 and Sch 4.
122 For the first four years of the programme, a derogation of 210 kg per hectare was available to the farmer.
123 See SI 1998/1202.
124 See SI 1998/3084 for approval of the Code.

Appletise Bottling, Northumbrian Water v Appletise Bottling[125] where an unconsented polluting emission damaged both controlled waters and storm drains resulting in a double prosecution. Undertakers have enjoyed something of a privilege in that though their discharges from sewage works were subject to the need for consent, the regime which governed the position before the Water Act 1989 (and now, of course, the Water Resources Act 1991), ie the Control of Pollution Act 1974, was somewhat lenient in that discharge consents usually required only a 95% compliance rate. Thus a treatment plant would not necessarily be in breach of its consent if on a few occasions it transgresses discharge limits. Thus it was possible for a sewerage undertaker to commit serious polluting incidents from time to time and to avoid legal liability. This loophole was closed as from September 1991 in order to comply with EC groundwater requirements.

Sewers and drains

The WIA 1991, Part IV, deals with sewerage services. Section 94 imposes a general duty on sewerage undertakers (effectively the privatised water companies) to provide a system of public sewers and to cleanse and maintain them, and to make provision for the emptying of sewers by means of sewage disposal works. In performing these duties undertakers must have regard to the needs to allow trade effluent to be discharged into public sewers and to dispose of such discharges.

The WIA 1991, s 111, places a general prohibition on the throwing, emptying, turning or passing, whether actively or by permission or sufferance, of any matter into any public sewer (or drain or sewer communicating with such a sewer) where that matter is likely to injure the sewer/drain, *or* to interfere with the free flow of its contents, *or* prejudicially to affect the treatment and disposal of its contents. Similar prohibitions are placed on the discharge into sewers of chemical refuse or waste steam, or liquids with a temperature exceeding 110°F which are 'a prohibited substance'. Such substances are those which either alone, or in combination with the contents of the sewer/drain in question, or when heated, are dangerous, or the cause of nuisances, or are injurious, or likely to cause injury, to health. Similar prohibitions are further imposed on the discharge of petroleum spirit or carbide of calcium. 'Petroleum spirit' means crude petroleum, oil or petroleum products or mixtures containing petroleum which give off inflammable vapours at temperatures of less than 73°F. It is an offence to contravene the provisions of the section. In determining for the purposes of actions whether any discharge will prejudicially affect the treatment and disposal of the contents of an affected sewer/drain the issue will turn on the balance of the available scientific evidence: see *Liverpool Corpn v H Coghill & Son Ltd*.[126]

Trade effluents

The foregoing provision is, however, expressly subject to the WIA 1991, Part III, which relates to trade effluents. WIA 1991, s 118 allows the occupier of any trade premises in a sewerage undertaker's area to discharge trade effluent via drains or sewers into public sewers *subject to* the undertaker's consent — unconsented discharges constitute offences. Likewise, WIA 1991, s 106 permits, *as to right*, occupiers of premises to have their drains and sewers connect with an undertaker's sewers and to discharge *surface*

---

125 [1991] 3 LMELR 132.
126 [1918] 1 Ch 307.

(including storm) water and foul water (including domestic waste) into those sewers. On the basis of a Scottish case concerned with a near equivalent of WIA 1991, s 106, the Sewerage (Scotland) Act 1968, s 12, it would seem that the fact that a public sewer is already overloaded will not necessarily entitle an undertaker to refuse a connection: see *Tayside Regional Council v Secretary of State for Scotland*.[127] Trade effluent is defined by WIA 1991, s 141 as liquids produced wholly or partly in the course of trade or industry at any premises, while trade premises are those used or intended to be used for carrying on any trade or industry, including those used for agricultural, horticultural, piscicultural, scientific research or experimental purposes. 'Trade' has been widely construed so that a launderette is 'trade premises': see *Thames Water Authority v Blue and White Laundrettes Ltd*.[128]

Trade effluent consents

WIA 1991, s 119 lays down the general procedure for obtaining the requisite consent. The relevant owner/occupier of trade premises must serve notice on the undertaker stating the nature and composition of the trade effluent, the maximum quantity of daily discharge and the highest proposed rate of discharge. However, some effluents are categorised as 'special', and where an application to discharge any of these is received the undertaker must (unless they refuse consent) further refer the matter to the Environment Agency asking whether the discharge should be prohibited or whether special conditions should be imposed on any consent. The would-be discharger must be informed of the reference: see WIA 1991, s 120. By virtue of WIA 1991, s 120(9) an undertaker commits an offence if they fail to make a referral to the Agency within a period of two months from the date on which the notice containing the application was served on them. Where a consent to make discharges of special category effluent has been granted in contravention of sub-s (9), the Agency may exercise its powers of review under WIA 1991, ss 127 and 131: see s 120(10).

This provision gives the Environment Agency considerable control over trade effluent discharges and enables a precautionary policy on water protection to be applied. It also implements the requirements of Directive 76/464 on dangerous substances, as defined by WIA 1991, s 138, the Trade Effluents (Prescribed Processes and Substances) Regulations SI 1989/1156 (as amended by SI 1990/1629 — the 'red list') and the Trade Effluents (Prescribed Processes and Substances) Regulations SI 1992/339.

Other effluents

WIA 1991, s 139 enables the Secretary of State by order to apply the powers over trade effluents to other effluents. It should also be noted that WIA 1991, Sch 8 generally preserves discharge authorisation and agreements made before the coming into effect of the Water Act 1989 as deemed consents. However, such 'old' authorisations, etc, are subject to the WIA 1991 powers of cancellation, replacement and variation, with the necessary provision for appeals against such changes being made: see further on s 132, etc, of the WIA 1991 below.

127 1996 SLT 473.
128 [1980] 1 WLR 700.

Sewerage undertakers powers

Sewerage undertakers themselves have powers under WIA 1991, s 121 to impose discharge consent conditions relating to the sewers into which any discharge of any trade effluent may take place, the nature and composition of discharges, maximum quantities of discharges and discharge rates. With regard to discharges of trade effluent from trade premises further conditions may relate to the daily timing of discharges; exclusion of condensing water from discharges; elimination or diminution of specified constituents of effluents where the constituent, alone or in combination with other matter, would injure or obstruct sewers or make the treatment or disposal of sewage from such sewers specially difficult or expensive or, in relation to sewer outfalls into harbours or tidal waters, would cause injury to navigation, etc; temperature of discharges, their acidity/alkalinity; payment for discharges; provision and maintenance of inspection facilities and meters and sampling and monitoring equipment; keeping of records of discharges, and the making of returns. Payment conditions must, under WIA 1991, s 121(4), reflect the nature, composition, volume and rate of discharges, the costs of undertakers in receiving discharges and any revenue they are likely to derive from effluents. Breach of discharge consent conditions constitutes an offence.

Persons aggrieved by refusals to give consents, or by failures to give them within due time (two months from the day after the date of service of notice of application to discharge) or by any discharge consent condition may appeal to the Director General of Water Services who has a wide discretion under WIA 1991, s 122 to grant consents, and impose or vary conditions. Under WIA 1991, s 137 the Director General may refer any issue of law on appeal to the High Court, this also applies to s 126 proceedings, see below.

WIA 1991, s 124 empowers sewerage undertakers to vary, annul or add discharge conditions by direction, though this is subject to a *general* restriction that such variations may not be made within two years of consent being given. Notice of proposed directions must be given to the owners/occupiers of relevant premises, and, under WIA 1991, s 126, there is a right of appeal to the Director General of Water Services against the direction in relation to which again the Director possesses a wide discretion. The time restriction on variation restrictions does not, under WIA 1991, s 125, apply to proposed changes considered necessary by the undertaker in order to provide proper protection for persons likely to be affected by relevant discharges. Such a course of action normally involves the payment of compensation to the discharger unless it is necessary to make the change in consequence of changes of circumstances otherwise than other discharge consents given which have occurred within the period of two years from the date of consent and which could not reasonably have been foreseen at the time of consent. (Similar compensation requirements relate to the powers of the Environment Agency to review discharge consents in certain cases, see WIA 1991, s 134, as amended.)

Note also the power in WIA 1991, s 128 to enable an undertaker to apply to the Director General for a postponement of a date specified for a discharge of trade effluent on the grounds that, inter alia, because of failure to complete works in connection with the reception and disposal of the discharge, a later date ought to be set.

Environment Agency powers

The Director General, it is clear, has extensive powers under the provisions examined above. They are, however, subject to the powers of the Environment Agency in certain cases falling within WIA 1991, s 123. Effectively where a s 122 appeal is made and the case is one in which a 'special category of effluent' reference should have been made to the Agency, the Director General may not determine the appeal unless he first submits the matter to the Agency and has received notice of the Agency's determination on the issue. The Environment Agency also has extensive powers to review consents relating to 'special category' discharges under WIA 1991, s 127. Constraints exist on the exercise of this power in that the Agency may not review a consent unless one of the following applies:

1   The consent has not been previously reviewed and was given before 1 September 1989 or in contravention of WIA 1991, s 133.
2   A period of more than two years has elapsed since the time when notice of the Environment Agency's determination on a reference relating to the consent was served.
3   There has been since the time of service of such a notice a contravention of any requirement of a consent.

These constraints do *not* apply where a review is carried out to enable the UK to comply with EC or international legal obligations or otherwise to protect public health or flora or fauna dependent on an aquatic environment.

Under WIA 1991, s 132 where any reference or review is made under ss 120, 123 or 127 (see above) or under ss 130 or 131 (see below) the Environment Agency must before making a determination allow relevant owners/occupiers of trade premises and the undertaker to make representations/objections to the Agency and must consider any such as are made. Once the determination is made the parties and the Director General must be informed by notice stating the conclusions and determinations of the Agency, and it is then the duty of the undertaker and the Director General under WIA 1991, s 133 to give effect to the Agency's determination. An undertaker who fails to perform this duty is guilty of a offence: see WIA 1991, s 133(5). Moreover, in order to secure compliance with a WIA 1991, s 132 notice, the Environment Agency is empowered by virtue of s 133(6) to serve notice on the undertaker and owners/occupiers of trade premises that any consent to make discharges of special category effluent or any agreement under WIA 1991, s 129 (see below) may be varied or revoked.

WIA 1991, s 129 confers a general power on undertakers to make agreements for the reception and disposal of trade effluents with the owners/occupiers of any trade premises within their areas. Such an agreement may authorise discharges otherwise needing consent. However, such an agreement must be referred to the Environment Agency under WIA 1991, s 130 where special category effluent is concerned for the Agency's determination as to whether the operations necessary under the agreement should be prohibited or whether any further requirements should be imposed. It is an offence for an undertaker to fail to comply with this statutory duty: see WIA 1991, s 130(7). Where the Agency becomes aware of an agreement relating to special category effluent which has not been referred to it, the Agency may proceed as if the reference had been made: see WIA 1991, s 130(8). The Agency's power under WIA 1991, s 131 to review such agreements is subject to the same constraints as the power to review consents contained in s 127. However, both these powers of review may be exercised by the Agency notwithstanding these constraints where an undertaker has failed to comply with the duty to refer the consent or agreement to the Agency: see WIA 1991, s 130(9).

In order that it may discharge its functions under the WIA 1991, Part IV, Chapter III, s 135A, inserted by para 113 of Sch 22 to the Environment Act 1995, confers a power on the Environment Agency to require of any person such information as the Agency reasonably considers it needs for this purpose. It is an offence to fail, without reasonable excuse, to comply with such a requirement or knowingly or recklessly to make a false or misleading statement when providing information. The penalty for a summary conviction is a fine not exceeding the statutory maximum, whilst a conviction on indictment may result in a fine or a term of imprisonment not exceeding two years, or both.

Information

WIA 1991, s 196 imposes a duty on undertakers to maintain publicly available registers of discharge consents, any directions given and all agreements made. WIA 1991, s 202 imposes a duty on undertakers to furnish the Secretary of State with such relevant information as he may reasonably require, though s 206 imposes restrictions otherwise on the disclosure of information. These provisions are very similar to the corresponding measures under the WRA 1991, as is the s 208 power of the Secretary of State to give directions to undertakers in the interests of national security, and the provision as to offences by bodies corporate, s 210.

Drinking water

WIA 1991, Part III, Chapter III, is concerned with the quality and sufficiency of supplies of water. WIA 1991, s 67 provides that the Secretary of State may make regulations as to whether water supplied to premises is/is not to be regarded as 'wholesome' by reference to prescribed requirements. 'Wholesome' so far as the courts are concerned appears to mean safe and pleasant to drink: see *McColl v Strathclyde Regional Council.*[129] The regulations may make both general and specific requirements as to the quality of water, substances present in it, and its characteristics. Sampling techniques may also be specified. The Secretary of State may also authorise departures from prescribed requirements, though these may be subject to conditions. The regulatory powers exist to fulfil obligations under Directive 80/778 on the quality of drinking water, earlier attempts by the UK to meet its obligations by administrative measures only, eg DoE Circular 20/82, having been of dubious legality. The current regulations are the Water Supply (Water Quality) Regulations SI 1989/1147 amended by SI 1989/1383 and SI 1991/1837. These provide mandatory standards for domestic drinking, washing and cooking water and water used for food production. The standards include the EC requirements together with further UK requirements. Monitoring and sampling requirements are also laid down, as are provisions as to information and registers to be made publicly available and annual reports. The regulations also make provision for certain relaxations of standards by the Secretary of State on an application by an undertaker, subject to a right for local authorities to make representations. It should be noted, however, that as from 1 January 2004, the 1989 Regulations will (in so far as not already revoked) be revoked by the Water Supply (Water Quality) Regulations SI 2000/3184.

The Private Water Supplies Regulations SI 1991/2790, which impose quality requirements on waters from private sources or waters which are supplied by an unlicensed supplier, are substantially the same as the 1989 Regulations discussed above, save for the monitoring requirements which they lay down. These divide private water supplies into either Category 1 or Category 2 supplies depending on whether the water is supplied for domestic or food production purposes, and impose a duty on the local authority to take and analyse samples from each category in their area. Where the private supply is found to be unwholesome or insufficient, the local authority may serve a notice on the owner/occupiers of the premises which is either using the supply or is

129 [1984] JPL 351.

the place where the source is located or on any party which exercises powers of management and control in relation to the source, specifying the remedial action that is necessary, see further below.

Statutory duty with respect to water quality

The WIA 1991, s 68[130] imposes a duty on water undertakers (the privatised water companies) to ensure that water supplied to any premises for domestic or food production purposes is wholesome at the time of supply and, so far as is reasonably practicable, to ensure in relation to each source of supply of water, or combination thereof, from which such water is supplied that there is no deterioration in the quality of supply from time to time. In *R v Secretary of State for the Environment, ex p Friends of the Earth*,[131] which was discussed earlier in this chapter, the undertakings which the Secretary of State accepted from Thames and Anglian Water in accordance with WIA 1991, s 19(1)(b) were that the water companies would meet their obligations under Directive 80/778 and comply with the duty under s 68(1) to supply wholesome water. However, as was also noted earlier in this chapter, in *EC Commission v United Kingdom*,[132] the European Court of Justice held that such undertakings represented an unlawful means of complying with Directive 80/778 and the UK government responded by making the Drinking Water (Undertakings) (England and Wales) Regulations SI 2000/1297. WIA 1991, s 68 duties may be enforced by the Secretary of State under WIA 1991, s 18.

Supplying water unfit for human consumption

It is an offence under WIA 1991, s 70 for an undertaker to supply water unfit for human consumption, though defences include that the undertaker had no reasonable grounds for suspecting water supplied would be used for human consumption, or that all reasonable steps were taken and all due diligence exercised to secure that the water was fit at the point of leaving the undertaker's pipes, or, if not fit, was not consumed by humans. The Secretary of State and the DPP only may institute proceedings under this provision. Severn Trent Water became the first water company to be convicted of charges brought under WIA 1991, s 70 in respect of premises in the Worcester area which were found to have contaminated water present. In *Drinking Water Inspectorate and Secretary of State v Severn Trent Water*,[133] the Crown Court found that Severn Trent's failure to take sufficient steps to avert contamination resulted in their supplying to three premises, a bakery, a children's home and Lea & Perrins, water which was unfit for human consumption. Accordingly, they were fined £45,000 and ordered to pay £67,000 costs. The case is of particular interest in the context of the WIA 1991 since it draws a distinction between the 'fitness' and the 'wholesomeness' of water. It would appear that water may be 'unfit' for human consumption for the purposes of the Act despite the fact that it is 'wholesome' within the meaning of the drinking water standard regulations and does not pose a risk to public health. In a further case, *Secretary of State for Wales v DWR CYMRU*,[134] Welsh Water was found guilty of an offence

---

130 For the equivalent provision in Scottish legislation, see s 8 of the Water (Scotland) Act 1980, as amended.
131 [1996] 1 CMLR 117.
132 [1999] ECR I-2023.
133 (1995) Independent, 25 April, (1995) 243 ENDS Report 45.
134 (1995) 242 ENDS Report 45.

contrary to the Water Supply (Water Quality) Regulations 1989, reg 28 where it failed to observe the conditions of approval for use of an epoxy resin material used for the internal relining of water mains. Despite the fact that no evidence was adduced to show that drinking water quality was affected once the main was returned to service, Welsh Water's failure to carry out the necessary checks in accordance with the conditions of approval ensured that the company could not be certain that consumers had not been exposed to any risk.

Where a water company has been convicted of a WIA 1991, s 70 offence, in determining the level of fine to be imposed, a court should have, inter alia, the following considerations in mind: the degree of culpability; the damage caused; the defendant's previous record; the balance that might have to be struck between a fitting censure and the counter-productive effect of imposing a substantial fine where a water company is endeavouring to carry out work in connection with the water supply; the attitude and performance of the company after the events in question; and the need to determine the penalty for any one incident without using the number of complainants as a multiplier.[135]

Common law liability

Outside the statutory framework, it appears that there may be residual liability in public nuisance for the supply of unwholesome water. This was the offence charged in *R v South West Water Authority*,[136] following the accidental and mistaken placing of aluminium sulphate into a tank of water intended for public supply in the Camelford area of Cornwall. A number of customers suffered various ill effects in consequence, and up to 5,000 people were affected in some way. The authority, which by then had ceased to exist due to the privatisation of water authorities under the Water Act 1989, was ultimately found guilty of committing a public nuisance in respect of its actions and accordingly fined £10,000 and ordered to pay £25,000 costs. The relatively low level of the fine despite the seriousness of the polluting incident was justified by the Crown Court on the basis that the authority's guilt was limited to their tardiness in tackling the pollution.

Regulations for preserving water quality

The Secretary of State has a further power under WIA 1991, s 69 to make regulations to ensure compliance with the s 68 duty to supply wholesome water. In particular regulations may impose obligations on undertakers, inter alia, to:
1   Monitor and record the wholesomeness of water supplies to premises.
2   Monitor and record the quality of water sources.
3   Ensure water sources are not used until prescribed requirements for establishing water quality have been complied with.
4   Comply with requirements as to water analysis.
5   Forbid the use of certain processes or substances, or to require them to conform to standards.
6   Publish information about water quality.
7   Act with regard to the use of specified processes and substances and products containing such substances as might affect water quality.

135 See *R v Yorkshire Water Services Ltd* (2001) Times, 12 December. See also *R v F Howe & Son (Engineers) Ltd* [1999] 2 All ER 249, referred to above at p 683.
136 [1991] 3 LMELR 65.

See, again, SI 1989/1147 and SI 1989/1384. The WIA 1991, s 86 enables the Secretary of State to appoint assessors (the Drinking Water Inspectorate) of water quality to assist him in his duties in this regard.

Waste, contamination, misuse etc of water sources

Special provision is made by the WIA 1991 for combating the contamination or waste of water. Under WIA 1991, s 71 it is an offence to cause or allow any underground water to run to waste from any well, borehole or other work, or to abstract from any such well, etc, water in excess of reasonable requirements. WIA 1991, s 76 further enables water undertakers if of opinion that there is, or is threatened, a serious water deficiency, to prohibit the use of hosepipes for watering gardens or washing cars, ie a 'hose pipe ban'. Such bans must be publicly advertised before coming into force, thereafter contravention of the ban constitutes an offence. WIA 1991, s 72 creates an offence of committing any act of neglect whereby the water in any waterworks likely to be used for human domestic purposes or food production is or is likely to be polluted. The offence does not extend to prohibit any method of land cultivation in accordance with the principles of good husbandry or the use by highway authorities of oil or tar on public highways. WIA 1991, s 73 further makes it an offence for any owner or occupier of premises to cause or permit (intentionally or negligently) any of his water fittings to be so out of repair or so misused as to lead to the contamination or waste of water, and s 74 supplements this by enabling the Secretary of State to make regulations concerning water fittings in order to prevent the waste or contamination of water, while s 75 confers emergency power on undertakers to prevent damage to persons or property or the contamination or waste of water.

Local authority functions

Local authorities (districts and London boroughs) are under a duty by virtue of WIA 1991, to be informed about the wholesomeness and sufficiency of water supplies in their areas, and they have certain other powers and functions, in the exercise of which they are subject to the direction of the Secretary of State: see WIA 1991, s 77(2). For this and other connected purposes the Secretary of State has power to make regulations under WIA 1991, s 77(3) imposing duties and conferring powers on local authorities with respect to information gathering and regulating the performance of their functions. In this connection regard should be had to SI 1989/1147, Part VIII where water undertakers are required to inform local and district health authorities of events threatening water supplies by giving rise to significant health risks. Authorities are furthermore required by WIA 1991, s 78 to notify undertakers of anything which appears to them to suggest that any supply of water is, or has been, or is likely to be unwholesome or insufficient for domestic purposes, that the unwholesomeness or insufficiency is likely to endanger life or health or otherwise to lead to the breach of the duty to supply wholesome water. If an authority then becomes dissatisfied as to remedial action on the part of the undertaker they must refer the matter to the Secretary of State because he is the enforcing body with respect to undertakers.

Local authorities, however, have remedial powers over private water supplies to premises within their areas. Under WIA 1991, s 80 where satisfied a private supply is not wholesome or is insufficient, they may serve notice on a 'relevant person', ie owners and occupiers of the premises and of the source of supply. This notice *must* give details of why it has been served and must specify necessary remedial works and the time within which representations and objections responding to the notice may be made. The notice *may*, inter alia, require the person served to take specified steps within specified periods, or it may designate certain action to be taken by the authority themselves. Requisite steps may include ensuring that an adequate supply of wholesome water to the premises is provided by an undertaker or some other person. Where such a 'private supply notice' is served and objections are received and not withdrawn the local authority, if they wish the notice to proceed, must submit the matter to the Secretary of State. He then has a wide discretion, under s 81, to confirm, quash or vary the notice, or to direct the local authority as to the issue of notices, and to this end he may cause a local inquiry to be held. Once a private supply notice is in force it 'runs with the land' and its subsequent enforcement and/or variation is a matter for the local authority: see WIA 1991, s 82. In connection with their functions under the 1991 Act authorities are also granted extensive powers of entry and to obtain information by ss 84 and 85.

The future

The key development in terms of water law and policy is clearly the adoption of the Water Framework Directive.[137] This directive, as has previously been noted, establishes a strategic framework for managing the water environment. Given that it must be transposed into national law by December 2003, the DETR (now DEFRA) and the National Assembly for Wales have put in place a process of consultation as to how best to implement the Water Framework Directive. The first consultation paper was published in March 2001 and it is envisaged that the second and third phases of the process will take place during 2002 and early 2003. While the second phase is likely to include the publication of some initial draft regulations and the third phase will invite views on the main package of implementing measures, the first consultation paper seeks to introduce the key provisions of the Water Framework Directive and to invite views on how implementation of its requirements might best be achieved.

With regard to transposing the directive into national law, the consultation paper notes that the existing legislative framework which includes, inter alia, the EPA 1990, the WRA 1991, the WIA 1991, the Environment Act 1995 and the Pollution Prevention and Control Act 1999 (and the associated secondary legislation) already provides many of the powers that will be required. However, it is also noted that additional legislation will be required to fill any gaps, eg the requirement to produce a river basin management plan, and that the working assumption is that this will take the form of secondary legislation.

In terms of the substance of the Water Framework Directive, it will be remembered that Art 3 requires the identification of individual river basin districts which will then become the main unit for managing the water environment. Allowing for the fact that certain catchments cross the borders between England and Scotland and England and Wales, eg the River Dee, the consultation paper proposes an arrangement which would result in a total of eleven river basin districts covering England and Wales. Since it is proposed that the Environment Agency will be the 'competent authority' in England and Wales for the purposes of the directive, it is worth noting that the identification of river basin districts may well have some future impact upon the Agency's present regional boundaries.

The problems which have arisen from time to time over the UK's implementation of certain EC Water Directives resurfaced once again in December 2000 when the European

137 Discussed above.

Court of Justice ruled that the UK must implement the Nitrates Directive[138] fully by applying it to all ground and surface waters so as to reduce the risk of eutrophication as well as to protect drinking water sources.[139] Given that a failure to comply with the Court's ruling could result in the imposition of substantial daily non-compliance fines, it has been necessary for the UK government to consider how to properly implement the Nitrates Directive. To this end DEFRA published a consultation paper[140] in 2001 in which opinions were sought on the two options open to the government.[141] The first option was to follow the approach adopted in countries such as Austria, Germany, the Netherlands, Denmark and Finland, ie apply an Action Programme throughout the whole of England. Option 2 was to proceed as before, ie designate specific NVZs, but on a wider scale than at present so that approximately 80% of the land in England would fall within a NVZ. Although it is stated that the government does not have a firm view on either option, the advantages and disadvantages of each are set out in the consultation paper. Thus in the case of option 1, the advantages are: that all farmers would be treated the same with no competitive advantages for some (ie those farming the 20% of land not falling within option 2); that it would provide for a simpler and less uncertain system where farmers would be clear as to what was required; that a country-wide application of Action Programme measures would limit the need for additional controls on agricultural diffuse pollution in the future; and that country-wide improvements in water quality would benefit the aquatic environment, nature and habitat conservation and associated industries such as fisheries and tourism. The disadvantages are that: it would affect all farmers in England regardless of the extent of the nitrate problem in the local area; and compliance costs as a whole would be higher than for option 2.

Option 2 is considered to have less advantages and more disadvantages than option 1. With regard to advantages, it is stated that: a targeted approach will result in the designation of NVZs on areas with the greatest nitrate concentrations in surface and groundwaters; and that compliance costs as a whole would be cheaper than for option 1. The disadvantages of option 2 are stated to be that: it may give the minority of farmers outside NVZs (ie the 20% of land not covered) a competitive advantage over the majority of farmers inside NVZs; the option may give rise to uncertainty for farmers in that following a four yearly review of monitoring data as required by the directive, it may be necessary to extend the NVZ designation to land not previously covered; and the option takes the minimum action to protect drinking water and the environment. It remains to be seen how the government will proceed in the light of the responses which it receives to the consultation paper. As is clear from the above, however, maintaining the status quo is not an option.

C PLANNING AND WATER POLLUTION

The legitimacy of using planning powers for purposes covered by water legislation is questionable. A restraint on development policy may be justifiable in order to preserve the existing high quality of water in a river or estuary, or to prevent further deterioration in an already polluted stretch of water. The Secretary of State for the Environment may be unwilling, however, to allow planning authorities to trespass on the preserves of

---

138 91/676.
139 See Case C-69/99 *EC Commission v UK* [2000] ECR I-10979. It should be noted, however, that implementation of the directive throughout the EC has not been good: see generally COM (97) 473 and para 2.24 of the DEFRA consultation paper.
140 'How should England implement the 1991 Nitrates Directive?' (DEFRA) 2001.
141 The consultation period was scheduled to end on 28 February 2002.

the Environment Agency and water undertakers, though collaboration between them is another matter. An example of this was the consultation between Leicestershire County Council and the Severn Trent Water Authority in the preparation of the Leicestershire Minerals Subject Plan. Consultation began some time before the plan was made to satisfy the water authority that the county council was aware of the need to protect water resources, means of water supply and land drainage issues. In particular the authority declared itself in favour of planning policies normally leading to refusal of planning permission in respect of an extraction that could prejudice water resources. The authority also acknowledged that, despite the existence of other statutory controls, planning control is an essential feature of the protection of watercourses and resources. This is especially true with regard to incorporating provision for pollution control in the after care requirements in a mineral planning permission, or, more appropriately, an obligation. DoE Circular 17/91 gives advice to planning authorities on developments involving water industry investment, including counselling 'sympathetic' consideration of proposals to enhance the treatment of sewage, and 'expedited' handling of applications in respect of water treatment works needed to meet legal obligations, eg under EC law.

In certain cases planning authorities are under an obligation to consult the Environment Agency before granting planning permission, see the Town and Country Planning (General Development Procedure) Order 1995, SI 1995/419, Arts 10(1)(k), (p)–(t) and (y) which apply to: development involving or including mining operations; the carrying out of works or operations in the bed of or on the banks of a river or stream; development for the purpose of refining or storing mineral oils and their derivatives; using land for the deposit of refuse or waste; development relating to the retention, treatment or disposal of sewage, trade-waste, slurry or sludge; using land as a cemetery; and, development for the purposes of fish farming.

D LAND DRAINAGE

The powers relating to the drainage of land are to be found in the Land Drainage Act 1991. Briefly, Part I of the Act states the various bodies involved in land drainage. The Environment Agency has general supervisory powers over drainage functions under the Land Drainage Act 1991, s 7, and without Agency consent water may not be discharged into a main river except by way of maintenance of existing works. The 'on the ground' work is carried out by internal drainage boards who, under the LDA 1991, s 1, supervise all drainage work within their districts, ie those areas as 'will derive benefit, or avoid danger, as a result of drainage operations'. Though such boards are initially ministerially appointed provision is made by LDA 1991, Sch 1 for their subsequent partial election, though the franchise is very limited. Relevant ministers (the Secretary of State and the Minister of Agriculture), the Agency and internal drainage boards are, by virtue of LDA 1991, s 61A (inserted by the Land Drainage Act 1994, s 1) under a general duty in relation to drainage board functions to further the conservation, and enhancement of natural beauty and of flora, fauna and geological and physiographical features of special interest; to protect and conserve historic and architecturally interesting buildings and to have regard to the effect any proposals would have on urban or rural habitats. There is also a duty to preserve and enhance recreational enjoyment. Internal drainage boards may also be subject to notification of the existence of an SSSI, see LDA 1991, s 61C (inserted by the Land Drainage Act 1994, s 1), and thereafter may not carry out works likely to damage flora or fauna, etc, without consultation with the appropriate notifying authority, eg English Nature. A similar obligation applies to land in National Parks and The Broads.

Even allowing for the foregoing environmental duties, boards have extensive drainage powers to maintain, improve and construct new land drainage works. In relation to 'main rivers' (ie those shown on a 'main river map') such drainage functions belong to the Agency by virtue of the WRA 1991, s 107. The drainage powers include that to dispose of spoil by deposition, see the LDA 1991, s 5, though compensation may be payable for any injury caused: see *Marriage v East Norfolk Rivers Catchment Board.*[142] Similar drainage powers are also conferred on local authorities, and the Agency has powers, as do local authorities, under LDA 1991, s 18, to carry out small area drainage works where it would not be practicable to constitute an internal drainage board. Drainage boards have powers also to control the erection of mills, dams, weirs and culverts likely to affect the flow of watercourses, (LDA 1991, ss 23 and 24), and to require works to be done to maintain a watercourse's flow, (LDA 1991, ss 25 and 26). Part IV, Chapter II authorises the levying of rates to finance drainage, while s 62 confers compulsory purchase powers on drainage boards, and s 64 grants them powers of entry. LDA 1991, s 66 enables boards to make byelaws in connection with their functions. Development by a drainage body consisting of works on, in or under a watercourse for its improvement, maintenance or repair have 'permitted development' status under the Town and Country Planning (General Permitted Development) Order 1995, Sch 2, Part 14, while Part 15 confers similar rights on the Environment Agency.

E RESERVOIR CONSTRUCTION

The WIA 1991, s 155 confers compulsory purchase powers on water and sewerage undertakers, the procedure in such cases being, generally, that under the Acquisition of Land Act 1981. Though, however, water undertakers have certain development rights under the Town and Country Planning (General Permitted Development) Order 1995, Sch 2, Part 17, Class E, the construction of reservoirs on land acquired generally requires planning permission.

The use of these powers has been controversial. It might be argued that water authorities are allowed to create large new reservoirs too easily and wastefully, swallowing up great acreages of land and dramatically changing landscapes. The Kielder reservoir in Northumberland covers 1,086 hectares, holding 4.1 billion litres of water. Rutland Water is even larger at 1,500 hectares. During the debates on the Water Bill in 1989, however, it was made clear in the House of Lords that a good case for compulsory acquisition would have to be made out by an undertaker, and that a public inquiry would examine any opposed acquisition. Water undertakers may prefer to acquire land by agreement in such circumstances.

Important safety provisions with regard to reservoirs are contained in the Reservoirs Act 1975, which applies to 'large raised reservoirs', that is those capable of holding 25,000 cubic metres of water or more *above* the natural level of any land adjoining the reservoir. The Act also applies to reservoirs altered so as to increase capacity to above 25,000 cubic metres, and to artificial lakes, etc, provided they are of appropriate capacity, *but not* mine or quarry lagoons within the meaning of the Mines and Quarries (Tips) Act 1969, or canals, etc. Under the RA 1975, s 2 local authorities, generally county councils as enforcing bodies, must set up public registers of relevant reservoirs, and must obtain relevant information from reservoir undertakers. Undertakers are under a duty to give information under the RA 1975, s 24, and s 21 further requires them to

---

142 [1950] 1 KB 284, [1949] 2 All ER 1021.

furnish authorities with information about reservoirs constructed, altered, abandoned, or brought back into use.

Reservoir undertakers are under obligations to ensure safety in the construction, alteration, supervision and regular monitoring of relevant reservoirs by the employment of qualified civil engineers, and authorities have general and specific enforcement powers in relation to the appointment of appropriate engineers, inspection and supervision of reservoirs, discontinuance, abandonment and reuse of reservoirs: see the RA 1975, ss 6, 8, 9, 10, 11, 12, 13, 14 and 19. Where a reservoir owner is unknown and cannot be found, or where he has no funds to maintain the reservoir as required by the RA 1975, authorities may carry out safety works under s 15, and s 16 grants powers to act in emergencies. The RA 1975, s 3, requires authorities to make reports on their functions to the Secretary of State.

Further reading

BOOKS
Bates, J, *Water and Drainage Law* (looseleaf), Sweet & Maxwell.
Hawkins, K, *Environment and Enforcement* (1984) OUP.
Howarth, W, and McGillivray, D, *Water Pollution and Water Quality Law* (2001) Shaw and Sons.
Krämer, L, *EC Environmental Law* (2000) Sweet & Maxwell.
Richardson, G, Ogus, A, and Burrows, P, *Policing Pollution* (1983) OUP.

JOURNALS
Land Management and Environmental Law Report/Environmental Law and Management
Bates, I, 'Water Quality: The New Regime' [1990] 1 LMELR 156.
Forster, M, 'Nitrate Sensitive Areas — Too Voluntary a Settlement'? [1990] 2 LMELR 48.
Forster, M, 'Enforcing the Drinking Water Directive' [1991] 3 LMELR 56.
Poustie, M, 'The demise of coal and causing water pollution' [1994] 6 ELM 95.
Warn, T, 'Discharge Consents: how they are set and enforced' [1994] 6 ELM 32.

Water Law
Howarth, W, 'Reappraisal of the Bathing Water Directive' [1991] 2 Water Law 51.
Howarth, W, and Somsen, H, 'The EC Nitrates Directive' [1991] 2 Water Law 149.
McGillivray, D, 'Discharge Consents and the Unforeseen' [1995] 6 Water Law 72 and 101.
Somsen, H, 'EC Water Directives' [1990] 1 Water Law 93.
Stallworthy, 'Water Quality: the Capacity of the European Community to Deliver' [1998] 9 Water Law 127.
Stanley, N, 'The *Empress* decision and Causing Water Pollution' [1999] 10 Water Law 37.

Journal of Environmental Law
Ball, S, 'Causing Water Pollution' [1993] 5 JEL 128.
Elworthy, S, 'Finding the Causes of Events or Preventing a "State of Affairs"?: Designation of Nitrate Vulnerable Zones' [1998] 10 JEL 92.
Howarth, W, 'Water Pollution: Improving the Legal Controls' [1989] 1 JEL 25.
Parpworth, N, 'The offence of causing water pollution: a New South Wales perspective' [1997] 9 JEL 59.

Journal of Planning and Environmental Law
Parpworth, N, 'Causing Water Pollution and the Acts of Third Parties' [1998] JPL 752.

Modern Law Review
Howarth, W, 'Poisonous, Noxious and Polluting' (1993) 56 MLR 171.
Howarth, W, 'Self-Monitoring, Self-Policing, Self-Incrimination and Pollution Law'
    (1997) 60 MLR 200.

OFFICIAL REPORTS
'Discharge Consents and Compliance: the NRA's approach to Control of Discharges
    to Water', NRA Water Quality Series No 17 (1994) HMSO.
'Implementation of the EC Freshwater Fish Waters Directive', NRA Water Quality Series
    No 20 (1994) HMSO.
'Implementation of the EC Shellfish Waters Directive', NRA Water Quality Series No
    16 (1994) HMSO.
'Bathing Water Quality in England and Wales — 1994' NRA Water Quality Series No
    22 (1995) HMSO.
'Community Water Policy', House of Lords Select Committee on the Environment, Eight
    Report, Session 1997–98, HMSO.
'Code of Good Agricultural Practice for the Protection of Water (The Water Code)',
    MAFF 1998.
'Policy and Guidance on the use of Anti-Pollution Works Notices', Environment
    Agency, 1999.
'Water Pollution Incidents in England and Wales 1999' (2000) HMSO.
'First Consultation Paper on the Implementation of the EC Water Framework Directive
    2000/60/EC', DEFRA and the National Assembly for Wales, 2001.
'How should England implement the 1991 Nitrates Directive?', DEFRA, 2001.

Index

Negligence—*contd*
property damage, concept of, 136
standard of care, 138
statutory authority, defence of, 141, 142
Noise
abatement-
injunction, 587, 589
notices-
appeals, 586
duty to serve, 584
non-compliance with, 587
offences, 595, 595
previous legislation, under, 590
works, execution of, 585
statutory provisions, 584
zones-
designation of, 594, 595
offences, 595, 595
orders, 594
practice, in, 596
ability to create, 579
aircraft, control of, 581, 606-613. *See also* AIRCRAFT NOISE
ambient, 579
anti-social behaviour, 600, 601
audible intruder alarms, from, 598
byelaws, 603
codes of practice, 597
common law provisions, 582, 583
commonly occurring, 580
compensation for, 618-620
construction site, from, 591-593, 605
defences to allegations, 588
definition, 580
effects of, 580
entertainment, 598, 599
European Community, in, 581, 582
frequency and intensity of, 580
harmful nature of, 579
house insulation grants-
aircraft noise, for, 616, 617
railway noise, for, 618
traffic noise, for, 617
industrial and commercial development, from, 605
Integrated Pollution and Prevention Control regime, 602
loudspeakers, from, 593
motor sports, from, 598
national ambient noise strategy, 601
National Noise Survey, 579
neighbour and neighbourhood, 602
night, at, 590, 591
norms, 581
nuisance, as, 582-584
offences, 595, 595
person aggrieved, summary proceedings by, 589
planning controls-
construction sites, 605
general principles, 604
guidance on, 603
industrial and commercial development, 605

Noise—*contd*
planning controls—*contd*
residential developments, 604
road and rail traffic, 604
sporting and recreation, 605
waste disposal sites, 605, 606
plant and machinery, from, 597
public law controls-
development of, 583, 584
premises, noise nuisance from, 584
rail, 616, 618
raves, from, 599, 600
reduction notice, 596, 597
residential developments, exposure for, 604
road and rail traffic, from, 604
sporting and recreation, 605
street, 587, 588
traffic-
control standards, 614-616
heavy commercial vehicles,. 614
house insulation grants, 617
motorcycles, 615
traffic regulation powers, control under, 613, 614
waste disposal sites, from, 605, 606
Non-governmental organisations
judicial review, standing for, 167-170
pressure groups, 165, 166
public participation, strategic lawsuits against, 173-175
Nuclear installations
consent for, 332, 333
inquiries, 334, 335
liability for damage from-
causation, 145, 146
compensation arrangements, 146, 147
congenital disabilities, 145
defence to claim. 145
grounds of, 144-146
licensed bodies, of, 144
limitation, 146
physical, 144
property, to, 145
specified types of damage, 144
strict, 144
UK Atomic Energy Authority, of, 144
licence for use of, 144
licensing, 332, 333
power stations, operation of, 333
Nuisance
atmospheric pollution as, 563
contaminated land, and, 477
environmental protection, as tool of, 131
noise as, 582-584
private-
abatement, duty of, 123, 124
actionable, requirements for, 118
claimant, 121, 122
damage, scope of liability for, 125-127
damages for, 127, 128
definition, 118
emanation from land, requiring, 119

Sea—*contd*
  mining, 641
  petroleum exploration and exploitation,
    641, 642
  pollution. *See* MARINE POLLUTION
  sand and gravel extraction, 642, 643
Sites of Special Scientific Interest
  area, increase of, 260, 261
  byelaws, 265
  consents, appeals, 261
  damage to, 259, 260, 264
  denotification, 261
  designation of, 51, 254
  disposal of interest in, 265
  evaluation of law, 265, 266
  ineffectiveness of regime, 259
  management agreements, 264
  management notices, 263
  management schemes, 262, 263
  new law, continuation under, 265
  offences, 264
  public bodies, exemption from provisions,
    261, 262
  Special Areas of Conservation, as, 267
  specified operations in, 261, 265
Smoke
  pollution by. *See* ATMOSPHERIC POLLUTION
  statutory nuisance by, 13
State sovereignty
  principle of, 64
Statutory nuisance
  abatement notice-
    appeal against, 11, 12
    clear and certain, to be, 11
    person on whom served, 11
    service of, 10
  best practicable means to counteract,
    taking, 12
  concept of, 9
  current law of, 9-14
  defence to proceedings, 12, 13
  definition, 130
  diminishing importance of, 9
  health, prejudicial to, 9, 10
  injurious to health, statement as to, 12
  inspection and investigation of complaints,
    9
  meaning, 9
  noise, by, 13
  private citizens, action by, 13, 14
  reasonable excuse for, 13
  single act as, 10
  smoke, by, 13
  statutory procedure-
    local authorities, action by, 10-13, 130
    person against whom action taken, 11-
      13
    requirement to follow, 10
Statutory registers
  compliance entries in, 153
  contaminated land, as to, 154, 490
  corporate accountability, as form of, 153
  enforcement entries, 153

Statutory registers—*contd*
  entitlement to search, 153
  Environment Agency premises, search on,
    154
  genetically modified organisms, as to, 154
  Integrated Pollution and Prevention
    Control, information as to, 537, 538
  legal right of access to, 154
  licence-specific, being, 153
  measure of compliance, entries as, 153
  pollution control, 677
  Pollution Inventory, publication of, 153
  prescribed processes, information as to,
    510, 510
  types of, 153
  use of, 153, 154
  water pollution, relating to, 695
Stewardship
  concept of, 18
  environmental protection and regulation,
    as moral basis for, 19
Stubble burning
  control of, 576, 577
Surveillance
  directed, 114
  intrusive, 114
  regulation of, 113, 114
Sustainable development
  Agenda 21, 70
  applications of, 23
  Bruntland definition, 41
  Commission. *See* COMMISSION ON SUSTAINABLE
    DEVELOPMENT
  communities, sustainable, 59
  constitutional significance, acquisition of,
    24
  ecological criteria, 41
  economic issues, 21
  economy, sustainable, 58
  Environment Agency, contribution of, 41
  environmental economics, relationship
    with, 20-22
  environmental law, as basic principle of,
    22
  environmental protection, approach to,
    59, 60
  evolution of concept, 20
  expression of, 23
  fishery conservation, 23, 24
  future development, 23, 24
  idea of, development, 20
  legal development, 22
  legislation, meaning in, 41
  market transformation, 58
  national strategic plans, 23
  natural resources, prudent use of, 41
  planning, and, 179, 180, 189
    influence on, 9
  reconciliation of objectives, 41
  resource allocation, 22
  strategy-
    first, 56
    principles, 57, 58